A Global History of Architecture

A Global History of Architecture

Third Edition

Francis D.K. Ching

Mark Jarzombek

Vikramditya Prakash

WILEY

Library of Congress Cataloging-in-Publication Data:

Names: Ching, Francis D. K., 1943- author. | Jarzombek, Mark, author. |
  Prakash, Vikramaditya, author.
Title: A global history of architecture / Francis D.K. Ching, Mark Jarzombek,
  Vikramaditya Prakash.
Description: Third edition. | Hoboken, New Jersey : Wiley, 2017. | Includes
  bibliographical references and index.
Identifiers: LCCN 2017004046 (print) | LCCN 2017005382 (ebook) | ISBN
  9781118981337 (hardback) | ISBN 9781118981610 (Adobe PDF) | ISBN
  9781118981603 (ePub)
Subjects: LCSH: Architecture--History. | BISAC: ARCHITECTURE / History /
  General.
Classification: LCC NA200 .C493 2017 (print) | LCC NA200 (ebook) | DDC
  720.9--dc23
LC record available at https://lccn.loc.gov/2017004046

Printed in the United States of America

SKY10030163_092821

Contents

CONTENTS

CONTENTS

CONTENTS

Preface

What is a global history of architecture? There is, of course, no single answer, just as there is no single way to define words like *global*, *history*, and *architecture*. Nonetheless, these words are not completely open-ended, and they serve here as the vectors that have helped us construct the narratives of this volume. With this book, we hope to provoke discussion about these terms and at the same time furnish a framework students can use to begin discussion in the classroom.

This book transcends the necessary restrictions of the classroom, where in a semester or even two, the teacher has to limit what is taught based on any number of factors. The reader should understand that there is always something over the horizon. Whereas any such book must inevitably be selective about what it can include, we have attempted to represent a wide swath of the globe, in all its diversity. At the same time, however, the book does not aspire to be an encyclopedia of everything that has been built; nor does it assume a universal principle that governs everything architectural. The buildings included are for us more than just monuments of achievement; we see them as set pieces allowing us to better appreciate the complex intertwining of social, political, religious, and economic contexts in which they are positioned. As much as possible, we emphasize urban contexts as well as materials and surfaces. We have also tried to emphasize quality as much as quantity. From that point of view, the word *global* in the title is not so much a geographic construct as an eruditional horizon. In that sense, this book is not about the sum of all local histories. Its mission is bound to the discipline of architecture, which requires us to see connections, tensions, and associations that transcend so-called local perspectives. In that respect, ours is only one of many possible narratives.

Synchrony has served as a powerful frame for our discussion. For instance, as much as Seoul's Gyeongbok Palace is today heralded in Korea as an example of traditional Korean architecture, we note that it also belongs to a Eurasian building campaign that stretched from Japan (the Katsura Imperial Villa), through China (Beijing and the Ming Tombs), to Persia (Isfahan), India (the Taj Mahal), Turkey (the Suleymaniye Complex), Italy (St. Peter's Basilica and the Villa Rotonda), France (Chambord), and Russia (Cathedral of the Assumption). In some cases, one can assume that information flowed from place to place, but such movement is not itself a requirement for the architecture to qualify as "global." It is enough for us to know, first, that these structures are contemporaneous and that each has a specific history. If there are additional connections that come as a result of trade, war, or other forms of contact, these are for us subsidiary to contemporaneity.

This is not to say that our story is exclusively the story of individual buildings and sites, only that there is a give and take between explaining how a building works and how it is positioned in the world of its influences and connections. We have, therefore, tried to be faithful to the specificities of each individual building while acknowledging that every architectural project is always embedded in a larger world—and even a worldview—that affects it directly and indirectly.

Our post-19th-century penchant for seeing history through the lens of the nation-state often makes it difficult to apprehend such global pictures. Furthermore, in the face of today's increasingly hegemonic global economy, the tendency by historians, and often architects, to nationalize, localize, regionalize, and even micro-regionalize history—perhaps as meaningful acts of resistance—can blind us to the historical synchronicity and interconnectivity of global realities that existed long before our present moment of globalization. What would the Turks be today if they had stayed in East Asia? The movement of people, ideas, food, and wealth has bound us to each other since the beginning of history. And so without denying the reality of nation-states and their claims to unique histories and identities, we have resisted the temptation to streamline our narratives to fit nationalistic parameters. Indian architecture, for instance, may have some consistent traits from its beginnings to the present day, but there is less certainty about what those traits might be than one may think. The flow of Indian Buddhism to China, the opening of trade to Southeast Asia, the settling of Mongolians in the north, the arrival of Islam from the east, and the colonization by the English are just some of the more obvious links that bind India, for better or worse, to global events. It is these links, and the resultant architecture, more than the presumed "Indianness" of Indian architecture, that interests us. Furthermore, India has historically been divided into numerous kingdoms that, like Europe, could easily have evolved (and in some cases did evolve) into their own nations. The 10th-century Chola dynasty of peninsular India, for example, was not only an empire but possessed a unique worldview of its own. In writing its history, we have attempted to preserve its distinct identity while marking the ways in which it maps its own global imagination.

Broadly speaking, our goal is to help students of architecture develop an understanding of the manner in which architectural production is always triangulated by the exigencies of time and location. More specifically, we have narrated these interdependencies to underscore what we consider to be the inevitable modernity of each period. We often think of the distant past as moving slowly from age to age, dynasty to dynasty, or king to king, and only of our recent history as moving at a faster pace. In such a teleological view, the present is the apex of civilization, and history becomes a narrative of progress that is measured against the values of the present. By contrast, we have tried to present every historical period in terms of its own challenges, and the history of architecture as the history of successive and often dramatic changes spurred on by new materials, new technologies, changing political situations, and changing aesthetic and religious ideals. These changes, spelled out differently in different times, have always challenged the norm in a way that we, in our age, would call modernity.

The Sumerian urbanization of the Euphrates River delta made the earlier village-centered economy of the Zagros Mountains obsolete. The introduction of iron in the 9th century BCE spelled the demise of the Egyptians and allowed societies such as the Dorians, the Etruscans, and the Nubians, who were once relatively marginal in the global perspective, to suddenly dominate the cultural and architectural landscape. The Mongolian invasion of the 13th century may have destroyed much, but in its wake came unprecedented developments. The Bantu expansion into southern Africa and the Polynesian expansion into the Pacific were just as dramatic in their own time as the admittedly more effective and rapid colonialization of the planet by the Europeans. By concentrating on the modernity of each historical example, we have used the global perspective to highlight the drama of historical change, rather than viewing the history of architecture as driven by traditions and essences.

Turning now to the term *architecture*, few would have any difficulty in differentiating it from the other arts, such as painting or sculpture. But what architecture itself constitutes is always the subject of great debate, particularly among architects, architectural historians, and critics. Some have argued that architecture arises out of an urge to protect oneself from the elements, others that it is an expression of symbolic desires, or that it is at its best only when it is embedded in local traditions. In this book, without foreclosing the discussion, we hope that the reader begins to see architecture as

a type of cultural production. In that sense, this book is a companion to *Architecture of First Societies* (Wiley, 2013), which looks in depth at the history of pre-agricultural worlds and the transition to agriculture.

Here, we have emphasized issues of patronage, use, meaning, and symbolism where appropriate, and have attempted to paint a broad historical picture of time and context while, at the same time, making sure we have covered the salient formal features of a structure. Of course, words like *culture* and *civilization* are, like the word *architecture*, open to contestation and will have different meanings in different contexts. Yet, despite such ambiguities, we believe that civilization is unthinkable without those buildings that are given special status, whether for religion, governance, industry, or living. Just like the processes of agricultural domestication, architecture emerged in our prehistory and will remain an integral part of human expression to the very end.

Because we have dealt primarily with buildings of quality, we do not have the space to paint a picture of the historical development of vernacular and domestic spaces. This is not because we do not recognize their importance, but because we wanted to remain consistent to a line of reasoning that allows us to see architectural history as connected to the history of ideas, technologies, theories, religions, and politics. Each chapter introduces the set of terms that shape the architectural production and meaning of that age. Changes in some places are perhaps more dramatic than in others, but in all cases we try to explain the causes. The ancient Egyptian pharaohs, for instance, during a period of time commissioned pyramids; but then they stopped and instead built huge temples. The reader needs to come to understand the political reasoning that necessitated this change. Not only did Buddhism morph as it filtered its way into East and Southeast Asia; so, too, did Buddhist architecture. The rock-cut temples of Ellora did not appear out of a vacuum, but the technology of rock-cutting had never been attempted at that scale and would die out by the 13th century. In that sense we ask readers to compare architecture not only across space, but also across time.

Organization of the Book

Rather than preparing chapters on individual countries or regions, such as India, Japan, or France, we have organized the book by "time-cuts." Eighteen chronological slices of time, beginning with 3500 BCE and ending with 1950 CE, comprise the armature of the book. Each time-cut marks not the beginning of a time period, but roughly the middle of the period with which each chapter is concerned. The 800 CE time-cut, for instance, covers the period from 700 to 900 CE. Yet we have not been strict about the scope of a particular time-cut. Whenever necessary for coherence, we have not hesitated to include material from before and after its prescribed limits. Each time-cut should, therefore, be seen more as a marker amid the complexity of the flowing river of history, rather than a strict chronological measuring rod.

We have begun each time-cut with an introductory essay addressing the historical forces graphing that period of time, followed by a map and a timeline locating all of the major buildings we discuss. Discussions of individual buildings and groups of buildings are in a series of small subsections marked by relevant subcontinental location—East Asia, Southeast Asia, South Asia, West Asia, Europe, Africa, North America, Central America, or South America.

Rather than arrange all the time-cuts in the same order, we have arranged each according to its own internal logic. Despite the difficulties this may pose, we have chosen this strategy to remind readers that the globe does not really begin in the East or the West but can indeed start and end anywhere. We have arranged the sequence of the subsections as needed to maintain continuity in the narrative of a particular chapter. Often this continuity is provided simply by geographical adjacency; in other cases, we have linked subsections to make a point about historiographical issues such as the influence and movement of ideas, or contrasts between kingdoms.

The individual subsections, which may be a single page or as long as four or five pages, are conceived as mini case studies, coherent in themselves. These can be assigned as independent readings. Besides ensuring that the relevant facts and descriptions of each significant project we address are adequately covered, we have emphasized the cultural and global investments of its creator. For instance, a discussion of the Italian High Renaissance consists of pages on the Piazza del Campidoglio, il Gesù, the Villa Farnese, Il Redentore, Palladian villas, and the Uffizi. The number of case studies accompanying each civilizational discussion is not uniform. Sometimes there are six; at other times, just one or two. The differences are largely a measure of our judgment of the importance of the material and the availability of literature on a topic. Indeed, there exists a great disparity in the availability of information. While we know much about the early civilizations of Mesopotamia; we know startlingly little about pre-Columbian civilizations. An archaeologist we spoke with estimated that only 15 percent of pre-Columbian sites have been excavated. And there are also many inaccessible archaeological sites in war-torn countries around the world, and even sites that cannot be excavated because of lack of funding or awareness. A fully fleshed-out picture of architecture's history is, therefore, still a dream that we can only aspire to.

The book's drawings are intended to be integral to the narrative. They not only illustrate the text, but also help tell a story of their own. Not everything in the text is illustrated by drawings, just as the drawings can be used to communicate things that are not referenced in the text. We have tried to make a virtue out of this fact by sharing the physical and epistemological space on each page as evenly as we could between text and image. The drawings also speak to the diminishing art of drawing in an age of photography and computer-enhanced plans. Though faculty may not want to organize

their syllabi by the time-cuts, they may find it useful to cut and paste selectively chosen subsections together to suit their historical narrative. Such selections could be made geographically or by other means. Once again, the fact that the individual subsections are conceived as case studies allows them to be read coherently, even out of sequence.

A book like this faces almost insurmountable problems in trying to establish a single standard for names, terms, and spellings, particularly those of non-Western origin. A particular mosque, for instance, might have different English, Arabic, Persian, and Hindu names. Which does one use? Should one say Nijo-jo or Nijo Castle (the suffix *–jo* in Japanese means castle)? Should one call a pagoda a *ta*, as it is called in Chinese, or should we persist with its conventional English name? Generally speaking, we have tried to use the names that are most common in current scholarship in English. It would be foolish to dispense with the Greek word for those Egyptian buildings that we call pyramids, named after the Greek bread called *pyramidos*, but, on the other hand, we would like to suggest that Angkor Wat be called by its real name, Vrah Vishnulok, to cite one counterexample. Once we have made a choice regarding the spelling of a particular proper noun, we have tried to remain consistent in our use of it. However, at several places, we have intentionally used non-English terms, even when there is a common English usage. This we have done whenever we have felt that the English is misleading (the English *pagoda*, for instance, has nothing to do with the *ta*) or when discussion of local linguistic practice is in some way illuminating. Our aspiration is to initiate movement toward a more diverse and appropriate vocabulary for the world's architecture. Language, like architecture, is a living thing with indistinct boundaries and, as such, reflects architecture's status as a multifaceted cultural signifier.

In conclusion, we would like to acknowledge that in preparing and writing this book, a process that we have enjoyed at every turn, we were continually reminded of our ignorance on many matters. Conversations with colleagues were particularly valuable, as were trips to some of the sites we cover. But in the end, a work like this can only be the beginning of a long process of refinement. So we ask all readers who wish to do so to contact us, to point out inaccuracies, to tell us about things that should be included in subsequent editions, or to open a conversation about history, the world, and our place within it.

3500 BCE

1.1 !Kung hut

INTRODUCTION

For a million years, humans lived off hunting, food gathering, and fishing. From the perspective of our advanced world today we tend to look back at this and wonder how we could even have survived given all the difficulties. We once labeled these people savages or barbarians, and then we called them primitives. More recently we call them hunter-gatherers, as if all they do is obsess about food acquisition. But the !Kung, who have lived in the Kalahari Desert in Botswana for hundreds of thousands of years, spend only about 40 percent of their time hunting and gathering. The rest of the time, they do what most of us might do: they socialize, dance, cook, and rest.

In the Kalahari, mongongo trees, which produce tasty and nutritious nuts by the thousands, proliferate in mile-long groves. Tubers can be dug from the ground, and animal herds migrate through the territory, easy prey for a canny hunter and his poison-tipped arrows. The !Kung live in camps that are rebuilt every year near seasonal water holes. Women make the huts around a common campfire, usually under the shade of a large tree. The huts are not really to live in, since people tend to live mainly outdoors, but serve as storage areas for tools and as shade on a hot day. The modern world has little respect for its venerable ancestors. Because of forced relocations, mining on their territory, and fences cutting across their land, the !Kung people's survival into the next decades is much in doubt. It is not the natural world that endangers them, but our civilized world.

As populations expanded, groups would bud off to form new communities in the next valley or further along the shores. In this way, the first groups of people left Africa some 1.5 million years ago with a second group, our human ancestors, following around 60,000 BCE to slowly yet persistently colonize the globe, reaching the southern tip of South America around 13,000 BCE. First Society people, however, were not nomads as is so mistakenly assumed. Instead they tended to live within prescribed and familiar territories, moving seasonally between winter camps near rivers and upland summer camps for hunting and fishing. The ancient people of Australia, for example, moved in predictable cycles: in some parts of the year they lived in relative isolation, and in other parts they would get together for large annual ceremonial and social events.

During the Ice Age (ca. 25,000 BCE– ca. 15,000 BCE), humans faced a global phenomenon the likes of which we have never seen since. The extreme cold, which sent massive, mile-deep ice sheets far to the south of the polar regions, impacted Europe in particular. But the people there did not leave. This was not because they were trapped. It was because those areas had become a hunter's paradise, with bears, lions, and, above all, huge herds of horses, reindeer, and mammoth moving across the grassy landscape. The Gravettian Culture was the first to master the cold. They developed leather-making and the needle to create fur-lined clothing, boots, and jackets. In great festivals, they congregated near caves where artists had painted brilliant images of animals on the walls and ceilings. What form of magic these places produced is still unknown, but the quality of the art staggers the imagination even today. The animals were painted not as carcasses but as living creatures moving and breathing, and were made by artists who had practiced their skills over a lifetime. As the weather warmed, the hunters moved to the east, crossed Siberia, and around 13,000 BCE crossed Alaska to enter the open plains of North America. Called the Clovis People, they hunted mammoth and then, when the mammoth were all hunted out, they switched to bison. Their sacred landscapes include Seminole Canyon in Texas, with its ancient rock art depicting shamans and sacred animal spirits.

1.2 **Haida settlement, Canada**

The warming of the weather raised the levels of the oceans, separating Japan from China, and England from mainland Europe. It created vast rivers, swamps, and forests teeming with animals and plants, drawing humans to the river shores. It was, one might say, an age of affluence. At Lepenski Vir along the Danube River, a settlement of triangular huts emerged. The people there caught sturgeon, a fish that averaged some 3 meters long. Why go hunting when catching one fish would feed an entire community? The nearby forests provided a wide assortment of berries, mushrooms, and nuts to complement the diet. Nor was this village a solitary community. Similar villages lined the shores, and their inhabitants traveled by boat to connect with each other for ceremonial events.

Half a world away, another affluent society emerged along the northwest coast of Canada. It was a favorable site for many reasons. It was in a pocket of relatively mild weather, the result of cross-Pacific winds; it was also sited along the migration path of whales, and salmon came in the thousands to swim upstream to spawn. Huge cedar trees, sacred to the Haida, provided material for houses and boats. The tree was not just "wood." Its red color and sweet smell were indicators of its connection to the world of the spirits. Linear settlements sprang up along the shore, composed of large, clan-based community houses facing the water. Each house was a sacred diagram designed in relation to the cosmos, which for the

Haida was divided into three shamanistic zones: the sky world, the earth, and the oceanic underworld. The building's frame system consisted of massive roof beams, often more than half a meter in diameter and spanning the width of the house, which ranged from 7.5 to 15 meters. These beams were supported by posts carved to represent important family ancestors or supernatural beings associated with the family's history. Walls were clad with split-cedar planks tied horizontally between paired upright poles.

It was not just rivers and shores that attracted human habitation to make the first settled communities, but also the emerging great rain forests. The Bambuti in Congo still today pay homage to a forest spirit, Jengi, whose power is thought to emanate through the world. Jengi is seen as a parental figure and guardian. Society is organized around individual households consisting of a husband, a wife, and their children, forming settlements that can number up to about fifty residents. The women build the huts that, in the shape of upside-down baskets, are made out of a frame of saplings and clad with leaves. Other rain forest cultures developed in Brazil, Central America, and Southeast Asia.

Beginning around 10,000 BCE in some places, the great First Society traditions that had sustained human life for so long began to change. Instead of hunting animals, humans began to herd them, and instead of gathering and tending plants, they began to domesticate a few chosen plants and grow them in organized fields. These changes altered

1.3 **Village scene**

1.4 **Pottery making**

the imaginaries of the spirit world. Cattle in particular were seen as living gods, requiring daily attendance and a culture of respect. They were not killed for food but were sacrificed to mark special events in the life of the community. Among the Dinka in the Sudan, a man knows his cattle by special names, sings songs to them, and sleeps next to them for long periods of time. Cattle are sacrificed only on special occasions, such as at weddings or funerals. Although only a few cattle-centric societies remain today, the impact of this worldview can be felt even in modern religions.

Just as important was the shift from gathering plants to farming. Rice in southern China and eastern India, millet in Africa and northern China, wheat and barley in the Levant, and corn in Guatemala—all rose from being just one of thousands of plants that humans tended to the precious focus of effort and devotion. The combined transformation of our relationship to animals and plants produced a new way of life: agropastoralism. While today we call this period the birth of agriculture, we have to remember that crops like rice and barley were not raised as food. They were gods. We have so secularized food production today that we forget that the birth of what we call agriculture coincided with profound transformations that deified certain foods and thus, it might be said, guaranteed the proper and complex work ethic needed for their production. The impact on women was particularly profound; harvesting, grinding, storing, and cooking were all largely women's work, as was pottery making, basket weaving, and, of course, the raising of children.

The emergence of pastoral and agropastoral cultures produced village societies organized around chiefs with more or less power depending on circumstances. Villages were well calibrated to meet the needs of the animals, to deal with the calendar of planting and harvesting, and to produce the necessary equipment for life, such as the bowls and containers that stored grain and water and that allowed fermentation and cooking to take place. These activities were all governed by ritual practices and unwritten rules of behavior that shaped the destiny of all. But village society could not spread just anywhere. It needed the right combination of good soil for farms, grasslands for cattle, forests for firewood, and upland areas for hunting—and, of course, water and salt.

The Mesopotamian highlands were perfect for such agropastoral societies, and beginning around 9000 BCE compact villages began to spread along the slopes above the great rivers

in the plains. A similar expansion took place along the Sahel in Africa, where sorghum was the main plant, as well as in the foothills of the Baluchistan Mountains (barley), in northern China (millet), and along the Yangtze River (rice). By 5000 BCE these places had also established themselves as profoundly different from the First Society worlds that neighbored them, even if they maintained some aspects of the older traditions. Whereas the agropastoral tradition in Mesopotamia, the Indus Valley, China, and Egypt remained confined by their ecological niches, a remarkable transformation took place in Europe, where between 9000 and 4000 BCE, agropastoral cultures moved slowly along rivers and shores to reach even northern Ireland. There the newcomers thrived and built one of the greatest structures of the time, Newgrange, a vast artificial mound with a sacred chamber in its interior that was designed to mark the first rays of the winter solstice.

1.5 **Herding**

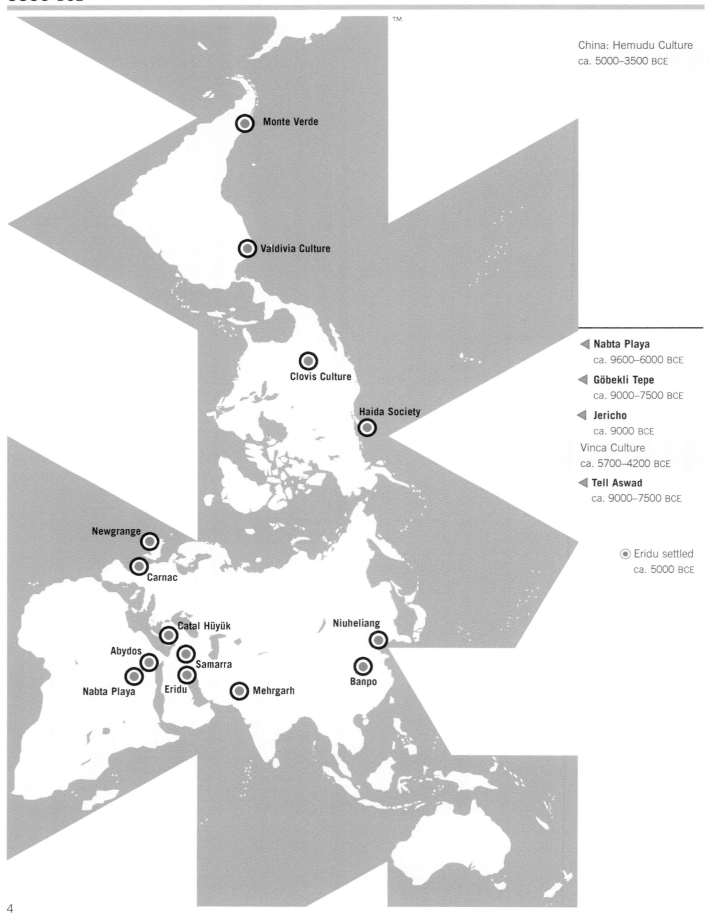

China: Hemudu Culture
ca. 5000–3500 BCE

Monte Verde

Valdivia Culture

Clovis Culture

Haida Society

◀ **Nabta Playa**
ca. 9600–6000 BCE
◀ **Göbekli Tepe**
ca. 9000–7500 BCE
◀ **Jericho**
ca. 9000 BCE
Vinca Culture
ca. 5700–4200 BCE
◀ **Tell Aswad**
ca. 9000–7500 BCE

◉ Eridu settled
ca. 5000 BCE

Newgrange

Carnac

Catal Hüyük

Niuheliang

Abydos

Samarra

Nabta Playa

Eridu

Mehrgarh

Banpo

China: Yangshao Culture
5000–3000 BCE

Hongshan Culture
4700–2900 BCE

Longshan Culture
3000–2000 BCE

▲ **Banpo**
ca. 4500 BCE

▲ **Niuheliang Ritual Center**
ca. 3500–3000 BCE

▲ **Yaoshan Ritual Altar**
ca. 3300–2000 BCE

Indus Valley: Early Harappan Period
ca. 5000–2600 BCE

▲ **Mehrgarh**
ca. 6500–2800 BCE

▲ **Harappa**
ca. 3000–1900 BCE

▲ **Dholavira**
ca. 2650–2100 BCE

4500 BCE   **3500 BCE**   **2500 BCE**

Late Neolithic Period
ca. 5000–2000 BCE

Early Bronze Age
ca. 3000–2000 BCE

◉ Bronze casting begins in the Near East.
ca. 3600 BCE

◀ **Catal Hüyük**
flourishes ca. 7400–5500 BCE

Mesopotamia: Ubaid (Eridu) Culture
ca. 5300–4300 BCE

Uruk Period
ca. 4000–3100 BCE

◀ **Tell es-Sawwan**
6000–3500 BCE

▲ **White Temple**
Begun ca. 4000 BCE

▲ **Temple at Uruk**
ca. 3400 BCE

▲ **Temple at Eridu**
4500–3800 BCE

◉ Invention of the wheel
ca. 3600 BCE

◉ Earliest readable documents in Mesopotamia
ca. 3200 BCE

Egypt: Pre-Dynastic Period
ca. 4500–3100 BCE

Early Dynastic Period
ca. 3100–2649 BCE

▲ **Tombs of Hor Aba**
ca. 3100 BCE

▲ **Royal Tombs at Umm el-Qaab**
3100–2890 BCE

▲ **Tombs of Hor Aba**
ca. 3100 BCE

Earliest tumulus tombs in Portugal
ca. 5000 BCE

Europe: Passage Tombs and Dolmens of Megaliths
ca. 3500–2500 BCE

▲ **Newgrange**
ca. 4000 BCE

▲ **Stonehenge**
Begun ca. 3000 BCE

▲ **Passage grave: Île Longue**
ca. 4100 BCE

◉ Saracen Ring added at Stonehenge
2500 BCE

▲ **Carnac Stones**
ca. 3500 BCE

◉ Cursus tradition in England
ca. 3500 BCE

RITUAL CENTERS

In the agropastoral environment, humans began to think and act differently than their First Society ancestors had. Forests had to be chopped down, clay had to be gathered for pots that then had to be fired in kilns, granaries had to established, animals tended to, wool harvested and made into cloth; plants that were once considered food were now thought of as weeds that had to be culled from gardens and farm plots. Decisions had to be made about priorities; children had to learn their respective roles as adults; and priests had to secure the privilege of the divine. Customs had to be followed about social ranking, finding a mate, and building a house. Herds could die because of disease or predators, and crops could be lost to pests or carelessness. Grains could rot, and neighboring tribes could attack. The marshaling of energies that the village required, the stratification of gender activities along with the creation of a new set of powerful gods in privileged communication with the elites, produced a type of cognitive revolution. The cohesiveness that this required is impressive, and in many parts of the globe the village world is still the glue that holds society together.

One of the first sites where we see the transformation is Nabta Playa in what is today southern Egypt, some 80 kilometers west of Abu Simbel. It is now an inhospitable desert, but in 9000 BCE it was next to a large lake with pastured shores. The site featured a circle of slender upright stones, the main stones being four pairs set close together. Compared to Stonehenge, built 6.000 years later, the circle is small, measuring roughly 4 meters in diameter, but its purpose was similar: to organize time according to the seasons. Two of the stone pairs are aligned north–south, the other two pairs northeast–southwest. They aided in the observation of the motion of the sun and probably of the constellation Orion. Priests and their associated clans probably came to live at Nabta Playa permanently, with the population swelling periodically with the seasonal arrival of herder tribes who would have come from far afield with their cattle for large celebratory

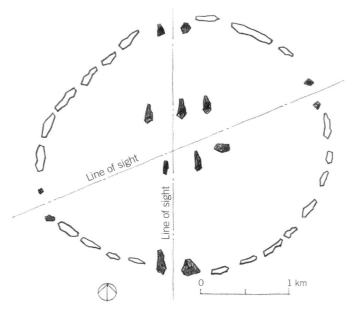

1.6 Plan: Nabta Playa, Egypt

events. By 3500 BCE, however, Nabta Playa had become increasingly arid: the lake dried up, and the site was abandoned. The exodus from the Nubian Desert to the Nile River played a large role in the development of social differentiation in the pre-dynastic cultures of the Nile Valley. One important link between Egypt and the ancient cattle cult of Nabta Playa was Hathor, the goddess of fertility.

Another ritual site was on top of a hill near the village of Urfa in southeastern Turkey. Here, too, the now arid site was once a lush forest. The oldest layer of the site appears to date back to around 9000 BCE. The structures, called Göbekli Tepe, consist of several circular dry-stone walls, each of which contains monolithic pillars of limestone up to 3 meters tall. Since there is no indication of any roof covering, it seems that the circles were open-air ritual chambers. They are now called temples, but it is unlikely that they were temples in the sense of being used by a priesthood with organized devotional practices. What went on in these spaces is not known, but they most certainly had links to ancestor cults and might have been used in conjunction with mortuary rituals. The floors consisted of a concrete-like substance made of burnished lime. A low bench runs around the inside of the circle walls. The pillars show detailed reliefs of foxes, lions,

cattle, wild boars, herons, ducks, scorpions, ants, and snakes, all executed with great skill, demonstrating that precision work—even without metalworking tools—was possible even at this early time.

If we add to these two sites the Niuheliang Ritual Center (ca. 3500–3000 BCE) in northern China, with its numerous platforms and structures, and, of course, Stonehenge (ca. 3000 BCE), we have four ritual centers—and there are certainly countless more—that served as gathering places and eventually as religious centers for newly settled communities. Niuheliang will be discussed in this chapter; Stonehenge, perhaps the last of the great early ritual centers, will be discussed in the next.

Around 3500 BCE something quite remarkable happened in four places on the earth: groups of people developed something that we today call cities. This transformation was not as natural as one might assume, even though it was dependent on several thousand years of village life and the necessary cohesion that came with it. In Mesopotamia, the farmers in the hills at first stayed away from the vast, overgrown, flood-prone swamps of the Tigris and Euphrates Rivers. But an intrepid group must have set out one day to try their luck. Finding a knoll, they dug up the reeds, planted barley, and carved out canals, activities that were hugely

1.7 Göbekli Tepe, near Urfa, Turkey

1.8 **Elam, a typical Mesopotamian city with walls and towers, as depicted in this bas-relief commemorating Assyrian king Ashurbanipal's conquest and destruction of the city in 647 BCE.**

labor-intensive. It was a success, built on the simple premise that by doing one thing well—growing barley—the inhabitants of an isolated place could trade for everything that they did not have. They created the wheel to speed up travel; they created writing to document trade transactions; they created city-scaled gods to protect them; they laid the foundation for laws and regulations; and they created walls to defend their precious grain surpluses on which the entire operation depended. The first cities of Mesopotamia were thus experiments in an extreme landscape. They were governed by an elite, with most of the work done by slaves from nearby conquered regions. Some cities thrived, some did not, but over time, the power and wealth that they created for themselves pushed their destiny forward. In Egypt, the story is similar, but here the rise of cities—more like sprawling villages—was the consequence of the rapid influx of refugees from the expanding Sahara Desert. Prior to about 5000 BCE the Nile was an unruly, lightly populated, swampy river, but with the drier climate that created the desert, thousands of people came with their animals and agricultural skills. Over time they refashioned the Nile into a fertile paradise. The intensity of this foreshadowed the rise of a controlling elite who became first chiefs, then gods.

In India along the Indus River, cities also emerged, spectacular in nature, because unlike in Mesopotamia and Egypt where the building material was largely mud-dried brick, here the inhabitants made kiln-fired bricks that could not only withstand the test of time but also allowed them to build close to the river, and to build pools, drainage systems, and multistory houses. Ships from these cities traded with the Mesopotamians to the north.

In China, the development of cities had a slightly different cast. Village communities had formed in the south in the swampy regions around Hangzhou Bay and the Yangtze River estuary, where rice could be planted. Villages were also forming in the north where people had long since discovered the value of millet, a hardy plant that grows on hillsides. Here people used a form of architecture well-known in the north since 25,000 BCE, the pit house. Dug partially into the ground with a superstructure of thatch held in place by posts and beams, these communal buildings were dry and warm and the focus of a range of ritual activities. Unlike the Mesopotamian cities, which were import-export centers, these dense villages were more self-sustaining as they attained the scale of cities. There were areas for the manufacturing of pottery and bronze, just as there were areas reserved for the elites.

These first cities produced a concentration of wealth and power that was to have significant implications for the destiny of humans and indeed for their definition of themselves as "civilized." But as much magic as they worked on the human imagination, these cities' experimental nature should not be forgotten. Cities were made; they were also made to be destroyed. The Chinese, in fact, would continuously destroy their cities; with a new dynasty, the old capital was often burned or leveled and the inhabitants forced to relocate. The Mesopotamians and Egyptians glorified their destruction of enemy cities, and so it went on—until even today.

Although urban densities were able to pull a large amount of resources into their orbits, around 3500 BCE they constituted only a tiny percentage of the world population, maybe as small as .001 percent. Most people lived in spread-out village societies, and many more lived in a world with no agriculture at all, as humans had for hundreds of thousands of years.

BEGINNINGS OF CHINA'S CIVILIZATIONS

In China, the shift to an agricultural/village world took place around 9000 BCE. There was, however, no single "origin" of Chinese civilization. Instead, there was a gradual multinucleated development taking place somewhat independently at first, with the emphasis to the south on rice and to the north on millet and pigs. Rice grew wild and was then domesticated on the swampy shores and in the delta of the Yangtze River. Millet, which prefers a cooler climate, grows wild on hillsides, where it over time was also domesticated. Pigs played a role in village life from early times and, along with sheep, were introduced to northern cultures by 5000 BCE, if not earlier. By 4000 BCE, especially in the north, small but well-organized regional communities emerged. These included the Hongshan Culture (4700–2900 BCE) to the north of Bohai Bay in Inner Mongolia and Hebai Province, and the Yangshao Culture (5000–3000 BCE) in Henan Province. Geographically between the two, and developing later, was the Longshan Culture (3000–2000 BCE) in the central and lower areas of the Yellow River. The emergence of walls around communities is a clear indication that the political landscape was very much in flux. To the north, villages were generally composed of pit houses that, whether large or small, trace their ancestry back to 20,000 BCE and possibly earlier. Pit houses were used throughout Inner Asia by steppe hunters. People to the south developed houses on stilts, a natural response to the swampy soil of the rice paddies.

Niuheliang Ritual Center

The Hongshan Culture, with its villages focusing on millet and sheep and pig grazing, was located along the Laoha, Yingjin, and Daling Rivers, which empty into Bohai Bay. Though scattered over a large area, the community's ritual life focused on a sacred landscape in which a mountain known locally as Pig Mountain must have played a part, as its silhouette is visible to the south. The ritual center consisted of at least fourteen burial mounds and altars over several hill ridges. It dates from around 3500 BCE, but its importance could well have been established earlier.

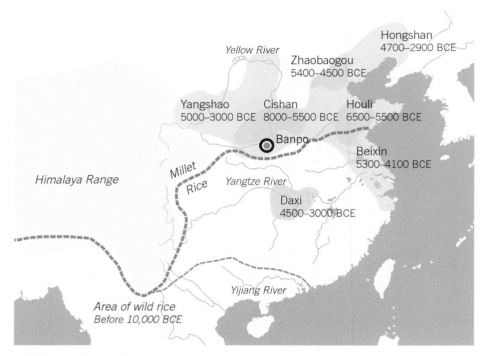

1.9 China's early agriculture

Though rituals would have been performed here for the elites, the large area of this sacred landscape implies that audiences for the ritual would have encompassed all the villages of the Hongshan Culture. The site might even have attracted supplicants from further afield. A key building was a structure that is called a goddess temple, though its purpose is not known. The walls, made of interwoven branches and covered with packed mud, leaned inward to form a tunnel-like space. Its main body was 25 meters from south to north, with secondary spaces projecting from that. On the outside, its surviving footings show that its surface was covered with geometric designs in high relief that were painted yellow, red, and white, all of which certainly suggests that it stood out in the landscape in a colorful way. To its north was a single detached room where excavations have uncovered clay body parts, including a head, a torso, and arms, belonging to an image of a protectress or goddess (from which the site got its name).

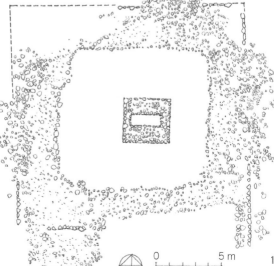

1.10 Plan: Cairn with stone tomb, Niuheliang Ritual Center, tomb site II

Another structure of interest to archaeologists is an artificial hill at the entrance to the valley. On the ground level, the mound is encircled by a ring of squared white stones. Another ring of white stones is embedded at the middle height of the mound; a third was placed near the top. Artifacts found near the top of the mound include crude clay crucibles used for smelting copper. Since the top of a hill is a surprising place to melt copper, the structure seems to have been meant for ritual events. Burial grounds on hills seem to mark the north and south extremes of the moonrise in the east. All in all, this center contains the essential elements of Chinese ancestor worship—burial cairns, platforms, and a ritual temple—as evidenced, for example, by the Ming tombs built five thousand years later.

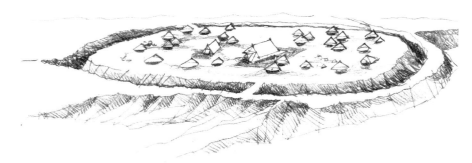

1.11 **Reconstruction of Banpo village, China**

In the valleys of the Yellow River we see the emergence of several compact villages, such as Banpo (near the modern-day city of Xi'an), which dates to about 4500 BCE and was part of the Yangshao Culture. It was surrounded by a ditch or moat 5 to 6 meters wide, probably for drainage and defense. The homes were circular structures of mud and wood with overhanging thatched roofs, all raised on shallow foundations with fire pits at the center. Entrance ramps sloped down into the dwelling. Such pit houses, with furs lying on the floors and hanging from the inner walls for insulation, were comfortable places to live. If the timber beams could be kept dry and the

thatch was properly maintained, a pit house could last twenty years. The dead were buried in the back of nearby sacred caves or in simple pits outside the village in a communal burial area. The remains of children, it seems, were interred in urns just outside their homes. Within the town there were large open plazas and storage holes, and at the center of the village was a large house, presumed a clan or community center, which was built of a heavy timber construction. One area of the village was dedicated to the production of pottery, indicating the emergence of craft specialization. Pottery was used not only in daily life but also in mortuary rituals.

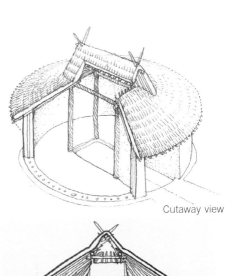

Cutaway view

Cross section

0   3 m

Plan

1.12 **Reconstruction of circular dwelling at Banpo**

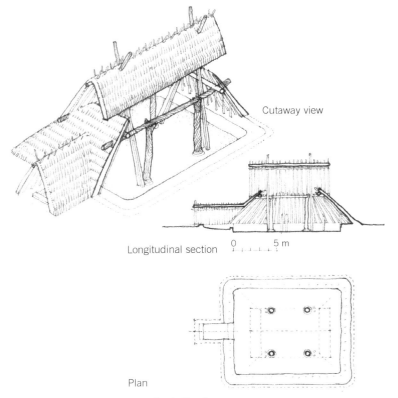

Cutaway view

Longitudinal section   0   5 m

Plan

1.13 **Reconstruction of meeting hall at Banpo**

In terms of religion, the Hongshan and Yangshao cultures were shamanistic. A shaman is an intermediary between the natural and the spiritual worlds who travels between these worlds in a trance. A tomb at Puyang, dating from about 4000 BCE, is likely that of a shaman priest. It was made in the shape of a single, squarish room with a lobed space at the rear. A man was buried in the pounded earth floor, flanked by a dragon on one side and a tiger on the other, both painstakingly and beautifully made of hundreds of shells. Dragons and tigers, still central to Chinese Confucian symbolism, are considered to be prospectors in both life and death. Hill ranges, especially those with prominent peaks, are considered to be dragons.

Along the Yangtze River, farmers had developed rice as their prime staple by around 5000 BCE, if not earlier. It was a labor-intensive crop that required level fields and the precise monitoring of water levels. The first culture to master rice farming was the Hemudu. Given the swampy nature of the land, the people at Hemudu built elevated houses that served for both living and storage. The houses were also ritual centers. This house type was introduced by rice growers to other parts of the world, most notably to Japan and the Philippines.

By the time of the Liangzhu Culture (3400–2250 BCE), located in the Yangtze River delta, we see the emergence of numerous small cities. Some, such as Shijiahe, had walls, others had none; some were regional centers with villages around them, others were more autonomous. A city near Yuhang, south of modern Shanghai, was quite large—3 million square meters. A roughly rectangular city, about 0.5 kilometers long, located a few kilometers east of the modern town of Pingyao, is believed to have been the capital of the kingdom. It had a fortification wall and a planned irrigation system.

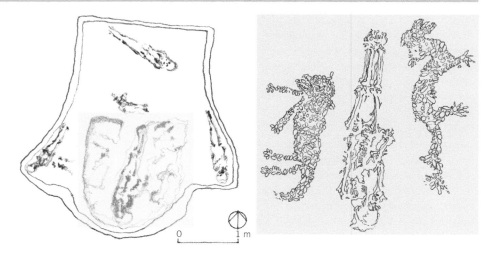

1.14 Dragon, human, and tiger figures found in tomb at Xisuipo, Henan Province, China

Rammed earth platforms on which palaces and temples were built were now a common feature of Chinese architecture. These platforms (known as *hang-t'u*) were created by pounding layers of 12 to 14 centimeters of earth onto each other with wooden or stone mallets, creating a very hard and long-lasting material. Since what was built on top was made of wood, nothing of this superstructure remains. A Liangzhu Culture ritual altar at Yaoshan, located to the west of Tai Lake, gives some indication of the religious edifices of the time. A ditch defines a sacred precinct extending over 25 meters square, at the center of which is a platform

measuring 6 by 7 meters constructed of rammed red earth, red being a particularly sacred color. Archaeologists found twelve graves, presumed to have belonged to priests, arranged in two rows within the platform. It is still unknown how this platform was used, though it most probably involved ancestor worship and ritual feast offerings. The use of jade for religious and devotional objects was by this time common to all of the Chinese cultures; the quality of Liangzhu jade was, however, quite remarkable. Though there were several sources, one was in the mountain deserts of modern-day Xinjiang Province in the northwest of China.

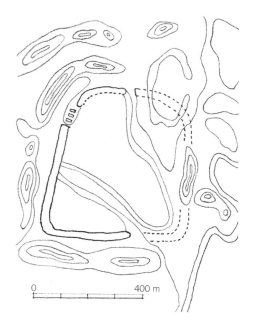

1.15 Walled city of Shijiahe, China

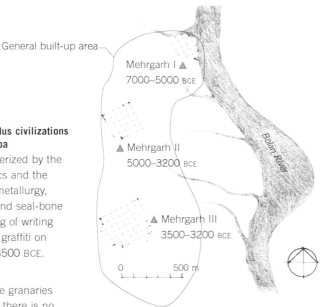

1.16 **Location of the Indus civilizations of Mehrgarh and Harappa**
This period is characterized by the elaboration of ceramics and the beginning of copper metallurgy, stone-bead making, and seal-bone carving. The beginning of writing is seen in the form of graffiti on pottery from around 3500 BCE.

1.17 **Site plan of Mehrgarh, Pakistan**

MEHRGARH AND EARLY INDUS SETTLEMENTS

Though evidence of the Neolithic occupation of India dates back to 10,000 BCE, settled cultures began to emerge around 7000 BCE, in the eastern hills of the Baluchistan Mountains in today's Pakistan. It was an agropastoral environment typical for the age, allowing farming along the slopes above the river, herding in the flat lands of the valley, and hunting in the hills and mountains. Around 6500 BCE, one community seemed to rise in importance and became the first in a long line of proto-urban environments that were soon to grow here. Known as Mehrgarh, it was strategically located overlooking the Kachi Plain southeast of modern Quetta near the Bolan Pass, an important gateway connecting South Asia to the rest of the continent. Its five-thousand-year history can be traced from a village to a regional trading center that covered, at the peak of its development, an area of 200 hectares.

By 3500 BCE, its occupants had mastered extensive grain cultivation. Dominating the urban landscape were mud-brick buildings presumed to be granaries, designed as multi-roomed rectangular structures with a long narrow corridor running more or less down the center. The absence of doors suggests that grain was fed from the top, as it would be into a silo.

Though the presence of these granaries connotes social organization, there is no evidence of dominant temples or ritual structures, nor are the granaries aligned with adjoining structures. And yet it is clear that the granaries were the center of social and ritual life. Outside one such granary, along its western wall, a large hearth has been found, complete with several hundred charred grains. Along the southern wall, archaeologists found the remains of the stone tools and drills of a steatite- or soapstone-cutter's workshop. On the eastern side, there were heaps of animal bones mixed with ashes, indicating the presence of intense butchering activity. Life, in other words, was organized around the sacred granaries. The granaries were also associated with mortuary practices: human bones, presumably those of priests, were found buried in its corridors and intermediary spaces. Archaeologists excavated about 360 such tombs, in which the dead, sometimes buried with tarred baskets, had funerary effects including skillfully crafted ornaments. These ornaments used materials brought from long distances, such as seashells, lapis lazuli, and turquoise.

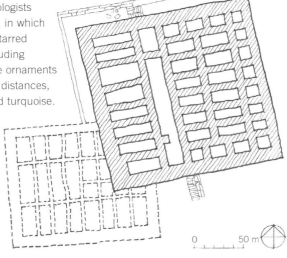

1.18 **Plan: Mud-brick granaries, Mehrgarh II**

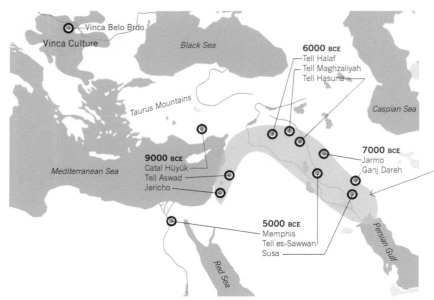

Vinca Belo Brdo
Vinca Culture
Black Sea
Taurus Mountains
Caspian Sea

6000 BCE
Tell Halaf
Tell Maghzaliyah
Tell Hasuna

7000 BCE
Jarmo
Ganj Dareh

9000 BCE
Catal Hüyük
Tell Aswad
Jericho

Mediterranean Sea

5000 BCE
Memphis
Tell es-Sawwan
Susa

Red Sea

Persian Gulf

Mesopotamia comes from the Greek words *mesos* and *potamas*, meaning "middle river," and refers to the fertile plain between the Tigris and Euphrates Rivers.

The Fertile Crescent is an agricultural region that runs along the foot of the Taurus and Zagros Mountains in a broad arc from the eastern shores of the Mediterranean to present-day Iraq.

1.19 Fertile Crescent: An early, dense network of cities and villages

THE VILLAGE NETWORKS OF MESOPOTAMIA AND THE BALKANS

The shift to village-world farming took place in the Levant around 9000 BCE. During a few centuries of cold weather, two plants in particular seemed to thrive, wheat and barley. The locals figured out how to tend these grasses into larger and larger patches. This, combined with the domestication of sheep and goats and the herding of cattle, produced a culture far different from that of their ancestors. Ritual practices changed, as did gender roles. Clan lineages became important, and with clans there emerged chieftains, who along with ritual specialists managed the complex sequence of activities. By 8000 BCE, a network of agropastoral villages had formed in the highlands of the Levant and from there spread eastward into the upland reaches above the Euphrates River and even northward into the Balkans.

Catal Hüyük

As village communities developed in the hills of the Levant and overlooking the Tigris and Euphrates Rivers, one commodity was sought after in particular: obsidian. This black volcanic rock with its sharp edges could be fashioned into small blades that were attached to sickles. The result was a much faster harvesting time. The problem was that obsidian was a rare commodity that came from the mountains in Anatolia.

A remarkable settlement developed as one of the main suppliers of obsidian. Known as Catal Hüyük, the city (near the modern city of Konya, Turkey) dates back as far as 7400 BCE; by the third millennium BCE it had a population of about eight thousand. The city was located in the center of a large, well-watered valley and next to a river that fed into a nearby lake. The lake and river have long since dried up. What has been recovered archaeologically is but a small part of the city that followed the slopes of the hill.

The city consisted of rectangular flat-roofed houses packed together into a single architectural mass with no streets or passageways. Astonishingly, walls made of mud bricks reinforced by massive oak posts were not shared, meaning that where we see a wall, we are really seeing two walls, one for each house. Why this developed has not been clearly answered. Inhabitants moved across rooftops and descended into their homes through the roofs via ladders. Light came through small windows high in the walls. If a family died out, its house was abandoned for a period of time, leaving gaps in the urban fabric, until eventually the space was reclaimed. The typical residence contained one large room connected to smaller storage rooms. The main room was

1.20 Typical Iranian mountain village

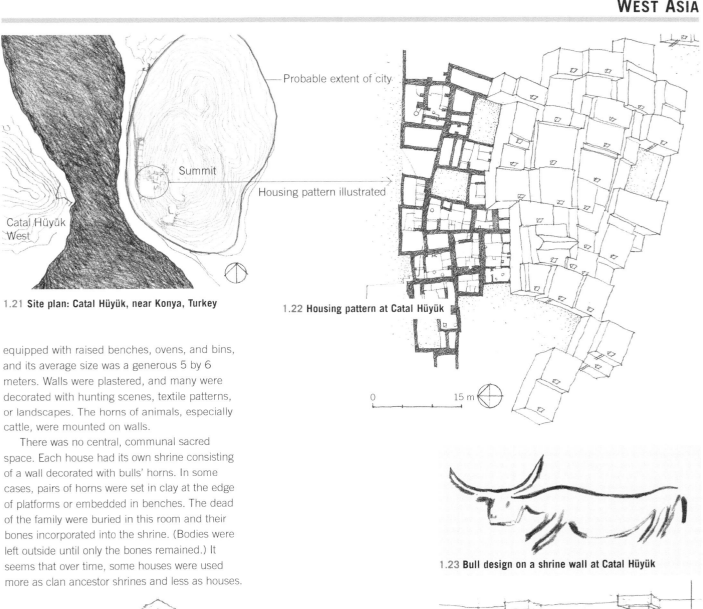

1.21 Site plan: Catal Hüyük, near Konya, Turkey

Catal Hüyük West

Summit

Probable extent of city

Housing pattern illustrated

1.22 Housing pattern at Catal Hüyük

0   15 m

equipped with raised benches, ovens, and bins, and its average size was a generous 5 by 6 meters. Walls were plastered, and many were decorated with hunting scenes, textile patterns, or landscapes. The horns of animals, especially cattle, were mounted on walls.

There was no central, communal sacred space. Each house had its own shrine consisting of a wall decorated with bulls' horns. In some cases, pairs of horns were set in clay at the edge of platforms or embedded in benches. The dead of the family were buried in this room and their bones incorporated into the shrine. (Bodies were left outside until only the bones remained.) It seems that over time, some houses were used more as clan ancestor shrines and less as houses.

1.23 Bull design on a shrine wall at Catal Hüyük

Ladder leads to roof opening, which served as the entrance to the house as well as a vent for smoke.

Sleeping platform

Oven

Open hearth

0   6 m

1.25 Typical house in Catal Hüyük

1.24 Reconstructed shrine at Catal Hüyük

1.26 Terra-cotta figurine of seated goddess from Catal Hüyük

The principal deity was the mother goddess. Figurine representations of her, made of a variety of materials, have been found throughout the village. One statue, remarkable for its bold three-dimensional design, is of a voluminous seated woman giving birth. The chair on which she sits has armrests in the shape of lions. The figurine represented fecundity and regeneration, and was part of the widespread mother-goddess worship typical of European and Mediterranean late Stone Age and early Bronze Age societies.

Catal Hüyük was at the northern end of a zone of developing urbanization that reached from Jericho (in Israel) to Tell Aswad (in Syria) and Susa (in Iran). Jericho was a major city—probably the largest in the whole area. Like Catal Hüyük, it had the benefit of local mines. Susa had the benefit of a well-established network of nearby villages in the Zagros Mountains, which constituted a close supply of metals. The Karun River, a river no less important than the Tigris and Euphrates, connected the city to the world at large; grains, figs, and lemons were raised in the river's broad valley.

Tell es-Sawwan

The climate in Mesopotamia back then was cooler than it is today, meaning that the verdant valleys of the Tigris and Euphrates Rivers were far different from the deserts found in the region today; in the highlands, forests were interspersed with steppes and savannas rich in flora and abounding with goats, boars, deer, and foxes. Farmers worked in the valley, but the community lived in the more easily fortifiable hills. Shepherds lived in the steppe regions between the farms and the deserts. In the areas around the Black Sea, one would have found a similar fabric of habitation, except there the locals discovered that their hills contained obsidian, copper, and salt, which became important commodities for trade. Around 5000 BCE the two worlds cohered into recognizable cultural formations: the Vinca in Romania and the Samarra in Iraq. A few places stood out, like Jericho (in Israel) and Tell Aswad (in Syria, 30 kilometers east-southeast of Damascus), which were larger than the rest. Also important was Catal Hüyük in Turkey, which was a key source of obsidian, a volcanic glass that was needed for sickle blades.

One of the most important groupings of villages dating from this period (6000–3500 BCE) was located just to the east of a rain-fed agricultural zone that arches northeastward from the northern tip of the Persian Gulf along the flanks of the Zagros Mountains. Among these settlements was Tell es-Sawwan, on the left bank of the Tigris near Samarra. It started as a small village that became fortified, growing over time into a substantial community. The plan shows a clear hierarchy, with the important buildings in the southern half. The central building is symmetrical and has a hall or corridor down the center; it was built at a later stage in the development of the village. Its purpose is unknown, but it was possibly a granary. There are about seven or eight houses that have nearby areas for sheep and goats. The basic building material was mud and timber; the mud was mixed with reeds and dried in a mold to create bricks, an innovation that remains a characteristic of the region even today. Rooms were rectilinear, measuring, on average, about 1.5 by 2 meters. The horizontal roofs were made of beams of oak on which were placed a layer of branches and reeds sealed with mud, bitumen, and gypsum. The interior wall surfaces were decorated with gypsum plaster, which had been developed as early as 7000 BCE and which was to remain a central part of building construction in the entire area. From the extensive outcrops of rock gypsum in northern Iraq and Syria, stone blocks were mined, stacked, and burnt to form an easily transportable white powder. This building material was not only used locally but also exported as a trade commodity. The development of trade in craft goods, pottery, building materials, and metal objects stimulated the economies of the region and played a central part in its drift toward craft specialization and urbanization. The Samarra Culture produced abundant grain, which was then exported to surrounding regions.

Though we often think of the Tigris and Euphrates region as the birthplace of urban civilization, the truth is that civilization—if that complex and awkward word can be used, at least in this area—was the product of a combined culture in which some people raised grain while others built mines. The oft repeated image of Mesopotamia as a "Fertile Crescent" is flawed if one does not add the Metal Crescent that embraced it. In Mesopotamia, grain and metal were mutually reinforcing commodities. The principal copper-producing areas stretched from the Caspian Sea through Anatolia and around the Black Sea.

An important early Copper Age society, known as the Vinca Culture, flourished from 5500 to 4000 BCE in an area that stretches from present-day Bosnia to Romania. Whereas the Mesopotamians developed mud-brick walls covered with plaster to protect the walls against moisture, the Vinca lived in freestanding rectangular houses with walls made of wattle and daub. The roofs were pitched and made of thatch. Their ritual world was intense. The Vinca had house shrines with an assortment of strangely carved deities that governed fertility and that spoke to the ancestors or gave omens.

1.27 **Vinca statuette**

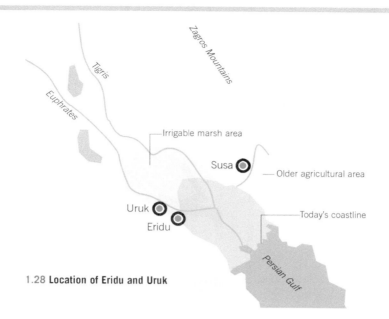

1.28 **Location of Eridu and Uruk**

The Taurus Mountains in eastern Anatolia, known for their tin mines, played an equally important part in the West Asian economy, since tin was needed, along with copper, to make bronze. Though there were many copper-producing areas, tin was more rare. An ancient tin mine was discovered at a site named Göltepe, which was a large village from around 3290 to 1840 BCE. The miners, using narrow shafts, brought cassiterite ore to the surface, where it was crushed, washed, and smelted with charcoal in small crucibles rather than in the large furnaces characteristic of copper-smelting sites. By measuring the enormous deposits of slag (600,000 tons in one pile), researchers have ascertained that this was a major site during much of the early and middle Bronze Age.

Metal began to play an important part in international relations in the third millennium BCE. Around 2350 BCE, Sargon of Akkad invaded Anatolia from his lowland base to secure trade routes. In records that have been found, he boasts that a single caravan carried about 12 tons of tin, which can make 125 tons of bronze—enough to equip a large army. Today it is widely accepted that mining was responsible for vast deforestation and played an important part in the desertification of western Asia.

Eridu and Uruk

With this in mind we can now better understand the rise of the first cities in the marshes of the Tigris and Euphrates areas. Though villages spanned the area from the Levant into northern Syrian and Iraq, few people ventured into these marshes, overgrown with tall reeds, useful for boats and thatching but little more. It was an extreme landscape that had no lumber for roof beams, and no metal or even stone. But around 5000 BCE we see the first attempts to transform this landscape. Societies gave up their partial dependency on an integrated farming-hunting lifestyle and concentrated on farming alone, the aim being to produce huge grain surpluses that would be traded for other things. These cities were not secular adventures. They were built at the command of the deities who in a sense sponsored these

surplus-making enterprises. In Mesopotamian mythology it was never the humans who created cities, but the gods themselves.

But back in the realm of the humans, the making of these places did go hand in hand with technical advances. The Tigris and Euphrates, unlike the Nile, flooded before the harvest, in April and May; this had made lower-lying reaches unusable for agriculture. But sedimentation brought by the rivers tended to build up natural levees that farmers could reinforce, allowing the canal bed to become somewhat higher than the surrounding countryside. Farmers could then make openings in the levees to feed water into the irrigation channels, as they still do today. Aerial photography has recently proven the extensive nature of these ancient canals and dikes, some of them more than 100 kilometers in length.

1.29 **Iraqi marsh**

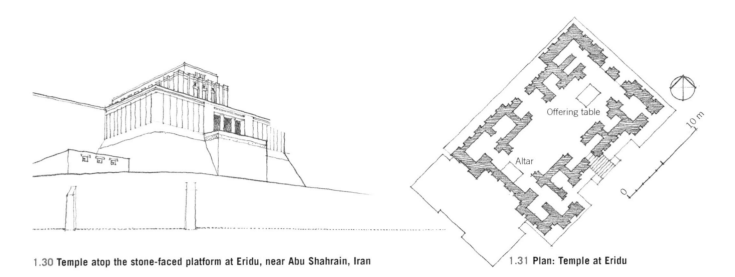

1.30 **Temple atop the stone-faced platform at Eridu, near Abu Shahrain, Iran**

1.31 **Plan: Temple at Eridu**

The relationship with the rivers was a delicate and dangerous one. The system was vulnerable to flood, war, and neglect. Records from Ur deal repeatedly with repair work. But the investment was worth the effort. In a few centuries the area became an economic engine unparalleled anywhere in the world except in Egypt. Though these cities are discussed in relationship to advances in agriculture, what we really see are cities serving by necessity as export and import centers.

Eridu and Uruk were, in a sense, *modern* cities dependent on a single economy of grain, requiring the control and movement of goods. It thus stands to reason that it was here that the wheel came into its full use to haul loads over long distances, and that standardized weights were invented at this time. Another innovation was one of the great civilizational achievements: writing, which was put to practical use to record trade transactions and keep up with inventory. Concomitant with this was the development of a legal and archival system. Evidence of the impact this made can be found in vestigial remnants of words deeply embedded in our present-day language. In Ur, the ancient title designating "king" is *lugal*, which is probably the origin of the Latin word *lex* ("law") and the English word *legal*. And another ancient Mesopotamian word, *pala*, referring to the garment of kingship, constitutes the root of our word *palace*.

We see the emergence of a complex religious world in tune with the equally complex life of urban civilization. The mother goddess, who had ruled in many places throughout Eurasia, now had to compete with an expanding list of divine presences—including powerful male gods who tied society firmly into a network of obligations. Significantly, the mother goddess Apsu, who controlled the oceans, was "killed" by her son Ea, earth, who divided her unruly waters into chambers. Concurrent with the shift was the emergence of a priestly class responsible for all aspects of society, from religion to administration to technology. The priestly class was responsible not only for the proper communication with the deities through food sacrifices and ritual events, but were also the architects of increasingly larger buildings to stage their power.

The culture that first began to master the Tigris and Euphrates Rivers as early as 5000 BCE was known as the Ubaid. Around 3000 BCE, they were superseded by the Sumerians, who were to no small degree the first modernizers, replacing old and well-established traditions with new and better-organized ones. Eridu was located on the banks of the Euphrates in the delta, which has since silted up so that the ancient site is now located 90 kilometers inland. Originally, however, Eridu had easy access to boats coming up from the south.

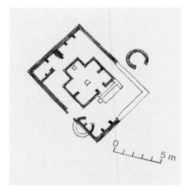

1.32 **Temple XVI–XVIII at Eridu**

The temple at Eridu was rebuilt seventeen times (4500–3800 BCE), with each effort built directly over the earlier one, and with each one being bigger and taller, resulting in a massive building, a veritable mountain of bricks. The earliest temple was a simple box with an altar at the back and an oven outside in the front, where sacred bread offerings were prepared. The last temple, positioned on an enormous plinth of clay bricks, was painted in vibrant colors and was visible for miles. It had a form defined by rhythmically spaced buttresses, and though roughly rectangular in shape, it had an irregular perimeter. A flight of steps at the center of the broader side led up to the entrance, where a shallow vestibule gave access to a large central room oriented lengthwise. Ancillary spaces, probably used as reliquaries, were located at the corners.

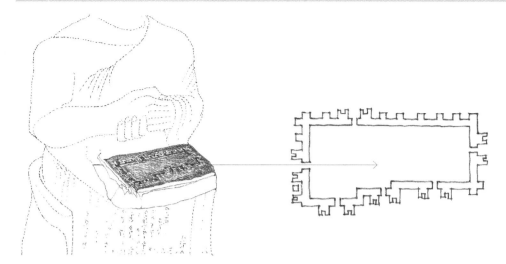

1.33 Statue of King Gudea at Eridu, with a temple plan carved on a lap tablet

The chief deity was Ea, son of the mother goddess Apsu; he was not only an earth god but also manifest in "sweet waters." He was seen as crafty, for he "avoids rather than surmounts obstacles, goes round and yet gets to his goal." Ea, who in some accounts made human beings by mixing his own essence with that of his brother, Enlil (the earth and storm god), was also worshipped as the god of wisdom and as a friend to humankind. Images of Ea show him wearing a cloak of fish scales, and fish bones have been discovered near the offering table at Eridu. A text written somewhat later states that

> When Ea rose, the fishes rose and adored him,
>
> He stood, a marvel unto the deep…
> To the sea it seemed that awe was upon him;
> To the Great River terror seemed to hover around him
> While the south wind stirred the depth of the Euphrates.*

*Thorkild Jacobsen, "Sumerian Mythology, a Review Article," *Journal of Near Eastern Studies 5* (1946): 140.

The Temple at Eridu served as a prototype for later efforts: a statue made about a thousand years later, in 2150 BCE, shows the plan of a temple with similar attributes. It is no sketch, but a precise plan with door and pilasters drawn in, all to scale. It is placed on the lap of King Gudea of Lagash and, in its accuracy and precision, leaves no doubt as to the planning that went into these early temple designs. Its position on the king's lap also proves that the plan was more than just a convenience of the builders: it was an expression of the claim to legitimacy of the monarch and his sacrosanct function.

Uruk developed into a significant, large city with a possible population of fifty thousand. It was dedicated to the god Anu, a sky god, an important and newly emerging deity linked to the number one, and thus to mathematics and trade. His temple, the so-called White Temple, begun around 4000 BCE and expanded over the next centuries, rested on a broad terrace on top of a tall artificial hill, irregular in outline and rising 13 meters above the plain, with its vast expanse of fields and marshes. Access was by a stairway on the northeastern face.

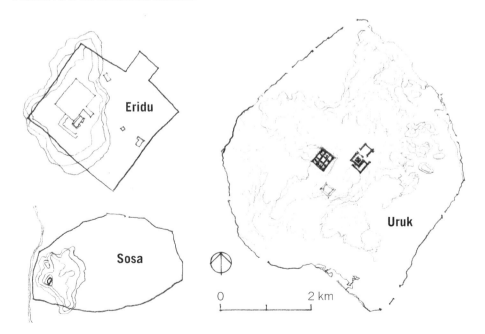

1.34 A size comparison of Eridu, Susa, and Uruk

1.35 Mosaics from the Stone-Cone Temple in the Eanna District of Uruk, near Samawa, Iraq

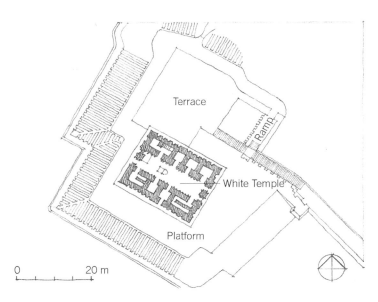

1.36 Plan: White Temple at Uruk

The White Temple's overall shape was simpler than that of the Temple at Eridu, but as at Eridu, one passed through a shallow vestibule into a great hall. In the White Temple, however, there was in one corner a platform or altar with a flight of narrow steps leading up to it. Toward the middle of the space was an offering table with a low semicircular hearth built up against it. To the west of the building there was another temple built out of stone that had been imported from the mountains to the west. Its purpose and the reason for its peculiar plan are not known.

During this time, Mesopotamian builders discovered how to use the kiln to harden bricks, roof tiles, and drainage tubes. The Mesopotamians may have acquired this skill on their own but more likely learned it from the Indus Valley civilization, with which they most certainly were in contact and which had developed brick very early on. As wood for kilns was scarce in the Mesopotamian marshes, bricks were a luxury item and were mainly used for palaces, temples, and gates; the Gate of Ishtar at Babylon is the most famous. The kilns devoured enormous amounts of wood, depleting wood resources and contributing, it is now thought, to the growth of the desert that is today pervasive in these parts. The use of brick in building foundations in Uruk indicated a building's status. The brick city wall was seen even by Mesopotamians as one of Uruk's wondrous aspects. Near the beginning of the epic of Gilgamesh, composed in the later third millennium BCE, we read:

Look at its wall which gleams like copper,
inspect its inner wall, the likes of which no one can equal!
Take hold of the threshold stone—it dates from ancient times!
Go close to the Eanna Temple, the residence of Ishtar,
such as no later king or man ever equaled!
Go up on the wall of Uruk and walk around,
examine its foundation, inspect its brickwork thoroughly.
Is not (even the core of) the brick structure made of kiln-fired brick,
and did not the Seven Sages themselves lay out its plans?*

*Maureen Gallery Kovacs, trans., *The Epic of Gilgamesh* (Stanford, CA: Stanford University Press, 1985), 3.

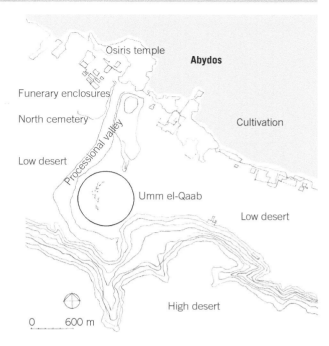

1.37 Early dynastic Egypt

1.38 Site of royal tombs at Umm el-Qaab, Abydos, Egypt

PRE- AND EARLY DYNASTIC EGYPT

North Africa was once a vast, fertile savanna of scrub forests and pasturelands that was populated by humans early on. It was here, as we have seen at Nabta Playa, that cattle were first domesticated. But in the sixth millennium BCE, a dramatic warming affecting the whole globe changed North Africa bit by bit into the endless stretches of sand that we now call the Sahara Desert. The populations moved either westward to Morocco, Spain, and beyond, or eastward to the banks of the Nile. The density of the Nile River population was unlike anything one would have seen anywhere else in the world at that time; that it did not overwhelm the social system was predicated on several conditions, one being that the local elites quickly learned to define themselves as divine, assuring the mechanism by which to protect and isolate their power. This meant that Egyptian religion never went through a chthonic phase based on the mother goddesses and caves that were common in many places in Eurasia and the Mediterranean and that would thrive in places like Crete and Malta for a long time. Egyptian religion was from the start a religion for the elite alone. There were no epic tales of communal destiny, but rather myths of heroic actions of kings who passed the torch

of succession to the next generation. This explains why a complex pantheon of gods, stretching from the bovine Hathor to the more abstract Ptah and Amun, could develop so quickly. It was only during the New Kingdom (1540–1069 BCE) that the features of this religion began to have a broader role in society.

Another factor that stabilized Egypt's existing social order was that the Nile flooded after the harvest in the middle of October; more people working the fields therefore resulted in the production of more food. But in contrast to the celebration of water and food, there was, for the Egyptians, the fearsome entombing power of the earth. Life and death, the river, and the mountains of sand became intimately and naturally connected to each other around the all-encompassing mythology of divine rulership.

The tombs of the First Dynasty (3100–2890 BCE) are located at Abydos, an important early city about 100 kilometers downstream from Thebes. The tombs are outside of town under the face of an imposing cliff. A gorge opens out dramatically through the cliff at that spot and, according to some scholars, this opening was regarded as the entrance to the netherworld. The site was accessed by a processional route from a

valley temple. The oldest tombs, of Narmer and Aha, are rather simple brick-lined rooms placed in the ground and covered with a wooden roof at ground level. Aha's tomb consisted of three chambers stockpiled with provisions for a lavish life in eternity. There were most likely large cuts of ox meat, as well as freshly killed waterbirds, loaves of bread, dried figs, and jars of beer or wine, each bearing Aha's official seal. Beside his tomb more than thirty ancillary graves for servants and animals were laid out in three neat rows. The tomb of Queen Merneith (ca. 2900 BCE), is, like its predecessors, largely sunken underground, except that now the storage rooms are part of the main structure, in the form of long, thin rooms.

The ancillary tombs are also integrated into the design as a type of frame set at a respectful distance from the tomb chambers. This framing is open on its southwestern side, presumably so that the spirit of the dead can exit through the gap toward the gorge. The tomb of the next ruler, Den, makes this connection to the cliff even more explicit. Though the main entrance is from the east, there is a special chamber next to the tomb with a separate staircase leading back up to the surface and to the west.

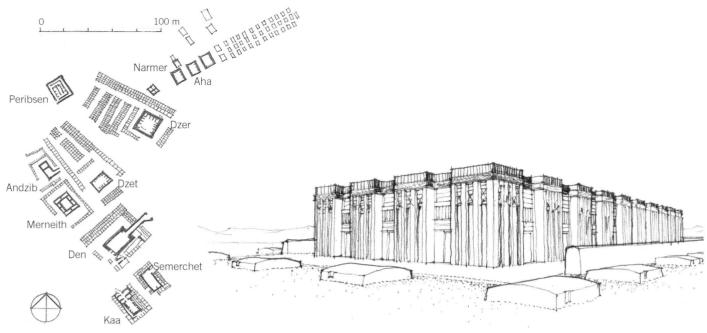

1.39 Royal tombs at Umm el-Qaab

1.40 Tomb of King Djed at Saqqâra

The design and the decoration of these tombs clearly anticipates the development of the mastaba (from the Arabic word for "bank"). The grandest was the tomb of King Djed at Saqqâra (ca. 3100 BCE), just outside of Memphis. Some argue that the complex niche pattern in the walls represented wooden or reed construction; others have suggested an influence from Mesopotamia or the Near East. Only the five central chambers, dug into the earth, constitute the tomb. The whole was roofed over and plastered to appear as a solid but colorful plateau set against the sand. There was a low bench surrounding the superstructure at the base of the main exterior wall; on this platform were laid about three hundred clay-modeled bull's heads provided with real horns. The facade was was painted white, whereas the innermost panels of the large niches were painted red.

In this early stage of Egyptian culture, there was no temple architecture such as one might find in the Mesopotamian cities, where religious practices, highly visible around the ziggurat temples, unified broad swaths of society. Instead, architecture, defining the interface between life and death, was reserved for the elite. Its place

in society was thus more limited, but its purpose could not have been more dramatic. Death for the Chinese involved the handing down of family memories and could be articulated spatially with house shrines and fragile wooden temples on earthen mounds. In Egypt, death—in religious terms—was a dramatic event only for the ruler, with his (or sometimes her) spirit rising majestically over the trivialities of domesticity and family in a specially constructed, simulated house with all the accoutrements of a comfortable life. What went on in that "house," and how the

spirit moved about, ate, and drank, was a matter of great concern, since it was thought to determine the flow of history in the present time and beyond. But the "house" was only half of the equation. Death in Egypt had an inside and an outside shape. Entombing the "house" at the scale of the landscape was the structure's outside shape. Eighty percent of King Djed's mastaba was nothing more than a mass of walls and spaces linking these two scales. The architect's job, in essence, was to bring the inner and outer manifestations of the ruler's death into unity.

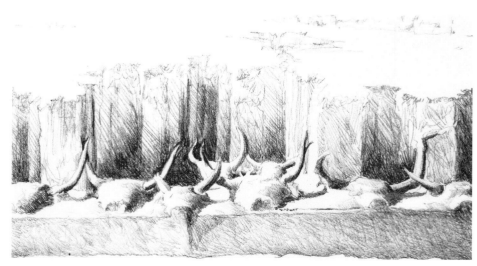

1.41 Bull horns at the base of Tomb 3504, Saqqara, Egypt

1.42 **Megalithic cultures, 4800–1200 BCE**

EUROPEAN DEVELOPMENTS

Europe's complex geography of shorelines, rivers, and mountain ranges made it unlikely that it would arrange itself into a single civilizational unit like those in Egypt, China, and India. Furthermore, because of the difficulties of transplanting grain northward into different climatic regions, Europe was only fully settled around 3500 BCE. Because European cultures developed without the history of agricultural domestication, their focus was not on family matriarchal histories through which such knowledge was, by necessity, handed down, but on the clans that could pull communities together for defense, war, and trade. This explains why

the Europeans did not develop a temple culture or, for that matter, a more complex priestly culture until much later.

But unlike in Mesopotamia, where death was still a relatively informal affair, or in Egypt, where death-as-eternal-life was in essence reserved for the elites, the Europeans magnified death around clan lineages, building a variety of stone and mound structures in places that preserved clan memories and that served as places for ceremony, gathering, and trade. Barrow tombs or passage graves, for example, consisted of a passageway made of large

stones, sometimes ornamented with carvings and paint and mounded over by tons of dirt and clay. Examples can be found throughout Europe—in Portugal, Sardinia, France, and England, and as far north as Norway—as well as in Morocco, and span the period from 5000 BCE to 2500 BCE. The Portuguese tombs are among the oldest. The ceilings of some of the central chambers were corbelled with stones placed closer and closer toward the center of the space till they meet at the top. An example of this can be found in the passage grave on Île Longue, South Brittany, France.

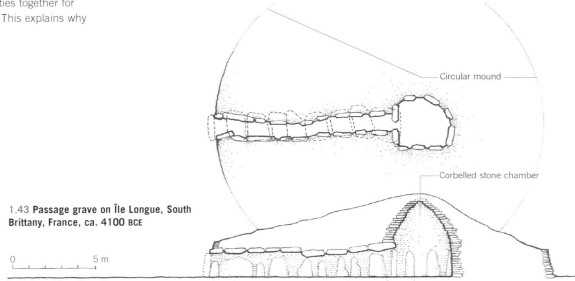

1.43 **Passage grave on Île Longue, South Brittany, France, ca. 4100 BCE**

0   5 m

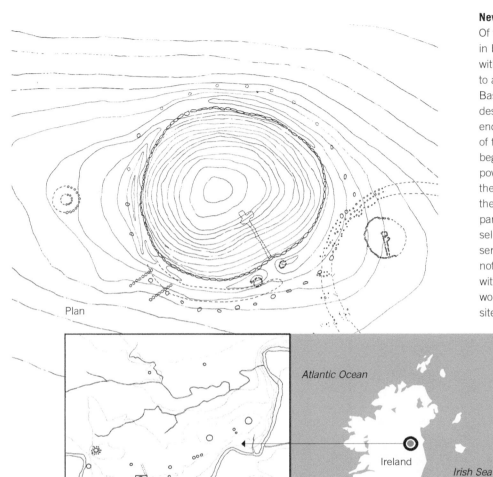

Plan

Newgrange

Of the various constructions that were made in Europe at the time, few could compete with the great mound of Newgrange, dating to about 4000 BCE. But this was no tomb. Basically it was a clock with one tick, designed to mark the winter solstice at the end of December, indicating the passage of the season and the promise of a new beginning, while also serving as a particularly powerful moment to access the spirit of the ancestors. Thousands of people from the various clans congregated at the site to participate in dances, revelry, the buying and selling of cattle, and, above all, memorial services for the deceased. The structure was not isolated but set in a sacred landscape with various mounds in the vicinity, and would be used for centuries to come. It was sited on the western slope of the river Boyne.

Atlantic Ocean

Ireland

Irish Sea

Site plan

1.44 Newgrange, Ireland
Source: Timothy Cooke, Geraldine Stout, and Matthew Stout, *Newgrange* (Cork: Cork University Press, 2008), 46.

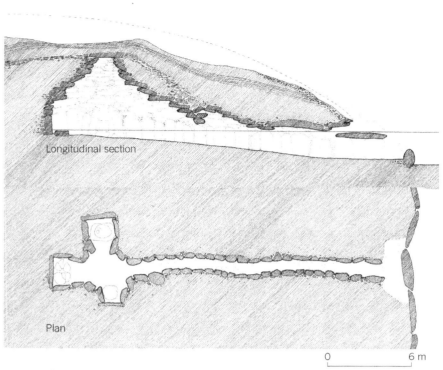

Longitudinal section

Plan

Cross section

0   6 m

Detail of Entrance Stone

1.45 Newgrange, Ireland

Source: Timothy Cooke, Geraldine Stout, and Matthew Stout, *Newgrange* (Cork: Cork University Press, 2008), 46.

The large mound is approximately 80 meters in diameter and is surrounded at its base by a kerb of 97 stones. The most impressive of these stones is the highly decorated Entrance Stone. The mound's entrance leads to a 19-meter-long passage constructed of large stones leading to a small, cross-shaped chamber. A corbelled roof covers the chamber. The massive stone structure was mounded over with tons of clay. The side of the mound near the entrance was covered with white quartz stones. It seems that people brought the stones from quartz veins in the hills some 160 kilometers to the south and threw the stones onto the mound as a ritual act. Sadly, the modern reconstruction placed the stones along a concrete wall, thus giving a false impression of a wall. At dawn on the winter solstice, a shaft of sunlight enters the inner chamber through a concealed opening in the roof of the entrance corridor. It is a remarkable piece of engineering that served as a powerful symbol of the inevitable victory of life over death, perhaps promising new life to the spirits of the dead.

Carnac

Carnac, named after a nearby French village, consists of a set of various alignments of more than 3,000 standing stones. What prompted people to drag multi-ton stones from miles away to this site? Did it have celestial purposes? Quite likely, but no one knows for sure. It could also be that clans brought their stones as a type of spiritual labor in memory of ancestors. At any rate, the site consists of different alignments, including the Ménec alignments (eleven converging rows of stones stretching for 1,165 by 100 meters), the Kerlescan alignments (a smaller group of 555 stones, further to the east), and the Petit-Ménec alignments (a much smaller group, further east again of Kerlescan). There are also several dolmens scattered around the area. A dolmen is a tomb monument composed of a set of vertical stones surmounted with a horizontally placed stone. Dolmens are generally considered to have been tombs; however, the acidic soil of Brittany has eroded away the bones. Some dolmens were buried under a mound of earth, but others were left without a mound. The Crucuno Dolmen is crowned by a massive, multi-ton capstone.

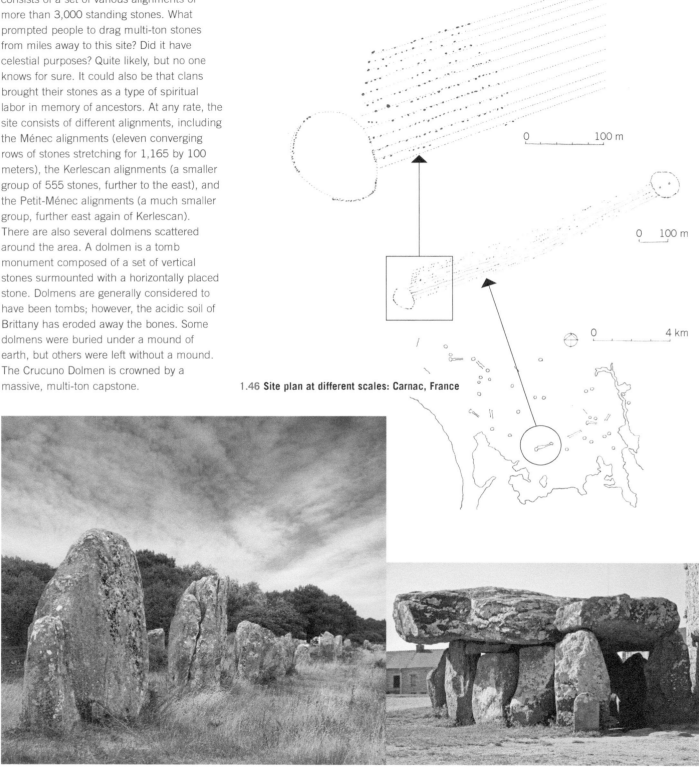

1.46 Site plan at different scales: Carnac, France

1.47 Stone alignment, Carnac, France

1.48 Crucuno Dolmen, Carnac, France

2500 BCE

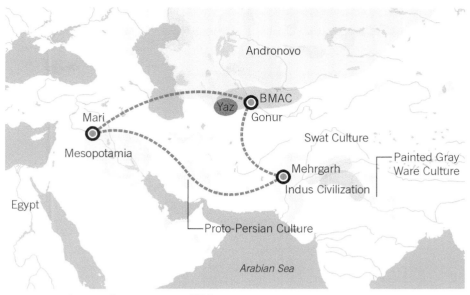

2.1 **Central Asia, emerging contacts, ca. 2500 BCE**

INTRODUCTION

By the beginning of the third millennium BCE, the various river-oriented civilizations were primed for rapid cultural development. There were at the time six principal cultural hubs: Egypt, Mesopotamia, Margiana, the Indus, China, and Europe. In all these places, elites emerged who ruled not just by force, but with some form of divine or ancestral blessing. Generally speaking, when things went well, this was attributed to the gods; when things went badly, this was seen as a sign of divine displeasure.

Mesopotamian cities were the most unusual since they were created in the context of an extreme landscape of marshes that were converted into agricultural land. The first Mesopotamian cities can be considered risk societies, based on the gamble that producing huge surpluses of grain would allow them to trade for commodities that were not readily available. The cities thus became ritual centers in their own right, where the relationship to the sacred was organized and mastered with calendric precision. The elites who governed the city were devotees of a complex pantheon of gods who in turn "governed" all aspects of nature, even human. The elites operated in close alliance with a priestly class for whom huge temples were built in the form of artificial mountains rising in colorful terraces. The ziggurats at Eridu and Ur were by far the most extensive buildings of the age,

testament to the wealth flowing to the cities. They were prestige buildings, made just as much by "deities" as by human labor. The cities that were built around them consisted of a dense fabric of houses. Most buildings were made of mud brick with wooden roofs. Outside the walls, along the canals, one would have found a vast network of small villages that were controlled by the temple. But these cities had limits on how far their authority could reach, and so they existed in tense alliances with similar cities up and down the river.

Egypt, less prone to invasion, developed a clear dynastic power structure and a consistent set of religious traditions from an early age. Furthermore, due to the seasonality of local agriculture, farm workers could be summoned by the pharaohs to perform forced labor on building projects. Zoser's mortuary temple, built on an unprecedented scale, was one of the first monumental stone buildings in the world. The mastery of stone masonry is one of Egypt's great contributions to architecture. The expansive mortuary complex answered to the intricate cosmology used by its Egyptian elites. The building was made for a dead pharaoh who was deemed to be still "alive" and thus in need of the illusion of rulership in perpetuity. His spirit was embodied in a statue, called the Ka statue, which was ritually fed and housed in a special chamber so that he could see the western sunset through a small hole.

Meanwhile, around 2500 BCE, people moved down from the Baluchistan Hills and settled in the river valleys that define the eastern edge of the South Asian subcontinent—those of the Indus and the now dried-up Ghaggar-Hakra Rivers. The Indus/Ghaggar-Hakra region was the first urban civilization in the true sense of the word. The reason for its success is obvious. The 900-kilometer-long valley is hemmed in to the north and south by vast stretches of dry and rainless mountains and deserts. One can imagine it as a linear oasis. Irrigation here was easier than in Mesopotamia, and the plentiful supply of trees allowed for the early development of fired bricks that withstood the ravages of water better than mud brick. More than a thousand cities and towns have been discovered spread over 650,000 square kilometers, an area roughly equivalent to that of modern-day France. Though these cities were distant from each other, they shared a common language and a standardized system of weights and measures. Thousands of terra-cotta seals depicting a wide range of human, animal, and mythical forms have been found, each with distinctive markings that are presumably letters of an alphabet. The inhabitants, about whom we still know very little, seemed to have called themselves something akin to Meluhha. That, at least, is what the contemporaneous Mesopotamians called them. Ships carried bricks, beads, lumber, metals, and lapis lazuli up the Persian Gulf to the cities of Mesopotamia, where such items were scarce. The nature of the return freight is uncertain, since few Mesopotamian objects have been found at the Indus. The area between Mesopotamia and the Indus was also urbanized with cities such as Tepe Yaha and Jiroft, in the once fertile and expansive Soghun Valley. Tepe Yaha specialized in mining a highly desired stone used to make ritual bowls. Not far away was Jiroft, an even larger city, which specialized in the production of highly prized, golden-flecked lapis lazuli.

This Zone of Interconnection was linked to a fourth civilizational area that had been developing around the Oxus River and was known as the Adronovo Culture. It was based at first around small villages, but two large cities were eventually built (in today's Turkmenistan and Uzbekistan) that were not only of great size but were designed with great geometrical precision. The area, drawing on the steppe landscape of inner Asia, was a center of extensive pastoral communities.

In China the first recorded dynasty, the Xia dynasty, emerged around 2100 BCE. We find there a horizontal civilization of villages and towns unified around palace centers. One of these was Erlitou (1900–1500 BCE). Lying on the Yi River, a tributary of the Luo River, Erlitou was located at the foothills of the mountains and served as an interface zone between the mountain area rich in ore and the plains rich in grain. The palace complex was surrounded by a 2-meter-thick rammed earth wall that set it apart as an ancestral ceremonial center for the elites. The elites made extensive rituals that required vessels and other instruments. This meant that craftspeople lived near the palaces. In this way, cities emerged not as temple economies as in Mesopotamia, but as a consequence of palace economies. In both cases, small elites ruled over large swaths of population because of their association with the gods and ancestral deities. But whereas in Mesopotamia important ritual events were something on the order of public spectacles, in China such rituals garnered esteem because they were highly private.

Meanwhile, Europe, between about 5000 and 3500 BCE, had slowly transformed into an agropastoral world of interconnected villages. Large polities never developed, meaning that there was no centralization of power and nothing that could be called cities. It was a world still governed by sacred landscapes and ancestor rituals. The most famous sites are Carnac in France, Stonehenge in England, and Newgrange in Ireland. But there were hundreds of lesser sites, from Scotland south to Portugal. Around 2800 BCE commenced the spread of the Beaker People, whose origins are still debated but who most likely came from the Balkans. They are named after their culture's distinctive pottery drinking vessels. Known for

their advanced metalworking skill, the Beaker People left their traces in various locations. They arrived in England, where they encountered such sites as Stonehenge, which they took over and redesigned, orienting it to the sun rather than to the moon. While physically this was largely a matter of fine-tuning, the cultural implications this reorientation presupposes are imponderable. Stonehenge, since 3000 BCE, when the first stone circle was built, became a huge ceremonial zone attracting people from far afield. There they awaited the sacred moment of winter solstice, when contact with ancestors was most propitious. Far to the south, on the island of Malta in the Mediterranean, emerged an astonishing culture that built large "caves" mounded over with tons of earth. The small island eventually had a dozen or so of these structures, probably used as places where supplicants, under the spell of singing and hallucinogenic drugs, would experience dream visions. Since there were many more of these temples than the local population could possibly need, it is quite likely that this was a sacred landscape that also served people from surrounding Mediterranean communities, who would arrive by boat. Stonehenge and Malta represent the last such sacred landscapes. In other places, the ritual world was being pulled increasingly toward the city. In fact, the great accomplishment of the Mesopotamian cultures was precisely to equate city with ritual center.

Apart from an agropastoral zone that stretched west to east just below the Sahara Desert, the rest of Africa was still First Society, as was all of the Americas. But the Americas should not be written off as a "hunter-gatherer" world. Many communities had developed into affluent societies. The Northwest Coast peoples in Canada, for example, thrived from about 3000 BCE until the arrival of the Europeans in the 19th century, one of the most enduring First Society cultures in the Americas. Another site of importance was in the area to the north of the Mississippi River delta. The yearly flooding of the river allowed large annual ceremonies to take place on a bluff overlooking the river, called Poverty Point, where a massive artificial mound, seemingly in the shape of a bird, was built. It seems that

2.2 **Zoser Pyramid, Saqqâra, Egypt**

different tribes helped build the mound with clay brought to the site in basketfuls from their home areas. To the east of the great mound there was a 300-meter-wide dance area surrounded by raised ridges on which temporary huts were erected. Communal construction of such large ceremonial sites became an important aspect of what is now called the Mississippi Culture, which lasted into the 16th century.

In Peru, we see a remarkable transformation. Intrepid farmers left their hillside terraces on the Andean mountain slopes for the arid valleys along the Pacific Coast. The intent was purposeful. The newly arriving farmers channeled the river waters to grow cotton for the making of fishing nets, and gourds to be used as floats. But they were not fishermen. The fishermen lived on the coast, and they traded with the newly arriving agriculturalists in a way that was mutually beneficial. It was a novel and extraordinary arrangement that first took place at what is now called Caral, about 200 kilometers north of Lima.

The Zoser Mortuary Complex and the temples of Malta bring to the fore a way of understanding the originating power of architecture—as models. Today we tend to think of models simply as practical devices used in the preparation of a design. Yet the history of architecture is filled with structures that serve as built models. The Zoser Mortuary Complex is entered through a portal that leads past a corridor of columns painted to look like gigantic reeds. The visitor literally passed through a scaled-up model of the swampy shores of the Nile, symbolizing not just the transition between life and renewal but also the difference between the human and divine scales. Egyptians continued to build such scaled-up models; their columns are all large models of flower bundles, richly painted and even emitting, in principle at

least, a divine fragrance. Architecture as model is even more obvious in Malta, where the temples are models of caves, purposely dark and mysterious. The Maltese also made some of the earliest known representations of buildings in history. The purpose of these small models, no more than a few centimeters across, is unknown, but it has been suggested that they served as tokens given to devotees after a visit. They were more than trinkets; they were living pieces of the temple, which in turn was itself a living entity; thus, a model was a sure way to link its owner to the life force of the temple. The use of architecture as model remained a key element of its core purpose. Even the stepped structures of Caral are models of sacred mountains, created to charge up or enhance the potency of the landscape.

2.3 **Mnajdra Temple, Malta**

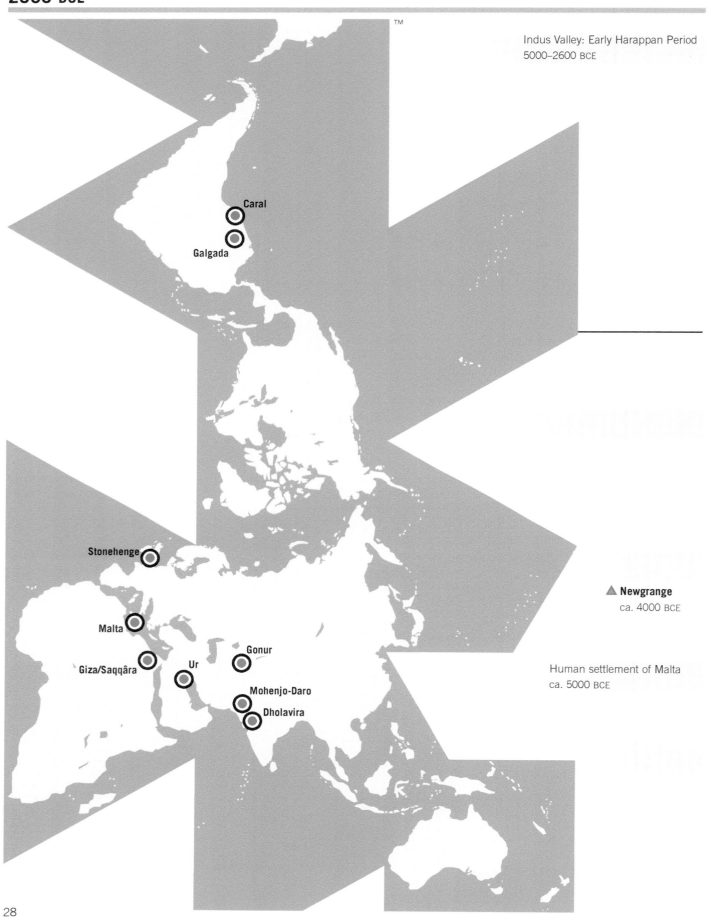

Indus Valley: Early Harappan Period
5000–2600 BCE

Caral

Galgada

Stonehenge

▲ **Newgrange**
ca. 4000 BCE

Malta

Gonur

Giza/Saqqâra

Ur

Human settlement of Malta
ca. 5000 BCE

Mohenjo-Daro

Dholavira

Ghaggar-Hakra Civilization
7000–1800 BCE
Mohenjo-Daro ▲ ▲ **Dholavira**
ca. 2600 BCE   ca. 2650–2100 BCE
▲ **Lothal**
ca. 2400–1900 BCE

Margiana and Andronovo Culture
ca. 2500–1400 BCE
▲ **Gonur**   ▲ **Arkaim**
ca. 2500–1700 BCE   ca. 1700 BCE

Mesopotamia: Early Dynastic Period
ca. 2900–2350 BCE
▲ **Temple at Uruk**
ca. 3400 BCE

Akkadian Dynasty
ca. 2350–2150 BCE
▲ **Akkad**   ▲ **Ziggurat at Ur**
ca. 2300 BCE   ca. 2100 BCE
Palace of Naram-Sin ▲ ▲ **Mari**
ca. 2170 BCE   ca. 2200–1800 BCE

3500 BCE   **2500 BCE**   **1500 BCE**

Early Bronze Age
ca. 3000–2000 BCE

Egypt: Pre-Dynastic Period
ca. 4500–3100 BCE

Old Kingdom
ca. 2649–2150 BCE

Middle Kingdom
ca. 2030–1640 BCE

▲ **Step Pyramid of Zoser**
ca. 2650 BCE
▲ **Bent Pyramid**
ca. 2600 BCE
▲ **Great Pyramid of Khufu**
ca. 2580 BCE

Brittany and British Isles: Megalithic building cultures
ca. 4200–2000 BCE

Beaker Culture
ca. 2800–1800 BCE

▲ **Stonehenge**
Begun ca. 3000 BCE

◉ Sarsen Ring added at Stonehenge
ca. 2500 BCE

◉ Bluestone circle added at Stonehenge
ca. 2300 BCE

Building of megalithic temples
ca. 3600–2500 BCE
▲ **Ggantija Temple**   ▲ **Tarxien Temple**
ca. 3600 BCE   ca. 3100 BCE

North and Central Andes: Early Ceramic Cultures
ca. 4000–1800 BCE
▲ **La Galgada**   ▲ **Caral (Supe Valley)**   ▲ **El Paraiso**
ca. 3000–1500 BCE   ca. 2600–2200 BCE   ca. 1800 BCE

◉ 3100 BCE
Mythic base date of the Maya long-count calendar

Mississippi Culture
ca. 3500 BCE–1500 CE

THE INDUS GHAGGAR-HAKRA CIVILIZATION

The Indus Ghaggar-Hakra civilization went through roughly four phases of development:

1. The urbanization of the Ghaggar-Hakra River valley, ca. 2800 BCE
2. The rising dominance of four cities—Harappa, Mohenjo-Daro, Rakhigarhi, and Ganweriwala—ca. 2500 BCE
3. The new urbanization of areas south and east, ca. 2200 BCE
4. The post-decline reurbanization of the Ghaggar-Hakra River, ca. 1700 BCE

The period around 2500 BCE was generally one of expansion and prosperity throughout West Asia and the Indus. Certainly the cities along the Ghaggar-Hakra River were being enlarged, and their builders became world masters of hydrology. Burnt bricks were used to construct huge platforms that served as the bases for the cities and for defensive walls, but also to control floodwaters. And most important, elaborate interconnected drainage systems were designed to disperse storm waters. A central drain under the main gate of Harappa still stands in place. Nonetheless, the Indus flooded many times, each flood burying the city under a thick layer of silt. Harappa was rebuilt at the same spot at least eight times. It is thought to have had a population of about fifty thousand.

There were also specialized cities, such as a port and mining towns. Dholavira had to solve a hydroengineering problem opposite of Harappa's: Because the city sits in a very dry area, the issue was not keeping floodwater out, but ensuring that enough water could be harvested for the dry season. The solution was a series of strategically located dams that controlled water during a flood and also directed some of the water to huge, rectangular, shallow man-made lakes that surrounded the city and that could be tapped in summer. In Lothal, a port city, water was let through a sluice into a vast rectangular tank that some speculate functioned as a dry dock for seafaring vessels.

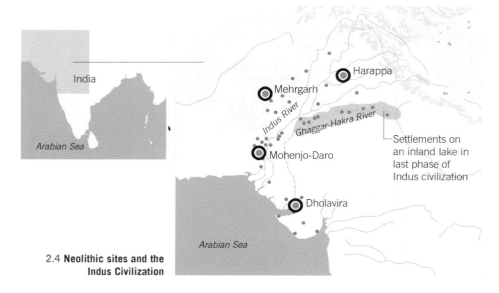

2.4 Neolithic sites and the Indus Civilization

The largest cities were divided into an upper town, which was on the highest ground and had large palaces and ceremonial spaces, and a lower town, which had most of the housing. The upper town usually had its own wall within the general wall that surrounded the whole city. At Dholavira the boundary wall was over 9 meters thick. Burials were often under mounds just outside the city. Though these cities clearly had a social hierarchy with a strong ruling class (confirmed by the fact that they were divided into sections with larger and smaller houses), there is little evidence of a centralized kingship, as there was in contemporaneous Egypt, Mesopotamia, and China. In the same vein, there are no large temples. As to their religious system, terra-cotta seals show a plethora of supernatural animals—unicorns in particular. There is also the depiction of a proto-Shiva-like divinity sometimes shown sitting in the lotus position. He wears bull horns on his head and seems to be worshipped by animals of all sorts. There is also a proliferation of sculptural figures dedicated to fertility and procreation.

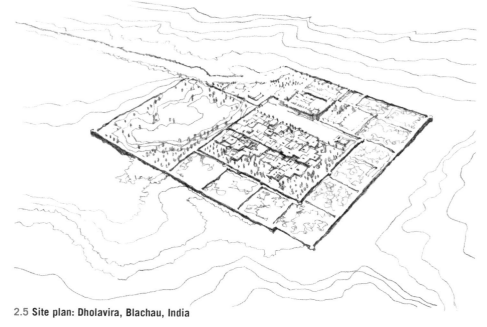

2.5 Site plan: Dholavira, Blachau, India

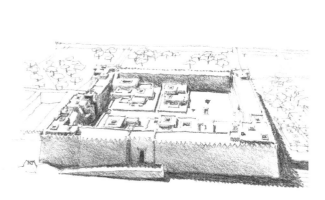

2.6 Reconstruction view of Dholavira

2.7 An entrance gate to Harappa, near Sahiwal, Pakistan

Early in the second millennium BCE, the Ghaggar-Hakra begun to dry up. The reasons are debated, but it seems an earthquake in the Himalayas caused one of its major tributaries to change course and drain into the Indus, depleting the Ghaggar-Hakra. Its waters collected in an inland lake that spawned a successful maritime community around its shores. Subsequently, the lake, too, dried up, bringing about the final phase: the abandonment of the entire Indus Ghaggar-Hakra region. Where the people went is still debated, but the majority probably dispersed eastward to the plains of the Ganges River. Some, however, may have gone westward and relocated as far away as Assyria, causing a ripple effect of disruptions that were felt all the way to Egypt.

Mohenjo-Daro

Mohenjo-Daro was the dominant city of the southern Indus. The Indus, which originates in the high Himalayas, is frequently subject to ice floes and landslides that can hold back its waters for a while but that eventually give way, resulting in huge flash floods. To guard against these, the two largest building areas of Mohenjo-Daro were raised high on a platform of bricks designed to disperse the floodwaters through a series of culverts. (The site of Mohenjo-Daro itself receives very little rain.) Under the main streets were drains running to settling tanks, which could be accessed and cleaned.

Mohenjo-Daro's neighborhoods were inward looking. The main streets were lined with the largely blank walls of houses, and even the secondary streets usually did not have any major houses opening directly onto them. Accessible by alleys only, the houses faced into open courtyards, with the larger ones often having two stories, the upper level built of wood. The number of rooms in houses varied from two to more than twenty. A good number of the rooms contained wells, and the larger ones had bathrooms and toilets.

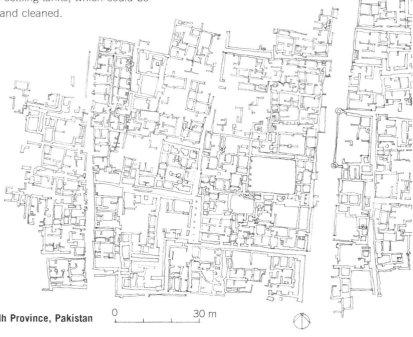

2.8 Urban fabric of Mohenjo-Daro, in Sindh Province, Pakistan

0   30 m

Great Bath

Granary

Stupa

Fortifications

0   100 m

2.9 Plan: The upper town of Mohenjo-Daro

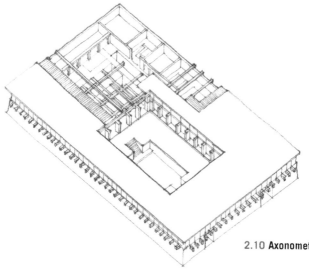

2.10 Axonometric of the Great Bath, Mohenjo-Daro

Located at the intersection of the major north-south and east-west streets, the Great Bath of Mohenjo-Daro, as it is called, was very likely the social and ritual center of the city. Its 12-by-7-meter pool, which was 3 meters deep, was accessed by means of symmetrical stairs on the north and south. The bath is surrounded by a narrow deep-water channel, and an outlet from one corner of the bath leads to a high-corbelled drain that eventually empties out into the surrounding lowlands. Burnt bricks lined the pool, while a layer of bitumen waterproofed it. Whereas the burnt bricks were certainly locally made, the bitumen must have come from Mesopotamia. It was, obviously, a highly valued commodity, and its use in the Great Bath is another indication of the importance of the building. The water tank was surrounded by a brick colonnade, behind which was a series of rooms of various sizes (one had a well). The whole structure had a wooden second story, although the central pool was probably open to the sky. Access was carefully controlled, with only one opening from the south. Ritual urns with ashes—presumably of important people—were found close to the entrance.

One can only guess at the social practices that led to such an institution, but the very presence of the Great Bath indicates the dominance of water and ritual bathing in the inhabitants' ideology, themes that seem to carry through into modern-day Hinduism. To the west of the bath is a building with doorless rooms crisscrossed by narrow ventilation channels. Archaeologists originally assumed this was a granary, but more recent evidence suggests that it may have been a general-purpose warehouse. Its proximity to the bath is not to be overlooked.

MARGIANA

Today, the northern foothills of the Turkmen-Khorasan Mountain Range near the Caspian Sea are a desolate and relatively depopulated area, but thousands of years ago they would have been steppe, providing a perfect area for grazing, combined with farming along the river. The region also lay at the center of far-flung trade connections linking all of Asia into a composite whole stretching from Egypt and Mesopotamia to the Indies and even to China. The area is known as the Margiana civilization, also called the Bactrian-Margiana Archaeological Complex (BMAC). Most of the BMAC lies in Russia and modern-day Turkmenistan.

The BMAC consisted of more than three hundred settlements in the valleys that form the headlands of the Oxus River. Gonur, along the Murghab River, seems to have been its capital. It consisted of a temple/citadel and a palace compound separated by about 300 meters. The palace, dating from about 2500 BCE, was almost square (measuring 120 by 125 meters) and was surrounded by a defensive wall with towers at regular intervals. Outside were several altars, low to the ground and open to the elements, suggesting that they were used for fire rituals. There is no evidence of any deity figures. To get to the throne room, one traversed two long audience halls and made two left turns. The residential part of the palace was at the center and had two courtyards to its west. There was also a chapel and a mortuary complex. Oddly, there was a suite of rooms with no access doors that was completely filled with clean river sand. The symbolic purpose of these extraordinary spaces has not been ascertained, but they may have been part of the first palace that had become ritually protected. A long stairway led to the roof over these rooms, an indication that the roof was used for ritual events. In the wall decoration of the palace, archaeologists have noticed strong similarities to West Asian, Anatolian, and even Minoan art. Clearly these were people with strong ties to West and Central Asia. Did they emigrate from there, as some believe? Or were they a part of a larger civilization development? The parallelogram-shaped temple district went through several stages of development, with the fort at the center belonging to the last stage.

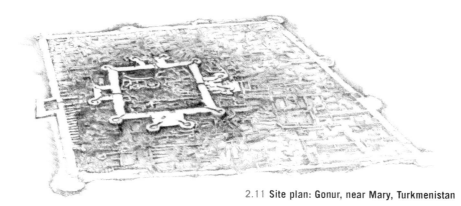

2.11 Site plan: Gonur, near Mary, Turkmenistan

To the west of the site was a large burial ground of about five thousand graves. It seems that bodies were not buried immediately after death but were first purified by fire. This startling discovery has led archaeologists to surmise connections to the later development of Zoroastrianism, which also emphasized the purification of the body before interment. The fate of this culture is much debated. Some hold that with the deteriorating ecology, the inhabitants of the area migrated to Mesopotamia and India, contributing to the general upheavals that these places experienced between 1600 and 1200 BCE.

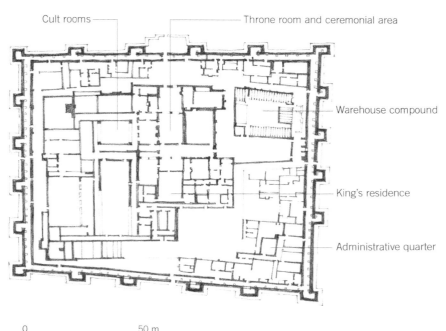

Cult rooms — — Throne room and ceremonial area

Warehouse compound

King's residence

Administrative quarter

0   50 m

2.12 Plan: The Citadel at Gonur

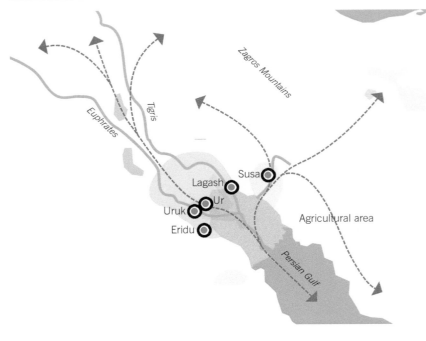

2.13 Early Lower Mesopotamia

Eridu, Uruk, Ur, Lagash, and, farther to the east, Susa, which lay on the Karun River, formed a larger economic environment, with trade developing toward India to the south; toward Sialk, a metal-producing city on the other side of the Zagros Mountains; as well as toward points northward. In Lagash, archaeologists discovered the remains of a storehouse that contained not only supplies of grain and figs but also vessels, weapons, sculptures, and numerous other objects connected with the use and administration of palace and temple. Though these cities seem small by today's standards, at the time they would have been the largest in the world, along with Memphis in Egypt. The economy of the Sumerians was thus twofold: a northward-looking Mesopotamian-based one, and a southward-looking trade economy with the proto-Persians and Indus River cities.

EARLY EMPIRES OF MESOPOTAMIA

No one knows when the Akkadians first began to infiltrate central Mesopotamia, nor what their origins were, but by 2300 BCE they were predominant in the vicinity of modern Baghdad and farther north along the rivers. Sargon, an Akkadian king who reigned from around 2334 to 2279 BCE, reshaped the Mesopotamian political landscape; his was the first known successful centralization of power in the region. The idea of village-based civic loyalty, so important to early Sumerians, was replaced by the concept of loyalty to a ruler, with Sargon taking measures that deliberately diminished the power of local chieftains. This new concept of kingship is expressed in the statue of a head representing an Akkadian ruler, found in the city of Nineveh. It is notable for its bold features, artfully braided beard, and majesty of bearing. The mouth, from which the pronouncements of law and rule issued forth, is as expressive as the eyes, which were once inlaid with stone, resulting in an active image in marked contrast to the quiet and contemplative stare of the Sumerian figures. Sargon's capital city, Akkad, was located on the Euphrates about 30 kilometers south of modern Baghdad.

Around 2150 BCE, the Akkadian dynasty was overthrown by tribes from the mountainous northeast that descended to the plains, contributing nothing to the civilization they ransacked. The survival of Mesopotamia was now suddenly dependent on kingdoms in the old Sumerian south. The Sumerians took up the challenge, drove the mountain people back, and reunited the realm under the kings of Ur. These kings, part of the Third Dynasty (2112–2004 BCE), accepted many of the innovations that had been created under Sargon. These Sumerian cities were not only in communication with cities along the Persian Gulf, such as those of the Elamites, but also perhaps with the hundreds of cities in the upper Euphrates region. The rulers of Ur defined kingship as a privilege that descended from heaven and was bestowed upon one city at a time, but only for a limited period. There was no notion of a single political entity comprising a nation in the modern sense. Rulers were, in essence, stewards of the gods who gave them protection and guidance. The temples, however, were the principal landowners, which, to all practical effects, meant that the priests controlled and organized the labor needed to build and maintain the irrigation canals and ditches. Priests were, in effect, the managers of the city's economy and infrastructure.

2.14 Statue of the head of an Akkadian ruler

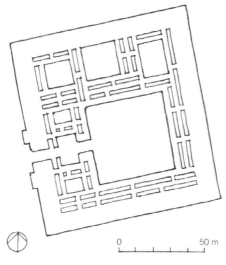

2.15 Plan: The Palace of Naram-Sin

2.16 **Group of statues from the Abu Temple, Tell Asmar, Iraq**

The political structure was thus a type of theocratic socialism in which all the people worked in their various capacities—from slave to priest—in the service of the city-state. The chief god was Anu. Below him was Enlil, the earth or storm god, and Ea, the water god whom we encountered in Eridu. Nanna, the moon god who ruled in Ur, was among a group of gods at a slightly lower level. He measured time and provided fertility. Senior members of the pantheon served as patron deities of individual cities, while deities of lesser rank were associated with smaller urban centers. There were over three thousand other gods and demons that governed even inanimate objects like pickaxes and brick molds. The flexibility with which the minor gods and goddesses came and went and syncretically changed their names makes it difficult to be specific about a Mesopotamian pantheon. Some of these deities were shared across various regions; some were part of local cults. This divine population was thought to meet regularly in an assembly and to arrive at agreements that bound all deities to the more senior deities. The temple was the actual domicile of the god rather than merely a place that permitted contact between the ruled and the divine powers, although one of the priests' principal jobs was the interpretation of omens, which had a powerful influence on every sphere of activity in Sumerian society.

Mesopotamian religion was heavy in superstitions and subscriptive behavior. Life after death was portrayed as a sad and pitiable state, and the dead as potentially hostile toward the living. Apart from rituals to appease the dead, burial architecture was thus rare. A person's association with the gods was based very much on the fulfillment of his or her duties in the here and now and on the principle of constant vigilance. For the manufacture of cult statues, for example, a text, slightly modified here, reads:

> When you make the statues of cornel wood in the morning at sunrise you shall go to the wood. You shall take a golden axe and a silver saw, and with censor, torch and holy water you shall consecrate the tree…. You shall sweep the ground, sprinkle clear water, set up a folding table, sacrifice a sheep and offer the shoulder and fatty tissue and the roast, scatter dates and fine meal, set out a cake made with syrup and butter, pour out beer, kneel down, and stand up in front of the cornel tree and recite the incantation: "Evil is the broad steppe." With golden axe and the silver saw you shall touch the cornel tree and cut it down with a hatchet; you shall damp it with water, then remove the set-out material, kneel down and break the cornel tree into pieces.*

*Frans A. M. Wiggermann, *Mesopotamian Protective Spirits: The Ritual Texts* (Groningen, Netherlands: Styx, 1992), condensed from pp. 7–9.

The person then carves the statues as if "clad in their own garment, holding in their right hand a cornel-stick charred at both ends and with their left clasping their breasts." After writing his name on the statues, the person was asked to bring the statues he had made to his house for the purification ritual, placing them "on a pedestal in a walking pose so as to repel the evil ones." He was then asked to touch various parts of the house while reciting incantations and performing other prescribed rituals. Statues such as these were set up in temples, creating a charged ocular and oracular environment, with the eyes of the supplicant seeking to establish an unblinking connection between the profane and the sacred. Coming back from the other direction were the silent commands of the gods, translated into words by the priests. This exchange played itself out most grandly in the ziggurats.

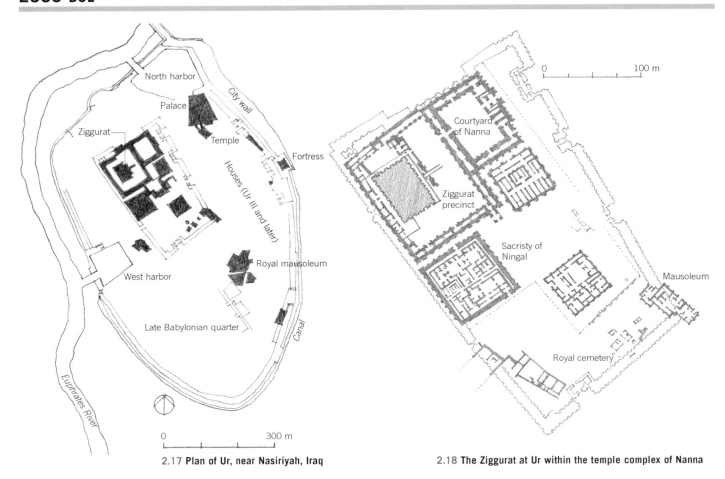

2.17 **Plan of Ur, near Nasiriyah, Iraq**

2.18 **The Ziggurat at Ur within the temple complex of Nanna**

Ziggurat at Ur

The Ziggurat at Ur was one of the most impressive structures of the time, and remains of it are still extant at Tall al Muqayyar in Iraq, about 42 kilometers south of Babylon. Some reconstruction drawings show it as a freestanding object similar to an Egyptian pyramid; it was in actuality surrounded by precinct walls to the east within which was a large square-shaped sanctuary dedicated to Nanna's divine wife, Ningal. A law court was close by. The whole was eventually enclosed by its own set of defensive walls.

The ziggurat measured 65 meters by 100 meters at its base, was 21 meters high, and consisted of three terraces, with the sacred shrine on the highest one. Though the ornamentation of the ziggurat cannot be confirmed, the building was not the volumetric heap of bricks that we see today in the 20th-century reconstruction.

Three monumental staircases rose up the northeast flank of the ziggurat, converging at a canopied vestibule at the top of the first platform, 20 meters up from the ground. From there, the central stair continued on to the next stage and then to the third. Though highly axial, the axis did not carry through to the surrounding architecture. Access to the court was not from the front but diagonally from a gate at one of its corners. The plain brick of the modern-day reconstruction can give a misleading impression of the structure. The sides would have been plastered smooth and painted to serve as a visual key to a cosmological narrative, the principal character of which was Apsu, the god of the primeval waters who fathered heaven and earth. Despite his importance, he was defeated and killed by Ea, who transformed Apsu into still or stagnant subterranean waters. The lowest terrace of the ziggurat, representing Apsu, was painted white. The next terrace, probably black, represented Ea floating on and dominating the water. The

top level would have been red, representing the sun-kindled air. The blue tiles that were found on the site are thought to have come from the temple at the top, which would have represented the blue heaven above the earth. What made this structure so innovative is that the elements—the stairs, the platforms, and the temple itself—were no longer arranged as a geographical mass, as at Uruk, but were brought into the embrace of a unified and dramatic color-coded design. Geographical simulation had been replaced by an architectural abstraction.

The start of a construction of such a scale was initiated by elaborate rituals in which the king fashioned the first brick and carried up the first basket of earth. This act of dedication was commemorated by the burial of peg-shaped copper figurines in the foundation. The hard work was done by slaves taken from conquered lands, a common practice of the time. The structure was made of square flat bricks mortared with bitumen. Reed matting soaked with bitumen was inserted horizontally at various layers to add cohesion and protect against vertical shear forces. The bricks were stamped with an inscription reading "Ur-Nammu, king of Ur, who built the temple of Nanna."

That ziggurats served as symbolic conjugal sites is proven at Ur, where the ziggurat was linked by a watercourse to a small temple 6 kilometers west of the city dedicated to the mother goddess Ninkhursag. She was represented by the cow, whereas Nanna, the moon god who ruled over Ur, was sometimes referred to as a bull. Once a year, Ninkhursag, the Lady of the Mountain, whether embodied in statues or by a priestess, would have been brought to the city in a procession and led up to the shrine on top of the ziggurat to consummate her marriage while sacrifices and chants proceeded outside. Similar notions exist in Hinduism and in ancient Greece, with the celebration of the mystic marriage, the *hieros gamos* (from *hiero*, "sacred," and *gamos*, "marriage"). Ninkhursag thus represented the older goddess tradition that had been preserved and incorporated into the more complex mythologies needed after the move into the Mesopotamian marshes.

The city of Ur was almost oval in shape, with the Euphrates River coursing around its sides. There were harbors on its north and west sides, with the temple complex clamped between them. The surrounding walls, as is the case in all Mesopotamian cities, were intended just as much to impress as to protect. From their ramparts one would have seen the vast stretches of cultivated fields in all directions, as well as the villages of farm laborers tending them. The presence of gardens and orchards near the walls was also common. Much effort was made in the design and outfitting of the gates, which were flanked by towers whose tops were decorated with bands of shields. The visitor, upon entering through the gates, would immediately confront the densely built-up jumble of the city. There was, however, little evidence of organized city

2.19 **Massing of the Ziggurat at Ur**

planning. Royal roads would be designed only later. Streets varied from narrow lanes to routes 2 to 3 meters wide and served not only as passageways but also as a convenient place in which to dump garbage, a practice that was still encountered even in medieval Europe. Because windows were rare, the narrow lanes formed curving chutes punctuated only by doors or enlivened by lean-tos where food or goods were sold.

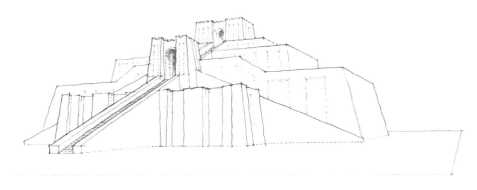

2.20 **Pictorial view from the northwest: Ziggurat at Ur**

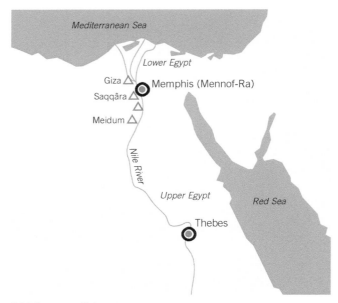

2.21 Egypt, ca. 3rd century BCE

2.22 Mortuary Complex of Zozer, Saqqâra, Egypt

EGYPT: THE OLD KINGDOM

Though later Egyptians described their early history as emerging after the unification of Upper and Lower Egypt, archaeological evidence suggests that unification was a protracted process that took place over several centuries. Out of this unification emerged what later Egyptians would themselves call the Old Kingdom, with its capital at Memphis. This new political unity, combined with the rapid development of a powerful bureaucracy, was the final stage of Egypt's transformation into a complex and vertically structured society with a population of several million farmers and slaves. It has been estimated that by the third millennium BCE, the Nile Valley produced three times its own domestic requirements. From very early on, plenty of labor was available—above and beyond the stage of self-sufficiency. Soon, huge workforces of slaves, laborers, technicians, bureaucrats, and cooks were employed solely for royal projects. And there was no shortage of building material. Stone was abundant up and down the Nile: the colorful red granite of Aswan, the white marble of Gebel Rokham, and the black basalt of Faiyum—not to mention the various types of soft sandstone brought downriver from Nubia. One tremendous obelisk of red granite 41 meters long still lies on its side in the quarry near Aswan. Stone may seem to be an obvious building material, but the

difference between a rock and a polished slab of marble is enormous and it was the Egyptians who first mastered this art.

By the Third Dynasty of the Old Kingdom, the political stability of Egypt was secure, with Zoser (2686–2613 BCE) creating building projects against which later rulers would measure their accomplishments. The Mortuary Complex of Zoser, located on a slight hill west of Memphis and just to the north of Saqqâra, was enclosed by a 277-by-544-meter wall laid out in precise orientation to the four cardinal points. The walls were of white stone and rose to an impressive 10.5 meters. They served the symbolic purpose of defending the mortuary complex from the chaos of the unordered world outside. There were fifteen gateways, three at the north and south walls, four on the east wall, and—oddly—five on the west wall, yet only a single one was a functioning entrance. The building is something of a mystery. Clearly the dead pharaoh was still considered to be alive, but since his perceptions were limited, his new divine world could be simulated in strategic pieces.

One entered the complex from the southern end of the eastern wall. The visitor passed through a 1-meter-wide hallway into a narrow corridor defined by two rows of columns attached to wall fins that projected into the space and supported a massive stone ceiling. These columns are probably

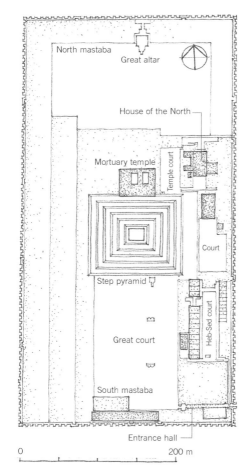

2.23 Plan: Mortuary Complex of Zoser

2.24 Section through entrance hall, Mortuary Complex of Zoser　　　**2.25 Entrance hall to the Mortuary Complex of Zoser**

the earliest monumental stone columns in the history of architecture. They are fluted and simulate a reed bundle, thus imposing on the visitor the difference of scale that separates the divine from the mortal world.

The shadowy entranceway led to the south court in front of the step pyramid. This was the Sed festival court, where ceremonial races were enacted. In the centuries before the Old Kingdom, the king had to prove that he was strong and capable of ruling by running a course for each of the provinces he governed. If he failed, he would be sacrificed in a religious ritual. From this derives the name Sed, or "slaughter festival." By the time of the Old Kingdom this practice had died out, but it remained an important element in the symbolic attributes of kingship. Zoser conceived the complex as a review stand for this event, which lasted five days, ending with a final ceremonial sprint. Originally it was to be held for every king in the thirtieth year of his reign, but that was not always the case. Ramesses II celebrated his Sed in grand style by inviting foreign dignitaries.

Since Zoser did not live long enough to perform this ritual, the court was designed so that he could perform it in death. This is confirmed by the complex's two mastabas: one on the south side, next to the wall—a type of fake mastaba—and the other, belonging to Zoser, to the north. The two structures have almost identical tomb designs, a room at the bottom of a 28-meter-deep shaft sealed by a 3-ton granite plug. In the southern mastaba, archaeologists found the wall decorated with small blue tiles with a glaze just as brilliant today as it was four thousand years ago. The tiles represent a reed matting set in stone posts designed to imitate the appearance of wood, the whole thing creating the illusion of an outdoor canopied room. Between the tile sections is a large stone relief of Zoser "running" the ceremonial race.

The northern mastaba was covered with a stone superstructure with four gently sloping steps. No sooner was that built than it was decided that the structure should be expanded yet again. It was transformed into a 60-meter-high, six-tiered structure by adding material in the northerly direction. The first mortuary temple behind this step pyramid was also rebuilt and expanded. To the east was another court, lined on both sides with chapels, one for each of the Egyptian provinces. Behind them rose the facades of ten tall dummy buildings, replicating

government buildings or, more likely, granaries. Slender columns, drawing on the imagery of reed bundles, ornamented their surfaces. On their other side are engaged columns with smooth-angled shafts holding bell-shaped capitals modeled on the shape of the papyrus flower. Like the reed-shaped columns, the papyrus also had symbolic value. The north part of the complex was dominated by a monumental altar to which offerings were brought each day, a metaphor for the offering place of the northern heaven. In a small chapel positioned against the north side of the pyramid was a life-size statue of Zoser, showing him wearing a priest's Sed festival cloak, a ceremonial beard, and a ritual headdress. Sitting in the dark chamber, he gazes through two small holes in the wall placed at the statue's eye level, through which he could watch the ceremonies taking place in the court. This is the Ka statue, and the structure was nothing without it, as it embodied the still-living spirit of the king. The statue had to be tended to and provided with food and drink. Though a Ka statue might have been placed near the altar, others were placed in the mortuary temple. If anything were to happen to the Ka statue, the spirit of the deceased would never gain entrance to the heavenly realm. The principle of living ancestors is an ancient one and is common to most cultures across Africa and Eurasia. Here, however, it is the pharaoh's Ka that reigns supreme in the ancestor world.

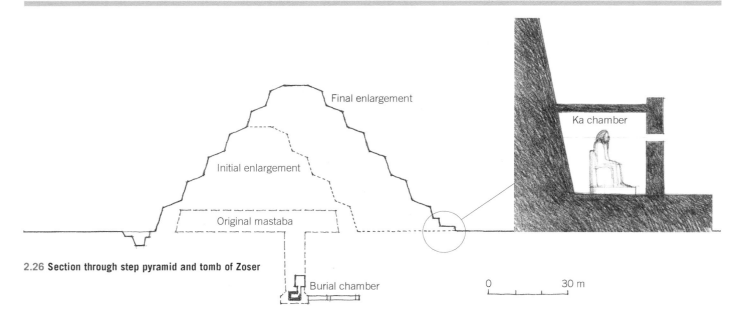

2.26 Section through step pyramid and tomb of Zoser

This building represents a shift in the idea of death and its associated religious practices. The low-lying mastabas of the pharaohs were no longer considered worthy of rulers, who now ranked among the gods. In classical Egyptian, the word for *tomb* actually meant a "house of eternity" or, more precisely, a "house for eternity." The pyramids were certainly built for eternity, but they were now defined differently, as "the place where one ascends." And this might explain the steps, since that was a literal form of the Egyptian glyph, namely a set of giant steps.

After Zoser, the pharaonic institution began to assert its cosmological narrative with ever-greater force and precision. One of the places where this manifests is a cult center for the falcon-god Menthu not far from Medamud, a provincial town 5 kilometers northeast of Karnak at Thebes. The sanctuary, which dates from about 2500 BCE, consisted of a roughly lozenge-shaped enclosure 83 meters at its widest, surrounded by a high wall with a gate to the east. The interior contains a grove of trees and two burial mounds that could be interpreted as the primeval mounds appearing above the waters of chaos.

With Snefru (2613–2589 BCE), who ruled during the Fourth Dynasty, one sees the maturity of the Medamud prototype. But it took Snefru several tries. His first project was the step-faced pyramid at Meidum. The location of the two tomb chambers was innovative. Separated horizontally in the Zoser temple complex, here they are placed one on top of the other, the lower one representing the chthonic aspect of the Egyptian religion. Snefru abandoned the building after fifteen years of work and started another, larger pyramid complex 50 kilometers north, near Dahshur. Originally planned to be a towering 150 meters high, it was too bold, and the ground gave way under part of it. In an effort to save the building, the designers added a kink or bend to reduce the weight and angle of the slope, which is why it is today called the Bent Pyramid.

The failure forced Snefru to ask his builders to return to the Step Pyramid at Meidum. They added a layer that transformed it into a true pyramid, but this time only after careful preparation of the ground. (In Roman times, the stone facing was removed to be made into stucco. Hence it is possible to see the original form.) Still, it was not enough for Snefru. He constructed a third pyramid two miles north of the Bent Pyramid. Not as steep as the earlier ones, it is called the Red Pyramid because of the reddish cast of the stone. This is where Snefru is actually buried. Construction was so well thought out that despite the weight of the 2 million tons of stones on the roofs of the chambers, cracks have yet to appear. The harmonious proportions of the form and the perfection of the system of tomb chambers made it the model for subsequent tombs.

2.27 Ka statue of Zoser

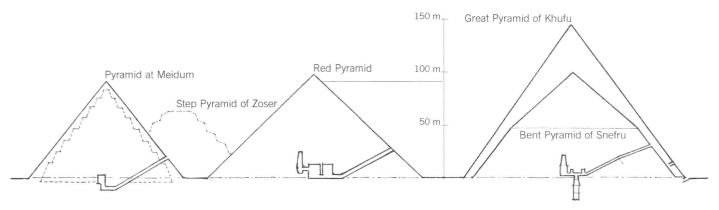

2.28 A scalar comparison of Egyptian pyramids

Pyramids at Giza

Pyramids are only the massive residue of an extensive ritual architecture that included temples, causeways, ports, shrines, and even special tombs for the sacred boats that carried the sarcophagus and other objects. The pharaoh's body would be brought on a funerary ship to a valley temple along the Nile River. The temple consisted of an intricate though largely symmetrical combination of galleries and courts, at the center of which was a monumental courtyard with twelve colossal statues in niches along its perimeter.

Behind the courtyard was a row of five chapels that held the sacred barges that had brought the sarcophagus and other objects down the Nile from Memphis. Once the body had been properly prepared, the coffin was sledded up to the mortuary temple in the shadow of the pyramid, where other rituals would take place, including daily prayers, incantations, and offerings. The coffin, attended by a lavish funerary cortege, was then brought into the pyramid and placed in the stone sarcophagus that was built into the burial chamber of the pyramid. The

pharaoh and the canopic jars that contained his entrails, along with assorted possessions, were placed in the tomb chamber, and offerings were made. Then the funerary party exited the pyramid and the entrance was sealed. At the cosmological center of this system was the belief in the sun god Re, creator of all things, who, according to legend, created himself out of a mound that emerged from the primeval ocean. Snefru's son Khufu (Cheops) identified himself with the sun god to such an extent that his successors referred to themselves by the new royal title, Son of Re.

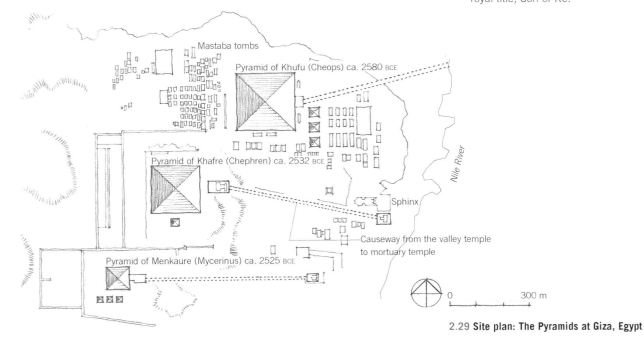

2.29 Site plan: The Pyramids at Giza, Egypt

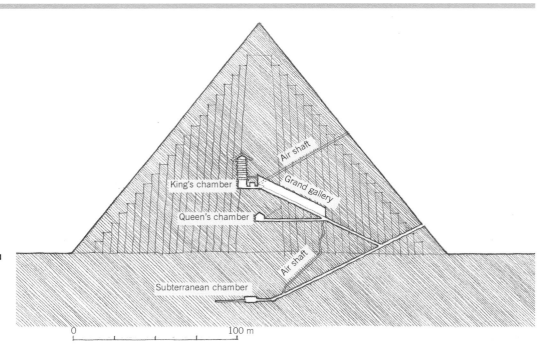

2.30 Section: Great Pyramid of Khufu

When engineers set about to build the Great Pyramid of Khufu (Cheops), they took no chances and chose a solid rock foundation. Its orientation, so close to true north, has raised the question of how the ancient Egyptians managed to achieve such accuracy. Six million tons of solid masonry, consisting of 2,300,000 individual stones, rested on that foundation. The core was mostly of yellow limestone quarried from the immediate area, while the stones of the casing are of a white limestone from quarries at Tura and Masara, on the east bank of the Nile on the outskirts of modern Cairo. The casing stones were fitted together with such precision that the sides would have been seen as a smooth sheet glistening in the sun.

Though the Egyptians were highly proficient mathematicians, the mathematical and astronomical systems used in the design of the pyramids is much debated. Furthermore, the exterior measurements of the pyramid are uncertain because the outer surface has been removed over the years. However, it is generally agreed that the sides of the pyramid are about 440 Egyptian royal cubits and that its height would have been about 280 royal cubits. The face of the triangle intersects the ground at an angle a little less than 51.5 degrees. This means that the height of the triangle along the surface to the top is phi (the golden section or ratio, 1.61803399) and that the vertical height of the pyramid at its center is the square root of phi. The angles of the internal passages, as well as the location of the various chambers, are also thought to have been defined mathematically. There is also solid evidence that the layout of the three pyramids is not haphazard, but that it too conforms to a unifying geometric plan.

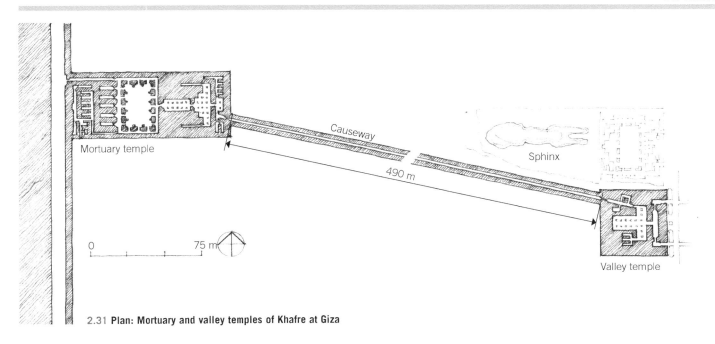

2.31 Plan: Mortuary and valley temples of Khafre at Giza

Mortuary temple

Causeway

490 m

Sphinx

Valley temple

0   75 m

The upper granite burial chamber stands isolated in the interior of the pyramid; five upper chambers with granite beams, weighing up to 40 tons each, serve to relieve the pressure. The uppermost burial chamber has a gabled roof of limestone blocks. From the middle of the south and north walls of the burial chamber, narrow mock corridors point toward the southern and northern skies to provide a direct route to heaven for the deceased's soul. The northern one, so it is thought, allows the regenerative north wind to flow down to meet the body of the king. The room below the burial chamber was meant to house the Ka statue of Khufu. Though the statue has been lost, early accounts describe it as a statue of green stone, standing inside the niche. This room was misnamed the queen's chamber by early explorers, but it cannot have served as a tomb since it was not provided with a stone sarcophagus and was not sealed by a portcullis (stone plug). A unique aspect of the pyramid is a subterranean chamber that was cut out of the solid bedrock. Unlike the precision of the structure above, it was designed with a rough and disorderly look. It is clearly cultish in nature, but its purpose remains unknown.

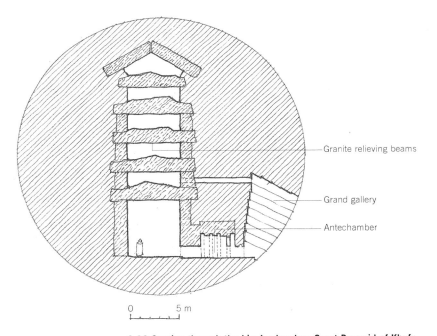

Granite relieving beams

Grand gallery

Antechamber

0   5 m

2.32 Section through the king's chamber, Great Pyramid of Khufu

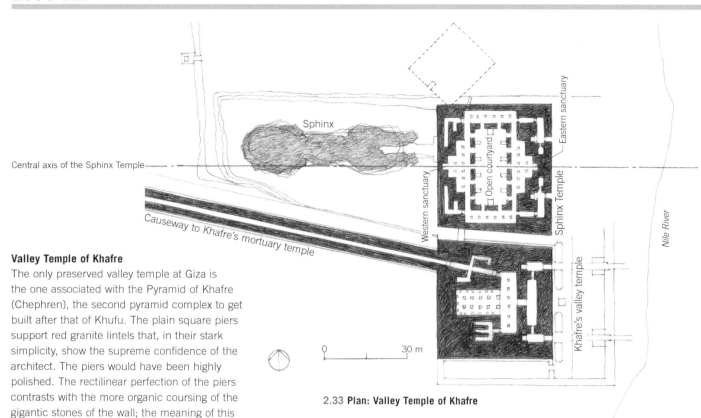

Sphinx

Central axis of the Sphinx Temple

Causeway to Khafre's mortuary temple

Western sanctuary

Open courtyard

Eastern sanctuary

Sphinx Temple

Khafre's valley temple

Nile River

0   30 m

2.33 Plan: Valley Temple of Khafre

Valley Temple of Khafre

The only preserved valley temple at Giza is the one associated with the Pyramid of Khafre (Chephren), the second pyramid complex to get built after that of Khufu. The plain square piers support red granite lintels that, in their stark simplicity, show the supreme confidence of the architect. The piers would have been highly polished. The rectilinear perfection of the piers contrasts with the more organic coursing of the gigantic stones of the wall; the meaning of this distinction is unknown. The floor was paved with alabaster. The main chamber housed twenty-three statues of Khafre. On the outside, the box-shaped form gives no indication of the complex internal layout. In fact, the space between the interior and the exterior is filled solid with enormous limestone stones; the interiors would thus have seemed to be carved from the earth itself. Next to this temple is the famous Sphinx, its purpose and meaning still a mystery.

2.34 Overview: Valley Temple of Khafre

2.35 Interior: Valley Temple of Khafre

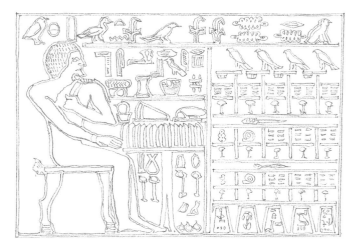

2.36 Egyptian slab stela
A slab stela shows a royal personage at a funerary repast sitting next to an offering table covered with the loaves of bread that have been brought to him. Next to him on the floor, on small platforms, are containers holding incense, ointments, figs, and wine.

ARCHITECTURE AND FOOD

For both Mesopotamian and Egyptian societies, food was the sustenance not only of humans but also of the gods. Offerings of food were laid out in front of the Ka statue in its niche to provide for the difficult journey ahead. They consisted of meat, roasted fowl, bread, fruit, vegetables, beer, and wine, all delivered out of the temple district's own gardens. The slaughter of the animals, out of sight of the gods, was supervised by the priests. From an anthropological perspective, one can say that this equation was necessary for social and political cohesion. There is also evidence of this in Mesopotamia, where the ziggurat was a type of elevated feasting platform. A text states, "In the first night watch, on the roof of the high temple of the ziggurat … when [the star of] the great Anu of heaven comes out," the feast was to be laid out upon a golden table for Anu and his wife Antum, as well as for the seven planets. The most exact instructions were reserved for the nourishment and entertainment of the gods. The flesh of the cattle, sheep, and birds, and beer of first quality, along with wine "poured from a golden ewer," was to be offered.

2.37 Statuette of a woman bearing offerings

Though both Mesopotamian and Egyptian food sacrifices emphasized breads, drinks, and the bounty of the land, the Mesopotamians rarely sacrificed animals, which were not plentiful in the alluvial plain. For the Egyptians, animal sacrifices were not uncommon, with offerings—especially of gazelles, antelopes, geese, ducks, and pigeons—coming mainly from hunting. The meat was offered in either boiled or roasted form. The shank and the heart were thought to have a particularly reviving effect for the Ka. Unlike the Greeks, the Egyptians did not perform the actual killing and bloodletting in "sight" of the gods; the meat arrived fully cooked. The difference is telling. The Ka is visualized as alive and sensitive, or at least as coaxed back to life by tasty morsels. The Greeks, as will be discussed later, saw the sacrifice very differently.

In Mesopotamia, food was prepared almost around the clock for the temple ceremonies. Documents list in great detail the preperations that were necessary, from fattened sheep and oxen to dates, figs, fruitcakes, birds, and vegetables. It was only at the time of the New Kingdom, the Mycenaeans, and later the Dorians, that one finds the multiple slaughter of large animals such as bulls. Furthermore, for the Greeks, the sacrificial animals could only be taken from domesticated herds, such as cattle and sheep. Sacrifice would remain important in Judaism and Christianity, but mainly in a symbolic sense. Hinduism is one of the few modern religions that still preserves ritual food offerings to the gods, though meat sacrifices are forbidden.

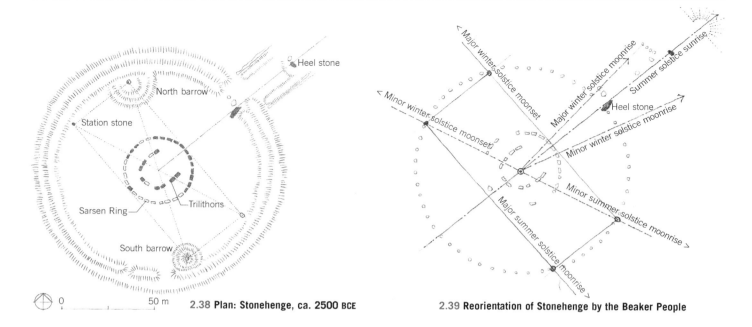

2.38 Plan: Stonehenge, ca. 2500 BCE

2.39 Reorientation of Stonehenge by the Beaker People

STONEHENGE

The structure of Stonehenge as we see it today is in fact a combination of the last two phases of its several revisions and dates from between 2500 and 1800 BCE, making it more or less contemporary with Ur in Mesopotamia and the end of the age of pyramids in Egypt. This is important because there is a tendency to overstate the primitivism of Stonehenge, when in actuality it was an advanced Bronze Age structure. Furthermore, Stonehenge must be contextualized as the last in a line of such artificially enhanced sacred landscapes, a history that stretched back at least two thousand years. Newgrange was a similar site in that it was an important regional ceremonial attractor, but it dates to a thousand years before Stonehenge. Today, because Stonehenge is isolated in the landscape, it is difficult to visualize the area as a sacred landscape. In the immediate area, hundreds of burial mounds would have been visible, some dating back to the fourth millennium BCE.

The first version of Stonehenge, dating to about 3000 BCE, was consistent with the circular henges of that age, except that this one was an impressive 100 meters across, with two or perhaps three spaces left open for access to the inside of the circle. Two alignments were built into it: one astronomical, at the northeast entrance toward the northernmost rising of the moon, and the other to the cardinal point to the south at the other causeway.

Around 2500 BCE, the Beaker People transformed Stonehenge from a local temple to a focal point for a larger civilizational entity. They filled the area for miles around with their circular burial mounds and founded a new city to the northeast of Stonehenge, now called Durrington Walls, which was defended by circular defensive walls 480 meters across. Their wealth shows up in their graves. In one grave, archaeologists found gold ornaments as well as bronze pins from Bohemia, blue faience beads from Egypt, and amber beads from northern Europe.

At the center of the Beaker People's cosmology was a connection between the smelting of ore and the sun. For this reason they had to redesign Stonehenge, transforming its orientation from the moon to the sun. To do this they rotated the axis an almost imperceptible 3 degrees eastward to coincide with the rising midsummer

sun, according to the research of Gerald S. Hawkins in collaboration with John B. White. The Beaker People also imposed four large stones that point to summer and winter risings and settings. Though the precise nature of how the stones worked is in dispute, Stonehenge's latitude, as it turns out, is the only one in Europe where this combination is even possible.

The most significant change attributed to the Beaker People was the addition of a ring of sixty large bluestones to the interior. The stones are not actually blue; they are a dark, heavy, medium-grained rock, harder than granite. The Beaker People also constructed, about 1 kilometer north of Stonehenge, what archaeologists call a cursus—a 3-kilometer-long, 100-meter-wide rectangular form, slightly beveled at the ends. Created by incising a ditch into the landscape, it lies in an east-west orientation. Though simply built, it is laid out with great precision. Its purpose is unknown, even though there are other cursi scattered across the region, some predating the arrival of the Beaker People. It certainly was not a running track, as the name unfortunately implies. One can surmise that since the eastern sector was associated with the sunrise and the western side with the sunset, the cursus played an important part in the ritual expressions of life and death. Was it a pathway for the soul?

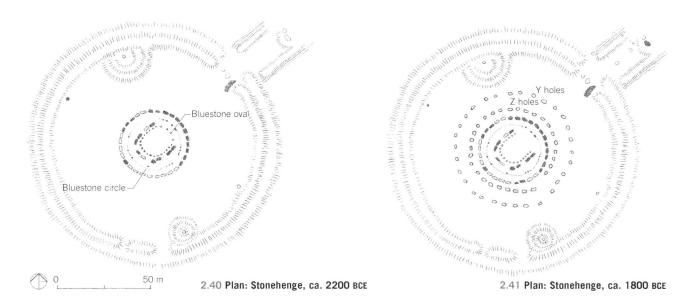

2.40 **Plan: Stonehenge, ca. 2200** BCE

2.41 **Plan: Stonehenge, ca. 1800** BCE

No sooner had the Beaker People completed their work, around 2300 BCE, than Stonehenge underwent yet another and even more impressive transformation. The new designers were working at the behest of a culture represented by chieftains whose numerous cemeteries were added to the landscape around Stonehenge. Their origin is even more mysterious than that of the Beaker People. The new overlords removed the bluestones and added the now famous Sarsen Ring of trilithons, *sarsen* being the name of the local sandstone boulders. The ring, 33 meters across, was composed of thirty enormous stones with an average weight of 26 tons. The transportation of the blocks from a site 30 kilometers away would have been a feat in itself. Particularly noteworthy was the effort made in the preparation of the stones. Moving in unison and using stone mauls swung on ropes, workers pummeled the surface of the boulders to pulverize protrusions, first with large mauls the size of pumpkins and then moving down to smaller mauls the size of tennis balls. When the surfaces were finally flat, other teams set to work rubbing the surfaces with large flat stones, back and forth like a woodworker with sandpaper. When they were done, the posts measured 4.1 meters high, 2.1 meters wide, and 1.1 meters thick. They were surmounted by thirty 6- to 7-ton lintels that formed a continuous circle around the top.

The precision was remarkable. The tops of the lintels, once they were in place, never varied more than 10 centimeters from the horizontal. Such carefully worked stone is not typical of other English henges, where stones were usually left natural, perhaps because they were seen as possessing a magical, chthonic presence. The Sarsen Ring was architecture of a particular type, for it was in reality something akin to carpentry in stone. Possibly the designers were replicating in stone a wooden prototype, or perhaps they were seeking to enhance the power of the stone structure by embodying in it the more familiar techniques of woodworking.

In the final phase of Stonehenge's transformation, some of the bluestones that had been removed were brought back to the site, with some being erected within the Sarsen Ring and others placed in a horseshoe configuration. Such a horseshoe was uncommon in England, but occurred more frequently across the channel in Brittany. The implications of this have yielded much speculation, but it is almost certain that southern England and French Brittany were at this time part of a single cultural province.

As a result of climatic cooling, so it is thought, the culture that built Stonehenge devolved into a hamlet society, with little capacity to continue the great architectural accomplishments of its predecessors. In the shadowy remnants, a druid culture emerged that contributed practically nothing to the architectural legacy of England.

How Stonehenge was used has been debated for well over a century, and new insights are still arising. It was once assumed that the site was a celestial clock—a clock with one tick, which pointed to the rebirth of the year. This is now seen as too limited an understanding of the site. It was a site of magic, a site where people would congregate to communicate with ancestors and to bury their dead, physically and ritually, while engaged in ceremonial socializing, feasting, and dancing.

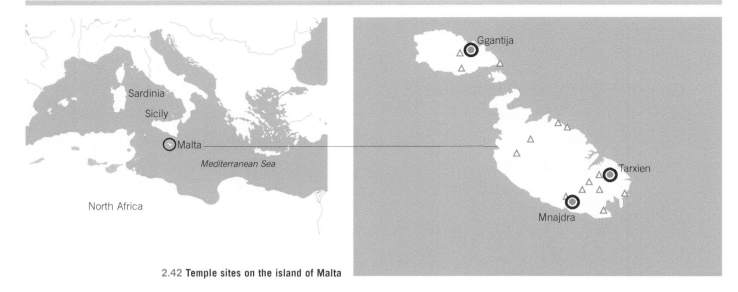

2.42 **Temple sites on the island of Malta**

MEGALITHIC TEMPLES OF MALTA

Around 4000 BCE, settlers arrived at the Maltese archipelago, a string of rocky islands between Sicily and the North African coast. There they set up farms and traded with Sicily and Sardinia for flint, obsidian, and other nonnative materials, tools, and foods. Today, without modern technology, the island would be relatively inhospitable, given that there are few trees and no natural water sources. But in ancient times there must have been natural springs and an environment suitable for agriculture, for the Maltese flourished for a thousand years, between 3500 and 2500 BCE, more or less contemporaneously with the Old Kingdom in Egypt.

In Egypt, there had been a rapid shift to a complex cosmology controlled by the elite. But in Malta, religion revolved around the ancient mother-goddess cult. Malta should not, however, be seen as more primitive, but rather as a place where the goddess cult not only survived but thrived. It is also unlikely that Malta was completely isolated. In fact, the large number of temples, far exceeding the needs of the local population, implies that the island was a type of religious destination. People came to the island for oracles and to communicate with ancestors. Ceremonies seem to have involved sleeping and dreaming.

The temples share common characteristics. The outer walls were made of raw, undressed megalithic stones set vertically in the ground and forming an oval. How the massive, multi-ton stones were brought to the sites remains a mystery. Archaeologists have found parallel ruts along which the stones might have been pulled, possibly on round stones used as rollers, but these ruts do not lead to the temple in efficient lines (they zigzag through the landscape), nor are they always parallel.

The interior spaces of the temples were defined by their own stones, meticulously dressed and set up to create lobed chambers, the surfaces of which were sometimes finished with plaster and then painted. The spaces between the outer and inner walls were filled with dirt and rubble, and the whole was mounded over to form artificial hills with interior caves. How the spaces were roofed is still debated. Corbelled Neolithic tombs can be found in Spain and Portugal, but given the absence of such stonework, it seems likely that the roofs were supported by timber beams. A model of a tomb, made by the ancient builders themselves, shows that these buildings conformed to a clear prototype. This small model, the size of a matchbox, is the earliest architectural model in the world. Its purpose is not known, but it is possible that it was a type of souvenir, proving that the recipient had indeed visited the temple and participated in its ceremony.

2.43 **Sleeping Goddess from the subterranean temple of Hal Saflieni**

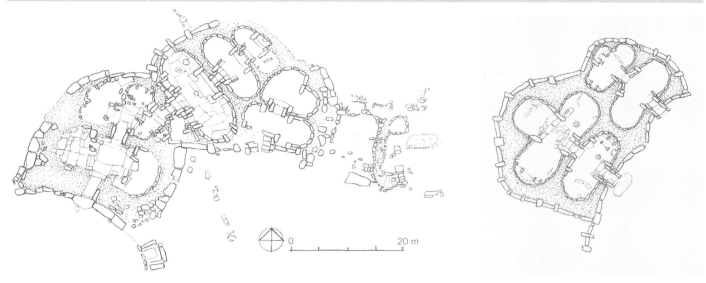

2.44 Plans of temple complexes on Malta drawn at the same scale and orientation: Ggantija (above left) and Tarxien (above right)

The nature of the rituals for which these structures were built has been lost to history. But statuettes of heavyset earth goddesses found on the sites are evidence of a cult dedicated to fertility, death, and renewal. The deities, some sitting upright, others lying asleep, look not unlike the plans of the temples themselves—squat, rounded figures harboring a mysterious, bodily inner world. Animal bones and statuettes testify to the ritual offerings and sacrifices that were likely associated with the cult. Many temples contained carved or freestanding stone altars, and most had libation stones with wells for liquid offerings to the earth. The later temples have a type of plaza in front of them that were equipped with stone benches, indicating that the temples were used for communal gatherings where people waited for priestly announcements or perhaps for their turn to enter.

The earliest temple on the Maltese archipelago is Ggantija, part of a cluster of temples situated on the island of Gozo. Used continuously for hundreds of years, it dates to around 3500 BCE. It was a double temple, nearly 30 meters long. The temple had a floor of crushed limestone slurry that formed a hard, concrete-like surface. The portals from chamber to chamber were huge post-and-lintel configurations of megalithic stones. The exterior was monumental and simple. The core cloverleaf configuration to the west was built first. Two more lobed chambers were then added along its entry passage. Later, a second temple was built adjacent to the first and enclosed within the original mound. The reasons are unclear. Perhaps the local population expanded and exceeded the original temple's capacity. Perhaps a plentiful harvest year prompted the farmers to renew their thanks to the earth goddess. Whatever

the reason, generations of Maltese continued to regularize and expand the design, testing, refining, and reproducing the archetypal shape at different scales, with different orientations, and with varying numbers of chambers.

The temple at Tarxien, built around 2500 BCE, is the most complex of the surviving temples. The imposing concave facade of the main temple was composed of finely coursed stone, with larger blocks at the base and smaller blocks at the roof, which corbelled outward to form a small cornice. Within, pairs of symmetrical chambers were built successively deeper over the centuries, one connected to the next by dual trilithon portals and connecting passageways. At nearby Mnajdra is a complex of three temples of the same period, overlooking an oval court. The southern temple is aligned such that the equinox sunrise illuminates its main axis.

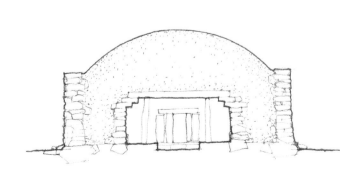

2.45 Section through a typical Malta temple

2.46 Temple complex at Mnajdra, Malta

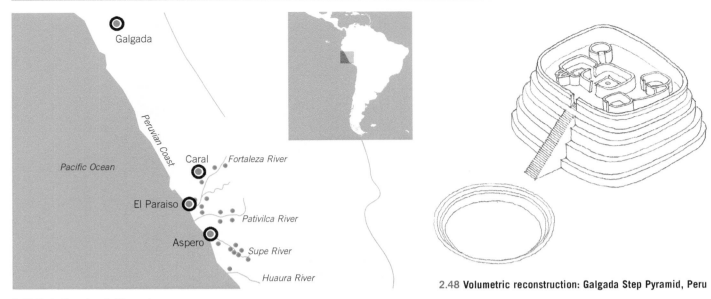

2.47 **Early Peruvian Settlements**

2.48 **Volumetric reconstruction: Galgada Step Pyramid, Peru**

THE FIRST CIVILIZATIONS OF SOUTH AMERICA

During the Ice Age, between 30,000 and 10,000 BCE, nomadic populations from China and Mongolia crossed the then existing Bering Strait land bridge, moving first into the Great Plains of North America and then south along the shore of the Pacific Ocean. By 10,000 BCE they had reached the southern tip of South America. (Recently, it has also been proposed that another stream of people may have come westward from Europe, following the edge of the Atlantic ice shelf. This is based on the similarities of arrowheads in both locations.) Throughout the Americas, the social structure of the native Americans remained that of hunter-gatherers until sometime between 5000 and 3400 BCE when, in Central America, the first attempts were made to create permanent settlements and cultivate crops such as corn, avocados, chili peppers, amaranth, squash, and beans. By 2500 BCE, villages appeared with shelters made of wattle and daub, and by 1500 BCE we see the first examples of pottery.

The peoples of the Americas can be classified according to their ecological zones. The oldest cultures were on the vast steppes of North America, but whether they had by this time developed the tipi as their distinctive habitation is not known. Affluent shore cultures had developed along the Pacific coast of Canada, along the southern stretches of the Atlantic coast of North America (from Georgia to Florida), in the great flood marshes of the lower Mississippi River, and finally in the great rain forests of Mesoamerica and the Amazon. By 3500 BCE, the Mississippi River delta people began constructing large mounds as part of their ceremonial culture. They were the first to construct such mounds in the Americas. Mound making was an attempt to construct ceremonial landscapes that brought in people from far away for ritual exchanges. It remained a tradition in the southeast areas of North America until the arrival of the European colonizers.

Around 3500 BCE important transformations were also taking place in the western uplands of the Amazon, and it is to this area that our story turns, since it holds the key to the transformations that were to take place first in Peru and then in Mesoamerica. The rain forests were home to an astonishing variety of plants and animals, making them an important incubator of

human social networks. People formed tribes, and developed a slash-and-burn gardening technique to better harness cashew, cocoa, and Brazil nuts, as well as the all-important manioc, used to make bread, soups, and fermented drinks. The process began slowly around 10,000 BCE as the rain forests began to expand. Groups pushed higher and higher into the mountains, where they encountered the potato, maybe around 5000 BCE. These people are not considered agriculturalists, however, because as far as we know they did not develop irrigation, one of the elements associated with agriculture. That changed around 3000 BCE, when a group of intrepid farmers settled in a high Andean valley that still today seems impossibly arid and remote, and began a farming community there based on irrigation. Using the slope of the valley to their advantage, they tapped the stream and fed the water horizontally to garden plots. Their method worked, and soon the dusty valley was turned into a gardener's paradise. Such activities were never just "farming" but were part of a sacred landscape; and it is now known how that landscape was defined. Archaeologists call the place La Galgada—and the settlement was no casual affair, but organized around a powerful family clan and its shamanistic leaders. And to emphasize

2.49 **Galgada ruins today**

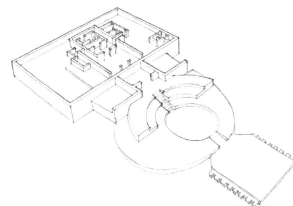

2.50 **Circular sunken plaza, Caral, Peru**

the authority of the clan lineage, the elders over time developed a unique architectural form, an ancestor mound. The clan leaders, who were also probably shamans, met in something akin to a sweat lodge, a flat-topped chamber that could hold about fifteen people. The idea of sweat lodges, a widespread phenomenon, developed in Siberia and was brought to the Americas by its ancient settlers. At Galgada, when the chief died, he was ritually wrapped in a fetus position and buried in the lodge, which was then mounded over and a new one built on top. Over the centuries, the mound grew higher and higher in the shape of a stepped mound. Its surface was plastered and probably painted red.

Though the history of agriculture is often told as a story of Peru, it is really a story of the Amazonians, who, with their thousands of years of experience, took the step to what we call agriculture by moving into the mountains and developing irrigation and controlled farming.

Caral

The experiment at Galgada was such that soon other groups were setting out to transform mountains into farmscapes. The most ambitious group tackled what might seem an almost impossible task—to transform the uninhabitable coastal Peruvian desert into a fertile plain. The shores had supported fishing communities for thousands of years. The fishing here is among the best in the world, but these fishing communities were isolated, and could only trade north and south. Enter the highlanders who arrived at the Supe River floodplain, and in a few decades made it into Peru's first great agricultural center. Known as Caral, it was first settled around 2600 BCE. The farmers brought with them two plants in particular, plants that they knew the fishermen would need—cotton and the gourd. Cotton was needed for fishing nets, and the gourds served as floats. In essence, the farmers supplied the fishermen with advanced equipment, and in return got fish. It was a brilliant arrangement, but it required a strict regime on the part of the Supe Valley farmers. At the center of the community were the shaman elites, who governed by a mixture of ancestral and divine right from a huge central plaza, roughly 500 meters by 175 meters, that was surrounded by

an extensive array of buildings, platform mounds, smaller mounds, and two major sunken circular plazas, all sited along a bluff overlooking the river and its agricultural fields. Brightly painted, the structures would have stood out against both the green fields below and the yellowish gray of the arid mountains above. The ceremonial center was probably activated by a special ritual class, with events certainly taking place daily. Some events probably involved the larger community in multiday festivals of dance, music, and feasting. Archaeologists have found flutes made of condor and pelican bones, as well as horns made of llama and deer bones. The site had formally arranged residential complexes for the elite. The rest of the inhabitants, namely the farmers, lived in a network of hamlets of thatch houses near the fields that were dispersed throughout the valley.

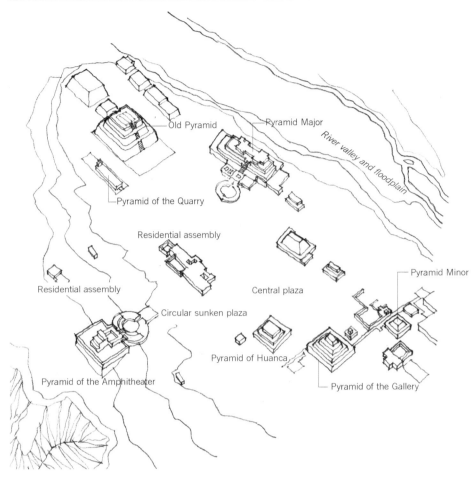

2.51 Central zone of Caral

Pyramid Major, Caral's dominant platform mound (160 by 150 meters and 18 meters high) is perched on the northern end of the site, at the very edge of the terrace from which it overlooks the valley. It was constructed in two major phases. First, the mound walls were built by filling open-mesh reed bags with cut stones. Five other platform mounds join with it to form a C-shaped plaza facing south. Just beyond its open mouth, at the center of a low mound, is a sunken circular plaza 50 meters in diameter.

If the main plaza, surrounded by mounds high above the valley floor, creates the impression of a vast bounded space reminiscent of a high valley plateau, then the circular sunken plaza, reminiscent of the later kivas of North America, repeats that space on a smaller scale, perhaps corresponding to the principles of the earth. Although the ceremonial structures of the early Andean civilizations have the outline of a pyramid and are usually called pyramids, it is more accurate to refer to them as platform mounds. This is because they were conceptually conceived as a series of platforms. (*Pyramid* is from a Greek word that describes Egyptian structures.) What the native Americans called their structures is unknown. The word *pyramid* will, however, be used here in cases where convention has already established it as part of a name.

2.52 Caral and its environment

1500 BCE

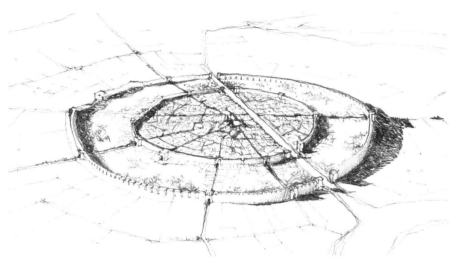

3.1 Reconstruction of the city of Mari, Syria

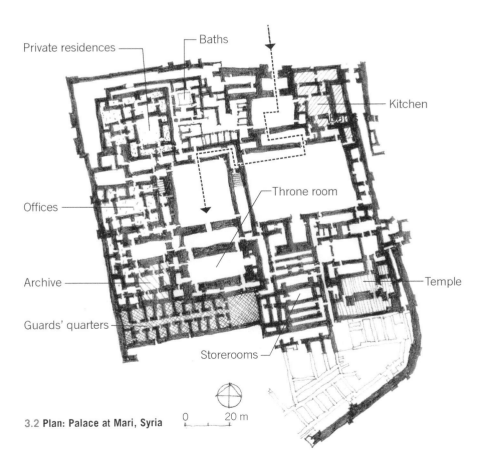

Private residences

Baths

Offices

Throne room

Kitchen

Archive

Temple

Guards' quarters

Storerooms

3.2 Plan: Palace at Mari, Syria   0   20 m

INTRODUCTION

How much different our world would be today had the camel and horse not existed. The impact of the camel was felt first. Traditionally, the great economic centers had all relied on boats or oxcarts as the primary means of transport. With the camel, traders could now cross the deserts and mountains that stretch thousands of miles east and west and cut Asia into separate north and south regions. By the middle of the second millennium BCE, caravans with as many as six hundred animals were plying trade routes across the desert plains. The first place to monetize this trade was a city called Mari. Located in modern-day Syria on the western bank of the Euphrates, it flourished as a trade center and city-state from 2900 BCE until 1759 BCE. It was located halfway between the Persian Gulf and the upland reaches of the river. In other words, it was designed as a short cut to the Mediterranean and thus was perfectly sited to collect and distribute goods. But this was not a city in the conventional old-Mesopotamian sense. It did not really produce anything but instead was an entrepôt city, a transshipment hub of the third millennium. That the city was a perfect circle makes sense.

The palace, thought to have been built by King Zimri-Lim (r. 1779–1757 BCE), had at its core a vast rectangular throne room, at the entrance of which was a statue of a maiden holding a jug of water from which water actually poured. It was meant to impress the visitor that here in the desert, water could be poured away. Behind the throne room, protected by a guardroom, were special storage areas where the king kept his most precious items. Nearby was an area for the bureaucrats who recorded what went in and out of the city. Contrast Eridu with Mari: the first was a ritual center designed for the agricultural production of surplus and dependent on an exchange economy primarily through boats (canals and seaports) and oxcarts, whereas the latter was dependent on the rapid turnover of goods. More than 25,000 tablets in the Mari archives have survived, including economic reports and juridical texts. The records describe an astonishing abundance of material and food going through the city, including prized spices such as coriander, cumin, saffron, and cloves; and even ice, a luxury item imported from the far-off mountains. The records also show that things did not always go smoothly. Letters describe the difficulties of moving a massive shipment of some 360,000 liters of barley. Another record tells how flour that had been shipped to feed an army had been destroyed by ants.

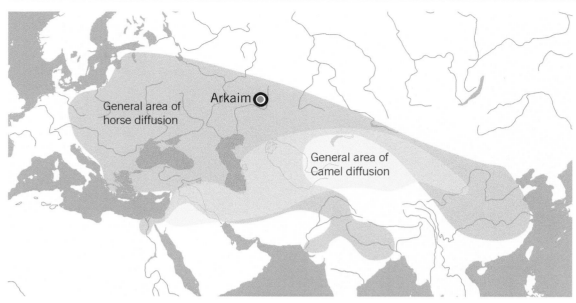

3.3 Inner Asia camel and horse diffusion areas to around 1300 BCE

3.4 Statue of a water goddess found in the palace at Mari

The camel at this stage of history was still a relatively local Mesopotamian phenomenon, but its use expanded eastward until it finally reached China, where its impact would be felt around 800 BCE during the Zhou dynasty. The new transcontinental network would become the economic engine of Eurasia until the arrival of colonialism in the 16th century.

In the second millennium BCE another quadruped entered the scene: the horse. Domesticated around 3000 BCE on the vast Eurasian steppe, the horse played a dynamic role in history well into the modern age. And this was not just because the horse was fast; it also conferred a significant military advantage in that riders with bows and arrows could now rule supreme. Indeed, in the middle of the second millennium BCE, Central Asia—from the Bactrian-Margiana Archaeological Complex society in Turkmenistan to the Indus Ghaggar-Hakra region in the south—went into a period of turmoil and decline. An ecological disaster—the drying up of the Ghaggar-Hakra River—certainly played a part in creating a political vacuum. But just as important during this period were large groups of horse-centric people that called themselves Aryas and are now known as Aryans, who moved into northern India. Since their structures were

built of wood rather than brick, very little tangible evidence of this period has survived. The newcomers brought with them not only horses, but also a sacred oral tradition of mythologies and legends. Around 1500 BCE these were assembled and written down. This was the beginning of the so-called Vedic period, named after a Sanskrit Indo-European word that means "knowledge."

West Asia also experienced a state of flux and instability. Assyria, Babylon, and other Mesopotamian cities were overrun by horse-mounted invaders of unknown provenance, the Mitanni and Kassite people, who had moved in from the north or east. A similar situation existed with the so-called Sea People, who conquered the Nile Delta (ca. 1300–1200 BCE) and from whom the Egyptians learned how to make chariots and better bows. Also among the newcomers to West Asia were the Hittites, who settled in Anatolia around 1600 BCE. There, in the north-central region, they founded Hattusas, a capital with numerous temples. They brought in scribes from Syria to maintain their records in cuneiform script, creating voluminous state archives. The Hittites and the Egyptians became the preeminent land powers in western Asia.

3.5 **Camel caravan in Mongolia**

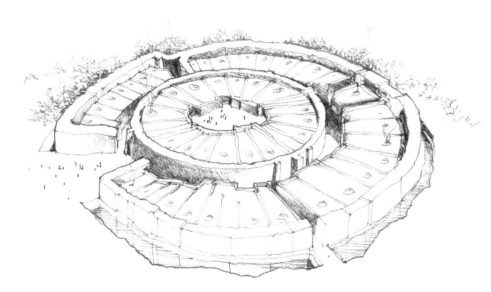

3.6 **Reconstruction of the town of Arkaim, Russia**

The time period between 1206 and 1150 BCE was a troubled one that saw the cultural collapse of the Mycenaean kingdoms, the Hittite Empire in Anatolia and Syria, and the New Kingdom of Egypt. Almost every city between Pylos and Gaza was violently destroyed, and many were left unoccupied thereafter. The Hittite capital was burned and abandoned around 1200 BCE, and was never reoccupied.

There is a possible explanation for the problems that beset kingdoms in the middle of the second millennium, namely the development of a technology to go with the horse: the chariot. The earliest known fully developed chariots come from burials of the Andronovo culture in Kazakhstan around 2000 BCE. These people engaged in bronze metallurgy on an industrial scale and practiced complex burial rituals that included the burial of chariots and horses. They were once largely pastoralists, but with a global warming and the growth of the steppe, they turned increasingly to horse herding. One can only assume that chariots were highly prized and a core element in newly developed mythologies relating to the spiritual world. Over time the settlements grew larger and developed into a series of towns, some circular and some square. Arkaim (ca. 1700 BCE), for example, had two protective circular walls, 160 meters in diameter and 4 meters wide, built with soil that was packed into timber frames before being faced with adobe bricks. The fortified town had four gates, the widest one being in the southwestern direction and the remaining three oriented to the cardinal directions. The community consisted of thirty-five houses built adjacent to the outer wall, each of them having an exit to the main street of the settlement. Most archaeologists believe that it was an administrative or ceremonial center with a set of core inhabitants—perhaps priests and bronze forgers—and that people would have gathered there for special occasions.

3.7 **Ramesses on his chariot, relief in Abu Simbel, near Philae, Egypt, ca. 1260 BCE**

3.8 **A Western Zhou chariot burial pit unearthed at Zhangjiapo, Chang'an County, China**

The chariot spread quickly, with the advantage going initially to the steppe people. The chariot was brought to Egypt by the so-called Sea People, who easily overcame the fabled Egyptian army. It was only when the Egyptians developed an updated version of the chariot under Ramesses II that they were able to turn the tables. Ramesses portrayed himself on a relief in his Abu Simbel temple proudly riding a chariot into battle against the Hittites. The chariot and everything that it implied in terms of prestige and power made it to China around the same time with the Zhou, who rose to defeat the earlier Shang dynasty. The Zhou were from the western province, hence the chariot. Several of their chariot burial sites have been found, such as the one in Hougang, in Henan province (ca. 1200 BCE). As a warrior class, the Zhou developed a social system generally known as feudalism, in which the nobles ruled over the peasants, while merchants were a social group outside the social pyramid and were hardly even considered people. There are certain undeniable similarities here to the chariot-based Vedic culture that was beginning in India around that same time.

The chariot was a symbol of prestige, the limo of the day. In both Hindu and Persian mythology, most of the gods are portrayed as riding them. Giant three-story chariots are still today pulled through the streets of Puri, India, in an annual celebration of Jagannath, "Lord of the Universe," a deity worshipped by Hindus mainly in northeast India.

3.9 **Vitthala Temple chariot, Vijayanagar, India, ca. 1500 BCE**

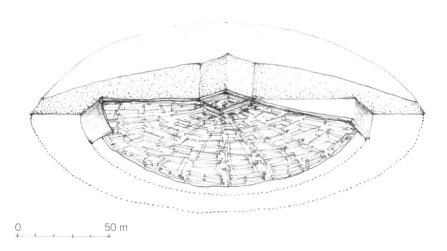

0   50 m

3.10 Wooden substructure with tombs for the chief, his wife, and their horses, Arzhan, Russia

In Greece, the earliest representations of horsemen in Mycenaean art is dated to about 1300 BCE, which makes sense in terms of its diffusion from Central Asia. But the Dorians, who invaded Greece around 1200 BCE from their steppe homeland, brought with them an even more elaborate horse and chariot culture. The god Apollo drove his chariot across the skies every day, carrying the sun with him. Over time, the steppe people who remained in Inner Asia and cohered into a group known as the Scythians came to prosper as both traders and metallurgists. On the open steppe they built clan burial mounds known as kurgans. Thousands of these were built between Europe and northern China, dating back to the third millennium BCE. Most were near a river, including the Maikop kurgan on the Belaya River, not too far from the Black Sea (ca. 2500 BCE); Kurgan 4 near the Volga River at Kutuluk near Samara, Russia (ca. 2400 BCE); and the Novovelichkovskaya kurgan (ca. 2000 BCE) on the Ponura River. The most specular kurgan, known as Arzhan (ca. 650 BCE), is located in a broad and beautiful valley in the Tuva Republic, Russia, some 60 kilometers northwest of Kyzyl. It is a stone structure, 4 meters high and 120 meters in diameter. The stones entomb a shallow structure with wooden walls, arranged in a spoked manner, which contains the burials

of several people and their horses, with even the horses spectacularly ornamented in gold jewelry. The central stone disk structure was surrounded by smaller disks, each one probably built by a clan in homage to their leader. It is quite likely that huge gatherings were held here to pay respect to clan leaders, conduct business, socialize, and feast.

Despite the disruptions, trade continued unabated, especially along the Mediterranean coast. Documents discovered at Ugarit mention a wide spectrum of goods—wheat, olives, barley, dates, honey, wine, and cumin, as well as copper, tin, bronze, lead, and iron—coming from as far away as Afghanistan and central Africa. Ugarit seems to have specialized in the Murex seashells that were used in the fabrication of greatly sought-after purple dye. Timber from the Levant's forests was another important Ugaritic export.

Meanwhile, in the Andes, the experimental transformation of the dry and barren Caral Valley into an agricultural paradise was being copied in the valleys to the north and south, including Supe Valley to the north. The ritual centers involved enormous U-shaped complexes, the elements of which would remain part of the Peruvian architectural language for millennia. Unlike Poverty Point, which was a communal effort, these Peruvian centers were built for powerful elites who ruled as gods over a subservient population of farmers. Success depended on the surplus production of crops like cotton, potatoes, and squash.

3.11 Helios the Sun God

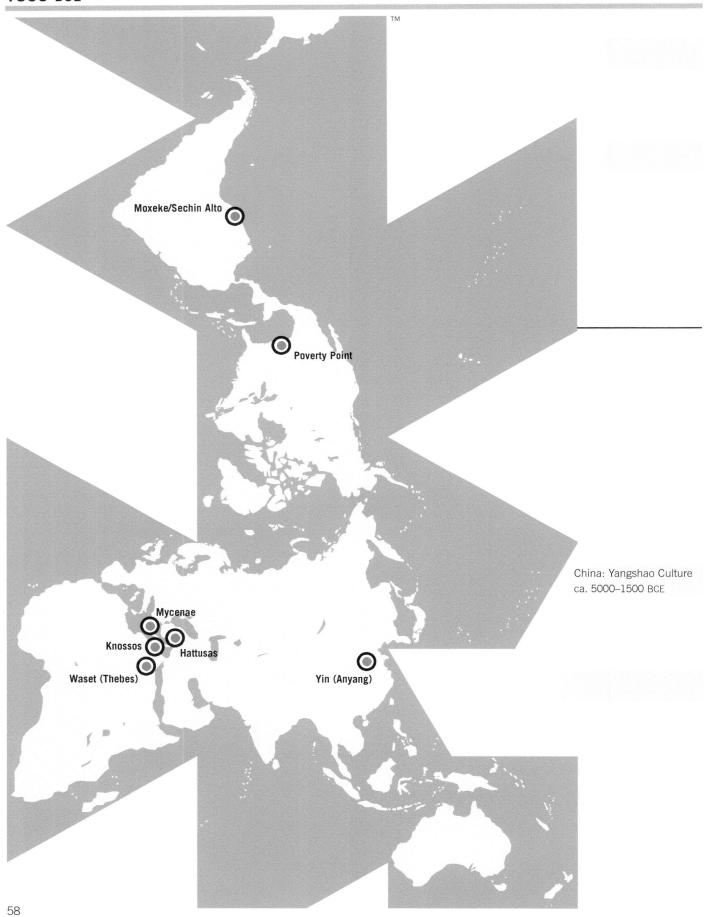

Moxeke/Sechin Alto

Poverty Point

China: Yangshao Culture
ca. 5000–1500 BCE

Mycenae

Knossos

Hattusas

Waset (Thebes)

Yin (Anyang)

™

Minoan Culture
ca. 3000–1200 BCE

Greece: Geometric Period
ca. 900–700 BCE

▲ **Knossos Palace**
ca. 1600 BCE

Egypt: Old Kingdom
ca. 2649–2150 BCE

Middle Kingdom
ca. 2030–1640 BCE

New Kingdom
ca. 1550–1070 BCE

Third Intermediate Period
ca. 1070–712 BCE

▲ **Great Pyramid of Khufu**
ca. 2590 BCE

▲ **Temple Complex at Karnak**
Begun ca. 1550 BCE

▲ **Valley of the Kings**
ca. 1500–1100 BCE

▲ **Mortuary Temple of Queen Hatshepsut**
ca. 1470 BCE

▲ **Temple of Luxor**
ca. 1350 BCE

▲ **Abu Simbel**
ca. 1264–1244 BCE

2500 BCE	**1500 BCE**	**500 BCE**

Early Bronze Age
ca. 3000–2000 BCE

Middle Bronze Age
ca. 2000–1600 BCE

Late Bronze Age
ca. 1600–1200 BCE

Iron Age
ca. 1200-580 BCE

Hittite Empire
ca. 1600–1180 BCE

▲ **Hattusas**
ca. 1600 BCE

Scythians
ca. 900 BCE–400 CE

Mycenean Culture
ca. 1600–1100 BCE

▲ **Treasury of Atreus**
ca. 1250 BCE

▲ **Babylon**
ca. 1800 BCE

▲ **Palace of Mycenae**
ca. 1300 BCE

China: Xia Dynasty
ca. 2070–1600 BCE

Shang Dynasty
ca. 1600–1050 BCE

Zhou Dynasty
ca. 1046–771 BCE

▲ **Zhengzhou**
ca. 1700–1400 BCE

▲ **Shang tombs at Anyang**
ca. 1400–1100 BCE

Southeast North America: Archaic Period
ca. 8000–2000 BCE

Southeast North America: Formative Period
ca. 1000 BCE–500 CE

▲ **Poverty Point**
ca. 1800–700 BCE

Casma/Sechin Culture
ca. 3600–200 BCE

▲ **Sechin Alto**
ca. 2000–1500 BCE

▲ **Moxeke**
ca. 1800–900 BCE

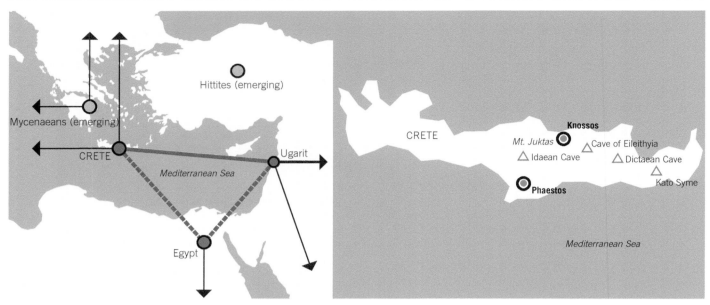

3.12 **Trade diagram, ca. 1600 BCE**

3.13 **Minoan sites on Crete**

THE MINOANS AND KNOSSOS

The turmoil in the Mesopotamian heartland and northern India benefited the economies of the eastern Mediterranean, especially the Minoans on Crete, who developed the world's first thalassocracy, a maritime trading economy. The Minoans stitched together the economies of West Asia and Egypt with the emerging markets of Greece and other parts of Europe. Their palace architecture (Knossos, Phaestos, Mallia, and Zakros) was conceived according to very different principles than that of Mesopotamia. The Minoans appeared not to have been overly concerned with defensive installations, which indicates that their trading practices were peaceful in nature. The Minoans also never came under the type of political stresses that necessitated complex cosmologies. Theirs was not an extreme landscape of deserts and floods. They thus emerged still clothed in ancient chthonic religious practices, which were more intimate and less formal than the rigid systems prevalent in Egypt and Mesopotamia; their holy places were connected to landscape features.

Over time, however, Cretan religion began to become more complex, and strong male gods emerged, in particular the Cretan Zeus, a fertility god who died annually and was reborn in a sacred festival. He took the

form of a bull, which was central to a festival known as the Thiodaisia, during which the cities renewed their oaths of alliance to each other. These rites included large-scale drinking and feasting, and were staged in the open landscape or in front of the major palaces in special theater-like settings. There was a joyful, life-enhancing quality to these festivals as well as to their artwork, as can be seen in the murals in their palaces. Three caves were particularly important in their cult: the Dictaean Cave on Mt. Dicte near the village Psychro, the Idaean Cave on Mt. Ida near Anogheia, and the Cave of Eileithyia, dedicated to the birth goddess. The Dictaean Cave, cold and moist even in the heat of summer, with a pool of water surrounded by stalactites, was the site of rituals dating back to the earliest time of Cretan habitation. The Cave of Eileithyia is now a Christian site and is still visited by Cretan women. A procession led up to the peak of the mountain to a special sanctuary where offerings were "fed" into a cleft in the rocks. Today an annual procession still makes its way up to the top of the mountain for the feast of Afendis Christos—an example of how Christianity often tried to nullify "heathen" cults by appropriating ancient rituals and customs. The cave most intimately connected with the Cretan creation myth is the cave on

Mt. Ida, where the earth mother Rhea gave birth to Zeus. Myth describes him as tended by nymphs and protected by youths against his father, Chronos. Zeus then fathered Minos, who became king of Knossos and of Crete.

3.14 **Ruin of ritual structure: Cave of Eileithyia, near Amnisos, Crete**

The Thiodaisia festival involved a dance in which performers somersaulted over a charging bull, as represented vividly on the walls of the palace. Men and women are both portrayed performing the jump, a man in one case in midair, waiting to be caught in the open arms of a woman. Given that the entire landscape was sacred, the Minoans did not build temples but rather palaces, the largest of which was at Knossos, built around 2000 BCE on top of a prior Neolithic settlement. It was rebuilt and enlarged in 1700 BCE after a large earthquake. The palace contained residences, kitchens, storage rooms, bathrooms, ceremonial rooms, workshops, and sanctuaries. There were sophisticated infrastructural installations, ventilation systems, and groundwater conduits. In storage basements, archaeologists have found elephant tusks from Syria and copper ingots from Cyprus.

Though we do not know what role the priest-king who ruled there assumed, it is clear that the palace, with its many different kinds and sizes of interior spaces, terraces, courtyards, and platforms, represented a mosaic of interwoven activities. It was part palace, part warehouse, part factory, part religious center. It was laid out around a large rectangular courtyard with several entrances converging onto it. The courtyard was surrounded by verandas at the upper levels, allowing views into its space. Because of the verandas, windows, porches, steps, and doors that folded open into the sides of the walls, the visual interrelationship between inner and outer space is particularly intricate—more so than in any other palace architecture of this period.

Flanking the courtyard was the throne room, which had built-in gypsum benches on the north and south walls with a place for the insertion of a wooden throne, which was replaced with a gypsum one later. The red stucco walls are covered with images of griffins, legendary animals with the head and wings of an eagle and the body of a lion that are thought to have symbolized strength and vigilance. The floor was painted red. The benches, though at seat height, were probably used to hold votive offerings. Opposite the throne was a water basin to which steps descended and which may have served for initiation rites. The low room, which was kept dark, was meant to simulate a sacred cave, according to some scholars.

Around the room were various storage rooms, which were repositories for the precious objects used in ceremonies. The whole complex of chambers—sixteen in all—was designed as a self-contained unit that had both a public entrance from the courtyard and a private staircase connecting to the floor above.

3.15 The double axe, or *labrys*, principal symbol of the Minoan-Mycenaean religion, standing erect on a bull's head

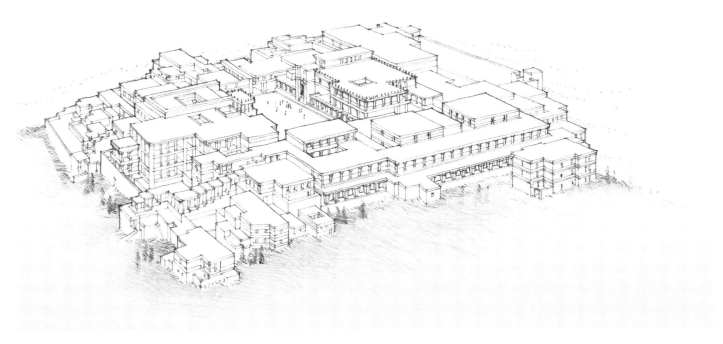

3.16 Overview of Knossos, near Heraklion, Crete

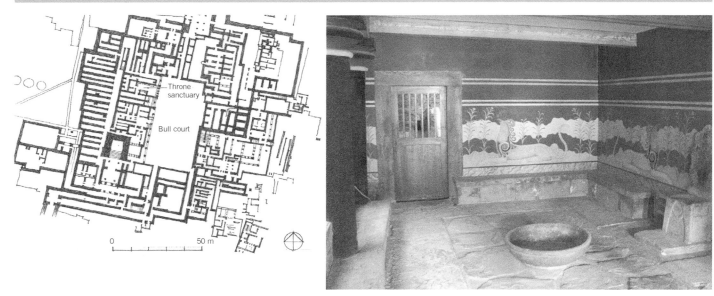

3.17 Plan of throne sanctuary at Knossos

3.18 Throne room, Palace at Knossos

Minoan columns are particularly distinctive. Made of wood, they tapered toward the bottom and were painted dark blue; the capitals, painted red, had the profile of cushions. In the principal rooms, the stone rubble walls were finished with a fine layer of plaster painted in a fresco-like technique; they depicted scenes of animals and plants, and nautical life of remarkable vibrancy and beauty. Minoan art was among the first to represent human movement. The main

colors used were black (carbonaceous shale), white (hydrate of lime), red (hematite), yellow (ochre), blue (silicate of copper), and green (blue and yellow mixed together).

Though palaces by definition require controlled access, entry into the Palace at Knossos was more than a sequence of gates and antechambers; it was a linearly extended spatial experience. The starting point was the west porch, which consisted of a single column standing between walls—an iconic representation of the mother goddess. From that point one walked south to a terrace

that offered a broad vista to Mt. Juktas. No visitor would have missed the reference to the Cretan Zeus here. Through an opening midway down the terrace, one turned away from the mountain and entered a series of state rooms that led to a great columnar hall illuminated by clerestory windows designed as a box within a box. The hall, in turn, opened up to a flight of steps flanked by a colonnaded veranda for spectators. At the top of the stairs was a lobby with two ceremonial doors right and left of the axis leading to another hall. At the back of this hall a door led to a staircase that descended at a right angle to the central courtyard. Nothing as spatially remarkable would be designed for a long time.

3.19 Court-level plan: Palace at Knossos

3.20 Schematic plan: Palace at Knossos

Descending the stairs, the visitor faced across the court to a goddess sanctuary, an imposing structure with a wide ceremonial staircase leading up through a colonnade to a landing in front of a pier-and-door partition. Inside was a spacious room 18.5 by 15 meters, with eight tapering pillars around a central square that was probably open from above. A statue was placed against the back wall, with the walls themselves richly decorated with scenes of boxing and bull-grappling, and more griffins. It is possible to imagine the central court as a plateau, positioned at the intersection of the sunken throne room on one side and the elevated cult space, with its skylight, on the other.

In the middle of the courtyard was a small altar for burnt offerings and, off to one corner, a large circular stone with concavities in it, probably also for offerings. It was perhaps in this space that the bull ceremony was performed, with the spectators viewing it from the numerous balconies and verandas.

Other palaces have been uncovered on the island, as have several peak sanctuaries, such as the one on Mt. Juktas, which was clearly linked to the cult practices at Knossos. It was the focus of pilgrimage ceremonies and was also probably associated with ceremonies legitimating the rule of the kings of Knossos.

The demise of the Minoans was largely due to volcanic eruptions on the nearby island of Thera (modern Santorini) around 1600 BCE. This created opportunities for the Mycenaeans on the Peloponnese, who set up posts on Crete and integrated Minoan cultural elements into their own aesthetic protocols.

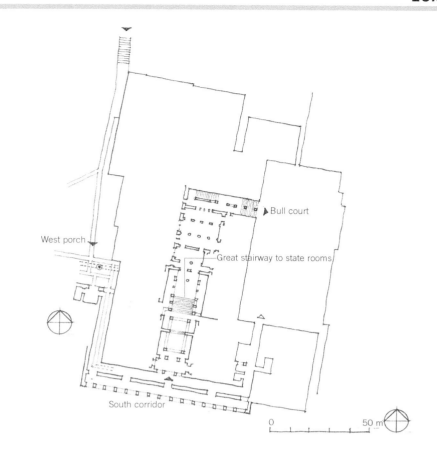

3.21 **Diagram of entry sequence: Palace at Knossos**

3.22 **One of the grand stairways at the Palace at Knossos**

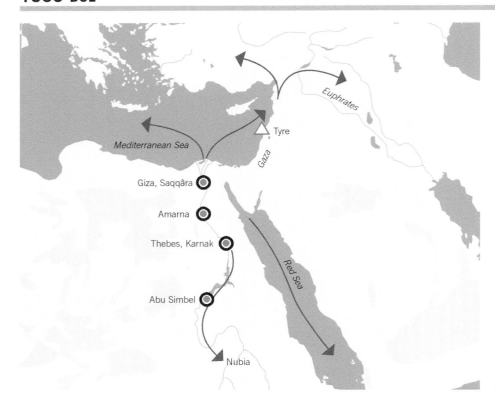

3.23 Egypt, ca. 1500 BCE

EGYPT: THE NEW KINGDOM

The Nile Delta of Egypt, around 1720 BCE, was invaded and occupied by the Hyksos, also called the Sea People, who ruled Lower Egypt from their capital, Avaris, until driven out by Ahmose I of Thebes in 1567 BCE. The origin of the Hyksos, and even their name, remains the subject of scholarly debate. In 1550 BCE, Ahmose I, founder of the Eighteenth Dynasty (called the New Kingdom, a rule of dynasties lasting until 1070 BCE), was able to throw off the Hyksos and regain control over the country. The Hyksos, despite being enemies of Egypt, brought to Egyptians some previously unknown things: not only the chariot, but also new techniques of bronze working and pottery, new breeds of animals, new crops, and a particularly powerful composite bow.

The return of stability in Egypt meant the vigorous trade in goods on which so many Near Eastern societies depended could recommence. Furthermore, with the continuing troubles in Mesopotamia, Egypt began to dominate the region. Seeking to

guarantee the borders against the all-too-volatile political environment, the Egyptians marched into Syria and besieged Nineveh and Babylon. No longer isolationists, as they had been in the Old Kingdom, they now became colonizers. Their turquoise mines in the Sinai were reopened, and Ekron and other cities controlled by the Philistines traded with Egypt in pottery and metals.

An important change that came with the reestablishment of unity involved religion: no longer only the purview of the elite, it now comprised larger sections of society. Festivals, processions, and celebrations that could draw thousands of participants were introduced. The New Kingdom saw the rise of large temple institutions that played an important part in hosting these mass celebrations. As a consequence the temple priests rose in power and played an increasingly large role in Egyptian politics.

Waset (Thebes)

During the period of the New Kingdom, the capital of Egypt was Thebes, where the family that had thrown out the Hyksos came from. The Egyptian name for Thebes was Waset, the "city of the scepter." It was located on a small rise of the middle of the Nile floodplain that became, during the inundation of the Nile, a quasi-island. Thebes was the Greek name for the city that eventually stuck. The prime deity of Thebes was the ram-god Amun-Re, the god of the sun and the heaven and the omnipresent father of the kings who guaranteed world order. The ascendency of Thebes mean that Amun-Re was elevated to the status of a national deity. At least a dozen temples were built over a five-hundred-year period, from about 1500 to 1000 BCE. The site spans both sides of the Nile and includes the Valley of the Kings, where many of the pharaohs were buried. Thebes had been used as a burial site since around 2000 BCE, but with its new prestige as imperial capital, it also became the royal site. The first temple at the site was erected around 1970 BCE and was a rather modest structure. Thutmosis I began enlarging the Karnak temple complex at Thebes around 1530 BCE. Queen Hatshepsut added her temple on the west bank (ca. 1470 BCE), and Amenhotep III started work on Temple of Luxor around 1350 BCE; the temple-building activity culminated in the efforts of Seti I and Ramesses II, who made significant additions to Karnak and Luxor around 1280 BCE. From then on the complex went through periodic expansions and transformations until the 5th century BCE.

At the ritual core of all of this construction was a simple, small chamber in the Karnak temple—essentially a sacred dry-dock, which held a barque through most of the year. The barque chamber Queen Hatshepsut built, which was dismantled by her successors, has been uncovered and reconstructed at Karnak, but not on the original site. The chamber was made of special red quartzite stone (thus its name, the Red Chapel) on a base of black diorite. The current barque chapel, built by Philip III of Macedonia around 340 BCE, follows the idea of the original and contains only two rooms: one where the offerings were presented, and one with a stone base on which the barque rested. On special occasions the barque was carried out of the temple in the context of a great popular celebration and taken to various sites depending on calendric requirements. Though a boat, this barque never got wet but instead was transported by priests on their shoulders. When it crossed the Nile, it was placed on a special boat.

3.24 **Barque chamber at Karnak**

3.25 **Relief carving showing the barque being ceremoniously carried at Karnak**

Some sixty festivals were celebrated in Thebes annually. Some took place within the temple confines; others involved moving cult images from temple to temple. The three most important of these traveling festivals involved Amun; his wife, Mut, the Egyptian mother goddess; and Mut's son, Khonsu, the lunar deity.

1. Preeminent was the Opet ("secret chamber") festival during which the statues of Amun, Khonsu, and Mut were escorted from Karnak to the Temple of Luxor. At a particular moment during the events, the deity "spoke" to confirm the legitimacy of the king. The god's legitimization of the king was reciprocated by gifts to the temple from the royal family. The festival took place during *Akhet* (roughly our September), the season when the Nile flooded, and lasted for eleven days, but as time progressed, the number of festival days grew. The journey from Karnak to Luxor was made over land along a processional street; the return journey was made along the Nile by boat.

2. The Beautiful Feast of the Valley coincided with a celebration of the dead in which Amun, Mut, and Khonsu would travel to the western shore to visit the gods of the West and the deified dead kings. The festival came to be associated with renewal and regeneration. It occurred during the second month of *Shemu*, the harvest season (roughly our April), and lasted for over twenty days.

3. Amun's cult image traveled every ten days from the Temple of Luxor on the east bank to the shrine of Medinet Habu (ca. 1460–1420 BCE) on the west bank. The original name was Djanet, and according to popular belief, it was the place where Amun first appeared.

The Karnak culture of processions was at the time unique in the world and would have a huge impact on subsequent religious world views. The processional rituals among Catholics, for example, is rooted in these ancient prototypes.

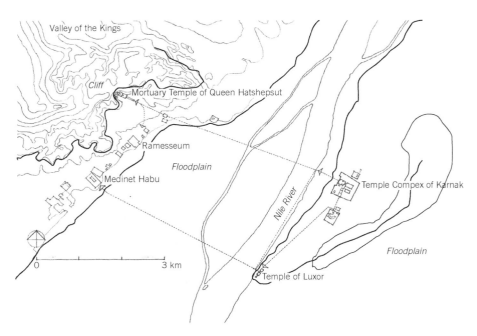

3.26 The principal temples and processional routes of Karnak

Karnak has two entrances: one for those arriving from the direction of the Nile, to accommodate the barque procession, and the other from Luxor. The Nile entrance had its own harbor. Both entrances are defined by a series of majestic pylons. To the north of the enclosure is a small sanctuary dedicated to Ptah, who was sometimes seen as an abstract form of the Self-Created One. He was intimately connected with the plastic arts and especially with the mysteries of architecture and stone masonry.

A pylon (from the Greek word for "gate") is a high, inclined, and slightly trapezoid-shaped wall with a large central entrance guarding a sacred precinct. It was often accented by tall flagpoles and obelisks whose tops were sheathed in gold plating. The two flanks of the pylon, formal and imposing, symbolized the mountain ranges that hem in the Nile. Their form was a purely symbolical expression of Egyptian power. Though all architectural forms of the period—such as the ziggurat in Mesopotamia, the *megaron* in Greece, and the processional paths in Egypt—had symbolical value, the pylon gates were among the earliest architectural forms that condensed wall, gate, and cosmology into a single declaration of power. The Egyptian word for pylon was *bekhnet*, which implies vigilance. Thus it relates to the watchtower-like nature, if not the actual function, of these structures. Flagpoles were placed along the front of the pylons, the poles and flags representing, for the Egyptians, the presence of a sacred precinct at the most basic level.

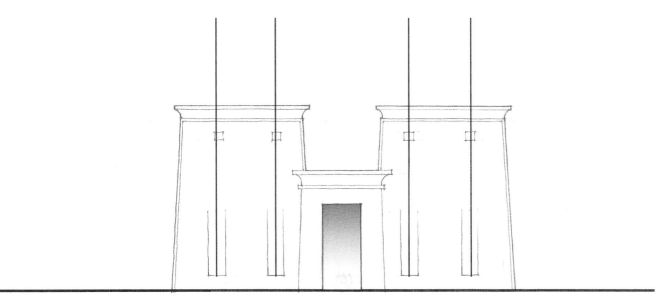

3.27 **Entrance pylon to the Karnak Temple of Khonsu, Thebes, Egypt**

Like huge billboards, the pylons also proclaimed, in image and text, important events in the role of the donor-king. On one, the seventh pylon of Karnak, a huge Thutmosis III is shown holding a club and taking a swing at a cluster of enemy soldiers—depicted smaller—whom he seemed to seize by the hair. Beneath his feet, in three rows, are the names of the conquered cities and peoples, also listed in three rows. The conquest of the Lybians, Hittites, and Bedouins are particularly vigorously portrayed. The pylons were most often covered with a fine layer of stucco and painted white, while the figures and other pictorial elements were rendered in vivid colors.

3.28 **Barque sanctuary of Temple of Khonsu**

The pylons are numbered in the order in which they are encountered when walking through the site. Here, the parts of the building are listed in order of their construction:

- Pylon 8, Hatshepsut, ca. 1479 BCE (Hatshepsut builds mortuary temple and Medinet Habu.)
- Pylons 5 and 6, Thutmosis III, ca. 1450 BCE
- Festival Hall, Thutmosis III, ca. 1450 BCE
- Pylon 7, Thutmosis III, ca. 1450 BCE
- Pylon 3, Amenhotep III, ca. 1350 BCE (Amenhotep III begins Temple of Luxor)
- Pylons 9 and 10, Horemheb, ca. 1300 BCE
- Pylon 2, Horemheb and Ramesses I, ca. 1300 BCE
- Hypostyle hall, Seti I and Ramesses II, ca. 1280–1270 BCE (Ramesses II added pylon and courtyard at Luxor.)
- Temple of Ramesses III, ca. 1150 BCE
- Temple of Khonsu, Ramesses III, ca. 1150 BCE
- Pylon 1, Thirtieth Dynasty, 350 BCE

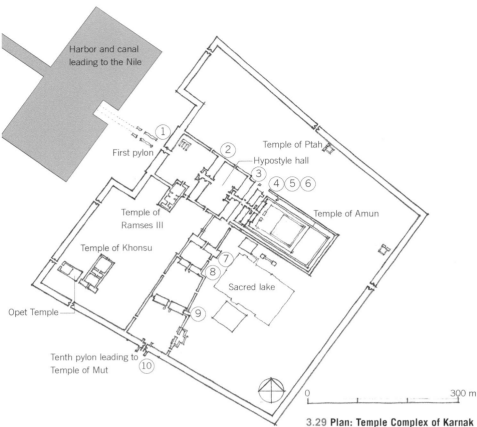

3.29 Plan: Temple Complex of Karnak

The first interior space of the Temple of Amun, located behind the second pylon, was the so-called hypostyle hall, or hall with many columns. The intervals between the enormous columns are proportionately small, dwarfing visitors, who feel as if they are walking among colossal giants. The columns, 24 meters high, are more than just the structural supports for the roof; they serve as superdimensional history books: the scenes painted on them refer to the religious practices and great achievements of the king. At the bottom they are decorated with images of papyrus and at the top with offering scenes. These details were not actually meant to be read by visitors: the screened light coming from the clerestory windows high up under the roof would have created a shadowy environment, with the bulk of the columns rising majestically into darkness. The columns are designed as flower bundles; indeed, they should be seen less as structural and more as a much-magnified floral arrangement giving off an imagined, but nonetheless real, sweet scent of flowers as an offering to the deities.

3.30 Hypostyle hall, Temple of Amun

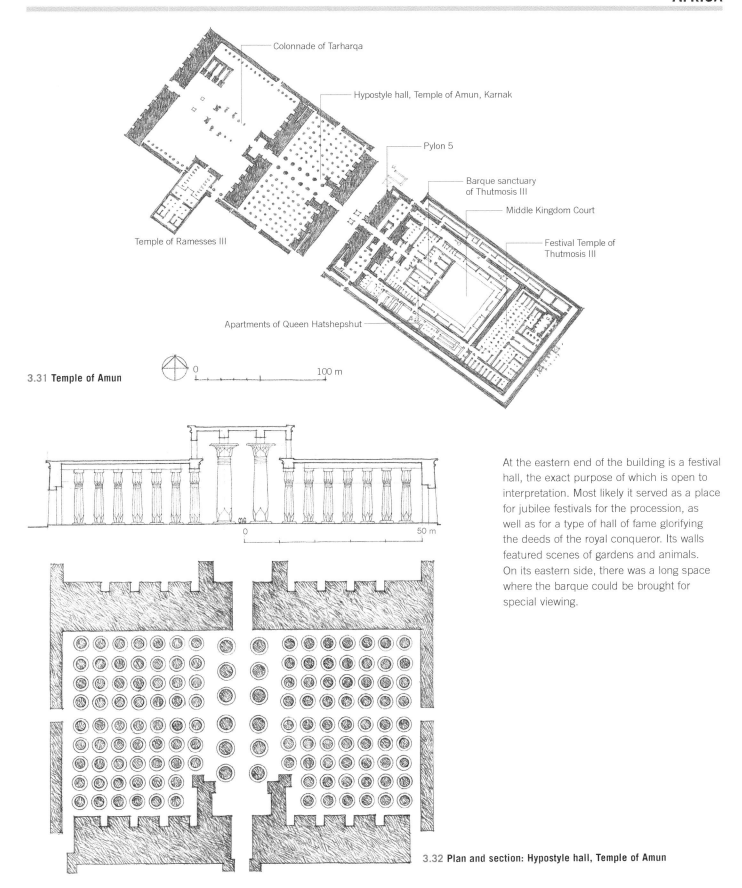

Colonnade of Tarharqa

Hypostyle hall, Temple of Amun, Karnak

Pylon 5

Barque sanctuary
of Thutmosis III

Middle Kingdom Court

Festival Temple of
Thutmosis III

Temple of Ramesses III

Apartments of Queen Hatshepshut

3.31 **Temple of Amun**

0   100 m

At the eastern end of the building is a festival hall, the exact purpose of which is open to interpretation. Most likely it served as a place for jubilee festivals for the procession, as well as for a type of hall of fame glorifying the deeds of the royal conqueror. Its walls featured scenes of gardens and animals. On its eastern side, there was a long space where the barque could be brought for special viewing.

0   50 m

3.32 **Plan and section: Hypostyle hall, Temple of Amun**

Mortuary Temple of Queen Hatshepsut

Queen Hatshepsut, daughter of Thutmosis I, the fifth pharaoh of the Eighteenth Dynasty, was a charismatic and controversial figure in her role as a female monarch. She ruled for twenty years, during a particularly strong moment in the Egyptian economy. It is presumed that after her death, Thutmosis III, her stepson, ordered the systematic erasure of her name from any monument she had built, including her temple at Deir el-Bahri. Some of her monuments were destroyed outright. Such destructions were not uncommon in Egyptian history. Her mortuary temple, however, played a key role in the processional events as the temporary resting place for the barque during the Beautiful Feast of the Valley.

The temple, built by Senmut, her architect, combined mortuary temple, processional way, rock-cut tomb, and ancillary chapels into one synthetic unity with no parallel in Egyptian architecture.

3.33 Mortuary Temple of Queen Hatshepsut, Deir el-Bahri, Egypt

The original Egyptian name of the temple was *djeser-djeseru*, or "the sublime of the sublimes," because it is located in an area that was called Djeseret, or "sublime place," which was dedicated to Hathor, a mother goddess as well as the goddess of love and beauty. A preexistent Hathor chapel on the site was positioned directly under an impressive cliff and built partially into Hatshepsut's temple. The temple was approached by a causeway and a canal that allowed the sacred barque to be brought from the Nile. The temple did not contain her tomb, which was located in the Valley of the Kings and is concealed behind the cliff that looms over her mortuary temple. The axis of Queen Hatshepsut's mortuary temple was precisely aligned to the east with the temple complex at Karnak across the river and to the west with Hatshepsut's tomb on the other side of the cliff in the Valley of the Kings, which was to become the main burial place for the Egyptian royalty for many centuries. There was also a valley temple next to the Nile, but that structure has disappeared.

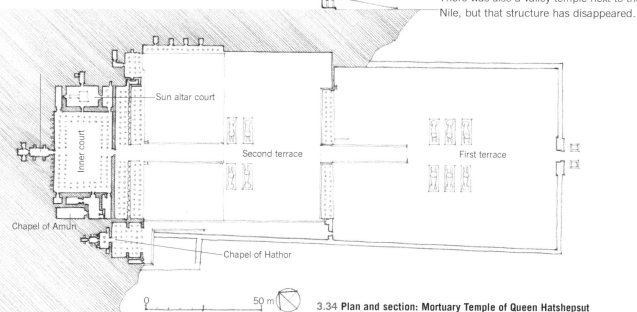

Sun altar court

Inner court

Second terrace

First terrace

Chapel of Amun

Chapel of Hathor

0   50 m

3.34 Plan and section: Mortuary Temple of Queen Hatshepsut

An innovation was the use of terraces leading upward to the foot of the imposing cliff face; an axis runs through the entire scheme with ramps connecting the various courts. The first terrace contained trees and gardens. The second level connects to a chapel of Hathor. On the opposite side is a chapel to Anubis, the jackal-headed god of the dead. The axis leads through a hypostyle hall to the last courtyard, with the cliff wall rising impressively above it.

To the left of the upper terrace is a faux palace for Hatshepsut's ancestors, and to the right an open-air sanctuary dedicated to Re-Horakhty. (Re, the sun god, went through a daily cycle of death and rebirth, dying at the end of each day and being reborn in the morning as Re-Horakhty.) The rooms for the barque, which terminate the axis, together with the room for the cult image, were carved out of the rock itself.

The plan displays a brilliant use of symmetry and asymmetry based on the integration of different elements. Particularly noteworthy are the columns along the front of the temple that are part of a wall and pier system that foreshadows later development. Also, instead of using the usual lotus motifs for the capitals, here the columns are fluted cylinders built out of drums.

3.35 Temple of Luxor, Thebes, Egypt

Temple of Luxor

One enters the Temple of Luxor through a rhomboid-shaped courtyard, built later by Ramesses II, that leads to a passageway of two rows of seven impressively scaled columns 21 meters high. That space opens to a court and a hypostyle hall, and finally to the sanctuary itself. A series of successively smaller telescoping rooms then leads to the sanctuary, where the barque was stored. From there, one gained access to a hall, placed at right angles to the axis, which was defined as the mythical place of the path of the sun. Three doors opened to rooms, one for each of the cult images of the divine triad: Amun; his spouse, Mut, the mother of gods; and their son, the moon god Khonsu. They all "gathered" here during the Beautiful Feast of the Valley.

Egyptian temples, unlike Mesopotamian temples—or even later, Greek and Roman temples—were not conceived as finalities. Instead, they could grow, be changed, get rebuilt, and even be allowed to decay over time. In the case of Luxor, rulers added courts and hypostyle halls as indications of their support and patronage. The Amun-Re Temple, for example, grew steadily toward the Nile, with new gateways being added and others redesigned. In this case, the temple is not axially aligned but follows the gentle easterly bend of the processional route, as it was extended in later building campaigns farther and farther to the northeast.

Nile River

Possible site of the enclosure wall (no longer extant)

Obelisks of Ramesses II

Entrance pylon of Ramesses II

Court of Ramesses II

Colonnade with scenes of Opet Festival

Court of Amenophis III

Barque sanctuary of Amenophis III

Sanctuary rooms for Mut, Amun, and Khonsu

0   100 m

3.36 Plan: Temple of Luxor

3.37 **Temple at Abu Simbel, near Philae, Egypt**

3.38 **View looking toward the sanctuary of the Temple at Abu Simbel**

Abu Simbel

Ramesses II (1290–1224 BCE) extended the sphere of Egyptian influence from the upper valleys of the Euphrates to the fourth cataract of the Nile. Nubian gold from the mines of Wabi el-Allaqui swelled his coffers. To protect the trade routes, he built a series of temple outposts that also served to spread Egyptian cosmological beliefs. His wealth enabled him to carry out numerous large-scale building campaigns, the most ambitious of which was the founding of the city of Ramesses (Pi-Ramesse). Close to the old Hyksos capital, Pi-Ramesse stood at the departure point of the increasingly important and well-fortified road to Palestine. The city was sprawling, crowded with temples to state gods, palaces, and military installations (including stables and weapons factories). Copper, the all-important raw material, was delivered here from the newly opened mines at Timma in Israel.

Ramesses II's temple at Abu Simbel (1260 BCE) represents the pinnacle of Egyptian rock-cut temples. The facade, carved directly into the sandstone cliff, takes the form of a pylon and is dominated by four colossal seated figures, 22 meters tall, all portrayals of Ramesses. On either side of the statues and between the legs of each are figures of Queen Nefertari and some of the royal children. Above the temples, Ramesses is shown sacrificing to the lord of the temple, Re. The cornice is decorated with a row of baboons, their arms raised in worship of the rising sun. The whole would have been brightly painted.

On the interior, the temple contains two pillared halls, storage rooms, and a sanctuary deep in the rock. The 10-meter-high walls are mainly covered with scenes and inscriptions relating to the king's military exploits against the Hittites and against the Kushites in Nubia. The axis ends in the sanctuary on the west wall with a row of four seated statues of Ptah, Amun, Ramesses, and Re-Harmachis. The small altar in front of them is where sacrifices were made when the light of the rising sun illuminated the sanctuary at dawn.

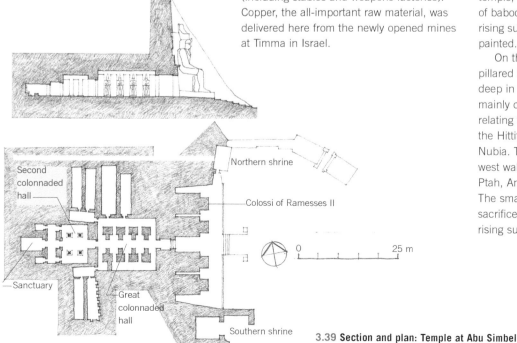

3.39 **Section and plan: Temple at Abu Simbel**

3.40 **Relief of a Djed column**

3.41 **Papyrus column, bundled shaft**

Egyptian Columns

The Egyptians were the first not just to develop advanced stone work, but also to develop the column as more than just a load-bearing device—it had symbolic importance. Reeds and flower stalks bundled around poles were used to demarcate sacred spaces. Mostly, the columns were covered with stucco and painted in vibrant colors. Because we tend to see columns as purely structural devices, we can easily forget that for the Egyptians, the column was a denotative form.

The most common plant themes were the palm, the lotus, and the papyrus. For lotus capitals, there was the so-called bud form, which was usually used in outer courts, and the open form, found in a temple's central area. At the Hatshepsut mortuary temple, one finds fluted cylindrical columns, representing bundled reeds, with plain square capitals that were to have a profound impact on the columns developed by the Greeks.

The preferred structural support for columns was bedrock, but where that was not possible, they rested on a broad base that in turn rested on a cone-shaped stone below the surface of the floor to further distribute the weight. Foundations were often made of compacted sand several meters deep, the sand creating an even distribution of the forces.

The Djed pillar was the archetype of the Egyptian column. It emerged in the early history of ancient Egypt and, though its meaning is much debated, it most likely derived from a harvest ritual and came to represent the creation myth. Its importance grew over time to represent the world holding up the sky, and as such it came to represent the idea of stability and permanence, important themes in Egyptian dynastic definition. The pillar as it was used in ceremonies was associated with the god Sokar in association with Osiris, the god of the dead.

3.42 **Papyrus column, bundled shaft with lotus bud capital**

3.43 **Hatshepsut mortuary temple columns**

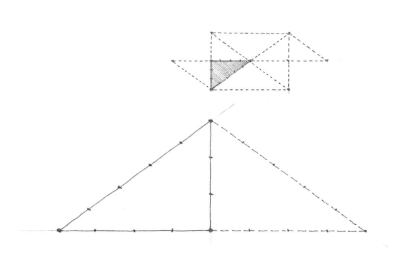

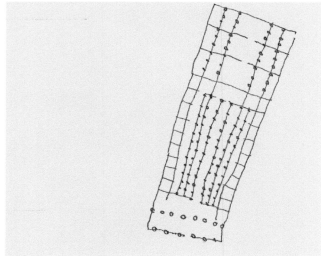

3.44 Laying out construction with knotted cords and pegs

3.45 Low relief of a pylon: An early example of an architectural design

Egyptian Design Methods

Texts relating to architecture, surveying, and town planning make it obvious that Egyptian architecture had risen to the level of a distinct craft. Architectural plans—drawn on stones, some of which have survived, and most certainly on papyrus, though none of these have survived—indicate a high level of coordination between planning a building and its construction. Beside the titles of royal architect, builder, and overseer of works, there were also priest-architects who had access to secret books that had plans and specifications for buildings and statues. There was even a goddess of architecture and reckoning, Seshat, who begins to appear in Egyptian records in about 2500 BCE. She is depicted as bearing a seven-pointed star or rosette on her head, sometimes above a wand. She was also the goddess of the art of writing.

The king himself played an important part in the planning and the symbolic execution of a structure. In one mural, Thutmosis II is shown performing the ceremony of staking out the ground plan of a temple using a special "plan net," a netlike webbing of rope with knots that marked off locations. The procedure consisted of stretching a net along the axis and then spreading it out to determine the basic points of the construction. To form a right angle, for

example, the Egyptians used a cord with twelve intervals that was wound around three stakes at units of 3, 4, and 5. For construction, plans were certainly produced. Sketches have even been found on the walls of a quarry. On the pylon of the Temple of Khonsu at Karnak is a low relief of a pylon that could very well be one of the first surviving architectural design projects.

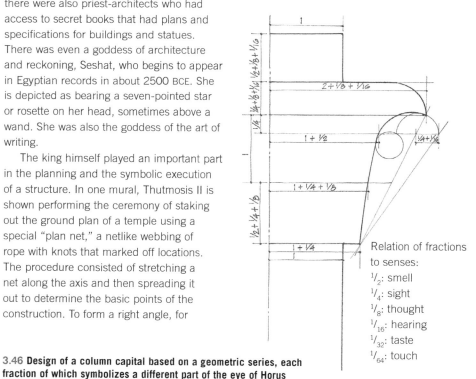

Relation of fractions to senses:
$\frac{1}{2}$: smell
$\frac{1}{4}$: sight
$\frac{1}{8}$: thought
$\frac{1}{16}$: hearing
$\frac{1}{32}$: taste
$\frac{1}{64}$: touch

3.46 Design of a column capital based on a geometric series, each fraction of which symbolizes a different part of the eye of Horus

Drawings from the roof of the hypostyle hall of Edfu and elsewhere give us some indication of how columns were designed using a complex ordering of ratios in which a cubit was used in conjunction with a geometrical series of fractions. For example, to a column 9 cubits high, the architect would add $\frac{1}{4}$ + $\frac{1}{8}$ + $\frac{1}{16}$, each fraction symbolizing a different part of the Eye of Horus. Unlike later Greek and Hellenistic assumptions that positioned mathematics in relationship to cosmological spheres, Egyptian mathematics was connected to the physiology of the body. The eye was seen as one unit, with each of the parts measuring a fraction. This unit was named after Hequat, who was a goddess represented by a frog; she was also the sign of fertility. The name is fitting, since Egyptian mathematics involves a system of leapfrogging over various fractions to achieve the desired answer. The carving of a column and capital was thus a shortcut for these operations.

Though we do not know for certain the geometry of the pyramids, it has been ascertained with a fair amount of probability that height-to-width was determined through the ratio of 4:1 pi or sometimes 3:1 pi. Egyptian mathematics, as discussed by Corinna Rossi in her book on the subject, was the most advanced in the world at the time. By 1700 BCE, the date of various papyrus scrolls dealing with mathematical topics, various complex mathematical systems were being devised.

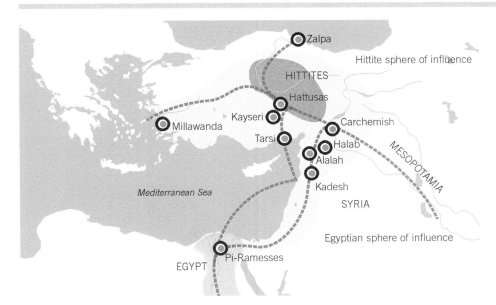

HITTITE EMPIRE

The Hittites settled in Anatolia around 1600 BCE, choosing the site of their capital, Hattusas, with an eye toward dominating the intersection of two important trading routes. One ran from the Aegean coast, from a harbor later to become Ephesus, to the Black Sea. The other ran southward, from the Black Sea port of Amisus (Samsum) to the headwaters of the Euphrates. To further stimulate trade, the Hittites permitted Assyrians to set up posts for their donkey and camel caravans in eastern Anatolia, such as the one at Kanesh, 20 kilometers northeast of Kayseri and only 100 kilometers southwest of Hattusas. At its height, the Hittite Empire stretched into the Levant, leading to conflict with the Egyptians and to the famous battle for Kadesh (1275 BCE) in northern Syria. After the battle, which was a draw, the two parties wrote up a treaty that guaranteed peace and security throughout the area, allowing the cities along the Syrian coast to grow in importance and also creating a power shift away from Mesopotamia toward the eastern Mediterranean. A cuneiform version of this treaty, found at Hattusas, hangs today in an enlarged copy at the United Nations Building to demonstrate the age-old importance of international treaties.

Though the Hittite economy was basically agricultural, the Hittites conducted a lively export in copper, bronze, and later, most prized of all, iron. Many of the mines were in the vicinity of Bokar-Maden in the Taurus Mountains. The main military strength of the Hittites lay in the intensive development of new weapons, such as the light horse-drawn chariot with its six-spoked wheels. It contributed greatly to speed and mobility in battle. The Sumerians had already had chariots pulled by wild asses, but their wheels were made of solid wood. Egyptian chariots held only two men, while those of the Hittites held three—the driver and two soldiers, one each for attack and defense.

The Hittites, similar to the Mesopotamians, had a vast pantheon of intermarried gods and goddesses, in the center of which was the male weather god, symbolized by a bull. His consort controlled the rivers and the sea but was also sometimes known as a sun goddess. Even though temples were important for the Hittites, they also had outdoor sanctuaries. In this they were much more like the Minoans than either the Egyptians or the Mesopotamians. One such sanctuary is Yazilikaya, a little over a kilometer to the northeast of Hattusas, to which it was connected by a processional way. It had a pantheon of gods chiseled into the face of the cliff, perhaps showing them arriving at the house of the weather god for the spring festival.

3.48 Relief depicting twelve gods of the Hittite underworld, Yazilikaya, Turkey

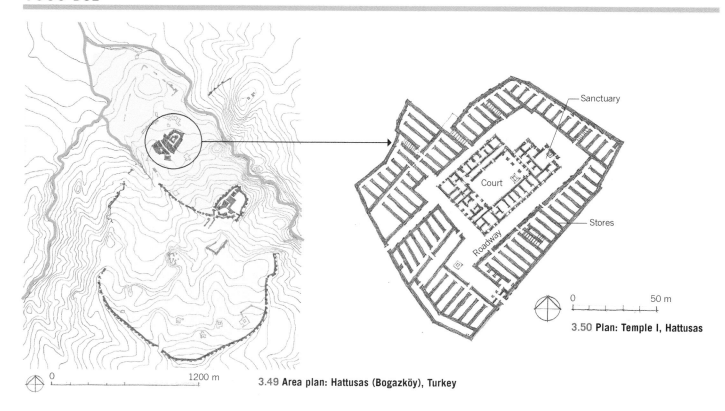

Sanctuary

Court

Stores

Roadway

0   50 m

3.50 Plan: Temple I, Hattusas

0   1200 m

3.49 Area plan: Hattusas (Bogazköy), Turkey

Hattusas

Hattusas (modern Bogazköy), situated at the juncture of two ancient trade routes in north-central Turkey, lies on the northern slope of a ridge where a high plateau begins to descend toward a valley. Of the many temples in the city, the most notable was the so-called Temple I, squarish in plan with an annex in the back. It took up an irregularly shaped city block and was composed principally of storage cells for sanctuary treasure and food. Archaeologists have found jars of Cretan and Mycenaean provenance there. The storage room walls were very thick, suggesting that the building was two or three stories high. The entire complex, including the vast number of storerooms, measures 160 by 135 meters. The temple was built of limestone, whereas the annex that contained the sacred statues was built of granite, indicating its special status as well as, most likely, the presence of Egyptian masons, since it is unlikely that the Hittites would have developed the skill of carving granite so rapidly on their own. The courtyard was entered through a symmetrically laid out gate, square in plan and divided into nine spaces. In the rest of the plan there was an

attempt to balance the right and left sides of the courtyard. In the northeast corner was a washhouse, while a portico at the far end gave access to the sacred spaces in the annex. The cult statues were in the larger of the two rooms to the northwest and were dedicated to the sun goddess, while the other room was dedicated to the weather god. All in all, the building is an aggregation of different elements: the gate, the court, and the annex.

The most important event at the temple was a springtime festival at which the combat of the weather god and a dragon was acted out or recited. During the festival, the king and queen, accompanied by jesters and musicians, would enter through the ceremonial gate on the eastern wall and proceed to a stone basin, where the king would perform a ritual hand washing using water poured from a jar made of gold. From there he would enter the temple courtyard through the monumental gate. A master of ceremonies then prepared the king and the assembled dignitaries for a feast, perhaps in the colonnade of the courtyard or in the throne room itself. The Hittites, like the Mesopotamians, employed no columns or capitals in their architecture. Instead, they

grouped rooms around paved courts. In contrast to Sumerian temples, which had dark and mysterious interiors because the rooms received daylight from windows high up in the walls, Hittite temples had tall windows starting close to floor level. Such windows were placed on both sides of the cult statue and would have bathed it in light. The Hittites also employed colonnades in a type of wall-and-pier system that enriched their spatial vocabulary considerably. And finally, Hittite architects strove for a deliberate tension between symmetry and asymmetry that has parallels with Minoan architecture.

There are other differences from Mesopotamian temples. The *cella* of a Mesopotamian temple communicated with the courtyard through an intervening antechamber or antechapel, so that the congregation in the court would have a clear view of the god's statue in its niche. In Hittite temples, the cult room was approached indirectly, through side rooms; the statue would therefore not have been visible from the court. This has led archaeologists to conclude that the *cella* was reserved for priests or a corresponding elite who alone were admitted to the sanctum.

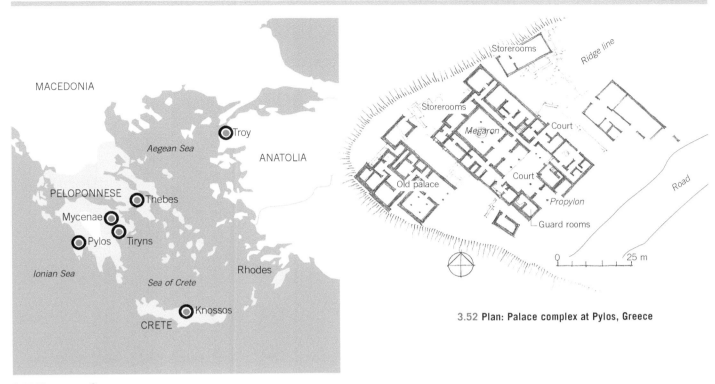

3.51 Mycenaean Greece

3.52 Plan: Palace complex at Pylos, Greece

MYCENAEAN CIVILIZATION

The Mycenaeans, from parts unknown, settled in Greece around 2000 BCE. There, like the Hittites, they quickly coalesced into a unified Bronze Age social order. The numerous harbors and islands of the Peloponnese lent themselves to a system of regional chieftains or kings operating under the umbrella of the lord of Mycenae, to whom they were connected by ties of blood, tribal loyalties, language, and old memories of origins as reflected in their myths. Commanding a powerful fleet, the lord of Mycenae could ensure his city-state's foremost position. After the decline of Minoan dominance over the Mediterranean, the reach of Mycenae extended to all the Aegean islands, including Rhodes and Cyprus. The Mycenaeans traded with Sicily, southern Italy, Egypt, Sardinia, and the countries bordering the Black Sea, leaving trading outposts along the way. Their form of power was a novelty in world history. They were not centralized and had no land-based army. But it was precisely this that propelled them into world events. Tribal affiliations created small but fiercely loyal fighters. They developed their own export commodities. Their carpenters,

for example, used ivory from Syria with great skill to adorn furniture. Their metallurgical skill was legendary; Mycenaean bronze swords have been found in Romania. There were obviously interactions with the Minoans, from whose long culture the Mycenaeans borrowed elements of wall decorations and building techniques. Mycenaean architectural sensibilities were their own, however, and centered on the *megaron*, or great hall.

Nestor's palace complex at Pylos, of which we hear much in Homer's *Odyssey*, was built between 1300 and 1200 BCE. Predominant is the *megaron*, a square room with four fluted columns in the center of which is an elevated hearth 4 meters in diameter; the room was vented by a clerestory ceiling. The floor was plastered and decorated with a grid, the fields of which were painted with nonfigural patterns.

The walls were covered with an elaborate series of frescoes showing animals, musicians, and individuals carrying offerings and a bull sacrifice. On the wall near the throne (*to-no* in Mycenaean Greek, whence comes the word "throne"), was a drawing of an octopus with special symbolical meaning. Did the slippery, multi-armed organism

resemble the adept, multi-zoned Mycenaean social structure? The throne was made of wood, plated in gold and ebony.

Behind the great hall were two storage rooms for valuables and containing large pots for storing oil. The residential quarters were in a discrete block at the eastern corner. There was even a room with a bath made of terra-cotta. Access to the *megaron* was more direct than the labyrinthine approach at Knossos. From the outside, one entered through an H-shaped *propylon* (the word literally means "before the gate") with a single column dividing the path into two, much as one would have found in Crete. It did not lead to a hall or corridor but into a courtyard, where a porch of columns and a set of doorways formed the entrance into the *megaron*. To the right of the entrance was the guard room, and to the left, the palace archives and records of trade transactions. Before entering the *megaron*, a visitor would first have been led to a room on the left side of the courtyard, which was a place for ritual preparation. The palace was located on a ridge with a protected port about 5 kilometers from the sea, right on the trade route that worked its way through the Peloponnese.

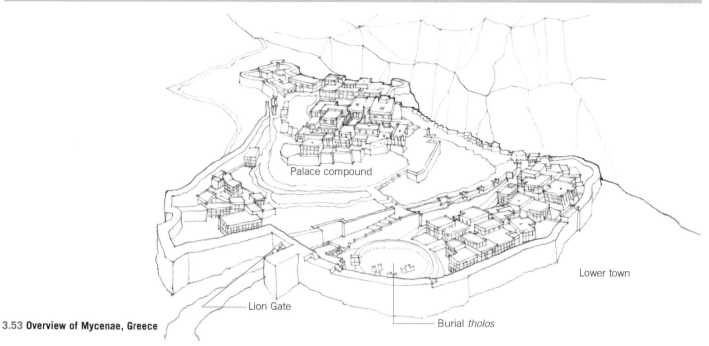

3.53 Overview of Mycenae, Greece

Palace compound

Lion Gate

Burial *tholos*

Lower town

Mycenaean palaces were much more than residences; as at Knossos, they were administrative centers and the locus of the region's industrial production. The Palace of Pylos, for example, employed around 550 textile workers and 400 workers in the metallurgical industry. There were also other types of artisans, such as goldsmiths, ivory carvers, stone carvers, and potters. These people lived in nearby hamlets.

The most dominant city of the time was Mycenae itself. Though today the city seems remote, this was not the case in 400 BCE. It straddled a shortcut through the Peloponnese between the broad and protected Argos harbor and a port on the Bay of Corinth, and thus connected Crete and the eastern Mediterranean with the markets in Italy and beyond. Situated on the side of a mountain, it was easily protected.

Mycenae was defended by thick ring walls that were built around 1450 BCE. Part of this formidable defense work consisted of a cyclopean wall named for the seemingly superhuman strength it must have taken to move these immense boulders. In other parts one finds regular rows of blocks of stone fitted without mortar. One enters the citadel through the famed Lion Gate, which might imply a connection to, or at least familiarity with, Hattusas.

Just to the right after entering the citadel is a large circular burial *tholos* placed on the flat top of a purpose-built conical hill, about 6 meters high. It has six chambered tombs containing gold, silver, and bronze burial treasures. Entrance to this circle was certainly restricted to the elite, who accessed it from a bridge that connected it to a set of ritual buildings, also placed on a high stone podium. There were no temples in the Mesopotamian sense. Sacred rituals were performed in buildings that were similar to houses, except that they were better ornamented and made with more refined material.

The lower town and the burial circle were originally outside the citadel walls, but were later encased by a more expansive perimeter wall. The palace, placed at the top of hill, was protected by its own set of walls. Unlike the Egyptian pharaohs, who were placed in pyramids, and later in secret caves, the Mycenaean dead were displayed within the city at a place where memory and narrative were most likely to converge. Later Greeks would call the gathering of people in commemorating places a *choros*. Indeed, Homer would emerge, long after the Mycenaean age had waned, recounting the tales of Mycenaean heroes, among them Agamemnon.

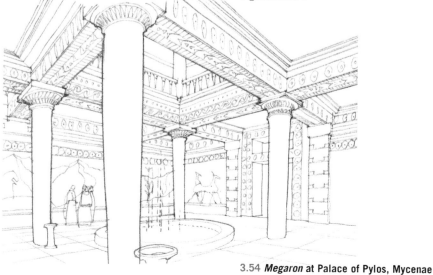

3.54 *Megaron* at Palace of Pylos, Mycenae

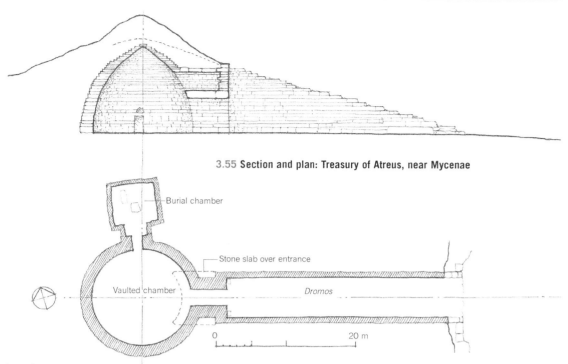

3.55 Section and plan: Treasury of Atreus, near Mycenae

Burial chamber

Stone slab over entrance

Vaulted chamber

Dromos

0   20 m

Treasury of Atreus

Beginning in the late Bronze Age, the kings were buried outside the city in great beehive—or *tholos*—tombs, monumental symbols of wealth and power. The one at Mycenae, the Treasury of Atreus, is the most famous and the most finely built. It consists of a great circular chamber, some 15 meters in both diameter and height, cut into the hillside and entered by a corridor—a *dromos*—about 36 meters long and 6 meters wide. The tomb was roofed by a corbelled dome made of finely cut ashlar blocks. A rectangular room, the burial chamber proper, was tucked in next to the central one. The whole was covered with earth to form a conical hill. The high facade at the entrance was flanked by two half-columns of green porphyry—a stone native to Egypt—carved with chevrons and spirals. Though fitted with Minoan-style capitals, their bulbous proportions foreshadowed the transformation the capitals would undergo subsequent to the Dorian invasion. The stone lintel above the door was elaborately decorated with running spirals and other patterns.

3.56 Plan: Treasury of Atreus

79

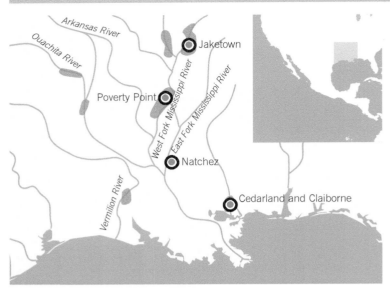

3.57 **Mississippi cultures**

3.58 **Pictorial view: Mound A (Large Bird Mound), Poverty Point, near Epps, Louisiana**

POVERTY POINT

First reported in 1873, the semi-elliptical ridges of Poverty Point were thought to be natural formations. It was only in the 1950s, when the site was viewed from the air, that archaeologists realized they were artificial constructions. Located in the lower Mississippi Valley of West Carroll Parish, Louisiana, near both the Gulf Coast and the confluence of six major rivers, Poverty Point is not a unique construction. Similar earth mounds had been built along the Mississippi River dating as far back as 4000 BCE. Humans probably moved into this area around 6000 BCE, and the reason is obvious: it was one of the richest areas in plants and wildlife in North America. There were seasonal migrating ducks, fish of various kinds, and deer in the forests, not to mention a wide variety of edible plants and nuts, including hickory nuts, pecans, acorns, and walnuts. All this made for an affluent world. The massive spring floods allowed people to communicate with each other via canoes. Trade was extensive and included chipped-stone projectile points and tools, ground-stone plummets, and beads made from shells and stones. There is clear evidence that trade reached as far north as what is now Michigan.

The mounds served as places for ritual gatherings that lasted for weeks and were an important part of First Society life. These gatherings entailed ceremonial gift giving, socializing, singing, and dancing. In that sense, this was not a village but a sacred landscape that served as a magnet for people from near and far, although the local tribe might have lived there the year round.

The site consists of six concentric semi-elliptical rings that enclose a vast open plaza covering an area of about 14 hectares. Aisle-like openings run between the rings, dividing them into six sections, which are thought to have stood over 2 meters high. It is thought that visiting tribes built their huts on these mounds for the festivals. In and around the complex were six to eight constructed earthen mounds. The main plaza faced east and overlooked the Mississippi River. This was the site of elaborate dance ceremonies. Someone looking along the aisles from the center outward would have looked toward the sun at the winter solstice in one direction, and toward the sun at the summer solstice in the other.

To the west of the site was a huge mound, built on a patch of black soil that was ritualistically covered with a layer of white sand, probably symbolizing the forces of life and death. The mound was made by the different tribes, each carrying clay in baskets from far away to the site. When finished, it had the shape of a west-flying bird, which most likely was meant as a communication device for the ancestor spirits. How the shamanistic rituals worked, whether on its summit or on its slopes, is unknown. Today the mound is overgrown with grass and trees, but originally its clay surface would have been bare.

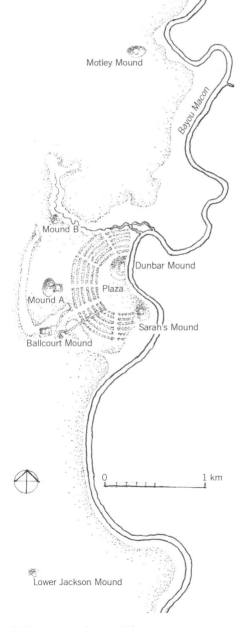

3.59 **Area plan: Poverty Point**

3.60 **Shang dynasty, China**

SHANG DYNASTY, CHINA

Ancient Chinese historians talk of the ten thousand kingdoms that existed before the Xia dynasty (ca. 2070–1600 BCE), and indeed, the rise of defensive fortifications around cities was a testament to intra-urban warfare. Among these numerous city-states, Xia came to control the territory on the Yellow River, paving the way for the rise of the Shang dynasty (ca. 1600–1050 BCE), whose first capital was Ao, known as Zhengzhou. The Shang, who continually moved their capital due to frequent natural disasters, left Ao around the 13th century BCE. Despite the capital's importance, centralization of state power had not yet been developed. Nonetheless, it was during the Shang dynasty that the royal person came to be viewed as a symbol of cosmic powers. While feasts for the dead were commonplace, during the Shang it seems that ordinary people were no longer believed to become spirit ancestors. In other words, the ancestors of the elite became the spiritual ancestors of all. And, since the royal ancestors were credited with supernatural powers, divining their wishes was a preeminent task placed in the hands of a priestly class. The theocratic order thereby established was to remain foundational to the Chinese definition of rulership. The king or his diviners would address an oral "charge"—a question—to the ancestors using a prepared turtle shell or cattle scapula while applying a hot poker to produce a series of heat cracks in the shell or bone. The diviners then interpreted these cracks as auspicious or inauspicious, after which engravers carved into the surface of the shell or bone the subject of the charge, sometimes the forecast, and less frequently the result. Apart from the living ancestors, there were an assortment of nature deities with various degrees of abstraction.

It was during the Shang period that there is the first clear evidence of the rise of cities in China. They dominated the great northern plain that was enclosed on the north, west, and south by mountains or deserts and open to the sea on its eastern rim. The Huang River and its tributaries flowed through the plain from the mountains in the west. In those days, the eastern parts consisted of extensive marshes, and the coastline was farther west than it is today. But the middle zone, well watered and with fertile soil, was an excellent place for agricultural exploitation. It comprises a territory known as the Middle Plain. In this, Chinese urbanism began in a way that was fundamentally different from in Mesopotamia, where cities began as risky endeavors in the marshes. They were dependent on extensive irrigation techniques, and their power could rise and fall with the next flood. The first Chinese cities were built in much less stressful situations, and the Chinese did not yet have extensive irrigation.

These cities were at their core ceremonial centers for the elite, and for the construction of buildings enormous sacrifices were made. So much power did the elites have that for the dedication of just one palace, 852 humans, 15 horses, 10 oxen, 18 sheep, 35 dogs, and 5 fully equipped chariots with horses and their charioteers were all entombed. The centers had earthen walls, usually of a roughly rectangular form. Though they were not purely rectangular, they were still governed by sacred principles. An important difference between these early Chinese cities and their Mesopotamian counterparts is that as ceremonial centers they contained, either inside the walls or nearby, workshop districts where the artisans lived who made the bronze, jade, and pottery objects that were necessary for the ritual practices of the elites. In some sense the city emerged as a production zone around the ritual center.

3.61 Reconstruction of a Shang dynasty palace

Zhengzhou was immense, with its east wall measuring 1.7 kilometers long. It was surrounded by small villages, workshop areas, and bronze foundries. In the northeast section of the city, just south of a small hill, was a district of palaces and temples where rammed earth (*han tu*) platforms of different sizes supported large wood-framed buildings, the largest of which was 60 by 13 meters and oriented to the cardinal points. That it is located just south of the hill is no accident, as that was and remained the preeminent position of Chinese palaces. Whereas the elite lived on houses built on *han tu* bases, the rest of the population lived in round or oval pit houses. *Han tu* platforms are almost always an indication of elite status.

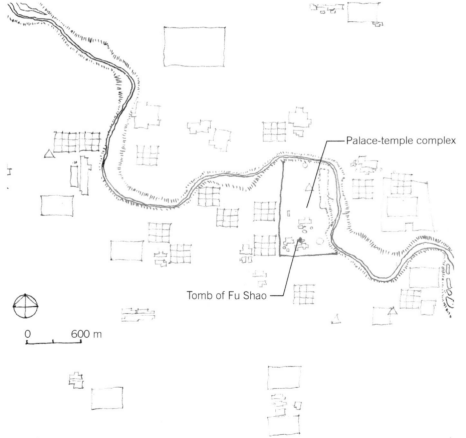

Palace-temple complex

Tomb of Fu Shao

0   600 m

3.62 Site plan: Yin, Anyang County, China

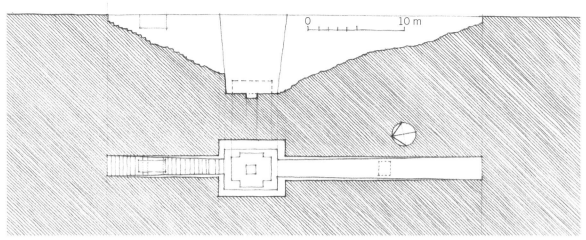

3.63 Plan and section: Tomb of Fu Hao, near Yin

At the beginning of the 14th century BCE, the Shang established their capital, Yin, about 2 kilometers (1.2 miles) north of the modern city of Anyang on the banks of the Huan River. It too was a vast walled-in ceremonial center with palaces and temples for ancestral worship. There was a special mortuary district for the elite, the tombs of which were miniature cosmic diagrams. At the center of a royal grave, for example, was a wood-chambered tomb, decorated and painted and placed some 12 meters belowground. Two and sometimes four ramps led down from the surface to the sides of the chamber, in the center of which the king was buried. In some tombs, guards were buried in the corners, each with a dog and holding a weapon. One tomb was for Fu Hao, one of the three wives of a Chinese king. *Fu* is a term equivalent to "queen"; *Hao* is her personal name. She was no ordinary queen, but rather a military commander. Her tomb was a square wooden room at the base of a pit 7.5 meters deep. The artifacts discovered in the tomb include 460 bronze vessels used for ancestral offerings. There were also about 16 human sacrifices as well as 6 dogs, including an armed man and a dog under the coffin to protect her in her afterlife. The tomb was located within the ceremonial enclosure at Yin (Anyang).

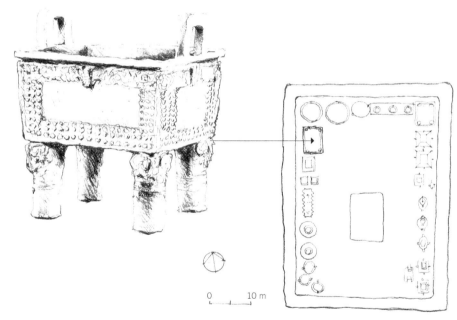

3.64 Interior plan: Tomb of Fu Hao

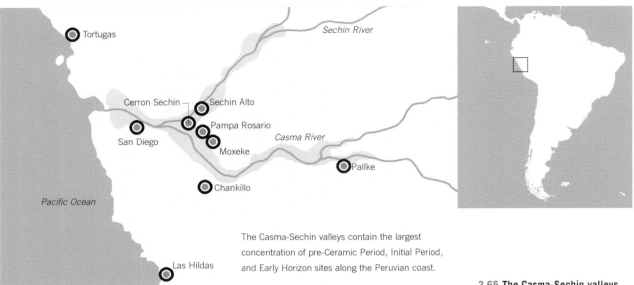

The Casma-Sechin valleys contain the largest concentration of pre-Ceramic Period, Initial Period, and Early Horizon sites along the Peruvian coast.

3.65 **The Casma-Sechin valleys**

CIVILIZATION OF THE HIGH ANDES

The transformation of arid Andean valleys into farmscapes that began at Galgada around 3000 BCE continued at Caral a few centuries later. But these grand experiments could not last forever. As Caral grew it became more vulnerable to floods, and over time the soil quality deteriorated. The valley's decline was certainly seen as a message from the gods. But the energy was not lost; it simply moved to the next valley, Sechin Alto, some 110 kilometers north of Caral. As at Caral, the culture in this valley arrived fully intending to transform the river into an agricultural universe. The people erected an astonishing 300-by-250-meter platform mound rising an imposing 44 meters above the surrounding plain. The mound contained 2 million cubic feet of fill, masonry, and conical mud bricks, making it the largest construction in the Americas at that time. It was augmented by an almost 1-kilometer-long series of axially aligned platforms, terraces, and circular pits.

As in the Caral Valley, the Sechin Alto had were no cities in the technical sense, but rather kilometer-long networks of hamlets and farmsteads spread out next to the fields where the slopes fan out before reaching the valley floor. As more fields were created, new micro-unities developed, related to one or another of the preexisting centers. How much friction there was between centers, if any, is not known. The people, as would have been typical throughout Peru, would travel to the centers on ritual days. Trade was key to the valley civilization's survival. Obsidian came from the highlands, and the wood used for roofs and doorways came from a tree that grows only between 1,500 and 3,000 meters above sea level. Salt was also important for the preservation of food and fish, with a major source located 115 kilometers to the north, near Salinas de Chao. Plant remains from this site include both the white potato and the sweet potato.

The site contains more than a hundred platform structures aligned with two major edifices separated by a distance of 1.3 kilometers. They are oriented 90 degrees to the Casma River valley and along the western side of a valley that opens into the Casma. Between the two structures are several large plazas, dominated by a structure known as Moxeke, some 170 by 160 meters at its base and 30 meters tall. It consists of stacked platforms and is rectangular in plan, with gently rounded corners. A staircase leads up to a walled square enclosure on a terrace halfway up. Behind this enclosure is another staircase, this one between two separate terrace mounds, both with ritual structures on their tops.

Just as the white stones of the Parthenon in Athens were once painted in various colors, so too were these structures. In Peru, the exteriors were painted in shades of red, the ancient color of ritual and death, but over time the color palette became more complex and was used to portray animals, people, and mythological scenes. Hindu temples might serve as living examples of how buildings were painted.

The outside walls of some of the terraces were ornamented with figures painted light red, emerald, white, and black. The size of the 3-meter-tall figures indicates that they were designed to be visible from quite a distance. Furthermore, their placement high on the mound front and extending around on either side serves to enhance their visibility to the audience in the surrounding plazas.

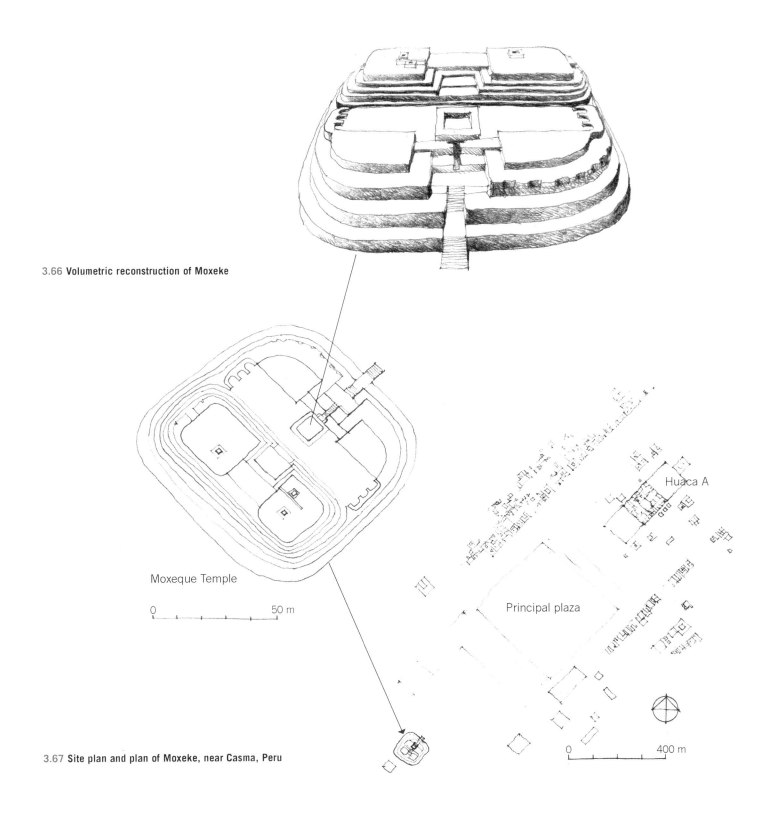

3.66 Volumetric reconstruction of Moxeke

Moxeque Temple

0   50 m

Huaca A

Principal plaza

0   400 m

3.67 Site plan and plan of Moxeke, near Casma, Peru

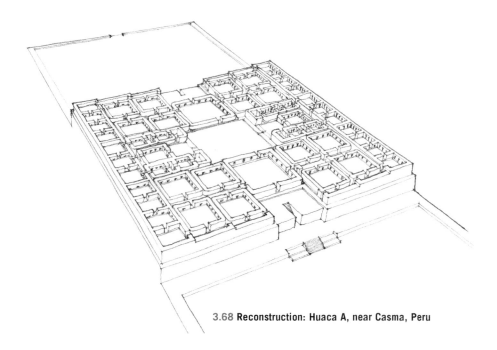

3.68 Reconstruction: Huaca A, near Casma, Peru

The valley contains a most unusual building, known as Huaca A, that is composed of 38 roughly square rooms packed into a large rectangular building about 150 meters long, with a courtyard in its center. The organization of the rooms is complex. The structure, symmetrical around both axes, consists of four approximately equivalent quadrants. Three large spaces define its dominant central axis, with smaller rooms to the sides. There are no shared walls between the room units. The units, each with walls about 2 meters thick, were constructed as if they were freestanding elements, even when placed next to one another. In some instances there no usable space between the units; in other instances, the rooms are separated by corridors. There is also a substantial increase in the elevation of room floors as one moves away from the center. The floor level of the corner rooms is 4 meters higher than the floor of the central court. There can be no doubt that the rooms held important commodities, since access to the various rooms was regulated by wooden gates and bar closures. The rooms are not freely interconnected; most of the large rooms are accessible only from the two large entrance lobbies. Similarly, the smaller rooms can be accessed only through a carefully designed system of corridors. The building was clearly meant to impress. Ascending the central staircase, one enters an atrium and is immediately confronted by an enormous frieze of a pair of felines, 10 meters long and about 6 meters tall, facing each other across the entrance. The three-dimensional aspect of the animals would have been enhanced by the curvature of the atrium's walls. A low bench, 120 centimeters wide and 25 centimeters high, further accentuates the frieze and may have served as a barrier to discourage too close an approach. It seems that the building was a sacred storehouse, given that the remains of a variety of plant foods such as peanuts, beans, and tubers were found in the niches. And since other items found there include turquoise beads, a wooden figurine, and finely made textiles, the storehouse was likely used not just for food but for commodities of all sorts. The building was clearly the focal point for the bureaucratic and ritualistic activities of collecting and redistributing food and craft items.

800 BCE

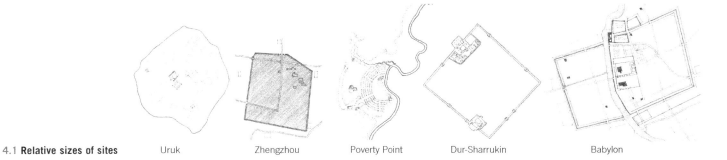

4.1 Relative sizes of sites   Uruk   Zhengzhou   Poverty Point   Dur-Sharrukin   Babylon

INTRODUCTION

By 1000 BCE the Peruvian coastal agro-ritual centers were in decline, perhaps because of the overworking of the land. A new center was founded, Chavín de Huántar, which was located in the mountains at the intersection of important trade routes and was from the beginning a ritual center, comparable in its lure and symbolism to Jerusalem. People came there for devotional reasons, bringing with them riches and gifts for exchange.

Meanwhile, in Mexico, the first great corn-centric cultures were forming. Maize, or corn, had been domesticated around 5000 BCE in the Guatemala forest region, with its cultivation spreading northward into Mexico. The Olmecs elevated it to the level of a major crop, which is now grown and consumed in many places around the world. They began to drain the marshy and unsettled lands of Veracruz and convert them into thriving agricultural zones. The resulting prosperous trading economy formed the basis for the first major ritual centers of Central America, such as San Lorenzo and La Venta.

In the Eurasian world, by 1000 BCE iron smelting had become fairly widespread, having been first developed by the Hittites. Its usage spread all the way to China. Iron weapons were presumably the cause of much of the period's upheaval and displacement. Iron also improved the plow, meaning that new areas could be tilled. Sicily, for example, was targeted by the intrepid Greeks, who wanted to avoid having to buy grain from the Egyptians. Iron also transformed construction processes, by speeding stone carving. Above all, iron changed the traditional balance of power between those who had metal and those who did not. The Egyptian and Mesopotamian urban cultures were on

the losing end of this equation, while the victors were from what had previously been their hinterlands: the Etruscans in Italy, the Dorians in Greece, and the Nubians in southern Egypt. It was within this context that the Dorians and Ionians extended their power by founding colonies in Sicily and Italy to secure newly developing trade routes. Magna Graecia, as it was called, was so strong that by 500 BCE it had become an economic and cultural continuity unto its own. It was thus in Sicily and Italy that one finds some of the first Greek experiments in stone architecture, as the Greeks in essence learned this technique from the Egyptians with whom they traded.

The 9th and 8th centuries BCE also saw the rise of the regional importance of Palestine and the Israelites in relationship to the Kush in Nubia and the Sabaean kingdom in Yemen. Kush, Israel, and the Sabaean kingdom formed an important economic engine all their own. Kush was a source of gold, and for a period its kings took control of Egypt. The Sabaean kingdom in Yemen had a monopoly on the production of frankincense, an oil derived from a plant that grew only there. Frankincense, which had a value similar to gold, was used in many religious ceremonies. In order to reach the markets, it was brought to Palestine, with its connections to ports and trade routes.

Between the 8th and 6th centuries BCE, the Assyrians and Babylonians established themselves as the leading powers of western Asia, but they had to do this by establishing control of the iron-bearing cultures to the north. Fully weaponized, they began to create extensive empires; but their policy of relocating large groups of people and their inability to establish coherent financial and trade policies meant that, as grand as they were, these empires were doomed to

be short-lived enterprises. The fall of the Babylonian Empire to Persia in 539 BCE marked the end of a Mesopotamian-centered culture that had, for over two millennia, been one of the dominating regenerating forces—culturally, economically, and politically—in Eurasia.

Further to the east, in India, the Vedic Indo-Aryan invaders who had imposed themselves as a ruling class had by this time occupied large sections of the Indo-Gangetic Plain, where they established sixteen *mahajanapadas*, or kingdoms. The city of Varanasi, on the sacred Ganges River, rose to become an important center of learning and a preeminent holy site that attracts devotees to this day. With a three and half thousand years of history, Varanasi can be considered today as one of the longest-lasting sacred sites in the world. Little architecture survives from this period, as buildings were largely constructed of wood.

In 1046 BCE in China, the Zhou replaced the Shang and built their capital cities, Hao (or Haojing) and Feng on flanking sides of the Feng River (west of present-day Xi'an). Though little has survived in physical terms, the Zhou fundamentally changed Chinese notions of governance by creating an ideology of imperial rule known as the "mandate of heaven," which was later to be extolled as the model of governance by Confucius and others. The Zhou also reinforced state-mandated principles of ritualized "tradition" as a way to assert the privilege of the elites. Despite this "mandate," the Zhou faced the typical unrelenting tension in the Chinese political world between imperial control and clan-based authority that would lead the empire into decline, once weakness was perceived.

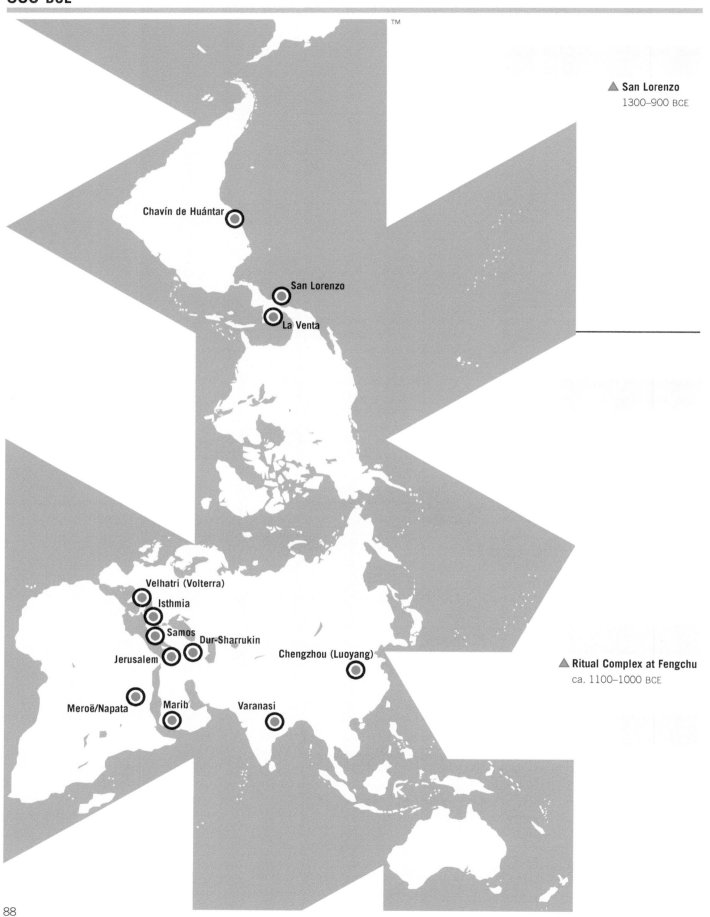

▲ **San Lorenzo**
1300–900 BCE

Chavín de Huántar

San Lorenzo

La Venta

Velhatri (Volterra)

Isthmia

Samos   Dur-Sharrukin

Jerusalem

Chengzhou (Luoyang)

▲ **Ritual Complex at Fengchu**
ca. 1100–1000 BCE

Meroë/Napata   Marib   Varanasi

Olmec Cultures
ca. 1500–400 BCE

▲ **La Venta**
1000–400 BCE

Chavin Culture
ca. 1000–400 BCE

▲ **Chavín de Huántar**
ca. 900 BCE

Etruscan Culture
ca. 750–90 BCE

▲ **Banditaccia**
8th to 3rd centuries BCE

▲ **Volterra**
5th to 4th centuries BCE

◉ Founding of Rome
753 BCE

Iron Age
ca. 1200-580 BCE

1000 BCE　　　　　　　　　**800 BCE**　　　　　　　　　**600 BCE**

Greece: Geometric Period
ca. 900–700 BCE

◉ ca. 776 BCE
Olympic games founded

▲ **Temple of Hera at Samos**
8th century BCE

Temple of Apollo at Thermos ▲
630 BCE

▲ **Mahram Bilqis**
9th century BCE

▲ **Temple of Poseidon at Isthmia**
7th century BCE

Kingdom of Kush
ca. 760–350 CE

▲ **Napata**
ca. 900-300 BCE

▲ **Temple of Solomon**
953–586 BCE

Western Zhou Dynasty
ca. 1046–771 BCE

Eastern Zhou Dynasty
771–256 BCE

▲ **Luoyang**
ca. 1040 BCE

Early Vedic Period
ca. 1500–800 BCE

▲ **Varanasi**
ca. 1000 BCE–present

Neo-Assyrian Empire
ca. 911–612 BCE

▲ **Dur-Sharrukin**
717–706 BCE

▲ **Babylon**
Rebuilt 605 BCE

89

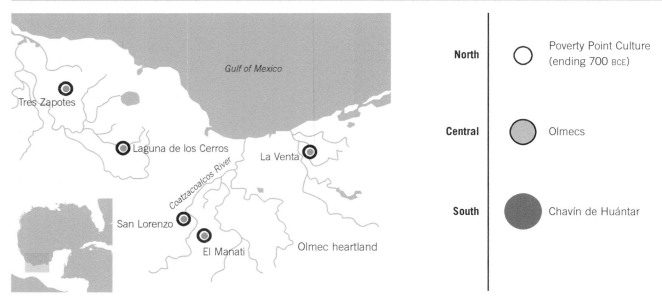

4.2 **Urbanization of the Americas, ca. 800 BCE**

4.3 **Trade in the Americas, ca. 800 BCE**

North ○ Poverty Point Culture (ending 700 BCE)

Central ◑ Olmecs

South ● Chavín de Huántar

THE OLMECS

In the Americas, by 7000 BCE a huge assortment of plants had come into being that required little more than rudimentary plant-tending to harvest. Among these were the potato, peanuts, cacao, beans, manioc, squash, and avocado. Nowhere else in the world did such a wide variety of plants appear in such close geographical proximity. Milling stones appeared along the southwest coast in Belize and in northeast Mexico. By 3000 BCE, hoes start to appear in Gulf Coast sites, and in Oaxaca and Puebla the first indications of settlements and village life emerge. The agricultural revolution had begun. If the people of the contemporaneous Mississippi culture had seemed affluent compared to their neighbors of the open plains, even they would have been amazed had they traveled to Mexico and seen the tended garden fields.

It might seem counterintuitive that in a land where so many different foods were so easily available that these same people would master the production of corn. Unlike wheat, barley, and rice, which in their edible forms are relatively similar to their wild forms, corn was the product of hundreds of years of genetic development. It seems that this took place in the area that straddles the El Salvador–Guatemala border, where a wild grass known as teosinte grows. What attracted people to the plant is not known, since it is inedible. Perhaps it was discovered that the seeds could be "popped" when

roasted. This might have had some ritualistic significance that focused growers on perfecting the plant until it finally yielded corn in the modern sense. At any rate, it is clear that that corn was not merely a plant—it was a god, which mean that planting corn was not only an agricultural process but a theological one. Soon, certainly before 1000 BCE, it was discovered that soaking the corn in lime or ash softened the kernels and allowed the pods to be made into cornmeal. The process created significant nutritional advantages over untreated maize.

Corn came in different types and sizes and was used in a variety of cuisines. One type was used for cornmeal; another for roasting; another for hominy, a type of grits; and yet another for bread. For corn bread, the corn was grated from the cob and made into a milky mush—which could also be combined with bean meal—and was slowly baked until it became a type of cake. Some types of corn were best when preserved, which was done in the sun or over a fire. Corn could also be used to make a fermented drink.

4.4 **A fired-clay Toltec votive vessel with an image of corn priest, dedicated to Xilonen, the Aztec goddess of maize, from around 1500 CE**

4.5 A characteristic motif of Olmec art was the were-jaguar, a human face with the mouth of a jaguar

4.6 Colossal monolithic head uncovered at San Lorenzo, Mexico

It was the Olmecs who set in play the corn-centric worldview that would become the marker of civilization in the Americas. They did so by making a risky move, leaving the wet forests for uninhabited marshes on the east coast of Mexico. The only wildlife of any size in these swampy areas were turtles and birds. The Olmecs' decision to build in stone was even more extraordinary, since the massive stones that they used had to be dragged for many kilometers from the mountains to the north. Two elements were, however, in their favor: One was salt from the shore, which they processed and used to trade for many things they needed. They also had bitumen from various oil seeps, which was useful to make watertight baskets and boats. It might be a stretch to compare the situation to the modern-day difference between a family farm and a corporate one, but holding this difference in mind, even in general terms, helps illuminate the drama set in play by the Olmecs. This was no gradual expansion of plant-tending lifestyles; it was a purposeful industrialization of the landscape. This means that the Olmecs settled in the region specifically to transform it from swamp to a corn-producing center, controlled by a cult of powerful personalities who were probably part shaman, part deity, and part ruler.

The religious life of the Olmecs centered on sacred caves, springs, and volcanoes. The volcano, a symbol frequently used in Olmec imagery, was associated with the world being born from below but was also viewed as the home of the storm clouds, lightning, and rain. It was depicted as a dragon with a gaping mouth representing the portal to the underworld. The sky was ruled by a bird monster or sun god whose energy powered the cosmos and made the plants grow. Underneath the dragon, the Olmecs visualized a watery void out of which the world was formed. The main deity in their mythology was the rain god, depicted as a jaguar, a shamanistic symbol of transformation. This jaguar could assume other forms—even human ones. The sexual union of a woman and a jaguar gave birth to a special class of gods that were represented in sculpture as having toothless gums, fangs, a snarling mouth, and a cleft head. The Olmecs learned to drag and float stones and columns of up to 40 tons over a distance of 160 kilometers. Most were chiseled into jaguars or human heads by Olmec sculptors. Unlike the angular and sharp features of the sculpture of later civilizations, the Olmec heads were round, soft, and very lifelike. They were also quite large—some of them over 3 meters high.

Ball playing was an important element of Olmec ritual, as evidenced by clay figures showing players wearing heavy leather belts and possibly headgear. It seems that the ball players also wore mirrors, giving us some indication of the magical nature of the games. Balls ranged from 10 to 22 cm and were heavy, 3 or 4 kilograms. In a modern-day game known as *ulama* that is played in some Mesoamerican villages, the play resembles a net-less volleyball, with each team confined to one half of the court. The ball is hit back and forth using only the hips until one team fails to return it or the ball leaves the court. But why the games were held and what they signified is not known. Were they to defuse or resolve conflicts, struggles to the death by captives, or symbolic activities associated with calendric events and shamanistic practices?

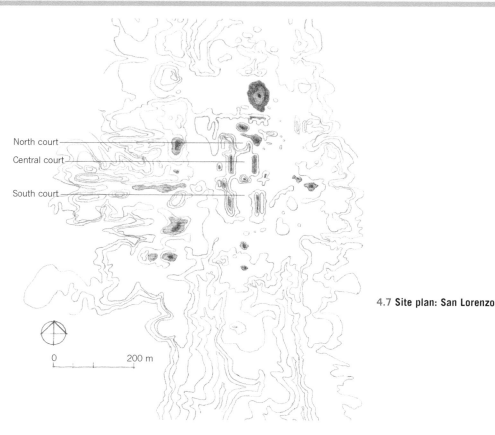

North court
Central court
South court

0   200 m

4.7 Site plan: San Lorenzo

San Lorenzo and La Venta

The site of San Lorenzo (founded around 1300 BCE), named after a nearby modern village, is located in the lower reaches of the Coatzacoalcos River. It was on a hill overlooking a large agricultural floodplain. The highest point of the hill was landscaped to create a plateau covering an area of about 7 square kilometers and resembling in plan the shape of a bird. Though the wooden and thatch architecture has long since disappeared, the use of basaltic stones, brought from the distant Tuxtla Mountains, for steps, columns, and aqueducts gives a vivid picture of the scale and grandeur of Olmec skills. The main ceremonial complex consisted of a series of earth platform mounds arranged north-south in a series of courts.

Though the mounds are not aligned according to a single design, huge monolithic heads stood in the middle of the courts. The central court also had a series of cut-stone cisterns that, given their location and drainage system, must have had had ritual purpose. One can assume that sites for a city in this era were not chosen for purely economic purposes. San Lorenzo was a ritual site, but what made it so special compared to other locations on the plateau? According to one argument, it was the only place along the river where the sunset aligned with the volcano Cerro Zempoaltepec at the winter solstice.

For unknown reasons, San Lorenzo went into decline. Many of the great colossal heads that had been so laboriously brought to the site were rolled down into the ravines that divide the edges of the terrace and were carefully covered up; within a generation or two, the jungle had totally reclaimed the site. It is unknown whether this was done to ritualistically deactivate the site or for other reasons.

A new center had by then already been built and prepared, and perhaps the priests of that center were eager to be the solitary overlords of the region. It is known as La Venta and is 80 kilometers northeast of San Lorenzo and closer to the shore of the Gulf of Mexico. La Venta was perhaps the first use of symmetry in the overall design in Mesoamerican architecture, with the site appearing to be oriented to the summer solstice sunset over the volcano San Martín to the northwest. Its pyramid, about 30 meters high and 150 meters in diameter—the largest of the Olmec pyramids—was constructed from 3,700 cubic meters of beaten earth and clay, with a rectangular base from which rose an unusual fluted, conical shape (although this could have been caused by subsequent erosion). It was not just the symmetry of the composition that was new. The designers used stone sculptures to create a narrative procession from south to north, while at the same time burying other sculptures and artifacts as a type of offering. The invisible and the visible were meant to work in relationship to each other. The aboveground sculptures are grouped at significant intervals along the axis.

Some of the altars of La Venta show a man exiting a cave holding an infant in his arms. The colors red and green played a critical part. And naturally, an important symbolic element was maize, celebrated by four stelae, placed at the foot of the Great Mound, that show stylized human embryos wearing maize regalia. They function as four human-maize seeds, or the originators of the human race.

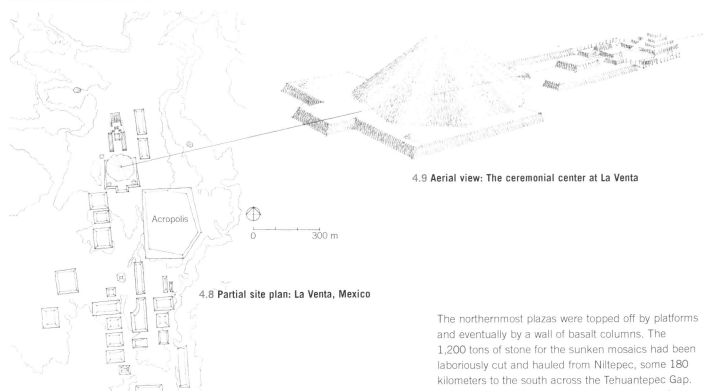

4.9 **Aerial view: The ceremonial center at La Venta**

Acropolis

0   300 m

4.8 **Partial site plan: La Venta, Mexico**

The northernmost plazas were topped off by platforms and eventually by a wall of basalt columns. The 1,200 tons of stone for the sunken mosaics had been laboriously cut and hauled from Niltepec, some 180 kilometers to the south across the Tehuantepec Gap.

La Venta, like San Lorenzo before it, was a place where a sacred landscape was produced ex nihilo. Sacred landscapes had historically been deeply connected to specific landscapes, but in these sites there was no such deep tradition. Here the sacred was fabricated and thus spelled the beginning of the end of the conventional shamanistic world.

The site thus revolved around the concepts of the timeless repetition of life and death. But how the Olmecs experienced this is conjecture. Was a yearly festival celebrated here? Was the site a type of religious sanctuary used only by initiates? Regardless, the site was a man-made spiritual landscape designed to serve both as a pilgrimage site and as a massive energizer that would keep the corn fields productive.

Most astonishing of all were several large buried plazas that constituted offerings in their own right, made up of hundreds of tons of greenstone blocks, placed in huge pits and imbricated with colored clays. Archaeologists speculate that they were created as effigies of a female life-force taking the form of artificial lakes and rivers that controlled childbirth and fishing. Part of the design included a pavement made up of a geometric pattern known as a quincunx that represents the surface of the earth with a diamond pattern fringe, referring perhaps to the flowering mantle of the earth. Over these offerings, the builders placed sand of different colors, phallic celts, and stone figurines.

4.10 **Mysterious buried "pavement," La Venta**

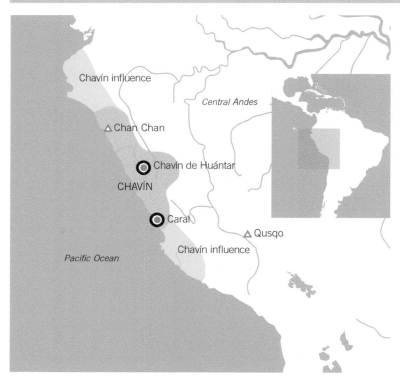

4.11 **Chavín culture along the Peruvian coast**

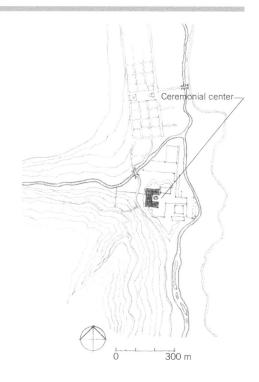

4.12 **Area plan: Chavín de Huántar, Peru**

CHAVÍN DE HUÁNTAR

By 800 BCE, the innovative Peruvian shore civilizations at Casma and Supe valleys had gone into decline and were conquered by invaders, probably from the highlands; no one knows for sure. The rise and decline of these civilizations within a relatively short time, along with the militarization of society, must have had a powerful impact on the psyche of the times and seems to have led to a shift in ideological focus. Power shifted to centers away from the coast to the rugged highlands, the most important of which was Chavín de Huántar, founded around 900 BCE. It is located halfway between the Supe Valley to the south and the Casma Valley to the north, at a place where the Mosna River narrows dramatically into a precipitous gorge. There, at the convergence point of two major passes crossing the snowcapped Cordillera Blanca, the Mosna meets the Wachesqua River at a triangular space wedged between descending mountain slopes that is the only flat area for miles around. Though seemingly remote, Chavín de Huántar was only about a six-day trek to the Pacific Ocean to the west and to the tropical forests to the east. The tight valley could never have supported the

population density of Casma; agriculture here was thus pursued by the more traditional means of small terraced plots.

The temple of Chavín de Huántar was, therefore, of a new type of institution deriving its economy almost entirely from the draw of its ceremonies and rituals. Unlike ritual centers in the Supe and Casma valleys, with their open plazas and relaxed and generously scaled monuments, here the temple was in fact less a temple than a type of machine designed to enhance and produce certain effects. The measure of divinity was not distance but psychological intimacy, and perhaps even fear.

The first structure that was built was a U-shaped platform called the Old Temple. Facing east, it consisted of a large circular sunken plaza, with stairs on axis and a centralized main staircase leading to the roof of the building, which acted as a raised terrace. The platform, built of dressed stone, rose 12 to 16 meters above the plaza. Its walls were adorned with numerous gigantic grotesque heads, carved in the round and inserted in the massive masonry. The carvings also show jaguars, strombus shells, and clawed hands as well as San Pedro cactus, an Andean hallucinogenic. They were

probably painted in black, white, and shades of red and blue. The surface of the temple was most probably painted both inside and outside, as evidenced by the great quantities of clay on the floors and the remains of red and yellow paint that appear on some side walls. Unlike the earlier centers, which had rooms on the top of the mounds but no interiors, here the main attraction was inside the temple, which, though built as a solid mass of stone, was honeycombed with labyrinthine passages. Roofed with large slabs of stone, these passages are no more than a meter wide and vary in height, but are large enough for a person to walk through. One passage oriented directly on axis with the round plaza contained a mysterious and imposing 3-meter-high slender granite stone known today as the Lanzón. It was not a natural stone, but a sculpture that is half cat and half human, the design of which is wrapped around the stone so that it is never entirely visible from one standpoint. Facing east along the axis of the Old Temple but invisible from outside, its right arm is raised with open palm of the hand exposed and its left arm is lowered with the back of the hand visible. This pose seems to express the role of the deity as a mediator of opposites or as a personification of the principle of balance and order. Its narrow, tapered upper section fits accurately through a tailor-made hole in the roof, indicating that the temple was designed around the statue. Why was this sacred relic hidden away in the depths of the temple, and in such a way that it could not be removed? There is a depression on the deity's head into which the blood of sacrificed victims may have been poured from the hole above. The entire structure was enlarged several times; the two principal additions affected the south wing, which ultimately formed a solid rectangular structure 70 by 72 meters in plan.

An aspect of the design that seems to have been at the core of the experience was sound. Water channels route water beneath the temple and would have been amplified in the passageways. The ducts leading to the outside were perhaps not for air, but to emit the sound. During the spring flood and when the underground channels were opened, the building would have probably come alive with its roaring. The aqueducts, coming from the direction of the setting sun, might symbolize the underground river along which the sun travels to be born again in the east. This

4.13 Section through central passageway of the Old Temple leading to the Lanzón at Chavín de Huántar

river was regarded as the continuation of the Milky Way. Strombus shell trumpets were also discovered in one of the galleries, and when recently played were found to produce intense auditory experiences. Perhaps the temple was seen as a type of "mountain," alive with the spirit of the deity—a spirit that could be "summoned" by the priests who controlled the building's inner mechanisms. Light might also have played a part. The corridors are connected to the outside by a series of perfectly straight narrow tubes often called ventilation shafts. Experiments have shown that they could have brought daylight into the corridors, but also perhaps flames at night, which would have produced unsettling effects.

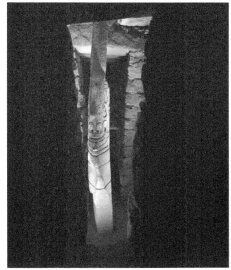

4.14 Lanzón, Chavín de Huantar, Peru

Chavín reflects the use and manipulation of nature in order to reinforce the power of the site and its authorities. The amplification of the rushing water to a roar played a part, as did hallucinogenic drugs. It is generally thought that an initiate would have been led down the corridor, which would have reverberated with echoes from the rushing water below, to witness the divinity and perhaps to hear its oracular declamations. This suggests that the religious leaders were not the proverbial chiefs over the land, but served an institution that was nothing less than a living deity. The priests fed it, monitored it, cared for it, and ritualistically activated it. Though Chavín eventually went into decline, its sanctity was never forgotten, even until the arrival of the Spaniards. Antonio de Espinoza, who visited the site around 1620, notes that the locals from all over the Inca kingdom came there to make offerings and sacrifices.

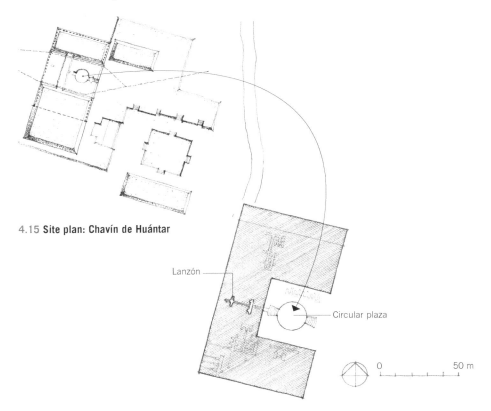

4.15 Site plan: Chavín de Huántar

Lanzón

Circular plaza

0   50 m

4.16 Plan: Old Temple at Chavín de Huántar

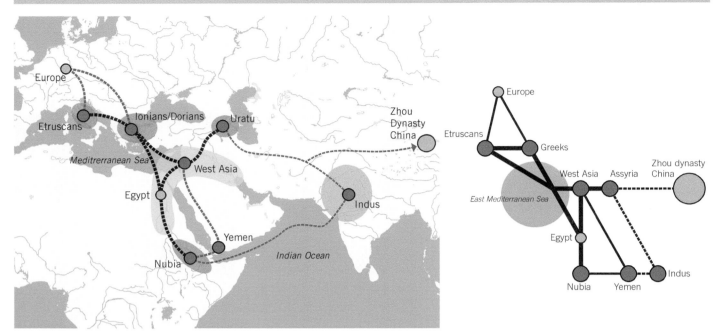

4.17 West Asian and African metal centers, ca. 800 BCE

4.18 Eurasian trade diagram, 800 BCE

THE IRON AGE

Scholars generally think that the forging of iron was developed by the Hittites, who kept the technique secret. Its development had taken thousands of years of familiarity with kilns, metals, and extraction methods, until high-temperature smelting could be mastered. But after the downfall of the Hittites in 1200 BCE, the art of iron forging spread, reaching China around 600 BCE.

Apart from China, there were five newly emerging metal-oriented societies: the Urartians in Armenia, the Nubians in the Sudan, the Etruscans in Italy, the Dorians and Ionians in Greece, and, somewhat later, the Mauryans in India. As these cultures were all marginal to the Mesopotamian/ Egyptian civilizations, the consequences were enormous. Iron, in other words, completely changed the political and civilizational landscape; areas once peripheral to the urbanized agro-centric, Mesopotamian/ Egyptian heartlands became important, if not dominant, players in the world economy.

Iron was used to make weapons, of course, but was also superior for crafting agricultural implements like plows and wheels. With iron plows, the plains of Sicily, the north coast of Africa, and even the high plains of eastern Anatolia became major grain-producing regions,

significantly lessening the need for grain from Mesopotamia and Egypt. Iron farm implements also had a profound impact on the development of agriculture in sub-Saharan Africa, where for the first time, large-scale agriculture and land clearing could be undertaken. The African connection—which was centered around Nubia and later Aksum—exhausted itself around 600 BCE largely because deforestation had led to serious environmental degradation, which made both mining and agriculture difficult and had permanent negative consequences for the economy.

The Urartians were conquered by the Assyrians in order to secure a steady supply of metal for their army. There is little left of Urartian architecture, apart from remnants, most of it having been destroyed by centuries of warfare. The Nubians, who produced extensive architectural works, continued Egyptian traditions. The Etruscans and the Dorians were, however, newcomers, having moved into the Mediterranean from the north. Their views on the world were different from that of the Egyptians and Mesopotamians, leading them to create a highly refined civic-legal description of the divine that was to impact European architecture for centuries. (Many Etruscan and Greek concepts were adopted by the Romans.)

In eastern India, the discovery of iron in the Barabar Hills was to have a global impact. In the 5th century BCE the rise of the Mauryan Empire began, first along the Ganges River and subsequently into Central Asia. By the 6th and 5th centuries BCE, the most powerful forces in the global economy emanated from India, Mediterranean Europe, and China, with Central Asia becoming important mainly as a transit region. Disadvantageously, this region could also be attacked from many sides; indeed, for the next thousand years, until the modern era when relatively fixed national boundaries were constructed, the borders in Central Asia were in continual flux as state after state attempted to secure a dominant role in cross-Asian trade.

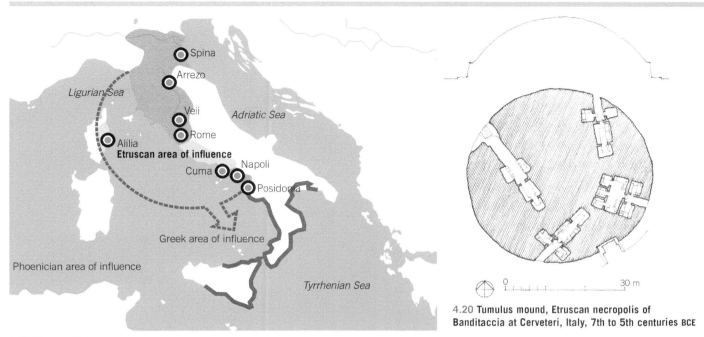

4.19 **Etruscan Italy**

4.20 **Tumulus mound, Etruscan necropolis of Banditaccia at Cerveteri, Italy, 7th to 5th centuries BCE**

THE ETRUSCANS

The origin of the Etruscans is hotly debated. Their language, which has only been partially deciphered, does not belong to the Indo-European language family. They settled predominantly in the north part of the Italian peninsula, between the Arno and Tiber Rivers and on the west side of the Apennine Mountains. This territory provided plenty of metal ore, such as copper, iron, lead, and silver, but the Etruscans appear to have acquired the skill to exploit these metals prior to settling in Italy; indeed, the presence of these ores might have attracted these settlers in the first place. For example, Volterra, one of their main cities, twelve of which formed the Etruscan League (Dodecapoli), was close to Colline Metallifere (Metalliferous Hills). The Etruscan city of Vulci, also part of the league, was especially noted for its bronze work.

It was not just the Etruscans' economic acumen that differentiated them from the surrounding tribes but also their fantastic belief structure, which relied heavily on omens. The Etruscan aesthetic, as displayed in the decoration of their graves, was spontaneous, vivacious, and open to the appreciation of other cultures—especially that of the Greeks, whose goods and vases they freely imported and copied. As a group, the Dorians, Ionians, and Etruscans all played an important part in restoring the Mediterranean to economic and cultural viability after the disruptions of the preceding centuries.

Despite the settlements of the Greeks in the south and center of Italy, the Etruscans were able to maintain their hold over the northern half of the Italian peninsula. There they had a vibrant interaction with Rome, the ascendant power, until they were finally absorbed into the Roman Empire, to which they contributed substantively. Many Etruscan cities, like Veii, north of Rome, were, in their heyday, as big as Athens, with a population estimated as high as one hundred thousand. Though the physical fabric of Etruscan

4.21 **Example of an Etruscan arch**

cities has largely been lost, much can be discerned from the multitude of tombs that dot the hillsides—veritable cities of the dead, all executed in skillful masonry and richly decorated interiors. Most of the tombs are in the shape of mounds, some 40 meters across, that contain decorated chambers.

Many Etruscan walls and gateways in Rome, Perugia, Cortona, and other places still exist today. At Velhatri (today's Volterra), sections of the formerly 7.3-kilometer-long enclosure, built during the 5th and 4th centuries BCE, as well as the Porta all'Arco and the Porta di Diana, still bear witness to Etruscan skills. The city gate of Perugia in particular exhibited a bold use of the arch, a building element that, along with the vault, was introduced by the Etruscans and became one of their main contributions to Roman architecture. In Rome itself, several famous structures, including the Circus Maximus and the Cloaca Maxima, the Roman sewage system still in use today, were built by Etruscan masons. The deft and unfailingly secure use of arches that emerged in Etruria was to have a tremendous impact on Roman architecture, as is evidenced by the Roman aqueducts. Even the Greeks had not equaled this skill, remaining content with what was basically a simple post-and-lintel system in the construction of their temples.

Etruscan Religion

The outward aspect of Etruscan religion was its scrupulous adherence to ritualistic formulas. And yet, through Etruscan art and painting, one senses a lively appreciation of individuality. This vibrancy did come at the expense of stylistic unity—something that lent their art an unmistakable, and in some sense unusual, receptivity toward outside influences. Elements of the Corinthian, Ionian, and Attic are all in evidence in Etruscan art and painting. This is also true of their religion—so much so that their own deities came to be fused with, and coalesced around, Greek ones, paving the way for the later Roman assimilation of Greek culture. Unlike the Greek pantheon, however, that of the Etruscans included supernatural and chthonic beings whose number and nature have not yet been determined. The Etruscans also had a complex system of augury (such as the study of the entrails—especially the liver) and of sacrificial animals. They studied and interpreted natural phenomena, such as comets or the flight paths of birds (a practice known as *auspicium*, or divination). A 3rd-century BCE bronze model of a liver recovered near Piacenza, Italy, was perhaps used to train Etruscan priests (haruspices) in the art of interpretation. The upper surface is divided into forty sections, corresponding to the celestial zones of the Etruscan pantheon; these have the names of gods, including many with whom we are unfamiliar, engraved on it. The particularities of the animal's liver told the priest which deity to invoke. It was probably meant to be aligned north-south.

One of the words used to describe this liver was *templum*, which could refer to the sky, to a consecrated area on earth, or to a much smaller surface, such as the liver of an animal used in divination, as long as the orientation and partition of the area followed the celestial model. A *templum* could thus be a physical space (in which case it would be marked or enclosed), but it could also be an area of the sky, in which the birds would be observed.

A *templum*, in other words, was a space where humans, represented by priests (augurs), could interact with the gods. In all ancient Mediterranean and Mesopotamian cultures, nature was associated with divine presences, but for the Etruscans, the gods

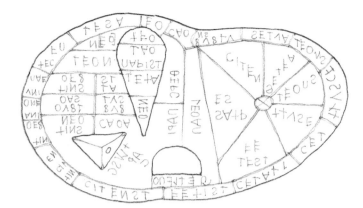

4.22 Bronze Etruscan model of a liver, 3rd century BCE

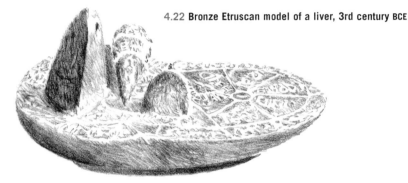

spoke through signs. This was not the case in Mesopotamian religions, where gods spoke more directly, through priests. For the Minoans, religion centered on nature's life cycles, with the gods representing the stories associated with those cycles. But for the Etruscans, religion was a practice of translation. Unlike the more fearsome and arbitrary gods of the Mesopotamians, Etruscan gods readily communicated their intentions. Disaster could come about just as much from the actions of the gods as from a misunderstanding of their messages.

The orientation of Etruscan temples was of critical importance and was determined by the intersection of two axes, one north-south, called *cardo*, and the other east-west, called *decumanus*. The idea was employed later by the Romans in setting up military camps according to strictly standardized rules and subsequently became fundamental to Roman town planning. Apparently these orthogonal lines were closely connected to Etrusco-Italic religious iconography. The observer's place was at the point where the two lines crossed; he stood with his back to the north. The eastern sector to the left (*pars sinistra*) was of good omen and superior gods; the western sector to the right (*pars dextra*) was of ill omen and for the infernal deities. The vault of heaven, thus quartered and oriented, was further subdivided into sixteen minor sections in which were placed the habitations of many divinities. This plan corresponds to the outer ring of sixteen compartments of the Piacenza liver.

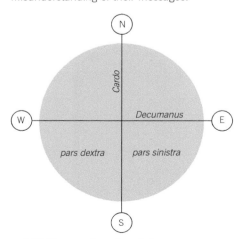

4.23 Diagram of *cardo* and *decumanus*

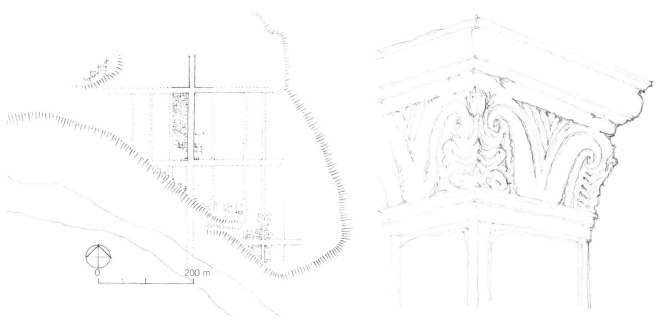

4.24 **Site plan: Marzabotto, Italy, 5th century BCE**

4.25 **Detail of an Etruscan capital**

The position of signs manifested in the sky, thunderbolts, flights of birds, and other portents, as studied by the augur, would indicate which god was responsible for a particular message and whether it was a good or a bad omen. This process was called *auspicium*, a word that was a combination of *avis* ("bird") and *specio* ("to see"). The priest and soothsayer watched the flight and feeding of birds, listened to their cries, and even examined their entrails. From this came words like *contemplatio*, meaning literally "with a template." There was also the distinction between whether the message was an order or a friendly reminder. All in all, the *templum* (as a type of three-dimensional template) stood between the ephemeral and the real, linking the invisible absolute realities of the divine with the real needs of the supplicants. The consecrated ground on which this took place was expressed in Etruscan language by the word *sacni* (becoming the Latin *sancti*). When the temple was finished, the opening was presided over by the augur in a ceremony called the *inauguratio*.

4.26 **Etruscan tomb, Tarquinia, Italy**

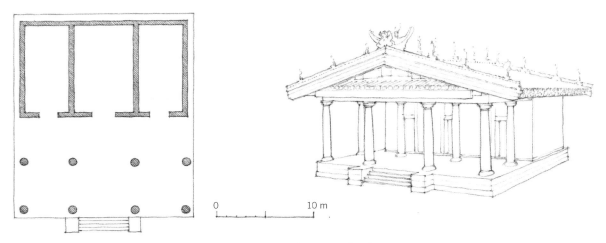

4.27 Plan and pictorial view: An Etruscan temple, based on descriptions by Vitruvius

Etruscan Temples

The form of Etruscan temples paralleled certain aspects of Greek temples, but there are several important differences. The Etruscans never made the leap to stone. Except at a very late period, the Etruscan temple was not thought of as requiring permanence. The podium that raised the temple above the surrounding ground level, however, was often of stone, with stairs or ramps leading to the top. The temple proper was built of mud, brick, and timber. Though similar to Greek temples in that respect, Etruscan temples were meant to be viewed mainly from the front rather than stand as objects in the landscape; they therefore have no rear facade. The pitch of the roof was relatively low, and they had overhanging eaves. The pediment was originally open so that the roof timbers could be seen. Also distinctive was the roomy colonnaded porch, known as the *pronaos* (meaning "in front of the naos") that stood in front of the *cella*. Etruscans often organized gods into a trivium, erecting temples with three *cellae*; their overall shape was rectangular, tending toward square. Etruscan temples introduced the principal of an axial connection between temple and altar, which the Greeks eschewed until very late, and probably then incorporated only under Italian influence. Also characteristic was the striking use of color for the various temple elements, and the way the mass was broken up by antefixae, *acroteria*, and sculptural groups.

The Etruscans experimented with a range of columns, including the Ionic, until, by the 5th century BCE, they developed the Tuscan column, as it was later called by Vitruvius. This was a smooth wooden column with diminution toward the top and a capital, akin to the Doric, consisting of a round cushion (echinus) and a square abacus. The bases, however, were inspired by the Ionic order (Doric columns had no bases). Because these structures were of wood, Etruscan temples had wide intercolumniations. The habit of ornamenting the temple with decorative terra-cotta elements may have been taken over from the Greeks, but was implemented by the Etruscans with particular showmanship. These elements were often on the ridges of the roofs, which were considered a type of landing place for the divine.

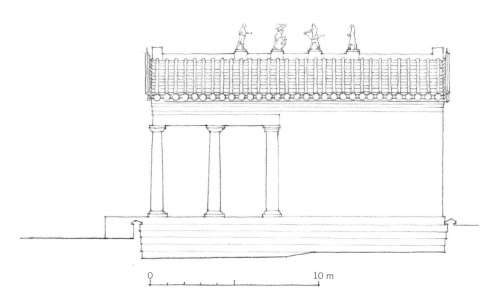

4.28 Side elevation: Portonaccio Temple at Veii, Italy, 515–490 BCE

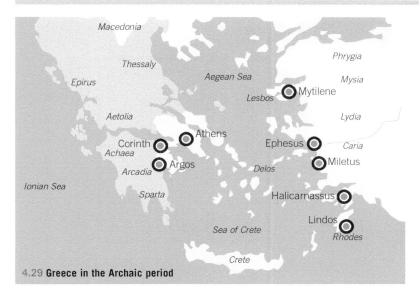

4.29 **Greece in the Archaic period**

4.30 **Geometric period Greek vase, typically serving as a monumental grave marker**

GREECE: THE GEOMETRIC PERIOD

Post-Mycenaean Greece was a period of migrations, confusion, and poverty. But over time, the Dorians in Greece and the Ionians along the Turkish coast came to develop common cultural practices that fused elements unique to them with residues of the Minoan and Mycenaean cultures. This explains some of the differences in their development from that of the Etruscans. The Minoans and Mycenaeans, having had no temples in the technical sense, held caves and mountains sacred, with worship augmented by shrines. Homer represents the gods as highly mobile creatures constantly visiting each other in their palaces. The early Dorian religious practices took place in natural settings, which made it easy to incorporate some of the features and even locations of Minoan religion into their own. These rites, as described by George Hersey, also often involved trees, or groves of trees, that were fenced off and decorated with materials used in sacrifices—bones, horns, urns, lamps, weapons, fruits, and vegetables. Trees held a special place in Greek culture, and almost every god was associated with one. Athena was, for example, associated with the olive tree. The altar dedicated to a god was set out in front of his or her particular tree or grove.

Participants in the rites would bathe and dress in special clothes and, accompanied by flutists, sing while processing to the place of sacrifice. They were led by a girl carrying a basket of grain on her head. Under the grain, and concealed from view, was the slaughtering knife. The sacrificial animal, decorated with wreaths on his horns, was then led up to the altar with a fire already burning on it. Gathering in a circle, the participants would wash their hands by pouring water from a jug, which they would also sprinkle on the animal. The barley grains from the girl's basket would be flung over the animal, altar, and earth. Once the knife was revealed, the priest would step forward, take it, and prepare for the sacrifice.

The beast, which had to be a prime specimen from the domestic herd, rather than a wild animal, had to be willing to submit to the sacrifice, so the priest placed a bowl of milk at the base of the altar. As the animal stepped forward, it would bow its head to drink, which was interpreted as a sign of submission. Another indication of its assent was its shivering in the sight of the god, a process helped along by the liberal use of cold water. As the blood was held to be precious, it was drained into conduits and pits beneath the altar. The animal was then carved up; special meaning was given to various parts, with the liver being, of course, particularly important for the augur. Some parts were chopped up and wrapped in fat to form a type of reconstituted body. Sometimes the skull was placed on a stake near the altar and draped in an animal skin. Representations of this type of sacrifice extended to trophies and spoils taken from the conquered in battle, to assuage the spirits of the dead.

4.31 **Statue of a calf-bearer**

After the animal was carved, the flesh was roasted and eaten. The communality of the meal bound together social units, from the family to the city. The gods received the act as devotional; as the smoke, immaterial, rose up from the altar, it was, so the Greeks thought, a sign of reverence. In exchange for this act of devotion, the humans could then read the message of the gods embedded in the physical shape of the liver. As mentioned earlier, the animals sacrificed to the gods had to be prime specimens from the domestic herd rather than wild animals.

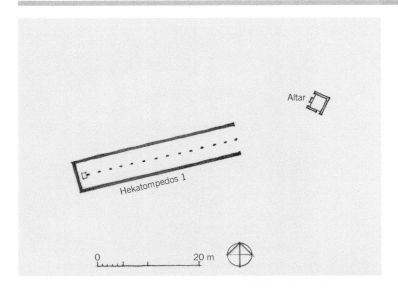

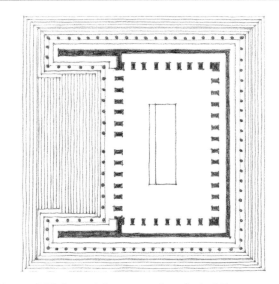

4.32 Plans: The Temple at Samos, Greece (above left). The Altar of Zeus at Pergamon (upper right) drawn at the same scale and orientation

The meaning of this sacrificial process is explained in the myth of Prometheus, who stole fire from the gods and brought it to mankind. In so doing, he made it possible for humankind to civilize itself. The gods did not take the fire back but punished Prometheus by chaining him to a cliff and having an eagle eat his liver. His liver would grow back every day, only to be eaten again. The sacrifice was thus part of a ritual remembrance of humankind's emergence into civilization and of their dependence on the gods for the regulation of their lives. But the sacrifice also marked the difference between humankind and gods, for unlike the gods, who existed in an ethereal form, humankind had to work and show sincerity to keep the communication alive. Only by making a sacrifice—in some ways a labor of love—could men demonstrate that they were thankful to the deities. That is why a skinny bull or decrepit goat would not do: the animal had to be the best of the lot.

Nevertheless, Dorians, Minoans, and even Etruscans had somewhat differing notions about sacrifice. Etruscan sacrifice was more formulaic and Minoan sacrifice more intimate than that of the Greeks. Unlike the Egyptians, Greek sacrifice was connected to the principles of farming and herding, rather than to the palace garden. Bread and meat were at the center of Greek sacrifice. Even in the Christian Eucharist, which developed later, the importance of bread and wine is encountered in veiled form, a comparison

that raises important questions about the influence of Greek practices on early Christianity. The importance of the Greeks' attitudes toward sacrifice might easily be overlooked because so many of their altars were removed when Christianity tried to destroy any evidence of heathen practices. In fact, in the early days of Greek religion, there were no temples, only altars built out in the open.

One of the earliest and most sacred of the Greek altars, on the top of Mt. Lykaion in the Greek Peloponnese, dates back to 3000 BCE—Mycenaean times. It eventually became associated with Zeus, the king of the Greek gods, but whether that was true in the earlier period is unknown. Below the summit there was a stadium, indicating the site's association with an athletic festival, a combination that was to become another important element of many Greek sanctuaries.

The Mt. Lykaion altar, like the Temple of Hera at Samos (8th century BCE) consisted of no more than a low enclosure of flat stones forming a rectangle of about 2 by 3.5 meters. Altars became larger as time progressed; the one on the Acropolis at Athens, for example, from the 5th or 4th century BCE, could hold a dozen bulls at one time. The Altar of Zeus at Pergamon, now in the Pergamon Museum in Berlin, was the most spectacular of all. Built from 197 to 159 BCE, it featured a flight of steps on its west side and flanking Ionic colonnades. It stands on a five-stepped,

almost square plinth. The altar proper was inside the court.

The altars were not necessarily aligned symmetrically on axis with the temple, especially during the Archaic period. At Samos, the altar, with its sacred tree, stood at first at an oblique angle, referring perhaps to a different celestial moment than that of the temple.

The emergence of the altar-plus-temple form coincided with the personification of gods in statues and, once again, seems to have been part of the assimilation process the Dorians underwent when they came into contact with older Mediterranean practices. Early Greek representations of their gods show influences from both the Mesopotamian and Egyptian cultures. But Greek representations were rarely as diminutive as the Mesopotamian and Minoan statues could be, nor as large as the Egyptians' often were. And perhaps therein lies the origin of the Greek advancement of the depiction of the human figure. The earliest three-dimensional representations of divinities, known as korai (draped female statues standing with feet together) were carved from wooden columns or planks at a roughly life-size scale. The Greeks called such statues *kolossos*, which had nothing to do with their size but denoted an image that was shaped like a pillar or column. The statues gradually came to represent gods in a more relaxed stance, one foot forward with the weight of the body balanced naturalistically on the rear leg.

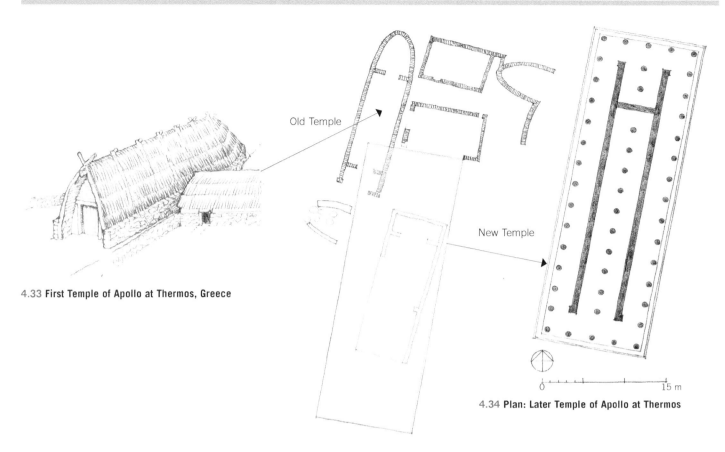

4.33 **First Temple of Apollo at Thermos, Greece**

Old Temple

New Temple

0   15 m

4.34 **Plan: Later Temple of Apollo at Thermos**

4.35 **Scene depicting early Greek sacrificial rites**

Emergence of the Greek Temple Form

The earliest temples, built of mud bricks and thatched roofs, were presumably modeled on chieftains' houses and consisted of a single elongated, windowless room—a *naos* or *cella* (from which the word *cellar* comes)—that was eventually divided into a *pronaos* and *naos*. An example is the Temple of Apollo at Thermos (ca. 950 BCE) in the area of Aetolia in western Greece, where a low stone wall supported a high, steeply pitched thatched roof. There were no side chambers, ancillary spaces, or storage rooms. Soon a continuous porch was added around the body of the building to form an oblong shape, which over time became regularized and systemized. Later (ca. 630 BCE) we see, in the successive rebuilding of the temple, the development of the temple form over time, ending in the regularized form of later temples. The last temple had an elongated form, with proportions of almost 5 to 1 and a row of columns down the center.

Though Greek temples can be found facing the various directions of the compass, more than 80 percent were laid out to face the sunrise, and most, more specifically, faced toward the sunrise on the actual day of their founding, which in turn coincided with the festival day of the divinity to which the temple was dedicated. From this custom arises the term *orientation*, primarily applied to the direction of the axis of a temple. Temples, however, were also sometimes oriented to elements in the landscape, to a solitary peak that suggested the presence of Zeus, or to double peaks, which, reminiscent of a bull's horns, were equated with Zeus. The Greek sanctuary was far from being a detached and spiritual sphere. Symbolically, it was representative of political, economic, and military life as well as the well-being of the city and the region. Many temples served as war museums, holding the spoils of conquest as well as serving as armories.

4.36 Slightly bigger than life-size female figure, mid-6th century BCE

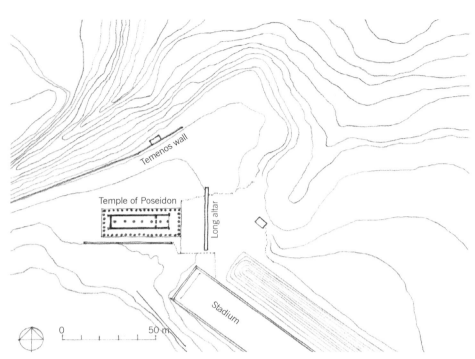

4.37 Site plan: Temple of Poseidon at Isthmia, Greece

The word *temple* is widely used to describe Greek—and often non-Greek—religious structures, though that word, which is derived from the Etruscan, came to be used only later by the Romans. For the Greeks, the structures were considered a type of house (*oikos*) for the deity, who was represented inside the temple by his cult statue, originally made out of wood. But unlike Mesopotamian and Egyptian temples, the Greek temple had no storage rooms, preparation rooms, courtyards, or ancillary spaces. The temple was an integrated architectural unit, the main purpose of which was to house the divine statue. The *cella* was used primarily to store gifts to the temple and even war booty. Unlike in Egypt, the statue was not mobile: it was not paraded from site to site. Furthermore, the main religious events took place outside the temple, in front of the altar, and not within. Of particular sacred importance was the idea of the *temenos*, the boundary around the temple precinct. It could only be crossed at one point, marked by a gate, or *propylon*. The *temenos* did not necessarily have to be a wall, and could be nothing more than a row of stones on the ground. Its sanctity was inviolate, as it was a piece of land cut off from secular reality and reassigned to the divine.

Temple of Poseidon

The Temple of Poseidon at Isthmia (ca. 700 BCE), not far from Corinth, is among the earliest known Greek temples. Its podium measures 14 by 40 meters, with a central row of five columns within the *cella* and two in the *pronaos*. The *cella* was of stone, but the columns and entablature were of oak; the roof was low pitched and covered in fired terra-cotta tiles—a Greek invention. This temple represents an important break in the development of temple design. Whereas the stones for Egyptian temples were of irregular size, the ashlar blocks of this temple were laid in regular courses all the way to the roofline—a standardization of masonry elements. Furthermore, in Egypt, a wall was typically composed of two separate walls, the gap between them filled with rubble. Here the wall is a single vertical element. As with Egyptian temples, however, the wall was covered with a thin coat of plaster that would present to the viewer a smooth, continuous surface broken only, in this case, by a series of pilasters that responded to the rhythm of the colonnade along the outside of the *cella*.

The site was fortified in about 1200 BCE, and ritual festivities were performed from the middle of the 11th century BCE onward. The Temple of Poseidon eventually attracted the Panhellenic Games, called the Isthmia, which took place every two years in honor of Melicertes-Palaemon, or Poseidon. The altar was a 30-meter-long structure in front of the temple, with the sports field and stadium just to the south.

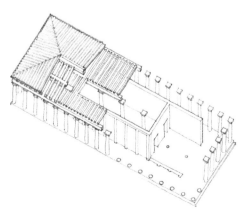

4.38 Pictorial view: Temple of Poseidon at Isthmia

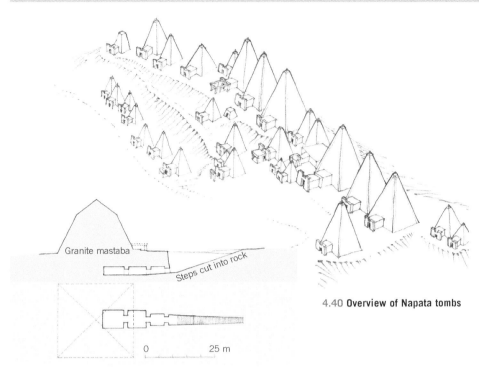

Granite mastaba

Steps cut into rock

0   25 m

4.39 Section and plan: Typical Napatan royal tomb, near Kuraymah, Sudan

4.40 Overview of Napata tombs

Iron played an important role, for the Kushites had learned the techniques of ironworking from their Assyrian enemies. Though the Kushites had iron, they did not have the fuel with which to smelt it. For that they had to turn southward, to the area around the city of Meroë, where the ancient, largely unexcavated slag heaps are still visible today. There the Kushite pharaohs promoted the Egyptian religion and embarked on programs of temple restoration.

At first, the center of the Kushite state was at Napata, lying just above the fourth cataract in the Nile River. Its focal point was the sacred flat-topped mountain of Jebel Barkal, which stands like a natural altar in the landscape a few kilometers from the northern bank of the Nile. In its shadow Ramesses II had already built several temples, one of which was the rather substantial Temple of Amun. The tombs at Napata are sited on both sides of the Nile; they are all that is left of the Nubian capital that once stood nearby. The early tombs were round mastabas. These gave way to pyramids mounted on high bases with distinctive porches. During the last phase, at the height of Kushite control over Egypt, the rulers simplified the form to a pyramid and porch. A group of these are located not too far from Napata, near the modern town of Nuri. They form a tight cluster, with the bigger ones loosely lined up in row.

KINGDOM OF KUSH

Egypt had only one main export, grain, and as the Greeks became more self-reliant, the Egyptian economy began to falter. It had no metal either, and in the end it fell victim to the Iron Age. Not only was it conquered by the distant Assyrians, Babylonians, Persians, Greeks, and Romans, but for a period even by the Nubians, who had been at the sharp end of the Egyptian spear for centuries. As a consequence of the imperial expansion of the New Kingdom dynasties of Egypt into Nubia, these subjugated peoples had adopted Egyptian religion, culture, and weapons of war. The Nubians served as valued mercenaries in the Egyptian army, worshipped Egyptian gods, and built pyramids in which to entomb their rulers. Nubia was rich in natural resources, notably gold, with mines numbering in the hundreds scattered over the desert. To extract the metal from the veins of the quartz rock, the rock was first cracked by means of fire, then crushed into a powder by mills, and finally washed to separate the ore, which was melted into small ingots. The system was hugely labor intensive but yielded, by one estimation, 40,000 kilograms of gold a year, an amount that would not be exceeded again

until the 19th century CE. With the demise of the New Kingdom, Nubia, also known as Kush, was free to assert itself and, during the reign of Piye (747–716 BCE), conquered Egypt and ruled there as the Twenty-fifth Dynasty.

4.41 Mortuary structure of Meroë, near Kabushiyah, Sudan

4.42 **The ruins of Mahram Bilqis, a Sabaean temple at Ma'rib, Yemen**

SABA/SA'ABIA

A much desired commodity during this time was frankincense, derived from the sap of the *Boswellia sacra* tree, which grew mainly in Yemen. Since its aroma was thought to be life-enhancing, it was used to anoint newborns. It was also used in burials to embalm corpses. The Egyptians used it to make the distinctive black eyeliner seen in many Egyptian paintings. The Egyptian queen Hatshepsut sent an expedition to Punt (believed to be either Somalia or southern Arabia) in 1500 BCE; it returned with thirty-one frankincense trees, as depicted on the walls of her mortuary temple near Thebes. The demand for frankincense was staggering. Cities like Sumhuram and Ubar in Dhofar (southern Oman) were reported to export the equivalent of 3,000 tons of it every year.

In the 9th century BCE, the leading supplier of frankincense was the Sabaean kingdom (southwestern Yemen), whose capital was at Marib. The oil was brought up to the Levant, its prime outlet to world markets. The Israelites served as important mediators in this trade. Though the Sabaean area is now barren, it was then a lush oasis irrigated by means of a massive dam, the largest engineering work in the world at that time. Marib's main temple, Mahram Bilqis, or "Temple of the Moon God," was situated about 5 kilometers from Marib. It was so famous that it remained sacred even after the rerouting of the spice trail caused the collapse of the Sabaean kingdom in the 6th century BCE. The dam, left in a state of poor repair, collapsed, causing the emigration of fifty thousand people and the abandonment of the city.

The temple was unusual, a rectangular structure with an inner peristyle. It was accessed at its north and south entrances by massive gates and towers. Once through the temple, one entered an oval, walled enclosure about 90 meters across. There is still much archaeology that needs to be done on this site. The enclosure probably defined a sacred garden, but its purpose and function are unknown. Even the dedication of the temple is uncertain; some say it was to a moon goddess, others that it was a sun temple. The building was not an isolated structure, but part of a large complex now buried beneath the sand.

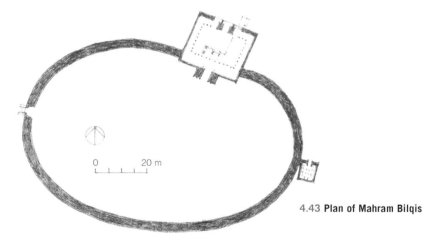

4.43 **Plan of Mahram Bilqis**

4.44 **Frankincense tree**

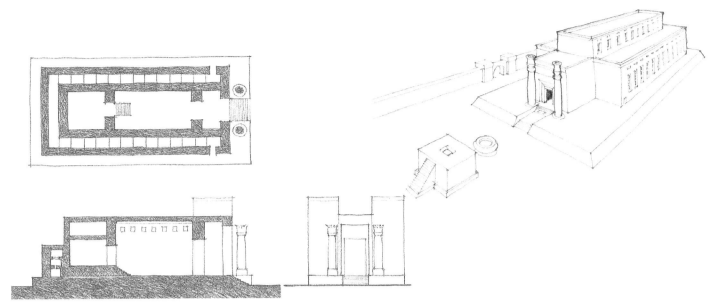

4.45 Conjectural plan, section, and pictorial view: Temple of Solomon, Jerusalem

TEMPLE OF SOLOMON

No other building from these ancient times quite compares to the Temple of Solomon, and the reason is not necessarily because of splendor or size. There were certainly buildings that were larger and more elaborately decked out. Rather it is because there is a precise description of it in the Bible in the book of Kings. One of Judaism's great contributions to the world was its concept of ethical monotheism, which became the basis of both Christianity and Islam.

The Jewish conception of religious space is a complex one. The Jahweh of the Israelites is an invisible, unrepresentable entity, a purely ethical force that is not permitted to be called by name. The mental image of the Israelites' self-identification was that of desert tribes living in tents in which permanent buildings played no role. Indeed, it has been held by some scholars that Moses refused to bring his charges across the Jordan into Canaan for fear that they would become concretized—that is, tied to property and agriculture.

After Moses's death, the Israelites entered Palestine and founded Jerusalem as their capital. A threshing floor was brought from the Jebusite "Zion" on Mt. Moriah as a place for carrying out the traditional sacrifices and as a place to display the sacred ark. As described in the Bible, the ark was a gold-plated, portable chest containing the two stone tablets of Moses on which were inscribed the Ten Commandments. On top of it sat figures of two winged cherubim facing each other, the only kind of bodily representation permitted. Their outspread wings formed the throne of God, while the ark itself was his footstool. Wherever the Israelites went, the ark was carried in front by priests, especially in wars where its leading presence was viewed as a blessing for the enterprise. It was veiled in badgers' skins and blue cloth so that even the Levites, who were the only ones allowed to handle it, could not see it. As a more symbolic statement of permanence, Solomon, King David's son, built the First Temple for the ark (dedicated ca. 950 BCE). It was built with substantial help from Hiram of Tyre, who delivered not only the famous cedars of Lebanon used in its construction but also, so it is suggested by specialists, his favorite architect, Chiram Abiff.

Because Solomon married the daughter of Amenhotep III, one could expect a certain amount of Egyptian influence at the Solomonic court. Even though the temple had an altar in front for animal sacrifices, the temple was not viewed as the residence of a god but as an elaborate container for the ark in the windowless Holy of Holies (Kodesh Kodashim). This room—in which, it was thought, one could speak to God directly—contained no furniture, but had, guarding the ark, two tall statues representing cherubim, whose outspread wings met in the center of the room. Over the centuries, many attempts at a reconstruction of the temple have been made from the descriptions given in the Bible. Details as to the temple's features are given in 1 Kings 6:19 and 8:6: "And the house, when it was in building, was built of stone made ready before it was brought thither: so that there was neither hammer nor axe nor any tool of iron heard in the house, while it was in building." The reason for the injunction against iron tools at the construction site—though they were certainly used in preparing stones before they reached the site—is the cause of much discussion. The reason probably has something to do with the fact that iron smelting was often associated with negative magic and thus was potentially polluting.

The temple was destroyed in 586 BCE by the Babylonians, and the Jewish population was taken into the Babylonian Exile (597–537 BCE). Today's Wailing Wall is a remnant of the foundations of the Second Temple (515 BCE), built by the Israelites after they had returned from their enforced exile to Babylon. It was that temple that was destroyed, in 70 CE, by the Romans. Hadrian built a temple to Jupiter on the site. That building was in turn demolished and replaced by the Dome of the Rock.

4.46 *Gui* vessel

4.47 *Zun* vessel

4.48 *Ding* vessel

ZHOU DYNASTY, CHINA

The Zhou tribes from northwestern China conquered the Shang. The Western Zhou (1046–771 BCE) and Eastern Zhou (771–256 BCE) periods are distinguished by the relocation of the capital city from Hao (near the present city of Xi'an) in the west to Luoyang in Henan Province. The move was apparently prompted by the need to stabilize the eastern provinces. The Zhou soon entered into a period of internal strife, known as the Warring States Period (475–221 BCE). Despite this, the Zhou made the transition to iron, developing cast-iron production (as opposed to forged iron in the West) around 500 BCE. They also established the first imperial cities, two of which—Xi'an and Luoyang—are still major urban centers today.

Though it might seem that China has been "Chinese" from early on, there were, prior to the Zhou dynasty, several regional and linguistic groups (somewhat similar to what one might have found in South Asia). In their conquests, the Zhou enforced the use of the Chinese language, part of an effort that they perceived to be a civilizing agenda. Those who did not want to succumb moved southward, displacing or integrating into local populations to become the ancestors of modern Thai, Laotians, and Burmese. Rites of worship, an ideology of harmony, and the sacrifices to ancestral deities all served to link political and religious authority. The Zhou articulated this as the "mandate of heaven" (*tianming*), which will be discussed in more

detail in a later chapter. It is thus safe to say that during the Zhou dynasty, many of the cultural and political ideals that were to pervade Chinese imperial society were established.

Underlying this mandate was the principle of ritual (*li*), a sign of aristocratic behavior. Several Zhou period texts, including *Zhou li* (Rituals of Zhou), *Yi li* (Ceremony and Ritual), and *Li jie* (Record of Ritual) detail the organization at the courtly duties that governed every rank and office. *Li* consists of the norms of proper social behavior as taught to others by fathers, village elders, and government officials.

At the core of the ritual were elaborate bronze vessels that were placed on platforms during ancestor ceremonies. The vessels were used as offerings, with different types

of foods requiring different types of vessels. There were vessels containing millet wine (*zun*), vessels containing food (*ding* and *gui*), and vessels containing water. Some vessels, with their long feet, made it possible to cook the food inside, making a fire of charcoal under the vessel. Ritual books minutely describe who was allowed to use what kinds and number of sacrificial vessels, with the *ding* being the most important and even used as a indicator of power. The king of Zhou could use 9 *ding* and 8 *gui* vessels; a duke was allowed to use 7 *ding* and 6 *gui* vessels; and so forth down the line. These elaborately scripted activities were meant to suppress the tension between imperial divine control and the agitation from the camps of the clan elites, who were continually jostling for power and prestige.

4.49 A modern food offering in a market stall in Bangkok

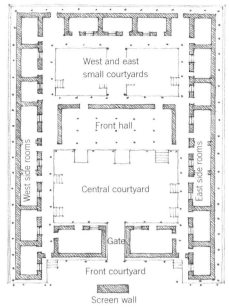

West and east
small courtyards

Front hall

West side rooms

East side rooms

Central courtyard

Gate

Front courtyard

Screen wall

0 _____ 15 m

4.50 Plan: Ritual complex at Fengchu, Shaanxi Province, China

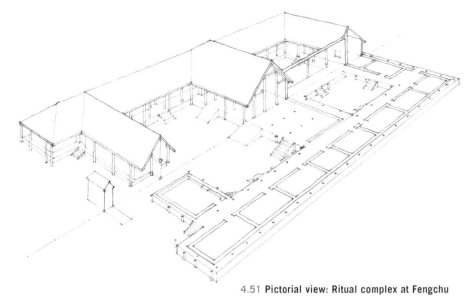

4.51 Pictorial view: Ritual complex at Fengchu

The Ritual Complex

Under the Zhou, ritual halls became part of the standard architectural vocabulary. These halls were places where the elite assembled according to their status in the social hierarchy. The vessels would be set out on the floor or low shelves in pre-established order, with the rituals themselves accompanied by chimes that marked noble rank. A chime of sixty-five bells, which would have required six musicians standing and kneeling on both sides of the instrument, was recovered from a Zhou dynasty tomb. The hall was positioned in a central court entered through a gatehouse. A reconstruction of the ritual complex at Fengchu (1100–1000 BCE) shows an axially symmetrical arrangement of one-story buildings. In front of the entrance there was a freestanding wall, which, as in later Chinese structures, served to prevent unwanted spirits from entering the complex. The ritual platform was accessible by three flights of stairs. The main construction was of wood, with bronze used to bind and reinforce structural elements at the joints.

Although the only physical evidence of Zhou cities are earth foundations, there is an important description of an ideal city, accompanied by an illustration, in the *Rituals of Zhou*. The description, known as the Wangcheng plan, is presumed to be of Luoyang, capital of the Eastern Zhou dynasty, but is better known as Wangcheng, or "Ruler's City":

The *jiangren*, or master craftsman, builds the state, leveling the ground with the water by using a plumb line. He lays out posts, taking the plumb line (to ensure the posts' verticality) and using their shadows as the determiners of a midpoint. He examines the shadows of the rising and setting sun and makes a circle that includes the midpoints of the two shadows.

The master craftsman constructs the state capital. He makes a square nine *li* of each side; each side has three gates. Within the capital are nine north-south and nine east-west streets. The north-south streets are nine carriage tracks in width. On the left (as one faces south, or to the east) is the Ancestral Temple, and to the right (west) are the Altars of Soil and Grain. In the front is the Hall of Audience and behind, the markets.*

*Nancy Shatzman Steinhardt, *Chinese Imperial City Planning* (Honolulu: University of Hawaii Press, 1990), 33.

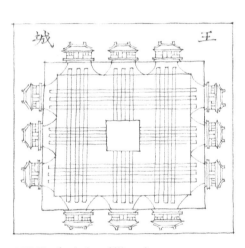

4.52 Idealized plan of Wangcheng

Site of later 6th-century BCE Zhou dynasty graves

Markets

Palace

Altars of soil and grain

Ancestral shrine

Luo River

4.53 City plan of Chengzhou (Luoyang)

Drawings of Luoyang from the 15th and 17th centuries CE illustrate its salient features, with the addition of the inner city walls. Not far from the temple one finds soil and grain altars, the private or sleeping chambers (*qin*), and the markets. Although no single Chinese city of later date seems to actually have been built according to the Wangcheng plan, it can be argued that most subsequent major Chinese cities developed along its basic principles. Wangcheng symbolizes the notion that the Chinese emperor is at the center of the world; in addition, the number nine, which sounds like the word *long-lasting* in Chinese, was habitually associated with the emperor. City walls were not only defensive but also a symbol of a ruler's power and nobility. The three words *cheng*, *du*, and *jing* are each commonly translated into English as "city," but *cheng*, as a verb, meant "walling a city." Later, in imperial China, *cheng* referred to a walled administrative city. Even in common parlance today, *cheng* is translated as "city wall" or simply "wall."

In 1038 BCE, the Duke of Zhou founded a new city, Chengzhou, to the north of the Luo River. It was intended to be the capital but did not become so until 770 BCE. The city, which closely resembles the ideas of the Wangcheng plan, had a palace at the center, three markets to the north and to the south, an ancestral temple, and, next to it, altars of soil and grain. It was destroyed in a civil war in 510 BCE and rebuilt with a modified design and with a new name, Luoyang, which is its current name.

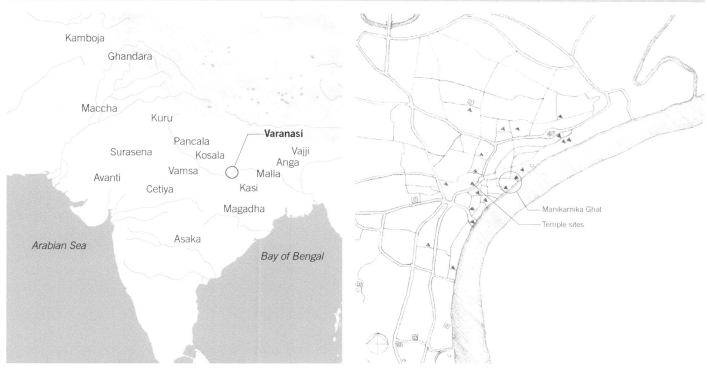

4.54 **The sixteen great kingdoms, or** *mahajanapadas*, **of India**

Manikarnika Ghat

Temple sites

4.55 Plan of Varanasi, India

THE ARYAN INVASION AND VARANASI

As the cities of the Indus Ghaggar-Hakra civilization were withering away, a group of migrants, originating in Central Asia, made their appearance. These Indo-Aryans, as they are now called, were expert horsemen, inventors of the chariot, and skilled in their use of iron. They settled first around five tributaries of the Indus River, but then, using iron to chop down the forests, moved into the fertile Gangetic Plains around 1200 BCE. Of the numerous cities that came to be built, little remains, since everything was made of wood. By the year 1000 BCE, sixteen kingdoms and semirepublics, known as *mahajanapadas*, had developed. Warfare among them was constant, with victors absorbing the vanquished and destroying their cities. By 500 BCE, four *mahajanapadas* dominated: Magadha, Kosala, Kasi, and the republican Vrajji Confederacy. Around 450 BCE, Magadha became the dominant power by defeating the Vrajji Confederacy as well as Kosala and Kasi. Kasi's capital, Varanasi, was spared the normal fate of a conquered city and granted special status as a pilgrimage site. It was here that codification of Aryan rituals, as elaborated in their oral treatises, took place. What emerged was not a single doctrine, but various philosophical schools ranging from the materialist to the atheist.

4.56 **A contemporary Vedic fire ceremony, Satara, Maharashtra, India**

4.57 **A cremation fire at Varanasi**

Varanasi was so important as a center of religious learning that in the 6th century BCE, the famed Shakyamuni Buddha made Varanasi his first stop after his self-enlightenment. Numerous other influential thinkers came to the city as well, including Adi Shankara (9th century CE), whose teachings and writings laid the foundations of Hinduism, which relied heavily on Vedic ideas.

Vedic rituals did not require temples or even the creation of statues. They were based on fire sacrifices of various kinds that needed only brick platforms. Fire was the agent that enabled the transformation of the sacrificial food (matter) into smoke and air (energy). The water of the Ganges is also sacred as another essential element of life. At dawn every morning, thousands of devotees gather on ghats—steps leading down to the shore—to face the sun that rises across the broad expanse of the Ganges River and is reflected in its waters. Half immersed in the river, they greet the sun by cupping the water of the Ganges into their palms and pouring it back into the river with arms extended. This is followed by a slow turn of 360 degrees while standing in place, a miniature act of circumambulation. A quick dip in the river completes the ritual. This ritual can be repeated many times or performed with greater elaboration that includes long chants and sequences of yogic postures.

Varanasi is built on the western side of the river on a high, natural berm at a curve in the river. Behind the berm, in a semicircular arch, lies the dense fabric of the medieval city, with twisting narrow streets and a multitude of temples, water tanks, and street shrines.

4.58 **Ritual ablutions at Varanasi**

The eighty-four ghats that line the river's edge are accessed at more than fifty locations along the berm. In the midst of all this, one can see rituals pertaining to every aspect of human life: the shaving of a newborn's head, the first blessing after a marriage, the penances of old age. The Manikarnika and Harishchandra ghats are particularly important, as they are dedicated to the ritual of cremations; it is from these ghats that the ashes of the dead are immersed into the Ganges River. To be born and, more importantly, to be cremated at Varanasi is to attain the highest aspiration of Hindu practice: *moksha* or nirvana—freedom from the cycle of birth and death.

Most of the temples and ghats that one sees today date from the 18th and 19th centuries CE. In the 9th century BCE, there was a much simpler—but no less symbolically powerful—relationship between land and water.

4.59 **The ghats of Varanasi**

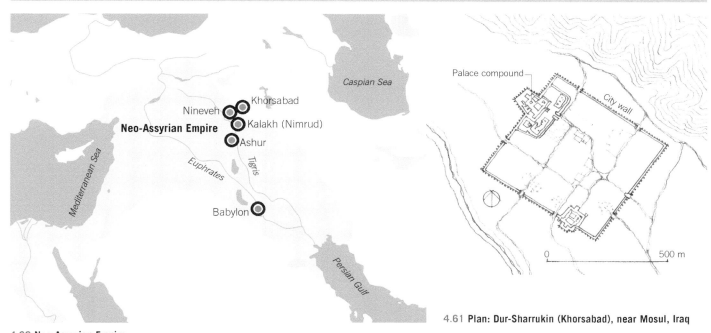

4.61 **Plan: Dur-Sharrukin (Khorsabad), near Mosul, Iraq**

4.60 **Neo-Assyrian Empire**

NEO-ASSYRIAN EMPIRE

The open terrain of the Mesopotamian heartland exposed the Assyrians, who controlled the northern river regions, to the seminomadic intrusions of the Kassites, the Hurrians, and subsequently, the Mitannians, whose kingdom was to extend over all of northern Mesopotamia. Assyria remained under Mitannian rule until early in the 14th century BCE, with only the core of its kingdom more or less intact, forming a narrow strip of land 150 kilometers long and only 40 kilometers wide along the western bank of the Tigris River. After the Mitanni defeat at the hands of the Hittites, the Assyrians reasserted themselves, invading Syria and compelling Mediterranean coastal cities like Tyre, Sidon, Byblos, and Arvad to pay tribute. In 663 BCE, the Assyrians were even able to sack the Egyptian city of Thebes. They were the first

to command a truly Iron Age army. Though linked to Mesopotamian religious practices, the neo-Assyrians, with the god Assur at the top of their pantheon, imposed a particularly strict rule of divinely sanctioned warfare. Their engineers built bridges, tunnels, moats, and weapons of various sorts. By the year 668 BCE, Assyria had control over Egypt and the Nile River valley.

Because Assyria's first capital, Ashur, on the west bank of the Tigris, was open to the western steppe, it was relocated by Assur-Nasir-Pal II to Old Kalakh, now Nimrud, 64 kilometers to the north. But shortly thereafter, Sargon II (r. 722–705 BCE) designed the remarkable Dur-Sharrukin (Fort Sargon) near the present-day village of Khorsabad. Located 24 kilometers northeast of Nineveh, the fortress/city controlled the main pass route coming down from the mountains to the north, and its founding was intended to fend off any threat of invasion by the northern tribes. It was also a place where precious iron ore could be funneled into the empire. In plan, the city was a squarish parallelogram, with the palace, temples, and government buildings all compressed into an autonomous unit straddling the walls. In all, it covered 300 hectares of ground.

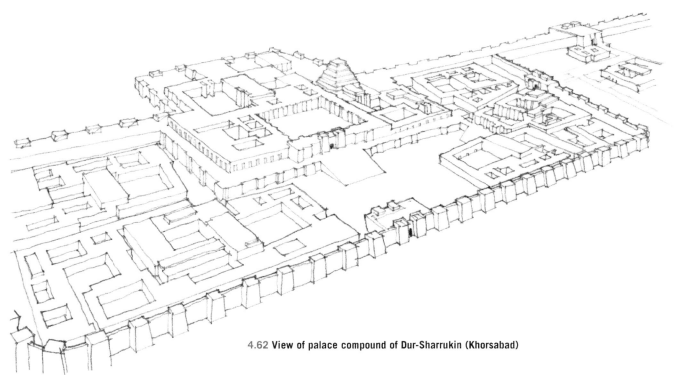

4.62 View of palace compound of Dur-Sharrukin (Khorsabad)

On the northwest side, half within and half without the circuit of the walls, protruding into the plain like a great bastion, stood the royal enclave. It rested on a 16-meter-high, 10-hectare platform overlooking the city wall and comprised more than two hundred rooms and thirty courtyards. The palace in the center opened around a large inner court. It contained the public reception rooms, which were elaborately decorated with sculptures and historical inscriptions representing scenes of hunting, worship, feasts, and battles. The harem, with separate provisions for four wives, occupied the south corner. The stables, kitchen, bakery, and wine cellar were located at the east corner. In the west corner stood the temple with a multistage ziggurat, its seven floor levels painted in different colors and connected by ramps. Below this enclave, on the inner side, was a zone surrounded by its own walls that held the administrative heart of the city and the sumptuous houses of high-ranking officials. For some reason, but likely because of its precarious position at the perimeter of the empire, Sargon's son and successor, Sennacherib, moved the capital back to the old established city of Nineveh.

The Assyrians, though possessing a formidable military machine, were unable to translate military success into economic stability. This was largely because they relocated vast numbers of people—estimates are as high as around six million—in their effort to thwart rebellion. Not only were the resettled peoples unfamiliar with their new lands, but many of their skills were no longer appropriate. In essence, the Assyrians obliterated their own tax base and quickly ran out of money.

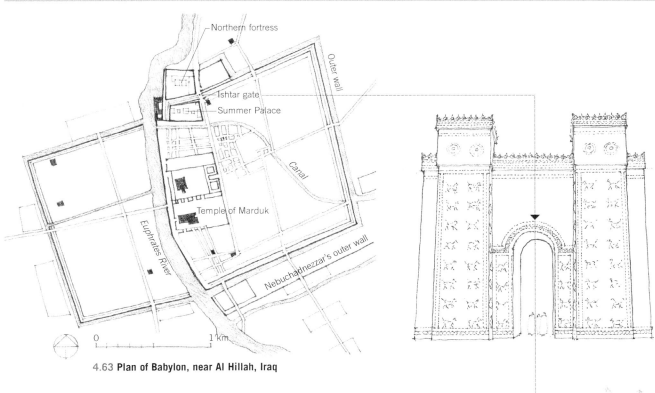

4.63 **Plan of Babylon, near Al Hillah, Iraq**

Babylon

Even at the height of Assyrian power, Babylon remained the ceremonial center of southern Mesopotamia. By the mid-7th century BCE, however, as Assyria went into decline, the city began to assert itself, sacking Nineveh in 612 BCE and initiating a new but brief era of prosperity—brief because the Babylonians more or less copied the failed economic scheme of the Assyrians. Nebuchadnezzar, who ruled between 604 and 562 BCE, started massive building projects. By 560 BCE, Babylon was certainly the most spectacular city in all of western Asia if not the world. Spanning the Euphrates, Babylon had two principal residential districts, with the palace and ziggurat compounds located along the shore. The palace reputedly had a garden on a high terrace some 18 meters above the river; a pump brought water up from the river.

The Ishtar gate, brilliantly decorated with animal figures in yellow and white glazed brick against a vivid blue background, conveys a sense of the splendor of the city. It was the terminus of a processional way that led from the palace to the temple of Ishtar of Agade (Bit Akitu) that was used during the New Year festival.

4.64 **Ishtar gate leading into Babylon from the north**

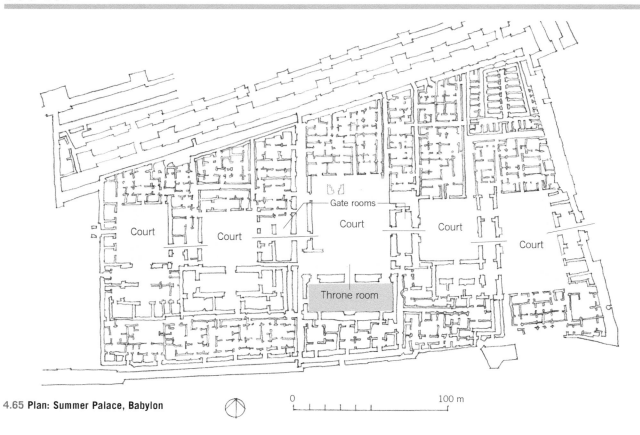

4.65 Plan: Summer Palace, Babylon

0   100 m

The Summer Palace was located on the northern side of the city between the Ishtar gate and the Euphrates. Similar to Assyrian tradition, the palace was not in the city but at its perimeter, an indication of its ambiguous status in relationship to the urban inhabitants. But unlike Assyrian practices, the religious precinct remained in the center. The palace was constructed on high terraces and overlooked the plain and river below, but whether it was the location of the famous Hanging Gardens is not known. There were five courtyards at the core of the palace that formed an east-west chain through the expansive complex, each courtyard serving a different register of rooms in the north-south direction. The throne room was located lengthwise to the largest courtyard. It might have been barrel-vaulted, given the size of the walls. Typically for the age, the courtyards were not symmetrically aligned with each other. Access from one to the other was through a type of gate room.

Babylonia's economic power was short-lived. The Greeks no longer needed Mesopotamian grain, having developed Sicily for that purpose. Persia to the east, having a more coherent sociopolitical system, was better able to control the emerging trade routes between east and west and soon became the dominant regional player. Babylonia was folded into the Persian Empire in 539 BCE.

400 BCE

5.1 **Parthenon, Athens**

INTRODUCTION

From China to Greece, religious, ethical, and social thinking was undergoing various evaluations that contrasted with centuries-old traditions that had accepted the notion that power was imposed from the top, by force or by ancestral privilege, rather than that it should be examined from a theorized point of view. In the 6th century BCE, however, we see the emergence of a more conscious attempt to think though the question of ethics and governance. In China, for example, Confucius (551–479 BCE) envisioned a world defined by reason and proper conduct, while Daoism, which existed alongside Confucianism, stressed a sort of quietist noninterference and the paradox of complementary opposites. In India, Buddha and Mahavira challenged the highly stratified world of Vedic orthodoxy, emphasizing the discipline of self-abnegation. Buddhism might have remained tangential to history had it not been made a state religion by Asoka (304–232 BCE), the creator of the first empire of South Asia. Since Buddhism at the time was largely an ascetic practice, Asoka did not order the construction of large temples, but set up pillars with the teachings of the Buddha etched onto them. In western and Central Asia we find Zoroastrianism, an ethically based religion that perceived the world as a struggle between good and evil. Man was viewed as a potential helper of God, capable of eradicating evil. And in Greece, Socrates, Plato, Aristotle, and others engaged in vigorous debates about democracy, law, and social philosophy. Athens, adopting democracy, became seminal in prefiguring the modern state.

Politically, however, the major player in western and Central Asia was Persia. Filling the vacuum created by the collapse of the Egyptian, Assyrian, and Babylonian empires, it extended its reach from northern India to Greece, giving rise to new architectural forms in the expansive capitals of Pasargadae and Persepolis. Persepolis was a showplace of prestige. It was not a city and not a fortress, but an array of vast palaces for feasting and banqueting, all set up on a terrace that made it visible to the thousands of people who came there annually to pay their respects to the great kings. The Mediterranean, however, remained firmly under Greek control, with the Greeks, in the 5th century BCE, developing an architectural vocabulary that was later to become foundational for Roman architecture. Still today, the Parthenon is celebrated as one of the greatest buildings in the world.

The famous battles between Greece and Persia can deflect us, however, from understanding the geopolitical energy that these two areas brought to the Eurasian world. Persia was the link between the Mediterranean Sea and India; and just as Greece was working to expand its trade relations with the agropastoral communities to their north, so too the Indians sought to expand their connections to the south of the subcontinent. These three regions—India, Persia, and the Mediterranean/Black Sea—were knit into a tight economic unit.

Persia's unsuccessful attempt to conquer Greece was to have unintended consequences. It stimulated the fantasy and ambitions of Alexander (356–323 BCE), who

conquered Persia and its territories. For a while it seemed that the Greek Empire would stretch all the way to the Indus River, but Alexander's ambitions were cut short by his death in Babylon in 323 BCE. The conquered lands, divided among his generals, turned into quasi-independent states and regional power centers. The strongest of these was Egypt, ruled by the Ptolemies, who governed from Alexandria. An equally important city-state was Pergamon in Anatolia. The tiny island trading city of Delos overtook Athens as the cosmopolitan trading hub in the Mediterranean. The impact of Greek culture, generally called Hellenism in lands far from Greece, was huge. It was an aesthetic that tended toward realism, delicacy, and emotional expression. The columns and entabluatures of 9th-century CE Khmer in Cambodia make it clear that, however remotely, Hellenism was still a factor in the architectural conversation. Khmer masons, probably from India, knew nothing of the Greeks, but the legacy persisted. The impact of Hellenism made its way to China as well, in the sculptural representations of Buddha.

In South America, the most important cultural developments were well-organized societies that inhabited the Peruvian lowlands: the Moche civilization to the north, and the Nazca tribes to the south. The Olmecs, who had been the most influential culture in Mesoamerica for some time, were in decline by 400 BCE, having been replaced by the Maya and Zapotec peoples, who were making the transition from chiefdoms to small states.

Achaemenid Empire
ca. 559–330 BCE

Alexandrian Empire
334–ca. 301 BCE

Seleucid Period
ca. 305–247 BCE

▲ **Pasardadae** ▲ **Persepolis**
ca. 546 BCE   ca. 518 BCE

▲ **Seleucid**
Founded 305 BCE

Greece: Archaic Period
ca. 700–480 BCE

Classical Period
ca. 480–323 BCE

Hellenistic Period
ca. 323–31 BCE

▲ **Temple of Poseidon at Isthmia**
ca. 600 BCE

▲ **Parthenon**
ca. 447–438 BCE

▲ **Athenas Polias at Priene**
334 BCE

▲ **Propylaea**
ca. 435 BCE

▲ **Temple of Apollo at Didyma**
ca. 313 BCE–41 CE

⊙ Socrates
Born 470 BCE

▲ **Erechtheum**
ca. 421–405 BCE

Sanctuary of Athena at Lindos ▲
ca. 190 BCE

▲ **Temple of Athena Nike**
ca. 427 BCE

600 BCE   **400 BCE**   **200 BCE**

▲ **Paestum**
Founded ca. 600 BCE

▲ **Miletus**
Founded ca. 500 BCE

▲ **Priene**
Founded ca. 334 BCE

▲ **Pergamon**
ca. 300–150 BCE

▲ **Second Temple of Solomon**
516 BCE

Egypt: Ptolemaic Dynasty
323–40 BCE

▲ **Temple of Horus**
Begun 237 BCE

Rise of great states in South Asia
8th to 6th centuries BCE

⊙ Gautama Buddha
Born 556 BCE

Mauryan Dynasty
ca. 323–185 BCE

▲ **Lomas Rsi Cave**
ca. 300 BCE

China: Eastern Zhou Dynasty
ca. 770–256 BCE

Warring States period
ca. 481–221 BCE

Qin Dynasty
ca. 221–206 BCE

⊙ Confucius
Born 551 BCE

▲ **Tomb of Zeng Hou Yi**
ca. 433 BCE

▲ **Xianyang Palace No. 1**
4th century BCE

▲ **First Emperor's Tomb**
246–210 BCE

⊙ Laozi, founder of Taoism
Late 4th century BCE

119

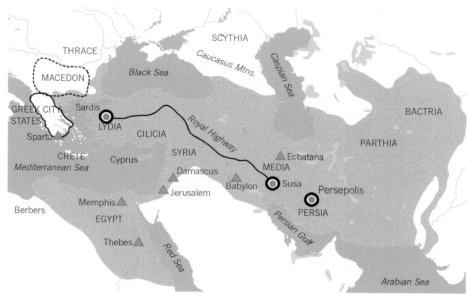

5.2 The Achaemenid Empire

THE ACHAEMENID EMPIRE

Settlers arrived on the Iranian plateau sometime before or during the fifth millennium BCE, with one of their ancient cities, Tepe Sialk (in central Iran, near the present-day city of Kashan), experiencing various occupations until about 800 BCE. By that time, the area had become known as Mede, and powerful kings extended control southward over the Elamite civilization located in the plains around Susa. With the weakening of the Assyrians to the west, one of the Median kings, Cyaxares (625–585 BCE), invaded and destroyed their capital, Nineveh, marching all the way to the gates of Sardis, where he turned back when a solar eclipse, interpreted as a bad omen, occurred. The capital of the Median kingdom at the time was Hagmatana ("Place of Assembly"), located under the modern city of Hamadan. The Median kingdom, however, underwent a transformation when the Persians, a branch of the Medians, took control under Cyrus the Great (559–530 BCE), who picked up where Cyaxares had left off and, in effect, united the Elamite, Median, and Babylonian realms into the Achaemenid Empire (also known as the First Persian Empire) that extended from Anatolia to the Persian Gulf. The ascendency of the Persians had important geopolitical consequences in that their lands were halfway between India and the Mediterranean. They were well aware of this, of course, and indeed, their existence depended on extending trade in these two directions.

Like all empires, the Persians went through their expansionary mode, with famous military campaigns by both Darius and his son Xerxes I (in 490 and 480 BCE, respectively) against the Greeks. Both campaigns were unsuccessful, but the Persian alliance with the Phoenicians, who contributed substantially to their fleet, brought prosperity to the Levant and its cities along the eastern Mediterranean coast. Phoenician cities like Byblos and Sidon experienced an economic upturn. The Persians, seeing for the first time the great buildings of Egypt and western Asia, were eager to match these accomplishments. From the Ionians, Persia not only collected taxes but also took their famously skilled craftsmen. An inscription of Darius's relates that the stonecutters who worked on his palaces were from Ionia, and the wood craftsmen were brought in from Lebanon, along with large boatloads of lumber.

By the year 500 BCE, the Achaemenid Empire had grown to become the largest and most important realm in Asia, especially under Darius (522–486 BCE), who extended the boundaries of the empire into the heart of Egypt; the Zhou dynasty in China, by comparison, was still relatively isolated. The numerous city-states in India were occupied fighting each other. The Persians seemed to have learned from the negative lesson of the Assyrians and Babylonians. Unlike them, Persian rulers attempted to gain the good will of their subject nations. Darius, for example, allowed Jews to rebuild the Temple of Jerusalem, which was finished in 516 BCE, the sixth year of his reign. Weights and measures were standardized, and an extensive road network was built—the first organized system of roads in history. The Royal Highway ran from Sardis, on the coast of Anatolia, to Susa, where it linked up, by means of western extensions, to the silk routes and to Pasargadae and Persepolis, the newly constructed Persian capitals. In fact, apart from the Greece, India, and Egypt, Persia was to a large extent surrounded by nomads and pastoralists, none of whom had extensive use of iron. It therefore stands to reason that Persia was eager to bring all of the Mediterranean into its realm of influence. Its failure to do so resulted in a double world: the linear geography of the Persians brought together by the Royal Highway, and the network geography of the Mediterranean controlled by the Greeks and Phoenicians.

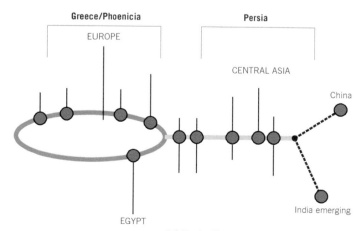

5.3 Trade diagram, ca. 400 BCE

Pasargadae and Persepolis

In 546 BCE Cyrus established Pasargadae as his capital, locating it at one of the starting points for the caravan route northward across the Great Salt Desert. The city's administrative core is remarkable for its spaciousness; palace, audience hall, altars, and pavilions, all distant from each other yet integrated into a parklike setting with trees, watercourses, and gardens. The Egyptians and Babylonians had palace gardens, but such an expansive landscape of palaces, gardens, and orchards was quite novel. It was also a sacred landscape, for to the north there was a sacred enclosure consisting of a walled precinct with a series of flat terraces supporting an open altar. Much later, the Persian garden was to become the prototype of Islamic gardens.

The Tomb of Cyrus the Great is located not far from Pasargadae. Its *cella* is 6 meters high and rests on a six-level stepped plinth that measures 13.5 by 12.2 meters at the base. The entire 13-meter-high edifice is of white limestone. Five huge slanted stones make up the roof. The monument, sitting boldly in the landscape, is an elegant combination of sepulcher and sanctuary. The building recalls similar, though more modestly scaled, Greek Ionian tombs. It was probably enclosed by a courtyard.

Pasargadae as a capital was relatively short-lived, for Darius designed his own capital city, Persepolis—"the city of the Persians," as the Greeks called it—located 10 kilometers to the southwest and closer to the fertile lands along the coast. It was an audacious move to a dramatic site at the edge of a large plain, the Marv Dasht basin, surrounded by cliffs. The palace is located directly under the west-facing slope of one of those cliffs. Construction went through several phases between 515 and 330 BCE. The first one involved cutting into the irregular and rocky mountainside to level a large platform 10 to 20 meters above the ground and measuring about 300 meters in length and 450 meters in width. The foundations contained complex drainage systems and water channels.

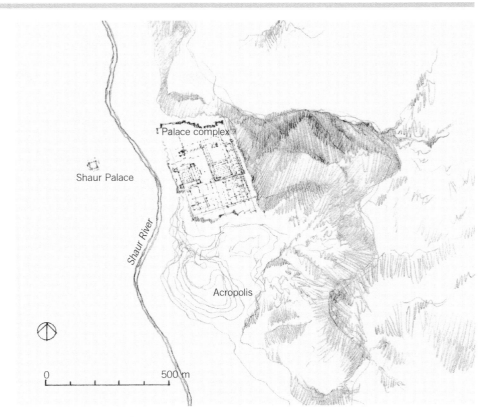

5.4 **Area plan of Persepolis, Iran**

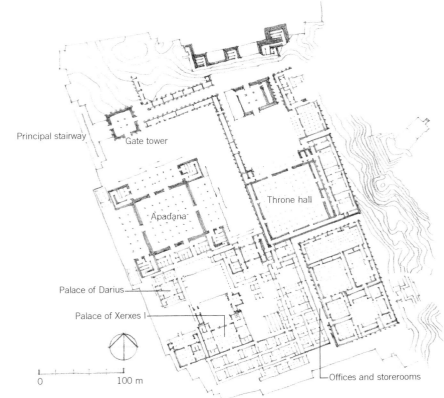

5.5 **Plan: Palace complex at Persepolis**

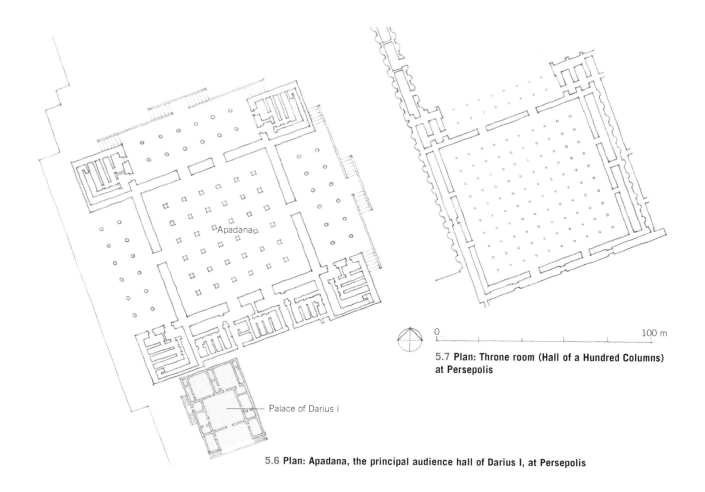

5.7 **Plan: Throne room (Hall of a Hundred Columns) at Persepolis**

0   100 m

Palace of Darius I

5.6 **Plan: Apadana, the principal audience hall of Darius I, at Persepolis**

The purpose of the vast foundation was make sure that the buildings placed on it commanded views across the valley. Of the buildings themselves little remains, since most of the walls were of mud brick, stuccoed and brightly painted. What we see today are the sections that were built in stone: the columns, foundations, and carvings.

The northern part of the terrace, which included the throne room (known also as the Hall of a Hundred Columns), measured 70 by 70 meters and represented the main section of the complex; it was accessible only to a restricted few. The southern section contained the palaces of Darius and Xerxes I, the harem, and a council hall. A huge, defendable independent structure at the southwest corner, with separate areas for different wares, served as the treasury. Records found show that in the year 467 BCE, no fewer than 1,348 people were employed in the treasury recording and documenting its holdings. The largest building, the Apadana ("castle" in Persian), served as the main reception hall; it had seventy-two awe-inspiring fluted and tapered limestone columns 7 meters high surmounted by bull- or lion-shaped capitals. The ceiling beams of cedar, ebony, and teak were gold plated and inlaid with ivory and precious metals. The general concept of a columnar hall dates to early Median architecture: a palace-citadel in Gobin Tepe from the 8th century BCE had a hall with thirty columns, as did Cyrus's palace in Pasargadae. This hall, however, was designed as a showstopper in scale and ornamentation.

5.8 **Part of the palace complex at Persepolis**

An innovative design feature was a stone-faced double staircase leading to the Apadana, the great audience hall. The walls depict rows upon rows of emissaries, soldiers, and chariot drivers. It is a virtual film strip from which we can see how the various peoples of the vast empire dressed and what kinds of ornaments, weapons, and hairstyles they sported. A group from India carries a bag of gold; a group from Africa carries tusks. These people are portrayed not as sad and subjected, but as if in a celebratory mood. One frieze shows a man, like an usher, holding another man's hand, guiding him along. At the head of the staircase was a gate, with black marble benches where visitors could wait.

The frieze helps us understand the meaning of this innovative structure. It was the backdrop to a great annual celebration—perhaps a new year celebration—with people arriving from all over to bring gifts, make treaties, and socialize. The flatlands to the west of the complex would have been filled with tents of various types. The central event for a visitor was to be received by the Persian ruler in the Apadana, which probably served as the setting for grand feasts, with hundreds of people sitting on the floor around large round platters, being entertained by musicians and dancing women. Persepolis might be imagined as a modern-day convention center, where business, socializing, and celebration are all intermixed.

5.9 **Staircase leading to the Apadana at Persepolis**

5.10 **Staircase frieze at Persepolis**

5.11 **Greek and Phoenician colonies around the Mediterranean, ca. 550 BCE**

GREECE AND THE MEDITERRANEAN

If Persia's empire was based on a comprehensive network of roads and the exchange of goods, the Greek enterprise was based on sea trade and manufacturing, particularly of bronze and ceramic bowls. Greeks plied the Mediterranean all the way to Gibraltar in the west and the Black Sea in the east, founding dozens of cities and trading posts. This trade network was a consequence of competition among Greek cities and of the gradual opening of the European hinterland to commerce. Massalia (now Marseilles, France), for example, was founded in 600 BCE as a trading outpost to facilitate commerce with the Gauls. Many of the city-states had their own colonies, with Miletus alone having no less than some ninety colonies spread around the Mediterranean. It was a brand-new economic model; one might call it the urban franchise model. When viewed together, the two contrasting systems—the landlocked one of Persia and the maritime one of Greece—constituted a large east-west geopolitical continuum that remained viable until the breakup of the Roman Empire in the 5th century CE.

The first Greek colonies were established around 770 BCE by the Euboeans on the island of Ischia (Pithekoussai) near Naples; at Cumae in central Italy; on the island of Naxos in the Cyclades; and at Leontini in eastern Sicily. Around 710 BCE, the Achaeans founded Sybaris and Croton in southern Italy. The Spartans founded Tarentum around 650 BCE, while Syracuse was founded by the Corinthians in 743 BCE. All in all, in a span of a hundred years, some thirty colonies sprang up. The settlers maintained close relationships with their mother cities and often appealed to them in times of war. But the colonies also began to flex their own military muscles. In 480 BCE Syracuse defeated Carthage in the Battle of Himera, and in 413 BCE it inflicted catastrophic damage on Athenian forces, which lost two hundred ships and thousands of soldiers.

The Greek Temple

Greek temple design changed considerably in the middle of the 6th century BCE, as wood was increasingly abandoned for stone. This may have been partially due to a desire for permanence, but it may also have been spurred by the influence of Egyptian architecture, with which the Greeks increasingly came in contact.

At the time, the northern part of Egypt had been divided among vassals of the Assyrian Empire. Around 664 BCE, an Egyptian prince named Psamtik was banished to the marshes. Plotting his return, he allowed the Dorians to settle in Naucratis, on the western edge of the Nile Delta, around 620 BCE on the promise that they help with his military ambitions, which were indeed successful. He was able to defeat his rivals, break with Assyria, and reunify Egypt. This opened a series of mercantile exchanges between Egypt and Greece that was profitable to both.

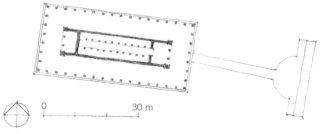

0   30 m

5.12 **Plan: Temple of Artemis at Corfu (Kerkira), Greece, ca. 580 BCE**
The earliest known Doric temple completely of stone

5.13 Temple of Segesta, Sicily, Italy

Naucratis became a type of duty-free zone, with the Greeks setting up factories to produce pottery and ornaments in an Egyptian style for the Egyptian market. They also imported silver, which was still rare in Egypt; in return they appear to have received Egyptian grain.

When the Greeks, accustomed to small wooden temples and simple outdoor altars, first encountered the enormous Egyptian stone temples and pyramids, they were certainly amazed, and lost no time in studying Egyptian construction techniques. They also had ample opportunity, since Psamtik had embarked on an extensive building campaign. The impact of these lessons must have been immediate, for there is very little evidence that the Doric order existed before the Greek experience in Egypt. The Greeks were, however, not unfamiliar with stone and had already begun using it for the walls of the *cella*, as is evident at the Temple of Poseidon at Isthmia. But to make columns and even the roof of the colonnade out of stone was a different matter.

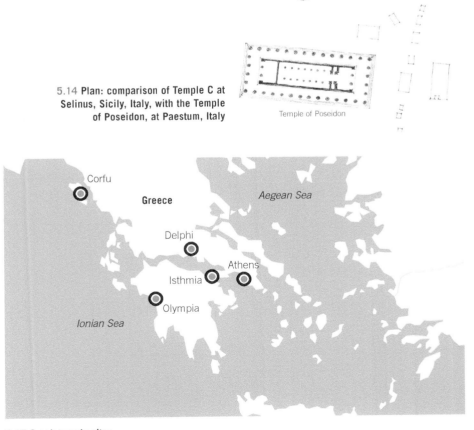

5.14 Plan: comparison of Temple C at Selinus, Sicily, Italy, with the Temple of Poseidon, at Paestum, Italy

5.15 Greek temple sites

5.16 A collapased column showing typical drums of which the column was made.

One can follow the development of the Doric order at the Temple of Poseidon at Isthmia, where, by the time of its completion around 600 BCE, the oak columns were replaced by stone columns. (A Roman visitor in 176 CE reported a peculiarity: one oak column was still standing.) Some of the first stone columns were huge monoliths; others consisted of superimposed drums of varying heights and diameters.

The wealth of the Sicilian colonies helps explain why many of the early Greek temples were not in Greece, but in Sicily and Italy. At Selinus, on the southern coast of Sicily, seven temples were lined up on the acropolis and a nearby ridge. They date from 570 BCE to 409 BCE. At Paestum in central Italy, there arose a temple of Hera (550 BCE), a temple of Demeter (520 BCE), and a temple of Poseidon (460 BCE). In contrast to the early temples at Selinus, the later temple of Poseidon in Paestum opened up the *cella* by means of an inner colonnade and achieved closer interaction between the body of the temple and the *pteron*, or columnar surround.

There was an important difference between Greek and Egyptian stone preparation. In Greece, stones were brought to the construction site in an almost finished state, whereas in Egypt, stones for columns arrived at the site still quite rough (apart from horizontal cuts), with much of the finishing taking place when the stones were in situ. This difference would have significant impact on Greek architectural developments, as it would allow for an ever-increasing elaboration of detail, proportion, and form.

Greek and Roman temples are described according to the number of columns on the entrance front, the type of colonnade, and the type of portico. The Parthenon, for example, is an octastyle peripteral temple with hexastyle porticoes at both ends. The Temple of Zeus at Olympia is a hexastyle peripteral temple with distyle in-antis porches at both ends. The basilica in Paestum is a rare enneastyle pseudodipteral temple with a tristyle in-antis portico.

Almost all surfaces of the temple—the steps, columns, capitals, walls, even the figures on the pediment—were painted in bright reds, blues, yellows, and black. What we know about the colors used for the temples comes from both archaeological and literary sources. The pigments were made from minerals, soot, ground stones, vegetables, and animal matter. The purple dye, for example, came from shellfish; the yellowish color that was applied to columns and beams came from saffron. The colors were sometimes applied with wax but usually on stucco.

Though today we may perceive Greek temples as isolated objects, they were actually framed in the landscape by a *temenos*, or sacred precinct, which could consist of something as simple as a row of stones but could also be a built-up wall. The *temenos* was the territory of the deity and had to be approached in a prescribed manner and entered only at a special place defined by a *propylon* (i.e., *pro-pylon*, or "before the gate").

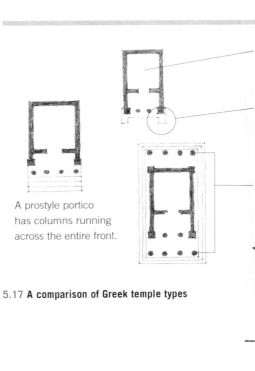

The *cella* ends with either columns in antis or a prostyle portico

Anta refers to the thickening of the projecting end of one of the lateral walls. If columns are set between them, then the colums are said to be in antis.

An amphiprostyle temple has prostyle porticoes at both ends.

A prostyle portico has columns running across the entire front.

5.17 A comparison of Greek temple types

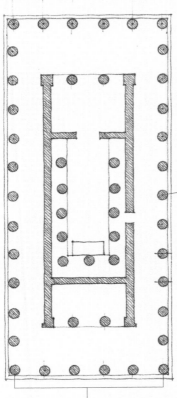

The most basic element of the temple was the colonnade. Though so common today that it might seem to be a natural architectural form, it was actually a unique innovation of the Greeks. Called a *pteron*, it was a sacred form always reserved for temples. *Pteron* means "wing" or "fin," but also "oar" and "sail." It perhaps refers to early awnings placed against buildings. But it also indicates that the Greeks saw the building as a dynamic location—as something that literally catches the wind and hears the voices of the gods. In addition, the *pteron* evoked the idea of a grove of trees, especially because columns were originally made of wooden trunks. The *pteron* has also been associated with stout soldiers forming a phalanx—a rectangular military formation—symbolically protecting the statue within the *cella*.

The following terms describe the type of colonnade surrounding the *naos* of a Greek temple:

- Peripteral: one row of columns
- Dipteral: two rows of columns
- Tripteral: three rows of columns
- Pseudodipteral: suggesting a dipteral colonnade, but without the inner colonnade

The following terms refer to the number of columns on the entrance front of a Greek temple:

- Henostyle: one column
- Distyle: two columns
- Tristyle: three columns
- Tetrastyle: four columns
- Pentastyle: five columns
- Hexastyle: six columns
- Heptastyle: seven columns
- Octastyle: eight columns
- Enneastyle: nine columns
- Decastyle: ten columns

5.18 Greek temple terminology

A corona is the projection at the top of a cornice; the word was associated with the forehead and with controlling things from above. It was also associated with the eagle, the bird of omen and Zeus's favorite bird. For these reasons it became the appropriate element with which to top off a temple.

On the abacus of a capital rests the architrave, the main stone or marble beam running from column to column. Above the architrave is the frieze, which consists of alternating triglyphs and metopes. Beneath each triglyph, on the face of the architrave, is a smooth band—the regula—on the underside of which hang six stone pegs, or guttae. There is normally one triglyph to each column and one to each intercolumniation. The metopes were often decorated with paintings or relief sculpture depicting stories of the local hero or episodes from the myths associated with the god to whom the temple was dedicated.

- Pycnostyle: 1.5 diameters
- Sistyle: 2 diameters
- Eustyle: 2.25 diameters
- Diastyle: 3 diameters
- Araeostyle: 3.5 diameters

Intercolumniation refers to the space between columns, expressed in column diameters. This systematization applies mainly to Hellenistic and Roman temples.

5.19 Elements of the Doric order

The temple rested on a *crepis*, the base of a building but also a shoe or sandal—a footing, in other words, proper to the divine presence. This foundation was constructed from roughly dressed masonry that was not concealed below the ground but was designed to appear as steps leading up to the platform on which the temple's columns rested.

The capital, which derives its name from the Latin word *caput* ("head"), was in Greek terminology the *kranion*, which refers to the top of the head or skull. The Doric capital, carved out of a single stone block, consists of a spreading convex molding, the echinus—a word that was applied to almost anything curved and spiny found in nature—and a low square block, the abacus.

The column shaft tapers from the bottom upward in the form of a delicate curve called an entasis, or swelling. The shaft of a Doric column almost always stands directly on the floor, without a base. Early columns from the 6th century BCE are often monolithic, but later the shaft came to be composed of superimposed drums, which were rounded by turning them on a lathe.

The drums were doweled together with wooden or bronze spikes enclosed in concavities at the center. The shafts were fluted after the columns were in place. There are usually twenty broad and shallow flutes that meet to form sharp edges, or arrises. The joints between the columns would have been concealed by marble stucco.

The steps were often too tall to ascend comfortably, so a flight of stairs or a ramp was provided at the entrance. This demonstrates that the steps had nothing to do with the necessities of construction, for they could easily have been designed with more risers. Instead, the steps were intentionally built to make the temple appear as if it were rising on a natural outcropping, cleaned and smoothed in preparation for the building.

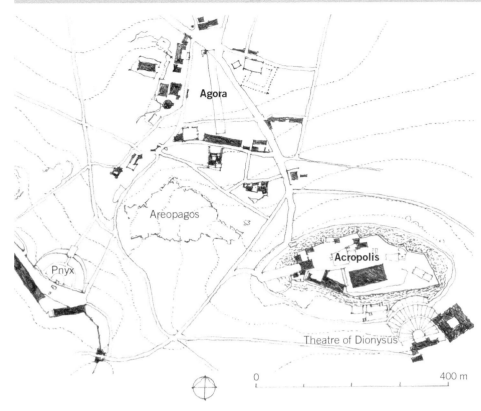

5.20 **Site plan showing the relationship between the agora and the acropolis, Athens**

The agora was also the site of the Leokoreion, a small shrine associated with a well in the northern part of the agora. It was named after the daughters of Leos, who were sacrificed to save the city from a terrible plague. Also on the agora was a stoa, a long colonnaded building with shops on the back facing the agora. These shops were for the more elite merchants. Council meetings were held in a building known as the bouleuterion. The law courts were located there as well. The central space was used for markets, ritual gatherings, or the making of speeches and pronouncements. But most importantly, the area served as a market. One could find almost anything in the agora: confectioners, slave-traders, fishmongers, vintners, cloth merchants, shoemakers, dressmakers, merchants selling cookware and other household goods. Socrates famously taught his students by walking back and forth along the Athenian stoa, questioning the market-goers on their understanding of the meaning of life and attracting a crowd of Athenian youth who enjoyed seeing the more pretentious of their elders made fools of. One listener was the young poet who became a student of Socrates under the name Plato.

Athens

The city of Athens had three main components: the acropolis, which was the great ritual and spiritual core of the city; the agora, which was its economic hub; and the urban fabric itself, where one found small shrines and temples. The agora, probably laid out in the 7th century BCE and developed in the 5th and 4th centuries BCE with the construction of temples to Hephaestus, Zeus, and Apollo, was a unique Athenian invention. It was a specially demarcated space outside of the core of the city that brought together the different dimensions of urban life. Though often called a public space, it was just as much a religious space as a social one. One of the key temples overlooking the agora was the temple to Hephaestus. Hephaestus was the god of the smithies, and his presence there was a testament to the role of bronze casting in the Athenian economy. It was set on a hill to the west, its elevated presence signifying its importance.

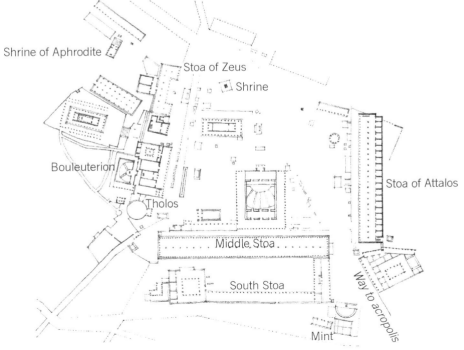

5.21 **Site plan of the agora of Athens**

5.22 Calvacade frieze, southern wall of the Parthenon, Athens

The ancient Dorians, when they arrived in Greece from the north, had sacred groves to which they would periodically go for ritual communal events. What they learned from the Egyptians was to dramatize these journeys into spectacular processions involving music and dancing. They did not, however, hold processions with the deity as the Egyptians did, and in this they held true to their fundamental belief in the deity being fixed in special, sacred places. Over time the number of these processions multiplied, with some becoming elevated to the level of state protocol. One was the Dionysia, a large Athenian festival in honor of the god Dionysus that was held in early spring. It involved a procession of phalluses and military equipment, and ended in theatrical performances. A few weeks later, there was the more official Panathenaic procession that started at the Leokoreion and ended at the acropolis. That it began at the Leokoreion was an indication of the procession's attempt to connect deeply to the principle of sacrifice and triumph.

The procession was an elaborate affair. For months before, a team of maidens from aristocratic families would weave a special new garment for the deity in the temple. By the late 5th century BCE the robe was as big as a ship's sail and was, in fact, fixed on the model of a ship mounted on wheels. This ship-cart had a crew of priests and priestesses wearing golden and colorful garlands. When all was set, a nocturnal festival took place, and at sunrise a new fire was fetched, carried in a torch race from outside the city—where sacrifice was made to Eros and Athena together—through the agora, and up to the altar of Athena on the acropolis. A procession then formed in which all members of the community had their place. The high point was the sacrifice, in which more than a hundred animals were slaughtered at the Great Altar, and the meat distributed to the whole populace in the agora. From 566 BCE onward an athletic contest was added to the program of activities, including foot races, wrestling, horse racing, boxing, and javelin-throwing.

The frieze of the Pantheon seems to portray such a celebratory procession. The narrative of the frieze begins at the southwest corner, where the procession appears to divide into two separate files.

What does it represent? According to traditional interpretation, it depicts the annual Panathenaic procession. But this view, though oft repeated, has been challenged by scholars who argue that it must be a representation of a mythological moment, not a real procession involving mortals. Since the pediments and metopes all illustrate mythological scenes, it is natural to reach for a mythological explanation for the frieze as well. John Boardman has suggested that the cavalry portrayed on the frieze depict the heroization of the soldiers who fell at Marathon in 490 BCE, and that therefore these riders were the Athenians who took part in the last prewar Greater Panathenaia. Chrysoula Kardar has ventured that the relief shows an imagined first Panathenaic procession as instituted under the mythical King Kekrops.

A perplexing issue is that the frieze's location high in the building's porch would have made it difficult to see. In the museum today, the figures are on eye level, whereas originally they were 7 meters up. This suggests that they were not meant to be "seen" in the conventional sense.

Thomas Bruce, the Seventh Earl of Elgin, dismantled about two-thirds of the frieze and had it shipped to England between 1801 and 1806, and today the so-called Elgin Marbles are in the British Museum, to the outrage of many. In looking at the frieze, one has to remember that it, as indeed the entire building, was painted.

5.23 Approach to the Parthenon from the Propylaea

The Parthenon

Because of the constant warfare in ancient Greece, almost every city was divided into a lower town and an acropolis, which literally means a "city on the height." The acropolis of Athens was no exception. It sits on a great isolated slab of limestone tilted toward the west side, from which it had to be approached. Already fortified with a wall by the Mycenaeans, it was held to be invested with divine presences from ancient times. The waters from a spring on its southern flank are today still considered to have healing powers. An olive tree rooted to a rock on its summit was dedicated to Athena. It was here that the Parthenon was built under the political leadership of Pericles. The building, replacing one that had been destroyed by the Persians, was designed by Ictinus (with advice from Callicrates and

Phidias) and built between 447 and 438 BCE. Designed as a monument to Athena and housing her sacred statue, it was bigger than any temple ever before built on the Greek mainland, its stylobate measuring 30.9 by 69.5 meters. Early accounts of the temple call it Hekatompedos, or "hundred-footer," referring either to its overall width or the length of the large eastern room of its *cella*, also known as the *hekatompedos*.

But size was not its only unusual feature: the east and west facades were lined with eight towering Doric columns, making the Parthenon the only octastyle peripteral temple built in ancient Greece.

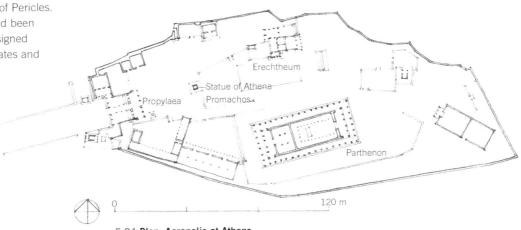

5.24 Plan: Acropolis at Athens

5.25 A conception of the interior of the Parthenon, based on the evidence

The interior of the *naos* has been variously reconstructed, in some places with a standard roof (as in figure 5.25) or with an opening in the center. It is clear, regardless, that the columns in the *naos* supported a second tier of smaller columns above, and that there was a shallow rectangle in front of the statue of Athena, possibly used as a reflecting pool, although such a pool would have been highly unusual. The building would have been painted inside and out, with the columns probably a reddish hue.

Underlying the construction is a system of refinements that control the delicate curvature of horizontal lines, the elegant convergence of vertical lines, and the nuanced size and spacing of the fluted marble columns. The stylobate was not a flat plane but rather like a section of a very large sphere; it curved upward toward the middle, rising 41 millimeters on its short sides and 102 millimeters on its long flanks. This curve was carried upward through the entire structure, imparting a subtle upward curvature even on the architrave, the cornice, and nearly every "horizontal" line of stone. Furthermore, every column was given an entasis, or a slight bulging of the middle of the column's shaft. The entasis measures only 20 millimeters of deviation from a straight line. Moreover, each of the forty-six perimeter columns was tilted slightly inward, with the corner column tilting on a diagonal. If the columns of the short sides were extended upward, they would meet around 4.8 kilometers above the roof.

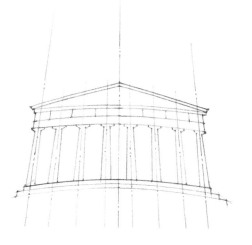

5.26 Diagram of the curved stylobate and inclined vertical axes of the perimeter columns of the Parthenon

5.27 **Detail of the pediment of the Parthenon**

While each of these refinements have functional advantages—the curvature to shed water, the angling to increase lateral structural support during earthquakes, and the corner adjustments to maintain proper column alignments with the metopes above—scholars, beginning with the Roman architect and historian Vitruvius, have argued that the nuances were mostly for aesthetic effect; and indeed, in no other temple was this visual tension as subtle and refined as in the Parthenon. It nevertheless seems astonishing that in contrast with other attempts at making grand statements, where architects sought height or the addition of special embellishments, here the architects sought a level of precision that was almost imperceptible, yet could not be matched anywhere else in the world at the time. How these astonishing curves were made is something of a mystery, since the building, like all Greek temples, is made of precut pieces allowing for few on-site adjustments.

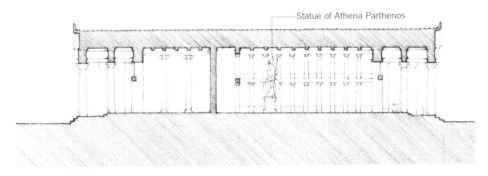

Section

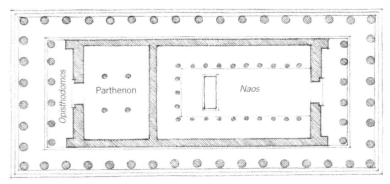

Plan

5.28 **Section and plan: Parthenon, Athens**

5.29 **Caryatid porch, Erechtheum, Athens**

Erechtheum

Unlike Egyptians, Greeks never added new elements to a temple. New structures, of course, could be added to the precinct, but the temple itself was not changed unless it was somehow destroyed and rebuilt. It would be wrong, however, to assume that Greek architects were unable to think beyond the inflexibility of the temple form. The Propylaea and the Erechtheum on the Athenian acropolis are examples of rather complex buildings whose architects had to accommodate a range of programmatic and ritualistic purposes. The Erechtheum wraps up different mythical narratives into a single composition. It was built on two levels with three porticoes of different designs; there were four entrances besides the subterranean one under the north porch. This irregularity was due to the necessity of designing a building around the spots that were essential to the narrative of the founding of Athens. Erechtheus, after whom the Erechtheum is named, was the mythical founder of Attica and the "earth-born king of Athens." At that time, it was believed that gods challenged one another to be honored by cities. Unfortunately, both Poseidon and Athena aspired to control Athens, so Erechtheus set up a contest in which each had to make a

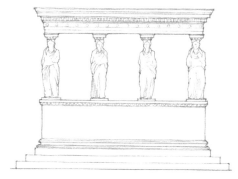

5.30 **Drawing: Caryatid porch, Erectheum, Athens**

gift to the city. Poseidon drew salt water by striking the ground on the acropolis with his trident, while Athena grew the first olive tree on its slopes. Erechtheus judged Athena's gift to be the most useful to the people of Athens, and the city was named in her honor.

The central elements of the drama can be read by entering first through the north porch dedicated to Poseidon. Its expansive design takes in the grand vista and can be seen from the agora below. On the floor to the left of the door, a type of window looks down at the bedrock, where one can see the indentations of Poseidon's trident. An opening in the roof above indicates the space through which the trident was thought to have flown. The great door leads to a narrow room that contained a shrine to Erechtheus. Under the floor was a cistern containing the salt water of Poseidon. A door to the right leads to the sacred court containing Athena's olive tree. Continuing on the axis made by the porch of Poseidon, one goes up the flight of stairs to the caryatid porch, which today sits isolated in the field of ruins.

Although the plan of the building may seem chaotic, the temple makes sense as a three-dimensional celebration of the founding myth of Athens. The north porch is the largest and projects forward two intercolumniations, the height of its roof being almost level with the eaves of the central block. The south porch is less than half as high, but it is raised upon a terrace. Instead of columns, there are caryatids—columns

5.31 **Erectheum from the south, as it stands today**

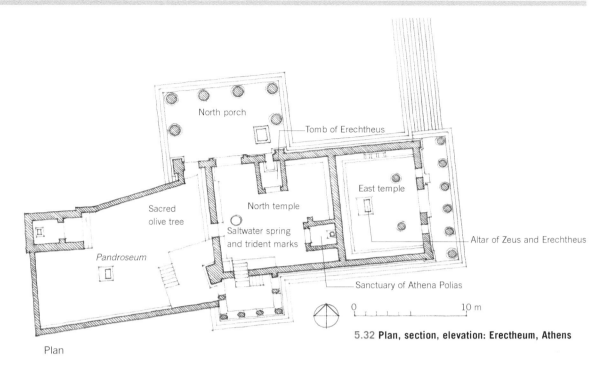

North porch

Tomb of Erechtheus

Sacred
olive tree

North temple

East temple

Saltwater spring
and trident marks

Altar of Zeus and Erechtheus

Pandroseum

Sanctuary of Athena Polias

0   10 m

5.32 Plan, section, elevation: Erectheum, Athens

Plan

in the shape of young women—carrying the load of the entablature on their heads. The east porch consists of six Ionic columns. The central block that holds all this together has two levels corresponding to the north and east porches. Three doors lead into it: the great door of the north porch, a plain opening at the bottom of the west wall, and a small door on the south side, to which a staircase leads down from the interior of the caryatid porch.

Rising up over the entire story and at a 90 degree cross-axis is the edifice of the victor, Athena, facing east. At the diagonal, upon descending the external stairs on the northern side and before entering the north porch, was an area dedicated to Zeus, the ultimate arbiter of the contest. His position seems to address the dynamic northeasterly pull of conical Mt. Lykabettos, for it, too, plays into the story. According to legend, Athena was absent from her city to retrieve a mountain to use on the acropolis. Her sisters were curious about the chest in which Athena was protecting the young Erechtheus and opened it, contrary to Athena's orders. She became so angry that she dropped the mountain. How this plays out in the design is unknown, but from the agora below the acropolis, the mountain and the Erechtheum are clearly in dialogue.

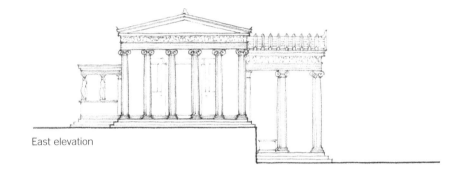

East elevation

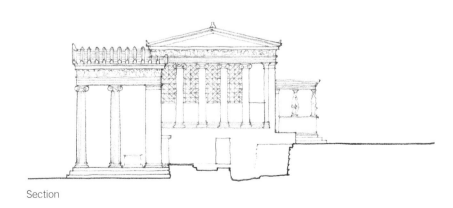

Section

5.33 Ionic capital from the temple at Neandris

5.34 Bronze female figure with headdress

5.35 Treasury of Siphnos at Delphi

Ionic Order

Though usually discussed after the Doric, the Ionic should not therefore be regarded as later. The development of the Ionic and the Doric orders paralleled each other, but stylistically there are notable differences. First, Ionic columns rest on molded bases that stand on square plinths. These moldings consist of combinations of tori, scotias, and rondels, often in pairs. The capital has different front and side views and is meant to be seen chiefly from the front and back. At the base of the capital there is a flat-topped molding with a profile like that of the Doric echinus, but it is usually carved with egg-and-dart moldings. Above this lies the volute, its loose ends winding down in dropping spirals on each side of the shaft and ending in buttonlike *oculi* (eyes). The entablature usually consists of three bands of fasciae of unequal height, each projecting a little beyond the one below it. Above it runs a band of egg-and-dart molding and over that a row of dentils, superseded by a projecting cornice often decorated with lions' faces and plant motifs.

The Ionic capital came into its own during the 7th century BCE. Unlike the Doric, the Ionic did not derive from a structural system, but perhaps from symbolic headdresses or from poles surrounded by bundled vegetation marking sacred areas. The capital consists of two large spirals that spring upward and outward from the shaft, as if a pliant stick were split at the ends and each curved outward halfway to form a spiral. The space between the spirals was decorated with a fanlike pattern. Capitals of similar form were found on the island of Lesbos.

Sima carved with lions' heads and floral ornaments

Cornice

Dentils

Egg-and-dart and bead-and-reel moldings

Architrave with three fasciae

Voluted capital

Egg-and-dart echinus

Fluted column shaft

Torus with horizontal flutes

Plinth

5.36 Elements of the Ionic order

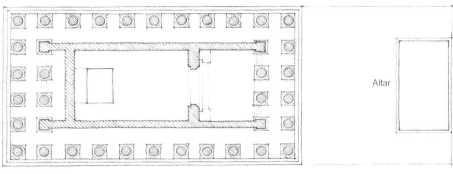

5.37 Plan: Temple of Athena Polias at Priene, Turkey

To construct the volutes, craftsmen devised a system of gridded holes into which pegs were inserted and around which a cord was wound and then, with a stylus attached, unwound. In essence, the spiral was a series of interconnected quarter circles and semicircles. They are not "organic" but precisely calibrated mathematical puzzles that come in a vast variety depending on how tightly wound the spirals are. One of the most elegant Ionic temples is undoubtedly the small Temple of Athena Nike (ca. 425 BCE) at the acropolis in Athens.

Though proportional systems were most certainly in play in the design of the Doric order, the formalization of the system began with the Ionic. A temple of the Ionic at its most classic is the Temple of Athena Polias at Priene (ca. 334 BCE) by the architect Pythius, who wrote a book explaining the proportions of this temple. The larger proportions were worked out in similar ratios of 1:2. The overall dimensions of the stylobate measured 19.5 by 37.2 meters, for a ratio of 11:21. The axial spacing between the columns was twice the width of the square plinths. The antae of the porch and the *opisthodomos* in the rear stood opposite the penultimate columns of

the ends and sides and enclosed a rectangle measuring 12 by 30 meters, for a ratio of 1:2.5. No longer did architects manipulate the form to adjust for optical illusions; geometrical precision was now in order. The Ionic was codified further around 150 BCE by the architect Hermogenes, also of Priene. He worked out a series of ideal proportions that were to influence Vitruvius a century later. According to this system, the height of the column varied inversely according to the axial spacing, so that the sum of axial spacings and height was always 12.5 column diameters.

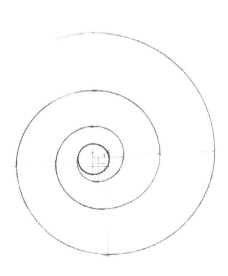

5.38 Development of the Ionic spiral

5.39 Temple of Athena Nike, acropolis, Athens, Greece

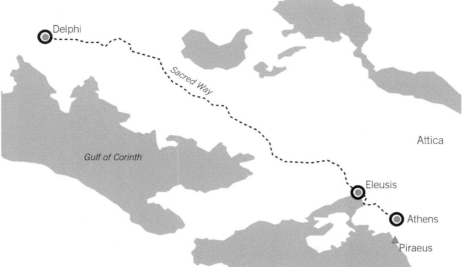

5.40 Sacred Way from Athens to Delphi

5.41 Plan: Telesterion at Eleusis, Greece

Telesterion at Eleusis

Festivals were an important part of Greek political and religious life similar to the Middle Kingdom practices of Egypt, except that Greek festivals were considerably more folksy in nature. The temple at Isthmia, for example, was the center of a festival that involved a major athletic contest. In Athens, festivals accentuated the flow of the year, and in fact filled 120 days, or one-third of the calendar year.

One of the oldest of these festivals, and one possibly once linked to the Eleusinian Mysteries, was the Thesmophoria, a harvest festival (*thesmoi* meaning "law," and *phoria* deriving from the word for "carrying"). It was celebrated by the married women of Athens whose husbands were Athenian citizens. The festival centered on the earth goddess Demeter, whose daughter Persephone had to spend one-third of the year in the underworld with her husband, Hades. During these dry summer months, Demeter abandoned her function as harvest goddess and mourned for her absent daughter. The women set up makeshift shelters outside the sanctuary, purified themselves, sat on the ground, and fasted in commiseration with Demeter. On the third day, a meat celebration was conducted named after Kalligenaia, the goddess of beautiful birth and an ancient term that alludes to the very antiquity of this rite, which quite possibly antedates even the Greeks: this

festival, if it can be called that, had at its roots the ancient Mediterranean-wide mother cult.

Another important Greek festival, one that exemplifies the very essence of Greek religiosity, was the celebration of the Great Mysteries at Eleusis, which took place in that city. Dating back some two thousand years, probably to Mycenaean times, this city was located some 25 kilometers distant from Athens and became part of the Athenian state festivals in the 6th century BCE. It was a seven-day celebration in the late fall, beginning on the fifteenth day of the Greek month of Boedromion. People streamed to it from all of Greece, and even slaves were admitted. This festival was so deeply entrenched in the folk practices and the communal memory that it continued on into early Christian times—until the early Christian fathers put a stop to it. The procession followed the sacred road from Athens to Delphi that had, according to myth, been traveled by Apollo. The route started at the sacred gate in the city walls of Athens and proceeded through Eleusis to the sanctuary of Demeter on the Thriasian Plain.

Every September a great torch-lit procession wound its way along this route. Two days before it was to begin, the *hiera* (sacred objects) were brought in baskets to Athens by young Athenians in military training. The initiates met their *mystagogus* (a person initiated previously who helped them

through the process) and took piglets down to the sea, bathed with them, sacrificed them, and purified themselves with their blood. On the fifth day, they made the long 25-kilometer march to Eleusis. The statue of Dionysus was carried at the head of the procession. Then came the priests with the sacred cult objects hidden in baskets and finally a huge crowd of *mystai* (initiates). The high point of the festival took place in the Telesterion at Eleusis, a square, windowless building arranged in its final configuration with tiers of seats to accommodate some three thousand people.

The Anaktoron at the center of the great hall housed the hiera, the inner sanctum that, though small and windowless, was precious and of venerable age. The renovations and additions that were made to the Telesterion changed only the space around it, not the Anaktoron itself. The building in its final form (ca. 435 BCE) was designed by Koroibos. In the 4th century BCE, a colonnaded porch known as the Stoa of Philon was added to the southeastern side of the building. Though the songs and offerings were public, the experiences of the *mystai* during the rites were secret, and access to the inner sanctum of the Telesterion was restricted to initiates. Despite how long they lasted and the huge number of people who took part, the secrecy surrounding these rites has been preserved; one can only guess what the mysteries involved.

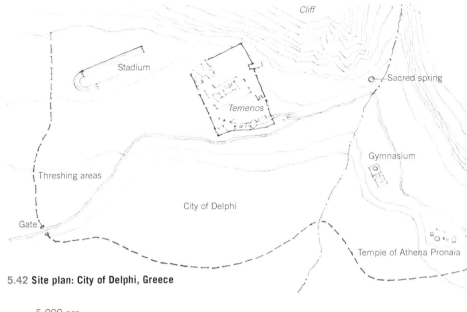

5.42 Site plan: City of Delphi, Greece

5,000 BCE
Mycenaean cult site (later Temple of
Athena Pronaia)
1500 BCE
Mycenaean cult site of earth goddess
(later Temple of Apollo)
650 BCE
First Temple of Apollo
550 BCE
Second Temple
5th century BCE
Stadium
Stoa of the Athenians
4th century BCE
Tholos
Theater
Third Temple

5.43 Plan: Temenos at Delphi, Greece

Delphi

Delphi was without doubt the most sacred of the religious sites in Greece, with its own festivals and celebrations. One approached it from Eleusis on the sacred route that crosses the Boeotian Plains, passes the city of Thebes, and courses its way through increasingly rugged and remote territory filled with history and myth. Finally, the dramatic scenery of the limestone cliffs, from which gushes the Castalian Spring with its great cleft, comes into view, the buildings of the sanctuary rising up against the base of the cliff. The early history of Delphi is the story of a struggle between different types of religious practices. Initially, the site was dedicated to the great mother goddess in the Minoan tradition. With the arrival of the Dorians we see their paternalistic practices superimposed on the existing maternalistic social structures. Nonetheless, despite the seizure of the shrine by the followers of Apollo, the new concepts did not totally obliterate the old; rather, the maternalistic elements were subsumed. The mother goddess was transformed into the serpent, Python, slain by Apollo, and said to be buried there, but she retained her ancient *temenos* close to the Temple of Apollo, near the Rock of the Sybil. The temple foundations come close to her spot but do not obliterate it. Apparently, the Apollo cult was forced to compromise with the older deities as two population groups made their accommodations.

5.44 Delphic Pythia sitting on a tripod, attended by a supplicant

5.45 **The ruins of Delphi from above the Temple of Apollo**

5.46 **Treasury of Athens, Delphi**

Temple of Apollo at Delphi

During the three winter months, Dionysus shared the temple sanctuary on the Parnassos slope with Apollo, a reference to some of the ancient chthonic elements connected with the cult of Persephone, who, according to the Orphic myth, was the mother of Dionysus. Out of the ecstatic dances and choruses of Dionysus, the Greek drama was born, and at Delphi, above the great Temple of Apollo, there lies on cross-axis to the temple and facing straight down the slope a brilliant example of such a theater. Filling and defining a natural concavity at the base of the cliff, the natural and man-made merge into one majestic swath—one great hymn to the creation cycle of life.

From just inside the wall of the *temenos*, the viewer would see the silhouette of the Temple of Apollo floating against the backdrop of the cliff. The path to the temple was not a direct one but rather snaked its way upward past the various treasuries—many of distant colonies—to emerge just below the broad terrace built up against the slope. A supplicant, guided by an assistant of the Delphian cult, would have been led to the temple terrace to await his turn with the oracle. He would have had the opportunity to look straight down into the ancient precinct of Gaia. He might have spent some time regarding the temple itself.

What is visible today is the last temple, the site having been occupied earlier by two previous Doric temples. The first one, a structure from the 7th century BCE, burned in 548 BCE and was replaced by a larger one in 525 BCE, which itself was replaced in the mid-4th century BCE. On the east pediment facing the altar in front of the temple, sculptures portrayed the arrival of Apollo at Delphi, shown with his mother, Leto; his sister Artemis; and his companions, the Muses. At the opposite pediment, Dionysus, Apollo's brother—both having been fathered by Zeus—occupied the center, establishing a principle of balance: Apollo representing music and poetry; Dionysus, wine and ecstasy. The Dionysian and the Apollonian were not perceived as opposites by the Greeks but rather as complementary; together they embodied the wholeness of life. Below the east pediment hung the golden shields from the spoils of the Persian War, a gift to the temple by the Athenians.

The most important festival associated with Delphi was the change of rule that took place between Apollo and Dionysus at the appointed time. It was enacted in the great open-air theater above the temple with its thronelike overview of the sanctuary and surrounding landscape. The sports events that accompanied these festivals took place in the heights above the *temenos*.

Once inside the temple, the supplicant would smell the meat burning on the hearth and see the smoke rising toward the opening in the roof, from which shafts of sunlight penetrated down into the gloom. Visitors also mentioned a perfumed smell. The supplicants would have seen tripods, statues, pieces of armor, even entire racing chariots, brought as donations from the entire world of Magna Graecia, and often from foreign countries as well. After depositing his own offering, the supplicant would be led toward the far end of the chamber, where steps descend to a sunken area a meter below the level of the floor. From there he made his way into the adytum, at the back wall of which was a bench close to the branches of a laurel tree as well as a golden statue of Apollo. There, the prophetess, on a tripod and hidden from him by a curtain, was positioned over a crack in the rocks from which, according to some visitors, emanated that sweetish smell. An attendant, drawing back the curtain, would relay the question of the petitioner, and from the depths, the prophetess received a reply to the question, often equivocal, which she conveyed back to the petitioner. Whatever the response—which often required a large amount of interpretation—it probably necessitated further donations. What caused the sweet smell has not been determined with scientific accuracy. Recent archaeological studies point to the possibility that it might have been ethylene, a common vapor in natural tar pits that produces euphoria, which is used today as an anesthetic.

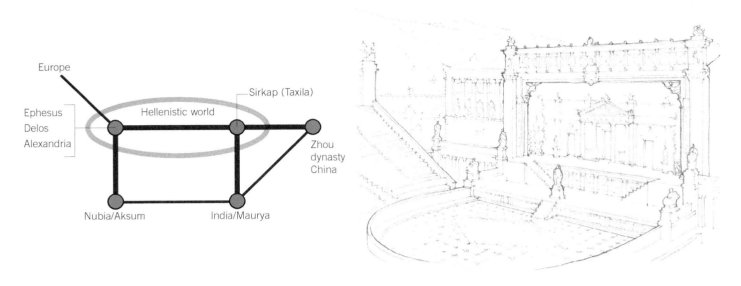

5.47 Eurasian trade diagram, ca. 300 BCE

5.48 **Dionysus Theater, Athens**

THE HELLENISTIC AGE

The legacy of Greek architecture would move in two different directions, with two different destinies. It would move westward when it was adopted by the Romans and spread into Europe, where, with the demise of the Roman Empire in the 5th century CE, it would slowly wither away, its ideas and ideals only revitalized beginning in the 15th century with the Renaissance. It would, however, also move eastward with Alexander the Great (356–323 BCE), son of Philip II of Macedon, and have a profound impact on Indian architecture and even on the architecture of the 13th-century Khmer Empire. The modern-day notion that "classicism" is at the core of "Western architecture" is a myth of the 19th-century Romantics. It was in fact in the non-European world that the legacy of "classicism" would be most palpably felt.

Alexander assumed kingship over the newly consolidated mainland Greece after his father's death and continued his expansionary policies. He crossed the Hellespont in 334 BCE, defeated the Achaemenid Empire, and on his way to the border of India founded many fledgling cities, stocking them with some of his Macedonian Greeks, who awaited—in vain, as it turned out—his return with new troops and settlers to sustain his eastern empire. Alexander's empire fell apart after his sudden and unexplained death in 323 BCE in Nebuchadnezzar's palace in Babylon. Strife broke out among his potential successors, but eventually three realms emerged: the Antigonid Empire (Greece), the Seleucid Empire (Mesopotamia and Persia), and the Ptolemaic Empire (Egypt, Palestine, and Cyrenaica). All are part of what is called the Hellenistic Age. As an art form, Hellenism had lost some of the discipline of its origins and in temple construction tended to gigantism and spatial experimentation; in sculpture, it is noted for the portrayal of emotions and empathy, as, for example, in the Dying Gaul.

Old cities like Athens, which for a while became part of the kingdom of Antigonus, were given new buildings. Some were paid for locally; some funds came from foreign donations. The enormous Temple of Zeus at Olympia in Athens, begun in 170 BCE, was paid for by Antiochus IV (d. 164 BCE) of the Seleucids of northern Syria. A new harbor, council hall, and residential quarter were added to the city of Miletus. Assos redesigned its central agora with a long two-story-high stoa. New cities were laid out, some as far away as Ai Khanum on the Afghan bank of the Oxus River.

Though planned cities go back millennia, the architecture of cities and the architecture of palaces or temples were until then, generally speaking, quite distinct. In Hellenistic cities, urbanism and architecture begin to overlap for the first time. Theaters, temples, villas, palaces, libraries, stadia, and streets are all equally important in such cities as Priene, Pergamon, Alexandria, Dura-Europos, Delos, and Rhodes.

The economic engine that drove this tremendous expansion was not Athens but Hellenistic Egypt, the newly restored economic marvel of the Mediterranean. By the time of Ptolemy III (245–221 BCE), Egyptian fleets controlled most of the shipping lanes of the eastern Mediterranean. Building on the old pharaonic tradition of state control, the Ptolemaic kings updated technologies and production systems, transforming the country with its population of seven million into a grain-producing machine of unprecedented proportions.

The Ptolemaic rulers introduced the water screw of Archimedes and built machines with drums or wheels driven by humans for raising water and pushing back the desert. Salt production was escalated. Mines and quarries, as well as the development of a state-run bank, were integrated into the system. It was in some respects one of the first examples of state-supported modernization.

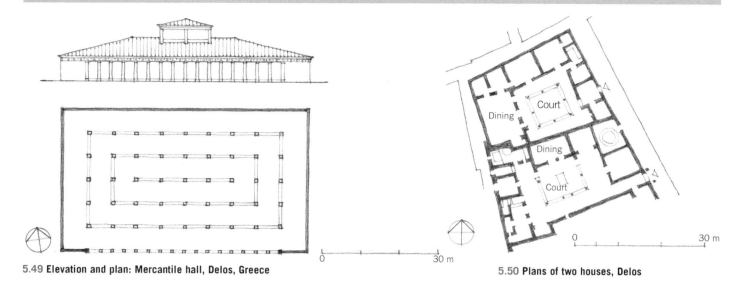

5.49 **Elevation and plan: Mercantile hall, Delos, Greece**

5.50 **Plans of two houses, Delos**

Delos

One of the places that most quickly adapted to the new world order was Delos. Though the island was small—one of the smallest in the Aegean—and though it had no local economy to speak of, it was almost equidistant from the various ports in the Aegean Sea. It entered into economic relations with Egypt and Macedonia to become the leading Mediterranean trading station. The tradition that had begun with the Minoans was perfected by the rulers of Delos. Money was made in the transfer of goods rather than in their manufacture and sale. Delos was also a holy place, considered the birthplace of Apollo and Artemis. It was, for a while at least, the perfect combination of the sacred and the economic. On one side of its harbor was a special landing place for pilgrims visiting the sacred sites; on the other side, one would have found a large and new mercantile harbor fringed with storage houses, wharves, and commercial buildings. The Egyptians, bringing their grain for redistribution, built shrines to their gods. Phoenicians came to sell ivory. Jews built a synagogue. The Italians were on the scene as well, building an agora of their own. A mercantile hall measuring about 60 by 35 meters was built in 210 BCE, with houses for the merchants laid out with unprecedented richness.

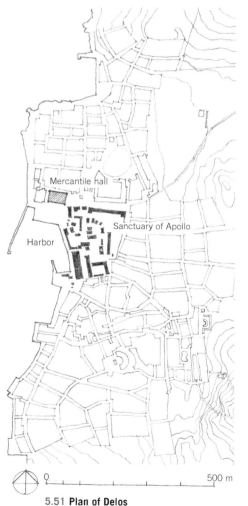

5.51 **Plan of Delos**

Priene

On the eastern coast of Anatolia, Miletus, Priene, and Heracleia were part of an inlet that has long since silted over. Together with Didyma and with the ancient sanctuary of Samos as a type of gateway, this area was another major religious and economic center. Priene, founded in 334 BCE, occupies a sloping ground beneath a fortifiable acropolis. The streets run east-west along level ground and are about 4.5 meters across. From south to north, with the ground rising steeply, the streets are mostly narrower. The principal civic elements of the city are embedded in the structure of this grid and yet in dynamic resistance to it. The agora, for example, juts out from the grid to the south and does not align with the side streets. Across from it is a three-block-long stoa. Up the hill a few blocks to the west is the platform with the temple of Athena, and a block higher yet but to the east was a theater with spectacular views into the valley below and the mountains across. Farther northward yet, where the city ends and the steep slope of the acropolis begins, is a sanctuary dedicated to Demeter. A stadium and gymnasium define the lower edge. The city, because of its composite character, might appear to have been built up over time, but it is in actuality a skillful play of solids and voids and of private and public zones, spread out over a difficult terrain.

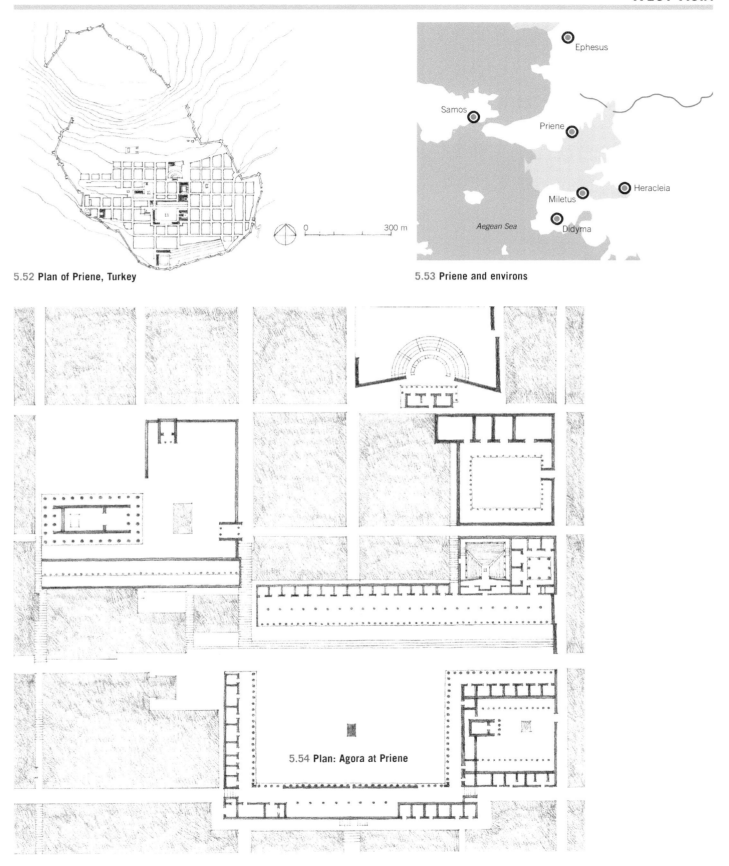

5.52 **Plan of Priene, Turkey**

5.53 **Priene and environs**

Ephesus

Samos

Priene

Heracleia

Miletus

Didyma

Aegean Sea

0   300 m

5.54 **Plan: Agora at Priene**

Pergamon

By the year 281 BCE, the city of Pergamon had become the center of a small but powerful city-state rivaling Athens and even Alexandria as a center of Greek culture. It is estimated that at its peak, it had a population of three hundred thousand people spreading from the mountaintop site to the southwest, across the Caicus Plain. Overlooking the city was an acropolis decked out with an assortment of structures that show the Hellenistic spatial aesthetic at its best. The object of the overall composition was not simply to work with the contours, almost instinctively, as was traditional in Greek planning, but to exploit them for their inherent sculptural qualities. At the heart of the acropolis stood a temple to Athena, the protectress of the city, dating from the beginning of the 3rd century BCE and most likely the oldest structure on the acropolis. It is one of the very rare Doric temples in Asia Minor and was no doubt built as an homage to the Parthenon. It was enclosed in a *temenos*, with stoas on three sides that clamp it into the hill. Just behind the stoa was the palace of Eumenes II. Behind another wing of the stoa but at a higher level was the famous library built around 190 BCE, which held up to two hundred thousand volumes. Still farther up is the military zone of the acropolis with its storehouses, officers' housing, barracks, and arsenal.

The theater, resting against the slope of the mountain, is one of the most spectacular in the Hellenic world. It was originally constructed in the 3rd century BCE, rebuilt around 190 BCE, and refurbished in Roman times. The cavea, or auditorium, forms part of the natural contour of the west-facing slope and has room for ten thousand spectators, with the king's marble box just at the center of the front row. A comparison of Pergamon with Priene is instructive, for it shows that, as important as the Hippodamian city grid plan was, Hellenistic town planners also saw its limitations and, as at Pergamon, adopted a method that followed the lay of the land and indeed exploited it with great skill.

5.55 Plan: Pergamon, near Bergama, Turkey

0 200 m

5.56 Remains of the theater at Pergamon

5.57 **Propylaea on the acropolis at Lindos, Greece**

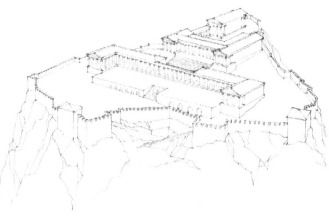

5.58 **Pictorial view: Sanctuary of Athena on the acropolis at Lindos**

Toward the south, at the edge of the acropolis and on a terrace 25 meters below the Athena temple is the Altar of Zeus, built for Eumenes II soon after his victory over the Gauls in 190 BCE. The Gauls had been sweeping southward from western Europe, and even though they would continue to harass the northern borders of Mediterranean countries for centuries, Eumenes II had managed to hold them at bay, at least for a while. The altar was a U-shaped, Ionic, stoa-like structure perched on top of a high socle, with a vast flight of stairs leading up its west side to the level of the colonnade. On its enormous socle level was a frieze representing the mythical battle between the Olympian gods and the ancient giants, symbolizing the triumphs of the Pergamon kingdom over the Gauls.

The altar stands in a courtyard atop an almost square plinth. It was surrounded by a colonnade that sheltered a wall on which there was another frieze celebrating the legitimacy of the Pergamon kings. This altar was not only the traditional end point of the sacrificial procession but also a political monument and even a war memorial. These are roles that had been in earlier days connected with the temple—the Parthenon being an excellent example. But here the altar reverted to an autonomous cultural object.

Sanctuary of Athena at Lindos

Though Pergamon is a masterpiece of adaptation to the landscape, resulting in a multifaceted architectural environment, another example is the acropolis of Lindos (ca. 190 BCE) on the island of Rhodes, built around an older temple to Athena (ca. 300 BCE). The first terrace is framed out over the landscape by an outward-facing winged stoa, opened at the center by a broad flight of stairs. The stoa's front row of columns holds its edge to form a screenlike passage across the front of the steps. The steps lead to the top level and to a broad porch that, in turn, opens into a courtyard with an altar in the middle. The old temple is sited to the left of the courtyard, in dynamic tension with the altar.

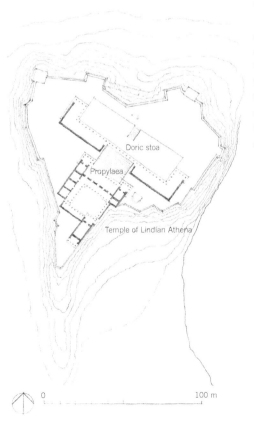

Doric stoa

Propylaea

Temple of Lindian Athena

0   100 m

5.59 **Plan: Sanctuary of Athena on the acropolis at Lindos**

5.60 Temple of Apollo, Didyma, Turkey

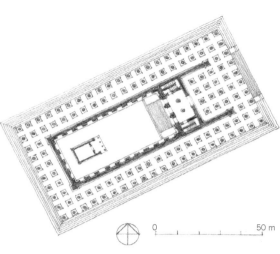

5.61 Plan: Temple of Apollo

Temple of Apollo at Didyma

It is difficult to speak of the Hellenistic temple as a single aesthetic form. In the cosmopolitan environment of western Asia, one sees different tastes in different places as well as variable influences. In Egypt, buildings of the Hellenistic era were designed in an Egyptian revival style. Such neoarchaisms were not outside the aesthetic interests of the Greeks. The Hellenistic aesthetic did, however, draw on centuries of experience in creating complex, composite relationships between space, landscape, and mythical narration—organizing it, as at Priene, into unified aesthetic expressions. One of the most spectacular of Hellenistic temples in this respect is the unfinished Temple of Apollo at Didyma, 14 kilometers south of Miletus. Sitting on a gentle hill and exposed on all sides, it contained the unusual feature of an open court, planted with bay trees, among which stood a shrine-like Ionic temple. Though several Greek temples—possibly even the Parthenon—had open interiors, this was something altogether different. The architects are said to have been Paeonius and Demetrios of Ephesus. Though much of the plan may have been laid out by them around 313 BCE, the work took well over three hundred years to complete and was abandoned in 41 CE.

The temple's Ionic double *pteron* stands on a stylobate accessed by seven huge steps. After ascending the steps, one enters the deep porch of the *pronaos*, behind which is an antechamber. The antechamber is actually higher than the *pronaos*, with its door serving as a window from which the oracles were delivered. Standing among the *pronaos*'s treelike columns—the tallest of any Greek temple's—the windows would have appeared to be the mouth of a cave. Access to the inner courtyard was by way of small doorways on either side of the window, through sloping, dark tunnels roofed with barrel vaults.

Penetrating through this dark "grotto," one enters the sacred grove. But this "inside" was in fact an outside. The artificial grove of trees, which is how the columns would have appeared from the outside, gave way to real trees on the inside. Furthermore, within that grove was another temple, with its axis oriented toward the entry; this small Ionic temple at the far end of the open *cella* faced a grand staircase leading back up to the antechamber, from which the priests could officiate. Folding one temple compound into another was a consummate example of Hellenistic brilliance.

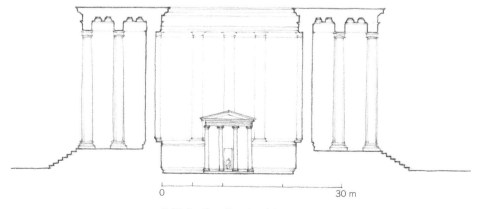

5.62 Section: Temple of Apollo

5.63 **Hypostyle hall, Temple of Horus, Edfu, Egypt**

5.64 **Pronaos at the Temple of Horus**

Ptolemies

Alexandria was one of the principal Hellenistic cities. Situated on the western extremity of the Nile River delta, the city was founded in 332 BCE by Alexander to serve as a regional capital. It soon became the largest city in the Mediterranean basin, and it was unlike any other, with libraries, museums, and a rich cosmopolitan culture. Though little is left of the ancient city, the Ptolemaic period left a vibrant record of its art and architecture in many parts of Egypt, including the construction of about fifty medium-size and large temple complexes, not to mention smaller architectural works. The Ptolemies and their queens had no misgivings about following Egyptian tradition, and set up statues of themselves as cult images. Nonetheless, Ptolemaic architects did not place windows on the top of walls, as the earlier Egyptians had done: their hypostyle halls are pitch black if one closes the doors. Ptolemaic architects also added ambulatories around the temple, making it an autonomous object within the confines of the outer walls. Much innovation focused on the elaborations of columns and their capitals. The capital could be round or single-stemmed, quatrefoil or even eight-stemmed. The plant motifs are palm, papyrus, lotus, and lily, even though the lily was not a native Egyptian species. The plants' leaves could then appear stacked variously, from two to five. The richness of form was augmented by lively coloring.

Temple of Horus

The Temple of Horus (begun 237 BCE) is an excellent example of these tendencies. The building not only had to reflect the needs of the cult of Horus but also had to serve as a pantheon for the cumulative aspects of Egyptian religion. The entrance is marked by a grand pylon 62.6 meters across and 30.5 meters high, leading to a court colonnaded on three sides—a very un-Egyptian motif, more Hellenistic in tone. The colonnade not only frames the entrance of the temple but also constitutes a type of extended porch that, along with the perimeter walls, forms a passageway. Past the two hypostyle halls is an inner court, in the center of which is the freestanding sanctuary of Horus. The court gives access to thirteen small chapels for the pantheon, all windowless and completely dark except for tiny slit entries. Great care was given to align the pylon with the noontime sun at the midsummer solstice. At that particular moment, the pylon does not cast a shadow.

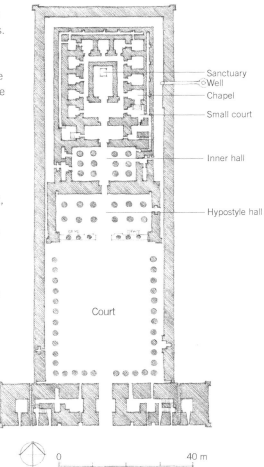

5.65 **Plan: Temple of Horus**

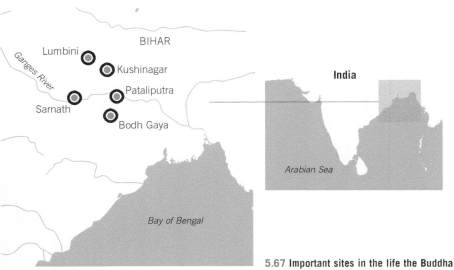

5.67 Important sites in the life the Buddha

5.66 Asokan pillar at Vaishali, near Patna, India

MAURYAN DYNASTY AND EARLY BUDDHISM

India, despite its vibrant culture, had remained relatively isolated from the Hellenistic economies that linked Delos and Pergamon in the west to China in the east. This situation changed rapidly when the Mauryan kings unified the Indian subcontinent, forming a new and potent economic force in the Asian world. Maurya had under its control not only a rich agricultural basin, but also the Barabar Hills to the south of the Mauryan capital Pataliputra, where copper and iron could be mined. Consequently, India could begin to compete in the global politics of iron and thus emerge from its relative isolation. At its height, the empire stretched northward along the natural boundaries of the Himalayas and westward to Kandahar, which had been founded by Alexander in the 4th century BCE. This brought India into full contact with Greek and Persian culture, and soon Indian spices, copper, gold, silk, and rice began to appear in distant places. The impact of this contact manifests itself in Indian buildings in a shift from wood to stone architecture, initially in the form of monumental columns and rock-cut Buddhist caves.

The rise of Buddhism can be traced to smoldering divisions within the Aryan polity during the Mauryan dynasty. Brahmins were the lawmakers, scholars, preachers, and advisers to the rulers, who occupied the highest position in the Vedic caste system. Since the caste system controlled the lives and destinies of everyone, there was little individuality. In the 6th century BCE, two men, Siddhartha Gautama (the Buddha, or "enlightened one") and Mahavira Jain, both from marginal clans, asserted the idea of an independent and individual journey to spiritual bliss, or nirvana, that contradicted not only the principles of warfare, but also the highly regimented Vedic rituals that required the leadership of the Brahmins. Nirvana was accessible to all, but it was not easy to reach, as it required a commitment to rigorous asceticism. The main difference between the two men was that while meditation-based practices were at the core of the Buddha's

5.68 Vajrasana ("Diamond Throne") at Bodh Gaya, India

teachings, Mahavira Jain insisted on a radical vegetarianism that included a prohibition on farming, since that inadvertently killed soil worms.

Buddhism might have remained just another intellectual stream of the Aryan world had it not been adopted as state law and moral order under Asoka (r. 272–231 BCE), the most famous of the Mauryan kings. After a particularly brutal battle, Asoka lost faith in the traditional Aryan order, and after more than a year of consultation with various philosophers, decided to convert to Buddhism. Asoka was not the first Mauryan leader to be interested in Buddhism. At the end of his life, Chandragupta Maurya, founder of the Mauryan dynasty, abdicated his throne and became a Jain ascetic. His son, Bindusara (r. 298–272 BCE) became a follower of an even more extreme ascetic movement known as the *ajivikas*. The ascetic interest of these rulers derived from the fact that they were not born into the Aryan Kshatriya (warrior) caste, but were low-caste upstarts who became Kshatriya after seizing the Magadha throne. The difference between Asoka and his predecessors was that he adapted Buddhist teachings into a new moral and social order for his empire that he called the *dhamma*. In essence Buddhism became a state religion.

Though most of Asoka's *dhamma* derives from Buddhism—including vegetarianism and belief in nonviolence—it was not identical to Buddhism. In fact, Asoka rarely mentioned the Buddha while describing his *dhamma*, which, significantly, included respect for all religions as a core part of its tenets. To promote his *dhamma*, which consisted of about thirty-three edicts, Asoka had them etched in stone tablets, on the side of prominent rocks, and inside cave sanctuaries, all in the vernacular language of his kingdom. He also carved them on the sides of pillars, about twenty of which have survived. One such pillar, in Lauriya Nandangarh (in Bihar), made from a single piece of polished sandstone, rises 12 meters above the ground and extends 3 meters into the earth. Though the pillar is surmounted by an ornate capital, it is the shaft with the inscribed edicts that is of primary significance. The Asokan pillars consist of a stylized lotus base that supports an ornamental drum on which there are sculptures of animals ranging from the bull to the lion signifying royal authority. Most famous is the pillar found at Sarnath, the site of the Buddha's first sermon, the lotus base and drum of which is topped by a capital of four lions. Surmounting all this, at least originally, was the Buddhist wheel of law, which has, in turn, been adopted as the symbol of the modern Indian nation.

To further promote the Buddhist order, Asoka convened a council of all significant Buddhist practitioners, whose mission it was to codify the Buddha's teachings. Asoka also memorialized the major sites associated with the Buddha—in particular his birthplace (Lumbini), the site of his enlightenment (Bodh Gaya), the location of his first sermon (Sarnath), and the place of his death (Kushinagar). He sent emissaries throughout the empire and abroad, including to Sri Lanka, Afghanistan, Persia, and Greece. Most importantly, he collected all the known relics of the Buddha and distributed them to about eight sites, at which the first centers of Buddhist learning were established. The Buddha was never represented as a human figure in Asoka's time. Representations of the Buddha began to be made in the 1st century CE and have become important in the Buddhist tradition ever since. Asoka did build the diamond throne at Bodh Gaya to stand in for the Buddha and to mark the place of his enlightenment.

5.69 **Plan, section, and interior: Lomas Rsi Cave, near Bodh Gaya, India**

Barabar Hills Caves

Buddhist ascetics were responsible for the first rock-cut caves in India, which date to the mid-3rd century BCE. They are located in the Barabar Hills of Bihar, 20 miles north of Bodh Gaya, at a prominent cluster of rock outcroppings in an otherwise flat landscape. There are four caves, consisting of two chambers each: a rectangular hall followed by a round room with a hemispherical ceiling. Inscriptions in three of them note that they were dedicated by Asoka for use by the *ajivikas*. Unadorned, with crisp rectangular openings punched into the rock, they are carved out of the granite with exacting precision and with a highly polished internal surface. One of them, the Lomas Rsi Cave, is incomplete. It was probably abandoned after the interior rock sheared and the roof partially collapsed. This cave has an entrance that clearly simulates a vaulted wooden and thatch structure of pavilion. Since the cave has no inscription, it probably dates to Asoka, though its exterior may well have been carved later.

Rock-cut architecture had a long tradition in Egypt, Anatolia, and Patra, so the technique was most likely brought to India through Persia, particularly after Asoka. The word *cave*, which is used to describe these structures, is sadly misleading, since they are constructed structures, and as such are a form of architecture. In the centuries to come, this simple beginning was to flower into a tradition of rock-cut buildings that spread throughout South Asia and China.

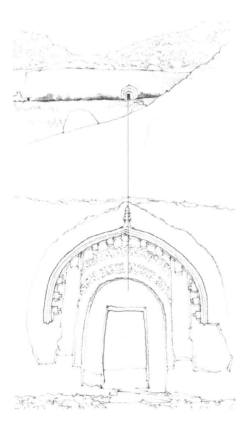

5.70 **Entrance, Lomas Rsi Cave**

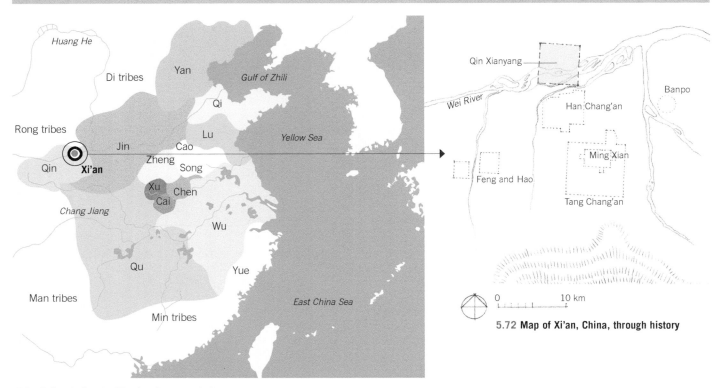

5.72 **Map of Xi'an, China, through history**

5.71 **China during the Warring States period**

CHINA: THE WARRING STATES PERIOD

In the Warring States period (481–221 BCE), the old league of cities ruled by the Zhou nobility was replaced by a system of territorial states (seven major and about seven minor ones) under the command of monarchs who seem to have engaged in feverish construction activity. They fortified existing city walls, multiplied enclosures and barricades, and established satellite towns, all primarily for the purpose of defense. Prior to the Warring States period, cities were cultic and political entities inhabited by the nobility and their followers. Populations were in the tens of thousands at most. During the Warring States period, as cities became capitals of states, their nature changed, becoming divided between a political center and an economic center, the two holding each other in mutual suspicion. This suspicion was articulated in laws that attempted to control the actions and influence of merchants. The result was that new and sharp boundaries were drawn within the city between the political district, which was protected with its own wall, and the merchants' district. New architectural elements appeared that, through height and verticality, emphasized the ruler's authority. Towers, pillar gates, and raised buildings were all used to demonstrate power. When Shang Yang began constructing the new Qin capital Xianyang, the first items built were the gate towers.

Stepped terraces—called *tai* platforms—surrounded on all four sides by the wooden columns and beams of the palace, could give the impression of multiple-storied buildings. In an age that lacked the ability to construct true multistoried buildings, this design allowed for structures that seemed to rise above the city. The ruler was both all-seeing and yet invisible. Furthermore, it was believed that the ruler should move in secret to avoid evil spirits and that he should live as much as possible in towers. For this reason, Shi Huangdi, the First Emperor, built elevated walks to connect all 270 of his palaces and towers. Anyone who revealed where the emperor was visiting was put to death. This withdrawal from the gaze of the populace, and even from the court, became an essential attribute of Qin and Han imperial personages. In Rome and India, a ruler's person had to be visible. But in China, his status was derived from being hidden and remote.

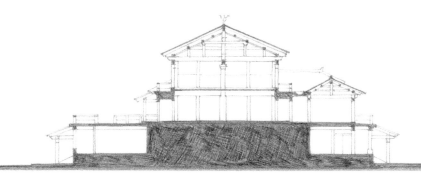

5.73 **The monumentality of palace complexes in the Warring States period**

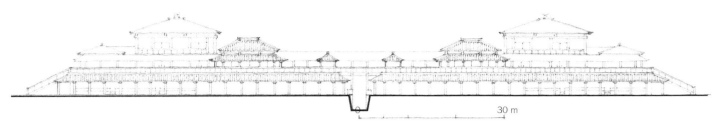

5.74 **Elevation: Xianyang Palace No. 1, Xi'an, China**

Xianyang Palace

Unlike the enclosed and understated ritual complexes of old, these new palaces projected themselves into space as imposing three-dimensional structures. In general, the higher the *tai*, the more assertive the claim to power by the ruler who had commissioned it. In a time when rulers and states were constantly at war, claiming authority through buildings was critical for a ruler's image. For instance, a Zhou king constructed an imposing platform at the site of his meeting with other lords. History reveals that his guests, struck with awe at the sight of this platform, agreed to join the Zhou alliance.

A dramatic terrace pavilion, the Xianyang Palace No. 1 consisted of a series of rooms and corridors built one on top of another around an earthen core, giving the impression of a multilevel structure of great volume and height. While this structure has been identified with the Xianyang Palace of Qin Shi Huangdi, first emperor of Qin, recent evidence suggests that it was first built during the Warring States period and subsequently integrated into Shi Huangdi's palatial complex. Located north of the Wei River, the palace's foundations are 60 meters long east to west, 45 meters wide, and about 6 meters high. The reconstruction suggests that the palace superstructure was symmetrical, having had two wings. The earthen core was surrounded by bays on all sides, creating the image of a three-story building of immense size. A drainage system guided water into underground pipes. The chambers were connected by intricate passages, and balconies were decorated with elaborate bronze accessories and colorful murals.

5.75 **Pictorial view: Xianyang Palace No. 1**

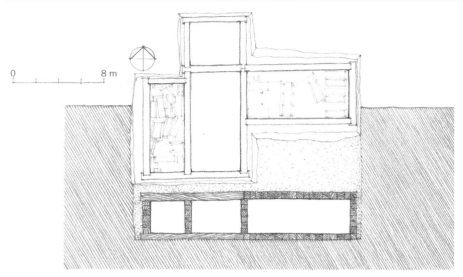

0   8 m

5.76 Plan and section: Tomb of Zeng Hou Yi, Sui Zhou, China

5.77 Coffins with window-like and door-like openings found in the Tomb of Zeng Hou Yi

Tomb of Zeng Hou Yi

The architecture of tombs and graveyards became increasingly important at this time. Texts compiled during this period distinguish between rituals performed within the city in ancestral temples and others performed outside the city at graveyards. The most visible remnants of Zhou architecture are, in fact, tombs, of which more than six thousand have been discovered. The tomb of Zeng Hou Yi (Marquis Yi of Zeng) attracted international attention when a large collection of bronze objects was found there, including a set of sixty-five ritual bells weighing a total of 2,500 kilograms. The tomb consisted of an irregularly shaped vertical pit, 13 meters deep and more than 200 square meters in area. It was divided into four chambers by wooden planks, with the principal chamber, on the east, containing the marquis's body.

The body was placed in a double-layered coffin. The space between the coffin and the chamber walls was filled with charcoal, clay, and earth to seal it as completely as possible. The eastern chamber also had coffins for eight women—possibly musicians who were sacrificed at the time of the burial (although human sacrificial internment was almost over by this time in Chinese history). The western chamber held skeletons of thirteen young women, who may have been the ruler's concubines. The remaining two chambers

were filled with ritual objects and weapons made of bronze, gold, copper, lacquer, wood, jade, and other materials.

A curious aspect of this tomb is that small window-like openings connect all four chambers. Even the marquis's outer coffin bears a rectangular hole, and his inner coffin is painted with doors and windows with lattice

patterns. Similar openings have been found in other Zhou tombs. According to Chinese Daoism, when a person dies, his *hun* (the spiritual soul) would leave, but his *p'o* (the earthly soul) would remain attached to his body. The series of openings in this tomb might be there to facilitate the movement of the *p'o* in its underground "palace."

5.78 Bianzhong bells found in the Tomb of Zeng Hou Yi, along with a 125-piece orchestra and 25 musicians

0

6.1 **The remnants of a Roman road, the Via Appia, south of Rome**

INTRODUCTION

Eurasia was dominated by China and Rome, interconnected by an increasingly vast system of land and sea trade routes known in their entirety as the Silk Route. In spite of its name, it wasn't only silk that moved westward; in actuality the Silk Route economy was a transcontinental trade in not just silk but also other luxury items such as rugs, gold, silver, craft objects, gems, ivory, and perfumes—all things that could be easily packed and transported on the backs of camels. The term *Silk Route* emphasizes the trade that went from east to west, but trade also went from west to east. The Chinese valued horses as well as woolen goods, carpets, curtains, blankets, rugs, and Parthian tapestries since they were unfamiliar with carpet manufacture and weaving. Also imported into China were military equipment, gold and silver, semiprecious stones, and glass items, all of which were rare in China. In addition to the trade in luxury items, there was bulk trade in grain, lumber, and building materials. This trade belonged to a different economic universe and was usually transported by boat along rivers and shores; here, the southern route through India and along the coast around Southeast Asia was preferred. That trade, along with cinnamon from the Indonesian spice islands, was to escalate in importance in the next centuries. The Chinese, in order to get rice and other bulk material, such as bricks and lumber, from the rural south to the urban north,

built a vast network of canals, some 1,776 kilometers in total length, called the Grand Canal. The oldest parts date back to the 5th century BCE, although the various sections were not connected until the Sui dynasty (581–618 CE). The Romans, meanwhile, are still famous for their roads today. Estimated at about 400,000 kilometers in total, these roads ranged from small local connectors to broad, long-distance highways built to link cities, towns, and military bases. The major roads were stone-paved and flanked by footpaths and drainage ditches.

The city of Rome developed from a relatively small town to a sprawling metropolis. Though the Romans planned the layout of their military camps with great ceremonial precision, the city of Rome developed with little top-down planning. At its center was the forum, the political core of the city. It was located in a valley surrounded by hills over which the city began to spread. Though almost all cities in the Mediterranean world were associated with deities and ritual, and linked to sacred acts when they were created, the Roman Forum was designed as a particularly intense site, from its mythical origins with Romulus and Remus to the Vestal Virgins who lived in a special residence and maintained the sacred fire. It was the site of the umbilicus of the earth and the site where the sacred law tablets were on display. And as the ceremonial center of the republic, (ending in 27 BCE with the establishment of the Roman Empire), it was politically far different from almost every model of rulership to date, with the exception of Athens. The transition to the empire was much contested, but it was more than just a grab for power by certain elites. The enormous sale of the territory did not match well with the still rather loose mercantile ethos of the republic. The shift began when Caesar invaded Gaul, not just for his personal glory but to gain access to some of the best farmland in Europe as well as to metal. For several centuries, the Romans had traded with the Gauls and Celts for iron, which they needed for their military. Despite early resistance to Roman domination, the Celts largely accommodated themselves to a Roman way of life that brought protection and prosperity.

Initially, the economic ascendancy of Rome cast a pall over western Asia, and very little of consequence was built during the 1st century BCE. But soon Rome was able to impose a cohesive appearance over its expanding domains. Roman emperors from Augustus to Trajan built impressive temples, forums, villas, and cities, all with the typical Roman imprint. Cities, roads, theaters, baths, markets, and military camps began to be built, from Hadrian's Wall in England (122 CE) to Timgad in Algeria (founded by Emperor Trajan ca. 100 CE).

Between the great centers of Rome and China, there stretched trackless steppe and desert; to get material across this area, the Chinese, like the Romans, had to rely on people who lived in gers, yurts, and tents, and whose survival depended just as much on their reliability as on their cunning and prowess. These nomadic cultures, however, get little credit for their efforts, as they were generally seen as rootless barbarians, but without them, there would have been no China and no Rome. For instance, it was the Xiongu khanate's confederation of tribes north of China that fed the ravenous needs of the empire. Such confederations would come and go over the centuries, but they were indispensable to the Eurasian economy.

The Romans, at their end of the Silk Route, had to deal in particular with the Parthians, the great horseback warriors who controlled the deserts of western Asia. The Romans tried to conquer them again and again in a series of battles that lasted over the entire period of their empire. But although the

6.2 The Colosseum, Rome

history books emphasize war and conquest, war or no war, it was the trade exchange that linked people across the landscape. A significant border city was Dura-Europos (in modern-day Syria), built on a bluff 90 meters above the right bank of the Euphrates River to control the river crossing on the route between the Mediterranean port city of Antioch and the inland caravan cities to the east. Initially founded in 303 BCE, Dura-Europos was redesigned in the 2nd century BCE in the Greek manner, with rectangular blocks around a large central agora. At the end of the 2nd century BCE it came under Parthian control and was known as a cosmopolitan center. It contained not only a well-preserved synagogue but also an early Christian church. The city was captured by the Romans in 165 CE and all but abandoned in the middle of the 3rd century CE. To enhance their trade position, the Romans tried to do an end run around the Parthians by making alliances with the Nabataeans, a caravan-based culture centered in Jordan; the Nabataeans controlled the routes to the south and to India. The Roman attitude toward the Nabateans was different than toward the Parthians. The Nabataeans were made citizens of Rome and were showered with privileges. The extravagant tombs the Nabataeans built for themselves are showpieces of architectural luxury and testaments to their important position in global trade.

The Roman attempt to control the eastern Mediterranean included the all-important Levant, and in 70 CE they conquered the city of Jerusalem and destroyed its famous Second Temple, an act still mourned annually as the Jewish fast Tisha B'Av. Back in Rome, Emperor Titus built an arch celebrating the sacking of Jerusalem and its temple. At the center of this prosperity was Rome, which underwent a profound transformation between 50 CE and 150 CE. It is clear that architecture in the Roman heartland in the 1st century CE was often magnificent in scale and material, but in design terms it was notably conventional compared to that found in West Asia at the time. The architecture at Petra, the Nabataean capital, parallels the spatial innovation seen elsewhere, such as at Herod's Palace at Masada, which works its way down a difficult slope.

The Romans built extensive villas, including a new palace for the emperor, the Palace of Domitian (also known as Flavian Palace), which was completed in 92 CE during the reign of Titus Flavius Domitianus and attributed to his master architect, Rabirius. The very word *palace* is thought to have derived from its location on the Palatine Hill. It consisted of a series of open courtyards that define imperial, ceremonial, and private activities. The plan is a master class in spatial organization.

This period also saw the construction of the Colosseum (72–80 CE), which could hold up to 80,000 spectators, and the rise of vast urban-scale entertainment. Unlike earlier such structures that were built into hillsides, this is an entirely freestanding structure, its monumental facade comprising three stories of superimposed arcades surmounted by a tall attic story. The building was used to host gladiatorial shows and a variety of other events, such as animal hunts that required a great variety of wild beasts, mainly imported from Africa and the Middle East, and battles that required elaborate sets with movable buildings. Apparently there were even simulated sea battles. The Colosseum was so vast that the building was also used as a quarry until well into the 15th century. Most significant in the transformation of Rome was the construction of the Imperial Forums, built between 46 BCE and 113 CE. These are a series of interconnected monumental plazas celebrating the accomplishments of emperors Caesar, Augustus, Nerva, and Trajan. This ensemble of forums was unique in the world, with an interconnected fabric of colonnades, temples, libraries, statues, altars, and public spaces.

In China, the Qin dynasty, systematically annexing all competing states, created a centralized government with a correspondingly large bureaucracy. For this achievement the Qin emperor Shi Huangdi is known as the First Emperor. It is, in fact, from the word *qin* (or *ch'in*) that the name *China* derives. Shi Huangdi's public works included the unification of diverse efforts at building defensive walls into a single effort, known as the Great Wall, that would be the hallmark of China's defense against the northern nomads for centuries to come. He divided China into a hierarchy of administrative units: commanderies, districts, and counties. The system was different from that of previous dynasties, which had loose alliances and federations. He also created a system of advancement in the bureaucracy based on merit instead of hereditary rights. His rule was brutal, however, and his dynasty collapsed with his death. The tomb that he built was at the time, and perhaps remains to this day, one of the most elaborate ever made anywhere in the world. It had at its core a room that contained a vast landscape model

of the empire. The building was surrounded by high walls of tamped earth, and the whole was covered with tons of earth to make a gigantic mound, in the vicinity of which were extensive pits that contained thousands of statues of soldiers and horses. This army was there to protect the deceased in the afterlife. The representations of both man and animal were so meticulous that we have an excellent idea of the clothing and even the bridles of the time.

The Qin dynasty gave way to the Han dynasty (206 BCE–220 CE). It was an age of economic prosperity, with the economy of the Silk Route drawing China ever closer to both the wealth and the problems associated with cross-continental trade. The dynasty had contact with the Kushans and the Parthians as well as with Burma and Japan. An embassy from Rome, perhaps of merchants, is recorded to have reached the court in 166 CE. But as was typical of the Chinese imperial system, court politics and power struggles between the various clans and military elites caused the Han's ultimate downfall. Their capital was Chang'an, the largest and wealthiest city in the world at the time. When the Han lost control of the city in 9 CE, they moved their capital to the relative safety of the east, to Luoyang. Chang'an (which means "Perpetual Peace") was destroyed in 24 CE (to be refounded and redesigned at an even greater scale in 582). Unlike almost every other civilization, the great cities of China were often destroyed not by foreign invasion but by inner rebellion or the transformation from one dynasty to another, when entire cities would be put to the torch. This is one of the reasons that so little Chinese architecture has survived the ages.

From a religious point of view, this period was one of extraordinary experimentation and transformation that developed out of Hellenistic experimentations. Old static religions were replaced by mystery cults and religions that emphasized personal salvation. Along with the established mystery cults at Eleusis and elsewhere, Judaic cults developed a new concept known today as heaven. Christians began following the teachings of Christ; and Mithraism, with its complex system of purification rites and ritual meals in underground temples, was popular

among Roman soldiers. The cult of Isis, with its emphasis on mother and baby, was also spreading throughout the Mediterranean.

In India, Buddhism began to develop into a set of codified written sutras around the 1st century BCE. These sutras allowed the teachings to be easily disseminated and translated. One of the key sites of the new religion was at Sanchi, where a stupa was built in the 3rd century BCE. It consisted of a simple hemispherical brick structure, crowned by a *chatra*, a parasol-like structure, the traditional symbol of high rank. It was covered with stone during the period of the Sunga Empire (187–75 BCE). The idea of a structure as a solid mass harkens back to Egyptian and Mesopotamian worldviews, but it also relates more possibly to traditions brought into India from steppe people who commemorated the dead by making stone heaps. During this time, however, Buddhism's importance as a stand-alone religion began to wane in India, even though it spread rapidly into other parts of Asia.

India was mainly controlled by the Satavahanas (230 BCE–220 CE), who were known for their commercialism. A contemporary text (ca. 60 CE) notes that ships were outfitted to bring "the products of their own places; wheat, rice, clarified butter, sesame oil, cotton cloth…and honey from the reed called sacchari [sugar]. Some make the voyage especially to these market-towns, and others exchange their cargoes while sailing along the coast." (*Periplus of the Erythraean Sea*, chapter 14). It was along the trade routes that Buddhism spread. The Satavahanas produced the first wave of Indian cultural expansion eastward into Southeast Asia, a process that would be known as Indianization and that would have profound consequences to political and urban development in lands from Burma to Vietnam.

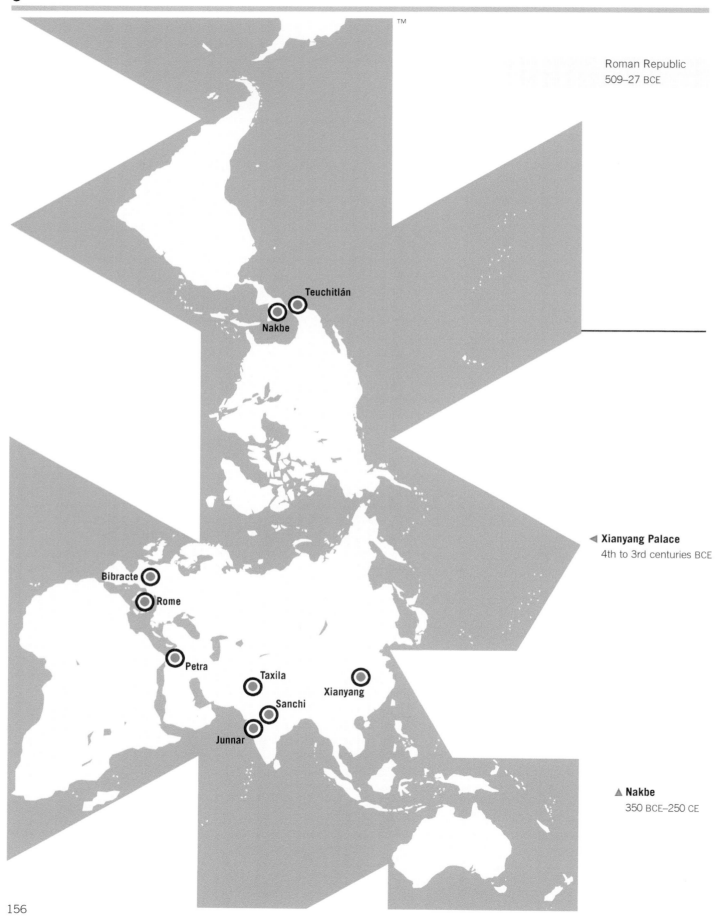

Roman Republic
509–27 BCE

◀ Xianyang Palace
4th to 3rd centuries BCE

▲ Nakbe
350 BCE–250 CE

Teuchitlán

Nakbe

Bibracte

Rome

Petra

Taxila

Xianyang

Sanchi

Junnar

Roman Empire
27 BCE–393 CE

▲ **Imperial Forums**
48 BCE–112 CE

▲ **Colosseum**
72–80 CE

▲ **Temple of Mars Ultor**
Begun 42 BCE

▲ **Domus Aurea**
ca. 65 CE

▲ **Temple of Fortuna at Praeneste**
40 BCE

▲ **Tabularium**
78 BCE

◀ **Pompeii**
From 6th century BCE

▲ **Mausoleum of Augustus**
28 BCE

▲ **Palace of Domitian**
92 CE

▲ **Bibracte**
ca. 1000–30 BCE

▲ **Petra Rock-Cut Tombs**
312 BCE–106 CE

▲ **Northern Palace at Masada**
30–20 BCE

200 BCE	**1 BCE 0 1 CE**	**200 CE**

4239: Egyptian calendar
3763: Jewish calendar
756: Roman calendar
752: Babylonian calendar
547: Buddhist calendar
1 of the Yuanshi era of the Han Dynasty: Chinese calendar

Parthian Empire
ca. 247 BCE–224 CE

▲ Taxila
150 BCE–100 CE

Qin Dynasty
221–206 BCE

Western Han Dynasty
206 BCE–9 CE

Wang Mang Interregnum
9–25 CE

Eastern Han Dynasty
25–220 CE

▲ **First Emperor's Tomb**
246–210 BCE

Mauryan Empire
ca. 323–185 BCE

Sunga Empire
187–75 BCE

Kushan Empire
2nd century BCE to 3rd century CE

▲ **Stupa Complex at Sanchi**
ca. 100 BCE

▲ **Rock-Cut Caves at Junnar**
100–25 BCE

Pre-Classic Mayan Culture
ca. 1000 BCE–250 CE

Teuchitlán Tradition
ca. 300 BCE–900 CE

▲ **Teuchitlán**
300 BCE–200 CE

Zapotec Civilization
ca. 700 BCE–1400 CE

▲ **El Openo**
300 BCE–200 CE

▲ **El Mirador**
150 BCE–150 CE

O

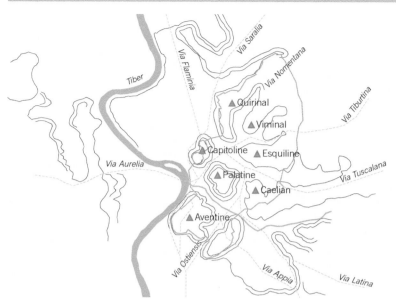

6.3 Map of Rome, ca. 4th century BCE

THE FOUNDING OF ROME

The founding of Rome remains shrouded in myth. From Plutarch, Virgil, Titus Livius (Livy), and other Roman authors, there emerge colorful tales that ascribe the founding to Aeneas's descendant Romulus. Aeneas, after fleeing the burning Troy and various adventurous voyages, arrived on the Latin shores, where he founded a dynasty with Livia, daughter of Latinus. From them sprang, generations later, the twins Romulus and Remus, with Romulus eventually founding Rome, an event that is said to have occurred around 750 BCE. The judgment of modern scholars is that the tales constitute a summary of folk memories enhanced by wishful thinking.

Nonetheless, archaeological evidence has not yet been able to undermine this general narrative. Around the 4th century BCE, Rome became conquest-oriented, and one by one the neighboring cities and tribes were brought under its control. When the Greek city of Tarentum in southern Italy (Apulia) fell in 272 BCE, Rome enslaved all its citizens. The fall of Syracuse in Sicily followed in 212 BCE. The sack of the Greek city of Corinth in 146 BCE brought Greece itself under Roman control, and with the conquest of Carthage on the north coast of Africa, Rome assumed uncontested control over the Mediterranean basin. The religious life of the Romans centered on the Temple of Saturn (498 BCE) and the Temple of Concord

(367 BCE) on the Capitoline Hill. Little is known about these temples, but they were most probably Etruscan in style. The civic heart was the Comitium (whence comes the word *committee*), a meeting place located on the forum just below the Capitoline Hill. It was a shallow circular amphitheater in front of the council chamber, or curia. Though not a building, it was nonetheless a *templum*, or sacred space laid out on a north-south axis.

Over time, a speaker's platform—the rostrum, named after the ships' prows that were hung there following the Battle of Antium in 338 BCE—was added. The forum (which

is the Latin word for "outdoor public place") was more than just an open space. It was a composite of several symbolic layers. A few feet away from the Comitium, for example, was the Umbilicus, the navel of the city of Rome. It was the symbolic center of the city; all distances in ancient Rome were measured from it. The Umbilicus had a cylindrical shape and was about 4 meters in diameter, but most importantly it had a door that allowed priests to ritually feed the "navel" over which it stood. Behind rose the Capitoline Hill, on the upper slopes of which stood a building called the Tabularium, constructed around 78 BCE. Built out along the cliff edge, it featured two stories of arcades overlooking the forum. The building housed the Roman law tablets. At the southern end of the forum was the Temple of Vesta, tended by the Vestal Virgins. *Vesta* means simply "hearth." The women who served the temple took a vow of chastity in order to devote themselves to the study and correct observance of state rituals. The premises were off-limits to males. The women's job was to make sure the sacred fire in the temple never went out; in the event that it did, they would sacrifice their lives. Initially there were two vestals; over time the number increased to six.

The most sacred site, however, was the apex of the Capitoline Hill, where the Temple of Jupiter Optimus Maximus was located (first constructed 509 BCE). The temple measured almost 60 meters square and had three shrines in typical Etruscan manner, with Juno Regina

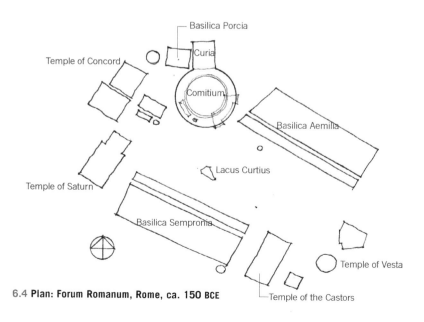

6.4 Plan: Forum Romanum, Rome, ca. 150 BCE

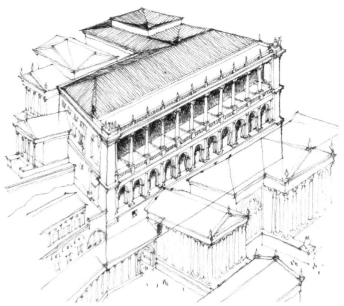

6.5 **A reconstruction of the Tabularium, Rome**

6.6 **A Roman sacrifice being prepared at an altar in front of a temple**

on the left, Minerva on the right, and Jupiter Optimus Maximus in the middle. Connecting all of this to the outside world was the Via Sacra, or "Sacred Way." It was the route of the Roman Triumph that began on the outskirts of the city and proceeded through the Roman Forum. It was eventually paved and during the reign of Nero was lined with colonnades. On both sides of the forum there was a building type invented by the Romans, the basilica. These were rectangular buildings somewhat similar to a Greek stoa, except that they had a central aisle that tended to be higher than the flanking aisles so that light could penetrate through clerestory windows beneath the roof of the higher center section. The buildings served as law courts and as places where legal matters could be transacted. Temporary partitions were set up for proceedings, as there were no wall partitions.

Though there is a debate about who exactly the Romans were, there can be no doubt that they were deeply rooted in Etruscan custom. This means that almost everything was connected to ritual observances, at the core of which was the sacrifice that served as a type of consummation of deals made between the supplicant and a specific god. Supplicants could be an individual or an entire city. Precise adherence to ritual was essential, since deviations could contaminate the results. Important sacrifices involved animal victims. Each deity had his or her own preference as to what was to be sacrificed. The sex of a chosen animal was also significant: male for gods, female for goddesses. So was its color: white beasts were offered to deities of the upper world, black to those of the underworld. The sacrifice for

Mars was usually a combination of an ox, a ram, and a boar. Sacrifices took place in front of an altar and were elaborate and messy routines. The head of the victim was sprinkled with wine and with bits of sacred cake made from flour and salt. The animal was then stunned with an axe or mallet before its throat was slit. It was then disemboweled, and the liver and other organs were inspected. If there was something wrong, this was considered a bad omen and the process had to be repeated with a fresh animal until it came out right. The vital organs were burnt upon the altar and the carcass was cut into pieces and eaten on the spot, with all participants in the ritual receiving a piece of the animal. For large urban-scale sacrifices, this could entail a large number of animals. All sacrifices and offerings required an accompanying prayer to be effective. Public religious ritual had to be enacted by specialists and professionals faultlessly; a mistake might require that the action, or even the entire festival, be repeated from the start. Even private prayer by an individual was formulaic, a recitation rather than a personal expression. The disasters of the early part of the Second Punic War were attributed by the Roman historian Livy to a growth of superstitious cults, errors in augury, and the neglect of Rome's traditional gods, whose anger was expressed directly in Rome's defeat at Cannae (216 BCE).

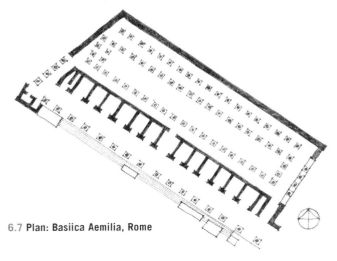

6.7 **Plan: Basiica Aemilia, Rome**

6.8 Sites of Roman cities and colonies

6.9 Ruins of the Temple of Fortuna showing a curved element

Temple of Fortuna at Praeneste

The temple at Praeneste (now Palestrina) was dedicated to the goddess Fortuna Primigenia. Her oracular answers were read by a gifted boy who randomly chose from among oak sticks inscribed with oracular pronouncements. The building stood over or near the site of a town 35 kilometers east of Rome that had been vanquished in 82 BCE and resettled by Romans who, because of the cool breezes, came to use it as summer resort. It was favored by the wealthy, whose villas studded the neighborhood. Since the Romans by this time had conquered Greece, they had come into contact with Hellenism and its tradition of spatial experimentation. It is possible that the structure, with its spectacular series of terraces, colonnades, exedras, and porticos on four levels descending down the hillside, linked by monumental stairs and ramps, was designed by an Anatolian or a Greek, given that architecture in Rome was still a rather new field. The uppermost terrace was crowned by a double L–shaped Corinthian colonnade that framed a semicircular theater, which was itself surmounted by a colonnade. Behind this, on the central axis, stood a small round temple, or *tholos*, cut partially out of the rock, indicative of a particularly sacred site. The upper terrace and the theater were used for festivals, dances, and rituals.

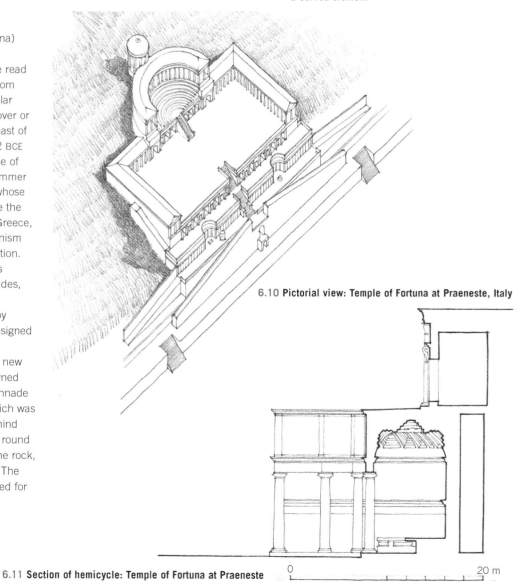

6.10 Pictorial view: Temple of Fortuna at Praeneste, Italy

6.11 Section of hemicycle: Temple of Fortuna at Praeneste

0   20 m

The building did, however, make a unique Roman contribution to the field of architecture. Except for the columns and other architectural elements, the structure, including the support vaults, was built entirely of concrete. Exploiting the potential of the new material, several kinds of vaults were used, including ramping and annular forms. That the facade of the upper level rested on a vault, rather than on the wall beneath it, would have been unthinkable in the days before concrete. Though concrete had been known to Romans since 190 BCE, it was not able to support great weight. But during the period of Praeneste's construction a new form of cement, known as pozzolana, came into use. It was made with volcanic ash from the Vesuvius area—especially from the city of Pozzuoli, from which it took its name. Roman architects might not have understood the chemistry, but they were well aware of its exceptional properties—especially of its ability to set underwater, which facilitated the design of ports and harbors. Though the famous Roman architectural theorist Vitruvius was still highly suspicious of the material when he wrote his treatise in 40 BCE, the architects of the Temple of Fortuna Primigenia showed no lack of confidence.

Roman concrete consisted of three parts: hydrate lime, pozzolan ash, and a few pieces of fist-sized rocks. The trick to a strong bond was not just in the mix but also in the proper application. A formwork was constructed of wood in the desired shape. Laborers hand-mixed the wet lime and volcanic ash in a mortar box with very little water to give a nearly dry composition. They carried it to the

6.12 *Opus incertum* concrete wall

job site in baskets, placing it over a prepared layer of rock pieces, and then pounded the mortar into the rock layer. This involved long lines of laborers, who had to act quickly. Once the process of laying the concrete had begun, it had to be carried through without pause in order to avoid seams. Pouring large structures was a complex, around-the-clock process. Modern concrete, being wetter, shrinks when it dries and is, therefore, actually less durable than that of the ancients. And though concrete workers today vibrate the wet concrete after they pour it to make sure it fills the formwork, Roman concrete was pounded—the pounding, as the engineer David Moore has discovered, being an important element in the chemical process that makes the material hard.

The earliest form of Roman concrete is known as *opus incertum*. *Opus* is the Latin word for "work," so *opus incertum* means something like "worked in," which makes sense since the concrete was layered with irregularly shaped uncut stones or fist-sized blocks of tufa. Tufa is a relatively lightweight stone and is thus easy to use. Over time, a more finished look was produced using more regularly shaped stones. A variant is known as *opus reticulatum*. *Reticulatum* is Latin for "netlike." This form of concrete wall consists of diamond-shaped bricks of tufa placed around a core of cement. The blocks were placed at an angle of 45 degrees to form a diagonal pattern. This construction technique was used from the beginning of the 1st century BCE until *opus latericium* became common in the imperial age. In *opus latericium*, the concrete wall is surfaced with brick.

The Romans also industrialized the production of bricks. Their armies operated mobile kilns so that they could build structures rapidly. In this way, they introduced bricks to many parts of the empire. Roman bricks are often stamped with the mark of the army legion that supervised their production. Sizes, however, were not uniform. Shapes included square, rectangular, triangular, and round, with some reaching over 1 meter in length.

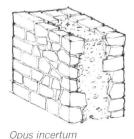

Opus incertum

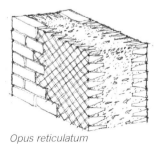

Opus reticulatum

Opus testaceum

6.13 **Three types of Roman concrete walls**

6.14 **Residential fabric of Pompeii, Italy**

6.15 **Plan: Portion of the Taxilan city Sirkap, Pakistan, at the same scale as Pompeii, for comparison**

The Roman Urban Villa

Until the 2nd century BCE, Roman houses followed the old Mediterranean plan, with rooms grouped around a tall, dark atrium. Eventually, however, with increased prosperity, private houses became ever more luxurious. Colonnaded gardens, inspired by Egyptian architecture, were added behind the house. Exedrae and libraries were installed, as well as fountains, summer dining rooms (some upstairs to allow views), and even private baths. Windows became bigger, and walls were ornamented with illusionistic pictures. In Pompeii, some families bought out their neighbors to increase their living space and create a grand house. Compare this with Sirkap, in present-day Pakistan, founded by the Greeks in around 190 BCE; while there is a similarly dense fabric of houses, there is little differentiation in their scale. But in Pompeii, after the abovementioned consolidation had taken place, a single villa could be as large as an entire city block in Sirkap. The owners of these houses, based on Etruscan traditions, placed great value on the social importance of feasting. Meals were elaborate affairs prepared by professional cooks and served on silver plates, with occasional bouts of drinking. In 182 BCE, the senate passed a law regulating the size of parties, but this did little to stem the tide. Villas grew to enormous size and can be found in the Campagna, or by the coast.

Villas were embellished with dining pavilions, towers, colonnades, fish ponds, and formal parks. During this time, wealthy Romans began sending their sons to Greece to learn rhetoric, leading to careers in law or politics. Also admired was Greek art and architecture, although there was less interest in Greek literature, music, and science. Sundials were brought from Greek cities in Sicily, but it took Romans a hundred years to learn that, having moved the sundials northward, they had to adjust their markings for the change in latitude.

The hearth was the very spiritual center of the home, and the woman of the house had the responsibility to guard over it. Just as Rome itself had its eternal flame burning in the Temple of Vesta, so too the hearth was meant to be kept alight. It was at the hearth that sacrifices were made to the gods and the spirits of a family's ancestors. Apart from Vesta, the other principal house deity was Janus, the god of doorways and the chief guardian of the house. Lares, who protected ancestors, was also important. Statues of Lares were placed at the table during family meals, and their presence was required at all important family events.

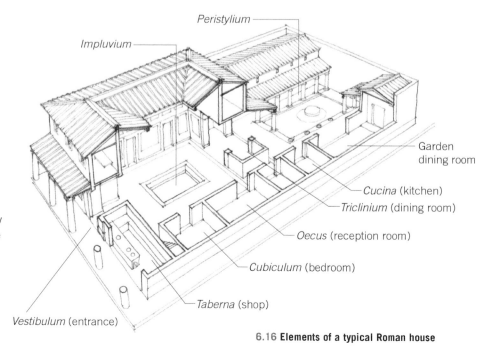

6.16 **Elements of a typical Roman house**

6.17 **Tomb of Marcus Vergilius Eurysaces, Rome**

6.18 **Monument of the Julii, St.-Rémy, France**

Republican Tombs

The rise of an affluent merchant class combined with Hellenistic emotionalism led to the emergence of a funerary architecture that became an autonomous form of architectural expression. Although tomb design can easily be dismissed as a minor architectural typology, it played a key role in offering a field of experimentation in which architects could work out, in miniature, certain architectural problems or themes. Roman temples in the time of the republic were, by contrast, quite conventional—and purposefully so, since they embodied the principle of tradition. Not so with tombs.

The tomb of Marcus Vergilius Eurysaces (30 BCE) is a case in point. A wealthy Roman baker, he asked the architect to design something on the theme of a *panarium* (a tube for storing bread). The exterior is decorated with rows of giant tubes—carved in stone, of course—with a lower range of standing tubes and an upper range where they are horizontal. The top has been lost, but it was most likely a pyramid. Grave monuments of the leading class were, of course, more monumental and dignified, conforming to the deceased person's status in life. The Monument of the Julii in St.-Rémy, France, for example, is sedate and consists of three superimposed zones: a socle, or foundation zone; a four-sided arch; and a delicate round tempietto on top.

6.19 **Tomb of Absalom, Jerusalem**

The so-called Tomb of Absalom in Jerusalem, 20 meters high, is a mixed construction. The lower part is carved out of the bedrock, while the roof is constructed of ashlar. For the lower part, a socle supports a cubic box, the faces of which are decorated with half-columns. Though the bases are Ionic, the entablature is Doric. On this there rests a plain and unornamented attic element that supports not a pedimented roof, as one might expect given the structure's temple-like appearance, but a drum on which rests a "tent." Such combinations are typical of the Hellenistic imagination. The tent indicates this might have been the tomb of a military commander. Although the tomb is traditionally considered to be that of King David's son Absalom, he lived in the 10th century BCE, so this cannot be accurate. Most scholars date the tomb to the 1st century CE. The box is broken by a hole, which is not a window, but was made by grave robbers.

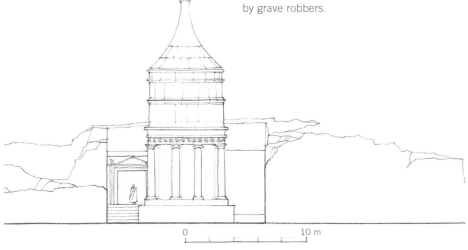

0   10 m

6.20 **Section: Tomb of Absalom**

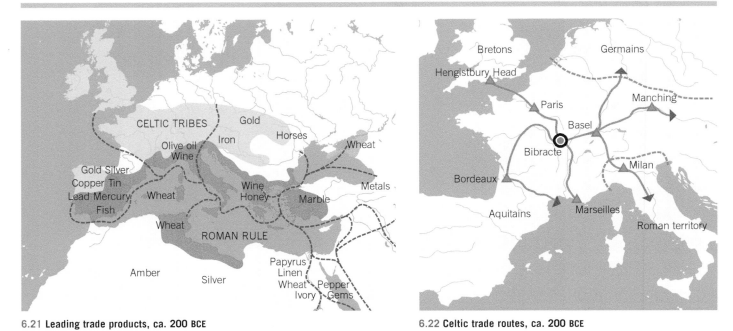

6.21 **Leading trade products, ca. 200 BCE**

6.22 **Celtic trade routes, ca. 200 BCE**

BIBRACTE

Originating from areas to the north and west of the Black Sea, the Celts began to spread westward across Europe around 1000 BCE and soon dominated the area from Switzerland and northern Italy to France and southern England. As a clan-oriented society interconnected by trade, the Celts were suited to the complex and disparate landscapes of the region. They were also excellent agriculturalists, organized around networks of small settlements and farms. Large cities developed during the 1st century BCE. These included, from east to west, some cities that are still inhabited, such as Kelheim in Germany, Bern in Switzerland, and Reims and Paris in France. Most others have long since disappeared back into the landscape, such as Hengistbury Head on the cliffs of the southern coast of England and Manching Oppidum in Bavaria. These cities, the first efforts at urbanization in Europe, were located on flat-topped hills or along ridges that could be easily defended by the addition of earthen berms. The Romans used the word *oppidum* to describe these cities, and the term stuck.

In the cities of Gaul, there was a shift from a largely agricultural and self-sustaining local economy to one based on regional and transregional trade and industrial specialization, such as metal and cloth making. The principal trading partner was, of course, Rome to the south. Most maps

depicting Europe at the time show only the Roman Empire, but viewing the Roman and the Celtic areas together provides a sense of the scale of Celtic territories. Celtic metalworking was facilitated by the presence of extensive forests, even though archaeologists believe that large parts of southern England, as well as locations elsewhere, became deforested as a result of these activities. The Celts also exported salt, tin, and amber. The principal import from the Greek and Roman territories was wine, transported northward with great difficulty in large amphorae. The Celts had a polytheistic and animistic religion, with shrines situated on hilltops, in groves, and on lakes. They worshipped both gods and goddesses, many associated with natural features like springs and mountains. The oak tree was particularly sacred. Their gods possessed particular skills, like blacksmithing, healing, and warfare. Some gods were local to a particular area; others were shared. Priests were not only religious officials but also judges and calendar keepers, as well as guardians of the communal memory.

Though life in these Celtic areas was hardly static, with raids, expansions, and contractions occurring in many places over the course of time, by the 1st century BCE the situation had become increasingly unstable. A set of tribes from Germany and Denmark began to move southward into areas held

by the Helvetii. The Helvetii themselves also were on the move westward, for unknown reasons; to the south, the Romans had begun to chip away at Celtic territory, taking Milan and Marseilles. In 51 BCE, following a brutal campaign, the Romans took Bibracte, one of the largest Gaulic cities, and by 79 CE, most of the Gaulic territory had been incorporated into the Roman Empire. Bibracte stood halfway on the trade route between Marseilles to the south and Paris to the north; the route to Paris continued across the English Channel to Hengistbury Head. Bibracte was also the jumping-off point eastward to Germany. The original name of the city was probably Éduens, the name of the regional tribe.

At over a square kilometer in size and straddling the ridge of one of the tallest mountains in the area, Bibracte was the same size as Rome, though considerably less dense—it contained space for farm animals, and the houses were rarely more than one or two stories high. The city had a population of several thousand, but there were numerous smaller satellite villages. Despite its mountaintop location, several artesian springs fed the city with water year-round. The city also served as a refuge for the local villagers in times of warfare, which might explain the construction of a second fortification ring in the 1st century BCE, about a hundred years after the construction of the first ring. These rings, which are log-reinforced earthen

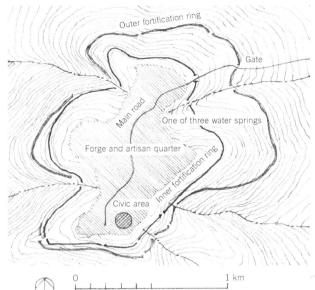

0   1 km

6.23 **Plan of Bibracte, France**

6.24 **A ritual basin, Bibracte**

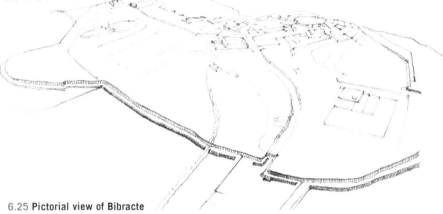

6.25 **Pictorial view of Bibracte**

berms some 5 kilometers in length, were not insignificant engineering feats. They required twenty thousand logs as well as tons of earth and rocks to be packed together to form artificial ridges. A wide road led through a gate to the center of the city, where the civic buildings were placed, including, at the city's peak, an open platform that served communal purposes. On that platform is a large oval-shaped stone well—called the Saint Pierre Fountain—which had a sacred function, perhaps even in regards to its unusual design. The houses were all of wood, though later houses, built by the Romans, were sometimes built of stone and stucco. The city has been only partially excavated, but a forge and its associated artisan quarter have been revealed along its main road.

In his *Roman History*, Cassius Dio wrote, "Caractacus, a barbarian chieftain who was captured and brought to Rome and later pardoned by Claudius, wandered about the city after his liberation and after beholding its splendor and magnitude he exclaimed: and can you then who have got such possessions and so many of them, still covet our poor huts?" But it was not the huts that the Romans coveted—rather, it was Gaul's extensive agricultural and mining network. At first the Romans were occupiers, but by the 1st century CE, the two cultures were highly interwoven. The Romans, however, preferred to build their cities on plains, as they were more conducive to the movement of their armies. For that reason, many of the Celtic cities died out and disappeared. One of the exceptions is Bern, Switzerland. Bibracte was more typical. It was eventually abandoned to the forest, with the nearby Roman town Augustodunum, today's Autun, taking its place as the regional center.

6.26 **Section through fortification wall of Bibracte**

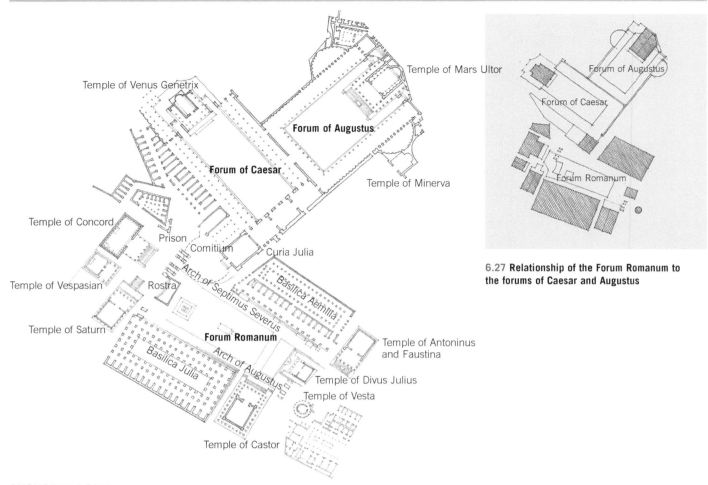

Temple of Venus Genetrix

Temple of Mars Ultor

Forum of Augustus

Forum of Caesar

Temple of Minerva

Temple of Concord

Prison

Comitium

Curia Julia

Temple of Vespasian

Rostra

Arch of Septimus Severus

Basilica Aemilia

Temple of Saturn

Forum Romanum

Arch of Augustus

Basilica Julia

Temple of Antoninus and Faustina

Temple of Divus Julius

Temple of Vesta

Temple of Castor

Forum of Augustus

Forum of Caesar

Forum Romanum

6.27 **Relationship of the Forum Romanum to the forums of Caesar and Augustus**

AUGUSTAN ROME

Rome's shift from republic to empire coincided with the trend of deifying rulers. Caesar was the first to experience such an apotheosis; after that, it became common practice for emperors to be equated with divinity. Emperor Augustus, who followed Caesar, changed Rome. It is said that he found Rome a city of brick, but that when he died, he left it a city of marble. This is not far from the truth, for in the forty years of his reign, Augustus practically rebuilt the entire city, and more than anything, he remodeled the Roman Forum.

To understand the magnitude of these efforts, we have to remember that before Augustus's long tenure (27 BCE–14 CE), Rome was an unattractive and even unsafe city. It had a population of one million; crime, corruption, speculation, and mismanagement caused the temples to be neglected and the public structures to crumble. Many parts of the city were nothing better than slums. Fires broke out continuously—in 16, 14, 12, and

7 BCE—while floods ravaged low-lying areas. Among Augustus's efforts was an attempt to bring order to the core of the city. After a major storm, he asked for a study of roof tiles. He also created a new water system, restored eighty-two temples, increased spending on public building and street repairs, and even established a fire brigade of six hundred slaves.

One of his first efforts was to complete the Forum of Caesar, which had been left unfinished at the latter's assassination in 44 BCE. Rectangular in shape, it was similar in scale to the old forum but enlarged to the north and connected to it by a portal. The Temple of Caesar, built in white marble, sat on a high podium at the narrow end of the forum. The building had columns on three sides, making it appear that the *pteron* and the *cella* had been snapped into each other. The fundamental idea of the composition was Hellenistic, but its simplicity and orderliness established it as a prototype. The new forum, encroaching on the old Comitium, had to

be moved further to the south. The senate house, where Caesar was murdered, was rebuilt so that it fit neatly along the new forum's perimeter, at the southern corner.

Another of Augustus's building projects was the Basilica Julia, which served as a courthouse that dealt in particular with wills and inheritance matters. Typical of the basilica building type, it had no walls, but had open colonnades on three sides, with one of its long sides reserved for shops. The building (101 by 49 meters) defined the western side of the forum. On the eastern side of the forum, Augustus rebuilt the Basilica Aemilia. It had a sixteen-bay, two-story facade, richly articulated with columns and marbles, and was considered one of the most beautiful buildings in Rome.

Forum of Augustus

Apart from the efforts in the old forum, Augustus decided to lay out a brand new forum (10–2 BCE), which was located to the east of the Forum of Caesar and along the city wall to the west. Since it was in a thickly settled area, houses had to be purchased and cleared away. One entered the forum from the south side, on axis with the temple, which was placed at the far end of the forum. It seems Augustus was not able to purchase all the land he needed, even though the area behind the forum was one of the poorer sections of town. A large wall was erected behind the building, both to serve as a firewall and to shield against the squalor on the other side.

The use of statues to depict great men was a unique Roman invention. The Greeks, of course, had elevated statue making to a high art, but their statues were largely used to portray gods or goddesses. It was the Romans who put statues to political purposes to represent the elite class. In all cases, statues were painted to make them more lifelike.

The northern portico frames a temple dedicated to Mars the Avenger (Mars Ultor) in accordance with a vow made by Augustus before the Battle of Philippi (42 BCE) in which Brutus and Cassius, the assassins of

6.28 Temple of Mars Ultor, Forum of Augustus, Rome

Julius Caesar, were killed. There are eight Corinthian columns in front and along the flanks. The plan is nearly square, measuring 38 by 40 meters. Omitting two rows of columns created space for a generous entrance. Inside the temple, in the apse, elevated five steps above the floor, were statues of Mars, Venus, and the deified Julius Caesar. But this building was more than just a temple; it was an imperial statement.

Augustus saw himself as the son of the union of Mars and Venus. The building also wanted to place that rather audacious claim in the context of Roman history.

Forming a cross-axis across the courtyard are two large exedrae. They held statues that told the narrative of Romulus and Aeneas, the great men of Rome's founding. The Augustan Empire was depicted as the culmination of this history, with Augustus himself presiding over this portrait gallery in the form of a bronze statue on a pedestal in the middle of the forum. Apart from the religious ceremonies that took place here, the forum became the starting point for magistrates departing for the provinces and the repository of the triumphal banners. It was also the place for senate meetings when reports of military successes were expected.

All in all, the design and imagery of the Forum of Augustus were carefully orchestrated to further the Augustan program, portraying the history of Rome as a divinely ordained expansion through just wars (Mars the Avenger) toward an orderly peace (Venus who disarms Mars) based on Roman virtues ("manly valor," symbolized by Romulus) and pieties ("filial, religious, and patriotic duty," symbolized by Aeneas), carried out through a long line of illustrious Romans (the statues of Republican dignitaries in the porticoes) culminating in the rule of Augustus, who presented himself as the new founder of "a new Romulus."

6.29 View eastward into the Forum Romanum

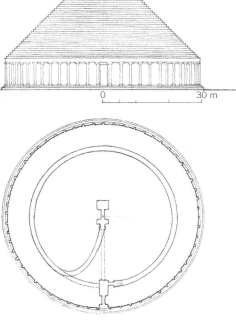

6.30 Kbour-er-Roumia (Tomb of the Christian Woman), Tipasa, Algeria

Tholoi Tombs

In Algieria, in northern Africa, one finds several tumulus tombs that obviously harken to ancient traditions. Particularly impressive is the Kbour-er-Roumia (where a Berber king and his queen were buried, 19 BCE), located west of Tipasa, Algeria. It has a diameter of 60 meters and rests on a low square base. A three-stepped *crepis*, or foundation, supports a ring of sixty slender Ionic half-columns that decorate a drum, from which rises a stepped conical hill terminating in a circular platform 32 meters above the ground. The top was ornamented by a sculptural element that has since disappeared. A spiral corridor gave access to the tomb's interior. Though such a tomb might strike one as alien and not in tune with classical sensibilities, the type actually served as model for the mausoleum of Augustus in Rome, which Augustus had built in 28 BCE shortly after his victory at Actium. This imposing structure, though badly ravished by time, has a tall circular base 87 meters in diameter that was covered with travertine. Flanking the entrance were two obelisks taken from Egypt, as well as bronze tablets summarizing the emperor's achievements. On top of the base there was a tumulus planted with cypress trees, at the top of which stood a cylindrical structure. The building was thus a blend of architecture and landscape, of building and mountain. In 410 CE, during the sack of Rome by Alaric I's Goths, the golden urns, containing the ashes of Augustus and his family members and deposited in niches in the inner sanctum, were emptied of their contents and plundered.

6.31 Plan and elevation: Kbour-er-Roumia

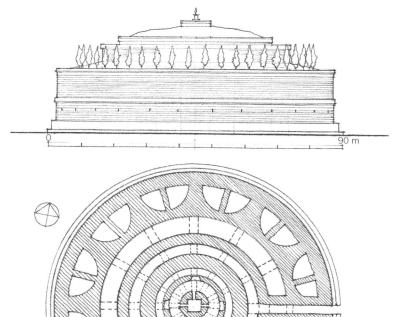

6.32 Plan and elevation: Mausoleum of Augustus, Rome

Vitruvius

The Augustan Age was a boon for architects, leading Marcus Vitruvius Pollio (ca. 70–25 BCE) to compose a treatise entitled *De architectura* ("On Architecture"), known today as the *Ten Books on Architecture*. Though the book contains a vast amount of useful information on construction materials, choice of site, and even the education of an architect, Vitruvius was generally critical of the architectural developments of his age. He was hesitant to accept concrete and felt that many of the new buildings commissioned by Augustus were built without guiding principles. In attempting to reestablish these principles, he argued that the three orders—Doric, Ionic, and Corinthian—should be governed by proportions unique to each. Vitruvius also differentiated between *firmitas*, *utilitas*, and *venustas* ("durability," "usefulness," and "beauty"). Each building, he argued, needed to be designed with these criteria in mind. A warehouse, for example, should be built with usefulness in mind, but not be unpleasant to look at, whereas a palace should be built with beauty in mind, but nonetheless designed for the ages.

The impact of Vitruvius on Roman architecture was minimal, but when a copy of his treatise was rediscovered in 1414 in the monastic library of St. Gall in Switzerland, it became the foundation of architectural theory in Europe for the next three centuries.

Following are some quotes from chapter 2, book 1 of Vitruvius's *Ten Books on Architecture*:

> Architecture depends on fitness (*ordinatio*) and arrangement (*dispositio*); it also depends on proportion, uniformity, consistency, and economy.

> Arrangement is the disposition in their just and proper places of all the parts of the building, and the pleasing effect of the same; keeping in view its appropriate character.

> Proportion is that agreeable harmony between the several parts of a building, which is the result of a just and regular agreement of them with each other; the height to the width, this to the length, and each of these to the whole.

6.33 Corinthian capital: Temple of Athena, Tegea, near Tripolis, Greece

6.34 Corinthian capital: Temple of Castor and Pollux, Rome

Corinthian Capitals

Among the major orders, the Corinthian capital was a latecomer. Its first appearance in architecture, so it is now thought, was at the Temple of Apollo at Bassae (420–400 BCE) in Greece, where Corinthian columns stand framed at the end of the *cella*. They appear for the first time on the exterior of the Temple of Zeus at Olympia (begun 170 BCE), a huge Hellenistic-era temple in Athens. The use of Corinthian columns remained intermittent until the age of Augustus, at which time they became synonymous with the young empire. Thus even though the Corinthian was created by the Greeks, the Romans used it to differentiate their imperial temples and buildings from Greek prototypes.

The conceptual origins of the Corinthian capital are obscure. Vitruvius tells the story of a Corinthian girl who died. Her nurse put various pots and cups into a basket and placed it on her tomb. The following spring, an acanthus root that had been under the tomb began to send sprouts through the basket. The architect Callimachus happened to pass by and decided to model a capital on the arrangement. There is no way of knowing if this is accurate, but the themes of purity and death were certainly important attributes of the column, and the acanthus had long been associated with immortality.

Unlike the Doric and Ionic, which could be transformed only in subtle ways, the Corinthian capital tolerated numerous variations that are usually described by the number of rings of acanthus leaves (typically two). From behind these rise the stalks, usually springing in pairs at the corners and curving into volutes (literally "turns") under the abacus. At the center of the abacus, one often finds a blossom. The Corinthian capital of the Temple of Athena in Tegea (350 BCE) is shorter and has stalks with greater definition than Augustan-era Corinthians (as at the Temple of Castor, from 6 CE), which emphasize the leaves. Sometimes an Ionic capital is added to the Corinthian to make what is known as a composite capital. At the Temple of Apollo at Didyma, the architect added a palmette between the stalks.

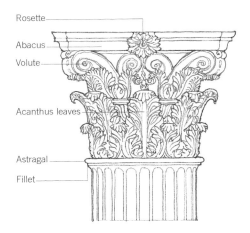

Rosette
Abacus
Volute
Acanthus leaves
Astragal
Fillet

6.35 Parts of a Corinthian capital

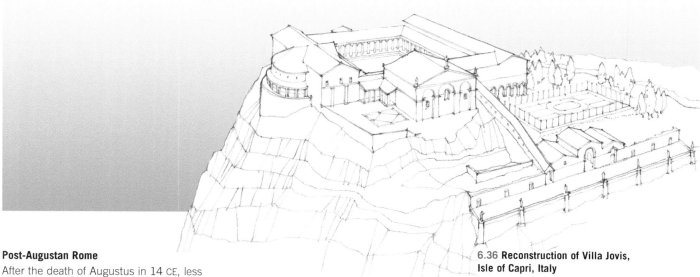

6.36 **Reconstruction of Villa Jovis, Isle of Capri, Italy**

Post-Augustan Rome

After the death of Augustus in 14 CE, less emphasis was placed on grand public monuments and more on lavish residences, picking up on the trend established in the closing century of the republic. Emperor Tiberius's main residence, for example, was the Villa Jovis ("Villa of Jupiter") on Capri, perched on top of a sheer cliff at one end of the island. It was built around 30 CE on an enormous vaulted concrete undercroft that served as a cistern, the only source of water for the villa. A semicircular hall and dining pavilion looked eastward, directly over the cliff's edge. A loggia was to the north of the courtyard, the baths to the south, and the service rooms and a kitchen were in the wing to the west. It was from this grand perch that Tiberius ruled the far-flung empire.

The great fire of 64 CE completely destroyed more than four of Rome's fourteen regions, clearing large areas of land in the city center. Nero, who was always rumored to have set the fire, immediately cleared a place for his new residence, a type of villa grafted into the urban landscape and the stage for complex rituals and ceremonies involving the imperial person. The grounds filled the valley between the Esquiline, Caelian, and Palatine hills. There was an artificial lake in the middle where the Colosseum now stands. Suetonius's description of Nero's palace complex gives some impression of the splendor. Its vestibule contained a colossal statue (40 meters high) of himself. The area covered by the vestibule was so great that it had a triple portico 1.5 kilometers long; it also had a pool that looked like a sea, surrounded by buildings that gave the impression of cities. There were rural areas with plowed fields, vineyards, pastures, and woodlands filled with all types of domestic animals and wild beasts. Walls were inlaid with gold and highlighted with gems and mother-of-pearl; the dining room ceiling had rotating ivory panels that sprinkled flowers and perfumes on those below.

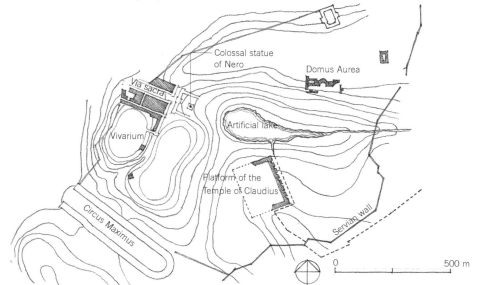

6.37 **Area plan: Nero's palace complex, Rome**

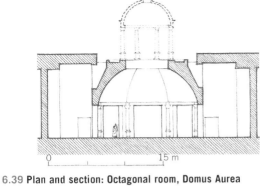

6.39 Plan and section: Octagonal room, Domus Aurea

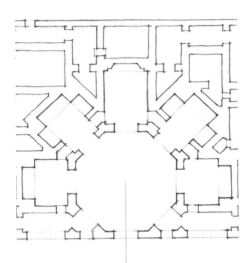

6.38 Interior: Octagonal room of the Domus Aurea

Only one wing of the palace complex remains, the Domus Aurea ("Golden House"), which rests against the side of the Esquiline Hill and is in itself a remarkable piece of architectural ingenuity. It is a combination of small scale and tactically applied axial units. To the east, an octagonal room is woven into a register of rooms to the rear. The vault of the octagonal room was designed so that light could filter in from behind the shell of the vault, which in turn is supported by eight brick-faced concrete piers originally dressed with marble and stucco. Though it begins as an octagon, the vault blends into a sphere at the top, where a wide oculus 6 meters across brings light into the room. Based on iconographic and literary evidence, some scholars have suggested that the oculus was covered by a lantern dome. Equally ingenious is the waterfall room on the vault's northern axis. Further to the east,

a large, open pentagonal court intrudes into the building from the south and pushes the rooms once again toward the service rooms to the back. On axis is a vaulted room flanked by a suite of supporting rooms. The western wing contains a particularly elegant sequence of spaces that, like pistons, connect the front with a courtyard to the rear, ending in a chamber with fountains. The long axis of the courtyard ends in a large vaulted dining room that also seems to back its way into the side of the hill. The brick walls that we see today would have been covered with marble and painted stucco.

This remnant of the palace shows the extraordinary spatial genius of Roman architects. Think of the wing's plan as four different buildings—see labels on the plan— lined up next to each other, but in such a creative way that the whole is seamless.

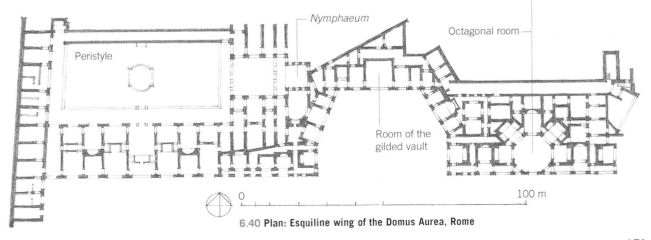

Nymphaeum

Peristyle

Octagonal room

Room of the gilded vault

0   100 m

6.40 Plan: Esquiline wing of the Domus Aurea, Rome

6.41 **Water garden, Palace of Domitian, Palatine Hill, Rome**

6.42 **View into court, Palace of Domitian**

Palace of Domitian

Following a period of violence and anarchy after the death of Nero, stability returned with the rule of Vespasian (r. 69–79 CE) and a century-long sequence of rulers whose policies, broadly considered, brought peace and unity to the ancient Mediterranean world. Peace for Romans, of course, came at a price for others. In 70 CE, Vespasian destroyed the Second Temple of the Jews in Jerusalem and forced the Jews into slavery. About ten thousand Jews were transported to Rome to be used as workers to help build the Colosseum. In the wake of these and other victories, Vespasian's son Domitian (r. 81–96 CE) began a new imperial palace (also known as the Flavian Palace or Domus Augustana), which, on the eastern ridge of the Palatine Hill, was to become the permanent residence of the emperors. It was still in use when Narses, the conqueror of the Goths, died there in 571. Domitian imposed his absolutist tendencies upon society to a degree previously unknown. Under his rule, the lingering pragmatism of Roman culture became increasingly infused with an ideology of Near Eastern flavor with implications of the quasi-divine nature of the ruler. The new palace had to reflect the new notions of power and majesty. The tight, almost chaotic jumble of conflicting axial realities that made Nero's palace so startling gave way to a more

controlled expressions when Domitian's architect, Rabirius, cut a great step into the hillside to create a split-level palace.

The palace was in the upper part, the residence in the lower. Though there is a great deal of spatial innovation, everything is thought through. There are no awkward or surprising collisions of space, as one finds in Nero's palace. The entrance is on an axis that leads through two peristyle courts and into a structure that is at first symmetrical but, at its right and left perimeters, connects fluidly into other spatial configurations. Helping to negotiate the spatial transitions is the ingenious use of curved and rectilinear geometries. The entrance, for example, is marked by a curved vestibule that leads through a series of spaces that expand and contract based on the theme of the vaults above and on openings of different sizes and qualities that lead to side rooms.

At the far end of the axis were two summer houses, located at the top of the large curve of a gallery overlooking the Circus Maximus. On the east side of the palace one finds another register of spaces dominated by a hippodrome, the floor of which is some 10 meters lower. A viewing box forms the terminus of a cross-axis connecting the garden fountain and the peristyle court. The *aula regia*, or audience hall, overlooked the forum.

A staircase leads to the lower level, where the residence of the emperor was located, just at the seam between the two buildings. Roman stairs were never very elaborate, and this was no exception. The principal rooms are arranged around the court with its fountain, while the emperor's private chambers are on the northwest. The central room projected out into the space of the courtyard's ambulatory. To the right and left were fountain rooms. The entire suite was separated from the retaining wall by a service corridor. To the northern side three remarkable rooms with niches, *aediculae*, and complex vaulting formed another unit—a palace within a palace.

To the west is another axis, but one that is enclosed. This is the part dedicated to the imperial state and is conventionally called Domus Flavia. A gate leads to a peristyle court. To the north are three state chambers: the basilica, the *aula regia*, and the *lararium*, or palace chapel. The basilica has attracted considerable attention because it seems to prefigure the form of the early Christian basilica. Though there are many potential sources for this kind of space, there is no doubt that its long architectural life as a proper setting for a supposedly all-powerful figure was guaranteed by its presence in this palace.

Next to the basilica was the *aula regia*, where embassies and audiences were held in a space calculated to dramatize Rome's claim to majesty and unity. It was a spectacular room, with surfaces covered in marble. Ornamental columns attached to spur walls projected into the space. Between the columns were alternating round and square niches, each with an *aedicula* inside, another feature that would become a trademark of Roman wall articulation. Opposite the court was a large *triclinium*, or dining hall. Doors in the sidewalls led out onto gardens with an ingenious display of fountains in the shape of an elliptical island rising from a pool.

6.43 Plan: Palace of Domitian, Palatine Hill, Rome   0   50 m

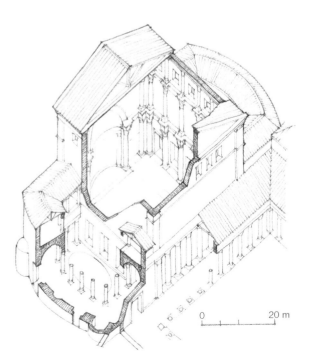

6.44 Pictorial cutaway: *Triclinium*, Palace of Domitian

The building is an example of the brilliance of Roman spatial practices. The designer starts with the courtyard of peristyle. Since the spaces attached to its four sides do not need to be the same, the designer then plugs in components to match the program. These components are usually locally symmetrical, but become less symmetrical the further one moves from the central axis. In this way, the designer creates "blocks" that can then be added to each other around regulating grids. The more this plan is studied, the more combinations can be made of these spaces, depending on whether they are read as recessive or dominant. For example, the southern end of the entrance peristyle hooks directly to another peristyle, which has three different suites of rooms on its three sides. The loggia overlooking the hippodrome is one such unit, the entrance to the palace on its opposite side is another such unit, and the complex set of rooms to the south yet another.

6.45 **Colosseum, Rome**

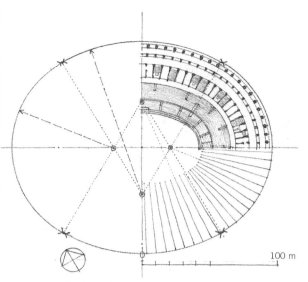

6.46 **Possible method for laying out the Colosseum**

The Colosseum

The Colosseum (72–80 CE), much like the Temple of Fortuna, derives its structural strength from its concrete vaults. If the building, after earthquakes, fires, and lootings, today still conveys its onetime grandeur and even retains, up to a point, its usability for open-air functions, we have the ancients to thank for their bold use of that material.

Though theaters were a common element in Greek and Roman cities, this was the first one that was designed as a freestanding object. An earlier design dating from 80 BCE in Pompeii and another from 56 BCE in Lepcis Magna in North Africa were similar in plan, but both were partially carved into the rock. The Colosseum sits in a shallow valley between three hills, making it visible from all directions, which gave it the status of a landmark from the very beginning.

It is elliptical in plan and could hold fifty thousand spectators, with boxes for the emperor and dignitaries at the centers of the longer sides. Gladiatorial combats and the exhibition of wild beasts did not stop with the Christianization of Rome. Romans remained Romans. While gladiatorial combats were abolished in 404 CE, games came to an end only in the middle of the 6th century. And it remained a place of public punishment well into the 8th century. The masses of stone that came down in earthquakes in 1231 and 1349 provided Rome with building material for more than four centuries.

If the undercroft shows once again the skill of the engineers in designing and organizing a building on this scale, its facade shows the architects' confidence in their use of the orders in relationship to the building's solids and voids. Though ornamentation is minimal, the system of attached columns and arched openings allows for a balanced interpretation of structure and mass. The 53-meter-high wall was divided into Doric, Ionic, and Corinthian layers. The fourth story had no openings, but brackets in the cornice allowed large masts to be clamped against the building to support awnings.

The capitals were stripped to their elemental form. While this may have been for economy, it also kept the columns from becoming merely ornaments. Instead, they seem to be infused with the same purposefulness as the vaults, even though they belong to a different structural system. Furthermore, the arches have an architectural profile created by the way a molding separates each arch from its supporting pier at the impost blocks and lightens the appearance of each arch from the heavy voussoirs of which it is composed. The columns look more structural than they are, and the arches less so. A less skilled hand could easily have tipped the balance the wrong way.

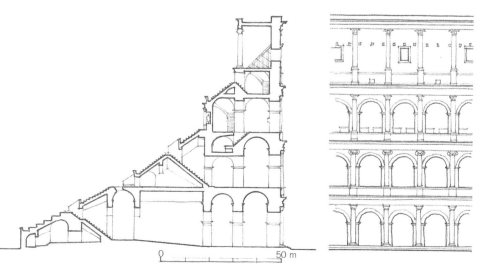

6.47 **Partial section and elevation: Colosseum**

The Imperial Forums

At the beginning of the 2nd century CE, under Trajan (r. 98–117 CE) and then Hadrian (r. 117–138 CE), Rome was at the height of its power. Trajan defeated the Dacians in Romania (101–6 CE) to dispossess them of their plentiful gold mines. Other campaigns led into Armenia and Mesopotamia. The wealth that flowed back into the capital restored the public treasury and insured vigorous implementation of architectural programs. And the rulers set a determined pace. Trajan rebuilt Ostia, Rome's harbor; established a new public bath; and repaired or extended existing streets. Above all, he ordered a new forum to be built. Attributed to the architect Apollodoro of Damascus, it was a complex larger than any of the other forums. Three hundred meters long, it covered more than three times the area of the Forum of Augustus. To prepare the site, the engineers had to chop away a section of a hill that connected the Quirinale to the Campidoglio. The Forum of Trajan was entered through a gateway located in a gently bulging wall. At the far end was the sideways-oriented Basilica Ulpia (107–13 CE), whose apses on both ends echoed the ones built into the colonnade of the forum that, in turn, emulated the ones in the Forum of Augustus.

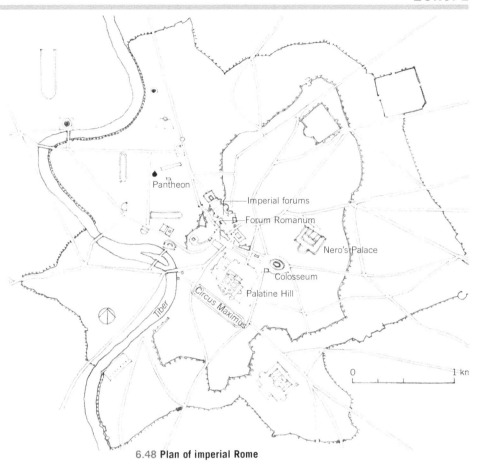

6.48 **Plan of imperial Rome**

Apart from the size of the basilica, it was designed in a traditional manner. Two rows of gray granite columns lined the aisles, with light filtering down, as usual, from a roof that covered the central space. The roofs of the side aisles were covered by concrete vaults rising directly from the architraves, while the roof over the central aisle was probably spanned with wooden timbers. Sculptures and relief panels show the campaigns and triumphs of the emperor. On the main axis just behind the basilica stands Trajan's Column, with a spiral sculptural relief reading from the bottom to the top that depicts the various important events of Trajan's campaign in Dacia. At the top was a bronze statue of Trajan himself. The column contained an interior staircase. The freestanding column, an unconventional feature in its own right, was also unusual for Roman architecture, insofar as it interrupted the axial flow to the temple. But it also highlights the central role of the forum as a war memorial. The column is flanked by libraries: one for Greek scrolls, the other for Latin. The whole complex ended with Trajan's temple, which was enormous, with columns measuring 2 meters across. The forum's unusual design may possibly derive from its emulation of the central administrative area of a military camp: Trajan's Column and the flanking libraries seem similar to the location of the general's standard and military archives, which were set up behind the basilica. Trajan was born in Spain and was raised as a soldier; the military iconography has thus been suitably translated into a civic monument.

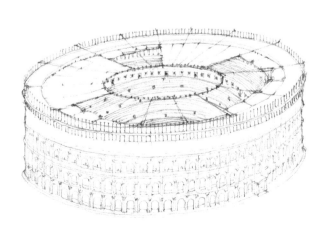

6.49 **Aerial view of the Colosseum**

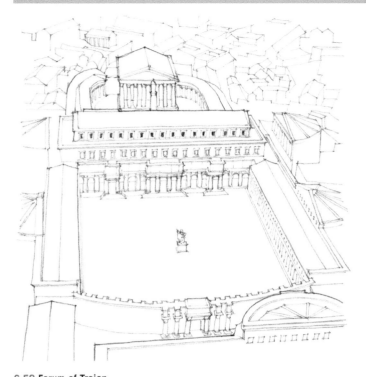

6.50 Forum of Trajan

Taken as a whole, the imperial forums constitute a remarkable urban composition. There are no streets and no spatial or axial connections between the spaces. The axis between the Temple of Trajan and the Temple of Peace (though not exactly axial) is purely planimetric. The elements are simply bonded to each other to create a sequence of open, colonnaded, and enclosed spaces. The words that come to mind when looking at this are *montage* or *assemblage*. The Forum of Nerva, sometimes called the *transitorium* (place of crossing), was the principal connection between the hill and the older forums. A road led to a semicircular piazza on the eastern side, the only place where the outside world infringes on the space of the forums. But even that receptacle forced the foot traffic to the left and around the side of the Temple of Minerva. Traffic, moving then diagonally through the space, exited at the other end on the right, leading to the street that ran along the curia wall. There was no attempt to make this forum into a street.

48 BCE	Forum of Caesar
2 BCE	Forum of Augustus
1 CE	Forum of Nerva, dedicated to Minerva
71–75 CE	Forum of Vespasian, or Templum Pace ("Temple of Peace"), erected after the bloody taking of Jerusalem and the end of the Jewish War.
112 CE	Forum of Trajan

6.52 Plan: Imperial forums

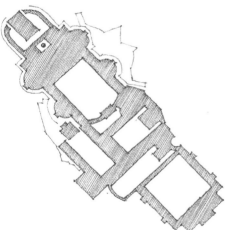

6.51 Figure ground: Imperial forums

ROCK-CUT TOMBS

The idea of making rock-cut tombs is an ancient one. Hittite rock-cut sanctuaries, for example, date back to 1250 BCE. Rock-cut tombs can be even found in Italy dating from the Etruscans. The custom was brought eastward by Darius I, whose own tomb (486 BCE) was carved out of the cliffs near Persepolis. The rock-cut tombs in Lycia on the southern coast of Turkey date from the 4th century BCE; on the front of many of them are temple facades in miniature. Though rock-cut architecture was made in imitation of traditional buildings, construction techniques were very different. Masons had to start from the top so that the discarded stones did not fall on the heads of their compatriots or damage the new building elements. Working from the top down required a different type of planning and thinking; since it was not possible to go back up for finishing touches, one horizontal layer had to be completely finished before the workers moved to the segment below. This applied even for interior spaces, which had to be chiseled from the vault to the floor. The technique was used not only for tombs but also for Buddhist and Hindu temples, and later even for churches. A large necropolis of rock-cut tombs exists in Cyprus near the town of Paphos. Several are designed in the form of an *impluvium*.

6.53 **Plan and Elevation, Lycian chamber tomb**

6.54 **Lycian tombs, Dalyan, Turkey**

6.55 *Impluvium* **of a rock-cut tomb, Paphos, Cyprus**

Rock-Cut Architecture
Some of the main sites, by date.

1450 BCE	Tombs	Thebes, Egypt
700 BCE	Tombs	Cyprus and Lycia, Turkey
500 BCE	Tombs	Etruria, Italy
486 BCE	Tomb of Darius	Persepolis, Iran
312 BCE–106 CE	Tombs	Petra, Jordan
300 BCE–200 CE	Tombs	Cyprus
250 BCE	Buddhist *caityas*	Eastern India
100 BCE	Buddhist *caityas*	Western Ghats, India
100 CE	Buddhist *caityas*	Northwestern India
100 CE	Houses	Tiermes, Spain
400 CE	Buddhist caves	Dunhuang, China
480 CE	Buddhist caves	Ajanta, India
600 CE	Hindu temples	Elephanta, India
650–750 CE	Hindu temples	Southern India
700–900 CE	Hindu, Buddhist, and Jain caves	Ellora, India
900 CE	Churches	Cappadocia, Turkey
1200 CE	Churches	Lalibela, Ethiopia

6.56 **Rock of Naqsh-i-Rustam, near Persepolis, Iran**

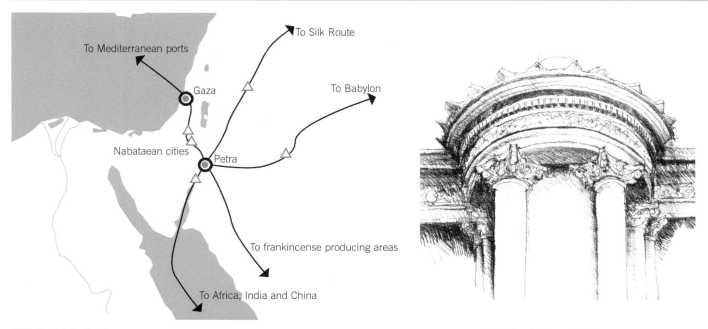

6.57 West Asia, 1 CE

6.58 Detail: Khasneh al Faroun, Petra, Jordan

Petra

The Romans tried repeatedly to control if not defeat the Parthians, the great warriors on horseback who controlled the deserts of western Asia. Their struggle lasted some three hundred years, over the entire period of their empire. In 113 CE, the Roman emperor Trajan even successfully overran the Parthian capital, Ctesiphon, but could not really hold it. This led the Romans to do an end run around the Parthians by making friends with the Nabataeans in Jordan, who controlled the routes to the south and to India. The Nabataeans were middlemen in the trade of luxury items, including frankincense, myrrh, gold, and camels, which they bred extensively. They moved in caravans and maintained a nomadic ethos that did not require the building of permanent houses. Eventually, however, the Nabataeans established several cities that linked Petra with the Mediterranean ports of Gaza. To secure their connection, after 106 CE the Romans, instead of invading the Nabataean area, offered them Roman citizenship, with its much-coveted privileges.

The Nabataean architectural legacy is best preserved in the city of Petra, meaning "rock" in Greek. On this site, temples, theaters, and hundreds of tombs—all cut into the rock of the steep mountains that surround the Petra Valley—still stand in testament to this largely forgotten culture. It is located in the area of Jordan called Edom, meaning "red," from the color of the Shara Mountains that ring the Petra Valley, which is only accessible through a 1.6-kilometer-long canyon. The site was fitted with well-developed systems of water control and storage, including rock-cut cisterns and ceramic pipes bringing water from remote cisterns that trapped the water of flash floods. These innovations enabled the city to prosper. The Romans even built a colonnaded resort with a theater and swiming pool.

The extravagant tombs that the Nabataeans built for themselves as showpieces of architectural luxury are a testament to their important position in global trade. Architecture in Rome, because of its location, tended to be relatively conservative architecturally, whereas in the former

6.59 Water channel, Petra

6.60 **Khasneh al Faroun, Petra**

Hellenistic areas, there was always a sense of experimentation; there, Roman architecture became less "Roman." This was certainly true in Petra. These were no temples, however, but tombs, the most abundant of which date from the early decades of the 1st century CE. Their facades reveal a range of cultural influences. Some are framed by pilasters and topped with stepping "crow's-feet" ornamentation, a motif of Assyrian and Babylonian origin. Others are massive, largely unadorned facades with small, clearly delineated entrances recalling an Egyptian pylon. Petra was thus a combination of caravan meeting center and memorial site, unique in the architectural world.

The beautifully preserved, deep-pinkish facade of El-Deir is a showpiece of the highest order. Its eight columns hold an astonishing upper floor with a *tholos* at the center, flanked by what seem to be the pieces of a broken porch front, the whole then "framed" by protruding walls.

Khasneh al Faroun was probably built for King Aretas III (87–65 BCE), but most scholars date it to the 1st century CE. Standing an astonishing 30 meters high, it recalls the massing and intercolumniation of Hellenistic temples. Twelve columns, six on the lower level and six above, are capped with Corinthian capitals and highly ornamented moldings and friezes. The upper columns are shorter than the lower, but from the perspective of a viewer on the ground, they seem well proportioned. The spaces between the attached columns contain high reliefs depicting Nabataean deities and animals. The griffins that decorate the frieze are derived from Mesopotamian lore. The facade's culminating feature is a round *tholos*, standing largely free and framed by broken pediments. Once past the entrance, the spaces are left plain, since they were largely tomb spaces. In 363 CE, an earthquake destroyed many buildings and crippled the vital water management system, forcing the abandonment of the site.

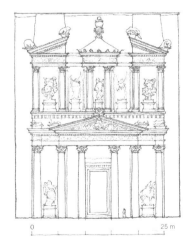

6.61 **Plan and facade: Khasneh al Faroun, Petra**

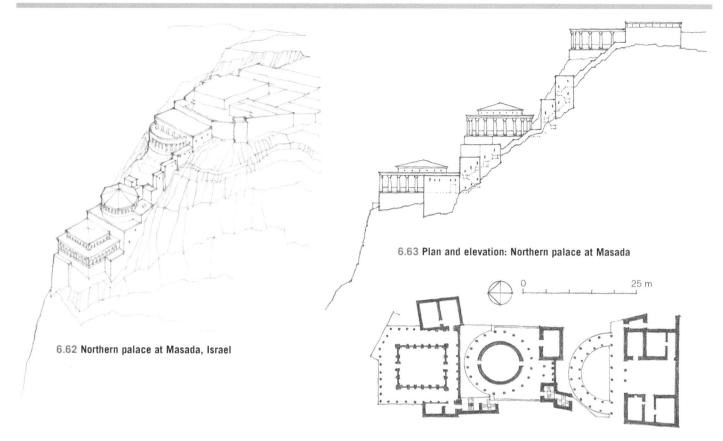

6.62 **Northern palace at Masada, Israel**

6.63 **Plan and elevation: Northern palace at Masada**

0   25 m

NORTHERN PALACE AT MASADA

Another striking example of Roman architecture is Herod's Palace (30–20 BCE) at Masada, a mountaintop fortress city rising above the shores of the Dead Sea in the Judaean Desert, 20 kilometers southeast of Jerusalem. This palace is a synthesis of Roman and Hellenistic design principles. The main residential part of the palace is at the top of the acropolis, while the rest of it descends down the steep northern slope of the cliff in a tour de force encounter between architecture and nature. On the upper terrace, rooms were grouped around a large hall that opened onto a semicircular pavilion or balcony, offering a fine view over the almost vertical drop of the cliff. Steps led down to the middle terrace, dominated by a rotunda and used, perhaps, as a dining room. Behind it, carved out of the cliff face, was a library and an enclosed room, possibly a treasury. Below that was another terrace, with a hypostyle hall and a bath complex. Herod built several other spectacular structures. The so-called Herodion, south of Jerusalem, built around 24 BCE as both a palace and a fortress, lies atop an 80-meter-high semi-artificial hill. Two concentric walls contained the palace.

6.64 **Masada, Israel**

TAXILA: THE GANDHARAN COSMOPOLIS

In the period from 150 BCE to 100 CE, the Gandharan region of the upper Indus Valley—now in Pakistan—was ruled by the Shakas from Sogdiana and the Parthians, who took over this region from Alexander's governors. The Shakas and the Parthians adopted Buddhism, cultivated Hellenistic workers, and brought their own Persian and Central Asian backgrounds to the mix, creating an architecture that was an international synthesis of varying tendencies. Located on a major tributary of the Indus River, the Gandharan capital city, Taxila (also called Sirkap), was positioned at the meeting point of three trade routes, one extending east to the Indian heartland, a second west to Bactria and Persia, and a third to Central Asia and the northern path of the Silk Route. Taxila was rebuilt several times, until an earthquake in the 1st century CE prompted a complete rebuilding.

The urban layout of Taxila is rigidly rectilinear in plan, with a 700-meter-long street running through its center. The whole was bounded by a high wall. Dense courtyard housing of various sizes is organized in blocks around a main street. A number of religions seem to have commingled in Taxila. The city was celebrated in the ancient world as a prestigious center of learning, and for the next eight hundred years or more Buddhist shrines continued to be built here. One of the city blocks was given over to what is known as the Apsidal Temple,

which is like a *caitya* hall of the type that was pervasive throughout South Asia at the time. But this temple was constructed as a freestanding object. Sitting in the middle of an open courtyard and measuring about 40 by 75 meters, the temple was raised on a high plinth and accessed by a large axial stair. The stair was flanked by two stupas on square bases. (Only the bases survive.) To the southeast of the city, on another plateau, is the large Dharmarajika Stupa. The mound on which it sits is surrounded by a multitude of monks' cells.

North of the city, on a high rocky outcrop, is a Jandial temple, a Greek peristyle temple complete with a *pronaos*, *naos*, and *opisthodomos*. The base of this temple, however, is thicker than structurally necessary, promoting speculation that there may have been another superstructure above the main walls and that the temple may have been a fire temple of the Zoroastrians.

6.65 Plan of a Jandial temple

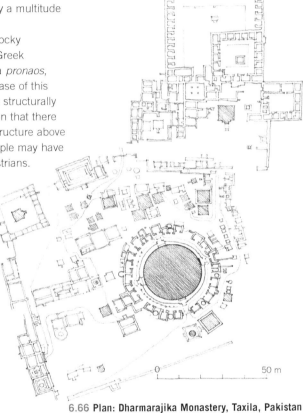

6.66 Plan: Dharmarajika Monastery, Taxila, Pakistan

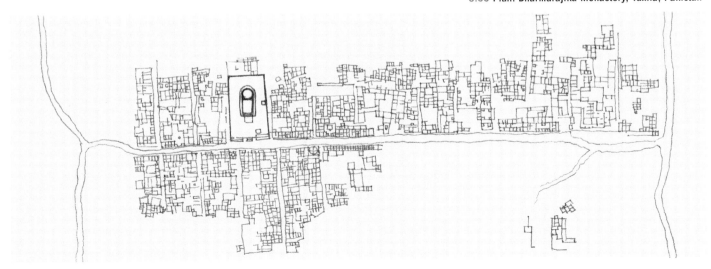

6.67 Plan of Taxila

O

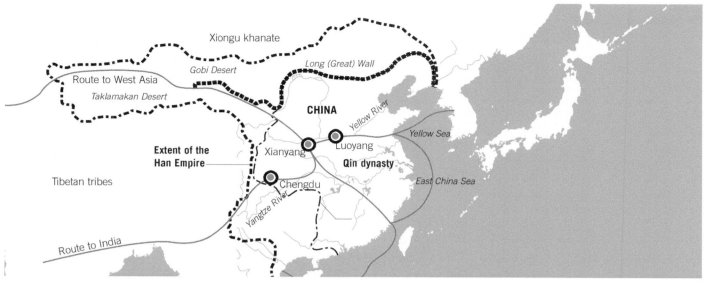

6.68 Qin dynasty, China

QIN DYNASTY, CHINA

After almost two hundred years of civil war, China was unified by the short-lived but supremely despotic Qin dynasty (221–206 BCE). The first ruler of the dynasty, Ying Zheng, renamed himself Shi Huangdi ("First Emperor") and justified his ruthless suppression of opposition on the grounds that he had a divine mandate to reunify China. After victory over the last of his enemies, Shi Huangdi put in place a centralized bureaucracy and administration that could account for the diverse sections of the empire. The system of writing was standardized, as was the language. A single currency was introduced—a copper coin with a hole in the middle so it could be strung on a string. Shi Huangdi also connected the existing defensive fortifications in the north of China to form the first Great Wall to fend off invading "barbarians" from the north. Despite these accomplishments, Shi Huangdi was unpopular in his time; he raised taxes, deprived the nobility of power, was ruthlessly intolerant of those who opposed him, and suppressed the writings of alternative philosophers. Although Shi Huangdi's short-lived dynasty was controversial, Qin (pronounced "chin") is the origin of the Western name China ("land of the Qin"). The Chinese themselves referred to their domain as the Middle Kingdom.

The ideal of a unified China, which was to persist throughout Chinese history, can be contrasted with the histories of South Asia and Europe, where, even though emperors were periodically able to conquer large territories, the idea of a single, unified empire was always keenly contested. It was only as a consequence of European colonialism in the 18th and 19th centuries that India, for example, became a single nation.

The Qin capital, Xianyang, about 28 kilometers west of present-day Xi'an, was built in a very unusual manner as a microcosm of the Chinese empire. Each time the Qin conquered a warring state, the palace of the enemy was destroyed, and a replica was built on the northern bank of the Wei River, facing the new palace to the south. These replica palaces were then connected by covered walkways and filled with musicians and singing women from the vanquished states. The emperor also resettled over one hundred thousand people from these conquered states to Xianyang. This policy was meant to reduce the possibility of rebellion by placing dangerous elements within the purview of the emperor.

Though the Qin palaces were destroyed in dynastic wars, they are described extensively in the literature, and excavations in the late 1970s discovered that these palaces are quite similar to those descriptions. One of the most impressive was the palace of Qin Shi Huangdi himself. It seems to have been

a two-level structure, with the upper level imposingly raised 6 meters above the lower. The upper level is L-shaped and extends 60 meters east to west and 45 meters north to south. At its center was the principal hall, with a large pillar right at its midpoint. A smaller hall to the southeast is thought to have been the emperor's residence. The L shape suggests that another, similar complex was to be symmetrically placed to the east. According to a description:

[He] had palaces constructed in the Shanglin Gardens, south of the Wei River. The front palace, Epang, was built first....The terraces above could seat 10,000, and below there was room for banners [20 meters] in height. One causeway round the palace led to the South Hill, at the top of which a gateway was erected. A second led across the Wei River to [the capital]*

When Shi Huangdi died, his ambitious building program in Xianyang had not been completed. The Han dynasty then proceeded to destroy it.

*Sima Qian, *Selections from Records of the Historian*, trans. Yang Hsien-yi and Gladys Yang (Beijing: Foreign Languages Press, 1979), 179.

6.69 Terra-cotta warriors in the Tomb of the First Emperor, near Xi'an, China

Tomb of the First Emperor

The Tomb of the First Emperor is located in Lishan, just south of Xi'an. Sited on a plain with a wall of mountains framing its southern view, it is probably the largest and most costly tomb in history, even compared with the Egyptian pyramids. Its outer perimeter wall, 6 meters thick and constructed of rammed earth, encloses an area of approximately 2 square kilometers. The main entrance is on the east. Within the perimeter there was a second walled enclosure with four more gates, one on each of the four sides.

Outside the eastern entrance, archaeologists have uncovered more than 8,000 life-size terra-cotta figures, grouped in battle order, rank by rank, some mounted on horse-drawn chariots, others in infantry groups armed with spears, swords, and crossbows (although the spear shafts, bows, and other wooden objects have decayed away). Vault no. 1 is the largest, measuring 60 by 210 meters. In eleven parallel trenches there are over 3,000 terra-cotta foot soldiers arranged as an infantry regiment, facing away from the emperor's tomb. In the eastern gallery are bowmen and crossbowmen in a formation of three rows, making a total of almost 200 sharpshooters. Most were armed with actual crossbows with a range of 200 meters. Archaeologists once believed that each warrior had individual traits—that they were portraits of the emperor's guard of honor—but it now seems that there are about one hundred different types of faces.

Vault no. 2 contains a formation of chariots and cavalry with supporting troops, all turned toward the east. There are 1,430 warriors and horses divided into four groups. Vault no. 3 seems to be the headquarters of the terra-cotta army, with a commander along with 68 officers. This vast buried army was meant to accompany the emperor in death and protect him. Other vaults contain acrobats, musicians, and craftsmen.

The 76-meter-high mound remains unexcavated but recent tests have shown that it is a building of extraordinary dimension and design, covered completely over by tons of earth. The building consists of two bracket-shaped structures of rammed earth that tower over a large central room that serves as the tomb chamber. The Shiji contains a description of this burial monument. For a long time it was thought to be an exaggeration, but now seems to be quite plausible:

Qin excavations and building had been started at Mount Li, while after he won the empire, more than 700,000 conscripts from all parts of the country worked there. They dug through three subterranean streams and poured molten copper for the outer coffin, and the tomb was filled with models of palaces, pavilions, and offices, as well as fine vessels, precious stones, and rarities. Artisans were ordered to fix up crossbows so that any thief breaking in would be shot. All the country's streams, the Yellow River, and the Yangtze, were reproduced in quicksilver and by some mechanical means made to flow into a miniature ocean. The heavenly constellations were above, and the regions of the earth below. The candles were made of whale oil to insure the burning for the longest possible time.*

*Sima Qian, *Selections from Records of the Historian*, trans. Yang Hsien-yi and Gladys Yang (Beijing: Foreign Languages Press, 1979), 186.

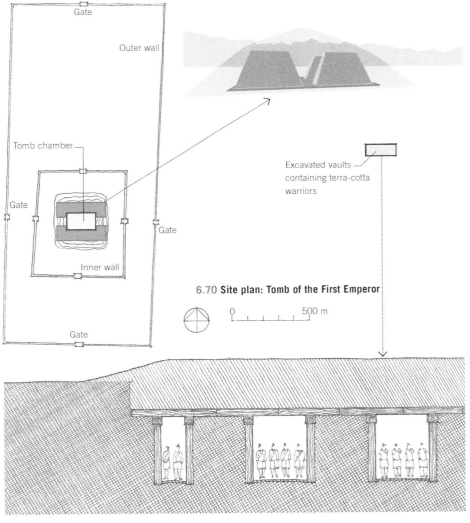

6.70 Site plan: Tomb of the First Emperor

0   500 m

6.71 Section through vaults: Tomb of the First Emperor

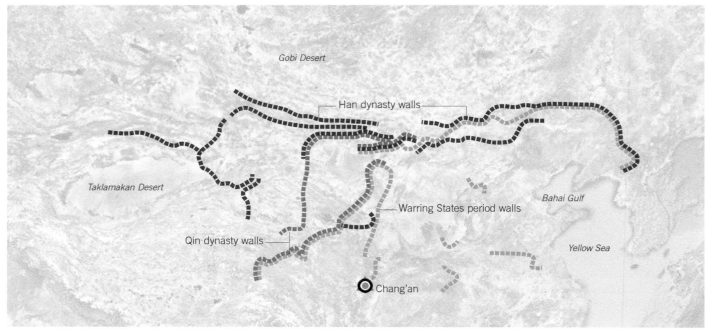

6.72 Construction of the Great Wall during the Warring States period, the Qin dynasty, and the Han dynasty

Great Wall of China

The empire created by Shi Huangdi had few serious enemies to its south, and to the west, the enormous Taklamakan Desert served as an impediment to all but the hardiest of traders. But to the north, the nomadic Mongol tribes were, for the Qin and Han dynasties, the quintessential "barbarians." The Mongols' skill with horses gave them a military advantage that would, under Chengiz (Ghengis) Khan, not only yield China to them but indeed take them to the very doors of Europe. The Chinese response to the Mongol threat was to reach for a radical option that could only be mounted by a highly organized empire—the creation of a vast defensive wall, the *wanli qangqeng* (10,000-li-long wall), popularly called the Great Wall. Small segments had been constructed along the northern frontier in the Warring States period under the Zhou, but Shi Huangdi conceived of connecting and extending these segments, a work that would be continued by the Han emperors. The resulting fortification is not a single continuous structure but a network of walls and towers.

To maintain its integrity, the Great Wall was constantly patrolled, and signal systems were set up to transmit messages from one watchtower to another. It was, however, a failed enterprise. Despite being repeatedly reinforced, the Great Wall was easily breached by northern nomadic civilizations, many of which went on to establish successful ruling dynasties in China, such as the Jin, the Liao, the Yuan, and the Qing. These supposedly "barbarian" dynasties, of course, had less interest in reinforcing the wall.

Extending from contemporary North Korea all the way to the Jade Gate in Gansu Province, the Great Wall had several architectural components:

- Border towns: Of varying shapes and sizes, these towns were small and defensible, complete with moats, walls, streets, dwellings, and watchtowers.
- Fortifications: Small forts, 50 to 150 square meters in area and protected by moats and high walls, served as military stations.
- Checkpoints: Two- to three-story watchtowers were built everywhere the wall encountered intersections or was open to movement.
- Beacon towers: Watchtowers on platforms, from which lookouts could spot approaching enemies and alert adjacent towers by smoke signals, were located about 130 meters apart.

Most of the Qin and Han sections of the Great Wall were made of pounded earth and paved with stones. Some parts, however, were made of Chinese tamarisk and reeds that were arranged in a checkerboard pattern and then filled in with sand and stone. While much of the ancient wall of Shi Huangdi has disappeared, most of what was built in the Ming dynasty (1368–1644), following a route different from that of Shi Huangdi's fortifications, survives today.

6.73 View of the Great Wall of China

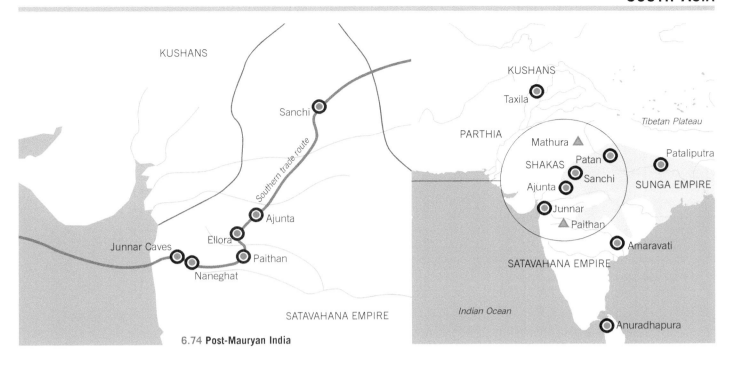

6.74 Post-Mauryan India

DEVELOPMENT OF MAHAYANA BUDDHISM

Late in the 2nd century BCE, Asoka's Mauryan Empire began to disintegrate, resulting in the formation of a series of smaller kingdoms: the Sunga in the west, the Satavahanas to the south, and in the north, the Shakas. This transformation paralleled an equally significant transformation within Buddhism that had important implications in the field of architecture. As originally conceived, Buddhist monkhood was strictly mendicant. Its members lived without money and survived by begging; they were not allowed to erect shrines, acquire property, or deify the Buddha. This form of Buddhism was subsequently referred to as Hinayana (or the "Lesser Vehicle"). In time, as Buddhism began to receive royal patronage and its practitioners became more diverse, a more monastic and populist form of Buddhism, known as Mahayana (or the "Greater Vehicle") emerged that required the establishment of institutions where monks could live and study.

The transformation can be tracked through the four great Buddhist councils called to reconcile differences in interpretation. King Ajatsatru convened the first Buddhist council in the 5th century BCE, soon after the Buddha's death, in order to record the extant sayings of the

Buddha (sutras) and to codify the rules of mendicancy. Continuing conflicts between the Hinayana and Mahayana schools of Buddhism prompted the convening of the second Buddhist council in 383 BCE, a third in 250 BCE, and a fourth around 100 CE, at which time three hundred thousand verses and over nine million statements were compiled and written in Sanskrit. These became the basis of Mahayana Buddhism, which soon began to flourish and spread into Central Asia, China, Korea, and Japan.

Significant parts of the Mahayana credo were articulated by Nagarjuna, the 2nd-century Indian philosopher and the most influential Buddhist thinker after the Buddha himself. Nagarjuna promoted what is known as the Middle Path, a compromise between the ascetic and the worldly sects of Buddhism. He argued that Asoka, as a virtuous Buddhist king, was a *cakravartin* and should thus be considered to have direct access to nirvana, or Buddhahood. Nagarjuna's definition of kingship served as a model for generations of rulers throughout Asia, including the 18th-century Qing dynasty emperor Qianlong and today's Dalai Lama.

Sanchi Complex
The Buddhist sanctuary known as Sanchi was founded by Asoka and flourished for thirteen centuries. The complex is located near the ancient town of Vidisa, along the fertile river valleys of the southern trade route (or *dakshinapatha*). It is located on a hill that rises sharply above the valley, making its stupas distinctly visible from afar. The surrounding hills are also surmounted by stupas, all of which establish the area as a sacred landscape. Originally the stupas were plastered and painted, and on festival days gaily decorated with flowers and other ritual offerings. Large groups of visiting monks and laity alike came to Sanchi in processions.

Stupas started out as reliquary mounds, or *caityas*, which can denote any sacred place—such as where a funeral pyre or consecration had occurred; they were usually marked off by a wooden railing. Asoka had the Buddha's bodily remains divided into eight parts and distributed throughout his empire as relics, with their locations marked by ceremonial mounds (*stupa* means "piled up").

6.75 Stupa II at Sanchi, near Bhopal, India

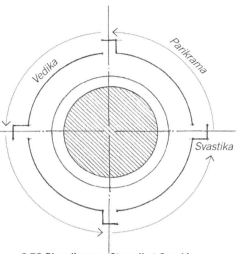

6.76 Plan diagram: Stupa II at Sanchi

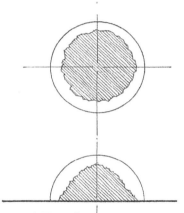

6.77 The idea of the stupa

Built by the thousands, stupas became the dominant symbol of Buddhism. Conceptually, a stupa is a cosmological diagram linking the body of the Buddha to the universe. The fundamental elements of a stupa are present in the oldest of Sanchi's stupas, Stupa II (ca. 100 BCE). The central mass consists of an earthen hemispherical mound faced with fired bricks, with a shallow berm (or *medhi*) ringing its base. This round structure is then surrounded by a stone balustrade (or *vedika*) that replicates a construction out of wood. Both the interior and exterior surface of the *vedika* are carved with shallow reliefs and medallions depicting scenes and events of Buddhist significance. The *vedika* has openings on four sides, aligned to the cardinal directions. These are accessed not on axis, however, but at right angles, through entrances whose openings face counterclockwise. The cross-axis of the cardinal directions, coupled with the directional openings, form a space-time cosmological diagram, or mandala, in the form of a *svastika* (or "swastika"). The directions represent space, and the entrances, replicating the movement of the stars, represent time. The purpose of the *vedika* is to also give spatial definition to the ritual counterclockwise circumambulation of *parikrama*. A Buddhist monk, or a pilgrim, in performing the *parikrama*, engages in a haptic reenactment of the fundamental order of space and time, and in the process, brings his or her body into harmony with that larger order. In Buddhism, as in Hinduism, *parikrama*, along with the mandala and the *svastika* (unrelated to its Nazi appropriation), are still fundamental to architectural expression.

Stupa I, known as Mahastupa, or Great Stupa, is essentially a magnification of Stupa II in plan and has a diameter of 36 meters. An Asoka pillar defines its southern entrance.

At the top of the stupa is another *vedika*—the *harmika*—that is inaccessible and serves only symbolic purposes. In the middle of the *harmika* is a finial, with three stone discs of diminishing size, called *chattris*, balanced on a columnar support. The *harmika* and the *chattris* collectively denote the stupa's vertical axis, echoing Asoka's pillar and completing the cosmic connections of the stupa. The other innovation at the Mahastupa are the monumental stone gateways called *toranas*. The *toranas*, imitating wooden construction, consist of two vertical pillars supporting three horizontal bars that are slightly bent at their center and that project well beyond the posts. The beams end in volutes that connote the sacred scrolls, the treasured objects of the Buddhist *sanghas*. Like the *vedikas*, the surfaces of the *toranas* are elaborately decorated, depicting Buddhist themes and events, completing the classic stupa as we know it.

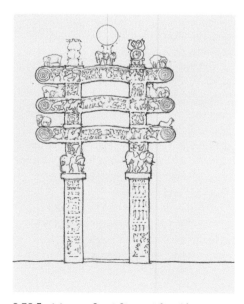

6.78 East *torana*, Great Stupa at Sanchi

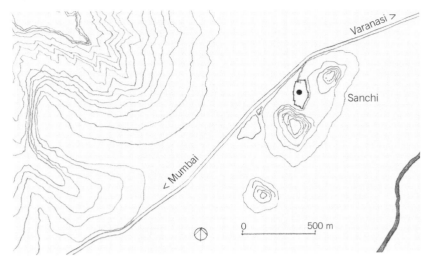

6.79 **Area plan of Sanchi**

6.80 **Steps leading up the Great Stupa, Sanchi**

Sanchi enjoyed extensive patronage and grew into a large monastic complex of Buddhist learning and worship that included subsidiary structures where the monks lived. Over time, a number of small stupas were added to the complex. The more important the person whose relics were contained in a stupa, the closer that stupa was to the Mahastupa. (During excavation in the mid-19th century, most of these relics were removed.)
The Hindus also recognized this site as important, and one of the oldest Hindu stone temples—from the 4th century CE—is found there, close to the southern entrance of the Mahastupa. A relief on the northern *torana* of the Mahastupa depicts a large ceremonial procession, complete with musical instruments and offerings and led by elephants, on its way to the Mahastupa. One has to imagine Sanchi thus—not as a remote monastery populated by mendicant Buddhist monks totally disassociated from ordinary life, but as a bustling center of religious activity where the monks and their patrons enjoyed extensive contact and communication.

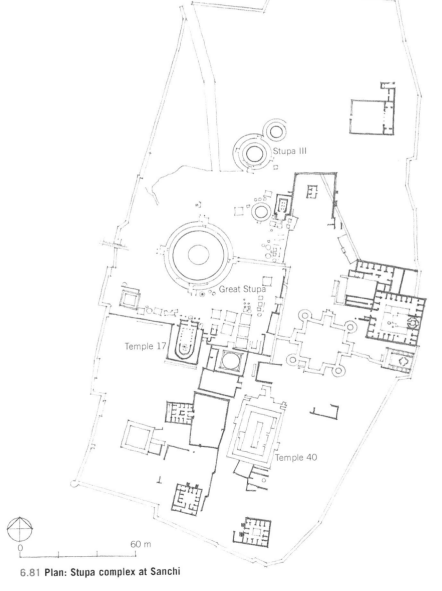

6.81 **Plan: Stupa complex at Sanchi**

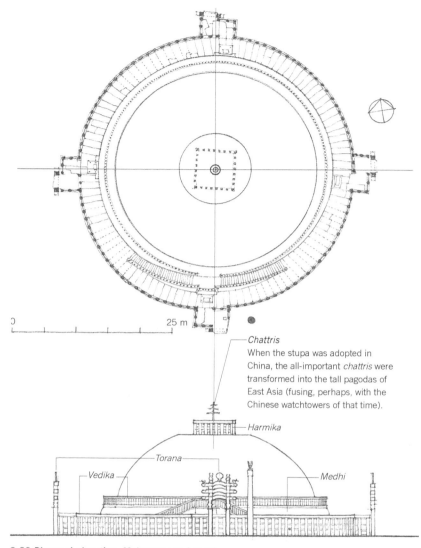

Chattris
When the stupa was adopted in
China, the all-important *chattris* were
transformed into the tall pagodas of
East Asia (fusing, perhaps, with the
Chinese watchtowers of that time).

— Harmika

— *Torana*

Vedika — — *Medhi*

6.82 Plan and elevation: Mahastupa at Sanchi

6.83 Mahastupa at Sanchi

Abhayagiri Vihara

A monastic complex designed around
similar principles to Sanchi was founded
in the 2nd century BCE on the island of Sri
Lanka. Known as the Abhayagiri Vihara, it
was located north of the Sri Lankan capital,
Anuradhapura, and became, by the 1st
century CE, a major Buddhist institution. At
its center was a huge *dagoba* 107 meters
in diameter and a colossal 120 meters
high. Around it were clustered an image
house, a series of assembly halls, general
purpose halls, a refectory with a communal
rice trough, bathrooms, and multistoried
residential dormitories, or *viharas*. In the 4th
century CE, Abhayagiri became the center
of Mahayana Buddhism, which opposed the
more officially sanctioned Theravada sects of
Sri Lanka.

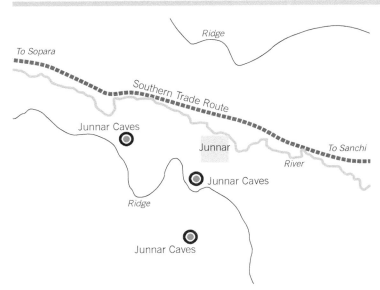

6.84 Junnar Caves area

6.85 View of Junnar Caves, near Naneghat, India

Junnar Caves

Rock-cut architecture has a venerable history dating back to the Egyptians and Abu Simbel (1264 BCE). It was a key architectural method in West Asia. The Lycians in Anatolia were also its masters, as were the architects in Petra. It was used for the first time in India around 250 BCE, and it is quite likely that the technique travelled there along the trade routes. But whereas Lomas Rsi Cave in the Barabar Hills (ca. 300 BCE) was an open cavity, the new caves were of two types: a *caitya*, or meditation hall, consisting of an apsidal hall focused on a stupa, and a *vihara*, or living quarter, consisting of a number of cells organized around a rectilinear, columnar court. By the 1st century BCE, rock-cut Buddhist architecture became increasingly elaborate in concept and execution. Such structures were excavated all over South Asia, but in particular in the passes of the Western Ghats, a mountain chain in western India running some 45 to 90 kilometers inland from the Arabian Sea. Their purpose was not remoteness, however, but rather to be close to the trade routes—and indeed, it was along the trade routes that a growing culture of Buddhist sites arose. The largest concentrations of caves are in Bhaja and Pitalkhora in western India. Because they are man-made, rock-cut structures, they should not actually be called caves, but this is how they are often referred to in India.

Caitya, which in Sanskrit means "that which is worthy to be gazed upon," indicates a sacred place or object. According to texts from about 200 BCE, wandering Indian ascetics often gathered near *caityas* to beg alms from local religious pilgrims and to pay homage to the deities residing therein. Later, the term *caitya* assumed the distinctive meaning of a meeting place or Buddhist pilgrimage site, probably with some temporary wood structures for visitors. Beginning in the 2nd century BCE, *caityas* were carved directly into the rock bluffs in a style that clearly alludes to these wooden prototypes. Over time, and more generally, the *caityas* were rectangular spaces that defined the stupa at its rear.

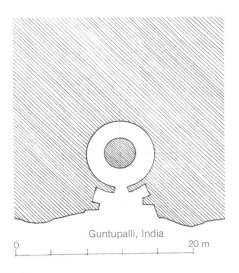

Lenyadri, India

Guntupalli, India

0   20 m

6.86 Plans of *caitya* halls: Lenyadri and Guntupalli, India

6.87 Plan of *caitya* halls at Tulija Lena, Junnar, India

6.88 Cross-section: *Caitya* hall at Bhaja, Maharashtra, India

6.89 Entrance to the rock-cut Buddhist shrine and *vihara*, Cave 12, at Bhaja, Maharashtra

The Tulija Lena (100–25 BCE)—one of some 200 rock-cut temples in the area around Junnar—is significant because a *caitya* hall there is completely round in plan. The *caitya* hall at Bhaja, Maharashtra (100–70 BCE), is, however, a more classic example in that the stupa chamber, with its *parikrama* path and antechamber, is fused into one large space while maintaining the distinctive presence of the *parikrama* path by creating a long, U-shaped colonnade that extends the entire length of the hall. The pillars are octagonal but otherwise unadorned. As is the case with all Buddhist rock-cut architecture, the *caitya* hall is carved out to faithfully imitate wood construction, complete with ribs, inward-leaning columns, and traces of joinery. Ribs of real wood added to the stone vault complete the image. Nonetheless, there is a good deal of debate about what kind of wooden architecture is represented here, since there are no horizontal beams as might have been expected. The meaning of these spaces is also unclear. The hall is more than just a shelter over the stupa built in rock-cut form, but possibly a type of memorial space, with the stupa—which is not built, but carved out of the rock—perceived as a living entity.

The entrance of the hall is in the form of a large opening with a horseshoe-shaped top, reflecting the vaulted ceiling of the hall. Around the central opening one sees a number of miniaturized faux building facades, representing perhaps a city or palace, complete with carved human figures leaning over railings.

6.90 Interior: *Caitya* hall at Bhaja

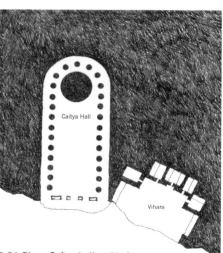

6.91 Plan: *Caitya* hall at Bhaja

6.92 **Urbanization of the Americas, 1 CE**

6.93 **Trade in the Americas, 1 CE**

THE MAYA
Shaft Tombs of Teuchitlán

At the turn of the millennium, Central America was dominated by the Zapotecs, who had replaced the Olmecs, now in serious decline. In the Yucatán Peninsula, in the meantime, the Mayan culture had begun to take root, developing monumental platform-and-pyramid complexes in the Mirador basin and Tikal. At the edges of these great civilizations, in the high lake valleys of western Mexico, we find a relatively minor but fascinating civilization at Teuchitlán, around the slopes of the extinct volcano Tequila. The remains today consist of funerary shaft tombs accompanied by corresponding surface-level ritual architecture created as integral parts of small chieftain settlements, the largest of which probably had about twenty to thirty thousand inhabitants. Though burial chambers were a constant in western Mexico, significant here is that no pyramids or images of the usual deities have been found. The origin of this particular culture and the reasons for their autonomous architectural development are not well understood. *Ancient West Mexico* (edited by Richard Townsend) contains some of the more recent studies.

For the residents of Teuchitlán, funerary tombs had a critical part in establishing the connection between the living and their ancestors. They were used by hereditary chieftains and their families and became the symbolic center of the society's communal life. The earliest type of tombs (1500–800 BCE) consisted of a round opening surrounded by a low platform, from which a short, stepped passage led into the mortuary chamber. Such small tombs from all periods are found everywhere in western Mexico. Little is known of the tombs from the period between 800 and 300 BCE, since none have been scientifically excavated, although tombs are found throughout the lake-basin district.

In the period 300 BCE to 200 CE, the shaft tombs used by hereditary chieftains and their families became the symbolic center of the society. Carved into volcanic tuff, the tombs are generally boot- or bottle-shaped. Vertical shafts are cut between 1 and 21 meters below the surface before opening into one or more side chambers in which the dead were interred, along with a large offering of hollow ceramic figures, shell jewelry, obsidian jewelry, ground stone, and other items. There is evidence that the tombs held burials from different times and were therefore reopened as necessary. A ceramic model from one of the tombs shows the house of the living above and the house of the dead below.

6.94 **Model of a temple sited on an elevated platform**

O

Of the shaft tombs of the period between 300 BCE and 200 CE, the largest, at El Arenal, has an 18-meter shaft and three burial chambers. Two other shaft tombs are located within the same ceremonial area. On the surface, the shaft emerged at the center of a circular stepped mound that was surrounded by an elevated circular patio, at the edge of which were eight to twelve evenly spaced rectangular platforms. Made of rubble and packed earth, the larger complexes of the later phase (300–800 CE) range from 28 meters in diameter at Potrero de las Chivas to well over 100 meters at Guachimonton, the largest of the Teuchitlán ritual sites. The circles were often found in groups of two or three, with some of the circles overlapping. Ball courts were also found in association with these circles. Later, in the period from 300 to 800 CE, shaft tombs became less important, and huge surface circles, along with ball courts, came to dominate the construction, to the point that their burial chambers are as yet undiscovered.

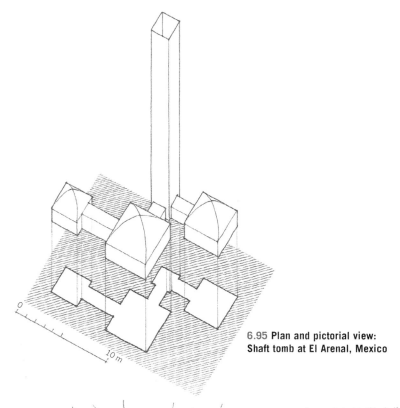

6.95 Plan and pictorial view: Shaft tomb at El Arenal, Mexico

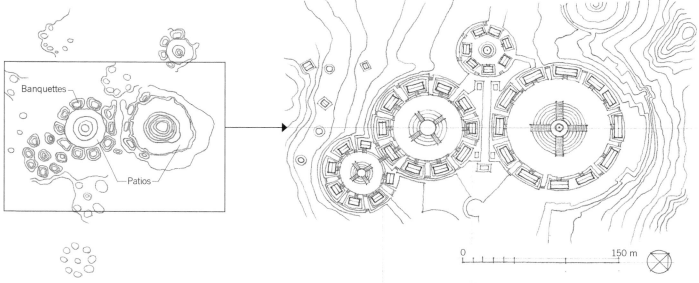

6.96 Site plan: Guachimonton precinct at Teuchitlán, near Ameca, Mexico

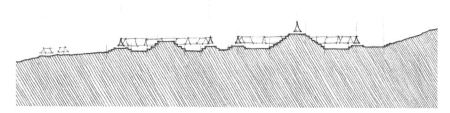

6.97 Plan and section: Central circular structures of the Guachimonton complex at Teuchitlán

The graves of El Arenal, like most shaft tombs, have been looted or destroyed. One that has been excavated intact at Huitzilapa is a shaft tomb 8 meters deep, with two burial chambers, several burials, and about sixty thousand artifacts. The tomb sits at the western end of the 50-by-200-meter settlement. At the eastern end is a large, elongated ball court. The center of the settlement is dominated by a religious complex consisting of eight platform mounds surrounding a circular pyramid. This complex abuts another, smaller circular complex to its west consisting of four platform mounds fronting onto a square court with a small circular pyramid in the middle. The shaft tomb is located in one of the mounds. Low abutments indicate that the four platforms were linked together in a ring at their base. The shaft tapers about one-third of its way down and then opens into two domical chambers, oriented north-south, which are entered through narrow openings and stairs. Within, six skeletons, one of which is clearly that of the chieftain, are laid out with their heads toward the entrance, surrounded by offerings.

Clay models found with the offerings testify to the self-consciousness of the designs, linking community festivals to the order of the cosmos, the rhythms of the seasons, and the cycle of life and death. The circle replicates the encompassing ring of the horizon; cardinal and intercardinal orientations are established by pyramid stairways along axes related to the path of the sun. The models show a tall mast rising from the central pyramid, which in mystical parlance would be the axis mundi, connecting the apex of the sky to the central point of the earth's surface and to the underworld nadir. These sites were also the location of observations and rites on the day of the summer solstice, the annual time of the sun's zenith passage, the beginning of the rainy season, and the renewal of the earth's fertility.

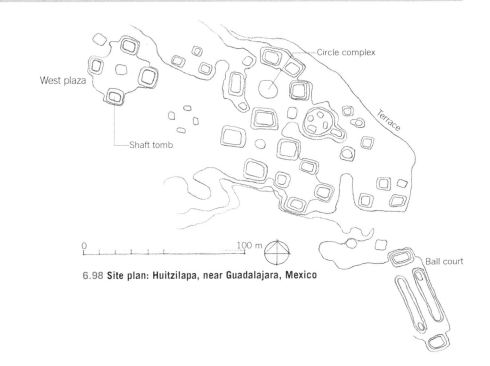

6.98 Site plan: Huitzilapa, near Guadalajara, Mexico

6.99 Pictorial view of Huitzilapa

Nakbe

The Mayan civilization, initially centered on the coastlines of Guatemala and El Salvador, spread northward between 250 and 900 CE into the Yucatán Peninsula. At its peak, it was one of the most densely populated and culturally dynamic societies in the world. Many of the pre-classical sites declined by the 3rd century CE, leaving the cities in northern Guatemala dominant. The Mayas developed a religious philosophy controlled by a professional priesthood built around the importance of astronomical manifestations that were part of the eternal struggle between the powers of good and evil. The benevolent gods brought thunder, lightning, and rain, and insured abundance, whereas the malevolent ones brought death, destruction, hurricanes, and war. The religion developed into a worship of time in its various manifestations; it was highly esoteric in nature, requiring priests, mathematicians, and prophets. Dancing was an important aspect of religious ceremonies, as was the giving of sacrifices. These ranged from food offerings and ornaments (like feathers and shells) to the practice of human sacrifice.

This specialized production and dependency on foreign trade might have been the reason for both the success and the eventual demise of the Mayas. Trees were felled to fuel the kilns in which limestone was burned. Deforestation, it has been suggested, led to a gradual erosion of both land and wealth. By 350 BCE, a centralized elite was able to control large labor populations whose rapid rate of production was aided by the development of standardized construction modules and faster stonecutting techniques. It is during this period that monumental Mayan architecture—at a scale never seen previously—emerged in the Yucatán Peninsula. An abundance of massive architectural assemblages, ranging from 40 to 72 meters high, are found in the Mirador basin. Since they are located in marshes, all the major building groups were raised on large platforms that were then connected by elevated causeways.

Located in the Petén region of Guatemala, habitation at Nakbe started around 1400 BCE, reaching its height between 600 and 350 BCE. Its central area was constructed on a massive man-made platform surmounted by three mounds. The mounds contained clusters of temples, with the tallest structure, at 50 meters, on the west platform; the one on the east platform was 30 meters high. Nakbe was linked by causeways made of white crushed rock to adjoining settlements, including the one at El Mirador, its rival to the north.

In general, the organization of early Mayan ceremonial complexes was devoted to creating distinct visual hierarchies by means of a system of interconnected raised platform terraces surmounted by temples. The central ceremonial complex at Nakbe consists of two major, connected, built-up platforms (the eastern one 32 meters high, and the western one 45 meters high), on top of which the principal structures are clustered.

6.100 Stela 1, the hero Twins, Nakbe, Guatemala

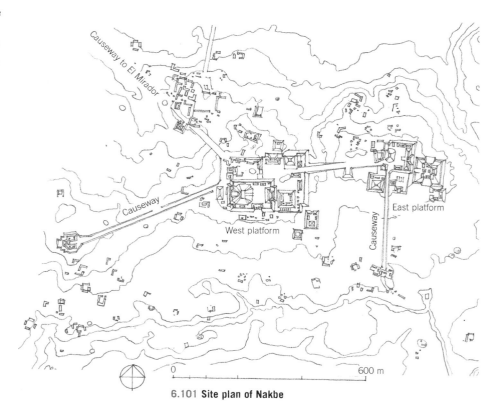

6.101 Site plan of Nakbe

The eastern platform has two parts. One is a cluster of low-platform structures on a terrace, creating a court that is anchored on its west side by a large freestanding pyramid. The other part has a larger pyramid, which is visible from the court, but whose access was restricted to priestly use. Thus a complex ceremonial whole was formed—with multiple hierarchically organized spatial and visual centers—that was used for a variety of ceremonial functions.

Across the causeway is the western platform, which consists of three terraced courtyards, the highest of which supports the large pyramid; as with the others, access is restricted through the small courtyard in front of it. Since the function of Mayan pyramids was to support the temple, they were always flat-topped. The pyramid itself consisted of tightly compressed layers of stones and clay sealed by a brick casing.

El Mirador

Just north of Nakbe, El Mirador (Spanish for "lookout") was an early Mayan city that reached its cultural high point between 150 BCE and 150 CE. Though the city was spread out over an area of 16 square kilometers, the center was a crowded constellation of sacred and secular buildings. Here the platforms have been built up successively over time, comprising the largest set of platforms found anywhere in the Mayan world. The entire site was dominated by the so-called El Tigre, a gigantic building complex covering 5.6 hectares, in which the emerging Mayan typology of the triple-summit structures can be seen. These generally consisted of a steep platform mountain having at its summit two smaller buildings facing each other in front of an axially placed stepped pyramid temple. Archaeologists believed that this arrangement represented the three stars in the constellation of Orion— known as Alnitak, Saiph, and Ligel—within which was supposed to burn the fire of creation.

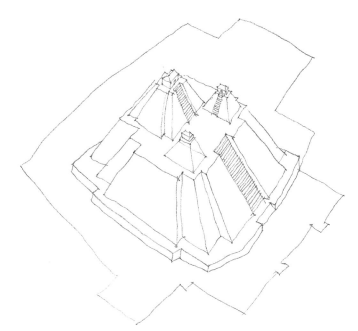

6.102 Reconstruction of El Tigre, El Mirador, Guatemala

6.103 Site plan: The west group at El Mirador

6.104 **El Tigre, El Mirador, Guatemala, as it stands today**

200 CE

7.1 Pont du Gard (Roman aqueduct), Nîmes, France

INTRODUCTION

In the year 200 CE, Rome, Chang'an, and Teotihuacán were the world's megacities; all three were the capitals of vast empires. Cities at this scale impacted the world even in far-off places. They required an extensive trade in luxury items, with everything embedded in a system of revenue production, collection, and control, not to mention an army and territorial mastery. Above all, there had to be an imperial awe. And in this respect, the idea of "tradition" in both Rome and China was not a phenomenon emerging naturally over time. It had to be enforced and re-enforced from the top down, against the rising tide of social and economic transformations.

Between 100 and 300 CE, the Roman Empire in particular grew into one of the greatest and most extensive empires in the world. For centuries, it had traded with the Celts to the north, mainly exchanging metals for Roman wine, but once Rome had conquered the Celts and Romanized them, the Romans discovered that the Germanic tribes to the east were much more difficult to pacify. The expansion of the territory paid off, however, in the short term. Wealth was lavished on temples, palaces, baths, aqueducts, libraries, courts, streets, theaters, and amphitheaters. The development of Roman architecture, the most extensive urban architecture of any civilization to that date, reached from England to North Africa and from Spain to the Levant, and would

have a profound impact on subsequent developments throughout Europe and beyond for centuries to come. The Han dynasty in China was also building cities, palaces, and tombs on a massive scale, helped by remarkable advances in technology and mining. But because their architecture was all built out of wood and tamped earth, comparatively little has survived the ages. Their western capital, Chang'an, served as the Silk Route's eastern terminus.

Both Rome and China, in facing the rapid changes that came with expansion and cross-cultural contact, came to place strong counter-emphasis on tradition, which was instrumentalized as a condition of state control. Traditions were promulgated and enforced as a way to define the principle of stability. Augustus, the first emperor, claimed that he needed to create an empire precisely to restore Roman tradition to its former glory. And in China, tradition was imposed and self-imposed on the Chinese through Confucianism, which promoted security and predictability for the elites.

Linking China and Rome were the Parthians, a horse-based tribal society of former nomads who established themselves as a ruling elite in Mesopotamia and Central Asia. Since they were not an architecture-oriented culture, they allowed local cults to continue. But they were keen traders and played an important part in maintaining the Silk Route; their capital, Hecatompylos,

7.2 Trade routes across Asia, 2nd and 3rd centuries CE

became one of its prime stopping places. The Parthians eventually lost control of the Iranian highlands to a new lineage that came to be known as the Sassanians, who unified their control under the heading of Zoroastrianism. They built numerous cities, many of them circular, presumably to give the inhabitants a defensive tactical advantage. Among these was Firuzabad, built under Ardashir I (r. 224–42 CE). It had a diameter of 2 kilometers, with two roads dividing it into four districts, which in turn were divided into five smaller sectors and thus ordered the entire city in twenty sectors. The detailed planning seems to have continued in the surrounding landscape. The Sassanians also built enormous citadels, such as the Falak-ol-Aflak Castle (226–651 CE), situated on the top of a large hill within the city of Khorramabad, Iran. This gigantic structure measured approximately 300 by 400 meters and had twelve towers and massive walls.

The religious innovations taking place in various parts of Eurasia, in combination with the cross-Asian circulatory system that was now abuzz with traffic, led to important transformations in western Asia with long-term ramifications beyond its immediate geographical range. The old Mesopotamian religions with their complex pantheons were superseded by Hellenistic and Iranian mystery cults, by sun cults,

by Zoroastrianism's fire worship—and by Christianity, itself an outgrowth of Hellenistic sensibilities. Generally, these new religious practices were more personal than their forerunners. Another emerging religion, Mithraism, was increasingly practiced by the soldiery in the far-flung provinces of the Roman Empire and would impact Christianity. Buddhism, which has to be understood as part of this search for ethical self-transformation, was also developing rapidly, moving deeper and deeper into China and Southeast Asia in the form of monastic schools located along the trade routes.

In Central Asia, the nomadic Yueh-chi from Mongolia established the Kushan Empire (1st century BCE to 3rd century CE) that stretched from parts of Afghanistan and Iran to Pataliputra in the central Gangetic Plains in the east and down to Sanchi in the south, the location of the greatest Buddhist sanctuary of the time. Though nomadic, they quickly adopted the typical cross-Asian organization of society, where they, as the aristocratic warrior class, were on top. Below them were the merchants, and below the merchants were the artisans and peasants.

The Kushans understood the uniqueness of their geographical location in the former Graeco-Bactrian world. They had three basic agendas: to actively promote trade along the Silk Route; to promote artisanal

production of luxury goods; and finally, to promote the expansion of agriculture in the otherwise mountainous and arid lands. India exported spices like pepper, ginger, and saffron, as well as sugar, dyes, perfumes, and gems. Trade was a hugely lucrative business for Kushans, who augmented this with commodities that they produced, like bronze, tin, and glassware. The new rulers also developed local industries like silversmithing for jewelry and ironsmithing for weapons. And finally, they made miles and miles of canals to irrigate mountain slopes and valleys. One of these is the Zang Canal, located in Surxondaryo, Uzbekistan, which drew water from Surkhan River. There were similar canals along the Amu Darya. The water irrigated the vineyards the Kushans planted, as wine, the drink of the Greeks, was now an important luxury export to India. This astonishing burst of activity, far from the traditional centers of civilization, resulted in an empire that was unique. It became a melting pot for people and ideas from India, Persia, China, and even the Roman Empire.

At first the Kushans absorbed the remnants of the Greek culture of the Hellenistic kingdoms, becoming at least partly Hellenized. They even spoke Greek. Some of the elites adopted Zoroastrianism from the Persians, others embraced some form of Hinduism, and yet others became Buddhist.

Whereas their first coins depict the Kushans dressed in heavy coats and big felt hats appropriate to the steppe, later coins show them dressed in Greek togas or lightweight tunics. The first documented translation efforts by foreign Buddhist monks in China were in the 2nd century CE, probably as a consequence of the expansion of the Kushan Empire into the Chinese territory of the Tarim Basin. Their most lasting contributions to architecture were the stupas that they began to erect along the trade routes. Few have survived, but the Kanishka Stupa—built for Kanishka I (ca. 127–40 CE)—on the outskirts of today's Peshawar, Pakistan, was described by Chinese pilgrims in the 7th century as the tallest stupa in all of India. It rose to about 200 meters and contained three bone fragment relics of the Buddha, which have now been transferred to Mandalay, Myanmar (Burma). Only a stump remains of the original building. Hans Loeschner suggests that it might have appeared similar to the stone relief from Butkara III in Swat Valley, which shows a stupa placed on a tall square base. In the corners there are four pillars with lions at the top, similar to many of the Ashoka pillar with lion capitals, such as the one at Vaisali, India.

One of the major impediments on the Silk Route was the Taklamakan Desert, a vast oval desert surrounded by mountains. However, rivers running down from the mountains provided enough water for caravans to move around the edges of the desert from one oasis to another. One of these was Khotan, the center of a small kingdom. The Chinese pilgrim Xuanzang passed through Khotan around 644 CE on his way back from India to China and wrote:

> This country is renowned for its music; the men love the song and dance. Few of them wear garments of skin and wool; most wear taffeta and white linen. Their external behavior is full of urbanity; their customs are properly regulated. Their written characters and their mode of forming their sentences resemble the Indian model; the forms of the letters differ somewhat; the differences, however, are slight….There are about a hundred sangharamas [monasteries/nunneries] with some 5000 followers, who all study the doctrine of the Great Vehicle.*

Si-yu-ki Buddhist Records, vol. 2 (London, 1884), 309.

7.3 A stupa from a cave mural in China

During this time, the southern maritime trade routes from Egypt by way of the eastern coast of Africa to India, Indonesia, and China were beginning to develop into a trade network as important as the land-based Silk Route. The Romans, seeking to circumvent the vicissitudes of the cross-desert trade, saw places like Petra as veritable port cities linking trade to India and beyond. And like Petra, Aksum in modern Ethiopia had become by this time a significant regional force, trading with India and, northward, with the Roman Empire. In summary, it can be said that the 3rd century CE saw the maturation of a new world order, namely that of transregional, transcontinental trade interdependency, especially in luxury goods. It was a world order that would continue to escalate with the emergence of the great Mongolian Empire in the 13th century.

In all of this, it is important to remember that the trading world that stretched from Rome through India and China was extraordinarily narrow. It did not yet include Southeast Asia; Africa, apart from the Ethiopian and Mediterranean coasts, was largely on its own, as was the Siberian north.

In Peru, one sees regional states emerging: the Moche in the north and, in the south, the Nazca, who produced large pilgrimage centers such as Cahuachi, where mysterious patterns on the ground

later appeared, celebrated today as the Nazca Lines. The purpose of these elaborate designs—whose full impact can only be appreciated from the air—remains unresolved, as do questions about the nature of the Nazcas' religious practices, to which they seem related. In Mexico, the superpower of the region was unquestionably Teotihuacán, the capital of an empire that encompassed most of Central America and that was the center of a trading network extending from the Mississippi Delta to the Peruvian coast. Teotihuacán was the largest and most influential city of pre-colonial America. All subsequent architecture in Central America was impacted by its legacy.

In the Americas, the Hopewell Culture became the first large-scale culture in North America, spreading a web of cities and villages along the Ohio River. It was a unique culture in that it specialized in ceremonialism. The Hopewell controlled land rich in salt, flint, and pipestone, and people from far away would come to gather or mine these materials. But to do this, they had to bring gifts and participate in elaborate ceremonial exchanges. The Hopewell built large enclosures, hundreds of meters across and shaped in various ways. They also lined the rivers and streams with ancestor mounds, producing a complex, sacred landscape.

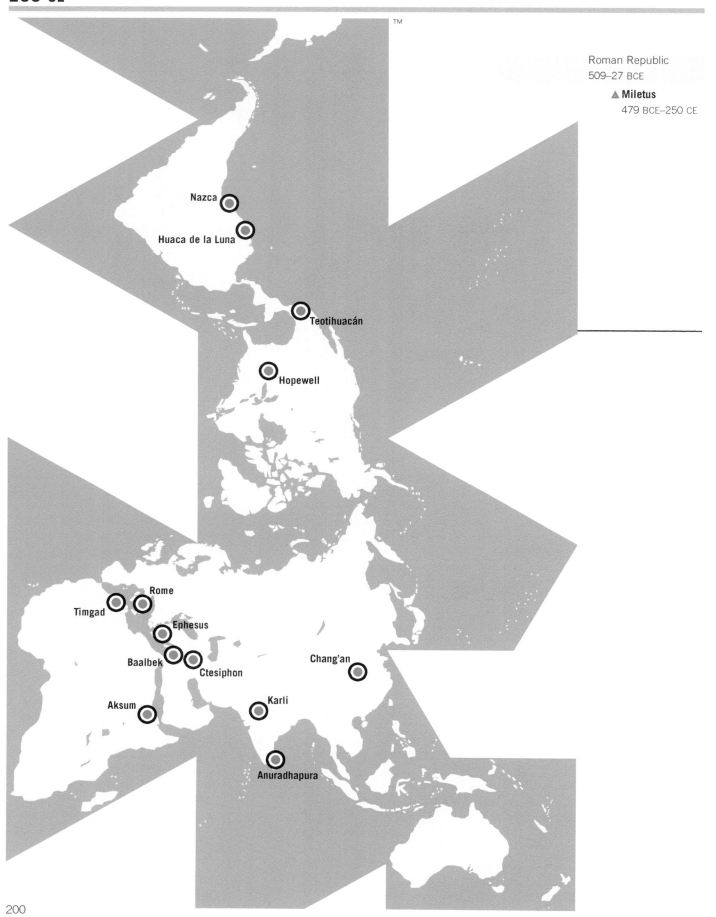

Roman Republic
509–27 BCE

▲ **Miletus**
479 BCE–250 CE

Nazca

Huaca de la Luna

Teotihuacán

Hopewell

Timgad

Rome

Ephesus

Baalbek

Ctesiphon

Chang'an

Aksum

Karli

Anuradhapura

Roman Empire
27 BCE–393 CE

▲ Forum of Augustus ▲ Forum of Trajan ▲ Pantheon   ▲ Bath of Caracalla
20 CE   112 CE   126 CE   212–16 CE

▲ Ephesus   ▲ Hadrian's Villa   ▲ Baths of Diocletian
270 BCE–420 CE   118–34 CE   298–306 CE

▲ Temple of Jupiter at Baalbek   ▲ Library of Celsus at Ephesus   ▲ Diocletian's Palace
Begun ca. 10 CE   115 CE   300 CE

Parthian Empire   Sassanian Empire
247 BCE–224 CE   224–651 CE

▲ Takht-i-Suleiman
ca. 300 BCE–110 CE

Aksum Prominence
1st centuriy CE

| 0 | 200 CE | 400 CE |

Kushan Empire: Central Asia and northern India   Satavahana and Ikshvaku Dynasties: Central and southern India
2nd century BCE to 3rd century CE   2nd century BCE to 4th century CE

◀ Amaravati Stupa   ▲ *Caitya* Hall at Karli   ▲ Jetavanarama Stupa
ca. 3rd century BCE   ca. 2nd century CE   3rd century CE

Wang Mang Interregnum   Eastern Han Dynasty   Sixteen Kingdoms Period: North China
9–25 CE   25–220 CE   25–220 CE

▲ Mingtang-Biyong Ritual Complex
ca. 1st century BCE–1st century CE

▲ Han Tombs
3rd century BCE to 3rd century CE

Teotihuacán Culture
ca. 150 BCE–650 CE

▲ Pyramid of the Sun   ▲ Pyramid of the Moon
ca. 200 CE   ca. 250 CE

Nazca Culture   Moche Culture
300 BCE–200 CE   ca. 200 BCE–700 CE

▲ Huaca del Sol and Huaca de la Luna
ca. 100 CE

Hopewell Culture
200 BCE–500 CE

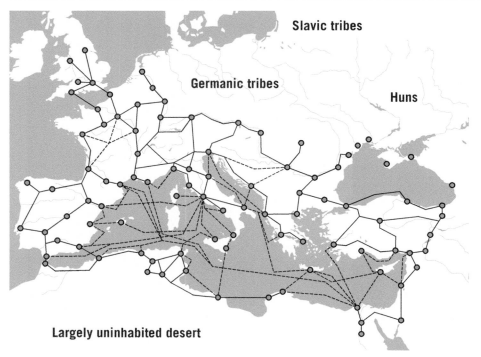

Slavic tribes

Germanic tribes

Huns

Largely uninhabited desert

7.4 Trade routes in Europe and western Asia, 2nd and 3rd centuries CE

ROMAN EMPIRE

The Roman Republic (509 BCE–27 BCE) focused largely on the Mediterranean, especially once Rome took over Greece in 146 BCE. But with the Gaulic Wars and the conquest of northern territories, Rome could combine trade over both sea and land. And though this was perhaps the vision of Caesar, the process of fusing everything into a single imperial unit, rather than a network of unequal principalities, would ultimately be completed by Caesar's successor, the emperor Augustus. The land/sea combination was the first such empire at that scale. By the 2nd century CE, the empire extended north all the way to England. Under Hadrian, North Africa was absorbed. Inroads were made into western Asia in order to secure trade links to the East. The eastern reaches of the empire were defined by older cities like Petra, Antioch, and Alexandria as well as by newly expanded cities like Palmyra and Duros Europus.

The development of cities was now at its peak, and the consequences can be seen throughout Europe and the Mediterranean. The list of Roman foundations includes Aosta, Bordeaux, Florence, London, Mainz, Mantua, Paris, Milan, Silchester (Hampshire, England), Trier, Cologne, Turin, Verona, and

Vienna, to name only a few. Many cities, like Florence, Milan, Paris, and Trier, still carry the imprint of the Roman grid to this day. Though the paradigm for the city was the *castrum*, or military camp, which was divided by two intersecting main streets, the *cardo* (north-south) and *decumanus* (east-west), this model was used mainly in the initial phases of the colonization in Europe and North Africa. In Europe, though some of the Gaulic cities remained in use, many, because they were on hilltops, were evacuated by the Romans, who preferred valleys and river towns, which were easier to defend and more amenable to Roman practices of camp organization. Bibracte, for example, was abandoned and the new city of Augustodunum, now known as Autun, was built in the nearby valley. The *castrum* model, however, was rarely used in the East, where cities were already well established. There, the Romans simply added to what they found. Regardless of whether the *castrum* model was used or not, the Roman method of creating cities can be compared with that of the Chinese. The Chinese were specialists in megacities, concentrating huge populations and bringing a large spectrum of activities into the confines of the city walls. Chinese cities were largely composed of one- or two-story houses and were thus not very

dense. The Romans specialized in compact, small-scale cities networked across the landscape. This allowed for easy expansion and was a critical element in their success. The Romans became experts in water management, building extensive aqueducts, many of which have lasted into the modern world. The Pont du Gard in modern-day southern France and the equally impressive Acueducto de Los Milagros in Mérida, Spain, are testaments to the boldness of these designs. The water fed not only great fountains but also magnificent public baths, which were among the largest public buildings in the world at the time.

North Africa is an excellent place to study Roman urban concepts; it supplied the capital with staple crops and luxury goods. Hadrian was eager to develop this area and offered free tenancy and a period of tax exemption to anyone who would agree to reside permanently on marginal land and put it under cultivation. It was a successful policy that encouraged the establishment of rural trading centers, many of which developed into urban environments. In some places a new town was founded, like Timgad, a gridded city roughly the size of Florence; in others, such as at Leptis Magna, an existing Phoenician city (east of Tripoli), the planners adopted a flexible and additive approach.

Roman cities were more differentiated than Greek cities, which were usually defined by a central public area and temple precincts. A Roman city had streets, squares, fountains, baths, gates, memorial columns, and public buildings that formed a type of armature around which the rest of the city grew. At the core of the city was the forum, the political and economic center of the city's activities. Public ceremonies and announcements took place there, and around it were ranged temples, offices, jails, butcher shops, and law courts.

At Palmyra and Ostia we can see the attempt to graft this armature onto places that had been founded at an earlier date, when they were more towns than cities. Djemila, in Algeria (96 CE), is typical; its elongated shape is a result of the terrain. The first part of the city to the north shows a relatively systematized layout, with the forum at the center of the town along the main road. But when that proved inadequate, a new forum, temple, and theater were built in a southward

7.5 Principal temple of Djemila, Algeria

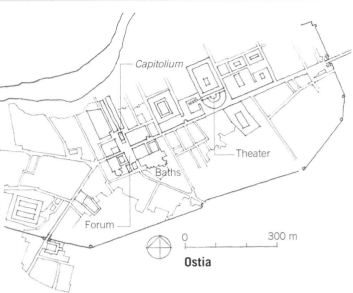

7.6 Plans of three Roman towns drawn at the sample scale and orientation

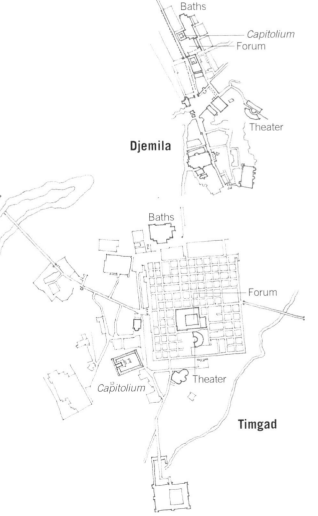

extension that followed the curves of an existing road. Though Timgad (100 BCE) is often given as a typical example of the rigorous application of the grid, the original town soon outgrew its borders. In fact, the elements of the armature that were originally left out of the design—the baths, the gates, even a *capitolium*—were grafted onto the fabric of the city once it had proven its success. A new arch, the Lambaesis Gate, demarcated the limits of the development. These urban extensions show a willingness to negotiate with the landscape and existing features such as roads. In some places, the Romans were even willing to work within the Hellenistic design mold; the most spectacular examples of this are at Ephesus and Miletus.

7.7 Main road of Timgad, Algeria

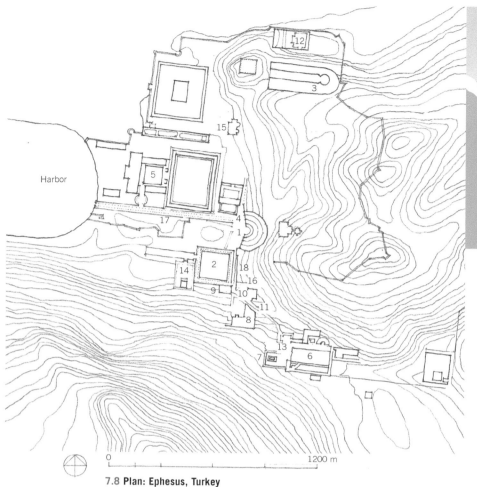

7.8 Plan: Ephesus, Turkey

0   1200 m

7.9 Area plan of Ephesus

Ephesus

Ephesus, a small town and religious center on the shores of the Cayster River near its mouth on the Turkish coast, was settled in the 9th century BCE and began to develop into an important port. Because the river was silting over, the city was abandoned and rebuilt at its current location 2 kilometers to the east around 270 BCE. It was designed not from the top down, as was Pergamon, but horizontally, in a protected, curving valley that opens in dramatic fashion onto the new harbor. By the end of the 5th century CE, the port of this city, just like that of the first one, silted up and the city fell into disuse. Today the harbor is 5 kilometers inland.

When the Romans took over the city in the first century BCE, they began the process of Romanization, adding temples, baths, fountains, paved streets, and libraries. When Augustus became emperor in 27 BCE, he made Ephesus the capital of the Roman holdings in western Asia Minor. Ephesus then entered an era of prosperity, becoming both the seat of the governor and a major center of commerce. According to Strabo, it was second in importance and size only to Rome. The Library of Celsus (ca. 115 CE) was built to store 12,000 scrolls and had an elegant facade with four sets of marble column pairs that framed *aediculae* and windows.

7.10 Theater at Ephesus

	Ephesus rebuilt	ca. 270 BCE
1	Theater	100 BCE
2	Agora	4 CE
3	Stadium	54 CE
4	Fountain	86 CE
5	Gymnasium	90 CE
6	Temple of Domitian	96 CE
7	State agora and odeum	100 CE
8	Nymphaeum	102 CE
9	Library of Celsus	115 CE
10	Temple of Hadrian	120 CE
11	Gates of Heracles	150 CE
12	Gymnasium of Vedius	150 CE
13	Pollio Fountain	150 CE
14	Temple of Serapis	170 CE
15	Palace of the Proconsul	300 CE
16	Baths of Scholastica	370 CE
17	Arcadiane	395 CE
18	Marble Way	420 CE

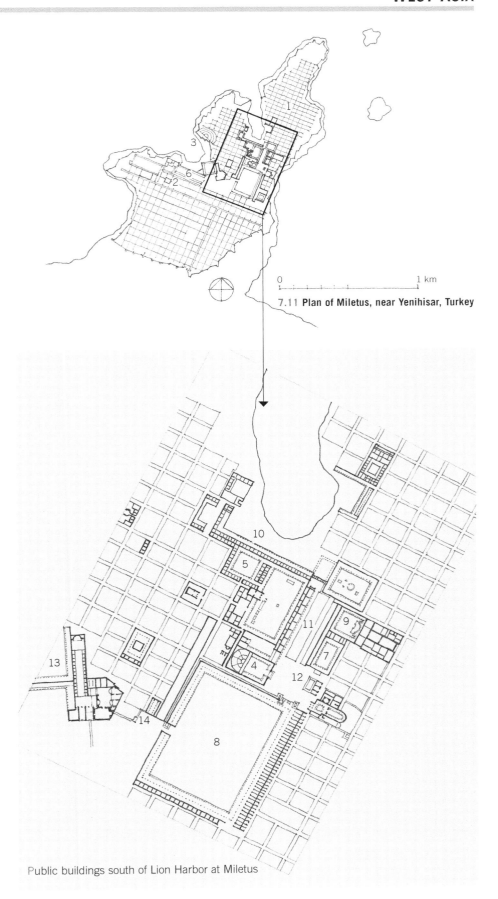

7.11 **Plan of Miletus, near Yenihisar, Turkey**

Miletus

Miletus, about 40 kilometers to the south of Ephesus on the western coast of Anatolia, went through three distinct phases. First it was a Greek colony; then it was a quasi-independent city-state, prospering during Hellenistic times; and finally, it became part of the Roman Empire. It was known as a religious destination as well as a health resort, and as an exporter of wine. The Roman designers worked sometimes with, and sometimes against, the established pattern; some of the older buildings, like the Bouleuterion (175 BCE), were preserved, while others were destroyed. The Romans inserted an intricate web of public buildings, streets, gates, and spaces that linked the old harbor with the new extension to the south. The dates show the pace of construction.

	Miletus founded	479 BCE
1	Northern street grid	470 BCE
2	Temple of Athena	450 BCE
3	Theater	450 BCE
	Rise to prominence	
4	Bouleuterion	175 BCE
5	North agora	170 BCE
6	Gymnasium	150 BCE
7	Stadium	150 BCE
8	South agora	150 BCE
	Imperial era	
9	Baths of capitol	50 CE
10	Harbor stoa, redesigned	50 CE
11	Processional way	150 CE
12	Nymphaeum	150 CE
13	Baths of Faustina	170 CE
14	Temple of Serapis	250 CE

Public buildings south of Lion Harbor at Miletus

205

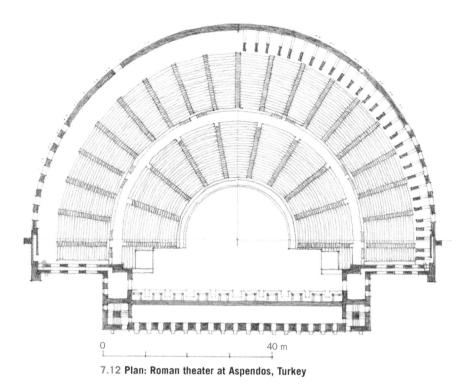

0   40 m

7.12 Plan: Roman theater at Aspendos, Turkey

The Roman Theater

Almost all Roman cities had a theater used for both popular and religious purposes. In the days of the republic, the Romans were somewhat skeptical of theaters—which were common in Greek cities—and concerned about their potentially corrupting influences. One decree forbade sitting at theaters, since it was deemed more manly to stand. As a result, theaters built during the republican period were temporary structures built of wood. The first permanent theater was ordered by Pompey in 55 BCE. Its design was what could be called transitional; it included a temple of Venus at the top of the seating area so that the rows of seats appeared to be steps leading up to the temple. Gradually this subterfuge fell away once theaters were built in the colonies, where the emphasis was on the theater as a public amenity.

Whereas Greek theaters were carefully and strategically inserted into the natural landscape and often had dramatic views, the Roman theater was conceived as an urban architectural element, its magnificence and splendor a token of Rome's imperial status. The slope of the seating was steeper than in Greek theaters, possibly for acoustic reasons. Initially, Roman theaters were hollowed out of a hill or slope, as at the theater at Aspendos, a Roman colony in Turkey. Over time, however, Romans viewed their theaters as regular urban structures. All of the theaters built within the city of Rome were made without the use of earthworks. Also unlike Greek theaters, the auditorium, though not roofed, was covered with awnings or velaria, which could be stretched out from tall poles to provide shelter from rain or sunlight. The buildings were usually semicircular. The stage building (*scaenae frons*) was usually three stories high, with the theater divided into the stage (orchestra) and the seating section (auditorium). In Rome, few theaters have survived the centuries. Arausio, the theater in modern-day Orange, France, is a good surviving example of a classic Roman theater, as is the theater at Aspendos, though of course they are missing all their ornamental grandeur.

7.13 Roman theater at Aspendos

7.14 **Pantheon, Rome**

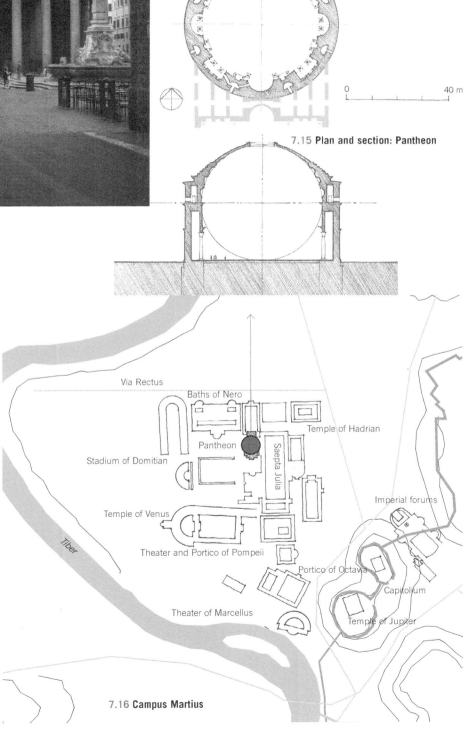

7.15 **Plan and section: Pantheon**

0 — 40 m

7.16 **Campus Martius**

Via Rectus
Baths of Nero
Temple of Hadrian
Pantheon
Saepta Julia
Stadium of Domitian
Temple of Venus
Imperial forums
Tiber
Theater and Portico of Pompeii
Portico of Octavia
Capitolium
Theater of Marcellus
Temple of Jupiter

The Pantheon

Hadrian (76–138 CE) had, of all the emperors, the deepest personal interest in architecture; he was also a poet and a painter—as well as a competent commander. His reign was generally a peaceful one, except for the role he played in the Bar-Kokhbar Revolt in Judaea. Reneging on his promise to let the Jews rebuild their destroyed temple, he planned to replace it with a temple to Jupiter and turn Jerusalem into a Roman city, the Aelia Capitolina, named after his own name, Aelia, and that of the Roman god Jupiter Capitolinus. The resulting revolution was brutally repressed. Hadrian's effect on architecture was felt in all corners of the empire, including Rome, where he built numerous buildings, but none more significant than the Pantheon (126 CE). It survived largely because it later served as a church. Although it has lost its original marble cladding and lacks the impressively dimensioned court that once framed the entrance of its facade, it is still an impressive building. However, what one sees today from the outside is nothing like the original, which was not a freestanding building but embedded in the urban fabric. Its principal view would have been from within a long, colonnaded forecourt.

7.17 Oculus of the Pantheon

The building was sited in an area north of the old city center known as Campus Martius ("Field of Mars") that, before the founding of Rome, had been used for pasturing horses and military exercises. During imperial times, it became the site of Rome's urban expansion, with baths, theaters, and temples, including a large open courtyard building known as the Saepta Julia, where Romans voted.

While the classical *cella* had always been a dark and mysterious place oriented east to the rising sun, this building rejects that tradition. Its bold, domed interior space was, for the Romans, an innovation. It derives conceptually from Greek and Egyptian mathematical interest in spatial geometry—concepts familiar to Hadrian, who had lived in Alexandria, a city famous as a center of learning. It was Archimedes, a Greek, who had solved the problem of measuring the volume of the sphere and cylinder in relation to each other. By way of contrast, Romans contributed practically nothing to analytical geometry. In that sense, the building is, one might almost say, un-Roman.

Smaller domed oculus structures had been built earlier, for bathhouses, like the one that still stands at Baia, on the north shore of the Bay of Naples. These places might have been a good place to work out

technical issues, but they were certainly not models in the symbolic sense. The octagonal room in Nero's palace brings us closer, in that it ended in an oculus and descriptions emphasize its symbolic purpose. Perhaps seventy-five years later, with Hadrian, Roman architects had an emperor who, like Nero, had a verve for architectural experimentation and an interest in the Hellenistic East, where

sun worship first came into its own in Egypt and Syria. Here, Jupiter is here represented not by a statue but by the abstraction of light itself.

Against the vertical alignment of the half-spherical dome is added the startling dynamic of the sun's rays as they move slowly through the space like a searchlight, illuminating one by one elements of the architectural interior—sometimes the floor, with its pattern of orange, red, and white marbles brought in from all over the empire; sometimes the orange marble columns; sometimes the coffering of the dome itself. The building probably had an astronomical dimension, but nothing about that is known for certain.

Unfortunately, no Roman text has yet been found that explains the interior in respect to the arrangement of the divine statues, the ritual practices undertaken in the building, or even the symbolism of the oculus. But it is likely that the building alludes to the unity of the divine and the imperial realms. Apart from sun temples that were beginning to be built in Syria (where Hadrian was the governor in 117 CE), there are mystery cults that emphasized light and darkness, like the Eleusinian Mysteries practiced in Greece, into which Hadrian had been initiated. In that sense the building can be perceived as an import of Eastern religious ideas into the very heart of Rome.

7.18 Interior of the Pantheon

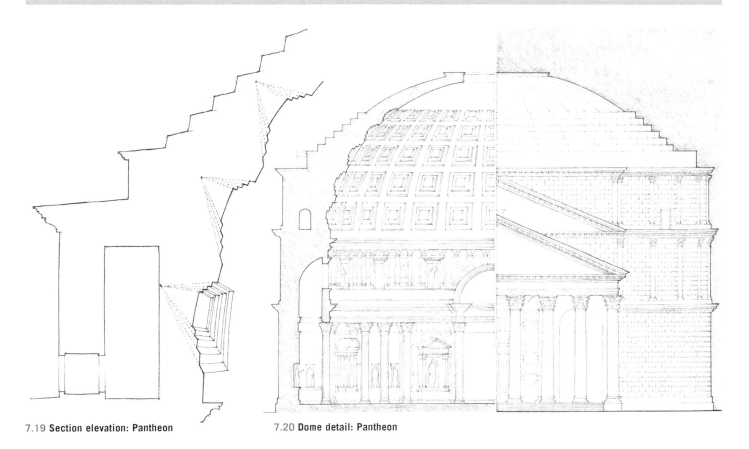

7.19 Section elevation: Pantheon

7.20 Dome detail: Pantheon

Originally, a flight of five steps as wide as the entrance portico led to the floor level of the interior. The monolithic shafts of the facade are of gray Egyptian granite; the four inner columns are reddish Egyptian granite; and the capitals Pentelic marble. The porch leads to a barrel-vaulted entranceway, flanked by niches. Between the porch and the rotunda are areas for stairways to reach the spaces that honeycomb the cylindrical structure. The threshold is defined by a huge block of Portasanta marble. The walls, carved out by alternating square and round niches, form four axial connections through the center space.

The niches of the interior are screened by columns and flanked by pilasters of yellow-orange marble under a continuous entablature. The apse is marked by freestanding columns, which interrupt the entablature running along the back of the niche. The dome presents itself on the interior as successive rings of coffering that diminish in size and depth as they near the oculus. They end, however, not at the mouth of the oculus but well short of it,

leaving a smooth, platelike area around the opening. The concrete surface of the dome visible today is not what contemporaries saw, however. The edges of the oculus, and the coffering as well, were probably gilded, with rosettes filling the centers of the coffers and creating a much more ephemeral and less structural impression than what can be observed today.

Though the Romans are often praised for structural innovation, they could easily make structure subservient to architectural vision. The lower half of the coffering, in fact, bears no relationship whatsoever to the structure behind it. In that sense, the architects were willing to work with the illusion of structure, or at least wanted to separate the visual vocabulary of a dome's "celestial" structure from the hard reality of the structural support. Even the coffering was designed from an optical point of view. The steps are shallower on their lower edge and steeper on the higher so as to appear the same height when viewed from the center of the floor.

The lower part of the structure is brick-faced concrete, with voids serving to reduce

the overall weight. Massive curving vaults direct the forces to the ground. For the dome, only concrete was used. The pour, made against a temporary wooden formwork, had to be seamless, placed bottom to top without pause in order to guarantee the cohesion of the whole. Organizing the production of the concrete, its immediate transport to the level of the dome, and its distribution to the right places by people carrying small batches was quite a feat. The width of the wall at the bottom is 6.15 meters. It thins to only 1.5 meters at the level of the oculus, which is 8.3 meters across and open to air and weather.

Despite the powerful evocations of the building, Hadrian's experiment would not be repeated. Though Roman architects continued to work with domed spaces, as in the Baths of Caracalla, the dome-and-oculus as imperial message was never repeated.

The original intermediary frieze was replaced in 1747 with one far less delicate in proportion. In the early 20th century, a small section of the original frieze was rebuilt based on Renaissance-era drawings.

Hadrian's Villa

Hadrian's other major contribution to architecture was an extravagant villa complex, a miniature world that he built for himself (118–34 CE) at the top of a hill about 25 kilometers east of Rome. It is not a single building, but a series of interconnected structures and gardens. Unlike the Palace of Domitian, with its compressed orderliness, the villa returns to the more freewheeling texture of Nero's palace. There are dozens of distinct elements separated from each other in the landscape and yet linked in surprising ways, so that the whole design unfolds only gradually. Some of the parts were meant to evoke memories of distant lands from Hadrian's far-flung travels. The residential parts were to the north. To the south was the stadium, followed by a series of baths ending in the spectacular structure known as the *canopus*, which was lined with copies of the caryatids of the Erechtheum in Athens.

The whole was meant to evoke the international—and particularly Greek and Egyptian—flavor of Hadrian's trips. In that sense the villa was a collection of memories and allusions. The *canopus*, for example, refers to a particularly bright star that was often used in navigation by Mediterranean sailors. It appears in numerous Greek legends and was also the name of an Egyptian port near the mouth of the Nile. The *canopus* at Hadrian's Villa is designed as a long lake decorated along its edges with columns supporting alternating arches and lintels. The Shrine of Serapis (Serapeum) on the southern end of the complex was built against a steeply sloping hillside, creating the impression of a grotto or miniature gorge with a waterfall at the back. It was dedicated to Serapis, the syncretic Hellenistic-Egyptian god who was the protector of the city of Alexandria. With water from an aqueduct above flowing through the gorge and around a crescent-shaped masonry reclining seat toward the long, riverlike pool, diners on the curved bench seats would have had a cool and enjoyable meal, even in the heat of summer. A small semicircular pool where food could be floated back and forth further added to its charm. The vault's surfaces were covered with blue and green mosaics. And the walls of the exedra were decorated with semicircular niches that held statues.

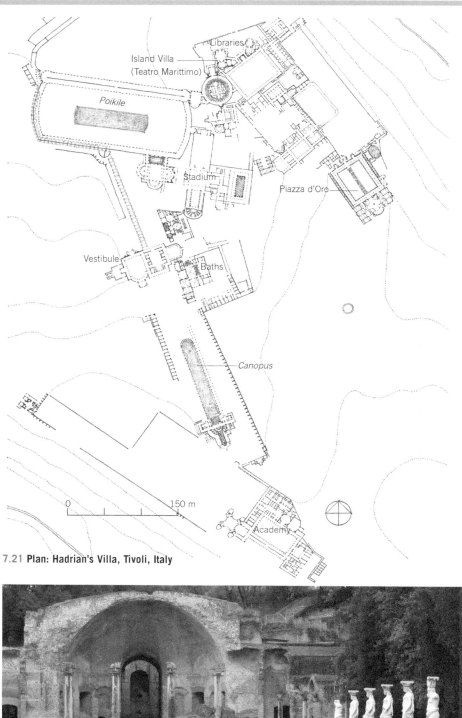

7.21 **Plan: Hadrian's Villa, Tivoli, Italy**

7.22 *Canopus*, Hadrian's Villa

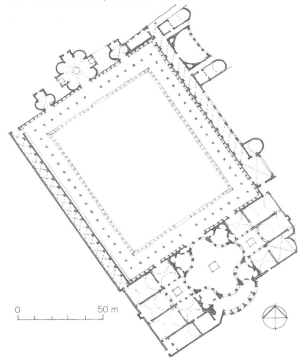

7.23 Plan: Island Villa, Hadrian's Villa

7.24 Island Villa, Hadrian's Villa

7.25 Plan: Piazza d'Oro, Hadrian's Villa

0   50 m

The so-called Island Villa, surrounded by a moat and a colonnade, is among the many astonishing elements of the villa. Access across bridges leads into an intricate architectural composition of concave and convex curves. The apparent symmetry at the center, typical of the spatial imagination of Roman architects, feathers out toward the perimeter, as if the architect had less and less control over the more marginal volumes—in a sense a metaphor for the Roman Empire itself. The two bedroom suites were on the east side; the dining room on the south. The western side was taken up by a small bathing area. At the center of the compressed peristyle court was a fountain, its sound filtering its way through the rooms.

The Piazza d'Oro, another element in the villa, was another tour de force of spatial imagination. It consists of a large, nearly square peristyle court, with a pool at its center. At the far end is a pavilion, or nymphaeum. Its main room is composed of rounded "walls" turned concave and then convex to form a flowing, four-armed space. These were not walls in the strict sense, but curved colonnades that allow one to view through them to the adjoining spaces. The room was open to the sky. The four ancillary spaces at the corners are all identical. The concave side leads to rooms with fountains in the floors, whereas the one on the principal axis leads to a curving space, the back wall of which is lined with fountains. Hadrian's Villa shows the Roman spatial imagination at its best. Order is balanced against complexity, as is architecture against landscape.

7.26 Fornix system of the *tabularium*

7.27 Arch of Septimus Severus, Rome

Roman Vertical Surface

Since the Egyptians covered their temple walls with images or historical reliefs, there was no opportunity for architects to think of the wall as anything other than a definer of space. In Greek architecture, walls were often hidden behind columns, and even though the Greeks invented the pilaster in the form of columns in antis, and sometimes even articulated walls with shallow panels, they never saw the wall as anything other than a wall. But by the time of the Colosseum, Roman architects were beginning to experiment with complex articulations of the vertical surface. For the first time, the wall became an architectural element per se. The technique of framing arches within engaged half-columns supporting an entablature, called the fornix system of ornamentation (*fornix* meaning "vault" or "arched room"), dates back to about 150 BCE. The Romans also invented the *aedicule*, a combination of niche with flanking columns connected by either a pediment or arch. In addition, they developed the dado, a boxlike stone under the column that allows it to be elevated.

The amphitheater in Nîmes, France, recapitulates the theme, as do numerous triumphal arches, such as the Arch of Titus (81 CE) in Rome. Eventually, *aediculae* and niches were added to the vocabulary, as can

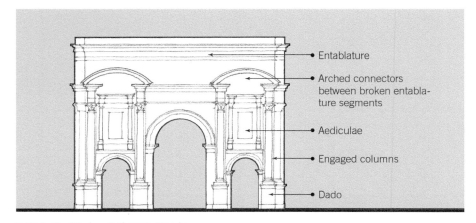

7.28 Arch of Trajan at Timgad, Algeria

- Entablature
- Arched connectors between broken entablature segments
- Aediculae
- Engaged columns
- Dado

be seen at the Arch of Trajan at Timgad (10 CE), a path-breaking design. The central arch is flanked by smaller arches surmounted by *aediculae* flanked by their own columns. The two sides are then organized by enormous columns that reach to the top of the *aediculae* and that, with the help of imposts, rise to a level where the arches can spring over them. The two side elements are united by an entablature that is reduced to a thin projection. It is perhaps a bit awkward, but certainly kinetic.

To get a sense of the level of experimentation that this opened up for designers, one can turn once again to the

rock-cut tombs of Petra in southern Jordan. The so-called Palace Tomb, for example, which has been variously dated to the second half of the 1st century CE or early 2nd century, shows a stratified design, with the lower register of four doors framed by round-headed and pedimented *aediculae* with unusual, abstracted capitals. The whole is tied together by an unbroken entablature on which rests a row of half-columns, the last ones being pilasters; above that is an accordion-style entablature with the pilaster order shadowing its way through to the top. The Tomb of Sextius Florentinus is particularly refined. Above the lower register is a pilaster order and a second set of capitals. This interpenetration of horizontals and verticals shows a capacity to see in the x- and y-axes simultaneously. Such a degree of visual complexity would not recur until the Italian Renaissance.

During the 2nd century CE, richly elaborated architectural fronts that had once been associated with the prosceniums in theaters sprouted forth in public spaces. This is true of the facade of the Library of Celsus at Ephesus (115 CE), which stands on the western end of a marble courtyard and is approached by a flight of nine steps. The three entrances, with large windows above them, are flanked by four niches that contain statues personifying the virtues of Celsus, Roman senator and proconsul of Asia. In front of the facade are four double-story pairs of columns; the capitals of the lower story are Corinthian, and those of the upper story, Ionic. In a further display of design skill, the architect changed the pairing between top and bottom. At the top, the columns are brought together with pedimental and rounded arches spanning the gaps. The end columns stand almost free against the facade.

Such displays were more than just architectural excess. They conformed to the Hellenistic desire for immediacy and were meant to express the qualities and generosity of the patron.

At the nymphaeum of Nîmes, France, the columnar elements form an exoskeleton against which presses the mass of the walls. The search for complex and imaginative formations reaches a climax at the stage for the South Theater in Gerasa, Jordan (modern-day Jerash). Though the first floor has been reconstructed without the second floor, it shows a row of paired columns on a socle forming a screen in front of pedimented doorways with *aediculae* between them. A similarly well-thought-out scheme prevails at the court of the Temple of Zeus at Baalbek. Two Corinthian columns in antis work with two pilasters to create the semblance of a screen unit. The *aediculae*, roundheaded at the bottom level and pedimented at the top level, are squeezed in between the pilasters, practically hiding the wall surface behind. The theme continues in the large niche behind the columns. The whole is tied together by a single unbroken entablature.

7.29 Library of Celsus, Ephesus, Turkey

7.30 South Theater, Gerasa, Jordan

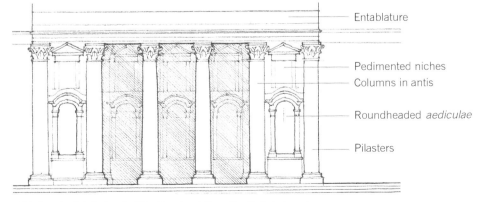

Entablature

Pedimented niches
Columns in antis

Roundheaded *aediculae*

Pilasters

7.31 Facade detail: Court of the Temple of Zeus, Baalbek, Lebanon

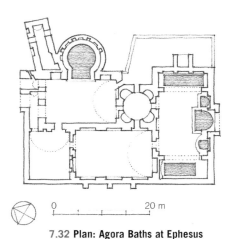

7.32 Plan: Agora Baths at Ephesus

Roman Baths

Although wealthy Romans had baths in their townhouses and country villas, the heating of a series of rooms, or even an entire separate building especially for this purpose, was usually reserved for public bathhouses, which were available in cities and towns throughout the empire. These baths, called *thermae*, were owned by the state and often covered several city blocks. Entrance fees were quite reasonable and within the budget of most free Romans. The area in these baths that was actually covered with water was relatively small, for the bulk of the structure was filled by exercise spaces, lounges, and places to stroll. Since the Roman workday began at sunrise, work was usually over a little after noon. At about 2 or 3 PM, men would go to the baths, staying for several hours of sport, bathing, and conversation, after which they would be ready for a relaxing dinner. Republican bathhouses often had separate bathing facilities for women and men, but by the time of the empire, the custom was to open the baths to women during the early part of the day and reserve them for men from 2 PM until closing at sundown.

The baths were secular spaces not associated with altars or divine patronage. Some of the thermal or mineral baths, however, might be associated with local river nymphs or the gods of medicine. Baths offered an environment that was both sensual and social. Some baths had lecture halls and libraries. The origin of these institutions goes back to the beginning of classical culture and the emphasis placed on physical fitness by the Greeks; bathing was viewed as a part of the hygienic rituals associated with sports. Gymnasiums, in which sports and education were combined, were reserved primarily for the sons of citizens and as a place for military training. Under Alexander the Great, however, the baths of Greek gymnasiums became a more social environment—and the Roman bath even more so. In fact, few citizens were so poor that they could not afford the entrance fee. Aware of the beneficial role these institutions played in the health, education, and entertainment of the people, the Roman state allocated considerable resources to their maintenance. Some of these baths, like the Baths of Caracalla and the Baths of Diocletian, were enormous structures, the largest public buildings in the world. Their lavish interiors were decorated with trophies, inscriptions, and sculptures reflecting the reach and power of the emperor.

The Baths of Caracalla (212–16 CE) are recognized as the best developed example of the Roman public bath. The main building (200 by 114 meters) was set in an enclosure (328 by 400 meters) that contained cisterns, running tracks, gardens, libraries, and shops. The facade was relatively austere and had only a few doors; by contrast, the internal spaces were open and sunny. The main pool was the *natatio*, or swimming pool.

7.33 Interior scale: Baths of Caracalla, Rome

Though it had no roof, the towering walls on all sides provided cooling shade in the afternoon. The *frigidarium* was at the center of the composition. It was covered by three cross-vaults that soared above the level of the surrounding rooms. Clerestory light would have filtered down into the space. The right and left rooms led to the *palaestrae*, the exercise courts. Then came the *tepidarium*, with small plunge baths of warm water on both sides. The climax was a circular *caldarium* 35 meters across, with large windows in the walls. Heat was supplied by hypocaust ducts from below.

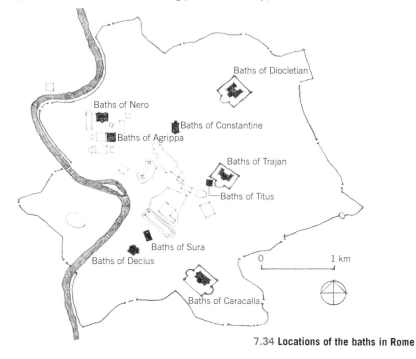

7.34 Locations of the baths in Rome

There are eight major public baths in Rome; they covered a significant proportion of the city by the time of the end of the empire:

25 CE	Baths of Agrippa
64 CE	Baths of Nero
80 CE	Baths of Titus
104 CE	Baths of Trajan
ca. 100 CE	Baths of Sura
212–16 CE	Baths of Caracalla
ca. 250 CE	Baths of Decius
298–306 CE	Baths of Diocletian
320 CE	Baths of Constantine

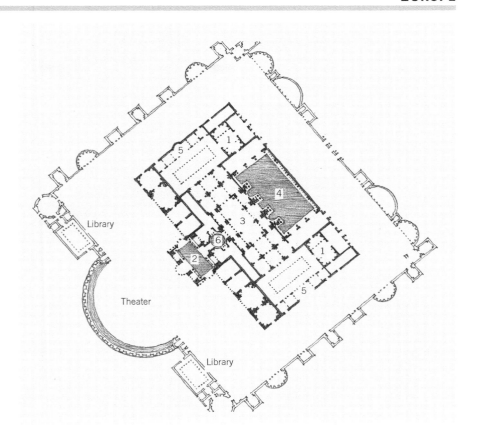

7.35 Plan: Baths of Diocletian, Rome

Parts of the Roman Bath

1 *Apodyterium*: Dressing room/locker room
2 *Caldarium*: Main hot room
3 *Frigidarium*: Main cold-water hall, often containing several unheated pools
4 *Natatio*: Large unheated swimming pool
5 *Palaestra*: Exercise yard
6 *Tepidarium*: Warm room and bath, often a type of "heat lock" between the *caldarium* and *frigidarium*

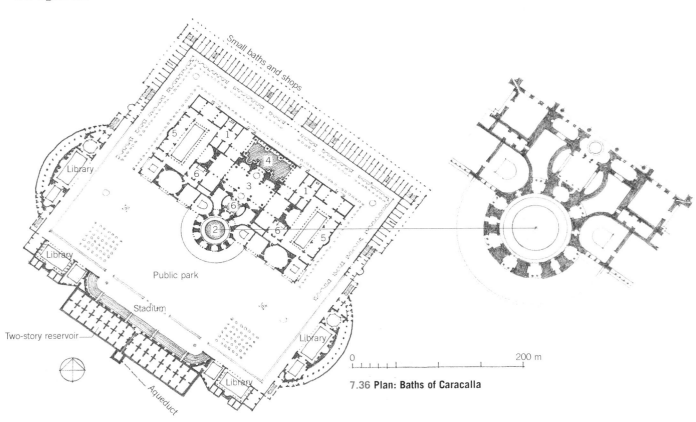

7.36 Plan: Baths of Caracalla

Diocletian's Palace

In 166 CE, Germanic tribes breached Rome's frontier along the upper Danube, and in 172 CE, the Moors from northern Africa invaded Spain. In 253 CE, the Franks from the middle and lower Rhine regions began to launch intermittent attacks on northern Spain. In 257 CE, the Goths raided Greece and Asia Minor. Although the empire was under siege, there were also problems within Rome itself. In the decades before Diocletian (r. 284–316 CE) became emperor, there had been no fewer than twenty successive emperors proclaimed by the senate, and at least as many usurpers and pretenders. To restore order in Gaul and to prevent usurpation of the throne, Diocletian drastically changed the governance of the empire, a move that had profound historical implications for the rest of Europe. He split the empire into two, and then into two again, with his friend Maximian serving as co-regent in the western part of the empire. The four rulers had their respective capitals at Nicomedia, Greece; Mediolanum (modern Milan); Treveri (today's Trier, Germany); and Sirmium (in modern-day Serbia). Diocletian governed the Asiatic part of the empire and Egypt from Nicomedia, using the Persian model of rulership, implementing other territorial partitionings of the empire, and separating military from civilian administration. Initially these efforts were successful. In 296 CE, Britain was restored to the empire; in 298 CE, the Persians were subjugated, and the Germans were expelled. Although previously somewhat tolerant of Christianity, which was growing in momentum, Diocletian issued an edict in Nicomedia in 303 CE in which he prohibited it. This brought about numerous executions, the confiscation of property, and the destruction of churches. On May 1, 305 CE, he abdicated and retired to the palace he had prepared for his retirement in Split (Spalato) on the Bay of Aspalathos, on the coast of what is today Croatia.

Diocletian and Maximian both built sumptuous palaces. The Piazza Armerina (Villa Romana del Casale) by Maximian, located in eastern Sicily near Catania, follows some of the conventions of Hadrian's Villa, though with less overall compositional quality. The various elements seem to be stuck together relatively arbitrarily around a large open courtyard. Nonetheless, the

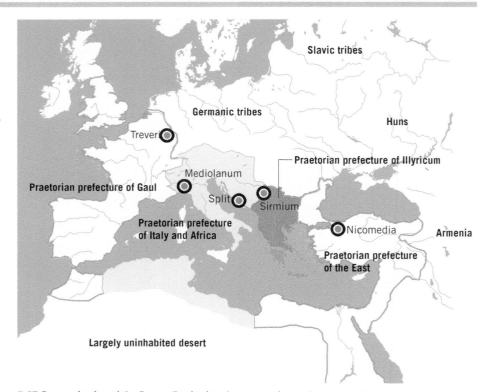

7.37 Reorganization of the Roman Empire into four praetorian prefects, ca. 405 CE

composition is not without order. From a curved entrance courtyard, the visitor turns right into a series of slightly disjointed spaces leading up to the audience hall at the east. The composition is tied together by a type of "street" running north and south linking the principal elements of the program. The composition looks relaxed, and purposefully so, as if it were built up over time. The villa contains spectacular floor mosaics. The

60-meter-long corridor, for example, depicts incredibly elaborate hunting scenes, and even animals such as panthers, lions, and antelopes being loaded onto ships destined for Rome, where they would be shown in the great amphitheatres.

In contrast to Piazza Armerina, Diocletian's Palace in Split, Croatia, is part fortified camp, part city, and part villa. It is, unlike the purposeful casualness of Piazza

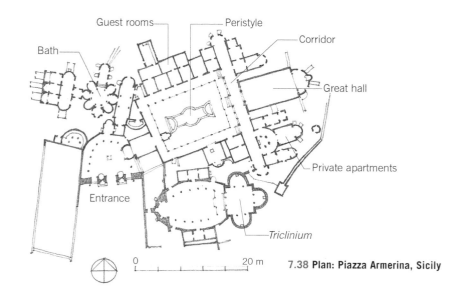

7.38 Plan: Piazza Armerina, Sicily

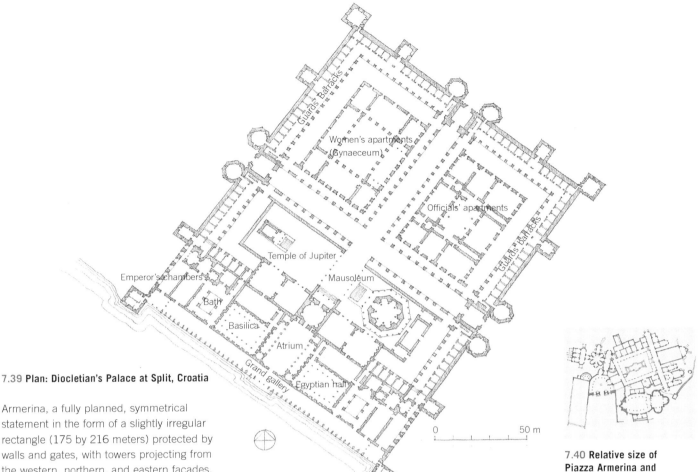

7.39 **Plan: Diocletian's Palace at Split, Croatia**

Armerina, a fully planned, symmetrical statement in the form of a slightly irregular rectangle (175 by 216 meters) protected by walls and gates, with towers projecting from the western, northern, and eastern facades. Only the southern facade, which rose directly from the sea, was unfortified, with a long colonnade running the whole length at the top level. The *decumanus* that links the east and west gates divides the complex into two halves. To the south were the emperor's quarters, both public and private. On the other half are kitchens, stables, and storage. The streets are lined with colonnades. Between the main crossing and the imperial apartments is a separate rectangular zone for the temple and the mausoleum, an octagonal, domed structure. The plan of the villa is powerful in its abstraction and in its zoning of functions. The weakest part is probably the area of the imperial apartments, which are reduced to a lining up of spaces on the great terrace. From east to west, there are the private suites with a bath, the basilica throne room, a large reception hall, and *triclinium*, followed by kitchen and service rooms.

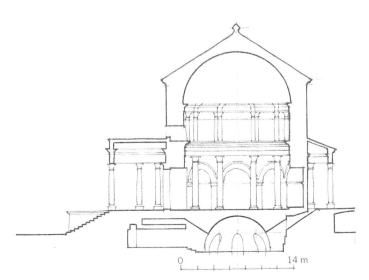

7.40 **Relative size of Piazza Armerina and Diocletian's Palace**

7.41 **Section through the mausoleum at Diocletian's Palace**

7.42 Location of Baalbek, Lebanon, West Asia

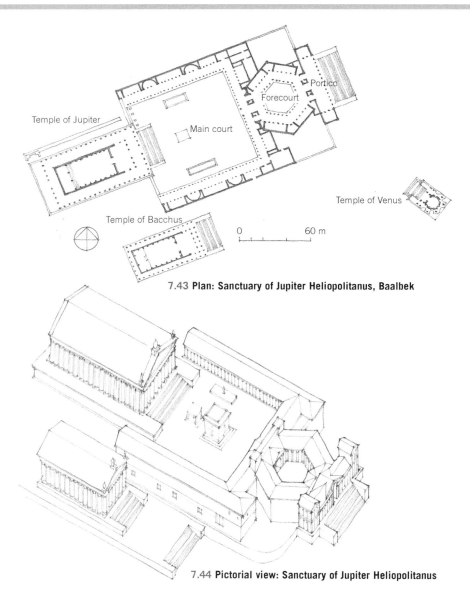

7.43 Plan: Sanctuary of Jupiter Heliopolitanus, Baalbek

7.44 Pictorial view: Sanctuary of Jupiter Heliopolitanus

Baalbek

The supreme deity of the Canaanites was El, the sun god who also carried the bull as an attribute. The fertility goddess Ashera was his companion. Worshippers were not allowed to pray directly to the couple but could use the mediating influence of their son, Baal, the master of rain, tempest, and thunder. This was typical of the Hellenistic era, which saw the emergence of several sons of deities. The principal site of the worship of Baal was near a natural rock fissure some 15 meters deep, at the bottom of which was a small rock-cut altar. Since the altar was difficult to access, another one was constructed above it on the hill. This was then augmented with protective gates and towers. Eventually a temple was added, built on a high undercroft. The Temple of Jupiter, the final temple on that site, was begun during the reign of Augustus (27 BCE–14 CE); it was constructed on a scale unknown in Rome until then. Some of the foundation stones weighed 800 tons and are some of the largest stones ever used in Roman times. Nonetheless, the temple was not as big as some of the enormous Hellenistic temples, such as the one at Dydima, which sat on a podium 17 meters high, with columns reaching another 22 meters. (Large size was valued in the colonies but looked down upon by the homeland as a sort of barbaric excess.)

The temple's entrance was demarcated by two buildings: a conventional U-shaped propylaeum that was plugged into the front of the temple (3rd century CE) and an unusual hexagonal building (2nd century CE). The latter had an open courtyard surrounded by porticoes with rooms against the walls that served various functions. It had a showpiece facade that was a building in its own right. Though symmetry was seen as part of the natural order of architecture, architects plugged different "buildings" into each other to produce creative and unusual structures like this one. Trajan visited the shrine around 115 CE to consult the oracle before attempting to conquer the Parthians, and it may even have influenced him in the

design of his forum back in Rome. In 195 CE, Septimus Severus (r. 193–211 CE) bestowed upon Baalbek the title *jus italicum*, moving it up to the most prominent class of Roman cities. Construction at the site continued during the rule of Caracalla (211–17 CE), a member of the Syrian dynasty of emperors.

Nearby is the Temple of Venus (3rd century CE), an extraordinary building composed of a round *cella* with a porch. The *cella* on the exterior is ornamented by columns attached to a scalloped entablature, creating a dynamic play between the round and rectilinear geometries. The building is a testament to the ongoing formal experimentations typical in the eastern part of the Roman Empire. Building activity in

Baalbek was still taking place when Emperor Constantine declared Christianity the official religion of the Roman state in 330 CE, thus putting an end to one of the largest and longest building projects in the Levant.

Inner Asia was defined by specific ecological realities. In the frozen north there lived First Society people who specialized in hunting and fishing. Along the vast steppe region that spans thousands of kilometers east to west and that in essence linked China to Europe, there clustered dozens of interrelated horse-centric tribes, who lived as traders and raiders. The closer these people got to the Silk Route, the more one tribe or another wrested control of the flow of wealth. Boundaries and allegiances were transitory across the vast distances of deserts and mountains. The Parthians and the Kushans, for example, were continually fighting not just an east-west battle for supremacy over the trade routes but also a northern battle against steppe newcomers. On the western edge of this great continuum, in what is now Germany and eastern Europe, there was a robust pocket of the only agropastoralists in the entire northern tribal belt. Once the Celts in France had become Romanized, this group of former kinsmen also came to feel the pressure from the nomadic steppe people. They were driven westward and finally broke through the Roman defenses to settle in Europe between the 4th and 6th centuries CE. From the perspective of the Romans and Chinese, all of these people were barbarians, living in villages instead of cities; living by raiding instead of farming; and housed in yurts and thatch instead of stone, brick, and mud brick. A description of the Huns by the 4th-century CE historian Ammianus Marcellinus describes them as such:

None of them plough, or even touch a plough handle; for they have no settled abode, but are homeless and lawless, perpetually wandering with their wagons, which they make their homes; in fact, they seem to be people always in flight. Their wives live in these wagons, and there weave their miserable garments; and here, too, they sleep with their husbands, and bring up their children ... nor, if asked, can any one of them tell you where he was born, as he was conceived in one place, born in another at a great distance, and brought up in another still more remote.

The irony was that the great urban civilizations of Eurasia were dependent on this vast community of horsemen; they were the oil in the Eurasian economic engine.

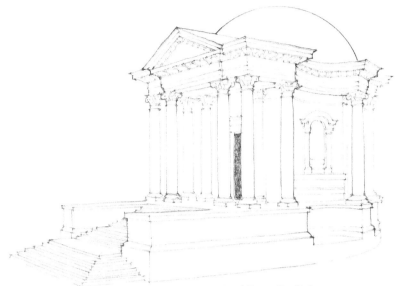

7.45 **Temple of Venus, Baalbek**

7.46 *Cella* **of the Temple of Bacchus, Baalbek**

7.47 Horse statuette of Parthian warrior

THE PARTHIAN EMPIRE

The Parthians took over the Hellenistic Seleucid Empire; originally they were nomads from northern Iran and Central Asia, but because of their trading skills, the Parthian Empire (247 BCE–224 CE) became the glue that held together the vast Central Asian trade networks. They brought with them, however, little in the way of architectural culture, and so for the most part adopted the Hellenist structures before them, blending them with their own particular aesthetic. As a result, there is remarkably little to show for some five hundred years of Parthian rule. Remaining consummate and feared horsemen, they governed as a military elite, leaving, by and large, the local administrations intact. There were, as a consequence, several regional capitals. Though warfare with the Romans and with nomadic invaders from the north was more or less constant, the 2nd century was a time when the caravan cities of Palmyra, Hatra, and Mesene (formerly Characene), situated at the confluence of the Tigris and Euphrates Rivers, grew in wealth and influence. It was also a time in which, given the lack of centralized authority, different religious practices began to flourish simultaneously. Iranian sun, fire, and mystery cults took the place of ancient Mesopotamian practices. Christianity, Judaism, and various baptismal sects expanded into Mesopotamia. Strong relations between the Parthians and the Chinese resulted in envoy exchanges.

When the Chinese envoy arrived at the Parthian border, he was greeted by an escort of twenty thousand horsemen. Parthian elites, on the whole, adopted Zoroastrianism (see 400 CE), an emerging religious practice based on fire worship. This they fused with certain Hellenistic practices, creating fire sanctuaries dedicated to specific divinities, saints, or angels. Parthian fire altars served as regional and national pilgrimage sites. One such site, Takht-i-Suleiman, in western Iran, around the rim of an extinct volcano with a lake at its core, was frequently visited by the royal elites. The most important Parthian founding was Ctesiphon (see 400 CE), on the east bank of the Tigris at its confluence with the Diyala River, 32 kilometers south of Baghdad. Originally a garrison city, it developed into a regional capital, as it was situated on the so-called Royal Road, which connected Susa with Anatolia. It is not clear when Ctesiphon became important, but it seems that the spoils of a large campaign against the Roman Empire in 41 BCE were invested in the new capital, which had become the winter residence of the kings after 129 BCE. The Romans sought to take the city and did so in 116, 165, and 198 CE, but in 224 CE, Ardashir overthrew the Parthian monarchy and established the Sassanian Empire, with Ctesiphon remaining one of its capitals.

AKSUM

By the 4th century BCE, the area of what is today northern Ethiopia had come to enjoy a strategic position in the developing sea trade routes between Africa and points east in Arabia, India, and even China. With the decline of Kush, perhaps because deforestation led to the loss of wood for smelting, this area, controlled by the Aksumites and with its own vast forest reserves (now, of course, completely nonexistent), was primed to become a regional powerhouse. Though Aksum was an inland capital, its port cities, Adulis and Matara, were cosmopolitan centers. The rulers imported silver, gold, olive oil, and wine while exporting luxury goods of glass crystal, ivory, brass, and copper. Other important exports to the Greek and Roman world were frankincense, used in burials, and myrrh, which had important medicinal properties. Both these highly valued products were obtained from the resin of particular trees that grew mainly in the mountainous regions of Aksum and southwest Arabia. The quality of Aksumite metalwork in gold, silver, bronze, and iron attests to the skill of their craftsmen.

The significance of Aksum in global trade should not be underestimated. With the Romans eager to seek alternative trade routes to the East to get around the Parthians, they had developed relationships with Petra.

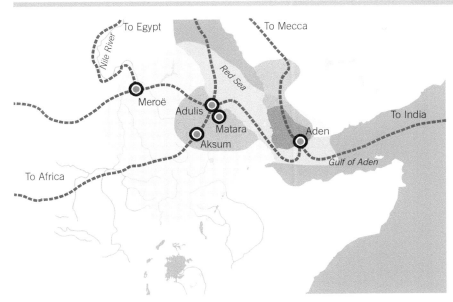

7.48 **Area of Aksumite influence, 200 to 500 CE**

Aksum, much like Petra, was a part of this southern trade network and should be understood in the context of developments in India. There is little of the original Aksum left today, apart from some impressive stelae, the largest being King Ezana's Stele, erected in the 4th century CE and named after the first monarch of Aksum to embrace Christianity. It is decorated at its base with a false door and apertures resembling windows on all sides. The city was originally impressively located in a gap between two prominent rock outcroppings. The remains of a vast palace and a smelting factory have recently been uncovered.

Across the Strait of Hormuz lay the Himyarite kingdom, or Himyar. It had formerly traded in frankincense, but the decline in demand for that product led to trade in ivory exported from Africa to be sold in the Roman Empire. Ships from Himyar regularly traveled the East African coast, where Himyar exerted a considerable amount of political control over the trading cities. Himyar was independent until taken over by the Aksumites in 525 CE. Aksum remained a strong empire and trading power until the 6th century, when deforestation led to its decline (much as it had in Kush)—a decline accelerated by the rise of Islam and the resulting shift in trade routes. The area's arid geography today gives little indication of this once lush and forested territory.

The Aksumite religion was related to Mesopotamian and Arabic religions insofar as it was polytheistic: Deities were perceived as controlling the natural forces of the universe. In the 4th century CE, King Ezana converted to Christianity and declared Aksum a Christian state—the first Christian state in the history of the world. The city contained several large palaces that, unlike the more rambling palaces of western Asia, tended to be highly symmetrical. They were approached by broad staircases that led to a forecourt with more stairs leading to a central throne or reception room. Construction material was stone and brick, probably covered with plaster. The roofs were wooden.

7.49 **Plan of an Aksumite palace**

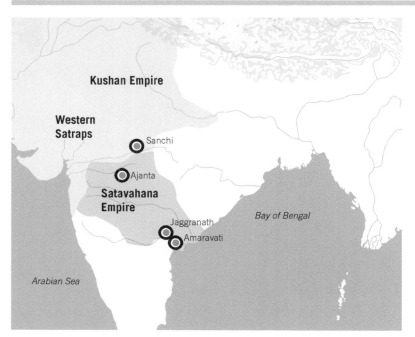

7.50 Satavahana Empire, 200 BCE–250 CE

7.51 **Detail: Capitals of the** *caitya* **hall at Karli, Maharashtra, India**

AMARAVATI STUPA

In the 2nd and 3rd centuries CE, South Asia was dominated by two major dynasties: the Satavahanas, who controlled central and southern India, and the Kushans, who, although having recently migrated to the region, ended up ruling a vast area stretching from Central Asia to northern India. The Kushans were Mongolians who emigrated to Gandhara in response to the building of the Great Wall by the Qin. It was a mutually reinforcing combination since both had their roots in trading communities. Both were predominantly Buddhist, although the Satavahanas were already witnessing a re-emergent Hinduism and the Kushans continued to practice aspects of their older, shamanistic beliefs. The Satavahanas called themselves the *dakshinapath-pati*—"the rulers of the southern trade route"—which linked Egypt, controlled by the Romans, with the Han rulers of China. The route went from ports along the Indian Ocean to the west, across India in a northeasterly direction, to ports on the Bay of Bengal. Buddhist monasteries became catalysts for this mercantile development, serving as resting places and transition points for the traders. The most famous of the Satavahana merchant constructions, the Amaravati Stupa (3rd century BCE), was dismantled

in the 19th century, its artwork distributed to the museums of Europe. Like the earlier ones at Sanchi and Bharut, the Amaravati Stupa, when first built under the Mauryas, was a simple mound, but it was significantly enlarged under the patronage of the merchants. The elaborately carved railings and gateways that have been preserved depict scenes of a bustling city. Turban-wearing people fill every panel; musicians play for well-endowed dancers; richly adorned women lean from barrel-vaulted balconies; horses, bullocks, and elephants crowd the streets, along with oxcarts. In the distance, large ships with open sails are ready to take to the sea.

7.52 **Carved slabs from the Amaravati Stupa, near Guntur, India**

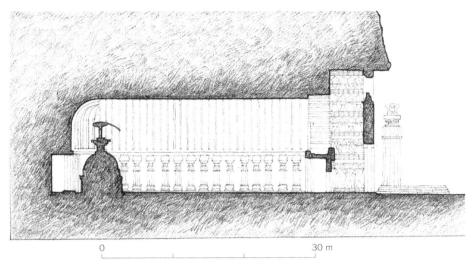

7.53 Longitudinal section: *Caitya* hall at Karli

CAITYA HALL AT KARLI

By the 3rd century CE, *caitya* halls were being built in several places in India. One of the largest and most impressive was made in 120 CE at Karli, on the western Deccan Plateau. About 40 meters deep and 12 meters wide, the Karli sanctuary is fronted by a recessed entrance of stone screens that has holes in it, indicating that originally, a larger wooden construction had been added to complete the building. Just beyond the screen, on the left, is a large pillar carved from the same matrix as the rest of the cave. The end wall of the entrance portico displays a stamped-out, repeated set of horseshoe-arched building motifs that sit atop a plinth composed of life-size elephants, as if they were supporting the weight of the superstructure. The central panel of the cave entrance is dominated by male-female couples, known as Mithuna couples, holding each other affectionately with a distinctive touch of sensuality. According to one source, Mithuna couples represent "the notion of the individual's reintegration with the universal principle." The entrance panels also contain bodhisattvas, but these were carved in the late 5th century CE, when the iconography was "modernized."

Karli is famous for its interior, in part due to its sheer size, but more so because of the balanced and measured nature of the overall composition of its elements through which Karli brings the *caitya* vocabulary to one of its finest resolutions. It is hard to imagine that this is a rock-cut building, carved in essence from the roof downward. The columns (fifteen on each side) have fluted, bell-shaped capitals on which rests a plinth that supports Mithuna couples on elephants looking down into the space.

Compared to earlier *caitya* sanctuaries, the width of Karli's central space is much more generous in relation to its height and depth. The Karli stupa at the rear is no longer the incidental center of a crowded array of elements, but the focus of a hierarchical composition. The stupa itself is relatively simple in form. An unadorned hemisphere sits atop a slightly tapered base, ornamented with carved *vedikas*. At the same time, it is much bolder than most earlier stupas, as its *chattri*, rising from a rectangular base, or *harmika*, expands into mushrooming tiers of horizontal bands. But then it suddenly projects into space on a high vertical *stambha*, upon which sits the final *chattri* that becomes the focus of the entire composition. The *chattri* catches the light in the dark surroundings and appears as a horizontal flash in the vertical composition. (The *chattri* denotes the umbrella of the Buddhist ideal under which the monk finds shelter and faith.)

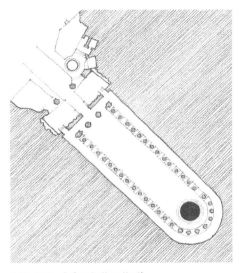

7.54 Plan: *Caitya* hall at Karli

7.55 Interior: *Caitya* hall at Karli

223

ANURADHAPURA

Sri Lanka may have been far from the Silk Route, but it nevertheless contributed to trade in an important way, since it was the primary regional source of gems, such as rubies, that served as lightweight and easily transportable currency. The island was also a source of pearls, from its western shores, and cinnamon, from the wet southern regions, the latter particularly important as incense in Hindu rituals. Most of these luxury goods could be produced with minimal governance by shore-based communities. With the arrival of Buddhism in the 3rd century BCE, however, the drier and more sparsely inhabited northern part of the island was turned into a rice-paddy village world dominated by powerful, palace-centered elites with strong mercantile interests. They transformed rivers into a series of interconnected shallow lakes, one feeding into the next, ending in a final, large lake restrained by a massive dyke. With sluices and canals, the water was then used to irrigate rice paddies. The first of these systems was followed by many others over subsequent centuries. Soon Sri Lanka was exporting not only rice but also its hydro-technological know-how throughout Southeast Asia. Anuradhapura was at the center of this effort and was, in fact, boldly built right below the dam of one of the first of these great artificial lakes. The Malwaty Oya River connected Anuradhapura to the city of Mahathia (modern-day Manner), a major port, trading with India, Rome, and Southeast Asia.

In the context of this booming economy that drew in traders from all around, a sapling from the original Bodhi tree from Bodh Gaia, India, was brought and planted in the palace compound at Anuradhapura, transforming the city into a spiritual center in its own right, one which has retained this status to this day. Of past grand palaces of wood, only the foundations and the stone columns of ground floors remain, but these are sufficient to give an indication of the impressive scale of these lofty, multistoried buildings. The city has at least five major stupas, each with its own monastic complex: Thuparamaya (245 BCE); Ruvanvelisaya (140 BCE), which stands 90 meters high; Lankaram (85 BCE); Abhayagiri (final form 4th century CE); and Jetavanarama (ca. 280 CE), the largest stupa of them all, at 115 meters in diameter and originally 120 meters high. The stupas were placed in square, walled compounds. The Sri Lankan architects developed an unusual stupa type, which was protected by a wooden domed roof supported on stone columns. It is typified at the Thuparamaya. The core was built in 245 BCE, but the superstructure was added in the 7th century CE.

7.56 Jetavanarama Stupa, Anuradhapura, Sri Lanka

7.57 Thuparamaya Stupa, Anuradhapura

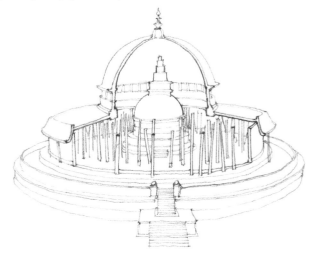

7.58 Pictorial section: Thuparamaya Stupa

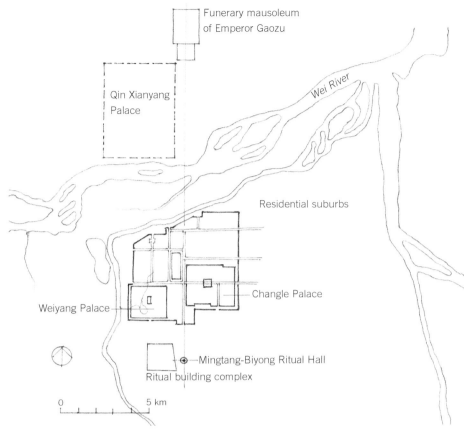

Funerary mausoleum
of Emperor Gaozu

Qin Xianyang
Palace

Wei River

Residential suburbs

Changle Palace

Weiyang Palace

Mingtang-Biyong Ritual Hall

Ritual building complex

0   5 km

7.59 Plan of Han Chang'an. The word *chang'an* means "eternal peace."

HAN DYNASTY CHINA

By the turn of the millennium, the Han dynasty (206 BCE–220 CE) ruled an area larger than the Roman Empire. The Han abandoned Shi Huangdi's absolutism for a more balanced philosophy of governance, even though they held on to the Qin idea of a unified and centralized China. Emperor Wudi (141–86 BCE) established new commanderies in Korea, and his conquest of Ferghana and neighboring regions in 101 BCE gave China control of the trade routes running through the Taklamakan Desert, its gateway to the west. In return for its silk and bronze, China received wine, spices, woolen fabrics, grapes, pomegranates, sesame, broad beans, and alfalfa. Under the Han, poetry, literature, and philosophy prospered, and the voluminous *Shiji* ("Historical Records"), written by Sima Qian (145–80 BCE), set the standard for later government-sponsored histories. By 100 CE, trade along the Silk Route began to flourish, with caravans reaching Luoyang almost every month. International diplomatic exchanges

became common, including those with Emperor Andun (the Chinese name for the Roman emperor Marcus Aurelius Antoninus) in 166 CE. By the 3rd century CE, paper was widely used in China, replacing bamboo, wood, and silk slips. Paper was exported to Korea and Japan in the 7th century, and then to Europe, most likely through Central Asia and Arab intermediaries, in the 12th century. The existence of water clocks, sundials, astronomical instruments, and even a seismograph in 132 CE attest to the Han's technological and scientific sophistication.

To the north of Han territories were the Xiongnu, who established an empire (209 BCE–93 CE) that stretched beyond the borders of modern-day Mongolia. The Xiangnu were part of another nomadic confederation known as Xianbei. By the 3rd century CE, these various confederations, known by the Chinese as "barbarians," were instrumental in establishing the eastern part of the Silk Route. So important was this to the Han worldview that they built their

new capital, Chang'an, at the far western edge of their traditional territorial control. To populate the city, around 200 BCE the Han forcibly relocated thousands of clan families in the military aristocracy to this region. The purpose was twofold: First, it kept all potential rivals close to the new emperor; and second, it allowed the emperors to focus their energy on defending the capital from invasion by the nearby Xiongnu. This astonishing break of geographical ties was also the first step in the creation of an artificial—one might even say universal and divine—imperial culture.

The site was just to the south of the by then destroyed Xianyang, the old palace city of the Qin. The Han even used one of the Qin palaces, the Xingle Palace, as its core, optimistically renaming it Changle ("Long Joy") Palace. The shape of the new city, with its twelve gates, was irregular, this having to do with its siting along the river and with certain astrological imperatives. About half of the city was filled in with huge palaces connected by two-story passageways with bridges crossing the streets. The passageways that linked the palaces allowed the emperor to move among the palaces unseen. As the city grew, a suburb developed to the east. To the west of Changle Palace, the Weiyang Palace was constructed, with an immense audience hall. (The word *weiyang* means "maintaining the dignity of the law.") Because the emperors lived there, this building had a particular prominence. Like the Qin palaces, these gigantic Han palaces were built of wood around a solid earthen core. The Han also constructed a major palace complex west of the city at Shanglin Park, along with an artificial lake, the Kunming Chi. The lake, which symbolized the world's oceans, had at its center the statue of a whale. Very little survives of the vast wooden constructions of the Han. However, funerary objects placed in royal tombs often contained models of structures for use in the afterlife. These models show multistory timber-frame watchtowers with corner piers and upper levels generally smaller than the lower ones, resulting in tapered profiles. At each level, widely overhanging roofs and balconies were supported by elaborate bracket sets and braces.

Mingtang-Biyong Ritual Complex

If the Qin capital was designed as a microcosm of the Chinese empire, nearby Chang'an was designed to represent nothing less than the heavens themselves. For the Qin, rituals tended to include disparate rites from China's far-flung geography. According to the *Shiji*, the sacrificial rituals, known as *zhi*, were meant to be performed on high grounds in forested areas, where offerings were made to the four deities of the directions, represented by the colors white, azure, yellow, and red. The Han multiplied the Qin rituals and offered sacrifices to the gods of heaven and earth, mountains and rivers, the sun and the moon, and the stars and the planets, and they built artificial replicas of natural altars in the capital itself.

All of this coincided with the emerging notion of imperial power. Unlike in Europe, where absolute power was an extension of aristocratic privilege and military might, the emerging Chinese tradition interpreted the power of the emperor as dependent on the will of the divine. His actions were seen as an integral part of the cosmic order. It was thus incumbent upon the emperor to perform a certain set of rituals in order to demonstrate that he was the rightful emperor—to validate his own position within the system, and at the same time, to validate the system itself. He was seen as the Son of Heaven, operating with the Mandate of Heaven (*tianming*). This mandate did not require that the emperor be of noble birth, and several dynasties were, in fact, founded by people of common birth. If, however, there were trouble of any sort, bad weather, a drought, or an invasion, these might be signs of divine disfavor that could lead to unrest. If the emperor was overthrown, this was seen as his having lost the Mandate of Heaven. A successful rebellion was thus interpreted as evidence of that divine approval had passed on to the successive dynasty. In principle, the system was an incentive for rulers to rule well and justly. The practice was a different matter.

In Chang'an, the ritual structures that were at the core of this mandate were to the south of the city. They were known as the Biyong ("Jade Ring Moat") and Mingtang ("Bright Hall," 141–86 BCE), and were designated as the intersection of heaven (circle) and earth (square), oriented around the four cardinal directions.

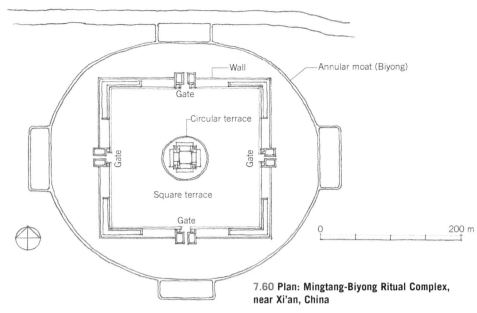

7.60 **Plan: Mingtang-Biyong Ritual Complex, near Xi'an, China**

The circular moat of Biyong that defines its outer perimeter is bridged by paths coming in from the cardinal directions and heading into a square enclosure, in the center of which, on a round terrace, was the main bi-level sacred hall, the Mingtang. The walls of the four outer chambers were painted with colors associated with each direction: east, green; south, red; west, white; and north, black. The structure was aligned with the mausoleum of Emperor Gaozu, the founder of the Han dynasty, which was located on the north side of the Wei River. (See plan on page 225.)

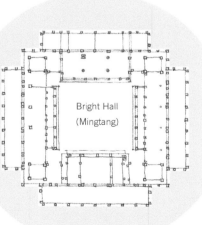

Bright Hall (Mingtang)

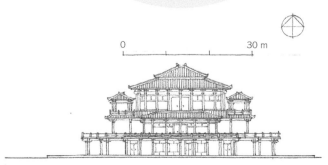

7.61 **Plan and elevation: Central structure of Mingtang-Biyong Ritual Complex**

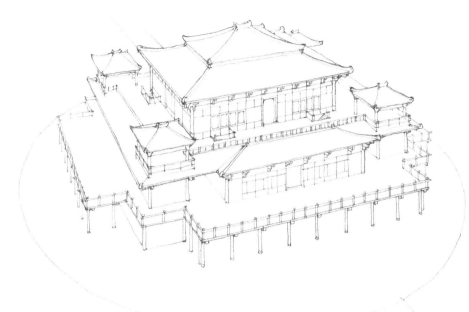

7.62 **Pictorial view: Central structure of Mingtang-Biyong Ritual Complex**

The building is a diagram of Chinese imperial philosophy. The human realm was seen as a land mass surrounded by water, with the empire in the center, and with peripheral territories occupied by barbaric people at the edges. At the conceptual center of it all was the emperor, who ruled by divine mandate and was the Son of Heaven. From this spot, the calendar was regulated and its knowledge disseminated.

Over the span of centuries, numerous such complexes were built in the various capital cities. Few have survived apart from the Altar of Heaven at the Temple of Heaven Complex in present-day Beijing. It was built in 1420 during the reign of the Ming dynasty Emperor Yongle and is a circular platform on three levels of marble stones. Twice a year the emperor and all his retinue would leave the Forbidden City to encamp near the altar. Ordinary Chinese were not allowed to view this procession or the following ceremony. After a highly prescribed series of preparations, the emperor would pray to heaven for good harvests. The ceremony had to be perfectly completed; it was thought that the smallest of mistakes would constitute a bad omen for the whole nation in the coming year.

7.63 **Altar of Heaven, Beijing, China**

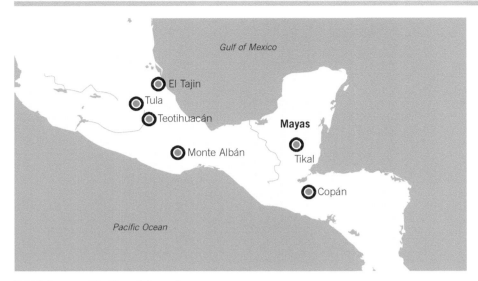

7.64 Influence of Teotihuacán's empire

TEOTIHUACÁN

Teotihuacán was the largest and most impressive of America's cities until modern times. Located in the highlands of central Mexico, Teotihuacán existed for a period of eight hundred years, growing from a large village of about 6,000 people into a metropolis of 150,000 to 200,000 inhabitants around 600 CE, with an urban core extending across 20 square kilometers. It was the center of an empire that dominated the culture and politics of even the furthest Mayan city-states and kingdoms. Third-century inscriptions on stelae at Tikal and Copán record that Teotihuacán controlled their dynasties. They may have also influenced the mound cultures of the Mississippi. In spite of its size and magnificence, little is known of Teotihuacán's multiethnic inhabitants. Evidence of a writing system is only just coming to light, most of it seemingly destroyed when the city fell. The city was a type of "forward capital," insofar as it was an exposed outpost on the northern edge of the Mesoamerican cultural realm. Beyond it to the north stretched the arid wastes of the Mexican plateau. The Aztecs were to eventually master that plateau with their water systems.

The Maya called the city Puh ("place of the reeds"), but the name Teotihuacán, "the place where men become gods," was given to it later by the Aztecs, who built their own capital, Tenochtitlán, farther to the south a millennium later. (The original name is not known.) By the time of the Aztecs, Teotihuacán, by then abandoned, was already a place of legend and mystery. Today, there are many ongoing debates about the nature of the city and the purpose of its structures. Though at its height Teotihuacán was roughly contemporary with the early stages of the Mayan cities located to the south, there were distinct differences between the cultures and, so it seems, only minor evidence of interaction.

Archaeologists believe that a four-chambered cave, discovered by local residents in the early years of the 1st century BCE, marks the beginning of Teotihuacán's rapid growth. Caves played an integral role in the Mesoamerican religions; they were considered places connected with the origin of gods and ancestors, as well as portals to the underworld, the world of demons and other potent beings. The Teotihuacán lava cave may have held particular significance, as its four lobes could represent the four parts of the Mesoamerican cosmos. It became the center of a spiritual landscape and a focal point of fire and water rituals. But whether this was the beginning of clan cohesion or a convenient prop for territorial control is not known. In the 2nd century CE, Teotihuacán's largest pyramid, the Pyramid of the Sun, was built directly over the cave.

The city, most of it laid out between 150 BCE and 150 CE, was organized into quadrants, with one avenue running east-west and the other, more important one, running north-south. The latter, called the Avenue of the Dead by the Aztecs, was aligned with the sacred mountain, Cerro Gordo, and pointed approximately 15 degrees east of north. The width of the avenue varied, ranging from 40 to 95 meters. A large, long channel underneath the avenue gathered rainwater from neighboring architectural units

7.65 Citadel of Teotihuacán, Mexico

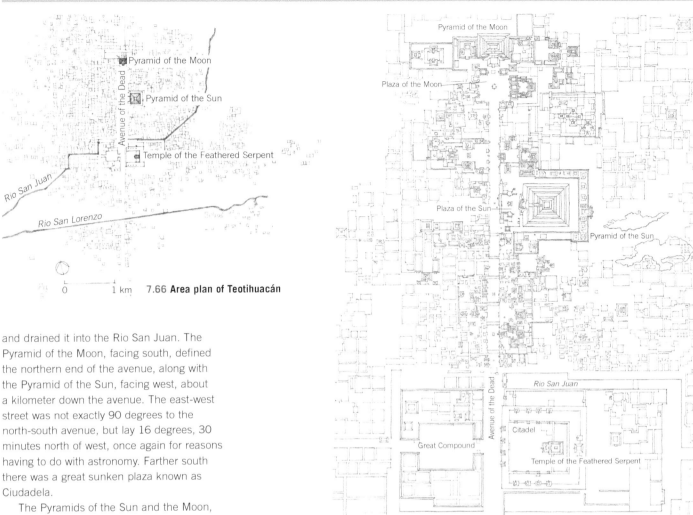

7.66 **Area plan of Teotihuacán**

0   1 km

7.67 **Plan: Central zone of Teotihuacán**

0   1 km

and drained it into the Rio San Juan. The Pyramid of the Moon, facing south, defined the northern end of the avenue, along with the Pyramid of the Sun, facing west, about a kilometer down the avenue. The east-west street was not exactly 90 degrees to the north-south avenue, but lay 16 degrees, 30 minutes north of west, once again for reasons having to do with astronomy. Farther south there was a great sunken plaza known as Ciudadela.

The Pyramids of the Sun and the Moon, echoing the shapes of the mountains surrounding the valley, were constructed by hauling millions of cubic meters of sun-dried bricks, all without the help of wheels and beasts of burden. Beneath the pyramids are earlier structures, perhaps the tombs of Teotihuacán rulers. The first to be built was the Pyramid of the Sun. One of the largest structures in the ancient Americas, it was 215 meters square and some 63 meters tall. The profile as it exists today is misleading and a product of the imagination of its reconstructors in the early part of the 20th century, who were eager to make it too pyramid-like. It originally consisted of four stepped platforms surmounted by a temple and an Adosada platform, which was built over what was the pyramid's principal facade. Its exterior was originally covered with a thick layer of smooth plaster and was probably painted red.

The Pyramid of the Moon at the northern end of the Avenue of the Dead was completed around 250 CE. Recent excavations near the base of the pyramid staircase have uncovered the tomb of a male with numerous grave goods of obsidian and greenstone, as well as sacrificial animals. One of the most significant tombs yet discovered at Teotihuacán, it might indicate that even more important tombs lie buried at the heart of the pyramid. At the foot of the Pyramid of the Moon, there is a plaza (204 by 123 meters) surrounded by platforms that in ancient times were stuccoed, painted, and topped with temples. A low platform at the center of the plaza and visible from all the surrounding platforms served as an important ritual site.

7.68 **The feathered serpent god (Quetzalcoatl), Teotihuacán**

Temple of the Feathered Serpent

After the Pyramid of the Sun and the Pyramid of the Moon were completed, construction shifted to the south, where a large ritual complex and palace compound called the Ciudadela—a sunken plaza large enough to hold most of the city's inhabitants—was centered on the Temple of the Feathered Serpent (Quetzalcoatl). Completed in the early 3rd century CE, the temple is flanked by two apartment compounds where the city's rulers may have lived, as well as fifteen smaller stepped pyramids—three at its back on the west, and four each on the other three sides.

The initial construction phase of the Temple of the Feathered Serpent appears to have been marked by several mass burials of people who were apparently sacrificed, their hands tied behind their backs, during the construction of the pyramid. They seem to have been killed as part of a warfare cult that, according to archaeoastronomers, was regulated by the position of the planet Venus in the heavens during its 584-day celestial cycle. The Temple of the Feathered Serpent may have marked the first use of the distinctive Teotihuacán architectural profile known as *talud-tablero*, in which a rectangular panel (the *tablero*) sits atop a sloping panel (the *talud*).

The surfaces were decorated with murals. All the platforms at Teotihuacán have this profile, and its presence at other sites is generally an indicator of Teotihuacán influence throughout Mesoamerica. The balustrade and *tableros* of the Temple of the Feathered Serpent featured large, tenoned serpent heads with low-relief bodies upon which elaborate mosaic headdresses appear at intervals. The headdresses, with their prominent eyes and fangs, were integral to the military iconography at Teotihuacán and were used throughout Mesoamerica.

By 200 CE, all major construction at the site had been completed, and the Puh Empire attended to building and improving the city's residential areas. Teotihuacán's complex urban grid was filled with single- and multifloor apartment compounds. This grid, the only one known in Mesoamerica before Tenochtitlán, the 14th-century Aztec capital, implies a high degree of social control.

From 200 to 600 CE, Teotihuacán continued to flourish, with long-distance trade becoming an important factor in its prosperity. But its success did not last. Around 750 CE the city burned to the ground, possibly torched by invaders from the city of Cacaxtla, 210 kilometers to the east.

7.69 **Detail: Temple of the Feathered Serpent**

7.70 South America civilization, ca. 200 CE

7.71 Urbanization of the Americas, ca. 200 CE

North Hopewell

Central Maya

Teotihuacán

South Moche

MOCHE AND NAZCA CIVILIZATIONS

Two South American civilizations rose simultaneously in Peru during this time: the Moche on the north coast, and the Nazca in the south. (They are known by the current names of the rivers in whose valleys their ruins are located.) Very little is known about their political and social organization. The Moche were, however, outstanding metalworkers, and both the Moche and the Nazca were potters and weavers.

The Moche Valley on the northern Peruvian coast had been occupied for a long time. The largest of the pre-Moche settlements were made by the Salinar (450–200 BCE). The period was one of turmoil, and for that reason large protected cities developed, one of which, known as Cerro Arena, sprawls for 2 kilometers along a ridge on the south side of the Moche Valley, overlooking a trade route. Its two hundred structures made of quarried granite range from small one-room residences to elaborate twenty-room buildings. Strangely, the Salinar seem not to have built any ceremonial structures.

About 100 CE, construction began on the ceremonial complexes of Huaca del Sol and, 500 meters away, Huaca de la Luna, in the center of the Moche Valley. About ten thousand people are believed to have lived in the neighborhood of these two huge platform mounds. As was the tradition in

Mayan structures, Huaca del Sol, sited along the river, was successively expanded; it was rebuilt in eight stages, the last in 450 CE. Little remains of their gigantic pyramid (345 by 160 by 40 meters), apart from one edge. But an analysis of the adobe shows that each brick had a mark on it, generally believed to be that of the bricks' builders and suppliers. This indicates the presence of a complex, highly organized building guild or similar social organization.

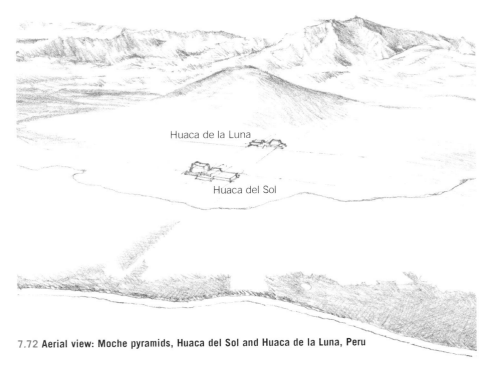

7.72 Aerial view: Moche pyramids, Huaca del Sol and Huaca de la Luna, Peru

Huaca de la Luna

Huaca del Sol

In building this giant structure, the builders decided not to construct a single piece, but instead placed segments next to each other, thus improving its resistance to seismic activity. In an earthquake, the independent sections might collapse, but the overall structure would remain intact. The sides of the stepped pyramid were decorated with colorful patterns and images. The whole was topped by small buildings that formed a sacred precinct. The original name of the structure is not known.

Nearby is Huaca de la Luna, sited at the northern base of a tall mountain. Built in six stages, its extension (290 by 210 by 22 meters) consisted of three platforms and four plazas. It is generally believed that Huaca de la Luna served as the region's paramount shrine and the setting for ceremonies of human sacrifice. In an enclosure behind the temple, archaeologists found the remains of over forty men, their bones buried in a thick layer of sediment, indicating that they were sacrificed during periods of heavy rain. Sacrifices in periods of drought were also evident. The principal deity behind this practice was a half-human, fanged god often shown holding a ceremonial knife in one hand and a severed human head in the other. The city's main buildings were located in the plain between the two temples.

Andean metalworking reached its height at this time. It had developed from a long-standing metallurgical tradition of the Lambayeque region, with its gold, silver, and copper mines. Gold had a special status, not as money, but as a symbol of power. Smiths developed elaborate techniques for making and working the alloys, including the equivalent of electrochemical replacement plating: they dissolved gold in acidic solutions so that it would attach to copper surfaces, thus creating stronger and longer-lasting alloys with shiny golden surfaces. The metal was used by priests in headdresses and as ornaments, and possibly on the surfaces of buildings as well.

By the 7th century, the site had begun to be abandoned. It is thought that a thirty-year drought, in combination with devastating mountain floods, weakened the legitimacy of the Moche rulers.

7.73 Examples of figures from the polychrome friezes on the courtyard walls at Huaca de la Luna

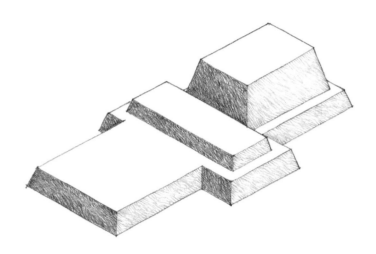

7.74 Massing of Huaca del Sol

7.75 **Aerial view: Nazca ground drawing, Peru**

Nazca Lines

Though the origins of the Peruvian cultures are far from clear, it seems that the Nazca culture dates back to around 3000 BCE. It was an oasis culture at the edge of a shore desert. The oasis allowed a thriving culture to develop. Citrus fruit and manioc were grown on the plains; corn was grown at high altitudes and stored in massive silos. The Nazca traded up and down the coast, as indicated by the presence in gravesites of a special oyster shell that came from Ecuador and was used by the elites as sacred ornamentation. At first the Nazca people made rock art, as was common to many cultures worldwide, but then, making use of the terrain, they began to draw figures in the desert. Though large, these images were easy to make by scraping or removing the dark volcanic stones from the otherwise white surface of the desert.

At first it was thought that the lines were astronomical in nature, but more recent excavations have shown that the lines were made to honor the gods as part of elaborate shamanistic rituals that focused on ancestral memories or weather deities. Though the images can famously be seen from high altitude, scholars are convinced that they were actually meant to be seen from the west-facing slopes of the hills that served as viewing areas for the rituals that certainly spanned many days and were possibly even performed with torches at night. The lines were not empty signifiers, but paths along which ritual participants would walk in the context of elaborate dance ceremonies.

The drawings were made in various phases from about 500 BCE to about 400 CE. At first the drawings showed figures with large eyes; then there was a phase when animals appeared, serving as orientation points for shaman "flights." Since the monkey, hummingbird, and spider were not local to the region but creatures from the rain forest to the east, the images may have been meant to communicate with these animals in the hope of bringing rain.

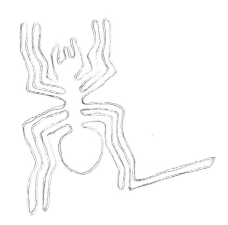

7.76 **Nazca ground drawing of a spider**

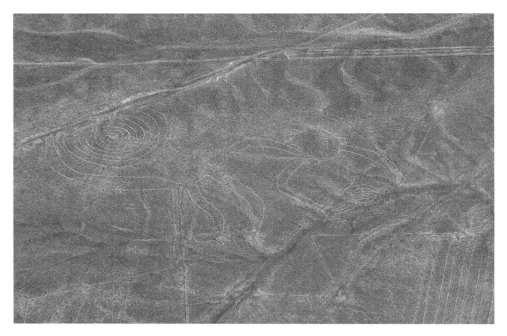

7.77 **A Nazca figure of a monkey**

Beginning around 200 CE, the area was drying out, and the desert began to spread up the once green and fertile slopes. The ceremonies that served as a struggle against the drought seem to have gotten bigger and bigger. Animal shapes gave way to huge geometric and linear designs, the scale of which indicates that all the Nazca people were now involved in these efforts, not just the shamans, possibly in order to add weight to the ceremonies. People came to the pilgrimage center of Cahuachi from far afield to participate in these elaborate rituals.

Cahuachi owes its significance to its geographical location: because of its geological path, the Nazca River goes underground midvalley and emerges at a point just below Cahuachi. In a water-scarce region, the reappearance of the river would have been viewed as miraculous. Cahuachi's adobe platform mounds are much smaller than those of their Moche neighbors, and they cap some forty low-lying hills overlooking the Nazca River. Even after the Nazca people abandoned the city in the 5th century, it remained an important site for rituals and burials.

NORTH AMAZON SOCIETIES

Along the border between Brazil and Bolivia, researchers have recently discovered evidence of mounds, earthworks, and even a ring of megaliths used for celestial calculations, dating to about two thousand years ago. The ring comprises 127 granite blocks, each about 3 meters high. This indicates that settled societies had by this time penetrated the Amazon rain forest along the various rivers where fertile floodplain soil for agriculture was available in abundance. The people who lived here seem to have specialized in planting fruit trees, capitalizing on the rich soil quality to survive during the dry season and in periods of drought. An extensive network of low, water-controlling dams indicates the practice of fishing on a large scale. In fact, experts now estimate that a significant portion of lowland forests in this area was organized to benefit humans. It has been suggested that the diseases that came with the arrival of Europeans wiped out this civilization, and that the forest consumed the physical traces.

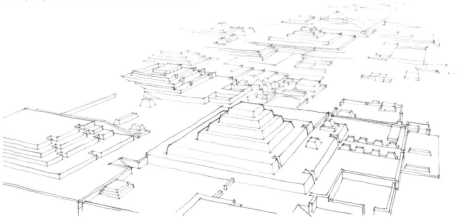

7.78 **Cahuachi, major pilgrimage center of the Nazca culture, Peru**

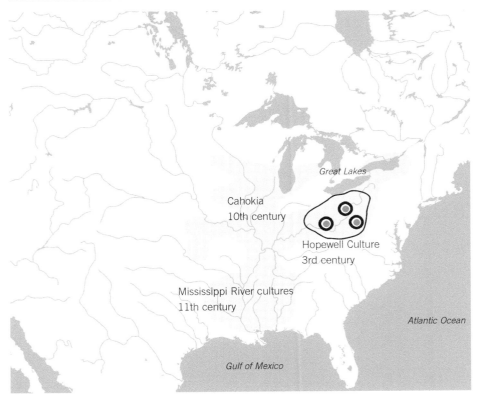

7.79 Hopewell Culture

7.80 Copper falcon and mica hand, Hopewell Mound Group, near Hopewell, Ohio

OHIO'S HOPEWELL MOUNDS

The term *Hopewell* refers to a culture that flourished along the rivers of the northeastern and midwestern parts of North America from 200 BCE to 500 CE. At its greatest extent, the Hopewell Culture stretched from western New York (including the shores of Lake Ontario) to Missouri and from Wisconsin to Mississippi. The largest communities were found in the Ohio region. The Hopewell were not an agricultural society, but lived in the traditional way of hunting, gathering, and gardening. Their affluence, however, came from their location, which supplied salt, flint, and especially pipestone, a highly prized soft stone that was used by Native Americans to fashion ritual smoking pipes. A man's smoking pipe was one of his most important possessions, since the communal ritual use of tobacco was an important social activity. Groups would travel from far afield to the Hopewell areas to mine and collect these materials in exchange for things that they brought, such as copper, obsidian, and craft goods. The economy of the Hopewell thus revolved around the intense ceremonialism of these exchanges. They built large enclosures in which their elaborate dances and ceremonies took place. One of the grandest was Newark Earthworks, which was a large enclosure along a bend in a river that was defined by linear mounds. It was designed in the shape of a water spider, which was sacred because it could navigate between the realm of the living and that of the ancestors. It is likely that during designated times, thousands of people would have arrived to participate in the ceremonies held here. Other enclosures in nearby settlements were in the shapes of circles, ellipses, and trapezoids.

7.81 Hopewell pipe

The Hopewell communities also built large mounds to mark the sites of their elaborate funerary rituals, usually along bluffs overlooking rivers, creating long stretches of sacred landscapes. At Mound City, as one of the Ohio sites is called, there are about twenty-three mounds, each built over the remains of a charnel house. Charnel houses were used for both cremation and for defleshing the body, before the whole structure was burnt down. The Hopewellians placed artifacts, such as copper figures, mica, arrowheads, shells, and pipes, in the mounds.

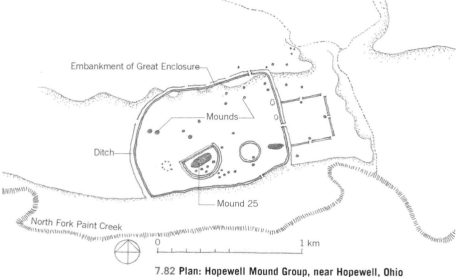

7.82 Plan: Hopewell Mound Group, near Hopewell, Ohio

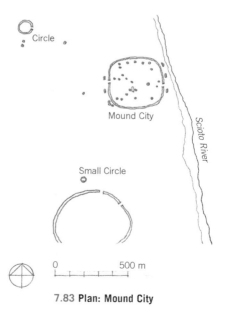

7.83 Plan: Mound City

400 CE

8.1 **Basilica of Santa Maria Maggiore, Rome**

INTRODUCTION

In Eurasia, the period between 200 and 400 CE was noted in particular by nomadic incursions from the steppe regions of Inner Asia. What prompted this exodus is not known, but the effects were clear. The Roman Empire was soon overwhelmed by people the Romans called "barbarians," but who were mostly agropastoralists—Saxons, Huns, Visigoths, and Franks, among others. In 441–442 CE, Saxons from Germany invaded Britain. The Visigoths took a more southerly route, invading Italy under Alaric I and sacking the fabled city of Rome in 410, settling down first in southern Gaul and eventually in Spain and Portugal, where they founded the kingdom of the Visigoths. The Franks were moving to the west, to eventually set up residence in the area of modern-day France. Meanwhile, the Huns who came to dominate central Asia, and unified under Attila, invaded the Eastern Roman Empire, which was beset by internal problems such as famine, plague, and earthquakes. In 451 CE, Attila's forces entered Gaul and later northern Italy. Indeed, the modern world of Europe was founded just as much on the legacy of the Roman Empire as it was by these various "barbarian" tribes who came to claim its land as their own. At first their contribution to architecture was minimal, as

these were chieftain cultures accustomed to village life and village needs. Houses were of wood and thatch. In some places they took over an abandoned Roman villa from which in fact the word *village* derives.

To protect the empire, Emperor Constantine founded a new city, Constantinople, which was built around a fusion of Christian and pagan motifs. Had that approach survived, Europe today would feel more like India, with its numerous complex hybrid religious practices. But upon Constantine's death in 337 CE, Christianity became an imperial religion, as effective in stabilizing the urban centers as in pacifying the encroaching tribal peoples, whom the Christians called "pagans," a derogatory term meaning something like country bumpkins, and from the Christian perspective untouched by the grace of God. A series of synods were held—from the First Council of Nicaea (325 CE) to others in 381, 431, 415, and 553 CE—that attempted to establish the principles for a unified state church. Policy was one thing, enforcement another. The Christianization of the empire would turn out to be a massive undertaking that would last some seven hundred years and would require not just that "heathen" altars and temples be meticulously destroyed, but that competing perspectives on Christianity be condemned as heresies and dealt with.

8.2 **Towers of Silence, Yazd, Iran**

In this world of religious intensification, Christianity injected an altogether new concept: the martyr. Since many Christians had died in Rome in the previous centuries, that city became a pilgrimage site even though it was by now little more than a village, located in the extensive ruins of the former world capital. People came from afar to visit the cemeteries where the martyrs were buried. To accommodate the influx, churches were built, often directly over the tombs. One of these was St. Peter's. In contrast to Zoroastrianism, Buddhism, and Hinduism, which made structures that were more or less open-air, these buildings, needing to enclose throngs of pilgrims, were large indoor spaces. The prototype came from the ancient Roman basilicas, or law courts, which were usually long walled and columnar buildings with heavy timbered ceilings. The symbolism of a building type dedicated to law was not lost on the early designers of these churches. In a world where security and lawfulness were at a premium, the Church could provide both, and with a message of divine deliverance to boot. In Roman times, lawyers, judges, and clients set up areas in the basilica's colonnades to transact business. There were no separate rooms in the building, and so there was a good deal of coming and

going. The apse at one end was often more a ritual formality than a site of worship. In the Christian basilica, the space was used altogether differently. Though the space was vast, its main purpose was to enclose the devotees and focus on the apse, which was now a highly charged space directly over the tomb. There were not chairs or pews as there are today. Furthermore, when there was no service, the space would often be used by merchants and traders.

St. Peter's was at the time the largest interior space in the world. Of all the churches from that era that have survived, only Santa Maria Maggiore (432–440 CE), though restored, gives us some sense of the quality of the interior. The columns lining the aisle were not custom made but taken from Roman buildings, the art and technology of making such columns having been lost. The church was built in honor of the Virgin Mary, who represented both the imperial ideals of classical Rome and those of the new Christian Rome.

In Central Asia, the story of incursions from the steppe culture is not dissimilar, except that here the deserts and mountains belonged to various tribes of the nomadic Huns, such as the Kidarites and Chionites, who set up camp in Afghanistan and

Turkmenistan to control the mountain passes between Persia and China. They encroached into Chinese territory, forcing the Jin dynasty to abandon its northern areas to a series of small, regional potentates. The Jin moved their capital to Jiankang, about 260 kilometers to the west of modern-day Shanghai. The division of China into northern and southern dynasties—parallel to the division of the Roman Empire between east and west—would last, in fact, until 581 and the emergence of the Sui dynasty, which for a brief time reunited China. But in the meantime, during this period large numbers of ethnic Han Chinese migrated to southern China (below the Yangtze River). This sinicization transformed the south from a land of farming communities into an area with increasingly large urban population centers.

In India, the Gupta Empire (320–550 CE) created a buffer zone for itself by subjugating the Persians to the north and the Kambojas to the east. But these efforts did not last long. Soon northern India was to be controlled by the nomadic Hephthalite Empire (408–670 CE), which was centered in Bactria in present-day Afghanistan and for a while dominated Central Asia. The Guptas seemingly showed little predilection for using horse archers, despite the fact these warriors were a main component in the ranks of their northern enemies. Nonetheless, in the 5th century, the Gupta Empire was the strongest urban civilization in Asia, its prosperity producing a period of magnificent accomplishments in sculpture and painting, as well as in science and poetry. The Gupta capital was Pataliputra, adjacent to modern-day Patna; but since it was built out of wood and on a river that frequently overflowed its shores, practically nothing is left, even though it was one of the largest cities in the world during this time, dominating the riverine trade of the Indo-Gangetic Plain.

Though shrines in India were then mostly made of wood, this period includes the first attempts to translate them into stone, such as Temple 17 at Sanchi. Its similarities to the Greek *naos* and porch are unmistakable. Perhaps more important was that during the Gupta period, popular worship was given formal sanction; temples and images dedicated to the various cults began springing up everywhere, releasing a new generation of architectural experimentation. The old Vedic world, which was not temple based, was now developing into small-scale shrine cults that would eventually cohere into what we today call Hinduism.

In Europe, the contestation between monotheism (i.e., Christianity) and the ancient animism of the Romans and their steppe invaders has parallels to the contestation between Buddhism and Vedism in India, except in reverse. In India, Vedic practices came to dominate because they incorporated the figure of the Buddha into their spiritual pantheon, mostly without sectarian violence. This was not the case in Europe, where Christianity, though it incorporated some local practices such as the Christmas tree, took an aggressive posture toward the tribal religions. Unlike the newly Christianized Roman Empire, where the political and religious elites sought to unify the religious message by identifying and repressing heresies, Hinduism unfolded in various directions, producing a complex tapestry of religious and architectural responses. Apart from Jainism and other more stand-alone religions, there is Shaivism, with its many different schools reflecting both regional and temporal variations and differences in philosophy, as well as Vaishnavism, which is often viewed as a synthesis of the worship of the gods Vishnu, Narayana, Vasudeva, and Krishna. While Shaivism developed mainly in the south and southeast; and Shaktism in eastern India

and in some parts of southwest Malabar; Vaishnavism, with its emphasis on Krishna, flourished mostly in the northern and central parts of India.

This period includes the first efforts to commemorate the pilgrimage site dedicated to the life of the great Buddha. The Mahabodhi Temple in Bodh Gaya was, however, no stupa. Though the current building is a 19th-century reconstruction, the basic idea of the building seems clear, even though its form may confuse an uninitiated observer. Unlike the stupa at Sanchi, which is a large hemispherical solid, this building looks like a Hindu temple. It has a tall tower, a *shikhara*, which would normally represent the geometrical model of Vishnu's mountain residence. The enclosed fence-shrine around the pipal tree, located just to the west of the east-facing temple, has similarities to the numerous sacred trees that are associated with Hindu temples. The same goes for the lotus pond, which is similar to the all-important water element in Hindu temples that represent the sacred ocean. Just as Hinduism was adopting the Buddha as an important deity on par with Vishnu and Shiva, Buddhist architecture here represents a type of syncretism of its own, combining different, often seemingly contradictory beliefs into a

8.3 Giant Buddha, Leshan, China

new whole. The uniquely Buddhist element of the Mahabodhi Temple is the requirement for circumambulation around the temple, which is not a Hindu practice.

During this time we see the expansion of Mahayana Buddhism along the trade routes between India and China. As Buddhism traversed the Kushan Empire (ca. 30–375 CE) and the Hephthalite Empire (408–670 CE), it came into contact with Hellenism and its legacy in figural sculpture. The Buddha began to take on human form and was represented in various ways as standing, seated, or even lying down. A grand example is the standing Buddhas at Bamiyan, Afghanistan, located at the intersection of the Eurasian trade routes. There, colossal rock-cut Buddha figures were carved out of the cliff face and then dressed and painted to give them a lifelike appearance. Other examples can be found at Unjusa, Korea (a Buddha in a supine position); and at Leshan, China, built during the Tang dynasty (618–907 CE), a seated Buddha 71 meters high. The largest Buddha statue in the world is the Spring Temple Buddha in Lushan County, Henan, China. The statue, finished in 2002, stands 128 meters high. Hinduism

also occasionally adopted the colossal form, as in, for example, the large reclining figure of Narayana, the Vedic supreme deity, at the Udaygiri Caves, quite likely carved in the 5th century CE in the Gupta period.

At Dunhuang (Mogao Caves), located at the western end of the Great Wall— where the Silk Route splits into its northern and southern arms, winding around the Taklamakan Desert—Buddhist monks built one of the largest cave complexes in the world. It represents part of the movement of rock-cut technology from India into China. Hundreds of caves, carved out of the sheer cliff face, show Buddha, usually seated, but sometimes lying down. The caves initially served as a place of meditation for hermit monks, but soon the priests who lived here came to function as a publishing house, copying sutras from India for distribution throughout China. By the 8th century CE the caves had become a place of pilgrimage in their own right. One could compare Mogao Caves with the martyrium churches in Rome. Pilgrimage had been one way in which humans accessed the divine, perhaps since ancient times when shamans would go to mountains to speak to the ancestors. But

with modern religions, pilgrimages became increasingly focused around specific sites and were increasingly part of the popular imagination. Places like Mogao and St. Peter's focused on the lives of holy men and the messages they embodied. The fact that one person died a natural death and another did not produced different types of ethical and moral stances.

The other major religion of the period was Zoroastrianism, the state religion of the Sassanians (ca. 230–650 CE), who dominated the Persian heartland and ruled from Ctesiphon, of which little of its ancient splendor is left apart from the vast central vault of a palace most likely built around 540 CE. It is known that artisans of the Roman provinces and masons from Byzantium helped in the building. Marble was brought in from Syria. Zoroastrianism, with connections to both the Hindu and Christian worldviews, stretched from West Asia to western China. The architectural legacy of Zoroastrianism is less secure since the religion was later repressed by both Islam and Christianity. Furthermore, most Zoroastrian buildings, like the Sassanian palaces, were built of sun-baked mud bricks that today are little more than dried-out wall stubs. Their surface decoration and painting have long since vanished. Nonetheless, across the deserts of Inner Asia, one can still find the occasional ruins of fire temples and dakhmas ("towers of silence"), where the dead are left exposed to be consumed by vultures. Zoroastrian tradition considers a dead body to be unclean, with the corpse demon rushing into the body and contaminating everything that comes into contact with it. To preclude this potential pollution, the bodies of the dead are placed atop a dakhma, exposing them to the sun and to scavenging birds. The towers are usually circular and have a flat unroofed surface with raised walls all about. The surface is divided into three concentric rings: the bodies of men are arranged around the outer ring, women in the second circle, and children in the innermost ring. Once the bones have been bleached by the sun and wind, which can take as long as a year, they are collected in a pit at the center of the tower, where—assisted by lime—they gradually disintegrate. This ritual precinct may be entered only by a special class of pallbearers. Of the various dakhmas that still exist, the now abandoned ones in Yazd,

Iran, are the grandest. The large circular enclosures at the top of the hill are visible for miles, as were the circling vultures that perched on top of the walls.

Japan, during this time, had its first encounter with centralized government, following the ascent of the Yamato clan. In this period, in terms of sheer scale, nothing competes with the Kofun in Japan. These are tomb mounds honoring elite personages that are clustered in a vast, sacred landscape. In plan, they have different shapes—keyhole, square-keyhole, round, and square—though the reason for the differences is not known. There are over 220 of these tombs built first in the Nara Basin and later in the Osaka Plain. The extraordinary quantities of weapons and armor discovered at Nonaka Kofun clearly indicates the relationship of the elites to military power, which makes sense given the uneasy times in China. In total, these structures constitute the most extensive mortuary landscape in the world, rivaled perhaps only by the Ming dynasty imperial tombs of the 15th and 16th centuries. Unlike the tombs of the martyrs in Rome, these tombs were embedded in the ancient shamanistic worldview. Perhaps

it might be valuable to compare these with other earthwork mortuary constructions, like the Egyptian pyramids, the great tumuli of the Europeans (from the 5th millennium BCE to the time of the Romans), the kurgans of the steppe people in Central Asia, and the mortuary mound of China's First Emperor. They all belong to the same ancestor-cult ethos, though some were made by tribal cultures and others by powerful elites as a way to cement and demonstrate their authority. The Japanese Kofun tradition and the Ming dynasty imperial tombs were the last great examples of this worldview in the form of monumental architecture.

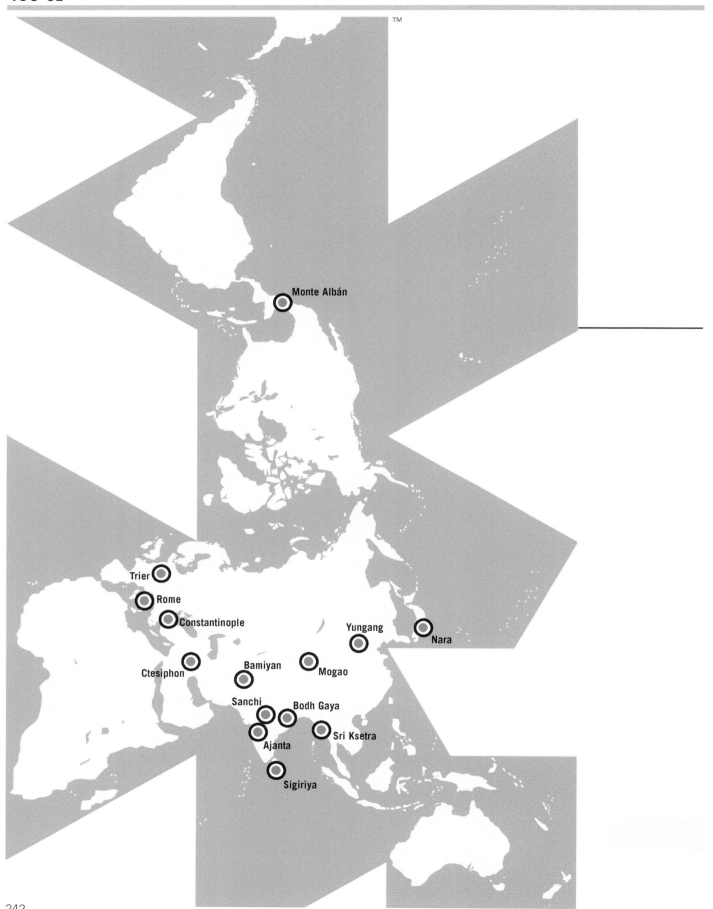

™

Monte Albán

Trier

Rome

Constantinople

Yungang

Nara

Ctesiphon

Bamiyan

Mogao

Sanchi

Bodh Gaya

Sri Ksetra

Ajanta

Sigiriya

Gupta Empire
ca. 320–550 CE

▲ **Temple at Bhitargaon**   ▲ **Mahabodhi Temple**
400–50 CE   Late Gupta period

▲ **Ajanta Caves**
Mid-5th to late 6th centuries CE

▲ **Temple 17 at Sanchi**
Early 5th century CE

China: Eastern Han Dynasty   Sixteen Kingdoms Period   Period of Northern and Southern Dynasties
25–220 CE   304–439 CE   386–589 CE

▲ **Mogao Caves**   ▲ **Yungang Caves**
4th to 14th centuries CE   Mid-5th to late 6th centuries CE

Parthian Empire   Sassanian Empire   Kushan Empire
247 BCE–224 CE   224–651 CE   2nd century BCE to 3rd century CE

▲ **Palace of Ardashir** ▲ **Palace at Shapur I**   ▲ **Bamiyan Buddhas**
ca. 224 CE   ca. 260 CE   6th century CE

200 CE   **400 CE**   **600 CE**

Funan City-States   Pyu City-States   Sri Lanka: Moriya Dynasty
est. 1st century CE   ca. 100 BCE–840 CE   463–691 CE

◀ **Sri Ksetra**   ▲ **Oc Eo**   ▲ **Sigiriya**
1st century BCE   1st to 7th centuries CE   5th century CE

Roman Empire   Western Roman Empire   Merovingian Dynasty in Central Europe
27 BCE–393 CE   393–476 CE   482–751 CE

▲ **Basilica at Trier**   ▲ **St. Sabina**   ▲ **St. Stefano Rotondo**
ca. 310 CE   425–32 CE   468–83 CE

▲ **Basilica of St. Peter**   ▲ **Santa Maria Maggiore**
ca. 320 CE   ca. 432 CE

▲ **St. John Lateran**   ▲ **Church of the Acheiropoietos**
ca. 314 CE   470 CE

Byzantine Empire
330–1453 CE

Church of the Prophets ▲   ▲ **Tomb of Theodoric the Great**
465 CE   ca. 520 CE

Church of Acheiropoietos ▲
470 CE

Japan: Kofun Culture
ca. 3rd century to 538 CE

Monte Albán Culture
ca. 500 BCE–900 CE

AJANTA CAVES

In 390 CE the Gupta king Vikramaditya arranged the marriage of his daughter Prabhavatigupta to Rudrasena II, the prince of the vassal state of Vakataka, through which went the *dakshinapatha*, the southern trade route. The Vakatakas' gratitude for their status as guardians of the *dakshinapatha* is recorded in their lavish patronage of Ajanta, the largest assemblage of Buddhist rock-cut *caityas* (meditation chambers) and *viharas* (dormitories) found anywhere in South Asia. These *caityas* and *viharas* are collectively called caves even though they are not caves but rock-cut architecture.

Like the Sunga period Sanchi complex, Ajanta was a kind of college monastery, affording accommodations for up to several hundred teachers and pupils. Chinese pilgrim Hsuan Tsang (Xuanzang) notes that Dinnaga, a celebrated Buddhist author of books on logic, resided there. Though his books are lost, the Ajanta Caves have survived; even their paintings are relatively intact. Though somewhat difficult to access, the location alongside the *dakshinapatha* meant that the caves could effectively serve the needs of both the Mahayana Buddhist monks and their students; the names of many of the latter are inscribed within the caves. As Mahayana practitioners, Ajanta's monks were allowed and encouraged to create Buddha figures and thus to propagate the concept that many had attained nirvana even before the historical Buddha. Since virtuous worldly acts were a way of attaining nirvana, or Buddhahood, the laity's patronage of the Ajanta monks helped them in their own quest for nirvana.

The Ajanta Caves are located along the sheer rock wall of a dramatic C-shaped chasm carved by the Waghora River. The Waghora, a mountain stream, forces its way into the valley and forms in its descent a series of waterfalls 60 meters high, which must certainly have been audible to the monks in the caves. The thirty-odd caves vary from 10 to 33 meters in elevation above the river. The *caitya* window, originally an imitation horseshoe-shaped wooden window, has now been transformed into an abstract representation of the Buddha, with a prominent topknot and elongated "ears" reminiscent of the ears of earlier statues of the Buddha.

8.4 **The cliff edge containing the Ajanta Caves near Aurangabad, India**

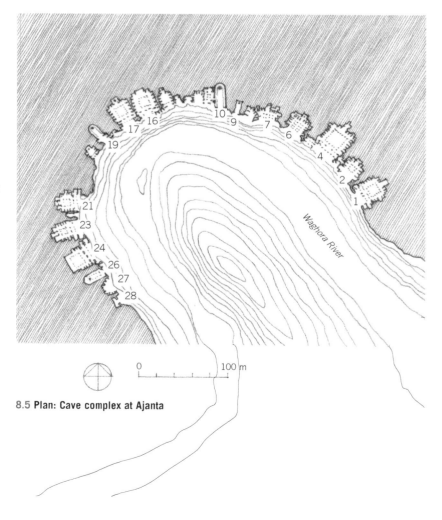

8.5 **Plan: Cave complex at Ajanta**

8.6 Paintings from Cave 2 at Ajanta

The Gupta Empire, with its capital at Pataliputra, is considered to be the classical age of Hindu and Buddhist art and literature. The arts, architecture, science, and literature were given strong support. The decimal system, which is still in use, was an invention of this period. Aryabhatta's expositions on astronomy in 499 CE, moreover, gave calculations of the solar year and the shape and movement of astral bodies with remarkable accuracy. Though the empire was relatively decentralized, one should consider the Gupta, the Sassanian, and the Byzantine empires as a continuous regional unit.

The columns are richly sculptured with floral and figural representations symbolic of the gardens where the Buddha preached and gained enlightenment. The column capitals and bases bulge like the folds of the corpulent Buddha. The stupas are also richly ornamented, with Buddha statues attached directly to their surfaces, presaging the eclipse of the stupa as the primary representational element, particularly in China and Southeast Asia. The oldest *caityas* (Caves No. 9 and 10, located almost in the middle) were relatively simple, with an apsidal colonnade marking the circumambulatory route around a largely unadorned stupa at the end. However, Caves No. 19 (450 CE) and 26 (490 CE), from the reign of Harisena, take on Mahayana overtones. Both have an elaborate forecourt open to the sky, with side chambers hewn directly out of the rock. Unlike the great *caitya* at Karli, whose entrance replicates a wooden assemblage of *caityas*, these are covered by large and small Buddha figurines and stupas. No longer imitation-wood stage sets, they are symbolic entities in themselves.

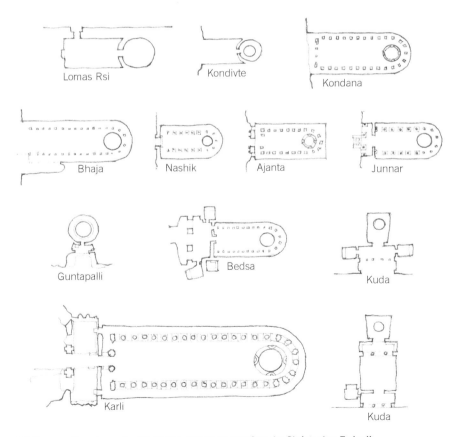

8.7 Comparative plans of *caitya* halls, based on drawings by Christopher Tadgell

As Mahayana Buddhism became ever more popular, it developed a more elaborate liturgical practice that supported a richer artistic program. Evidence of this can be seen in Ajanta's *viharas*, which served as the monks' residences. Over time, the *viharas* at Ajanta changed from simple dwellings for the monks to full-fledged ceremonial spaces, but the basic form, a rectangular colonnaded hall preceded by a portico and surrounded by cells, persisted. The Ajanta *viharas* have a broad veranda, the roof of which is supported by pillars that open into a central pillared hall averaging about 6 by 10 meters. The cells open to this hall. The number of the cells vary according to the size and importance of the *vihara*. Some of the cells associated with particularly significant monks were transformed into shrines with their own votive Buddha statues (as at Caves No. 2, 6, and 17). Some *viharas* even acquired multiple stories (Cave No. 6) and circumambulatory routes (usually defined by a colonnaded passage). As they began to house more ceremonies, they also became more ornamental and decorative, with images depicting scenes from the life of the Buddha and from Buddhist treatises painted onto the walls. A certain nonmonastic sensuousness pervades the images, which are not confined to designated panels. Despite the dim light, every surface of the *viharas* was painted over. Art, sculpture, and architecture, in other words, comingle to create a seamless, sensory experience. Structural expression is denied. Like the imitation-wood construction present in the older *caityas*, the essential symbolic message of the Ajanta *viharas* was to display the profound beauty of the life and world of the Buddha and, at the same time, underline its character as an illusion, or *maya*—a fundamental doctrine of Mahayana Buddhist practice on the path to nirvana.

8.8 Plan: Cave No. 2 at Ajanta

0   10 m

8.9 Interior of Cave No. 26 at Ajanta

8.10 Interior of Cave No. 19 at Ajanta

8.11 Interior of Cave No. 2 at Ajanta

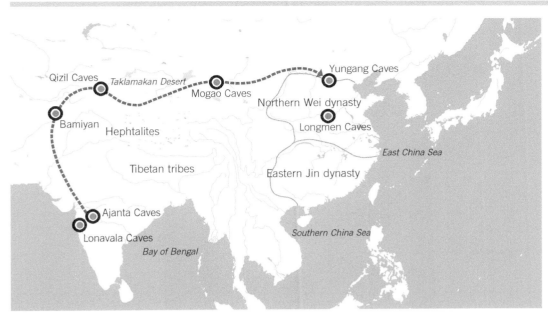

8.12 Buddhism in Central Asia

ESTABLISHMENT OF CHINESE AND CENTRAL ASIAN BUDDHISM

By the 6th century CE, Mahayana Buddhism had made its way into China and Korea, and from there crossed into Japan. Never accompanied by the sword, Buddhism was spread along the trade routes, benefiting from the symbiotic relationship between monastic monks and itinerant traders. Traffic between China and South Asia in the 7th century CE was heavy. (In Chinese literature, it is India—not Europe—that is referred to as the "Western Kingdom.") Besides silk, which was the prime luxury commodity, South Asian kingdoms imported camphor, fennel, vermilion, fine leather, pears, and peaches from China. The Chinese, who were much more self-sufficient, seemed to be interested mostly in Buddhism. The Han emperor Ming-di was the first to officially invite Indian Buddhist monks to China to translate Buddhist sutras into Chinese. In 64 CE, after the long and arduous journey, Dharmaratna and Kasyapa Matanga arrived in Luoyang, the new Han capital, with a white horse laden with sutras.

The Han emperor built a monastery for them called the Baima-si (or the White Horse Monastery). Although the current structure dates mostly from the 14th century, Baima-si is by reference the oldest surviving temple of China. In the millennium after the arrival of Dharmaratna and Matanga, hundreds of Indian monks came to live in China. Not as many Chinese traveled to India, although those who did were very well known, even in their own time, because they kept extensive records of their travels and actively interpreted Buddhism for the Chinese. These include Faxian in the 5th century CE and Hsuan Tsang (Xuanzang) and Yi Jing in the 7th century CE, both of whom made the long and arduous journey to South Asia and back. Although Buddhism spread rapidly across East Asia, its translation into relevant Chinese concepts took time.

Buddhism, however, was only one among many competitive intellectual traditions prevalent in China at the time. Not everyone was convinced that Buddhism was an improvement over local Confucian and Daoist principles. Confucianists, for instance, challenged Buddhism's inability to set out principles of an organized social and political order—which was, of course, Confucianism's strength. (Buddhism, in contrast, is introspective and personal.) Competition between these two divergent philosophical traditions remained a hallmark of Chinese history for the next two thousand years. There were several attempts at mediation—most famously the Qing emperor Qianlong's creation of a Tibetan Buddhist model of governance, with the emperor in a central role, in the 18th century. In general, however, Buddhism governed the temples and monasteries, while the court still operated on Confucian principles. As a result, East Asian Buddhism has a flavor different from the Buddhism of South Asia and even Southeast Asia.

In 400 CE, Buddhism was supported by the Northern Dynasties (386–581 CE). In the Southern Dynasties (420–589 CE), Confucianism was still dominant, even though some learned monks attempted to make Buddhist ideas compatible with Daoist philosophy.

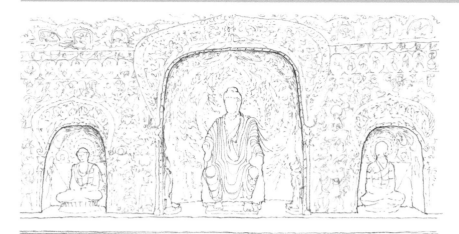

8.13 **Mogao Caves: West wall of Cave 285, Dunhuang, China**

Mogao Caves

Carved out of the cliffs on the western bank of the Dunhuang River, the five hundred or so Mogao Caves document the first millennium of Buddhism in China, from roughly 300 to 1350 CE. As one would expect, the caves are located at an important junction in the Silk Route, right at the western end of the Great Wall. The Silk Route breaks into its northern and southern paths at Dunhuang. West of Dunhuang begins, or ends, one of the most arduous parts of the journey, through the harsh Lopnar and Taklamakan Deserts. Abandoned in the 14th century, the Mogao Caves were rediscovered in the early 1900s, yielding a spectacular find of fifty thousand manuscripts in just one of the caves. Intentionally sealed in the 11th century, this cache held thousands of copies of sutras, letters, contracts, poems, prayer sheets, and various official documents. In some cases, there were multiple copies of the best-known sutras, handwritten with brushes dipped in lustrous black ink on paper, establishing that Mogao was a critical center for the dissemination of Buddhist knowledge. Large quantities of these manuscripts were distributed to Japanese and European museums before the Chinese government intervened and took the rest to the national museum in Beijing. The work of properly translating these manuscripts and understanding their significance is still ongoing.

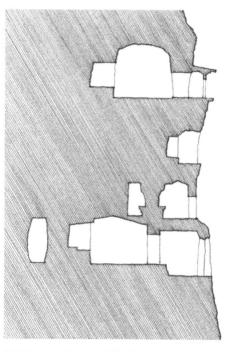

8.14 **Section through cliff at Mogao Caves**

The architectural significance of the Mogao Caves lies as much in their individual characteristics as in their collective presence as a marvelous city of caves. Visible from a distance in the arid landscape are three to five tiers of caves carved into a long cliff face, all fairly close to one another. Some are small niches with room enough for a single monk to sit in meditation, whereas others have lofty ceilings and are large enough for a procession of a hundred or so worshippers. Changes in dynasties marked new beginnings in different parts of the Dunhuang cliff. The earliest caves were simple chambers with niches and sculptures of the Buddha.

By the Northern Dynasties period, the caves became more complex and took the form of short corridors leading from the entrance hall to a transverse chamber with a simulated gabled roof. Opposite the entrance, the principal Buddha image was placed against a central pillar, allowing the worshippers, as at Ajanta, to perform *parikrama*, or circumambulation, around the central image. Cave No. 285 (539 CE) has its sidewalls lined with niches in which monks could sit and meditate. Cave No. 428, the bequest of the governor of Dunhuang, Prince Jian Ping, (565–76 CE), is one of the most elaborate of this period, with each of the four niches of the central pillar featuring statues of the Buddha and three bodhisattvas. The "gabled" roof is divided into panels by bands painted brown that mimic the structure of a wooden hut.

Like contemporary caves in South Asia, most of the Mogao cave walls are covered by paintings describing the life of the Buddha and various manifestations of Buddhist doctrine. The predominant colors are blue, green, red, black, white, and gold. Stylistically, the art is an amalgam of Indic, Central Asian, and Chinese influences, although the overall style is far more South Asian than is later Chinese Buddhist art and architecture.

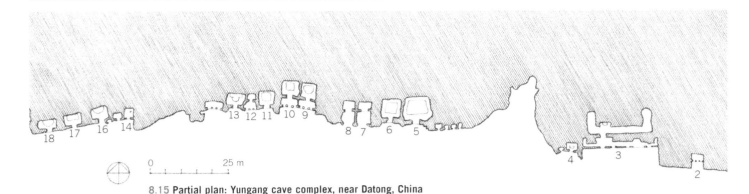

8.15 **Partial plan: Yungang cave complex, near Datong, China**

Yungang Caves

Some 1,000 kilometers east of Mogao, in present-day Shanxi Province, the Yungang caves were constructed in the late 5th to early 6th centuries CE under the imperial sponsorship of the Northern Wei dynasty (386–534 CE). Unlike the Mogao Caves, which were inhabited by monks on a trade route, those at Yungang were a new type of cave, being built adjacent to the Wei capital of Datong. They had only a small resident monk population and were meant for worship, primarily by the urban population of Datong. A Northern Wei minister ordered the construction of the first five of the caves. These contained colossal statues of the seated Buddha, in the manner of the Bamiyan, and reflect Hellenistic ideas about human representation. In an environment in which imperial patronage of the Buddha was fiercely contested, these caves may have been intended as representations of the five Northern Wei emperors as a way to compete with Confucian ideologies or even the self-deified emperors of the Southern Dynasties.

While most of the caves at Yungang are focused on the image of the Buddha, one of the caves (No. 29) has a vertical column rising from the floor to the roof, articulated as a multistory tower with a series of projecting eaves. Small images of the Buddha are located between the floors. This is an early manifestation of the Chinese pagoda (or *ta*) conceived, in Mahayana Buddhist thinking, as a magnification of the *chattris* of the South Asian stupa. Under Mahayana Buddhism, the esoteric abstractions of the stupa were slowly replaced by a more graphic and literal iconography. First, the figure of the Buddha was considered to be equivalent to the stupa, an idea that was often expressed by superimposing a Buddha figure directly onto

the stupa, as at Ajanta. In China, as the *ta* emerged as the dominant form, the figure of the Buddha was inserted into the pagoda, either as a single colossal standing figure or with several at each level. (See the discussion of the Mu-ta and the Guanyin-ge in 1000 CE.)

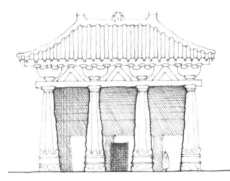

8.16 **Cave No. 10, Yungang**

8.17 **Interior, Cave No. 10, Yungang**

8.18 **View of some of the more than five hundred Mogao Caves**

8.19 **View of Bamiyan, Afghanistan**

Kushans of Bamiyan

Bamiyan was at the center of the 5th-century CE Eurasian world. Trade routes from China, India, and West Asia came together in this valley, located in the middle of contemporary Afghanistan. The site was protected by a large Buddhist monastery, with more than a hundred caves of various sizes carved out of the sheer cliff face of the nearby mountains. In their midst, separated by about 1 kilometer, the Kushan emperor Kanishka initiated the construction of two gigantic Buddha statues, known as the Bamiyan Buddhas. They were completed in the 4th and 5th centuries CE, under the Sassanians. Colossal Buddhas, never built in India, were a Kushan invention that was widely imitated throughout China, Korea, and Japan for centuries to come. In March, 2001, the Bamiyan Buddhas, among the first of their kind, were destroyed by the Taliban, who perceived them as idols.

The Bamiyan cliff rises sharply at the northwestern edge of its wide and expansive valley. To the north toward China and to the east toward India, the valleys approaching Bamiyan are narrow and sharp. The traders coming upon Bamiyan would have encountered a dramatic change in landscape. The traders' attention, however, would have been focused on the imposing sandstone cliff that rises sharply at the northwestern edge of a wide valley. As seen from across the valley, the 1.6-kilometer-long cliff, pockmarked by the caves, rises to a peak in the middle. Behind it, one after another, rise successive layers of the Himalayas, with the most distant ranges perpetually clad in snow.

Even from this distance, the Bamiyan statues would have been clearly visible and would in that sense have conversed with the distant Himalayan peaks.

The bodies of two Bamiyans were first cut directly from the stone and then molded with a mixture of mud and straw to create the folds of the robes, the hands, and the details of the face. The drapery was made by suspending ropes from the stone surface of the upper body. At the base the ropes were held in place by wooden pegs and then covered over with mud plaster. The entire surface was originally painted in gold and other bright colors. The outward expression of the statues, in particular the folds of the garments, has a Hellenic character. Precedents for colossal statues date from pharaonic Egypt and the Roman Empire. Most of the smaller caves at Bamiyan were covered with paintings, very similar in style to those found in the caves at Ajanta.

8.20 **Bamiyan Buddha**

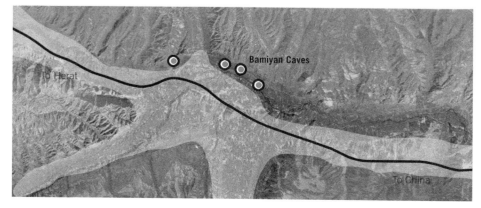

8.21 **Bamiyan and environs**

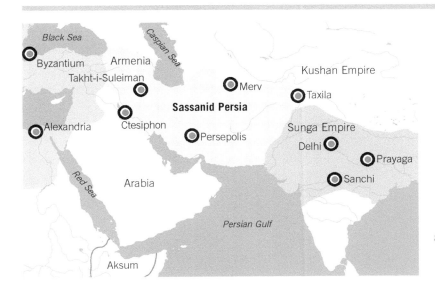

8.22 **Central Asia, ca. 400 CE**

THE SASSANIAN EMPIRE

With the weakening of the Parthian rulers, the Sassanians asserted themselves. They were led by Ardashir I (r. 226–41 CE), a descendant of a line of priests serving the goddess Anahita in Istakhr, Persis (Pars). Unlike his predecessors, Ardashir had a strong interest in architecture and urbanism, and founded numerous palaces and cities. The Hellenistic tradition of monumental architecture was revised and given its own Persian perspective. Ardashir rebuilt Ctesiphon, but little remains, as it was constructed using traditional mud brick. Elements of a palace made by Ardashir's successor, Shapur I (r. 241–272 CE), imply that the palace was a massive complex lying about three-quarters of a kilometer from the western shore of the Euphrates near a large loop in the river. Facing west, the Taq-i Kisra is an open vault flanked by massive walls decorated bottom to top with blind arcades, probably painted originally in vivid colors. The vault, known as an *iwan*, was a building innovation of the later Parthian era that is found in these Sassanian palaces and was to remain an important typological element in Persian architecture. Only parts of the impressive vault remain. Spanning 28 meters, it was probably the largest vault in ancient history. It is thought that the arch was built without wooden supports during its construction. The thin, unfired mud bricks are laid on a slant, the weight transferred to the massive sidewalls. Architecturally, the arch is a pointed ovoid peculiar to Mesopotamia.

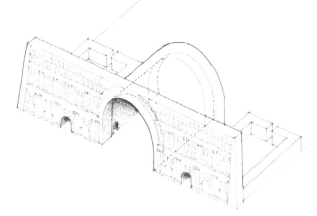

8.23 **Pictorial view: Taq-i Kisra, the *iwan* of Khusrau I, Ctesiphon, Iraq**

8.24 **The only visible remains of Ctesiphon today is the great arch, Taq-i Kisra, of Khusrau's palace.**

8.25 **Firuzabad and its area, Iran**

8.26 **Central fire at the *atash-gah* in Surakhani, Baku, Azerbaijan**

Visitors to the hall during the reign of Khusrau I (r. 531–79 CE) tell that the vast floor was covered with a splendid "winter carpet" of heavy woven silk adorned with gold and jewels. Its pattern was supposed to represent a pleasure garden with running brooks and interlaced paths. Though never equaled, it became the model for garden carpets. The carpet was confiscated by Arab conquerors when they took Ctesiphon in 638 CE. Scornful of the display of royal luxury, they cut it up and divided it among their warriors. But the idea of a carpeted floor was soon to become a permanent fixture of Islamic mosques. The desolate area of these ruins gives little indication of the once lush orchards and rose gardens that surrounded the building.

Ardashir's capital was Firuzabad, located in an easily defensible valley. At the front of Ardashir's palace was another open *iwan*, flanked by side chambers. To the rear were three domed rooms, and behind them, a courtyard and garden. The palace lay to the south of Ardashir's planned circular city, over 2 kilometers in diameter, at the center of which was a large tower that, so it is thought, served as a Zoroastrian fire temple. The Parthians established other cities as trading centers, such as Hecatompylos (Šahr-e Qumis) in eastern Iran, but little remains of their past splendor.

Zoroastrian Fire Temples

It is presumed that Zoroaster (Zarathustra) lived around 600 BCE, but no one knows exactly when or where he lived or died; there remain only traditions. And there is just as much ambiguity about the fire temples that were built for the faith he developed. Fire was ranked according to its uses, from the lesser fires of potters and goldsmiths, through cooking fires and hearth fires, up to the three great symbolically perceived eternal fires of the farmers, warriors, and priests. Zoroastrianism was opposed to the use of images, and during the Sassanian period, cult statues were removed, although anthropomorphized divinities remained.

Further, Zoroastrianism does not prescribe worshipping in a temple. Traditionally, Zoroastrians worship individually at home, or in the open, facing a source of light. When they wished to worship as a community, they did so in open-air gathering areas around a podium where a fire was lit. These gathering areas were usually on hillsides or hilltops. But as the rituals and practices became canonized, the corresponding religious architecture was standardized, and a complex network of temples resulted. The role of the fire in the religious services was mainly symbolic and served the purpose of consecration, much as the cross does in a Christian context. Each king in the Sassanian world had his own royal fire. There was a prescribed ritual for reigniting the home fire from the city fire and the city fire from the

royal fire. Rituals, together with the rites of purification, were in essence all part of state bureaucracy. Some have drawn parallels to the Hindu caste society and to Mandarin China.

It is difficult to construct a clear architectural history of the fire temples since only about sixty ruinous examples remain for the entire 1,200-year period from 550 BCE to 650 CE. At their peak, fire temples ranged from Azerbaijan to Osh, Kyrgyzstan, on the Chinese border. Pockets of Zoroastrian belief still linger at Stakhra, 20 kilometers south of Persepolis, and even as far afield as Taxila in Pakistan. Some of the fire temple ruins belong to the Sassanian era (224–642 CE), during which Zoroastrianism flourished as the official religion, but others date to the earlier Achaemenian, Seleucid, and Parthian periods. Many fire temples were built in the vicinity of geothermal springs. This is certainly the case in Azerbaijan, where burning eruptions of gas from the numerous mud volcanoes still light up the sky today and are linked to the fire temples at Nush-Dzhan-Tepe, Adurgushnaep, Surakhany, Pirallahi, Hovsany, Shakhdag, and elsewhere. An important fire temple site is Takht-i-Suleiman ("Throne of Solomon"), near Mt. Zindan in southern Azerbaijan. Tradition has it that it was thought to be the birthplace of Zoroaster. It is a spectacular site, consisting of the much worn crater of a former volcano that still spews out blasts of sulfuric air. Though little remains today, descriptions indicate that

8.27 **Fire temple in modern-day Iran**

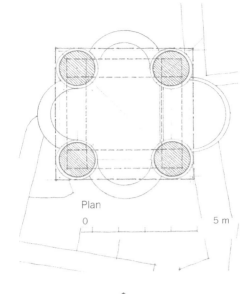

Plan

0   5 m

the temple was in use for several hundred years, beginning from around the 5th century BCE. It rose to particular prominence under the Sassanians.

An early fire temple is located near Ani, Armenia. It has four massive pillars and no walls. At a later period the structure was converted into a Christian chapel by the insertion of curved walls between its four columns. The massiveness of the columns suggests a stone roof, but the shape of the roof in the reconstruction is speculative.

The demise of Zoroastrianism was sudden. To the west, Christianity vigorously suppressed it. Islam effectively chased it from the realm, destroying its temples and dispersing its congregations. Today, most remaining believers live in Hindu areas in India, with a large community, for example, living in Mumbai. There are also residual communities in Iran, where there are important fire temples in Yazd, Kerman, and Tehran.

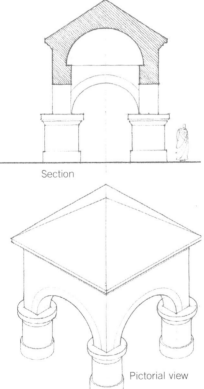

Section

Pictorial view

8.29 **Possible fire temple at Ani, Armenia**

8.28 **A Zoroastrian fire ceremony**

8.30 Temple 17, Sanchi, near Bhopal, India

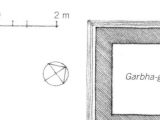
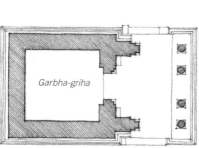

0   2 m

Garbha-griha

8.31 Section and plan: Temple 17, Sanchi

HINDU RENAISSANCE

As Buddhism was gaining new converts across East Asia, India saw it gradually waning. This transition took place during the Gupta Empire, when Buddhist practices began to fuse with the surviving Vedic practices of pre-Buddhist times, creating a new and well-organized religion that we now call Hinduism. The Gupta revival of a transformed Vedic Hinduism was a skillful exercise in adaptation and invention. It was not a simple revival of pre-Buddhist Vedic practices. Rather, Vedic institutions were reinvented to serve the purposes of their new champions. Old fire sacrifices were transformed into courtly ritual; oral Vedic literatures were rewritten to integrate contemporary social and cultural norms; and Vedic gods were supplanted by new, more agential and personal gods—particularly Shiva and Vishnu. Sanskrit became the language of the court and the medium of an official high culture that revolved around the reinvented institution of the temple.

Though the new Hinduism challenged Buddhism theologically, the latter's institutions and practices were assimilated into the Hindu temple. Unlike the Mauryas and the Han Chinese, the Gupta maintained subject kings as vassals and did not consolidate every kingdom into a single administrative unit. This enabled them not only to maintain and profit from the

trade routes that were still controlled by the Buddhists but also to exploit Buddhist institutions for Hindu purposes. Buddhist practices were not prohibited—in fact, their institutions continued to thrive. The interblending of Buddhist and Vedic cultures was described by Fa Hein, the famous Chinese pilgrim to the Gupta state from 399 to 414 CE. He talks of a magnificent procession of about twenty wheeled stupas with figures of seated Buddhas attended by standing bodhisattvas coming to the Gupta capital of Pataliputra, where it was received by the Hindu Brahmins and ushered into the city with great ceremony. By this time, the Buddhists were themselves routinely making stone images of the Buddha. In some instances, a Buddhist *caitya* hall would be reused for Hindu gods. And in a stroke of genius, the Buddha himself was deified as another manifestation of Vishnu from the Hindu pantheon.

The basic configuration of the Hindu temple can be seen at the so-called Temple 17 at Sanchi and the Kankali Devi at Tigawa, both from the early 5th century CE. Both consist of a flat-roofed *garbha-griha* and *mandapa*, linked by a simple stepped stylobate and architrave. The *garbha-griha* (literally "womb chamber") is usually square and unadorned. The *mandapa* is essentially a place for the worshipper.

In Hindu worship, the *antarala* (doorway or threshold) between the *garbha-griha* and a *mandapa* marks the all-important moment of transition at which the worshipper and the deity come into direct visual contact and enact the critical transaction called *darsana* ("beholding of an auspicious deity"). Indeed, the whole temple can be considered a two-way portal between the worlds of the worshipper and the deity. In essence, the deity descends into the lingam or statue while the worshipper ascends to the sacred threshold. The deity is considered to be a guest in the world of the worshipper. In a ritual called *puja*, the worshipper offers the deity food (and, at times, such gifts as clothing and ornaments) on a tray. The pandit, or priest, who stands at the threshold and mediates the ritual takes the food from the tray and touches it to the mouth of the deity. He keeps a portion for the temple, returning the rest, with some additional special food from the temple, called *prasada*, for the worshipper.

Another example of an early Gupta period Hindu temple is the brick and mud-mortar temple at Bhitargaon (400–50 CE). Here the *garbha-griha* is surmounted by a large tapering superstructure, called the *shikhara*. The *shikhara* marks the vertical axis in the form of the cosmic mountain. Its purpose is to enable the worshipper to visualize the order of the complete universe as described

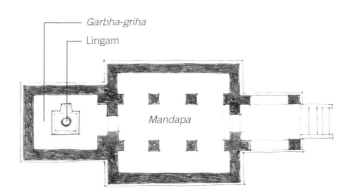

Garbha-griha

Lingam

Mandapa

8.32 Plan: Mallikarjuna Temple, Aihole, India, ca. 8th century CE

by Hindu cosmogony. A *shikhara*, therefore, is a three-dimensional model of the Hindu cosmos. All temples culminate in a finial, the conceptual center of the structure. From there, the "cosmos" splays outward, cascading down the building along radial lines. The actual geometries of the *shikhara* are determined by its mandala, or astrological diagram. They can best be understood, as Adam Hardy has recently described, as complex assemblages of mini-temples, or *aediculae*, intended to depict the composite nature of the Hindu cosmos. *Shikharas* are conceived of as solid and are for the most part, even though for structural reasons some may have internal hollows.

8.34 Three-dimensional model of the Hindu cosmos
Based on Adam Hardy, *The Temple Architecture of India* (Hoboken, NJ: John Wiley & Sons, 2008).

8.33 Lakshman Temple, Sirpur, India

8.35 Mahabodhi Temple, Bodh Gaya, India

MAHABODHI TEMPLE

Bodh Gaya, the garden in Gaya near Patna where the Buddha is said to have attained enlightenment while sitting under a pipal tree, is one of the most venerated pilgrimage destinations of the entire Buddhist world. The Mahabodhi (literally "Great Buddha") Temple at this site was begun by Asoka, who ordered the construction of a simple stone platform, known as the Vajrasana ("Diamond Throne"), to mark the spot where the Buddha supposedly sat. In accordance with the nonrepresentational requirements of Hinayana Buddhism, Asoka had no other representation or temple built at the site. The pipal tree itself is said to have been cut down by zealots, first in the 4th century BCE and then again in the 7th century CE. But a sapling from the original tree, taken to Sri Lanka by Asoka's daughter in the 4th century BCE, still thrives. In the late Gupta period, the Mahabodhi Temple (late 5th or 6th century CE) was constructed next to the tree. The temple has been renovated repeatedly over time, and it is difficult to be absolutely certain what part of it is original to the Gupta period. Nonetheless, its contours today are not that different from its description by Hsuan Tsang (Xuanzang) in 637 CE.

Hsuan Tsang recorded that the Bodhi Tree was enclosed by a strong, high brick wall (originally built by Asoka) 500 paces in circumference. Rare trees offered shade, while fine grasses, flowers, and strange plants covered the ground. The main gate opened east toward the Niranjana River, while the south gate connected to a large lotus tank, the sacred tank where it is believed that the Buddha spent a week. The north gate opened into the grounds of a large monastery. Inside there were innumerable stupas and shrines, built as memorials by sovereigns and high officials. In the center of the Bodhi Tree enclosure—defined by a stone *vedika* or fence (like the one around the Great Stupa at Sanchi)—was the Vajrasana, sandwiched between the Bodhi Tree to its west and, to its east, the Mahabodhi Temple, 48 meters high and 20 paces wide.

The temple was made of bricks coated with lime. It had tiers of niches with gold images, its four walls were adorned with exquisite carvings of pearls, and at its top was a gilt-copper stupa. Hsuan Tsang also recorded separately that south of the Bodhi Tree was an Asokan pillar more than 30 meters high. The Mahabodhi Temple is today clearly similar to this description. It is

surrounded by four subsidiary shrines at its corners that were added in the 19th century. The central chamber houses the image of the enthroned Buddha of the temple. The brick *shikhara* contains another *cella* at the upper level with a secondary image of the Buddha.

Along with the Bhitargaon Temple, the Mahabodhi Temple is among the oldest multistory brick temples in South Asia. Although they went out of fashion in India once stone temples began to be constructed, it is also possible that the development of the Buddhist pagodas in China may have in part been inspired by Hsuan Tsang's description of this temple, which was widely circulated. The temple is not dissimilar to the Hindu temple Bhitargaon (400–50 CE), and indeed the Buddhist use of Hindu forms demonstrates the experimental overlap of forms during this time.

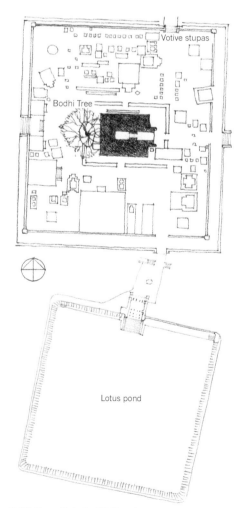

8.36 Plan: Mahabodhi Temple

SIGIRIYA

On the island of Sri Lanka, in 477 CE, Kasyapa Matanga assassinated his father, Dhatusena, and usurped the throne. But because his brother, Mogollana, challenged his accession and escaped to India to amass an army, Kasyapa Matanga left the capital city, Anuradhapura, and built for himself a defensible palace-fortress atop Sigiriya—a striking tabletop rock rising 370 meters over the plain. When Mogollana returned to Sri Lanka and defeated Kasyapa Matanga in 495 CE, he reinstalled himself at Anuradhapura, leaving Sigiriya to became a Buddhist monastery; it remained active until the 14th century.

The palace and gardens would have ranked as among the most magnificent at that time anywhere in the world. They were constructed on three levels: atop the impressively scaled rock, at midlevel on a shoulder of the rock, and on the plain surrounding the rock. An ingenious stair, hacked out of the cliff, connected the various levels. The top level, with its commanding views was designed as a series of interconnected pavilions, cisterns, pleasure pools and gardens. Artesian wells supply water year-round, thus making the whole palace possible. The midlevel structures were built around a series of rock-cut caves that were used by the Buddhist monks. At the base of the hill, a huge rectangular garden, irrigated by a system of hydraulics, is enclosed within ramparts and moats. A man-made lake just to the south of the rock feeds the moats and its related canals. The lower garden is a Zen-like blend of a strict geometrical plan overlaid by the boulders and other natural forms that are sprinkled across the site. Five gates regulated entry. Entering from the west, there was first a square garden with a central island that was linked by causeways and surrounded by L-shaped pools. This was followed by a long garden, divided into two levels that included pools with fountains fed by shallow serpentine streams. The sequence concludes at the stairs that lead up the rock and through a boulder garden leading to the gigantic rock-cut claws of a lion—thus its name, Lion's Gate. The western face of the rock was covered by paintings depicting the pleasures of royal life. Most of these paintings were destroyed once the palace became a monastery, so that they would not disturb meditation.

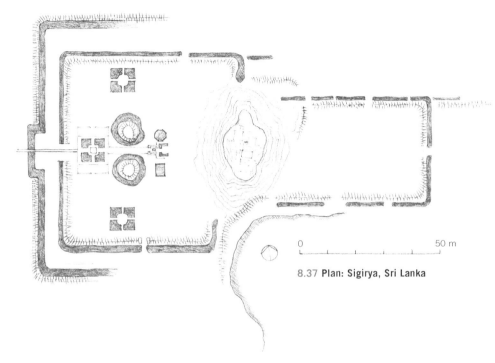

0   50 m

8.37 **Plan: Sigirya, Sri Lanka**

8.38 **View of Sigirya from the garden**

8.39 **Lion's Gate, Sigirya**

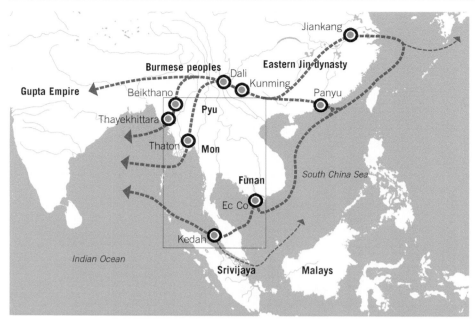

8.40 Trade routes in Southeast Asia, ca. 400 CE

THE PYU, MON, AND FUNAN

Southeast Asia was influenced by two related factors: the Indianization of its culture and the trade routes that ran from the Bay of Bengal to southern China and around the Malaysian Peninsula. China, under the Han dynasty (205 BCE–220 CE), sought to control the southern Silk Route, which ran through the cities of Kunming and Dali to Burma (modern-day Myanmar) and India. Around 200 CE, the Chinese established Pany (now Guangzhou) on the Pearl River delta for the purpose of expanding this system of trade routes, a policy furthered by the Jin dynasty—especially because in the 4th century CE, northern China was largely overrun by nomadic tribes. The Jin capital at the time was Jiankang (present-day Nanjing). The Indianization of Southeast Asia, which began in the 1st century CE in Burma and reached the southern coast of Vietnam by around 300 CE, was a complex process that involved both Buddhism and Hinduism. With these new religions came a temple architecture that intermixed Indian concepts with local traditions of woodworking. Driving this was a luxury trade in Southeast Asian commodities: pearls, diamonds, and gold as well as a long list of scented woods and other forest products.

Among the earliest Buddhist civilizations to develop in that way were the Pyu, in the central and northern regions of Burma and usually dated from about the 1st century BCE to the 9th century CE, and the Mon, who were located farther to the south in Burma and in Thailand. The Pyu controlled the trade along the Irrawaddy River, which was one of the prime routes between India and China. This area is quite dry, and agricultural production would have been poor had it not

been for highly effective irrigation systems that distributed water from the numerous streams. The Pyu constructed low weirs just below natural bends in streambeds; these directed part of the water into diversionary canals that then followed the contours of the landscape to deliver water to the fields. The Pyu established several major towns and cities, the principal ones being Sri Ksetra (Thayekhittaya), which controlled the trade routes to the south; and Beikthano and Halin (Halingyi, near Shwebo) in the north.

Sri Ksetra, which translates roughly as "affluent holy area," is an oval-shaped city, controlling access to the Irrawaddy River delta. The city is quite large—about 3.5 kilometers across—and was at its height during the 5th through the early 9th centuries CE. It has some of the earliest Buddhist shrines in Burma. Bawbawgyi, located just outside of the town, is 60 meters tall and has a bell-shaped body that is hollow up to about two-thirds of its height. In this respect it differs from most stupas in Burma, which are typically solid and cannot be entered. There is an opening at the base on one side and another aperture high up in the opposite wall. The interior contained a ceramic vase in which there were twenty sheets of gold and silver embossed with excerpts from Buddhist manuscripts. The exterior visible today may not reflect the original, which was probably plastered and painted.

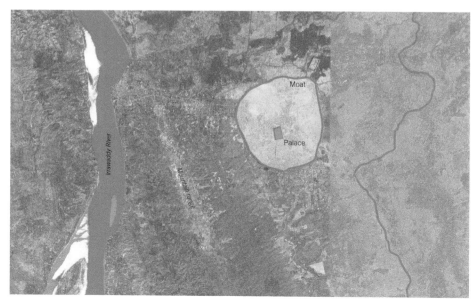

8.41 Area plan: Thayekhittaya (Sri Ksetra), Myanmar

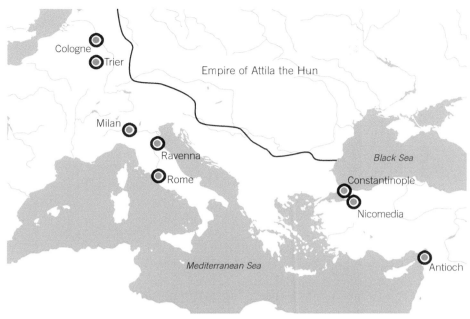

8.42 Roman capitals, 4th century CE

EMERGENCE OF CHRISTIANITY

When Constantine officially recognized Christianity in 326 CE, it did not instantly spell the end of paganism, and many traditions were carried over. Nonetheless, Christianity's monotheism, with its stress on ethical values, imparted an authenticity to religious practice that previously had been equaled only by Judaism, of which it was an offspring. Initially, Christianity might have appeared to be just another of the numerous Hellenistic religions and cults, such as the cults of Isis and Dionysus, Mithraism, the Gymnosophists of Upper Egypt, and the Theraputae of Alexandria. Few could have predicted the way Christian beliefs would sweep across the Western world as it spread in the footsteps of Roman occupation and took hold in Rome itself. Constantine, prodded by a dream, converted on his deathbed. From then on, the Roman title Pontifex Maximus signified that the Roman emperor was simultaneously the head of the Church and the vicar of Christ. As for the Church's competitors, they were folded bit by bit into the Christian world—or condemned as heresies. The religious pluralism that flourished in the 5th century CE, and out of which Christianity itself had emerged, ended by the end of the 6th century CE. Judaism alone was given some leeway, but it, too, was under pressure. Christians were forbidden to marry Jews, and

synagogue building stopped for the most part. Debates raged about the nature of Christ and his cosubstantiality with God, about the Trinity, about Mary, about the wording and the nature of the Eucharist, and about many other issues.

The choice of architectural style must also have caused considerable discussion. One thing was clear: it was impossible for the new religious architecture to follow in the footsteps of temple architecture. The wide variety of building types from the early days of Christianity are a result of the search for a proper fit between architecture and liturgy. In an earlier age, a tomb could not possibly have been mistaken for a basilica or a bathing establishment. Roman architecture created clearly defined architectural environments for the various urban functions. But by the 3rd century CE, distinctions were rapidly disappearing and being reformulated, as with Maxentius's "basilica," which was modeled on an imperial bath building. In early Christian architecture, when house-churches were no longer needed, this trend accelerated as various forms were studied and reevaluated for their compatibility with developing liturgical needs.

The impact of Christianity on Roman buildings was, of course, a negative one. The imperial forums were abandoned, and more often than not, stones from Roman

buildings were fired in large kilns to make lime for mortar. As late as 1606, Pope Paul V demolished the Temple of Minerva in the Forum of Nerva to obtain building material for the construction of a fountain. Christian fanatics went to Baalbek to destroy idols, but they were initially beaten back; pagan rituals continued there until about 380 CE. But bit by bit, the Christian emperors tightened their grip. The sanctuary at Baalbek was eventually destroyed and its remnants redesigned as a relatively humble church. The liquidation of sculptures was so complete that not a single example has survived. So devastating was the destruction of the pagan world that it took a thousand years, until the 15th century, before interest in its existence was anything more than fleeting.

To add to the complexity of the times, when Constantine left Rome in 326 CE and formally dedicated Constantinople as the "new Rome" in 330 CE, the city of Rome became a backwater almost overnight. Constantine founded his new city not so much as a Christian one, but rather as a place where Christianity and paganism could coexist. This was not possible in Rome, where Christians demanded complete allegiance from their sovereign. Seen from the perspective of Rome, the construction of Constantinople was a disaster. But seen from the perspective of the eastern provinces, it was a natural re-ascendancy. Unlike the European parts of the empire, which were spread out and had many different tribes laying claim to various regions, the east was naturally cohesive. The division of the empire had other consequences as well, for suddenly there was not one capital, or even four, but actually six: along with Constantinople, there was Antioch, Nicomedia, Milan, Trier, and Cologne, all of which were now refurbished as imperial residences. Milan was an imperial residence from 353 CE onward and suddenly became a major architectural center. Five new churches were built; three of them stand to this day, at nearly their full height.

In 380 CE, however, Emperor Gratian made Trier his residence, bringing the flow of money to the north. Emperor Honorius favored Ravenna and transferred the Imperial See there in the early 5th century CE; it became the residence of the Christianized Ostrogoths under Theodoric (490–526 CE) and his successors. Sumptuous new

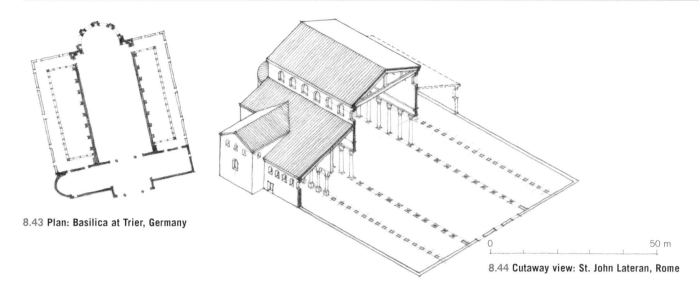

8.43 Plan: Basilica at Trier, Germany

0   50 m

8.44 Cutaway view: St. John Lateran, Rome

buildings were soon on the drawing boards. Of Constantine's considerable building activities in Constantinople, however, little remains. Most of what is known of the architecture from this early period of Christianity derives from the remnants that have survived in Syria and Egypt, and in Jerusalem itself.

Without an imperial presence, Rome had to fend for itself. In 410 CE, the city was sacked for three days by a band of Visigoths. The emperor of the West, Honorius, sat helplessly in Ravenna, and the emperor of the East was even farther away, in Constantinople. For protection, the Romans hired Odoacer, a German chieftain, but in 476 CE, he proclaimed himself king, defeated the Roman general Orestes at Piacenza, took Ravenna, and deposed Romulus Augustulus, barely more than a child, who was the last official emperor of the West until the coronation in 800 CE of Charlemagne.

The Roman administration of Italy continued to function under Odoacer, who retained the chief officers of state. In 488 CE, Zeno sent Theodoric the Great, king of the Ostrogoths, into Italy to expel Odoacer. In 493 CE, Odoacer consented to a treaty and was invited to a banquet where he and his officers were assassinated, leaving Theodoric master of Italy. Theodoric eagerly imported the most skilled masons and mosaic artists from the east, while adopting the conservative Roman basilica-style plan for his churches. But this did little to calm anxieties in Constantinople, and in 534 CE, Justinian sent an army to bring Italy and North Africa into his sphere of control. In 536 CE, even

Rome was taken, but in 568 CE, the Visigoths were back and laying waste to northern Italy. As water poured into Rome from the aqueducts that had fallen into disrepair, the unused land reverted to swamps, spreading malaria that made large parts of the area surrounding Rome into the disease-ridden plain that it remained until the 20th century. In 680 CE, the bubonic plague broke out. Rome's population dropped from about a million at the time of the Roman Empire to as low as thirty thousand by the 6th century CE. The large parts of Rome that were now abandoned or used as farms came to be called the *disabitato* ("uninhabited areas").

It has long been held that early Christian architecture evolved out of the atrium, or *tablinium*, of the Roman houses where early Christians met. Admittedly, until the 4th century CE, Christian architecture as such did not exist, as services were held in houses and in catacombs. But the argument that the basilica emerged out of the Roman house, persistent in ecclesiastical circles, creates the illusion of a linear evolution of form that the physical evidence does not support. The basilica that imposed a pattern on church buildings by Constantine was the Church of St. John Lateran, transformed from an imperial palace in Rome in 314 CE. For this church, the basilica was a logical choice. Though little of the original building is left, its form is well established. It consisted of five aisles, the central one higher than the others to let in light from a clerestory. Two rows of fifteen huge columns created the 75-meter-long colonnade. The whole was

8.45 Interior: Basilica at Trier

covered with a wooden roof. At the end was a large apse where the clergy would sit. They were separated from the populace by a columnar screen. The transept that one sees today is a medieval addition. There were no columnar embellishments, and the facade—indeed, the entire outer surface—was of little architectural significance. In fact, it would be several centuries before the idea of a representative facade, which had previously been nurtured by the Romans, would return as an important design element in Western churches.

Though the exterior of the building might seem primitive, the interior was opulent. The roof beams shimmered in gold foil, and the walls were ornamented with mosaics high above the red, green, and yellow marble columns of the nave. Seven golden altars and offering tables stood in the sanctuary, which was lit by chandeliers of gold and silver. A hundred years later, Rome saw the construction of St. Sabina (425–32 CE), a mature and stately replica of St. John Lateran. Its larger windows show a greater familiarity with masonry construction.

Martyria

Though the city of Rome was no longer a political or economic power, it became an important religious and pilgrimage center much like Jerusalem, for it had the burial places of St. Peter, St. Paul, and other martyrs. In making their tombs an important part of veneration, the notion of a dark and uneventful Hades, and the idea of death as a privileged realm of pharaonic afterlife, were obliterated. Tombs were perceived as a site of reawakening on the day of the Last Judgment, when all of humanity was to be judged. Visiting a tomb was in a sense an anticipation of this event. The cult was to become such a strong part of Christian religious folk practice that a church's possession of even a piece of a saint's or martyr's body, such as a finger, displayed in a reliquary, bestowed an aura of sanctity to the edifice. This went so far that body parts and even entire bodies were snatched away, such as that of St. Mark of Venice, which was taken from Alexandria.

The precedent for this type of veneration can be found in Buddhism, which, around the 1st century BCE, had already begun reliquary practices—certainly an innovation in the history of religion. This folk practice, which apparently arose spontaneously, was soon recognized as a boon by the Church establishment, as it attracted the pious, and as such was a public demonstration of Christianity's validity. Indeed, the new notion of history made by simple people doing heroic things—far different from history as mythology or history as royal lineage—would have a profound impact on later developments.

St. Peter's in Rome

Since many of the graves in Rome were at the outskirts of the city or in cemeteries outside the walls, the Christianization of Rome created an entirely new geographical profile previously unheard of in the history of Western urbanization. The city and its image were no longer dominated by a forum, agora, or palace, but rather by the dozens of monasteries, baptisteries, and churches scattered in clusters in the farthest reaches of the city and its environs. Whereas the Church of St. John Lateran in Rome is a basilica that had been established by imperial fiat as the official ecclesiastical seat of the pope, the bishop of Rome, it continues to serve as the political, religious, and administrative center of the Church.

Constantine founded the original church over the tomb of St. Peter around 320 CE. Though a basilica, St. Peter's had a slightly different shape than St. John Lateran, reflecting its status as a martyrium. A broad flight of stairs led to the atrium, built on a vast platform over the sloping ground. The platform itself was constructed over a Roman necropolis, with the tops of the various tomb structures cut off and the intermediate spaces filled in. The church itself, because of its use, was 112 meters in length—considerably longer than St. John Lateran. The nave can be described as a covered street with colonnades on both sides. The columns were not built for the church but were taken from pre-Christian Roman buildings. The nave became a place where those who could afford the cost could be buried, and the floors were soon carpeted with graves. Part street, part graveyard, and part sanctuary, on feast days it became the site of boisterous family celebrations (a practice that was eventually banned).

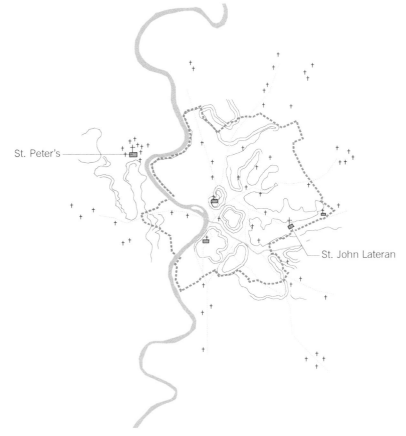

8.46 Christian sanctuaries outside the city walls of Rome

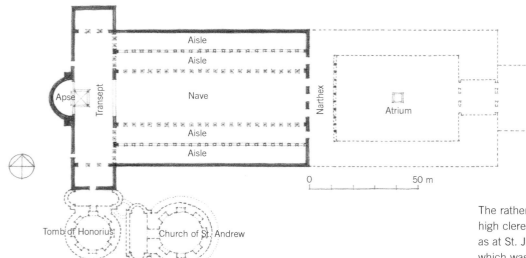

8.47 Plan and cross-section: St. Peter's, Rome

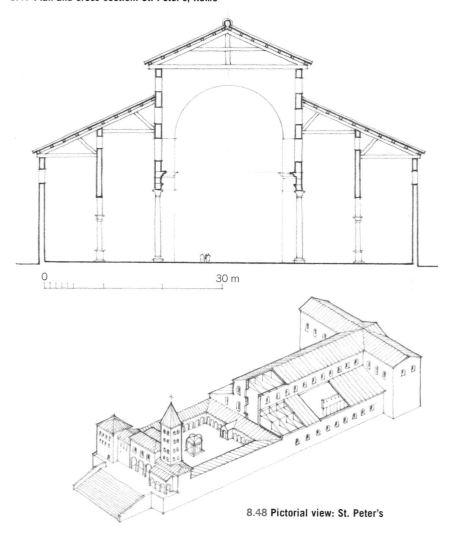

8.48 Pictorial view: St. Peter's

The rather dark nave, illuminated only by high clerestory windows, led not to an apse, as at St. John Lateran, but to a large transept, which was a unique space. At its focus, over the tomb of St. Peter in the crypt below and just in front of the apse, was a *baldachino*, or canopy, resting on four columns. Though today the nave-and-transept combination might seem common, that was not the case in the 4th century CE. The transept only became ubiquitous after the Carolingians made it a central part of their churches in the 9th century CE. At St. Peter's, the transept differentiated the more popular martyrium church from an imperial basilica like St. John Lateran. The building's significance lies in part in the difficulties involved in its construction. The use of concrete had by that time been forgotten, and vaulting was thus impossible. The art of stone masonry itself was diminished; even for a building commissioned by the emperor, the columns had to be taken from Roman buildings. Despite these limitations, and perhaps even because of them, the building achieved directness and majesty—it was one of the first buildings in the evolving Mediterranean world that was meant from its inception to highlight the mass appeal of the new religion. This was no dark and intimate "house of the gods" in the Hellenistic tradition, nor was it a place of personal reflection in the Buddhist sense. Rather, it was a space in which large-scale communal ritual overlapped with the message of imperial glory.

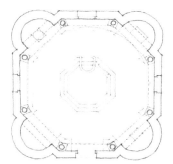

8.49 **Plan: Baptistery at Ravenna, Italy**

First Baptisteries

In Antioch, St. Babylas (378 CE) was composed of four aisle-less arms with timber roofs converging on the center square. A baptistery was built against one of the side arms and a sacristy against the other. These were, of course, new types of spaces, and they challenged the architectural form of the basilica, which was in its Roman days a structure without side rooms. Fitting these spaces into the basilica scheme was to become a main design problem in the coming millennium; at St. Babylas, they are simply stapled to the side of the building. At St. John in Ephesus (450 CE), they are bent around the northeast corner, whereas at St. Mary in Ephesus (400 CE), they were appended to one side of the atrium.

Baptism is one of the seven sacraments every member of the Christian community is subject to—as well as the first and most important one. Without being baptized, even an innocent baby may, after death, remain in limbo, as it has not been cleansed of original sin (according to St. Augustine). Because baptism symbolizes entry into the community of the Church, baptisteries were given special architectural importance. Some baptisteries were square, others rectangular; some had apses, others none; some were vaulted, others not. Soon, however, baptisteries became recognizable architectural elements. The baptistery at Ravenna (400–450 CE) has an octagonal plan that came to be emulated throughout Italy and elsewhere. The baptistery at Nocera (5th century CE), east of Naples, has a cupola that rises directly from a circular drum buttressed by the walls and arches of an ambulatory defined by column pairs. It is similar to St. Costanza in Rome (330 CE), which was, however, not a baptistery but rather a tomb that was converted to a church in the 13th century.

8.50 **Interior: Baptistery at Ravenna**

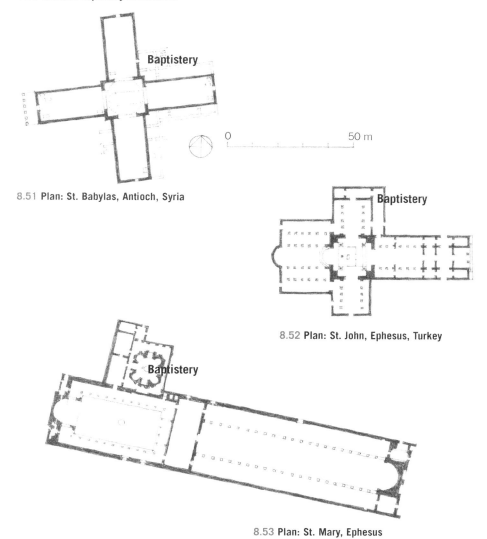

8.51 **Plan: St. Babylas, Antioch, Syria**

0   50 m

8.52 **Plan: St. John, Ephesus, Turkey**

8.53 **Plan: St. Mary, Ephesus**

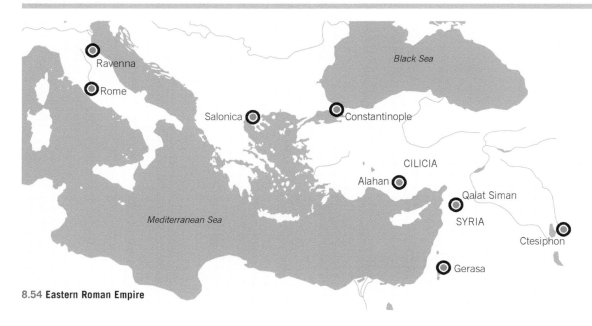

8.54 Eastern Roman Empire

POST-CONSTANTINIAN AGE

Splitting the Roman Empire into four parts under Diocletian in 293 CE was envisioned as the creation of a partnership that would increase responsiveness in case of a local crisis within the empire. When the Christian emperor Theodosius reformalized that division into east and west one hundred years later, in 395 CE, it ultimately led the empire into a schism. The rapidly shrinking importance of the western empire forced it into dependency on the East—and not without a good deal of resentment. Rome was sacked in 410 CE by the Visigoths and again in 455 CE by the Vandals, who had set up their kingdom in North Africa. And when central and northern France was lost to the Franks after 460 CE, northern Italy was opened to invasion by various groups, including the Ostrogoths; they converted under Theodoric (495–526 CE), who set up his rule in Ravenna. In the East, the Christian empire remained relatively unscathed. Nonetheless, the 5th century CE was very different from the Constantinian age that preceded it. The unity in theology and in architecture that Constantine had sought to impose on his dominions broke down, leading to an era in which each region began to develop its own particularities.

In the East, *martyria* became large freestanding structures. In the West, martyrs' graves were enclosed within churches. The architects in some places preferred columns, in others piers. Some architects used transepts; others did not. The location of rooms like the sacristy, the archives, and the library added further variations.

The Church of the Acheiropoietos in Salonica (470 CE) is almost classical in its clean lines and broad command of space. The White Monastery (Deir-el-Abiad, ca. 440 CE), not far from the city of Suhag in Egypt (about 500 kilometers south of Cairo), takes

on an Egyptian flavor in its compact, boxlike shape; its various rooms include an unusual triconch at the head. The narthex is placed not to the west, but along the south, with the baptistery at one end. The Church of the Prophets, Apostles, and Martyrs in Gerasa, Jordan (465 CE), is a brilliant essay on the theme of a square within a square. In Rome, St. Stefano Rotondo (468–83 CE) embodies a complex intersection of cross and rotunda. St. Stefano notwithstanding, the Roman churches tended to be the most conservative. St. Sabina (425–32 CE) and Santa Maria Maggiore (ca. 432 CE) preserved the Constantinian tradition of a colonnaded basilica.

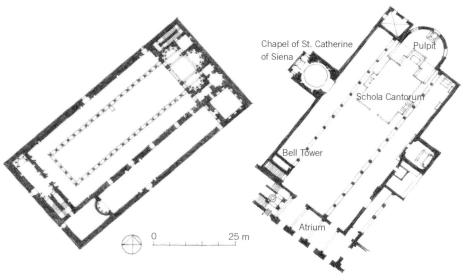

0   25 m

8.55 Plan: White Monastery (Deir-el-Abiad), near Suhag, Egypt

8.56 Plan: St. Sabina, Rome

Chapel of St. Catherine of Siena

Pulpit

Schola Cantorum

Bell Tower

Atrium

8.57 Ostrogoth and Visigoth territories

TOMB OF THEODORIC THE GREAT

The Ostrogoths, a tribe from the Russian steppes, had moved into Europe and settled in northern Italy. They established a relatively short-lived state under their king Theodoric the Great (454–526 CE) that included, at its zenith, Italy and the Balkans; its capital was at Ravenna. In 402 CE, Ravenna had become the capital of the Western Roman Empire. The transfer had been made primarily for defensive purposes: the city was surrounded

by swamps and marshes. But the move failed to hold back the Germans, who took the city. This led the Byzantine emperor Zeno to commission Theodoric to conquer Italy. But once installed, Theodoric created his own kingdom and purposefully sought to revive Roman culture and government as best as he could. Theodoric converted to a form of Christian belief called Arianism, which held that Jesus was not equal to God, as mainstream Christians believed, but somewhat lesser. This caused a major controversy and increased the rift with the Byzantines. Theodoric commissioned architects to build a palace that, though it has not survived, is known through frescoes to have had a colonnaded front with a four-columned, pedimented center.

The calm manner in which the large ashlar stones and arches are articulated in the tomb that Theodoric built for himself (ca. 520 CE) suggests the presence of Syrian stonemasons. It is located 1 kilometer from the center of Ravenna, beyond the ancient town walls, in an area used as a graveyard by the Goths. Though the foundation was of concrete, the construction itself is of dry masonry, indicating that no mortar or cement was used. The lower story forms a decagon containing, in each of its sides, a recessed rectangular niche with an arched head. Internally, it has the shape of a cross with equal arms. The upper floor is similar, except that it has a circular

8.58 Tomb of Theodoric the Great, Ravenna, Italy

interior. It is thought that the upper floor had a continuous balcony all the way around, the columns resting on the top of the wall of the lower part. Since there are no stairs leading to the upper floor and traces of an access stairway have never been found, it is presumed that the upper room was the funeral chamber, to which the remains of the king were perhaps brought by a temporary stairway. The dome, 10 meters in diameter, consists of a huge single piece of Istrian limestone with twelve handles on the top, used, no doubt, to lift the stone into place.

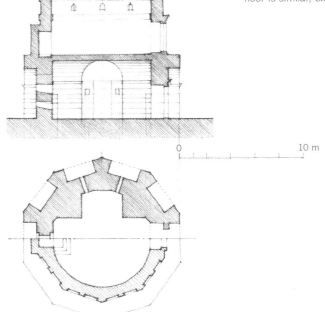

0   10 m

8.59 Plan and section: Tomb of Theodoric the Great

8.60 Mosaic depicting the palace of Theodoric the Great in his palace chapel of San Apollinare Nuovo, Ravenna

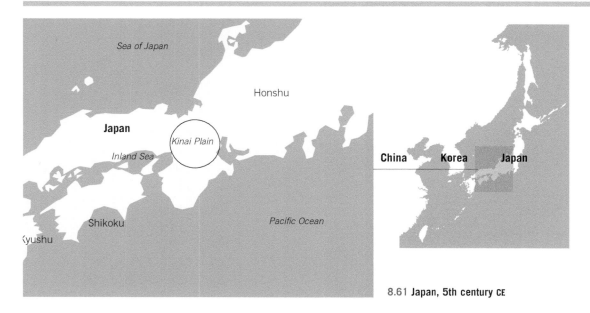

8.61 Japan, 5th century CE

KOFUN PERIOD: JAPAN

In the late 5th century CE, Japan's Yamato clan managed to wrest control over much of Honshu and Kyushu islands, thereby establishing Japan's first royal family, a bloodline that has continued unbroken to this day. The Yamato centralized the government and, most importantly, organized the production and collection of rice. Each new king built a new palace and was buried in his own huge earthen tomb. The tombs that the elites built for themselves, known as Kofun, were usually in the shape of a keyhole. The round part held the tomb. They were generally 100 meters long, with the largest, the Hashihaka Tomb in Nara, measuring almost 280 meters. The round part was designed as a truncated cone that intersected with an elongated stepped pyramidal form. The reason behind the complex geometry is not known; dozens of variations exist. The wooden coffin was usually buried directly at the summit, often in a pit lined with stone slabs and rocks. Later, stone coffins were used, and, finally, in the late Kofun period, stone chambers with horizontal entrance passages were constructed. These allowed reentry into the chamber, leading to their development as family repositories with multiple burials.

The horizontal strip at the top of the rectangular portion was used for rituals and ceremonies. These vast and costly structures were, in essence, platforms that guaranteed that the spirit of their owners, as viewed from a shamanistic perspective, would have clear access to ancestor spirits.

The first set of these tombs, which date to the late 3rd century CE, are in Sakurai, Nara, where the imperial capital was located. A second group was then built on the Osaka Plain a bit further to the west. Since these structures are surrounded by moats, the area was subject to vast canalization to channel the water to the various tombs.

8.62 Aerial view: The burial mound of Emperor Nintoku, Osaka, Japan

8.63 A *haniwa*, or funerary statue

8.64 Reconstruction of Goshikizuka Kofun, Kobe, Japan

Today the mounds are overgrown with trees, but originally the tops were filled with clay figures, called *haniwa*, that both served as substitutes for burial sacrifices and marked the borders of the gravesite. The slopes were lined with stones and ornamented with cylinders 40 to 50 centimeters in diameter and about a meter tall, which served as stands for weapons and armor. They were also lined with clay soldiers and horses, neatly arranged in rows, that were meant to be guardians for the journey to the spirit world. The appearance of horses and chariots shows the dissemination of the steppe imaginaries and the introduction of the horse as a symbol of power. In southern India this period sees the emergence of the first ceramic horse statues, also having to do with the arrival of a militarized elite, but whether there is a connection or not is unknown. Certainly the Chinese were already making ceramic horse statues during the Qin dynasty.

Kofun tombs disappeared in the 6th century CE, probably because of the reformation that took place in the Yamato court with the introduction of Buddhism.

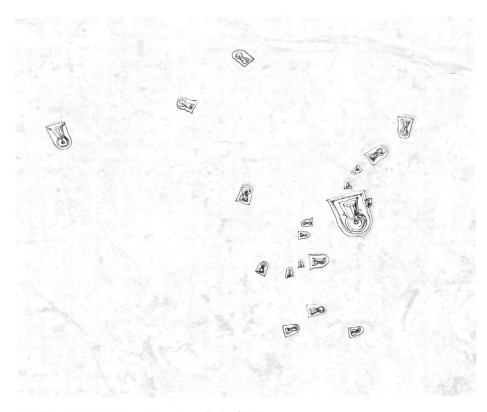

8.65 Mozu-Furuichi Kofungun in southern Osaka, Japan

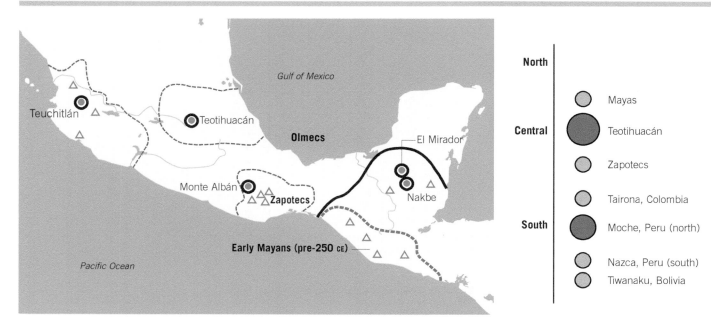

8.66 **Urbanization of the Americas, ca. 400 CE**

8.67 **Trade in the Americas, ca. 400 CE**

North

Central

South

○ Mayas
● Teotihuacán
○ Zapotecs
○ Tairona, Colombia
● Moche, Peru (north)
○ Nazca, Peru (south)
○ Tiwanaku, Bolivia

ZAPOTECS OF OAXACA

In a valley formed by the convergence of three mountains 480 kilometers south of Mexico City lies the dramatic and spectacular Zapotec capital, Monte Albán. The entire semiarid valley of Oaxaca was inhabited by the Zapotec people from 1500 BCE up until the Spanish invasion. By 1000 BCE, a Zapotec elite had emerged, with connections to the Olmecs in the north. By 500 BCE, the valley had an estimated twenty-five thousand residents, making it one of the largest population centers in America. It was supported by several types of irrigation projects, including artificially terraced hillsides watered by canals fed from permanent springs. The ubiquitous forest of today is far different from the tended former landscape of the Zapotecs.

The Zapotecs believed that the universe was divided into four great quarters, each associated with a color—red, black, yellow, or white. The center was blue-green, which they considered a single color. The east-west axis of the sun was the principal axis of their world. Their religion was animistic. They believed that everything was alive and deserving of respect. As in Hindu cosmology, the Zapotecs distinguished living things from inanimate matter by the possession of a vital force called *pee*, or wind, breath, or spirit. *Pee* made things move to show that they were alive—like a bolt of lightning, clouds

moving in the sky, a tremor of the earth, the wind in one's hair, and even the foam on a cup of chocolate. Inanimate things could be engaged with technology, but those with *pee* had to be approached with ritual and sacrifice, especially involving something living, like a beating heart. Zapotecs recognized a supreme being—without beginning or end—with whom no human came in contact. It was never represented. Humans did, however, interact with natural forces, the most powerful and sacred of which were Cociyo (lightning), the angry face of the sky, and Xoó (earthquake), the angry face of the earth—two of the four quadrants. Even time was alive and considered cyclical. The Zapotecs had two calendars—a solar calendar with 18 months of 20 days, plus 5 days to bring it to 365; and a ritual calendar, or *piye*, composed of 20 hieroglyphs or "day signs," which combined with 13 numbers to produce a cycle of 260 days.

Social structure was stratified into two layers: the commoners and the nobility. They had different origins. Commoners were born of commoners; they lived, worked, and died. Members of the nobility were descended from venerated ancestors; they conducted wars, brought home captives, and were buried in tombs from which they ascended to the sky to become "cloud people." Men had multiple wives, and under ideal circumstances, primogeniture was the law.

8.68 **A "dancing" figure showing the mutilated remains of an enemy king**

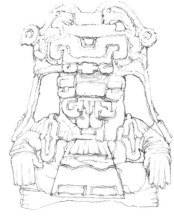

8.69 **Xoó: Lightning and earthquake motifs in Zapotec culture**

Monte Albán

Around 500 BCE, the Zapotec elite constructed a new administrative center, picking a previously unoccupied escarpment located dramatically in the heart of the valley of Oaxaca. The valley is composed of three sub-valleys that join together in the shape of a Y, with the 400-meter-high, 4-kilometer-long escarpment more or less in the center and visible from miles around. The city, known as Monte Albán, was built along the terraced slopes. It has long since disappeared; however, the temple precinct at the top of hill remains. Its oldest structure is the Temple of the Dancers (Monumento de los Danzantes, ca. 400 BCE), which consists of a triple set of platforms in the southeastern corner of the site. It is decorated by a series of "dancing" figures, so-called because they depict men in strange, rubbery postures as if they were acrobats of extraordinary ability. Despite the name, they are probably not dancing. Given their closed eyes and exposed, mutilated genitals (a sign of ritual humiliation), these figures are believed to represent the earliest set of rulers subjugated by the Zapotec elite. Between 100 BCE and 200 CE, Monte Albán rulers expanded their control throughout the Oaxaca Valley and constructed a grand plaza by leveling an area of 300 by 200 meters. It was oriented to the cardinal directions and paved over with white stucco.

8.70 **Monte Albán, near Oaxaca, Mexico**

The huge terraced platforms that are part of palace enclosures are on the northern and southern ends of the plaza. The northern platform, which was repeatedly enlarged and modified, has two sunken patios, each with steps and platform mounds on axis. The southern platform, which was smaller, was built by incorporating older platforms into its design. The period 200 to 700 CE finds the Zapotecs at the height of their prosperity, and this is the phase to which most of the surviving structures can be dated.

In the center of the plaza is a group of three conjoined buildings facing east-west; they were indisputably the focal temples. While the platform of the central temple has steps on both sides, it actually opens only to the east and consists of a double chamber separated by a partial wall and columns. Later Zapotec temples had two chambers: an outer, less sacred chamber to which worshippers could come, and an inner, more sacred chamber where the priests performed their rites. Those rites included burning incense and both animal and human sacrifice. Priests also performed autosacrifice, offering their own blood by piercing parts of their body. Some rituals involved the use of hallucinogenic mushrooms and other drugs.

There are three large complexes on the western side of the plaza, known as L, M, and IV, consisting of more platforms, temples, and enclosed forecourts. One platform contains an internal stairway leading to the top of the building; the stairway is reached by an underground tunnel that passes beneath the plaza to the central range of buildings, allowing the priests to reach them unseen.

8.71 **Aerial view of Monte Albán**

One structure detached from the main group, Building J, is a rarity in Zapotec architecture: it is set at a 45-degree angle to the site's main axis. Its ground plan resembles an arrowhead, with the steps forming the blunt end. It opens to the northeast and may have been oriented to the bright star Capella and used for astronomical purposes. A vaulted tunnel crosses the front part of the structure and leads upward.

Monte Albán re-creates the Zapotec conceptual order on several different scales. It is primarily the place of privilege at the center of the cosmological landscape. The complex also replicates, on a diminished scale, the very relationship of the escarpment on which Monte Albán was built to the larger valley of Oaxaca, with the main ceremonial temple in the middle surrounded by a "mountainous" ring of platform mounds. The sunken patios in the north platform repeat the order of a valley surrounded by pyramids, again with a central platform. Unlike the artificial mountain volcanoes of the Olmecs, the Zapotecs created here a miniaturized landscape that is both a sacred geography and its representation.

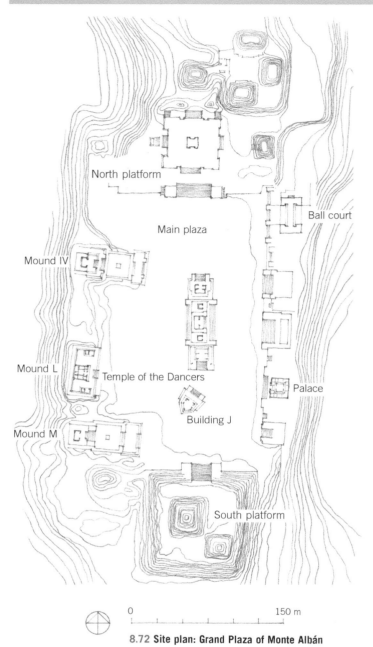

North platform

Main plaza

Ball court

Mound IV

Mound L

Temple of the Dancers

Mound M

Palace

Building J

South platform

0   150 m

8.72 Site plan: Grand Plaza of Monte Albán

8.73 Ball court, Monte Albán

600 CE

9.1 **Interior: Hagia Sophia, Istanbul, Turkey**

INTRODUCTION

The economic world of 600 CE was restricted in scope. India and China were prospering, however, and Southeast Asia, Korea, and Japan were emerging as economic forces. That narrow part of the world produced perhaps 90 percent of the architectural innovations of the time. Europe was in a state of disarray as its lands were being carved up by various tribes—the Visigoths, Franks, Lombards, Saxons, Avars, and Danes, among others. Most of these were agropastoral village societies that produced small fortified settlements of wooden construction. This left the eastern part of the former Roman Empire, Byzantium, as a relatively isolated hotspot of cosmopolitan, urban life. Byzantium had a leader of extraordinary charisma, Justinian (482–565), who violently suppressed dissent while pursuing a policy of Mediterranean conquest. During his rule a host of astonishing buildings appeared: the Church of the Holy Apostles (534), SS. Sergius and Bacchus (ca. 535), the Church of Hagia Irene (ca. 530s), and a 140-meter-long cistern. But nothing compared to the Hagia Sophia, which was begun around 532. This remarkable building, its inner finish considerably diminished today, was the greatest engineering marvel of the age. The dome, the first to rival that of the Pantheon, was completely of brick, concrete having by now become a lost art. But its structural sophistications were designed to be invisible to observers, who marveled at its gilded inner surfaces shimmering in the mottled light from distant windows and suspended candelabras.

9.2 Interior of St. Hripsime Temple, Echmiadzin, Armenia

The Byzantine Empire, however, was not on sure footing. A "black death," the Plague of Justinian (541–542 CE), killed perhaps 40 percent of Byzantium's inhabitants and caused the deaths of up to a quarter of the human population of the eastern Mediterranean. Vast stretches of territory were left uninhabited. The long-term effects were enormous. Justinian's death in 578 CE added to the problems of an empire that was in more or less continuous battle with the Persians and then the Arabs. The withdrawal of large numbers of troops from the Balkans to defend the southern borders opened the door even more for the southward expansion of Slavic peoples into the Mediterranean zone. In 568 CE the Lombards invaded Italy with little opposition from Byzantium, and thus began the fragmentation of Italy. By 650 CE Byzantium had lost all of its southern provinces and could from then on only bask in its former glory.

Throughout this period, the Armenians, remote from the pestilence of the ports, were pushing ahead with an amazing building campaign. They alone in the world were still building high-end stone masonry buildings with techniques from the Greeks. These buildings include the Church of Saint Gayane and the Cathedral of Mren, both from the 630s and both three-nave domed basilicas with an octagonal drum resting on four internal pillars. But the greatest of these Armenian buildings was Zvartnots Cathedral (643–652 CE), located at the edge of the city of Echmiadzin. It had an extraordinary plan. The core consisted of four lobes emanating from triangular-shaped piers. The whole was surrounded by a thirty-two-sided polygon, which appears circular from a distance. Its elevation is not known, but it is surmised to have risen three stories. Apart from copper, the Armenians had little to offer economically, so most of their wealth came from overland trade. They were an important, stable link between East and West. One could compare them with the Srivijayan Empire in Southeast Asia, which served as the link between India and China.

Meanwhile, the Persian Sassanians in the Iranian heartland were no longer in a position to contribute to the building arts. Their land was in disarray largely because of rigid social stratification, the increasing power of the provincial landholders, and a rapid turnover of rulers, all of which allowed the restive Arab tribes to seek greater autonomy. By 640 CE, the Arabs, newly united by Islam, began to assert themselves and make impressive territorial claims. By 651 CE, the Sassanian Empire had collapsed and was replace by the Rashidun Islamic caliphate (632–661 CE), which soon stretched cross a vast territory from Afghanistan to Morocco, and which was succeeded by the even more wealthy and powerful Umayyad caliphate (661–750 CE).

In India, the situation was altogether less volatile. Despite the decline of the Gupta dynasty in the 6th century CE, the newly emerging small kingdoms all tried to assert their regional control, leading to a period of prolific temple building. One of these kingdoms was the Pallavas in the south. The Pallava's wealth was generated from trade to the east through their port city of Mamallapuram, a sacred city and pilgrimage site. Mamallapuram came to host an amazing sequence of rock-cut temples carved along the slope of a nearby hill, connected to an artificial (though now largely dry) channel that represents the Ganges River. It was designed as a model of the Hindu sacred landscape and so was just as much a religious as an economic destination, as was typical in the Hindu world.

In 700 CE in Mamallapuram, one of the first stone-built buildings in India, the Shore Temple, was constructed. It is a type of elaboration of Dharmaraja Ratha, located about 5 kilometers away, which was not stone-built but one of several rock-cut experimental temples known cumulatively as Pancha Rathas (ca. 650 CE). These were carved, one next to the other, to study, so it seems, different potential temple forms. The Pancha Rathas experiment is unique in the history of architecture. But what prompted the change from rock-cut to built-up? Was there some connection to the Armenians, who were the best stonemasons in the world at the time, and who in these times of trouble were certainly leaving their homeland looking for work? Or was it a more homegrown transformation?

9.3 Shore Temple, Mahabalipuram, India

During this time, the process known as Indianization was expanding India's economic reach into Southeast Asia, which was slowly being transformed into a series of regional rice-producing centers. Indianization describes a process where monks, engineers, and officials created temple/city communities that slowly drew converts from among the locals, who eventually created nascent states. In Myanmar (Burma) along the Irrawaddy River, we see, for example, the rise of the Sri Ksetra kingdom, which was settled by adherents of Theravada Buddhism, indicating a close connection to Sri Lanka, one of the earliest centers of rice paddy irrigation in the world. The lucrative trade also led to the creation, around 500 CE, of the Srivijayan Empire near present-day Palembang, Sumatra, in Indonesia. The Srivijayan controlled the Straits of Malacca, through which all ships traveling between India and China had to pass. Along with the Srivijayan, other states emerged, such

as Dvaravanti (more or less in modern-day Thailand), the Chenla (more or less in modern-day Cambodia), and the Champa (more or less in modern-day Vietnam), each of which was beginning to develop an extensive rice-producing export economy and an architecture of sacred landscapes to go along with it.

Based on the regional strength of this economy, T'ang dynasty China built one of the greatest cities of the time, Daxing. The first cities of China were what one might call palace cities linked to a court culture and the needs of the court. The development of the centralized imperial government in the Han dynasty (206 BCE–220 CE) and later in the T'ang dynasty (618–906 CE) gave rise to large capital cities that were metropolitan in nature, with population concentrations of one million or more people. These megacities have to be seen somewhat differently from cities in other places of the world. The concentration of large populations into a city was a way to keep power under imperial control. This is true for many large cities, but unlike the ancient city of Rome—which expanded over time into a dense urban labyrinth with almost no planning, despite what one might assume about the Romans—the Chinese capitals were designed from the outset as a spatial imprint of imperial rule. They were low in density, composed mainly of mud-brick and thatch structures with gardens, pigsties, and animal pens. In many parts the city would have appeared as a compressed village.

For this reason, when there was a change of imperial control, capitals were usually destroyed and depopulated. Hundreds of thousands of people were displaced and resettled in new capitals. This created huge temporal disruptions in Chinese history. With the collapse of a single unifying power, as during the Three Kingdom period 220–265 CE between the Han and T'ang dynasties, three new capital cities were built. This gave the Chinese a lot of experience in designing cities at a great scale. The history of the Daxing site is complex, for Daxing is actually the third capital city on that site. The first city, Xianyang, to the north of the Wei River, was founded by the Qin dynasty (221–206 BCE). Because the city lay south of the Jiuzong Mountains and north of the Wei River—both sunlight-rich (yang) orientations—it was named Xianyang, meaning "fully yang" or "the side that is full of sun." When the city was destroyed in a flood in 202 BCE, the new capital, Chang'an ("Perpetual Peace"), was built to the south of the river by the Han dynasty. It was destroyed in 24 BCE. Subsequent dynasties moved the capital to Chengdu, Pingcheng, and Luoyang. During the T'ang dynasty (618–907 CE), Chang'an was made the capital again, this time at a scale that was grand even for the Chinese. It was not sited over the ruins of the old city, but just to its south. Its name was Daxing ("Great Prosperity") (580–904 CE). Colloquially, it was called Chang'an, leading to some confusion, but it was built ex nihilo. Very little is left of Daxing except for a few pagodas. It is a sad fate for one of the great cities of history. Today the sprawling modern city of Xi'an lies over the ancient capital. One of the few remnants of Daxing is the Giant Wild Goose Pagoda (649–683 CE) that was originally built at a height of 54 meters

9.4 **Sacred Grove at Futarasan Shrine, Nikko, Japan**

and had a rammed earth core with a stone exterior facade. After it collapsed, it was rebuilt in brick (704), although an earthquake in 1556 reduced its height from ten stories to seven stories. One of the pagoda's many functions was to hold sutras and figurines of the Buddha that were brought to China from India by the Buddhist translator and traveler Hsuan Tsang (Xuanzang). To feed the population, the Chinese built canals that linked in the north-south direction its various east-west flowing rivers. The Sui dynasty (581–618 CE) made major contributions to that effort. It was not just rice that was brought in from the south, but also vast amounts of bricks and lumber.

The arrival of Buddhism in Korea in the 4th century and in Japan in the 6th century brought with it the arrival of the monumental architectural forms that had been developed in China. Monks, architects, engineers, and even bureaucrats arrived hand in hand. One of the earliest Buddhist structures in Japan is Yakushi-ji (Healing Buddha Temple), built in Fujiwara-kyo, Japan's capital in the Asuka period (538–710 CE), when Japan was ruled by great clans and their extended families.

But whereas the story often focuses on Buddhism, since that left a relatively permanent architectural record, the emergence of Japan must be viewed in larger geopolitical terms. It paralleled the emergence of Southeast Asia as a rice producing/exporting area. In both cases, rice was elevated into the status of a deity, and in both cases powerful leaders emerged who mastered the politics necessary to control the intermixed realities of devotion, production, storage, and trade, while at the same time living at the behest and blessing of deities whom they served. But whereas by the 9th century the Khmer in Cambodia would force the forest to yield to the needs of a Hindu-based agricultural worldview, in Japan an assimilation occurred between the still-new rice-centric culture and the ancient local traditions associated with Shintoism. Shintoism was not replaced; it simply expanded to include a new and powerful deity known as Inari, the rice god. Rice granaries, elevated on platforms, became a form of sacred architecture, and with the rise of imperial clans the granary rose to the level of state symbol, with no building representing this better than the Ise Shrine.

The word *Shinto*, which can be translated as "the way of the gods," was coined in the 19th century to identify it as a religion distinct from Buddhism. Prior to then Shintoism was so fundamental to Japanese life and culture that it had no name apart from the names for the various cultic procedures, ceremonies, and shamanistic rituals. It was a belief system that stretched back to early humanity and was characterized by the worship in Japan of kami, which can be defined as the "spirits" of mountains, rivers, lightning, wind, waves, trees, and even rocks. Kami and humans exist in a shared continuum. Nonetheless, the kami, as innate supernatural forces residing in all things, are above the actions of man. Certain localities, such as sacred groves, or special stones are viewed as particularly propitious for the meeting of humans with the spirit of kami and are therefore held to be sacred. There are several such groves still existing in Japan, such as the 20-hectare wooded area Atsuta-ku in the city of Nagoya. Unlike modern monotheistic religious practices, Shintoism does not require those respecting its premises to be believers or practitioners. There are no sacred writings, nor is there an organized theory of death. The spirits of the dead go to the mountains, above the sky, below the earth, or beyond the horizon. Living beings from this world may visit those from the other worlds in border areas such as cliffs, caves, and coastlines. The deceased generally do not become kami unless there are special circumstances associated with their death.

Shinto's earliest formation has left no architectural expression at all. But this changed in the 7th century with the arrival of Buddhists and their highly developed architectural culture of temples and shrines. Shinto devotion learned the lesson and so was born the transformation of the village granary, already sacred, to imperial symbol. Most famous of all is the Ise Shrine. Located in a sacred forest, it was seen as integral to the imperial cult and serves in that capacity even today. It is not one building but several related structures all connected to a complex set of calendric rituals. Only the emperor and the priests were allowed entry. The buildings were unique in that they were required to be rebuilt every twenty years using the sacred trees from the holy mountain at the base of which the shrine sits. For that reason, we have a clear indication of ancient architectural practices. Since this is the only building in the world of such prominence that is repeatedly rebuilt in this way, it poses a question about the nature of time and architecture. In a sense the buildings are permanent, not in terms of their material but because of the ritual rebuilding requirements.

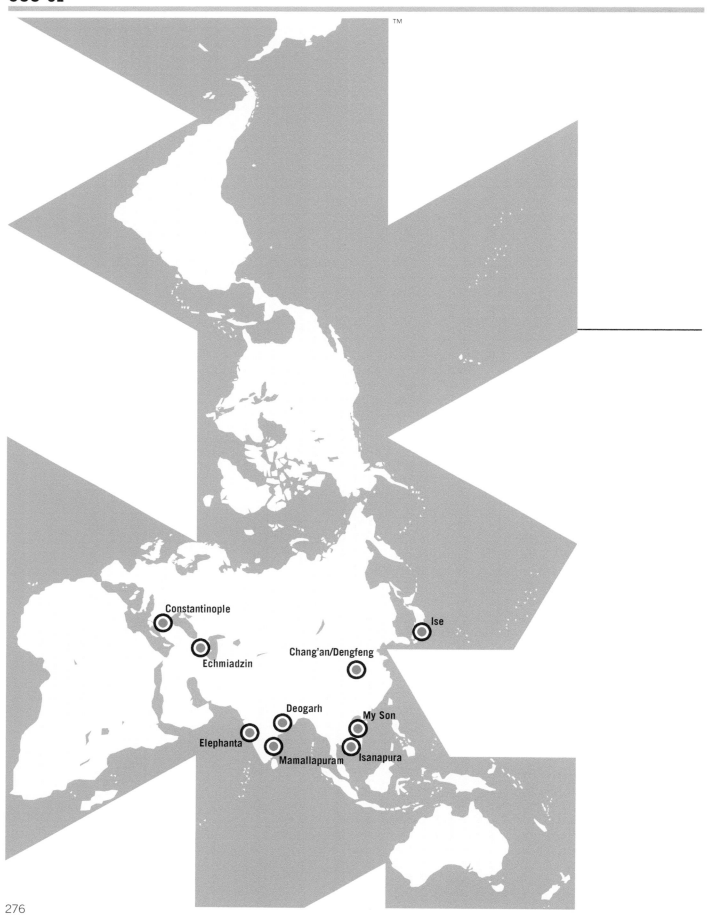

Byzantine Empire
330–1453 CE

▲ **SS. Sergius and Bacchus**
527–36 CE

▲ **Hagia Sophia**
532–37 CE

▲ **Zvartnots Cathedral**
Begun 643 CE

▲ **St. Vitale, Ravenna**
538–45 CE

▲ **St. Hripsime Church**
7th Century CE

India: Rise of regional states
500–1300 CE

▲ **Vishnu Temple at Deogarh**
Early 6th century CE

▲ **Five Rathas**
7th century CE

▲ **Shore Temple at Mamallapuram**
700–728 CE

▲ **Cave of Shiva at Elephanta**
540–755 CE

400 CE   **600 CE**   **800 CE**

▲ **My Son**
4th to 14th centuries CE

Period of Northern and Southern Dynasties
386–589 CE

T'ang Dynasty
618–907 CE

▲ **Songyue Temple Ta**
523 CE

▲ **Daming Palace**
Begun 634 CE

▲ **Wild Goose Pagoda**
7th century CE

Kofun Culture
ca. 3rd century to 538 CE

Asuka period in Japan
ca. 538–710 CE

Nara period in Japan
710–794 CE

▲ **Horyu-ji Temple**
7th century CE

▲ **Ise Shrine**
Rebuilt every twenty years since ca. 690 CE

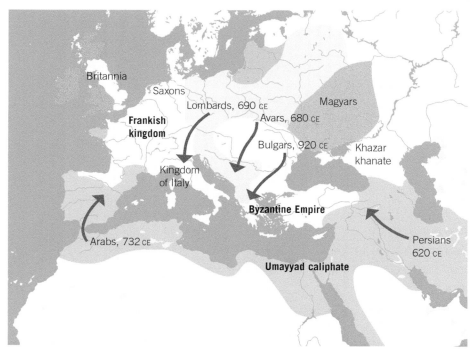

9.5 Justinian Europe, showing movements ca. 600 CE

AGE OF JUSTINIAN

The time period between Constantine the Great (272–337 CE) and Justinian (483–565 CE) was one of consolidation. For Justinian, the Romanum Imperium was to be identified with the Christian *oikoumene* (the known inhabited areas of the world), and the triumph of Christianity was as sacred a mission as the restoration of Roman supremacy. To this end, he reintroduced Roman law, but with the dogmatic primacy peculiar to the Christian religion. All other religions were denied legal protection. Pagan temples were torn down and strict laws passed to consolidate and unify the Christian domination of the empire. In 529 CE, Justinian closed the Academy in Athens, largely to stem the multiplication of ideas and theories in theological debates and to enforce a unified doctrine. Many of its scholars had to seek refuge in Persia, taking with them the fruits of Greek learning.

Justinian was able to recover Italy and Africa. Bridges, fortifications, aqueducts, churches, markets, and whole cities sprang up in the wake of his conquests. But the situation was tenuous. Eastern Europe was still in turmoil, with the Avars and Bulgars moving into Greece and the Lombards into northern Italy. The newly Christianized

Frankish kingdom, along with Italy, formed only a thin civilizational wedge into a still barbaric Europe. Newly developing, however, were trade links up the Volga River into the Russian steppe, facilitating trade that had become disrupted by the advances of the Islamic armies.

An excellent example of Justinian's architecture can be seen in Constantinople in the church dedicated to Sergius and Bacchus, two soldiers in the Roman army who were martyred in the early 4th century CE and became the official patrons of the Byzantine armies. Certain changes to its environs should, however, be kept in mind. The building, now a freestanding structure, was originally part of a larger complex that included Justinian's private residence and palace. Furthermore, the slightly thicker walls to the south belonged to another church dedicated to St. Peter and St. Paul, begun in 518 CE and built by Justinian's uncle, Justin I. When Justinian became Caesar in 525 CE, he appended the new construction onto that one.

The two churches were connected at ground level by means of three large arched openings that later changed into windows when the Church of SS. Peter and Paul was removed. (Such church composites

were not uncommon in the East, though they were rare in the West.) The narthex on the west extended across both churches, which shared a common atrium in front. To the north was a monumental entrance, presumably from the former palace, creating a cross-axis from north to south linking the two buildings. For reasons unknown, the Church of SS. Peter and Paul fell into disrepair and was demolished; by the 16th century, it was gone, as were most of the remnants of Justinian's palace.

SS. Sergius and Bacchus's original context is important, as it explains some of the curious—and also sometimes overlooked—aspects of its design. To provide an entrance for the priests from the southwest into the apse at the back of the church, the eastern facade was tilted a bit, with the space left for a porch perhaps still visible in the setback of the facade at that corner. The resultant tilt impacted the orientation of the apse and thus of the central nave. To the west, the tilt was not implemented because the narthex had to align with the Church of SS. Peter and Paul. The plan is distinguished by its extraordinary openness. Unlike Western churches, which channel the churchgoer into the nave from the west, here is a system that permits more fluid pathways into and through the church. Another remarkable feature of the plan that applies to both SS. Sergius and Bacchus and the Hagia Sophia is that there are no separate rooms to the right or left of the altar—rooms for the preparation of the sacred meal and where the bishop dons his garb. Such spaces, the *prothesis* and the *diaconicon*, respectively, are typical in later Byzantine churches, but they are not present in early Justinian ones. The result in both buildings is that the central structure holding the dome is freed from the surrounding architecture in a way that is uncharacteristic of Byzantine design.

It would be a mistake to project current medieval liturgical uses in Greek Orthodox churches onto these spaces, even though there are clearly numerous similarities. In Justinian's day, the populace gathered closely around the ambo in the nave. In addition, the preparatory rites of the *prothesis* (in a room for the preparation of the sacred meal) for the First Entrance that are common today were not practiced; the entrance ritual was

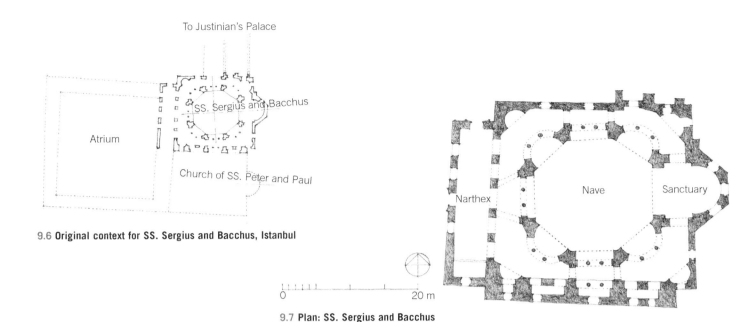

9.6 Original context for SS. Sergius and Bacchus, Istanbul

0   20 m

9.7 Plan: SS. Sergius and Bacchus

more straightforward but also grander. The people gathered in the courtyard, and there they made their offerings of bread and wine to the church. Once the bishop had blessed the entrance and had himself entered, he was followed by the deacon, who carried a bejeweled and bound volume of the Gospel—which stood for Christ himself—accompanied by candle-bearers, incense-bearers, and a subdeacon carrying a cross. The rest followed. The First Entrance had numerous symbolic meanings, including the rejection of disbelief, and signified the first appearance of God and the conversion to faith. In Rome, the order is reversed: the priests enter first and await the arrival of the bishop. In Constantinople, the bishop would go past the ambo and into the sanctuary—defined by the short barrier of the iconostasis—to the altar where the Gospel would be placed, and then to a semicircular tier of benches called the *synthronon*, where he would give the initial blessing signifying the glorification of Christ.

If the emperor, who was the head of the Orthodox Church, was present, he would arrive earlier than the bishop and join him at the narthex, at the head of the procession. His honor guard, consisting of soldiers and cross-bearers, would have preceded him into the church to define the path. After leaving

a gift of gold at the altar, he would proceed to the south aisle, where his throne was located. The interaction between emperor and priesthood was an essential and defining moment in the integrity of the empire and the Church, with their meeting and common participation in the ceremony a sign of the unity of the earthly and divine realms. At SS. Sergius and Bacchus, the emperor's spot was in the northeast of the gallery, from where he could overlook the proceedings.

Today, a table or niche on the north side serves as the *prothesis*, but there is no evidence that this custom existed in Byzantine times. It seems that the act of bringing offerings of bread and wine by the congregation started outside the church, in a special room of a building called the *skeuophylakion* that was used to hold the sacred vessels in which the food was transported. In other words, during the service, the wine and bread brought by the congregation was prepared out of sight and, in the process, "became" the flesh and blood of Christ, and was then carried into the church. The bishop made his entrance already vested—thus the absence of the *diaconicon*, a room where the bishop dons his garb, which came only later. The atrium served as a place for people to gather. The

narthex was a more formal space used to organize the procession once it had arrived. Once the procession had commenced, the congregation could also enter, which it did by streaming into the space from the various entrances, in a manner of popular commotion.

Following the blessing, the readings took place from the altar and from the ambo, the Gospel having been carried to the ambo with great solemnity and excitement. After the reading and the sermon came the Great Entrance, or as it was called at that time, the Entrance of the Mysteries, during which the Eucharistic bread and wine were transferred from their place of preparation to the place of offering on the altar. The bread and wine were brought in through a side door. The space inside the church was used to segregate men from women, but exactly how this was done remains unclear.

9.8 Narthex: Hagia Sophia, Istanbul, Turkey

9.9 Exterior: Hagia Sophia

Hagia Sophia

The Hagia Sophia ("sacred wisdom," 532–37 CE) in Constantinople was, from the date of its opening, considered one of the greatest buildings in the Western world. Little is known for certain about its predecessor, which was dedicated by Constantine in 360 CE but damaged in civil strife. For the new church, Justinian called in Anthemius of Tralles and Isidore of Miletus, who produced a daring and lofty domed structure still largely intact today. Sheathed in marble and gold, its splendor made it one of the most talked-about buildings in the Christian world. One visitor, Procopius, writing in the 6th century, when the building was newly finished, stated, "The dome must surely seem not to rest upon solid masonry but to cover the space beneath with its golden dome suspended from heaven." Some skeptics thought they had been right when an earthquake destroyed the dome in 557 CE, barely twenty years after its dedication. But Justinian, undaunted, had a new dome built, though the second one was more steeply pitched.

The structural system is simple but ingenious. A 30-meter square forms the center. At the corners, piers rise up to support four arches, between which are pendentives that hold a dome scalloped with forty ribs. Windows line the base of the dome, making it seem to float. The east and west arches are closed off with a screen of columns and windows. The undersides of the east and west arches, however, seem to have blown away, allowing one to look into vast, three-apsed buildings on both sides. The only difference between east and west is that on the eastern side, the final 8 meters of the apse boldly project from the perimeter wall that otherwise, like a box, contains its precious spatial cargo. The apse that projects from the wall is known as a *synthronon* and is where the bishop sits. The deep galleries on the north and south, which form spacious corridors parallel to the nave, help create the sense of drama that pervades the building. From a structural point of view, they serve to divide the buttressing into segments.

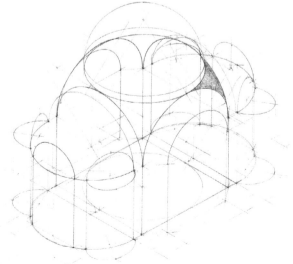

9.10 Spatial composition: Hagia Sophia

The vaults, made of brick, are thin and lightweight. There is still considerable uncertainty about the statics that govern the building's integrity, because the semi-domes are too thin to be of much assistance. But the combination of supporting half-domes, quarter-domes, and massive piers were enough, and in the days before computers and earthquake impact studies, the audacity of the system is remarkable. Later, from the 8th century on, various types of buttresses were added to the exterior to prevent problems.

The use of windows is similarly complex. The window at the east end of the apse, the lights along the base of the dome, and those on the north and south all allow light to stream directly into the nave. But the other windows are all invisible from the nave and produce various backlit qualities. For example, under the north and south tympana, the colonnaded columns stand in the shadows, backlit from the windows in the outer wall. The large windowless openings under the supporting arch at the west end are filled only with grille work. Impressive as the complex structural system of the Hagia Sophia is, the architects made every effort to make it all appear effortless. The marble cladding and the mosaics would have obliterated any sense of oppression or weight. From the dark-gray marble of the pavement, the green marble with white veins, dark-blue marble with yellow veins, and reddish columns, to the silver and gold of the mosaics, the eye moves from surface to surface as if structure simply did not exist.

The first dome was covered with a gold mosaic. The second one had a large figure of a cross embedded in its decoration. The windows were filled with glass tinted blue, red, green, brown, yellow, and purple to add to the effect. The light was thus a subdued one. Even the patterned marble floor, unlike the floor of the Pantheon, denies a sense of stability and has been described by ancient commentators as a wavy sea. Though a good many of the marble panels have survived, few of the mosaics have, since most were taken down or plastered over during the building's conversion to a mosque. (The Hagia Sophia was secularized in 1935.)

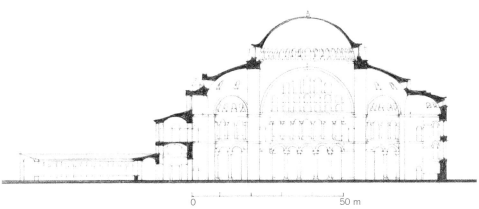

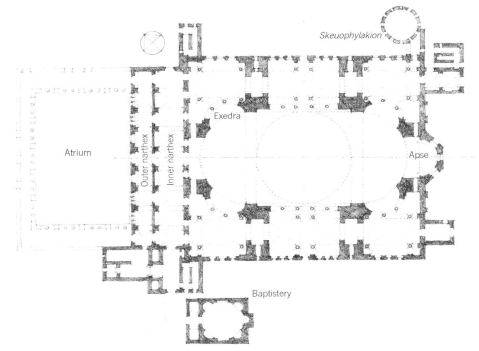

9.11 **Plan and section: Hagia Sophia**

Despite its inner drama, the building from the outside, with its staggered heaping of volumes, does not give the visitor the expectation of such a grand interior space. In fact, once one passes through the narthex, the space rises forcefully, creating the feeling of being at the bottom of a vast canyon, with the church floor a type of stage on which the Entrance of the Mysteries was performed. Nighttime illumination must also have been impressive. From the base of the dome, brass chains swept down to support a metal ring equipped with flat silver disks pierced to hold glass vessels for oil lamps. Within this vast candelabrum hung another, smaller crown of lights, while higher up, a great silver disk acted as a reflector.

The church was sited just north of the palace complex at the terminus of the main avenue that ran through the city. Apart from the Hagia Sophia, very little of the palace survives today. The atrium, where congregants gathered, is also no longer extant.

9.12 View of the semi-dome, Hagia Sophia

9.13 Palace area of Constantinople

9.14 **Detail of capital, Hagia Sophia**

Byzantine Capitals

There are two types of capitals used at the Hagia Sophia: composite and Ionic. The composite capital that emerged during the late Byzantine Empire, mainly in Rome, combines the Corinthian with the Ionic. Composite capitals line the principal space of the nave. Ionic capitals are used behind them in the side spaces, in a minor position relative to the Corinthian or composite orders (as was their fate well into the 19th century, when buildings were designed for the first time with a monumental Ionic order). At the Hagia Sophia, though, these are not the standard imperial statements. The capitals are filled with foliage in all sorts of variations. In some, the small, lush leaves appear to be caught up in the spinning of the scrolls—clearly, a different, nonclassical sensibility had taken over the design. At SS. Sergius and Bacchus and other churches of the time, we see the full emergence of this experimentation.

Post-Renaissance classicism in Europe dismissed these efforts as radically outside the norm of the "classical" tradition. But the classical tradition was more open to experimentation than one might at first think. Furthermore, after the fall of the Roman Empire, in which standardized models were often used, local craftsmen were invited to test their skills. That many of these craftsmen were using northern motives or were themselves Christianized Visigoths is more than obvious. The Visigoths invaded Byzantine territories in the 5th century, with many of them staying on to be conscripted into the Byzantine army. They tended to use vine and plant motifs for their ornamentation, as can be seen in their belt buckles. Most of the Visigoths eventually went on to settle in southern Spain.

The capitals at St. Vitale in Ravenna show wavy and delicate floral patterns similar to decorations found on belt buckles and dagger blades. Their inverted pyramidal form has the look of a basket. At the Basilica Eufrasiana in Parenzo, Croatia, along the Adriatic Sea, we find a double-tier design, with birds at the corners and delicately carved grapevines below. At Salonica, Greece, we encounter capitals that also consist of abstract curved patterns, in conjunction with some that have leaves that look as if they are being tossed around by the wind. The capitals at SS. Sergius and Bacchus have a delicate stenciling that allows the swirling tendrils of acanthus to stand out against the blackness of a deeply cut background.

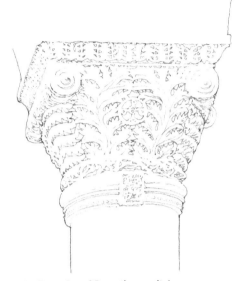

9.15 **Examples of Byzantine capitals**

9.16 **A Visigoth ornament**

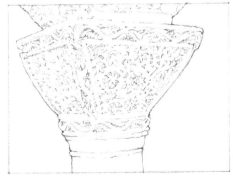

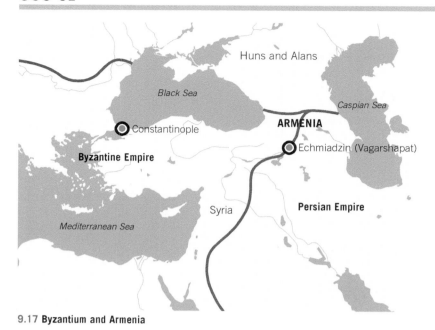

9.17 Byzantium and Armenia

ARMENIAN ARCHITECTURE

The area defined by the Caspian Sea to the east and the Black Sea to the west was an important geographical hub. Merchants could unload goods from China on the shores of the Caspian, where they would be taken through Armenia to the Black Sea, from which almost any destination in Europe was reachable. The trip from China to Rome would have gone through fewer contested territories in the year 600 CE than it does today; the location was, however, the cause for both the rise and the fall of the Armenian kingdom. Descended from the Urartu, the Armenians were in turn controlled by the Persians, by Alexander the Great, by the Romans, and then by the Persians again. Despite all this, the Armenian desire for autonomy was strong, and the period between the 4th and 9th centuries saw Armenia at its creative best. In the 6th and 7th centuries, with Arab regions to the south and Viking areas to the north still in disarray, Armenia was a safe link between East and West. But by the 10th century, with the expansion of Islam and Christianity into large, far-flung yet interconnected domains, trade increased—to the detriment of Armenia, which was able to survive only until 1375.

The significance of Armenia in the history of architecture lies, once again, in the high quality of its stonework. In Constantinople, stone had given way to brick. (The Hagia Sophia is basically a brick building.) The use of concrete, furthermore, had been forgotten by this time. Only the Armenians had maintained the classical Hellenistic tradition of clean surfaces, volumetric complexity, and a strong focus on a compact, object-like effect of the building in space. This would have an important impact on the later development of church architecture in Europe, when Armenian masons were in demand in the west, particularly in France.

The history of Armenia's Christian architecture begins in 301 CE, when Dertad III (the king of Armenia under Roman suzerainty) was converted to Christianity by St. Gregory the Illuminator, a native Armenian who made Christianity the state religion. In general, the Armenian liturgy resembles that of the Eastern Church, except that its language is classical Armenian rather than Greek. The distinctive look of Armenian architecture developed quite rapidly. Buildings tended to have forms that were simple and solid-looking. From the earliest date, they were volumetric and planimetric masterpieces. Furthermore, the carving and placement of the stones was excellent; indeed, at the time, these buildings would have been far superior to other stone buildings in Europe and Asia. Though Byzantine architecture introduced the dome as an important potential element in Christian architecture, the Byzantine dome was not visible externally. Armenian architecture, by way of contrast, pushed the dome up over the mass of the building. Though the dome itself was covered with a light wooden conical roof, the silhouette achieved would have a profound impact on future church design.

The Armenian word *gmbet*, usually translated as "dome," means more precisely "the vault of heaven." The vision of Gregory the Illuminator (b. 239 CE), the patron saint of Armenia, also played a part in the acceptance of the dome. He wrote that he saw a figure of light descending from heaven associated with a magnificent building that had the form of a dome on four columns.

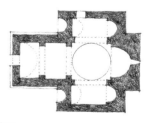

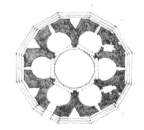

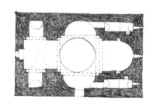

9.18 Typology of Armenian churches

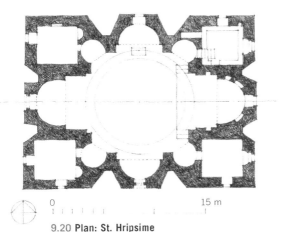

9.20 **Plan: St. Hripsime**

9.19 **St. Hripsime, Echmiadzin, Armenia**

St. Hripsime

One of the most refined examples of Armenian architecture can be found in Echmiadzin. St. Hripsime was the second church built by St. Gregory the Illuminator during the first quarter of the 4th century. It was replaced in 395 CE by a small chapel. The present edifice was built in 618 CE. The building is constructed of dark, ash-colored tufa bonded on the interior with concrete-like mortar. The whole rests, like a Greek temple, on a stepped stylobate. The small windows emphasize the mass and solidity of the structure.

The interior is organized on a quatrefoil plan, with niches in the cardinal directions. In addition to these, there are niches on the diagonal corners, creating a fluid and dynamic interior space. The diagonal niches, having the form of three-quarter cylinders, may also have been intended to strengthen the abutment of the dome. They give access to four subsidiary chambers that flank the eastern and western niches. Though the building is biaxially symmetrical, the eastern apse is emphasized by the raised altar section that protrudes into the central space. Barrel vaults intervene between the axial niches and the central square. These vaults, which are wider along the main axis, accentuate the east-west direction. The whole composition is bound together to form

a well-proportioned rectangle with large triangular recesses on the exterior that impart a rhythmic impression of the composition. The dome rests on a sixteen-sided windowed drum that has twelve windows at its base. Four of the windows are now obscured by small cylindrical towers that were added later as buttresses. The entrance porch on the west is also a later addition. The beauty of the St. Hripsime edifice derives from the simplicity and harmony of its different parts.

9.21 **Interior: St. Hripsime**

285

9.22 **Zvartnots Cathedral, Echmiadzin, Armenia**

Zvartnots Cathedral

Among the many inventive designs of Armenian churches during this period, one stands out particularly: the Church of Zvartnots near Echmiadzin. Begun in 643 CE after Armenia's recovery from an Arab invasion in 640, it served for a time as the seat of the Armenian church. Though only the foundations and columns remain, it can be reconstructed with reasonable accuracy. From the outside it consisted of three telescoped cylinders, 37 meters across at ground level. The external walls were enlivened by blind arcades. The cylindrical exterior disguised a remarkable interior. Four wedge-shaped piers framed four large exedrae, three of them composed of six columns and the fourth closed off to form the apse. The piers rose to form arches that supported a dome on squinches. At the ground floor, the space between the exterior and interior served as an ambulatory, in essence producing a building within a building. As with all Armenian churches, the windows were small but well integrated into the composition. Here, however, the interior was proportionally quite tall, unlike most Armenian churches, which seem to strive for a balance between the horizontal and vertical. The church was recognized in its day as a marvel. There are clear similarities to the church of SS. Sergius and Bacchus (527–36 CE) in Constantinople. But that building, a brick structure, apart from the columns, was squat and was integrated into a palace compound. Zvartnots, by contrast, was not only larger in footprint and built of stone, but designed to be clearly visible against the landscape. Furthermore, the carving of the capitals and detailing of the arches was of the highest order.

VISHNU DEOGARH AND ELEPHANTA

After the collapse of the Gupta Empire, the Gangetic Plains were controlled by the Hephthalite Empire, which originated in the area that is now Afghanistan and Turkmenistan, and soon dominated central Asia. The power vacuum left most of India to fracture itself into numerous small nations, such as Harshavardhana (606–47 CE) in the north, and, moving southward, the Chalukyas, the Pallavas, the Cholas, and the Pandyas. During this period, with Buddhism marginalized, Hindu architecture in South Asia entered an experimental phase, and rock-cut temples competed for prominence with the new structural-stone and brick temples. Although an invasion of north India by the Huns dispersed the Buddhist monks from Kashmir, they continued to prosper in major universities such as those at Nalanda, Ujjain, and Sirpur. Typical for the syncretism of the time, Sirpur had shrines dedicated to Hindu deities such as Shiva and Vishnu adjacent to compounds dedicated to the Buddha. One of the oldest statues of a female deity, Haritiki, has been found at Sirpur.

An interesting comparison can be made between two 6th-century Gupta period temples: the Shiva shrine on Elephanta Island, a rock-cut structure built by Shaivite monks for their own use, and the Dasavatara Vishnu Temple at Deogarh, a brick-and-stone structure built for a large devotee population.

9.23 **A Hindu mandala**

9.24 **Vishnu Temple, Deogarh, India**

Elephanta is a Hindu shrine adapted from the older Buddhist rock-cut structures, while Deogarh is a new invention—a shrine constructed with stones to appear as if it is monolithic (i.e., rock-cut). The latter has a representational mountain as its *shikhara*, while the former has a real mountain in which it is embedded. Both begin with a square *garbha-griha*, but while Deogarh would have had originally held an image of Vishnu, Elephanta still has the Shiva Lingam at its center. From the middle, four axes radiate out, defining access paths. Deogarh, however, is accessible only from the west (the direction of Vishnu) and has three implied doors (*ghana-dwaras*, literally "blind doors") along its remaining cardinal directions.

Elephanta is open on all four sides, though east is its primary direction of access. Deogarh's main shrine is at the center of a nine-square mandala, with four subsidiary shrines interlocked at its corners. Elephanta has a much more complex geometry, with four sets of nine-square mandalas interlocking to define two major axes of access, one from the west and the other from the north. The north-south axis, aligned with the main entrance, terminates in three gigantic Shiva sculptures in deeply recessed niches. This triptych, much celebrated in the annals of art history, occupies the entire width and height of the end wall, and, compared to the rough-hewn character of the rest of structure, was carved with greater care.

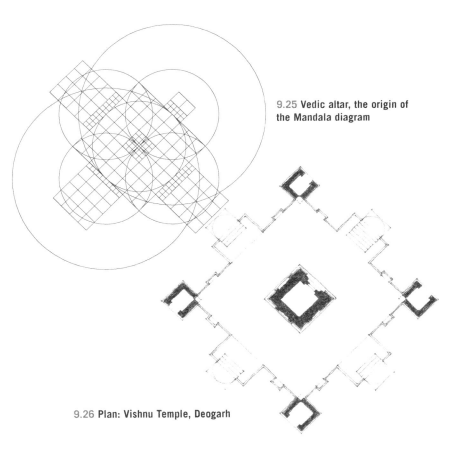

9.25 **Vedic altar, the origin of the Mandala diagram**

9.26 **Plan: Vishnu Temple, Deogarh**

9.27 *Garbha-griha*, Cave of Shiva, Elephanta, near Mumbai, India

9.28 Lingam, Cave of Shiva at Elephanta

The cerebral exploration of interlocking geometries based on mandala diagrams was to become the defining characteristic of Hindu temple form in the centuries to come. Mandalas are derived from original Vedic altars and are used in both the Hindu and Buddhist religions as diagrams to map the cosmos for astrological observations. These diagrams are abstract, without scale, and can take any number of forms derived from a combination of superimposed squares and circles.

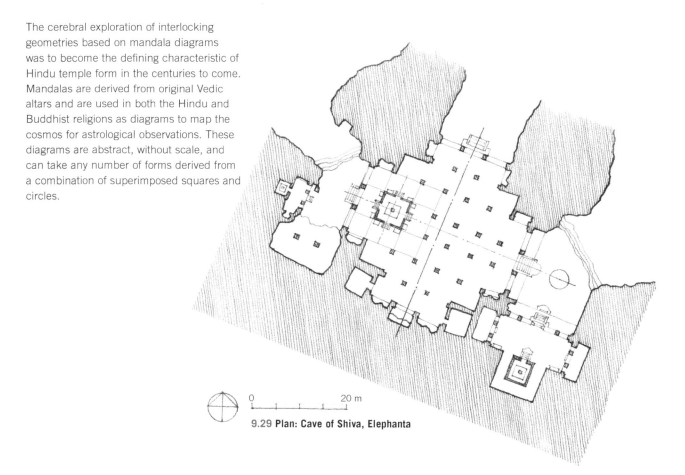

0   20 m

9.29 **Plan: Cave of Shiva, Elephanta**

9.30 **Five Rathas, Mamallapuram, India**

THE FIVE RATHAS

Contemporary with the Chalukyas, with whom they had frequent commerce, the Pallavas were one of the most distinguished dynasties of South Asia. The second Pallava ruler, Narasimhavarman II, built at Mamallapuram, one of India's largest port cities of the time, a series of monuments that made it one of the great spiritual hubs of India. The hill overlooking the shore was transformed into a "model" of the Hindu universe. A channel of spring-fed water, "the Ganges," was created, winding its way down the slope and passing numerous finely carved rock-cut temples. At the bottom of the hill, the channel opens into a waterfall that spills over a large and richly decorated bas-relief rock face known, fittingly, as the Descent of the Ganges.

The rulers, however, were eager to experiment with temples that were not rock-cut, but built up from stone. For this, so it seems, they held a competition, asking their designers to produce models from which temples could later be constructed. The results are known as the Five Rathas (mid- to late 7th century). They are a group of five miniaturized rock-cut temples accompanied by life-size sculptures of a bull, an elephant, and a lion. Every temple is a thought of as a miniature, or model, of the Hindu cosmic order. And the "decorative" module of a temple on a *shikhara* is also a miniature of the temple of which it is a part. In other words, on every scale—from the mini-temple on a *shikhara*, to the temple itself, to the full-scale reality of the Hindu cosmos—the same form repeats itself, as in fractal geometry. Beyond being a symbol of cosmic order, the temples also project to the worshipper a sense of personal wholeness.

9.31 **Elevation of Dharmaraja Ratha, Mamallapuram**

9.32 Shore Temple at Mamallapuram

Shore Temple at Mamallapuram

The Shore Temple at Mamallapuram (700–728 CE), so called because it overlooks the Bay of Bengal, is one of the oldest structural stone temples in southern India. It is attributed to the Pallava king Narasimhavarman II. Originally, it was part of a series of temples that belonged to a former port city that has long since disappeared into the waves, leaving the building isolated on the beach. The temple is modeled on the Dharmaraja Ratha, one of the Five Rathas, located a few kilometers away. The Dharmaraja Ratha, a rock-cut structure, is in turn clearly modeled on a wooden temple, suggesting that as with the ancient Greeks, here a stone building replicates a wooden one. The superstructure of the Dharmaraja Ratha is a series of stacked planes, each a representation of a sacred city. The Shore Temple expands on that theme, with each rising layer representing the intensification of the divine.

The temple is actually an amalgam of three different shrines, and in this respect is quite unusual. The main shrine is dedicated to Shiva and faces east. The second shrine, with a smaller *shikhara*, is also dedicated to Shiva, but faces west. Between the two, attached to the back wall of the smaller Shiva shrine and entered from the east, is a small third shrine with no superstructural presence, dedicated to the reclining Vishnu.

The Vishnu shrine, probably the oldest on the site, is on axis with the larger Shiva shrine, although there is no direct communication between the two. The Shore Temple's configuration of the two Shiva shrines, which are separated and yet linked by the small Vishnu shrine, represents an effort to balance the multiple competing liturgical requirements. Most later Hindu temples, dedicated to more than one deity, are lined up hierarchically or organized radially around a dominant center.

Although most of the exterior arrangements of the temple have eroded, there is ample suggestion that water may have been channeled into pools in the temple and may indeed have also entered into the Vishnu shrine—which would have been appropriate, since the reclining Vishnu figure is described in mythology as lying in the primordial ocean. The *shikharas* are similar to those of the nearby Five Rathas, with a strict pyramidal outline and a pilastered wall. The individual tiers of the Shore Temple's *shikharas* have been kept distinct and separate, with the deep overhanging eaves casting dark shadows without blurring the levels. Both *shikharas* resolve themselves into octagonal capstones with long finials. Just to the north of the temple, there is a sacred pool that replicates the primordial ocean. Because of climactic changes, it is no longer filled with water.

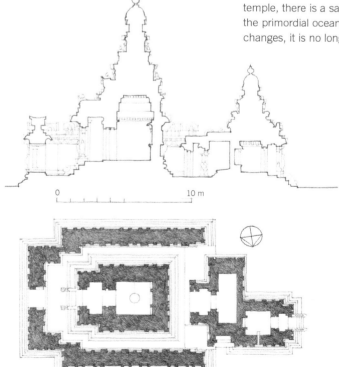

9.33 Plan and section: Shore Temple at Mamallapuram

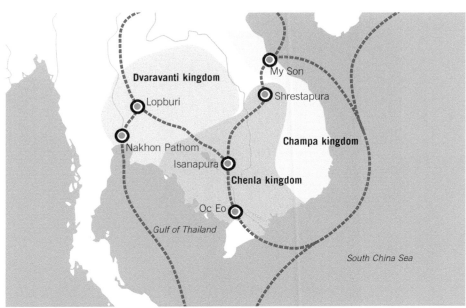

9.34 **Zone of development in Southeast Asia, 600 CE**

SOUTHEAST ASIA

Between 300 and 600 CE, there was a marked transformation of the Irrawaddy and Mekong river hinterland in areas that are today Thailand and Cambodia. River water and floodwaters were brought under control, and increased centralization allowed for the exercise of authority. In the Mekong River area, *barays* were created. These water pools, formed by large enclosed dikes, were flooded naturally by the Mekong River, and after the floodwaters receded, retained water in the basins for irrigation during the dry season. By means of this hydroengineering, rice production increased and new cities sprang up.

Among the larger of these new cities were Nakhon Pathon and Lop Buri in Thailand, and Isanapura and Shrestapura in Cambodia and Laos. All were carved out of the jungle and surrounded by newly created agricultural zones. It is clear that the Southeast Asian hinterland was becoming interconnected with trade routes that worked their way both east-west and north-south, with China consequently gaining in importance. Politically, the area was divided between the Dvaravanti in Thailand, the Chenla in Cambodia, the Champa along the Vietnamese coast, and the emergent Srivijaya kingdom in Malaysia and Indonesia. These kingdoms were heavily influenced by Indian religious ideas. The Dvaravanti were Buddhists, whereas the Chenla, developing

Sambor Prei Kuk temple complex

9.35 **Area plan: Isanapura, Cambodia**

from the Furnan, were Hindus. This Indianization was not met by a similar cultural movement from China, for complicated reasons that have something to do with China's complex trade policies. Furthermore, the idea of temple-cities—which were relatively small in scale and had developed in India as an economic unit that could be stamped onto the landscape—found no parallel in China, where cities were large administrative entities that could not be easily replicated in foreign lands, much less in the dense rain forests of Southeast Asia. By contrast, the temple-city that developed in India was a perfect instrument of agricultural/economic expansion.

In 618 CE, for example, the Chenla king Isanavaram I (r. 616–35 CE) established Isanapura—the suffix *pura* means "city"—as the capital of his kingdom, 20 kilometers northeast of Kompong. (The city is now called Sambor Prei Kuk.) It was about 2 kilometers square and contained approximately 150 temples, all dedicated to Shiva or one of his numerous forms. Though the city has not been thoroughly studied archaeologically, the brick temples show considerable sophistication. Among the three main temples, one—called the North Group—consists of a 100-meter-square platform about 1 meter high on which rest five shrines, a standard prototype for Hindu temples that represents the five peaks of the mythical Mt. Meru, the abode of the gods. The central shrine contained the Shiva Lingam, but unlike most shrines, it is open on all four sides. It rests on a terrace about 50 meters square. Small shrines define the corners. The whole is contained by an enclosure wall.

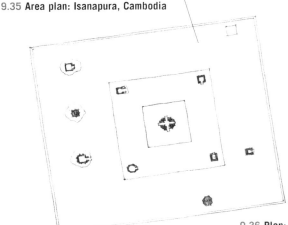

9.36 **Plan: Prasat Sambor (North Group), Hindu temple complex of Sambor Prei Kuk, Isanapura**

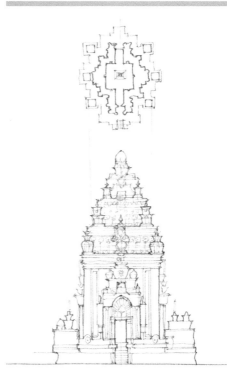

9.38 My Son temple

9.37 Elevation and plan: My Son temple, near Da Nang, Vietnam

My Son

The idea of a sacred landscape also took root in the Champa kingdom. The coast of Vietnam that it controlled had for centuries been developing as an important regional economic zone, its numerous bays and inlets accommodating trade with Chinese and Indian vessels. Initially, the Champa, as a set of federated cities, were closely tied to Chinese cultural and religious traditions, but in the 4th century CE there was a strong infusion of Indian culture. Sanskrit was adopted as a scholarly language, and Hinduism—especially Shaivism—became the state religion. Toward the end of the century, in a somewhat unusual move perhaps reflective of Chinese notions of kingship, a valley known as My Son (69 kilometers southwest of Da Nang) was set aside for religious purposes and as a memorial site dedicated to the noble achievement of the royal dynasty. My Son ("Beautiful Mountain") is located near the Thu Bon River and to the west of Indrapura, now known as Hôi An, a city that at that time possessed a large harbor and was an important trading center. The valley, hidden from the plain and with only one entrance, is surrounded by hills and mountains. The site was envisioned as a

sacred one. The highest mountain of My Son, the Rang Meo, or "Cat's Teeth Mountain" (800 meters), symbolized Mt. Meru, the residence of the god Shiva, the main deity worshipped by the Champa.

The earliest temples, built from wood, have not survived. Brick masonry was introduced toward the end of the 7th century. The temples all followed a similar Indian model: a square ground plan with a platform and shrine proper, and a high, stepped roof. The external surface was often plastered and painted. Eventually, stone was also used for decorative purposes around lintels and door jambs, as well as for columns and pilasters. There is a blind portico facing east, also lavishly ornamented. The interiors are plain, with small niches for lamps. The Shiva Lingam, symbolizing the divine force, was situated on a plinth in the center. A decorated frieze connected the tower with its roof (*suarloka*). Each tower had three stories, forming a stepped pyramid that represented Kailasa, the abode of Shiva. Many of the roofs were originally covered with gold or silver leaf. In front of the *kalan* stood a smaller gate tower (*gopura*), built from brick, with stone pillars. Most of the temple complexes also had long buildings

(*mandapas*) with tiled roofs adjacent to the gate towers, used for religious ceremonies. In many cases there were smaller, two-roomed temples (*kasagraha*) around the *kalan* for the worship of lesser deities. Each complex was surrounded by a thick wall of brick, but these have almost entirely disappeared over the centuries.

As was the case in all Hindu temples, only the Brahmin were allowed to enter the *cella*, or inner sanctuary, and minister to the god with food, music, and other offerings. Pilgrims could pray outside, leaving their gifts with the religious authorities.

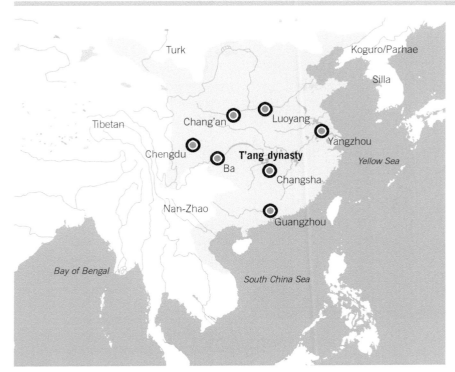

9.39 T'ang dynasty, China

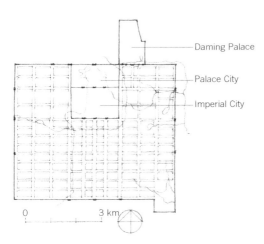

9.40 Plan: Chang'an, the T'ang capital, China

SUI AND T'ANG DYNASTIES

The Sui (581–618 CE) and the T'ang (618–907 CE) succeeded in establishing centralized dynasties that made determined investments in public works—in particular the building of canals and roads. Their engineering achievements can be seen in the segmental stone-arch bridge they built over the Jiao River near Zhaozhou on the main north-south trade route. The Jiao River was more than 40 meters wide at this point. The steep approaches of their older, semicircular bridges were impractical for wheeled vehicles, while their post-and-lintel technology was not sufficiently advanced. The problem of sinking stone piers into the swiftly flowing river made a multiple-arched structure impractical. Li Chun, the engineer of the Zhaozhou Bridge, constructed it using a series of twenty-eight adjacent arcs, each containing forty-three wedge-shaped stone voussoirs tied together with nine reinforcing iron rods to pull the stones together. Over the next four centuries, T'ang engineers constructed bridges using not only the segmental arch and open spandrel construction but also arched, suspension, and cantilever technology.

Daxing (Chang'an)

Located at the terminus of the Silk Route, Chang'an ("Forever Peace") was first established by the Han dynasty in 200 BCE. But in 24 CE, in the middle of the Han reign, Chang'an was looted, burned, and reduced to a provincial city; Luoyang was reestablished as the Han capital. In the 4th century CE, however, Chang'an experienced a revival as a center of Buddhist learning. And late in the 6th century, the first emperor of the Sui dynasty reestablished Chang'an as an imperial capital. The Sui rebuilt the city a few kilometers south of the old Han city and called it Daxing ("Great Prosperity"). This was the city that, under the T'ang, was to become famous as China's *urb primus* of the 1st millennium CE. Developing both external and internal trade was a high priority under the Sui, and then the T'ang linked Chang'an with Luoyang, Yangzhou, Chengdu, Guangzhou, Youzhou, Bianzhou (now Kaifeng), and Mingzhou (now Ningbo). Guangzhou and Mingzhou were ports that serviced Korea and Southeast Asia, respectively. An ancient form of bill of exchange known as *feiqian* ("flying money") was introduced by the T'ang. Merchants who sold their goods in Daxing could get *feiqian* drafts with which they could draw money in other places.

In 750 CE, Daxing (Chang'an), with a million residents, was the largest city in the world. A stela inscribed in 781 CE documents the introduction of Nestorian Christianity by Syrian priests in 635 CE. The last of the Sassanian princes, Firuz, found refuge there around 670 CE. Manichaeism arrived with the Persians fleeing Islam around 694 CE. However, Chang'an remained predominantly a place of Buddhist scholarship. Thousands of Buddhist scholars and pilgrims, such as Faxian, came to live in Chang'an, with its hundreds of Buddhist monasteries. In 840 CE, the Japanese pilgrim Enin found monks from southern and northern India, Sri Lanka, Kucha (from the Tarim Basin), Korea, and Japan—as well as China—building pagodas, temples, and monasteries. The Wild Goose Pagoda of Hsuan Tsang (Xuanzang) was constructed in the 7th century to hold all his manuscripts. Enin also noted that among the city's prized relics were four teeth of the Buddha, from India, Khotan, and Tibet—and the fourth, reputedly, from heaven. During festivals honoring these dental relics, each monastery was bedecked with offerings such as medicines and foods, rare fruits and flowers, and various kinds of incense. Individual donations were commonplace. One donor gave a hundred bushels of rice and twenty bushels of millet; others provided biscuits or cash.

293

9.41 Wild Goose Pagoda, Xi'an, China

Chang'an became a model for city planning, not only for later Chinese capitals like Beijing during the Ming and Qing dynasties but also for the capital cities of Korea and Japan, such as Nara, Heian-Kyo (Kyoto), and Kyôngju. Construction was overseen by the engineer and planner Yuwen Kai (555–612 CE). Kai had already engineered the Grand Canal (605–6 CE) to facilitate the transport of grain from the alluvial southern plains to the relatively impoverished (but militarily strong) northern areas. Although overscaled, Chang'an's master plan was based on Zhou period descriptions of the Wangcheng ideal city (see "800 BCE"). But whereas ancient texts described the model city as surrounded by a square wall, with the emperor's palace at the center of the city, the market to the north, and the temple to the imperial ancestors and the shrine of the earth to the south, the planners of Chang'an placed the palace—Daming Palace ("Palace of Great Brilliance")—in an enclave outside of the square, along the north wall. The Taiji Palace ("Palace of the Supreme Ultimate"), which consisted of palaces and halls for imperial meetings, was located at the north end of the central north-south axis, occupying no less than 5 percent of the entire city. Just south of it was the Imperial City (offices of the government and national ceremonial halls). The Imperial City, which was the administrative heart of the empire, was also

where the emperor conducted his ritual sacrifices at the imperial ancestral temple and at the imperial heavenly altar.

The rest of the city was divided up on a grid pattern. Enclosing an area some 8.65 kilometers by 9.72 kilometers in size, the city's outer walls were punctured by three gates, one each on the western, southern, and eastern walls. The southern gate, Mingde, was the main entrance and opened onto a monumental street 220 meters wide, while the streets leading from the other gates measured about 140 meters wide.

Water played an important part in the design, with several streams running through the city. One went through the west market and another through the east market. There were five transport and sanitation canals running throughout the city—which had several different water sources—that delivered water to city parks, the gardens of the rich, and the grounds of the imperial palaces. The canals were also used to transport crucial goods throughout the city.

The residential part of the city was divided by east-west and north-south avenues into 108 neighborhood blocks called *fangs*. The roads were lined with water drainage channels on both sides, and shaded by rows of trees. The residential areas were further accessed by alleys. In spite of its population, the colossal spread of the city ensured that the density of the *fangs* was not very high,

especially compared to that of Teotihuacán and Rome at their heights. The *fangs* contained temples, commercial buildings, public parks, and housing. Each *fang* was a mini-city with its own inner transportation network, walls, gates, and corner towers. There were two major commercial areas in the outer city, referred to as the west and east markets, each occupying two *fangs*. These markets were the subject of many literary descriptions, often devoted to the global range of goods available there. The areas around Quijan Lake and the Xingqing *fang* were famous scenic districts. In the southeastern part of the city was a ward that was home to a large monastery with ten courtyards and the Wild Goose Pagoda (652 CE). This same city ward also had a large bathhouse, an entertainment courtyard, and an additional monastery, as well as a mansion that had its own bathhouse. The Wild Goose Pagoda had five stories, with a rammed earth core and a stone exterior facade. When this collapsed, the structure was rebuilt in brick in 704 CE, which with renovations still stands today, one of the few surviving edifices from that period. The building had special significance, since it held the the sutras that were brought to China from India by the noted Buddhist translator and traveler Hsuan Tsang.

Daming Palace

The authority of the emperor was represented by the palace, constructed axially at the head of the city. In the long reign of Gao Zong (650–83 CE), the power of the emperor was further magnified by the creation of another palace beyond the boundaries of Chang'an. The Daminggong (*gong* means "palace"), or "Palace of Great Brilliance," is in its own special compound covering 3 square kilometers. It was organized axially in a series of interconnected courts forming a four-part complex:

1. Entry square, about 500 meters square
2. Hanyuan Hall (Hanyuandian) in front (south side) of the entry square
3. Xuanzheng Hall at the back (north side) of the square
4. Northern third, containing the emperor's court, reception areas, residences, gardens, and temples

9.42 Pictorial view: Hanyuan Hall, Chang'an (Xi'an), China

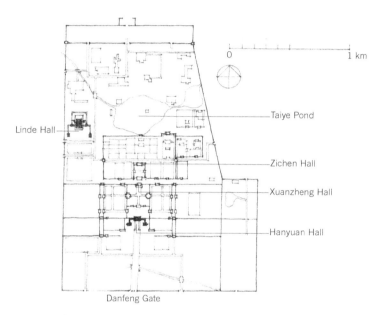

Linde Hall

Taiye Pond

Zichen Hall

Xuanzheng Hall

Hanyuan Hall

Danfeng Gate

9.43 Plan of Daming Palace, Chang'an

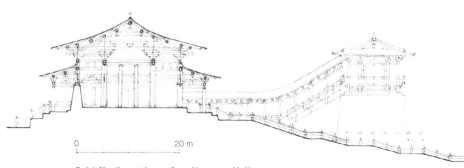

0   20 m

9.44 North-south section: Hanyuan Hall

First in Daming Palace's axial sequence was the Hanyuan Hall, or the "Enfolding Vitality Hall," the main gate where imperial rites were performed. This huge, imposing gate faced a gigantic square where ceremonies with a large number of participants and spectators were held. Fifty-eight meters wide, the Hanyuan Hall, quite large in itself, had a vast stair at its center, the Dragon-Tail Way, that was a classic example of the Chinese horizontal elongation of space. The gate's 11-by-4-bay structure supported a double-hipped roof and was flanked by high pavilions on either side that were raised, on their own bases, higher than the main hall. Three hundred meters beyond was the Xuanzheng ("Political") Hall, from whose sides extended walls that defined the palace complex. Here the emperor held court on the first and fifteenth day of each lunar month. Beyond its arcades lay all the main offices of the imperial bureaucracy. Two gates led to the internal compound of the palace, which consisted of a series of pavilions strung together by rectilinear arcades. Beyond the palace lay the Taiye Pond and a large open area with pavilions and garden compounds. West of the main palace area was the Linde ("Unicorn Virtue") Hall, which was used for banquets and less formal receptions. It consisted of three interconnected structures that abut one another on their long sides to form a larger complex 58.2 meters wide and 86 meters deep, accompanied by a panoply of surrounding arcades and pavilions. Literary sources record that theatrical performances were held in the arcades and polo matches took place in front of the first hall.

9.45 Songyue Temple Ta, Dengfeng, China

Songyue Temple Ta

Architecturally, the Chinese translated the South Asian stupa into the *ta* (or *pagoda*, a Portuguese-derived word). While the stupa is a round earthen mound, the *ta* is a tower. Both the *ta* and the stupa serve the same purpose: to house a buried relic at their core. The stupa emphasizes the fullness of the mound's body and focuses on the mystery within its earthen core; the *ta* magnifies the vertical axis and makes a display of the many levels of heavens inhabited by many Buddhas.

Though the form may have been inspired by Han Chinese watchtowers, the *ta* never functioned as such. Rather, it served as a beacon visible from a distance. The *ta* was no mistranslation, however; it was how the Chinese chose to represent the stupa. This may be because stupas began during a phase of Buddhism that deemphasized representation, while the *ta* emerged after the establishment of Mahayana Buddhism, which permitted representation. The *ta*, in fact, symbolizes outright the multi-heavened cosmology of Mahayana Buddhism. In the stupa, this cosmology is referred to through the small *chattris* (umbrellas) at the summits. The *ta*, essentially, is a *chattri* magnified to huge proportions. Even Hsuan Tsang (Xuanzang), who had seen and carefully recorded innumerable stupas in India, specifically chose the form of a *ta* when building his own monastery in Chang'an, the Wild Goose Pagoda (652–704 CE), a seven-story, 20-meter-high structure originally made of mud and brick.

The Songyue Temple Ta (523 CE), in Dengfeng, Henan Province, is China's oldest and largest surviving *ta*. Located in the middle of a river valley, it is a twelve-sided, 40-meter-high polygon consisting of fifteen bodhisattva levels, surmounted by an obtuse finial. The whole is made of brick, including the corbelled overhanging eaves of the main body. The overall form is parabolic, with a slight suggestion of entasis. The unornamented lower story of the base has an entry facing south. The second story is slightly cantilevered, with engaged columns at the corners and lotus-bud capitals that seem to be of Indian origin. The four sides face the cardinal directions and have openings leading to a central space; the other sides have arched niches, like the Mahabodhi Temple complex in India. The arches are decorated with lion motifs.

The Songyue Temple Ta was originally plastered, possibly white, and would have stood out against the hills. As it is, the pagoda, along with others with which it forms a family, sits in dramatic relation to

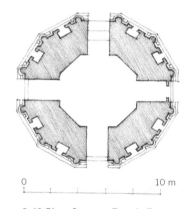

9.46 **Plan: Songyue Temple Ta**

its surroundings. Unlike most later pagodas, the Songyue Temple Ta is inaccessible. The individual stories—much too small to ever have been intended for human occupation—are entirely representational, complete with a door and two windows carved into each of the twelve sides at each story.

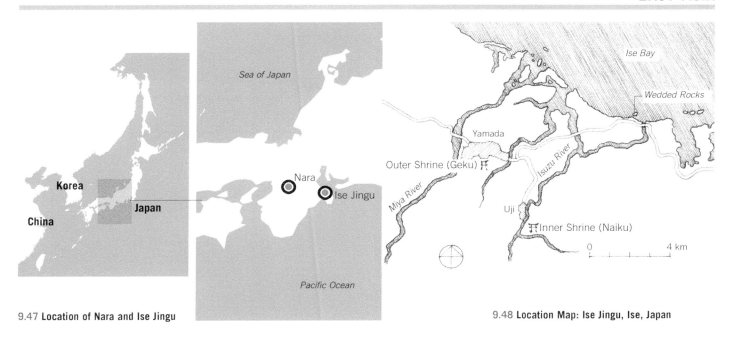

9.47 Location of Nara and Ise Jingu

9.48 Location Map: Ise Jingu, Ise, Japan

NARA PERIOD: JAPAN

By the 8th century CE, the various clans of Japan had cohered into a single political unit under an emperor; the northern islands were the last to be brought into this unity. Rice was the principal commodity. Japan's native religion at the time was Shintoism, a form of animism in which every aspect of nature was revered. There were no creeds or images of gods, but rather a host of kami, or sacred spirits. Kami were both deities and the numinous quality perceived in objects of nature, such as trees, rocks, waters, and mountains. The kami are still venerated at more than one hundred thousand Shinto shrines throughout Japan and are considered to be creative and harmonizing forces in nature. Humans were seen not as owners of nature, or above and separate from it, but as integral participants in it—and indeed derived from it. The Buddha was received as a "great kami," but a kami could also be attributed to the spirits of deceased emperors, heroes, and famous persons. In the 6th century, the emperor came to be deified as a living kami, and his divinity surpassed that of other kami. One honored kami in the form of food offerings, music, dance, and the performance of traditional skills such as archery and sumo wrestling. Ceremonial purity was strongly encouraged, and bodily cleanliness was an absolute necessity.

Only priests could approach the kami during special rites, since they alone were the mediators between the human and the kami. The earliest Shinto sanctuaries were simple piles of boulders or stones that marked the sacred places where the kami were thought to reside. Kami could also live in a constructed shrine, usually a simple, unadorned structure before which there stood a detached portal, known as a torii.

Ise Jingu

The unification of Shinto's animism with the spirit of the emperor set the stage for a remarkable building, the Ise Jingu ("Shrine"), dedicated to the tutelary kami of the Japanese imperial family. It has no parallel in the entire history of global architecture. Every 20 years for the last 1,500 years, the shrine has been rebuilt, identical to the one before, but with virgin old-growth timber.

The Ise Jingu that stands in Japan today was built in 2013. In a sense, then, it is practically new. Yet, at the same time, it can be dated to the year 690 CE. The sacred necklace of *magatama* (jewels representing the soul spirit, which enter the body of the possessor) is the symbol of succession from the sun goddess and is the emblem of the emperors of Japan even today. This necklace is kept at Ise. As such, Ise Jingu is Japan's most revered shrine.

Set deep in a sacred forest at the mouth a river valley south of the town of Ise, the shrine consists of two primary structures—the Inner Shrine (Naiku) and the Outer Shrine (Geku)—as well as a wide array of lesser sanctuaries distributed around a narrow, verdant coastal plain on the east coast of the Kii Peninsula in southern Honshu. The area, relatively warm even in winter, is crossed by the fast-flowing Isuzu River. Naiku is dedicated to Amaterasu Omikami ("Heaven-Illuminating Great Kami"), the traditional ancestral deity of the imperial house, and Geku is dedicated to Touke Okami ("Abundant Food Great Kami"). Originally unconnected, the two were joined into an institutional unit in the 9th century. Of the two, the Inner Shrine became the more important, its complex now containing about 120 separate shrines, including a number of tiny sanctuaries dedicated to the spirit of a single rock or the deity of a bubbling spring, as is Shinto practice.

9.49 Area plan: Ise Inner Shrine

9.50 South gateway to the Ise Inner Shrine

The path to the Naiku is carefully scripted, marked today by a series of torii (derived from the Sanskrit *torana*, for "gate"). One accesses the precinct by crossing the Uji Bridge, which is constructed from fragrant cypress wood, over the sacred Isuzu River. From the bridge, the pilgrim proceeds to the right along a broad street covered with gravel and flanked by carefully tended gardens. The path eventually turns east and rises up the gentle slope through another torii, surrounded by a forest of sacred cedars and zelkova elms. Finally, the path curves to approach the Naiku from the south. The double platforms on which the temple rests is terraced out over the sloping site and supported by giant stones.

The final approach is made by way of twenty-one stone steps that bring one to the top of the terrace and the outermost fence. A fine silk curtain hanging across the entrance and moving in the breeze is all that marks the beginning of the prohibited zone. The innermost shrines are open only to the temple priests or the imperial family, and even then only in a highly regulated and hierarchical fashion. The emperor has access to the innermost shrine, the Shoden, and the rest of the family's distance from the Shoden is a measure of their distance from the throne. Everyone else worships from the outside. The Naiku contains three structures organized axially—the central shrine, the Shoden; and, behind it on either side, the two treasuries. The 15-by-10-meter Shoden is raised off the ground by columns set directly into the ground (without a foundation). It is a meticulously crafted and ornamented wooden structure three bays wide and two bays deep, built entirely without nails. It has a deeply thatched reed roof and an entrance on its long side accessible via an external flight of stairs. The building, though empty, is modeled on a granary and is the symbolic residence of the rice kami.

Straight, squared timbers are used for the rafters that descend sharply from the ridgepole. The side gable ends have no openings. At the middle of each gable end is a freestanding solitary pillar that supports the ridgepole.

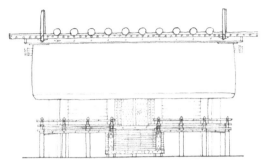

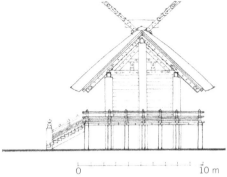

9.51 Elevations and plan: Shoden, Ise Inner Shrine

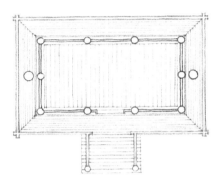

9.52 Kami shrine, Ise, Japan

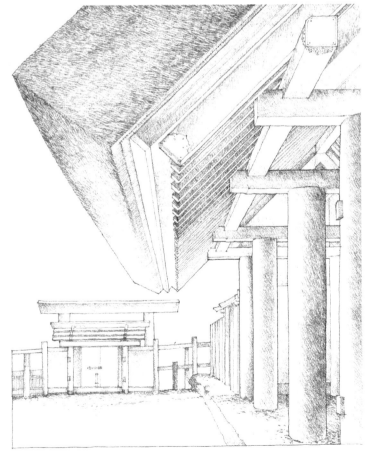

9.53 Inner precinct of the Ise Inner Shrine

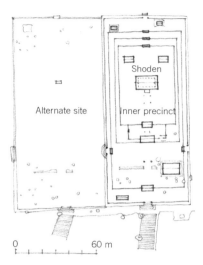

9.54 Plan: Ise Inner Shrine

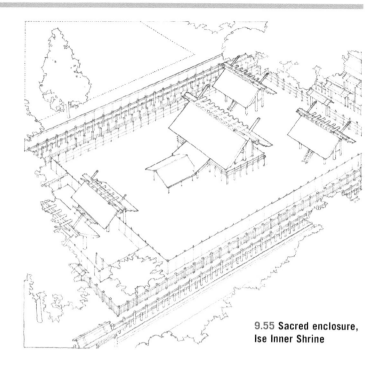

9.55 Sacred enclosure, Ise Inner Shrine

The elaborate ritual process of rebuilding the Ise every twenty years is known as *shikinen sengu* ("the transfer of the god-body to a new shrine in a special festival year"). The reconstruction alternates between two adjacent sites. While one site is in use, the other is left empty, covered by white gravel. When the floor of the previous Shoden is relocated, a small wooden pillar, known as the *shin-no-mihashira*, or "heart pillar," is left buried in the old shrine compound, and a small shed, the *oi-ya*, is built over it to protect it from the elements. The lumber consists of hundreds of trees that are taken from a sacred grove in the mountains and transported to the site with much fanfare and reverence. The old lumber, still sacred, is disseminated to be used in the repair of other Shinto shrines around Japan.

The idea of renewal might also be tied to Shinto beliefs and could be described as the desire to show reverence to the Great Kami by revitalizing its earthly residence. In a metaphysical sense, a belief in the transience of material objects as opposed to the permanence of form—a metonym for the nature of the kami—is ritually enacted. Most fundamentally, perhaps, the rebuilding renews the social contract with the imperial family, the core of whose legitimacy lies in the long line of its unbroken ancestry.

Following is a simplified list of the ceremonies that are required to make the transfer from the old to the new sanctuaries:

2005
- Ceremony to offer prayers to the kami who resides at the foot of the mountain in order to obtain permission to enter the mountainside and to cut the sacred wood

2006
- Ceremony to mark the start of pulling the timber into the sanctuary
- Ceremony marking the arrival of the wood to be used for the *shikinen sengu*

2008
- Ceremony to offer prayers of consolation to the kami who dwells at the site where the new sanctuary is to built

2012
- Ceremony to erect the first pillar for the main sanctuary building
- Ceremony to install metal plates to ward off evil spirits, under the gable at either end of the main sanctuary's roof
- Ceremony to lift the ridgepole of the main sanctuary building
- Ceremony for the thatching of the roof

2013
- Ceremony to place the white pebbles on the sacred ground around the new sanctuary
- Ceremony to place the sacred wooden box for holding the symbol of the kami in the main sanctuary
- Ceremony to purify the building with sacred water
- Ceremony to celebrate the completion of the sanctuary building, and to offer prayers to the kami who dwells at the foundation of the newly reconstructed sanctuary to make the ground stable
- Ceremony to confirm that the newly made clothing offered to the kami by the emperor is in accordance with tradition
- Ceremony to decorate the inside of the building with a part of the new apparel and sacred treasures
- Ceremony to transfer the symbol of the kami from the old to the newly constructed building
- Ceremony to serve the first sacred food to the kami in the new building
- Ceremony by the imperial envoy to offer sacred silk to the kami
- Ceremony to transfer sacred treasures from the former sanctuary to the new one
- Ceremony by court musicians

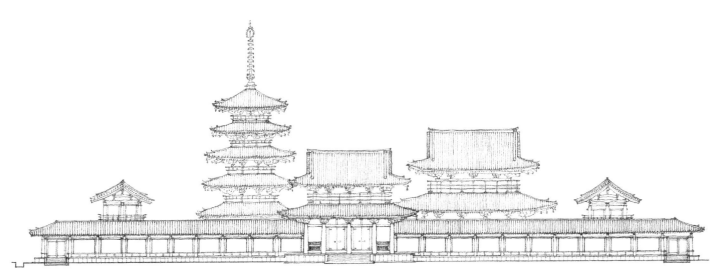

9.56 **Elevation: West precinct of Horyu-ji Temple, Nara, Japan**

Horyu-ji

Following the so-called Taika reform (645–49 CE), the Japanese royalty came to prefer the Chinese rather than the Korean precedents to culture and architecture. This is reflected in Horyu-ji (*ji* means "temple") at Nara, built late in the 7th century, where the axiality of the components was abandoned. The golden hall and the pagoda were placed next to each other, the height of one balancing the width of the other. The cloister was wide enough to give both sufficient breathing room. The eastern wing of the precinct has one extra bay to accommodate the width of the golden hall. This created a dynamic balance between the verticality of the structures and the general horizontality of the forms. Inside the golden hall is the triad of the Buddha Sakyamuni with two attending bodhisattvas, made by the celebrated sculptor Kuratsukuri no Tori in 623 CE to commemorate the death of Prince Shotoku. The Four Heavenly Kings were made around 650 CE by the sculptor Yamaguchi no Atai Oguchi.

The five-by-four-bay proportions of the hall make it appear almost square. It is a two-story structure with two deep, overhanging eaves, upturned at the ends, complemented by a shallow porch eave on the lower level that was built later. It sits on a low base, with small stairs on all four axes and a hipped gable roof marking the crest. As in Greek architecture—and in most contemporary wooden temples—the columns at Horyu-ji display entasis, with their greatest dimension in the middle and their smallest at the top. The middle gate roughly repeats the organizational scheme of the golden hall, but on a simpler scale. It is four bays wide and three bays deep, and because it has a row of columns down the center, one enters the complex slightly off axis.

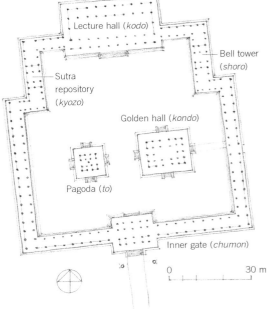

9.57 **Plan: West precinct of Horyu-ji Temple**

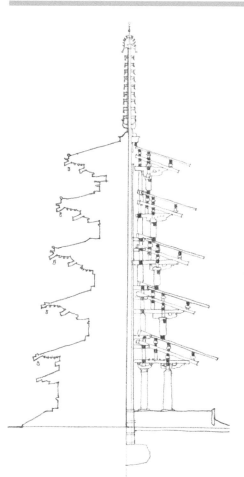

9.58 Section: Pagoda, west precinct, Horyu-ji Temple

9.59 Courtyard of west precinct, Horyu-ji Temple

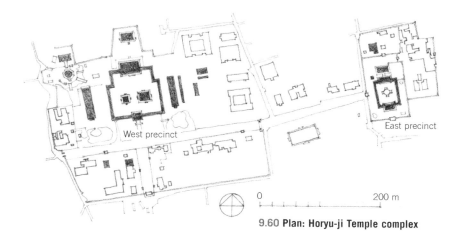

West precinct

East precinct

0   200 m

9.60 Plan: Horyu-ji Temple complex

The five-story pagoda of the west precinct is based on the three-bay square module. In the center is the ceremonial axis mundi column, which is presumed to be spliced somewhere in the middle. Each succeeding story recedes as it rises. They culminate in a tall finial with a traditional arrangement consisting of an upside-down bowl and lotus flower, preceding the seven *chattris* of the upper worlds, and finishing with water-fire and illumination finials. The original precinct was expanded by extending the northern end of the enclosure to include a lecture hall (*kodo*) in the early 8th century.

800 CE

10.1 **Umayyad Mosque of Damascus, Syria**

INTRODUCTION

The period between 800 and 1000 CE saw dramatic transformations across the African/Eurasian world. Most significant among these were the expansion of Islam across northern Africa and the further development of Indianization in Southeast Asia. Just as Indianization tightened the maritime economic connection between China and India, Islamization unified the land-based connections from Baghdad in Iraq to Córdoba in Spain. The water highway and the desert highway redefined the very paradigm of African and Eurasian civilization. To this must be added another sweeping change, the Buddhafication of northern China, Korea, and Japan. Normally, these transformations are viewed as separate and are treated as such. From a global perspective, however, they are interlocked, and together they set the foundations for the modern world.

To put all this in architectural terms, the Mosque of Córdoba in Spain (begun in 784) is contemporaneous with Borodudur (ca. 800) in Indonesia and Todai-ji (ca. 730) in Japan, each the result of the respective processes of Islamization, Indianization, and Buddhafication. In other words, the new emirate of Córdoba, the Sailendra dynasty in Java, and the Nara in Japan were similar in that they were important new links in the transcontinental economic system. For the first time in history, the furthest points east were connected to the furthest points west. Contemporaneous also was an array of new, large, planned cities: Baghdad in Iraq, Hariharalaya ("City of Shiva and Vishnu") in Cambodia, Samye in Tibet, and Heijo-kyo in Japan, all of which would soon rival more established urban centers like Chang'an and Constantinople. In this crosscurrent of cultural exchange and tension, architecture was not simply copied and exported but underwent a wide range of innovations.

As far as the development of Islam was concerned, nothing like it had ever been seen in human history. Christianity, by comparison, despite repressions during the Roman Empire, eventually in the 4th century became an imperial religion, and it spread in jumps and starts. The nomadic groups that had swept into Europe settled and converted, often en masse. In 863, for example, the Bulgars (who settled in modern-day Bulgaria) converted by the thousands, allowing Byzantium to develop trade relations with its northern neighbor without conquest. Buddhism spread differently, namely along trade routes, and was almost totally peaceful. But Islam, with its fervor and expanding military strength, worked its way to North Africa and beyond with astonishing rapidity, reaching southern Spain in 711.

10.2 **Borobudur, Java, Indonesia**

It was not just the excitement of religion that drove this powerful force. Islam's expansion was funded by the extraordinary wealth coming from India and Southeast Asia. With the deterioration of the northern Silk Route across Inner Asia because of regional infighting and a warming period that dried up springs and wells in the Taklamakan Desert, India had become the 9th-century global powerhouse. India was unique in the world in that it had a dual capacity to unify trade in bulk items, such as lumber and grain, with trade in luxury goods, such as gold, silver, diamonds, and gems. The Silk Route may have been named for a commodity that came from China, but just as important now—if not more so—was what was coming out of India and Sri Lanka, namely gemstones like rubies, sapphires, emeralds, and diamonds. Hsuan Tsang (Xuanzang) (602–64 CE, a Chinese Buddhist monk and scholar, traveled to Sri Lanka and reported seeing a ruby on the spire of the temple at Anuradhapura whose magnificence illuminated the sky. Ratnapura—literally "Gem City"—is the capital of Sabaragamuwa province and even today is a hub for gem traders. India also exported sugar, cotton, and ivory. This vast diversity of exports differentiated India's economy from that of China, which tended to focus only on silk, bronze, and porcelain

as export commodities, and produced a complex, interwoven import-export ecology that was unique in the world. There is no doubt that India was the richest and most politically stable area at the time, and that this area with its various kingdoms served as the motor to the Eurasian economic system.

Across India and Sri Lanka, hundreds of sacred sites were being established. Hinduism, or some variant of it, was now adopted by almost all of the regional powers, with rock-cut architecture reaching new heights. Though the Elephanta Caves rank high among these accomplishments, the most impressive of all was Kailasa Temple in Ellora, India, which was built by the Rashtrakuta dynasty. Carved inside and out in a rock-cut manner, Kailasa is without doubt one of the greatest examples of that technique in the history of architecture. Designed to recall Mount Kailash in the Himalayas, it was dedicated to the god Shiva. But rock-architecture with its eight-hundred-year history in India was soon to be a thing of the past. The 9th century saw the transition to stone masonry temples.

Though Indian influence through Buddhism had worked its way north into the mountains, its more important orientation was eastward in the process known as Indianization, which had begun some four

centuries before. Merchants, bringing with them Buddhist and later Hindu monks and priests, had actively set out to transform Southeast Asia from a village economy to an economy driven by state bureaucracies, trade, and rice production. The Indianization of Southeast Asia was not met by a Sinicization from the other direction. Chinese cities were massive enterprises designed as a means to consolidate power. It was a model that was impossible to replicate without complete control of the surrounding land. In India, however, cities were often built around temples and their economies and bureaucracies. It was a model that could be easily replicated since it was designed to grow from village-scale to city-scale. And indeed, this economic/social/ religious package was eminently successful in transforming the region into one of the world's major economic hotspots. Pyu (in modern-day Myanmar), along the Irrawaddy River, had already developed as a rice-exporting Buddhist state in the 5th century and, based on precedents from the Gupta in India, was beginning to develop its unique form of Buddhist stupas. To the south on the island of Java, the Srivijayan Empire was rising to become an important regional force, but of a new sort that did not need huge armies or expensive flotillas. Trade and tolls generated from the ships going back and forth from China and India were the source of its wealth. Its rulers, eager to accommodate both Buddhists and Hindus, built huge sanctuaries for the devotees of both religions. Of these Borobudur was the most spectacular, and certainly ranks as the most impressive architectural accomplishment of its age. It was innovative in many ways. Built entirely of stone, it fused the Hindu idea of a sacred mountain with the Buddhist idea of a sacred mandala, becoming nothing less than a three-dimensional mountain/mandala that epitomized the tight relationship between Buddhist metaphysics and mathematics. In 850, the Srivijayan built a parallel building, but dedicated to the Hindu deity Shiva. Known as Prambanan, it was unlike any temple in India, rising from the misty valley floor like a steeply cliffed, craggy mountain.

In Cambodia, at the eastern front of the Indianization process, there was an even more startling transformation as the forests were clear-cut for vast rice paddies fed not by monsoon floods but by water from large *barays*—kilometer-long artificial lakes that were designed to hold water for the dry season—water that could then be tapped to create a second growing season. The Khmer, who were largely Hindu, had perfected this technique and were now the veritable kings of

rice, becoming the bulk supplier of the grain to both China and India. They had little to offer in terms of luxury items, apart from rare feathers and lumber. Everything else they had to import, including bronze, cooking vessels, and gold and silver for their buildings. All this depended on mastering the landscape. Hariharalaya ("City of Shiva and Vishnu"), a perfectly square city some 2 kilometers on a side, with its own vast *baray*, was a testament to this new, extreme economy. It was without doubt one of the greatest urban experiments of the age. Located deep in what had been forest, it was designed as a brand-new, sacred Hindu landscape with a great temple dedicated to Shiva. At its geometrical center was a step temple, Bakong, which was not just a temple on earth but a new spiritual center of the world. This great experiment in hydrology and religion was to develop into what is now colloquially known as Angkor, a vast sprawling city of temples, palaces, and canals, the size of modern-day Boston. The vast deforestation of the surrounding area would eventually have negative effects, but for the time being, the wealth of the Khmer—rooted precariously around a single export product—made it into a regional powerhouse. It was, one might say, new wealth.

The rise of Southeast Asia occurred at the same time as the T'ang dynasty's loss

of Chinese control over the northern trade routes, and indeed Southeast Asia benefited greatly from this disruption. The great metropolis Chang'an, the nominal capital of the T'ang, was in decline and the empire was increasingly ruled by local military governors and warlords. The problems in the north meant that large numbers of people were leaving there for the more stable south. In the 7th century, northern China held 75 percent of the country's overall population; by the 9th century that number was reduced to 50 percent. There was also, in this turbulent time, an attempt to turn the clock back to ancient, pre-Buddhist religions. In 845, the emperor shut down 4,600 Buddhist monasteries along with 40,000 temples and shrines, forcing 260,000 Buddhist monks and nuns to return to secular life. Not even the Roman repression of the Christians was on this scale. The repression was so vast that few buildings from this era have survived into modern times, apart from the Nanchan Temple (782 CE) and the Foguang Temple. The issue was not religion as such, but the attempt by the government to keep Buddhist monasteries from becoming a type of alternative government, with their own power structure and fundraising capacities. As is often the case, what may have seemed like a good idea on paper had terrible

10.3 **Dome of the Rock, Jerusalem**

consequences, in this case the destruction of the social network, which only further weakened the T'ang and led to their ultimate demise. There can be no doubt that the spectacular rise of the Khmer to the south and of Japan to the east, both rice suppliers, had much to do with the weakening of the Chinese economy, which forced the Chinese to become rice importers.

The irony was that Buddhism was gaining strength in—and transforming—Mongolia, Korea, and Japan, precisely because of its capacity, like most modern religions, to organize society around a set of common ideals. In Tibet, the new city of Samye (775) was laid out as a circular, mandala city with a square temple complex at the center. But in Tibet, and elsewhere as it moved north, Buddhism encountered resistance—not from the government elites but from below, from the deep-seated attachment to shamanism, which had roots in ancient social norms. In Tibet, a ruler named Lang Darma (r. 838–842) persecuted Buddhists, and after his death Buddhism declined. And when it was revived in Tibet in the late 10th century, it was a different Buddhism, one that had adopted shamanic and folk elements. In many cases, Tibetan Buddhist religious functionaries took over the roles normally held by the shaman. Buddhism won support by converting the spirits of wind and earth into various types of protector figures. In Japan also there was

a type of rapprochement with shamanistic worldviews as Buddhism and Shintoism developed hybrid forms. In all of this, Buddhist architecture went through a critical period of experimentation. As to the stupa, what in India had been just a roundish mound was now taking on a wide variety of shapes, to eventually become a tower.

Japan during this century was now emerging as a geopolitical force with the founding in 708 of Heijo-kyo, its first permanent capital. That it was modeled after Chang'an was no accident, for it was designed as the ambitious eastern terminus of the Silk Route, and indeed, it hosted merchants from as far off as India. The political times were, however, unsettled, with Japan suffering from a series of disasters and epidemics. In the context of these problems, Emperor Shomu, doing the opposite of the Chinese, who were suppressing Buddhism, issued an edict in 741 to promote the construction of provincial Buddhist temples throughout the nation. Of these, Todai-ji served as the central administrative temple for the other provincial temples. Todai-ji contains the largest bronze Buddha statue in the world, a testament not just to the skill of the artisans but to the wealth and indeed bravura of a new generation of Japanese rulers.

This cross-regional economic zone from Japan and China through Southeast Asia to

India produced a huge outlay of trade and wealth. The emerging Islamic caliphates extended the reach of this wealth westward. An early mosque was Umayyad Mosque of Damascus in Syria (715); it was built on the site of a former Roman temple complex that had been previously converted to a Christian church. The design is conditioned by these earlier realities; the Corinthian columns on the interior, for example, were taken from the ruins of the Roman temple. A mosque is designed for congregational worship. At some moments it is filled and at others quite empty. Borobudur was designed to facilitate the search for nirvana. Apart from sutras that individuals know by heart, there is no sacred text that guides a devotee. A mosque is designed to orient the believer to Mecca and is a place where the imam can hold forth on the Qur'an.

In Jerusalem, the Umayyad built a particularly innovative structure, the Dome of the Rock (691). Though one of the holiest sites in Islam, it is not technically a mosque. It was built around the rocky apex of a hill, from whence Mohammed is said to have left the earth to commune with the divine during one of his dreams. It was probably built by Byzantine masons, and its architecture and mosaics were clearly patterned after Byzantine churches, though its great dome, now gilded, was of wood and not heavy brick. This building is unusual in that one can enter its perimeter, but not set foot in the interior space, the floor of which is the exposed rock itself. It is unique in the world in this respect. One can compare it with Borobudur, another building designed as a sacred destination. That building, once one reaches its apex, has at the top a massive stupa that is, of course, inaccessible except to the mind's eye. At the Dome of the Rock, the central space is also inaccessible, though it is defined not by a solid mass but by a soaring, domed space.

After the fall of the Umayyads, who ruled from Damascus, the next Muslim dynasty, the Abbasid, built a new capital, Baghdad (founded 762), located just north of the former Sassanian capital of Ctesiphon. Like Hariharalaya and Samye, this city too was an example of theocentric urbanism. If Hariharalaya was the city of Shiva and Vishnu, and Samye was the Buddhist mandala of enlightenment, Baghdad was a deliberate reminder of an expression in the Qur'an referring to paradise. Baghdad was soon to become one of the great cities in central Asia; by the 10th century, the city's population was over a million.

The Abbasids, despite their wealth, were not able to control the vast Islamic regions, and thenceforth the history of Islam became a history of regional powers, often with conflicting theological perspectives. One of these new powers was the Tulunids, who became the first independent dynasty to rule the newly Islamic Egypt. The Tulunids built the impressive and well-proportioned Mosque of Ibn Tulun (879). It was intended as the focal point of Ibn Tulun's capital, and in fact was built next to Ibn Tulun's palace (no longer extant). Its design featured a large courtyard with one covered hall on each of the four sides, the largest being on the side of the *qibla*, the direction to Mecca.

Europeans were not a particularly significant part of this global economy. Admittedly, the feudal system had stabilized things following several centuries of turmoil, but it was built around the principle of economic regionalism, as opposed to cross-continental economic interdependence. A strengthening monastic culture enhanced stability, but whereas in India the Hindu temple was an economic unit, often associated with a city and with the ideals of wealth, the European Christian monastery was by definition anti-urban and committed to the ideals—if not the practice—of poverty. St. Augustine and other theologians saw the city of Rome as decadent, which explains to some degree the need for remoteness and isolation. There are similarities with Buddhism, but Buddhism emphasizes the personal attainment of nirvana, whereas in Christian monasteries, attainment of a state of blessedness was a distinctly communal effort enforced by a set of complex regulations handed down from higher authorities. We are fortunate to have a surviving plan of a monastic compound at St. Gall in Switzerland that serves as a plan/diagram of the inner workings of the monastery. The plan lays out a complex spatial organization delineating secular and religious zones as well as the different activities that define the monk's daily life.

The status of Europe was soon to change with the rise to power of Charlemagne as head of the Franks, who had just converted en masse to Christianity. Building for himself the Palace of Aachen in what is now Germany, Charlemagne was able to unify the Franks and bring his rule in alignment with papal ambitions, creating a new entity called, on paper at least, the Holy Roman Empire. Since the Franks were largely simple, agropastoral villagers, it stands to reason that the sumptuous palace at Aachen was designed by imported architects, most likely from Armenia and Constantinople, since they were the most skilled stonemasons in the world at the time.

But Europe was in no position to benefit from any of the transcontinental wealth that was flowing to its south along the Mediterranean. Large-scale Viking attacks devastated the northern territories and extended along the coast of France. Even Rome was sacked by the Saracens in 846. As a whole, Europe was, therefore, a rather backward place architecturally, as most of

10.4 Church of San Salvador de Valdediós, Spain

its buildings were made of wood or stone rubble, compared to the advanced stonework of Borobudur or the Hindu temples of India. One need only look at the churches of San Salvador de Valdediós and San Julián de los Prados, both in Spain, to recognize the difference. These are hardly world-class structures. Windows are small and unevenly spaced. Most of the building is made from stone rubble. Compare it to the well-formed proportions and meticulous stonework of the Armenian church of Saint Hripsime, or to the Shore Temple in Mamallapuram, India, or the Bhringesvara Shiva Temple in Bhubaneshwar, India, both of which demonstrate meticulous stonework and complex curving surfaces.

That said, one has to remark again on a fundamental issue. Borobudur is a building that is experienced outdoors, meaning there is no inner space. It is a custom-built mountain; the same can be said of the Shore Temple in Mamallapuram. There is an inner sanctum, but it is not a public space. Neither of these buildings center on a congregational ethos. The Mosque of Ibn Tulun in Cairo certainly does, but it too is in essence an outdoor building. Though there is a roof over part of the structure, apart from the perimeter

wall there are no inner enclosures. Christians alone—with an architecture that draws on its sources in the Roman basilica—had by now developed the idea of a completely enclosed indoor space, with structures built of wood and stone. These early churches were not, however, for the people. Most Christians, if they did worship regularly, did so in more modest buildings. The early stone-built churches were for the elites and the nobility, for whom Christianity brought a special standing in the community.

Think of the 9th century this way: The wealth-generating horizon of rice and high-end luxury goods was restricted to a narrow east-west belt that curved from southern China through Southeast Asia and India to Baghdad and Cairo, with heavy emphasis on India. Adding dimensionality to this was a radical intensification of architecture and engineering around the production of rice in Indonesia, Cambodia, Korea, and Japan. The combined energy of this trade produced inextricable changes at the various peripheries, where the first states, Japan to the east and Tibet to the north, arise. Soon arrows would be pointing even further afield, to Scandinavia and southward across the

great Sahara Desert. Within two hundred years these "peripherals" would be firmly connected to the larger transcontinental world of economic wealth.

In all of this, one must not forget that northern and Inner Asia, separated from the south by vast stretches of trackless deserts, forest, and tundra, were still inhabited by First Society cultures. But even here things were by no means static. In northern Canada the Dorset hunting culture was being replaced by a highly skilled, oceangoing, seal-hunting culture known as the Thule and later as the Inuit. They would develop a unique architectural form known as the igloo. An even more significant transformation was taking place in the southwest of the United States, where corn had been introduced around 100 BCE. Beginning in the 7th century, the Hohokam began to build extensive irrigation networks along the lower Salt and middle Gila Rivers. They were the only American culture to use irrigation north of Mexico. They also integrated corn with the development of native plant species like mesquite to develop an extensive and complex agro-spiritual landscape that would culminate in the construction of sacred ritual

10.5 **Toltec Temple of Tlahuizcalpantecuhtli ("Lord of the Morning Star"), Tula, Mexico**

cities in Chaco Canyon between 803 and 1130. By this time, corn was also starting to make its appearance in the eastern part of North America, with dramatic implications to come in the subsequent centuries.

In Mexico, after the collapse of Teotihuacán around 600 CE, competition ensued among several important political centers in central Mexico, leading to the emergence of the Toltecs (ca. 800–1000). They constructed a vast ceremonial center with a large stepped pyramid, known as Tula de Allende. To the south, in the Mayan heartland, two great cities emerged: Palenque in Mexico and Copán in Honduras. Meanwhile in Bolivia, of the various regional powers that emerged in previous centuries, Tiwanaku rose to particular importance. Around 700 CE, three centuries into the existence of Tiwanaku, all construction efforts were suddenly concentrated on making what was to become the largest structure in the Andes: the Akapana, an astonishing building, carved so precisely from stone that even today it elicits a sense of wonder. It was to the Americas what Borobudur was to Eurasia, the most advanced stone building in the world. For its construction, the earlier monuments

of the city were torn down and their stones reused. It was a huge, multifaceted platform mound or stepped pyramid of earth faced with cut andesite, a hard volcanic rock, with a sunken open chamber at the summit. It was ultimately left unfinished when the city, for unknown reasons, was abandoned.

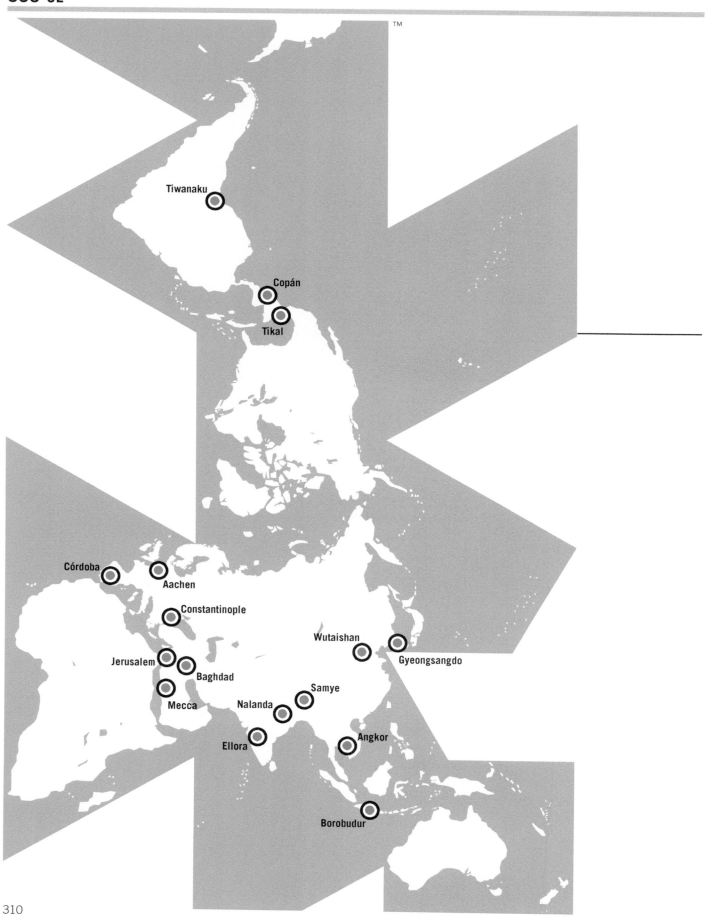

Tiwanaku

Copán

Tikal

Córdoba

Aachen

Constantinople

Wutaishan

Gyeongsangdo

Jerusalem

Baghdad

Mecca

Nalanda

Samye

Ellora

Angkor

Borobudur

Umayyad Rule
651–750 CE

Abbasid Caliphate
750–1258 CE

▲ **Dome of the Rock**
632–91 CE

▲ **City of Baghdad**
ca. 762 CE, capital of Abbasid Caliphate

▲ **Great Mosque of Samarra**
852 CE

▲ **Umayyad Mosque**
706–15 CE

▲ **Great Mosque of Córdoba**
784-87 CE

South Asia: Pallava Dynasty
to 740 CE

Chola Dynasty
ca. 860–1279

▲ **Kailasnath at Ellora**
600–1000 CE

▲ **Virupaksha Temple**
733–44 CE

▲ **Mahavihara of Nalanda**
6th to 7th centuries CE

▲ **Rajasimhesvara Temple**
Early 8th century CE

▲ **Somapura Vihara**
7th century CE

600 CE	**800 CE**	**1000 CE**

Pre-Angkor Period in Cambodia
ca. 550–802 CE

Angkor Period in Cambodia
802–1431 CE

▲ **Borobudur**
ca. 760–830 CE

▲ **Bakong Temple**
ca. 811 CE

▲ **Phnom Bakheng**
ca. 900–921 CE

▲ **Samye**
787–91 CE

▲ **Candi Prambanam**
835–56 CE

Silla Dynasty
668–935 CE

▲ **Buseoksa Temple**
676–1000 CE

T'ang Dynasty
618–907 CE

▲ **Chang'an: The T'ang Capital**
581–906 CE

▲ **Nanchan Temple**
782 CE

▲ **Foguang Temple**
857 CE

Merovingian Dynasty in Central Europe
482–751 CE

Carolingian Dynasty
751–911 CE

Holy Roman Empire
962–1806 CE

▲ **Abbey of Fulda**
790 CE

▲ **St. Gall**
816–36 CE

Abbey Church of St. Riquier ▲
Completed 799 CE

▲ **Palatine Chapel**
792–805 CE

Mayas: Dynastic City-States
ca. 250–900 CE

▲ **Palenque**
ca. 600–800 CE

▲ **Copán**
ca. 600–900 CE

▲ **Tikal Temple Complex**
700–900 CE

Southern Andes: Peak of Wari and Tiwanaku cultures
6th to 10th centuries CE

◄ **Tiwanaku**
First settled 1000 BCE

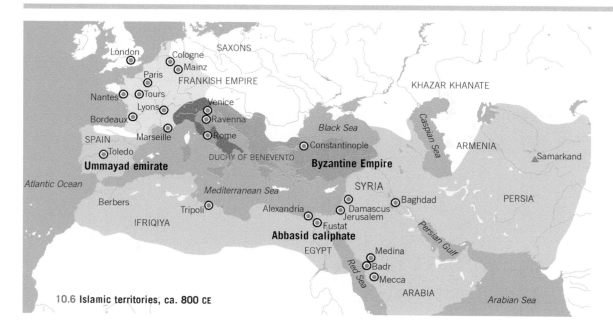

10.6 Islamic territories, ca. 800 CE

RISE OF ISLAM

Arabia, on account of its extreme climactic and geographic conditions, was at the periphery of the great cultural centers of the age. It was mainly inhabited by nomadic Bedouin Arabs who served as traders or lived off the land's meager resources. The center of Arabian religion, which focused on nature and heavenly bodies, was in Mecca. Mohammed (ca. 570–632 CE) began a bitter and prolonged struggle with Arab tribes and their polytheism, advocating instead a brand of monotheism based on universalist and egalitarian sociopolitical ideas that conflicted with traditional tribal politics.

Born in Mecca, Mohammed was an orphan raised by his uncle. When he was forty years old, he retreated into a cave near Ramadan, where he received his first illumination. After further revelations, he began preaching monotheism. Successful in attracting followers, he eventually conquered Mecca and transformed it into Islam's holiest city, which all adult Muslims are required to visit at least once in their lives. He died in 632 CE after having converted most of Arabia to the new creed. Beyond being a prophet, Mohammed was also a farsighted statesman, a political arbitrator, and a gifted military commander, setting the stage for a fusion of religion and politics that was to define Islamic culture for centuries to come. By 711 CE, Muslim Arab armies were attacking northern India to the east as well as North Africa to

the west, and by the end of the 9th century, Islam had grown into the largest political entity west of China.

Since Mohammed made no arrangements for a successor, dissension arose after his death as to how to govern this vast territory, and the conflict between the Abbasids and Umayyads created a divide in Islam that persists to this day. The Abbasids, descendants of Mohammed's uncle, al-Abbas, based their claim to the caliphate on the theological aspects of their rulership. The Shi'ites joined with the Abbasids in the 8th century, as they, too, believed that the caliphs ruled by divine designation and thus possessed spiritual authority. The Umayyads also saw themselves as heirs to the Islamic state but interpreted the caliphate as a constitutional necessity working for the temporal welfare and protection of the community. The conflict between the theological and political interpretation of rulership continues to be contested. It was initially the Umayyads who were dominant, governing from their capital in Damascus. Able administrators, they ruled for a brief but important period over the whole of the Islamic realm—the only time that it was so unified.

Muslims do not require a building, or even a consecrated space, to worship; rather, Islam is based on five "pillars," the most important being the five daily prayers performed while facing Mecca. The month of Ramadan is also important; during that time, Muslims commune with themselves,

give thanks to God through fasting, and make donations to the needy, fulfilling the commandments of the third pillar.

The typical mosque has a courtyard through which one enters and that contains a well or fountain for washing the hands and feet. In the first centuries of Islam, the hall of worship was, in most instances, a space consisting of rows of columns so that the congregation could face the *qibla* wall—a wall that stands at right angles to a line drawn to Mecca. The imam, or prayer leader, stands in front of a mihrab, or niche, in the middle of the *qibla* wall. In some mosques, the bay just in front of the mihrab is elevated and roofed with a dome. To the right of the mihrab is a stepped pulpit, the minbar, made of wood or stone, from which the imam can deliver a sermon (*khutba*), usually on Friday. Almost all mosques have a minaret from which the faithful are called to prayer. There is no prescription as to where these should be located or how many there must be.

Tarik Khana (ca. 760 CE) in Damghan, northern Iran, is one of the oldest extant mosques. Its rectangular shape encloses a courtyard and prayer hall. Massive round brick columns almost 2 meters in diameter support arcades of tunnel vaults. The Aksa Mosque in Jerusalem (702 CE) shows the development of an axis and transept emphasizing the *qibla* that becomes even more pronounced in the El-Hakim Mosque (991 CE) in Cairo.

Umayyad Mosque

Though the Arabs were initially illiterate, their conquests put them in contact with a multitude of civilizations, many features of which they began to assimilate, much as the Romans had done with Greek and Asian cultures—except that the Arabs' transition occurred with astonishing rapidity and determination. From the Indians, who at that time were leaders in the field of mathematics, they adopted numbering systems; from the Persians, skills in construction; from the Byzantines, skills in vaulting; and from the Armenians, skills in stonemasonry. The center of this learning was Damascus, built up by al-Mansur, an Abbasid caliph, who lavished the wealth and power of the new empire on the city.

Later, Caliph al-Ma'mun ordered a library to be built to house translated books from Greece, Byzantium, and India, as well as the growing collection of works by Arabic scholars. Known as the House of Wisdom (opened 1004 CE), it became the most outstanding single repository of knowledge since the Great Library of Alexandria. Libraries were set up in other cities as well. Soon Arab scholars were making breakthroughs in everything from medicine and chemistry to optics and philosophy. In 807 CE, Sultan Harun al-Rashid (766–809 CE) sent Charlemagne a brass clock with a moving ball and brass horsemen who stepped out of windows on the hour. There was then nothing remotely similar in all of Europe.

The Umayyad Mosque in Damascus (709–15 CE), another monumental work of Islamic architecture, was built on a religious site dating back to an ancient Aramaic temple dedicated to the god Hadad. The Romans built a Temple of Jupiter on the site, a building that was, in the 4th century, transformed into a church (the Cathedral of St. John) situated on the western side of the temple. The church was then incorporated into the design of the mosque, which consists of three parallel ranges of space facing onto a large, enclosed courtyard.

After the Islamic conquest of Damascus in 661 CE during the reign of the first Umayyad caliph, Mu'awiya ibn Abi Sufiyan, Muslims at first shared the church with Christians. The caliph eventually negotiated with Christian leaders to take over the space; in return,

10.7 Courtyard, Umayyad Mosque, Damascus, Syria

he promised that all the other churches in the city would be safe and that a new church, dedicated to the Virgin Mary, could be erected. Damascus itself was completely rebuilt in the shape of a rectangle bisected by a Hellenistic-inspired colonnaded road running north and south and crossing at the center, where the principal buildings were positioned.

The plan of the mosque is a 97-by-156-meter rectangle with three gates that connect the building to the city from the northern, eastern, and western sides. The mosque is defined by three halls, or *riwaqs*, that run parallel to the *qibla* wall. They are supported by two rows of stone Corinthian columns. Large and classically proportioned arches support a second, smaller colonnade, on which the massive wooden beams of the roof

rest. The location of the mihrab is enhanced in the center by the octagonal, 36-meter-high Nisr Dome ("Dome of the Eagle"). In the eastern part of the mosque, a small marble structure between the columns of the *riwaq* holds the tomb of St. John the Baptist, who in Islamic tradition is known as the prophet Yahya. The building was richly outfitted with marble paneling and mosaics. In the beginning of the 8th century, Caliph al-Walid ibn Abd al-Malik addressed the citizens of Damascus thus: "Inhabitants of Damascus, four things give you marked superiority over the rest of the world: your climate, your water, your fruits, and your baths. To these I wanted to add a fifth: this mosque." Originally, the mosque was abutted by a palace on its southern flank, with a special entrance next to the mihrab.

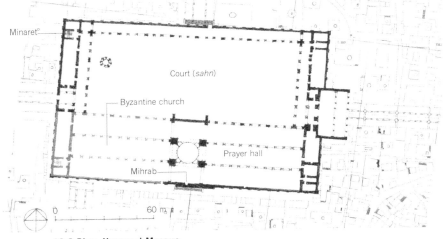

10.8 Plan: Umayyad Mosque

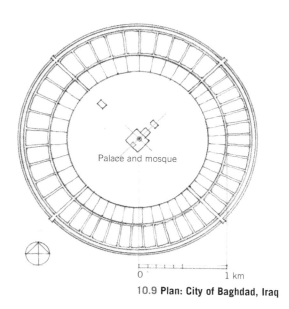

10.9 **Plan: City of Baghdad, Iraq**

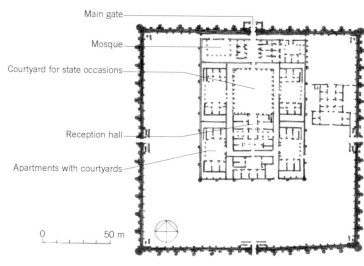

10.10 **Plan: Palace of Ukhaidir, Iraq**

Baghdad

The Umayyad dynasty, which had its center in Damascus, fell in the mid-8th century. The new rulers, the Abbasids (r. 758–1258 CE), eventually became the champions of Sunni orthodoxy—a policy that helped them to unify an increasingly cosmopolitan Muslim empire. They constructed a new capital city, Baghdad, to the west of Damascus and on the banks of the Tigris River. Engineers from the entire Islamic world were called to the site to help in its planning and construction from 762 to 766 CE.

The layout, one of the most remarkable examples of town planning in history, was a simple circle about 3,000 meters across. The walls were built of bricks and ornamented with colorful tiles. Two rings of residential zones lined the inside walls, leaving a vast area open in the middle for the palace and mosque. The walls were punctured by four gates. Though there are other smaller, regional examples of circular cities, this was by far the most elaborate. The city prospered, and with a population of about two million, it became a center of science, literature, and art, like Damascus. However, nothing of the city remains: it perished as a consequence of numerous sieges and inundations. The Abbasid dynasty ended when Baghdad fell to the Mongols in 1258.

Made possible by the wealth of the Abbasid rulers, palaces of great size sprang up throughout the region, such as the fortified Palace of Ukhaidir in the desert about 200 kilometers south of Baghdad. It consists of a rectangular enclosure approximately 175 by 170 meters, with a gateway at the center of each of the round towers at the corners and semicircular towers spaced regularly between them. The main entrance led to an autonomous royal enclave (approximately 60 by 80 meters) positioned close to the north wall. It had a large courtyard and a barrel-vaulted *iwan* throne room, behind which was the royal apartment. Around that complex were four residential suites, each with its own courtyard. The palace possessed its own mosque; a bathhouse was located in the southeast of the complex. In the space between the palace and the outer walls, there would have been gardens. Though today only the mud brick of the interior construction remains, these surfaces would have been lavishly decorated with carved stucco and paintings, often of flowers and vines arranged in panels.

Great Mosque of Samarra

In 836 CE, the Abbasid capital was moved to Samarra, some 40 kilometers north of Baghdad. Samarra soon ranked among the greatest of the early Islamic cities. Though it remained the capital only until 892 CE, it prospered for centuries, reaching an area of 50 square kilometers. The caliph's residence itself took up 173 hectares on a cliff overlooking the Tigris River. Equally impressive were the two mosques, the Great Mosque of al-Mutawakkil (848–52 CE) and the Mosque of Abu Dulaf (860 CE), both designed to look like desert fortresses. The bastioned walls of the Great Mosque of al-Mutawakkil measured 240 by 156 meters, and for centuries it was the largest mosque in the world. There were sixteen doorways that fed into the vast interior. On the inside, four hypostyle structures (one prayer hall and three porticoes) were arranged around a large courtyard. Unlike in Damascus, where the three minarets were placed in the corners of the enclosing wall and one in the middle of the wall, here the minaret was a freestanding element placed on axis in front of the principal north entrance of the mosque. It had a helicoidal shape that reached 50 meters to the summit, with an external staircase.

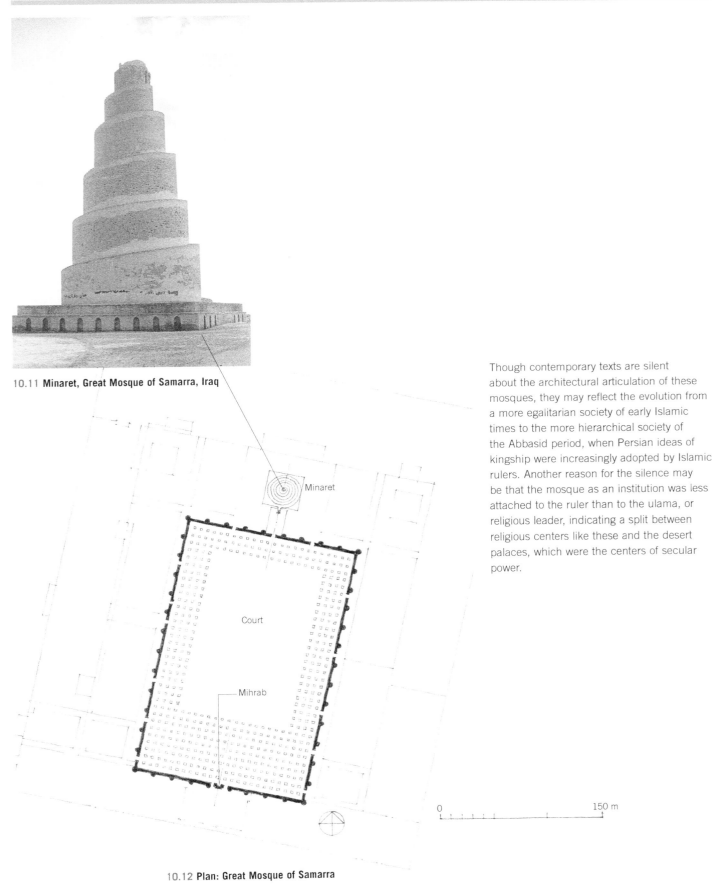

10.11 **Minaret, Great Mosque of Samarra, Iraq**

Minaret

Court

Mihrab

0   150 m

Though contemporary texts are silent about the architectural articulation of these mosques, they may reflect the evolution from a more egalitarian society of early Islamic times to the more hierarchical society of the Abbasid period, when Persian ideas of kingship were increasingly adopted by Islamic rulers. Another reason for the silence may be that the mosque as an institution was less attached to the ruler than to the ulama, or religious leader, indicating a split between religious centers like these and the desert palaces, which were the centers of secular power.

10.12 **Plan: Great Mosque of Samarra**

10.13 Spain (Al-Andalus)

10.14 Roofscape, Great Mosque of Córdoba, Spain

Great Mosque of Córdoba

Arab forces occupied Alexandria in 643 CE and crossed the Straits of Gibraltar in 711 CE. From there, they made forays over the entire Mediterranean into Italy and France, driving out the monks from Monte Cassino, south of Rome, in 883 CE. By the mid-7th century, however, the Muslim world had lost any real political unity: the Abbasid caliphate began to disintegrate, and in the mid-10th century, rival caliphates established themselves in Cairo and Córdoba. Originally, the Spanish territories were administered by a provincial government established in the name of the Umayyad caliphate based in Damascus. But when that dynasty was overthrown, its last surviving member, Emir Abd al-Rahman I, fled to Spain. Under him, Córdoba became the quasi-autonomous capital of a vibrant Islamic culture. By the end of the 10th century, it had become the largest city in Europe, with a population of about one hundred thousand. It was also an important center of Arabic learning, making crucial contributions to European civilization.

The first building of significance designed under Abd al-Rahman I was the Great Mosque of Córdoba (784–87 CE). Only the southwest part, the original prayer hall, still survives more or less unaltered. The mosque, modeled loosely on the Umayyad Mosque in Damascus (706–15 CE), included a walled-in courtyard opening onto a hypostyle structure consisting of twelve bays with ten columns

each. The columns taken from Roman buildings were chosen for their whitish tone. The capitals are spoils taken from destroyed churches and Roman civic buildings. Indeed, the unusual siting of the mosque at the perimeter of the city may be due to its being built over the ruins of a Roman warehouse. The principal shape of the arches above the columns is, however, unique—a high horseshoe arch with a nested free-spanning arch below it. The voussoirs, alternately of red brick and white stone, create dramatic three-dimensional diagonal vistas. The building signals that the rulers had come to terms with certain aspects of the existing architectural tradition, which they incorporated with great ingenuity into their design. The horseshoe-shaped arches are thought to have been adapted from the remains of local Visigoth architecture. The minaret, topped with a domed pavilion, was one of the first tower minarets in Islam. The mosque does not face Mecca, but the reason is not clear.

10.15 Dome structure, Great Mosque of Córdoba

10.16 **Hall of the Great Mosque of Córdoba**

10.17 **Entrance facade, Great Mosque of Córdoba**

Over time, the structure was lengthened and widened, but always with reverence for the initial design. The addition of al-Hakam II (964 CE) is the most elabaorate of the extensions. Unlike the previous extension that featured white columns, this one featured black and red columns placed in an alternating scheme. Craftsmen made capitals on a simplified Corinthian model. Al-Hakam II's addition also included a new mihrab with a remarkable set of three domes added to the last bay. The central dome is spectacular. Unlike Roman domes, which were primarily spatial elements, or Byzantine domes, which were props for spatially ambiguous mosaics, this dome emphasized a combination of geometric logic and decorative detail. It seems to rest on the square base as an elevated building supported by column bundles from which spring a set of intersecting arches that in plan form two intersecting squares. The result is an octagonal frame that holds a petaled, umbrella-shaped dome, trimmed in white at its base. This is not a dome in the sense of a unified object, but a series of spatial layers that act horizontally and vertically. Light filtering in through the screens of the lower register of arches contrasts with the dark niches at the corners. The mosaics, executed by Byzantine craftsmen, complete the design with plant and vine motifs.

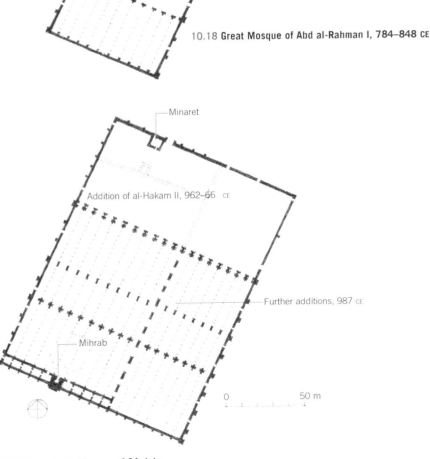

10.18 **Great Mosque of Abd al-Rahman I, 784–848 CE**

Minaret

Addition of al-Hakam II, 962–66 CE

Further additions, 987 CE

Mihrab

0   50 m

10.19 **Plan: Great Mosque of Córdoba**

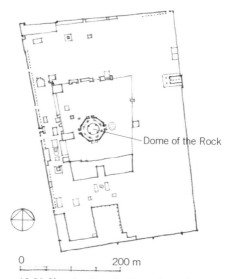

10.20 Site plan: Temple Mount, Jerusalem

10.21 Dome of the Rock, Jerusalem

Dome of the Rock

With the Islamic conquest of Palestine and Jerusalem in the third decade of the 7th century, Caliph Abd al-Malik brought in the best masons and craftsmen available to design the Dome of the Rock, or in Arabic, the Haram al-Sharif ("Noble Sanctuary"), which is today the oldest Islamic building to have survived intact in its original form. Completed in 691 CE, it encloses a huge rock at its center, the highest point of Mt. Moriah, from which, according to tradition, the prophet Mohammed ascended to heaven at the end of his Isra' (or Night Journey) to Jerusalem. In the older, Jewish tradition, this is the Foundation Stone, the symbolic underpinning upon which the world was created, as well as the place of Abraham's binding of Isaac. This same location is also where numerous important events in the life of Christ are believed to have occurred. The site is therefore holy to the Jewish, Christian, and Islamic religions.

The building, which is Byzantine in conception and Sassanian in ornamentation, can be entered on all four points of the compass. The central space, however, is inaccessible. The dome reaches 20 meters across the rock and is borne on a drum that rests on a double system of pillars and columns, the middle one circular, the outer one octagonal. The two rings, composed of piers and columns, are rotated so that the four piers of the inner ring face the arches of the outer octagonal ring, creating a dynamic interplay between square and circular geometries.

The dome and drum are not of brick or stone, but of wood. The dome is covered today with golden copper-alloy plates, and the drum with shimmering mosaic patterns of blue, red, green, and gray. The interior, in the Byzantine manner, was decorated with mosaics, with a marble veneer in the lower section. Though technically not a mosque, the building is much more. It is not only a geometrical and paradisiacal enclosure and a celebration of a spot of particular reverence but also a parallel to the Ka'aba in Mecca. Unlike that building, which can be circumambulated but not entered, this one can indeed be entered—yet because of the presence of the rock, the center of the building remains inaccessible. Furthermore, one gazes not at a rock, but at the peak of the mount; the architecture thus creates the feeling of suspending the viewer in space around that peak.

The history of the building site has been much debated. It was first consecrated by the Israelites when they built the First and Second Temples. After the Second Temple was razed by the Romans in 70 CE, Emperor Hadrian built a temple to Jupiter there that was perhaps connected to an octagonal structure that served as the foundation of the Dome of the Rock—but this has not yet been archaeologically proven. The crusaders consecrated the building as a Catholic church, but with their defeat, the site reverted back to Islam.

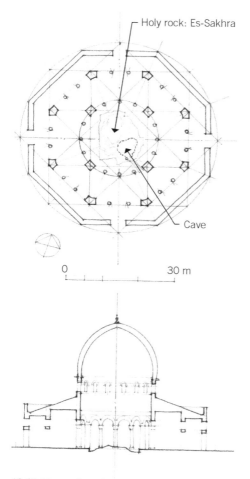

10.22 Plan and section: Dome of the Rock

10.23 **Mahavihara at Nalanda, Bihar, India**

MAHAVIHARAS AT NALANDA

Mahavihara (literally "great *vihara*") was the term used to designate the huge Buddhist universities that were established by the Guptas in the 5th century and that flourished until the 12th century. The most famous of these was Nalanda. Almost every Buddhist pilgrim to India made a stop at Nalanda. Mahaviharas like Nalanda were multidisciplinary universities devoted not only to the preparation of Buddhist practitioners but also to the study of secular disciplines. Officially established by the Gupta king Kumara Gupta I (415–55 CE), Nalanda boomed in the reign of Harshavardhana. Nalanda had more than two thousand senior monks and about ten thousand disciples. Theravada, the school of Buddhism followed mainly in Sri Lanka, Burma, Thailand, and Cambodia, developed here. Besides the various schools of Buddhism, including Hinayana, Mahayana, and Tantric, courses on the Indo-Aryan Vedas, *hetu vidya* ("logic"), *shabda vidya* ("grammar"), and *chikitsa vidya* (medicine) were also taught at Nalanda. The Chinese pilgrim Hsuan Tsang (Xuanzang) spent most of his time at Nalanda studying law.

Aryabhatta, the 5th-century astronomer and mathematician (b. 476 CE in Kerala, India) came to Nalanda as a boy to study astronomy. He was one of the earliest people to support the theory that the earth is a sphere, preceding Copernicus by a millennium. His main work, known as the Aryabhattiya, was translated into Latin in the 13th century. It included methods of calculating the area of a triangle, the volume of a sphere, and square and cube roots. Aryabhatta also wrote about eclipses and proposed the sun as the source of moonlight. Another 7th-century Indian astronomer, Brahmagupta, calculated the circumference of the earth as 5,000 *yojanas*, or about 36,000 kilometers, only 4,000 short of its true distance. The number zero, called *sunya*, (meaning "void" or "empty") was invented at this time. *Sunya* passed into the Arabic as *sifr*, meaning "vacant." In about 1200 CE, this word was transliterated into Latin, but its original meaning was lost, resulting in the word *zephirum* (or *zephyrum*).

Nalanda consisted of ten quadrangles covering 14 hectares, all lined up in a block and packed next to each other. Made of brick, each *vihara*, 50 to 60 meters long, had a central courtyard (some with a shrine) ringed by two or three stories of cells for the monks, who lived about thirty to a floor. The *viharas* faced a row of freestanding stupas (sometimes described as *caitya* temples) also made of brick, each with long central stairways leading to a platform on which stood the main shrine, with subsidiary shrines at the corners. In its time, the street between the *viharas* and the stupas would have been packed with monks and their disciples.

After Harshavardhana, the Pala kings of Bengal maintained Nalanda for four centuries, until the 11th century. In fact, the surviving ruins date from the Pala period. The Palas were also the patrons of several other monastic universities, such as at Vikramsila and Somapura. So numerous were the *viharas* that the name of the modern state in this region, Bihar, is a contraction of the Sanskrit for "Land of the Viharas."

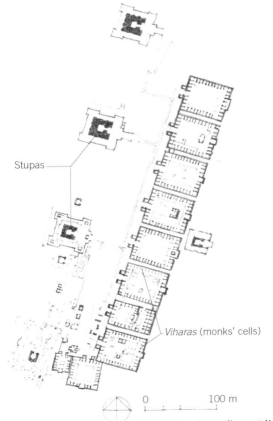

Stupas

Viharas (monks' cells)

0   100 m

10.24 **Plan: Mahavihara at Nalanda**

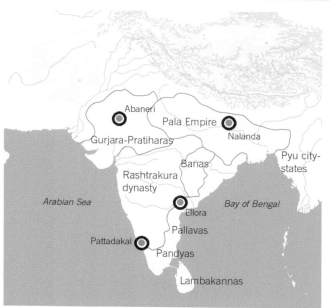

10.25 **India ca. 800 CE**

Basic Vocabulary of Hindu Architecture

Garbha-griha: Literally, "womb chamber"; innermost sanctum

Lingam: Literally, "phallus," but also "mark" or "sign"; the symbol for Shiva. (Shaivite temples face east; Vaishnavite temples face west.)

Shikhara: Literally, "mountain peak"; the rising tower of north Indian temples

Gopuram: A monumental tower at the entrance of south Indian temples

Pradakshina: Circumambulation

Prasada: Literally, "palace"; temple precinct

Mandapa: A pillared hall in front of the temple and sometimes connected to it; if a temple has more than one *mandapa*, each is allocated a different function and given a name to reflect its use.

RAJASIMHESVARA AND VIRUPAKSHA TEMPLES

While India was ruled by a series of diverse kingdoms, the competition in south India between the Chalukyas and the Pallavas intensified. Victorious kings routinely carried the other's masons and temple builders back home with them. The consequence was a cross-fertilization of temple design. As a temple inscription notes, the Rajasimhesvara Temple (700–730 CE)—built by the Pallava king in his capital, Kanchipuram—was the model for the Virupaksha Temple (733–44 CE), built by the Chalukyan queen at Pattadakal. Workmen from Rajasimhesvara also worked on the Virupaksha; the two make for an interesting comparison.

10.26 **Rajasimhesvara Temple, Kanchipuram, India**

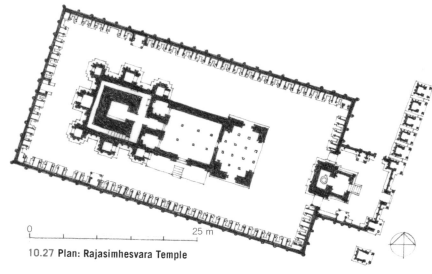

10.27 **Plan: Rajasimhesvara Temple**

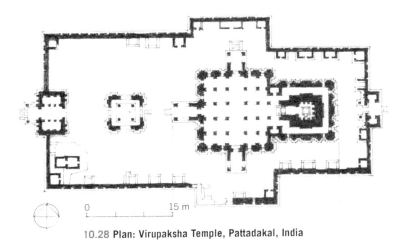

10.28 Plan: Virupaksha Temple, Pattadakal, India

The two temples' similarities involve their size and organizational type, rather than their appearance and formal order. Though most Hindu temples face east, Virupaksha, being a Shiva temple, faces west. The *garbha-grihas* of both temples are surrounded by a well-defined and fully enclosed *parikrama* path, but Rajasimhesvara has nine subsidiary shrines arrayed in constellation around it, while the Virupaksha establishes the presence of subsidiary shrines through articulations of the outer wall. Both have attached *mandapas*, but while Rajasimhesvara's two enclosed *mandapas* set up a single longitudinal axis, Virupaksha's single *mandapa* is fully pierced and sets up a cross-axis with spatial dynamism. Both temples are located with their own precincts of roughly equivalent size, and both have large entrance *gopurams*. But while Rajasimhesvara's precinct is packed with a phalanx of subsidiary shrines, and in fact has the beginnings of a second precinct enclosure also made of subsidiary shrines, Virupaksha's precinct has only an episodic collection of subsidiary shrines attached to it and breaks to respond to the cross-axis of the *mandapa*. The Virupaksha, being a Shiva shrine, also has the requirement of a Nandi pavilion for Shiva's bull; the pavilion sits as a separate element in its forecourt.

Unlike earlier Hindu temples in which the *garbha-griha* is framed by its plinth and precinct walls, here the outer frame and the inner *garbha-griha* are locked into each other by means of spatial intermediaries, including the *mandapa*, that allow for both axial and circumambulatory readings. Overall, the geometric order of the Virupaksha is more

articulated than that of the Rajasimhesvara, as is evidenced in the ordering of the twelve freestanding columns of the *mandapa* that are extended into the edges, either by pilasters or by columns, and arranged to clear the path of the cross-axis. The inner columns of the Rajasimhesvara, by contrast, are laid out by a simple arithmetic geometry.

10.29 Virupaksha Temple

10.30 **Two views: Temple of Kailasnath at Ellora, near Aurangabad, India**

KAILASNATH AT ELLORA

Control of the Deccan Plateau was wrested from the Chalukyas around 750 CE by the Rashtrakutas, who ruled for about two centuries, until 973 CE. The Rashtrakutas quickly established their military superiority and captured the all-important trade routes that connected the western region to the rest of the subcontinent, in particular, the *dakshinapatha*, or southern route. On the *dakshinapatha* at Verul (contemporary Ellora), the Rashtrakuta ruler Krishna I ordered the construction of what was to become the largest rock-cut temple ever. Fifty meters wide, more than 90 meters deep, and 20 meters high, Kailasnath is in the middle of the 3-kilometer-long wall of basalt that has thirty-four caves carved out of it (twelve are Buddhist, seventeen Hindu, and five Jain, dating from 600 to 1000 CE). Kailasnath is conceived as a representation of the mythological mountain abode of Shiva, Mt. Kailash. Unlike the Buddhist rock-cut structures that essentially had always been elaborations of a cave, Kailasnath is an independent entity, a freestanding colossal sculpture revealed from the matrix. Since it is still surrounded by the rock from which it was hewn, there is a palpable sense of excavation to Kailasnath, as if it were still a work in progress.

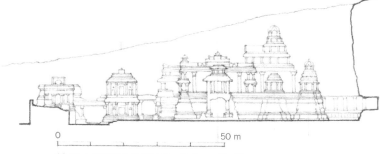

0   50 m

10.31 **Longitudinal section: Kailasnath, Ellora**

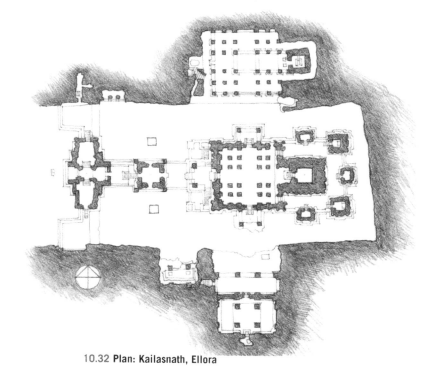

10.32 **Plan: Kailasnath, Ellora**

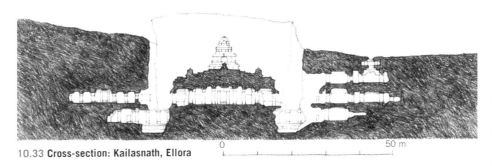

10.33 Cross-section: Kailasnath, Ellora

0   50 m

Two "victory towers" have been left on either side of the mass of the Nandi chamber. They not only provide the vertical axis of the composition, but their length also visibly measures the mass of the rock that has been excavated. From outside, the temple is almost entirely obscured by its two-storied entrance *gopuram* (flanked on either side by Shaivite and Vaishnavite figures) on the west that leads, through a vestibule, into the main space. The ground floor is dominated by the immense presence of the excavated mass, since the body of the temple at this level is mostly solid and cannot be entered. Toward the back, the perimeter is ringed by a colonnade of square pillars whose only purpose seems to be to support the overhanging rock. In the midst of an elaborate sculptural program, the lower rock mass of the main shrine has life-size elephants carved into it, as if they were supporting the temple above.

Access to the main level of the temple is from a pair of symmetrical stairs on the west that emerge into the entrance vestibule of the shrine. The *mandapa* has sixteen columns clumped into groups of four, creating a cruciform central space that opens into smaller porches on the north and south. The *garbha-griha* has no inner *parikrama*; it is instead on the outside, defined by five subsidiary shrines. Bridges connect the main shrine with the Nandi chamber and the entrance *gopuram* as well. The *shikhara*—or tower—of the main shrine has a four-tiered pyramidal shape resolving into an octagonal finial. The subsidiary shrines use the same vocabulary. Toward the north, on the cross-axis with the *mandapa*, there is another rock-cut temple, Lankesvara, complete with a sixteen-pillared *mandapa* and *garbha-griha*, that almost rivals the main shrine. And to the south there are two additional shrines, also rock-cut, one of which extends almost 25 meters into the rock.

Most discussions of Kailasnath's construction process assume that gigantic trenches were dug into the rock to clear out the main mass of the temple; this would have been followed by a process of excavating and sculpting. A counterintuitive possibility is suggested by the subsidiary shrines—in particular the one to the north—which are excavated so deep into the rock; the same process might have been employed for the main shrine. Since Kailasnath is derived from rock-cut cave temple precedents, excavating the sacred cave and then, in an act of superseding the infinity of the mountain around the traditional caves, "uncovering" the exterior in the form of a complete temple, makes sense conceptually as well. There would have been no room for error, since

rock cannot be replaced. Making the temple had to have been an act of skilled and deliberate craftsmanship. The Rashtrakutas would, of course, also have been very familiar with the constructed temples of the Chalukyas, their predecessors, and the Pallavas and Pandyas, their contemporaries to the south. The reason for their decision to dedicate the full extent of their resources to the creation of a gigantic rock-cut structure is unknown, but it must have had to do with reasserting the value of the traditional way of making a monumental ritual structure in the face of the imminent modernity of the structural stone temple.

10.34 Detail: Temple of Kailasnath, Ellora

10.35 Detail: Temple of Kailasnath, Ellora

SAMYE, TIBET

A century after the introduction of Buddhism into Tibet, King Trisong Detsen formally established Buddhism as the state religion by building the Samye Monastery. Its full name is Bsam yas mi 'gyur lhun grub gtsug lag khang, or the "Temple of Unchanging Spontaneous Presence" (founded 775 CE, constructed 787–91 CE). The first Tibetan monks were ordained here, and it was the seat of Tibetan Buddhism until the establishment of the Potala Palace by the fifth Dalai Lama in the 17th century. Located in the Chimpu Valley just south of Lhasa, the monastery was laid out in the form of a mandala, with a circular perimeter wall about 300 meters in diameter; the main temple, the Utse, representing Mt. Meru, is in the center. The wall is topped by 1,008 tiny chortens with gates at the four cardinal points. The four continents in the ocean around Mt. Meru are represented by temples at the cardinal points, each flanked by two smaller temples to symbolize islands. The Utse has three main stories, each of which was designed in a different traditional architectural style—Indian, Chinese, and Tibetan. The first floor is dominated by the main assembly hall; the second is basically an open roof area where monks and locals carry out the craftwork for the temple; and the third is the palace of the Dalai Lama, with a small anteroom, throne room, and bedroom. Four chortens at the corners of the Utse are brightly colored black, white, red, and green. Each has stairs and small chapels. There is a *nyima* ("sun") temple in the north and a *dawa* ("moon") temple to the south. Though all Buddhist temples are modeled on an imaginary mandala, this one has the mandala as its basic plan, writ large in the landscape.

10.36 Samye Monastery, Dranang, Tibet

10.37 Samye Monastery

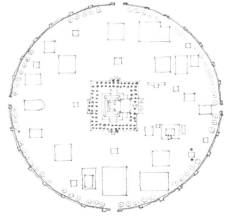

0   200 m

10.38 Plan: Samye Monastery

10.39 **View of Borobudur, near Yogyakarta, Indonesia**

INDONESIA AT A CROSSROADS

By the 9th century, the entire region of Southeast Asia had begun to cohere as a series of relatively stable states linked by trade and religion. Guangzhou was the primary entry point into China. Kunming, a quasi-independent state (to become the Kingdom of Dali) was the primary land-based entry point. Particularly important was the development of trade around the Straits of Malacca. Ships no longer unloaded at Kedah for the portage across the peninsula. With the sea route now becoming the norm, Sumatra and Indonesia quickly became a strategically important area. The rulers of the Srivijaya Empire made their wealth less on export than on transit tariffs, since almost all shipping trade had to go through the Malacca Straits.

The Hindu-Buddhist kings of 9th-century Indonesia used their new wealth to catapult their kingdom into a conceptual center of the Hindu-Buddhist cosmological universe. Within the short space of a hundred years, they built not only one of the finest Buddhist stupa shrines ever, Borobudur, but also, a scant 20 miles away, one of the largest and most complex assemblages of Hindu temples of the time, the Prambanam complex.

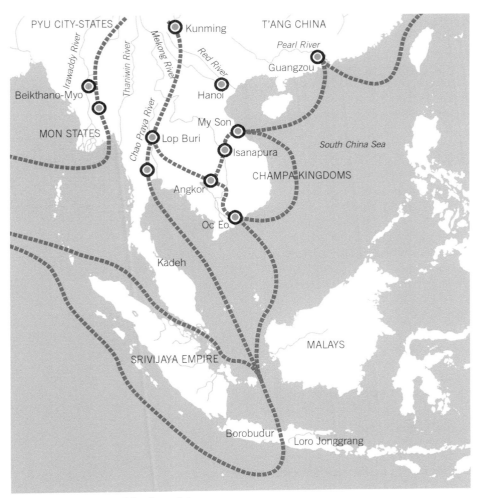

10.40 **Rivers and cities of Southeast Asia**

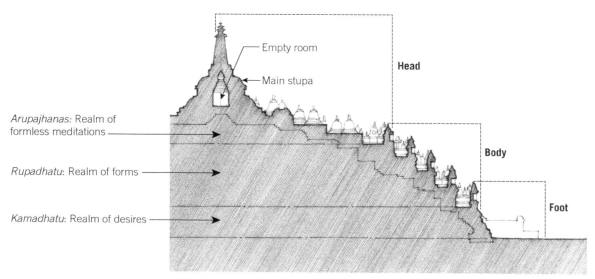

Empty room

Main stupa

Head

Arupajhanas: Realm of formless meditations

Rupadhatu: Realm of forms

Body

Kamadhatu: Realm of desires

Foot

10.41 Partial section showing the three levels of Borobudur

Borobudur

The great "cosmic mountain" at Borobudur (ca. 760–830 CE) was started in the reign of the Shailendra king Indra and completed in that of Samaratunga. Though based on earlier experiments, Borobudur is unique in its formal organization and articulation. It is approximately square in plan (122 meters north to south and 116 meters east to west), and it is roughly aligned to the cardinal directions. The plan follows a typical Buddhist mandala diagram, with a biaxial symmetrical order composed of a series of jagged terraces giving way to round ones in the middle.

To make the building, the architects chopped down the top of a sizable hill, leaving a stepped-shape stub on a terrace. On the face of the rock, the designers basically added a layer of stone to create the effect of a terraced mountain.

Borobudur is at one level a quintessential stupa, having been built onto a solid mound; at another level, it is a three-dimensional pedagogical diagram. The building is neither a temple nor a monastery. Rather, it is something of a mountain-scaled university to which one goes not to invoke divine beings but to participate in a didactic journey, to learn—by moving through its spaces—a progression of lessons by means of which the successful student can attain a state of *bodhi,* or perfected wisdom, just as the Sakyamuni Buddha did 2,500 years prior. The essential

10.42 Aerial view of Borobudur

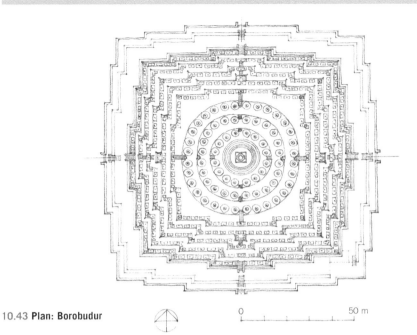

10.43 Plan: Borobudur

0   50 m

experience consists of an orchestrated sequence of four galleries followed by three terraces, preceded by one large plinth, or pre-terrace. The first four terraces are square, and the latter three are round. The whole culminates in the central stupa, which is completely solid and cannot be entered. As the Buddhist pilgrim approaches it, the complete profile of Borobudur is clearly visible, its levels of galleries and rounded stupa terraces placed hierarchically around the central stupa, forming the outline of a gently swelling mountain. The destination, the central stupa, seems evident. As the pilgrim gets closer, however, the central stupa disappears and seems to retract into the monument, and it is replaced by a forest of smaller stupas and sculptures on a more human scale. Since nirvana is not a place or a thing, it has no physical dimension that can be described. Rather, it is an inner state that must be achieved by the pilgrim by means of a personal journey. As governed by the mandala, this journey must be completed by a pilgrim in sixty conceptual steps.

The journey begins by circumambulating the four lower galleries, which have two rows of sculpted panels on each side, recounting sequentially stories from the life of the Buddha. These narrow galleries are staggered to block all lines of sight, in order to focus the pilgrim's attention on the panels. Only after having cleared these four levels can pilgrims ascend to the round upper levels, where there are no enclosing walls. Instead, they encounter the bell-shaped hollow stupas, each one of which contains a different sculpture of the seated Buddha displaying one of the mudras, the characteristic symbolic gestures of Buddhism. The openings on the lower stupas are diamond-shaped and large, while those on the ones above are square, smaller, and fewer in number. While each side of the *candi* ("temple") in the lower level is one step, each bell-shaped stupa takes a whole step toward the end. At the final stage, pilgrims arrive at the stupa, whose solidity symbolizes the *shunyata*, or "nonpresence," aspired to by the Buddhist pilgrim who seeks nirvana. The lowest terrace of Borobudur, probably added to stabilize the structure, was constructed at a later date; it hides a row of friezes behind it. One of the unresolved controversies surrounding Borobudur is whether it was originally planned with a large stupa in the middle that would have dominated the whole edifice.

The Shailendra kingdom also constructed a series of Hindu temples, the most impressive of which is Candi Prambanam, known popularly as Loro Jonggrang ("Slender Virgin"). Built around 850 CE, Loro Jonggrang's three central shrines, facing east, are dedicated to the Hindu trinity, Brahma, Vishnu, and Shiva, with Shiva at the center. Three subsidiary shrines, for the corresponding animal "vehicles," or *vahanas*, of the temple deities, face westward, toward the main group.)

The shrines sit on a platform, accessible from all four sides. Around the platform, 224 small shrines are arrayed in concentric rings, with extra widths for passages leading to the center. A wall encloses the complex with access gates on each side. Prambanam's shrines are articulated as two-story structures divided by a band of molding. Their profiles are most like those of the Pallavas of southern India, which emphasize slender verticality with distinct and clear horizontal layers, as in the Shore Temple. Prambanam's two-storied base, however, is significantly taller than its South Asian precedents. The plans and tripartite elevational orders of Hindu and Buddhist structures of Southeast Asia were—probably quite purposefully—very similar. The two cosmologies were often articulated in parallel as well. As a consequence, it is not unusual to mistake a Hindu temple for a Buddhist one, and vice versa, especially in contemporary Cambodia.

HINDU KINGDOMS OF CAMBODIA

In 802 CE, Jayavarman II, who had united the various Chola kingdoms in Cambodia and southern Vietnam, became king and supreme ruler over his vast new territory. The coronation ceremony took place on Mt. Mahendraparvata overlooking the Angkor Plain. It was, for the region, a new type of kingdom. The traditional trade route from Kunming had gone through Burma and through cities on the Irrawaddy River, like Biethano-Myo. And the shipping lanes that developed around 400 CE hugged the coast to the benefit of cities like Oc Eo. The Khmer controlled a large inland area that they made fertile with their irrigation technology. In a century, it was to make them the wealthiest kingdom in Southeast Asia. The rise of the Khmer was also spurred on by the trade between China and India. The rule of the Song dynasty (960–1279 CE) conforms quite closely with that of the Khmer, and with the Chola in India (860–1279 CE). Both China and India exerted powerful economic influences in the Southeast Asian areas, although, from a cultural point of view, it was India that won out, with its variants of Buddhism and Hinduism spreading throughout the region. To the east, in Vietnam, were the Champa, whom the Khmer tried several times to conquer in order to gain access to their ports. To the south was the Srivijaya Empire, founded in the 8th century on the island of Sumatra, which controlled the Straits of Malacca. Also to be factored in is the Dali kingdom in Yunnan Province in southern China. From 900 until 1253 CE, when it was conquered by the Mongolians and brought back into the fold of the Chinese Empire, it was an autonomous state; with the disruptions of the trade routes that came with the Mongolian expansion into Asia, the southern route, which went right through the Dali heartland, proved to be a viable alternative. The Khmer sold specialty items such as spices and wood to the Chinese, in exchange for metal items such as bronze pots, as well as silver and gold. Above all, however, they were producers of rice, and it was in fact rice as bulk exchange item that drove the founding of the cities at Agkor.

10.44 **View of Bakong Temple Mountain, near Siem Reap, Cambodia**

10.45 **Area plan: Angkor, Cambodia**

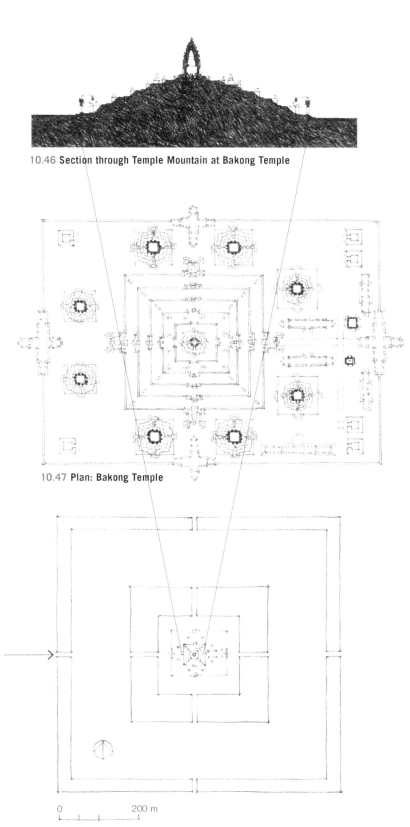

10.46 **Section through Temple Mountain at Bakong Temple**

10.47 **Plan: Bakong Temple**

0   200 m

10.48 **Plan: Bakong Temple and its precinct**

Hariharalaya

The first city that was laid out, called Hariharalaya, was designed as a perfect square about 3 kilometers on a side. The name *Hariharalaya* is derived from the name of the Hindu deity Harihara, who was prominent in pre-Angkorian Cambodia. The name *Harihara*, in turn, is a composite of *hari* (meaning "the Hindu god Vishnu") and *hara* (meaning "the Hindu god Shiva"). The name thus means something like "the City of Vishnu and Shiva." The city was not as dense as medieval European cities, since its built-up areas were interspersed with gardens and small fields. It was however, an extremely orderly layout, with the areas surrounding the city dedicated to rice cultivation.

That Jayavarman II chose this site to the north of the Great Lake for his capital was no coincidence. Apart from a steady supply of water for rice growing, the place was seen as a local holy land that, with relatively modest enhancements, could be transformed into *the* holy land of the Khmer. Angkor spiritual geography, as would have been typical in Indic mythology, was defined around three primary elements: the mountain, the river, and the ocean—or Mt. Meru, the Ganges River, and the Indian Ocean. Each had its own translation in the local Angkor geography.

Mahendraparvata (Mt. Meru)

Mt. Meru, the abode of the gods, lies at the center of the physical and spiritual universes. For the Khmer, its incarnation was Mahendraparvata, "the Mountain of Indra, the King of Gods." Known today as Phnom Kulen, it is located about 25 kilometers to the northeast of Angkor. Jayavarman II built several temples on the mountain to house the lingam. It was also from this mountain that the stones for the Angkor temples were quarried. In that sense, the stones possessed a spiritual charge.

Siem Reap (Ganges River)

The mountain is the source of the Siem Reap River, which in its numerous offshoots drains most of the plateau before reaching the Great Lake. It is the water from this river that feeds the complex system of canals and *barays*. The river was identified with the goddess Ganga.

Indratataka (Sea of Indra)

The "ocean" was built in Jayavarman II's city immediately after he became king. This vast *baray*, the largest of its kind at the time, was called Indratataka, or "Sea of Indra," and was 3.8 kilometers long and 0.8 kilometers wide.

Bakong

Jayavarman II may have founded the city, but his state temple was some 20 kilometers away, back in Phnom Kulen. For this reason, his court remained at Phnom Kulen until 802 CE, when he finally moved to Hariharalaya. The next king, Indravarman I ("Protected by Indra"), built a new state temple, but in the very center of the city. The temple (881 CE), which had long avenues extending from it in the cardinal directions, sat in a moated enclosure that would have contained palaces and royal storehouses. Dedicated to Shiva, it measures 900 by 700 meters and consists of three concentric enclosures separated by two moats. The innermost enclosure, which measures 160 by 120 meters, contains eight towers and the central temple, which has a single tower on its top platform. The plan of the temple is square and consists of five levels. Though not complicated compared to subsequent temples, the design is quite refined. The levels become successively shallower, and the staircase narrows as it ascends. The culminating tower is thought to have replaced the original one, since its architectural style corresponds to that of the 12th-century temple city Ankgor Wat.

Stone was used for the platforms, whereas brick was used for the architectural parts. The brick was covered with bas-relief carvings in stucco depicting scenes from Hindu mythology. Large stone statues of elephants are positioned as guardians at the corners of the three lower levels of the pyramid. Statues of lions guard the stairways.

What often makes Khmer temples seem alien to Western perceptions is that they are not set *against* the landscape. They are both a form of architecture based on a complex application of geometry and site planning, and a constructed landscape; all these temples are not only set in a sacred landscape but are themselves copies of the symbolic landscape of mountain and ocean. The moats that surround the temples do not serve a protective purpose but represent the primeval oceans in which the treasure of immortality was hidden. The water also visually echoes the temple's image, making the temple-mountain appear linked with its inverted reflection. On a practical level, these waters are integrated into the *baray*

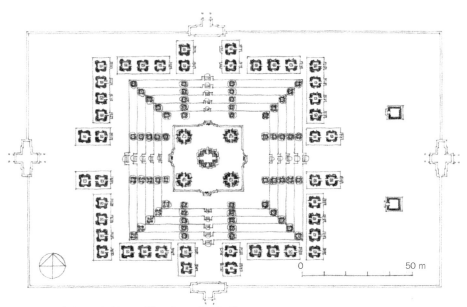

10.49 Plan of Phnom Bakheng, Siem Reap, Cambodia

system, literally nourishing the land. This mutually reinforcing relationship between a symbolic landscape and its real-life model is continuously at play in these temples.

The temple represents a combination of these five principles:

1. The sacred mandala/mountain/ocean of Shiva and the Hindu pantheon
2. An intensified model of the sacred landscape in which they are sited
3. The home of the god(s)
4. The omnipotence of the king
5. The economy of the Khmer people

Around the year 900 CE, King Yasovarman I ("Protected by Glory"; r. 899–917) created yet another new city, along with a new state temple and a new and significantly larger *baray*. The city, Yasodharapura ("Glory-Bearing City"), was, like its predecessor, perfectly square, but it was much larger: about 4 kilometers on a side. The new state temple, Phnom Bakheng, located at the center, was known originally as Yasodharesvara—the "Lord of the One Who Bears Glory."

It is also referred to in inscriptions as Phnom Kandal ("Central Mountain"). Yasodharesvara is built on top of a sizable 60-meter-high rock outcropping, the top (and perhaps even the slopes) of which had been shaved down to suit the design. Whereas Bakong was more of an artificial mountain than a real one, Bakheng was a mountain augmented by a temple to become a type of super-temple/mountain. The whole was surrounded by a moat measuring 650 by 436 meters. Avenues radiated out in the four cardinal directions from the mount, with a causeway running in a northwest-southeast orientation from the old capital area to the east section of the new capital's outer moat and then, turning to an east-west orientation, connected directly to the east entrance of the temple. The temple faces east, measures 76 meters square at its base, and is built in a pyramid form of six tiers. At the top level, five sandstone sanctuaries stand in a quincunx: one in the center and one at each corner of the level's square. The quincunx represents the five peaks of Mt. Meru.

10.50 **Buseoksa Temple, Gyeongsangdo, Korea**

KOREAN BUDDHISM

By the end of the 7th century, the Silla dynasty (668–935 CE), which had initiated the introduction of Buddhism into Korea, controlled most of the Korean Peninsula. It defeated the Kaya Federation in 562 CE, and thanks to an alliance with the Chinese T'ang court, it also succeeded in conquering the kingdoms of Paekche in 660 CE and Koguryô in 668 CE, thereby unifying Korea for the first time under a single kingdom, with its capital at Kyôngju. Even after the Chinese troops had withdrawn into Manchuria, the Silla maintained close ties with T'ang China through trade and diplomatic exchanges. The Silla made Buddhism the state religion, causing it to spread rapidly as far as Japan. Nonetheless, the introduction of Buddhism into Korea was met with some resistance, which was only resolved when native gods were in essence seen as apparitions into which Buddhist gods had temporarily projected themselves. Certain shamanistic gods, for example, were made into bodhisattvas incarnate. A similar tension persisted in Japan between Shinto traditions and the new modern Buddhist concepts.

As Mahayana Buddhism evolved in India and China, several different sects accessible only to initiates evolved in Korea as well, particularly those influenced by Tibetan and Chinese esoteric or Tantric Buddhism.

Among the various temples that were built during this period was Buseoksa Temple (676–1000 CE), which was the center of Silla Buddhism. It was established by the monk Uisang, the founder of the Consciousness-Only School, an idealistic system of thought in which sense perceptions have no objective reality. Instead, it is the mind or the consciousness of the perceived that holds and contains the universe. Buseoksa, or "Temple of the Floating Stone," is so named because of a large rock beside the western hall that appears to float above the stones underneath, perhaps symbolizing its defiance of gravity.

The monastery rests on a forested slope defined by a series of terraces accessed by paths, stairs, and gatehouses. There are 108 steps between the Cheonwangmun Gate and the Anyangmun Gate, the number of steps representing redemption from agony and evil passions through 108 cycles. The Anyangmun Gate is actually a pavilion floating out over the edge of a terrace; the terrace is entered from underneath. *Anyangmun* means "entrance to heaven," and the gate is the culmination of the spiritual path. With spectacular views into the valleys and landscape beyond, it sits opposite the Muryangsujeon Hall, with its Buddha; it dates from about the year 1000. (The temple was burnt by the Japanese in 1593 and restored from 1969 to 1973.)

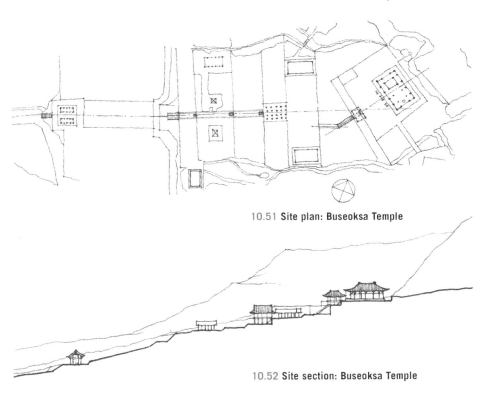

10.51 **Site plan: Buseoksa Temple**

10.52 **Site section: Buseoksa Temple**

10.53 **Main hall, Nanchan Temple, Wutaishan, Shanxi Province, China**

FOGUANG MONASTERY

The Nanchan and Foguang monasteries, built during the Sui and T'ang periods and located far north of the capital on Wutai Mountain in Shanxi Province, are among the few wooden monasteries to have survived into modern times. The Foguang Temple (857 CE) was the more ambitious construction of the two. Unlike the three-bayed hall of Nanchan, with its simple hip-and-gable (*xieshan*) roof, the Foguang hall is seven-by-four bayed and has a roof format known as first-class hip style. The columns divide the hall into an inner and outer *cao* ("space"). Just as they transformed the stupa to a *ta*, or pagoda, the Chinese also transformed the monastery format; in this case, it clearly derived from the palatial architecture of the time. Monasteries generally consisted of a Buddha hall framed by a courtyard within a colonnaded enclosure, with a north and a south gate. The larger ones had east and west gates as well. The courtyards were named after their principal buildings—for example, the pagoda courtyard, the *chan* ("meditation") courtyard, the *vanaya* ("discipline") courtyard, the *purea* ("land") courtyard, and so on. The overall styles of Nanchan and Foguang temples, however, are very similar, with low-pitched roof slopes, deep eaves, and dominating brackets.

The Foguang Temple almost did not survive. In 845, as part of the persecution, the original 5th-century structure, an important stop for Buddhist pilgrims, was burned to the ground, with only the small yet elegant Zushi pagoda surviving from the temple's early history. Twelve years later, however, in 857, a woman named Ning Gongyu provided funds for a reconstruction led by a monk named Yuancheng. (The current building is a reconstruction from the 1970s.)

Chinese wood roofs are described by the number and types of bracket sets and beams deployed. While bracket sets are a complex addition to the number of horizontal, vertical, and diagonal composite elements, called *dou-gong*, the beams are designated by their position and the number of rafters they span. *Dou-gong* bracket sets differ in size and number depending on their position and location, the size of the roof, and the stature of the building. Bracket sets of this complexity never developed in India, Mesopotamia, or areas to the west, where walls played a more important role in the structural stability and expression of a building. In the West, wood beams needed to be attached with skill, but architects did not have to worry about a building twisting, which is a common problem with structures set up on columns or posts. The brackets keep the top part of the building stiff against rotational forces while supplying enough flexibility in case of earthquakes. The technology was developed early on by the Chinese, but it was by no means static. It went through several developmental stages. By the 15th century, engineers had learned how to simplify the bracketing systems and began using them more for the purposes of tradition than out of structural necessity.

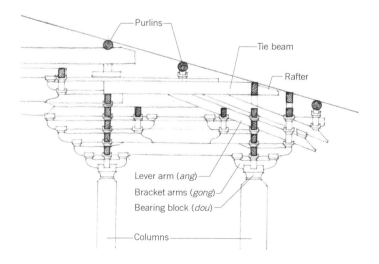

10.54 **Detail of bracket system: Main hall, Foguang Temple, Wutaishan, Shanxi Province, China**

10.55 Main hall, Foguang Temple

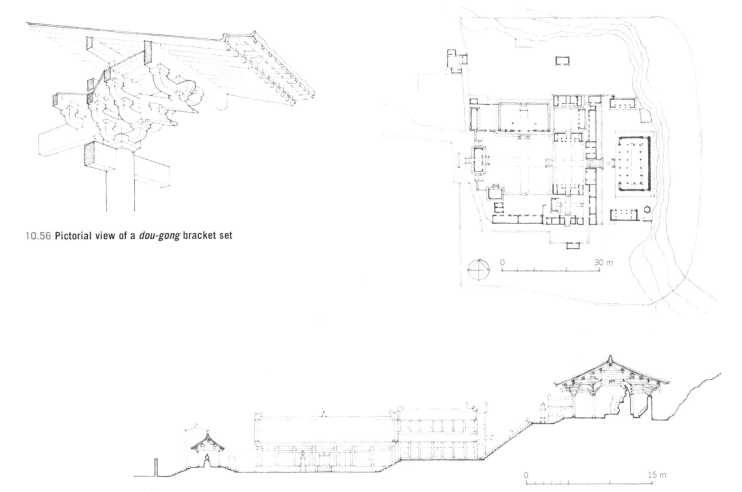

10.56 Pictorial view of a *dou-gong* bracket set

0   30 m

0   15 m

10.57 Site plan and section: Foguang Temple, Wutaishan, Shanxi Province, China

EUROPE AND THE CAROLINGIANS

Around the year 800 CE, the architectural hot spots were in Indonesia, China, and the Islamic world. In Europe, the situation was still bleak. Stability had improved somewhat with the Christianization of the Franks when Clovis I adopted Catholicism in Reims, France, around 496 CE; as was then the practice, all the Franks then adopted Catholicism as well. The king of the Visigoths, Theodoric I, along with other Germanic tribes, finally stopped the invasion of the Huns in Chalons, France, south of Reims, in 451 CE. But the onslaught of steppe tribes was not over yet. With their families and herds, the Lombards had moved into northern Italy. The Ungars and Bulgars were on the move as well, dispersing into Greece, and some even into Italy. This meant that a huge swath of territory, from the tip of Greece northward all the way to the Baltic Sea, was still in a state of flux. The settlement of the Franks, who had moved into France from the lower Rhine only a few centuries earlier and who were now starting to farm the land previously known by the Romans as Gaul, was the only bright spot.

Though they had been Christianized by the 7th century, the Franks had rarely had periods in which there had been just one ruler. Furthermore, southern Spain had been lost to the Islamic armies, as had the Christianized areas of the eastern Roman Empire in Syria. The Armenians, with their vibrant architectural culture, were also dispersed, many fleeing westward to Constantinople and Italy. Byzantium itself was under continual threat of invasion by Islamic armies, and even the Mediterranean was largely controlled by Islamic ships. Nonetheless, the Franks eventually consolidated their hold to become the dominant force in Europe. Together with the Byzantines, the Christian civilizational area formed a tenuous U, from Denmark down through France and Italy, around Greece, and into Anatolia. The invasion of northern Italy by the Lombards threatened to cut Italy off from France, but in 774 CE, Charlemagne, by then king of the Franks, conquered the Lombards and brought them into the Christian fold. The Frankish, Italian, and reduced Byzantine areas now formed the core of the Christian world.

Charlemagne (747–814 CE), was by all accounts an unusual man. The eldest child of Pepin the Short (r. 751–68 CE), he introduced new financial regulations, took a serious interest in scholarship, and promoted the liberal arts at his court. With all this in mind, Pope Leo III realized that in order for Europe to survive, he would have to share power with Charlemagne. Thus was born the idea of the Holy Roman Empire. To their mutual benefit, it in essence had two rulers: a religious one and a secular one, the military power of the latter protecting the existence of the former. On Christmas day of the year 800 CE, in Rome, Leo crowned Charlemagne emperor of the Holy Roman Empire. It was a unique arrangement for its age, and one that would have long-term consequences. The title would be handed down and fought over for centuries and officially dissolved only in 1806.

Long before Charlemagne's coronation, the Carolingian Church had established a close relationship with Rome, but it was only with the coronation that the Roman liturgy became the norm. For this, Charlemagne turned to the monastic rules of St. Benedict (489–543 CE), who had lived three centuries earlier. He had formulated his rules during an age in which temporal rule had broken down. As a counterbalance to the chaos, Benedict envisioned the monastery as a devout Christian family of men. The monks' waking hours were devoted primarily to worship and manual labor. But over the centuries, the system was inconsistently applied. Charlemagne reaffirmed the rules as a way to regularize monastic life from the patchwork of devotional practices it had become, while simultaneously bringing the Church closer to imperial policy by making it the basic financial, territorial, and educational institution of the land. Christianity, which had formerly lived within the limited confines of what was left of the Roman Empire, was now becoming a broad European phenomenon.

A new unified era was thus created. The seat of religious power was still in Rome, however, and therein lay a peculiar ambiguity about the location of power that was to beset European politics for centuries and would not be resolved until the Enlightenment in the 18th century. But at the time of Charlemagne, the careful balance between the secular and the religious was still perceived as a mutually beneficial cooperation. The type of government Charlemagne set up developed into a feudal system, with a strict hierarchy linking serf, landlord, and count to the king. (It did, however, lack a firm centralized administrative structure.) Charlemagne moved from place to place to assert and expand his authority. The result was an important expansion of architectural works that imprinted his rule on the landscape. In Italy, just north of Rome, he rebuilt the monastery at Farfa as a southern outpost of the empire, while to the east, he relied on the monasteries at Lorsch and Fulda.

Plan of St. Gall

A 9th-century plan for a medieval monastery at St. Gall in Switzerland provides direct insight into the organization of the medieval monastery. Drawn with red lead on smooth calfskin, the plan provides a remarkably comprehensive snapshot of an institution of about forty buildings inhabited by about 110 monks, with an equal number of laypeople who served as support staff. The site is organized into three zones: to the west, at the bottom of the plan, are the areas open to the lay population; the monastery proper is in the middle zone; and to the east, at the top, are the garden, infirmary, and cemetery. To the left of the road that accesses the church entrance, a reception hall and a dormitory for pilgrims was foreseen. To the north of the church there were special buildings for the abbot and novices. St. Gall was a nave church, with no transept. Its rounded entrance was flanked by freestanding towers. These were not bell towers—those were a later development. At the top of one tower was an altar to St. Michael, and on the other was an altar to St. Gabriel, the celestial guardians representing the forces of light against those of darkness and evil.

Though the draughtsman did not show the thickness of the walls, he did show doors, chimneys, and ovens and labeled each room. He even labeled the vegetables that were planted in the garden, such as onions, leeks, radishes, and fennel. The monk's cloister, the spatial core of the plan, was an open yard about 30 meters square, with arcaded walks giving access to surrounding buildings such as the dormitory, the refectory, and the

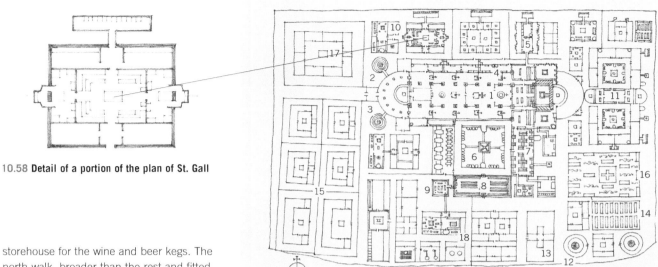

10.58 **Detail of a portion of the plan of St. Gall**

10.59 **Plan of St. Gall, St. Gallen, Switzerland**

storehouse for the wine and beer kegs. The north walk, broader than the rest and fitted with benches, was used as a chapter house for daily meetings. It was connected to the east wall of the church by a special entrance that allowed the monks access to the altar, which was screened off from the public. The plan was drawn using a module of 40 Carolingian feet, the *numeri sacri*, as that is the dimension of the crossing of the church's altar. The church length was five times that amount, or 200 feet, and the depth of the side aisles half that amount, or 20 feet. By means of further halving, the draughtsman arrived at 2.5 feet, the smallest base measure applied in the plan.

1. Church
2. Tower of St. Michael
3. Tower of St. Gabriel
4. Guest lodgings
5. Abbot's house
6. Cloister
7. Monks' dormitory
8. Monks' refectory
9. Kitchen
10. Brew house
11. Novitate and infirmary
12. Henhouse
13. Granary
14. Monks' garden
15. Monks' orchard and cemetery
16. Sheep, goats, and cows
17. Unknown function
18. Workshops

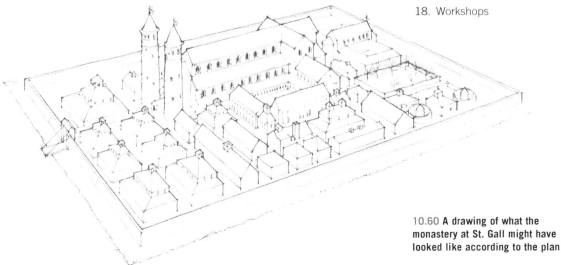

10.60 **A drawing of what the monastery at St. Gall might have looked like according to the plan**

10.61 **Pictorial view: Abbey Church of St. Riquier, near Amiens, France**

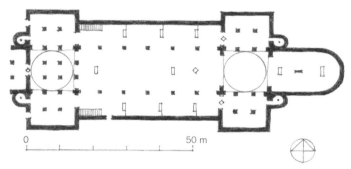

10.62 **Plan: Abbey Church of St. Riquier**

10.63 **Interior of the dome, Palatine Chapel, Aachen, Germany**

St. Riquier

In the 9th century, a series of large abbey churches were built northward from Italy as a way to spread the message and influence of the Church of Rome. These buildings tended to be stark and simple volumetrically. Windows were small, round-headed, sparsely ornamented, and positioned high in the wall. Walls were built of coarse or loosely finished stone that required a good deal of thickness for stability. It was an architecture that did not tax the spatial imagination yet one that yielded stable, solid forms and dark, mysterious interiors. The transept, a minor element in the 5th-century basilica churches of Rome, became integral to the design. But vaulting at the time was to a large extent a thing of the future: most Carolingian buildings had wooden roofs supported by trusses.

The Abbey Church of St. Riquier in northern France, not far from Amiens, though it is no longer extant, can be reconstructed from descriptions and old views. Completed in 799 CE, it followed the basic plan, with towers soaring from cylindrical bases. The external appearance was of clear geometry, solid walls, and small windows. The building was accessed in the Roman manner via an atrium as well as transept entrances. The atrium stood in front of a massive structure surmounted by a cylindrical tower. The monastery had a population of about three hundred monks and one hundred novices, in addition to the servants and serfs. The abbey was dedicated to the Holy Trinity and was connected to two smaller sanctuaries dedicated to St. Benedict and the Virgin Mary, all connected by walls and porticoes. Conforming to the new liturgy, there was a processional path through the church, which was designed to allow the various altars to be visited in sequence. (The church contained a collection of twenty-five relics.) This processional movement through the church was to become a mainstay of medieval religious practice. Also new was the addition of an autonomous spatial zone behind the altar that accommodated the monks. This church-behind-a-church, or choir, was to become an important element in the church design of the Middle Ages. Also significant was the design of the tower over the transept crossing.

Palatine Chapel

Aachen had been founded by the Romans as a spa because of its thermal springs. It was laid out as a square with baths, a palace, and a garrison. Destroyed in the 5th century during the invasions by the German tribes, it was more or less abandoned as a ruin. Because the Frankish kings moved their court from place to place, they had no need for a capital complex, but when Charlemagne came to power in 768, he decided to settle down in order to govern his kingdom from one place.

The architect, Odo of Metz, kept the basic layout of the Roman roads that divided the site into four parts. To the north he placed a basilica/council hall and to the south the Palatine Chapel, connected by an enclosed

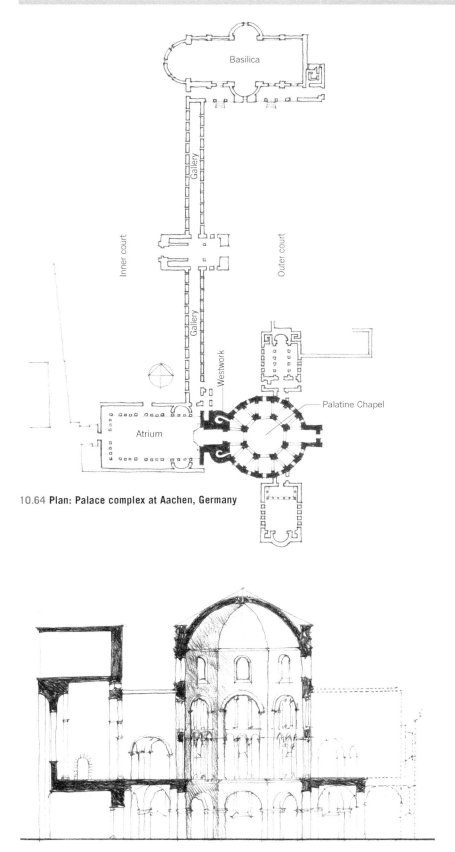

10.64 Plan: Palace complex at Aachen, Germany

10.65 East-west section through the Palatine Chapel

gallery. The chapel consists of a tall octagonal shaft of space surrounded by annular galleries. Unlike earlier buildings in which the walls were of stone rubble stuccoed over, here the whole is designed with elaborate marbles augmented by mosaics. The craftsmen were certainly brought in from Byzantium or Armenia, along with the columns and marbles that came, with the Pope's permission, from Rome and Ravenna.

At the ground floor, the octagon is defined by plain undivided arches, the voussoirs decorated gray and white, holding a cornice that separates the lower zone from the upper arches. Above the cornice, openings consist of elegant arcade screens set between tall arches leading up to a groin vault. To fight the lateral thrusts of the 16.5-meter-wide, segmented dome, the architects added lateral vaults at the gallery level that seem to have been inspired by observing Roman theater construction. The design, in its simple organization of piers and columns, has the appearance of a Carolingian attempt to revive Roman aesthetics. The use of variegated marbles for the paneling and the voussoirs also reflect an awareness of St. Vitale in Ravenna, with which this building most certainly sought to compete, although at St. Vitale the shimmering and curved surfaces create a more ephemeral effect. Nonetheless, at the Palatine Chapel we see the beginnings of an internal facade and of the search to bring unity to the various architectural elements—the openings, cornice lines, revetments, and columns—while still providing for liturgical needs. The king sat in the west on the upper level, on a throne made of white marble plates. He had a view on the three altars: that of the Savior right in front of him, that of the Virgin Mary on the first floor, and that of Saint Peter in the far end of the western choir.

As the burial place of Charlemagne and the setting for imperial coronations, the Palatine Chapel became, in time, a dynastic shrine and an icon of imperial power. It was likely also viewed as an incarnation of the heavenly Jerusalem: it cannot be a coincidence that the circumference of its inner octagon comes to 144 Carolingian feet, just as the walls of the heavenly Jerusalem described in the book of Revelation come to 144 cubits.

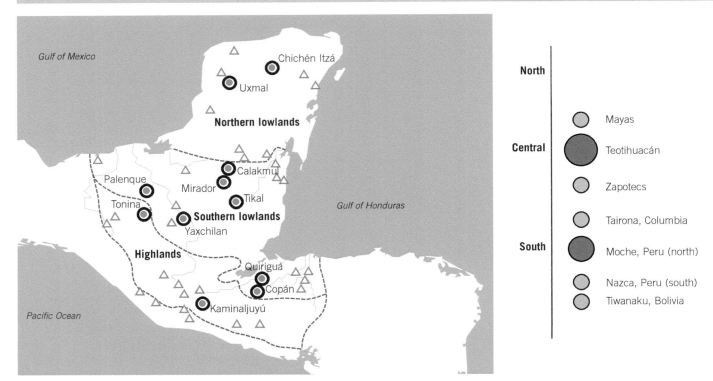

10.66 Mayan sites

10.67 Urbanization of the Americas, ca. 600 CE

North

Central

South

○ Mayas

● Teotihuacán

○ Zapotecs

○ Tairona, Columbia

● Moche, Peru (north)

○ Nazca, Peru (south)

○ Tiwanaku, Bolivia

TIKAL

Tikal's recorded history begins in 292 CE, when Balam Ajaw ("Decorated Jaguar") came to power. At its peak around 700 CE, Tikal was home to about eighty thousand people. Surrounded by cornfields cultivated with intense labor, the houses of its residents were spread evenly over a 16-square-kilometer area. They were clustered into groups of about four to seven, all raised on high platforms and organized around a courtyard. A high level of civic organization and hydraulic engineering was critical to Tikal's survival. The swampy land had to be sectored by raised causeways that provided access to the cultivable land and also allowed for travel and transport. For dwellings, more permanent stone platforms had to be built, and for fresh water, stone-lined cisterns were constructed. Tikal was built on a set of hills, located on the watershed between the Gulf of Mexico and the Caribbean Sea. Perched at the high point of the region, therefore, Tikal's temples enjoyed a commanding view of their surroundings.

Though the central buildings of the Mayas were used for ceremonial and religious functions and also sometimes as markets, the city itself was spread out in the form of an urban settlement. The Mayan cities were organized around neighborhoods, each with its own residences for the elite. Whereas the priestly class and ruling elite lived in the palaces associated with the shrines, the rest of the Mayas visited the centers sporadically for distinct ritual purposes. Though temples were constructed with specific orientations and functions in mind, ceremonial centers as a whole were not expanded according to preplanned rules or geometries, giving them a somewhat ad hoc appearance. There may, of course, have been reasons for the slightly disjointed and angular arrangement of buildings and open plazas, but these have been lost to time.

The North Acropolis, Tikal's oldest complex, was "reskinned" many times. When a ruler of some significance died, he was buried in the acropolis, and a new stone layer was added to it. The new mass was carefully set to ensure that the addition did not damage the older structure. Small vaults were built for the burials, each with its own shrine. Stairs provided access to these chambers for ancestral rites, which had to be performed by later rulers. A section through the acropolis, therefore, is a veritable textbook of Tikal's thousand-year history. The plaza is a flat stone platform approached by climbing six wide steps. A set of stelae describing Tikal's rulers and dating their achievements are lined up along its northern edge. Temples I and II were constructed simultaneously from 734 to 736 CE by Yik'in Chan K'awiil. (K'awiil also built Temples IV and VI.) The Tikal ruler Jasaw Chan K'awiil I died in 734 CE and was buried beneath Temple I in a spectacular ceremony.

Unlike most Central American platform mounds, whose colossal size completely dwarfs the shrine that sits atop them, the shrines of Tikal dominate their substructures. The width atop the shrine of Temple I is just a little less than that of the structure's base. This makes for an extremely steep profile. As a consequence, the visual focus of the entire composition is the shrine's entrance, which is wider than the steps leading to it. Nowhere else in Central American architecture does one find this particular set of architectural proportions at work. Unlike the clay and stone interiors of earlier Mayan pyramids, the interior of this one was built with large blocks of stones, carefully and accurately fitted in the supporting walls. To keep water from leaching into the interior, the surface was sealed with mortar. The brickwork that covered the entire pyramid served more for decoration than for protection.

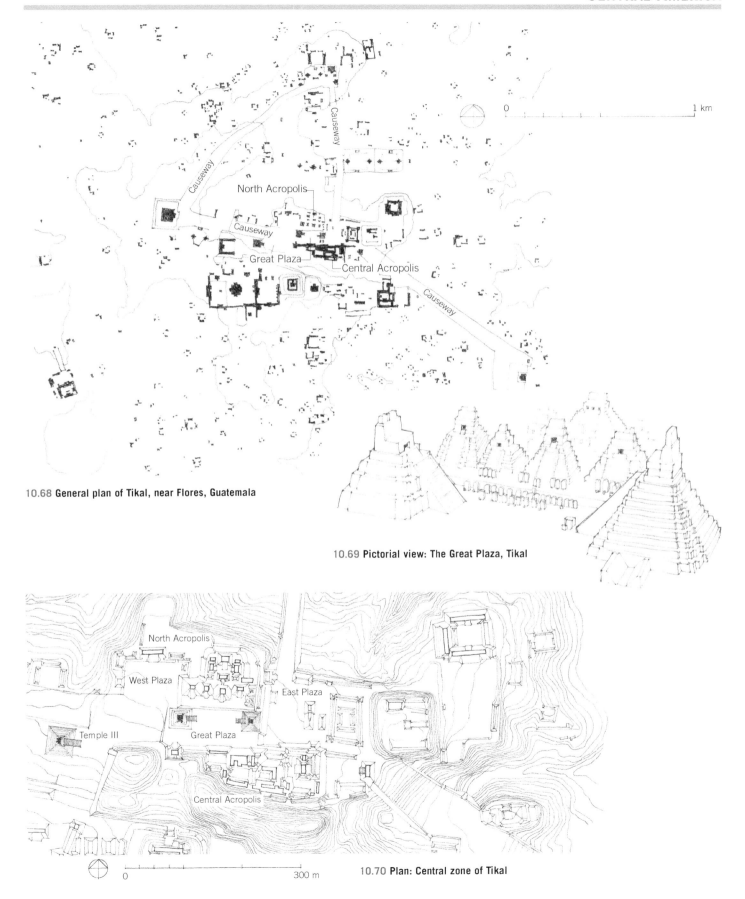

10.68 General plan of Tikal, near Flores, Guatemala

10.69 Pictorial view: The Great Plaza, Tikal

10.70 Plan: Central zone of Tikal

Southeast of the Great Plaza is the so-called Central Acropolis, which held the royal courts and residences. It consisted of a series of courts connected at the corners, with simple adjoining buildings sitting on platforms. The palace courts, although they adjoined the central ceremonial complex, were visually screened off from their surroundings. They were entered at the corners. Tikal's urban core is a spectacular assembly of more than a hundred stone temples. The Mayan engineers constructed Tikal's base by building up the higher zones into platforms with mud and stone. Three zones in the middle were linked over time by causeways to form a triangle. Additional causeways connected to adjoining platforms and the rest of the urban area.

The largest of these zones is focused on a giant stone platform, the Great Plaza. To its north is the North Acropolis, which faces the Great Plaza. Its eastern and western ends are anchored by the so-called Temples I and II, respectively. Farther west and slightly to the south is Temple III, and even farther west, connected by a causeway, is Tikal's largest temple, the 70-meter-tall Temple IV.

Astronomy determined the location of the main temples. They are linked by sightlines. Standing on top of Temple I looking west, the peak of Temple III marks the setting of the sun at the equinoxes. From the same position, a sightline to Temple IV marks sunset on August 13, the day the world began, according to the Mayan calendar. Farther north, two adjacent platform mounds, called the Twin Pyramid complex, are oriented exactly along the cardinal directions. Their collective steps add up to 365, corresponding exactly to one calendar year. They were constructed at the end of a twenty-year period of the Mayan calendar, signifying the successful completion of that period.

10.71 **Temple I (Temple of the Great Jaguar), Tikal**

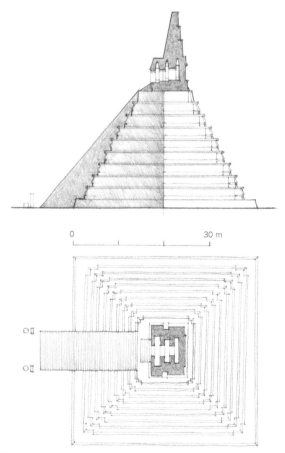

10.72 **Plan and section-elevation: Temple I (Temple of the Great Jaguar), Tikal**

10.73 Temple of the Inscriptions, Palenque, Chiapas, Mexico

MAYAN CITY-STATES

In the 8th and 9th centuries, the Mayan city-states of the Yucatán dominated the peninsula. In the period from 600 to 750 CE, the city of Palenque, located in the foothills of the Chiapas *altiplano*, began to expand under the leadership of the king Pacan and his two sons. Palenque is set into the hillside and laid out to take advantage of the contours and natural cleavage formed by the Otulum River, which passes through the city; water from it was diverted to the Palenque's central palace, the city's most remarkable building, via a long corbel-vaulted tunnel. The Palenque architects set corbeled vaults parallel to one another, which not only created greater interior spaces, unlike the solid masses of most Mayan buildings, but also stabilized the whole structure. This is one reason Palenque's buildings have aged so well. Their rooftop ornamental superstructure was also made as a roofcomb, which further reduced the structure's overall weight.

Palenque's palace sits on a broad platform that is centrally located to visually command the site. On one side, the palace dominates the edge of the Otulum River; on the other, its platform and profile define the edges of Palenque's central plaza. The palace complex opens toward the hills, although the monumental stairs are on the north and west sides. This indicates that access to the palace, as one might expect, was carefully regulated. The interior is dominated by two courts that take up half the complex and are separated by a long double-vaulted building that was the palace's original core. The south half of the palace is labyrinthine, with a dense network of interconnected chambers.

Palace

Temple of the Inscriptions

Temple of the Sun

Temple of the Foliated Cross

0   300 m

10.74 Plan of Palenque

341

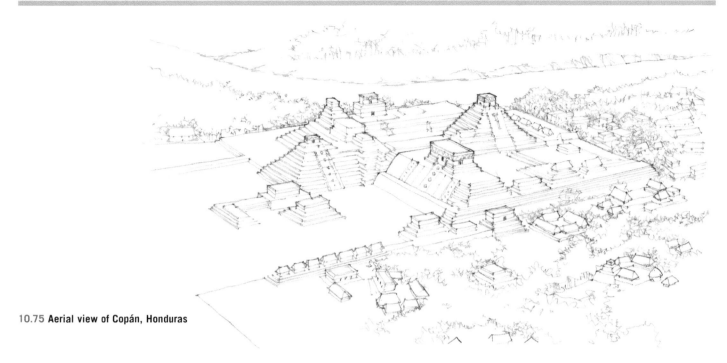

10.75 Aerial view of Copán, Honduras

Visually, the palace's most recognizable structure is the four-story tower that rises just outside the west courtyard. It is unique in Mayan architecture, and its purpose is still undetermined. To the southwest of the palace complex is the so-called Temple of the Inscriptions (683 CE), which is famous because its foundation contains the tomb of K'inich Janaab Pakal. Unlike most tombs in the base of pyramids (as at Tikal, where they are completely interred within their superstructure), Pakal's tomb remained accessible from a stairway at the top of the temple. In the access stairway can therefore be found the explicit spatialization of one of the cardinal ideologies of Mayan religious practice: that rulers and generations to come ruled because of their connection to their ancestors, and that honoring and maintaining an ongoing relationship with those ancestors was critical to their being and welfare. The stelae on Pakal's sarcophagus show him passing through the underworld in the process of becoming an ancestor. During the 8th century, the city came under increasing stress, in concert with most other classic Mayan city-states, and there was no new elite construction in the ceremonial center. Palenque was eventually abandoned.

Copán

Located in a mountain valley of the Copán River on the western edge of Honduras, Copán is the southernmost of the major Mayan cities. One of the largest Mayan centers, Copán was the capital of a state covering several hundred square kilometers between 400 and 820 CE. The site is about 600 meters above sea level, above the jungles and rain forests of the lowland Mayas. Although occupied for about two thousand years, the main visible buildings were built in the period between 600 and 900 CE. The excavated ruins cover about 16 hectares and consist of the main acropolis and five plazas. Like the ancestral complex of Tikal, the main structure at Copán is an agglomerative megacomplex, built over a period of six hundred years, consisting of a gigantic platform with an assorted collection of masonry temples, palaces, ball courts, plazas, tombs, carved stelae, and altars, dating mostly from 695 to 800 CE.

Like Monte Albán in modern-day Oaxaca, Mexico, the surrounding mountains of the Copán River valley offered rich possibilities for dramatic landscape alignments. In particular, the Copán ball court, which sits between the main plaza and the acropolis, is aligned so that a view through it, which is

10.76 Ball court, Copán, Honduras

also the main view from atop the acropolis, seems to exactly echo the angles of the steep hills beyond. The Copán main group, as is typical of Mesoamerican ceremonial centers, is oriented to the cardinal directions along the longer north-south axis, with the heavier concentration of built-up terraces and palaces to the south and a main plaza to the north. The main plaza is entered from the east. A subsidiary plaza leads into the vast rectangular space of the main bounded plaza, with a low, three-level platform mound in the middle. A ball court and subsidiary platform abut the south end of the main plaza, just before a monumental set of stairways leads up to the higher levels of the royal complex. A platform pyramid sits in the middle of the high terrace, which is edged by a series of palaces and tombs. The northern edge of the main plaza extends out into a T, forming another pyramid. The steep western stairway is a famous hieroglyphic stairway whose 2,200 glyphs relate the story of the last Copán dynasty.

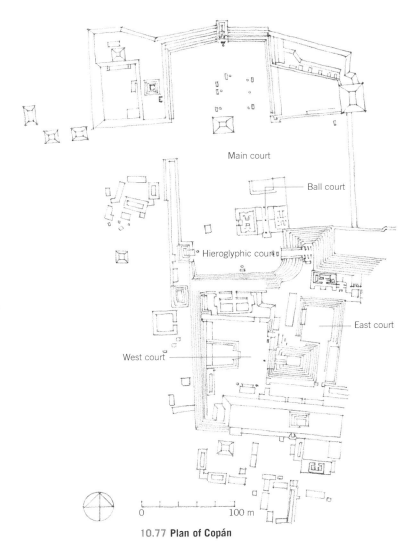

Main court

Ball court

Hieroglyphic court

East court

West court

0   100 m

10.77 Plan of Copán

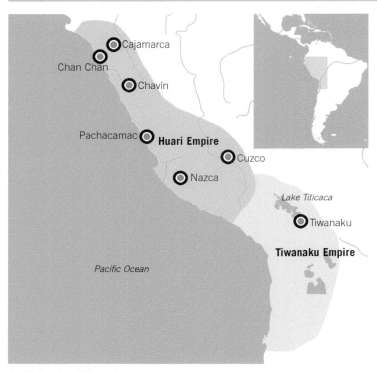

10.78 Huari and Tiwanaku empires

TIWANAKU

Tiwanaku lies in a highland valley in the southern Andes 3,660 meters above sea level, near the south shore of Lake Titicaca. Inhabited from roughly 1000 BCE to 500 CE, it was not only the capital of a network of cities but also the regional ceremonial center, maintaining its preeminent position until about 1000 CE. It was not so much the city that was important but the lake, which was seen as the place of origin from whence the primeval couple were sent out to call mankind forth from the springs, rivers, rocks, and trees. Lake Titicaca was known as a *taypi*, a zone of convergence between the principles of *urco* (the west, high, dry, pastoral, celestial, male) and *uma* (the east, low, agricultural, underworld, female). If Tiwanaku was the central representation of the *taypi*, the elite who lived there were viewed as the guardians and representatives of this sacred order.

The ceremonial center was surrounded by an immense artificial moat filled with water diverted from the Tiwanaku River, which evoked the image of the city's core as an island. The level of the lake itself would have been higher. Now the ruins are 10 kilometers from the shore, but the shore would have been closer to or possibly at the very foot of the site, which featured several temples, gateways of monumental scale, platforms, and sunken courts. The two most important structures are the Akapana (ca. 700 CE) and the Puma Punku, which was built somewhat later.

The Akapana was a low-terraced platform mound with a base 200 meters square and a height of 17 meters. It is an earthen mound, faced with a mixture of large and small stone blocks. Vertically placed stones, approximately 3.5 meters on center and joined with characteristic Andean precision, mark the edges of the six terraces that work their way up to the summit. The topmost terrace was covered by a thin layer of bluish-green gravel, brought in from the Quimsachata mountain range just south of Tiwanaku. On the summit was a sunken court with a complexly engineered drainage system connecting it to the Tiwanaku River and ultimately to Lake Titicaca. Associated with the Akapana are four temples—the

semi-subterranean, the Kalasasaya, the Putuni, and the Kheri Kala. Like the other platform mounds within Tiwanaku, it has a central sunken court. The Akapana is axially linked to the Kalasasaya—a large, terraced platform (measuring 120 by 130 meters) with a megalithic staircase on the south centered on the Portal of the Sun, and a monumental stone sculpture, the so-called Ponce Monolith. The Kalasasaya had its own central sunken court. On the morning of the spring equinox, a sunbeam bisects the semi-subterranean temple and appears in the center of the Kalasasaya's staircase. But how exactly these buildings functioned as astronomical observatories is unknown. In front of the northwest corner of the Kalasasaya is a small structure known as Chunchukala, which has a hole in one of its walls similar to the shape of a human ear, which permits one to hear sounds that are made far away. This "sound amplifier" must have something to do with the oracular nature of the ceremonies performed here.

10.79 Megalithic entrance to the Kalasasaya Mound, near La Paz, Bolivia

Even more spectacular is Puma Punku ("Puma Door," ca. 536–600 CE), which was built to the southeast. It is an earthen platform mound with three levels of stone-lined terraces and retaining walls. Its walls are thought to have been adorned with polished metal plaques, brightly colored ceramics, and fabric ornamentation. One ascends to the top terrace through a series of huge gates. The top, as at the Akapana, has a sunken courtyard with a temple overlooking it, though its final form is not fully known. The stonework is some of the best in the world, prompting many discussions about the techniques used to cut and polish the stone. One stone slab measures 7.81 meters in length and weighs 131 metric tons. There are many such slabs with precisely cut niches and revetments.

This great city and its temples were abandoned rather abruptly some time around 1000 CE. Scholars speculate that an extended drought led to political instability. Puma Punku was abandoned before it was finished.

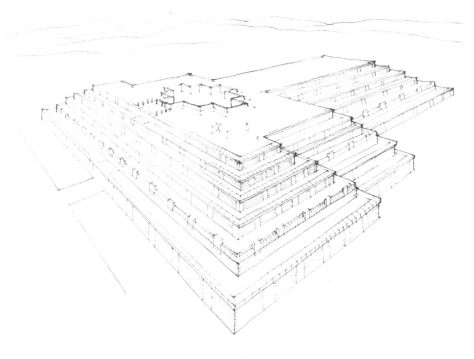

10.80 The Akapana, the main temple of Tiwanaku, near La Paz, Bolivia

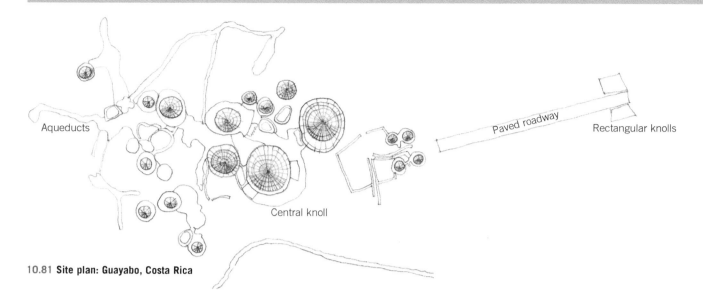

10.81 Site plan: Guayabo, Costa Rica

Labels: Aqueducts · Paved roadway · Rectangular knolls · Central knoll

QUIRIGUA

Cauac Sky became king of Quirigua in 725 CE, while it was still a part of the state of Copán, but after he defeated and captured Eighteen Rabbit, king of Copán, in 738 CE, Quirigua became independent. The city, which rests in the floodplains of the Motagua River, has at its core a gigantic rectangular plaza, oriented north-south and studded with some of the largest Mayan stelae and monoliths ever discovered. Its main platform mounds and palace group are clustered at its south end. A freestanding, solitary pyramid sits off-center at one end of the great plaza; its other side lines up with a much smaller, better defined plaza, with a ball court in its center. A monumental flight of stairs at the southern edge of this ball court plaza leads to the main set of terraces and platform mounds that support the principal palaces. The Jade Sky Palace at the southernmost and highest point of the complex lines up on axis with the great plaza, forming its visual terminus, although access to it is carefully regulated. Both the palaces front their own private raised plaza, which they share with another, the so-called Palace 1B5. The embankments and shape of the western edge of the acropolis indicate that the Motagua may have flowed along its edge at one time, so that the palaces would have directly overlooked the river.

GUAYABO

South of Mexico, in Costa Rica, archaeologists have uncovered traces of a significant urban settlement near the town of Guayabo. Human occupation of the site dates back to 1000 BCE, but the most recent studies reveal that Guayabo reached its peak from 300 to 700 CE. The culture was influenced by the Mayan's and belongs to the southernmost edge of what is known as Mesoamerica. The city consisted of large, conical wood-and-thatch houses with several internal stories built on stone foundations. Paved roads connected the city to the fields and the aqueducts that brought water into the city center.

10.82 Pictorial view of Guayabo

1000 CE

11.1 **Courtyard of a caravanserai**

INTRODUCTION

The difference in Africa and Eurasia between 800 and 1200 CE is huge. By 1200, a band of economic wealth had spread from Japan in the east to Spain in the west and from Sweden in the north to Ghana and Ethiopia in the south, with even the east coast of Africa as far south as Zimbabwe becoming connected to the great continuum of trade. Old-wealth worlds, like those of south China, India, and Constantinople, were now linked to the new-wealth worlds of the Japanese, the Khmer, and the Islamic caliphates. Added to this were emerging-wealth worlds like those associated with Ghana, central Europe, and the Vikings. Even the remote islands of Hawaii had now been settled by intrepid oceangoing people. This vast realm of connectivity would separate urban and village cultures from the residual pockets of First Society people and the haves from the have-nots for centuries, a division that would be markedly transformed only in the modern era.

The critical element in this story is the competition between the traditional, land-based route that went through Afghanistan and the Taklamakan Desert and the southern, sea-based route, the importance of which had begun to be apparent already in the 7th century. On the ocean, ships could carry well-calibrated loads, tariffs could be levied at docks, and state bureaucracies could organize labor and production. To transport goods along the northern route was a riskier operation. Vast stretches went through unclaimed or lawless territories. Foods could perish in the heat; delicate porcelain objects could shatter when repeatedly loaded and unloaded. Furthermore, as goods moved, their price increased incrementally but steadily as they passed from hand to hand. Inner Asia, apart from some mined resources, carpets, and leather goods, had little to offer as trade. For these and other reasons, the southern route, with its cargos of lumber, rice, sugar, pepper, and cinnamon, had begun to take precedent over the traditional, land-based route. The world was also undergoing a perceptible warming period. In some areas this meant long growing seasons, but in Inner Asia it meant the drying out of wells and streams, making cross-continental travel difficult. The consequences were visible at Chang'an. In 904, the T'ang dynasty abandoned the once-great city and forced its million or so residents to move to Luoyang, the new capital on the east coast. The T'ang dynasty itself would come to an end in 907.

The steppe region between the 6th and 10th centuries was in continual flux as one nomadic culture after another tried to assert control over the fabled Silk Route. In the 10th century, the area saw the arrival of various Turkish tribes from Inner Asia, the first of which created the Ghaznavid dynasty (977–1186), which was ruled by a clan of Turkish Sunni Islamic generals who wrested

11.2 Step well, India

control of the region from the Zoroastrian Sassanians. With their cousins now ruling in Persia, the Turks to the north began to move south into the region in several waves over the next century, building up to the moment when Seljuk converted to Islam around 985 and headed south to defeat the Ghaznavids and take over Persia, adopting its cultural perspectives. The newly formed Seljuk Empire soon controlled a vast area stretching from the Hindu Kush to eastern Anatolia and from Central Asia to Persian Gulf. All told, the impact of the various Turkish tribes was profound, for they had accomplished a rather important geopolitical mission, relinking the economy of the Indianized world with the economy of the Islamic world. In doing this, they added security to the northern routes across the steppe. Once this great economic continuum had been established, it would remain Africa's and Eurasia's prime economic engine until the age of colonialism made it obsolete.

More quickly than one could imagine, areas peripheral to this continuum were pulled into its orbit. Tibet was now an independent region linking India and China. The Vikings set up camp on the Caspian Sea, linking the east-west trade with their networks to Russia, Scandinavia, and other parts of Europe, making the Normans the envy of all the Europeans. The port of Pisa was bustling with trade from Cairo. For the Europeans it was indeed a breakthrough moment. And in Africa, trade routes manned by new formations of camel-centric cultures were forged across the desert to Ghana for its salt and gold.

The Seljuks were in a way the right people at the right time with Isfahan, almost at the geographical center of this expanding universe, rising to be one of the great entrepôt cities of all time. They founded the Great Mosque of Isfahan, rebuilding an earlier mosque and creating, in fact, a new typology, the four-*iwan* mosque, so called because its

vast central courtyard was faced on all sides on axis by a large open space, the *iwan*, roofed by elaborate *muqarna* vaults with their complex geometric faceting. The building's columns, vaults, and walls are made almost entirely of brick. When the Seljuks arrived in Anatolia, however, they began to use stone, following the local tradition of advanced stonework. With Konya as their new capital, the Seljuks built hundreds of caravanserai to facilitate trade. Sultan Han, not too far from Konya, was particularly elaborate. With a single, richly ornamented entrance, it was a place where caravans could be refurbished, animals rested, and drivers afforded a good rest and haircut. From the 11th to the 13th centuries, hundreds of caravanserai were built or refurbished, significantly improving the flow of trade.

India in this period, prospering as it had for centuries because of its trade to the east, saw the rise of numerous religious temple institutions, the intensification of agriculture, and the expansion of commercial activities and networks. The Rajputs rose to prominence in the northern part of the subcontinent, and the Cholas in the south. The Cholas became the first and really the only Indian empire with a strong naval presence, sending ships to Malaysia and Indonesia to assert their regional dominance. They began to build a new capital city, Gangaikonda Cholapuram, of which little remains today apart from an impressively scaled Shiva temple. As for the Rajputs, their sumptuous palaces were often graced by elaborate step wells, where the ladies of the court could gather in the cool shade. One of the most impressive was Rani-ni-Vav (ca. 1050) at Anhilwara (modern-day Patan), Gujarat, India. It was a vast, sunken, paradisal retreat. To the south, the Chandela Rajputs produced a remarkable set of temples dedicated to the Tantric school of Hinduism. The Tantric practitioner seeks to use prana (energy flowing through the universe, including one's body) to attain goals that may be spiritual, material, or both. This brand of Hinduism had developed around 300 CE. Of the over eighty-five temples that were built by the Chandelas, only about twenty-five now stand in a reasonable state of preservation, scattered over an area of about 20 square kilometers. The Lakshmana Temple and the nearby Kandariya Mahadeva Temple (1050) are the most refined. They rest on a high terrace and are accessed by an axial staircase that leads to an elevated interior floor with balconies. Their external surfaces portray tantric practice, including the sex acts that were seen as a natural way to access the supra-mundane through the mundane.

Jainism was another important subsect of Hinduism, its origins dating back to about the 5th century BCE. It prescribes a path of nonviolence toward all living beings and emphasizes spiritual independence and equality between all forms of life. Jains make considerable efforts in everyday life not to injure plants any more than necessary. Of their numerous temples, the Vimal Vasahi Temple (1031) on Mt. Abu is a masterpiece, made completely out of white marble. The ceilings feature engraved designs of lotus buds, petals, flowers, and scenes from Jain and Hindu mythology. In the sacred city of

Bhubaneswar, the rulers built a similarly refined temple, the Lingaraj. *Lingaraj* means "King of Lingam," a being worshipped by devotees of both Shiva and Vishnu. In Sri Lanka, King Vijayabahu I, who defeated the Chola invaders in 1070 and reunited the country, declared Polonnaruwa the capital city and began a major reworking of it. By the 12th century trade and agriculture were flourishing, with advanced irrigation systems being developed to provide water during the dry season.

Farther east along the trade routes is the land of the Khmer. Hariharalaya (known now more colloquially as Angkor) had by this time become nothing less than a boomtown—a religious rice-growing industrial complex—with new city districts being built, along with bold new temples, to accommodate a population approaching a million. The temples at the core of all this include Phnom Bakheng (900), Pre Rup (960), Banteay Srei (967), and Phimeanakas (980). Each represented an economic unit unto itself. The Angkorites fully understood their geopolitical situation. They expanded their power northward to connect to China and to better control access to the overland trade routes.

In China, given the restless expansion of the northern steppe cultures, the T'ang gave way to the Song dynasty (960–1279), who retreated south of the Yangtze River to establish a capital at Lin'an (now Hangzhou). Soon, Hangzhou rose from a middling city of only regional importance to become one of the world's largest and most populous cities. Arab, Persian, and Korean merchants lived there. The Chinese also underwent a population boom, with the population doubling during the 10th and 11th centuries. This growth came through expanded rice cultivation in central and southern China, which was developed to offset imported rice from Southeast Asia. With Buddhism repressed, imperially sanctioned temples reemerged, drawing on ancient animistic belief systems; one of these was the Sage Mother Hall (ca. 980–1100), built around a sacred spring. Buddhist pagoda towers continued to be built, but in the countryside rather than within a city's walls, largely to avoid competition with the attempt by the imperial authorities to impose their cosmic-derived ideology on the city.

To the north, the new Mongolian-based overlords did not lack architectural ambition. On the contrary, the Liao dynasty (907–1125) employed captured carpenters to build the impressive Yingxian Timber Pagoda (1056), also known as Mu-Ta, meaning "Timber Pagoda." Since timber buildings are so vulnerable to the vicissitudes of time, this building, one of the oldest surviving in China, gives us valuable insight into a structure built completely without nails.

The Mongolianization of northern China secured Buddhism in this area and strengthened its position in Korea and Japan, where Buddhism underwent yet another of its numerous transformations. Less a religion than a path to religion, Buddhism tolerates and even welcomes different experiments in making that path possible. One of these is known as Pure Land and is based on the premise that the way to let go of the worries of daily life is to imagine a land of beauty that surpasses all other realms. Since a devotee did not need to live in meditative isolation, Pure Land appealed to a more general public. In China, Pure Land practices never became a stand-alone sect, but in Japan, Pure Land came to exist independently as one of several sects. The earliest surviving example of a temple dedicated to this new sect is the Phoenix Hall (Byodo-in) in Kyoto. Unlike a Christian church, where images of paradise might be painted on the walls, or an Islamic garden, where paradise was imagined through poetic inscriptions, here paradise was presented in situ, with the building itself, reflected in a pond, being the focus of meditation. The Phoenix Hall can be compared with Kandariya Mahadeva Temple: Both reach out to people who are not priests or ritual experts. Both are buildings that bring the supplicant past the everyday into a higher realm through meditation and ritual practices. For both, the building serves not just as a site of ritual but as a visualization for meditation.

Meanwhile, Constantinople had become the largest city in Europe, with a population of about a half a million. To its north, the conversion of the Bulgarians, Serbs, and Rus to Orthodox Christianity brought some stabilization to the restless area, even though it did not stop a major Rus attack on Constantinople in 941, probably over trading rights; the Rus used a navy of ten thousand

11.3 **Sage Mother Hall, Jinci Temple, Taiyuan, China**

vessels to devastate the Asiatic shore of the Bosporus. But Islamic armies controlled the Byzantine's eastern border, and Islamic navies controlled much of the Mediterranean. Adding to the increased isolation of the Byzantines was the final separation of the eastern and western churches in 1054. From then on, the Christian church had two distinctly different rules of authority, one emanating from Rome and the other from Constantinople. One of the few major architectural commissions of the time was the church of Christ Pantokrator ("Ruler of All," ca. 1120, now the Zeyrek Mosque) that was commissioned by a Byzantine empress. It had a library and a sixty-bed hospital, and was home to over eighty monks. But if the destiny of the Byzantines was on a downward slope, the Russians to the north were in expansion mode. Now almost completely Christianized, they linked the Silk Route with northern Europe and Scandinavia.

Kievan Rus had by now established itself as an important regional powerhouse. Several churches were built, such as the Cathedral of St. Sophia, the Holy Wisdom of God in Novgorod, and the Church of the Tithes or Church of the Dormition of the Virgin (ca. 990) in Kiev.

Farther south, in the Islamic world, were the Fatimids, who belonged to the Ismaili branch of Shi'ism and claimed to be descended from Fatima bint Muhammed, the daughter of the prophet Mohammed. In 909, the Fatimids established the Tunisian city of Mahdia as their capital, and when they conquered Egypt in 969 they established Cairo as the capital. They were known for their exquisite arts; there are many surviving traces of Fatimid architecture, the defining example being the Al-Azhar Mosque (972) and its associated university. It was the first university in the East and perhaps the oldest in history. The Fatimids used it for official

pronouncements and court sessions. Initially built as a prayer hall with five aisles and a modest central courtyard, the mosque has been expanded multiple times. Though none of the original minarets or domes has survived, the plan, despite the later additions, is unmistakable. It was a rectangular box with a doorway in each of the walls other than the *quibla* wall. The columns were taken from various Roman or Byzantine-era ruins. The plan features an axial hallway that cuts through the grid in front of the *quibla*, thus giving it special prominence in the plan.

To the east, along the Mediterranean, the Almoravids, a Berber Sunni dynasty from Morocco, formed an empire in the 11th century, founding their capital at Marrakech in 1062. The Almoravids were crucial in maintaining Islamic control over southern Spain when they defeated a coalition of the Christian, Castilian, and Aragonese armies at the Battle of Sagrajas. This enabled them

11.4 **Speyer Cathedral, Speyer, Germany**

to control an empire that stretched 2,000 kilometers north to south. Their rule was relatively short-lived. They failed to quell the Masmuda-led rebellion initiated by Ibn Tumart that led to the rise of the Almohads. The Almohads—who were also Sunni—came from Tin Mal, a village that became the spiritual capital and the artistic center of the Almohad Empire.

For the first time since the fall of the Roman Empire, Europe was being connected to global horizons. The region was the equivalent of what today would be called a developing area. The Saracens had been driven beyond the Pyrenees; the Slavs had been forced back to the Oder River; the Magyars had been expelled from Germany and Italy; Danes had become Christians. With the relative relief, regional lords surfaced who established themselves and claimed their own sovereignty. Abbeys, usually in remote locations, were still important political sites,

such as the Abbey of Sant'Antimo, begun before 1118 just south of Siena. More than just an abbey, it was an institution that had authority over thirty-eight churches, from Pisa to Grosseto, and controlled about a thousand farm estates throughout Tuscany. Built of white stone, it was sited in a field purposefully planted with tarragon, an herb that is rare in Italy but frequently used in French cuisine, and as such an indicator of the building's connections to Charlemagne. But the architecture of Sant'Antimo was increasingly a thing of the past. Boxy churches with small windows, primitive stonemasonry, and wooden-beamed ceilings were giving way to more ambitious designs. The transition began with the Ottonians in Germany. They sought to define themselves as extending the imperial lineage of Constantine and Justinian. They even brought in artisans from Constantinople, and the results show themselves at the Church of St. Michael

(ca. 1010) in Hildesheim, made of cleanly dressed stone. The building was up the hill of the nearby market town and was indicative of a closer relationship between the Church and daily life. The style of building, with its clearly legible geometries and volumes, including tube-like towers, is known as Romanesque, largely because it derives consciously from the Roman basilica with naves, side aisles, and wood roofs.

In Italy, the Tuscan region, profiting from the flow of goods brought to the Mediterranean by Islamic traders, was at the start of a building boom, with the port city of Pisa leading the way. Pisa built a cathedral (1063–1180), a large baptistery (1152–1363) and a tower, the famous Leaning Tower of Pisa (1173–1372), all of which was rounded off with the addition of the Campo Santo, also known as Camposanto Monumentale ("monumental cemetery"), an expansive, rectangular cloister (begun in

1278) that is said to have been built on a shipload of sacred soil taken from Golgotha, Israel, and brought back to Pisa from the Fourth Crusade. The ensemble was one of the great religious sites in Europe at the time. The building was paid for by the spoils taken from Mahdia, a Tunisian city that was the capital of a regional Islamic power. It was attacked by Pisa and its allies and then forced to pay a high ransom—a sign of the growing dominance of Christian powers in the Mediterranean.

One can compare Pisa with St Mark's Basilica in Venice that was consecrated in 1084. The latter is clearly Byzantine in conception, with its great billowing vaults covered with golden mosaics. The Cathedral of Pisa is "Latin" in conception, essentially copying the basilica model that came out Rome with columns running down the aisles. Whereas St. Mark's was a brick building and more interior than exterior, the buildings at Pisa were surfaced all around with shimmering white marble ornamented with thin horizontal bands of black stone. Such revetment has a tradition that goes back to Roman times, and indeed, some of the stones were scavenged from Roman-era ruins. It is clear that the patrons wanted a building that in its extravagant exterior

11.5 Pueblo Bonito

finish would herald itself as a freestanding monument of their success.

The Romanesque style of St. Michael and the Cathedral of Pisa was, however, being creatively transformed in Germany and France, as is already visible at Speyer Cathedral (consecrated in 1061). There we see a building that is not only taller but has a whole new interior organization. Instead of the nave being a wall held up as a variation of columns or arches, here the piers have partially melded into the wall. On the surface of the pier, two columns are placed on top of each other, almost as if they were a single very tall column. The top of the column connects directly to a rib of the vaulted ceiling that then connects to a

vertical pier on the other side of the nave. The eye could move up across and down in a single sweep. The ancient and venerable prototype of post and beam has now been replaced by an aesthetic of a completely different order. The idea of a column as an independent architectural entity would only make its return in Europe only with the Renaissance. The Normans in England made particularly important contributions. They had left northern France to conquer England and then sailed around Spain to conquer southern Italy and Sicily. There, they encountered Arab architects and Byzantine artisans. The impact is clearly evident in the difference between the cathedral at Cefalu (1131) and the later cathedral at Monreale. The former is a veritable fortress with a dark and gloomy interior. The Cathedral of Monreale (1174–85), commissioned by Henry II (r. 1154–89), has an interior with golden mosaics that completely cover the walls of the nave, aisles, transept, and apse. The mosaic cycle is second only to the Hagia Sophia in size, and much better preserved. In the apse, a magnificent portrait of Christ Pantocrator ("Ruler of All") gestures in blessing and gazes serenely off to one side. The Normans brought their Arab craftsmen back to England, and quickly their architecture began to transform, as can be seen in Durham and Canterbury Cathedrals. At the piers, what had been two columns placed one on top of the other at Speyer now becomes a single, tube-like column rising from the floor to the base of the vault. The result was a revolution of sensibilities that was to contribute to the emergence of the Gothic style.

In the Yucatán Peninsula the Mayan civilization was at its height. In the valley of Oaxaca the Zapotecs continued to build new cities, moving their political center from Monte Albán (ca. 700 BCE–700 CE) to Mitla (ca. 700–1400 CE), transforming the fortified village into a major religious and economic hub. The city was still being expanded when the Spaniards arrived and destroyed it in the 16th century. To the north, the Toltecs were in the process of building a powerful new dynasty destined to define the form and shape of the cultures that the Spanish conquistadors encountered five hundred years later. But this was not happening in isolation. Trade with the Southwest Puebloans was now well established, in particular because of the turquoise mines in their territory. Turquoise, not readily available in Mexico, was a prized commodity, as it was used for sacred masks and other ritual objects. The Puebloans, in the arid landscapes of the Southwest, had developed a thriving agricultural communal lifestyle, with people living in dwellings made of stone and mortar that allowed for two-story construction. Settlements had round, belowground kivas that were used for ceremonial purposes. Some kivas were as large as 17 meters in diameter. The Puebloans were not centralized into kingships as the Mayans were, but constituted an association of clans unified around powerful communal and seasonal activities, at the core of which was Chaco Canyon. Roughly 9 kilometers long, it contained several ceremonial sites, though how they functioned individually and as a group is not known. The complex contained the largest buildings in North America until the 19th century. Meanwhile, Peruvians were undergoing transition; the kingdoms of Wari and Tiwanaku had died out, to be replaced by dozens of smaller regional powers, among which were the Chimú, with their capital at the city of Chan Chan, a large adobe city in the Moche Valley. The culture arose around 900 CE in roughly the same territory where the Mochica had existed centuries before. The city is composed of nine independently walled citadels that housed the elite and their ceremonial rooms, burial chambers, temples, and reservoirs. Most of the city's population—artisans and farmers—lived outside the quadrangles in modest quarters of less durable construction. As with most Peruvian cities, it was at the center of a vast network of canals that irrigated the surrounding land.

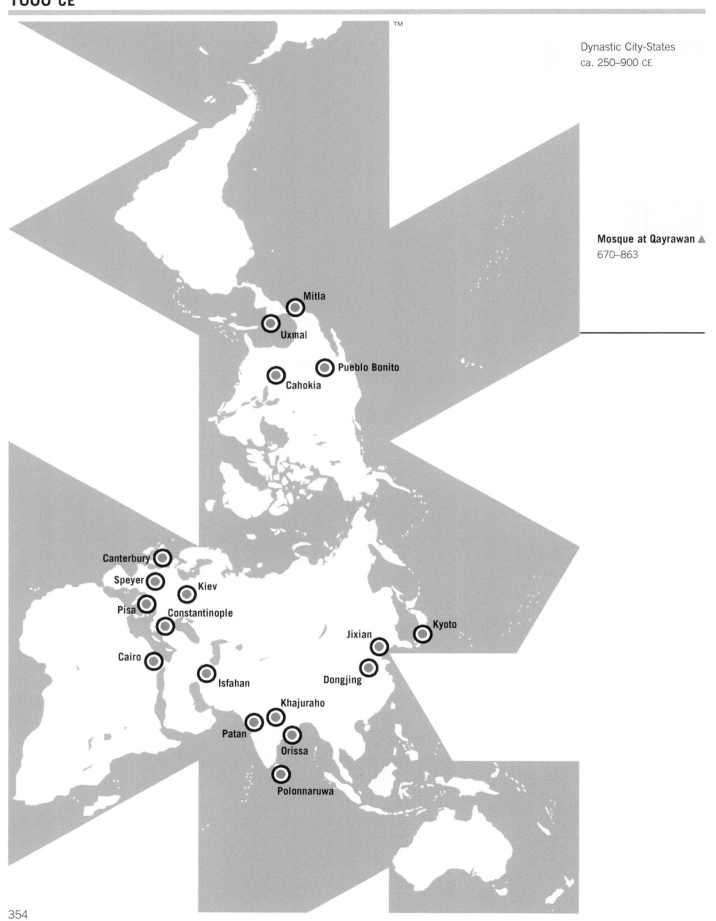

Dynastic City-States
ca. 250–900 CE

Mosque at Qayrawan ▲
670–863

Mitla

Uxmal

Pueblo Bonito

Cahokia

Canterbury

Speyer

Kiev

Pisa

Constantinople

Cairo

Isfahan

Jixian

Kyoto

Dongjing

Khajuraho

Patan

Orissa

Polonnaruwa

Toltec-Chichén City-State
ca. 1000–1200

▲ Mitla   ▲ Uxmal
750–1521   800–1000

Pueblo Cultures   Mississippian Cultures
ca. 600–1600   ca. 800–1600

▲ Cahokia   ▲ Pueblo Bonito   ▲ Serpent Mound
ca. 700–1300   Begun 920   ca. 1060

Fatimid Caliphate   Seljuk Empire
969–1171   1037–1157

▲ Great Mosque of Isfahan   ▲ Al-Azhar Mosque   ▲ Mosque of Tinmal   Sultan Han ▶
8th to 16th centuries   970–72 CE   1153–54   1229

---

800 CE   **1000 CE**   **1200 CE**

South Asia: Rise of regional states
ca. 500–1300

▲ Rajarajeshwara Temple   ▲ Sun Temple at Modhera   ▲ Lingaraja Temple
Late 10th century   1022–27   ca. 1100

Lakshamana Temple ▲   ▲ Khandariya Mahadeva Temple   ▲ Jain Temples on Mt. Abu
ca. 950   1000–1025   10th to 16th centuries

▲ Parakramabahu Palace
12th century

T'ang Dynasty   Northern Song Dynasty   Southern Song Dynasty
618–906 CE   960–1127   1127–1279

▲ Dulesi Monastery   ▲ Iron Pagoda
ca. 984   1049   ▲ Mu-Ta Yingxian Timber Pagoda

Japan: Late Heian Period   Byodo-in ▲   1056
ca. 900–1185   1053

Byzantine Empire
330–1453

Cathedral of Ani ▲ ▲ Sanahin   ▲ Church of Christ Pantokrator
989–1001   10th to 13th centuries   1118–43

Kievan Russia   ▲ Church of the Tithe
ca. 860–1240   989–96 CE

Ottonian Dynasty
936–1024

St. Michael in Hildesheim ▲   ▲ Speyer Cathedral   ▲ Abbey Church of St. Foy
1001–33   1040–1137   Begun 1050

Norman rule in England   ▲ Canterbury Cathedral   ▲ Durham Cathedral
1066–1154   1042–1185   1093–1133

Italian City-States
Late 11th to early 16th centuries

▲ Cathedral of Pisa   Baptistery of Parma ▲
1063–1180   1196–1270

▲ Santiago de Compostela
1075–1128

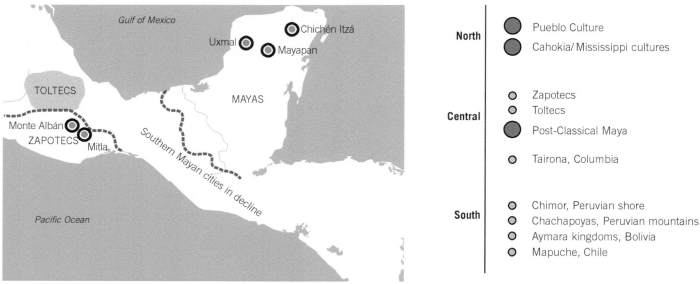

11.6 **Urbanization of the Americas, ca. 1000 CE**

11.7 **Trade in the Americas, ca. 1000 CE**

North
- Pueblo Culture
- Cahokia/Mississippi cultures

Central
- Zapotecs
- Toltecs
- Post-Classical Maya
- Tairona, Columbia

South
- Chimor, Peruvian shore
- Chachapoyas, Peruvian mountains
- Aymara kingdoms, Bolivia
- Mapuche, Chile

MAYAN UXMAL

Uxmal was one of several Mayan city-states competing for territory, but by 900 CE it had become the regional capital and most likely the largest of the Mayan cities. A network of stone roadways, called *sakbehoob*, connected Uxmal to Nohpat and Kabah. Chichén Itzá was a major ally. Uxmal's elite lived in a sprawling palace complex located on the area's highest ground. A stone wall with regularly spaced openings enclosed the area. At the southern end of the complex, built into a small mound, was the main platform mound, wedged between a gigantic platform with the so-called Governor's Palace to its east and a series of rectangular courts to its west. The platform mound faced north, its broad stairs visible from a great distance. The northern edge of the palace complex was dominated by a huge quadrangular palace, called the Nunnery (890–915 CE). To its immediate east, the largest structure, a steep platform mound with a rare oval-shaped base, was the so-called Temple of the Magician. Scores of other buildings, arranged in quadrangles of various size and shape, were distributed through the complex; most were residential units, and a few were platform mounds. Similar structures outside the wall were dispersed across a much larger urban residential area. The currently used

names for many of the structures were coined by the conquering Spanish and do not indicate the actual functions of the buildings.

Chan-Chaak-K'ak'nal-Ajaw (9th century), who ruled the city, commissioned the Governor's Palace, the Nunnery quadrangle, and very likely a rebuilding of the Temple of the Magician. The latter, originally built in the 6th century, was reconstructed at least four times. While the exact reasons for its unusual shape are still uncertain, its dramatic profile dominates the setting, contrasting with the orthogonal geometries of the Governor's Palace and the Nunnery quadrangle. Its limestone core was originally covered with smooth plaster and painted red with accents in blue, yellow, and black.

North group

Nunnery

Temple of the Magician

Cemetery group

Ball court

Governor's Palace

Great Pyramid

0   200 m

Pyramid of the Old Woman

11.8 **Uxmal palace complex, Mexico**

11.9 Temple of the Magician, Uxmal

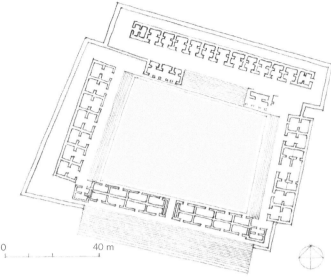

0   40 m

11.10 Plan: The Nunnery quadrangle at Uxmal

The Governor's Palace, standing as a clearly defined entity in its own right, was both the royal residence and a sort of council house. Its huge terrace was linked to the main platform mound at the corner, signifying their continuity. Although the platform was accessible only from the west, from the middle of the complex the main structure of the Governor's Palace, an astonishing 100-meter-long building, faced east, away from the center, and overlooked a distant vista from across a vast platform. The rising sun would have brightly illuminated its twenty-four rooms, which were clustered into three compartments. Narrow passages with steep triangular roofs separated them. Each room was a set of two, one opening onto the front, and the other behind it, against a blank back wall. The broad frieze on the Governor's Palace is its chief glory. Made from over twenty thousand individual stones depicting serpents, thatched huts, masks of the rain god Chak, human busts, and geometrical motifs, the frieze is a kaleidoscope of Mayan mythology. A gigantic stone sculpture above the main entrance shows Lord Chak on a throne surrounded by serpents. The friezes on the four buildings of the Nunnery quadrangle together depict the Mayan cosmography, or the order of the universe as conceived by the Uxmal. The southern building—also known as the *itzam nah*, or "conjuring house"—bears the icons of the Lords of Xibalba, the underworld.

The south building of the Nunnery quadrangle aligns axially with the ball court, the symbolic gate to Xibalba. The eastern frieze depicts the cyclic themes of world creation, while the western frieze depicts scenes of war, sacrifice, death, and rebirth. Together, the eastern and western friezes symbolize the diurnal and annual journeys, or "lives," of the sun, and its compact with the earth, inhabited by humans. The northern building, erected on the highest platform of the quadrangle, has a frieze that depicts celestial figures symbolic of the world of "heaven." In the middle of the quadrangle stood a stone column, representing the *wakaj-chan*, or "world tree," and an altar representing the first stone of the cosmic hearth.

11.11 Ball court at Uxmal

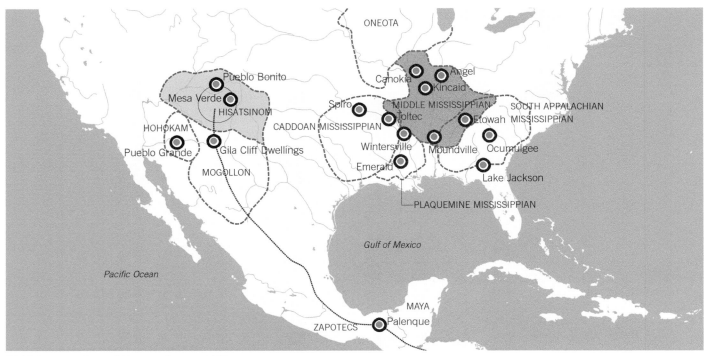

11.12 **North America and Mesoamerica, ca. 1000 CE**

CAHOKIA

By the 11th century, Hopewell Culture cities had fallen on hard times. The new power centers were now farther west along the Mississippi River. This change coincided with the emergence of a chiefdom society that adopted a comparatively large-scale, intensive, maize-based agriculture. It had taken about a thousand years for corn cultivation to make it this far north, and its impact was quite dramatic. For the first time there is a clear settlement hierarchy and the construction of truncated pyramid mounds, with temples or burial buildings atop such mounds. Soon a network of larger and smaller city cultures developed in a large triangular area down the Mississippi River at its western edge and eastward into Georgia along other rivers.

One of the most important of the new cities was Cahokia (ca. 700–1300). Its residents benefited from the Mississippi's alluvial deposits as well as from the trade that brought copper from the upper Great Lakes, mica from the southern Appalachians, and seashells from the Gulf of Mexico. Twenty thousand people lived in Cahokia at its peak in the 12th century, making it the largest city north of Mexico.

At the center of its vast religious precinct was the so-called Monks Mound. Begun around 1000 CE, it was surrounded by terraces and smaller mounds roughly on axis. It was a huge mound—30 meters high, 291 meters long, and 236 meters wide—made by carrying tons of earth a basketful at a time. The Cahokians, who seemed to have

known of Central American advances in astronomy, built several calendrical circles with posts of red cedar. A circle of 24 posts was enlarged to one of 36, then to one of 48, and finally to one of 60. Their last and largest circle was built to an arc of only 12 posts, but if completed, it would have had 72 posts. At the equinoxes, the post marking

11.13 **Aerial view: Cahokia, near St. Louis, Missouri**

sunrise, due east, aligns perfectly with the front of Monks Mound. Because the city was located in the Mississippi floodplain and not on the surrounding bluffs, the city was designed to be partially flooded during the spring flood season. It is thought that elaborate ceremonies were conducted at that time with people arriving from up and down the Mississippi. But whether the city was controlled by a single chieftain-priest or was shared by several groups is not known. The city was abandoned in the 15th century. Overhunting, environmental degradation because of the overplanting of corn, and social conflict may have all played a part. Whereas Mississippi cultures in Ohio faltered, they continued to thrive farther south in Georgia and Alabama until the arrival of the Europeans.

SERPENT MOUND

In Ohio, where there had once been the Hopewell Culture, a new and more modest culture emerged, known by archaeologists as the Fort Ancient Culture (1000–1650). Settlements composed of circular and rectangular homes constructed of twigs and thatch and situated around an open plaza were enclosed by stockades, suggesting an increase in the level of conflict that perhaps accounted for the breakdown of the Hopewell Culture. Settlements were rarely permanent, usually shifting to a new location after one or two generations when the resources surrounding the village were exhausted. The diet was composed mainly of maize, squash, and beans, supplemented by hunting and fishing in nearby forests and rivers.

Though this culture was a step down from Hopewell Culture, it nonetheless managed to construct some remarkable earthworks, including Serpent Mound (ca. 1060), in Adams County, Ohio. The mound consists of a low berm made of stones and compacted clay placed on a promontory that rises 30 meters over a small river. Measured along its coils and curves, it stretches 400 meters. The head of the serpent was placed at the crest of the bluff. Several theories have been proposed as to the meaning of the mound. For some American tribes, the serpent was considered evil, but for others, it was thought of as beneficial. In all cases, however, the snake was considered a potent force. (The Hopi snake dance was used principally as a prayer for rain.) Astrological alignments have been proposed, and indeed, the snake's head is aligned to the summer solstice and the various curves to other celestial events. The village was located across the river from the mound.

11.14 **Serpent Mound, Adams County, Ohio**

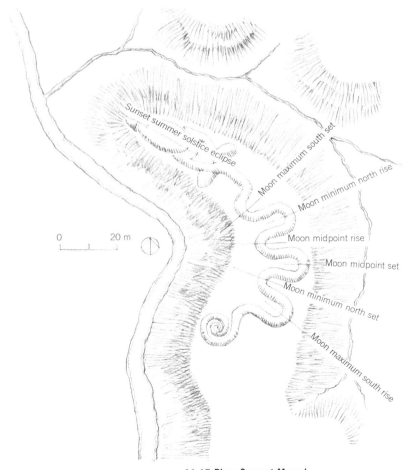

11.15 **Plan: Serpent Mound**

PUEBLO BONITO

Modern borders encourage viewing the ruins of the southwestern United States separately from those of Mesoamerica. In reality, the settlements in places such as Chaco Canyon and Mesa Verde made up the northern frontier of the Mesoamerican world and were not separated from its influence. However, because of their unique climatic circumstances, the Puebloans developed a very self-defined culture. By 600 CE, the area came to be occupied by three distinct groups: the Hisatsinom (also called Anasazi) to the north and the Mogollon and Hohokam to the south, the latter seemingly having originally been Mayas. They had begun to change from a migratory farming culture to a sedentary one. One of the reasons for the change was the adoption of corn, not just as a food but as a principal deity. The Puebloans integrated corn with a range of local plants that they also cultivated. The result was a rapid increase in population beginning around 700 CE due to improved weather conditions and more copious rainfall—the dry and arid conditions of today were not those of the 9th century. By 1100, there were twelve major Pueblo cities and hundreds of small clutches of houses—one of the most impressive urban structures north of Mexico, bespeaking a high level of social organization.

One of these groups has traditionally been known as Anasazi, but since that is a Navajo word meaning "ancient enemy," the Pueblo people prefer to use the Hopi word *Hisatsinom*, meaning "the old ones." What they called themselves is not exactly known. The largest Hisatsinom settlement was Pueblo Bonito (Spanish for "beautiful town"). Located beneath a massive cliff, part of which has since caved in, the city had a D-shaped plan, with masses of rooms and circular ceremonial structures called kivas surrounding two large plazas. The rows of rooms each rose one story before stepping back from the one below, giving the whole an impression of a terraced amphitheater. Indeed, it has been suggested that one of the city's functions was to provide a place for viewing ritual dancing.

11.16 **Pueblo Bonito, Chaco Canyon, New Mexico**

Kivas, a local building type with a very long history and broad distribution, were an essential part of the Hisatsinom culture and architecture. They originated as circular storehouses, often nothing more than deep-pit houses, plastered on the inside with smooth adobe. But they soon became semi-subterranean temples, serving as communal spaces for the performance and viewing of ritual dances. Each kiva was the province of a social unit, and there were several kivas in each village. They were only for men; women were allowed in only on special occasions. In Pueblo Bonito, among the regular-size kivas, were two that were over 18 meters across and that probably served the entire city. Though these kivas were built aboveground, the subterranean effect was maintained by constructing rooms all around and filling in any empty space with earth. Kivas were equipped with a central fireplace, a low masonry bench around the wall, and four wooden posts. Some kivas had an underfloor ventilating system and a subfloor vault to the west of the fireplace. Their flat roofs had a smoke hole in the center and served as an entrance by means of a ladder. The sandstone masonry walls at Pueblo Bonito consisted of a loose rubble center-faced on both sides with artfully placed sandstone bricks.

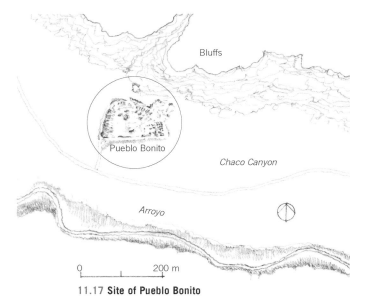

11.17 **Site of Pueblo Bonito**

Construction of Pueblo Bonito began in about 920 CE, and the city was modified over the course of three centuries. Early research attempted to relate its construction directly to more contemporary Pueblo architecture, whose structure reflects the social order of its inhabitants. The evidence, however, indicates that this was not the case at Pueblo Bonito. Nonetheless, its construction would have required a complex coordination of labor and materials. Tens of thousands of pine beams, used for wall supports and roof structures, came from a forest 90 kilometers away. Pueblo Bonito's overall orientation is north-south, which became typical of all structures erected by the Hisatsinom, but the architecture integrates the midpoint and extremes of the cycles of the sun and the moon into its layout. Though the highly disciplined architecture could suggest a strong hierarchical social order, the Hisatsinom are believed to have had a fairly egalitarian society. Pubelo Bonito was one of several large constructions in Chaca Canyon. Its purpose is not known for sure, but it is thought that the site was a ceremonial center for people who travelled from far afield for certain calendrical events, the canyon itself being a type of sacred site.

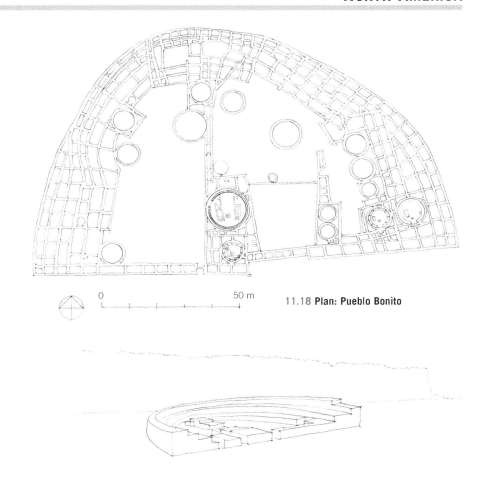

0   50 m

11.18 Plan: Pueblo Bonito

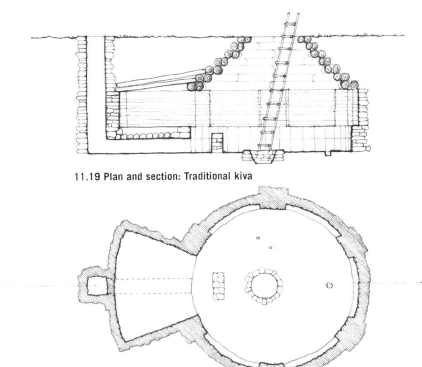

11.19 Plan and section: Traditional kiva

The Hohokam also soon began to design cities, such as Casa Grande (in Arizona, ca. 1100), having developed canals to bring water to their fields. Archaeologists have discovered hundreds of miles of these canals in the Gila River valley, as well as the Salt River valley of Phoenix and elsewhere. By the 13th century, long periods of drought brought that culture to an end and changed the social landscape of the region. They were replaced by the Pima and Tohono O'odham tribes. It was the Pimas who called their predecessors the Hohokam, meaning the "vanished ones."

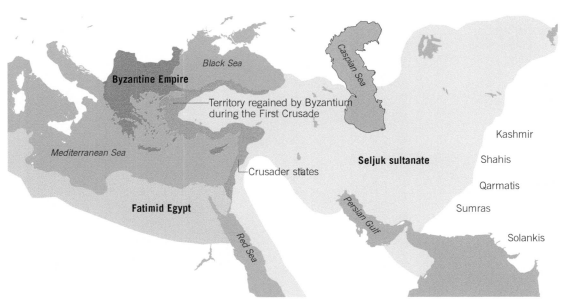

11.20 West Asia, ca. 1000 CE

SELJUK TURKS

Turks in the 10th century were a pastoral people living in Central Asia east of the Caspian Sea. Abandoning their homeland, they moved into Afghanistan and Iran. Accepting the faith of Islam along the way, they created a number of Turkish-Islamic states, one being the Ghaznavids, who settled in what is now western Afghanistan. Another tribe, the Seljuks (named after a tribal leader), drove further westward, into Iran, Syria, and eventually the ethnically diverse Anatolia, held nominally by the Byzantines. The Seljuks consolidated their power over eastern Anatolia in 1071; their presence was a major factor in bringing about the Crusades. Despite the problems with the Crusaders, the Seljuk period was one of relative calm, with Persia seeing one of its most prosperous periods.

The stability and success of the Seljuk regime was the achievement of the politically skilled Vizir Nizam al-Mulk, a cultured Persian, a brilliant administrator, and a significant political philosopher, whose *Book of Government, or, Rules for Kings* is a classic of Islamic literature. At its peak, the Seljuk Empire spanned a region from northern India to the Aegean Sea, allowing the ancient trade routes of Anatolia to be connected with those to China. The strengthening of the Silk Route not only brought in enormous wealth but also promoted the development of industries, like the manufacture of paper. Paper originally

had to be imported from China, but in the 8th century, it was being produced in Baghdad and Damascus and exported to Europe.

The Seljuks distinguished themselves from earlier Islamic societies by their strict military hierarchy and attendant financial and landholding prerogatives, which were closed to all but a few exceptional local recruits. The principal elements of their political program were the mosque; the madrasa (Arabic for "school"); the *ribats* and *khanqahs*, which were the Sufi lodgings; and the mausoleum, which commemorated their deeds.

The Seljuk architecture of Iran is characterized by elaborate brickwork and the development of the four-*iwan* plan. The Seljuk rulers in Anatolia used a vocabulary characterized primarily by stonework. Tiles were important decorative elements of Seljuk architecture. The technology for tile-making emerged out of a century-old tradition in Iran and Iraq, which was brought to Anatolia by the Seljuks. The tiles consisted of an underlying paste with a high silicate content, over which a thick mixture containing kaolin and feldspar was spread. Monochromatic tiles were used for fill and borders; others were designed as large custom-made plaques for a particular place in the composition.

During Seljuk times, textile and leather exports were also important, as they were shipped to both Europe and the East. Once a year there was a vast commercial fair called Yabanlu Pazan ("Bazaar of the Foreigners")

held for forty days not far from Kayseri, in the center of Anatolia, at a place where several caravan routes converged.

11.21 Seljuk design
Representations of the human form are banned in Islam, but images of birds and animals as well as sphinxes and centaurs—often linked to ancient totemic worship still prevalent in Anatolian lands—were frequently embedded in the composition of Seljuk art. Calligraphic inscriptions of Qur'anic verses were often used along the cornices or to frame portals.

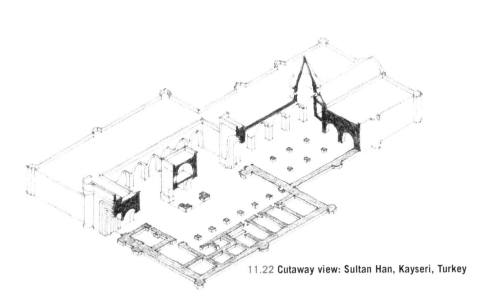

11.22 **Cutaway view: Sultan Han, Kayseri, Turkey**

11.23 **Entry portal, Sultan Han, Kayseri**

Sultan Han

Among the finest and most characteristic of Seljuk buildings are the caravansaries (derived from two Persian words meaning "a palace for caravans"), or *hans*, constructed during the 13th century to encourage trade throughout the empire; several dozen of them survive in good condition. These buildings, some 119 of which are known to have been erected, were made to shelter and protect not only the caravan drivers but also their camels, horses, and donkeys, along with their cargoes, and to provide needed services. Though caravan resting places had existed for centuries, this was the first large-scale systematization of mercantile transport across a desert. The services offered were free of charge for the first three days. One of the basic rules was that travelers who came to the establishment were to be treated equally, without regard to race, creed, or social status.

Though plans of caravansaries vary, they were typically square or rectangular buildings with thick stone walls and a large courtyard in the center surrounded by one- or two-story arcades; they accommodated bathing services, storage, a treasury, and stables, and had rooms for physicians, cooks, blacksmiths, and musicians as well as drivers. Though the exterior walls were plain and devoid of decoration, the portals were often elaborately embellished with bands of geometrical designs and Qur'anic inscriptions. At the center of the caravansary was usually a small mosque or prayer room, raised aboveground level on a stone platform. At the far end of the courtyard, opposite the main portal, was a large vaulted hall, usually with several aisles. Lit by narrow windows in the stone walls, it served as a shelter for goods and men during bad winter weather.

The Sultan Han, the grandest caravansary of all, covering 4,500 square meters, is west of Aksaray, a center in the Cappadocia region on the Konya Highway. Designed by a certain Muhammet of Syria, the doorway is particularly spectacular. Made of marble, the outer frame is covered with a delicate floral pattern. The tympanum over the door, which has an abstract geometrical pattern, looks as if it were eaten away by the encrustations of an open conically shaped stalactite vault. There are two parts to the design: a courtyard building and a hall. The courtyard building contained a bath and kitchen, and a room for special dignitaries. At its center was an unusual, square-shaped mosque. The large hall at the rear, entirely covered in vaults, consisted of one principal aisle and two symmetrical side aisles. There are windows at 4 meters high in each of the bays. The animals remained in the raised areas closest to the sidewalls; the middle was reserved for the travelers and communal functions. In this building we see the strong tradition of advanced stonemasonry that goes back to the Armenians and earlier.

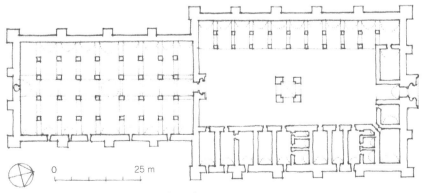

0   25 m

11.24 **Plan: Sultan Han, Kayseri**

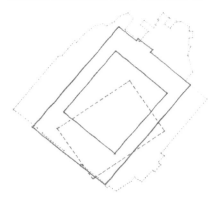
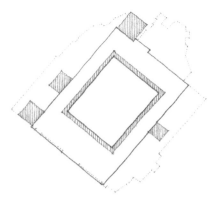
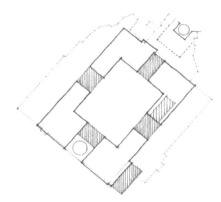

11.25 **Development of the Great Mosque of Isfahan, Iran**

Great Mosque of Isfahan

The Great Mosque of Isfahan (Masjid-i Jome, or Friday Mosque), in the northern part of the city, was one of the most influential of all early Seljuk religious structures. Though the building is known as a four-*iwan* type because the *iwans* face each other across an open courtyard, the building is, in actuality, the result of numerous architectural transformations. The primary building substance dates to a mosque built in the 840s CE that stood over an even earlier mosque, built in 772 CE, which in turn was built over the foundations of a Christian church. The mosque was a conventional hypostyle-courtyard mosque, typical of early mosques. But beginning around 870 CE, it was thoroughly revised. The central space was reduced somewhat by the addition of a new facade running around all four sides. An elegant *qibla* dome was built and, to the north, an annex with a domed sacred area, the original purpose of which is not precisely known.

In the time of Sultan Sanjar (1096–1157) four *iwans* were added to the courtyard, in essence imposing them on top of the older system. The old columns were thickened or removed, as was required; the original columnar rhythms are still best visible in the areas to the right and left of the northern *iwan*. In the 1350s, buildings were joined to the outer flanks of the structure, a madrasa was added to the western flank, and a *musalla* (a temporary place in which worshippers congregate to perform their prayers) to the eastern one, to name only the most prominent changes made to the building over time.

In its original pre-Islamic form, the *iwan* was a type of stage for the enthroned king, but the Seljuks used it for several purposes; in a madrasa, for example, it was a lecture room. At the Isfahan mosque, the *iwans* are grand portals, becoming the very symbol of the mosque on the other side. The Isfahan *iwans* are not identical. The main one, at the southwest, leads to the dome in front of the *qibla*. The side *iwans* have no particular relationship to the spaces behind them and lead nowhere except through doorways at the sides.

To the north, the *iwan* with its barrel vault points in the direction of a *haram*—a special sanctuary where contending parties could meet to settle disputes—which had originally been freestanding on three sides but was eventually roofed over and connected to the neighboring buildings. The particular reason why the mosque orientation was interrupted by the use of the four *iwans* is not known, but the building is an ideal space composed of principal elements, with the *iwans* a symbolic armature arranged in precise relationships to each other.

11.26 **Courtyard, Great Mosque of Isfahan**

11.27 *Iwans*, Great Mosque of Isfahan

11.28 Close-up of *muqarnas*, Great Mosque of Isfahan

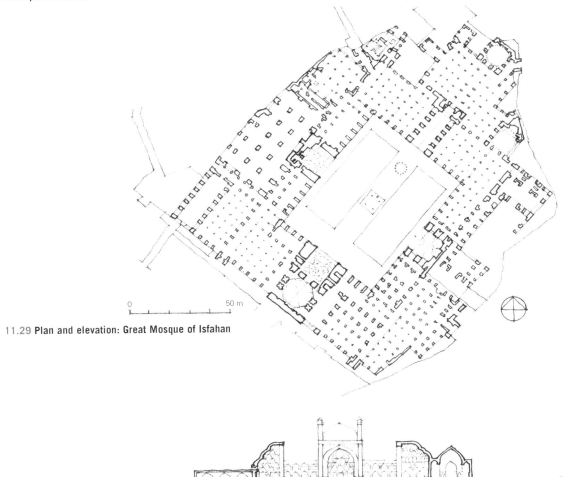

11.29 Plan and elevation: Great Mosque of Isfahan

0   50 m

11.30 **Gök Madrasa, Sivas, Turkey**

11.31 **Courtyard, Madrasa al-Firdus, Aleppo, Syria**

First Madrasas

If the caravansaries were the central element of the Seljuk economic policy, the madrasa was an important element of Seljuk political ideology, initially serving to promote the Islamization of the Anatolian population, which until the 13th century had been predominantly Christian. The madrasa served subsequently to enforce and unify the Seljuk's Sunni beliefs. The madrasas were thus an important element in the campaign against the Shi'ite Fatimids of Egypt. Though many mosques had spaces and annexes that were used for classes as well as for residences for students and teachers, separate institutions for higher studies were still relatively rare prior to the Seljuks.

Madrasas were built in almost all parts of Asia Minor, but their origin is unclear. Some link it with the Buddhist *vihara*—and given that the eastern areas of Islam had been saturated with Buddhism for centuries, there is some plausibility to that argument. Another possibility is its association with the courtyard house, a tradition that goes back to ancient times. A madrasa was usually founded by a sultan or nobleman, who would generously endow it to meet its expenses. As with the caravansaries, the Seljuk madrasa followed a standard form. They were rectangular, compact, and relatively windowless, appearing as solid objects in the landscape.

Portals, however, were often grandly and richly carved. Most, like the Ince Minare Madrasa (1260–65) in Konya, Turkey, had a central courtyard lined with classrooms around a central *iwan* opposite the entrance. Others, like the Madrasa al-Fridus (1235–41) in Aleppo, Syria, had no *iwan*.

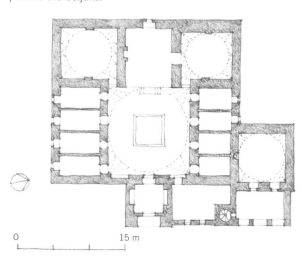

0   15 m

11.32 **Plan: Ince Minare Madrasa, Konya, Turkey**

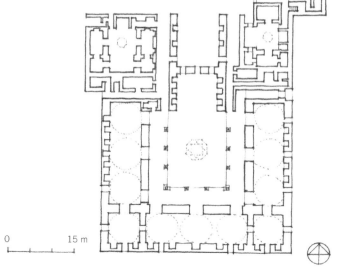

0   15 m

11.33 **Plan: Madrasa al-Firdus, Aleppo**

11.35 **Hall of the Abencerrajes, Alhambra, Spain**

11.34 **Mausoleum of Koutloug Aka, Samarkand, Uzbekistan**

MUQARNAS

Muqarnas, also called stalactite or honeycombed vaulting, are one of the most common features of Islamic architecture between the 11th and 15th centuries. They appear around the Islamic world, including South Asia, in a variety of materials, including brick, stone, stucco, and wood. The term's origin and meaning, as well as the historical development of the form, are not known for certain and are much debated. They originally developed out of squinches that eased the transition between the square and circle of a dome, but they became an articulation of the fascination among Islamic artists for complex geometrical patterns, which were being applied to the surfaces of doors and window moldings. Though they do not have an explicit symbolic value, they allude to the geometry of the heavens and the wonders of God's creations.

An early example is the Shrine of Imam Dur, in Samarra, Iraq (1085). The building consists of an elongated cube on which rests a series of octagonal tiers that telescope and rotate toward the final dome. Among the more developed examples is the dome (*qubba*) of al-Barubiyyin in Marrakech, Morocco (1117), another early example of a complex dome structure. Its eight-pointed star seems to almost float free from its enclosing frame. The four corners have *muqarnas* of their own, producing a dynamic three-dimensional effect. One of the most spectacular of these domes is in the Alhambra palace in Granada, Spain, over the Hall of the Two Sisters (1356–59), which projects both chaos and order at the same time.

11.36 **Two-dimensional fan-shaped radial *muqarnas* quarter vault design from the Topkapi Scroll**

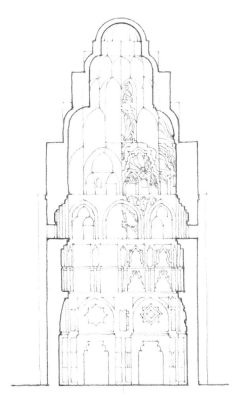

11.37 **Section: Shrine of Imam Dur, Samarra, Iraq**

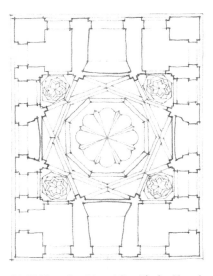

11.38 **Plan of *qubba*, al-Barubiyyin, Marrakech, Morocco**

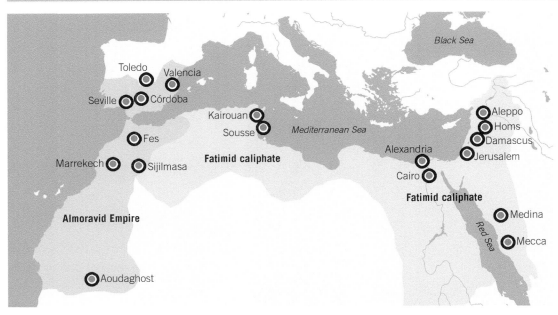

11.39 **North Africa, ca. 1000 CE**

THE FATIMIDS

The Fatimids, who had established themselves in Tunisia, eventually lost Algeria and points to the west. But they were successful in their expansion to the east, sweeping through the Nile Valley, across Palestine, and into southern Syria to control a considerable part of the Middle East for more than two hundred years. Most Egyptians at that time were Sunni Muslims, whom the Fatimids—Shi'ites of the Isma'ili sect—opposed. The Fatimid caliphs, who considered themselves to be divine rulers sent by God to ensure the prevalence of Islamic justice, refused to recognize the legitimacy of the Sunni Abbasid caliphates ruling from Baghdad. It was the Fatimid vision and mission to convert the whole Muslim world to its faith and overthrow the Sunni caliphate. One of its principal architectural expressions was the construction of the city of al-Qahira, which became the heart of the modern city of Cairo, a few kilometers to the north of the old early Islamic town. At the core of the city, which was bisected by a main road, was a palace district with an east and west palace separated by a large square; nearby were the office of the state bureaucracy and the military. Though descriptions testify to the sumptuousness of the Fatimid palaces, little of that palace architecture survives, but a sense of Fatimid era architectural

skills can be gained by studying the facade of the Aqmar Mosque in Cairo (1125). Based loosely on the triumphal arch motif from classical times, it has a central portal flanked by tall niches that are surmounted by *muqarna* panels and by blind niches. An inscription runs across the top. Moldings and decorative friezes are used to tie the parts together.

Al-Azhar Mosque (970–72 CE) was built to the southeast. Though it has been much renovated and enlarged, the mosque still

maintains its North African hypostyle hall with wooden roofs. A striking feature is its central axis, which breaks the rhythm and emphasizes the *qibla*. The minaret is placed on axis on the south side of the courtyard. The mosque in its final form, with various functions appended to its rectangular hall, almost became a city unto itself. The building consists of an open courtyard with the main prayer hall to the east. The western part of the building contains several madrasas, or schools. An ablution hall is to the north and

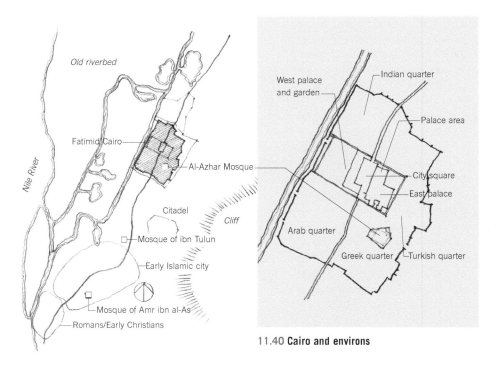

11.40 **Cairo and environs**

11.41 **Al-Azhar Mosque, Cairo**

11.42 **Interior of Al-Azhar Mosque**

student rooms to the south. The building is named "the radiant" in honor of the prophet Mohammed's daughter, Fatima al-Zahra, from whom the Fatimid dynasty claims descent.

In 1005, Al-Azhar was endowed by the Fatimids with thousands of manuscripts that formed the basis of its collection and its learning. In 1009, however, the newly founded al-Hakim Mosque became the sole location for the caliph's sermons. The Ayyubid dynasty (1174–1250) and then the Mamluks (1250–1517), who later took the reins of power, and who were Sunni as opposed to Shi'a, showed differing degrees of deference to the Fatimid mosques and provided widely varying levels of financial assistance to the school and to the upkeep of the mosques. With the change of power, Al-Azhar became a Sunni institution, much of its manuscript collection was dispersed, and professors were forced to find other means to earn their livings. Al-Azhar nevertheless remained a place of learning throughout this period, and private lessons were often still offered. Today, Al-Azhar remains a deeply influential institution in Egyptian society and a symbol of Islamic Egypt.

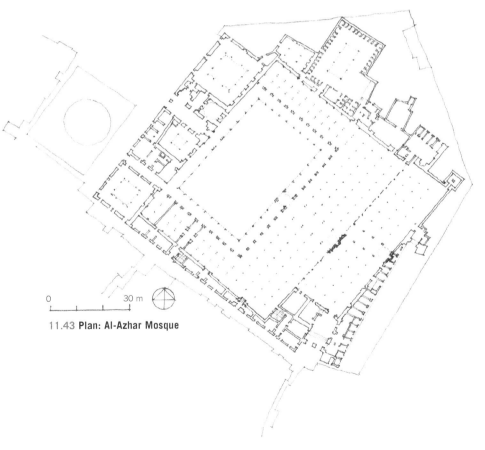

0   30 m

11.43 **Plan: Al-Azhar Mosque**

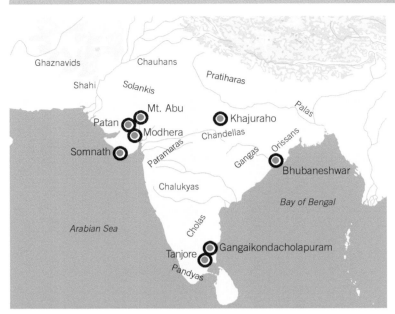

11.44 South Asia temple sites

RISE OF THE RAJPUT KINGDOMS

Between 800 and 1000 CE, the Gurjara-Pratiharas from the west, the Rashtrakutas from the Deccan Plateau, and the Buddhist Palla kings from the east were locked in a battle for control of the central Gangetic Plains. Kanauj, through which all of the major trade routes south, east, and north passed, was the prized possession. The three contenders, by turn, had all managed to capture Kanauj, but two centuries of warfare weakened all three to such a degree that they all eventually collapsed. The resultant power vacuum in northern India led to a series of new kingdoms. Some of these, like the Chalukyas, were former vassal states that now declared independence. More significantly, a large number of semitribal and tribal communities that had previously been subjugated emerged as kingdoms in their own right. These are known collectively as the Rajput kingdoms because of their shared caste identity (*raj-put* means "royal son"). Among these, the Solankis (western and central India), the Chandellas (north-central India), and the Orissans (east and central India) were eminent temple builders. The capital of the Solankis, Patan, was the largest city in India and the tenth-largest city in the world.

Most of the tribal communities were of the lowest caste, so their new kings had to acquire the Kshatriya, or warrior caste. To accomplish this, the kings laid claim to a mythical lineage and, more importantly, began to build and support temples as a way to legitimate their rule. The result was one of the largest temple-building campaigns in India, with new forms coming into being. Regional deities and gods were accepted into the expanding Hindu pantheon, and worship was conducted in regional languages. Other than the introduction of Islam, which was yet to come, the patchwork of regional identities that is modern India was established at this time. Contemporary India still has twenty-two official languages (and over five hundred dialects) with clear geographical divisions. It is therefore useful to think of India as one does of Europe: as an interrelated network of distinct regional areas. While the various regions share certain cultural aspects, their identities are as diverse as those of European countries. The same applies to their architecture. To think of a unified Indian architecture is as useful and as useless as thinking of "European architecture."

Rani-ni-Vav at Patan

Access to and distribution of fresh water played a critical role in all of Indian society, where water had both an economic and a symbolic value. But Solanki wells were no simple affairs. The step well called the Rani-ni-Vav, or "Queen's Step Well," was built at Anhilwara (Patan) in the 11th century, in memory of Bhimdev I (1022–63) by his widowed queen, Udaymati. It consists of a long stairway leading down to the water table. The entire excavation is lined with a multi-tiered colonnaded "facade" supported by elaborately carved stone columns and beams. It was partially roofed, with light filtering even into the deepest parts 28 meters below the surface. The reason for such splendor was that the Rani-ni-Vav (*rani* means "queen"; *vav*, "well") served as a supplementary palace for the queen and her attendants. The natural temperature of the earth, combined with the evaporative effects of the wind passing over the water, turned the step well into a subterranean world of cool repose during the blistering summer months. Since the well went so far down, its walls had to be buttressed against implosion. This was achieved by building heavy stone buttresses at the well's mouth and bracing its interior.

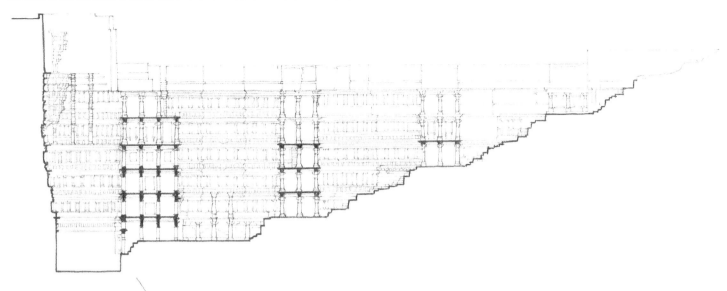

11.45 Section and partial plan: Rani-ni-Vav, step well at Patan, India

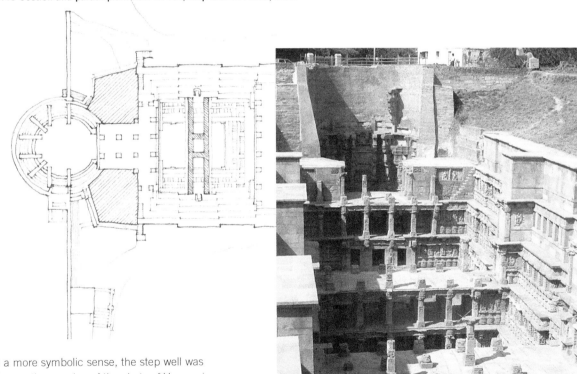

In a more symbolic sense, the step well was also another version of the ghats of Varanasi or the water tank of the Sun Temple at Modhera, except that the step well was fully inhabitable. Much of Solanki architecture was eventually destroyed by invading Islamic armies. The Rani-ni-Vav survived intact because it was intentionally filled in with earth by the retreating Solankis.

11.46 Rani-ni-Vav, step well at Patan

Sun Temple at Modhera

Of the various Rajput kingdoms, the Solankis, who ruled in Rajasthan and Gujarat, were among the most zealous temple builders. They traded not only with the other kingdoms of South Asia but also with Central Asia. Though principally worshipers of Shiva, they claimed lineage from Pandu, a mythological king during ancient Vedic times. Through that connection, they legitimized their tradition of solar cults. The Solanki royal temple, dedicated to Surya, or the sun, was made from golden sandstone in a tripartite axial arrangement. The main shrine is in the west, a rectangular water tank in the east, and a *mandapa* in between, all integrated into a single composition. The *mandapa* is connected to the steps surrounding the water tank by a freestanding gateway, or *torana*, that marks the top of a flight of steps. While the aesthetic expression of all the temple's elements is in itself quite remarkable, it is the delicate richness with which all the columns, brackets, cusped and wavy arches, and roofs are carved that stands out. Their distinction lies in how they function optically to connect the building's elements. Standing on the western edge of the tank and looking eastward toward the main temple, the view seems to be of one building composed of the steps leading upward to the *mandapa*. But the conical top belongs to the shrine in the distance, and the entrance of the *mandapa* is actually the *torana* in the foreground.

11.47 Sun Temple at Modhera, India

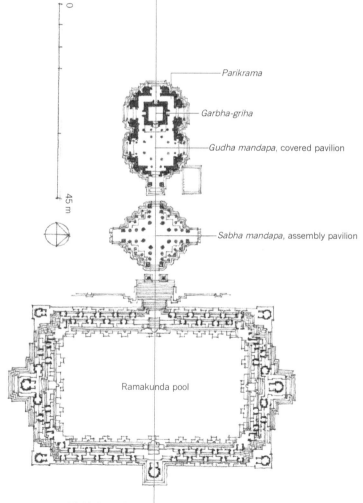

11.48 Plan: Sun Temple at Modhera

That this effect is deliberate is evidenced by the access steps, which are a separate element excavated from the ground between the edge of the tank and the torana, thereby establishing an optical connection between the two. There is also an echo effect between the implied triangular profile of the temple and the inverted V of the steps, and between the conical dome above and the steps at the base of the inverted V, which widen out into the tank. The entirety creates an uncanny reflective effect, even when there is no water present.

11.49 **Detail: Sun Temple at Modhera**

11.50 **Ramakunda pool, Sun Temple at Modhera**

11.51 **Lakshmana Temple sikhara**

11.52 **Lakshmana Temple at Khajuraho, India**

Chandellas

In a brief period of about 175 years, the Chandellas, who called their kingdom Jejakabhukti, built more than eighty temples in and around their capital of Khajuraho (ancient Khajjuravahaka). The crispness of their architectural forms and the close continuity in their order and language

indicate that there must have been a core group of architects, or perhaps even a single architect-in-charge. Two of the main royal temples of the Chandellas were the Lakshmana (ca. 950 CE) and the Khandariya Mahadeva (1000–1025).

Dedicated to Shiva, the Lakshmana rises on a high platform, ensuring that, like all other Khajuraho temples, it is visible in the surrounding flat countryside from afar. Independent subsidiary shrines are located at the four corners of the platform, suggesting a sense of enclosure and defining a sacred precinct without the actual existence of a wall. Access is highly dramatic, via an axially

placed stair to the platform and another set of stairs to the temple. The profile of the temple was itself something of a "stairway to heaven." The temple consists of three *mandapas* preceding the main *shikhara*. The *mandapas* are articulated in horizontal layers, while the main *shikhara* emphasizes the vertical. One of the key architectural issues is that the *mandapa* is no longer just a flat roofed box in front of the temple: it now has its own pyramidical roof that competes with the *shikhara* of the main shrine. From this time on, one of the main characteristics of Hindu temples is their silhouette.

One distinguishing feature of the Khajuraho temples is the manner in which their architects orchestrated the front elevations—not mathematically or geometrically, but perspectively. The front elevations of the *mandapas* are designed so that at eye level they all appear to nestle into each other perfectly. (This is similar to the design of the Sun Temple at Modhera.) The objective was not just aesthetic. The superstructure of every Hindu temple is conceived as a model of the universe; its purpose is to disclose to the believer the inherent order and beauty of that universe.

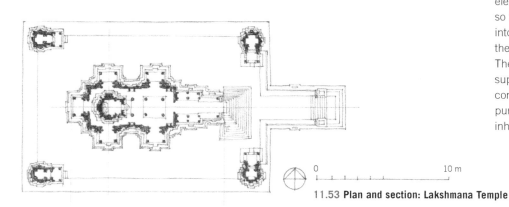

0   10 m

11.53 **Plan and section: Lakshmana Temple**

Unlike many Hindu temples, the Khandariya is lit by large openings located well above eye level. The effect is particularly spectacular in the circumambulation route, where the light coming from a high source casts dark shadows between the folds of the sculptures, bringing them into sharp relief. The openings are furnished with platforms and steps for attendants and musicians.

The Khajuraho temples are famous for their so-called erotic sculpture. Sexual acts of almost every kind are carved with the same attention to detail and fullness as all the other sculptures, underscoring the Chandellas' interest in Tantrism. This sexual sculpture, while present in abundance, is neither highlighted nor hidden; it is both an important part of the assemblage and a part of the wider variety of life depicted in the sculptural program.

11.54 **Khandariya Mahadeva Temple, Khajuraho, India**

Khandariya Mahadeva Temple

The Khandariya Mahadeva Temple (1000–1025), like the Lakshmana, sits on a high platform that it shares with another, smaller temple, the Jagdambi, dedicated to the goddess Parvati. There are no corner shrines, so the profiles of the Khandariya and its partner are silhouetted against the sky without distraction. Balancing the composition between the two temples is a small shrine resting on its own plinth. At 30 meters, including the 4-meter-high platform on which it rests, the Khandariya rises higher than all the other temples, but its strength lies not in its size, but in the quality of its architecture. Its profile is designed to represent the rhythms of a jagged mountain range, both in its outlines and in the composition of its parts. Unlike the Lakshmana, the Khandariya's four *mandapas* are articulated with distinctive mini-*shikharas* that cluster around the main *shikhara*. These mini-*shikharas* produce the sense of a rising wave while still being fully geometrical. The slight widening at the base, the strong horizontal protrusions of the porches, and the tightly bound faceting at the intersection of the *shikhara* and the *mandapa* make for an extraordinarily powerful composition. Because of their height, the porches give the visitor a sense of elevation above the quotidian. The interior of the sanctuary, however, is appropriately deep and dark, like a cave.

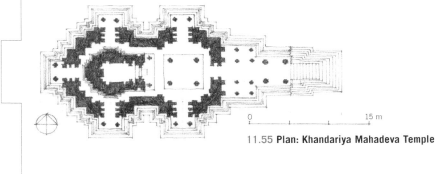

11.55 **Plan: Khandariya Mahadeva Temple**

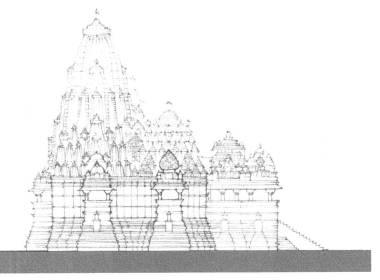

11.56 **Elevation: Khandariya Mahadeva Temple**

11.57 **Tantric sculpture from Khandariya Mahadeva Temple**

Tantrism

The Chandella Rajputs, who were Gond tribesmen brought from obscurity into the caste through the bhakti cults, remained invested in aspects of their old animism—particularly in the rites associated with female fertility. Their practices therefore found sympathy among Tantra (anglicized as "Tantrism") practitioners, who held that veneration of the female deity was critical to attaining nirvana. Tantrics believed that through ascetic practices and esoteric rituals they could use the inherent divine power (*prana*) that flows through the universe (including one's own body) to attain spiritual goals. For this reason, Tantric worship makes elaborate use of mantras, or symbolic speech made up of words or phrases that are repeated over and over. Tantric practices required secret initiations by a guru or leader. A woman had to be present at every ritual because the female was the initiator of the action; the male could only be activated through union with a female. Routinely condemned by more orthodox Hindus, the Tantrics gained widespread acceptance among the nobility of the time, particularly the Rajputs. Tantrism was also an important force in contemporary Buddhism.

An example of an early Chandella Tantric structure is the Chausat Yogini Temple (mid-9th century), located 1 kilometer from Khajuraho. Its name literally means the "temple of sixty-four women saints." One of many such temples found in northern India, it

11.58 **Plan: Chausat Yogini Temple at Khajuraho, India**

consists of an empty quadrangular enclosure surrounded by sixty-four small shrines, each with its own individual pyramidical *shikhara*; the main opening is on one of the smaller sides to the north. The center of the Chausat Yogini is visibly empty or open, in contrast to a typical Hindu temple dedicated to a male deity, in which the dominant temple would be in the middle. Unlike the Vaishnite and Shiavite temples, the Chausat Yogini Temple is oriented north-south.

11.59 **Chausat Yogini Temple**

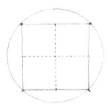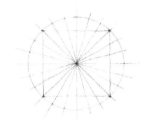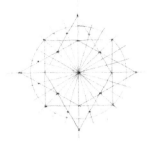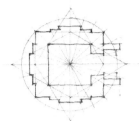

11.60 **Geometric evolution of an Orissan temple plan (after Andreas Volwahsen)**

Vastu-Shastras

In the 10th and 11th centuries, a series of technical manuals was published under such titles as *Vastu Shastra* ("Construction Treatise") and *Shilpa Shastra* ("Sculpture Treatise"); they provide insight into the highly codified language of temple design and construction. From these texts we know that a temple's overall design was handled by a chief Brahmin, known as a *sutradhar*. He based his work on an astrological diagram called a mandala, a graph that mapped the positions of stars, planets, deities, and the sun with respect to a particular site. Its design is based on the overlay of a square and a circle. The *sutradhar* chose from hundreds of mandalas, depending on the deity of the temple and the religious persuasion of the community. The temple's actual form was derived through a series of geometrical maneuvers designed to express the potency of the various planets and deities occupying the grid of the mandala. Radiating lines, the weight given to the primary directions, and special triangles all determined the location of the building's various parts. A complex system of faceting, known as *rathas*, determined the detailed articulation of the temple's surface. The purpose of the *rathas* was to enable multiple deities to share a single surface—in the vertical and horizontal plane—by suggesting superimposed layers. The final form was inevitably a heavily faceted pyramid. Once the design had been determined, it was

relayed to the master builder, whose craft was handed down through oral tradition. Sculpture and paintings were then finished by independent *shrenis* ("artisans").

The cosmic order expressed by a temple offers a vision of a pyramidal universe cascading downward in conceptual waves from a single point of origin that in itself is without form or substance. The objective of the worshipper, in apprehending this vision, was to devote himself or herself to ascending to that formless center, a task assisted by devotion to the temple's resident deity.

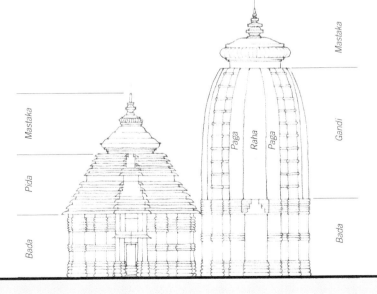

11.61 **Orissan temple elements**

Orissa and Lingaraja Temple

Another important kingdom was Orissa, located in eastern India south of Bengal, whose fertile rivers and ports were key to its wealth. Over the centuries, various dynasties ruled from its capital, Bhubaneshwar, which came to be home to about seven thousand Hindu temples, many of which were distributed around a sacred pool. A few hundred still stand. As Hinduism matured, the ruling dynasties grew in power, and their ritual practices became more and more elaborate, the temples of Bhubaneshwar grew in size and complexity. The temples were unique, as the *mandapa* was given its own pyramidical roof that had to be harmonized with the rising *shikhara* of the *garbha-griha* (which the Orissans call *rekha deul*). The emergence of this attempt at integration is seen at the Rajarani Temple (ca. 1000 CE).

11.62 Rajarani Temple, Bhubaneshwar, Orissa, India

Jagmohan   *Rekha deul*

11.63 Plan: Rajarani Temple

Rathas are the projections and recesses that form the *pagas*.

11.64 Lingaraja Temple, Bhubaneshwar, Orissa, India

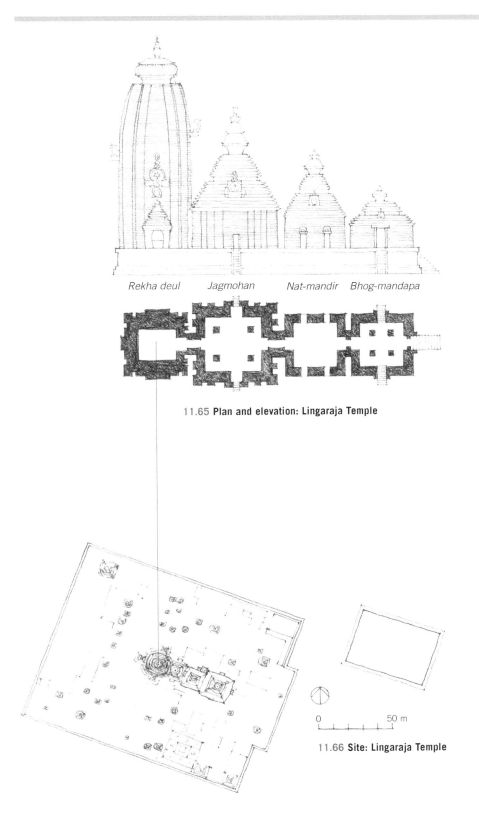

11.65 Plan and elevation: Lingaraja Temple

Rekha deul   Jagmohan   Nat-mandir   Bhog-mandapa

0   50 m

11.66 Site: Lingaraja Temple

As the "king" of the Bhubaneshwar temples, the Lingaraja (literally, "Phallus King," ca. 1100) was distinguished not only by its size but also by the presence of a row of three *jagmohans*. The rituals that would normally have been conducted in a single hall were here separated, enabling several rituals to occur simultaneously and creating the sense of a mini-pilgrimage in their performance. These *jagmohans*—a primary *jagmohan*, a *nat-mandir* ("dance hall"), and a *bhog-mandapa* ("collective ritual performance hall")—were about the same size, though each has a distinctive plan suited to its function. The *jagmohan* has a fully articulated exterior, making it a shrine in itself. The *nat-mandir* is airy and open so that its activities could be seen and heard in the surroundings. The *bhog-mandapa* duplicates the *jagmohan* and was probably added later to facilitate rituals by larger groups that could not access the innermost shrine. The Lingaraja's 37.5-meter-high *rekha deul*, which dominates the silhouette, has a distinctive profile, first rising almost vertically and then, only toward the top, curving inward, before yielding to a recessed neck that supports a wide *amalaka* resting on the backs of lions (an indication of royal patronage).

The Lingaraja sits in the middle of a quadrangular compound dotted with numerous small subsidiary shrines that were added over time to the main sequence in order to increase its potency. This proliferation is common in active Hindu temples and is described as the *parivar* (literally, the "family") of the main shrine, which is expected to change and grow in time as does a prosperous family around a reigning patriarch. Though the Lingaraja is now decommissioned, the nearby Jagannath Temple in Puri, also built by the Gangas in the 12th century, is still in use, and as a result, its *parivar* has grown. The compound is now completely saturated with subsidiary shrines, many built recently.

11.67 A Teaching Session (detail from a Shravanabelagola painting)

Jains

Many of the ministers employed in the Rajput courts were neither Hindus nor Buddhists but Jains, who were often the best financial experts and bankers available—an unintended consequence of their religion. Jainism originates in the teaching of Mahavira, a contemporary of the Buddha from the 6th century BCE. (*Jain* is a corruption of the Sanskrit word *jina*, meaning "conqueror," the title given to Mahavira in Jain texts.) Like the Buddha, Mahavira preached a doctrine of asceticism and meditation, but Mahavira insisted that all forms of life were equivalent and that respect for life was essential for the purification of the human soul. Strictly ascetic Jains, known as Digambaras ("sky-clad," or naked), were thus expected not only to be vegetarians but also to eat only a fruit or vegetable that had broken off its plant of its own accord. Root vegetables like potatoes and beets that entailed killing the whole plant were also prohibited. Nor could Jains be farmers, since working the land inevitably harmed insects and worms. As a consequence, they turned to professions such as jewelry making, trading, and banking and were thus highly sought after by the courts. They also often became great librarians and patrons of the arts.

Like the Mahayana Buddhists of Central and East Asia, the Jains built colossal monolithic statues of their Tirthankars (literally, "ford finders," or "those who cross the river of human misery") and spiritual leaders. In 966 CE, Chamundaray, a Jain minister of the Ganga dynasty, built at Shravanabelagola, Karnataka, a 17-meter-high statue of a naked Gomteshwara Bahubali, the first man said to have attained enlightenment through Jain practice. It sits on top of a hill visible from a distance. Every twelve years the statue is covered with milk, yogurt, ghee (clarified butter), and saffron, as well as with gold coins.

Like the Buddhists, the Jains challenged Hindu caste hierarchy and refuted Vedic orthodoxy, particularly the Brahmin's claim to privileged access to higher knowledge. So Jain ideas and institutions, like those of the Buddhists, were severely attacked by the Hindus in the 9th and 10th centuries. Followers of the Shaivite and Vaishnite bhakti cults blamed them for negating life and being too abstract and impractical for the common man. But unlike the Buddhists, who wilted under the critiques and eventually disappeared from India, the Jains managed to survive the rising tide of Hinduism (and later iconoclastic Islam), in part because of their economic and political clout.

11.68 Statue of Gomteshwara Bahubali

Today there are almost three million Jains in India, mostly in the western provinces and in Karnataka. That Hindu India today is largely vegetarian is mainly due to their influence. The Jains believe in the leadership of twenty-four Tirthankars who, after having totally conquered vices such as anger, pride, and desire, are said to have appeared on earth to show Jains the way to the true religion. The original twenty-four Tirthankars were expanded to fifty-two and then seventy-four after the 12th century.

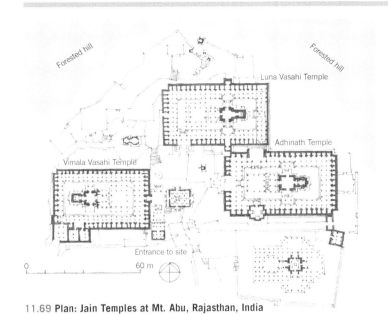

11.69 **Plan: Jain Temples at Mt. Abu, Rajasthan, India**

11.70 **Interior, Vimala Vasahi Temple at Mt. Abu**

Jain Temples at Mt. Abu

From the 10th through the 16th centuries, Jain ministers employed in Rajput courts used their wealth to build a set of five temples at Mt. Abu, Rajasthan, 170 kilometers north of Ahmedabad. Known collectively as the Dilwara Temples after a nearby town, they are clustered on a hill located on the high plateau summit of the mountain. Each temple sits high off the ground on its own terrace and is accessed on its flank by steps spilling out from a multitiered porch. The plans are modeled on Hindu precedents, with a main *garbha-griha* preceded by a *mandapa*. The central deity of the site is Adinath, one of the Tirthankars; shrines to all the Tirthankars were added to each temple later on. As a result, the individual temples came to be surrounded by a quadrangle composed of rows of mini-shrines. The *mandapas* of the mini-shrines were joined to form a cloister. Into the residual space between the quadrangle and the temple, the architects inserted a pavilion held up by highly ornate columns of lavish sculptural detail. The temples, of local white arasa marble, are carved as if made of wood. The columns and ceilings of the open pavilion are the climax of the sculptural program.

At the Vimala Vasahi, twelve multifaceted piers, linked by flying arches, hold up a domed ceiling. Sixteen female figures, personifying various aspects of learning, are attached in a ring around the perimeter. The exterior wall, by contrast, is restrained in its ornamentation, masking the rich articulations of the interior.

11.71 **Dilwara Temple at Mt. Abu**

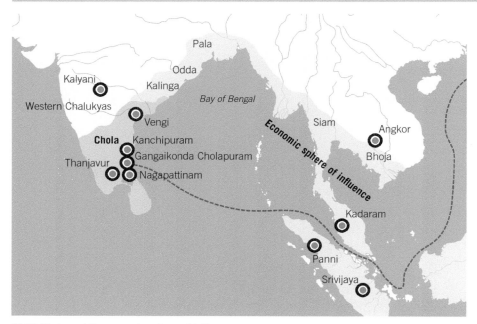

11.72 Chola and its economic sphere of influence

CHOLAMANDALAM

India's south came to be dominated by a single power, the Cholas, who combined military strength with an effective strategy of wealth generation and governance to bring about a social and economic revolution of their own. Building for themselves a new capital at Thanjavur, they eventually came to control all of peninsular India, becoming the largest power on the subcontinent. They lost no time in embarking on an aggressive campaign of temple building, not only to spread Shaivism but also to consolidate their economic base. Raja Raja Chola I (r. 985–1004) turned his attention to the trade routes and soon brought the Arabian shipping lanes under his control. Sri Lanka became a vassal state. His son, Rajendra I (r. 1014–44), with his eye on the lucrative sea trade with China, sent his fleet to conquer Malaya and Shrivijaya, leaving the Cholas the controlling superpower of Southeast Asia. The Cholas, who called their sphere of influence the Cholamandalam, the "Chola Vision-World" possessed the largest naval force India was to have until modern times.

The Cholas chose the image of Shiva Nataraj, who orders the movement of the world with his dance, as their representative royal deity. The temple itself was an extension of the royal ordering of the world. The word "temple" in Tamil is *kovil* (*kov* meaning "god-king," *il* meaning "home"); it connotes both temple and palace and thereby serves a range of functions, from the religious to the judicial. For every economic unit (like a village or a district), the Cholas built a temple. While the temple's basic endowments of agricultural land or villages were made by the king, the actual land for the building was donated by the local elite. Donations for building materials were made by the merchants. Provisions such as images, lamps, and oil were obtained through individual donations. Temples were also run like a corporation. They had the authority to make land grants and to invest their assets as they considered fit. They even became banks, with major contributions and investments inscribed on the walls of the temple for all to view. In this way, the Chola temples became the financial centers of the community. Village assemblies were held in them, and they were often responsible for the education of upper-caste boys. The temple's administration, however, was controlled by the king, and Brahmins were the only ones allowed to conduct rituals. Temples maintained a huge permanent staff that included musicians, artists, artisans, and dancers (including *devadasis*, women dancers dedicated to the temple for life.) The community's cultural institutions, in other words, were also the preserve of the temple.

Dakshinameru (Rajarajeshwara Temple)

While regional temples served the more quotidian purposes of governance, Rajaraja I's royal temple at Thanjavur, the Chola capital, embodied a vision of kingship at the scale of an empire. Rajaraja I projected himself as a *cakravartin*, a king destined to bring order to the world, a demigod in the grace of Shiva Nataraj. He called his temple Dakshinameru, the "Mt. Meru of the South," distinguishing his world from that of the north. (Dakshinameru is now generally known as the Rajarajeshwara or the Brihadeshwara Temple). Major ceremonies of royal initiation and legitimation were held there, linking deity and king. The daily

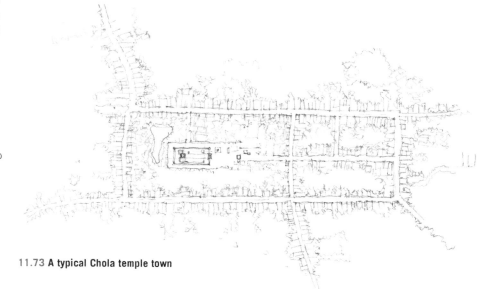

11.73 A typical Chola temple town

rituals of the deities mirrored those of the king, including his morning round of the sacred enclosure and his sunset retreat to his bedroom. Dakshinameru maintained a staff of six hundred *devadasis*, treasurers, accountants, record-keepers, watchmen, musicians, readers of texts, and craftsmen of every sort—in addition to scores of Brahmin priests. To this day it remains the largest temple in India.

Situated next to a river that was channeled to form a moat symbolic of the cosmic ocean, its outer enclosure was built like a fortress. It was entered on axis through a five-story *gopuram*. A second, three-story freestanding *gopuram*, set on a long, low platform, gave access to the main quadrangle. The towering, sixteen-story mass of the main *shikhara* dominates the view, with pilasters, piers, and attached columns articulating the entire surface. In the interior, the circumambulation route that goes around the massive lingam in the *garbha-griha* is repeated on the upper story, which is inhabitable. This is a rarity in Hindu temples, an allusion to the idea that Rajarajeshwara offered access to the realm of the gods. The ground story (which symbolically corresponds to the earthly realm) is articulated as two stories, indicating more than one celestial dimension of the royal temple. The main temple is preceded by two cojoined, dimly lit hypostyle halls: the *antarala*, or vestibule, where the priest would be, and the *mandapa*. In the *mandapa*, the columns are exquisitely and intricately carved—showing the potential for refinement—whereas in the *antarala*, the columns are left as massive and plain monoliths: the first manifestation of form emerging out of the formless.

11.74 **Dakshinameru (Rajarajeshwara Temple), Thanjavur, India**

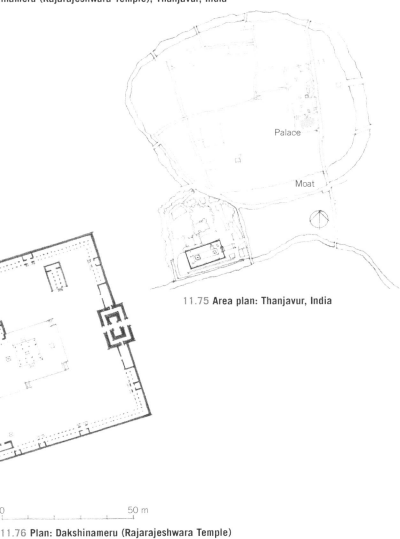

11.75 **Area plan: Thanjavur, India**

0   50 m

11.76 **Plan: Dakshinameru (Rajarajeshwara Temple)**

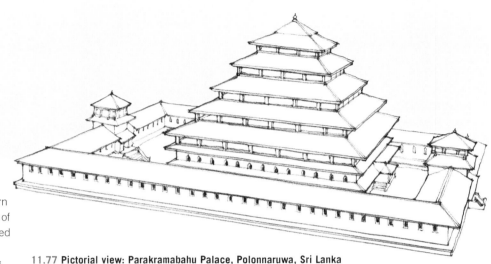

11.77 Pictorial view: Parakramabahu Palace, Polonnaruwa, Sri Lanka

POLONNARUWA

By the end of the 12th century, the northern part of Sri Lanka, with its elaborate system of artificial lakes, dams, and canals, constituted one of the most sophisticated hydro-engineering landscapes in the world. Along with exporting pearls and gems, Sri Lanka had become one of the leading maritime ports in South Asia. Following a period of conflict with empires from India, eager to wrest control of its markets, the old capital, Anuradhapura, was replaced by a new one, Polonnaruma, where the king built his palace compound directly to the west of a massive artificial lake. An extensive pleasure garden and audience hall were placed directly on top of the 2-kilometer long dyke that held back the water, an indication of the ruler's supreme confidence in the engineered landscape.

Among the numerous shrines, pools, and gardens, Vatadage (which means "circular relic house") was one of the most important constructions. At its core is a conventional stupa, about 5 meters high and painted white. It is located, however, within a walled cylindrical chamber of brick, the whole resting on a high, finely decorated stone plinth, with access via four cardinally oriented stairs. The circular wall, which was probably stuccoed and painted, is ornamented on the outside by an elegant blind, columnar stone screen. This screen, along with a ring of tall stone columns on the inside of the chamber, has led to conjecture that the whole structure was once roofed over. It is an unusual design found almost exclusively in Sri Lanka. One can imagine the building as a stupa that has been encased in elements symbolic of a palace.

0   30 m

11.78 Plan: Parakramabahu Palace

This would conform with the largely theocratic world view of the ruler, who was the arch-protector of the spiritual legacy of the Buddha. The building is surrounded by a low stone wall that permits only one entrance from the north, further setting it off from its surroundings. By thus enclosing the stupa, the designer took it out of the public realm, both physically and visually, and indeed this building probably housed for a while the tooth of the Buddha, a venerated relic that came to be associated with the king and the legitimacy of his rule. The cylindrical brick structure that surrounds the inner stupa is similar to a water tank, ruins of which can be found in various parts of the kingdom. Is it then possible to see the Buddha relic as blessing and protecting the great hydrological systems that defined the success of the kingdom?

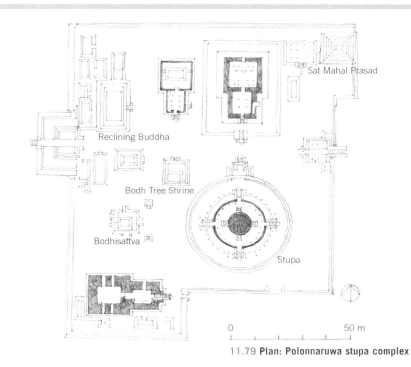

Sat Mahal Prasad

Reclining Buddha

Bodh Tree Shrine

Bodhisattva

Stupa

0   50 m

11.79 **Plan: Polonnaruwa stupa complex**

11.80 **Polonnaruwa stupa**

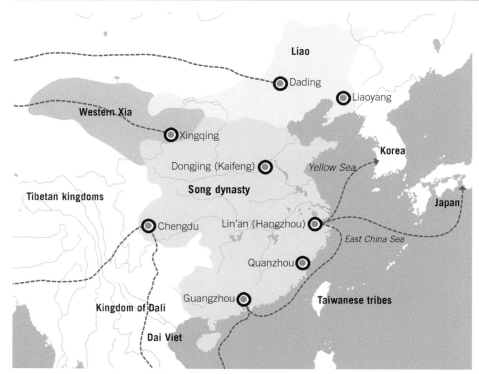

11.81 **Song dynasty China**

SONG DYNASTY CHINA

The Song dynasty (960–1279) reunited most of China proper. The Song period divides into two phases: Northern Song (960–1127), and Southern Song (1127–1279). The division was caused by the forced abandonment of north China in 1127 by the Song court, which could not push back Jin invaders. As to Chang'an, the Uyghurs helped recapture the fabled capital from rebels, but they refused to leave until the emperor paid them an enormous sum of tribute in silk. The abandonment of northern China was caused in part to floods in 858 along the Grand Canal that inundated vast tracts of land and terrain of the North China Plain; in 873 a disastrous harvest shook the foundations of the empire and made it all the more dependent on imported rice from Southeast Asia. Whereas the Northern Song capital was moved to Dongjing (now Kaifeng); the southern capital was established at Lin'an (now Hangzhou). Though much weakened, the economy was still powerful, and the use of a new type of early-ripening rice from Southeast and South Asia created abundant food surpluses. Confucianism was reinforced, and foreign relations were established with India, Indonesia, and Fatimid Egypt.

The 11th-century Song dynasty cities were the largest and most complex cities in the world. Among these, Dongjing, with close to a million residents of diverse faiths, was perhaps the largest. Unlike the cities of the T'ang, Song dynasty cities were more than just administrative centers; they also served as a locus of trade, industry, and maritime commerce. Dongjing lay at the intersection

of four major canals connecting to other cities and feeding into the Yellow River. Because the city was not divided into activity-specific wards, merchants could set up shop anywhere they pleased. Paintings from the time reveal that all the major streets and intersections were alive with activity. (A Song scroll, *Upper River during Qing-Ming Festival*, contains a detailed description of bustling Dongjing.)

Though Chinese authorities often preferred highly regulated cities, Dongjing shows the development of more flexible, wardless cities such as Lin'an, a center of culture on the southern coast of China during the 10th and 11th centuries and—following the defeat of the Song by the Jin in 1123—the capital of the Southern Song dynasty. Song cities were very cosmopolitan, with large populations of non-Chinese merchants. The new concept of a cultural entertainment area, a *wazi*, became popular, especially with the creation of night markets. The Song created extensive road networks between their large and small cities. The use of paper money facilitated the mercantile economy. The cultivation of tea and cotton became widespread; gunpowder was used for the first time.

One of the leading scientists and statesman, Shen Kuo (1031–95), a mathematician, astronomer, cartographer, and encyclopedist, also served as finance minister. Through experimentation with suspended magnetic needles, Shen discovered magnetic declination toward the North Pole—and the concept of true north, a revelation that made the compass useful for navigation. He also wrote extensively about movable type printing, which had been invented by Bi Sheng (990–1051).

11.82 **Site of Sage Mother Hall, Jinci Temple, Tayjuan, China**

Under the Song dynasty, Daoist and Buddhist traditions became closely aligned. But it was Confucianism, influenced by Buddhist practices, that reemerged as a major ideological force. Though having different emphases, the two were not seen as discordant.

Sage Mother Hall

Song cities, as had been traditional since the Han dynasty, had elaborate open-air sacrificial altars used for imperial sacrifices to the heaven, earth, sun, and moon. There were also magnificent roofed *ci*, temples with columnar interiors that were constructed for commemoration and veneration, often in connection with Confucian learning. During the Song dynasty, such structures also served as sites of imperial sacrifices. One of these was the Jinci, built at the site of three springs that had been worshipped since ancient times, and famous in Chinese literature for its pastoral beauty. It is located at the base of a mountain 25 kilometers southeast of Taiyuan, an important regional city. Whereas most Chinese temple compounds followed a conventional pattern of south-facing halls preceded by courtyards, the entirety framed by a wall with a gate, this sanctuary, dedicated to the springs' spirit, was built with the landscape in mind. Though numerous buildings have been added to the site over time, it originally consisted of a southeast-oriented series of buildings and bridges that crossed two canals, all set between two springs with the Sage Mother Temple set directly behind the middle and third one. The sanctuary was seen as a celestial court reigned over by a supreme goddess. For that reason, the Sage Mother hall (1038–87) at the apex of the composition was built in the imperial style: it has a timber-framed, double-eave hip-and-gable roof with dramatic, five-*puzo* eaves.

Since the Sage Mother was seen as important in providing rain as well as spring water, the lotus terrace, the first structure in the sequence, was, so it is thought, the site of ritual offerings and ceremonies dedicated to rain. This open-air platform is followed by a roofed offering hall that leads to the remarkable Spirit Bridge, which traverses one of the springs. It actually consists of two bridges that cross each other at 90 degrees, meeting at the center. They are set

in front of the hall itself, which is a single-story building; but because it was built with an encircling veranda with its own set of brackets, it appears as if it were two stories. The eight dragons of gilded wood that wrap themselves around the front columns are a marker of the Sage Mother's identity as water goddess and as a provider of rain. Columns were eliminated to allow for more room in the veranda, where it is two bays deep. The wall of the open U-shaped enclosure of the shrine has embedded within it, as is typical, the columns that support the roof. The inner walls, which were completely painted with themes associated with the goddess, had life-size statues of attendant women standing along them. The Sage Mother is clothed in elaborate robes but is in a seated Buddha position—no accident, as hers was meant to compete with Buddhist shrines.

11.83 Detail, Sage Mother Hall

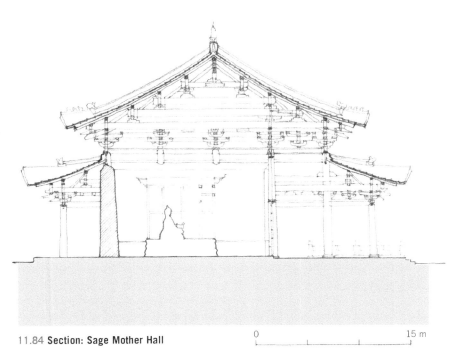

11.84 Section: Sage Mother Hall

0   15 m

The Iron Pagoda

The architecture of the *ta*, or pagoda, developed rapidly under the Song. Pagodas had first emerged during the Han dynasty (202 BCE–220 CE) as wooden structures, and then during the T'ang dynasty (618–907 CE) as stone and brick buildings that could more easily survive lightning strikes. Though Buddhism in China had waned after the late T'ang period, during the Song dynasty Buddhist pagoda towers continued to be built—often in the countryside instead of within city walls, perhaps so as to not compete with the cosmic-imperial authority that was represented by the cities' drum and gate towers. An exception to this is the Iron Pagoda of Youguo Temple in Dongjing (present-day Kaifeng), which gets its name not because it was made of iron but because the color of the building resembles that of iron. It is an octagonal brick structure about 57 meters high built around a solid core, with a spiral staircase circulating between the core and outer shell. The use of brick allowed the architects to achieve an elegant, thin shape that would not have been possible in wood, even though the building was designed to imitate a wooden structure with densely positioned eaves (*miyan*) and wooden brackets (*dou-gong*). The glazed bricks on the exterior are richly decorated with images of the Buddha, monks, singers and dancers, flowers, lions, and dragons and other legendary beasts. Under the eaves, 104 bells ring in the wind.

LIAO DYNASTY

A tribal clan known as the Khitan created the Liao dynasty (947–1125), which stretched from Korea and Mongolia in the north to Beijing in the south. The Liao was the first of China's several so-called foreign dynasties. In response to the dual nature of the area—with nomads to the north and settled Chinese populations in the south—the Liao created a double government, building a series of cities through which this duality was expressed. Its capital, Shangjing ("Supreme Capital"), near the modern city of Lingdong, was located at the headwaters of the Shira Muren River, a site hallowed by the Khitan people. It served as the administrative center of the empire and included a commercial district, called the Chinese city, made of permanent materials; the ruling Liao, however, continued to live

in their traditional yurts in their own part of the town. Eventually, more than thirty walled cities were built, including four subsidiary capitals for the four regions of the empire, serving as centers of commerce; the southern capital was a predecessor of Beijing. The cities were square (or almost square), with a separated walled palace city within the city adjacent to the north wall. The Liao embraced Buddhism with such vigor that it is estimated that 10 percent of the population were monks and nuns. Nonetheless, most Khitan still adhered in one way or another to the traditional animistic religion in which the sun was worshipped. Thus, the Khitan emperor faced the east, where the sun rises, rather than the south, as Chinese emperors did.

Though the Khitan accommodated themselves to the Song dynasty architectural and urban traditions—as they had no such traditions themselves—they transformed Chinese building conventions to develop their own style. The buildings they commissioned were made by Chinese and Korean craftsmen. Nonetheless, their buildings were in many respects different, if not superior, to those of the Song. Whereas the Song aspired to a clarity of structure, the Liao reveled in the complexity of brackets and joinery that made their buildings more durable and lent them a majestic tone. One of their innovations was to remove central columns in the halls to allow more space for the statue of the Buddha. This partially explains the need for a more complex roof structure, which had to span greater distances. It was during the reign of the sixth Liao emperor, Longxu, also known as Shengzong (971–1031), that the most Liao wooden architecture was constructed.

Mu-ta

More than one hundred early pagodas from the Song, Liao, and Jin dynasties have survived into modern times because most were made of brick. Of the timber buildings, few have survived, apart from the Liao structure known as the Yingxian Timber Pagoda, built in 1056. It is often referred to simply as Mu-ta, or the "Wooden Pagoda." The Mu-ta was built to commemorate Xinzong (1031–55), the seventh Liao ruler. Access to the 67-meter-high *ta* was through a monastic enclosure with a monumental

11.85 Silhouette, Iron Pagoda, Kaifeng, China

mountain gate (*shanmen*) and a large, 55-meter-long forecourt that is no longer extant. The building was elevated on four "moon terraces" (*yuetai*), each with a pair of side stairs. The *yuetai* were a standard feature of Liao buildings but at the time were not used in Song architecture.

The lowermost story of the building consists of three independent rings of wooden pillars. The smallest pillars in the outermost ring support the lowest eaves. The two interior rings form the inner and outer *cao*, with a giant seated Buddha figure in the center. With the exception of the lowermost level, where the columns are encased in a wall to create an enclosure, all the upper stories are open. There are three primary levels, each being a temple unto itself and each with a Buddha statue.

A skyscraper of sorts in its day, the Mu-ta was one of the most advanced structural achievements of its time. Like the Guanyin-ge of Dulesi Monastery, each story of the Mu-ta is a separate structural entity (none of the pillars rises more than a story) tied together by fifty-four different types of bracket sets. On the exterior, each story of the Mu-ta is represented by eaves, held up by a neat arrangement of structural *dou-gong*. In the interior, however, the structure is held together by a complex mesh of posts and beams, radial *dou-gong*, and cross-bracing that ultimately fashions a thick nest in the form of a torus between the external skin and the central space. It is this mesh of cross-reinforcements that has enabled the Mu-ta to endure for a millennium unharmed by numerous earthquakes.

Dulesi Monastery

In about 984 CE, Hebei, a Liao nobleman from Jixian, built a Buddhist monastery, Dulesi ("Solitary Joy"), dedicated to Guanyin, the bodhisattva of compassion and mercy. Dulesi Monastery was rebuilt several times, but its central structures, the main gate (*shanmen*) and the prayer hall (Guanyin-ge) are original to the Liao. (The suffix –*ge* refers to multistory buildings that are accessible only from the front and that, like this one, house colossal statues.) Thirty meters separate the *shanmen* from the Guanyin-ge. The line of sight is such that the top of the roof of the 22-meter-high Guanyin-ge is distinctly visible from the entry portal of the

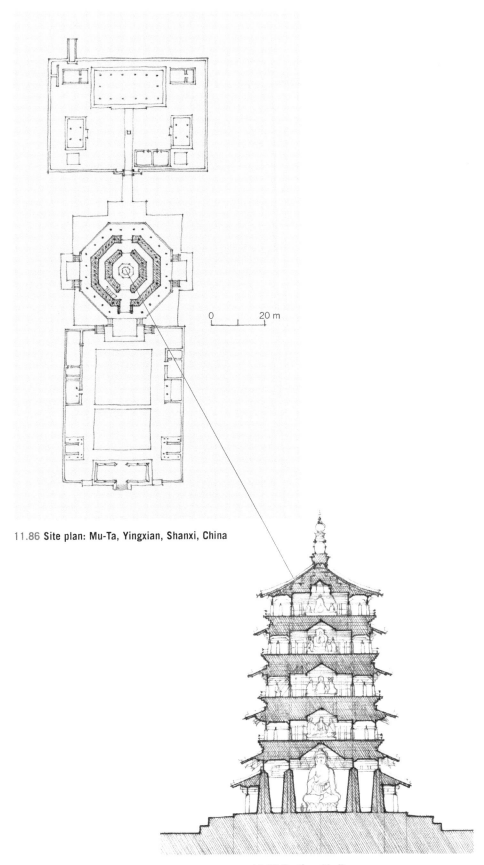

11.86 Site plan: Mu-Ta, Yingxian, Shanxi, China

0   20 m

11.87 **Section: Mu-Ta**

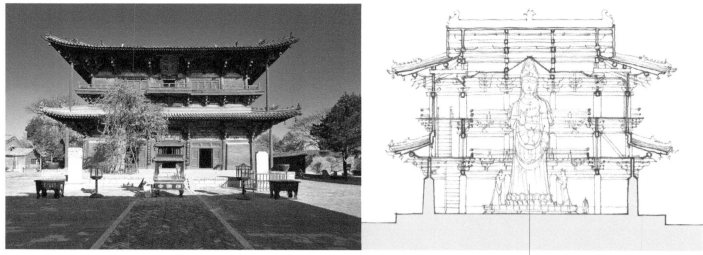

11.88 Dulesi Monastery, Jixian, Hebei Province, China

11.89 Section through Guanyin-ge, Dulesi Monastery

shanmen, allowing the entire structure to assert its full impact upon entry. As in the Mu-ta, each story of the Guanyin-ge is a distinct structure wedged into the one below. It is a three-story building, though on the outside it appears to have only two stories so that Guanyin's eyes can be seen through the upper-level windows when one enters the compound.

Wood roofs are described by the number and types of bracket sets and beams deployed. Bracket sets are classified by the number and complexity of their horizontal, vertical, and diagonal elements. Beams are designated by their position and the number of rafters they span. In the *shanmen*, four four-rafter beams and four two-rafter beams hold up the roof. The structure uses an astonishing twenty-four different types of bracket sets, the most complex ones at the corners. The building is raised on a polished stone base about 1 meter in height. The plan is divided by columns into an inner, triple-high space and a circumambulatory vestibule, known as the outer and inner *wai* and *nei cao*, respectively. The second-floor ambulatory is accessible by stairs. In addition, the Guanyin's eyes align with a masonry pagoda—the White Pagoda (reconstructed 1058) located 350 meters away on axis. This visual connection was a reinterpretation of the Mahayana Buddhist practice of superimposing statues of Buddhas on stupas to emphasize the commonality between the two.

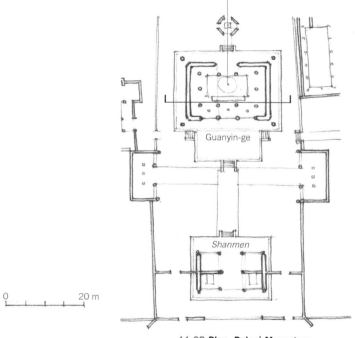

0   20 m

11.90 Plan: Dulesi Monastery

Located just outside their cities, Liao tombs consisted of multichambered underground burial vaults and several aboveground platforms on which descendants could perform sacrifices to appease the spirits of the dead. Accessed by a long "spirit path," a paved road leading to the tombs, they were flanked by larger than life-size statues of mythical and real animals and other ceremonial objects meant to guard and guide the spirits. Interiors were painted to imitate the interiors of tents and wooden structures. Curiously, the Liao tombs all contain one panel with the painting of a woman in the act of stepping through a door; their meaning

remains unclear. Bodies were drained of fluids and filled with vegetable products, embalmed, and often covered with a suit made of fine metal.

The Liao dynasty began to decline in the 12th century. In 1120, the Song made an alliance with the newly founded Jin dynasty and attacked the Liao regime. In 1125, the last emperor of Liao, Tianzuo, was captured by the Jin army, ending the Liao dynasty. The Jin, who were related to the Mongolians, turned out to be more formidable than the Song anticipated, and they soon controlled much of the former Liao area in northern China.

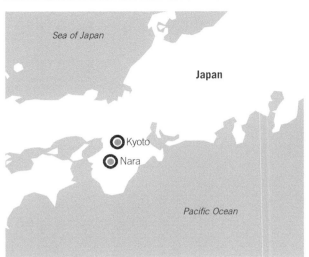

11.91 **Japan: Location of Kyoto and Nara, Japan**

11.92 **Phoenix hall at Byodo-in, near Kyoto, Japan**

PURE LAND BUDDHISM

Around the year 1000 CE, as power shifted from the upper classes to the aristocracy, a new form of Buddhism known as Pure Land Buddhism came to dominate Japan. Since Pure Land Buddhism was open to all, it offered a means by which the Japanese aristocracy could gain access to Buddhist teachings without having to live in monasteries. Originally developed in India in the 2nd century CE, Pure Land Buddhism was based on the concept that a devotee could attain rebirth in a *sukhavati* ("equanimous or pure land") of his or her choice by following a designated set of personal meditations. These meditations were to focus on a particular set of visualizations—a set of prescribed scenes that took the worshipper to that place through a series of steps. Its core teachings were contained in the "Visualization Sutra," a sermon believed to have been given by the Buddha to the virtuous Lady Vaidehi, who sought to be released from her world full of material attachments and demons. Because of its association with Lady Vaidehi, Pure Land Buddhism was promoted, in particular, by women. Pure Land visualizations were usually depicted in paintings, sculptures, and mandala diagrams. The act of transcribing sutras and redrawing visualizations was enough to earn a devotee merit. These transcriptions were ultimately done as architecture by remaking plans implied in mandalas into real buildings. This made the temple itself into an object of worship.

In 1053 a nobleman, Fujiwara no Yorimichi (990–1074), converted a preexisting villa in Uji, near Kyoto, into a transcription of the Taima mandala. This visualization is known as the Byodo-in, the "Temple of Equanimity." In Buddhism, *byodo* ("equal") refers to the condition of possibility that is open to all. The Phoenix hall (Hoo-do) is all that remains of the original temple. Hoo are mythical phoenix-like birds, sculptures of which top the roof of the hall.

The Taima mandala depicts the Buddha seated on a C-shaped platform on a lake surrounded by bodhisattvas. Built on an artificial island in a lake, the Phoenix hall replicates the Taima mandala in plan, with winglike extensions on the right and left. The Phoenix hall was meant to be viewed primarily from across the lake, as a visualization for a devotee to focus on during meditation.

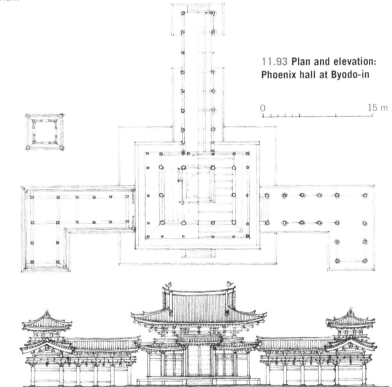

11.93 **Plan and elevation: Phoenix hall at Byodo-in**

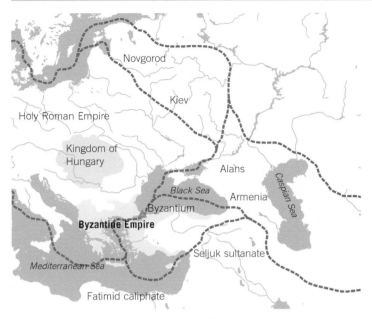

11.94 Byzantium and eastern Europe, ca. 1000 CE

BYZANTINE REVIVAL

By the year 1000 CE, the Byzantine Empire had rebounded under Basil II, due to successful military campaigns and a restructuring of its administration. Among the reasons for its new success was the rise of trade with Novgorod and Kiev, which created a circular trade flow that included Armenia while avoiding still-volatile central Europe. Church building also began to rebound. Formally, little changed: the central element was still a dome resting on four columns placed in a square. New, however, was the desire to create compound churches by adding new ones to older ones through opening a passageway between them and uniting them by means of a new narthex. This can be seen at the Church of Christ Pantokrator (known in Turkish as Zeyrek Camii), a complex of three churches (1118–43) in Constantinople that was completed by Emperor John II Komenos. The south and north churches were built first by Empress Eirene. After her death, John decided to join the two churches with a third dedicated to the archangel Michael that also served as a mortuary chapel for his family clan, the Commenus. Over the centuries, many Byzantine emperors were buried there. The building thereby became much renowned in Constantinople. It was, as was customary, associated with a monastery and a hospice—in this case one for old men. The south church is a four-column type. The columns, now gone, were of red marble. The north church is similar, with a dome carried on a high drum. The middle church also had a dome, creating a complex labyrinthine interior. The building was made of brick with a plastered wall that was painted.

11.95 Interior, Church of Christ Pantokrator

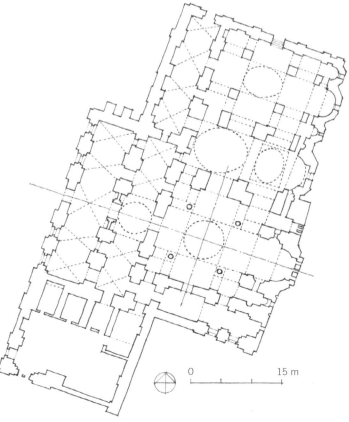

0   15 m

11.96 Plan: Church of Christ Pantokrator, Constantinople, Turkey

Kievan Russia

Centralization of power under the Rurikovichi dynasty, of presumably Norse origin, accelerated the decline of the patriarchal clan organization in Kievan Russia and gave rise to the development of a trading class ruled by noblemen. Kiev soon became the center of a great waterway system of rivers, principally the Dnieper, linking Scandinavia and Byzantium. This allowed for a consolidation of trade routes—the Dnieper and the Volkhov Rivers connecting the White Sea to the Black Sea, and the Volga River connecting the Caspian Sea to the north, serving as the highways of the age. Trade in furs, hides, wax, honey, wheat, spices, metals, and fabrics contributed to the increase in the wealth of the cities along these routes. Though the Hungarians made an alliance with the Latin Church, the Slavs and Rus converted in the 10th century to the Eastern Church centered in Constantinople. The decision, according to legend, was inspired by the beauty of the Hagia Sophia and the elaborateness of the religious rituals as reported back to Russia by emissaries sent to compare the two religions. The connection to Byzantium is borne out architecturally: the first masonry structure in Russia, the Church of the Tithe in Kiev (989–96 CE), was erected by Byzantine masons. Though little of it is preserved, 20th-century excavations revealed fragments of mosaics and fresco decorations and allowed for a reconstruction of the plan—an inscribed cross—that served as a prototype for Russian medieval masonry churches. Another important church of the time was the Hagia Sophia in Novgorod, a stone building consecrated in 1052 by the Novgorod prince Vladimir Yaroslavovich. The church became a main center of Christian spirituality in northern Russia. Though influenced by Byzantine architecture, Russian churches began take on a unique style. Unlike Byzantine churches, which do not have particularly pronounced silhouettes, Russian churches often had domes set high on tall drums. Furthermore, four domes were set in a tight cluster around a central one. The churches were bulky with small windows, making the interior all the more mysterious. A narthex helped negotiate the transition between outside and inside.

Vladimir-Suzdal was a principality that succeeded Kievan Rus as the most powerful Rus state in the late 12th century; it lasted until the late 14th century. Its fortification possessed a so-called golden gate (1158–64), one of the best-preserved instances of the ancient Russian city gates. It was modeled on similar golden gates in Jerusalem, Constantinople, and Kiev. It is probable that the masons were invited from Byzantium, as they used Greek measures rather than Russian ones. The structure was topped with a church dedicated to the Deposition of the Virgin's Robe.

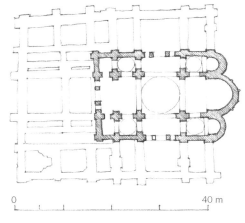

0   40 m

11.97 Plan: Church of the Tithe (Desyatinaya)

11.98 Elevation: Church of the Tithe (Desyatinaya), Kiev, Russia

11.99 Golden gate, Vladimir, Russia

Armenia

An important influence on Byzantine architecture came from the direction of Armenia. During the period of the Arab caliphate (654–861 CE), all church building in Armenia had stopped, but when its independence was regained, Armenia saw a reawakening of its architectural culture until 1045, when it was invaded from the north by the Turks. But in 1080, Prince Ruben founded a new kingdom in Cilicia and Armenia (sometimes known as the fourth Armenian kingdom). The close relations this kingdom established with European countries played an important role during the Crusades. Intermarriage with European crusading families was common among its aristocracy. Many French terms entered the Armenian language. To the north of this Christian realm was the empire of the Khazars, and to the south, the Islamic caliphate of Baghdad.

By the 10th century, Ani had risen to become one of the leading cities of West Asia. Located on what is now the border between Turkey and Armenia, it is sited on a long promontory defined by the Akhurian River. Its defensive walls were built in 963 CE, but the city quickly outgrew them to reach a population of about one hundred thousand. Though the city was taken by the Byzantines in 1045 and then the Seljuks in 1064, it was restored to local rule under Zak'are Mxargrjeli in 1199 and flourished until being sacked by the Mongolians in 1236. Its chapels and churches numbered in the hundreds. The Cathedral of Ani (989–1001) deserves to be listed among the principal monuments of the time because of its pointed arches and clustered columns and piers. It was spectacularly sited at the center of town on a bluff overlooking the Arpa and Akhurian Rivers. The architect responsible for the building was Trdat, whose fame was such that he was summoned to Constantinople to repair the dome of the Hagia Sophia, which had been damaged by an earthquake in 989 CE. Continuing the tradition of Armenian architectural innovation, Trdat rested the dome of the Cathedral of Ani on a drum with four pendentives descending between the arches, which rest on four piers. Smaller arches span the side aisles. Because the dome is independently supported, the rest of the structure is larger than the size of the dome would permit. This creates a more airy relationship between dome and perimeter than was the case in earlier Armenian churches, which were more compact.

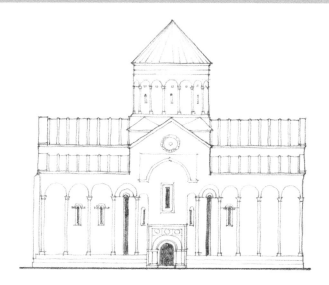

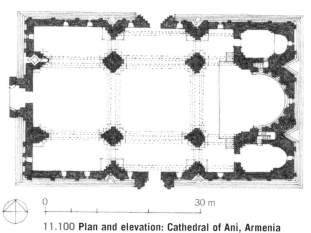

11.100 **Plan and elevation: Cathedral of Ani, Armenia**

11.101 **Cathedral of Ani**

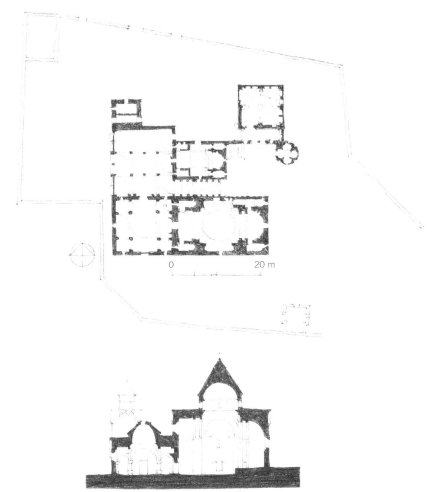

11.102 **Plan and section: Sanahin complex, Lori, Armenia**

11.103 **Interior of Sanahin church**

Sanahin Complex

A well-preserved monastic compound, Sanahin (also known as St. Amenaprkitch), 2 kilometers southeast of the town of Alaverdi, is an example of an Armenian monastic institution. Unlike Byzantine aggregates, in which buildings tend to fuse into each other, the complexes in Armenia maintained volumetric and functional clarity. The churches (begun 934 CE) have between them a barrel-vaulted corridor, or *academia*, where pupils could sit on stone benches while the teacher walked up and down the space, as was the custom in peripatetic schools. Appended to the front of both churches are *gavits*, dating from about 1210, which came to be used around that time. In these vaulted spaces, novices could assist during Mass. Their principal utilization, however, was as meeting halls; and laws and ordinances were carved on the internal walls. They also served as places to bury nobility.

The Church of the Holy Cross on the island of Aght'amar (consecrated 921 CE), originally unencumbered by ancillary buildings, makes its impression through symmetry and equilibrium. Unlike Byzantine churches, which were composite in nature, Armenian churches aimed to maintain a tight bond between interior and exterior. The sacristy and the vestry, instead of being separate spaces to the right and left of the altar, are therefore embedded in the mass of the wall. The interior, however, was never just a reflection of outer form. The church, as is also typical of Armenian architecture, presents the buildings in simple elemental forms: cubes, cylinders, cones, and pyramids. The dome is conical on the outside but hemispherical within. Walls are made of an aggregate of pebbles and mortar much like concrete, and dressed with blocks of closely fitting pink sandstone. The plan, with its four apses, is known as a tetraconch, even though the east and west exedrae are deeper than those on the north and south. The exterior is decorated with bands of bas-relief sculpture depicting biblical scenes. The lighting on the interior is indirect, and the windows are small. The main light source is around the drum, above which the dome seems to float, as if it were on a ring of light. The wide side apses swell the space outward at ground level, with small concavities at the corners, between the piers, adding further illumination. The entire interior was originally painted with religious scenes.

OTTONIAN GERMANY

For several decades under Charlemagne (742–814 CE), virtually the entire Western world—such as it was defined at that time—had been brought together into a single political entity governed by a homogenous group of bishops and judges, scions of the dominant families. But with the division of Charlemagne's empire after his death, Viking raids in the north, and Muslim incursions in the south, the quality of life in Europe deteriorated. Communities were scattered, libraries destroyed, and monasteries ruined. By the year 1000 CE, however, the situation had begun to improve, partially because by then the feudal system had been established throughout most of Europe. Society fell roughly into three groups; the serfs, attached to the land; the members of religious establishments; and the aristocracy, who had hereditary power and collected the taxes and took responsibility for the military protection of the land.

The balance of power shifted from France to Christianized Germany under the Ottonian dynasty (919–1024). The princely realm of Germany, like that of France, had no capital city in the modern sense. Rulers moved from place to place, adjudicating legal cases as they went, trying to hold together the network of relationships on which the kingdom depended. The absence of a capital city differentiated the European notion of governance at that time from almost every other state in the world.

The Ottonian rulers seem to have admired the life and culture of Constantinople. Mothers and wives of the aristocracy were often Greek princesses, and the emperor took over the Eastern notion of *basileus*, or sovereign, complete with the concomitant conception of authority and its emblems of power—the golden cape and the sphere held in the right hand. These Eastern connections brought with them artisans as well as Byzantine and Armenian architects and stonemasons, whose quality of workmanship had a positive impact on Ottonian architecture. Near Quedlinburg in Gernrode stands the only fully preserved church from the early Ottonian period, the Collegiate Church of St. Cyriakus. Different from Carolingian architecture, Ottonian churches, though still volumetrically powerful, demonstrate much more skilled stonework, along with a desire for verticality. Like Carolingian churches, Ottonian ones consisted of volumetric masses.

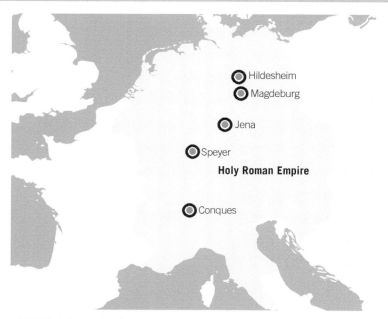

11.104 **Holy Roman Empire**

11.105 **St. Cyriakus, Gernrode, Germany**

As a way to cement imperial control over their territory, the Ottonian kings combined the founding of monasteries with the founding of market centers. But the uncluttered external surfaces and the integrated relationship between the crossings and transepts of St. Cyriakus in Gernrode (960 CE) and St. Michael in Hildesheim (1001–33), for example, impart to these buildings a complex simplicity that earlier Carolingian churches, such as St. Riquier, lacked. St. Michael was sited not far from the newly developing market city of Hildesheim, defined by its broad street onto which the shops faced. The church was not in the city proper, as that was not yet very common; instead, it was in its own precinct outside of town. Unlike Roman churches, the entrance of St. Michael was broadside, from the south, leading up from the marketplace.

Stretching between two almost identical transepts, the nave has a ratio of 3:1, the rhythm established by piers with two columns interspersed between them. The building, which has no westwork, reflects the gradual reduction of its importance. The crypt, with its ambulatory, is at ground level, with the high altar located above. The cloister to the north has been lost over time. The roof was supported by wooden trusses.

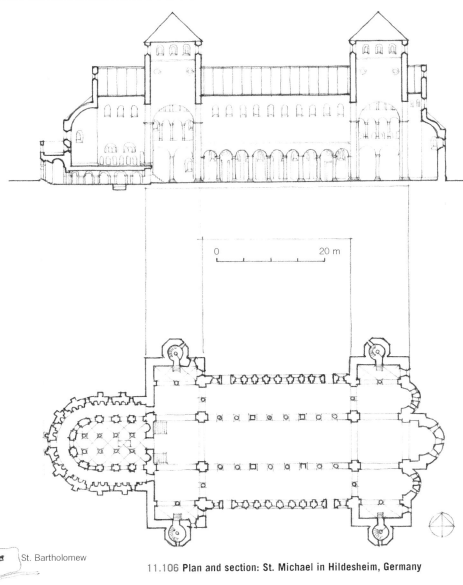

11.106 Plan and section: St. Michael in Hildesheim, Germany

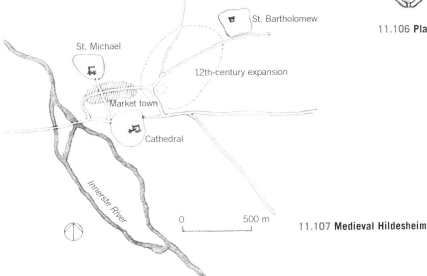

11.107 Medieval Hildesheim

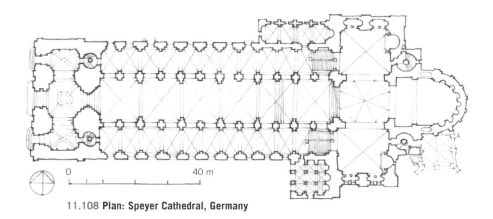

11.108 **Plan: Speyer Cathedral, Germany**

The word *cathedral* derives from a Greek word that designates a professor's chair from which a lecture was given. Early Christian bishops used a cathedra not only as a symbol of their power but also as a place from which to preach, even though that practice was eventually abandoned. The first use of the word in regard to architecture dates from around 800 CE. A cathedral, in that etymological sense, is thus an elaborate framing device for a bishop's chair. Some ancient chairs still exist, such as the so-called Chair of St. Peter, which is preserved in the Vatican Museums.

Speyer Cathedral

Despite the problems of the times, increased trade and competition among cities led to a rapid increase in architectural production and to an experimentation with new forms. Particularly important was the introduction of stone vaulting. The implications were profound—spatially, structurally, and symbolically. To support the vault, the builders could have decided to build thicker walls, but instead they interpreted the side aisles as structural buttresses for the vault, transforming the interior of the building into a tripartite space visually coordinated with the vaults over the aisles.

One of the earliest churches built in the new manner was the Speyer Cathedral, begun around 1040, with the vaulting completed around 1137. Abandoning the squat compositions of Carolingian and Ottonian architecture, the nave elevation of Speyer was defined by a series of high arches reminiscent of a Roman aqueduct. Windows at the top brought light into the nave. Even more significant was the presence of a single attached column that rose some 32 meters from the floor to the base of the vault—higher than any other vault at the time. The crossing is defined by an octagonal tower. The tall proportions allow the building to seem more compact and controlled, and to some eyes, more Roman, especially when compared to

Hildesheim's static arrangement of volumes. There can be no doubt that the third Abbey Church of Cluny, begun about 1088, was erected in open rivalry to Speyer. The interior nave of Speyer has since been rebuilt, but St. Étienne in Nevers (1063–97) is more or less comparable.

Despite its innovations, Speyer can also be seen as the end stage of the Romanesque style, for at that very same time, a remarkable new development was taking place at the Abbey Church of St. Foy at Conques, begun around 1050. As at Speyer, the tall, soaring barrel-vaulted nave creates the impression of a single structure, as opposed to a box with a roof on it. As at Speyer, the high side aisles serve as buttresses for the vault. And as at Speyer, the nave, at least in the lower part, combines its structure with arcaded openings. But the architects of St. Foy added buttresses on the outside to further strengthen the walls. Though small, they are enough to affect the clear differentiation between wall and column that defines Carolingian and Romanesque architecture. The wall begins to look more and more like a series of piers.

11.109 **Abbey Church of St. Foy, Conques, France**

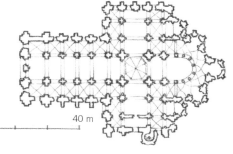

11.110 **Plan: Abbey Church of St. Foy**

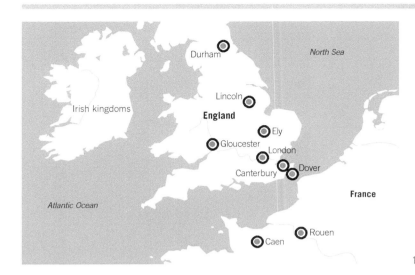

11.111 Norman England

THE NORMANS

In 911 CE, Charles the Simple validated the Norman possessions around Rouen, France, which the Normans had begun to occupy in the 9th century. The Normans, with amazing adaptive energy, renounced paganism and absorbed local customs and language. They also furthered the development of the Romanesque style, of which the Cathedral of Caen is the prime example. In 1001, Richard II, duke of Normandy, invited the Italian abbot William of Volpiano—accompanied by a colony of Benedictines, with their well-established traditions of design and masonry construction—to restore the Abbey of Fécamp. Soon a uniquely Norman style developed that incorporated Norse decorative motifs while drawing on the Islamic influences brought to England and France from the Norman holdings in Sicily.

A warrior people from the northern French coast, the Normans overran England and southern Italy and settled in Scotland, Wales, the Byzantine Empire, and (after the First Crusade) the Levant. Norman power was extended by strategic marriage alliances. In a series of waves, the Normans conquered parts of southern Italy and Sicily (1061), and then England, following the Battle of Hastings (1066). The new rulers transformed the entire religious, mercantile, and political geography of England. But their holdings were far-flung, from England and northern France to southern Italy and Sicily; the Normans consequently became a clearinghouse of different stylistic and cultural trends that bridged many classic divides.

Most importantly they transformed the village- and agrarian-based geography of the Saxons into one based on towns in the middle of large farming districts or boroughs, with castles at their centers to serve as the basic instrument of government. Unlike in Germany, where castles were generally on defensible ridges or mountains, in England, where mountains are not a prominent geographical feature, they were built at the core of the urban layout. Town markets were created and an aristocracy took shape, promoting an international luxury trade in commodities such as fine cloth and wine. It has been estimated that about four to five hundred new towns were laid out in this manner, creating a pattern of urban centers that was to survive virtually unchanged until the Industrial Revolution and, in parts of England, survives even today.

The Normans introduced not only a strong mercantile society but also a change in the notion of kingship. Roger the Great, in the chronicles of the time, is represented as the royal deputy of Christ. The small Saxon churches that dotted the English landscape could no longer measure up to such grand claims. Most were torn down, and in their stead the Normans designed a religious landscape around powerful state-supported bishoprics, each of which needed a sumptuous cathedral. Architects and masons were brought in from the continent, as were successive waves of continental monks—Benedictines, Augustinians, Cistercians, Cluniacs, and Carthusians—who were just as important from an economic point of view as

from a religious one, as their well-organized farms produced surpluses for the markets. The Cistercians, for example, were associated with irrigation and large-scale sheep farming. By the end of the 12th century, six hundred new monastic institutions of varying practices had been set up.

Durham Cathedral

Durham Cathedral is important for its architectural features, specifically its rib vaulting (the first of its kind in England), its pointed arches, and its high standard of masonry. Durham shows the specific Anglo-Norman style as a blend of the English decorative tradition with Norman architectural skills, and it marks the transition from a more monumental and simple scheme, as is seen in Gloucester Cathedral (begun 1089). The choir and the nave of the three-aisled church were built between 1093 and 1133, but the west towers were not completed until 1220. In comparison with the nave of Gloucester, which also has heavy round columns carrying the arcades, Durham, in the manner of Speyer, introduces the idea of attached half-columns that guide the eye to the ceiling.

The loftiness of these churches had always been a feature of Romanesque architecture; what is novel here is the structural openness of the walls. A basic principle of Norman building was the reduction of solid walls to a thick but open skeleton of arches. The arches were not just interruptions in the wall; they were defined in a regularized way, with surrounds framed by attached half-columns and horizontal string courses. The openings

11.112 **Durham Cathedral, England**

11.113 **Partial section through the nave of Durham Cathedral**

do not deny the weight and mass of the wall, as would become the tendency later, but rather, illuminated from behind, they seem to release their load gradually as the wall ascends.

The columns are decorated with zigzag and chevron motifs and make extensive use of color, specifically black and red, which was an influence from Islamic architecture that came to the country through the Crusades and the Norman-Arab connections in Sicily and northern Africa. Geometric patterns and other features of the inner decoration can later be found in other cathedrals in northern England, suggesting that the same masons moved on to work in Scotland.

Durham Cathedral is considered a forerunner of what is now called the Gothic style, largely because of the fusion of the ribbed vault and the pointed arch, which are considered essentially Gothic features. The building does not have buttresses and so appears from the outside quite boxy, unlike later Norman cathedrals such as Canterbury Cathedral, where buttresses contribute to a vertical articulation. The so-called Galilee Chapel (1153–95) in front of the west facade is unique, with its five parallel halls and longitudinal arcaded walls without any subdivision into bays. This layout resembles one encountered in Islamic mosques and once again shows the cross-fertilization of ideas introduced from the Mediterranean.

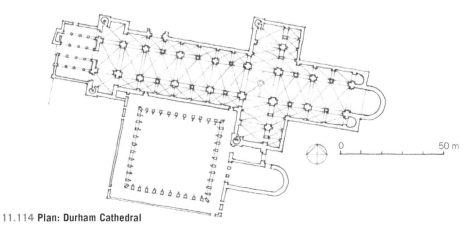

11.114 **Plan: Durham Cathedral**

11.115 **Nave of Durham Cathedral**

Canterbury Cathedral

Among the new bishoprics, Canterbury was the most important, as its bishop served as vice-regent of the king. When Canterbury Cathedral was destroyed by an accidental fire in 1067, one year after William the Conqueror landed on the south coast of England, Lanfranc, the first Norman archbishop of Canterbury, initiated a rebuilding that was based on the new cathedral of St. Étienne in France. When a fire destroyed the choir in 1174, the architects, William of Sens and William the Englishman, erected a new choir and a presbytery that doubled the length of the church. The newer part existed on a higher elevation, with the stairs serving to separate the more sacred areas to the east. The project shows how England adopted French construction techniques—specifically the flying buttress and the six-partite vault—while the nave itself remained from the time of Lanfranc. (The nave was, however, rebuilt in the late 14th century.) The church houses, among other sacred objects, the relics of St. Thomas, which were originally placed at the center of the round chapel at the eastern end of the building. The cloister and monastic buildings are placed on the north—instead of, as is more frequently the case, on the south of the church. Compared to Durham Cathedral, which has no buttresses, giving it a resolute boxy form, the wall surface at Canterbury has more vertical articulation.

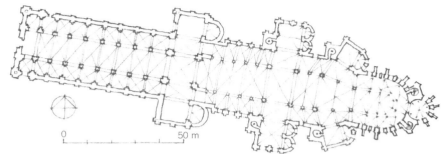

11.116 **Plan: Canterbury Cathedral, England**

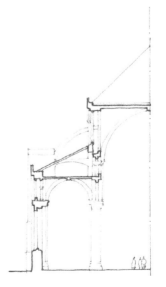

11.117 **Partial section: Canterbury Cathedral**

11.118 **Interior vaulting: Canterbury Cathedral**

Cefalù Cathedral

When Roger d'Hauteville conquered Sicily in 1060, he found a culture that had been under Arab influence since the late 9th century. The Normans not only availed themselves of the practical and technological innovations of the Muslims but also integrated Muslims into their administration and army. Soon Apulia, Capua, Sicily, and finally parts of northern Africa came under Norman domination. As a consequence, the Normans controlled the trade route to the Bosporus.

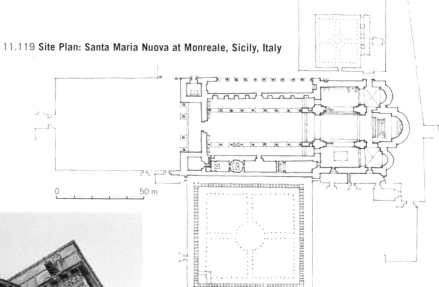

11.119 Site Plan: Santa Maria Nuova at Monreale, Sicily, Italy

0   50 m

11.120 Exterior detail: Santa Maria Nuova at Monreale

The first major Norman church in Sicily was built at Cefalù (begun 1131); it followed a typical early Norman footprint, with a nave with side aisles, a wooden ceiling, and a massive transept in the east. It is a heavy and somber building that contrasts sharply with Santa Maria Nuova at Monreale (from the Latin *mons regalis*, "royal mountain"), south of Palermo on the slopes of Monte Caputo, that was started only a hundred years after Cefalù. Islamic influences are apparent in the outside decoration of the apse, with its intertwined arches and terra-cotta ornamentation. The Great Mosque of Córdoba (10th century) and the Bab Mardum Mosque in Toledo (around 1000 CE) show similar interlocking arches. The cathedral also shows Byzantine influences, such as the exquisite mosaics that cover the interior walls of the cathedral and are second in quality only to those in the Hagia Sofia in Istanbul.

This stylistic synthesis is also evident in the areas of western Italy that the Normans controlled. Amalfi became a seafaring republic, rivaling Genoa, Venice, and Pisa, from the 9th to the 11th centuries. At its height it had trade representatives in Mahdiya, Tunisia; Kairuan (Cairo); Alexandria; Beirut; Jerusalem; Antioch, Syria; and Constantinople. At the Cathedral of Amalfi, the original Norman building underwent various expansions, including the Cloister of Paradise, which is clearly influenced by Islamic motifs.

11.121 Aerial view: Cefalù Cathedral, Sicily, Italy

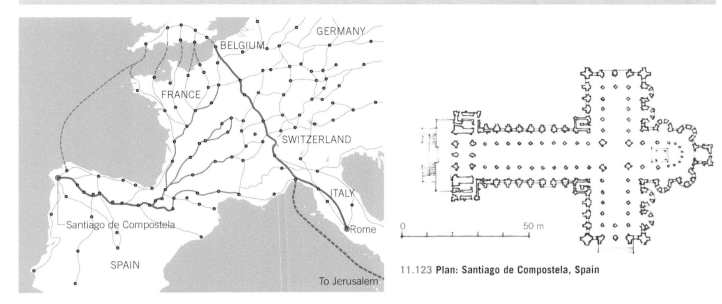

11.122 European pilgrimage routes

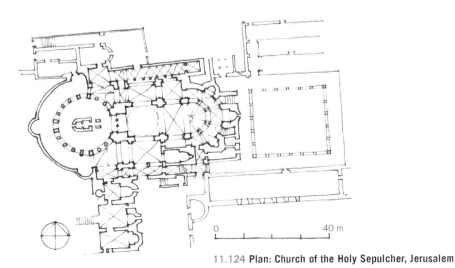

11.123 Plan: Santiago de Compostela, Spain

PILGRIMAGE CHURCHES

The 11th and 12th centuries saw a growth in the popularity of religious pilgrimages, usually to sites where miracles were believed to have occurred. Pilgrims sought out these churches mainly for the relics they housed, which were thought to emit a benevolent or curative aura. Possessing relics—a finger, a foot, or even a head of a saint—became central to a particular church's identity, and churches vied with each to collect as many such relics as possible. Major ones were the tomb of St. Peter in Rome, the tomb of St. James at Santiago de Compostela, and the Church of the Holy Sepulcher in Jerusalem. Most pilgrims traveled of their own volition, but some pilgrimages were acts of penance imposed for exceptional misdeeds. The trips, exhausting and often dangerous, became the source of stories and ballads, such as Geoffrey Chaucer's *Canterbury Tales*. Other accounts give us some of the earliest descriptions of church architecture in the West.

The most venerated pilgrimage site was the Holy Sepulcher in Jerusalem. The original church, constructed by Constantine, was consecrated in 335 CE to protect a tomb thought to have been that of Christ. Constantine's church was torn down by the Persians. The Crusaders then began a church that, with changes and additions, is the basis for the church as it stands today.

Originally, the entrance from the main street led to a courtyard and then to a basilica with two side aisles. This opened onto an inner atrium (the holy garden) and the rotunda (the anastasis), which had a conical roof. The shrine itself, a rectangular structure, was destroyed by fire in 1808; the current one dates from shortly thereafter.

Descriptions of the Holy Sepulcher from visitors led to the construction of models in the West, such as St. Bénigne at Dijon (1001), Neuvry-St.-Sépulchre (1045), and the Church of La Vera Cruz in Segovia (1208). As none of these replicas are alike, it is clear that a precise imitation was not as important

as other features. Among these copies is the frequently restored Church of San Stefano at Bologna. Erected in the 5th century, it was rebuilt in 1180 in the shape of a dodecagon. The tomb chamber has an altar on top and is approached by two staircases.

The churches begun in the 11th century were significantly different from their Romanesque counterparts. Whereas in the earlier churches the nave was for the public and the apse for the monks or priests, the newer churches, which had sacred relics, were built for movement through the church and around the back of the high altar, where many of the relics were displayed.

11.124 Plan: Church of the Holy Sepulcher, Jerusalem

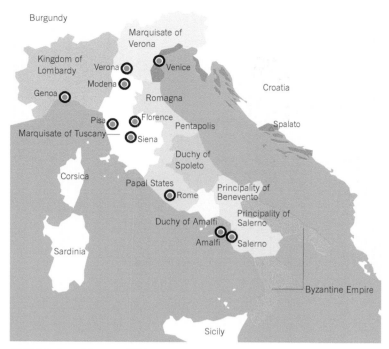

11.125 **Italian states, ca. 1000 CE**

11.126 **Modena Cathedral, Italy**

TUSCANY

Charlemagne traveled to Italy only four times, each trip lasting less than a year, setting a precedent of absentee monarchism that persisted for centuries. This allowed north Italian states, seen by the kings as the southern fringe of their empire, to survive as neither independent nor fully integrated into the empire. Nevertheless, their cities were bustling places. Lucca was growing so fast that houses were being built along the approach roads; soon a good portion of the population lived outside the walls in so-called bourgs. And between the cities, villages—called variously *vici*, *loci*, *casalia*, or *villae*—came to be established. As a result, monasteries—with some exceptions—were unable to develop the hold on the local population that they had in northern Europe. To be sure, the cities did not look very impressive. Roman civic buildings and temples had been left to rot, or they were used as quarries. Churches built after 600 CE were small. Only a limited amount of farming occurred within city walls. The forums had lost their civic value and become marketplaces. In 1006, a series of disastrous famines and plagues killed thousands of people. The weak centralized power of the emperors combined with the rising status of the cities; consequently, more and more

power was ceded by the emperors to the city bishops in order to maintain control.

The bishops of Modena, Reggio, Bergamo, Cremona, and other places were given unprecedented powers. In 904 CE, the bishop of Bergamo, for example, was granted the right to build city walls and to rebuild them with the help of the citizens. The result of this transfer of authority was dangerous to the imperial state, as bishops were not able to maintain their hegemony over urban society. Cities now began to vie with each other, however, in the construction of cathedrals and baptisteries that showed off the wealth of the city and the status of the church. The principal churches during this time were in Venice (begun 832 CE), Pisa (begun 1063), Modena (begun 1099), Cremona (begun 1118), Verona (begun 1139), and Siena (begun 1196).

The architect of the Modena Cathedral was Lanfranco, called *mirabilis artifex, mirificus aedificator* ("marvelous creator, wonderful builder"), about whom, however, little is known except that he came from Como, where a school of builders had been established. Compared to other Romanesque buildings of the time, Modena Cathedral is lighter and the lines stripped to their essentials. The building was clad in white Istrian stone and articulated by blind arcades. The central

division is emphasized by a rose window and a baldachino-style central portal. The rose window on the facade was added in the 13th century. The work is ornamented with sculptures by the stonemason Wiligelmo; it depicts, among other things, Adam and Eve working the land to gain redemption. The portals also portray biblical and mythological events, including monsters and centaurs that warn not only of the diabolic threats awaiting man outside the city of God but also the threats that come from outside the Christian world, a reminder that Sicily had already fallen, first to Islamic troops, then to Arab colonizers. The archbishop's palace and administrative center was connected to the cathedral by means of a private passage. The building was commissioned by Queen Matilda di Canossa (1046–1115). One of the most powerful women of the Middle Ages, she had a fortress in the heart of the Emilian Apennines and was a strong supporter of papal policy against the emperors. Matilda ruled over Tuscany, which extended from Siena and Pisa to Modena in the north. She commissioned, or had a hand in the commissioning of, several other buildings in the Po River valley, including the Rotunda of San Lorenzo in Mantua (1083) and the Benedictine abbey of San Benedetto in Polirone (1077), as well as Cremona Cathedral (1107–17) and Piacenza Cathedral (1122).

11.127 **Detail: Cathedral of Pisa, Italy**

11.128 **Cathedral of Pisa**

Cathedral of Pisa

Construction on the Cathedral of Pisa began in 1063 after the victory of the Pisan fleet over the Saracens near Palermo. Pisa could now attempt to fulfill its ambition to become the Venice of the western Mediterranean and to develop a greater visual presence. The cathedral was consecrated in 1118, but it was completed only after considerable alterations in the 14th century. Stylistically it is a variation of the Mediterranean basilica plan, with influences from Armenia, Syria, and Islamic architecture. The building also had imperial Lombard overtones, especially in its facade, with its four registers of freestanding gallery work. The granite columns in the nave were taken from Roman temples on the isle of Elba; the capitals range from imperial Roman to Byzantine temples. The walls have marble paneling inspired by Byzantine practice, and the shape and manner of construction of the dome, rising on the inside from very high and narrow pointed arches, looks Islamic.

The building does not follow the trend of the great pilgrimage churches, in which structure and surface were becoming increasingly unified. In fact, it defied that trend in its celebration of surface. The elegant and costly marble sheathing that wraps around the exterior has little if any correlation to inner structure. The massive volume of the building becomes light and airy even though the openings are few and small, in the typical Romanesque manner. The plan is also far different from French cathedral architecture, which aspired to a unity of form and structure. Here the double-aisled nave is intersected by a transept formed by two single-aisled minor basilicas, set front to front, with a domed crossing between. Each of the minor cross basilicas is provided with an apse of its own. The plan is thus a type of composite of basilicas that, on the exterior, gives the illusion of a nave with transept.

The baptistery in front of the cathedral was begun in 1153. In 1173, the foundations were laid for the campanile, known now as the Leaning Tower of Pisa. In 1278, the tombs that cluttered the area around the church were gathered together and placed into a separate structure, the Camposanto, to the north of the church.

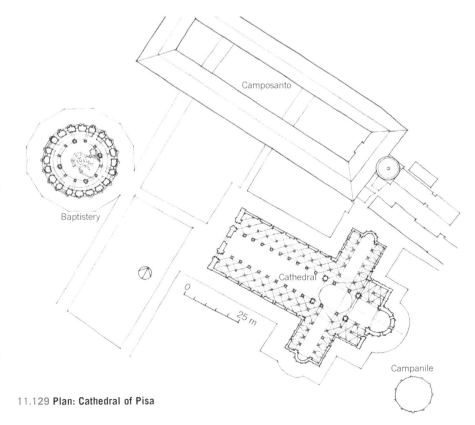

11.129 **Plan: Cathedral of Pisa**

11.130 **Baptistery of Florence, Italy**

11.131 **Baptistery of Pisa, Italy**

Baptistery of Parma

Parallel to the emergence of the Italian urban cathedral was the urban baptistery, conceived as a bold freestanding structure in the piazza in front of or next to a church. The typically octagonal shape had its roots in early Christian mysticism and imperial Roman symbolism. By the 10th century, with the revival of learning, came a rise in numerology—a science of its own at the time, built on the numbers embedded in the concept of the Trinity, the twelve apostles, the Holy Spirit, the number of perfection (3 x 4 x 5), and so forth. The number 8 and the octagonal form were especially important. In an inscription on the cathedral baptistery in Milan, the connection between number, geometry, and architecture is aptly expressed:

> He erected an eight-choired temple for use by the saints, and an octagonal font is worthy of its number. This number proved fitting for the elevation of a housing of the holy baptism, which gave back to the people true deliverance, raising them again in the light of Christ, who loosened the bonds of death, and [who] from their graves raised the lifeless.

Architecturally, the most significant baptisteries are at Florence (1060–1150), Pisa (1153–1265), and Parma (1196–1270). The Baptistery of Parma, modeled on the Rotunda of the Anastasi in Jerusalem, has corners that look like giant-order piers, with loggias and a blind arcade on top spanning the interstices. The lower level consists of generous arched openings and blind arches. The eight great piers and the sixteen columns on each register are standard referents to the Holy Sepulcher in Jerusalem. Although the imposing mass of the building is Romanesque, its sculptural decoration reflects French Gothic elements. This is most clearly seen in the prominence accorded the Virgin Mary—the main portal is dedicated to her—and in the changed representation of Christ from a severe judge to a more humane figure, which was the sign of the new religious mentality.

11.132 **Baptistery of Pavia, Italy**

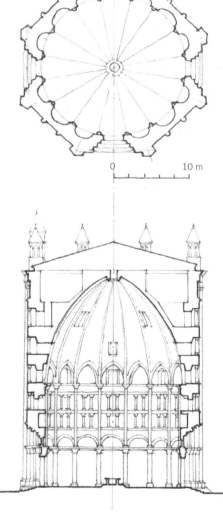

11.133 **Plan and section: Baptistery of Parma**

1200 CE

12.1 **Angkor Wat, near Siam Riep, Cambodia**

INTRODUCTION

To argue that the 13th century is the threshold of the modern world might seem strange at first, but imagine the economic world of Africa and Eurasia and think back a mere few hundred years. The southern route from Japan and China through Southeast Asia to India was now booming. At the head of it was the bustling Song dynasty seaport at Quanzhou—some 600 kilometers south of the Song capital at Hangzhou—with its extensive shipbuilding industry and its innovative dry-dock system. Enormous naval ships were built that could carry a thousand soldiers. The Song, despite the loss of the northern areas to the Jin, still produced over 100,000 metric tons of iron a year, using coal instead of charcoal in its blast furnaces. Much of this iron was reserved for military use in crafting weapons and armor, but some was used to fashion the many products needed to fill the demands of the growing domestic market. On the Quanzhou docks were bales of silk and crates of porcelain for the international luxury markets in Asia and Europe, but also tons of copper and iron needed for ritual objects in the temples in Southeast Asia. When Marco Polo visited the city, he commented on the ships filled with boxes of pearls (most probably coming from Hepu in southern China) and jewels. The city was ringed by walls, and the surrounding countryside was lined with canals to control flooding from the Jin River. The Song elite, fueled by wealth from global trade, brought the villa garden to spectacular and ostentatious heights. Emperor Huizong (1082–1135) had a garden called the Basin of the Clarity of the Gods, a large artificial lake surrounded by terraces. To pay for all of this, the Song used a new monetary device, paper money. It worked at first; printing money was easy and cheap. But the results soon led to a series of inflationary cycles that were to haunt the Chinese until they eventually abandoned paper money for silver.

The flow of trade between China and India benefited Southeast Asia and the Khmer more than anyone else. They consolidated power in Cambodia to control overland access to the independent kingdom of Dali, which functioned as a type of inland port into southern China. The Khmer built vast *barays* (large, man-made lakes) fed by kilometer-long canal systems to accelerate the production of rice, their prime export commodity. The *barays* were linked to gigantic religious complexes, the most elaborate of which was called Vara Vishnuloka (now more commonly known as Angkor Wat), one of the grandest of the many Khmer temples and on par in detail, engineering, symbolism, and sheer bravura of scale with Borobudur.

But squeezing more and more rice from the sandy soil of central Cambodia was a risky enterprise dependent as much on managing the intricate canal systems as on the weather. Ultimately, deforestation would exact its price. A series of devastating floods would bring the civilization to its knees, and by the 15th century the city of Angkor had all but been abandoned to the forest; but in the year 1200 this was not foreseen.

In India, two of the leading entrepôt cities were Kalinganagar (modern-day Srimukhalingam), the capital of the Eastern Ganga dynasty, located on the eastern coast; and Nabadwip of the Sena Empire, located north of modern-day Kolkata on the west bank of the Bhagirathi River. The economy was booming and construction of large-scale temples was a regular occurrence. These include the Hoysala Empire's Ishvara Temple (1220) in Arasikere and the enormous Konark Sun Temple of the Eastern Ganga dynasty. The latter was built in the form of the chariot of the Sun God, Surya, and supported by twelve pairs of elaborately carved stone wheels, some of which are 3 meters wide, that are "pulled" by seven pairs of stone-carved horses. At the nearby sacred city of Puri, elaborately decorated, three-story-high chariots of wood dedicated to Lord Jagannath

("Lord of the World") are pulled each year down a sacred road between two sets of temples, a ritual that probably began in the 9th century CE. Konark temple, by contrast, does not move, but stands as a type of mega-model of the divine solar chariot. Visible for miles around (though the main tower has since collapsed), it asks the question at what scale a building exists. Most buildings, even if large, are built to a scale comprehensible to the human, but this one was designed at something that might plausibly approximate the scale of the divine. Angkor Wat, by comparison, is also huge, yet despite its size, it seems to have been designed as a scaled-down model of a divine mountain. These structures recall the Egyptian hypostyle hall and the columns modeled on papyrus bundles, scaled at the dimension of the divine.

To the northwest of India was the Turkish-based Khwarazmian dynasty in present-day Iran, which ruled from Urgench, Uzbekistan. The Syrian geographer Yaqut, who lived in the city in 1219, considered it to be the most extensive and the richest of all the cities he had seen. Khwarazmian architects developed a double-domed cupola that featured extensive use of patterned brickwork and carved terra-cotta. Sadly, not much is left

of this once impressive city, as most houses were of mud brick.

One of the Ghaznavid generals established a sultanate in northern India, setting up his capital in what is now Delhi. There, his descendants built the mosque known as Quwwat-ul-Islam (Glory of Islam) on the site of a former Hindu temple. The architects used columns from the temple, but not as a sign of respect. Quwwat-ul-Islam is best known for its tower of victory, Qutb Minar (begun 1192), celebrating the Muslim conquest of India. Henceforth, Islam would be an integral part of the northern Indian subcontinent.

It was not just South Asia, from India to southern China, that was booming; Africa was opening up to international trade. Since around 6000 BCE, the Sahara Desert had been an unbreachable barrier between the Mediterranean and lower Africa. But the camel was introduced by the Arabs in the 8th century CE and camel-based cultures arose that moved east-west and north-south. Driving this trade was the discovery of vast salt deposits in Niger that are still being mined today. More important was the discovery of gold in Ivory Coast, in the upper reaches of the rivers that flowed down to the Atlantic. The rise of the empire of Ghana

12.2 Lalibela, Ethiopia

in modern-day Mali was a consequence. In 1252, the Florentines almost certainly used gold from Ghana when they struck their first gold coin—the florin, a coin that was to dominate large-scale transactions in Europe for several centuries. The trade routes went through Timbuktu and Djenné, the southern reach of Islam. Mosques were built, monumental in nature, out of mud and with a sense of form and proportion unlike anything seen before. The Djenné mosque is set up on a vast platform next to the city's market. Its tall, sparsely fenestrated walls are stabilized by rippling buttresses set between towerlike forms. From Mali, trade routes pointed to the Atlantic Ocean, leading to the rise in modern-day Nigeria of the Yoruba kingdoms of Ifè and Oyo. Though little remains of its architecture, Ifè is known for its naturalistic bronze, stone, and terra-cotta busts, which reached the peak of artistic expression between 1200 and 1400 CE.

The great mediators of the Sahara Desert were the Tuareg, who were nominally Islamic, and who developed a unique type of residence that could be disassembled and placed on a camel's back. Their houses can be compared to the *gers* (sometimes also called yurts) of the Mongolians some 9,000 kilometers to the east. The camel trains

in Inner Asia connected to both the Viking boats leading northward to Scandinavia, and past Cairo to the Tuareg people of the Sahara Desert leading to Ghana, creating a new system of overland trade networks that connected north and south and east and west over vast stretches of inhospitable territory for the first time in history. The Vikings and the Tuareg were the avant-garde of the great expansion of trade into the north and south, respectively. The stave churches in Scandinavia, built when the Vikings converted to Christianity, can be discussed together with the great mud mosques at Timbuktu and Djenné. Trade ships of Indian and Arab merchants were common sights off the coast of East Africa. The Arab traders established Islam early on, the result being a new and unique culture in East Africa known as Swahili. From the 13th to 17th centuries, the town of Gedi, for example, on Kenya's coast, was a thriving Swahili community, with its inhabitants trading with people from all over the world. Findings from archaeological digs include beads from Venice, a Ming vase from China, an iron lamp from India, and scissors from Spain. The new affluence explains the emergence of several East African kingdoms, in particular in Ethiopia, when King Lalibela built a city with an astonishing set of

churches, some of the last great examples of rock-cut architecture in history. Lalibela, as the city came to be called, was designed as a religious destination, attracting pilgrims who still flock to the city today. One can compare the site to Kailasa Temple, Ellora, built some four hundred years earlier, and indeed it is possible that Indian rock-cut specialists were directing the work at Lalibela. Both sites are models of sacred landscapes. Kailasa Temple models Mt. Meru and the Ganges River; Lalibela models Jerusalem and the River Jordan, a river that does not run through Jerusalem.

Further south is Zimbabwe, another source of gold. The Zimbabweans were Bantu agropastoralists who had pushed southward from their ancient homelands in Cameroon to colonize the great savannas of Africa, pushing the aboriginals into the forests and deserts. They set up large chiefdoms that traded ivory, gold, animal pelts, and tortoise shells.

The Mediterranean world was an economic engine unto itself. In Egypt, the Turkish Mamluk sultanate served as a hinge between two continents, and to the west, Córdoba, Spain, flourished like never before. The Mamluks built some of the most astonishing mosques to dot the Cairo

12.3 **Tomb of Sultan Qalawun, Cairo, Egypt**

cityscape. They are not the usual rectangle, but take the shape of the urban block and were designed to capture views along the streets. The domes are masterpieces of ornament and geometry, rising majestically over the tombs of the dynasty rulers. The Tomb of Sultan Qalawun, one of the great artistic and architectural achievements of the age, is one of several tombs, schools, and mosques lined up along one of the principal roads in the city, producing an architectural ensemble unique in its time.

The Islamic rulers in Spain were not to be outdone. Though being pushed out by the Christians, they constructed one of the world's most beautiful palaces, the Alhambra. With its slender columns, terraced gardens, water fountains, and elaborate vaults inscribed with poetic references to paradise, there was nothing else like it.

The rest of Europe, long a global backwater, was now beginning to prosper as well. Infrastructure was being improved for the first time in centuries. For example, bridges were being constructed, such as Pont Saint-Bénézet at Avignon to connect the city to the trade routes north—routes that led deeper into into France, where various towns were given special prerogative to hold fairs. These included Provins, together with Troyes, Lagny, and Bar-sur-Aube. Merchants converged here from all over Europe and the East to sell their wares. The towns also became important centers of banking; the Provins denier, for example, was one of the few currencies accepted widely throughout Europe.

Christian monasteries established in the 13th century number close to one hundred, and indeed the 13th century saw an extensive building boom in churches, monasteries, and cathedrals that yielded the Gothic style, which featured tall proportions, external buttressing, thin stone vaults, and elaborate decorative work. Examples include the cathedrals at Amiens and Cologne. In England, the new style can be seen at the cathedrals at Oxford, Wells, Salisbury, and Lincoln. This architecture separated structure from space, putting the former on the outside of the building, so that the interior could take a unified form. Without doubt, these were the most spectacular interior spaces the world had ever seen.

The 13th century saw dramatic changes in the Christian worldview, with the image of both Christ and Mary changing considerably. The figure of Christ nailed to the cross had usually been portrayed as stiff and remote. Now his body softens and droops; his suffering becomes more realistic. A similar change took place with Mary, who emerged at the center of a cult featuring her and the baby Jesus. For the first time, Christianity opened itself up to women, and indeed the church began to canonize an increasing number of women. The cult of the Virgin Mary was inspired by the writings of theologians such as Saint Bernard of Clairvaux (1090–1153), who identified her as the bride of the Song of Songs in the Old Testament. The Virgin was worshipped as Queen of Heaven, and as the intercessor for the salvation of humankind. This movement found its grandest expression in the French cathedrals, many of which are dedicated to "Our Lady." Entire cities, such as Siena, placed themselves under her protection.

Chartres Cathedral is an example of the pull of this form of worship. Even though its host city had a population of only about 7,000 and was not well located with respect to trade routes, it was the center of a miracle cult associated with the Virgin. People flocked there from far away.

The consequences of the Virgin Cult were profound, for most of the religions of the day were still largely controlled by men, with male saints. Even Buddhism still had a resolutely male-centric perspective. But while the cult of the Virgin Mary put a female in the upper reaches of sanctity, the 12th century also saw the emergence of courtly love as expressed in songs and poems. Castles may still have been designed around functional requirements, but they were now host to elaborate courtly activities. One of the main problems, however, was that with the Viking threat now over, soldiers roamed the landscape looking for "work." The Church sought to intervene in the resultant conflicts by emphasizing the value of peaceful activities as sanctioned by the martyrs, whose spirits abided in the form of relics. Thus, saintly relics became an integral part of devotional practice, and the attendant populism produced a whole new religious architecture based around pilgrimages to visit relics. The wealth that these pilgrims generated was enough to finance numerous cathedrals whose prime purpose was to serve as stations on the way to the Cathedral at Santiago de Compostela, Spain, built over the site where the remains of St. James were said to have been found in the 9th century. These churches include Vézelay, Le Puy, Arles, and Saint-Gilles. In the northern countries, the Hanseatic League was created as a commercial and defensive confederation of merchant guilds and their market towns that dominated trade along the coast of northern Europe. It stretched along the Baltic Sea from Novgorod to London, with its primary focus being Lübeck and Hamburg, both of which were to become important economic hubs in the next centuries.

As a response to the new excess in wealth and power, there arose a monastic movement, the Cistercians, that aimed to restore the principles of poverty. Cistercian monks purposefully sought out unwanted areas and reinstated the principles of work and devotion. Soon the Cistercians, spreading all over Europe, became a political force to be reckoned with by the emperors and bishops. The Cistercians rejected the airy Gothic spires, stained glass, and sculptural elaborations for an architecture that was intentionally simple. For the first time in history, we see an anti-architecture architecture, the best surviving example being the Abbey at Fontenay (1118), France. (The Shinto Shrine, by way of comparison, was designed as a building with an archaic quality that was to be preserved through its periodic rebuilding.) Fontenay Abbey was meant to evoke simpler times and to serve as an accusation against architectural extravagance.

In Italy, during this period there are the first stirrings of a political transformation that would have huge consequences as the centuries progressed. The cities of Verona, Padua, Vicenza, and the Republic of Venice created the Lombard League (1164) in an attempt to assert their independence from imperial German control. Their efforts succeeded to the extent that, in 1183, the German Empire signed the Peace of Constance with the Italians. The treaty

12.4 Town Hall, Padua, Italy

gave the cities local jurisdiction over their territories and the freedom to elect their own councils and to enact their own legislation. The cumulative result was that a new and remarkable society emerged with a mix of aristocrats and urban merchants. Most important of all, a new designation arose known as the *popolo* ("people"). For the first time since the days of ancient Rome, Italy had a political class, which was to play an increasingly large role, even conceptually, in modern history. The architectural consequences were immediate. Cities built town halls, the first such structures in modern history. They also built a new type of public space called a piazza, while at the same time competing to build large urban cathedrals. The wealthy built increasingly large private palaces. Some of the cities became great military powers, particularly Venice and Genoa, which built up vast naval empires in the Mediterranean and Black Seas. Padua was one of these cities as well. After a devastating fire in 1174, it rose to particular prominence. An impressive town hall, called Palazzo della Ragione ("Palace of Justice"), was built at the center of town with a huge assembly hall, some 81 meters long and 27 meters wide. Vaulted in wood

like an upside-down ship's nave, it was at the time the largest interior space in Europe, and possibly in the world. Its long side faced the town square and was lined by a two-tiered, arched loggia. A university was also founded (1222) in Padua, and it was to become one of the leading academic institutions in Europe, especially in law. Town halls were built in various cities across northern Italy: Palazzo della Ragione in Bergamo (ca. 1190), Broletto in Como (ca. 1215), Palazzo del Popolo in Todi (ca. 1220), Palazzo Vecchio in Florence (ca. 1300), and Palazzo dei Consoli in Gubbio (ca. 1340). In Siena, an enormous town hall, the Palazzo Pubblico (begun 1297), was built in front of a magnificent semicircular piazza. Siena is one of the best-preserved Italian cities from this era, frozen in time because of the Black Death that coursed through Italy in the 14th century, killing off a large proportion of its population.

If the northern Italians were slowly getting out from under the feudal system, in Japan feudalism was just getting started. The Kamakura period (1185–1333) marks the governance of the Kamakura shogunate, whose first shogun, Minamoto no Yoritomo, established its headquarters in Kamakura. Lords required the loyal services of vassals,

who were rewarded with fiefs of their own. The fief holders exercised local military rule. But their rule was not spread over all of Japan: to the north, during the 12th century, the Northern Fujiwara, who ruled over the Tohoku region, created a capital city, Hiraizumi, to rival Kyoto to the south. Despite its lack of high-quality rice-growing areas, the Fujiwara derived their wealth from gold mining and horse trading, and as middlemen in the trade in luxury items from continental Asian states. The Northern Fujiwara also developed an ambitious Buddhist temple-building program on Mount Kanzan, not far from Hiraizumi, which consisted of temples, pagodas, repositories, and gardens. Known as Chuson-ji, it featured a large pagoda at the top of the mountain with small reliquaries every 100 meters along Osho Kaido, one of the main roads that connected the northern provinces with Edo (modern-day Tokyo) to the south. Jodo-shu ("The Pure Land School"). Though its teachings first became prominent in China in the 5th century CE, it was brought to Japan by a monk called Honen, who gathered disciples from all walks of life, developing a large following, notably women, who had been excluded from serious Buddhist practice up to this point. One of

12.5 **Sanju-sangen-do, Kyoto, Japan**

the buildings that has survived and that best represents the Pure Land School is the temple Sanju-sangen-do ("Hall of 33 Bays") in Kyoto (1164). A linear building a whole city block long, its numerous doors could open onto a large courtyard to allow devotees to admire the thousand life-size statues of the deity Kannon that stand on both the right and left sides of the main statue, a bodhisattva of compassion. The emergence in Buddhism of a feminine deity related to compassion and motherhood also has many parallels with the emergence in Europe of the cult of the Virgin Mary.

It was in this extraordinary context that Asia saw perhaps the most remarkable event of all, the invasion of the Mongolians. In the previous century, it was the Turks who had mastered Central Asia; now it was their comparatively poor cousins of the steppe to the east. In 1220, the unified Mongolian army crossed the Syr Darya River, beginning their invasion of Central Asia. The Mongolians defeated the Song dynasty in 1279, allowing Kublai Khan to establish his own Yuan dynasty. By 1280, the Mongolians had created the largest empire ever seen in history. Masters of rapid equestrian attacks, the Mongolians were at first eager to confiscate goods

and haul them, along with thousands of captive artisans, back to their camps in Mongolia. But because the history of their invasion was almost completely written by the conquered—there are no surviving accounts from a Mongolian perspective—we have to take a more balanced view. The Mongolians were consummate traders and basically continued what the Seljuks and Turks had already begun. They also put their unique stamp on the cross-continental trade, not only developing Samarkand but also purposely demoting the southern route. The heady days of the Khmer and Pagan were over, and indeed the entire region went into steep decline. Angkor Wat was soon abandoned and given over to the forest, to be rediscovered only at the end of the 19th century. In India, the loss of the southern route to China had the effect of creating infighting, with a noticeable drop in architectural production in the early 14th century.

The first Mongolian capital was Karakorum, a vast city of yurts in western Mongolia, but Karakorum was too far from the center of political gravity in China, so the khan commissioned the building of a new capital city, Shangdu (meaning "Supreme Capital" and also called Kaipingfu),

some 1,200 kilometers to the southeast of Karakorum. It was designed by the Chinese architect Liu Bingzhong (1252) in a profoundly Chinese manner, with an outer city and an inner city, and a roughly square layout. In 1264, Kublai Khan gave Liu Bingzhong the task of designing yet another capital city that today is more commonly known as Beijing. It was broad in scale, strict in planning and execution, and named Dadu. It had large areas that mimicked the open steppe where the Mongolians could ride their horses and live in their yurts.

Consider all the areas just discussed, and then take everything that is *not* included: the rain forests and deserts of central and southern Africa; northern Asia and Siberia; and Australia. These regions would remain more or less independent from this economic continuum until the arrival of the colonial age or even later, but now that Europe and the northern and eastern parts of Africa were part of the global economic continuum, the map began to stabilize. Within this area, the historical narratives are still of war, conflict, and disruption, but they are just as much about power, personalities, and religion as about the need to control trade routes, markets, and sites of production in a rapidly changing landscape.

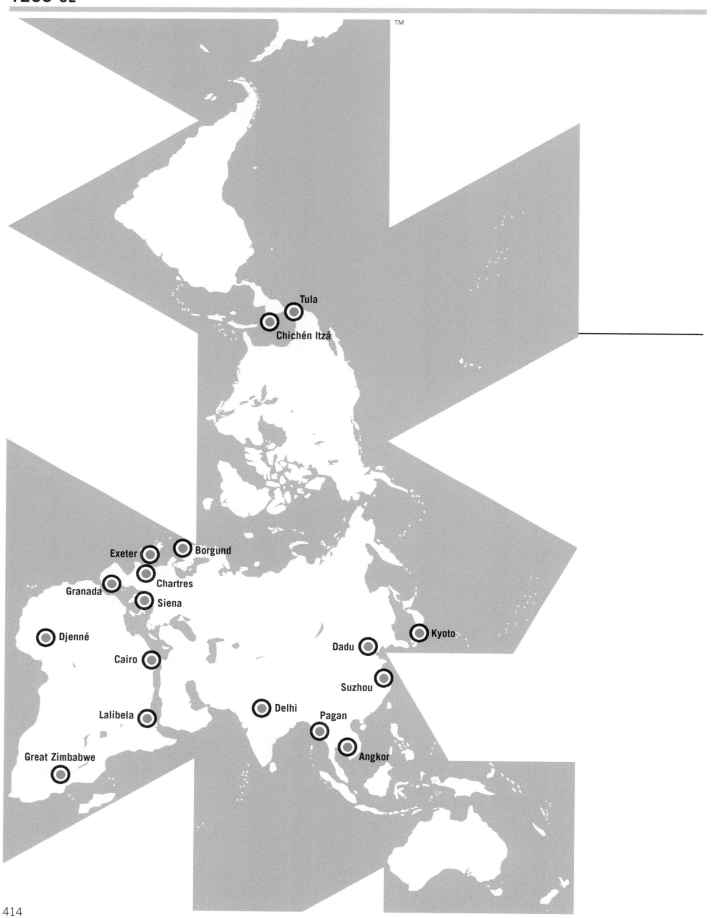

Khmer Kingdom: Angkor Period
802–1431

▲ **Angkor Wat**
802–1220

▲ **Lokesvara Temple**
Completed 1191

Kingdom of Pagan
802–1431

▲ **Ananda Temple**
1090–1105

▲ **Shwezigon**
Late 11th century

Japan: Late Heian Period
ca. 900–1185

Kamakura Period
1185–1333

Nanbokucho Period
1336–1392

▲ **Itsukushima Shrine**
6th to 13th centuries

Northern Song Dynasty
960–1127

Southern Song Dynasty
1127–1279

Yuan Dynasty
1279–1368

◉ *Yingzhao Fashi* **published**
1103

▲ **Dadu**
Rebuilt 1264

1000 CE   **1200 CE**   **1400 CE**

India: Hindu States
10th to 12th centuries

Delhi Sultanate
1210–1526

▲ **Quwwat-ul-Islam**
ca. 1192–1315

▲ **Sun Temple at Konark**
Late 13th century

Zagwe Dynasty
ca. 1137–1270

Mamluk Sultanate
1250–1517

▲ **Great Zimbabwe**
ca. 1250–1450

▲ **Churches of Lalibela**
13th century

▲ **Mosque of Djenné**
13th century

Holy Roman Empire
962–1806

▲ **St. Denis**
1144

▲ **Chartres Cathedral**
1194–1220

▲ **St. Croce, Florence**
Begun 1294

Crusades
1096–1270

▲ **Notre-Dame, Paris**
1163–1250

▲ **Notre-Dame of Reims**
1211–90

Black Plague
1347–52

▲ **Fontenay Abbey**
Founded 1119

▲ **Amiens Cathedral**
1220–35

▲ **Exeter Cathedral**
1280–1300

Olaf Tryggvason, King of Norway
995–1000

▲ **Borgund Stave Church**
12th century

▲ **Palazzo Publico, Siena**
1297–1310

Nasrid Sultanate
1298–1492

▲ **Alhambra**
13th to 14th centuries

Toltec-Chichén City-State
ca. 1000–1200

▲ **Tula**
ca. 950–1150

▲ **Chichén Itzá**
ca. 7th to 13th centuries

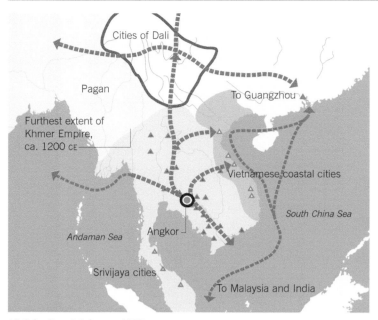

12.6 **Southeast Asia, ca. 1200 CE**

12.7 **Vrah Vishnulok (Angkor Wat), near Siem Reap, Cambodia**

VRAH VISHNULOK (ANGKOR WAT)

The Song dynasty (960–1279) in China and the Chola in India (847–1249) exerted powerful economic influences in Southeast Asia, even though it was India that won out from a cultural point of view, with its variants of Buddhism and Hinduism spreading throughout the region. Another factor in the area's geopolitics was the Dali kingdom in southern China's Yunnan Province. From 900 CE until 1253, when it was conquered by the Mongolians and brought back into the fold of the Chinese empire, it was an autonomous Buddhist state and served as part of an overland route to southern China. Its primary city, Kunming, had long been the main stopping point along the route to India by way of Burma. The disruptions of the Silk Route that were the result of the Mongolian expansion into Asia made this alternative route especially important. In the 9th century CE, Dali, a nearby city, took control of Kunming, unified the area, and built new temples and palaces.

A more distant development was the integration of the East African coast into the circuits of Arab and Indian traders, which created a continuous fabric of ocean ports from Africa to China. These regional and global events were highly advantageous to the Khmer, who were now at their height militarily and economically; they sat at the center of north-south and east-west trade in addition to having become one of the great rice producers in all of Asia. They had mastered rice production in the forest by cutting down the trees and establishing large rice-producing fields watered by an extensive system of irrigation canals. They could produce rice twice a year, basically making it into a bulk commodity to be sold to India and China.

By the 11th century, Yasodharapura, the Khmer capital located just north of the Tonle Sap Lake, had grown into a major city with about a million inhabitants; it was certainly the largest city in South or Southeast Asia, and maybe the second or third largest in the world.

King Rajendravarman (r. 944–68 CE) extended the city to the east with the construction of new temples. King Suryavarman I (r. 1001–50) added new palaces to the north and a vast new *baray* some 7 by 2 kilometers to the west. He also created a large new temple, Baphuon (ca. 1060), just outside the gates of Yasodharapura. Baphuon became the center of a new square city, about as big as, and overlapping, Yasodharapura. But all these temples paled in comparison to the one now known as Angkor Wat, built by King Suryavarman II (1113–50).

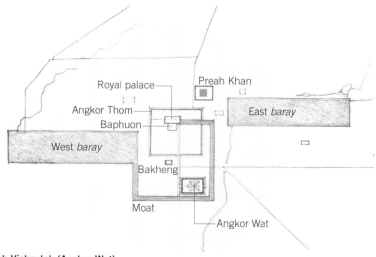

12.8 **Area plan: Vrah Vishnulok (Angkor Wat)**

For its construction, a large part of Yasodharapura had to be cleared. The temple's probable original name, Vrah Vishnulok, was dedicated to both Vishnu and Suryavarman himself; its *garbha-griha* once held a statue of Vishnu represented as a facsimile of Suryavarman. There is much that is still unknown about the temple—archaeological work on the Khmer civilization is still in its infancy. The building's astrological notations (such as the columns on its balustrade, which are equal in number to the years in a Hindu age), as well as its esoteric astronomical measurements, are still being decoded. It is therefore generally assumed that the building is a map of cosmological space and time as understood by the Khmer.

The outer surface of the shrine did not look as it does today. Along with its four corner towers, it is presumed to have been gilded and would have shone brightly, especially when illuminated by the western sun. The stone would have been covered with a thin layer of stucco and painted. A causeway in the form of a raised path 9.4 meters wide and 350 meters long leads across the "ocean" and then across an open field to the front of the temple compound. The causeway terminates at the bottom of an elevated cruciform altar in front of the entrance to the temple. This was as far as commoners could go. Both the causeway and the altar are edged by a balustrade designed as long serpents, a reference to Shesha Naga, the celestial serpent with seven heads. A critical role in the story of the cosmic ocean is played by Shesha, for it is on the coiled body of Shesha that the sleeping Vishnu dreams the universe. While he was dreaming, a lotus on a stalk emerged from Vishnu's navel, on which sat the god Brahma, who actually created the universe. The word *shesha* means "remainder," and Shesha is supposed to be made of what remains after each cosmic cycle comes to an end. The destruction of everything produces a remainder, which is the critical scaffold from which the "dream" of life comes into being. The Shesha Naga was one of the most prominent symbols of the Khmer.

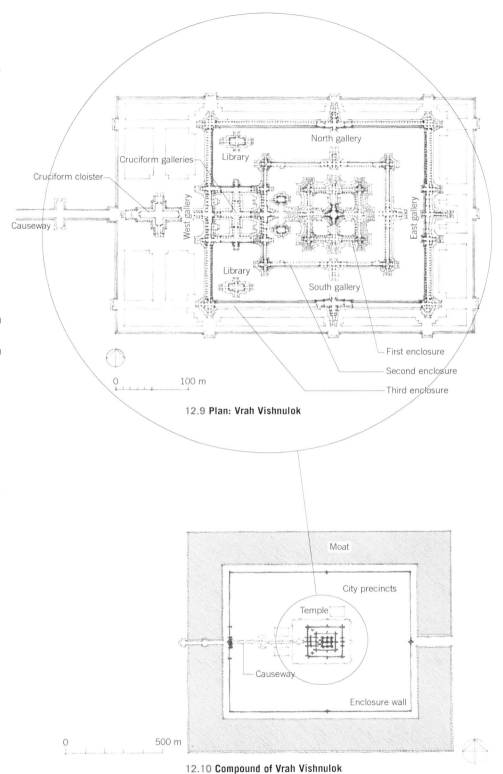

12.9 Plan: Vrah Vishnulok

12.10 Compound of Vrah Vishnulok

12.11 Third enclosure gallery, Vrah Vishnulok

After the Naga altar is a three-portaled gate that gives access to the third enclosure. The spaces beyond this were reserved for royalty. Along the walls of this enclosure, facing outward and protected by a colonnade, bas-reliefs tell of the various manifestations of Vishnu; they are interspersed with illustrations of the life and family of Suryavarman II. This is where the primary symbolic message of the temple—Suryavarman II as a manifestation of Vishnu—is made clear. Unlike Buddhist structures, in which one moves clockwise, the narrative works counterclockwise, starting from the northwest corner. The bas-reliefs were painted in strong hues and would have been visible from the ground below through the colonnade.

From here one moves up through the different levels, each a smaller version of the cosmic order of ocean and island precinct, one "world" resting on another. Unlike Bakong (see "800 CE"), which consisted of a series of terraces, the vertical scale of Vrah Vishnulok escalates and intensifies as it nears the central precinct in the final level, which looms above and is accessible only by a long and very steep flight of steps. It contains the central shrine, the climax of the whole arrangement: a tower that rises 43 meters above the floor of its gallery (that is itself 23 meters higher than the level of

the moat). It is surrounded by four smaller corner towers. The main *garbha-griha*, with its statue of Vishu/Suryavarman II, was originally accessible from all directions. There was also a 23-meter-deep well at its center into which offerings could be thrown. Wells, found in most Khmer temples, are not only a connection to the water-based authority of the Khmer rulers but also an inverted mirror of the cosmic mountain symbolized by the tower.

The influences of the 9th-century CE Temple of Prambanam are obvious, except here the various peaks are tied into a single, extraordinarily complex composition. Furthermore, movement into the structure is not only axial but also from the corners, which gives Vrah Vishnulok a more multidimensional aspect than earlier temples. But the use of square piers and Greek and Persian decorative motifs in the galleries indicate that Vrah Vishnulok's details might also be viewed from within the sphere of Hellenism. The cruciform structures known as libraries that flank the causeway seem particularly Hellenistic, right down to their use of attached pilasters on the entrance porches. A good deal of scholarly work still needs to be done to properly understand this building's importance as it relates to the flow of architectural thought through South and Southeast Asia.

Angkor Thom and Preah Khan

In 1181, King Jayavarman VII converted to Buddhism and embarked on a rebuilding of Yasodharapura. He relocated its center from Bekong to a new temple called Indrapattha, known today as the Bayon, located just outside the old city walls. Instead of the whole body, only the face of the Buddha was graphed onto the many towers of the temple, a reinterpretation of Mahayana Buddhist practice. The gigantic face sculptures give Bayon a unique, enigmatic character. Jayavarman VII's new city, known today as Angkor Thom, was smaller than Yasodharapura—3 kilometers square instead of 4—and it probably served primarily as a palace compound, since it incorporated the palaces that had been built there by previous kings. Among the other astonishing buildings erected by Jayavarman VII is a Buddhist university to the north of the city, originally called Lokesvara but known today as Preah Khan. At its height, the Lokesvara temple complex had one thousand students and teachers. Surrounded by a moat, this huge complex comprises a vast axial network of corridors, chapels, libraries, and pavilions, unified by the two axes that lead through numerous thresholds to the central sanctuary. The principal inner surfaces were covered with stucco (some traces still remain) and

12.12 **Quasi-Hellenic details in the interior of the Library at Vrah Vishnulok**

12.13 **Lokesvara temple (Preah Khan), near Siem Reap, Cambodia**

were presumably painted with didactic images in vibrant colors. One of the more interesting structures is a two-story building with round columns, perhaps dating from the 13th century.

Environmental degradation as a result of deforestation led to a rapid collapse of the Angkor aqua-engineering systems in the middle of the 14th century. The dangers of a single-commodity economy were now apparent. Without its steady flow of rice, the economy collapsed, and the inhabitants abandoned the city. The kingdom was easily sacked by the Thais and its vast wealth plundered. The collapse of the Khmer was also a consequence of the rise of the Mongolians, who organized their trade routes through Samarkand, much to the detriment of Southeast Asia.

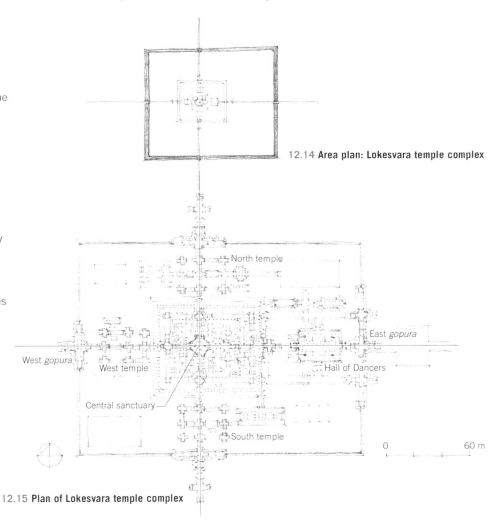

12.14 **Area plan: Lokesvara temple complex**

North temple

East *gopura*

West *gopura*

West temple

Hall of Dancers

Central sanctuary

South temple

0   60 m

12.15 **Plan of Lokesvara temple complex**

12.16 View of Pagan, near Nyangu, Myanmar (Ananda Temple in left foreground; Shwezigon Pagoda in background)

KINGDOM OF PAGAN

The Khmer and the Kingdom of Pagan were the principal powerhouses of Southeast Asia. In the 12th century, the Pagan came to dominate the Puy cities and ruled over an area roughly equivalent in size to modern-day Myanmar (formerly Burma). Its capital was at Arimaddanapura ("City of the Crusher of Enemies"), now known as the city of Pagan. For two centuries, Pagan waged war with the Cholas in peninsular India while maintaining a close but carefully guarded relationship with India's eastern kingdoms. Unlike the Khmer Empire, which was first Hindu and then Buddhist, or the Srivijayan Empire, which was both Buddhist and Hindu, the Pagan practiced Theravada Buddhism, a traditional form that spread from Sri Lanka. Between the 12th and 15th centuries, Pagan kings constructed more than two thousand structures, stupas, and temples. Despite their Buddhism, the Pagan kings, like the Khmer, adopted the Hindu idea, modern for its time, that the Buddha was a manifestation of Vishnu and that a virtuous king could also be a manifestation of Vishnu. Unlike Khmer temples, however, the temples of the Pagan kings were not dedicated to themselves as manifestations of Vishnu, but to the Buddha.

Arimaddanapura was located on a bend of the Irrawaddy River to the west of an extinct volcano that had significant symbolic import. The earliest buildings were terraced stupas derived from Indonesian prototypes. The Shwezigon Paya (the word *paya* can be translated as "pagoda," "stupa," or "*zedi*"), for instance, is a solid-core stupa that rises steeply, like a stepped pyramid, through five square terraces, culminating in a stupa form so completely merged with the umbrellas of its *chattri* above that the base forms an almost conical shape. Steep flights of steps at the center of the base's four sides gave pilgrims access to the terraces that, like those at Borobodur, contain didactic panels depicting tales from the life of the Buddha and other Buddhist texts. Though the stupa is intended to be conceptually solid, there is within it a complex network of narrow, interconnected corridors that were designed to enable postconstruction

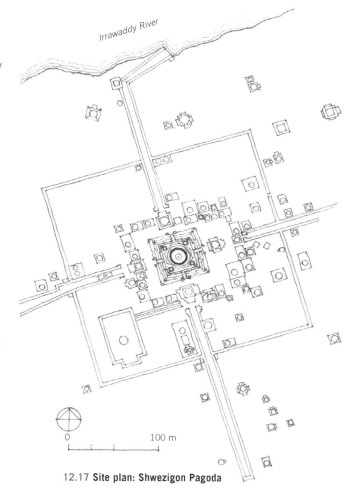

12.17 Site plan: Shwezigon Pagoda

12.18 **Shwezigon Pagoda, Pagan**

donors to gain merit by paying for dedicatory tablets embedded in its walls. The temple is presumed to have contained an important relic in its core, but it has not yet been found and is presumed stolen. Since the stupa was considered an extension of that relic, latter-day worshippers hoped to gain nirvana by embedding objects in its "force field."

Around 1100, soon after his ascension to the throne, Kyanzittha (1084–1113) began construction of several large stupas, among them the Ananda Temple (1090–1105). Though it has the customary square terraces, complete with glazed terra-cotta didactic tablets and corner stupas, it has no external staircases. From the square, ground-level substructure, the building rises in an escalating rhythm to the base of the superstructure and *shikhara*. In this building, the didactic galleries have been incorporated into the body of the temple in the form of two tall concentric ambulatories that are entered through broad, spacious porches at the center of each side. In no other Pagan temple is there so extensive a program of Buddhist education. Light comes through the thick walls into the outer ambulatory from high windows in a regular rhythm. Passageways cut directly in front of the windows allow light to filter further in. Nonetheless, at the core, the illumination is still rather sparse, and the atmosphere is meant to contrast with the light that comes dramatically into the space from hidden clerestory windows. This light illuminates the Buddha statues located in niches in the central core, facing out in all four directions. The clerestory light illuminating the innermost sanctum is a distinct Pagan invention. Almost all of the stupas were made of bricks produced locally from the alluvial soil.

0   20 m

12.19 **Elevation and plan: Shwezigon Pagoda**

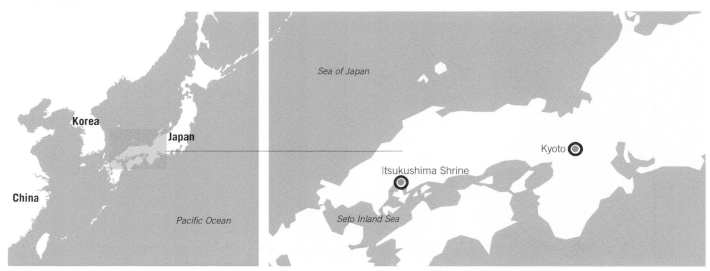

12.20 **Location of Kyoto and the Itsukushima Shrine, Japan**

SANJU-SANGEN-DO

In Japan, frequent wars, natural disasters, and attempted Mongolian invasions in 1274 and 1281 created a feeling of instability, which the Buddhists associated with the predicted end of the reign of Buddhism. This led to a period similar to that of the rise of the bhakti cults in South Asia. Charismatic Buddhist monks traveled the countryside popularizing Pure Land Buddhism, which promised enlightenment for anyone who devoutly repeated the name of the Amidaba Buddha.

An arresting example of the architecture of Pure Land Buddhism was built in Kyoto in 1164 by Taira no Kiyomori (1118–81), an important general. Known as Sanju-sangen-do ("Hall of 33 Bays"), the structure was 120 meters long, an entire urban block, and designed to display a thousand life-size statues of the thousand-armed Kannon (a bodhisattva goddess of mercy), five hundred on either side of a large central Kannon image. The statues are arranged in multiple rows and densely packed on bleachers rising toward the back wall. Twenty-eight additional "attendants," many of them directly derived from the contemporary Hindu gods of India, are lined up in front. The forest of statues, which can be presented to the public through large doors, makes a strong impression.

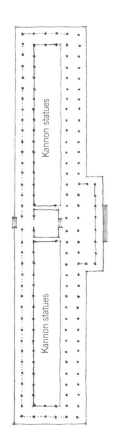

Kannon statues

Kannon statues

12.22 **Plan of Sanju-sangen-do**

12.21 **Sanju-sangen-do, Kyoto, Japan**

12.23 **Interior: Sanju-sangen-do**

12.24 Itsukushima Shrine, Hiroshima Prefecture, Japan

There are two sanctuaries: the *honsha* (the main shrine housing female deities), which faces out toward the water, and on the east, roughly perpendicular to it, the *maro-do jinja* (the shrine for male guest deities) facing west, or inland. The timber columns are all coated with vermilion lacquer and are a study in simplicity.

Torii gates have both Buddhist and Shinto associations. A torii is a reinterpretation of the Buddhist *torana*, or gateway. In Shintoism a torii also symbolizes the call to the god to come forth and grant the worshipper's prayers. Another meaning of *torii* is "bird perch," a term referring to a mythological story in which the gods attempt to lure the sun goddess, Amaterasu, from the cave in which she had hidden with the sounds of songbirds.

ITSUKUSHIMA SHRINE

Shintoism had by no means been weakened by this period. In fact, Taira no Kiyomori also built a Shinto shrine on Itsukushima, one of the many islands in the Seto Inland Sea. A sacred site since the earliest times, it was home to Ichikishima-Hime-no-Mikoto, the kami "who ensures safety at sea," and her two sisters. The original shrine dating back to the 6th century CE was rebuilt on a grand scale in 1168. In the main sanctuary, Kiyomori presented thirty-three illustrated scrolls of the Buddhist Lotus Sutra to the shrine, making Itsukushima a seamless blend of Shinto and Buddhist practices and architecture. The shirine is located on a island, which could be approached only by the devout. Even today, though it is now open to the public, there are certain restrictions. A solitary vermilion torii stands knee-deep in the sea at high tide, with the green mountain island as a backdrop. At high tide, it appears to float, and it is then that its Shinto character merges with Pure Land Buddhism's ideas, which would describe it as floating on the infinite ocean on a lotus plant. The beach shrine, built into a protected cove, is connected by a roofed passageway that zigzags between the two sides of the inlet. The passage, with its changing views, frames the dynamic relationship between water and land as the tide rises and falls.

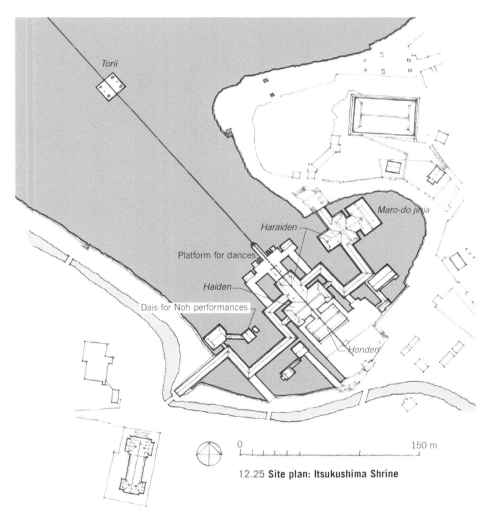

12.25 Site plan: Itsukushima Shrine

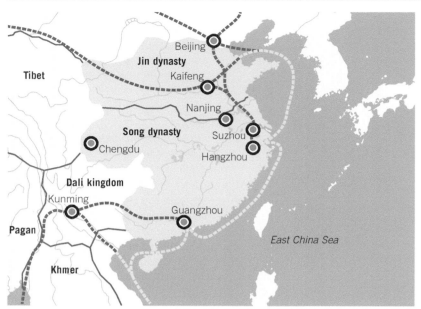

12.26 Song dynasty China

SOUTHERN SONG DYNASTY

The Mongolian Jin and Jurchen dynasties to the north cut off trade along the Silk Route, forcing the Song to move their capital to Hangzhou, south of modern-day Shanghai, their former capital, Nanjing, having been devastated by Jin dynasty raids. This move forced the Song to give up lucrative farming land for a terrain of mountains, lakes, and rivers that was inhospitable to widespread agriculture, making them dependent on imported rice from Southeast Asia. The Song thereupon created a vibrant maritime trading network to India. Ships were built, harbors improved, and warehouses constructed. As wealth poured in, powerful mercantile families began to establish large estates distinguished by elaborate private gardens. A garden at Dezhou, for instance, was renowned for its four distinct landscapes. Another garden had an artificial lake, with an island emerging from marshes and surrounded by artificial mountains and piles of rocks on which a palace was built. Little West Lake, a private garden in Lin'an, went so far as to "borrow" the views of an actual mountain outside its boundaries, splicing its view into its composition. The same is true for Genyue (1117–22), a Northern Song garden in Bianliang (modern Kaifeng) that is focused on a high peak, Longevity Mountain, in its northeastern corner. A multitude of lower peaks, called Ten Thousand Pines, are also visually "borrowed." Interspersed in the garden are about forty structures, including verandas, lodges, towers, platforms, and rustic huts, all linked by pathways that move up and down and wind around, framing the architectural structures within and against each other and the landscape.

There are several estates in Suzhou, which became an important center for China's silk industry during the Song dynasty. The Garden of the Master of the Nets dates from this period. (Its name came from a subsequent owner of the garden.) It has three sections focused around an inner garden designed to enhance and intensify the essential qualities of the landscape and achieve a perfected, "natural" experience that was, nonetheless, imbued with didactic messages. In that sense the garden was both a visual and literary experience. The Song dynasty period, known for its literary achievements, was one in which storytelling became a popular form of entertainment. The stories told by professional entertainers were printed in storybooks, called *huaben*, which later inspired China's longer didactic novels dealing with the battle between the virtuous and the unscrupulous that teach the consequences of behavior. This was related to the ideals of Confucianism and, during the Song dynasty, neo-Confucianism, an aggregate of Buddhist metaphysics and Confucian ethics that taught that through reason and study, the whole world could be understood.

12.27 Garden of the Master of the Nets, Suzhou, China

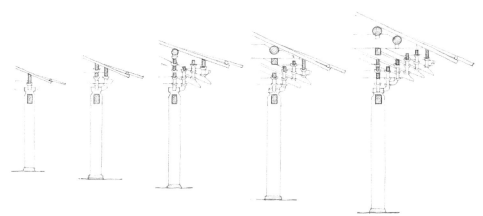

12.28 Hierarchy of the *dou-gong* (bracket system) according to the *Yingzhao Fashi*

Yingzhao Fashi

The Song emperor Huizong (r. 1100–1125) was an enthusiastic patron of the arts. A catalog of his paintings, the *Xuanhe Huapu*, published in 1123, lists over six thousand works in his collection. Art academies were established in his reign, which saw an increased interest in ancient history and culture; collecting antiques also became popular. Huizong also commissioned the *New Yingzhao Fashi* (1103), a detailed manual of architecture and construction. It was called the "new" *Yingzhao Fashi* because the previous one, dating to the T'ang, had become outdated. The manual was not, however, intended as an aesthetic or philosophical document, but rather to help the imperial administrators regulate, and reign in, the construction industry.

Aesthetically, architecture under the Song and the Jin (and later under the Yuan) had become very ornamental and complicated. The size of the *dou-gong* decreased with respect to the overall column heights, but it increased in complexity and showmanship. The placement of columns was even occasionally disrupted to accommodate more ambitious spatial arrangements. While all these transformations made for a much richer and more expressive architecture, it also resulted in a great deal of waste and corruption. Because construction was controlled by powerful guilds that carefully guarded their knowledge, passing it on only in oral verse, buildings routinely ran over budget. The imperial court found that it could not reasonably predict the cost to complete

buildings. Furthermore, the high demand for timber was causing rapid deforestation in the Song territories, and with the northern forests in the control of "barbarians," the court feared that it would soon run out of timber. The *New Yingzhao Fashi* aimed to solve both these problems. Li Jie was an intellectual, a painter, and an author of books on geography, history, and philology. In addition, as a superintendent for state buildings in the Ministry of Works (*Gong Bu*), he had carried out several building projects, which made him an ideal person for the job. For three years Li Jie systematically interviewed leaders of the construction guilds,

documented their building principles and processes, and added his own rationalizations and explanations. He finally presented his findings in 1105 in the form of regulations that the government administrators could use to monitor construction expenditures. Li Jie's *Yingzhao Fashi* consists of thirty-four chapters organized into five parts: basic data, regulations, labor work, materials, and drawings. Each part is subdivided into the following fourteen sections: moats and fortifications; stonework; structural carpentry; nonstructural carpentry and joinery (doors, windows, partitions, screens, ceilings, staircases, etc.); wood carving; turning and drilling; sawing; bamboo work; plastering, painting, and decoration; brickwork; brick and tile making.

The *Yingzhao Fashi* described eight types of buildings but was concerned primarily with imperial and governmental buildings, and not with buildings for commoners, since only the former would be paid for by the administrator. Most of the drawings are plans (determining the basic size of a building), sections (determining quantities), and wood sections (instrumental in determining costs). All these were regulated by a proportioning system, known as the *cai-fen*. A *cai* was 10 *fen*, and a *zu-cai* was 21 *fen*. The standard proportions were in the ratio 2:3. Thus a standard wood section would be 10 by 15 *fen*.

12.29 Detail of a garden scene from the Song dynasty

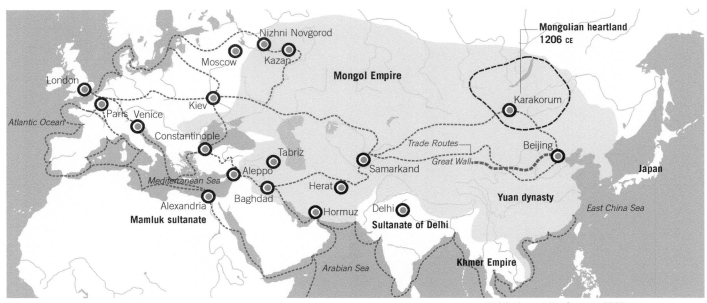

12.30 Mongol Empire, ca. 1200 CE

MONGOL EMPIRE

By 1206, Temüjin, called Genghis Khan ("Mighty Ruler") had united the dispersed and infighting Mongolian tribes, sending his armies south and west to create an expansive empire. Following his death in 1227, his son Ögedei advanced even farther west, taking Kiev in 1240. Kublai Khan, another grandson of Genghis, completed the conquest of China in 1279, establishing the Yuan dynasty. The result was the largest empire in history, covering 20 percent of the earth's total land area and holding sway over a population of more than one hundred million. Though it was not to last, it had important and numerous long-term effects.

Many accounts of the Mongolians focus on their ferocious fighting style and barbarous looting of cities, palaces, and libraries. But most of the information that has been handed down about the Mongolians was written by the people who were conquered and who were not inclined toward more neutral assessments. One of the reasons for the Mongolians' success was their military style. Most armies fought with slow masses of soldiers. Many soldiers were farmhands with minimal skills and training. Mongolian soldiers, all excellent horsemen, had not only mastered a dynamic mode of attack but were also seasoned to cope with the brutal conditions of the steppe. A diet of meat and yogurt made them taller and stronger than many of their enemies. Furthermore,

unlike in the West, where there were small groups of elite soldiers and large masses of untrained combatants, the armies of the united Mongol tribes consisted of the entire adult male population under the age of sixty. Living in tents designed to allow the soldiers to follow the movement of their grazing horses, they had no urban culture and were interested primarily in the trappings of movable wealth, which they distributed with democratic evenhandedness to all the tribes. When Genghis Khan died, he was buried in a secret, unmarked location in the desert of Mongolia, according to Mongolian tradition. (A team of archaeologists have recently located a site in Mongolia that is most likely Genghis Khan's tomb.)

The *ger* ("dwelling place"), the Mongolian yurt, was easily transportable and yet solid enough to withstand ferocious winds. The basic element is an expanding wooden lattice that forms the circular walls. Poles from the sides rise up to connect to a compression ring, thus forming the roof structure. A band of rope is drawn around the top of the wall to bind it together. A fireplace was set out in the center. The wood structure is then covered with various amounts of felt, depending on climatic conditions. (Felt was made by pounding and rubbing wool—the Mongolians had no weaving skills. In fact, all their clothing was bartered for, bought, or came from war booty.) The yurt's entrance faced south. The altar and place of prestige

were placed on the north, facing the entrance. Living, cooking and eating took place in between. The whole structure could be assembled or disassembled in a day and packed onto camels for transport.

Yuan Dynasty China

When Kublai Khan (1215–94), Genghis's grandson, ascended the throne of China, he chose the Chinese name *Yuan* ("original" or "prime") for his dynasty. By 1279, with the surrender of the last of the Song territories, all of China was under the Yuan. The Mongols divided society into four classes, with the highest reserved for themselves and the lowest for the southern Chinese from the former Song regions. Outsiders enjoyed the middle status in China, between the Mongols and the native Chinese, to the great irritation of the Song. Lamaist Buddhists—from Tibet and Nepal—and Daoists found particular favor with the Mongols, much as they had with the Mongolian-related Jin two hundred years earlier. Muslims were welcomed and happily tolerated at the western border. Under the Yuan, one of the oldest mosques of China, the tomb of Tughluq Temur, was built in 1363 in Huocheng, Xinjiang.

The Mongolian capital was Karakorum, and it was from there that Genghis Khan would rally his troops. Genghis's son and successor, Ögedei, erected walls around the city. Though nothing remains today, we know from descriptions that the city was square, with gates in the cardinal directions, and that it had Arab and Chinese quarters, several temples and mosques, and even a Nestorian church. When Kublai Khan claimed the throne of the Mongol Empire in 1260, he relocated his capital first to Chengdu and later to Dadu (present-day Beijing). While the Yuan introduced global civilization to China and modernized its military and its economy, they had no architectural culture. As a result, in building the new capital city, they adhered to the planning principles described in the *Rituals of Zhou*, which was a good political move, as it made them appear considerate of Chinese tradition. They also ordered the construction of numerous altars and temples throughout China dedicated to ancestors and local deities.

Dadu (from the word *ta-tu*, or "Great Capital") was known to the Mongolians as Khanbalig, the "City of the Great Khan." It was square with an orthogonal arrangement of streets typical of earlier Chinese capitals. The urban center, consisting of a palace and imperial quarters, was located south of the city center, with residential areas predominantly occupying the northern part. The name for the palace was *ta-nei*, or "great interior." It was surrounded by a 6-by-5 kilometer area reserved for the Mongolian overlords, who camped there in their yurts. To the south, in a separate rectangular precinct, was the "outer city" for the native Chinese, who lived in houses. A vast building served as the official site for ceremonies. Within it, Kublai Khan, like the Liao kings before him, lived in resplendent tents traditional to the Mongolians. Marco Polo, a visitor in his court, describes Kublai Khan's palace built in the Chinese manner:

> You must know that it is the greatest palace that ever was. The roof is very lofty, and the walls of the palace are all covered with gold and silver. They are adorned with dragons, beasts and birds, knights and idols, and other such things. The hall of the palace is so large that six thousand people could easily dine there, and it is quite a marvel to see how many rooms there are besides. The building is altogether so vast, so rich, and so beautiful that no man on earth could design anything superior to it. The outside of the roof is all colored with vermilion and yellow and green and blue and other hues, which are fixed with a varnish so fine and exquisite that it shines like crystal and lends a resplendent luster to the palace as seen for a great way around.

Geomancy required that the palace face south against the slope of a hill, but since no hill was on the site, one was made—the Green Hill, about 100 meters high and 2 kilometers in circumference. It was planted with trees from every part of China and is thus a type of map of the Chinese world. Surrounding the hill was an enormous Divine Menagerie—a park for deer, stags, and other animals—with paved roads that led to a large lake with islands and pavilions. Little apart from the landscaping survives today, since it became the site of the vast Forbidden City, which was built after all the Mongolian buildings were torn down. Two particularly critical issues for the new city were water and grain: for such a big city, it was located far from the fertile grain regions in the south. These two problems were solved by the construction of a canal from the nearby Pei Ho River to the east, which allowed grain to be brought directly to the city gates.

The Grand Canal that wound its way northward from the fertile grain-producing areas of the south to the large cities of the north was one of the most important engineering works in the world. The goal was to make the movement of goods and grain independent of ocean transport. The first canal was begun in 613 BCE. In 206 BCE, the Lingqu Canal, which connected the Xingjiang and Lijiang Rivers, was constructed. Another 200-kilometer section, completed in 589 CE, linked the newly constructed capital of Luoyang (Dongdu, or Eastern Capital) eastward to the confluence of the Wei and

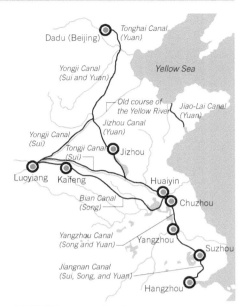

12.31 Chinese canal system

Yellow Rivers, thus overcoming the silting that plagued them. The Yuan dynasty continued these efforts, streamlining stretches of the canal by eliminating bends and consolidating the Jizhou and Huizong river systems, thus reducing the distance to be traversed from the southern end of the canal to the capital, Dadu, by almost 700 kilometers. The Ming dynasty (1368–1644) also committed large resources to canal maintenance and construction, keeping the canals clear of obstructions so that ocean transport was not required for grain distribution. The development of water locks and dredging techniques kept the canals in working order.

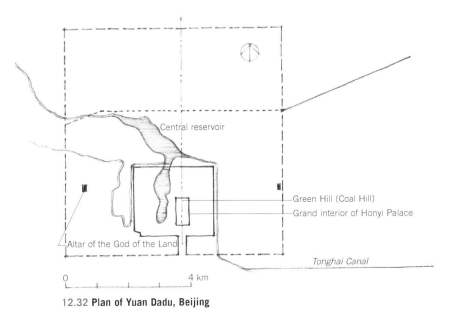

12.32 Plan of Yuan Dadu, Beijing

DELHI

In the 12th century, South Asia was transformed by the arrival of the Islamic armies. They were led initially by Qutb-ud-Din Aibak, a Ghaznavid general from Afghanistan, who defeated the Rajput king and took over his territories in north India in 1192. His efforts were superseded in 1296 by Ala-ud-Din Khilji (r. 1296–1316), who seized Ranthambhor, Chittorgarh, and Jaiselmer from the Rajputs and crushed the Solankis and the Pramars, going far south to conquer the fortress of Devagiri from the Yadavs.

Historians do not all evaluate the Islamic rulers' relationship to their Hindu subjects equally. Islamic rulers often massacred Hindus and systematically destroyed and desecrated Hindu temples. However, the Hindu population as a whole continued to thrive under Islamic rule, merging with it in many ways at the level of popular culture and thus underlining the more tolerant and even enlightened aspects of Islamic rule—particularly that of the Moghuls. (One of the eventual consequences of these underlying tensions was the partitioning of South Asia into India and Pakistan in 1947 by the British on the eve of their departure, an act whose ramifications are still in play.)

Qutb-ud-Din Aibak established his capital in Lahore but then moved to central India, taking over a Chauhan settlement called Tomar to build Qila Rai Pithora, the first capital on the site of modern Delhi. Delhi was reestablished as a capital seven times on new sites in the same general region. These are:

1. Qila Rai Pithora, by Qutb-ud-Din Aibak (1192)
2. Siri, by Ala-ud-Din Khilji (1296–1316)
3. Tughlaqabad, by Ghias-ud-Din Tughlaq (1321–25)
4. Jahanpanah, by Muhammad bin Tughluq (1325–51)
5. Feroz Shah Kotla, by Firuz Shah Tughluq (1351–88)
6. Purana Qila, by Sher Shah Sur (1538–45)
7. Shahjahanabad (now referred to as "Old Delhi"), by Shah Jahan (1638–49)

Early in the 20th century, Edwin Lutyens added New Delhi into the mix. All these are now integrated into modern Delhi.

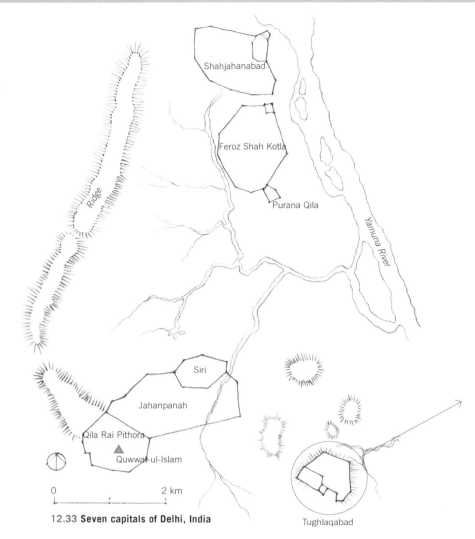

12.33 Seven capitals of Delhi, India

12.34 View of Tughlaqabad, Delhi

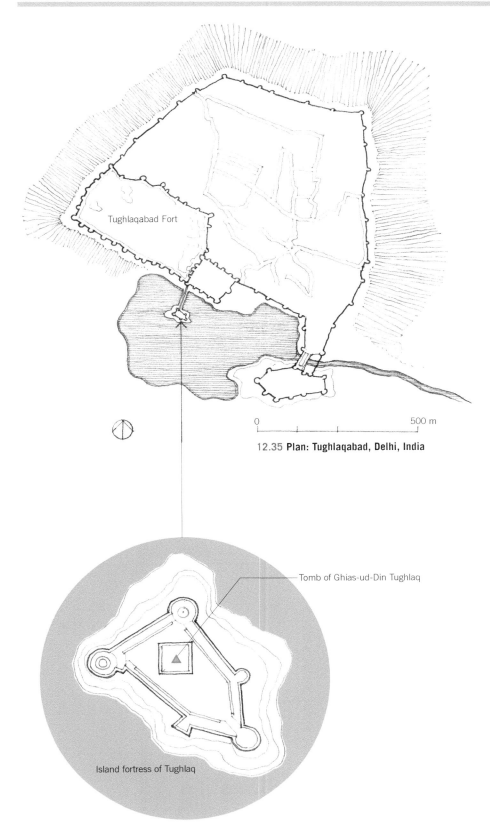

12.35 Plan: Tughlaqabad, Delhi, India

Tughlaqabad Fort

Tomb of Ghias-ud-Din Tughlaq

Island fortress of Tughlaq

0   500 m

Tughlaqabad

Ghias-ud-Din's Tughlaq's city, Tughlaqabad (1321–25), was the largest of Delhi's fortress cities and a remarkable piece of engineering. To site his city, Tughlaq picked an irregular plateau that was difficult to work because it was very rocky but had the advantage of jutting prominently above the gentle westward slope of the floodplain of the Yamuna River. Tughlaq delineated his fort, which was made with local stone, in the shape of an irregular parallelogram with frequent circular turrets. The ground dropped quickly around the fort. Within, on the southwest side, he built his palace, enclosed within another fortified rectangle. At the junction of the palace and the rest of the fort was a sub-palace, a separate defensible entity in itself. One of the Yamuna River's drainage canals originally went right past the southern walls of Tughlaqabad; Tughlaq converted this canal into an artificial lake by building a dam linking a rocky outcrop just south of the city to the city itself. Tughlaqabad thus had valleys on three sides, and a lake toward the fourth. Within this lake Tughlaq built yet another fortress, in the form of an island, linked to the main fort by a 220-meter-long elevated causeway. The lower level of this island fortress consisted of a network of arched rooms with carefully controlled access. This was the treasury. On the roof of the treasury, Tughlaq built his tomb, a spectacular visual in the middle of the lake. There were additional hidden tunnels and causeways in the palace complex, adding to the secretive nature of the whole construction.

Quwwat-ul-Islam

The mosque of Quwwat-ul-Islam speaks unambiguously of its iconoclastic ambitions. It was begun in 1192 by Qutb-ud-Din Aibak, who placed it on the rise of land in the center of the city, the site of a former Hindu temple, and used as his raw material the stones from the city's twenty-seven Hindu and Jain temples. The pillars from the temples were used at times upside down or placed one on top of the other to raise them to the necessary height. The main *qibla* wall, on the west, consists of five corbelled ogee arches, presumably made by Hindu masons.

12.36 Temple columns, Quwwat-ul-Islam, Delhi, India

Qutb's successor, Iltutmish (r. 1211–36) extended the qibla wall of the Quwwat-ul-Islam Mosque by three bays on either side and built a colonnade that enclosed the Qutb Minar on one side and his own tomb on the other. Iltutmish's was the first Islamic tomb in India. Built just west of the *qibla* wall, a small structure with a square base transforms into an octagonal dome on squinches.

A hundred years later, Ala-ud-Din Khilji (r. 1296–1316) decided to expand the complex by doubling the length of the *qibla* wall to the north. He also started construction of monumental *minar*, intended to be twice the height of the Qutb Minar, but which was never built beyond its first story. In 1311, Ala-ud-din Khilji constructed a gate, called Alai Darwaza ("Gate of Allah") to the south of the mosque. This elegant cubic structure, with the proportions of a Roman triumphal arch, was constructed by Indian masons taking directions from their new Islamic rulers. A central arch dominates each facade. To the sides of the arches, windows in the lower register and blind windows above articulated in red sandstone are set against a white sandstone background. The dome sits atop squinches in a plain interior illuminated by small deep windows. The Alai Darwaza, exhibiting influences derived from Seljuk artisans, was among the first monuments in South Asia to signal the arrival of a distinctly South Asian Islamic architectural way of building, which was eventually perfected by the Moghuls.

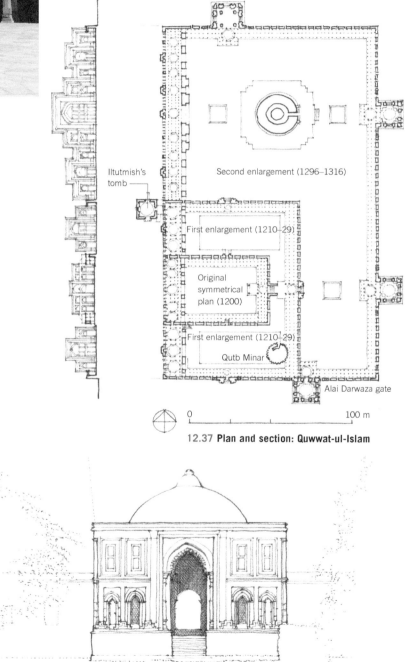

Iltutmish's tomb

Second enlargement (1296–1316)

First enlargement (1210–29)

Original symmetrical plan (1200)

First enlargement (1210–29)

Qutb Minar

Alai Darwaza gate

0   100 m

12.37 Plan and section: Quwwat-ul-Islam

12.38 Alai Darwaza gate, Quwwat-ul-Islam

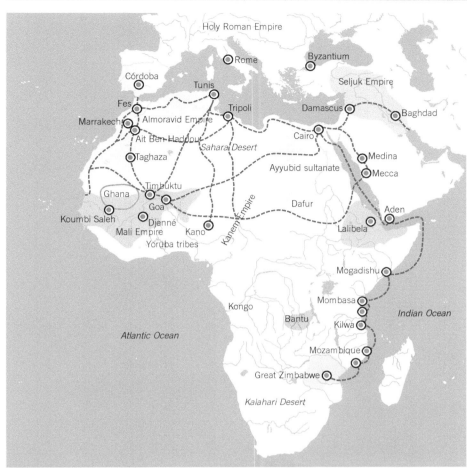

12.39 Africa, ca. 1200 CE

Its palace is situated on the rocky promontory of an island in Mso Bay. Husuni Kubwa, which means "large fortified house" in Swahili, had several courtyards for different functions, with a distinct progression from private to public. The king's private courtyard had a sunken pool with an audience court next to it. There was a protected harbor to the west.

North Africa was dominated by the Ayyubid sultanate in Egypt and the Almohads in Morocco and Spain. The once powerful Ghana Empire was in decline. The Almoravids, constituted of Saharan Berbers, had taken control of the trade routes through the Sahara and captured Koumbi Saleh, the capital of Ghana, in 1067. By the 13th century, however, a new power emerged: the Mali Empire. Centered to the north of Ghana, it was composed of several states that took control of the gold mines. Before the discovery of gold in the Americas, almost half of the gold in Europe came from Mali. The Mali Empire also controlled the salt trade in that region.

AFRICA

Prior to the 13th century, southern and eastern Africa were remote outposts in the global trade networks. But in the 1200s, the East African coast developed into an extensive trading zone linked to Arabian and Indian port cities and thus became the major distribution center for the African continent. East Africans sold gold, ivory, and slaves in exchange for metals, rice, and other commodities. One consequence of the cultural exchange was the emergence of the Swahili language, which combines African and Arabic linguistic elements.

Preeminent among the ports at this time was Kilwa, off the south coast of Tanzania. It was established in the 11th century by believers of Shirazi Islam, an East African variant of Middle Eastern Islam. The rulers controlled the sources of gold in nearby Mozambique. (In the 16th century, this provoked the interest of the Portuguese, whose subsequent arrival spelled the end of African control of the trade routes.)

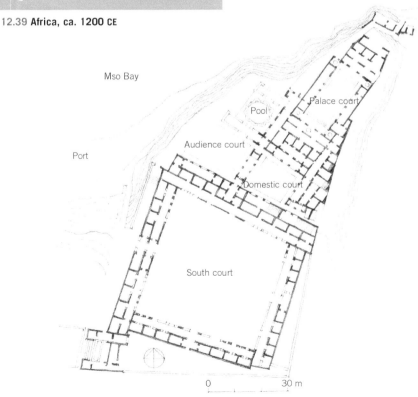

12.40 Plan: Palace of Husuni Kubwa at Kilwa, Tanzania

Mamluk Sultanate

The Mamluks, who ruled Egypt from 1260 to 1517, were not Arabs; instead, they were originally Turkish, Kurdish, and Mongolian slaves who had been raised as fighters in the army of the Ayyubids, who were themselves Kurdish Turks from Syria. The word *Mamluk* comes, in fact, from an Arabic word meaning "the owned." But with the collapse of Shi'ite Ayyubid rule in Egypt, General Baybars al-Bunduqdari (r. 1260–77) established Mamluk dominance over Egypt, pushing back the Mongolians as well as the Christian Crusaders in the Levant and Syria, and regaining control over the holy cities of Mecca and Medina. Under the previous Ayyubids, the center of power had been in Damascus, but under the Mamluks, Cairo's importance was restored; indeed, from a geopolitical perspective, Cairo was the prime link between India and Europe. Though a military elite, the Mamluks were savvy traders, establishing ties with Venice and Genoa as well as with Constantinople. Mamluk bureaucracy consisted mostly of Coptic Christians and Jews, who had filled such administrative roles for centuries.

During the 13th and 14th centuries at least five major madrasas were built in Cairo along a street close to the sultan's palace. Each of these was associated with a mausoleum. Normally, tombs, even for the rich, would be located outside of the city, but if the sultan gave an endowment to a madrasa he was granted an exception. Each madrasa is thus associated with a sultan's tomb. The buildings, sitting shoulder to shoulder, constitute one of the more important street environments of the age. As madrasas had to face Mecca, all the structures abut the street at about a 10-degree angle. The architects showed great adeptness at integrating the program into the complex and cramped urban site. Most impressive is the Tomb of Sultan Qalawun (1284–85). Though the life of a sultan was continually beset by the possibility of internal rebellions testing his authority, he proved to be a capable ruler open to trade even with the Christians with whom he was fighting. He made trade alliances with the Byzantine Empire, Genoa, and the Kingdom of Sicily.

The plan echoes the octagonal plan of the Dome of the Rock. The wall of the mausoleum is divided into a series of pointed arched recesses, the hoods supported on marble columns. The portal, a remarkable piece of Gothic marble work, is a trophy seized from a church in Acre, the last Crusader stronghold in Palestine. The tomb chamber is an almost square plan, with four piers and four columns arranged in the form of an octagon supporting arches that in turn raise a high drum and above that, a dome. The rose granite pillars have Corinthian

capitals. The walls are richly decorated with marbles and mosaics. At the mausoleum's rear there was a hospital. The madrasa, which specialized in Sunni jurisprudence, has its own courtyard with student cells. Another important monument from this era is the Mosque of Sultan al-Nasir Muhammad (1318), built in the great citadel that protects the city. Though conventional in plan, the columns and capitals are mostly spoils taken from other buildings, including churches and even the ruins of ancient Egyptian buildings.

Madrasa of Sultan al-Kamil

Madrasa of Sultan Barquq

Madrasa of Sultan al-Nasir Muhammad

Tomb of Sultan Qalawun

Madrasa of Sultan Qalawun

Tomb and madrasa of Sultan al-Salih Ayyub

0   40 m

12.41 Cairo madrasas

12.42 View of dome, Tomb of Sultan Qalawun, Cairo, Egypt

12.43 Tomb of Sultan Qalawun

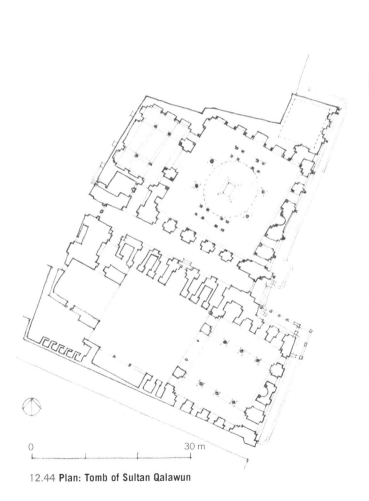

12.44 Plan: Tomb of Sultan Qalawun

12.45 Interior: Tomb of Sultan Qalawun

0   30 m

12.46 Bieta Giorgis, Lalibela, Ethiopia

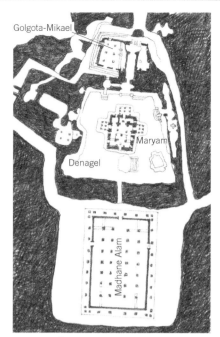

12.47 Partial plan: Rock-cut churches of Lalibela

Lalibela

The collapse of the Aksumite Empire around 400 CE left the Horn of Africa in the hands of various regional forces, but in the 13th century, the return of commerce to the shores and the transformation of Ethiopia into a Christian kingdom visited by pilgrims from far afield brought prosperity back to the region. The Zagwe dynasty (founded ca. 1137) capitalized on this, reaching its peak under King Lalibela (r. ca. 1185–1225), who is credited with building a set of eleven churches cut out of solid red volcanic rock in his new capital city, Roha, now called Lalibela (340 kilometers north of Addis Ababa). The city is located on a high ridge above the Takkaze River. Under threat from the forces of Islam from the north, the Zagwe had retreated into these ridges, from which they continued to control the Red Sea ports that linked central and southern African trade routes to the shipping lanes to India and beyond.

The ridge, despite its height over the valley, had the added advantage of featuring several artesian springs that had both agricultural and symbolic value. The churches are highly unusual in their overall conception. Not only do they constitute a holy land unto themselves, but they are also a type of map of the holy city of Jerusalem, which King Lalibela had never seen, but imagined from descriptions in the Bible. The churches are divided into northern and eastern groups by a rock-cut channel called Yordannos ("River Jordan"). Bieta Madhane Alam is the largest and most impressive of these churches.

The lack of documents makes the history of rock-cut architecture difficult to trace, but given that it had a strong presence in India, where Hindu and Buddhist sanctuaries were built out of the side of cliffs from 200 CE to at least 900 CE, it stands to reason that the techniques and indeed perhaps even some labor came from India, where the tradition was dying out. There is no firm way

of proving this, but the relatively sudden appearance of this form of building in Ethiopia lends credence to the argument. Indeed, the narrative of Lalibela, namely that it is organized around a sacred river, in this case the "River Jordan," has parallels to places like Mahabalipuram in southern India, where temples were organized around a "River Ganges." Each of the churches is associated with a square water tank filled by the pressure from an artesian spring. These tanks are planted with papyrus to emulate the Nile River. They are not baptismal pools in the conventional sense; rather, they symbolize fertility. During Easter, the site attracts pilgrims from far and wide.

Because the churches are carved down into the bedrock, the level of these pools, governed by the pressure of the water in the rock, had to first be determined, as that then determined the height of the individual church. Of the twelve churches, Bieta Giorgis (St. George), carved into the shape of a

12.48 Section: Rock-cut churches of Lalibela

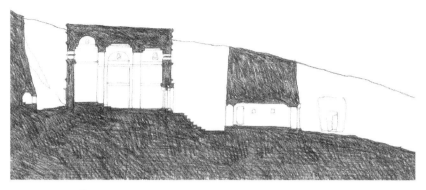

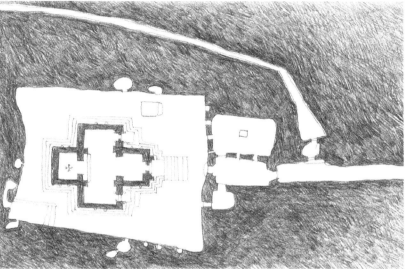

cross, is situated somewhat apart from the other churches to the west. Following a deep, narrow trench, visitors descend in a wide arc past a sacred spring, to its ground level. The building is approximately 12 meters in height, length, and width and rests on a triple-stepped platform. Though carved out of the living stone, it mimics a conventionally constructed building, replete with window framing, vaults, and delicately chiseled acanthus leaves and gargoyles. The interior has a cruciform floor plan with a dome above the sanctuary in the eastern arm of the church.

Rock-cut architecture continued on as a living tradition in Cappadocia, Turkey, where churches and even residences were carved out of the rock, probably for defensive reasons. The first churches of Cappadocia date to about this same period. Lalibela and Cappadocia are the last great examples of rock-cut architecture in the world.

12.49 Plan and section: Bieta Giorgis, Lalibela

0   10 m

12.50 Cappadocia, Turkey

12.51 **Great Zimbabwe, Masvingo, Zimbabwe**

Hill complex (acropolis)

Valley complex

Great Enclosure

0   30 m

12.52 **Site plan: The Great Zimbabwe**

Great Zimbabwe

The Great Zimbabwe ("Great Palace") is a fortress complex dating from the 10th century; it is located on top of a granite bluff as well as in adjacent valleys in Zimbabwe, not far from Masvingo. The complex housed a large population as well as the royal court, markets, warehouses, and religious shrines. The number of ruins in its vicinity is substantial, but they have yet to be thoroughly studied. The kingdom acquired its wealth from the abundant gold reserves in the region and from the good agricultural land. These drew Indian and Islamic traders down the eastern coast of Africa. The traders set up ports that usually became independent kingdoms. Most of the goods from Zimbabwe were brought 400 kilometers to the east to the port town of Chibuene, Mozambique, where archaeologists have found the remains of structures that served to smelt gold, probably obtained from Zimbabwe. Other commercial settlements, including Sofala, became important centers for the Arab, Persian, and later Portuguese trade in slaves, gold, ivory, and other commodities.

At the heart of the Great Zimbabwe is the palace itself. The Karanga ethnic group, whose ancestors are now thought to have built the structure, called it Mumbahuru, meaning "House of the Great Woman." The building was not constructed as an isolated object in space but as an extension of the natural landscape. The blocks of the walls that define this structure were skillfully laid without mortar and ranged from 1 to 5 meters thick. Curved walls are stronger than ones with corners, which is partially why it has survived the ages. Its oval-shaped walls enclosed a large area, within which were other stone-wall enclosures that contained an outdoor living space (*kgotla*), a garden, and a place that was presumably used to keep livestock. The *kgotla* is also a place where descendants can establish communion with one another and with their ancestors. The visual focus of the building is a 6-meter-wide by 10-meter-high conical tower, the original purpose of which remains unknown. The palace was sited between two rock outcrops. At their summits are thick, curving stone walls placed in relationship to large boulders, indicating that the area was a sacred landscape.

12.53 **The wall of the Great Zimbabwe**

12.54 **Sankoré Mosque, Timbuktu, Mali**

12.55 **Mosque at Djenné, Mali**

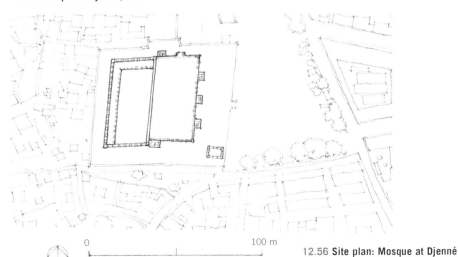

0   100 m

12.56 **Site plan: Mosque at Djenné**

Mosques of Mali

Timbuktu was one of Africa's leading cities as well as one of the intellectual and spiritual centers for the propagation of Islam. It has three great mosques—Sankoré, Djinguereber, and Sidi Yahya—which form part of an Islamic university. By the 14th century, many books were written and copied there. The city lies at the intersection of the east-west and north-south trans-Saharan trade routes and was (and still is today) an important market for rock salt. The Djinguereber Mosque (first built in 1327) is the oldest of the mosques. Except for a small part of the northern facade, which is of limestone, the building is made entirely of sun-baked mud bricks called *ferey* that are coated with a mud plaster to give the building a smooth, sculpted look. The thickness of the walls depends on their height. There are three inner courts, two minarets, and a hypostyle hall with twenty-five rows of pillars that creates a space for two thousand people.

Thirty-five kilometers to the southwest of Timbuktu is Djenné, which was not part of the Mali Empire but an independent city-state. It is the home of a large mosque that was first built in the 13th century, though the current structure dates from around 1907. The *qibla* is dominated by three large, boxlike minarets jutting out from the main wall, and eighteen buttresses. Each minaret contains a spiral staircase leading to the roof topped by a cone-shaped spire with two ostrich eggs. The logs that protrude from the building serve as scaffolding but have clearly been integrated into the design. Half of the mosque is covered by a roof, and the other half is an open-air prayer hall. The mosque's roof is supported by ninety wooden pillars. Roof vents allow hot air to rise out of the building. These buildings require continual maintenance, in which the entire community participates in preparation for the annual festival.

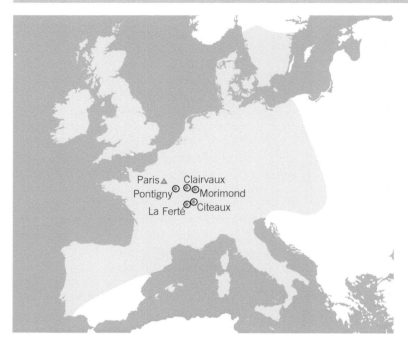

12.57 **Area of Cistercian monasteries**

12.58 **Interior: Fontenay Abbey, near Montbard, France**

FONTENAY ABBEY

Against the backdrop of 11th-century religious populism and the increasing laxity of the religious elite, especially in the monasteries, a countermovement sprang up, headed by St. Bernard of Clairvaux. He urged a return to the austere rules of the early monastic days of St. Benedict, who had conceived of the church as a workshop for prayer. Among the most prominent of the new reform orders were the Carthusians, founded in 1084, and the Cistercians, founded in 1115. The Cistercians had four so-called daughter houses: Clairvaux, Morimond, Pontigny, and La Ferté. These in turn promoted the creation of other daughter houses—so many, in fact, that by the close of the 12th century there were 530 Cistercian abbeys in Europe, forming a powerful monastic network. Though Cistercians had a large number of recruits from the feudal nobility, one of the reasons for their success was that they conceived of manual labor as a form of prayer, and therefore opened their doors to artisans and peasants. The workmanship in their buildings—even in places that are normally not visible, like certain roof sections—was therefore executed with attention to the minutest detail. Such details were not meant for the eyes of men but for the all-seeing eye of God.

The monasteries were organized as a farm, with all the monks participating in the chores. Cistercians soon became known for their innovations in farming and herding. Their vineyards in Burgundy and the Rhineland became legendary.

Under St. Bernard's influence, all the details of monkish existence were rigidly prescribed, and there were frequent inspection visits. Cistercian monasteries were not sited along pilgrimage routes but in inhospitable, often swampy and inaccessible land. They had no crypts or towers and were built on rigorous geometrical principles, sometimes by the monks themselves. They had simple vaulted naves; lighting was dim and limited by rule to only five candles. Wall surfaces were clean and simple. Sculptural embellishments were forbidden. The capitals of the columns were kept as plain as possible. Bold proportions and architectural bravura were not tolerated; even ornamental pavements were frowned upon. The plans had square east ends in defiance of the ambulatory design of the great cathedrals.

12.59 **Monastery, Fontenay Abbey**

Even though they were slow to explore its possibilities, the Cistercians' adoption of the ribbed vault around 1150 was an act of major architectural importance because they disseminated this feature across Europe. The building that best represents the Cistercian aesthetic is the Fontenay Abbey near Montbard, in the département of Côte-d'Or in France; founded in 1119, it is the oldest ensemble still in existence. Since there is no clerestory, the interior gets most of its light from facade windows and from windows at the crossing and in the sanctuary. A tunnel vault with transverse arches defines the space of the nave. The building, though its design was controlled by a proportional system, was conceived in opposition to the technical virtuosity and decorative program of the great cathedrals. On account of the tunnel vault, the nave possesses remarkable acoustical qualities. The refectory was placed in the customary Cistercian position opposite the fountain house on the south side of the cloister, with its axis perpendicular to the church.

Several factors determined the monastery's location. Because it was remote from cities, distractions were few. But the Cistericans were not idle monks, and this particular monastery was based around metal production: it was just as much an

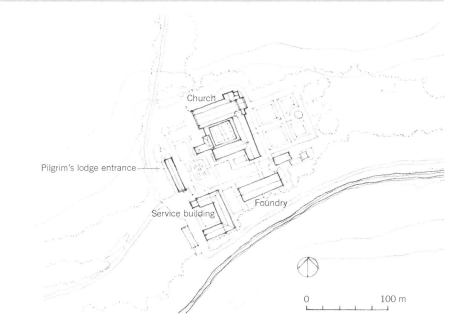

12.60 **Area plan: Fontenay Abbey**

industrial complex as a monastic one. Ore in the rocky hills just to the east of the monastery provided the raw materials, and a small but fast stream that ran through the valley could drive the forge's watermill, which in turn powered a gigantic hammer that pounded the metal. The tools that were made at the forge not only served the monks but were also sold in the surrounding region. Apart from the large forge, one of France's most productive at the time, the complex included the monastic compound itself, a hostel for pilgrims, and an herb and medicinal garden.

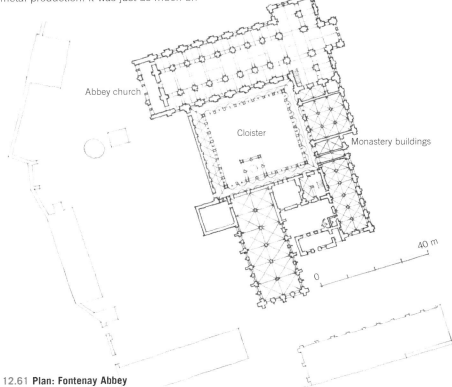

12.61 **Plan: Fontenay Abbey**

12.62 **Interior: Fontenay Abbey**

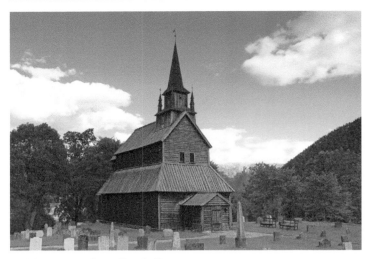

12.63 Kaupanger Stave Church, Norway

12.64 Borgund Stave Church, Norway

MEDIEVAL SCANDINAVIA

The conversion of the Norse and the Swedes to Christianity was not due to missionary activity, as in Ireland, but came about through the efforts of the local kings. Olav Trygvason, for example, who was king toward the end of the 10th century, was the first to build churches in Norway, probably with the help of a master builder brought over from the British Isles. Gradually, however, local craftsmen, with their shipbuilding skills, were drawn in. The churches are very distinctive. A low wall of flat stones raised the building above ground level. The rest of the church was in wood, with columns and planks, the two basic structural elements, all dovetailed, pegged, and wedged—never nailed. At the bottom of the columns, a sill beam was designed with a groove in it into which the lower ends of the wall planks fit. To tighten the structure above, a continuous belt of cross-braces was sometimes added. Some churches had porches on at least three sides that served as a place for processions to gather, or where lepers, who were otherwise excluded from the sanctuary, could listen. The interiors were very dark, with small strips of light occasionally forcing their way from openings in the west gable or from peepholes in the walls. Religious services were intimate and illuminated by candlelight. Small gold-covered reliquaries, often looking like small churches, held bone fragments from saints and would have shimmered on the altar in the dim light.

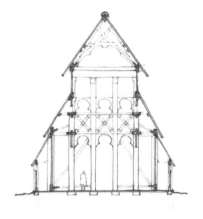

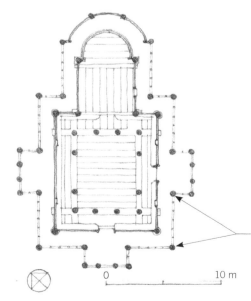

Particularly distinctive were the elaborately carved portals decorated with motifs of vines and coiled serpents. The portals were originally painted in black and white and vibrant shades of red and green; the visual effect of the buildings would have been more pronounced than today. The buildings were imbued with symbolic import. The portals, for example, represented the defenders of the faith and were narrow so that the devil could not accidentally accompany one into the church. Once totaling in the hundreds, as these were village churches, today there are only about twenty of these unusual buildings extant in various states of authenticity.

12.65 Plan and section: Borgund Stave Church

The word *stave*, from the Nors *stavr*, refers to the load-bearing posts that make up the structure.

0   10 m

12.66 **Europe during the High Middle Ages**

was to foretell the program of the interior. For Suger, the use of precious materials in the furnishings of the church was also important, as it served as a presentiment of the splendors of heaven.

For all these reasons, St. Denis broke new ground and is thus heralded as initiating the Gothic style. For the first time, features such as cross-rib vaulting and flying buttresses (although present in prior churches) were combined into an integrated stylistic statement along with sharply pointed spires, a rose window, clustered columns, pointed arches, and a stress on luminosity.

EUROPE: THE HIGH MIDDLE AGES

During the 13th century, the skyline of European cities underwent a profound change as the spires and towers of some six hundred major churches and cathedrals marked the location of cities in the landscape. This energetic building activity was driven by a combination of religious fervor and increasing wealth. Income from the selling of indulgences by the Roman Church was an important source of financing. It was a dubious practice that in the 16th century was to awaken the ire of Martin Luther and eventually lead to the Reformation. Another source of income was sending relics on tours. The bishops of Chartres, for example, sent the cathedral's relics as far away as England to solicit contributions.

The shift in focus dates to the Synod of Arras (1025), during which it was decided that sculptural programs could serve to help the illiterate visualize what they could not understand through the written word. Statues, once used only sparingly, and usually in relation to aristocratic worship practices, now stood row upon row along church facades. Compared with the Norman facade of St. Étienne (1067–87) in Caen, France, with its small windows and imposing, solid-looking wall of stone, the Basilica of St. Denis, with its broad and decorated portals, seems to almost float above the ground. The church was begun by the Normans but was transformed by Abbot Suger (1081–1155). Actively engaged in France's political life, Suger

played a leading role in running the kingdom while King Louis VI was away on a Crusade. He wanted cathedrals to accommodate large crowds that could then move easily past the relics. He thus created for St. Denis a space behind the high altar known as a chevet (French for "headpiece"), where the church's more precious relics could be displayed. It served not only to display the relics but also to reinforce the spatial significance of the high altar. Suger also redesigned the cathedral's facade, introducing a triple portal that served as a symbol of the Trinity. The Trinity had become important to theological speculation in the second quarter of the 12th century, and its reinstatement signified support for an orthodox interpretation of the Bible and for papal authority. The tympanum over the central door of St. Denis was the most important element of the facade, as it portrays Christ sitting in judgment. The sculptures were once again a concession to the unlettered, for few in the general population at the time could read and write. In this, St. Denis reflects a change in religious attitudes. Whereas Romanesque cathedrals were designed primarily for the elite, St. Denis and later cathedrals were buildings meant to appeal to the popular imagination. On a more elevated plane, Abbot Suger held that the religious experience was one of transcendence, symbolized by disembodied light. The rose window in the center of the facade, for example, was one of the first of its kind—a grand wheel of light and color. The function of the facade, so Suger held,

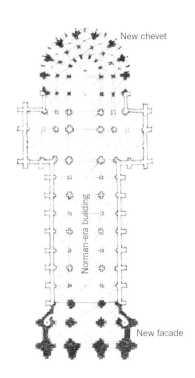

12.67 **Reconstruction: Basilica of St. Denis, France, at the time of Abbot Suger**

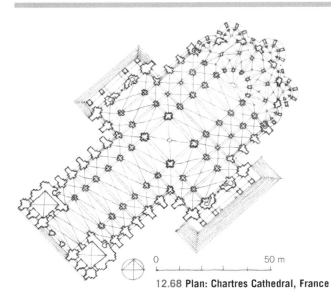

12.68 Plan: Chartres Cathedral, France

Cathedral Design

In the 13th century, cathedral building was by far the largest construction enterprise ever attempted in Europe. Chartres Cathedral, for example, was able to hold more than eight thousand people. Technologically complex and often dangerous, construction frequently took many decades and sometimes hundreds of years. Unlike Carolingian churches, with their imposing westworks, and Ottonian monastic churches, which were associated with market towns and might not have had a facade at all, the facades on this new generation of cathedrals served as sacred thresholds to a mystic interior.

Among the various aspects of church design that changed during this period was the emergence of the interior elevation of the nave as an architectural unit in its own right, with architects seeking to balance the interplay of horizontal and vertical elements. At Notre-Dame in Paris (1163–1250), there are four discrete horizontal levels: the ground-level arcade, over which run two galleries—the tribune and the triforium—above which runs an upper, windowed story or clerestory. The windows of these cathedrals were not transparent but filled with stained glass, bringing into the interior a muted, shimmering light. To obtain the soaring height that the Gothic age aspired to, flying buttresses made their appearance. While they achieve the desired result on the inside, they tended to pose a problem on the exterior. At first the flying buttresses were purely structural supplements, as at St.-

Germain-des-Prés, where they were added as reinforcements around 1180, but thereafter they were integrated into the plan from the start. Flying buttresses consist of a tower that supplies the necessary counterweight and an arch that transfers the lateral loads to the tower. Because of the flying buttresses, a church interior could become a spatial unit, although this occurred at the expense of the exterior's legibility.

The epitome of the new style was Chartres Cathedral (1194–1220), where on the outside the nave is almost completely obscured behind an intimate tangle of buttresses. The interior, on the other hand, is almost canyonlike. The nave elevation has only three levels, permitting a strong vertical extension of the bays. To compensate for the added height, two flying buttresses, one over the other, bring the load to the tower. The vaults, another important Gothic element, were composed of stone ribs with thin brick vaults in between, stretched like taut skin. The east end, with its rounded ambulatory, is modeled on St. Denis but goes further, adding five semicircular chapels. The piers were also innovative. Earlier piers often were composed of a cylindrical core at the level of the arcade and thin colonettes above. Here a continual line from the vault to the ground reduces the visibility of the column at the arcade level. Proportion and geometry were used throughout to organize all of the elements, from the small to the large. The length of the church, for example, is related to the transept in a ratio of 2:3; the length and width of the transept is 1:2.

The town of Chartres was, at the time, quite small, but among the wealthiest in Europe, with an important trade in textiles and metalsmithing. However, financing for the cathedral came not only from the local region but from nearly all sectors of France, as St. Marie of Chartres had almost attained the status of a national deity.

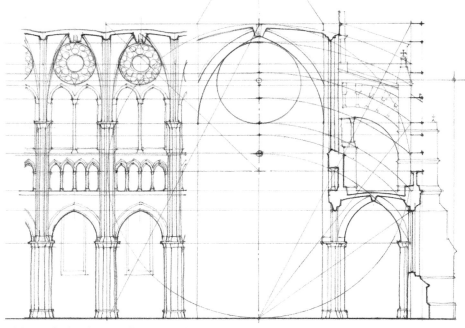

12.69 Partial interior elevation and section: Chartres Cathedral

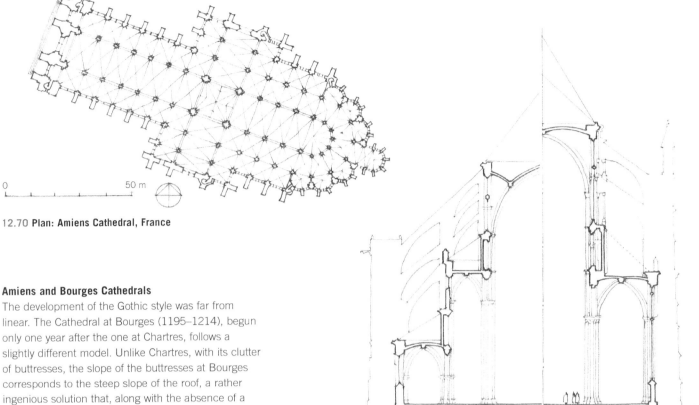

12.70 **Plan: Amiens Cathedral, France**

Amiens and Bourges Cathedrals

The development of the Gothic style was far from
linear. The Cathedral at Bourges (1195–1214), begun
only one year after the one at Chartres, follows a
slightly different model. Unlike Chartres, with its clutter
of buttresses, the slope of the buttresses at Bourges
corresponds to the steep slope of the roof, a rather
ingenious solution that, along with the absence of a
transept, allows the nave to be read on the outside as
a unified form. The chevet at the end rises in three
stages, with small high-peaked chapels seemingly
suspended between the buttresses' piers. The interior,
with its tall arches, is not as canyonlike as Chartres
because the tall arches create the illusion that the wall
of the side aisle is the actual side of the nave.

At Amiens Cathedral (1220–35) the architects
were more conservative than at Bourges, following
the model of Chartres, with its calmer interior and
soaring verticality. Amiens's impression of verticality
is further enhanced by the integration of the crossing
piers into the overall design of the nave's facade.
The division of the upper window into four segments
rather than the usual two increases the impression
of verticality. Its tall nave arches and high clerestory
windows combine elements of Chartres and Bourges
while to some extent preserving the unity of the nave.
The calm effect of the interior combines well with the
luminosity of the chevet. A comparison of the sections
of Amiens and Bourges shows that the interior of
Amiens creates a greater vertical effect, which is due
to the lower arches along its nave and the absence
of a second aisle, and is aided by better illumination.
The consequence is that the buttresses of Amiens
needed to be much higher to offset the weight, which
annihilates the corporeal presence of the building that
is still legible at Bourges.

12.71 **Half-section: Naves of Bourges and Amiens Cathedrals**

12.72 **Amiens Cathedral**

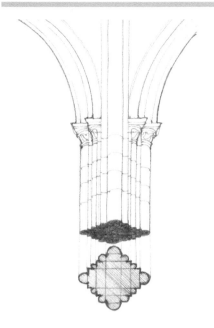

12.73 **Gothic compound pier**

12.74 **West front, Amiens Cathedral**

12.75 **Cathedral of Notre-Dame of Reims, France**

Whereas Romanesque churches had round columns in the nave, in Gothic churches from Speyer onward, columns that were composed of a columnar core with colonettes attached to it began to appear. The colonettes facing the nave continue upward to reach all the way to the vault, whereas the colonettes on the inside become part of the ribs of the vaults in the side aisles. As a result, Gothic supports were neither columns nor piers; rather, they were columnar bundles working not only in the vertical dimension but also in plan, as they would seem to be squares rotated 45 degrees, creating diagonals through the building.

Notre-Dame of Reims

By the second decade of the 13th century, the space of the church had changed from a place emphasizing the enactment of liturgical processes into a more public space where relics could be viewed and worshipped. On a philosophical level, the discussion changed from issues of liturgy to an emphasis on the transcendent and dematerialized quality of light (God) and geometry (the ordered universe). Robert Grosseteste, an English theologian and Bishop of Lincoln, who read Greek and was familiar with Arabic scientific commentaries, argued that all of human knowledge stemmed from the spiritual radiance of light. Rose windows appeared in almost every church, sometimes opening so

wide that they touched the framework of the buttresses, as at France's Auxerre Cathedral (completed ca. 1234). Along with these new ideas was the emergence of the cult of the Virgin Mary. The mother of Christ, Mary had until then played a minor role in the Christian liturgy; she now captured the popular imagination, and we begin to see her image standing alongside those of the saints. At the Cathedral of Notre-Dame of Reims (1211–90), figures of Mary were visible in every part of the church, standing in not only for the saints but also for the Christian church itself. The building was, in comparison to Amiens, more airy in its detailing. The tall windows right and left of the rose window, which allow a view through the building, make the upper part almost seem weightless. The rosette barely fits in the narrow space allocated to it, and indeed the nave, though similar to that of Amiens, is considerably narrower in proportion.

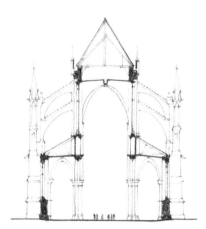

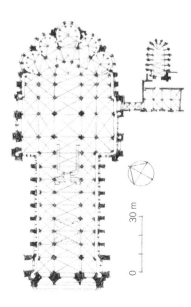

12.76 **Section and plan: Cathedral of Notre-Dame of Reims**

12.77 **Entrance facade, Exeter Cathedral, England**

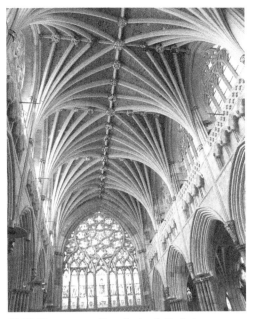

12.78 **Tierceron vaulting, Exeter Cathedral**

Exeter Cathedral

The transition from the Romanesque to the early Gothic lies to some degree in the systematization of the nave elevation and in the integration of the nave with rib vaulting. By 1300, architects, increasingly confident, began to explore the decorative qualities inherent in structure, creating styles that historians variously call Decorated, Perpendicular, or Flamboyant Gothic. Scholars have long wondered if the emergence of this new stylistic direction coincided with increased contacts with the East. It is known, for example, that England's Edward I (r. 1272–1307) sent an emissary to Persia. At any rate, Exeter Cathedral (1280–1300) shows a decorative unity and a fullness that earlier cathedrals did not have. The lower facade has become a veritable curtain displaying the figures of the saints. (The innumerable saints often have a special day allocated to them, and a child born on a specific saint's day would often receive that saint's name.) The gallery of saints at Exeter, with its abstract crenellations, stands as an almost independent screen in front of the building. On the inside, the crisply folded geometries of early 13th-century vaults have been replaced by the rippling shapes of fan vaulting, the origin of which is not known.

Buildings in this style do not represent a deterioration of the Gothic style, as is sometimes held; rather, they demonstrate a desire to integrate decoration and structure. One factor that contributed to the change was the fashion for more luminous interiors and more frequent use of white or clear glass, which enhanced the subtleties of a building's surface treatment. Furthermore, in England at least, cathedral builders did not aspire to the great heights that were typical of French churches, preferring instead wider windows, lower buildings, and taller steeples. Early 14th-century English cathedrals therefore tended to have more coherent and yet more dynamic silhouettes. This can be seen at the presbytery of Gloucester Cathedral (ca. 1350). Unlike those parts of the building that were already finished, the new extension, actually a structure unto itself, has huge windows that are clearly visible on the outside. The buttresses are kept tight to the body of the church. On the interior, facing the apse, the lightness and paperiness of the architecture has been so dematerialized that nothing is left except a thin filigree grid of supports. The new direction received its grandest manifestation at the Cathedral of Milan (begun 1387), a wide building with a vast orchestration of vertical elements in white marble, reaching a crescendo in an octagonal tower that rises almost magically from the center of the building.

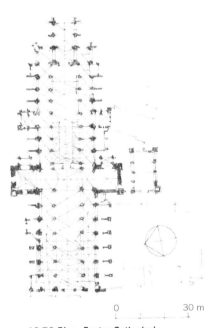

0 ———————— 30 m

12.79 **Plan: Exeter Cathedral**

445

12.80 View of Gubbio, Italy

12.81 Town Hall, Gubbio

Italian Town Halls

In Italy, in the wake of faltering imperial control, a population explosion, and an expansion of markets, the artisans, guild members, and merchants known collectively as the *popolo* banded together with men of rank and property to dominate the political system. The rise of the *popolo* was rapid. In Milan, in 1190, the *popolo*, the main source of communal revenues, were entitled to only one-fifth of government positions. By 1198, they were the dominant political force in the city. Often the first acts of the *popolo* were to pass tax reform, systematize the law courts, and set up controls on public monies. Beginning with Pisa in the 1080s, Bologna in 1123, and Florence in 1138, these fledgling city governments laid the groundwork for an urban consciousness that was to become the hallmark of Italian politics for the next two centuries. The formal acceptance of this new arrangement came in the form of the Peace of Constance (1183), a much overlooked treaty that paved the way for the modern notion of civic governance. With the German emperors no longer in a position to assert their power, they gave the northern Italian cities the right to elect their own consuls, to govern their own lands, and most importantly, to make their own laws.

Central to the new notion of governance was a town hall in front of a public piazza (*campo*) where people could assemble. There was often also a special building for the head of the militia and police. For the first time in centuries—perhaps since the days of the Romans—buildings were conceived and constructed as an ensemble with a public space. The earliest town halls date to the end of the 12th century and are at Brescia, Verona, Modena, Pavia, and Bergamo. These were followed in the 13th century by town halls at Volterra, Todi, Como, Ferrara, Siena, and Gubbio, among others. Most of these halls followed a simple prototype: a large meeting hall on the upper floor, with large windows facing the piazza and a balcony from which proclamations could be read. The ground floor was often open or had a loggia where silversmiths, gold traders, or other highly skilled craftsmen and merchants could work under the direct protection and supervision of the city. In the urban complex of Gubbio, the town hall and palace face each other across a piazza that is raised on a high undercroft looking out over the valley below. The new town halls were coordinated urbanistically with the cathedral buildings that were begun first at Pisa in 1063, followed by Modena in 1099, Verona in 1139, and Siena in 1196. The situation was, however, rarely peaceful. Milan, Brescia, and Piacenza were often at war with each other, as were Pisa, Genoa, and Lucca.

Siena

In the 13th century, Siena, one of the most important cities in Italy, controlled the southern Tuscan wool industry and dominated the trade routes between France and Rome. It was also home to Italy's richest banks. Siena's power reached a zenith with the defeat of a much superior Florentine army at the battle of Montaperti in 1260. The city then embarked on unrivaled urban redevelopment, building a cathedral, a *campo*, and the town hall. The *campo* was constructed more or less at the center of the city, on unclaimed land that sloped steeply into a ravine. A large terrace was built over the ravine to form the *campo*. At the steep end, a town hall was constructed—the Palazzo Pubblico (1297–1310)—with four stories facing the *campo* and elegantly proportioned reception and councilor rooms, many decorated with frescoes recounting important events in the city's history. The curve of the piazza is lined with a continuous row of palace fronts, most dating from the 14th century. Opposite the town hall is the Loggia della Mercanzia (1417), for the merchants. The Duomo (1196–1215) a few blocks away dominates the town's silhouette. As was common in Italy, areas of towns were organized around mendicant churches. In this case the principal ones are San Domenico (1226), Sant'Agostino (1258), and San Francesco (1326–1475).

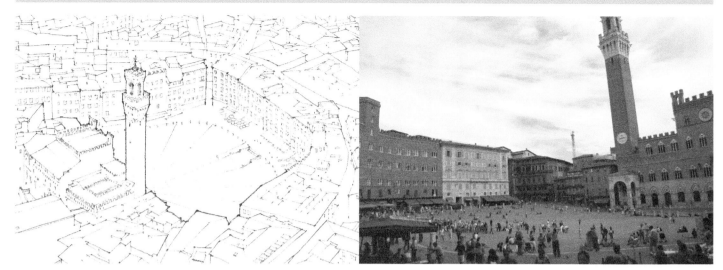

12.82 **Aerial view: Piazza del Campo, Siena, Italy**

12.83 **Palazzo Pubblico, Siena**

The city's prosperity came to an abrupt halt with the arrival of the Black Plague, which reached Siena in 1348; by the end of that year, two-thirds of Siena's one hundred thousand citizens had succumbed. The city never recovered; what we see today is a snapshot of a late medieval Italian city.

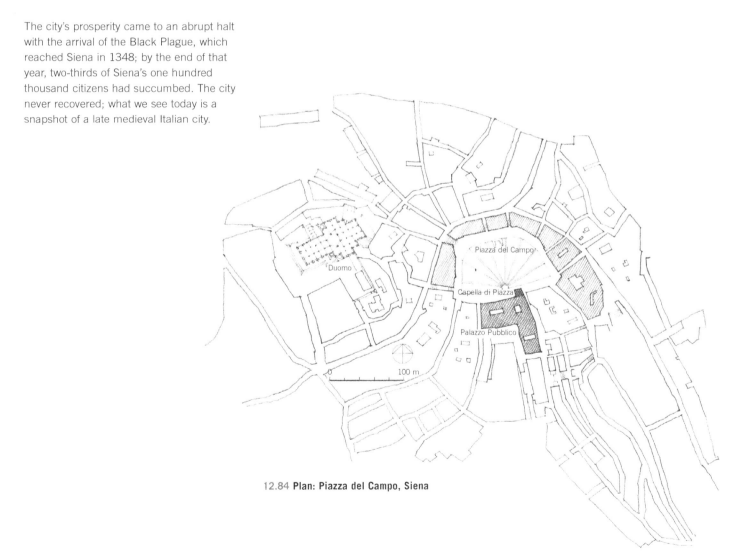

12.84 **Plan: Piazza del Campo, Siena**

12.85 Nave of St. Croce, Florence, Italy

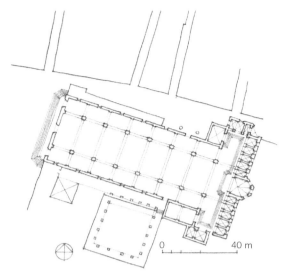

12.86 Plan: St. Croce

Mendicant Orders

At the beginning of the 13th century, the Roman Church saw its theological interpretation and hierarchical structure threatened by a series of so-called heresies, several of which revolved around an interpretation of the Gospels that held that access to the divine was through personal emulation of the deeds of Christ rather than through the complex liturgical demands of the church. Small wonder that this reading of the Gospels displeased the church fathers, who initially felt threatened by it. St. Francis of Assisi was on the verge of being branded just such a heretic in 1206 when he abandoned his privileged worldly life, became an ascetic, and preached the gospel of poverty. But Pope Innocent III, eager to bring the poverty sects under his control, allowed St. Francis to preach and informally approved his efforts in 1209 (and then officially in 1223), hoping to avoid a possible schism. Thus was born one of several mendicant orders that radically transformed church history and was to lead, some centuries later, to the Reformation triggered by the preachings of the German monk Martin Luther.

In the early Middle Ages, reclusive monastics preferred their monasteries in the quiet isolation of the countryside as a counterweight to what they saw as the decadence of Roman cities. As a result, inhabitants of cities and villages often had to walk long distances to go to a church

and were thus remote from the cosmic principles that united them as members of the Christian faith. The mendicant orders responded by setting up their monasteries in the hearts of cities or just outside their gates to make themselves humbly serviceable and approachable; in many places, religious services were both physically and conceptually within reach of the majority of Christians for the first time. Mendicant monasteries were not sites of calm reflection as Cistercian monasteries were, but served more as dormitories for the monks, who would leave in the morning to perform various duties. The Franciscans became specialists in architecture and construction, helping to build fortification walls and infrastructure. The Dominicans, another mendicant order, were known as doctors, lawyers, and teachers, and many became well-known philosophers. They were also closely associated with the development of Scholasticism during the 13th century and were prominent at the great universities of Europe. In a sense, the 13th century can be seen as the second Christianization of Europe. If the first was fought in the name of (often forcible) conversion and was largely dynastic in structure, the second was based on broad outreach and popular appeal.

Because mendicants had sworn an oath to poverty and consequently had no money, their churches were usually built for them by citizens. At first many were simple structures or converted barns. By 1250, there were

Franciscan communities in almost every city in France, Germany, and Italy. Mendicant churches were by definition simple and austere. The great ebullient forms of the cathedrals were spurned. The Dominican Church in Toulouse (1275–92), for example, had no flying buttresses and was built entirely of brick. At the Franciscan church of St. Croce (begun 1294), the architect Arnolfo di Cambio spurned vaulting and re-created the vast emptiness of Constantinian naves in a spare Gothic idiom. In many Italian towns, mendicant churches to this day are large plain brick buildings.

12.87 Dominican Church, Toulouse, France

12.88 Nasrid sultanate

NASRID SULTANATE AND THE ALHAMBRA

In 1260, the Mongolians destroyed Aleppo and Damascus, massacring fifty thousand inhabitants. With the Arabian heartland in turmoil, there were only two places in the Islamic world where architecture could develop: northern India (which would eventually come under the sway of the Mongolian Timurid) and the Spanish-Moroccan area, which was far removed from Central Asia. The latter was extraordinarily prosperous, even though by the 11th century the unity of Spain and Morocco, as established by the Almohads, had dissolved. The various rulers, caught up in civil wars, became increasingly vulnerable to Christian armies and indeed were slowly losing ground. It was in this context that the Emirate of Granada emerged, whose ruler built for himself the Palace of Alhambra (Red Castle), laid out in 1238 by Mohammed I (r. 1238–73). It is first and foremost a fortification, defined by a defensive wall circuit mediated by towers and gates atop a natural acropolis surrounded by rocky terrain and the River Darro, which guards its northern side. The citadel looks down on and protects the city that developed to its north on the far side of the rising slopes on the opposite side of the river.

The Alcazaba, the triangular citadel on the westernmost tip of the complex, enclosed within its own wall circuit, exemplifies the military aspects of the complex. It served as an armory and was heavily fortified with a watchtower. The palace was located just to the west of the citadel against the northern edge of the protective wall. It was entered by a gate at the eastern end of the southern wall circuit. A second entrance, Bab al-Shari'a, the "Gate of Justice" (*shari'a* is the Arabic term for the body of Islamic religious law), stands at the western end of the same wall and is noteworthy for the carving of an outstretched hand in the keystone and that of a key above the portal. Various interpretations have been made of these symbols, which are probably intended to demonstrate the rulers' authority. The palace has views down to the town and the distant landscape.

Given the decline of Mohammed I's fortunes—indeed, the palace lasted only ninety years before it was taken by the Christians—the architects had to make do with limited means, and the palace, despite its opulence, was actually quite small. Furthermore, stone was limited to columns and important ornaments, while much of the decoration of the walls and even the vaults was in the form of intricately carved and painted stucco (sadly reduced to all-white in the reconstructions). These designs combine geometric patterns, naturalist floral motifs, and a highly developed style of calligraphy through which Qur'anic verse and poetry became a visual art. The elaborate forms seen on the palace walls are often stylized script mirrored and transformed into an angular or curvaceous composition.

12.89 Column capital, Court of the Lions, Granada, Spain

12.90 Court of the Myrtles, Alhambra

12.91 Gate of Justice, Alhambra

The original purpose of most rooms can be extrapolated from the inscriptions on their walls. The palace was designed as a dense network of rooms, mediated by two large patio-gardens placed at right angles to each other and defining two separate areas, a public/political zone and a private zone. The Court of the Myrtles, with its long reflecting pool, served as the center of the political activities. It focused on the Hall of the Ambassadors, a square room with a high and richly ornamented ceiling. The Court of the Lions, by contrast, was the private court for the queen and a place for banquets. It was the more elaborate of the two courts. Delicate rose-white columns with subtle axial connections set up a colonnade around the entire court, which has four channels of water representing the four "rivers of paradise" extending cardinally within the columnar portico to a fountain held up by stone lions. Ashlar stones were used at the gates and to reinforce the corners of the walls. The outside walls were stuccoed and sometimes painted to simulate stone or brick. The marble columns are sometimes structural, sometimes decorative. The whiteness and thinness of the columns give them an elegant quality unknown even to the ancient Romans. Though the shafts of the columns were left plain, the capitals were painted in bright colors. The harsh, white marble flooring of the Court of the Lions visible today is a recent

addition. Originally the court was more of a garden planted with ornamental orange trees.

Representation of the human form is forbidden in Islamic religious buildings, but geometrical designs are commonplace. Squares and rectangular formations produced by the rotation of a radius from the base of the bisecting hypotenuse form the basis of most of the Alhambra's construction, in both plan and elevation. The two-dimensional ornament covers the colorful tile work that rises up from the bottom of the wall to about 4 feet. Geometric complexity is particularly evident in the ceiling of the Hall of the Two Sisters, an intimate banqueting room.

As the *muqarnas* rise to the center of the vault, they obliterate the structural character of the space even though they are governed by an intricate and complex geometry of their own. The mixture of hard and soft shadows makes the vault seem strikingly ethereal.

From 1492 to the 18th century, the Alhambra was the residence of the Spanish governors. In the 16th century, Charles V constructed a massive palace for himself that was grafted onto the fabric of the old structure; the grandeur of the original Islamic architecture contrasts strongly with the dull militarism of the newer building.

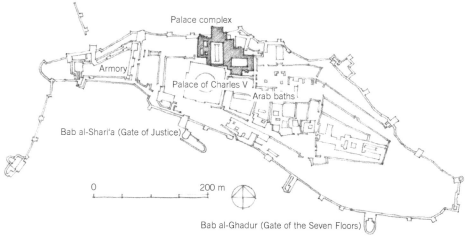

12.92 Plan: Alhambra

12.93 **Hall of the Ambassadors, Alhambra**

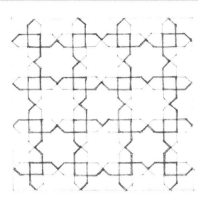

12.94 **Geometric motif, Alhambra**

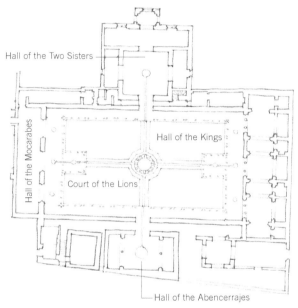

Hall of the Two Sisters

Hall of the Mocarabes

Hall of the Kings

Court of the Lions

Hall of the Abencerrajes

12.95 **Plan: Court of the Lions, Alhambra**

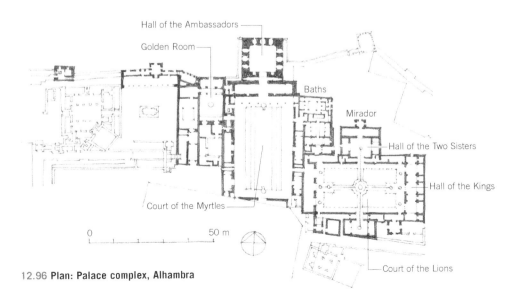

Hall of the Ambassadors

Golden Room

Baths

Mirador

Hall of the Two Sisters

Hall of the Kings

Court of the Myrtles

0   50 m

Court of the Lions

12.96 **Plan: Palace complex, Alhambra**

451

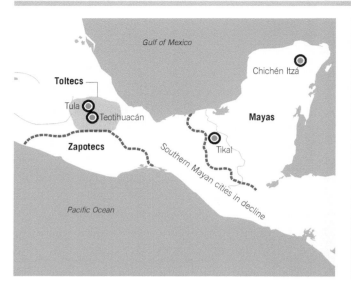

12.97 Mesoamerica, ca. 1200 CE

12.98 Giant Toltec figures at Tula, near Tula de Allende, Mexico

TOLTEC EMPIRE

From the 9th to the late 12th centuries, the Toltecs, with their capital at Tula, located farther north than any previous pre-Columbian Central American capital, were the determining force of the region, taking over the role that had once been Teotihuacán's. They adopted an aggressive militaristic stance and practiced human sacrifice extensively. No subsequent dynasty failed to claim Toltec ancestry. Their myth of Quetzalcoatl (the "Plumed Serpent") was the likely cause of the Aztec's acceptance of the Spaniard Hernán Cortés in the 16th century, when the latter's arrival was mistaken as the prophesied return of Quetzalcoatl.

Tula had a population of about forty thousand by 1100 CE. The Toltec architects designed within established methods, such as placing buildings around large plazas, using many-tiered platforms as bases, building newer structures atop older ones, and painting colorful motifs on building surfaces. Their main sacred complex sat on a high artificial terrace, with the central plaza occupying an area 100 by 100 meters partly enclosed by pyramids, palaces, and ball courts. The substructure to Tula's pyramid was covered with thick white stucco, which may have symbolized the underworld. Although the temple at the top of the pyramid was destroyed, the stone columns that supported the roof still remain; they were carved with images of Toltec warriors. Unique to Tula was the Coatepantli, or Snake Wall—a

freestanding structure that encloses a passageway north of the base of the pyramid. Both sides of this passage are carved with identical friezes—bands of geometrically stylized snakes framing the central panels and depicting partly skeletonized men apparently being devoured by serpents. Only two other *coatepantli* representations are known to exist—at Tenochtitlán and Tenayuca—suggesting that they were a feature of Mesoamerica only from 900 to 1500 CE.

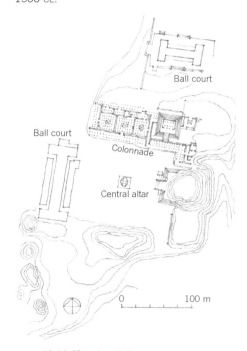

12.99 Site plan: Tula

CHICHÉN ITZÁ

The architectural ideas of Tula were reproduced and refined in Chichén Itzá, the main city-state of the Yucatán Peninsula in the 12th century. Because the city is very far from Tula, the mechanics of the influence between the two are still a subject of discussion. The sudden efflorescence of Toltec architecture in Chichén Itzá has led some to speculate that the exiled Toltec ruler, Topiltzin Quetzalcoatl, may have settled there. Although sacrifice and a militaristic stance were central to the Itzá elites, their ceremonial complex was much more about the cosmic calendar and its measurement and meaning.

The complex is organized around two *cenotés*, the Mayan word for the deep, water-filled sinkholes that the Itzá associated with the underworld. These sinkholes are scattered across the Yucatán. The name *Chichén Itzá*, in fact, means "the opening of the wells of the Itzá." Since the soil and rock in the region is porous and does not hold water well, the eerie underground pools had both a practical and a religious meaning. Of the two in the city, the southern one was used for drinking water, and the northern one, connected to the surface by a ceremonial path, was used for sacrifices. The main structure, however, was the *caracol*, or observatory; it is circular, on a trapezoidal base, and raised on a rectangular platform. Its walls have tiny openings that allowed the priests to track the movement of various

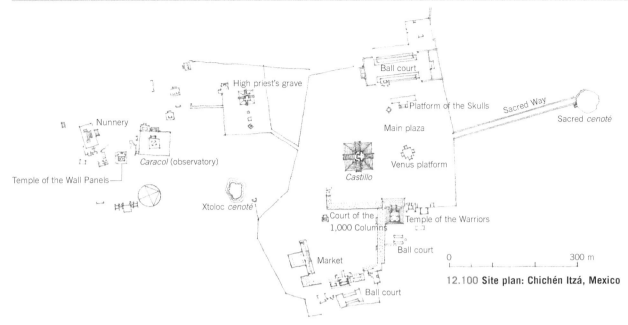

12.100 **Site plan: Chichén Itzá, Mexico**

stars and, in particular, the planet Venus. The northern complex is designed around an impressive biaxially symmetrical platform mound, known as the *castillo*. It hides within it an older platform mound, whose temple was accessed by a single stair. The temple, complete with its sacrificial sculpture, the *chacmool*, was carefully interred in the reconstruction, or the symbolic "reskinning," of the platform mound.

Besides being a sacrificial temple, the *castillo* also functioned as a solar calendar. It has 91 steps on three sides and 92 steps on the northern side, for a total of 365 steps, one for each day in the solar year. It is almost exactly aligned to the cardinal directions to enable the observation of solar events on solstices and equinoxes. The *castillo's* best known calendar effect occurs on the equinoxes, when the balustrade of its northern stairway casts seven isosceles triangles as shadows that link together to form the body and tail of a serpent, with its head sculpted at the base of the stair. This is presumably a depiction of the ceremonial descent of Kukulkan, the Itzá's name for Quetzalcoatl, from the sky.

Kukulkan's descent is also presented in the Temple of the Warriors, marking the western edge of the plaza, a structure remarkably similar to the one in Tula. A forest of pillars, carved with warriors and originally roofed over with perishable materials, forms a long pre-chamber, presumably to restrict access to the main pyramid, where the rulers

would have held audience. A single flight of stairs leads to a temple whose threshold is marked yet again with a *chacmool* and two columns depicting Kukulkan's descent. In the back is a bench where the king may have sat as captives were sacrificed against the *chacmool*.

On the western edge of the plaza is the city's principal ball court, the largest known in pre-Columbian America. It is 146 by 36 meters, its hoops 8 meters high, making it almost the size of an American football field—so large that it is hard to imagine its being used for sport; it may, in fact, have been intended to depict a more ceremonial ball court of the gods. There are several other smaller ball courts in Chichén Itzá.

12.101 *Castillo*, **Chichén Itzá**

12.102 **Ball court at Chichén Itzá**

12.103 **Temple of the Warriors, Chichén Itzá**

The impaled heads of defeated warriors were displayed on a special construction in the middle of the plaza, just east of the ball court. At the middle of the northern edge of the plaza lies the entrance to the path that leads to the sacred *cenoté*. As was the rest of the Yucatán, Chichén Itzá was suddenly abandoned in the middle of the 13th century, for reasons that are still not fully understood. However, the *castillo* and its path to the sacred *cenoté* continued to be used by local inhabitants until the Spanish conquest of the region.

The *chacmool* was a Tula invention. These post-Classical Mayan stone statues depict a human figure reclining face up, its legs drawn in, its elbows on the ground, with its upper back raised and its head turned to a near right angle. It holds a vessel, disk, or plate on its stomach, where offerings may have been placed or sacrifices carried out. (It is presumed that the hearts of sacrificed victims were placed in the vessel.) Although the origins of the *chacmool* are undetermined, they proliferated during Tula times. Twelve have been found at Tula, fourteen at Chichén Itzá, and two more in the Aztec capital, Tenochtitlán. The ancient name for this type of sculpture is unknown.

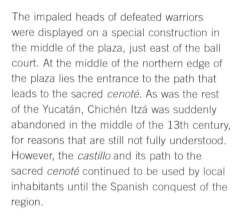

12.104 *Caracol* (observatory), **Chichén Itzá**

12.105 **A** *chacmool*, **Chichén Itzá**

1400 CE

INTRODUCTION

The year 1400 more or less marks the end of the great migratory conquests from the Russian steppes into Europe. The arrows on the maps showing the Gauls, the Huns, the Turks, the Mongolians, and other tribes from the steppes are no longer there; the Eurasian world for the first time in a thousand years was not beset by migratory invaders. Civilizations responded by building walls, from the Long Wall in China to the Roman Wall at Limez. Then, as now, the impact of these walls was more symbolic than functional—they defined limits and boundaries, rather than successfully keeping the "barbarians" at bay. The impact of the invaders had not been all negative; within a short time period, the respective tribes had adapted and started to make their own contributions, from the Huns in eastern Europe, who converted to Christianity; to the Yuan in China, who merged their Buddhist-shamanistic ways with Confucian thoughts and manners; to the Khanates in West Asia who adopted and transformed the new ways of Islam. The steppes invaders also cleaned up and linked the short- and long-distance land-based trade routes, particularly along the Silk Route, so that within a brief span of time, renewed civilizational and aesthetic imperatives were underway.

It is perhaps a great irony of history that the famous European oceangoing explorations and migratory conquests also began in this century, beginning with Columbus's unexpected encounter with the Americas. The colonial age ultimately decimated the commercial viability of the Silk Route, but remember that the initiative to search for an alternative ocean route to India and the East was not initiated as a great voyage of "discovery." Rather, it was the Spanish crown's desperate effort to find an alternative to the high prices charged by the new gatekeepers of the Silk Route, the Ottomans. Spices from the trade route were necessary not for occasional exotic fare, but to preserve meat. Ferdinand and Isabella, bankrupt from their long wars against the Moors, financed Christopher Columbus, an Italian, to counter the forces of the Ottoman Empire that, in collaboration with the northern Italians, had a stranglehold on Silk Route trade. The Ottomans, upset over the loss of Andalusia, were particularly hostile to the Spanish. The northern Italian city-states and universities, in correspondence with those of the Islamic world, had long known that the world was round and thus that a sea route to India from the West was a near certainty. The only remaining doubt was about its distance. Geometry suggested that no 15th-century European ship was robust enough to undertake that journey. It was only an error in translation that convinced Columbus that he could reach India in about the half the time that it would have actually taken. While his Italian compatriots, who profited significantly by the Silk Route spice trade, were not interested financing his missions, Columbus found his backers in the Spanish, who were willing to take an unlikely gamble.

Some scholars date from 1492 the Anthropocene age, the present geological period in which human activity has come to decisively affect climate, the biosphere, and geology. One marker of its onset is the titanic encounter, engineered by humans, between the microbes of Eurasia and the Americas that occurs at this moment. While 95 percent of the 20 million or so inhabitants of the Americas died from exposure to Eurasian diseases, particularly smallpox, a negligible number of Europeans died from American diseases, mostly syphilis. It seems that the long commerce between the distinctive communities of Eurasia and Africa, and the even longer tradition of close living with animals, had made Eurasians much more resilient to disease than their American counterparts. The Black Plague, for instance, had just ravaged its way across Eurasia, killing almost 10 percent of the population from China to Europe, which of course countered the effects of global trade—but it also ultimately improved the immune systems of the survivors.

This microbial imbalance, aided of course by Spanish and Portuguese determination to exploit, permanently negated any counterfactual possibility of a grand merger of civilizations, producing instead an essentially unilateral history of conquest and colonization. This was a significant loss because the American civilizations, at that time, were booming. By the middle of the 13th century, most of North America was inhabited by dozens of tribes whose villages dotted the landscape. Meanwhile, in Central America, the Toltecs had been displaced by a new migrant group from the north, known as the Mexica (from whom comes the modern name *Mexico*), who settled into the central valley of Mexico, establishing new cities. After two centuries of conflict, the city of Tenochca concluded a military alliance with the Acolhua of Texcoco and the Tepanecs of Tlacopan, forming a powerful bloc linking most of central Mexico. Their capital was Tenochtitlán, the site of contemporary Mexico City, a dramatic city on an island within a lake, connected to the mainland by causeways. Cortés's descriptions of Tenochtitlán, even as it was being decimated by disease, were depicted in one of the most circulated woodcuts of the time in Europe.

Farther south, the Chimú kingdom controlled the territories of coastal South America in the 13th and 14th centuries. Here they had exploited the arid climate to build the largest city ever made purely from adobe, an ancient type of sundried brick made of clay, sand, and water with some straw mixed in. In the middle of the 15th century, the Chimus were displaced by upstart rulers from the highlands of Peru, the Inca, with their capital in Qosqo (Cuzco). In their short life before they fell to the Spanish, the Inca dominated the trade routes of coastal South America, constructed long rope bridges, and built roads and cities with some of the most intricate and precise random rubble masonry ever to be seen in history. The Incas did not use the wheel, and the llama was their only real beast of burden, and it seems a not very hardy one at that. But their techniques of weaving, which were also complex systems of accounting and timekeeping, and their grasp of the interrelated mechanics of land and water—what today might be called ecology—enabled them to build cities that were not just spectacularly sited but also integrated into their natural context in ways that we are only beginning to fully understand. Their concepts of terracing, water management, and mass-based building evidence an epistemic universe that is still beyond our grasp.

The Italian world of the 15th century, retrospectively dubbed the Renaissance, was transformed by the Ottoman capture of Constantinople in 1453, led by Mehmed II. Propped up mostly by the Venetians who benefited significantly by funneling their trade through the strait of Bosphorus, old Byzantium ultimately fell to the ever-expanding reach of the Ottomans. After dominating Silk Route trade into Europe for centuries, the loss of Constantinople precipitated the decline of Venice. But that also opened up opportunity for the other cities of northern Italy, such as Florence and Siena, which now began to actively flex their economic muscle and to contemplate independence and self-determination. The Medici family came to dominate the banking systems of Europe and controlled a major share of the Silk Route trade into Europe. Numerous scholars and artisans fleeing Constantinople found new employment and audiences in the houses of northern Italy. With them came the old knowledge of the classical world that had long been preserved in the Islamic world, and which found, alongside the castigation of the Church, a receptive audience in the city-states of northern Italy.

Reacquaintance with classical knowledge imported from the Islamic world ignited the search for more—which was found in the old lost libraries of Europe, particularly Switzerland. These, then, were the circumstances that led to the intellectual expansion and reimagining of human possibilities that we now call the Renaissance. This is the milieu in which Brunelleschi, Alberti, Leonardo da Vinci, and their ilk emerged as scholars and original thinkers. As they reread old Greek and Roman texts, they faced the standard problem that all modernities face—that is, how to reinvest in the past in a way that suits the needs, purposes, and imaginaries of the present. Theirs was a Christian world that no longer knew concrete, and it was perhaps fortunate for them that the Italianate orthodoxy prohibited adoption of the styles and structural achievements of the Gothic cathedral, so they found space to test ways of adopting pagan Greek and Roman intellectual, artistic, and building design concepts for new, "modern" Christian projects. Thus we get the proliferation of urban cathedrals in new formal typologies,

some with new structural inventions to meet grand ambitions, such as the gigantic dome of the Duomo in Florence. The Italians also began investing in their cities, building not only grand palazzi but also urban amenities, such as the Foundling Hospital in Florence, to counter old Christian biases against cities as dens of disease.

Meanwhile, the bounty of gold and silver extracted from the Americas enabled the Spanish crown to not only consolidate its hold at home but also to curry favor in Rome. In competition with the northern city-states, the papacy undertook a vigorous new reconstruction of the Vatican building in an attempt to bridge the gap between their ancient world order and the newfangled knowledge of the time. This is when artists such as Bramante and Michelangelo received their grand papal commissions and built their formidable aesthetic reputations.

Competing with the authority of Rome, as usual, was France, whose King Francis I quickly seized the opportunity to build a strategic alliance with the Ottomans to create a new gateway to the Silk Route for Europe. He also patronized the northern Italian cognoscenti to populate his own court, famously having Leonardo da Vinci move to France to spend the last years of his life there. Fear of disease prompted the French court, unlike nobles in the Italian walled cities, to live a largely rural life, building country châteaux where they sought to control their lands and armies via vast and busy networks of communication. Later, these networks and protocols of communication and governance would also prove useful in organizing French colonies in the New World.

The Mongol invasions transferred the center of the Islamic world from its original base in West Asia further to the east, in the new post-Mongol kingdoms of the Ottomans in West Asia, the Safavids in Persia, and the Timurids in Uzbekistan and Afghanistan. The outlines of what we recognize today as the complex forces at play in the West Asian geopolitical sphere—from Afghanistan to Egypt—were established at this time.

The Ottomans were tribesmen who negotiated the border between the Christian world of Byzantium and the pre-Mongol Islamic states and who took advantage of the post-Mongol chaos to unite various tribes and establish a new state. "Ottoman" is the anglicization of the House of Osman, which

is known in modern Turkish as the Osmanli Empire. Osman Gazi ben Ertugrul (1258–1326), the founder of the Ottoman Empire, was yet another of the central Asian migrants who came from Turkmenistan in the middle of the 14th century to fight in local Anatolian battles. Osman's descendants captured Balkan territories, united local tribesmen, and put a decisive end to the Crusades.

Although Mehmed II firmly instituted Sunni Islam in Constantinople after capturing it in 1453, he also aggressively adopted Byzantine courtly life, administrative policies, and aesthetics across his empire. There was broad tolerance of non-Sunnis and even non-Muslims, and by the 17th century the Ottomans controlled most of the Arabic Islamic world along with the Balkan regions and Greece. Istanbul became the largest city in the world outside China. With this power, the Ottomans engaged in a vigorous process of building mosques along the trade routes; the mosques were Byzantine by formal reference, with a focus on domes and minarets.

To their east the Ottomans were in competition with the Safavids of Persia, who were also taking over from Mongol regents. The Safavids established descent from Safi al-Din, who was actually a mystic Sufi. But the Safavids aggressively adopted Shi'ite policies, including zero tolerance of nonbelievers. The Safavids governed their territories directly, and as a consequence, unlike the Ottomans, they were unable to expand their territories, but they maintained a firm grip on those they did control. Within their realms, the Safavids undertook construction of mosques and palaces of exceptional beauty.

To establish a counterclaim to the Ottomans as the locus of the Islamic world, Timur, who claimed direct descent from Genghis Khan, not only launched a major invasion of West Asia but also embarked on a major building campaign in his capital, Samarkand. With new bazaars, caravanserais, and mosques, Samarkand's location at the usual crossroads of the Eurasian traffic between China, India, and West Asia made it into one of the most cosmopolitan cities of the time. Samarkand's mosque achieved a distinctive style by marrying the dome (lifted on a high drum) with the *iwan*, while adorning every surface with blue tile patterns that reflected the sun and helped keep the buildings cool.

The competition for influence between Samarkand and the Ottoman caliphs was mirrored in the geopolitics of South Asia, with the Southern "Deccan" Islamic kings working hard to establish their fidelity to the distant Ottoman sultans (which is why they are known as the Deccan sultanates), while those further north in the Indo-Gangetic Plains leaned toward Timur (who invaded in 1398) and the khans. The northerners, however, had to compete heavily with Hindu kings and repeatedly suffered reversals in fortune, so that their architectural accomplishments, though spectacular, were few and far between. The Deccan sultanates, on the other hand, enjoyed relatively steady reigns, which, in competition with each other, generated a fascinating plethora of diverse architectural achievements, all of which happily married imported Ottoman styles with local building techniques and styles in the service of new Islamic courtly and liturgical functions. Although the Portuguese found a sea route to India around South Africa in 1496, just four years after Columbus's fateful discovery, new European presence in India was restricted to trading and building coastal seaports.

Meanwhile, in Southeast Asia, the Khmers had gone into decline, and while their grand sites were largely abandoned, the idea of great empires was now firmly established in the Southeast Asia peninsula. The Majapahit and the Thai established new kingdoms that continued the Khmer rereading of Hindu and Buddhist institutions and temples, in dialogue with those of Sri Lanka and eastern India.

At the eastern end of the Silk Route, the Chinese were undertaking a revival of their own. After three centuries of "foreign" rule by the Mongolian Yuan dynasty established by Genghis Khan, the Han Chinese Ming came into power in 1368. Although at first the Ming sought to consolidate a rural base, they quickly converted back to controlling the empire from their capitals with the help of their bureaucracy. The Ming actively projected the Yuan as foreigner-barbarians and worked hard to revive old Confucian practices. And yet, as we see time and again in history, the Ming did not hesitate to "modernize" the past and adopt practices of the Yuan that they found expedient. Thus, for instance, initially the Ming built a brand-new capital at Nanjing as per tradition, proclaiming the establishment of a new

order. But then the third Ming emperor, Zhu Di (r. 1403–24), moved the main capital back to Dadu, the old Yuan capital, which was still flourishing, now renaming it Beijing (meaning "Northern Peace"). Here the Ming built the Forbidden City as we know it today, incorporating a complex taxonomy of sight, visibility barriers, and access mediated through gates, courtyards, axial pavilions, and supporting quarters. Outside the Forbidden City, the Ming built the twin Temples of Agriculture and the Temple of Heaven Complex, which connected the terrestrial realm to the celestial one. While they criticized the Mongols for living in "tents" in the imperial cities, the Ming sought to revitalize their own old building techniques, emphasizing the development of the bracketing system along with techniques of glazing in construction and lacquering in furniture.

By the middle of the 15th century, the Ming had built up a stable government based on renewed cultivation and trade, with a population estimated at between 120 and 200 million people. They cultivated the supportive Joseon dynasty in Korea and invested heavily in undertaking global sea voyages to explore first Southeast and South Asia, and then the ports of East Africa and West Asia. These seem to have been voyages of ambassadorship rather than of conquest, so the sense of the usual threat from across the Long Wall quickly occupied the government's attention at the cost of further naval exploration. Later, the Ming empire was to significantly benefit from the discovery of the Americas, as vast quantities of gold and silver were used to purchase Chinese goods to be shipped back to Europe. Peppers were added to Sichuan cuisine, and the mass cultivation of potatoes and corn enabled large populations to be fed.

With the development of water-powered pounding mills, China had captured the energy of water by the 1st or 2nd century CE. This, together with the later invention of a water-turned wheel for irrigation, gave China an economic lead, beginning in roughly 1000 CE and continuing over the next 500 years. During these centuries, the Chinese economy achieved levels of productivity that Europe only started to attain in the 1500s. It was therefore not surprising that when trade began between China and Europe, fueled by American silver brought to China by the

Europeans, the Chinese economy was more productive than those of Europe.

But colonial contact proved to be a double-edged sword; as the Chinese economy became more dependent on overseas currency, it also became susceptible to it, and the Spanish (and Japanese) used silver control policies to squeeze the Ming. Considering the kind of trade taking place across the world in the 1600s and 1700s and the fact that Chinese finished goods were going to Europe in return for silver, this shouldn't be too great a surprise, especially since the first real urban commercial dynamism within Eurasia had taken place in China several centuries prior, in the Song dynasty.

Across the East China Sea, the Japanese also sought a revival of older world orders and older ties. Another unsuccessful attempt by the monarchy to regain control in 1333 prompted the new shogun (military dictator) Takauji, as a gesture of reconciliation, to reinstate Kyoto as the imperial capital and to reestablish connection with the Chinese Song dynasty, which had been severed since Kublai Khan's unsuccessful invasions of Japan in 1274 and 1281. Out of this reconnection emerged the signature Zen school of imperial Buddhist practice, which invented the miniaturized, abstract meditation gardens born from the necessity of building "nature" out of confined urban lots. Thus came into being the singular beauty of sites like Ginkakuji and Kinkakuji—the Golden and the Silver Pavilions—built for retiring shoguns in their search for the extraordinary.

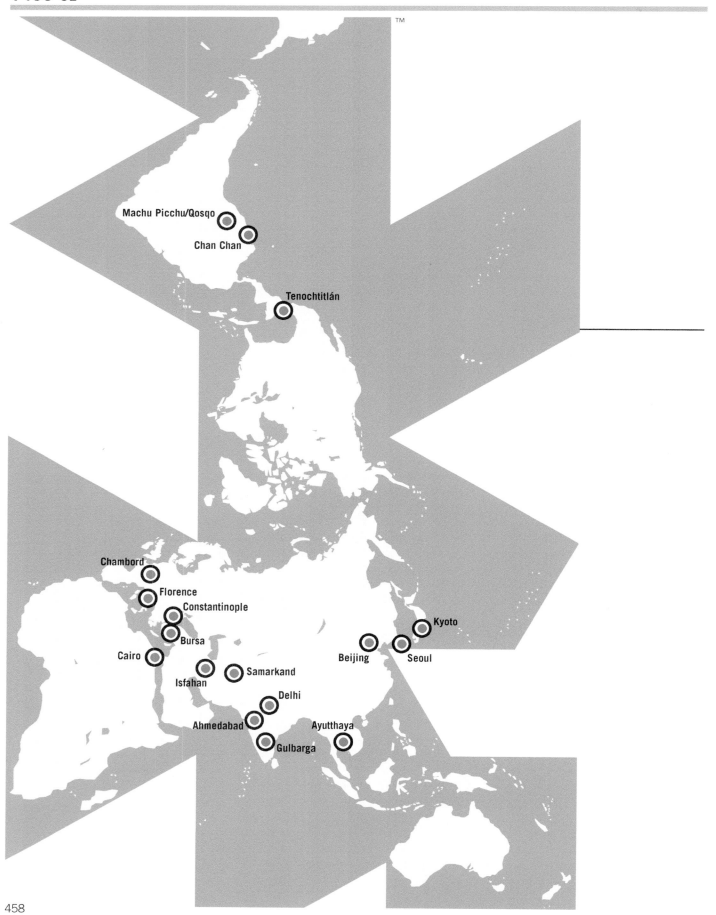

Machu Picchu/Qosqo

Chan Chan

Tenochtitlán

Chambord

Florence

Constantinople

Bursa

Cairo

Isfahan

Samarkand

Delhi

Ahmedabad

Gulbarga

Ayutthaya

Beijing

Seoul

Kyoto

Aztec State
ca. 1248–1521

▲ **Tenochtitlán**
ca. 1325–1521

◉ 1492
Columbus arrives in America

Conquest Period
1500–42

Inca Empire
ca. 1200–1532

◀ **Chan Chan**
ca. 1000–1400

▲ **Qosqo**
15th century

▲ **Machu Picchu**
15th to 16th centuries

China: Yuan Dynasty
1279–1368

Ming Dynasty
1368–1644

▲ **Forbidden City**
1420–1908

Joseon Dynasty
1392–1910

▲ **Gyeongbok Palace**
1394

▲ **Changdeok Palace**
1405–12

1200 CE   **1400 CE**   **1600 CE**

Japan: Kamakura Period
1185–1333

Nanbokucho Period
1336–1392

Muromachi Period
1392–1573

▲ **Kinkakuji**
1397

▲ **Ginkakuji**
1482–90

Black Plague in China
1330s

Black Plague in western Asia and Europe
1346–51

▲ **Bibi Khanum Friday Mosque**
1339–1404

Delhi Sultanate
1210–1526

Timurid Dynasty
ca. 1370–1507

▲ **Friday Mosque of Gulbarga**
1367

▲ **Jami Masjid of Ahmedabad**
1423

Ottoman Empire
1281–1923

▲ **Topkapi Palace**
Begun ca. 1459

▲ **Beyazit Medical Complex**
Completed 1488

Egypt: Mamluk Sultanate
1260–1517

▲ **Complex of Sultan Hassan**
1356–63

▲ **Mausoleum Complex of Sultan Qaitbay**
1472–74

Italy: Papal and Autonomous City-States
12th century to 1870

▲ **Cathedral of Florence**
Begun 1294

▲ **Medici Palace**
1444–ca. 1460

▲ **St. Peter's Basilica**
Begun 1506

▲ **Sant'Andrea at Mantua**
1472–94

France: Valois Rule
1328–1589

▲ **Château of Chambord**
Begun 1519

13.1 The Americas, ca. 1400 CE

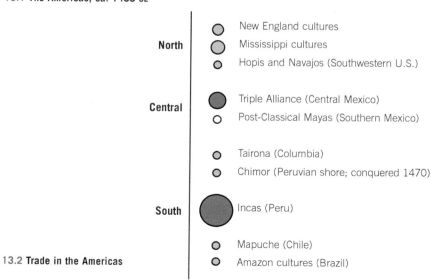

North	New England cultures
	Mississippi cultures
	Hopis and Navajos (Southwestern U.S.)
Central	Triple Alliance (Central Mexico)
	Post-Classical Mayas (Southern Mexico)
	Tairona (Columbia)
	Chimor (Peruvian shore; conquered 1470)
South	Incas (Peru)
	Mapuche (Chile)
	Amazon cultures (Brazil)

13.2 Trade in the Americas

THE AMERICAS

The Americas in the 15th century were far different from the Americas in the 17th century after about 90 percent of the continents' population had died of disease. In the 15th century, from eastern Bolivia through Peru to Central America into the western United States, eastward to Mississippi and Georgia, and north to what is now New England, there was what the first Europeans sailing down the coast of New England described as an almost continuous fabric of habitation. There were major cities that served as capitals of empires, like Qosqo in Peru and Tenochtitlán in Mexico; there were secondary cities that served as regional centers, like Chan Chan in Peru; Oraibi, a Hopi city in the United States; and other large cities in Georgia. In between, there were thousands of smaller villages. The spread of diseases was so rapid that some cultures disappeared even before they themselves encountered the Europeans. There is considerable debate about the specifics of this terrible loss of life and culture, but the basic parameters of the tragedy are not in dispute.

Hopis

In the 14th century, the Native Americans in North America were largely seminomadic, except for the major city-dwelling areas in the Mississippi/Georgia region extending to the Atlantic coast, and in the Southwest in areas controlled by the Hopis, who had been town dwellers for many centuries. The Hopi village of Old Oraibi in Arizona was founded around the year 1100. Clearly, the Hopis' notion of urban culture had much in common with earlier urban cultures in the area dating back to the Hisatsinom and Hohokam. In the period from 700 to 1130 CE there was a rapid increase in population in this area due to consistent and regular rainfall. In the late 13th century, however, a severe drought, which seems to have put an end to the nearby Hohokam culture, forced the Hopis to abandon the smaller villages and consolidate their population in larger urban centers. When the Spanish arrived, nine major towns existed: Sikyatki, Koechaptevela, Kisakovi, Sichomovi, Mishongnovi, Shipaulovi, Shungopavi, Oraibi, and Awatovi.

13.3 **Urbanization of the Americas, ca. 1400 CE**

Hopi is a shortened form of *Hopituh Shi-nu-mu*, "The Peaceful People" or "Peaceful Little Ones." The name reflects a concept deeply rooted in the culture's religion and spirituality, and even in its view of morality and ethics. To be Hopi is to strive toward a state of total reverence and respect for all things, to be at peace with these things, and to live in accordance with the instructions of Maasaw, the Creator or Caretaker of Earth. The Hopis, like most Native Americans, assume the souls of the dead go to another part of the universe, where they have a new existence, carrying on everyday activities as if they were still alive. Village life revolves around a series of ceremonies that are performed not only for the benefit of the village but also for the entire world. These ceremonies take place according to the lunar calendar and are observed in each of the Hopi villages. As with all Pueblo cultures, most of the ceremonies take place in kivas. *Pueblo* is a Spanish word derived from the Latin word *populus* (people), and in this case means "village." Hopi cities were located at or near the edges of north-south running, flat-topped mountains known as mesas. The difficulty of transporting water up to the towns kept their populations small, but their location did allow for protection, with access paths to some pueblos purposely following narrow ravines. Houses were made of stone and mud and were often several stories high. The walls were constructed of undressed stones bound with mud plaster. Wooden beams rested on the tops of the walls to form flat roofs, which were strengthened with grass thatching, a layer of plaster, and a covering of dry earth. The upper apartments were reached by outside ladders.

Acoma Pueblo was founded in the 12th century by the Acomas, who controlled a large area to the south and east of the Hopis. Though seminomadic, they eventually began to develop pueblo towns in the Arizona canyons. In the 17th century, the Navajos built even more pueblos, especially in their homeland in the northwestern corner of New Mexico, as part of their defenses against the Spanish invaders.

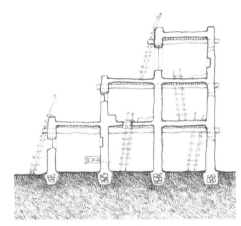

13.4 **Section through a Hopi house**

13.5 **Pueblo architecture, Arizona**

New England Societies

By the 14th century, the area in the United States known as New England was home to dozens of Native-American tribes. The area, when seen from a larger temporal perspective of the Americas, had been only relatively recently settled, perhaps as a consequence of the decline of Ohio's Hopewell society around 500 CE, the population of which dispersed in various directions. By the 16th century about 100,000 people lived along the coasts, estuaries, rivers, and lakes from Maine to the Carolinas in settlements and villages organized around tribal affiliations. Contrary to European belief, the area was not a sparsely populated wilderness. Armed conflict was not unknown between the tribes, though such conflict was less about territory than about prestige. The absence of pigs and sheep—as was true throughout the Americas before the arrival of Europeans—meant that there were no fences, something the colonists misread as implying that the Native Americans had no concept of land ownership.

Villages were led by a sachem, the equivalent of a chief or king. Each tribe had slightly different habits depending on location and circumstances. Some were seminomadic, moving from winter to summer; some were not. Some planted in organized fields; others relied more on hunting and fishing with supplemental agriculture. Trade was important, as it allowed a certain degree of specialization and exchange between areas. The forests were tended and underbrush cleared so as to improve hunting. Trees were pruned to create orchards of hickory, chestnut, and walnut, which produced edible and nutritious nuts. The area around the village would have been cleared for corn.

Iroquois villages were organized around clusters of houses (*wetus*) made of poles, with bark serving as walls. In winter the *wetus* were covered with rush mats that were impervious to water; in summer they were covered by thin sheets of flexible chestnut bark. A low fire burned in the middle and was vented through an opening in the roof. The structures were well suited to the environment; one early colonist noted that they were warmer and less leaky than the houses of the English. The villages were protected by palisades of wooden poles, but

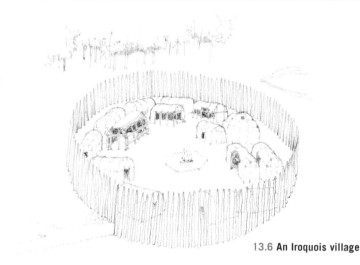

13.6 An Iroquois village

moats and berms, such as were used in the larger villages and cities farther south in Alabama and Georgia, were not used. In 1616, an epidemic brought by Europeans decimated 90 percent of the population on the Eastern coast in about three years. The result, from the European perspective, was a pristine land relatively untouched by humans. Plymouth Colony was established in 1620, for example, in an area that had been severely depopulated.

13.7 A *wetu*

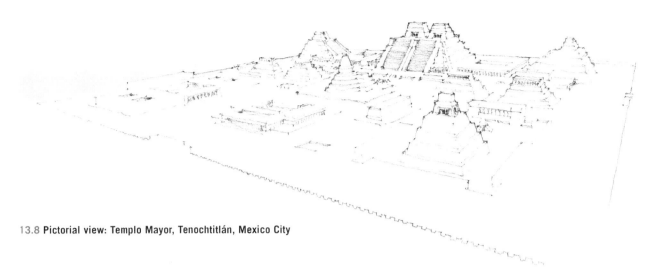

13.8 Pictorial view: Templo Mayor, Tenochtitlán, Mexico City

Tenochtitlán

The fall of the Toltec capital of Tula (located about 100 km north-northwest of Mexico City) led to the founding of a number of semiautonomous urban centers around Lake Texcoco. The city of Tenochtitlán (now Mexico City) was founded by one of these groups, the Mexica, on an islet in the western part of the lake in the year 1325. By the 14th century, war between the states had become systemic, leading in 1428 to an alliance between three of them that became the basis of the Aztec Empire. (Historians shy away from the term "Aztec" because it only came into use in the 19th century.) At its height, the empire stretched across central Mexico from coast to coast. In 1521, the Triple Alliance was defeated by the Spanish conquistadores and their native allies under Hernán Cortés, who described the city before he destroyed it; his text and drawing were presented to the Spanish king and widely circulated in Europe, thanks to the printing press. Cortés told of a city of 200,000 inhabitants on an island in the middle of a lake, connected by causeways to the shore. Gigantic stone towers dominated the city's center, at the intersection of the causeways.

The Mexica were originally poor and peripheral to the political world of that region, but under their general Tlacaélel, who masterminded the Triple Alliance, the Mexica altered their identity and religious worldview. Politically, they modeled themselves after the Toltecs and claimed descent from Teotihuacán, in order to appropriate their imperial claims. In terms of religion, they saw the sun as engaged in a violent and perpetual struggle for existence, a struggle that had to be nourished by human sacrifice. Several thousand were killed every year in ritual sacrifices. Though later European conquerors purported to be shocked at this, Europe in the 17th century was in fact a significantly more brutal place; tens of thousands of people were hanged, quartered, burned, or impaled—often in great public spectacles—during the various wars of religion.

The Mexica settled next to a swamp, but were able to drain the area to create a 10-square-kilometer lake with an island-city at the center that was linked to settlements on the mainland by three raised causeways. It grew to become an enormous city, much larger than any European city of the time. A gridded network of streets and canals teemed with boats transporting goods and people to its markets. Two aqueducts brought fresh water into the city. The ceremonial center consisted of two stepped pyramids rising side by side on a huge platform painted red and blue; nearby were palaces painted a dazzling white. Not far away were schools for sons of the nobility, houses for priests, a ball court, an intimidating *tzompantli* (skull rack) displaying the severed heads of the sacrificed, and several other pyramids and temples, all surrounded by protective enclosures.

The main temple (Templo Mayor) had large incense braziers, with serpent heads and cauldrons on all four sides in front of it to receive offerings. It rose in four platforms, representative of the celestial levels of the cosmos, until it reached the top level with its two temples dedicated to Tlaloc and Huitzilopochtli. Two parallel stairs led separately up to the summit. Huitzilopochtli, whose temple was to the south, was the Mayan warrior god who fought his brother Centzon Huitznahua and his sister Coyolxauhqui immediately after birth. He defeated them and threw their dismembered bodies down the mountain, a sacrifice marked by a round tablet at the foot of the stairs. Between 1325 and 1521, Templo Mayor was reconstructed seven times, with the older temple encased intact within each new larger building. Of all these, the second building has survived intact, including its two temples, complete with the stone to which prisoners were tied before being sacrificed.

Like their predecessors, the Mexica were dedicated observers of the sun, the stars, the cycles of nature, the passing of the seasons, and the death of plant and animal life. And like their predecessors, their architecture and rituals were intended to maintain the integrity of the cosmic order. The science of observation was certainly very sophisticated, though today it is still incompletely understood. Templo Mayor pointed 7 degrees south of east, so that on the equinoxes the sun rises exactly between the temples of Tlaloc and Huitzilopochtli. A monolithic calendar stone 1.2 meters thick, 3.6 meters in diameter, and weighing over 24 tons was found in 1790 under the main square. On its face is a representation of the sun god.

13.9 Calendar stone from Tenochtitlán

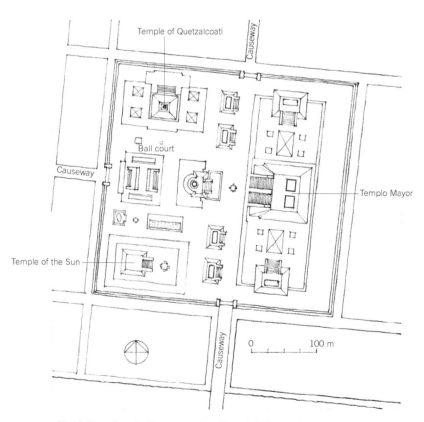

13.10 Plan: Templo Mayor complex, Tenochtitlán, Mexico City

13.11 **Chan Chan, near Trujillo, Peru**

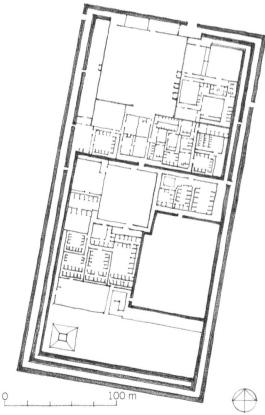

0   100 m

13.12 **Plan: Rivero Citadel at Chan Chan**

Incas

In the coastal valleys of northern Peru, the collapse of the Wari kingdom around the year 1000 led to the emergence of the Chimu (850–1470; also called the Chimor), who in time came to control the entire northern coast of Peru from the modern border of Ecuador to Lima. Their capital, Chan Chan, was spread out across a large plain of the coastal desert. Because Chimu kings after they died were not considered legally dead, new kings built new palaces, which would remain the extended family's base after that king in turn died. But Chan Chan was soon subsumed into the world of the Incas. Not much is known of the prehistory of the Incas except that, like the Mexica, they were originally a small peripheral kingdom that became much more successful than those around it. The Incas borrowed the Chimu approach to royalty, with the exception that their king, or *inca*, was divine. One of their *incas*, Pachakuti, who ascended the Incan throne in 1438, quickly built an empire that brought the area of present-day Peru, Bolivia, northern Argentina, Chile, and Ecuador under Inca control. He did this by means novel to the South American political scene. In the previous era, regional expansion had been limited given the difficulty of marshalling large armies and moving them from place to place—there were, after all, no horses. The Incas expanded by more or less peacefully assimilating neighboring areas into their regime, offering stability and inclusion in exchange for services. Soon they were able to command enormous teams of people— many purposefully displaced from their homelands—to build roads and palaces, and work in craft industries and on farms. Consolidation of the empire was more or less complete by 1520. There was no money, no markets, and no land ownership; all land belonged to the king. It was a centralized system akin to modern socialism, except that the ruling *inca* was a god. The result was that in just over a hundred years the Incan empire became the most powerful the Americas had ever seen, before they were conquered by the Spanish and depopulated by disease.

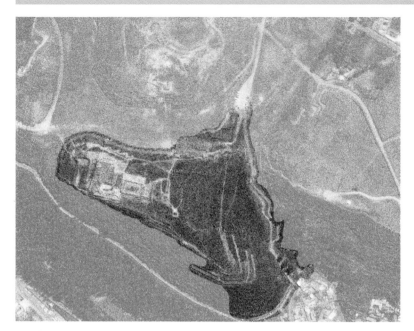

13.13 Plan: Upper temple area, Qosqo (Cuzco), Peru

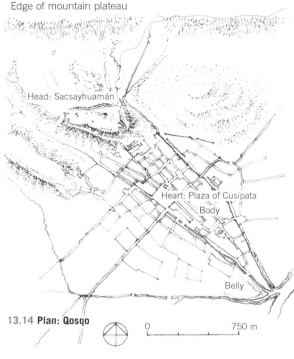

Edge of mountain plateau

Head: Sacsayhuamán

Heart: Plaza of Cusipata

Body

Belly

13.14 Plan: Qosqo 0   750 m

Their capital was Qosqo, located in the western fringe of the Peruvian highlands. Four major roads of the empire terminated in its center, the Plaza of Cusipata. Under Pachakuti, the first of the great Inca rulers, Qosqo was transformed from a village of clay and straw into a city of stone. Wedged between the Tullumayo and Huatanay Rivers, the city's plan notionally formed the body of a puma or jaguar. The head was represented by the fortress, the heart by the central plaza, and the tail by the confluence of the two canalized rivers. The Chunchulmayo, further south, was called the "gut river," as it represented the belly of the puma. The Plaza of Cusipata was surrounded by the main civic structure of Qosqo, the palaces, and three temples dedicated to the Sun (Qorikancha), the Creator (Kiswarkancha), and the Thunder (Pucamarka). The plaza was filled with pure white sand taken from the coast, and across the facades of the palaces were enormous plates of polished gold, reflecting the setting sun. The plaza was the center of the Inca cosmos, with the four highways radiating from it demarcating the four sectors of the empire. Also radiating out from the city was a spiderweb of forty-one crooked spirit paths that connected holy features of the landscape, like springs, caves, shrines, and stones. The Inca calendar counted forty-one weeks, each eight days long.

Qosqo seems to have had no defensive wall, but at its "head" on the hilltop overlooking the valley is an impressive structure, Sacsayhuamán, presumed to have been a fortress. It could also have been a temple to the sun, a water reservoir, or all of the above. It has three platforms, one on top of the other, followed by a triple row of toothed walls made from gigantic blocks of granite. The walls were precise works of engineering. Some of their granite blocks weighed up to 200 tons

and were shaped on site to fit exactly to their neighbors. Why such precision was demanded remains unknown. In many instances, the massive stones simply shield the body of the earth. In all cases, water was drained with great care, with individual stones being shaped and aligned to create a ceremonial series of water spouts and channels. There was also a large circular meeting plaza with ceremonial buildings perched at the lip of the cliff overlooking the city.

13.15 Aerial view: Qosqo

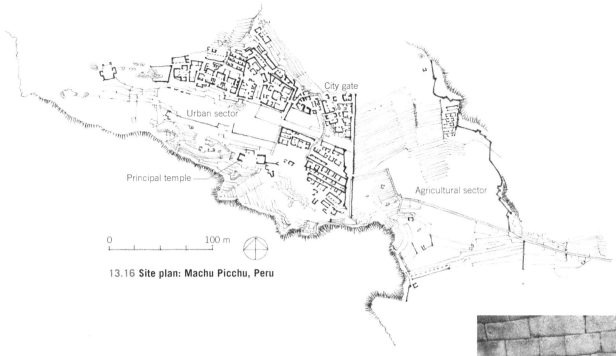

City gate

Urban sector

Principal temple

Agricultural sector

0   100 m

13.16 **Site plan: Machu Picchu, Peru**

Machu Picchu

Machu Picchu, 70 kilometers northwest of Qosqo (Cuzco), is located between two steep peaks, 2,750 meters above a gorge carved by the Urubamba River. It is the only Inca settlement to have survived intact, having been completely missed by the Spaniards. It was probably inhabited late into the 16th century, when it was gradually abandoned and forgotten. There are other Inca sites in this remote area, but these have yet to be fully explored or understood. Some two hundred buildings arranged on a series of parallel terraces on both sides of a central plaza constitute the core of the small settlement that housed at most about a thousand people.

Access to the site was difficult; it was a long trek up the steep gorges and entry was possible only from one carefully guarded checkpoint. Because it was a magnificent site for solar and stellar observation, some have argued that the city was a royal retreat or perhaps even a special temple reserved for the elite. Key to the success of the site was the artesian spring that supplied the inhabitants with water year-round. The genius of Machu Picchu lies in the terracing and partitioning of the site, which fills a roughly east-west-lying saddle between the two peaks. The saddle rises sharply in the south,

and after a crest and a short flat plain slopes gently down toward the north and the east. It resembles a wave, with a stable spot at its precarious top. To shore up the land and to create spaces to build on, the Incan planners constructed terraces carefully, following the contours. At the eastern end, there is a sector of terraces, presumably for cultivation, with a complex network of irrigation channels.

A long central plaza, gently terracing down toward the east, sets the stage. On either side of this plaza, accessed by a complex network of streets and stairs, lie the main buildings, most of which are single-room dwellings, clustered around courts when possible, but usually arranged along narrow pathways limited by the terrace widths. They are all made of the characteristic finely fitted stone masonry, with wedge-shaped windows and monolithic lintels, and equipped with water drainage and harvesting systems. The granite used in the construction was quarried locally. Gable ends testify to perishable roofs long gone. There is, however, no evidence of any adobe construction, suggesting a highly elite and ceremonial function for the city. Nestled within this network are some surprising anomalies: a semicircular, turret-like structure unexpectedly abuts the residential fabric, and a series of baths line the central north-south pathway.

13.17 **Stonework at Machu Picchu**

13.18 **Passageway: Machu Picchu**

The high southwestern edge of the saddle is reserved for a temple, accessed by a long stair from the east. At the foot of the stair lies what is assumed to be a temple, with three C-shaped rooms looking into a central court. At the top of the stair lies the main temple, the sacred center, dedicated to the sun. Three steps into an antechamber lead up to the final terrace, at the center of which lies a huge granite monolith known simply as the Intihuatana, or the "Hitching Post of the Sun."

The Intihuatana stone is something of a miniature Machu Picchu, with a series of small "terraces" culminating in a dramatic outcrop, resembling the peak just beyond. Intihuatana stones are believed to have once been dispersed throughout the Incan world, but they were destroyed by the Spanish, who considered them idolatrous. Their exact meaning is uncertain, but they were likely miniaturized replicas of a sacred peak to which the sun could be imagined to be tethered by a rope, enabling its circular journey through the upper and lower worlds. Perhaps Machu Picchu's peaks were as close as the Inca thought they could get to that sacred peak.

13.19 **Machu Picchu as it stands today**

13.20 **Close-up of the urban sector of Machu Picchu**

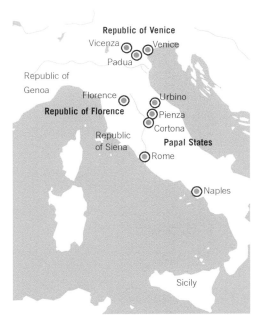

13.21 **Italy, ca. 1400 CE**

Ca' d'Oro (1428–30), named after the gold leaf of its exterior detailing, was among the best of the palaces built along Venetian canals. The palace was built for Marin Contarini, a Venetian aristocrat and one of Venice's leading cloth and spice merchants.

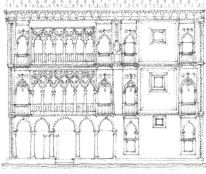

13.22 **Facade: Ca' d'Oro, Venice, Italy**

The facade of Ca' d'Oro consists of three superimposed galleries. Whereas the tracery of the loggias on the piano nobile and second floor had quatrefoil openings over the columns, the lower colonnade is noticeably more classical with its simple rounded and pointed arches. Though the exact origin of the quatrefoil shape is not known, the form was used on the Doge's Palace next to the Basilica di San Marco and was clearly meant to show its owner's status as a member of the merchant elite. Throughout the facade, at corners and edges, and defining various architectural elements, decorative bands make the facade appear as if it were almost a curtain, woven into place. The building, like almost all structures in Venice, had to be set on thousands of oak piles sunk deep into the sand and mud of the lagoon.

REPUBLIC OF VENICE

The Black Plague (1350–1425) carried off 35 to 65 percent of the rural and urban population of Italy. Only a handful of European cities rebounded, among which were Venice, Florence, Milan, Naples, and Genoa. If one followed the Silk Route westward across Asia, through the lands of Timur and the Ottomans, one would come to the European gateway, Venice. Almost all goods traveling to Europe had to pass through the port of Venice, which controlled coastal trade south through the Aegean Sea to Cyprus, and north into Asia via Constantinople. Taking advantage of four centuries of living at the edge of papal Italy, Venice had marshaled its port location to put itself at the center of Mediterranean trade. By 1423, the state budget of Venice was equivalent to that of France and England. The city, a thalassocracy, was ruled as a republic after its last autocratic doge had died, its new form of government being fiercely republican. Over time, Venice acquired considerable Mediterranean trading posts, including Crete, Cyprus, most islands of the Aegean, and coastline stretches of Dalmatia, in addition to terra ferma properties such as Bergamo and others up to Lake Garda and beyond. This expansion of its territory naturally put Venice in opposition to the objectives of the Ottoman Empire and the Mamluks of Egypt.

13.23 **Ca' d'Oro, Venice**

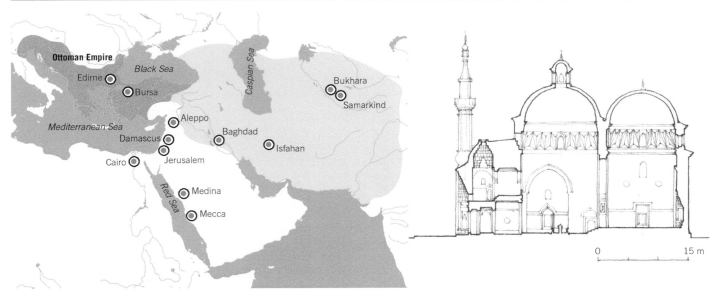

13.24 West Asia and the eastern Mediterranean, ca. 1400

13.25 Section: Yesil Cami complex, Bursa, Turkey

OTTOMAN EMPIRE

Central and western Asia in the early post-Mongolian era were dominated by three new powers—the Fatimids in Egypt, the Timurids in Persia, and the Ottomans in Anatolia. The latter replaced the Seljuk Empire, which had been weakened by Mongolian attacks. The Osmanlis, or Ottomans, as they came to be known in English, were a Turkish tribe that captured Bursa from the Byzantines in 1326 and used it as their capital. In 1371 they reached Serbia, and in 1453 they conquered the main prize, Constantinople, bringing the Byzantine Empire to an end. The Ottomans were soon so strong that no single European country could challenge their position, despite repeated coordinated attacks through the following centuries.

Ottoman mosques were not designed as introverted, walled rectangular enclosures, as they had been under the Seljuks. Instead they took up the theme of the dome from the Byzantines, resting it on a square structure that was entered through a three-bay loggia with a minaret to one side. This prototype was expanded with side rooms, vestibules, and loggias. Sometimes the dome was given an enclosed forecourt. One of the best examples is Yesil Cami Mosque in Bursa (1412–19). From an ornate marble portal a visitor passes a low, square vestibule that leads by way of a short barrel-vaulted corridor to the central hall. The main prayer hall, or *iwan*, behind

the hall is raised from the central hall by four steps, the side *iwans* by one step each. Both domes sit on belts of "Turkish triangles" that negotiate the change from square to circles. At the center of the main hall, which has an oculus, is a pool. The royal family would have ascended the stairs near the entrance to gain access to the royal box. It is composed of two sections: a domed antechamber that opens onto a barrel-vaulted rear chamber that, in turn, looks onto the interior of the mosque. Whereas Seljuk buildings tended to be

conceived as static rectangular objects that were brought into relationship to each other only by way of addition, Ottoman structures, from early on and in step with the advanced architectural thinking of the 15th century in India and Italy, were designed as institutional complexes that brought the building and public space into dialogue. At the Yesil Cami Mosque, the various parts of the institution—the madrasa, imaret (hostel for pilgrims), hamam (bath), and *türbe* (tomb)—are integrated into the city.

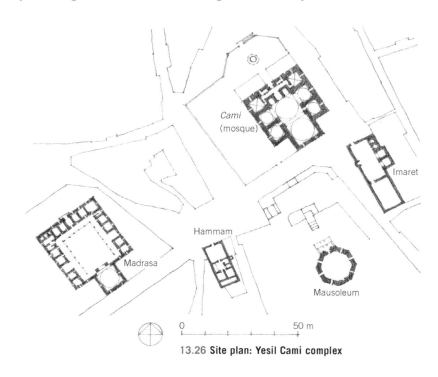

13.26 Site plan: Yesil Cami complex

13.27 Beyazit Medical Complex, Edirne, Turkey

13.28 Courtyard, Beyazit Medical Complex

Beyazit Medical Complex

In the spring of 1484, the thirty-seven-year-old Ottoman ruler, Beyazit II, on his way with his army to the Balkans, ordered the construction of the Beyazit Medical Complex (completed in 1488) in Edirne (close to the modern border between Turkey and Bulgaria). The five principal elements of the composition were carefully walled off because of the number of horses, mules, and camels that would have been grazing nearby on the shore of the river. The buildings form an irregular U-shape, with the mosque and its court at the center, facing in the direction of the street. The mosque is square in plan, half the width of the 50-meter-broad courtyard. The dome, lofty and rising dramatically over the entrance, was illuminated by a large central wheel carrying three tiers of oil lamps, all suspended by a single chain from the center of the dome. Flanking the mosque are two square *tabhanes* (temporary lodgings) with nine domes, each *tabhane* having four corner rooms opening onto *iwans* off a central court. This plan is distantly related to concepts from Central Asia. The minarets are set in the angle corners of the *tabhanes* protruding from the walls of the courtyard. It is generally thought that these spaces served as temporary lodgings for members of the dervish orders. Beyazit had mystical leanings and was described as a man who loved simplicity, peace, and retreat. The dervish orders were also increasing in number in the

15th century. To the east of the mosque were two buildings that served as refectories and kitchens. The hospital on the western side of the complex is a hexagonal structure, with its own small courtyard and forecourt. The hexagon was domed, and had a fountain in the center to soothe the nerves of the ill. It is quite possible that musicians played here or possibly that the ill rested on the long, carpet-covered sofa in the principal *iwan*, which forms a stage at the far apse end of the hexagon. The whole complex employed 167 people and was staffed by three doctors, two eye specialists, and two surgeons, as well as a dentist.

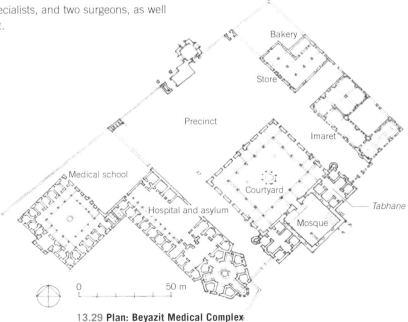

13.29 Plan: Beyazit Medical Complex

13.30 Topkapi Palace, Istanbul, Turkey

Topkapi Palace

On May 29, 1453, Sultan Mehmed II captured Constantinople after a fifty-three-day siege. For the Europeans it was a major defeat, as it brought to an end the Byzantine Empire and all that it represented. For the Arab armies it was a long-sought-after prize, as it provided them with a major metropolis. Almost immediately, work was begun on the construction of mosques and other buildings, including the vast Topkapi Palace (begun 1459) that served as the main royal residence and seat of the imperial Ottoman administration from the second half of the 15th to the mid-19th century. The palace was in the middle of a roughly triangular shaped site that was surrounded mostly by water on the north and east, while to the west a high wall separated it from the rest of the city. Its plan could be seen as a haphazard aggregation of buildings. But this would not be accurate, since it was planned according to a logic related to the definition of a sultan. He was seen as being beyond any relation of reciprocity, and ceremonies stressed the unbridgeable gap between master and subject, thus the insistence in this palace on the privacy of the sultan. The Moghuls, elaborating on Timurid and Mongolian models, had more accessible private zones, much as in Europe, where the ruler could entertain guests. The Topkapi Palace, however, with its clearly delineated boundaries, was designed to instill a sense of sanctity and respect as much as fear and awe.

The main entrance of the palace was just behind the Hagia Sophia, now converted to a mosque. The Imperial Gate, the first of three main ceremonial double gates, led to the first court, which contained workshops, storage areas, dormitories, kitchens, a bakery, and baths. It also contained a mint and various offices of the government. This court served as a waiting area for dignitaries as well as a staging area for processions and special ceremonies. Visiting ambassadors had to walk past the thousands of richly clad soldiers and courtiers standing in mandatory silence, an intimidating backdrop for diplomatic negotiations. The courtyard was also used for executions, which the sultan could observe from a window in the Tower of Justice.

At the second gate, the visitor would have had to dismount to gain access to the next court, called "the arena of justice," and the beginning of the palace proper. It was uncluttered by freestanding buildings and unified by a continuous marble colonnade. It housed the Tower of Justice, the Council Hall, and the treasury clustered at the far left corner of the court. A loggia, raised on a platform in front of the Council Hall, overlooked the space. On the inside of the hall, from the back, the sultan could watch the proceedings from behind a curtained window. The hall was low and unassuming, because it was modeled on a tent known as the "consultation tent," which was used by the imperial council during military campaigns.

The Third Gate (The Gate of Felicity) was especially sacred. On particularly important occasions, the sultan would greet visitors under its airy canopy. Behind the gate was the Chamber of Petitions, a square, one-story structure that served as an audience hall, a building technically within the private precinct but still conceptually a part of the second courtyard. The third court was raised on high retaining walls, with the land sloping down below it toward the north. The throne room was located at the far left corner. The buildings in this court were designed to take in the vistas of the surrounding landscape. The sultan, from his belvedere, could watch his flourishing capital and the port. The residential quarter was located to the east of the second and third courts in a compact mass huddled close to the walls of the court. Special areas housed pages and slaves—males, females, and eunuchs—who were all part of the sultan's retinue. This quarter also housed the harem. In the northernmost corner were the royal apartments.

Topkapi Palace is not organized along an axis, nor are the buildings grand in the traditional sense. Rather they are organized through diagonal vistas and angled approaches, with the open areas of the courtyards meant to contrast with the ad hoc intimacy of the residential quarter.

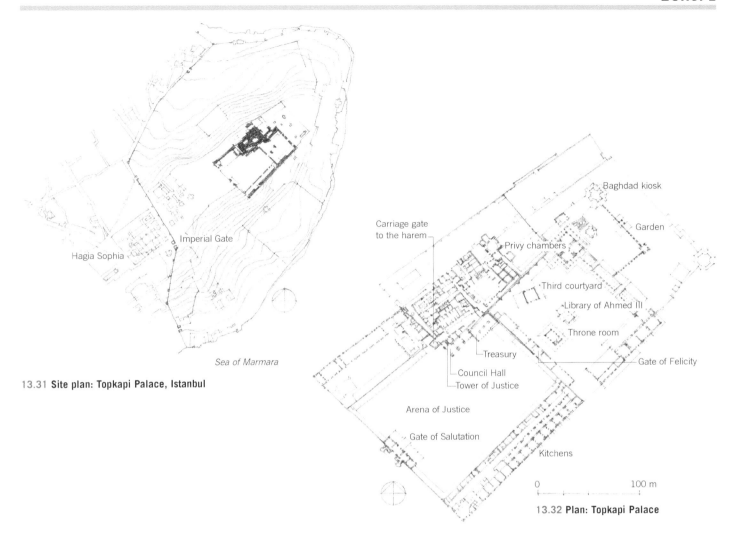

13.31 **Site plan: Topkapi Palace, Istanbul**

Hagia Sophia

Imperial Gate

Sea of Marmara

Carriage gate
to the harem

Baghdad kiosk

Garden

Privy chambers

Third courtyard

Library of Ahmed III

Throne room

Treasury

Gate of Felicity

Council Hall

Tower of Justice

Arena of Justice

Gate of Salutation

Kitchens

0   100 m

13.32 **Plan: Topkapi Palace**

13.33 **Throne room, Topkapi Palace**

13.34 **Detail, Topkapi Palace**

ITALIAN RENAISSANCE

The term *Renaissance* (from the French *renaissance*, "rebirth") was coined in the 19th century to describe the cultural and intellectual changes that took place in Italy during the 15th century. Inspired in part by the arrival of scholars fleeing Constantinople, who had preserved old classical knowledge in contact with the Islamic world, the Italians began to uncover and study Roman and Greek texts and buildings to relearn what had been lost to Europe in the Middle Ages, and then to find ways of applying this learning to their own times. One of the most influential discoveries of this process, for instance, was the discovery of perspective, the appearance of which had been approximated by painters like Giotto di Bondone (1267–1337), but which was first described mathematically by Leon Battista Alberti (1404–72) in 1435. With perspective began the process of locating the human eye, both literally and conceptually, at the center of our epistemic universe. Ultimately, one can argue, this led to the European Enlightenment of the 18th century.

Although the Renaissance is linked to what is called, also retrospectively, the Age of Discovery, we must remember that the initial voyages of discovery by the likes of Christopher Columbus, Vasco da Gama, and Amerigo Vespucci were sponsored not by the Italians, or the Ottomans, or the French—the new centers of the Mediterranean world—but by the Spanish and the Portuguese, who were at the edges of the intellectual revolution that was the Renaissance. For the Spanish and the Portuguese, the voyages were at the outset motivated singularly by economic imperatives: to find cheaper routes to the spice trade with Asia, or "the Indies."

Whereas in painting there is a clear progression that demarcates the Renaissance from the Middle Ages, the difference in architecture is less obvious. Medieval practices continued to intermingle with classically inspired ideas for a century. Nonetheless, the interior of the Pazzi Chapel, begun by Brunelleschi in 1429 but finished by other architects, set the tone for a type of architecture that emphasized the use of columns, pilasters, and entablatures, all unified by a proportional system that governed the heights, widths, and intercolumniations of the pilasters. Though the detailing of the columns and bases was

inspired by Roman buildings, Brunelleschi was still not using the orders in their distinctive categories of Doric, Ionic, and Corinthian. That emerged only somewhat later and was first insisted upon by Leon Battista Alberti in his treatise *De re aedificatoria* (1452), now known as the *Ten Books on Architecture*. Renaissance architecture is thus just as much about changes in practice as about the emerging theories of the discipline. Key was the discovery (ca. 1415) of a copy of a manuscript of Vitruvius's *Ten Books on Architecture* in the library of St. Gallen in Switzerland. Alberti studied the manuscript and used it as an inspiration for his own work. Covering a wide range of subjects, from choice of materials to the history of architecture and from different types of buildings to the philosophy of beauty, Alberti's treatise was written not only for architects but also for patrons eager to understand the logic of representation through buildings.

There are other phenomena that are part of what is understood by the words "Renaissance architecture." The difference between the architect and the craftsman was now accepted, and architectural drawings were now more common. Sebastiano Serlio (1475–1554) wrote a treatise, of which five books were finished, that was more visual than Alberti's treatise, which had no illustrations. Serlio's book had dozens of drawings, showing a variety of built and unbuilt projects. It was enormously popular among the many patrons and architects eager to emulate the splendors of antiquity.

Questions about the nature of ancient Roman architecture and about the proportional systems that the Romans used were not easy to resolve and led to a wide range of interpretations. Some architects, like Brunelleschi, were less Roman than others, and, in fact, it was only with Neoclassicism in the 18th and 19th centuries that rigorous adherence to antique models was seen as a virtue. Nonetheless, the Renaissance did require a rigorous attention to proportion, and as a result, facades become flatter and volumes more regularized. The vertical dimension began to be articulated by horizontal layers of columns, entablatures, and cornices. Niches and aediculae now entered the architect's vocabulary as secondary elements to be placed between pilasters. Windows were framed and often pedimented.

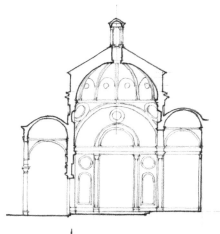

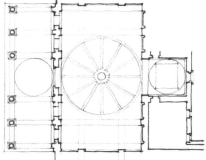

13.35 Plan and section: Pazzi Chapel, Florence, Italy

13.36 Interior of the Pazzi Chapel

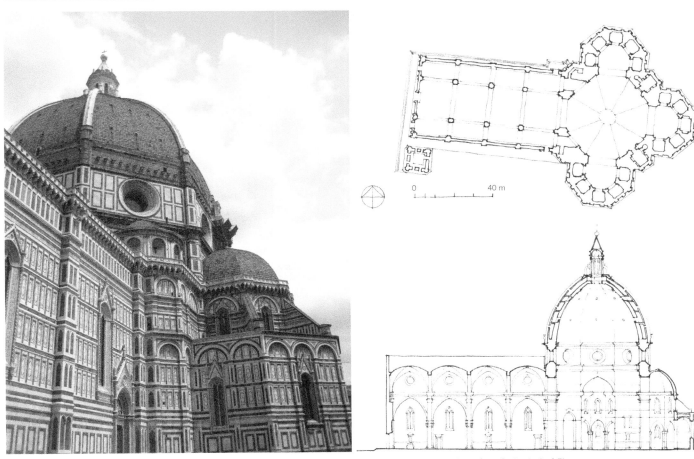

13.37 Cathedral of Florence, Italy

13.38 Plan and section: Cathedral of Florence

0   40 m

Cathedral of Florence

The Cathedral of Florence, begun in 1294, was among the last of the great Italian city cathedrals to be built. The plan, designed by Arnolfo di Cambio (1232–1300), was unusual, calling for a broad nave leading to an octagonal, domed apse. The design specifications for the building explicitly banned exterior buttresses so as not to reference the French cathedrals, and the craft of Roman concrete had been long forgotten, yet the city council wanted a dome as wide as that of the Pantheon in Rome. The Florentines were temporarily stymied, but construction continued.

Finally, in 1418, a competition was announced, among the earliest public competitions in the history of architecture. Brunelleschi won by proposing an ingenious system by which the dome could be constructed with only limited use of wooden

scaffolding. To deflect the lateral thrusts, Brunelleschi made a curving rib-lattice structure of brick laid in herringbone fashion to ensure cohesion; a large metal chain laid at the base of the dome protected against outward expansion. This solution did not require a support structure during the initial construction phase because each vertical extension of the dome as it was being built, and as it spiraled closer to the center, would cohere with what was below. A centering platform was constructed only in the last phase, but it was suspended from the partially completed dome. The dome terminated with an oculus about 7 meters in diameter, surmounted by a heavier than normal lantern (built in 1446) whose weight guaranteed that the ribs were in compression. The ingenious design rested not only on the manner in which the dome was built but on the combination of the double dome, which

reduced the weight; the lantern, which added compression to the dome helping coherence; and the chain at the base, which protected against lateral forces.

Double-shelled dome construction of course had a long history in the Islamic world, as for instance in the mausoleum of Oljaytu (1302–12) in the city of Soltaniyeh, Iran. Although such examples may not have provided direct precedent, it is clear that the concept was in circulation in Eurasia at that time. Double-shelled domes dominate subsequent architecture in innumerable variations, such as those of the Mughal tombs in India.

Florentine Loggias

The narrow streets of Italian cities consisted of hard materials, stone and brick, and because many of these cities were confined by city walls, open spaces were at a premium. Parks and gardens did not exist. Loggias, roofed over open outdoor spaces, were highly valued and served both functional and symbolic purposes. Unlike an arcade, which covers pedestrian traffic, a loggia is a place to assemble rather than to traverse. The Loggia dei Priori (now called Loggia dei Lanzi; 1376–82) was to serve visiting dignitaries and ambassadors, and even permit the celebration of coronations and marriages of distant kings. It was constructed perpendicular to the entrance of the Palazzo della Signoria, or the town hall, and consisted of three lofty arches rising from a stepped platform. The columns, sitting on a short, ornamented plinth, are composed of pilasters bound together into one massive shaft 10 meters in height, terminating in a rich and beautiful capital of the Corinthian order. This was probably the first attempt to re-create the Corinthian order since the time of the Romans.

Another type of loggia was for public services, like the one next to the Baptistery, which was used by the clergy to give out alms. But the most spectacular loggia was the one at the Foundling Hospital (Ospedale degli Innocenti; 1419–24; finished 1445), built by the Silk Guild, one of the most important guilds in Florence. Ever since 1294 the guild had committed itself to the care of infants (*innocenti*). Though it had set up wards and hospitals, this building was specifically for abandoned children. A special door was built in the facade with a rotating panel so that a child could be deposited anonymously. By the year 1640, more than 1,600 infants and children lived there, along with 40 priests, nurses, and administrators. The loggia that constitutes the building's facade was designed by Brunelleschi, and even though its prototype was medieval, its style was markedly new. The columns, modeled carefully on classical precedent, are the earliest examples of archaeologically correct Corinthian capitals in the 15th century. However, had Brunelleschi wanted to be more truly Roman, he would not have set the columns on thin plinths only

13.39 **Foundling Hospital, Florence, Italy**

5 centimeters high. The facade consists of a long unbroken entablature. The arches are semicircular rather than pointed. Rondels, depicting babies in swaddling clothes, decorate the spaces between the arches. The vaults, also spherical, were originally covered with a sloping wooden roof. The attic level was added later.

San Lorenzo

The drama of this building, begun in 1421, turns on the question of appearances. The stark contrast between the *pietra serena* (dark stone) and the whitewashed walls, creating the impression of a structural system in which the pilasters are meant to be read as load-bearing, though in reality they are not. Unlike French and English Gothic architecture, where the load-bearing function of architectural elements disappeared in column clusters, here the difference is clearly spelled out between what carries the load—or at least seems to carry it—and what does not. Even so, this is not a pure Roman-inspired building, for the prototype for the colonnaded nave is found in the early Christian basilica. The restraint and orderliness of the nave was also akin to Franciscan churches of the late 13th century, and the Latin cross plan, with

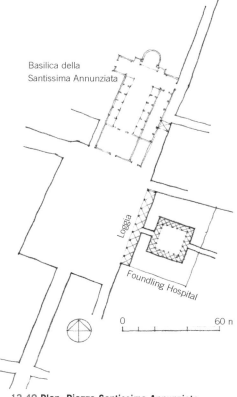

Basilica della
Santissima Annunziata

Loggia

Foundling Hospital

0   60 n

13.40 **Plan: Piazza Santissima Annunziata**

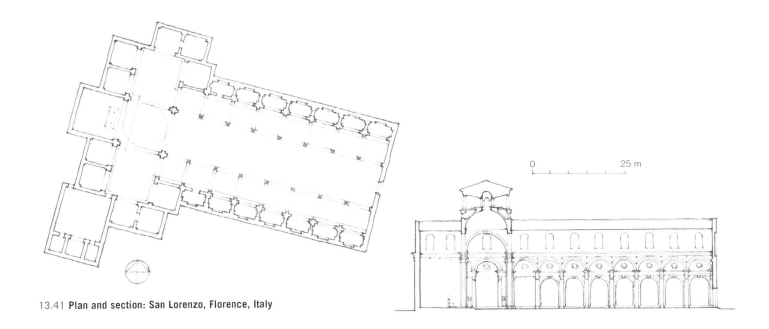

13.41 **Plan and section: San Lorenzo, Florence, Italy**

0   25 m

square chapels on the side, harkens back to the Cistercians. In that sense, one can see this as a complex fusion of early Christian, Cistercian, and Franciscan motifs, but built according to classicizing rules. Working within the constraints of that classical system forced Brunelleschi to confront the problem of "turning the corner," one of the persistent issues in classical architecture. On inside corners, only a few leaves of a pilaster are visible, implying the presence of a structural support hidden in the wall. Furthermore, the giant-order pilasters, in turning the corner between the transept and the nave, are partially obscured by the lower-order ones. Yet another problem is that the pilasters along the wall stand higher than the columns, because the floor of the chapel is three steps up from the floor of the nave. This means that they should have been thinner, but that would have looked odd. To solve the problem without raising the nave columns on bases, Brunelleschi had the pilasters reach directly to the entablature; but on the columns in the nave, he added a dosseret above each capital to equalize the distance. They are decorated with patterns that reduce their structural appearance.

Nonetheless, the idea of freestanding columns, arches, spherical vaults, and the use of classically inspired capitals, lintels, and cornices was quite revolutionary for the time.

13.42 **Nave of San Lorenzo**

13.43 **Medici Palace, Florence, Italy**

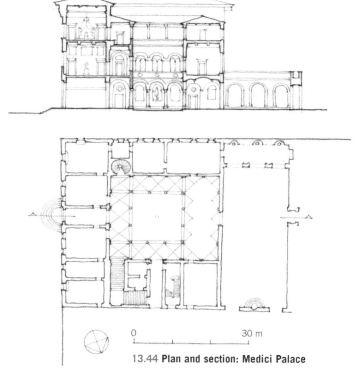

13.44 **Plan and section: Medici Palace**

Medici Palace

The Medici family, eminent bankers who built a fortune off trade on the Silk Route—particularly from silk itself—were the de facto rulers of Florence. Medici Palace (1444–ca.1460) was designed by Michelozzo di Bartolomeo Michelozzi (1396–1472), though heavily influenced by Brunelleschi's principles. The building is not what might be called classical or Roman, for it continued the prototype established in the 14th century of three-story buildings. This one, however, is topped by an enormous classically inspired cornice that was meant to optically tie the volume together, though it makes the top floor appear to be almost crushed. The ground floor is heavily rusticated in imitation of the fortresses built by Emperor Frederick II in the middle of the 13th century. The windows have round-headed openings with strongly marked voussoirs placed symmetrically in the design; a string course separates the ground floor from the *piano nobile*. The story above that is entirely smooth, creating a

strange effect in combination with the heavy cornice. If the outside has a deliberately medieval aspect, the plan shows a new type of architectural thinking. The courtyard is arcaded on three sides, connecting on the fourth side to a reception loggia by means of which one can gain access to the garden behind the palace. Because of its scale, elegance, and built-in loggia, the courtyard has the appearance of a private piazza, which is what it was. Interesting here is the relationship between the courtyard and the staircase, which leads up from the right side of the courtyard; the staircase allows direct access to the reception rooms on the *piano nobile* so that privileged visitors could avoid the lower floor's service areas. The location and character of this staircase—which introduces an asymmetrical element into the composition of the plan—was to become another issue that Renaissance architects were to struggle with. Family bedrooms were usually on the third floor, while the attic rooms were allocated to the domestics.

13.45 **Rusticated facade, Medici Palace**

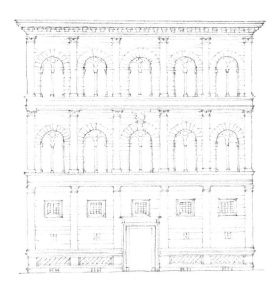

13.46 **Elevation: Rucellai Palace, Florence, Italy**

13.47 **Rucellai Palace**

Rucellai Palace

Wool merchants, the Rucellai family held important political posts in Florence under the Medici. Their palazzo was designed by Leon Battista Alberti, a scholar with a law degree from the University of Bologna. He worked as an advisor and official in the papal office, a position that was, in essence, his day job. His real passion was studying the classics, producing treatises on topics that were of interest to him, such as painting and architecture, as well as writing dozens of small plays.

The Rucellai Palace (1446–50), designed by Alberti, gave the Florentines their first taste of a truly "humanist" facade. It is, however, more show than reality, because this facade is little more than a stone veneer placed over a medieval palace. Nevertheless, it was a portent of things to come. All three horizontal zones of the facade are articulated by pilasters that, together with the unbroken entablatures that mark the different stories, form a grid over the entire surface. Window openings are placed within each intercolumniation. There were, of course, no readily available models of a multistoried Roman building, so in some sense this is a conjecture.

The initial design called for five bays; later, further bays were added to the right side of the facade. The pattern of the voussoirs, stones, and pilasters are grooved out of the variously shaped stones of the veneer. Unlike at San Lorenzo, where the pilasters appear as part of the structural system, here the pilasters, being of the same material as the wall, read less forcefully and as less "real." On the other hand, what is demonstrated is a desire to unify the facade in its two-dimensionality. A coherence of this kind had until then been reserved for church facades and not been applied to palace design.

Renaissance architecture struggled to strike a balance between the real and the suggested. This played itself out in the facade, which was an unheard of "design problem" in the Middle Ages. Even though the relationship between the facade and what was behind it remained important, the facade from then on was an architectural issue all its own. At its best, it symbolized and summarized the three-dimensional architectural program of the building it represented.

13.48 **Site: Rucellai Palace**

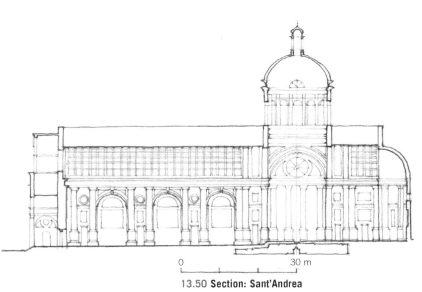

13.50 Section: Sant'Andrea

13.49 Sant'Andrea, Mantua, Italy

Sant'Andrea at Mantua

At Sant'Andrea at Mantua (designed ca. 1470, built 1472–94), Alberti abandoned the long tradition of side-aisled churches for a single barrel-vaulted nave with side chapels. Such a broad, open space could be easily justified for a church that was to hold large crowds of pilgrims during the annual showing of the blood of Christ. The blood, actually a dried substance held in a vial, is located in the crypt beneath the church and is retrieved during the ceremony through an opening in the floor. If the contents of the vial turns to liquid, it is seen as a good omen. The facade, one of the first true church facades of the Renaissance, faces onto a small piazza and is based on the theme of a Roman triumphal arch. The theme of triumph is carried into the interior elevations of the nave. Alberti's use of the giant order was novel for the Renaissance. The problem was how to coordinate the facade with the height of the barrel vault of the nave behind it. Alberti made no attempt to compromise the two disparate elements in the front, so he created an arched opening that shields the upper-level window. The barrel vault on the interior was another Albertian novelty. Since there

are no side aisles, the arches set between the giant order of the nave elevation simply open onto side chapels, which are also barrel-vaulted. The giant order, though not itself structural, at least marks the presence of buttress piers that support the vault. Integrating the buttressing into the building in this way shows Alberti's talent in exploiting structural elements for spatial organization. The same is true for the minor order pilasters in the side chapels that, together with the ribs, mark out the geometry of the space. This is far different from Brunelleschi's "structural system," which is basically applied

to the wall's surface. Strangely, the unity of the two scales at Sant'Andrea is avoided to some degree on the facade, where the lesser order is pulled away from the giant order by a few centimeters, perhaps to accommodate the necessary width of the opening, thus once again showing some of the difficulties of working with the classical system. It is not known if Alberti's design called for a dome. The current dome (built 1732–82) was designed by Filippo Juvarra. The building, apart from the facade, does not set itself free from the maze of its medieval urban surroundings.

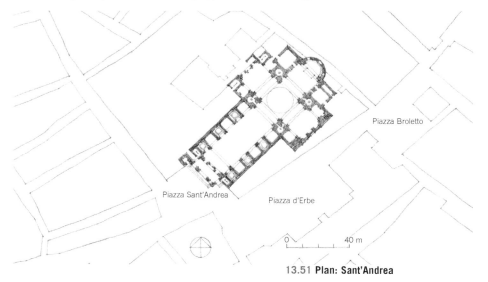

13.51 Plan: Sant'Andrea

13.52 Villa Medici, Poggio a Caiano, Italy

Villa Medici

Though urban palaces were the norm for the elite, the Medici were among the first to create a villa that was not just a fortified stronghold. As ubiquitous as this building type became over time, in the 15th century it was quite unusual. One of the important aspects of villas are the gardens, and their inclusion into the design was something of a novelty. During the Middle Ages, gardens as places of pleasure were rare; in the tight maze of medieval cities space was restricted by city walls, leaving little room for pleasure gardens. Furthermore, because of their association with pleasure, gardens were frowned upon. No doubt, visitors telling of the great gardens at the Alhambra in Spain played a part in establishing their legitimacy. At any rate, by the middle of the 15th century, the idea of having a place outside of town, perhaps in the hills where it was cooler in the summer and where the family could gather, became the norm for the elite. The word *villa* to describe these places came into use only in the late 16th century, when the villas themselves became more elaborate. In the 15th century, they were still—at least partially—working farms that supplied the family, but that were also outfitted with a manor house and garden.

Impacting this development was the revival of the old Roman notion of the bucolic country retreat as a place where one could enjoy music, poetry, and good company and play the gentleman farmer away from the mercantile world of the cities. A treatise that Alberti wrote entitled *Villa* helped define the parameters of this lifestyle. For the new elite, the villa served more practical goals as well: the artworks, sculptures, gardens, and buildings were all very much part of a system of wealth and prestige.

One of the several villas used by the Medici family, the Villa Medici at Poggio a Caiano was among the most important of that period. Standing on the top of a small hill a few kilometers west of Florence, it had a wide view over the plain between Florence and Pistoia. Originally a fortress, it was rebuilt, beginning around 1485, into a villa by Giuliano da Sangallo. It also seems to be the earliest attempt to re-create a classical *villa suburbana* as described in texts by Pliny and Vitruvius. The villa rests on a large vaulted platform containing the service rooms and spaces needed for the farm. It is a two-story building with an H-shaped plan, set sideways to the axis. The whole, including its gardens, was framed by an enclosing wall. The curved double staircase replaced the

initial design, which had a straight stairway leading to the top of the entrance platform. Functionally, the main rooms are aligned along the central axis with a large, barrel-vaulted room at the center, straddling the two arms of the H. There were apartment suites with antechambers and bedrooms located at each corner. The loggia, with its temple-front design at the entrance, was built for Giovanni de' Medici (son of Lorenzo, 1475–1521), who became Pope Leo X. The building was often used as a summer residence by the Medici family and increasingly for official receptions and the welcoming of important personalities, such as Charles V, who stayed there in 1536. In the 1570s, frescoes alluding to the history of the Medici family were added to the walls of the great hall.

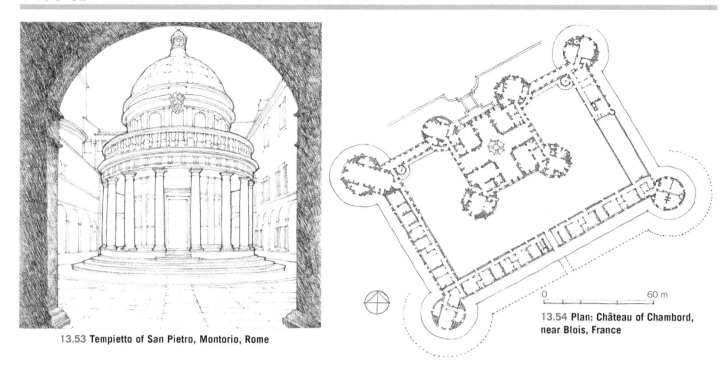

13.53 Tempietto of San Pietro, Montorio, Rome

13.54 Plan: Château of Chambord, near Blois, France

Tempietto of San Pietro

Architecture, with its equipoise of harmonic relationships and strict geometry, revealed the perfection and omnipotence of God's truth and goodness, according to the Renaissance architects. In this quest they found inspiration in part in the circular temples of the Romans, which inspired, for instance, the Tempietto of San Pietro in Rome (1499–1502), a *martyrium* commissioned by Ferdinand and Isabella of Spain. Designed by Donato Bramante (1444–1514), it is a small gem. A ring of Doric columns topped by a balustrade surrounds a cylindrical volume that rises over the one-story-high colonnade topped by a dome. The crypt gives access to the site where St. Peter was said to have been crucified. It is missing a circular courtyard that was meant to have been built around it.

The dome is such a ubiquitous element of the classical European tradition that it is easy to forget that it was initially a revolutionary innovation. Its history as a symbolic form begins with churches in Armenia, where domes signified the heavens. Armenian churches had tall dome structures visible from outside the building, but the dome itself was rarely expressed as such and instead was usually hidden underneath a conical external form. Similarly, the dome of the Pantheon was impressive from the inside, but had no exterior legibility. The domes of Islamic mosques and tombs were often hidden behind frontispieces.

By contrast, the dome of San Pietro in Montorio is not only the culmination of the composition, it was also designed to be seen and comprehended from both the outside and the inside. Later domes, like the one over St. Peter's Basilica in Rome designed by Michelangelo Buonarroti (1475–1564), were derivatives of this idea, even though for structural—and aesthetic—reasons, the outer and inner domes were rarely built as a single unit, but instead as two domes.

FRENCH CHÂTEAUX

In France, the 15th century and the first half of the 16th century was a period of relative economic weakness compared to the situation in Italy. The Black Plague had killed thousands, and due to the Hundred Years' War large tracts of farmland were left fallow. Furthermore, the struggle between the aristocratic classes had left the royal finances in disarray. High taxes fed a spirit of revolt. A turning point in France's fortunes came with the ascension of Francis I (r. 1515–47), who, though not a particularly astute military planner, did capture tracts of land in northern Italy, and in the process became a great admirer of Italian art and learning. In 1516 he invited the renowned Leonardo da Vinci to spend the rest of his life in his court, offering him his own little palazzo, Clos Luce, near the royal castle at Amboise, to which it was connected by an underground tunnel.

13.55 **Château of Chambord**

An urban culture such as was familiar to Italians did not exist in France. The kings did not even live in Paris, which was not to become the capital until the 17th century. Instead, in a tradition dating back to Charlemagne, they moved from place to place, living in an assortment of châteaux, usually close to hunting grounds. Whereas a villa is primarily a summer residence, a château is the residence of the lord of the manor—a country house for nobility and gentry. It is also often associated with a forest preserve used for hunting, an activity that only nobility were permitted to engage in. Between 1527 and 1547, Francis I built no fewer than seven châteaux near Paris. Some were hunting lodges; others were places of residence. Chambord (1519–47) was the largest and most elaborate château of its age; it was so huge that it was uncomfortable to live in, and Francis himself inhabited it for only a few weeks. It is believed that Leonardo da Vinci had a hand in its design, but since Leonardo died in 1519, in the year it was begun, he could only have been involved in its planning stages. Construction went on even though the royal treasury was empty.

The building consists of a square castle, or *donjon*, with round towers at the corners, the whole structure framed by a larger, rectangular building, still partially unfinished. The *donjon* is not in the center but on the inside of the square court, clamped against the northeastern side of the larger structure. The double helical staircase that rises through the center of the building, and which is attributed to Leonardo, leads to the roof of the building, a world unto itself. With its complex coves and turrets and views of the hunting grounds, it was used as a place for social events and outdoor entertainment. In a layout that was unique to the French, the central residential structure had four apartments, one in each quadrant.

13.56 **Staircase, Château of Chambord**

MAMLUK SULTANATE

The Mamluks of Egypt (to be distinguished from the Mamluks of Delhi; *mamluk* means "slave" or "owned," so these are kingdoms created by former slaves) maintained a turbulent rule from Cairo—battling the Mongols, trying to conquer Cyprus, and balancing a peace with the Ottomans. With a ready supply of well-trained masons, the Mamluks extended and enhanced the tradition of Fatimid palace architecture, establishing a series of important religious institutions along the main road leading to the citadel of Cairo. The greatest example is the Complex of Sultan Hassan, a colossal project begun in 1356. It contains a cruciform congregational mosque with four madrasas and a mausoleum of an imperial scale, as well as an orphanage, a hospital, a bazaar, a water tower, baths, and kitchens. It was meant to house some four hundred students. The religious spaces are organized symmetrically to fit into the awkward site, which is defined by two major streets. The portal of the complex, rising 37 meters high, is crowned by a *muqarnas* cornice. The decorations include such Chinese motifs as chrysanthemums and lotus flowers. The open central court was paved and has a fountain at the center. The four madrasas are located in the corners between the arms of the *iwans*; each has its own small courtyard. The southeast *iwan*, the largest of the four, was spanned by an enormous vault, considered at the time one of the wonders of the world. The mihrab and surrounding *qibla* wall are paneled in marble slabs of contrasting colors. Doors flanking the mihrab lead to the tomb beyond. In it, the walls are paneled with marble and the *muqarnas* of the dome are gilded, and the whole is illuminated by hundreds of specially designed glass lamps. The building not only makes maximum use of the site but redefines the Central Asian four-*iwan* mosque, making it more intimate yet also more monumental.

13.57 Courtyard door (left) and entrance portal (right), Complex of Sultan Hassan, Cairo, Egypt

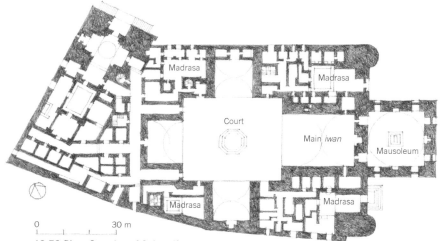

13.58 Plan: Complex of Sultan Hassan

Madrasa

Madrasa

Court

Main *iwan*

Mausoleum

Madrasa

Madrasa

0   30 m

13.59 Complex of Sultan Hassan

Mausoleum Complex of Sultan Qaitbay

The capacity of the designers to impose order onto complex urban sites was a unique aspect of Mamluk architecture in Cairo. No two buildings are alike, testifying to the fluid imagination of the architects. But the asymmetry of these buildings was not always a matter of necessity, as one can see at the Mausoleum Complex of Sultan Qaitbay (1472–74). Sultan al Ashraf Qaitbay (r. 1468–96) was known for the efficient manner in which he ran the country and the stability he created. He was particularly interested in architecture, promoting more than sixty projects, not only in Cairo but also in Mecca, Medina, Damascus, and Jerusalem. The mausoleum complex, with no other buildings surrounding it, houses a madrasa and the burial *qubba* of the sultan. Architecturally, it balances the minaret tower on the right with an open loggia on the left. The dome is made up of three separate elements: the square-planned building at the bottom; an intermediate volume with vigorously shaped scrolls at the corners that make the transition to an octagonal platform; and finally the dome, resting on a drum on that platform. Compared to the simple windows on the body of the building, some designed to look like they were carved out of the wall, the dome was given a particularly refined and elaborate decoration in which two patterns, an interlaced geometric star pattern and a floral arabesque, are combined. On the interior is found *pietra serena* paneling, a surface treatment similar to those found in northern Italian churches.

13.60 Dome, Mausoleum Complex of Sultan Qaitbay, Cairo, Egypt

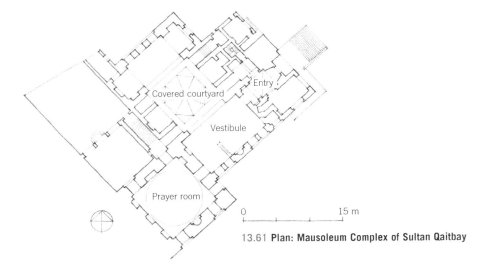

13.61 Plan: Mausoleum Complex of Sultan Qaitbay

TIMURID DYNASTY

The occupation of Persia by the Mongolians and the fall of Baghdad in 1258 unleashed a period of disarray and confusion. One of the earliest post-Mongolian states to emerge was created by the Turkish-speaking Timur (1336–1405), who proudly claimed descent from Genghis Khan. An ambitious and notably cruel commander, Timur defeated the Mamluks of Egypt, the early Ottomans, and the Delhi sultanates to create an empire that unified Persia, Iraq, Transoxiana, and parts of South Asia. While not themselves heterodox or Shi'ite, the Timurid rulers accorded respect to the Shi'ite figure of Ali, the prophet Mohammed's son-in-law, whom they considered the founder of their civilization's mystic brotherhoods. Furthermore, with a generosity unthinkable in later generations, Empress Gohar Shad built her Shi'ite subjects a splendid shrine in the city of Mashhad, still now a major pilgrimage center in modern Iran. Timur set up Samarkand, already a major metropolis along the Silk Route, as his capital. It soon possessed large suburbs with fountains and canals. In the factories, the citizens wove silk and cotton, worked leather, and decorated copper; Chinese craftsmen produced here the first paper outside of China itself. The 13th-century population exceeded half a million.

Consistent with Timur's passion for grand structures, imposing appearances became the main priority of his architectural program, with the facade developing into a virtual freestanding architectural form. High drums and external domes stabilized by brick ribs were often placed over the structural inner domes. The combination of portal and dome produced buildings of great spatial drama, such as Samarkand's biggest mosque, known as Bibi Khanum Friday Mosque (1339–1404) which was entered through a high portal with round corner towers, its arches spanning nearly 19 meters. The principal elements of the plan—the entrance portal, the mosque, and the lecture halls—are all enlarged into monumental forms and then framed by the repetitive elements of the mosque. The colossal entrance portal protrudes from the exterior wall, with two minarets projecting out even further. The cylindrical shafts of the minarets, rising from the ground rather than emerging from the top of the *iwan*, and sitting on decagonal socles, provide the earliest surviving example of minarets flanking a

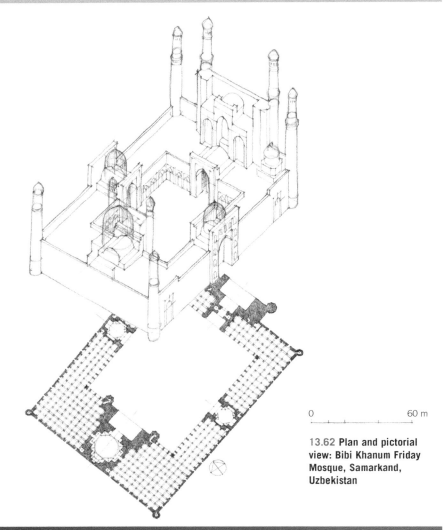

0　　　　　　　60 m

13.62 Plan and pictorial view: Bibi Khanum Friday Mosque, Samarkand, Uzbekistan

13.63 Bibi Khanum Friday Mosque

portal. Behind this lay a spacious courtyard, at the back of which stood the dome-covered main building of the mosque, towering 44 meters in the air. The basic plan is the four-*iwan* type that had been developed in an ad hoc way in Isfahan some four hundred years earlier. But this building was a unit from the very start, and its hypostyle hall forms the connective tissue holding together the monumental elements.

Of a similarly grand scale is the Ulugh Beg Madrasa in Samarkand (1417–20), which opens up to the main square on axis to the Bibi Khanum Friday Mosque. It is one of the largest madrasas in Central Asia, with an enormous entrance portal flanked left and right by dome-covered lecture halls with four axial niches. Slender round minarets mark the corners. The square courtyard has four *iwans* and a large mosque at the rear, with additional lecture halls to the right and left. The building became the prototype of many later madrasas. The domed corner rooms served as classrooms, while the court was enclosed by two stories of individual cells. The four colonnaded *iwan* porches, axially disposed and deeply recessed, served as meeting and discussion areas. The walls were decorated with marble panels and blue and purple bricks.

The Timurids developed a new type of dome support. Instead of the square hall and octagonal squinch, which had been developed in Islamic architecture over the previous centuries, the dome was set on two pairs of overlapping arches. The dome was thus smaller than in the older system, but the whole now had a dynamic plasticity, both outside and inside. This technique had originated in Armenia, where it had been known since the 12th century. From there it spread to Russia, and it is quite possible that captured Russian or Armenian building masters might have been responsible for this aspect of Timurid architecture.

Though decorative tiles were used in Islamic architecture from early on and had also been developed by the Seljuks, the complete sheathing of buildings in colored tiles, characteristic of Persian architecture today, dates only from this period. Prior to the 13th century, most monumental decorations were made of stucco that was painted or gilded. Only under the House of Timur in the late 14th century did the various ornamental motifs appear, fired in ceramic tiles, that utterly blanketed the structures. Though the color blue predominates, the range of possible colors was quite wide, including turquoise, white, yellow, green, brown, aubergine, and black.

13.64 **Ulugh Beg Madrasa, Samarkand, Uzbekistan**

13.65 **Timurid dome of Bibi Khanum Friday Mosque**

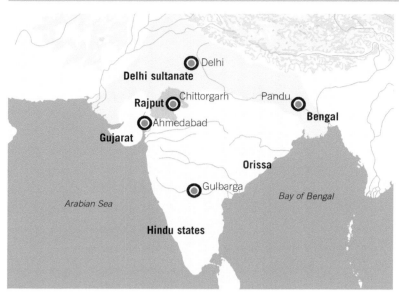

13.66 India, ca. 1400 CE

DECCAN SULTANATES

In 1400 central India was controlled by
a familiar patchwork of diverse regional
kingdoms, but this is the first time that most
of these were ruled by Islamic kings, known
as the Deccan (Southern) Sultanates. Most
of the Deccan sultans were affiliated with
the Ottomans in Turkey for political reasons.
Qutb-ud-Din Aibak's Mamluk dynasty
(1206–90) had controlled the entire Indo-
Gangetic Plain of northern India from their
capital in Delhi. Their successors, the Khilji
dynasty (1290–1320), did spectacularly
better and brought central India—that is, the
entire Deccan Plateau, from Gujarat in the
west to Pandua in the east and Gulbarga in
the south—under their control. The Khilji's
successors, the Tughlaqs (1320–1413),
however, were unable to manage this vast
empire and bungled a series of ill-conceived
administrative projects. Timur, the Mongol
sultan of Samarkand opposed to the
Ottomans, took the opportunity to launch
an invasion in 1398, and decimated the
sultanates. He did not stay to rule, however,
and in the ensuing chaos, the governors and
regents of the Deccan Plateau, many of them
Khilji appointees, declared independence,
establishing the Deccan Sultanates. The
sultans took pains to distinguish themselves
from the weak court in Delhi and instead
turned to West Asia, not only for trade but
also for occasional help in shaping their
material culture and architecture.

Pandua

Shamsuddin Ilyas Shah (r. 1342–1358) was
one of the regents of the Deccan Sultanes
who declared independence in the area of
Bengal and established his own dynasty. The
Ilyas Shah dynasty constructed a new capital
in Pandua, where it built a set of unique
mosques and mausolea.

The Shah dynasty sultans started out
building fairly conventional stone-clad
buildings. But stone is scarce in Bengal, and
it rains incessantly. Brick had always been
the local material of choice, as can be seen in
the Buddhist monasteries of the Pala kings.
Even mosques such as the Adina Mosque in
Pandua (1364) were made of brick and then
clad in stone. So in 1425, when the Sultan
Jalal al-Din Muhammad Shah (r. 1414–32)
began construction on his mausoleum, he
decided to make it out of brick. This square
building with corner turrets and an octagonal
room surmounted by a hemispherical dome
has an unusual twist to it. Inspired by the
curved roof of local vernacular bamboo-and-
hay structures, Muhammad Shah's architects
incorporated a curved cornice into the profile
that not only helps shed water but also gives
the mausoleum a unique shape. The Pandua
curved roof became iconic; from this time
onward all significant Bengal buildings began
incorporating the curved cornice, creating
a uniquely Bengali style that was imitated
around South Asia in later centuries.

Jami Masjid of Ahmedabad

In 1398, Ahmed Shah (r. 1411–42), a former
governor of Gujarat, declared independence
from the Tughlaqs, and in 1410, he founded
Ahmedabad on the Sabarmati River as his
new capital. Ahmedabad went on to become
prosperous, particularly under Fath Kahn
Mahmud (1459–1511), who expanded the
kingdom in all directions. Under the Delhi
sultanate and the Tughlaqs, it had been
standard practice to demean demolished
Hindu temples by reusing their columns,
upside down or in pieces, to hold up a
new mosque. The curious characteristic of
Ahmed Shah's architecture is the manner in
which this mark of repression became the
expressive language of the new architecture.
For his new Jami Masjid (Friday Mosque),
built in 1423 in Ahmedabad, Ahmed Shah
embraced the new aesthetic created by the
demeaned Hindu columns and authorized
the construction of new columns not
unlike the ones that were pillaged, thereby
legitimizing this new architectural hybrid.

13.67 Inner court, Jami Masjid of Ahmedabad, India

13.68 Court arcade, Jami Masjid of Ahmedabad

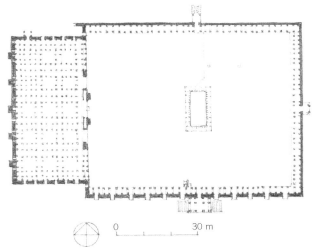

0   30 m

13.69 Plan: Jami Masjid of Ahmedabad

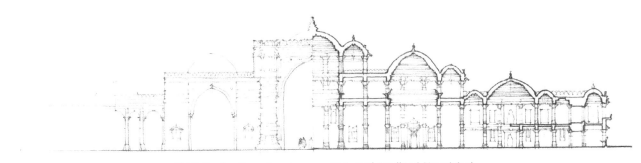

13.70 Section through main prayer hall, Jami Masjid of Ahmedabad

13.71 **Interior arcade, Friday Mosque of Gulbarga, India**

Friday Mosque of Gulbarga

In Gulbarga, the capital of the Bahmanid sultanate (1347–1542), Sultan Muhammad I remained strongly aligned with the Ottoman sultans. He preferred his imported architecture as puritanical as possible. He used Rafi bin Shams bin Mansur, an architect from Iran, to build his Friday Mosque (1367). Without any courtyard or *iwan*, the mosque with its central hall (66 by 54 meters) is covered with sixty-three small cupolas; the *qibla* wall to the west features a high dome surrounded by twelve smaller, lower domes. An unusual aspect of the interior is the extremely wide span of the arcades, with very low imposts that were to become more common in south Indian Islamic architecture later on but were unheard of at this time. There is a Persian mood and even a basilica-like feel to this mosque.

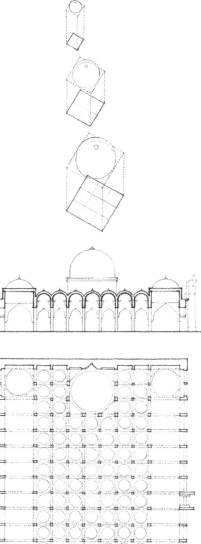

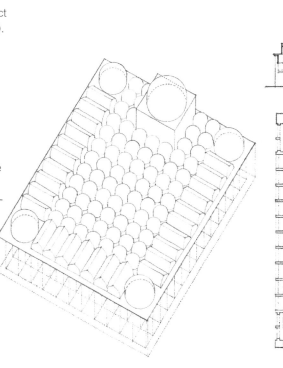

13.72 **Plan, section, and pictorial view: Friday Mosque of Gulbarga**

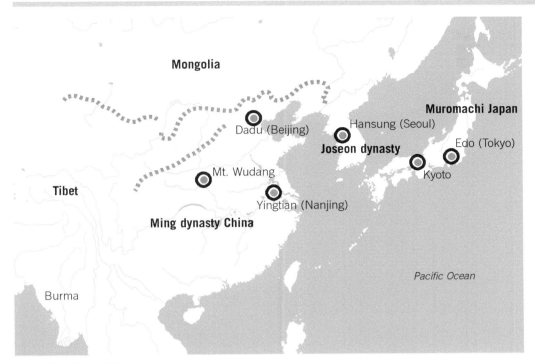

Mongolia

Dadu (Beijing)

Hansung (Seoul)

Muromachi Japan

Joseon dynasty

Edo (Tokyo)

Mt. Wudang

Tibet

Kyoto

Yingtian (Nanjing)

Ming dynasty China

Pacific Ocean

Burma

13.73 **Ming dynasty China**

MING DYNASTY CHINA

In 1368, Zhu Yuanzhang defeated the last Mongolian Yuan emperor and established the Ming ("bright" in Chinese) dynasty. The Ming (1368–1644) were Han Chinese and projected the Mongolian Yuan as foreign barbarians, reviving the "insider-outsider" conflict signified by the Long Wall. And yet, even as they tightened controls over the citizens and reinforced Confucian practices, they also continued the modernization programs of the Yuan and expanded their urban centers. Initially, the Ming established a new capital at Nanjing, in accordance with tradition; but then the third Ming emperor, Zhu Di (r. 1403–24), known by his royal name as the Yongle Emperor, broke with tradition and moved the capital back to the city of Yuan Dadu, renaming it Beijing (meaning "Northern Peace").

Zhu Di was a controversial emperor. Relentlessly ambitious, he exterminated his rivals ruthlessly and often doled out cruel punishments to criminals and detractors. At the same time, he consolidated Ming rule and undertook massive building projects. To revive Confucianism he ordered the transcription of all known classical texts into a single volume, sometimes referred to as the Chinese encyclopedia. He repaired and reopened the Grand Canal, the

1800-kilometer-long 6th-century CE canal connecting Beijing to Hangzhou. Running north-south, against the predominant east-west direction of the rivers of China, the Grand Canal was a critical transportation highway and had been neglected by the Yuan. Beijing, the capital, was located in northern China, in an area that was not nearly as fertile or as irrigated as the lands of the south. But the army and emperor were situated here to defend against invaders from the north, the primary direction from which they came. Thus, while the demand for grain was great in the north and particularly in Beijing, grain production was more than 1,500 kilometers away. But while the south produced a significant surplus of grain, until modern times grain was always very expensive to transport because it has great bulk and degrades easily. The Chinese solution was to create a water-based transportation highway, the Grand Canal, which served all kinds of commercial traffic. Zhu Di vociferously denigrated the Mongolians. At the same, he was protective of all non-Confucian religions and was most likely himself a Buddhist. Muslims enjoyed significant freedom in his time, and after the death of Timur (who had sworn to invade China) he maintained diplomatic missions with the rulers of Samarkand and the Safavids of Persia.

Forbidden City

The Forbidden City, the enormous palace complex built by Emperor Zhu Di in Beijing, is still one of the most celebrated icons of imperial China. Consisting essentially of one long south-to-north axis, this palace-cum–governmental complex functioned through a series of thresholds, each of which gave access to different levels of government. At its center were the diptych of the Hall of Supreme Harmony and the Hall of Preserving Harmony, with the diminutive Hall of Central Harmony in the middle. Beyond these, at the core of the imperial compound, was the Palace of Heavenly Purity—the residence of the Son of Heaven and the conceptual center of the empire. Since the emperor embodied both the authority of government and its justice system, access to him had to be both carefully circumscribed and, at the same time, projected well beyond his actual physical presence. This, in essence, was the dual purpose of the Forbidden City.

13.74 **Meridian Gate, Forbidden City, Beijing, China**

13.75 **Plan: 15th-century Beijing**

The Palace of Heavenly Purity consists of three pavilions on axis, on an I-shaped, single-stepped marble platform, preceded by a terrace facing south. It is surrounded by a wall. Sixteen pavilions, housing the royal concubines, extended beyond this innermost sanctum to the east and west. Imperial gardens and additional palaces for members of the royal family make up much of the remaining structures. South of the palace, a set of three halls perched on a three-step, I-shaped marble platform repeated the order of the innermost palace. This second set of buildings is the terminus and focus of the public sequence of the Forbidden City, and the conceptual center of the empire.

The emperor met daily with his officials in the Hall of Supreme Harmony. Only the highest officers had access to this hall, which was also the emperor's throne room. The halls behind it, the Hall of Central Harmony and the Hall of Preserving Harmony, only served supporting functions. Although the height, spans, and ornamentation of the Hall of Supreme Harmony are magnificent, the impact of the hall comes from the manner in which the deep overhang of the roof projects its presence into the vast space of the courtyard that precedes it. Here grand spectacles and marches could be staged. In front of the emperor all supplicants had to kowtow—that is, they had to prostrate

themselves, facing north. Only the emperor faced south, looking down upon them—an arrangement magnified by the orchestration of the roof and the courtyard. The Forbidden City housed the imperial bureaucracy and its millions of records. The daily communiqués that arrived from the most distant parts of the empire were catalogued, interpreted, and presented to the emperor and his counselors for action when necessary. The offices of the bureaucracy were located in the corridors on either side of the Hall of Supreme Harmony. Five marble bridges symmetrically straddle the Jinshahe, or "Golden Water River," that winds its way around the Forbidden City. Just beyond them, farther south, lies the imposing Meridian Gate, the designated entrance into the Forbidden City, which aligns with the city's enclosing wall and moat (with turrets in the corners). This was where high-ranking civil and military officials gathered to wait for the emperor and where large triumphant ceremonies were conducted.

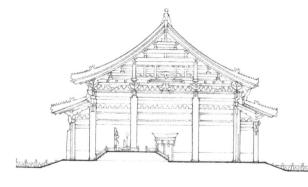

13.76 **Section: Hall of Supreme Harmony, Forbidden City**

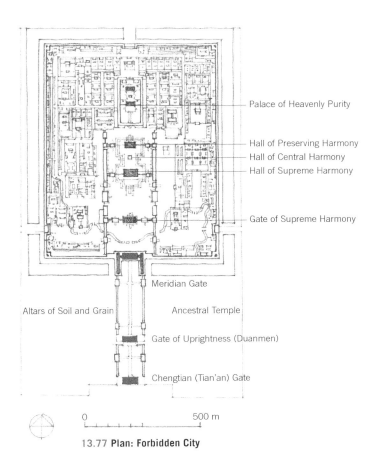

Palace of Heavenly Purity

Hall of Preserving Harmony
Hall of Central Harmony
Hall of Supreme Harmony

Gate of Supreme Harmony

Meridian Gate

Altars of Soil and Grain   Ancestral Temple

Gate of Uprightness (Duanmen)

Chengtian (Tian'an) Gate

0   500 m

13.77 Plan: Forbidden City

13.78 Hall of Supreme Harmony, Forbidden City

The U-shaped form (with five entrances and a tall platform with high pavilions) of the Meridian Gate connected the Forbidden City to the palaces beyond. The Gate of Uprightness, or Duanmen, was followed by Chengtian, from where the emperor issued imperial edicts, and then finally by the Great Ming Gate, or Da Mingmen, the main entry into the imperial city. As a visitor travels along the main axis of the Forbidden City toward its center, the elevation increases, each increase being an indication of the power of the emperor. The first three gates rise high above the ground on imposing blank walls, giving the viewer the impression of being far below the zone of privilege. Beyond the Gate of Supreme Harmony, where the view opens up, with the Hall of Supreme Harmony is raised handsomely as an object in space on its three stately terraces, and the highest point in the Forbidden City is attained. The south view from the top of the third terrace was the emperor's privileged view, enabling him to see over the walls. From here all the gates and the length of the city could be apprehended in a single glance. Color played an important role. The podiums on which the buildings stood are a brilliant white; the wooden pillars are a dull red (whose coloring agent also serves as a preservative); finally, the roofs are tiled in imperial sun yellow.

That these palaces survive is itself of historical significance, as it was ancient practice in China for new dynasties to burn the capital of the former dynasty. This is one of the reasons there are so few historical structures, apart from temples, in China today. But in 1616, when the Manchu set up their dynasty on the ruins of the defeated Ming, they did not destroy the capital. For five centuries, therefore, from about 1420 to 1908, the city was the hallowed seat of twenty-four emperors. The buildings that we see today are not the original Ming-era buildings, but most are relatively accurate reconstructions made by the Qing dynasty in the 17th and 18th centuries.

13.79 Purple Heaven Hall, Mt. Wudang, China

Mt. Wudang

Zhu Di, the Yongle Emperor, believing that his ascent to the throne had been aided by Zhenwu, a mythical Daoist warrior, in 1412 dispatched some 300,000 workers to Mt. Wudang, Hubei, where the Daoists believe Zhenwu attained immortality. Mt. Wudang is in an area of precipitous cliffs and dramatic views, often covered in mist. Its thick forest is filled with caves, springs, and grottoes. Zhu Di's workers built a 60-kilometer-long pilgrimage path made of stone that winds its way up to the peak, aided by thirty-nine delicately constructed bridges. Along the way are nine temple complexes, two monasteries, and thirty-six hermitages, some perched over and along cliffs. The Purple Heaven Hall, Mt. Wudang's largest monastery, is farther up the slope. Two terraces (only one short of the Forbidden City's Hall of Supreme Harmony) elevate the elegant double-eaved, hip-and-gable, five-bay hall. One of the main martial arts schools of China, Wudang kung fu, is associated with this area. Five hundred meters higher, the route culminates at Tianzhufeng ("Heavenly Pillar Peak"), on the top of Mt. Wudang. Here sits the small Golden Hall (1416) with its roof and the prominent parts of its three-bay structure executed in bronze. Within is the statue of the barefoot, long-haired Zhenwu, surrounded by his Daoist retinue. Above them, a bracket set more complicated than any found in the *Yingzhao Fashi* was built to signify their stature and royal favor.

Temple of Heaven

Periodically, determined by a set calendar, the emperor was required to travel out of the Forbidden City to altars located at the southern edge of the city. Thus a balance was maintained between the imperial authority of the Forbidden City and the celestial authority of heaven. The Imperial Ancestral Temple and the Altar of Soil and Grain, located just beyond the Meridian Gate, to the east and west of the major axis, were the oldest of the structures. The Altars of the Sun and Moon were located to the east and west of Beijing, and the Altar of Earth to the north.

The south was reserved for the most important altars of all, in the Temple of Heaven complex: the Altar of Agriculture, intended to ensure the timely cycle of production, and the Circular Mound Altar, the enabler of the Emperors' mandate. The Circular Mound Altar, also called the Altar of Heaven (Yuan Qiu Tan) is a three-tiered circular platform (the circle representing the shape of heaven) located in a square enclosure (the square symbolizing the earth). The altar, basically a type of ritual platform, was illuminated by hundreds of lanterns, and incense burned everywhere. In the middle, facing south, was a tablet representing heaven, moved there especially for the emperor's visits from its resting place in the Imperial Vault of Heaven just beyond to the north. Before it, the emperor prostrated himself and kowtowed to the heavens more than fifty times in a carefully scripted ritual,

witnessed by all present, that only he could perform. Heaven's displeasure with the emperor, manifested by bad omens and natural or political catastrophes, was always considered a sign of the withdrawal of his mandate to rule.

Just north of the Mound Altar is the Imperial Vault of Heaven, and farther north is the Hall of Prayer for Good Harvests (Qinian Dian). Elevated on three terraces of white marble, this temple has a triple set of conical roofs over a round space that is unique in Chinese architecture. The sacrifice there occurred on the winter equinox, and the emperor prepared for the event by fasting for three days, living in the Abstinence Palace located at the western edge of the complex. At three in the morning on the day of the equinox, the emperor traveled to the Circular Mound Altar, approaching it from the south—that is, facing north, in the position of a supplicant. The Abstinence Palace is one of the few Ming buildings made with stone vaults. Only the buildings for the dead (the Ming tombs) and this one were considered "unworthy" of a wooden roof, yet they were built with extraordinary care, showing that though stone architecture was not a tradition in China, it could be produced very skillfully.

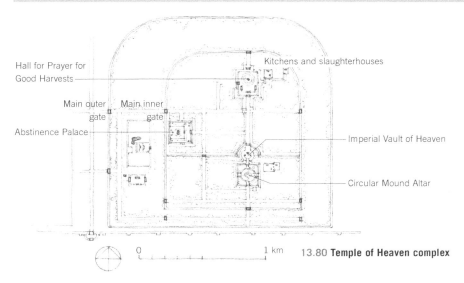

Hall for Prayer for
Good Harvests

Kitchens and slaughterhouses

Main outer   Main inner
gate   gate

Abstinence Palace

Imperial Vault of Heaven

Circular Mound Altar

0   1 km   **13.80 Temple of Heaven complex**

13.81 Imperial Vault of Heaven, Temple of Heaven complex, Beijing

13.82 Circular Mound Altar, Temple of Heaven complex

Dabao-en Temple, or the Porcelain Tower of Nanjing

The Porcelain Tower of Nanjing (Dabao-en Temple) was designed during the reign of Zhu Di, the Yongle Emperor (r. 1402–24), shortly before its construction in the early 15th century. The Yongle Emperor followed traditional rituals closely and held many popular beliefs. He did not overindulge in the luxuries of palace life, and used Buddhism and Buddhist festivals to help calm civil unrest. He stopped the warring between the various Chinese tribes and reorganized the provinces to best provide peace within his kingdom. Yongle was said by Ernst Faber to be an "ardent Buddhist."

In 1403 the Yongle Emperor, after experiencing a vision of the Avalokiteshvara Buddha, invited Deshin Shekpa, the fifth Gyalwa Karmapa of the Kagyu school of Tibetan Buddhism, to Nanjing. The visit of the Buddhist Karmapa revalidated Buddhism in Ming China and helped the Yongle Emperor secure a popular base for his rule. To mark this visit, the Yongle Emperor ordered the construction of the Dabao-En Temple, or the Temple of Giving Thanks, which was made of wood and covered in brightly colored porcelain. The tower—30 meters in diameter, rising 79 meters in 9 stories—was part of a massive Buddhist monastery on the banks of the Qinhuai River in Nanjing. One of the tallest structures in China, the tower was illuminated at night by lamps, which, reflected by the porcelain, gave it a luminescent quality that earned the building an international reputation. Extensively described by Western emissaries, the Porcelain Tower, as it came to be known in the West, inspired the blue-tiled roof of the Trianon de Porcelain built by Louis XIV in 1675. The tower was destroyed during the Taiping rebellion in the mid-19th century.

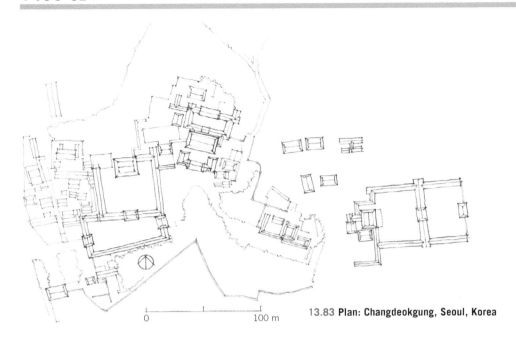

13.83 **Plan: Changdeokgung, Seoul, Korea**

0   100 m

JOSEON DYNASTY

In 1392 Yi Songgye, with the aid of the Ming dynasty, seized the Korean throne and established the Joseon dynasty (also known as the Chosun dynasty), which lasted until 1910. Korea was known under the Joseon as Daejoseonguk (the "Great Joseon Nation"). Though the Mongolians were defeated, aspects of Mongolian culture, here as elsewhere, remained embedded in Korean society. As in China, Confucianism was reestablished as the state religion. A new capital, Seoul, was built, situated not far from the peninsula's largest river and at the focal point of overland transportation routes. Several palaces were built in Seoul, the most important being Gyeongbokgung ("Palace Greatly Blessed by Heaven"—*gung* meaning "palace"—in 1394) and, a kilometer to the east, Changdeokgung ("Palace of Prospering Virtue," begun 1405, rebuilt 1592). For the siting of the palaces, the surrounding topography was carefully studied from the standpoint of both Confucian ideology and feng shui. Feng shui was also very much respected in the making of the principal roads connecting the main gates of the city by way of the four cardinal directions. Straight lines were not always the rule, as can be seen in the east-west and north-south thoroughfares, which are slightly curved.

According to feng shui, a building should face southward and should have mountains on the left and right, symbolizing an azure dragon and a white tiger, respectively. Changdeokgung was thus situated in the north sector of the city, in the foothills of Paekak Mountain, facing south to the northern mountain peak called Nam Mountain. The deity on Paekak Mountain was female, whereas the deity on Nam Mountain was male. Paekak, which symbolized royal authority and was the most highly valued in terms of feng shui, was closed to the common people and protected from any private use. Nam Mountain, however, was open to the common people. Because there was no natural mountain to the east of the palace, an artificial hill was created to compensate for the shortcoming in topography. In its original form, the palace had about five hundred buildings. They were burned during the Japanese invasions of 1592. About ten 19th-century reconstructions exist. Changdeokgung had a public portion (toward the south) and a more private part (toward the north) consisting of several stroll gardens strung together by a series of carefully composed follies for repose. One of these is particularly famous. Organized around a shallow quadrangular water tank, with a high ridge on one side and several

small pavilions distributed along the tank's edges on the other three sides, the folly is skillfully understated, as if it were nothing more than a reinforcement of natural elements already present in the landscape. The throne hall (*injongjon*), facing east and surrounded by its own wall, was a large two-story building built in 1405. It sits on the top of a series of low stone platforms that seem particularly well proportioned in respect to the slope of the eaves. Stone tables in the courtyard indicate where each rank of official should stand for formal ceremonies. The bays are 5 meters square except for those on the central axis, which are 6.7 meters square. The throne sat on a high platform at the back of the middle bay. It was connected in the north to the government building, where the king worked, and in the south to a portrait hall, or Sonwonjon Shrine, where the former kings' portraits were enshrined. On each king's birthday a memorial rite was held there, emphasizing the principle of continuity.

13.84 **Kinkakuji, Kyoto, Japan**

MUROMACHI JAPAN

After two centuries of domination by aristocratic regents and military rulers, Emperor Godaigo (r. 1318–39) enlisted the help of Ashikaga Takauji (1305–58) to reclaim the court in 1333. But when Godaigo refused to name Takauji as shogun after his victory, the latter forced the emperor into exile (1335) and placed his own representative on the throne. As shogun, Takauji made two decisions that changed the course of Japanese history: he reinstated Kyoto as the capital and reestablished links with the Chinese Song dynasty, links that had been broken since Kublai Khan's failed attempt to invade Japan in the 13th century. Profits from the China trade were important to the shogun's power. Song culture infused itself into Japanese society and with that came a blending of cultural elements that laid the foundation for a form of Buddhism known as Zen, the Japanese pronunciation of the Chinese kanji for *chan*. *Chan*, in turn, was a transformation of the Sanskrit *dhyan*, or meditation. Zen emphasizes sustained meditation rather than visualization as the way to nirvana. The Zen monasteries were built in the traditional Karayo style.

13.85 **Site plan: Kinkakuji**

Kinkakuji

In 1394, the Muromachi shogun Ashikaga Yoshimitsu (1358–1408), Takauji's grandson, gave up his government position to become a monk and retired to his private estate, the central focus of which was a three-story viewing pavilion known as Kinkakuji, or the "Golden Pavilion." It sits at the edge of a carefully designed reflection pond. The first story contained a public reception room with a loggia along the water that served as access point for pleasure boats, its clearly defined wooden structural elements contrasting with the white plaster walls. The second floor served as a place for private discussions; it was protected by the gentle sweep of an upward-turning eave. The views of the landscape from the balcony were carefully designed, as was the rest of the estate, with small islands in the foreground framing and enlarging the background. As in China, the surrounding distant landscape was also incorporated into the visual composition of the garden. Finally, the third story, Yoshimitsu's private refuge, resolves the pavilion in an upward-turning roof with a pronounced swell that culminates in a bronze phoenix finial. Yoshimitsu originally wanted to gild the pavilion (thus its title), but for most of its life it remained in wood. In 1950, the pavilion was destroyed by a mad arsonist. When it was reconstructed in 1955, its upper two stories were gilded to honor Yoshimitsu's original intentions.

13.86 Teahouse, Kinkakiju, Kyoto

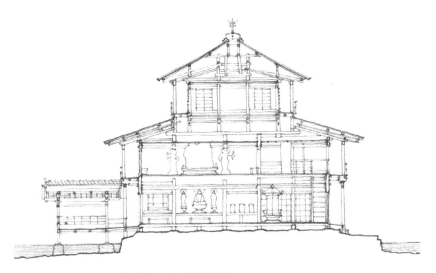

13.87 Section: Kinkakuji

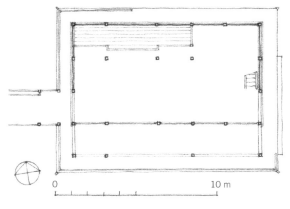

0   10 m

13.88 Plan: Kinkakuji

Ginkakuji

Ginkakuji ("Silver Pavilion") was built as a retirement villa by Yoshimitsu's grandson, the shogun Yoshimasa, in 1482. Yoshimasa intended to cover two stories of his pavilion with silver, but this intention was never realized. In Yoshimasa's original design, the two-story pavilion stood at the edge of a pond set off against small bridges, tiny islands, and exactingly planted and pruned shrubs, all designed to generate carefully framed views that recalled descriptions from Japanese literature. Ginkakuji's fame lies in the additions made by Zen Buddhist monks during the Edo period in the 17th century, the palace having been turned over to Zen Buddhists after its patron's death. Since sand had to be stored on site to maintain the gardens, the Zen monks decided to use it to build two sculpted mounds next to the pond and in stark contrast to it. One is low and carefully raked to form a plateau, and it is called the Sea of Silver Sand, so named for its appearance in moonlight. The other mound rises as a perfectly shaped, truncated cone, arresting at first glance if only for its sheer size. The cone evokes the profile of Mt. Fuji, but may also refer to the sacred mountain in the middle of a Buddhist mandala. From different points of view around Ginkakuji, the cone, uniform in color and outline from all directions, functions as an object of constancy in the changing panorama. The two mounds set in play a drama of visual tension, the exact meaning remaining open to interpretation This type of meditational paradox is typical for Zen Buddhism.

In a sense, Ginkakuji is more successful as a Zen garden than Kinkakuji. The assembly of its views is more restrained and subtle, and since they are bound by a much smaller space their experience is far more intimate and immediate. Together, however, they define the aspirations of the Muromachi warrior aristocracy as it changed under the influence of the Song and Zen.

13.89 Ginkakuji, Kyoto, Japan

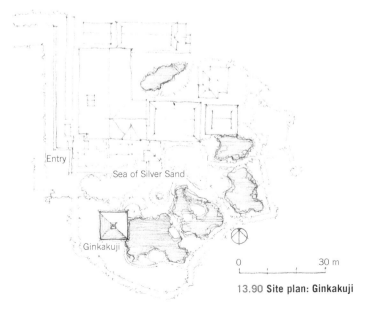

Entry

Sea of Silver Sand

Ginkakuji

0   30 m

13.90 Site plan: Ginkakuji

13.91 Southeast Asia, ca. 1400 CE

13.92 Ayutthaya temple complex

AYUTTHAYA

The collapse of the Khmer Empire, combined with the related unraveling of the Srivijayan Empire in Malaysia, reduced the importance of Southeast Asia in the global economy. The Majapahit Kingdom, which ruled from Java, and the Thai kingdom, with its capital in Ayutthaya, were the two dominant forces, both maintaining strong trade links with India and China.

The Thai kingdom was not a single, unified state, but rather composed of self-governing principalities and tributary provinces owing allegiance to the king. The name of the capital city derives from the Hindu holy city Ayodhya in northern India, which is said to be the birth place of the Hindu god Rama. King Ramathibodi, who established Ayutthaya, was Buddhist, however, and made Theravada Buddhism the official religion of the state, indicating the close continuity between Hindu and Buddhist practices at the time.

The kingdom's wealth derived not only from its control of trade routes but also from its introduction of a new strain of rice. Thai farmers had traditionally planted the glutinous rice that is still the staple in the north and northeast regions of the country. But in the floodplain of the Chao Phraya River, farmers turned to a variety of rice—so-called floating rice—a nonglutinous grain introduced from Bengal. It grew faster and more easily, producing a surplus that was sold abroad,

even to China. An extensive set of canals was dug to bring the rice from the fields. Though inland, Ayutthaya was essentially a port located on an island of the Chao Phraya River at the intersection of the Lopbur and Pasak Rivers. The island was crisscrossed by a network of canals that ran alongside a rectilinear road system. Over time, five hundred temples, stupas, and palaces were built on this island by successive generations of kings. Initially, Ayutthaya's temples derived their form from the architecture of the Khmers, but at a smaller scale and with a more deliberate staging of ancillary parts. The central stupa of Wat Rat Burana (1424) was not only surrounded by a geometrically configured cosmos of stupas, but also had colonnaded arrival halls to its east and west.

Ramathibodi II (r. 1491–1529), immediately after his coronation in 1491, initiated the construction of a spectacular triple-stupa funerary structure, Wat Si Sanpet, to contain the remains of his father and brother; the third structure, built by his son after his death, contained his own remains. These three stupas, with their tall spirals on bell-shaped bodies, copied the Pagan prototype. An arrival hall to the east and a cruciform temple to the west framed the centerpiece of this unique compound, which was also surrounded by numerous small stupas, each with its own small funeral temple for the extended families of the kings. As such, Wat Si Sanpet was a singularly royal precinct, and, atypically, had no residential or meditation halls for Buddhist monks.

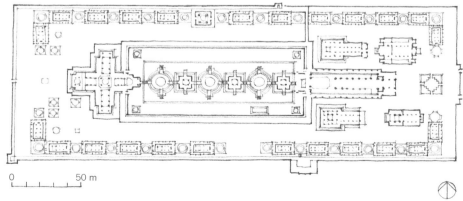

0   50 m

13.93 Site plan: Wat Si Sanpet, Ayutthaya temple complex

1600 CE

ARCHITECTURE OF THE EURASIAN POWER BLOC

In the 17th century, the Eurasian world, from Japan to western Europe, was a contiguous economic power bloc connected by well-established cross-country and coastal trade. From one end to the other, wealth and ideas traveled in the baggage or minds of traders, migrants, and armies. This was the Old World order that was now increasingly undermined by the newly arising, more efficient ocean trade. Eventually, sometime in the 19th century, the efficiencies of the ocean routes, the unprecedented advantage of untrammeled access to the American continents, and industrialization would make colonial Europe the unrivaled power of the world. Until then—until the complete collapse of the Silk Route—the power centers of Eurasia still dominated the old economies of the world.

Imagine a traveler in 1652 starting a trip through Europe and Asia to study the latest developments in the field of architecture. Starting in Japan, he is led through the Ninomaru Palace in Nijo Castle, located in the heart of Kyoto, the capital of shogunate Japan. He then visits the austere Katsura Imperial Villa and is introduced by his hosts to the newly developed intricacies of the Zen tea ceremony. Crossing into Korea, he visits the Gyeongbok Palace in Seoul, led there by a Mongolian commander serving in the Manchu empire, which had reduced Korea to a vassal state. Traveling into the heart of Manchuria through Mukden, its capital, he visits the then still relatively recent Forbidden City that is being refurbished by the new Manchu rulers who had just taken over Beijing. The times are just stable enough to travel to the nearby and equally forbidden Ming tombs. On the way, he discusses with his guides the pros and cons of the Ming Chinese international seafaring voyages, compared to the new ones being undertaken by the Europeans, and whether or not they should be resumed. He then works his way southward into the highland plateau of Tibet to visit the dramatic Potala Palace, built on a steep rocky crest for the fifth Dalai Lama, whose supporters had carved out an important political territory in the Lhasa Valley. After a tricky passage through the high Himalayas, he descends down into the fertile plains of the Ganges River. He now travels through areas controlled by the Timurid descendants of the Mongols, the Mughals of India.

He makes his way past Man Mandir, one of the grand 16th-century palaces of the city of Gwalior in central India, and on to Delhi and its expansive palaces. He inspects the great planned city, Fatehpur Sikri, capital of the Mughal Empire from 1571 to 1585, laid out by Akbar himself, and then heads up the Yamuna River to see the just-completed Illumined Tomb, later to be known as the Taj Mahal. Here he hears of new Portuguese settlers living in a small coastal town called Goa, having arrived there from the sea using a route never known before. He then heads north through the Khyber Pass to Kandahar and crosses into Persian territory, following the trade routes, where he sees the vast urban extension of Isfahan with its enormous city square, sumptuous mosques, and broad royal gardens. Here he meets traders from as far away as England, India, and China. From Isfahan, he crosses mountains and deserts into areas newly controlled by the Ottomans and, following the old Seljuk caravan routes, makes his way to Antioch on the Mediterranean, where he boards a ship to Constantinople. This city, taken by the Ottomans in 1453, is in the process of being rebuilt by its new lords. He admires the great Hagia Sophia, but his guide points out to him the superiority of the mosques recently built by Mimar Sinan (1489–1588), the great architect and engineer. The defeated Byzantine Church, he hears, has joined the Roman Catholic Church and is building Italianate churches in Kremlin, but is no threat to the Osmani. New Constantinople is thriving! But in the streets he also hears murmurs of competition from new ocean routes to the Indies.

It is in Constantinople that he meets the tribesmen of central Africa, and he learns of their conversion to Islam and the thriving trade they now carry on with the states of northern Africa. He makes a mental note to visit the great adobe mosques of which they speak.

From Constantinople he departs on a merchant ship for the somewhat faded port of Venice and is told there of economic hardships and of Dutch competition from the New World, in spite of which he is led to see the latest churches by one Andrea Palladio, a renowned scholar of antiquities, whose main projects he is told are on the mainland, built for the newly prosperous farming communities of Vicenza. He then follows a group of pilgrims to Rome, a city awash in Spanish gold and silver, mined from the Americas. The Pope is building a fancy new piazza on the old Roman Capitoline Hill to impress the visiting Holy Roman Emperor, Charles V. He is also still working hard on St. Peter's Basilica, determined to build a structure that exudes its claim as the sole center of Christendom, after the loss of Constantinople. Palazzi and churches galore are under construction, building the reputations of artists and architects. This is the Counter-Reformation world of the Italian Baroque, where the search for the orders of the Renaissance has given way to the Baroque pleasures of formal invention, and where the old papal authority of Rome is struggling to reinvent itself in the face of the challenges of the Protestants.

In Rome our traveler also visits Il Gesu, the church of the men called Jesuits, from whom he hears of their churches in the far-flung corners of the New World, and of the plight and devotion of the natives there. But our traveler also hears of newer claimants to the New World, so he heads to Amsterdam, a world metropolis with neither grand palaces nor dominating churches but with a bustling port, testimony to Dutch mercantile prowess. He visits the new city hall and bank with the world maps inlaid in marble on the floor. The Protestant movement is well under way here, and he takes time to visit his first Protestant churches, plain and austere, and is told of terrible religious wars.

Finally our visitor makes his way to France, where old money is still building rural mansions such as the Château de Chambord of Francis I on the Loire River, whose double helical staircase may have been designed by Leonardo da Vinci. Our traveler also visits the Place Royale in Paris, stopping along the way to admire the great cathedrals. And finally, he crosses the English Channel, and visits the newly built Banqueting House. It is one of the first buildings in England to be designed in the modern Italianate manner, and the structure represents an ambitious but—from the point of view of the Chinese, Mughals, Ottomans, and Dutch—still relatively marginal power, for England's major export commodity is still wool, and its foreign policy is still driven more by piracy than by politics.

Standing at the cliff shores of England, he looks across the Channel toward France. But then a galleon returning from the New World catches his eye; he looks across the Atlantic, and wonders what that world across the waters must be like.

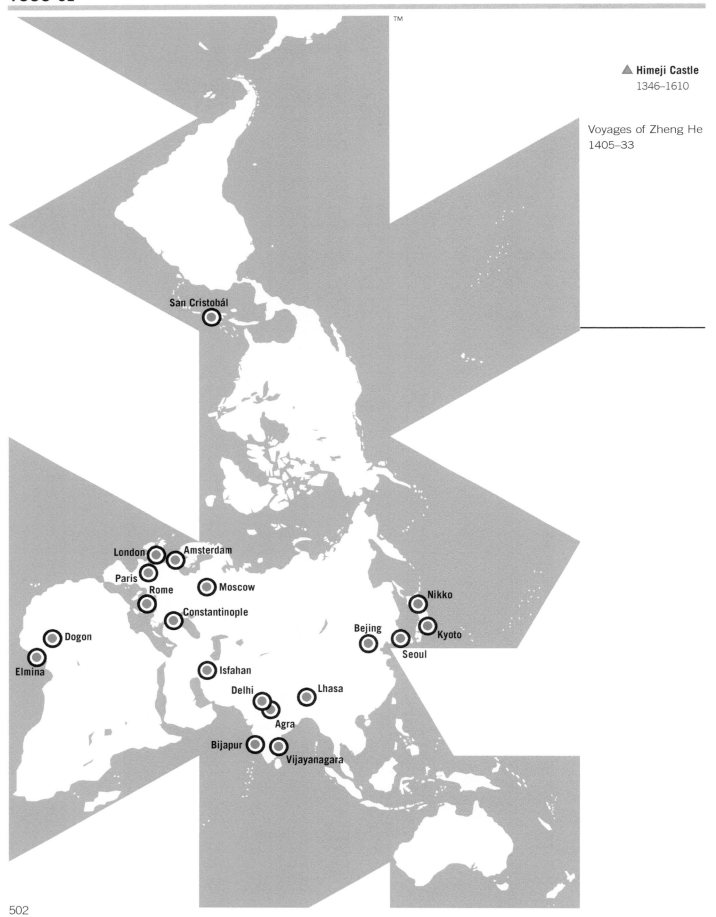

TM

▲ **Himeji Castle**
1346–1610

Voyages of Zheng He
1405–33

San Cristobál

London　Amsterdam
Paris
Rome　　Moscow
Constantinople
Nikko
Dogon
Bejing　　Kyoto
Elmina
Seoul
Isfahan
Delhi　　Lhasa
Agra
Bijapur
Vijayanagara

Momoyama Period
1573–1615

Tokugawa Shogunate
1603–1867

▲ Ryoanji Temple
ca. 1480

▲ Nijo Castle
1601–03 ▲ Katsura Rikyu
Begun ca. 1615

China: Ming Dynasty
1368–1644

▲ Ming Tombs
1409–1644

▲ Potala Palace
1649–94

Mughal Dynasty
1526–1858

Humanyun's Tomb ▲ ▲ Fatehpur Sikri
1565   1569–74

▲ Taj Mahal
1632–53

▲ Buland Darwaza
1573

▲ Gol Gumbaz
1627–56

1500 CE	1600 CE	1700 CE

Ottoman Empire
1281–1923

▲ Suleymaniye Mosque
1550–57

Russian Empire
1547–1917

▲ Cathedral of the Archangel Michael
1505–09 ▲ Church of the Ascension
1529–32

Migration and establishment of the Dogon people
15th and 16th centuries

Italy: Papal and Autonomous City-States
12th century to 1870

▲ St. Peter's Basilica
1506–1615

▲ Sant'Andrea al Quirinale
1658–70

▲ Campidoglio
Begun 1538

▲ Villa Rotunda
Begun 1566

▲ Il Gesù
1568–84

▲ Fort William
Begun 1699

▲ Elmina Castle
Begun 1482

▲ Santo Domingo
1547–60

Netherlands: United Provinces
1581–1795

▲ Zuiderkerk
1603–11

▲ Amsterdam Town Hall
Begun 1648

France: Bourbon Rule
1589–1792

▲ Place Royale
Begun 1605

England: Elizabethan Age
1558–1603

▲ Wollaton Hall
1580–88

▲ Banqueting House
1619–22

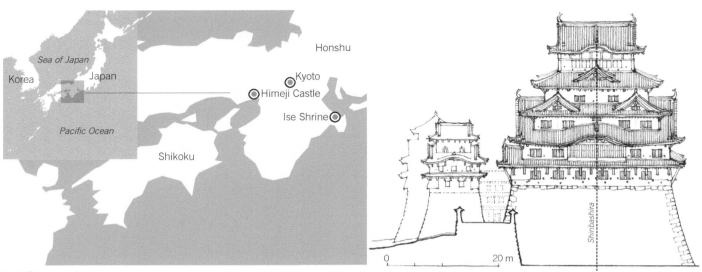

14.1 **Tokugawa Japan**

14.2 **Elevation of Great Tenshu, Himeji Castle**

TOKUGAWA SHOGUNATE

By the early 17th century, the shogun commanders had unified and pacified the country after a century of upheaval and civil war. They continued to patronize Zen Buddhism and reconstructed the major shrines and temples of Kyoto, such as Nishihonganji, Choin-in, and Kiyomizudera. In 1577, the shogun Oda Nobunaga (1534–82) sent his trusted lieutenant and subsequent shogun, Hideyoshi, to construct a castle in Himeji, some 150 kilometers west of Kyoto, to control the routes connecting the newly acquired western territories. Two gently sloping hills overlooking the north end of Japan's Inland Sea serve as the locus of the castle compound, which consists of a *honmaru* (inner citadel) and its defensive terrace. Resting on the top of a sloping stone base some 14 meters high, the main tower (known as the Great Tenshu) rises seven floors, a wooden skyscraper of its time. The entire structure is held together, from basement to the uppermost seventh story, by two massive pillars, which pass through and lock together each level of the building. The east pillar is made from a single trunk of silver fir 28.4 meters tall, while the second is a composite. This technology was taken from pagoda designs. Mastlike pillars at the center, known as the *shinbashira*, or "heart pillars," hold the structure together. The Himeji, in fact, is a type of bulked-up, inhabited pagoda—a symbolic allusion that certainly would not have escaped a visiting warlord.

Its exterior elevations consist of a carefully orchestrated rhythm of triangular and flaring gables, creating a visual signature for the Tenshu that eventually came to be imitated in all subsequent castles built in Japan. The walls are white, whereas the roofs are covered with gray tiles embellished with white plaster to secure them against the winds.

14.3 **Himeji Castle, Himeji, Japan**
The suffix -*jo* means "castle" in Japanese; Himeji Castle is thus known as Himeji-jo. (The suffix -*ji* means temple.)

In Japanese, the relationship between power and architecture is often codified in language. *Mon*, or gateway, is part of the word *kenmon*, which describes a person of authority. It literally means "power gate." The word *mikado* ("honorable gate") is used in reference to the emperor. A *kinmon*, or "prohibited gateway," could only be used in the imperial palace where access was restricted. By the 9th century CE, the building of gates had already been forbidden to people of low rank.

Nikko Toshogu

It is testament to the power and ambitions of the Tokugawa shoguns that Tokugawa Ieyasu, soon after his death, was deified as a tutelary kami, or a living spirit, of Japan in 1617. As such, Ieyasu was considered divine and on par with the emperor. As is appropriate to a kami, Ieyasu was buried high on the sacred mountain Nikko. His mausoleum and shrine, known as the Nikko Toshogu, was built by his grandson, Iemitsu (1604–51), the third and most powerful of the Tokugawa shoguns. The Toshogu occupies the side of a hill and was built in the *gongen-zukuri* form, with extended verandas carried on bracket sets and paired triangular and cusped gables at the front. The access gate opens onto an irregularly shaped compound with a series of subsidiary buildings. From there the path tends to the left before turning north again to face the main shrine somewhat up the side of the hill. A torii marks the path that leads to the first terrace. Another stair through another gateway leads to the second terrace. From there, twelve steep steps lead up to the Yomeimon, the gate of the inner shrine. This was as far as the daimyo—the feudal overlords—were allowed to go to pay obeisance to Ieyasu. Only priests and members of the Tokugawa family were allowed to enter the shrine itself, just as the imperial family had sole access to Ise's inner shrine.

In the Yomeimon, the visitor encounters a spectacular display of color and structure. Two layers of highly ornamented bracket sets support a balcony and a tiled Heian-style, hip-and-gable roof. The pristine surfaces of the frame, painted with white lime, are accented with gilded metalwork. Phoenixes, peonies, dragons in clouds, and imaginary

14.4 **Yomeimon, Toshogu Shrine, Nikko, Japan**

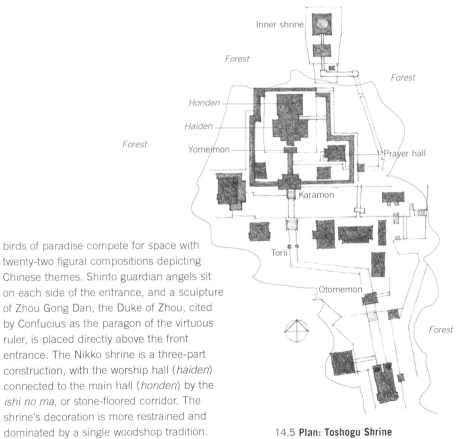

14.5 **Plan: Toshogu Shrine**

birds of paradise compete for space with twenty-two figural compositions depicting Chinese themes. Shinto guardian angels sit on each side of the entrance, and a sculpture of Zhou Gong Dan, the Duke of Zhou, cited by Confucius as the paragon of the virtuous ruler, is placed directly above the front entrance. The Nikko shrine is a three-part construction, with the worship hall (*haiden*) connected to the main hall (*honden*) by the *ishi no ma*, or stone-floored corridor. The shrine's decoration is more restrained and dominated by a single woodshop tradition. Forked finials (*chigi*) and billets (*katsuogi*) ride on the ridge of the *honden*, as was typical of all Shinto shrines.

Nijo-jo

If Himeji embodied the military authority of the shogun vertically, Ninomaru Palace (1569) in Nijo Castle (1601–3), located in the heart of Kyoto, was designed to stage that authority socially through a carefully orchestrated syncopation of waiting rooms and meeting halls. Built by the shogun Tokugawa Ieyasu, Nijo-jo was the palace where all the generals of the region had to come to pay obeisance. From 1624 to 1626, the palace was redesigned in preparation for a visit by the emperor Go Mizuno in 1626, the first visit by an emperor to a shogun's palace. The new design was coordinated by Nakai Masatomo, the master carpenter by title responsible for government projects in Kyoto.

A high stone wall with a moat surrounds the 500-by-400-meter site and contains two compounds, each within its own perimeter walls: one for a castle (now destroyed) and the other for the palace. The palace was capped by a series of massive clay-tiled roofs joined at various angles. Most of the woodwork was left unpainted. Entry is through a gate in the southern compound wall that leads into a courtyard with two further gateways, one to the stroll garden on the left and the other to the palace, directly ahead but just off axis. The wall behind the gate steps back, suggesting the presence of hidden depths to the court, whereas the wall to the garden is angled, using perspective to create the illusion of a larger space. The Tozamurai (waiting rooms and government

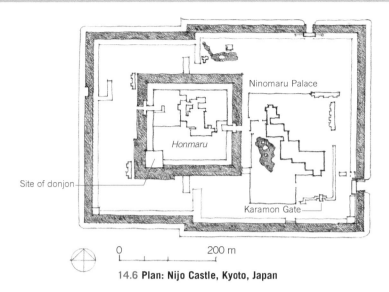

14.6 **Plan: Nijo Castle, Kyoto, Japan**

offices), the Shikidai (secondary audience space), and the Ohiroma (main audience space) are the palace's three main buildings. Added to these are the Kuroshoin, meant for informal audiences with the shogun, and the Shiroshoin, the royal residence. There was also a service building in the back (at the north) with kitchen and baths, connected to the main structure by a network of corridors. In plan the palace functions as a series of layers organized by a diagonal spine—a corridor that defines the edge between the garden and the internal spaces.

The main spaces of the four buildings are connected to this corridor. Movable screens can be used to close or open any part of the palace or its corridors. Every plank of

this garden corridor was fitted with tiny iron springs that distinctly creaked, even at the lightest of steps, so that when the screens were closed the occupants of the internal spaces would always know if anyone was outside, or if the shogun approached.

A visitor entering through the Kuramayose would be brought to one of the three waiting rooms of the Tozamurai. With the view of the garden screened off, the visitor would be confronted with a large painting of life-size crouching tigers and panthers lurking in bamboo groves. Here the hustle and bustle outside could be heard but not seen as the visitor waited to be called for his audience. This was the theater of intimidation. Most visitors would have their audience in the

14.7 **Garden entrance to Nijo Castle**

14.8 **Garden of Nijo Castle**

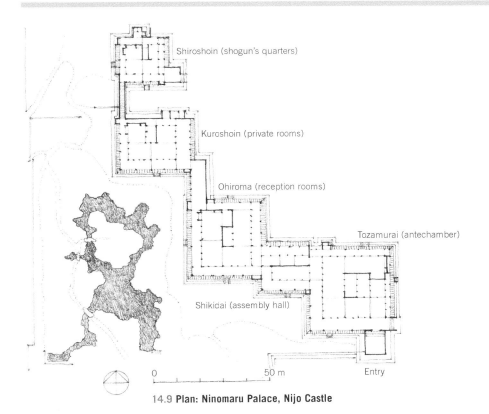

14.9 Plan: Ninomaru Palace, Nijo Castle

Shiroshoin (shogun's quarters)

Kuroshoin (private rooms)

Ohiroma (reception rooms)

Tozamurai (antechamber)

Shikidai (assembly hall)

0   50 m   Entry

14.10 Ninomaru Palace

Shikidai with one of the shogun's councilors. The room, long and narrow and offering only a partial view of the garden, focused on the councilor, who would sit at one end. Behind him the knotted branches of two large pine trees, evergreen and symbolic of the perennial authority of the shogun, were painted with bold strokes jumping freely across the structural elements in defiance of any containing frame. The three spaces of the main audience hall, the Ohiroma, were organized in an L-shape to build in visual hierarchy. The visiting councilors sat in the *gendan no ma* (lower chamber), separated from the *jodan no ma* (upper chamber) by a single step. Lower-ranking visitors sat out of sight in the third chamber. The shogun entered from the north and sat in the middle of the northern half of the *jodan no ma*, facing south. There was thus considerable distance behind him and the visitors.

Behind and to his east was the *chigidana* ("staggered shelves"), gilded in gold, with a painting marking the place of authority. Directly behind him was a display space with a twisted bonsai pine, its highest branch rising vertically on center. When all the screens were shut, backlight from the sun would illuminate the shogun against the screen. Directly to the shogun's left, on axis, was an elaborately decorated door; above him, the coffered roof was raised; and to his right, if the screens were open, he would be able to see the island in the middle of the lake—the only spot in the entire palace from which this was possible. Thus, although the shogun sat on the floor on a mat at a spot that was not distinguished in any way, it was staged from every direction so that the moment he occupied it, his significance immediately became clear.

14.11 Suminoe pine, Katsura Imperial Villa, near Kyoto, Japan

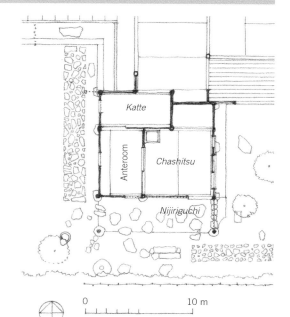

14.12 Plan: Taian Teahouse, Yamazaki, Japan

Katsura Rikyu (Katsura Imperial Villa)

In contrast to the Shogun military commanders who, in developing their political ambitions, created sumptuous displays of power, the older aristocratic families, now largely disempowered, began to adopt an introspective and pseudo-rustic aesthetic influenced by the ideals of Zen Buddhism. The most celebrated example of this new aesthetic—now considered by many modern architects to be the essence of Japanese architecture—is the Katsura Detatched Palace, also known as the Katsura Imperial Villa. It was built by the nobleman Hichijonomiya Toshihito (1579–1629) and his son Toshitada (1619–62). Underlying the design is the ceremonial teahouse. In the 17th century, serving and drinking tea had become the center of lavish rituals at courtly ceremonies, with the focus on the display of quality tea ware and the presentation ceremony often upstaging the tea itself. In the latter part of the 16th century, Sen no Rikyu (1522–91), a patron of the Zen monks in Ginkakuji, transformed the ceremony into a simple, precisely choreographed, and highly personalized exercise known as *wabi-cha*. His famous dictum was "one moment, one meeting." The goal of his ceremony, which contrasted with the extravagance of the shoguns, was to be free from all distractions—past and future—and to lead to a state of immediacy. Rikyu designed one of the first known neo-rustic teahouses, Taian, in Yamazaki, south of Kyoto, but the form found

its ultimate expression at the Katsura Imperial Villa, a 7-hectare estate on the western bank of the Katsura River, located in a suburb of Kyoto. The main building comprises three interlinked *shoins* (or sections) referred to as the Old, Middle, and New Shoins, staggered at the western edge of an irregularly shaped pond with several islands. The Old Shoin, farthest to the north, was built by Prince Toshihito and the other two by his son, Prince Toshitada. The New Shoin, along with a

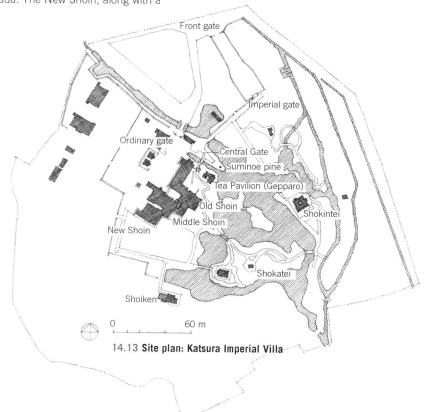

14.13 Site plan: Katsura Imperial Villa

14.14 Garden gate, Katsura Imperial Villa

special gate and access path, was built on the occasion of the Emperor Go Mizuno's visit to Katsura in 1663. Seven teahouses are distributed in the garden in a semicircular arc and linked by a stroll path. In its outlines, therefore, Katsura is nothing more than a nobleman's country villa with a stroll garden, but it was also an ideological statement about the superiority of aristocratic society.

The palace has two main entry gates. The entrance into Katsura is through a simple bamboo gate located at the far end of an austere but immaculately constructed bamboo fence. Nothing of the interior is visible from the outside. Even upon entering, the view is carefully screened by a hedge. Katsura's next gate was built for imperial visits. Yet it, too, was patently unassuming and opened onto a straight, unedged gravel path lined with trees, leading to yet another gate. From there the gravel path turns right for 50 meters or so, the longest stretch of straight path at Katsura. Although the entire garden is to the left and the villa ahead, the view down this imperial approach is carefully screened by bushes and trees. Small openings reveal views of the garden, a glimpse of the main teahouse, a look at the boathouse, a bridge over a water view. When a visitor reaches the villa, there is a sharp turn to the left and a view along a promontory, edged by a thick hedge, with a miniaturized Suminoe pine tree. The framed view of the tree draws attention to, and blocks the view of, the garden beyond. The miniaturization of the tree also makes the promontory seem longer than it is and introduces the notion of self-consciously constructed symbolism in the landscape.

Entry

Tea Pavilion (Gepparo)

Old Shoin

Middle Shoin

Music room

New Shoin

14.15 Plan: Katsura Imperial Villa

14.16 Stepping-stones, Katsura Imperial Villa, near Kyoto, Japan

To the right of the promontory, over an arched wood and earth bridge, is the Central Gate, a visitor's first encounter with the architecture. A simple freestanding wall with a rectangular opening extends out to the west from a subsidiary building which contains the commoner's entrance. The gravel path terminates with a single large, uncut stone at the threshold, followed by four dressed stones arranged in a square. From there, a loose arrangement of uncut stepping-stones crisscrosses the straight path made from cut stones and signals one of the signature themes of Katsura's walkways: the studied orchestration of stepping-stones to generate a haptic and tactile experience. From the Central Gate, stepping-stones lead to the entrance of the Old Shoin, called the Imperial Carriage Stop. Here, another freestanding wall with an opening, projecting out from the Old Shoin to the north, offers an alternative route, a second carefully staged path leading east to the Gepparo, the teahouse closest to the *shoins*. The stepping-stones winding through the opening have the quality of mysterious footprints and invite the visitor to follow them. The final step up into the Old Shoin is another uncut stone dramatically set against the straight lines of the wooden steps of the entrance porch. Another of Katsura's signature themes is the elaboration of the villa as a simple hut. Every entrance into the villa is from large uncut stones, and every exterior post on the garden side sits directly on a stone foundation. All the wooden posts and beams were left unpolished, some with their bark intact.

The geometry that governs the plan of the three *shoins* is derived from the dimensions of the tatami and the sliding shoji screens covered with translucent rice paper. The spaces are orchestrated as a series of interconnected rooms, with all the important rooms facing east onto the garden. The supporting rooms are to the west and are connected to secondary structures. The Middle and New Shoins are connected by an intermediate section called the Music Room. An external veranda runs along the eastern edge of the villa, edged by sliding screen doors that can be opened and shut to modulate the light and to connect the exterior and the interior.

The spatial and visual focus of the Old Shoin is an east-west cross-axis formed by the pantry, the Spear Room, and its main space (the "second room") with an external bamboo deck called the Moon-Viewing Platform. (The Katsura River was known as a scenic place for moon viewing in August.) A miniature stone pagoda in a clearing on the southern edge of the Island of Immortals is the view's stable point amid a dense arboreal landscape. Its focus is the still water of the pond, which at night reflects the rising moon in the east, and by day, the trees along its irregular edges. In autumn the trees are ablaze with color, and in winter, white with snow.

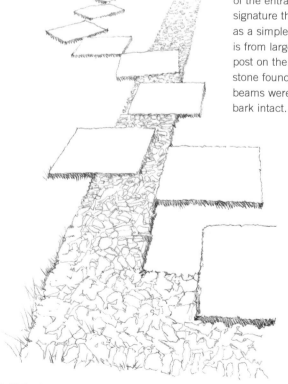

14.17 Garden path, Katsura Imperial Villa

14.18 Detail: Katsura Imperial Villa

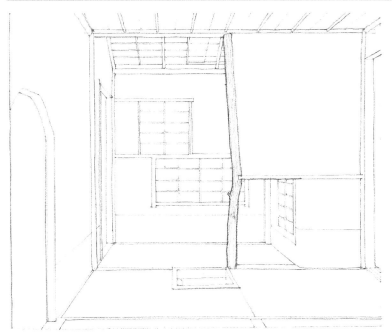

14.19 Interior of Tea Pavilion (Shokintei), Katsura Imperial Villa

14.20 Ceiling structure of the Gepparo, Katsura Imperial Villa

Katsura's "main event" is the stroll garden. Its design is credited to Kobori Enshu (1579–1647), a tea master and garden designer, though this is not certain. Many walks are possible. The main walk circumambulates the pond in a clockwise direction, beginning to the north of the Old Shoin, winding around the shore, to the main teahouse (the Shokintei), on to the large island with the Shoiken and Orindo teahouses, then across the riding ground and moss garden, and back to the Middle Shoin. It is the journey, rather than the destination, that is important.

Much of the path is made of stepping-stones of uncut rock. Although each stone is completely horizontal and never more than a comfortable stride from the next, they do not form a continuous walkway and can suddenly make unexpected twists and turns. This forces visitors to become aware of not only where they are walking, but of the very act of walking. When the dressed stones of the straight paths surrounding the *shoins* meet the stepping-stones, the latter dance around and through the former with a studied irreverence. But when they encounter the cascade of pebbles—the "sand" of the shore—they march through them like a determined walker on the beach. Sometimes they seem to have inherent purposes: the stepping-stones march straight across the

wet moss garden next to the Middle Shoin; whereas the straight path is forced to skirt around the edge. At other times, they seem more functional. Along the way, stone lanterns mark places of rest. One of the most famous uses of such a lantern is at the terminus of the spit of land that projects into the pond. The lantern, known as the Night-Rain Lantern, marks the terminus of the path not to be taken.

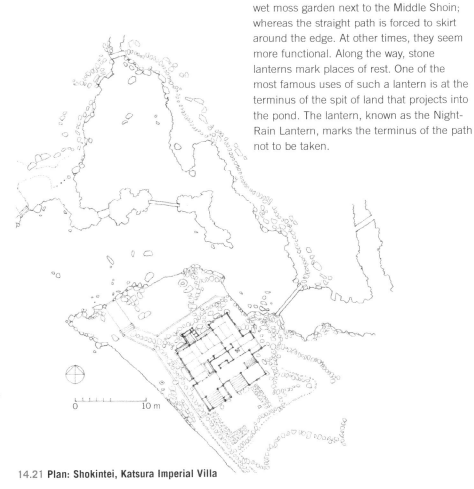

14.21 Plan: Shokintei, Katsura Imperial Villa

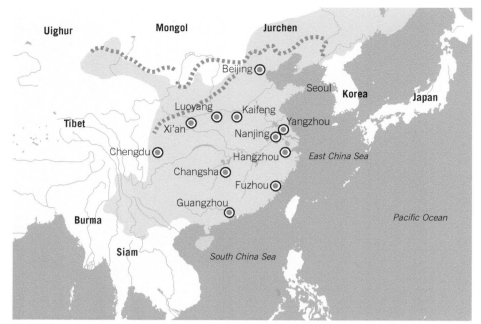

14.22 Ming dynasty China

The first Ming tomb built here was that of the third Ming emperor, Zhu Di, known as the Yongle Emperor, in 1409. Zhu Di moved the Ming capital to Beijing and built the Forbidden City. The Ming, continuing T'ang and Zhou funerary practices, designed their tombs to consist of three parts—a long Spirit Path leading up to the tomb, a shrine for ceremonies and sacrifices to the dead, and the burial mound itself. However, unlike their predecessors, the Song, the Ming did not build a separate Spirit Path for each tomb; instead, they clustered all their tombs in a single valley off one Spirit Path with a single approach. The Ming also did away with the practice of sacrificing for the emperor's "accompanying" concubines and servants and therefore did not need a separate chamber for them.

MING TOMBS

So efficient was the Ming bureaucracy that the fact that the reportedly indolent and pleasure-seeking seventh Ming emperor, Wanli (1573–1620), seems not to have affected the prosperity of his empire. Official ceremonies and presentations were simply made to an empty throne in his stead. A large proportion of Wanli's time, along with an estimated eight million *taels* of silver, was spent in the design and construction of his tomb, which began in 1585, when he was only twenty-two years old. Much more than personalized egocentric attempts to guarantee an afterlife, tombs, and in particular royal tombs, were an integral part of the Chinese cosmology. Spirits of dead ancestors of even the common people had to be fed and cared for, or else they were liable to visit misfortune upon future generations. The emperor's death, however, was particularly special, as he became part of heaven itself, and his tomb's architecture represented that transition. Many of China's royal tombs, going back to that of the First Emperor, Shi Huangdi, have still not been excavated.

The thirteen Ming tombs, of which only Wanli's has been excavated, are among the most famous and best preserved. They are clustered in the valley of the Tianshou Mountains, about 80 kilometers northwest of Beijing.

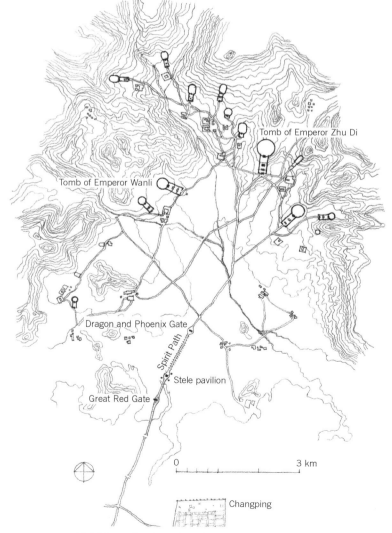

14.23 Area plan: Imperial Ming Tombs, near Beijing

The Yongle Emperor appropriated an area of about 330 square kilometers, which was defined by a perimeter wall that encompassed a large area, including a valley, the base hills of a mountain range, and rivulets feeding into a river running to the south. This area was protected by a prohibition against the cultivation or cutting of trees; a village was established near the entrance to house the people employed to maintain the land. About 1 kilometer beyond the *pai lou* was the Great Red Gate, the official entrance to the tomb grounds. (*Pai lou* is the generic term for gateways commemorating people who have led virtuous lives.) The building, square in plan, has a solid base cut through with tall tunnel vaults in its axes that, at their center, frame a huge 10-meter-tall monolithic stele held up on the back of a tortoise. Poems, written by later emperors in praise of their ancestors, were carved on the stele. At this gate, the emperor dismounted and proceeded on foot. Just to the side of the gate, there was a pavilion, no longer extant, where the emperor and his retinue of about 1,000 attendants rested and changed into the appropriate robes. From there, the emperor began his long walk down the Spirit Path.

As in earlier tombs, the main feature of the Spirit Path is its array of statues of mythical and real beasts and eminent nobles and generals, aligned on both sides. Twelve pairs of animals and six pairs of men symbolize an eternal guard, arrayed in the same manner in which the honor guard was prepared in the Forbidden City for ceremonial occasions. The animals are in pairs, one resting and one standing. At the end of this segment of the Spirit Path there is a small three-portal gate, the center portal of which is blocked to prevent the passage of evil spirits.

After passing through the sides of the gate, the Spirit Path continues in a gentle curve to the left and leads to a triple bridge across the river, straight to the Yongle Emperor's tomb. Subsidiary paths to the other tombs fan out from the main path like the branches of a tree. The tombs are a long distance from the main entrance, a walk of almost 6 kilometers from the *pai lou*. This walk, through a flat plain filled with carefully chosen fragrant trees, was often the subject of painting and poetry. As in the Forbidden City and Chinese imperial architecture in

14.24 **Drum Tower of Spirit Path, Ming Tombs**

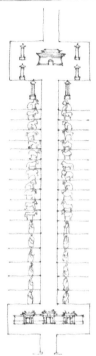

14.25 **Spirit Path, Ming Tombs**

14.26 **Spirit Path, Ming Tombs**

general, the path, as a monumental extension of space in the horizontal axis, was made at a scale appropriate only to the emperors. The horizontal extension of space was considered to be the measure of a building's significance. The Spirit Path thereby repeats the axis of the Forbidden City. But in another sense, it is the Forbidden City, with its fake mountain at the northern end, that copies the sacred axis embodied in the Spirit Path.

Conceptually, the Ming tombs are a part of the same spatial-symbolic order of the Forbidden City and the Altar of Heaven. This order is in part feng shui but is mostly a spatialization of a social and spiritual order focused on the emperor; the symbolic order of Beijing was designed to enable the institution of the emperor, as a governmental and spiritual center, to be functional and visible. In the tombs, however, there were no quotidian needs, no citizenry to be governed. Here, it was only the reigning emperor and his relationship with the ancestors, represented in the city by the empty space of the Altar of Heaven, which had to be spatialized, making for the purest representation of the intersection of the terrestrial world and the heavenly one. Each succeeding emperor was expected to visit the tombs of his predecessors on each of the anniversaries of their deaths. Site selection was critical. The Yongle Emperor picked a site for his tomb that nestled at the base of the intersection of two low mountain ranges at the end of a hilly spur that points into a valley. This fit the dictates of feng shui, which required that two mountain ranges (the tiger and the dragon) provide a protective backdrop to the site to block evil northern spirits. (In the Forbidden City, the mountain is represented by the small artificial hill just beyond the north wall.)

14.27 **Axial approach to the Ming Tombs, near Beijing**

14.28 **Underground chamber, Tomb of Emperor Wanli, Ming Tombs**

As he did at the Altar of Heaven, a visiting emperor would have approached the site from the south, the direction of supplication. The entrance was marked by a stone ceremonial gate with five portals, composed of six monolithic columns adorned with animals derived from syncretic sources representative of the Ming Chinese world—native Chinese, Buddhist, and Indic. Unlike the Chinese convention that gave every important building or structure a name that was then written on a tablet over its central entrance, the tablet on this particular gate was left empty, for it would have been inappropriate, so it was held, for mere mortals to announce the presence of the "sons of heaven."

14.29 **Stele guarding the entrance to the tomb of Emperor Wanli**

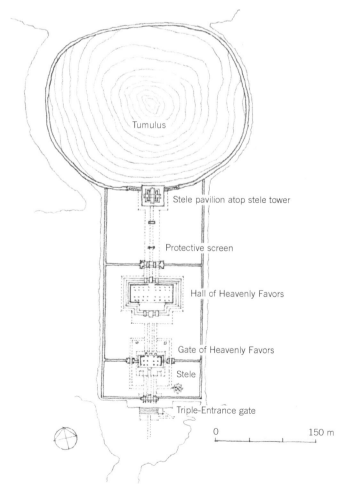

14.30 **Plan: Tomb of the Yongle Emperor (Changling)**

Tumulus

Stele pavilion atop stele tower

Protective screen

Hall of Heavenly Favors

Gate of Heavenly Favors

Stele

Triple-Entrance gate

0   150 m

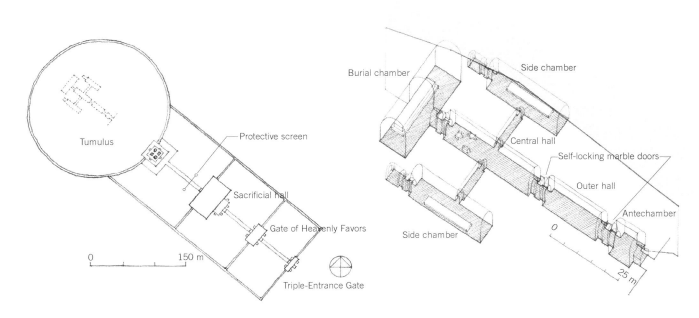

14.31 Plan: Tomb of the Emperor Wanli (Dingling)

14.32 Underground chambers at Dingling

The thirteen tombs consist of a sequence of rectangular enclosures for rituals and sacrifices, terminating in a round or oval burial mound. The enclosures signify the terrestrial and the circular mound, the heavenly. Where the wall of the last enclosure and the wall of the circular enclosure meet, one finds a Stele Tower with a pavilion on top of the base that gives access to the mound. Most of the tombs have only one or two enclosures, and only the largest three—Changling, Yongling, and Dingling—have three.

Changling, the oldest and largest, begins with a triple-entrance gate leading into an enclosure that originally held a structure in which the emperor and his retinue could adjust their clothes. This led through a gate into the main court for sacrifices, which contained the Hall of Heavenly Favors—almost identical to the Hall of Supreme Harmony in the Forbidden City—enabling the emperor to be honored in death as he was in life. Three marble terraces support the great hall (67 by 30 meters), with three stairs leading to it. Inside, sixty columns, each nearly 13 meters high and made from a single trunk of old-growth timber called *machilus nanmu*, support a double-eaved

roof without any diagonal struts. The *dougong* on the exterior is ornamental, not structural. The coffered ceiling is painted in blue, green, red, and gold. The Hall of Heavenly Favors and the Hall of Supreme Harmony are the two largest halls in China.

The tomb mounds are defined by fortified earthen mounds with 3-meter-wide walls, buttressed on the outside to hold in the earth with no visible entry markers. They are planted with thujas and oak trees (since the roots are believed to be able to nourish the dead). At the apex of the hill, one finds a small tumulus in the shape of a cone or long ridge. The tumulus is only representational; the actual tomb is far below the surface. Seen from the approach axis, the stele gate, the mound, and the mountain profiles are all part of one symbolic entity. The tumulus of Emperor Wanli's tomb, for example, lines up directly with the peak beyond. The approach to the offering table, which stands just in front of the base of the stele tower, is not flat but actually a series of transitions marked by gates and thresholds.

The tomb of Emperor Wanli, located 27 meters below the surface, consists of three sacrificial enclosures and four interconnected barrel-vaulted chambers. Three run parallel

to each other and one at right angles at the head, and that is the main chamber. Whereas the side chambers were empty and probably intended for concubines and family members, the central one contained three thrones for ritual objects. The burial casket of the emperor, the empress, and the highest concubine (elevated to empress when her son became the next emperor) were found intact in the main burial vault.

The vaults were all made of pure white marble, polished smooth. This tradition, which goes back to the tombs of the Han emperors, shows that although the Chinese had certainly mastered masonry skills, they chose to use them only for their tomb structures. One of the few places where a stone vault was used in a building above the terrain was in the Fasting Palace of the Altar of Heaven, where the emperor prepared himself for the all-important calendrical rituals. That room was, in essence, a type of tomb, for the emperor was expected to use it to purify himself through abstinence and fasting.

14.33 Potala Palace, Lhasa, Tibet (China)

POTALA PALACE

Buddhism was introduced into Tibet by Mahayana monks travelling from India and Nepal in the 8th century CE. By the 10th century, Nepal had begun to thrive as a regional power, capturing significant territories in Mongolia and China. The growth of Tibet was, however, checked by the Chinese well into the 15th century. Although China's non-Han dynasties—the Liao and, in particular, the Mongol Yuan—supported Tibetan Buddhism, they made sure the Tibetans were politically subservient. The Ming paid only lip service to Tibetan Buddhism since their focus was on the revival of a Confucian and Daoist state. As a consequence, Tibetan Buddhists split into a number of competing sects, variously identified by the color of their habit as the red, white, and yellow sects. But when the Ming dynasty began to lose power, the Uigher Mongols under Altan Khan, the descendants of the erstwhile Yuan dynasty, converted to the Tibetan yellow sect; after that, Tibetan Buddhism or Lamaism spread quickly among the Mongols of Central Asia. In 1641, Altan Khan's grandson, Gushri Khan, defeated all the other Tibetan sects and proclaimed Ngawang Losang Gyatso (1617–82), the fifth Dalai Lama, not only the spiritual head of Tibetan Buddhism but also, for the first time in Tibetan history, the political head of Tibet. Just then the Mongolian Manchus had taken over from the Ming, and one of their first diplomatic acts was to invite the fifth Dalai Lama to the Chinese court, where he was received with full honors.

One of the fifth Dalai Lama's first acts was to establish a new capital and build a new palace that was identifiable as the seat of both the spiritual and political power of the Buddhist world. This was the Potala Palace, a vast and majestic palace-mausoleum located on a hill in the middle of the valley of Lhasa, Tibet's "forbidden city."

The Lhasa River is a tributary of the Tsangpo, which becomes the Brahmaputra when it swings south around the Himalayas and into India. At an elevation of 130 meters above the valley, two steep, rocky outcrops tower above a widened riverbed at the bottom of a ravine. On the higher and larger of these, known as Red Hill, sits the Potala Palace, 360 meters long, 110 meters wide, and reaching a maximum height of 170 meters. It is oriented east-west, with the front facing south toward the inner city. The setting is dramatic. A jagged towering mountain range forms a towering bowl. In the middle, the rocky outcrop and the swiftly flowing Lhasa are at the center of what literally seems like the roof of the world.

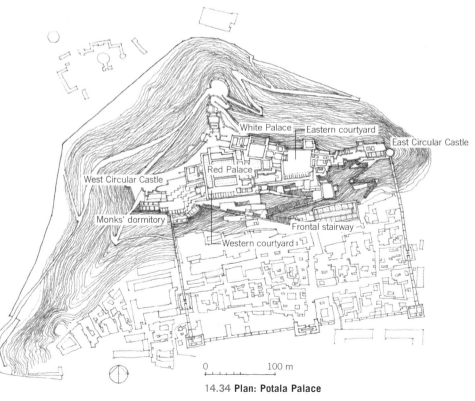

14.34 Plan: Potala Palace

The Potala Palace is the sacred center of Tibetan worship. It signifies Mount Meru, the conceptual organizing center of the Buddhist cosmos. As such, the palace is just as much a pilgrimage site as a royal residence.

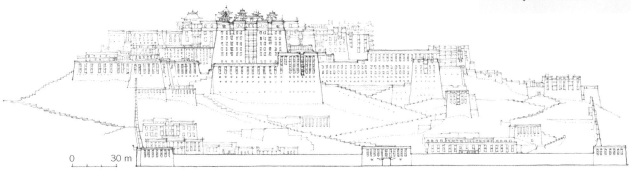

14.35 **South elevation: Potala Palace**

Since it was meant to be defensible, the palace's primary massing is that of a fort. Thick, battered brick walls, painted white, rise steeply from the rock surface in a series of terraces that take over the entire summit of the Red Hill. The walls step back and forth to accommodate the changing contours and to generate openings for the access paths.

Solid and impenetrable at the bottom, the walls' higher reaches are punctuated by dark windows, which are few and simple at first but, at higher elevations, become larger and more richly embellished. The walls are topped by a prominent red coping. The visual terminus is a series of small, golden, Chinese-style roofs that are not so large as to be the solitary focus but prominent enough to ensure that the eye comes to rest on them, providing a speck of metallic brilliance in a landscape dominated by gray rock. Long ramps, visible from the distance, wind their way up the side of the hill. Their slow ascents mark them as self-conscious processional paths, leading to a place of pilgrimage.

The current palace was built in two major phases. First the main ramparts and the western part of the main palace, known as the White Palace, were built. This was partially rebuilt and a Red Palace was constructed that became the primary residence of the Dalai Lamas.

The White Palace houses large ceremonial halls for prayers, rooms for visiting dignitaries, and offices, while the Red Palace houses the audience hall as well as burial stupas for the dalai lamas. The roof of the palace opens onto a flat terrace where there are Chinese-style pavilions, gilded in copper, one for each dalai lama. At the foot of the Potala Palace, a square walled enclosure contains a network of governmental buildings.

Access to the Potala Palace begins at the end of the lower quadrangle, at a column erected to mark the completion of the Red Palace. The first ramp leads to subsidiary structures in the west, but then it switches back and heads up toward the White Palace. After another switchback, it comes to a point where the entrances into the palace, which have been hidden until now, suddenly reveal themselves, nestled between the staggers of the walls. A stair to the east leads to the entrance of the White Palace and another, directly opposite, to the Red Palace. The high walls of Potala Palace itself are at hand, and for the pilgrim this is the first arrival threshold; several more follow. The usual entrance is through the White Palace. A tall rectilinear opening, with three open stories above, leads into a dark space with four columns.

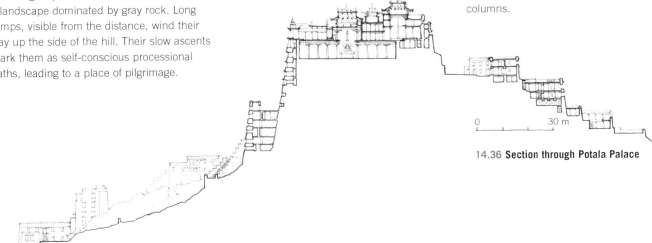

14.36 **Section through Potala Palace**

14.37 **Potala Palace, Lhasa, Tibet (China)**

From there the path turns left, proceeds down a narrow corridor, turns right, and arrives at a small curved court, where the second threshold to the palace is located. A flight of stairs and a two-column vestibule lead to another corridor, from which a left turn drops one into the eastern courtyard, the ceremonial arrival space of the Potala Palace. This is the pilgrims' third and final threshold. This courtyard is surrounded by a two-story enclosure and dominated by the canted mass of the White Palace at the northwestern corner. A central stairway leads into the six levels of the White Palace, highlighted by characteristic Tibetan windows made from brightly painted wooden frames and elaborately carved sunscreens. The elaboration and size of the windows increase with each story, the highest one terminating in the cornice. Internally, the main structural frame is made from wood, with rooms organized around a courtyard on the upper levels. This mode of construction and elevational representation is typical of Tibetan architecture, a consequence of its long intercourse with Nepalese architecture and culture.

The Red Palace contains pillared prayer halls and the salt-dried and embalmed remains of eight dalai lamas, marked by eight white stupas called *chortens*. The largest and most elaborate of these is the stupa for the fifth Dalai Lama.

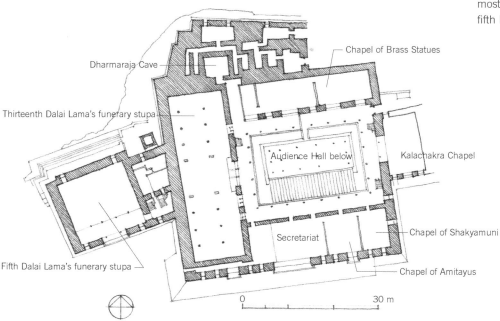

14.38 **Plan: Third floor of the Red Palace, Potala Palace**

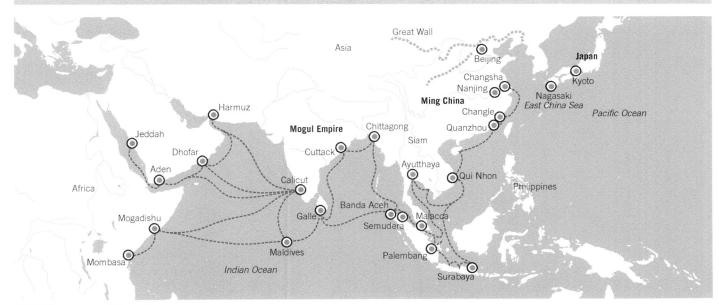

14.39 The voyages of Zheng He

VOYAGES OF ZHENG HE

The first Ming emperor, Taizu, also called the Hongwu Emperor, sponsored a series of naval voyages between 1405 and 1433, with at least seven of those traversing the "western ocean," which could be either the Indian or Pacific Ocean. The voyages were commanded by Zheng He (1371–1435), a Muslim eunuch from China's Yunnan Province whose father and grandfather had made the hajj to Mecca and who, therefore, knew of Islamic cartographic advances. Zheng He's mission was not economic but diplomatic, seeking to establish ties with other nations. Some of the voyages had as many as three hundred ships and 27,000 sailors in all, and they reached as far as Mombasa in Africa. Fantastic descriptions of the fleet are still evident in temples in Ayutthaya in Thaland.

The Chinese economy was integrally tied to trade, and these voyages were meant to expand China's trading horizon. The Chinese also traded with the Dutch, who controlled Java, as well as with the Spanish and Portuguese. It is estimated that as much as one-third of all the silver extracted from South America was brought to China to pay for porcelain, silk, and other luxury goods. To feed this export economy, huge kilns were built at Jingdezhen in Jiangxi Province, which produced an estimated 100,000 small ceramic pieces and 50,000 larger pieces annually. Still preserved as ceiling decorations in the Santos Palace in Lisbon are 260 Chinese plates and bowls.

In 1449 the Mongolians ambushed an expedition led by Emperor Zhengdong, wiped out the Chinese army, and captured the emperor. Stability returned only in 1457 when Zhengdong recovered the throne. The Mongol threat, yet once again, shook the Ming court. They resolved to disband the expensive explorative sea voyages and to concentrate instead on fortifying against the Mongolians. In 1474 the Ming general Wang Yueh insisted on and received approval to extensively rebuild the Great Wall. Almost forty thousand troops were set to work to build not only vast segments of the wall but also its accompanying fortifications, signal towers, and stockades. The Ming Great Wall occupies the rest of the last range of hills before the mountains level off in the northern deserts of Mongolia. And so the long-term possibilities of Zheng He's naval expeditions were traded for the immediate and urgent securing of the Great Wall system.

14.40 Ming dynasty treasure ship in comparison with Vasco da Gama's *São Gabriel*

14.41 Development of the Mughal Empire

14.42 Humayun's Tomb, Delhi, India

MUGHALS

The Delhi sultanates, with their various competing interests, fell prey to an outside conqueror, Babur, a descendant of the Timur line. He established the Mughal dynasty which, by the time of his death in 1530, stretched from the Deccan to Turkestan. Babur's oldest son, Humanyun, lost the throne in 1540 to Sher Shah Sur, an Afghan and former ally who, though he ruled for only fifteen years, established a centralized system of administration on the foundations of which later Mughals expanded. Humanyun regained the Delhi throne by 1555 but died a year later. He was succeeded by the eighteen-year old Jalal-ud-Din Akbar (1556–1605), who laid the foundation of—and consolidated—the Mughal Empire. His grandson Khurram Shah Jahan (1628–57) was the beneficiary. The former was an uneducated and idiosyncratic idealist, the latter an indolent and cultured aesthete; both used their vast wealth for two of the finest architectural creations of South Asia: the city of Fatehpur Sikri and the Taj Mahal.

Humayun's Tomb

Humayun's principal wife, Begai Begum, brought in Mirak Mirza Ghiyas, a Persian architect living in Bukhara, to design her husband's tomb (1570). It was located to the east of a tomb designed for one of Sher

Shah's noblemen in 1547. Humayun's Tomb was to become the prototype that influenced the design of the Taj Mahal some fifty years later. Faced with red sandstone, it sits in the middle of a large, square garden divided into quadrants by causeways, which are further divided into nine smaller sections in the manner of the *chahar baghor* four-garden plan of Persian provenance. Set into the axis of each causeway is a water channel with small, square lily ponds at the intersections. The eastern wall was built directly on the Yamuna River. (Over time, the river moved farther to the east.) Its main gate was on the south, although entrances were built in the center of all four walls. The tomb has two platforms, a low first platform with chamfered ends, followed by the second main platform, which contains secondary arcaded and vaulted chambers.

Stairs from the central arch lead to the upper platform. The tomb itself is an octagon with eight surrounding chambers on two levels. A bulbous dome, covered in marble, sits on a high drum. Passageways connect all the chambers, an unusual feature that may be associated with the Sufi practice of circumambulating the burial chamber. A tombstone marker indicating the actual tombstone below sits under the main dome and is raised on gigantic piers. The entire interior is plastered and painted in white and a delicate orange-red that closely matches the red sandstone used on the exterior.

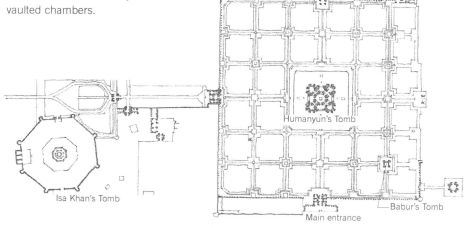

14.43 Plan: Humayun's Tomb

0   200 m

Fatehpur Sikri

Begun in 1561 and abandoned a mere fourteen years later due to lack of water, Fatehpur Sikri's origins lie in Akbar's close connections with Sufiism. Salim Chisti, a Sufi mystic, lived on a stony escarpment 48 kilometers west of the capital, Agra. Akbar traveled to Salim Chisti on foot to beg for the gift of a son, who was born a year later. To give thanks and to live in close proximity to his mentor, Akbar decided to build a new mosque and palace complex on the long and narrow stony escarpment, known then simply as *Sikri* (from *shukri*, or "thanksgiving" in Persian).

The first structure built at Fatehpur Sikri was the Jami Masjid, or Friday Mosque. Because the mosque had to be oriented due west, it is at an angle to the escarpment. The multiple courts of the royal palace that were built next were also are aligned with the Jami Masjid rather than with the escarpment, so that the whole complex staggers down the axis of the ridge. The spatial implications resulting from the shift in orientation are immense. All the courts are interlocked with skill. Because the centers of the courts are not aligned with each other axially, as is the case in most courtyard-based complexes, it makes for a dynamic diagonal sequencing of spatial experience full of unexpected spatial expansion and contraction. Axial expectations are manipulated to heighten the surprises. For instance, the view into the Pachisi Court from the center of the court at Birbal's House aligns with one of the arms of Anup Talao. This sets up the expectation that Anup Talao must also be the center of its court. Walking straight down the axis into the Pachisi Court, however, reveals that Anup Talao is instead at one end of its court, revealing the diagonal character of the axis.

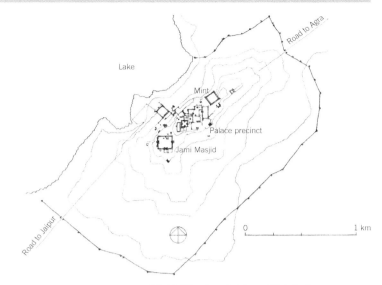

14.44 Site plan: Fatehpur Sikri, India

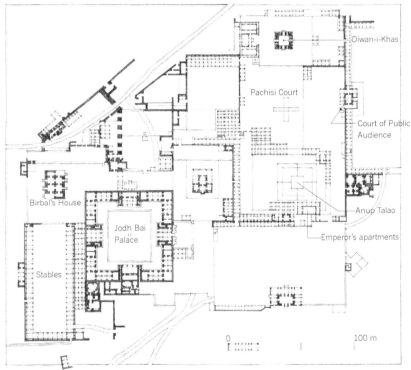

14.45 Plan: Palace precinct, Fatehpur Sikri

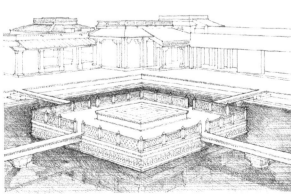

14.46 **Anup Talao, Fatehpur Sikri**

14.47 Exterior elevation: Buland Darwaza, Fatehpur Sikri, India

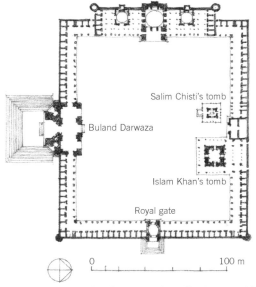

14.48 Plan: Jami Masjid, Fatehpur Sikri

Buland Darwaza

The Buland Darwaza (1573) is an ingenious work at the intersection of architecture and urban design. It was built in the Jami Masjid of Sikri, which until the late 19th century was the largest mosque in South Asia. The 165-by-133 meter Jami Masjid has a huge courtyard, with gates on three sides and, to the west, the *qibla* wall, centered on an *iwan* with a central dome flanked by two smaller side domes. The *mihrab* and the western wall are elaborately decorated with inlay work of stone mosaic and glazed tiles with azure blue and gold inscriptions. Except for the *qibla* wall, the rest of the mosque is made of red sandstone with occasional marble inlay. The sandstone, faceted like wood, is used in the columns structurally and not as cladding, an innovation that gives to the colonnade a delicacy denied to clad stone piers. Indeed, structural red sandstone columns are used throughout Fatehpur Sikri, and where thicker walls were necessary, they were all clad with the same red sandstone (with the occasional marble and semiprecious stone inlay), giving the entire complex a unified impression.

In 1573 Akbar rebuilt the southern gate of the mosque after his much sought-after victory over Gujarat. Renamed Buland Darwaza, or Victory Gate, the 54-meter-high gate is so tall that it ran the risk of overwhelming the *qibla* wall of the mosque, to which it is just an entrance. The skill of Sikri's designers is evident in their handling of the building's section, which ensures a majestic reading on the outside but not on the inside. First, they exaggerated the external height of the Darwaza by building a lofty flight of stairs in front of it to take advantage of the mosque's location at the very edge of the escarpment. Its impact on the mosque is mitigated by the stepping down of the section; while the exterior elevation rises to the full height, the interior elevation finishes below the height of the *qibla iwan*.

14.49 Section: Buland Darwaza

14.50 Interior elevation: Buland Darwaza

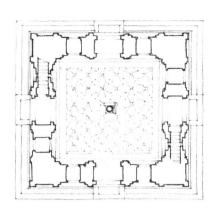 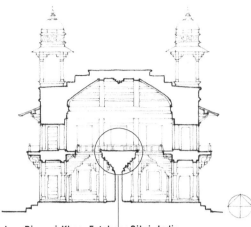 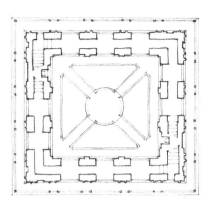

14.51 Ground-floor plan, section, and upper-story plan: Diwan-i-Khas, Fatehpur Sikri, India

Diwan-i-Khas

Akbar's Diwan-i-Khas is a singular building in the history of architecture. It was conceived by Akbar, who was an exceptional and, in many senses, a very modern thinker. Although he was illiterate, he was very curious about the empire he had just created. He surrounded himself with philosophers and aestheticians, and searched for a philosophical and religious practice that could, to his mind, resolve the multiplicity of and contradictions among beliefs in his world. Akbar constructed a new syncretic and pluralistic cult, or religious practice, called the Din-i-Ilahi, or Divine Religion, with a fairly generic creed of abstinence, meditation, beneficence, politeness, and mystical monotheism. In 1582, at Fatehpur Sikri, Akbar officially proclaimed the birth of Din-i-Ilahi and called a general council meeting of members of all faiths to resolve all their religious differences. The core of Din-i-Ilahi was Sulh-i-kul, or tolerance of all thoughts that benefit mankind. Akbar proposed himself, as a unique ambassador of God, as the central institution for resolving religious differences.

The concepts of Din-i-Ilahi are manifested in the Diwan-i-Khas, the royal audience hall. It is the solitary object-in-space building in the main court, a two-story square box with four *chattris* at the corners, made entirely out of red sandstone. A deep overhanging *chajja*

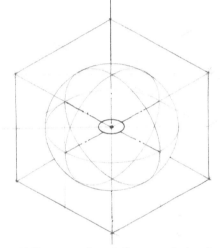

14.52 The emperor's seat, the conceptual center of Diwan-i-Khas

14.53 Emperor's seat, Diwan-i-Khas

casts a prominent shadow over the upper-story elevation. At 13.18 meters, the width of the building is the same as its height taken to the top of the *chattris*, making it symbolically a perfect cube. The drama of the Diwan-i-Khas is its interior. In the double-height space of the interior, located in the center of the overall volume and supported by a single pillar with a mushroom top of sandstone brackets, is a round platform that seems to hover in midair. It is connected at the corners with narrow bridges forming a cruciform pattern. A balcony runs around the interior at the second-story level. It functioned as an idiosyncratic audience hall, with the emperor listening to supplicants from above and consulting with ministers from the various philosophical and religious positions sitting at the ends of the bridges. The emperor's position, held up by a single column, was at the very center of the building, both in plan and section. Indeed, the emperor would sit at the very center of the cube and conceptual sphere implied by the building. This is a spatialization of the position occupied by the emperor, who was at the center—that is, equidistant for all philosophical positions—in Din-i-Ilahi. As a direct spatialization of a philosophical ideal, the Diwan-i-Khan can be described as a theoretical project. It had no known precedent and was never copied again.

14.54 Taj Mahal, Agra, India

14.55 Area map of Agra

Rauza-i-Munavvara (Taj Mahal)

Having inherited a vast and prosperous empire, Shah Jahan (1628–58) enjoyed the dividends of peace. He was dedicated to poetry, art, literature, and most of all to architecture, expending vast resources to build palaces, mosques, and tombs all across his empire, especially in Delhi, where he built a brand-new city called Shahjahanabad. In the latter half of his reign, however, the bulk of Shah Jahan's energies were devoted to the creation of the funerary tomb for Mumtaz Mahal, his favorite queen and granddaughter of the fabled Nur Jehan. The tomb was known to the Moghuls as the Rauza-I-Munavvara (or the Illumined Tomb), because of the luster and transparency of its marble. Later it was also referred to as Rauza-I-Mumtaj-Mahal, which the English contracted to Taj Mahal in the 19th century.

Mumtaz Mahal died unexpectedly in 1631 while giving birth to her fourteenth child. Twenty-thousand workmen labored for fifteen years on her tomb. On every death anniversary of Mumtaz, Shah Jahan staged the Urs celebration at the Taj Mahal. (Urs celebrations involve prayers and song in praise of the deceased, usually a saint.) The first Urs occurred on June 22, 1632, even before the tomb was completed. Shah Jahan was also buried on Mumtaz's right, feet facing south, and closer to the Ka'aba, as required by Islam. The Taj Mahal thus is truly the tomb of both Mumtaz Mahal and Shah Jahan.

Controversy surrounds the question of who was the architect of the Taj Mahal. The historical records list several people responsible for the tomb, or parts of it. Ismail Khan from Turkey may have designed the dome. Qazim Khan from Lahore cast its gold finial. Chiranjilal, a local lapidary from Delhi, was the chief sculptor and mosaicist. Amanat Khan from Shiraz was the chief calligrapher. Other specialists included sculptors from Bukhara, calligraphers from Syria and Persia, inlayers from southern India, stonecutters from Baluchistan, and so on. Thirty-seven men can be counted in the creative nucleus. In this sense, the Taj Mahal was a global project. Yet given that Shah Jahan personally supervised the design and approved every aspect of the project, he must be recognized as its chief architect.

Although the bulk of the building material is from South Asia, the Taj Mahal's ornamental materials came from all around Eurasia. Its marble and red sandstone came from the hills of Makrana, near Jaipur, Rajasthan. From central Asia came nephrite jade and crystal; from Tibet, turquoise; from upper Burma, yellow amber; from Badakhshan in northeastern Afghanistan, lapis lazuli; from Egypt, chrysolite; and from the Indian Ocean, rare shells, coral, and mother-of-pearl. In addition, topazes, onyxes, garnets, sapphires, and bloodstones were among the forty-three types of precious and semiprecious stones from all around India were used.

The main tomb is on the southern bank of the Yamuna River on a vast platform, 103 meters square and 7 meters high, erected on arches. To its west stands a diminutive mosque, made of sandstone, with three modest marble domes. To its east is an identical structure, placed there to provide symmetry. Reflected in the wide waters of the Yamuna, which flows slowly in Agra, the Taj Mahal seems to be an apparition of domes and minarets rising above the plain. The side usually depicted today is actually the building's rear; the Mughal emperors accessed it from the water, arriving by means of a special barge. It docked at the northeastern edge of the platform, from which a stair leads up to the tomb.

Land-based access to the Taj is from its southern garden. The simple and discrete red sandstone walls of its perimeter betray little of the drama that awaits inside. A small gate in the middle of the wall leads into a quadrangular enclosure with spaces for maintenance workers and shops. Stepping out beyond the wall is the main gate of red sandstone and marble, a rectangular *iwan* surmounted by a string of closely spaced *chattris*. In the center, a single large pointed arch opens onto the entrance bay that telescopes down into the actual entrance arch itself. From here the main body of the Taj Mahal is perfectly framed.

The tomb sits at the end of a 300-meter-square garden divided into four quadrants (each twice subdivided into further quadrants) known as the *char bagh* (meaning "four gardens). It is a representation of the Islamic Garden of Paradise. Four channels, representing the four rivers of Paradise, flow out from the center. The Islamic Garden of Paradise is a reinterpretation of the Garden of Eden from the Old Testement. Deciduous and evergreen trees fill the garden.

Once through the gate, the full frame of the Taj Mahal jumps into focus. The tomb of Mumtaz Mahal and Shah Jahan is placed at the end of the 92-meter-square garden that serves as its foreground. Even at that distance the Taj Mahal fills the frame. The backdrop, given the hidden presence of the Yamuna River, is empty—or, rather, always filled by the color of the sky. Water channels, with fountains down their middle, are wide and generous. They reflect the tomb and further magnify it. The slender three-story minarets create an implied cube that contains the Taj Mahal, making the tomb three-dimensional. The double dome of the tomb, however, rises above the minarets, so that it is only the dome and the outer dome (conceptually the dome of heaven) that rise above the frame created by the minarets.

The translucent white marble that covers the entire surface of the tomb absorbs and reflects the light. In the mornings and evenings, it has a reddish hue; during the day, it is a subdued white with a slight bluish tinge; and on moonlit nights, it is a brilliant white. On bright days, the light blurs the edges of the tomb, making it shimmer. Since every surface is covered in the same white marble, even the shadows are softened. At dusk and dawn, the Taj Mahal appears to float weightlessly, an ethereal, uncanny apparition.

14.56 **View of the main gateway to the Taj Mahal**

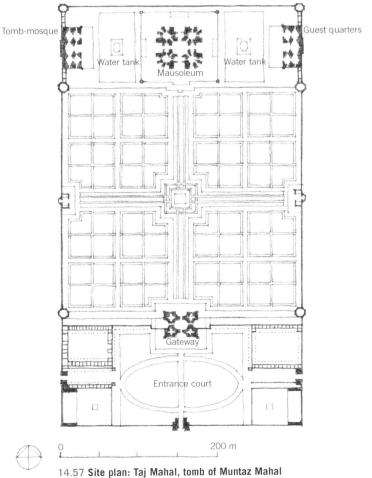

14.57 **Site plan: Taj Mahal, tomb of Muntaz Mahal**

14.58 **Taj Mahal, Agra, India**

14.59 **Faux tombs of Mumtaz and Shah Jahan, Taj Mahal**

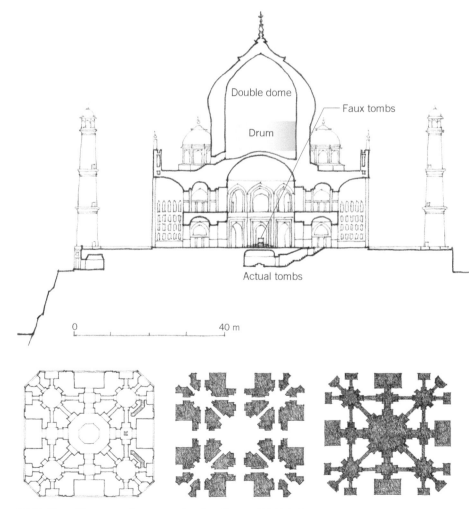

14.61 **Plan with mass and space rendered as figures, Taj Mahal**

In plan, the Taj Mahal's central chamber is surrounded by four corner spaces connected by corridors to permit circumambulation. At the ground-entrance level are the tomb markers of Mumtaz and Shah Jahan, with the actual burials in a crypt directly below (accessible by a stair). The section reveals that the outer bulbous dome is raised exceptionally high on a drum well above the inner dome, so that the volume contained in the upper dome is actually equivalent to the volume below. Because of the high drum, the outer dome rises well above the central *iwan* of the elevation, making it the undisputed center of the composition (unlike, for instance, Humanyun's Tomb, where the side chambers compete with the central dome, making the overall structure more squat than tall). The side *iwans* are considerably lower; they are faceted only on the outer side, and not on the inner as at Humanyun's Tomb; and the articulation of all horizontal elements has been decidedly subdued in favor of the vertical. Indeed, a distinguishing characteristic of the Taj Mahal's massing is that in elevation, all the elements are clustered and hierarchically arranged to ensure that they do not compete with each other and instead build up the centrality of the main dome. Even the *chattris* are clustered right next to the central dome, almost as if they were supporting domes themselves. Drawing an imaginary line along the edges of the central dome and the *chattris* yields a triangle or pyramid, framed by the four minarets.

VIJAYNAGARA

The brothers Harihara and Bukka escaped from captivity under Ala-ud-Din Khilji, to establish a new kingdom in the mid-14th century that resisted the rising tide of Islamic rule for 250 years. Consolidating Chalukyan, Hoysala, and late Chola territories, Vijayanagara built up its wealth by investing in Cholan decentralized temple-based administration and by irrigating new lands. A complex of canals, ducts, small dams, and aqueducts irrigated the surrounding lands, brought water to the city, and fed the palace's tanks and baths. A network of roads radiated outward from Vijayanagara. Commerce between the Portuguese, who captured Goa in 1510, and Vijayanagara was particularly important.

The capital was located to maximize defense. Rocky hills that were difficult to traverse and the impassable Tungabhadra River provided defense from north and west, the primary directions of a potential attack. The city itself was located on an uneven plateau, and the urban area was built into the gullies and valleys of the terrain.

Vijayanagara's temples and palaces were aligned to the cardinal directions, but three long market streets emanating from the temples are all mysteriously aligned about 2 degrees south of east. The main temples are freestanding on the southern bank of the Tungabhadra, but the palaces and the city are enclosed in a fortified wall. The palace complexes are bound in their own enclosures. A "hundred-columned hall" and a huge platform, the Mahanavami Dibba, were designed to stage frequent ceremonies for the presentation of tribute by vassals. An elaborate ceremonial tank and bathing pool, both fed by aqueducts, were part of the main palace. The tank was in fact disassembled from an unknown location, probably Chalukyan, and reassembled in Vijaynagar. A long passage way sliced between two palaces gave public access to the Ramachandra Temple, the oldest and most sacred temple in Vijayanagara.

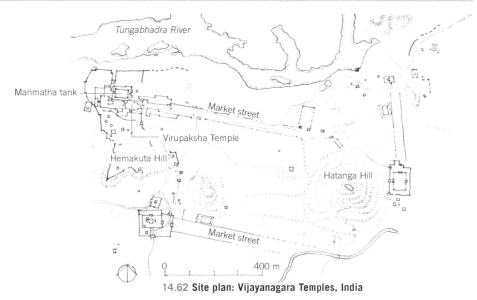

14.62 **Site plan: Vijayanagara Temples, India**

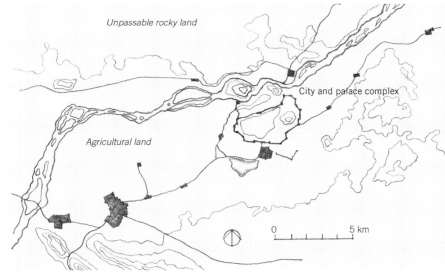

14.63 **Area plan: Vijayanagara, India**

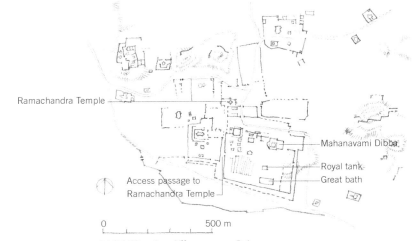

14.64 **Site plan: Vijayanagara Palaces**

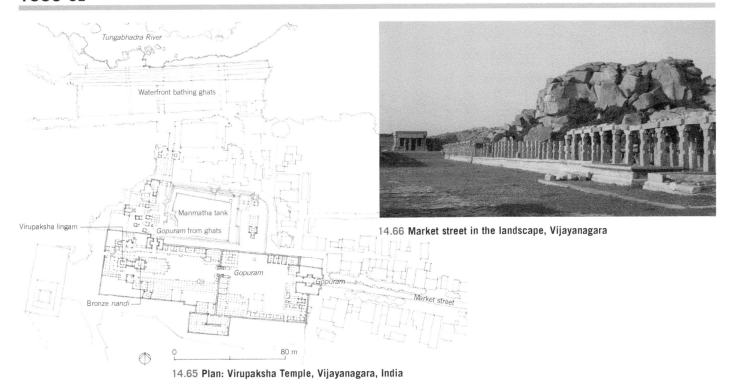

14.66 **Market street in the landscape, Vijayanagara**

Tungabhadra River

Waterfront bathing ghats

Virupaksha lingam

Manmatha tank

Gopuram from ghats

Gopuram

Gopuram

Market street

Bronze nandi

0   80 m

14.65 **Plan: Virupaksha Temple, Vijayanagara, India**

The Virupaksha, Vijayanagara's most important temple, started as a small 10th-century shiva shrine, with nearby ghats on the Tungabhadra. Over time it grew into a gigantic urban complex in itself, extending to both the water in the north and the market street to the east. The *nandi* enclosure was added in the 15th century; the open *mandapa*, surrounding cloister, and the two *gopurams* were built early in the 16th century by Krishnadevaraya (r.1509–29), Vijayanagara main period of growth. Krishnadevaraya also formalized the tank and expanded the ghats. All the subsidiary shrines were integrated into the complex over time. The Virupaksha, like all other temples, opens into a long market street, effecting a direct connection between commerce and religion. All the temples also visually connected with each other and with significant hilltops that themselves had small temples on them.

14.67 **Royal tank with aqueduct, Vijayanagara**

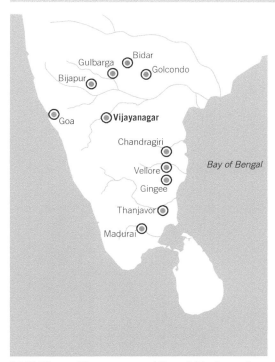

14.68 Bijapur, Vijayanagara, and the neighboring region

14.69 Tomb of Ibrahim II, Bijapur, India

BIJAPUR

An alliance of the armies of Golconda, Bijapur, Bidar, and Gulbarga defeated and laid waste to Vijayanagara in 1565. The Bijapur dynasty, founded by Yusuf Adil Shah (r. 1489–1510), benefited the most from the fall of Vijayanagara. Yusuf built Bijapur into a citadel with 10 kilometers of walls and six gates. Whereas his buildings were rather austere, those of Ibrahim Adil Shah II (r. 1580–1627) are sumptuous and celebratory. Ibrahim II lavished attention on the tomb and mosque complex he originally built for his wife but that eventually held his own tomb and those of the rest of his family as well. The mosque and mausoleum square off on a single platform placed asymmetrically within a larger enclosure. The freestanding mosque has five arches three bay deep, with a bulbous dome over the central bays. A deep parapet supported by closely spaced brackets rounds out at the corners in a profusion of brackets; these spin tall, thin minarets that culminate in small bulbous domes—almost complete spheres—supported like balls on a bed on a bed of flower petals. The central dome similarly appears to be a complete sphere, supported by tall lotus petals. The four corner minarets define a spatial field twice the height

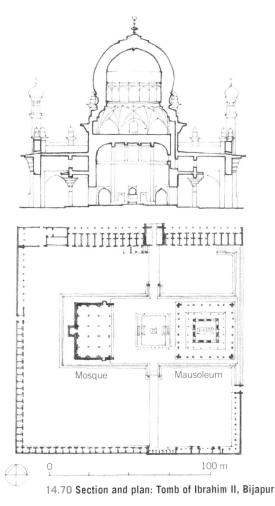

0   100 m

14.70 Section and plan: Tomb of Ibrahim II, Bijapur

Mosque   Mausoleum

14.71 **Gol Gumbaz, Bijapur, India**

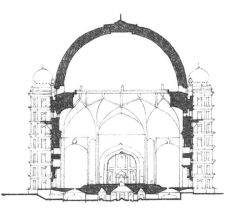

14.72 **Section: Gol Gumbaz, Bijapur**

of the primary building, at the center of which is the central dome with its own miniature corner minarets. Ibrahim II's tomb, on the east side, abuts the edge of the compound. Although it has seven arches on each side in a varying rhythm of widths, the tomb's overall vocabulary harmonizes with that of the mosque.

The most unusual of Bijapur's buildings is the Gol Gumbaz, the largest single-chambered building ever constructed. It was a tomb built by Ibrahim II's successor, Muhammad Adil Shah (r. 1627–57), for himself. Eight intersecting pointed arches, springing from two rotated squares, support both a round platform and the gigantic hemispherical dome. Built of horizontal brick courses cemented with thick layers of lime mortar, the dome is 3.5 meters thick at the base. It has six small openings, and a flat section at the crown. Its supporting walls are largely plain and unornamented. The main entrance to the west, and there is an unoccupied niche in the eastern wall. In the middle, directly below the intersections of the arches, is a simple platform with the tombs of Muhammad and his family at the center. Outside there are four corner turrets, more like stubs, with simple domes.

ISFAHAN

In Persia, throughout the 16th century various dynasties vied for control, with the Safavids (who originated in Azerbaijan), led by Shah Ismail I (1501–24), finally winning out in 1501. The population of Persia until that time had been chiefly Sunni, but Ismail enforced adherence to the Shi'ite sect and began a campaign of conversion and unification. He also sought to retake what had been lost between 1501 and 1587 to the Ottomans. Close ties with China and Europe were characteristic of the period. Iraq remained united with Persia until 1653, with the Shi'ite pilgrimage centers prospering. Under Shah Abbas (r. 1587–1629), Isfahan—located almost in the center of Iran, between Tehran and Fars—was made the capital in 1598. It was rebuilt into one of the largest cities of the world and the focus for all the artistic energy in the country. Transferring the capital away from the insecure borderland to the center of the country was part of Abbas's policy of state consolidation. Isfahan, with a population of about half a million, soon became a grand cosmopolitan center visited by English and Dutch merchants and European artists and diplomats—the latter hoping to secure alliances with the Safavid

court against their common enemy, the Ottomans. A famous rhyme, *Isfahan nesf-eh jahan* ("Isfahan is half the world"), was coined in the 16th century to express the city's grandeur. The new layout exemplified the most extensive urban planning in the world west of China.

Previously, the central square of the city lay next to the old Friday Mosque, believed to have been built on the site of a Zoroastrian fire temple. Though many of the old buildings in that area were restored by Abbas, he instructed his planners to create a new urban center to the south of the old city center and named it Naqsh-e Jahan ("Design of the World"). It consisted of a vast, rectangular open space that served as the city's new civic and commercial center. To its west was a monumental boulevard, Chahar Bagh Avenue, some 4 kilometers long, with canals, fountains, and trees, and flanked by palaces of the nobility. The boulevard stretched across the Zayanda River over a 300-meter-long multitiered bridge that connected the city to several garden estates (*chahar bagh* means "garden retreat") to the south. These estates were large, walled enclosures with pools, promenades, and pavilions. The central element in the composition—and the

14.73 Main square of Isfahan, Iran

link between the commercial district and the avenue—was the Imperial Palace in its own walled precinct, the Naqsh-e Jahan garden.

The new square—still today one of the largest in the world (512 by 159 meters)—was the symbolic center of the Safavid dynasty and its empire. It was used for festivals, markets, and games of polo. At night, fifty thousand earthenware lamps hung from poles in front of the buildings to illuminate the square. It was designed with two stories of shops around its perimeter. The long, modular facades decorated with polychrome glazed tiles were broken only by the monumental entrances to four buildings: the Masjid-i-Shah Mosque in the south, the Sheikh Lotfollah Mosque in the east, the Ali Qapu Palace in the west, and the Great Bazaar to the north. A royal mint and a royal caravansary were also included in the ensemble, as well as baths and a hospital.

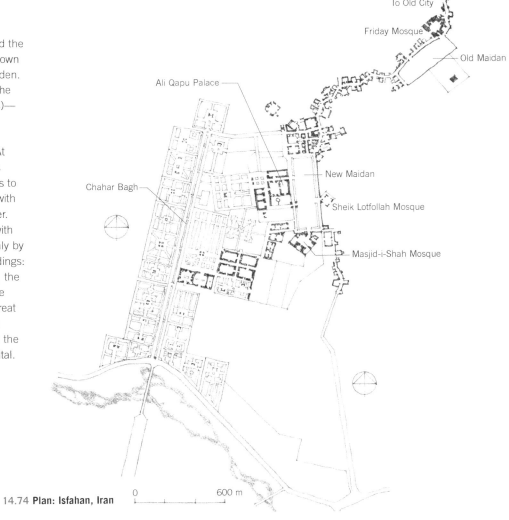

14.74 Plan: Isfahan, Iran

14.75 **Masjid-i-Shah Mosque, Isfahan, Iran**

14.76 **Interior: Masjid-i-Shah Mosque**

The Masjid-i-Shah Mosque, begun in 1611, is set at a 45-degree angle to the square so as to face in the direction of Mecca. Its main portal mirrors the entrance to the bazaar to the north. The mosque uses the four-*iwan* scheme, with a central courtyard 70 meters square and surrounded by two-story arcades noted for a calm balance between volumetric organization, decorative detail, and unifying symmetry. The plan is, in fact, distinguished from many other such buildings by its unusual concern for such symmetry. The domed sanctuary is flanked by rectangular chambers covered by eight domes that serve as winter prayer halls. These halls lead to rectangular courts surrounded by arcades that also serve as madrasas. The entrance portal is a tour de force of tile decoration, executed in a full palette of six colors (dark blue, light blue, white, black, yellow, and green). Glittering tiers of *muqarnas* fill the half-dome, some panels of which are decorated with stars and vines scrolling from vases.

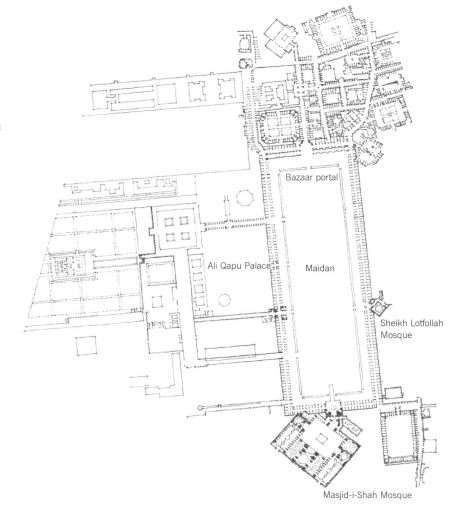

Bazaar portal

Ali Qapu Palace

Maidan

Sheikh Lotfollah Mosque

Masjid-i-Shah Mosque

14.77 **Plan: Main square, Isfahan**

14.78 **Ottoman Empire**

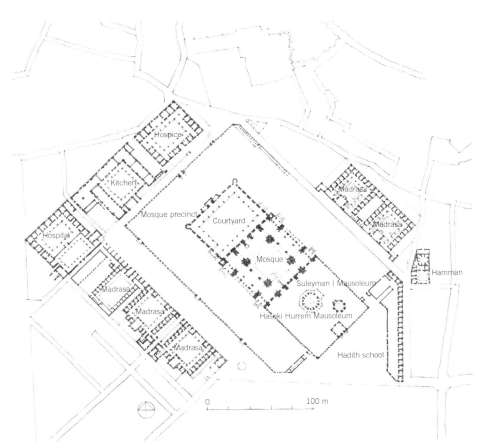

14.79 **Plan: Suleymaniye Complex, Istanbul**

SULEYMANIYE COMPLEX

The Ottoman sultan Suleyman I (r. 1520–66), also known as Suleyman the Magnificent, not only expanded the reach of the Islamic armies but also sought to turn Constantinople into the center of Islamic civilization through a series of building projects, including bridges, mosques, palaces, and various charitable and social establishments. He had the benefit of an extraordinarily gifted architect, Mimar Sinan (1491–1588), a contemporary of both Michelangelo and Andrea Palladio, with whom he is often compared. Sinan constructed nearly two hundred buildings in Constantinople alone, changing the face of the city and thereby creating its unique silhouette of mighty domes and slender minarets. As an officer in the military and a trained engineer, Sinan assisted in the building of defense works and bridges, and converted churches into mosques. With the capture of Cairo, he was promoted to chief architect and assigned the task of putting an Ottoman stamp on that city.

Though Sinan was consumed by the ambition to create a domed building modeled on the style of the Hagia Sophia, his signature achievement was to fuse Seljuk features, with their emphasis on portals, with the stone mastery of Anatolia and the structural logic of the Byzantine domes into a seamless and novel unity. This is nowhere better expressed than in Sinan's masterwork, the Suleymaniye Complex, begun in 1559, commissioned by Suleyman the Magnificent in the wake of his military successes in Iraq and the Balkans.

The walled complex (216 by 144 meters) was terraced up a hill to take advantage of the view overlooking the Golden Horn to the north, and it contains, among other things, four madrasas, a medical madrasa and a hospice, a caravansary, a bath, and a bazaar. The spatial composition of the mosque is obviously modeled on the Hagia Sophia, and in this it was similar to a trend already epitomized by the designer of the Beyazit Mosque (1501–6), except that with Sinan as the architect, the composition is considerably tighter.

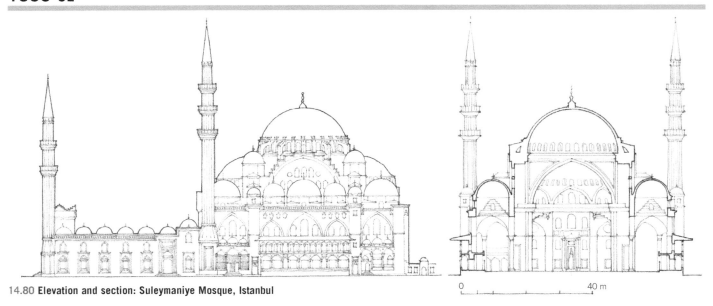

14.80 Elevation and section: Suleymaniye Mosque, Istanbul

0 _____ 40 m

The building is also, in many respects, very different from its Justinian model. It is dominated by a dome 48 meters high, with two flanking half-domes on the principal east-west axis and arches on the cross-axis. The weight descends to the ground by means of four massive columns of granite. On the exterior, the forecourt has a colossal portal with a tympanum framed by half-columns and minarets at the corners. Construction was organized by a court management office that, in consultation with the sultan, planned and oversaw the building project. Workers were Muslims as well as Christians and were organized according to their

skills. The decorative tiles were made in Iznik, the carpets in Anatolia and Egypt, and the colored and clear glass (the latter a technological innovation of the time) in Venice; the limestone and granite came from the quarries on the Sea of Marmara, and the lead for the window grilles and doors from the Balkans.

While the Hagia Sophia was dark on the inside and designed to have a mysterious effect, Sinan's building is lit from floor to dome in equal measure and pervaded by a sense of clarity and discipline. The windows are numerous and wide, and since the galleries are pushed back, sunlight entering

through the windows of the sidewalls reaches directly into the central space. The architectural volumes are clearly legible and enhanced by a corbelled gallery at the level of the springing of the arches (somewhat similar in effect to the arch style at Santa Maria del Fiore in Florence), thereby unifying the central unit underneath the domes. By comparison, at the Hagia Sophia, the surface mosaics and gilding tend to blanket the form. Sinan's mosques served as models for Sultan Ahmed's mosque, built by Mehmet Agha, a student of Sinan; it is known as the Blue Mosque (1606–17).

14.81 Vaulting in the Suleymaniye Mosque

14.82 Suleymaniye Complex

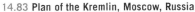

14.83 **Plan of the Kremlin, Moscow, Russia**

14.84 **Cathedral of the Assumption, Moscow**

KREMLIN'S NEW CHURCHES

The Byzantine Church, in a desperate move to relieve Turkish pressure on Constantinople, agreed to reunite with the Roman Catholic Church (Union of Florence, 1439). The Russian Church, a delegate of which was present at the signing in Florence, chose, however, to repudiate the treaty and to maintain the Russian Church as defenders of the Orthodox faith. This sense of renewal, along with the consolidation of central Russian lands in the face of the disintegrating Mongol Empire, spurred an unprecedented building campaign, especially under Ivan III (r. 1462–1505). Despite the Russian insistence on a decoupled relationship with the West on matters of church doctrine, Ivan III sent an envoy to Italy in 1475 to seek out Italian architects who could assist in the planning and execution of his various construction projects. None was more important than the redesigning of the Kremlin, the hilltop fortification compound at the center of Moscow that the city rulers had used as their place of residence since the 12th century.

The most important Italian architect to arrive was Aristotile Fioravanti (1420–85), who had worked in the service of Francesco Sforza in Milan. He designed the Cathedral of the Assumption or Repose of the Virgin (Uspenskii Sobor), a church that became the location for the crowning of Russian rulers and the investiture of the patriarchs of the Russian Orthodox Church. Though the design

was closely monitored by the Russian clergy, ever on guard against any possible heresy or the slightest sign of "Latinity," the church brilliantly fuses Italian and Russian motifs. The cathedral was designed as an open nine-square grid added to the front of the iconostasis, which was incorporated into the gridded system. Pilasters thicken the walls to give the volume a typical Italian flavor. The strict lines of the cornices dampen the profile of the semicircular *zakomary* gables. The groin vaults support tall drums and gilded domes. The typically Russian pentacupolar silhouette brings the Italian and Russian elements together. Fioravanti's technical expertise allowed him to provide better-finished limestone walls and better bricks and mortar, yielding a thinner but more durable structure.

One of the final churches begun by Ivan III was the Cathedral of the Archangel Michael (begun 1505) on a site 100 meters to the south of the Cathedral of the Assumption. It was to be used as the burial site for Russian rulers. The architect, Aleviz Novyi, had arrived in Moscow in 1504 after completing a palace for the Crimean khan, Mengli-Girei, at Bakhchisarai. He was possibly Alvise Lamberti da Montagnana, a student of Mauro Codussi, the noted Venetian architect. The architecture clearly reflects a Venetian style, as opposed to the Lombard style of Fioravanti. The facade is of a standard tripartite division, whereas the side facade has an ababa rhythm.

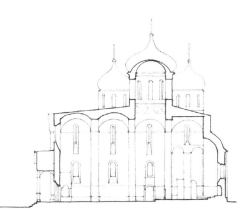

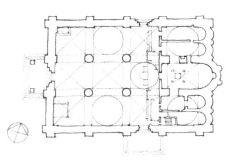

14.85 **Plan and section: Cathedral of the Assumption**

Instead of unadorned piers, as at the Cathedral of the Assumption (in the city of Vladimir, 1158–60), there are two registers of pilasters, some of the earliest examples of the neoclassical style in Russian architecture. Much like the Cathedral of the Assumption, there is a fusion of khanate and classical motifs, especially in the series of shell arches that form the crown of the building.

Indeed, it was the intent of Ivan's architects to remain firmly rooted in the Russian tradition, and classicism was therefore sublimated into regional idioms to maintain, for political purposes, a continuity with the past. Thus, here were the beginnings of the dialogue between classicism as a kind of universal idiom and regional expression—a dialogue that persists into the present in various forms.

Church of the Ascension

Following Ivan IV's conquest in 1554–6 of the Khanate of Astrakhan at the mouth of the Volga on the Caspian Sea, one of the most important Eurasian trading arteries came into Muscovite possession. Just as importantly, the conquest gave a boost to the Russian Orthodox Church, which had been facing challenges to its wealth, institutions, and even to its doctrines from various religious groups. The new churches being built at the time are known as tower churches and have become some of the more distinctive examples of Russian architecture. One of the most noted examples is the Church of the Purification (latter half of the 17th century), which was built in Aleksandrova Sloboda, in the compound from which Ivan himself ruled.

Built over an earlier structure, it consists of a two-story polygonal arcade supporting tiers of *kokoshniki* (a decorative form), an open octagon, and on top, a tent roof with cupola, soaring to a height of 56 meters. The building thus moves away from the religious traditions embedded in the pentacupolar motif toward a dynastic message, reaching its apotheosis at the Church of the Ascension at Kolomenskoe (1529–32) some 10 kilometers southeast of the Kremlin in Moscow. This was a two-tier arcaded church reached by external staircases, on top of which rose an astonishing structure consisting of the body of the church, three tiers of flattened *kokoshniki*, and an octagonal drum supported by a tent tower on top.

14.86 **Church of the Archangel Michael, Moscow**

14.87 **Church of the Ascension, Kolomenskoe, Russia**

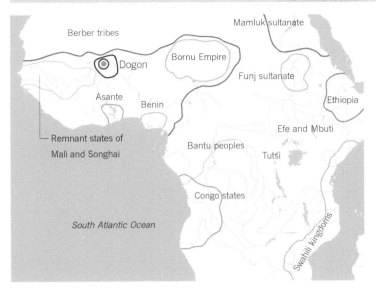

14.88 **Africa, ca. 1600**

14.89 **Dogon communal structure, Mali**

DOGON OF MALI

In the 17th century, the African continent below the Islamic north consisted of a complex web of social and political organizations. Some societies, like the Asante, Yoruba, and Tutsi, maintained large states; others, like the Mbuti and Efe of central Africa and the Kalahari Desert, continued a life of hunting and gathering. Despite the tendency to see African society as a collection of self-contained and self-supporting tribes, in reality, various groups had long and extensive contacts with one another through trade. Neighboring societies may in fact have borrowed elements of each other's rituals over the centuries, making it impossible to trace the precise origin of particular rituals. During the 1700s, aggressive Islamization from the north deeply impacted and changed West African nations, such as the Bambara, but full Islamization, still a matter of political friction to this day, was never achieved; often, a hybrid religious culture wasa created instead.

Western Africa was for a while dominated by the Mali Empire and then the Songhai, both of which had strong trade connections to the north. But when the latter were defeated by Moroccan forces, the area was left to various regional powers, and the center of political and economic gravity moved to the coast (to the Asante kingdom in Ghana and, farther east, to Benin, in the modern state of Nigeria) and eastward to the Bornu Empire in Niger. The Mossi retained control of the Mali heartland in central Burkina Faso.

Between the 12th and 17th centuries, difficulties with the Mossi and with Islamic slave raiders forced several groups in Mali to move east, to more defensible positions along and below the Bandiagara Cliffs, a 150-kilometer-long sandstone escarpment in south-central Mali. The name *Dogon* was given to these people by the French in the early 20th century, even though they are not a homogeneous group but a mosaic of different cultures, as is clear from their language, which consists of numerous dialects. In their new homes, the Dogon encountered a preexisting culture, the Tellem, whom they accepted into their society. Even today, the Tellem are the smithies for the Dogon, and they are responsible for making the important ancestor statues that are commissioned by Dogon elders for their ceremonies. The Tellem are held in awe because of their magical powers, but they are seen as lesser in the highly stratified society of the Dogon. Despite differences, the various groups have lived in remarkable peace over the centuries.

In Dogon society, an individual's status is determined by position within family groups and by hierarchies based on age and rules of descent. Religion involves the worship of ancestors as well as spirits. The Dogon believe, however, in one god, Amma, who is all-knowing and all-powerful and who upholds the balance between the living and the dead. Each clan has its own altar (*taba*) to Amma.

14.90 **Dogon houses, Mali**

The Léwé cult, dedicated to agricultural renewal, is the principal cult that reenacts the departure from the ancestral homeland. Its main symbol is the snake that comes out of the earth of the ancestors and that accompanies the tribes on their journey. These and other ceremonies are overseen by priests. All the rites and ceremonies involved masking, performed by males personifying supernatural beings and speaking their special language.

Dogon society is spread out over a vast area of cities, villages, and clan compounds. Some of the larger cities have more than 5000 inhabitants and are composed of densely packed compounds. These compounds (called *ginna*) have different typologies, but they mostly consist of walled enclosures and squarish towers topped with conically shaped straw roofs. Another type is composed of two rectangular volumes separated to make a courtyard with an entrance at one end and a cylindrical kitchen at the other. In the cliffs, the compounds have a more compressed, beehive-style arrangement. All compounds have granaries, divided up for different purposes. They are usually tall cylindrical structures with a door at the top and small portals below.

The word *ginna* also applies to the house of the oldest in the clan, who descends from his clan's ancestral founder. The house will be larger and more complex than the others in the compound and will be based on the symbolism of the number one and the number seven, which is the sum of the female number four and the male number three. At the social apex is the priest (*hogon*), whose house is appropriately large and visible, its facade painted with totem images. Civic buildings are known as *toguna*. They are basically artificial forests composed of high piles of sticks and straw held up on posts of wood, or sometimes stone. They are low to the ground, so it is not possible to stand up under them: they are places for sitting and talking.

14.91 Plan and section: a typical Dogon housing cluster

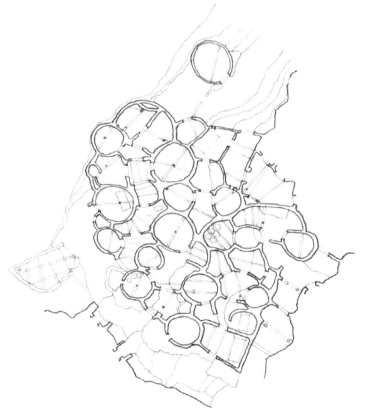

14.92 Plan of a Dogon city

14.93 Villa Foscari, Mira, Italy

PALLADIO

Venice's opposition to the Ottomans, accompanied by the opening of the new ocean trade routes, resulted a dramatic decline in its share of the spice trade from the Silk Route. Genoese ships, preferred by the Spanish, replaced the Venetian galleys; Antwerp had become Europe's most important port, and Portugal, using its new shipping lanes around the Cape of Good Hope, had brought the cost of pepper down considerably. In 1505, for example, pepper imported from Venice over the old route cost 20 Flemish *groats* per pound, while Portuguese pepper cost only about 16 *groats*. For a while, Venice managed to hold on to its economic position largely because of its mainland farms. (It has been estimated that by 1630 about 35 percent of patrician income came from Venice's mainland estates.) But eventually, the long-maturing crisis approached a climax, and by 1670 Venice was a shell of its former self.

In the interim brief window of opportunity, Andrea Palladio (1508–80) rose to prominence, designing most of his buildings not in Venice where trade was in decline, but on the farming mainland, in Vicenza. Palladio was trained as a mason, but under the influence of the humanist poet Giangiorgio Trissino, who became his first patron, he visited Rome with Trissino and made extensive studies of the ancient buildings, publishing his findings in 1554 in the treatise *Le antichità di Roma*. In 1545, he was given his first major commission, the rebuilding of the Basilica in Vicenza.

The villas Palladio designed for the great Venetian farming families were far different from those of the popes in Rome or the Medici in Florence, which were designed for urban grandness and privacy. Palladio's villas were working farms that had to simultaneously be both functional and dignified by access to the orders of antiquity. This made Palladio a protomodernist, in that he created buildings for common use. Among the numerous villas he designed, the most distinguished are Villa Barbaro (1549), Villa Foscari (La Malcontenta, 1560), and Villa Emo (1599). All except Villa Barbaro have splendid, elevated temple-front facades giving access to a great hall. Their layouts are always symmetrical and simple, and the rooms, too, are governed by simple proportions (1 by 1, 2 by 3, 3 by 4, etc.). Windows and internal doorways are often aligned, adding even more cohesion to the interiors. Villa Foscari became a model for palaces, villas, and houses throughout Europe and the Americas. The inner planning was based on a large cruciform hall that reaches from front to back. Its dramatic temple front, very three-dimensional, faces the Brenta River. Being so intimately connected with this gentle river imparts a special atmosphere of practicality to the villa. Not only could its owners easily commute to the Venetian lagoon, but its farm products could be transported to market. The villa was commissioned in 1550 and has in modern times again returned to members of the Foscari family, who have carefully restored it.

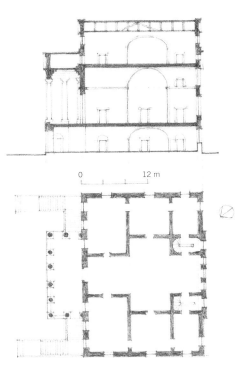

14.94 Plan and section: Villa Foscari

14.95 **Villa Rotonda, near Vicenza, Italy**

Villa Rotonda

Villa Rotonda (1566), though having many of the attributes of a working farm, was designed for the papal prelate Paolo Almerico as a type of retirement estate. The building's design is unusual for Palladio; it is symmetrical around both axes and stands on the top of a low hill artificially enhanced with retaining walls. At the center of the building was a rotunda—originally planned with an open oculus—with identical suites of rooms at each of the four corners. Each of the four facades had a temple front. The principal material was brick covered with stucco painted white. Given its cost in times of economic stress, stone was used sparingly, reserved for the capitals and for the ornamentation around windows. The villa, elevated on a basement disguised by its stairs, is itself built out on an artificial terrace. The entrance facing the northwest loggia is recessed into the hill so that from the villa looking back over the entrance, one sees the chapel on the opposite side of the small road. To the north are orchards going down toward a river. Cut out of the woods to the south is a *giardino segreto*, which can only be reached from the basement. Only on the east side is the view of the landscape unobstructed.

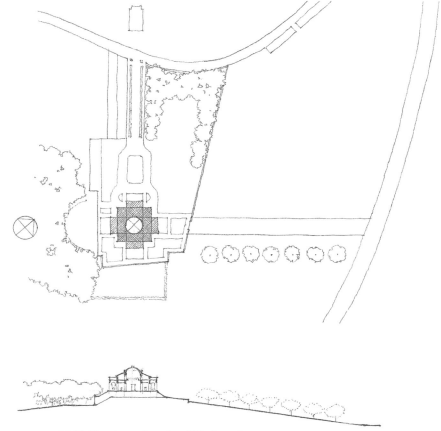

14.96 **Site plan and section: Villa Rotonda**

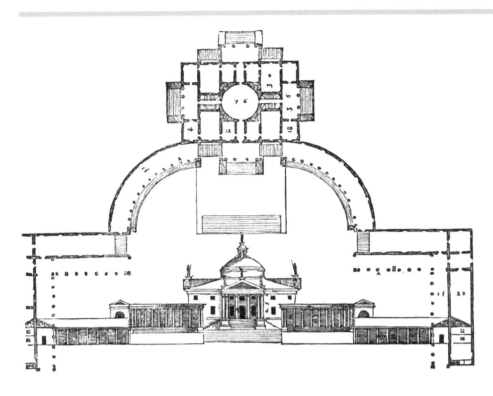

14.97 **Villa Trissino: From *The Four Books on Architecture*, Andrea Palladio**

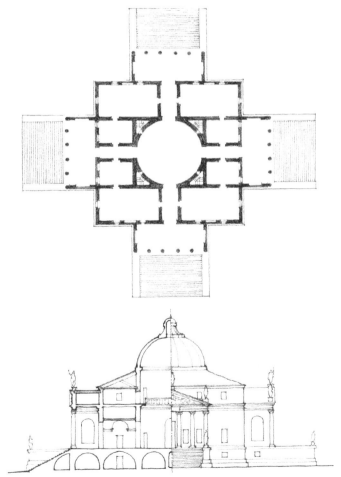

14.98 **Plan and section-elevation: Villa Rotonda**

Palladio was the most systematic and system-conscious of the great Renaissance architects, as evidenced by his *The Four Books on Architecture* (1570). Leon Battista Alberti and Sebastiano Serlio had been forerunners with treatises of their own, but Palladio's approach was different. Alberti, in his *Ten Books on Architecture* (1452), attempted a comprehensive study of the field of architecture and dealt with everything from the different types of buildings to where best to get building materials. There were no drawings. Serlio, in his *Five Books on Architecture* (first volume appearing in 1537), had plenty of drawings, but his purpose was to show how the classical system could be put to use to generate an almost infinite variety of plans. This was in contrast to Palladio, who emphasized the systematization of the ground plan and its relationship to the section and elevation of a building. Whereas Serlio's treatise allowed the patron a wide variety of options, Palladio's designs were much more circumscribed. Yet what made Palladio's architecture so influential was that despite its rigor it never produced uniform or boring buildings. Method and system did not overshadow creativity. Also important for Palladio was the relationship between the building as an object and its broader framing. Courtyards and perimeter walls were integrated into the composition.

BAROQUE ITALY

The Baroque style emerged in Rome essentially as a counterstatement to the Reformation; the architects who had contributed most to bring it to its ripe and full-fledged characteristics were Giovanni Lorenzo Bernini (1598–1680) and Francesco Castelli Borromini (1599–1667). It is important here to differentiate Roman Baroque from European Baroque. Baroque Rome waned after 1648 under Pope Alexander VII. From that time forward the papacy was no longer a major power in European politics. With the ascendancy of France and Austria, the Baroque style began to change, assuming a more urban form and, insofar as it was now also applied to châteaux and princes' castles, acquiring elements such as public parks and waterworks. Approaches often extended far into the landscape with elongated perspectives. In France it is exemplified by the Place Vendôme in Paris and the Château de Vaux-le-Vicomte (1656–61) by André Le Nôtre; in Austria, by the castle of Schönbrunn Palace (1695). Eventually the Baroque became an architecture of the late 17th-century European capitals—Rome, Paris, London, and Vienna—giving to these cities a profile that remains very much part of their identities today. On the negative side, many venerable old buildings of the Middle Ages were given new Baroque facades or makeovers, their interiors upgraded to conform to the "modernizing" trend of the Baroque.

The decade of the 1620s was a particularly promising moment in church politics. The heroes of the Counter-Reformation (many of them Spanish) were canonized—Charles Borromeo in 1610; Ignatius de Loyola, Francis Xavier, Filippo Neri, and Teresa of Avila, all in 1622; and Gaetano da Thiene in 1629. This, in itself, was a signal for new churches and chapels to be built, in honor of the new saints.

In church architecture, the Greek cross, which was sometimes favored in the Renaissance because of its symmetry, was rejected for the conventions of the Latin cross, which was liturgically more satisfying for Counter-Reformation purposes, as it allowed for a clear separation between clergy

14.99 Palace of the Senators, Campidoglio, Rome

and laity, this being one of the distinctions between Catholic and Protestant churches of the time. The preference, as established at Il Gesù, was for a longitudinal nave unencumbered as much as possible by side aisles. Transepts were minimized or nonexistent, allowing the use of rectangles and ovals, which also helped to create a sense of community that these churches were to inculcate. Baroque architects preferred curves to straight lines, deploying niches, walls, pilasters, and attached columns in a seamless way that made architecture seem pliant and rubbery—not framing the liturgical but part of it. They also had an appreciation of rhythmic movement through space, and intensified visual dynamics with the use of painting as well as sculptural putti (winged babies), which often inhabit the higher reaches of the space, sitting on ledges and entablatures. While in medieval cathedrals stained glass modulated the light, Baroque churches had plain glass devoid of tracery and the windows were often unseen, designed to create a mysterious and diffuse light. One often finds a Baroque church quite luminous upon entering—without first noticing any windows at all.

Campidoglio

The European 16th century was marked in the main by the Reformation and Counter-Reformation triggered by a recalcitrant monk in Germany. When Martin Luther (1483–1546) nailed his *Ninety-Five Theses* to the church door in Wittenberg in 1517, he only wanted to reform corruption in the Catholic Church. He had no idea that he was about to change the course of history. The rebellion against the church spread and soon embroiled Europe in terrible wars for most of the next two centuries. Additional reform movements emerged—such as the Calvinists, who believed in a form of predestination—but the various versions of counter-movements are for the most part summed up as "Protestant," a word derived from "protest." The response of the Catholic Church was called the Counter-Reformation, in which architecture played an important role, with great emphasis put on representation.

Following the embarrassing sack of Rome by the Holy Roman Emperor Charles V's troops in 1527, Pope Paul III (Alessandro Farnese; r. 1534–49) initiated a series of bold building campaigns to restore a sense of prestige, chief among them the construction

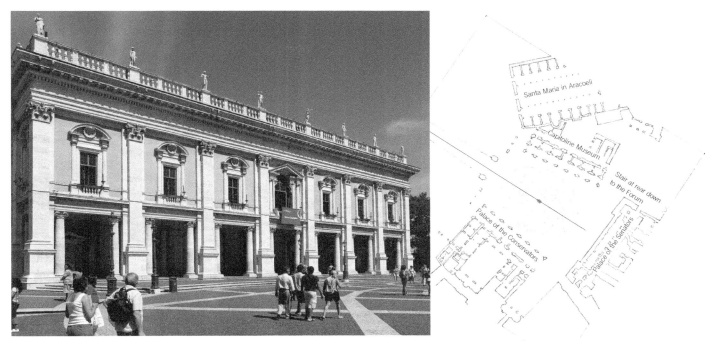

14.100 **Facade, Capitoline Museum, Rome**

14.101 **Plan: Piazza del Campidoglio, Rome**

of a piazza on Capitoline Hill, the nominal site of the Roman Senate. Though the area was of no particular importance to the political ideology of the papacy, Paul III wanted the Campidoglio to impress Charles V on his visit to Rome in 1536. The papacy, after all, depended significantly on the beneficence of the Holy Roman Emperor, who had recently redoubled his wealth with riches looted from the Americas.

Michelangelo Buonarroti (1475–1564) was put in charge of the transformation (begun 1538). He transfigured the disorderly complex into a symmetrical composition with a trapezoidal piazza and three palace fronts. The Via Sacra crossed the piazza, then descended a broad gentle stairway also designed by Michelangelo. In the name of symmetry, Michelangelo added a building, known as the Palazzo Nuovo (1646–50), with no programmatic requirements. This building, serving only as a framing device for the piazza, was erected by Carlo Rainaldi according to Michelangelo's designs. Although it looked like a habitable palazzo, it was in reality little more than a facade. For the first time Michelangelo used the giant order for the pilasters supporting an unbroken entablature, with a balustrade above the cornice to lend monumentality to the facade.

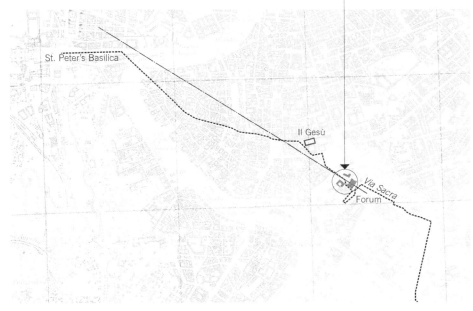

14.102 **Location map: Piazza del Campidoglio**

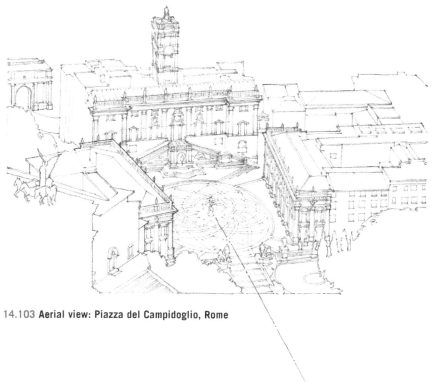

14.103 **Aerial view: Piazza del Campidoglio, Rome**

14.104 **Arcade, Capitoline Museum**

The trapezoidal shape of the piazza was unusual, and even though it was predicated to some degree by the existing context, it introduced a new and more dynamic notion of public space than had been common in the Renaissance, which tended to favor more static rectilinear schemes. At the center of the piazza is a shallow oval indentation, out of which rises a slight swelling of the ground, its surface ornamented with a rotating twelve-pointed blossom pattern hinting at a zodiacal symbolism. The ideological content of the piazza was brought to the fore by the sculptural program. A sculpture of the emblem of Rome, a she-wolf nursing the twins Romulus and Remus, was placed over the entrance of the Palace of the Conservators. The most prominent sculpture, however—indeed, the centerpiece of the piazza—is an equestrian statue of Marcus Aurelius, which was reluctantly incorporated into the scheme by Michelangelo. It is one of the best-preserved bronzes from Roman times and had been brought up from the Lateran Palace to emphasize the new civic nature of papal power. It escaped being melted down only because it had been mistaken by the Church as representing Constantine the Great, held to have been the first Christian emperor. But now in the 17th century, after the Renaissance, the pope bolstered his power by identifying himself, with a pagan Roman emperor. Michelangelo's ambitious project took several centuries to complete—the final flooring was put in only in 1940, under Mussolini, to Michelangelo's design.

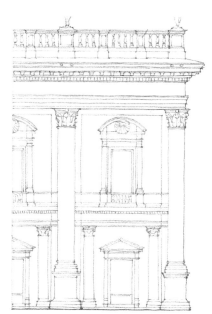

14.105 **Partial facade: Piazza del Campidoglio**

14.106 **Model for St. Peter's Basilica, Rome, made by Antonio da Sangallo the Younger**

14.107 **Medal showing Bramante's intentions for St. Peter's Basilica, 1506**

St. Peter's Basilica

The decisive loss of Hagia Sofia in Constantinople to the Ottomans in 1453 made St. Peter's in Rome the solitary center of the Christian world. This, accompanied by new wealth from the Americas, the rediscovery of classical orders, and the usual papal ambitions, instigated a colossal rebuilding of St. Peter's that took almost two centuries to complete in its core, and was ongoing even into the 20th century.

In 1505, Pope Julius II decided to tear down and rebuild St. Peter's, appointing Bramante, who had just finished designing the Tempietto of San Pietro in Montorio. Bramante (who worked on the project from 1505 to 1514) made a series of plans, some of which still survive, allowing a close look at his design progress. The buildings he proposed were suitably ambitious; his first plan (ca. 1505) shows a four-sided building sitting in a large courtyard open on all four sides. Each arm of the Greek cross ended with an apse projecting outward from the surface of the building. Four large towers were to rise from the corners. Bramante's building had remarkably little wall surface, with the architectural structure being a

residue between the spaces. The center was defined by a semispherical dome resting on columns. The building had no front, but was meant to be approached from all sides. The Greek cross format exerted a strong fascination for Renaissance architects both as an icon, as it was for the Eastern Church, and as a materialization of the mathematical ideals. One of the important champions of the centralized church was Leonardo da Vinci, who experimented with a wide range of possibilities, most consisting of a square, almost cubical box with apses on all four sides. In some, the apses take on complex shapes that allow for different formal arrangements between primary and ancillary spaces. All are surmounted by a dome, usually a replica of the Duomo of Florence.

Little was done, however, until the project fell into the hands of Michelangelo Buonarroti. By then the decision had been made to transform the building into a combination centralized-longitudinal church. By that time the piers of Bramante's building had been erected, and Michelangelo had to use them. He did, however, tear down some of the walls that had already been constructed.

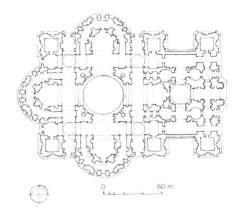

14.108 **Plan of St. Peter's Basilica by Bramante**

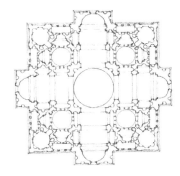

14.109 **Plan of St. Peter's Basilica by Sangallo**

14.110 St. Peter's Basilica, Rome

Michelangelo died without seeing his dome visualized. Giacomo della Porta, who inherited the project, changed Michaelangelo's intent and created an ogival form akin to the Duomo of Florence. He also raised the dome unto a higher drum so that it could be seen better from the piazza in front of the building. The windows between strongly buttressed fins are disguised by attached column pairs. When Michelangelo died, the front facade had yet to be designed. A series of architects were put in charge of the work, but until 1605 the front of the old basilica, astonishingly enough, was still in place and was serving as the entrance. Finally, a facade designed by Carlo Maderno was built, which elaborated on the themes of Michelangelo's building. The success of its composition is debatable. The *aediculae* appear as if they barely fit in their respective spaces; the enormous attic story looms over the facade; and of the five entrances, three have the lintels favored by Michelangelo, and two are round-headed, appearing awkward and small.

Compared to Bramante's, Michelangelo's plan is strikingly simpler. No longer was there a proportional declination of space from large to small. Instead, there was a single square with four apsidal ends to the Greek cross. A longitudinal orientation was created by the addition of a colonnaded portico across the front. The correlation between inside and outside was obscured, however, by the fattening of the mass to the right and left of each of the external apses, creating the appearance of a continuous succession of pilasters. In comparison with Bramante's design, which was intended to be read from the top down, its form dissolving into filigree patterns of niches, columns, and vaults, Michelangelo's building strives from the bottom upward, with the strained relationship between the outside shape and the dome hinting at the mystery of the divine presence within. The walls were not the result of volumetric elements added together, as they were for Bramante, but a dynamic balance between form, structure, and space, with an alternating rhythm of dilation and contraction. Bramante's building would have appeared as a static mass, while Michelangelo's appears as an undulating cliff surface that moves both toward and away from the center, especially when seen from the rear.

14.111 Dome of St. Peter's Basilica

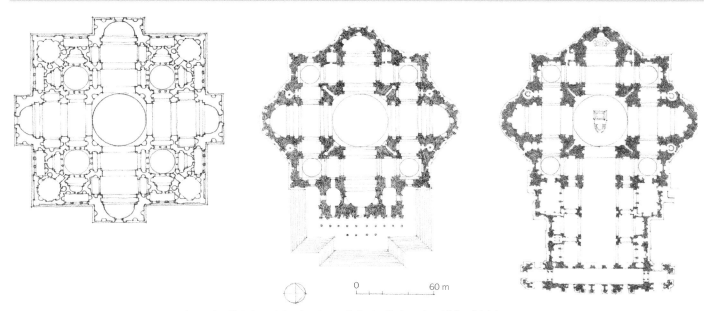

14.112 **Bramante's plan for St. Peter's (above); Michelangelo's plan (center); Carlo Maderno's addition (right)**

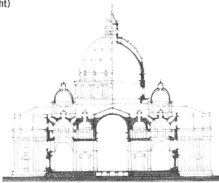

14.113 **Section: St. Peter's Basilica**

14.114 **Interior, St. Peter's Basilica**

14.115 **Facade: St. Peter's Basilica**

14.116 **View from the dome, St. Peter's Square, Rome**

In 1626 Pope Urban VIII called upon Giovanni Lorenzo Bernini to begin work on the great baldachino over the papal altar of St. Peter's. So impressed was he that in 1629 he appointed Bernini the official architect of St. Peter's. But the scheme to redesign the grand piazza in front of St. Peter's (1657–66) came from Alexander VII. A number of factors had to be taken into consideration. The old entrance to the Vatican was 120 meters northeast of the portico and had to be retained. Also, a covered processional way for state visits to the pope had to be constructed, and the loggia for the time-honored papal blessing over the central entrance had to be kept within view of the greatest possible number of people, especially for the Easter celebration. finally, there was a great Egyptian obelisk that had been brought to Rome in 37 CE that had to be moved to its present site (which occurred in 1586). Bernini's solution was to create and interlink two piazzas: a trapezoidal one in front of the church and a great oval one opposite the facade. The trapezoidal space consists of corridor wings connected to the facade of St. Peter's. In this way the basilica seems to be brought forward and its height accentuated.

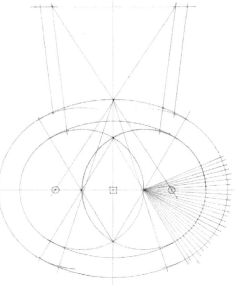

14.117 **Bernini's geometric solution for laying out St. Peter's Square**

14.118 **Aerial view of St. Peter's Square**

After experimenting with a circle, Bernini eventually made the piazza an oval. Yet the space is so vast that it is perceived as circular, with the preexisting obelisk serving as its center, and that may indeed have been Bernini's intent. The colonnade consisted of two rows of column pairs that were designed to flare out from the center; and with the side arms being farther from the center, circularity was emphasized. The solid strength of the columns contrasts with the verticality of the slender (if mismatched) Corinthian columns of the facade.

The site program required an important asymmetry in the plan to accommodate a suitable entrance into the Vatican Palace. Bernini solved this by incorporating the entrance into the northern colonnade. The entrance opens to the Scala Regia (1663–66), which serves to bring dignitaries up to the papal palace. The aisled and vaulted stairway is an architectural triumph over the awkward siting. Though the space provided was neither straight nor wide nor adequately lit, Bernini overcame each obstacle by using tricks of perspective that resulted in an impressive and dignified approach to the papal apartments.

When Bernini died in 1680, the connection of the great oval to the street leading up from the Tiber River had not yet been determined. Bernini had planned a building that would partially close off the piazza, creating a greater sense of enclosure, but it was never built. In 1935, under Benito Mussolini, the area was cleared out and given its current monumental design.

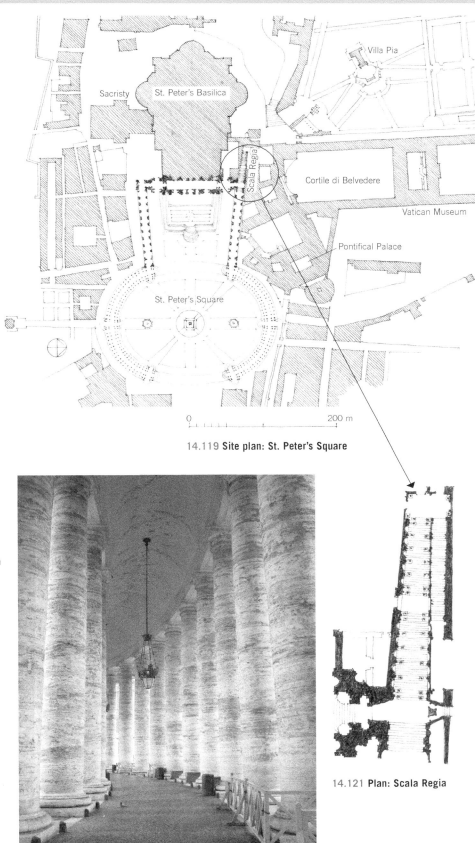

14.119 **Site plan: St. Peter's Square**

14.121 **Plan: Scala Regia**

14.120 **Colonnade, St. Peter's Square**

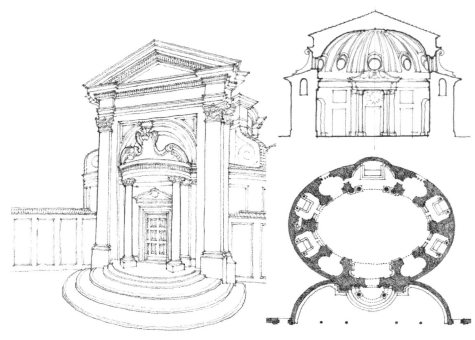

marble columns. The other four saints were positioned in the squarish niches on both sides of the principal cross-axis.

The color scheme and the use of light are striking. The Corinthian pilasters that mark out the principal spatial configuration are in white, whereas the spandrels, lesser pilasters, and freestanding columns on the side of the central apse are covered in delicate, white-speckled, rose-tinted marble. Light from a concealed window streams down into the apse, illuminating a spectacular picture frame supported by cherubs and solar rays, all in gold. The dome over the oval glistens with golden decorations evoking the heavenly space to which St. Andrew ascends. It is patterned between the ribs by finely worked hexagonal coffers. Perched over the windows at the base of the dome are figures of putti and the fishermen who were St. Andrew's companions.

14.122 Sant'Andrea al Quirinale, Rome

14.123 Plan and section: Sant'Andrea al Quirinale

Sant'Andrea al Quirinale

Up until the late Middle Ages in Europe, little if anything was known of architects or leading masons in respect to their life and training. By the early 15th century, however, the leading artists and architects began to come into focus. Biographies of Fillippo Brunelleschi were written, indicating his level of fame. Michelangelo and Leonardo da Vinci were already famous by the end of their lifetimes. Giorgio Vasari (1511–74) compiled the first history of Renaissance artists in his *Lives of Seventy of the Most Eminent Painters, Sculptors, and Architects*. But no artist of his time achieved as much popular fame or as many accolades as Gian Lorenzo Bernini (1598–1680). When he was called to Paris by Louis XIV to submit a design for a contemplated new east wing for the Louvre, people lined the streets to see his carriage pass by.

The core architectural works of Bernini are San Tommaso da Villanova at Castel Gandolfo (1658–61), Sant'Andrea al Quirinale in Rome (1658–70), and Santa Maria dell'Assunzione at Ariccia (1662–64). All three have simple geometrical plans based on the architect's unqualified reverence

for the Pantheon. Although Sant'Andrea is a transverse oval, its referent remains a classical one. The building had to be pushed back to allow for a small piazza in front of the church where carriages, which had become increasingly large over time, could pull up to the front. (The courtyard has since been removed.)

The church sits directly opposite the Palazzo del Quirinale, which initially was an official apostolic residence but now is the home of the president of modern Italy. Intended as part of a monastic complex set up by the Jesuit order to train novices, the building was dedicated to recently appointed saints of the Jesuits—Andrea Avellino, Francis Xavier, Stanislaus Kostka, and Ignatius Loyola. It was thus, in Bernini's eyes, a type of pantheon of the Jesuits. The massive Corinthian pilasters form the entrance, out of which projects a curved entrance canopy. The convex curve of the projecting porch is cradled in the middle of a concave-shaped piazza that mirrors the shape of the central oval in the interior. On the interior, a series of niches fill the body of the wall, with the central apse dedicated to St. Andrew and marked by flanking pairs of

Il Gesù

The major institution set up by the Church to fight the Reformation was the Society of Jesus, also known as the Jesuits. It was formed in 1534 by Ignatius Loyola (1491–1556), a Basque, and six of his followers, all students at the University of Paris in France. Loyola, a major force behind the Counter-Reformation, founded the Society of Jesus "to enter upon hospital and missionary work in Jerusalem and to go without questioning wherever the pope might direct." The principal difference between the Jesuits and other orders that had traditionally emphasized communal religious devotion was Loyola's relaxation of a prescribed monastic life and an emphasis on a more active apostolic mission. Prayer and meditation had to be balanced with service and teaching. The Jesuits hoped to unify religious teaching with academic learning. Classical learning with bible studies was required. By 1575 they had established fourteen educational institutions in France with about one thousand members and with some of the colleges having a student population of more than eight hundred. The Jesuits also set up colleges in India, Africa, and the Americas. In 1592,

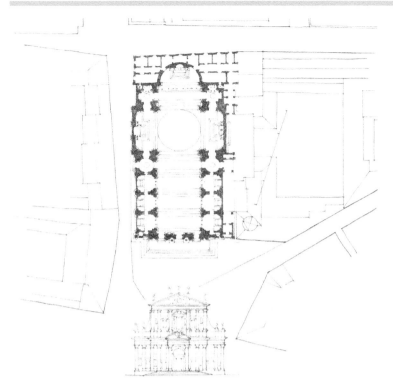

14.124 Plan and facade: Il Gesù, Rome

14.125 Entrance facade: Il Gesù

when Cardinal Odoardo Farnese visited the Jesuit college in the Piazza Altieri in Italy, twenty-seven languages were being spoken in the refectory.

Marguerite of Austria—wife of Octavio Farnese, the nephew of Alessandro Farnese (Pope Paul III)—paid for the building and for the use of the pope's architect, Giacomo Barozzi da Vignola (1507–73), to design Il Gesù, the Jesuit mother church, in Rome. The site for the church was a prominent one, just below the Campidoglio at an important intersection of the papal route through the city. Vignola's design was eventually modified, however, by Giacomo della Porta, whose facade was finished in 1577. In its plan and structure, Il Gesù was more influential than any other Roman church of the late 16th century, although the Jesuits' colonial churches continued to develop in their own way. In response to the Counter-Reformation's call for simplification, Il Gesù has a simplified plan with no narthex, a single nave without aisles, and transepts that are abridged. The interior walls were also sparsely adorned. Side chapels, sold to individual families, ensured proper endowments.

The facades of Jesuit churches spelled out the transition to the Baroque. New formal problems were tackled and solutions proffered that were soon to be taken up by the great Baroque architects. For example, here we see for the first time in Il Gesù the lower order, based on the theme of pilaster pairs elevated on high dadoes, with a similar dado zone separating the upper and lower orders. The central axis is emphasized by framed niches, as well as by the attached columns to the right and left of the door.

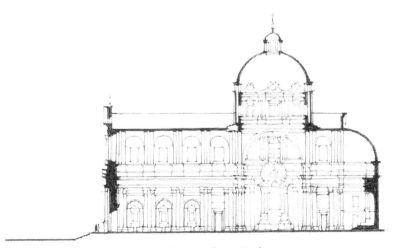

14.126 Longitudinal section: Il Gesù

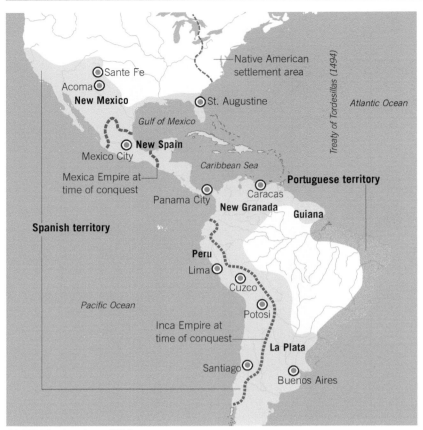

14.127 The Americas, 1600 CE

SPANISH INVASION OF AMERICA

Following a series of plagues in 1362, 1363, 1367, and 1374, the expensive campaigns of Ferdinand V and Isabella I of Castile (r. 1474–1516) against the Moors had so decimated the Spanish treasury that a century and a half of great cathedral building had come to a halt. Unable to afford the highly taxed merchandise and spices delivered overland by way of the Silk Route, the Spanish by the end of the 15th century were willing to risk sailing westward to open up a sea route to eastern markets. Christopher Columbus's discovery of the Americas in 1492 created excitement and hope, although initially it brought little to the Spanish coffers. Matters improved only when Charles V (1500–58) was crowned Holy Roman Emperor in 1519. The huge empire of the Incas in South America, subdued by Francisco Pizarro, yielded more gold than did the conquest of Mexico by Hernán Cortés. Not content with robbing the Incas of their gold, the conquistadores began searching for gold, using tens of thousands of slaves. Rich deposits of silver were found in the

city of Potosí in present-day Bolivia in 1545 and at Zacatecas (in what is now Mexico) in 1548. By 1650, Potosí was the largest city in the Americas, with a population of 160,000. Soon Spain became the world's leading silver producer (the Spanish crown received one-fifth of the silver) and ultimately produced 50,000 tons of silver, a quantity that doubled the previously existing stock of silver in Europe. The result was that the entire economic structure of Europe, and indeed the world, had to bend to this new reality. Vast quantities of silver were used to buy goods from China, where silver was the official currency. And it was not only silver that contributed to Spain's newfound wealth; the salt flats in Portugal and in the Caribbean belonged to the Spanish crown as well, and they delivered most of the maritime salt consumed in the West.

The money from these enterprises filtered its way through the European markets, even though Europe's commercialization and industrialization based on the New World were still a while away. Along with the wealth came food; tomatoes, potatoes, peanuts,

cocoa, maize, pineapple, chile peppers, vanilla, and tobacco were all American foods that were introduced into the European and eventually the global diet by colonization. For a long time before the potato and tomato became a staple of European cuisines, they were thought to be poisonous. Inversely, wheat, rye, oats, coffee, lemons, oranges, millet, yams, cotton, indigo, tea, rice, bananas, some beans, and other products of the Eurasian and African worlds were brought to the Americas, along with horses, sheep, pigs, goats, chickens, donkeys, rats, rabbits, cats, dogs, and guinea hens, most of which were introduced as part of the transplantation of farming and animal husbandry systems. A few American animal species were introduced to Europe as well, particularly the llama and the turkey—the latter eventually making it back to the Americas, at least in name. But it was arguably the "gift" of the European diseases—particularly smallpox, influenza, typhus, chicken pox, cholera, and measles—that truly tipped the scales in favor of the Europeans, as these diseases wiped out the native populations and yielded the American continents to relatively easy and inexpensive colonization. The native Americans seemed not to have had any diseases that impacted the Old World.

Spain ruthlessly exploited its new American colony, an effort that went hand in hand with the forced introduction of Christianity. At the center of Spain's colonial system was a form of feudalism, in which Spanish settlers (*encomiendos*) were entrusted with large tracts of land, the *encomienda*, along with a population of not more than three hundred Indians. The natives retained possession of the land, which, however, officially belonged to the crown of Castile. The *encomiendos* were given the right of taxation and were allowed to demand labor services from the population. According to a papal bull of 1493, the Spanish *encomiendos* were supposed to keep order and convert the Indians under their care to Catholicism. This, at least, was the theory; in practice, the system soon became corrupt and a tool for oppression and slavery. The *encomiendos* introduced European beasts of burden, farming techniques, and manufacturing processes, along with extensive mining facilitated by an unlimited supply of forced labor. New towns were created to support the *encomienda* economy and to connect it to the ports. A Spanish colonial town was laid out on a regular grid with a plaza in the center. Church and administrative buildings usually faced onto the plaza.

Hard on the heels of the conquistadores were Catholic friars—Franciscans, Dominicans, and Augustinians—with the assignment to claim the natives for Christ. They built churches, and in an effort to facilitate the task of converting the indigenous people, often intermixed the conventions of church liturgy with local pre-Columbian practices. The friars were also the first to actually defend the rights of the natives as children of God. Central to that effort was Bartolomé de Las Casas, a former *encomienda* turned Dominican friar who vehemently protested the *encomiendos'* cruel and harsh treatment of the natives to the Spanish crown. "Are they not human, children of God, deserving of our protection?" demanded de Las Casas. In response, the Spanish crown enacted a series of laws that prohibited the enslavement of the native peoples. But soon after, the viceroy was assassinated, and the new laws were withdrawn. The Spanish referred to their work as "conquest," but from the perspective of the natives of pre-Columbian America, it was, of course, an invasion.

Atrios

The Spanish-American churches built by the friars emphasized simplicity and directness. Straighforward boxes with thick walls, often buttressed on the exterior, provided a sturdy frame for the Franciscan house of God. Windows were few and usually very high. The walls were unsegmented and left bare, or were at best painted with simple illustrations in a style not unlike that of the pre-Columbian platform mounds. A simple stone table, raised up by a few steps, served as an altar, behind which might be a *reredos*—an ornamental screen—often painted with pictures illustrating Christ's trials.

The real innovations were on the exterior. To accommodate large groups of worshippers, the friars developed the concept of the *atrio*, a large open court, walled along the edges, that used the facade of the church as a backdrop; there was an outdoor

chapel to conduct Mass at the west end. In its entirety, the *atrio* was reminiscent of the plazas that fronted the pre-Columbian pyramids which were familiar to the native population. Within, the friars devised processions, complete with stopping places for the Stations of the Cross that began at the church and rotated counterclockwise around the *atrio*. The so-called stations were altars that represented the events that occurred as Jesus was brought to his crucifixion in Jerusalem. Worshipers would stop at each, thereby reenacting the way stations of Jesus's suffering in a form of spatial prayer that had also become common in Europe during this time. Hundreds of such *atrio* churches were built by the Franciscans in the 1560s and 1570s, with some of the classic examples at Cuernavaca, Cholula,

and Atlatlahucan. The Catholic Church, however, became very uncomfortable with some of the lenient practices of the friars, which they held to be unorthodox. The *atrio* churches contravened the basic principle of the house of God as a building with a roof. The friars also favored processional activities that often incorporated certain pre-Columbian songs and dances. Catholic icons often resembled older native images. All this made the Church in Rome nervous, opposed as it was to such hybridizations. In 1574, the monk's sacerdotal privileges were revoked, the building of monasteries was stopped, and the *atrio* churches were declared unfit for service. Their spirit, deeply ingrained in native consciousness, nevertheless, survived within the Latin American church, imparting to it its unique character.

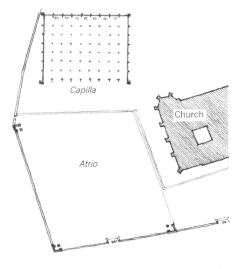

Capilla

Church

Atrio

14.128 Plan: Example of an *atrio*

14.129 Example of an *atrio*

14.130 Elmina Castle, Elmina, Ghana

COLONIAL FORTS

To enforce the policy of extraction as well as to protect ports and trade routes, colonial powers embarked on a worldwide fort-building campaign. Many hundreds, if not thousands, were built—sixty alone along the West African coast. Unlike the old forts of Europe, which were set up to defend against marching armies and long sieges, colonial forts were designed to withstand raids, assaults, and bombardments of short but potentially intense duration. They did not have much manpower to defend them, so they had to be built to withstand attacks, to enable clear line of sight for firing at enemy vessels, and to hold prisoners securely.

Portugal's Elmina Castle in Ghana, on a promontory overlooking the mouth of a river, set the pattern for subsequent buildings. The rectangular castle was located in the protected core of a set of perimeter walls. A church and an administrative center faced each other across the inner courtyard. Corner bastions projected past the surfaces of the building so gunners could protect the entrances and flanks. In 1637, it was taken by the Dutch, who rebuilt and expanded it as a slave collection point. By 1700, new technologies and military strategies required a different type of fort. Success no longer lay in the height of the walls but in the ability to shoot sweeping fire from within the fort while deflecting mortar and cannon shot coming from outside. Fort cannoneers did not

want to lob the ball high, as it would merely plunge into the earth. Instead, the cannonball was shot low to the ground so that it would bounce and ricochet through enemy lines. Artificial sloped terraces known as glacis were built around the fort to expose attackers to cannon shot. When combined with ditches and bastions that provide raking angles, the geometry of an 18th-century fortification becomes quite complex, as can be seen in Fort Manoel (ca. 1682). It was located on Manoel Island in Marsamxett Harbor to the northwest of the city of Valletta, in Malta. Fort Manoel was used as a model for forts built throughout the world, particularly by the English and the French. For example, the English Fort Commenda, in Ghana, begun in 1686, is a similarly advanced but somewhat simpler version. These forts would remain the norm for the next two hundred years, until the advent of aerial bombardment. One of the most complete 17th- to 19th-century fortification systems still extant can be found in Valetta, Malta.

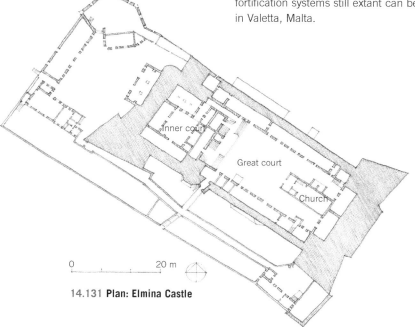

14.131 Plan: Elmina Castle

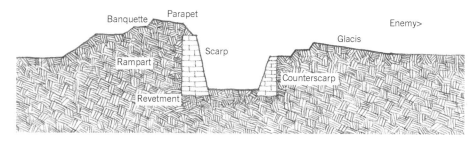

14.132 Section through fortification, Elmina Castle

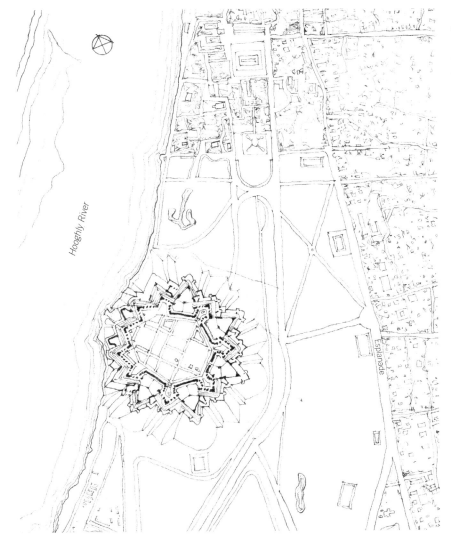

14.133 **Plan: Fort Commenda, Ghana**

Tower

Cistern

0   20 m

14.134 **View: Old Fort William, Kolkata, India**

Fort William, the British fort in Kolkata, was started in 1699 to protect passage on the Hooghly River, which was navigable from the ocean. The original fort faced the river to receive the ships sailing from the Bay of Bengal. In 1758, the fort was rebuilt to face all directions. An irregular tetragon, the fort had corner turrets where the guns were mounted, most of them facing the river. The riverside wall was solid masonry with occasional embrasures for heavy guns, while the main entrances opened toward the east, facing the mainland. Within, the soldiers' barracks, armory, and governor's palace were irregularly placed. The land around Fort William was cleared for unobstructed sightlines. This allowed for the spectacle of the Esplanade, the main street on which the large houses of the colonists were staged.

Hooghly River

Esplanade

14.135 **Plan: Fort William**

AMSTERDAM

Though Holland had the fastest-growing economy in Europe at the time, having become the mercantile hub of the Spanish Empire, this was not reflected in its architecture. Because the Dutch were for the most part Calvinists and their beliefs dictated simple structures, they did not build churches until they had gained independence from Spain. Following the destruction of Antwerp by the Spanish, Amsterdam, a relatively unimportant city until 1579, quickly became one of the leading international ports of Europe, developing a cityscape that included the town hall in Dam Square (now the Royal Palace), the Westerkerk, and the Zuiderkerk, as well as a large number of canal houses commissioned by leading mercantile families. Dutch naval power began rising rapidly in the late 16th century, and the Netherlands became the leader in global commerce during the second half of the 17th century. Its principal rivals in the contested ocean routes for sugar, slaves, and spices were initially the Spanish and the Portuguese, but by the end of the 17th century it was the English who had risen to naval preeminence.

The first church in Amsterdam specifically built for the Protestant community was the Zuiderkerk (1603–11). It is a simple six-bay rectangle that is pseudo-basilican in plan: although it has a nave and side aisles, it has no apse, thus reflecting the more community-oriented nature of its religious services. The minister gave his sermons from a pulpit attached to one of the columns more or less in the midst of the congregation. Music and especially communal singing were important parts of the liturgy. There is no crypt, since relics and their worship are not part of the Protestant religion. The building has a wooden vault with a tower squeezed into one of the corners. Although the building is relatively simple, the tower is as extravagant as any of that era. On the interior, the columns are dark and contrast with the whitewashed walls in a manner that was clearly meant to imitate 15th-century northern Italian Renaissance churches. In this way the style harkened back to an ideal of a simpler late Medieval or early Renaissance life, presumed to have been untainted by the grandeur and corruption of the church of Rome. The Zuiderkerk was

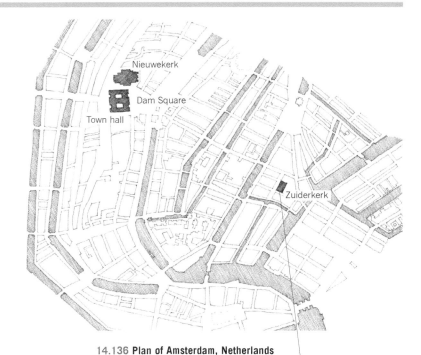

14.136 Plan of Amsterdam, Netherlands

followed by the Westerkerk (1620–31), which created a more unified whole with a clear division between the main axis—with the tower serving as entrance—and the cross-axis with the pulpit.

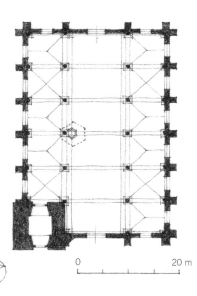

14.137 Zuiderkerk, Amsterdam

14.138 Plan and section: Zuiderkerk

0   20 m

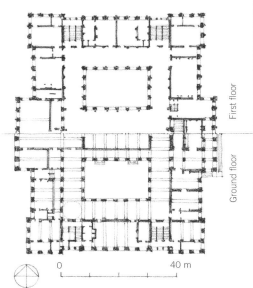

14.139 **Plan: Amsterdam Town Hall (Burgerzaal)**

14.140 **Amsterdam Town Hall (Burgerzaal)**

Amsterdam Town Hall

Early in the 17th century, with the formation of the British and the Dutch East India companies and the establishment of French Port Royal in Nova Scotia, newer powers entered the global colonial fray to compete with the Spanish and the Portuguese. For the Dutch, recently liberated from Spain, their colonial efforts began with the fur trade, but quickly gained a mercantile, banking focus. It was not gold that the Dutch were to extract from the colonies but cocoa, tobacco, and sugar—addictive cash crops that could be grown in vast quantities and transported overseas with few losses, and which would bring more profit than all the bullion of the Americas combined. In this way the Dutch, with the French, were responsible for transforming the Americas into a cash-crop economy that exploited the unique advantage of the vast stores of "empty" land that fell into European hands. In the long run, it was this mercantile economy that flooded European markets with vast amounts of cheap consumable products and transformed modern European culture, putting it on the path to rationalization, industrialization, and the Enlightenment.

In Amsterdam—the new center of the Dutch world and a city dedicated to making money—palaces, monasteries, and castles were not part of the cultural fabric. Instead, rows and rows of townhouses faced onto a relatively straight arrangement of parallel streets and canals. By the end of the 17th century, the city's population had grown from 20,000 to 200,000 in the span of just over one hundred years. The city's exchange bank, Wiselbank, founded in 1609, was for a long time the largest public bank in northern Europe. By the end of the 17th century, over 16 million Dutch florins were on deposit in its vaults—including the florins of other European governments. The bank was on the first floor of the new town hall (begun 1648), designed by Jacob van Campen. On the facade of the building, a statue of Atlas lifts the globe on his shoulders above a pediment in which the nations of the world offered up their goods to an allegorical Amsterdam. Inside, the marble floor of the huge barrel-vaulted town hall, or Burgerzaal, lit from the sides by two courtyards, was inscribed with maps of both the heavenly and the terrestrial worlds. Though the building is almost 100 meters long, its facade looks like two palaces stacked on top of one another.

Amsterdam's town hall was as an expression of the city's ascension in world politics, and it presaged the role civic architecture was to have in future European urban profiles. The town hall was one of the first applications of Italian Renaissance style to a monumental civic structure, and it was in many respects to remain the model for town halls well into the modern era. The building faced onto one of the few public squares of the city, called the Dam, which had as its focus a tall square building known as the Wage (or the public weigh-house). Here and in the nearby markets, as a description put it in 1664, almost the whole world seemed to be assembled to buy and sell—Poles, Hungarians, Frenchmen, Spaniards, Muscovites, Persians, and Turks.

14.141 **Place Royale, Paris**

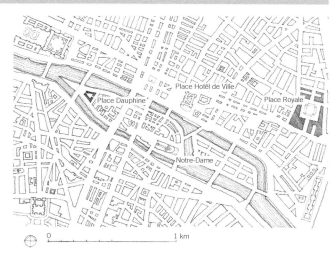

14.142 **Plan: 17th-century Paris**

PLACE ROYALE

When Henry IV came into power in France in 1589, Paris was hardly the city that it is today. Despite the nominal authority of the crown, France essentially functioned as a highly decentralized confederacy of autonomous provinces. Paris had suffered several setbacks, such as the absence of the kings, who preferred to live in their countryside châteaux, and the general downturn of the economy in the 16th century. In Paris, there was not even a royal palace. With an estimated population of 20 million in the 1600s, France was, however, the most populous country in Europe and the third most populous country in the world—only China and India had greater populations. Despite a massive increase in urban population, France remained a profoundly rural country. Economically, the glut of gold and silver from the Americas had led to inflation and a vast underclass that would haunt French politics for another century.

In deciding to make Paris a capital city and the seat of a newly forming centralized nation-state, Henry IV initiated a series of urban projects that were also intended to boost the city's economic condition. One such project was the triangular-shaped Place Dauphine (1609–14), designed to provide accommodations for bankers and merchants. To make its importance highly visible, it was located at the westernmost tip of the Île de la Cité; its narrow entrance formed, however, a tranquil and enclosed precinct within. Another experiment in urban design

and mercantile enhancement was the Place Royale (today the Place des Vosges), begun around 1605 on open land at the edge of the city. It was originally planned with three sides for shops and apartments and the fourth for a range of workshops for the manufacture of silk. Though some silk was still imported from China, much of it now came from Vigevano, Italy, where silk production was mastered in the late 15th century. Henry IV was eager to reduce France's dependence on foreign production, but French silk production never succeeded because of the climate, and eventually the whole square became a

residential address attracting the cream of Parisian society. Presiding over the square at both ends were special pavilions for the king and queen, as the square was intended as a setting for royal pageants. It was inaugurated in 1611 when a masque and a tournament were held there in celebration of the marriage of Louis XIII to Anne of Austria. As a setting it was well suited to the nobility and the rich bourgeois who had taken up the fashion of strolling and riding in carriages. Originally, therefore, the square was not paved but covered with a lawn and fenced in, an idea unknown to the Italian Renaissance.

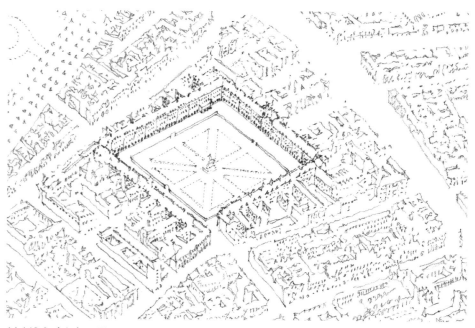

14.143 **Aerial view: Place Royale**

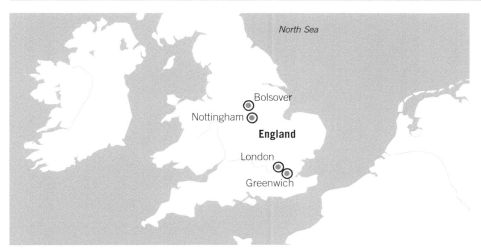

14.144 **Elizabethan England**

ELIZABETHAN ENGLAND

Though England, too, benefited from the shift away from the Mediterranean to the Atlantic, its growth in the first half of the 16th century had been hampered by complex internal conditions, poor management, and restrictive policies. Its maritime economy consisted mainly of fishing, smuggling, and plundering. It was at best a regional force. This began to change during the reign of Queen Elizabeth I (1558–1603). She adopted modern notions of management, transforming feudal magnates into officeholders. Overseas foreign investments resulted in a growing propertied class, with wool and textiles becoming an increasingly large part of the economy, along with the production of lead, salt, and soap. The population increased from 3 to 4 million between 1530 and 1600, providing a large reservoir of potential indentured labor. The English destruction of the Spanish Armada in 1588 established the country as a sea power and opened up an opportunity for the English to pursue Atlantic trade, putting them on a path to becoming the colonial superpower of the world.

14.145 **Plan: Wollaton Hall, near Nottingham, England**

Wollaton Hall (near Nottingham, 1580–88), the home of an important coal magnate, was already a splendid showcase for the new industry. It sported at the top a special "prospect room" that had no particular purpose other than to show off its towering fenestration. This type of fenestration can be contrasted with that of Titchfield Priory (Hampshire, 1537–40), which still has Gothic medieval windows in the surviving gatehouse.

14.146 Wollaton Hall, near Nottingham, England

English architecture, however, had a long way to go. Houses were relatively plain and rugged, and showed no fine paintings, apart from portraits. Nonetheless, the change in English culture was rapid and profound. Old houses were set out with chimneys, walls were paneled, windows glazed, and old timber-framed buildings were faced with stone. A particularly important innovation at the time and one that affected the development of Elizabethan-era architecture was the use of coal in glass firing. And here, once again, immigrants played an important role. Jean Carré, who was from the highly contested area of Lorraine and whose patent for plate glass was granted in 1567, was attracted to England along with other glassmakers from Lorraine. Soon furnaces were being built in scattered parts of the country, and prices began to fall almost at once. The market responded with enthusiasm.

14.147 Interior, Banqueting House, London

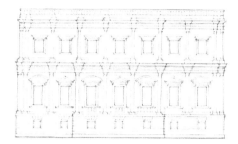

14.148 **Plan and elevation: Banqueting House**

14.149 **Church of Santo Domingo, San Cristobál de Las Casas, Mexico**

Banqueting House

Inigo Jones's second visit to Italy from 1613 to 1614, during which he studied the buildings of Andrea Palladio in particular, prepared the young architect for his most ambitious project, the Banqueting House. The first Banqueting House, appendaged to the Royal Palace in London, was built in 1581 and served for dining and theatrical entertainment. A second one was built in 1606 but was destroyed by fire in 1619. The Banqueting House designed by Jones in 1619 was less a place for banquets than a royal audience hall, reflecting a greater emphasis on royal authority. This was the first public structure in the mature Palladian style in England. At the ground floor, the windows between the pilasters are an alternating sequence of triangulated and segmental pediments, while at the upper floor the windows are all unpedimented, yielding an intricate yet calm design. The central three bays are emphasized by the use of attached columns, and the corners by pilaster pairs.

The whole is raised on a low rusticated basement that matches in height the balustraded frieze on top. The building's importance lies in the symbolic significance of its Italian motifs—an attempt to extend the architectural language born during Europe's mercantile revolution in the 15th century. But whereas Italian architecture developed in a culture of regional princes and rich merchants, it was now being associated with the centralization of the state. European sensibility was slowly transforming from more regional to more global.

CHURCH OF SANTO DOMINGO

One of the largest Spanish churches from this era is the Church of Santo Domingo in San Cristobál de Las Casas, Mexico. Built between 1547 and 1560 on the orders of Bishop Francisco de Marroquin of Guatemala, its present 17th-century facade is typical of the Mexican Baroque. The imperial double eagle, the coat of arms of the Emperor Charles V, can still be seen above the central portal and on the sides. The interior is lavishly decorated and contains a number of sculptures and wooden altars covered with gold leaf.

The city San Cristóbal de Las Casas was laid out on a grid according to the principles of the Law of the Indies, a series of laws that regulated social, political, and economic life in conquered areas. The grid facilitated land exploitation. A commons was always established in a city's center, in front of a church or cathedral. (The Church of Santo Domingo, however, was founded separately, to the north of the city center.)

14.150 **Plan: Dry garden at Ryoanji, Kyoto, Japan**

RYOANJI

The Zen monks invented the dry meditation garden as a practical necessity. Earlier Japanese garden design had been based on Song Chinese examples, which were built on large estates with long stroll paths that had views created from the natural landscape and constructed ponds, islands, mountains, and even rivers, complete with waterfalls. While the miniaturization of natural elements was a part of the design strategy, these gardens relied on size for their effect. In the 15th century, however, when the shoguns began to reduce plot sizes to accommodate larger populations in their cities, such full-fledged gardens were impossible. The newer generation of gardens, made by Zen masters, were designed around the principle of carefully staged views. In the process, they created dry gardens, so called because they employed abstract means of representation—using, for example, white pebbles and moss to signify large bodies of water. The Zen monks particularly enjoyed creating visual koans, or quizzical conundrums, that could be meditated upon.

Ryoanji, the Temple of the Peaceful Dragon, contains the most famous of Japan's dry gardens, created around 1480 by an unknown designer on the estate of Hosokawa Masamoto, located in the northwestern foothills of Kyoto. The southern half of the estate contains a pond with an island and a circumambulatory stroll path, to which was added a rectangular dry garden with a bed of white gravel, carefully raked to form east-west running bands. Within it were placed fifteen natural stones, clustered in five groups. The gravel around them is raked in the manner of ripples in a pond. The precise meaning of this koan is left open to interpretation. Perhaps the white field is an ocean and the rocks islands. The rocks could also stand for a tigress leading her cubs across a river. Ultimately, the garden is not meant to convey a singular interpretation but to serve as an aid to meditation, with the empty space between the stones just as important as the stones themselves—perhaps even more so.

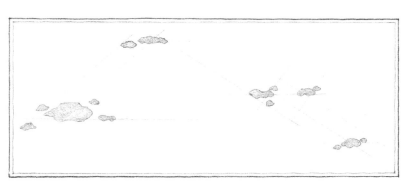

14.151 **Dry garden at Ryoanji**

1700 CE

INTRODUCTION

By the early 18th century, cities like Samarkand, Bukhara, Aleppo, Istanbul, Venice, and Florence, once at the heart of Eurasian trade, were becoming increasingly marginal to the new world economy centered on the maritime ports established by the European colonial powers. This phenomenon was global, spawning major new metropolises such as Hong Kong, Shanghai, Singapore, Bombay (now Mumbai), Calcutta (now Kolkata), Madras (now Chennai), Cape Town, St.-Louis (Senegal), Rio de Janeiro, Buenos Aires, Boston, and New York. It is not surprising, then, that the architectural survey of this time shows a world in which some areas were rapidly transforming under the modernizing sway of colonization, while others, in spite of the colonial frenzy, still clung to the old ways as long as possible.

This tumult of transformation centered on the Americas. Two hundred years after their conquest by the Europeans, the indigenous civilizations of the American continents had been almost completely destroyed. In their stead, a brand-new and revolutionary system of wealth generation was invented—the hacienda, or plantation, where vast tracts of land were used to grow a single or a few crops that could be shipped back to Europe for profit. Plantation culture not only transformed America; it also drastically impacted Africa, where an infrastructure was built to support the slave trade—including the development of internal exploitative cultures to facilitate the capture of slaves. Slavery put in place the hard divisions of racism in America, particularly after it was legalized into a race-based, hereditary institution in the late 17th century.

The plantation economies had the most transformative effect on Europe, where the massive influx of colonial wealth and goods radically remade urban culture. As colonial merchants plied European streets with coffee, sugar, tobacco, and tea, they created new urban institutions, such as coffeehouses, along with new building types, such as bourgeois apartments (or *hôtels*), parks, and theaters. This urban culture, which in so many ways still exists today, was instrumental in the rise of the bourgeoisie and preliminary to the discourses and ferment that led to the European Enlightenment in the late 18th century. If today the coffeehouse is essentially a place of recreation and quiet study—

perhaps the new library of our times—it is interesting to look back and see that it started as a site of novelty and exploration, a place to experience the new products of the colonial world.

The massive size of the colonial plantations, and the correspondingly massive volume of products that were grown, processed, shipped, distributed, and consumed—along with all the economic side eddies that this system generated—created an economic engine of unprecedented scale for Europe. It required a reimagining of governance and management that resulted in a new administrative culture focused on rationalization and efficiency. Although the Spanish were first in this reorganization, the French soon took the lead. Jean Baptiste Colbert, a renowned workaholic who served as the minister of finances from 1665 to 1683 under Louis XIV, took upon himself the task of overhauling and rationalizing the French government and bureaucracy. His administrative machinery gave the French, and subsequently the Dutch and English, who followed suit, a decisive advantage over the Spanish and Portuguese in the colonial competition.

Rationalization and efficiency, as the new administrative mantras of the times, also affected the culture. In architecture, the ongoing adaptation of the styles of antiquity for modern purposes was subjected to rationalization. The culture of science began to assert itself, particularly the questions of astronomy necessary for naval navigation. Although reason—beyond rationalization—had yet to become the dominant discourse of philosophy, its ideas were already being addressed in works such as those of Galileo and Copernicus. The push toward science was furthered in particular by the innumerable nautical and territorial maps that had to constantly be made and updated; the success of the colonial missions relied on their accuracy. As countries carefully guarded their knowledge of new cartographic information, it is no surprise that the French, Dutch, and English disputed the location of the prime meridian.

The European upper classes largely expended their new wealth building fantastic new palaces and the like, the most celebrated example being Louis XIV's extravaganza at Versailles. The fusses and frills of the Baroque continued to hold court in these palaces, as they did in the numerous Baroque churches and abbeys that were built across Europe. The Russians, under Czar Alexander, forced their way to the Baltic Sea in search of a viable port. Here, instead of launching a massive colonial campaign to compete with the British and French, they built a massive new capital city called St. Petersburg, founded in 1703 and modeled after French and Italian Baroque precedents. St. Petersburg was a project both heroic and extravagant, a self-conscious attempt to "catch up" with other countries that were considered more advanced by simply importing their culture and knowledge via a massive systematic transfer—thus mistaking symptom for cause. Such efforts would be repeated many times over in years to come, particularly by nations that were late to the colonial enterprise.

In England, the revolution wrought by the creation of the Church of England continued to play itself out with the radical Puritan call for de-Catholicization, which for a short while starting in 1688 even resulted in the overthrow of the monarchy. Its subsequent restoration resulted in the prosecution of the Puritans, many of whom then left for New England to join descendants of the *Mayflower* passengers. In the new world they sought to build their Puritan churches with renewed vigor, but their congregations included dissenters, such as Roger Williams, who left to found his own colony in Providence, Rhode Island, with religious toleration as one of its cornerstones. In keeping with their larger ethic, the Puritans, like the adherents of the Church of England, followed the austere renderings of a neo-Palladian architecture that relied on proportion and order for effect, rather than on style and gesture as in the Baroque style.

By the early 18th century, the Whigs had emerged as a force in English politics; they were strong supporters of English mercantile expansion (with protections in place) and advocates of constitutional monarchy. It was under the Whigs, and in their wake, that Sir Christopher Wren built his neo-Palladian churches in the aftermath of a great fire. The English picturesque garden now emerged— influenced though it was by descriptions of Chinese gardens—as an irregular landscape

with distributed follies that sought to unite the experience of the peripatetic visitor with surrounding nature. These gardens, along with philosophical propositions such as *cogito ergo sum* (I think, therefore I am), were at the genesis of the Enlightenment's autonomous subject.

The African slave trade was going full steam in the 1700s. Most of the slaves came from West Africa, and as a consequence, social structures in the region were devastated.

Meanwhile, the mineral wealth extracted from America continued to find its way across the Pacific to China, where it was exchanged by the Chinese for luxury goods such as porcelain and lacquerware. In the 17th century, China was in transition from the rule of the Ming to the Qing dynasty. The Ming, unable to capitalize on their early gains, had overprinted the Middle Kingdom's paper currency (the world's first), which led to serious inflation. In consequence, silver began to circulate as the de facto currency of the realm, which promoted coastal piracy.

Into the gap stepped the Manchu, Jurchen Mongolians from the northeastern frontier of China, who took over Ming China without a major battle and formed the Qing dynasty. Although theirs was still the largest economy in the world by far, the Qing quickly realized that they desperately needed silver to stabilize the currency. They also had to legitimize themselves as rulers, since they were a small and foreign minority. Not only did they manage to stabilize the currency, but they were also able to establish—first under the rule of the Kangxi Emperor and then under his grandson, the Qianlong Emperor—an administrative order that merged Confucian and Han Chinese systems with a transnational Manchu perspective that was keenly aware of the wider world beyond the Middle Kingdom. With their wealth, the Qing vastly expanded their borders, built vast and lavish palaces and gardens, established new cities, and, most importantly, renewed infrastructure. They also produced a new and comprehensive manual on building construction.

Even though a great quantity of Qing architecture still stands, it is not best served by a detailed analysis of its formal properties.

Formal orders and the quest for their perfection were an obsession in Europe at that time, but in China these things had been settled for some time and were no longer the defining question. Rather, the focus was on standardization, efficiency, and integration with the larger administrative machinery of the empire.

Qing China functioned as an efficient pre-modern empire and quickly became the cynosure of European intellectuals. Colonial ships carried missionaries to China, who settled there and subsequently produced detailed accounts of life and order under the Qing. These illustrated accounts made their way to Europe, where they were avidly read and citied by Enlightenment thinkers, particularly those who were keen to demonstrate nonreligious moral and political orders. It is in this sense that European stroll gardens such as Stowe in England, which were trying to establish the new human subject who was comfortable in nature rather than differentiated from it, can be seen as a reading of Chinese garden precedents. The Qing bureaucracy, or *jinshi* system, based on open competitive exams, was the role model of the European civil services. On the Chinese side, the Qing invited the Jesuits to court to learn from them and even built one of their palaces in European Baroque style.

The Koreans, strong supporters of the Ming, were forced to recognize the Qing authority in China; but once they did, they quickly adopted to it.

In Japan, the Tokugawa shoguns were also in the midst of redefining their culture at this time, creating a world that followed a strict code of behavior. The Bakafu code, as it was known, was in many respects astonishingly modern, as the rising middle class sought ways to articulate institutions suitable to its needs despite the restrictions placed on it by the shoguns.

The original colonial project to find an ocean route to the Indies for the spice trade continued to be pursued by several European powers—the Portuguese in particular, but also by the Dutch and the French—via private companies with monopolistic charters. The Portuguese built forts across the Amazon delta, and then across South and East Asia. In this way, the Portuguese colonial port network established the first infrastructure of today's global cities of Asia. The Dutch did the same, but their focus was on the fertile spice islands of modern-day Indonesia. The French, too, built trading posts worldwide, but their main interest, in competition with England, was in New England, Canada, and along the Mississippi. In these areas the French traded in fur, a commodity with a vast market in the frigid lands of northern Europe, where there were few forests left.

In India, European colonial companies traded and built ports with the consent of the Mughals, who remained formidable through the 17th century. Aurangzeb (r. 1658–1707) vastly expanded the Mughal Empire, bringing erstwhile vassal states directly under Mughal control. But unlike his predecessors and his Qing contemporaries in China, Aurangzeb adopted a much less tolerant attitude toward the diversity of India's peoples and cultures, and consequently his death in 1707 initiated a series of revolts. Shuja-ud-Daula in northern India, the Nawab of Oudh in Bengal, the Sikhs in Punjab, the Rajputs in Rajasthan, and the Marathas in the Deccan wrestled for power. At the same time, European colonizers began to build on their coastal footholds and start to acquire hinterlands. As a result, though this was a turbulent period in India, from a cultural and architectural perspective it was also a time of tremendous exploration. Jaipur, a beautiful new city, was laid out by Sawai Jai Singh, a former Mughal general, along an important trade highway. The Sikhs, a reformist movement, took root in northwestern India and established a formidable kingdom. Darbar Sahib ("Golden Temple") in Amritsar was their most important shrine. The Mallas of Nepal, meanwhile, enjoyed relative immunity from these global events next door, but their royal square in Patan embodied its own global history.

In contrast to the energy on both sides of the Atlantic, in China, and in India, building activity in West and Central Asia slowed down. The Ottomans held strong throughout the 17th century and in 1683 laid siege to Vienna again (after the first unsuccessful siege of 1529) but were conclusively defeated. In 1722, the Safavids of Persia were overrun by the Afghans. During the 18th century, the Ottoman Empire continued to reign from Istanbul, but it was now buffeted by the new wealth of the Atlantic trade. As in China, vast amounts of silver began to be smuggled into the Ottoman Empire, and a significant black market emerged. The resultant inflation destabilized their realms and rebellion ensued. The Mamluks of Egypt, their most prized possession, declared independence in 1768, and thereafter the Ottoman Empire began to go into decline.

Most books dealing with Islamic architecture end around 1750, after which time architecture that is retrospectively described as purely Islamic was no longer done on the same scale. Instead, new building forms emerged as a consequence of the Islamic world grappling with the colossal changes taking place around it. The result was hybridized architectural forms, a mix of divergent influences—an alternate modernity of its own kind.

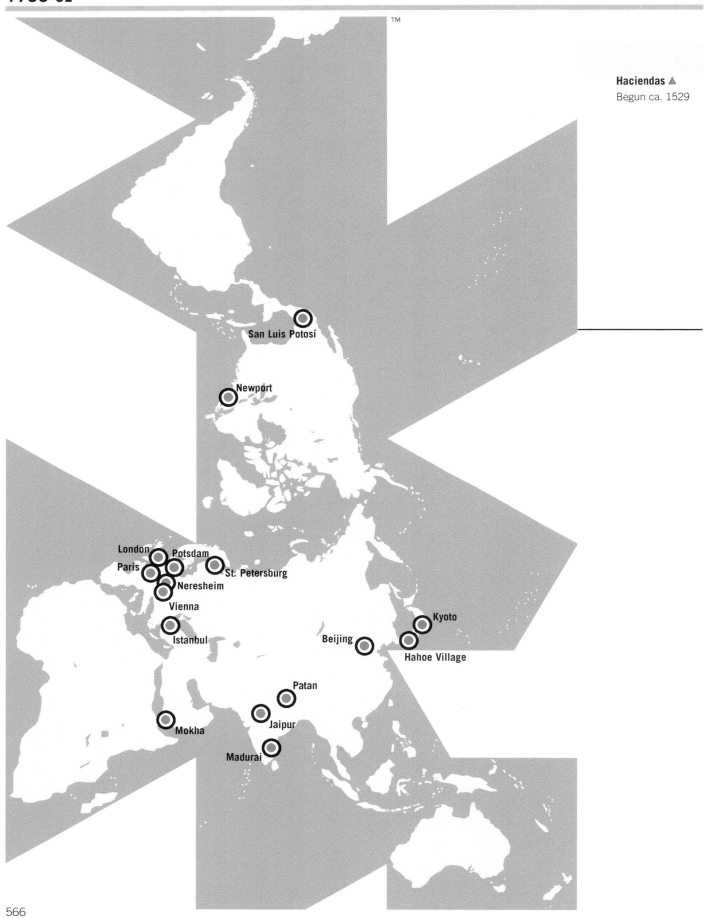

™

Haciendas ▲
Begun ca. 1529

San Luis Potosí

Newport

London Potsdam
Paris
St. Petersburg
Neresheim
Vienna
Istanbul
Beijing
Kyoto
Hahoe Village
Patan
Mokha
Jaipur
Madurai

Central America: Viceroyalty of New Spain
1535–1821

France: Bourbon Rule
1589–1792

▲ **Hôtel de Sully**
1624–29

▲ **Hôtel des Invalides**
1671–76

▲ **Versailles**   ▲ **L'Observatoire de Paris**
1661–1778   Begun 1671

▲ **Place Vendôme**
Laid out 1702

▲ **Sans Souci**
1757

The Baroque Era
Late 16th to early 18th century

▲ **Winter Palace**   ▲ **Vierzehnheiligen**
ca. 1730   1743–72

Sir Isaac Newton's *Principia* published ◉
1687

◉ Thomas Savery invents the steam engine
1696

◉ Abraham Darby produces high-quality iron
1711

1600 CE   **1700 CE**   **1800 CE**

◉ Benjamin Huntsman develops the
crucible method for making steel 1740

England: Stuart Rule
1603–1714

Hanoverian Rule
1714–1901

▲ **St. Paul's Cathedral**
1675–1709

▲ **Stowe Gardens**
Begun ca. 1712

▲ **St. Mary Woolnoth**
1716–24

▲ **Chiswick House**
1723–29

▲ **Stratford Hall Plantation**
1738

▲ **Shirley Plantation**
1738

▲ **Touro Synagogue**
1759–63

Qing Dynasty
1644–1911

▲ **White Stupa, Beihai**
1651

▲ **Yuanmingyuan**
1720s

Mallas of Nepal: ▲ **Durbar Square**
Rebuilt 17th century

Ottoman Empire: ▲ **Nurosmaniye Mosque**
1749–55

Japan: Edo Period
1615–1868

▲ **Sumiya**
1670s

South Asia: Mughal Dynasty
1526–1858

▲ **Meenakshi Sunderesvara Temple**
1623–59

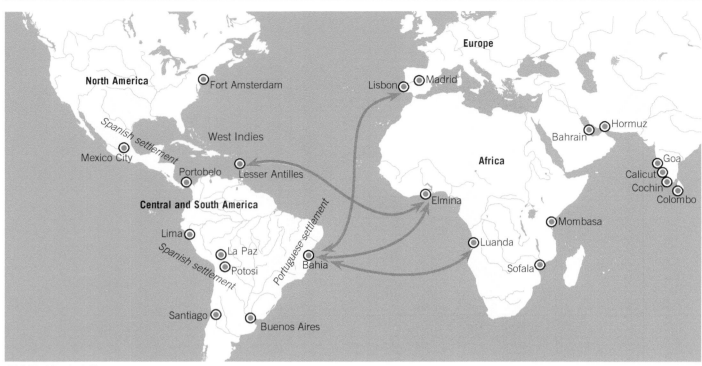

15.1 World colonialism

COLONIALISM

By the end of the 17th century, what had begun as risky sojourns to distant lands in search of less expensive spices developed into a struggle among the various European nations for control of coastal trading posts across the globe and with them, wherever possible, the hinterland that supplied those ports. The principal competitors were Portugal, Spain, Holland, France, and Britain.

For the first two centuries of its history (roughly the 16th–18th centuries), the colonial project was focused on the competition to exploit and develop the Americas. Spain, Portugal, and then France, England, and Holland all competed aggressively for a piece of the American pie—first for its mineral wealth and then, more profitably and impactfully, for its land. At the same time, all these European powers except Spain also developed trading ports around the rest of the rest of the globe, particularly along the coasts of South, Southeast, and East Asia. But at this time, these ports had only a fraction of the value of the American territories. It would not be until the 19th century—as most of the colonies in the Americas became independent and European wealth, particularly that of England, increased exponentially with industrialization—that the

colonial enterprise became fully global.

Initially, the Portuguese focused on developing the Amazon coast, and the Spanish conquistadores maintained their aggressive focus on annexing the territories of Central America and Andean South America. But then, as the gold and silver began to run out, they invented the plantation and its hacienda culture focused on the large-scale production of sugar, coffee, and cocoa using indentured labor. Most of the mineral wealth was gone or tightly controlled by the time the French, Dutch, and British got into the game, so they too ultimately focused on exploiting the plantation economies. At first the British, Dutch, and French developed footholds in the New England area, far from Spanish territories, and competed mostly for fur trade with the indigenous people. But as these footholds evolved into full-fledged colonies, they gained economic strength with the establishment of tobacco plantations, most of them British, in Virginia and territories farther south.

Before colonial plantations, in Europe sugar was a highly luxurious commodity accessible only to the upper classes, coffee was an exotic Arabic drink, and cocoa was mostly unknown. The plantations enabled sugar to be sold on the streets. Together with

coffee, cocoa, and tobacco, this chartered an urban addictive culture that is still with us. The plantations powered mercantile capitalism, the core of which was the large-scale, cheap production of a single crop destined for mass consumption. Racial slavery was its by-product.

The plantations were massive, as land was essentially "free." Large tracts of land under single control meant that large amounts of cash crops could be produced efficiently. The principal problem was the availability and supply of labor. At first European settlers worked the land themselves, encouraging locals to migrate. But this quickly became a poor economic proposition, although there was a massive migration of Irish populations (forced from Ireland by the policies of James II) to the Caribbean and Virginia. In 1619 the Dutch brought slaves from Africa to North America to work on the plantations. The native American populations had already been decimated, and native slaves often escaped, disappearing back to their tribes. But African slaves, in a completely foreign land with no hope of ever making it back to their homelands, were both more reliable and more easily obtained, with a steady stream of ships bringing new slaves to American shores. This is what led to the African slave "solution."

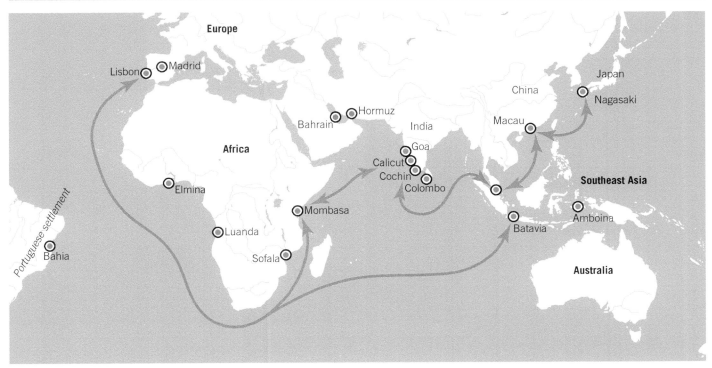

World colonialism (continued)

Initially, policies of the Spanish crown identified the locals as heathens and sought to destroy or convert them. By this system conversion was a process of acceptance; however exploitative it was, it provided potential paths to freedom. When the first Africans were brought to the Caribbean in the 1520s, they too were given the option of conversion. Racial slavery—the idea that African labor could be owned, and that children of African women inherited the slave identity of their mother and were slaves regardless of their father—was only developed as an institution on the British tobacco plantations of Virginia around landmark court cases in the middle of the 16th century. After that, the African slave trade increased significantly.

Slavery had existed across Eurasia and Africa since the beginning of history. The Egyptian pharaohs, the Greeks, Romans, Phoenicians, Persians, Seljuks, Indians, and Chinese all practiced slavery in various forms, particularly as it concerned subjugated and conquered peoples. In Africa, too, slavery preexisted colonial trade. But the new colonial model, dependent on cheap labor, magnified it to such a degree that the history of Europe, Africa, and the Americas was irrevocably altered. It is estimated that more

than 20 million people, and possibly as many as 40 million, were forcibly removed from Africa; all the colonizing powers participated.

The legacy of the plantation system was unambiguously negative and had consequences that are still playing out today. In Mexico, even by 1910, 70 percent of all arable land was held by just 1 percent of the population, and similar situations existed in South American countries. Almost every country or region that was colonized by the plantation system had to struggle later to create secular, scientific, and cultural institutions on par with those of the Europeans.

While critics of the slave trade could be found everywhere—particularly in England—from its earliest days, all European powers exploited the plantation and its system of slave labor. The situation in New England was arguably somewhat better: There were no large chiefdoms, as there were in Louisiana and Georgia, to stand up to the invaders, and this allowed settlers to nourish the illusion that they were occupying virgin territory. In addition, the influx of Europeans was extraordinarily diverse. By 1700, from Maine to Virginia, villages and towns had a mixture of Dutch and English Puritans, French Calvinists, Catholics, Swedes,

Spanish Jews, and English Anglicans. By the early 1700s, a traveler would have found courthouses, schools, churches, roads, and two universities—Harvard, founded in 1636, and Yale, founded in 1701. Although New England ships participated and profited extensively in the slave trade, slave ownership itself was relatively unusual. This New England exceptionalism in colonial America set the stage for conflict with the southern British settlements.

While the colonial project in the Americas quickly became a settler project, in most of the rest of the world the Europeans were primarily interested in setting up trading outposts. The Portuguese expanded from their ports along the Amazon coast by quickly establishing ports on the coasts of India, China, and points between in Southeast Asia. The English, French, and Dutch followed the Portuguese lead, developing competing ports on the Bay of Bengal coast of India, in southern China, and at intervals along the route through the Straits of Malacca. The Dutch focused their interests in Indonesia, and the English exploited their superior naval navigation skills to claim the territories of Australia and New Zealand, although it was the Dutch who first discovered them.

Outside of Australia and America, European colonial enterprise at this time focused on trade with local powers. Colonial forts, with their backs to their hinterlands—where they depended on treaties for their safety—faced their guns toward the sea to ward off attacks from competing European ships. Old European rivalries and alliances were replayed on these distant shores, and it was not unusual for European war treaties to dictate the loss or gain of distant colonial forts. The Asian powers, particularly the Mughals in India and the Ming and Qing dynasties in China, quietly tolerated and profited from these coastal activities, as long as the Europeans stayed within the terms of their treaties. It was the old Eurasian world as usual, but now along ocean-faring seaways. Ultimately, this seemingly small change would tilt the balance decisively in favor of the European colonists.

The largely Arabic and Islamic countries of West and Central Asia were of limited interest to the colonial powers. The Ottoman Empire was seen primarily as a convenient bulwark against czarist Russia. Persia was of even less consequence to the Europeans and slowly shrank under Russian pressure. The area did not receive any strong interest from Europeans until the discovery of oil in the 20th century.

15.2 Hacienda Tabi, Mexico

It is no accident that just as the colonial project was unfolding and flooding Europe with great wealth, the 18th century saw a philosophical movement emerge that challenged the arbitrariness of power and attitudes toward "primitive cultures." Known as the Enlightenment, it tried to imagine alternative civil and institutional models in tune with new thinking about the rule of law, even though it did not reject colonialism as such. Its successes and failures in that respect are still being debated. The Enlightenment ideals were widely discussed in the cities of France, England, and Germany, though they were also tested, contested, and remade in the colonies. Though usually described as "European," the Enlightenment can in fact be considered a global colonial construct.

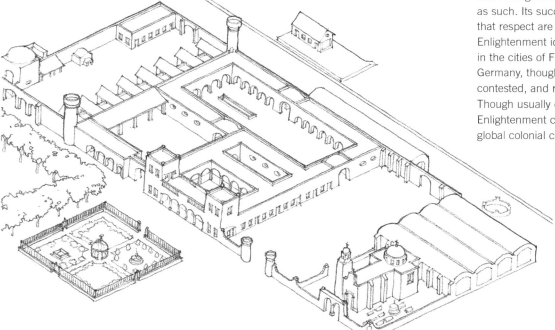

15.3 Pictorial view: a typical hacienda

Haciendas

The hacienda system is thought to date to 1529, when the Spanish crown granted Hernán Cortés the title of Marquis of the Valley of Oaxaca, in the present-day state of Morelos, Mexico. The grant included all the Native Americans then living on the land and the power of life and death over them. The Native Americans, like the slaves who soon arrived from Africa, were bound to a particular hacienda for life, as were their descendants. By the 18th century, the system, stretching from Mexico to Argentina, was the primary means of export production and in some cases the core of urban developments. The hacienda was developed throughout the Americas, and later other parts of the colonial world developed the plantation system.

Haciendas came in various sizes, and some were gigantic. Peotillos, 55 kilometers from San Luis Potosí in Mexico, for example, controlled an area of 193,000 hectares. The word *hacienda* comes from an Old Spanish term (*facienda*) derived from the Latin *focere*, which means "to make something," and most haciendas specialized in one or two products, always an export-based cash crop. In areas where water was abundant, sugarcane was grown, which gave rise to rum and liquor production. Other haciendas focused on livestock, cacao, coffee, tobacco, cotton, rubber, and a variety of woods. Since the hacienda was often remote from metropolitan centers, it had to accommodate a wide range of functions. It had its own marketplace, cemetery, and jail. Layout followed a common scheme involving courtyards for different purposes: for the workers and their families, for workshops, and for warehouses. The main residential building fronted onto a plaza, known as a *patio de campo*. The link between the *patio de campo* and the more restricted private areas of the master was through a corridor known as a *zaguán*.

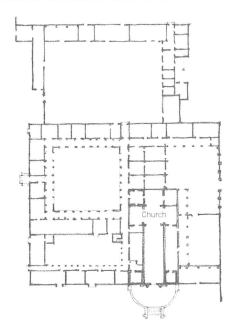

15.4 Plan: Brazilian hacienda, Santa Catalina

In Brazil, the development of sugar and coffee plantations generated a proliferation of *fazendas* (the Portuguese equivalent of *haciendas*) as early as the 17th century in the northeast of the country. As in other places, the high death rate of the native population created a need for African slaves, and eventually over 3 million were brought to the country. Thus a new type of construction was added to the architecture of the *fazendas*—the *senzala*, or slave quarter, which was divided into small spaces to house the slaves and their families. The symbolic and economic center of the *fazenda* was the large patio where the coffee was dried. The master's house was located on one side of the square, usually positioned on higher ground overlooking the entire area.

15.5 Example of a Brazilian hacienda

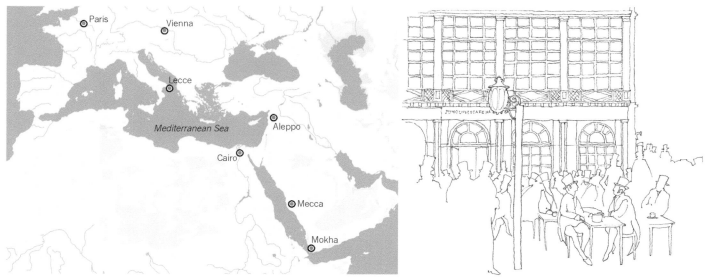

15.6 Africa, West Asia, and Europe, ca. 1700

15.7 Kaffeehaus Jüngling, Vienna, ca. 1838

New European Colonial Urban Culture

The expanding middle class, with its ravenous taste for novelty food items and luxuries supplied by the colonies, rapidly reshaped European culture. The diet changed considerably, with tomatoes, potatoes, and corn becoming the new staples; chocolate, imported from the Spanish Americas, became a luxury item; and sugar from the Caribbean became an indispensable consumer good in a very short time. Coffee, however, came to Europe first from Africa by way of Arab traders. It is thought to have been first produced in Ethiopia and Yemen. The drink caused a great deal of controversy in the Islamic world, because some authorities thought coffee was intoxicating and therefore should be forbidden. As a result, its consumption was initially associated with subversive political activity, perhaps because it was drunk in the new all-male coffeehouses, where intrigue might be brewed along with the beverage. From the beginning, then, the social significance of drinking coffee derived from the fact that it was consumed in public by an exclusively male clientele in this new kind of establishment, the coffeehouse, usually located on major commercial arteries. The coffeehouse of Ipshir Pasha in Aleppo (1653) is a rare early coffeehouse to have survived to present times. It consists of a courtyard and a covered hall, with windows overlooking the street to the south. Domes of varying shapes cover the hall.

The end of the Turkish trade monopoly over coffee came in 1616, when the Dutch East India Company illegally exported and planted seedlings in Java and elsewhere. From these plantations vastly larger amounts of coffee could be manufactured and exported at cheaper prices, flooding the market. The French subsequently founded coffee plantations in the Caribbean, leading to a rapid expansion of the drink's popularity.

The first Parisian café was opened in 1672. The Kaffeehaus Juengling in Vienna, from about 1750, had a completely glazed two-story wooden facade overlooking a piazza provided with tables and illuminated by a large lamp (such outdoor lighting being at the time quite a novelty). By 1800, there were more than three thousand coffeehouses in England.

Tobacco was brought to Europe by the Spanish army, and smoking was eventually taken up by men of the upper classes who were under the impression that it enhanced their reasoning capacities. Thus, along with coffeehouses emerged gentlemen's smoking rooms. The European habit of simultaneously drinking coffee and smoking stems from this era, when mass-produced colonial products transformed European culture. Sugar in particular starred in the newly emerging rituals of consumption. It was put into tea and coffee (first in France, so it is thought), thus combining—with a piece of chocolate—a culinary experience that was both addictive and gave consumers a

sense of cosmopolitanism and global access. Professional sugar bakers of the time, called *konditors* in southern Germany, often created a whole "sugar course," in which an entire meal was replicated in sugar for the guests to view and nibble on before it was taken away and the real meal served. No European city was complete without its *konditorei* serving sweets to ladies on cozy couches, forming the counterpoint to the bars for men, where coffee and liquor were consumed standing up. These socializing habits formed in the days of colonialism still continue today.

Mealtimes also began to change to accommodate the transformation of taste. Until then, the principal meal, dinner, was served at midday, but the custom of drinking tea and eating chocolate in the afternoon caused it to be shifted to later in the evening. It soon became the custom to start the day with coffee and chocolate, a repast now called breakfast. Whereas coffeehouses were associated with boisterous male conversation and business deals, tea became domesticated into a ceremony presided over largely by women, who often served it on tea sets made of silver or porcelain, both colonial commodities. (In 1717, 300,000 kilograms of tea were imported; 1.4 million kilograms were imported by 1742.) Furniture was designed to accommodate the new rituals, including high-backed padded chairs and a "conversation chair" that allowed one to lean back in a more relaxed position.

15.8 **East Facade of the Louvre, Paris**

THE LOUVRE AND THE *HÔTEL*

After the English defeated the Spanish Armada in 1588, France acquired the formerly Spanish Isle of Bourbon for use as a commercial base in the Indian Ocean; took over the mouth of the Senegal River in Africa, where it became involved in the slave trade; and set up sugar plantations in the Caribbean. French fur dealers also settled Canada, founding Quebec City in 1608, and traveling south down the Mississippi until they reached its mouth, where they founded New Orleans in 1718. The first major colonial export from North America was fur. (Large animals had been hunted out of existence in Europe centuries before.) Fur became the new fashion requirement for the elites. The money flowing into France, however, created an inflation that made the poor significantly poorer. For the elite, however, it brought unimaginable wealth, which was spent in lavish constructions beginning around 1660.

Unlike previous French kings, who had preferred to live in rural châteaux, Henry IV (1553–1610) periodically moved the court to Paris. To accommodate him, Louis Le Vau (1631–70), France's leading garden and château designer, took over the job of updating the Louvre, an old 12th-century fort, into an urban palace. He worked in collaboration with Claude Perrault. In 1664, a competition was held for the east facade of the Louvre, and the final design was a synthesis of the ideas of Perrault, Le Vau, and possibly others. Given the project's complex

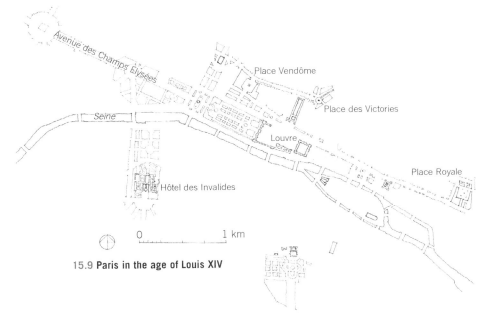

15.9 **Paris in the age of Louis XIV**

history and the number of architects involved in the final design, it is an astonishingly successful building. The high ground floor, with its narrow, minimally detailed windows, serves as a podium for the main floor, with ranges of coupled, freestanding columns that form a screen for the building behind, creating a linear loggia. A central pedimented projection was integrated, with the columnar screens to its flanks. Unpedimented "pavilions" with pilasters instead of columns define the far ends. Such an arrangement

was quite novel. It could be compared with Palazzo Porto-Breganze, designed by Andrea Palladio (built by Vincenzo Scamozzi, 1575), which is more unified in appearance; or the Villa Barbaro (1549–58), where the pieces are more differentiated. The Louvre is also significant in the history of technology. The columns carry straight entablatures that are actually a series of disguised arches held together in part by tie rods.

With Henry IV's move to Paris, the wealthy wanted to live as close as possible to the Parisian court, however temporarily. The result was the *hôtel*, a temporary lodging designed around a specific set of spaces. A porte cochere allowed carriages to enter the *cour d'honneur*, where the ritual of arriving, dismounting, and entering was played out. The stables were located to one side of the courtyard, along with special rooms for the carriages. The *corps de logis* (principal living quarters) faced the court. To the rear of the *corps de logis* was a garden, perhaps with a gallery, a long windowed room for taking in the views and conversing. Visiting rooms, ballrooms, and dining rooms, part of the *appartements de parade*, were on the main floor. The family living quarters, which were usually above, consisted of an antechamber, in which to meet visitors; the bedroom (*chambre*); and sometimes a more private room for conversation or study, known as the cabinet. Servants lived under the roof. In the arrangement of the elements, symmetry was preferred, at least for the entranceway and courtyard, with much creativity going into establishing the necessary imprint in the often irregular urban sites with which the architects had to work. One of the best examples is the Hôtel de Sully (1624–29) by Jean du Cerceau. It was lived in by Maximilien de Béthune, Duc de Sully (1560–1641), superintendent of finances under King Henry III and later Henry IV's prime minister.

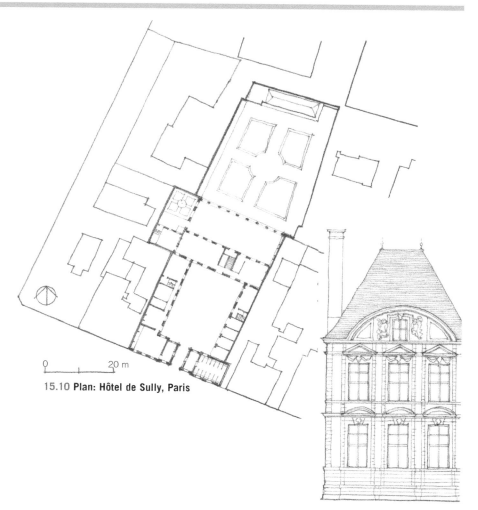

0   20 m

15.10 Plan: Hôtel de Sully, Paris

15.11 Hôtel de Sully

15.12 **First floor plan: Hôtel Crozat, Paris**

0 ⊕ 10 m

15.13 **Plan: Place Vendôme**

Most of the early 17th-century *hôtels*, though located near the Royal Palace, were built wherever land was available and were thus relatively isolated from each other. As the century progressed, architects sought to integrate hotels into real estate packages known as royal squares. Though these squares were called royal, they were usually built on the initiatives of private individuals or municipalities—even though the climate for their creation was fostered by the king—and they therefore had to be consonant with the principle of royal dignity. The first in Paris was the circular Place des Victoires (1684–87), with an equestrian statue of the king in the middle. This was followed by the Place Vendôme (commissioned in 1677), whose facades were all designed by Jules Hardouin-Mansart (1646–1708) and his disciple Pierre Bullet. Both *hôtels* have rooms in a remarkable variety of sizes and configurations; but typical of French design was the absence of corridors (except in the servants' quarters) to link the rooms, which were organized sequentially along the main facade.

15.14 **Place Vendôme, Paris**

15.15 **Château de Versailles, France**

CHÂTEAU DE VERSAILLES

The bulk of Henry IV's building expenditure, however, was on his extravagant rural residence, the Château de Versailles, an old hunting lodge about 20 kilometers southwest of Paris. The redesign of the building into a grand palace by Louis Le Vau and Jules Hardouin-Mansart went through several phases, beginning in 1661 after André Le Nôtre had begun work on the gardens and fountains. The architects solved the problem of what to do with the old building by wrapping a new building around it. The original palace still stands, but it is embedded within the fabric of a new structure that consists of a series of forecourts, creating a telescoping U around a central court at the top of a gently sloping hill. Processional avenues leading to the château were central to the spectacle and ceremony of the design. Three avenues lead through the countryside to the front gate, but only the central and northern avenues lead to Paris; the southern avenue, 1 kilometer long, was added for the sake of symmetry. Arriving carriages passed through the first gate and were stopped at the second; from there, all but the most distinguished had to proceed on horse or foot to the last gate, which led into the inner courtyard.

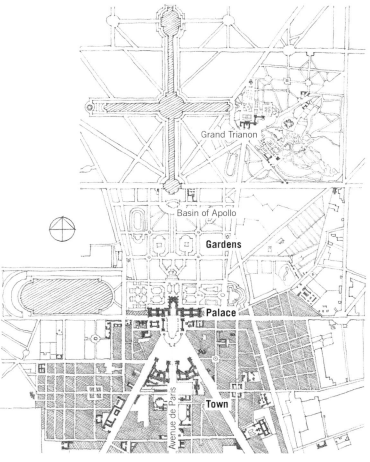

15.16 **Plan of Versailles**

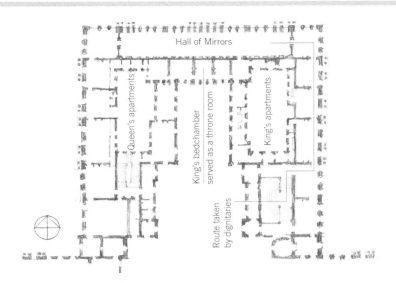

Hall of Mirrors

Queen's apartments

King's bedchamber served as a throne room

King's apartments

Route taken by dignitaries

15.17 **Development of the Palace at Versailles during Louis XIV's reign**

15.18 **Hardouin-Mansart's chapel at Versailles**

On the ground floor of the palace were apartments, mainly for the royal guards and administrators. One room to the right, however, was specially prepared for the reception of important visitors. It contained the grand double Stairway of the Ambassadors, resplendent with colored marble and wall paintings. The stairway led to the principal reception rooms where the king lived. There were no corridors. The apartments were arranged enfilade—that is, the doors of the rooms were lined up to provide a vista along the length of the suite. At the heart of the composition was the king's bedroom, located at the conceptual center of the palace's universe. The bedroom was not a private room, but a place where the king met friends and even important dignitaries.

At first the gardens were designed for traditional uses, like walks and pleasurable conversation, but Louis XIV introduced the idea of the garden celebration, or *fête*, which included horsemanship events, banquets, plays, music, and fireworks. These events, recorded in publications, were part of the king's publicity and propaganda apparatus to enhance the fame of Versailles. A century later, however, they served contrary to their purpose as the same propaganda was used to trumpet the extravagance of Versailles and whip up revolutionary fervor against royalty.

15.19 **Hall of Mirrors, Palace at Versailles**

15.20 Aerial view of St. Petersburg, Russia

Work had progressed far enough by 1712 for relics from the Vladimir-Suzdal Monastery to be sent to the St. Alexander Nevsky Monastery, named after the 13th-century national hero St. Alexander Nevsky who received his name after beating the Swedes on the Neva River. St. Petersburg now had its founding myth and was an instant religious as well as secular center. To speed things along, Peter, in 1714, even forbade masonry construction throughout the rest of Russia to ensure a supply of qualified workers and materials for St. Petersburg.

ST. PETERSBURG

Of the many Baroque projects of the period, none rivaled that of St. Petersburg in scale and complexity. At the start of the 17th century, Russia was a backward country, at the mercy of conflicting forces. There were urban riots in 1648, a revolt in 1662, a rebellion in 1669, and an uprising in 1668. Czar Peter Alexeyevich Romanov I (1672–1725), known as Peter the Great, reestablished order, modernized Russia, and pulled the country out of its isolation. Singlehandedly, he turned the Orthodox Muscovite state into a secular, Westernized empire—against considerable opposition from many levels of society. This was realized through massive forced-labor enterprises as well as a series of wars that consumed as much as 90 percent of the state budget. The result, however, was an empire that stretched from the Baltic to the Caspian Sea. After his victory over Sweden in a war that lasted twenty-one years, Russia could again sail down the Neva River to the Gulf of Finland. To safeguard his access to the Baltic Sea, Russia built the Peter and Paul Fortress, the cornerstone of which was laid in 1703. The project eventually grew into one of the biggest building sites in Europe. Forty thousand peasants were conscripted, along with Swedish prisoners of war.

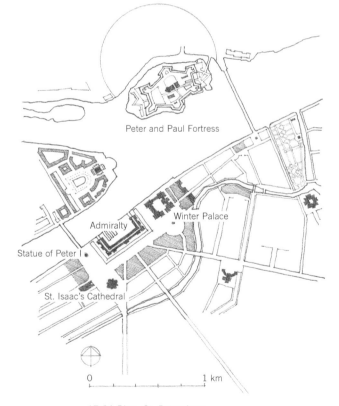

15.21 Plan: St. Petersburg

15.22 **Winter Palace, St. Petersburg**

15.23 **Winter Palace, St. Petersburg**

The completion of Versailles in 1710 prompted imitation by other European royals. Peter the Great's Winter Palace in St. Petersburg was initially a modest affair designed by Domenico Trezzini in 1711, but it was quickly expanded. Its present form began to take shape in the 1730s, designed by Bartolomeo Rastrelli, who imagined its twin facades—facing the square on one side and the Neva River on the other—as relentless Elizabethan Baroque facades, 250 meters long and broken only by two symmetrical projecting bays. The windows of the lowest story are taller than the rest, and each window is separated from the next by pilasters. In plan the palace is an elongated rectangle, with an enclosed court. Most of the building was used for courtly functions, with the apartments of the royal families situated toward the back, looking onto an enclosed garden. Catherine II greatly enlarged the Winter Palace when she asked the French architect Jean-Baptiste Vallin de la Mothe, who designed the Imperial Academy of Arts in St. Petersburg, to add a new private wing, where she amassed an extensive art collection. This came to be known as the Hermitage. The storming of the Winter Palace in 1917 was a signature moment of the Bolshevik Revolution, valorized extensively in Soviet painting, literature, and film.

15.24 18th-century Europe

15.25 Observatoire de Paris, France

RATIONALIZATION AND THE AGE OF REASON

While the Spanish thought that stockpiling gold and silver was the way to build wealth, the French, Dutch, and English, focused on economic efficiency as a means of wealth generation. Their success lay in combining absolutism with highly rationalized governmental processes and investment in a national knowledge base. The rationalization of the national economy was the undertaking of Jean-Baptiste Colbert (1619–83), one of Louis XIV's chief advisors. He was responsible for many of the bureaucratic innovations that, though cumbersome, created the base for France's economic prosperity and particularly its ordering of colonial territories and extraction processes. Thanks to Colbert, there was a new understanding that there was a nexus between global trade and the national economy. Colbert also appreciated that economic power was dependent on knowledge. He therefore commissioned extensive studies of, for example, shipbuilding, navigation, and armaments to ensure that the French fleet remained the strongest in the world. He also founded the Royal Academy of Science (1666) and the Academy of Architecture (1671), among other institutions, to serve and advise government administrators and ministers.

In economics, rationalization is defined as the act of bringing order to ad hoc workflows by defining appropriate rules or processes. It is thus not surprising that rationalization is linked to the so-called Age of Reason, for the scientific work of early scientists and philosophers of this age was also the search for the underlying processes and rules that defined the apparent ad hoc phenomenon of the world. Galileo and Tycho Brache were both looking for mathematical explanations for the movements of planets. Both knew René Descartes (1596–1650), the French-Dutch philosopher, with his famous declaration of the primacy of reason, "*cogito, ergo sum*" ("I think, therefore I am"). Condemned by the Catholic Church, which purported to rule by God's design, the rationalist world was conceived in the crucible of the colonial experience. One saw the publication of René Descartes's *Discours de la méthode* (1637), Thomas Hobbes's *Leviathan* (1651), as well as the *Théorie de la construction des vaisseaux* (Theory of the Construction of Ships, 1667) by the Jesuit priest Pierre Hotte, a professor of mathematics who sought to improve the art of shipbuilding. The slide rule, the barometer, the thermometer, and the compound microscope all came into being in the first half of the 17th century. Generally speaking, 17th-century science stressed mechanics as a governing principle in the same way that governments began to stress and extend their bureaucratic reach, both ultimately promising efficiencies of production. The world was suddenly filled not only with agency but also with the means to control and define agency and to give it spatial extension and measure.

Observatoire de Paris

Colbert realized that key to colonial dominance was precise knowledge of astronomy. For this purpose he initiated the construction of the Observatoire de Paris in 1671, through which ran the French Meridian, the basis of French nautical maps that was in competition with the meridians at Greenwich and Antwerp. Although Greenwich was adopted as the international reference in 1884, the French continued to use their own until World War I absolutely necessitated a single reference.

The Observatoire's architect was Claude Perrault (1613–88), whose brother Charles was secretary to Colbert. A fervent believer in the exalted position of his times, Perrault was familiar with Greek and knew Latin. His 1673 translation of Vitruvius's *Ten Books on Architecture* was authoritative and well-annotated, and became the standard work on architecture in Europe. Though Perrault's own taste influenced the illustrations, he attempted to adhere as much as possible to the information in Vitruvius' text, setting an example for accuracy and attention to detail that was to become an essential aspect of the neoclassical mentality. His images emphasized the undecorated aspects of antiquity, resisting the temptation, prevalent at his time, to dwell on ornamentation and decoration. A particularly heated debate revolved around the question of whether the perception of beauty was a result of custom or a spontaneous response. Perrault

15.26 **Courtyard, Hôtel des Invalides, Paris**

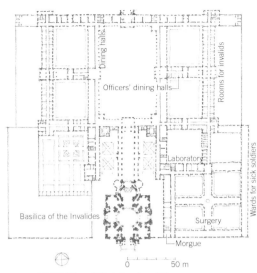

15.27 **Plan: Hôtel des Invalides**

argued that beauty was not a fixed property to be revealed by the artist but a variable depending on custom, pointing out, for example, that one can find neither two buildings—nor two authors—that agree on all subject or always follow the same rules.

The Observatoire was quite austere by the standards of the day. There were no orders, no columns, and no pilasters. Simple string courses demarcating the stories and openings are either slightly recessed from the smooth wall surface or surrounded by barely projecting moldings. Each side of the octagonal corner towers was aligned with the sun's position at solstices and equinoxes, and the eastern one was unroofed for the use of a telescope within. The building was put together with the greatest skill, and the staircase, with its complex three-dimensional curving surfaces—all in stone—still astonishes today. The roof was used as a platform from which astronomical measurements could be made. A hole in the center of the floors of the main chambers allowed the sun's zenith to be calculated.

Hôtel des Invalides

Hospitals had first appeared in Europe as a by-product of pilgrimages and of the Crusades. There were several important hospitals in Italy. The Knights of St. John were well known for their hospitals on Rhodes and elsewhere. By the 18th century, however, hospitals were flooded not only with the thousands of soldiers who fought in the almost endless cycle of battles, but also

by the poor and the indigent, who formed an increasingly large lower class. Plagues and epidemics added to the problem. In Paris, a cholera epidemic in 1519 and the plagues of 1580, 1596, 1606, and 1630 struck down thousands. But because hospitals remained associated with religious orders and charitable institutions, there was practically no distinction between a hospital, a pesthouse, and a poorhouse. Conditions were so terrible that the sick were often unwilling to leave their houses for a hospital, concerned that while they were sequestered, their property would be pillaged or their income threatened. To combat these conditions, Henry IV decreed the construction of the Hôpital St.-Louis (begun 1607). It was outside the city walls and easily accessible from major roads. The wards consisted of wide, open corridors with patients' beds placed against the walls. Four of these corridor buildings were linked to form a large courtyard.

At the end of the Thirty Years' War in 1648, much of Europe was flooded with former soldiers, many of whom had lived their entire adult lives in the military and had difficulty adjusting to civilian life, suffering from a form of PTSD. The Hôtel des Invalides (1671–76) aimed to address this problem in that it served as a military retirement dormitory. Behind its moat and expansive entrance lies a large court, while ranges of buildings to the right and left are grouped around smaller courts. The north

facade is articulated in typical French fashion by central and end pavilions that project forward. Apart from the entrance porches, there are no columns or pilasters on the main facade. The court has two stories of arches on piers relieved only by the pedimented pavilions at the center along the axis. There were special areas for sick and wounded soldiers, for pauper soldiers, and a barracks for older veterans. There were surgery areas and large mess halls where soldiers ate, with their officers at the head table.

Hospitals in England, built from public funds, tended to be simpler and less generous by comparison. There was considerable ambivalence among the English upper classes and Tories about spending money in a way that many thought would seem to reward poverty. Chelsea Hospital (begun 1682) shows, however, the first awareness of French innovation regarding the problems of former soldiers. Designed by Sir Christopher Wren, the cells were placed in ranges, back to back. At the end of the range, a larger room was set out for the sergeants. Instead of an enclosed quadrangle, the wards faced each other across a courtyard open to the Thames River, with a great hall and chapel linking the wards at the far end. The hospital's governor and lieutenant governor lived in detached pavilions at the corners. The differences between the two hospitals speaks volumes about the English and French attitudes about society and hierarchy at the time.

15.28 **Painted vault of Vierzehnheiligen, near Bamberg, Germany**

15.29 **Elevation and plan: Vierzehnheiligen**

15.30 **Nave of Vierzehnheiligen**

Johann Balthasar Neumann and the New Neresheim

Largely rural and possessing only three towns with a population over 100,000, Catholic Bavaria in southern Germany had not only withstood the Reformation but was also resistant to the aristocratic urban Catholicism of nearby Austria. Here a few architects assisted by painters, stucco workers, and sculptors created a unique style of church architecture, without a dome. Johann Michael Fischer (1692–1766) and Johann Balthasar Neumann (1687–1753) were the most prolific architects. Neumann's most extraordinary work is perhaps the Church of Vierzehnheiligen (1743–72) at a Franciscan monastery near the town of Bamberg, Germany. It had become a pilgrimage church in the mid-15th century, following what was said to be a miraculous apparition.

Neumann's last and most comprehensively conceived major project was the church of Neresheim (1747–92). It was integrated into the fabric of a Benedictine monastery and includes at its choir end an old tower from an earlier Romanesque church. Oval and circular vaults are supported on an undulating frame of columns, pilasters, arches, and piers. Though the space may read as decorative and plastic, Neumann was an officer in the engineering corps, and his buildings were just as much a testament to his engineering as to his design skills. He used wall piers or short sections of wall turned at right angles to the nave as primary load-bearing elements, eliminating the necessity for a solid continuous outer surface. Notwithstanding the cheerful interior, the exterior shell of the church was relatively plain. The oval at the crossing is placed lengthwise to the longitudinal interior, stretching between the part of the church that was used by the community and the choir at the rear reserved for the monks. The oval is counterbalanced by smaller ovals that evoke the tradition of the transept without interfering in the spatial liturgical rituals, which did not require such spaces. The ovals are connected by curving vaults that leave one in doubt as to how they work structurally, with light from the large windows visually dissolving the borders of the different spatial elements.

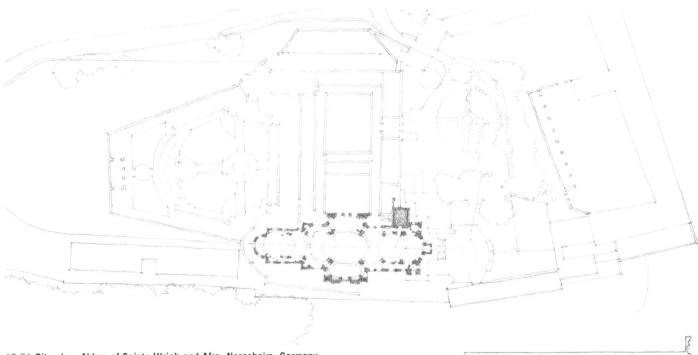

15.31 Site plan: Abbey of Saints Ulrich and Afra, Neresheim, Germany

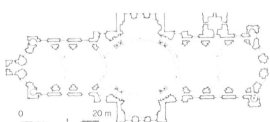

15.32 Plan and section: Church of Neresheim

0   20 m

15.33 Interior: Church of Neresheim

CHINA AND THE EUROPEAN ENLIGHTENMENT

The Jesuits, with their emphasis on education, were at the forefront of bridging the Chinese and European worlds. In 1601, the Italian Jesuit Matteo Ricci (1552–1610) arrived in Beijing and established a Catholic mission. For the next two centuries the Jesuits, as well as members of other Catholic orders, built close links to the Qing court while converting approximately 250,000 Chinese to Christianity. Because of their strong interest in education and their own high levels of education, many Jesuits became trusted members of the Qing court and were given important positions, such as control of the Board of Astronomy.

These Europeans wrote home detailed accounts of what they saw, which were published as books, usually in French or Latin, in Paris, the European center of Jesuit activities. These included *Confucius, the Philosopher of the Chinese* (1687); *Description of China* (1735), in 4 volumes; the long series *Edifying and Curious Letters*, in 34 volumes (1702–76); *General History of China*, in 13 volumes (1777–85); and *Memoirs on the History, Sciences, Arts, etc., of the Chinese*, in 16 volumes (1776–1814).

The Chinese political system was studied and cited by many European thinkers, such as Voltaire (1694–1778), Francis Quesnay (1694–1774), and Gottfried Leibniz (1646–1716), at a time when Europeans were beginning to develop alternatives to monarchic and church procedures in their own political systems. The German philosopher Leibniz, who was considered an "expert" on things Chinese, argued that a truly universal new civilization could be achieved by merging the best elements in Chinese and Western culture. He published this argument in a little book of 1697, *Novissima Sinica* (Latest News from China). Of particular interest to European philosophers was the concept of the mandate—the idea that the emperor ruled only by divine mandate, and that when things went wrong, it was a signal that the mandate had been revoked. As Derk Bodde has argued, the European Enlightenment thinkers particularly admired China as a land where governmental power was negotiated not through the traditions of a feudal aristocracy, as in Europe, but by the mandarins, a group of highly educated scholars, who gained their official positions only after proving their worth by passing a series of state-administered examinations. It became their aim to create an "enlightened despotism" that would rule for the benefit of the people as a whole, rather than merely for a small, privileged group. They argued this concept, particularly in the work of the economists known as the Physiocrats, whose leader, Francis Quesnay, wrote *The Despotism of China* (1767) as an example of a truly enlightened despotism. Quesnay influenced the ideas of Adam Smith (1723–90), the seminal thinker of modern economics.

The most famous of the Enlightenment thinkers to learn from Qing China was Voltaire, for whom China was the one country where the ruler was also a philosopher (Plato's "philosopher-king"). He was impressed by the idea that the Chinese were not forcing their own religious ideas upon other people. "One need not be obsessed with the merits of the Chinese," he wrote in 1764, "to recognize … that their empire is in truth the best that the world has ever seen." In 1755, Voltaire wrote the play *The Chinese Orphan*, adapted from an old Chinese play, as a rebuttal to Rousseau's (1712–78) "back-to-nature" theories that decried history, the arts, and other cultural constructs on the grounds that they corrupted the natural goodness of human nature. By contrast, Voltaire argued that superior civilizations can overcome barbarism, citing the example of the Chinese civilization's triumph over the invading Mongols.

The Gongyuan and the Jinshi

Of particular importance amongst the administrative buildings distributed around the Forbidden City was the Gongyuan, or the Examination Yard, where the highest exams for entering the imperial bureaucracy were held. Admittance to the Mandarin cadres required three levels of examinations: first in local counties, second in the provincial capitals, and the final in the national capital, held only once every three years. Those who passed this final weeklong exam earned the title *jinshi* (known in English as Mandarin).

The Gongyuan was a huge walled enclosure, inside of which were thousands of small brick cells laid out in straight rows. This eliminated cheating. Still, candidates were searched, carefully supervised, and not permitted to leave until the exam ended. The exams demanded high standards of literary style and calligraphy, as well as detailed knowledge of the Chinese classics.

From the Gongyuan, the lucky few who passed were allowed into the Forbidden City, where they participated in a daylong exam in the first of the great halls, which was attended by a large assembly of civil and military officials in full regalia. Of these examinees, the top three finalists were presented directly to the emperor and allowed to exit from the central gate first, followed by all the others who had passed the tests. The *jinshi*, who might have started out as a peasant's son, was quickly were incorporated into the imperial administration.

In the 18th century, as the European Enlightenment thinkers were looking for more egalitarian, merit-based models to replace the orders of the Church and the court, they turned to the Chinese *jinshi* system. The idea of a civil service that would be selected via competitive exams open to anyone derived from studies of this Chinese bureaucracy. The first written civil service exams were held in European universities in 1702. The French established their civil service in 1791, after the French Revolution. The British established their civil service exams in 1806, initially only for recruitment to the British East India Company. The United States began to require exams for some administrative positions after 1885. Contemporary licensing exams, such as those required to be registered as an architect, structural engineer, lawyer, or chartered accountant are also a legacy of the original Chinese system.

Bible, in which earth was naturally barbaric. It also projected a vision of harmony between nature and the "natural" proportions of the classical orders.

The English nationalist garden emerged with the early 18th-century rise of the Whigs, trenchant critics of the Tories and strong believers in constitutional monarchy. No clergymen or saints were among those chosen to be represented in the Temple of British Worthies at Stowe. Rather, the Elysian Field honored poets such as Shakespeare, John Milton, and Alexander Pope; architects such as Inigo Jones; and explorers such as Thomas Cook, among others. Over the next two centuries a large number of follies were added and destroyed, including a Shell Bridge, a Grotto, a Season's Fountain, a Temple of Friendship, a Chinese House, and others.

15.34 **Stowe Gardens, Buckinghamshire, England**

Stowe Gardens and the Temple of British Worthies

Along with lacquered tables and teaware, European merchant ships brought home folios and travel accounts of Chinese gardens. Sir William Temple, an aristocratic British essayist writing on the gardens of Epicurus in 1685, extoled what he called the Chinese concept of *sharawadgi*, or irregular landscape scenery carefully arranged, in critique of the axial symmetries and carefully pruned formal orders that characterized European gardens at that time. Temple is credited with originating the concept of the British picturesque stroll garden of the 18th century, which, like the Chinese garden, relied on irregular movement, artfully placed follies and pavilions, borrowed scenery, and studied asymmetry for effect.

William Kent's "Elysian Field" of 1738 at Stowe House exemplifies this trend. Elysium, a Homeric description of the garden where worthy souls found eternal life, was transformed into an instrument of nationalist consciousness in the form of the stroll garden at Stowe. In combination with neo-Palladian follies, and with the invention of the ha-ha trench that enabled seamless visual continuity between the designed garden and its larger surrounding environment, Stowe Gardens offered a new vision of nature and of man's place in it—an alternative to that of the

15.35 **Site plan: Stowe Gardens**

15.36 **Temple of British Worthies, Stowe Gardens, Buckinghamshire, England**

15.37 **Temple of Ancient Virtue, Stowe Gardens**

15.38 **Temple of Modern Virtue, Stowe Gardens**

Key to the success of Stowe and gardens like it, such as that at Chiswick, was that they could be experienced not only by their owners and friends but also by a wide range of personages drawn from the upper and middle classes. At the time, garden tourism was on the increase and already an important part of upper-class social life.

Stowe conceptualized a new, secularist vision of English nationalism. This idea of a harmonic natural landscape, however artificially contrived, designed around a dignified, civilizational armature, arguably also parallels the English colonial experience in the Americas. The French initially encountered strong resistance from the Indians and never had enough colonists to suppress them, so they began to study and analyze their habits to gain their cooperation in trade and then lead them into conversion. The British experience was different. Except in the Carolinas, they faced little organized resistance among the Indians, who were less socially unified than those in the French settlements in Canada and along the Mississippi River. Whereas contact with the Indians led the French to study and question the origins of civilization, the English, at least those back home in their gardens, began to muse on the mythological underpinnings of European identity and its role in the larger global theater that was only just beginning

to fit within a single frame. It may have been in the English gardens, with their often pedagogical and ideological emphasis, that the first traces of what later was termed Eurocentrism began to appear.

Sans Souci

The first detailed accounts of Chinese life that arrived in the 1520s were written by missionaries sent to China, India, Indonesia, and Japan. In 1585 Pope Gregory XIII instructed the Spanish priest Juan Gonzalez de Mendoza to set down all that was known about China. *The History of the Great and Mighty Kingdom of China, and the Situation Thereof* was the first widely read treatise on the subject; de Mendoza mentions palaces and gardens, and describes houses so grand that they reminded him of Rome. But these bits of information were (and remained) saturated with myths and legends. The first book with a more substantial content was *The History of That Great and Renowned Monarchy of China* (1655), written by Alvarez Semedo, who had spent twenty-two years in China. This was followed by a book by the Dutchman Jan Nieuhof, who took an interest in Chinese architecture. As a European accustomed to palaces in stone, he did not understand the Chinese custom of wooden architecture for its palaces and therefore found it lacking. But he did produce several

engravings of pagodas and palaces that fascinated his readers.

Soon European courts began to adopt certain Chinese themes in their gardens. In 1675, for example, Louis XIV built the Trianon de Porcelain, which, though in shape and form Western, had a roof with blue-and-white patterned tiles, creating what was thought to be a reasonable approximation of the porcelain pattern used on the famous pagoda at Nanjing.

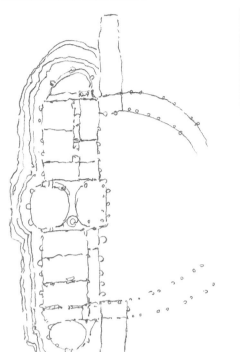

15.40 **Chinese Teahouse, Sans Souci, Potsdam, Germany**

15.39 **Sketch of Sans Souci by Frederick the Great, 1744**

15.41 **Chinese Teahouse, Sans Souci**

The building did not last long, in part because of leaks in the roof, but it set in motion a series of Chinese-styled pavilions, or what the Germans called *Porzellankammern*, the most famous being the Chinese Teahouse at Sans Souci palace in Potsdam (1757), built by the Prussian emperor Frederick the Great (Frederick II). The palace, which served as the emperor's summer retreat, had a vast park that contained several pavilions, one of which was the Chinese Teahouse. The gilt columns, which support the roof, are in the form of palm trunks opening out in luxuriant sprays of shoots as they meet the entablature. Life-size gilt Chinese figures sit at the base of the columns, playing musical instruments and engaging in animated conversation. Chinese pavilions, as well as Turkish tents, soon became common in pleasure gardens of the time. Chinese porcelain was also making its way through the markets of Holland, adding more fuel to the fire, with members of the gentry creating collections of their favorite pieces.

15.42 Qing dynasty China

QING BEIJING

The Ming dynasty's rule in China came undone in the 17th century. The reign of Zhu Yijun (known as the Wanli Emperor, r. 1573–1620), who gained the throne at the tender age of nine, proved to be disastrous, as he was incapable of dealing with the vast and complex administrative machinery that managed the empire. The consequence was inevitable; power brokers and local lords used the opportunity to carve out competitive mini-empires for themselves as the emperor became increasingly reclusive. Lawlessness increased, and Japanese and even Chinese pirates frequently raided coastal towns. At the same time a huge influx of illegal silver was arriving from the Americas by coastal routes. Indeed, the Chinese demand for silver was at the core of the growth of mining in South America. Silver became the alternative to Ming printed currency, which resulted in drastic inflation. The price of grain rose, and the poor went hungry and were unable to pay taxes. Vigilante bandit groups began to roam the countryside. Finally, a famous bandit, Li Zicheng, or the "dashing prince," made camp outside Beijing in 1644. In response, the Ming army commander, who had been sent to defend the northeastern border where the Manchu were assembling to attack,

made the fateful decision to instead invite them to enter the Middle Kingdom to defeat Li Zicheng. Thus, in 1644 the Manchu took over the Ming dynasty without ever having to fight for it.

The Manchu, who ruled under the title of the Qing, were Jurchen descendants who took on the Mongol title "khan." Although only a million strong in a kingdom of 250 million native Chinese, the Manchu proved equal to the task of governance, and quickly established stability. One of their first acts was to establish a strong regulatory framework for coastal trade. With that in place, they moved to establish internal order. The core of Manchu administrative policy was to simultaneously adopt established Confucian and Ming courtly practices while accommodating regional differences. They maintained a strong grip on central administrative control, but like the Mongols and the Yuan before them, they tolerated multiple religious and cultural practices. They settled into the Ming capitals, built similar tombs, restored and expanded the palaces and administrative wings, and, in Beijing, undertook a reorganization of the inhabitants, pushing the old Han Chinese to the south to make room for their own bannermen. The Qing also built scores of new towns and

administrative centers around the Middle Kingdom, making sure to distribute their own clansmen in these areas. The Dalai Lama was invited back, and stupas were built to mark his visit.

The Qing had a strong appetite for silver, which they used to mint currency. For geographical reasons, China was poor in minerals. They had some gold, very little silver, and some copper. And yet at the same time they had a vibrant economy that was very commercial in that it relied on active exchange of goods. Centuries before anyone else, during the Song period, the old Chinese solution had been to print money. Printed currency worked very well until the Yuan and particularly the Ming did what many governments in trouble do—they overprinted their currency, which resulted in loss of public confidence in the printed currency. The Qing solution to this was to mint currency in silver. After they exhausted the silver supply in Japan, South America's silver became the main source. It was transported to China on European vessels. Between 1500 and 1800, South America produced about 85 percent of the world's silver; about 40 percent of it went straight to China.

The Qing also embarked on a remarkably successful military campaign that resulted in the largest territorial expansion the Middle Kingdom had ever seen. The island of Taiwan (1683), Inner and Outer Mongolia (1697), Dzungharia (1757), and East Turkestan (1759), besides their own Manchurian homeland, became territories. Korea was made a vassal state in 1637, and Tibet a protectorate in 1751. Part of this aggressive expansion involved the genocide of the Dzungharia tribes, about 600,000 strong; 80 percent were killed on orders by Qing and Mongolian soldiers, and more by a subsequent outbreak of smallpox.

To accommodate the vast diversity that the Middle Kingdom now incorporated, the Qing, particularly in the sixty-one-year rule of the Qianlong Emperor (r. 1735–96) developed a pan-Asian conception of empire, a model of unity in diversity similar to that developed by the English after they became a major world power. Confucians, Buddhists, Muslims, and even Christian visitors were accepted and accommodated, and at the same time kept in check and abeyance. All decrees were issued in multiple languages. Underlying it all was deep investment in Tibetan Buddhist ideology, with its long history of accommodating multiple Asian peoples and histories. The Qianlong Emperor thought of himself as a *chakravartin*, the Buddhist ideal of royalty based on the canonical memory of Emperor Asoka.

The 268-year reign of the Qing was dominated by the sixty-year rule each of two monarchs: the Kangxi Emperor (r. 1662–1722) and his grandson, the Qianlong Emperor (r. 1736–95). Their reigns set the course that created the political, economic, and cultural legacy that was ultimately inherited by contemporary China. Their reigns, in this sense, defined the early modern period of China.

Crowned when he was only eight years old, the Kangxi Emperor's objective was to settle the uncertainties stemming from the end of Ming rule and overcome deep-rooted biases against foreigners. He quickly began to recruit Han scholars from southern China with the explicit goal of melding Manchu political authority with Confucian ideology, while incorporating Ming courtly and administrative processes and protocols.

Nanjing was demoted by the Qing to a regional capital, which made Beijing the all-important center of the empire. The Qing also expanded their own historical capital, called Mukden, in the northeast, building a new palace, tombs, and all the institutions of governance. But Mukden never rose to the status of a full-functioning capital. The six ministry buildings for Personnel, Revenue, Rites, War, Punishments, and Works; the Hanlin Secretariat; the Censonrate; the Directorate of Astronomy; and the Offices of Sacrifices and Ceremonies were all located in the Inner City, immediately south of the palace. The living areas around the Forbidden City were reserved for the so-called Eight Banners ("Eight" referred to the Jurchen tribesmen who had come together to form the Manchu army). Subsequently, the Eight Banners simply became the eight elite armies that the Qing came to rely on—to which Han and regional Chinese were liberally introduced in time.

After this, Nanjing became a center of Jesuit missionary activity; it was once the home of the Christian missionary Matteo Ricci and by this time was more open to

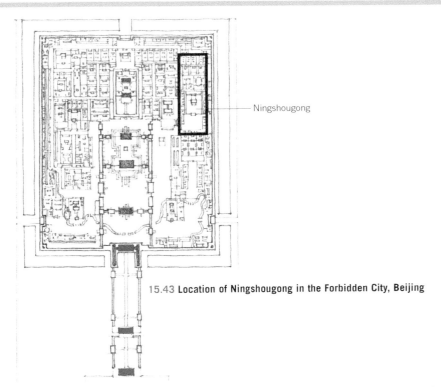

Ningshougong

15.43 **Location of Ningshougong in the Forbidden City, Beijing**

Western influence than Beijing. For instance, it was Nanjing painters who first incorporated Western ideas of shading and perspective in their depictions of local scenery.

Unlike all previous Chinese dynasties, the Manchu did not automatically burn and pillage the Ming capital and establish a new one at another location. Instead, they reoccupied the Forbidden City at Beijing. One of the Emperor's first decrees was to rebuild the parts of the Forbidden City that had been burned by the retreating Ming. His only specification was that ducts be built into the Hall of Supreme Harmony so that heat could be pumped into it. To stamp their identity onto the city, the Manchu renamed all the major gates and pavilions and changed the ceremonies associated with the Temple of Heaven to reflect the new Manchu cosmic order. Non-Manchu, Han Chinese men were required to shave their foreheads and wear their hair in a long ponytail called the *que*. Differences between the Qing and the Han also played out in the urban fabric. In 1649, the Northern City, the traditional heart of Beijing, was reserved only for Manchu. As a consequence, all the Han Chinese had to move into the Southern City, which had always been underdeveloped, but it developed into the commercial heart of the city as a consequence of the influx.

New temples and monasteries were built. Theaters, teahouses, shops of all kinds, guild halls, academies of classical learning, and public buildings were constructed. As wood became scarce, many of the residential and other secular structures were made from stone and brick.

By the middle of the 18th century, over forty new palaces had been built in the Forbidden City and in the privileged areas to its northwest. Unlike the Ming emperors, who confined most of their court activities to the Forbidden City and concentrated all major activities in Beijing, the Qing were avid travelers and built palaces and temples in distant parts of their empire. One of best-known Qing palace complexes is the Ningshougong ("Palace of Tranquil Longevity," 1698–1772), built by the Qianlong Emperor Ningshougong. Conceived as a mini Forbidden City within the Forbidden City, it consists of two sections: first a set of three ceremonial pavilions (the Gate of Tranquil Longevity, the Hall of Imperial Supremacy, and the Palace of Tranquil Longevity), followed by a denser living quarter consisting of a series of small and larger buildings arranged around a network of garden courts. The entire palace was completely screened from the rest of the Forbidden City.

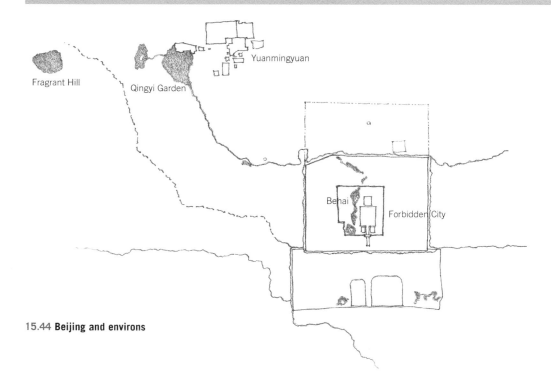

15.44 Beijing and environs

Beihai

In 1651 the Qing Shunzhi Emperor invited the fifth Dalai Lama to visit Beijing, as the Ming Yongle Emperor had before him. To commemorate the visit, Shunzhi ordered the construction of three Tibetan-style white stupas, two of them in the Imperial City. One of these is the bell-shaped White Stupa, the gigantic landmark of the Western Park or Beihai. East of the Forbidden City but within the city walls, Beihai had first been developed by the Yuan and the Jin, and under the Ming, waters were dammed to create three artificial lakes, with an island in the middle lake. Shunzhi placed the White Stupa on the highest point of the artificial hill on the island, so that it was clearly visible from a distance.

Yuanmingyuan

The area to the northwest of Beijing was a largely flat plain with a gentle gradient toward the southeast, where the Yuan, Jin, and Ming had built summer retreats. The Qing converted these into huge garden-palace complexes, exploiting the numerous springs and rivulets that traverse the area. Waterways and reservoirs were built to ensure a perennial flow and distribution of water. The largest of these gardens was the Yuanmingyuan ("The Garden of Perfect Brightness"; *yuan* means "garden"), built in the 1720s. Although its palaces and pavilions were similar to the axial courtyard structures of other palaces, such as those in the Forbidden City, their distribution and layout is more relaxed. Entered from the south, the Yuanmingyuan was dominated by a palace with a small lake in front and a larger lake in back to frame it. The back lake had nine islands, each designed with its own pavilions, palaces, and scenic spots. North of this complex was a dense fabric of secondary buildings, laid out in a closely packed system of interconnected islands. The eastern half of Yuanmingyuan was composed around the large Fuhai Lake, in the middle of which were three small interconnected islands, representative of the three mythical Islands of the Immortals, supposedly located in the East China Sea. Fuhai Lake was also surrounded by a string of nine connected islands with pavilions and hills designed for scenic views and strolls. Yuanmingyuan had 350 buildings organized into 123 building complexes. Furthest east was the Chunjua Garden, with a palace in the middle of a large island. Emperor Qianlong added a long horizontal strip to the north, for which he commissioned six European Baroque–style palaces, designed by the Jesuit missionaries resident in his court.

15.45 **Pyoungsan Academy, near Hahoe Village, Korea**

15.46 **Site plan: Pyoungsan Academy**

Ancestral hall

Library

Ritual preparation hall

Teaching space

Guardians' library

Students' residence

Students' residence

Reading and teaching

0   25 m

JOSEON DYNASTY OF KOREA

In Korea, the elite of the Joseon dynasty (1392–1910) had long supported China's Ming dynasty, but as Ming influence waned in the 17th century, the Manchu forced the Joseon to shift alliances. Following Manchu establishment of the Qing dynasty in Beijing in 1644, the Joseon and Manchu developed strong links.

The Koreans adopted the Chinese bureaucracy, as did the Japanese, complete with the system of exams. Pyoungsan Academy, picturesquely located along a bend in the Nakdong River in south-central Korea, was a private Confucian high school for the sons of that region's *yangban* elite (the *yangban*, meaning "two groups," were civil and military officials). The academy was erected in honor of Ryu Seong-ryong, who served as the prime minister during the destructive invasions led by the Japanese feudal lord Hideyoshi. The building, modeled on a *chôngjas*—a pavilion that members of the *yangban* class had begun to erect, often along a stream or river at a particularly attractive scenic spot—is an enclosed precinct rising up on a gentle slope.

15.47 **Section: Pyoungsan Academy**

The visitor passes through a gate with a vista up the slope under the *chôngjas* and into the main court above, where the path leads. The view centers on the spot where the teacher would sit, with windows providing views into the landscape. Flanking the court are student quarters. Access to the *chôngjas*, which seems to almost float above the earth, is along a simple, narrow, elevated wooden plank. Behind the school is the shrine in a separate enclosure and, to one side, a library. The caretakers' house is in a separate enclosure attached to the walls of the school. The teacher did not live at the school but in the nearby village.

15.48 **Durbar Square, Patan, Nepal**

MALLAS OF NEPAL

Nepal was the midpoint along the north-south highway linking Tibet to India. Buddhist monks traveling through here spread Indian- and Tibetan-style Buddhism in Nepal, creating a unique blend of the two. After Islamic invaders occupied northern India in the 10th century, fleeing Hindu priests, royalty, and merchants added a new Hindu layer to Nepalese culture and civic polity. In the 13th century, these Hindu kings established the long-lasting Malla dynasty, which ruled Nepal until 1482, after which it was divided into three independent kingdoms run by related Malla dynasties, with capitals in Patan, Kathmandu, and Bhaktapur. In the 17th century, the Mallas of Patan renovated and reconstructed their main royal court, known as the Durbar Square. Its oldest structure, the Manidhara Fountain, was built in the 6th century CE as a rest area for pilgrims. Under the Malla, the square grew in importance when royal palaces and temples were added to it. The eastern edge of the square was lined with a string of palaces abutting one another. On the western side an irregularly shaped open space is home to several freestanding temples. Dispersed throughout are many small shrines. At its northern end, just beyond the palaces, the Manidhara Fountain forms its own urban place. It is the delicate balance between structure and space that imparts to Durbar Square its unique urban character.

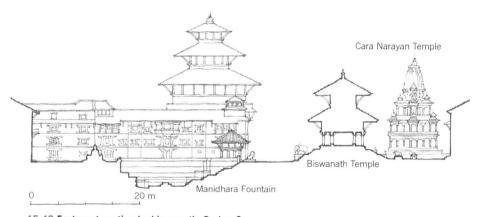

15.49 **East-west section looking south: Durbar Square**

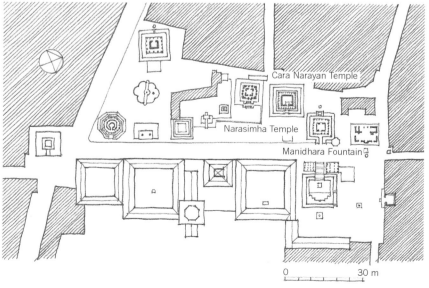

15.50 **Plan: Durbar Square**

15.51 Facsimile of Tobei Kamei's block print of the Shimabara geisha district, Kyoto, Japan

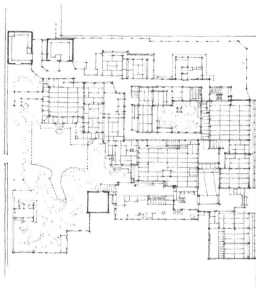

15.52 Plan: Sumiya, Kyoto, Japan

KYOTO'S ODOI AND SHIMABARA

A ten-year civil war (1467–77) between various lords that ended in stalemate also left Kyoto abandoned and a wreck. At its conclusion, a new shogunate was established, inaugurated by some of the most famous of Japan's shoguns—Oda Nobunaga, Toyotomi Hideyoshi, and Tokugawa Ieyasu. The ensuing peace was a period of rapid reconstruction, military consolidation, and economic development that enabled trade and commerce to thrive, in particular with China. The Dutch and Portuguese also established trading ports in Japan, although the Chinese ships were given priority since the silver trade with European merchants was blamed for the instability that imperiled Ming China. The shoguns' vision of Japanese society, like that of Qing China, was thus hostile to the laissez-faire ambitions of the new mercantile world and responded by tightening the strictures of the Bakufu code, a highly ceremonial, hierarchical code of conduct that prescribed everyone's designated place in the social fabric.

Like the Qing, who had to both align themselves with and distinguish themselves from the Han-dominated Confucian China that they ruled as a minority, the Japanese shoguns also had to thread the needle of distinguishing their authority as de facto heads of state from that of the emperor and the imperial order that was still nominally the social center. And so, the Tokugawa

redesigned the imperial capital, Kyoto, to meet the strictures of the Bakufu code and to define their own identity.

Pre-shogunate Kyoto's primary urban division lay between the imperial spaces and all the rest. Temples, the houses of nobles, shops, and entertainment areas could all be found in the same neighborhoods. Kyoto's shogun appointed governor, an erstwhile Buddhist priest named Maeda Gen'i (1539–1602), built a new north-south thoroughfare that cut through the old blocks, just as Hausmann would later do in 19th-century Paris. This opened up new street frontage, which was occupied by commercial establishments and houses. The street was also used to stage important processions in visually competitive displays of strength between the shogun and the emperor.

In 1591, the shogun Hideyoshi defined the borders of the city by building an earthen rampart 9 meters at the base, between 3 and 6 meters high, and topped by a wood and bamboo fence called the *odoi*. A mini-moat 6 to 18 meters wide was excavated outside. The world within the *odoi* was called the *rakuchu*, or the urbanized world, and the rest the *rakugai*, or the outside world. All forms of internal enclosures and fortifications were then demolished, erasing all signs of the localized authorities. Some of the major Buddhist temples were moved to outside the city walls, especially to the eastern hills. The members of the warrior class were

made to settle right next to the Nijo Castle and the Kyoto Governor's Palace, located just north of the castle. The members of the aristocracy were relocated to the peripheries of the imperial palace. Special quarters for the lowest classes—the *eta* ("the stained") and the *hinin* ("the nonhumans")—were designated at the margins of the city.

Kyoto's prostitutes were a constant threat to the Bakufu code, since they conducted their business in the mixed public space of the street. In 1640 they were confined to a single area that came to be called the Shimabara. Located in the southwest corner of the city far from its core, it was enclosed with its own wall complete with a moat, the purpose of which was not to prevent anybody from coming in but to keep the prostitutes from leaving. A single gate on the east side controlled all movement in and out. With the merchants, warriors, and aristocrats sharing the same space and the same prostitutes, the Shimabara quickly became a place of sanctioned transgression. The more exclusive establishments of the Shimabara, the *ageya* ("pleasure houses") catered to clients with high tastes. Accordingly, these places adopted architectural forms and decorations normally prohibited to those of lower-class status that were here appropriate to the high status of the clientele. This double standard was managed by making the exterior simple but creating individual spaces in the interior that were modeled on the residences of

15.53 Sumiya, Kyoto

15.54 Architectural drawing of street in Edo (Tokyo) with shops, 1876

the upper classes, and even those of the shoguns. Indeed, to respond to the varied status and tastes of the clients, the interiors were often extremely eclectic, with individual entertainment rooms right next to each other built in completely different styles.

The only surviving example of a 17th-century *ageya* is the Sumiya ("Place of Peace and Long Life"), controlled by the Nakagawa family, who administered it for thirteen generations from its very beginning in 1641. From the street its facade is simple but cleverly designed. The outer walls of both its ground and upper story are recessed by half a bay and fronted by wooden screens that ensured no one could look in, but that the guests could see out. They were also removable, so that when street entertainers came calling or during festivals when the streets of the Shimabara became one big theater, the guests of the Sumiya could look straight out without hindrance.

In the interior are a range of styles taken from those of the military mansions, town homes, and teahouses. They were, however, willfully decorative and colored with great variety and exaggeration. The main reception rooms for guests were located behind the exterior facade on the eastern edge of the building. This position corresponded to the typology of the houses of rich merchants. As in Shinden-style palaces such as Ninomaru at Nijo Castle and the Katsura Imperial Villa, the entertainment rooms located near the garden were stepped back to ensure that each room had a special relationship to the garden, with individually framed openings designed for each space. The second floor had smaller rooms for the more intimate relationships between the geisha and her clients.

EDO (TOKYO)

In 1603, the first Tokugawa shogun decided to rule from a new city, Edo (now Tokyo). Conceived as a spiral, with accommodations made for geography, it was developed with both security and symbolism in mind, with its thirty-two major gateways guarding the various lines of approach to the center. Their locations were correlated with the twelve signs of the zodiac, integral to the Chinese astrological and calendrical system. The populace was not allowed to freely intermix, and each class was placed in different sections of the city. The vassals were located to the northeast of the castle. Lower-ranking samurai were located in a section all to themselves; the merchants and artisans lived in the outermost, southwest parts of the city. Silver brokers lived in one neighborhood, gold brokers in another, and so forth.

15.55 Original spiral plan of Edo

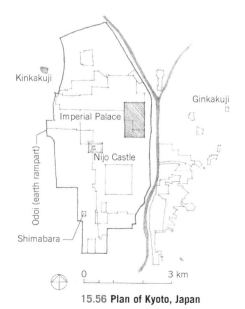

15.56 Plan of Kyoto, Japan

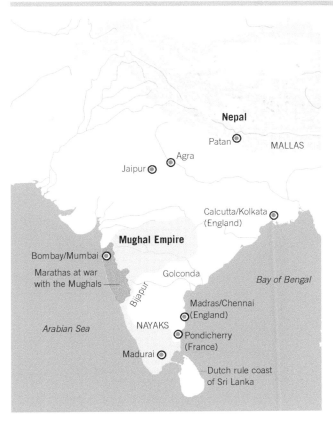

15.57 Mughal Empire, India

15.58 Meenakshi Sunderesvara Temple at Madurai, India

NAYAKS OF MADURAI

The Nayaks, though nominally under the rule of Delhi, continued the Chola and Vijayanagar practice of treating temples as surrogate courts. In fact, the temples of Madurai and Tanjore became veritable cities unto themselves. Their gates were rarely closed, and urban life moved in and out at will. The Meenakshi Sunderesvara Temple (1623–59) has two main shrines, the larger one dedicated to Shiva in the manifestation of Sunderesvara ("the beautiful one") and the smaller to his wife Meenakshi ("the fish-eyed one"). Nonetheless, the temple's main deity is Meenakshi, a local regional goddess who is important to the Tamils. Though she was married to Shiva after the rise of the bhakti cults, she maintained her dominance over the populace. Spatially this duality is represented in procession. Although Sunderesvara's shrine has a well-defined axis leading to it, it is Meenakshi's more informally defined access path that has the important historical locations along it, most importantly the Lotus Tank—the mythical origin of the temple—and a corridor with painted panels depicting stories from Meenakshi's life.

As it grew, the temple became a series of enclosures that nestle a diverse array of functional and ceremonial spaces, such as pillared halls, open courts, inhabitable corridors, and shrines, all designed to accommodate the temple's diverse civic and religious functions. In addition, it has markets, private shrines, places for resting, dwellings for priests, and ceremonial sites; a museum was added recently. Chief among the rituals is an elaborate annual procession meant to be visible to all, particularly the lowest castes, who were not allowed into

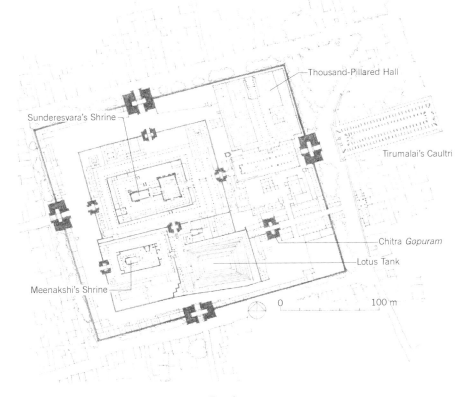

15.59 Site plan: Meenakshi Sunderesvara Temple

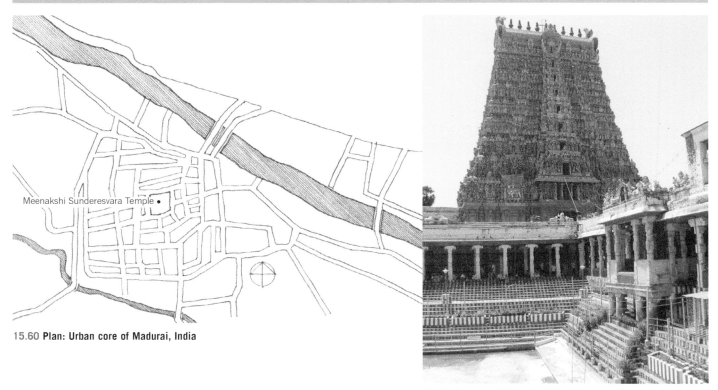

15.60 **Plan: Urban core of Madurai, India**

15.61 *Gopuram* of Meenakshi Sunderesvara Temple at Madurai

the temple. This procession celebrated Meenakshi's divine wedding to Sunderesvara (Shiva). Over a nineteen-day period in April and May, Meenakshi is taken out in procession in a mobile structure, into the crowded city streets, where she ceremonially defeats all the gods and earthly kings in one battle after another until she finally meets Sunderesvara, whom she almost defeats before suddenly realizing she is prophesied to marry him.

Seen from a distance, the Meenakshi Sunderesvara Temple's silhouette is defined by its *gopurams*, or gateways, the highest ones reaching 50 meters. Made of brick, they are largely solid and are ornamented with a myriad of vividly painted mythical deities and creatures. The *gopurams*

increase in height the farther they are from the center. The gold-covered *shikharas* over the shrines are actually the temple's smallest superstructures. In part, the *gopurams*' function is to announce the temple's presence to the city, and when seen from a distance, they create a visual wave radiating out into the landscape. In other words, the mandalic universe that is usually condensed into the figurative representation of a Hindu temple's *shikhara* was, under the Nayaks, expanded so far outward that it encompasses the geography of the entire city itself. And because Madurai sits in a river valley surrounded by a ring of low-lying hills, the hills can be imagined as the next layer of *gopurams*, implying mythical unseen mountains beyond.

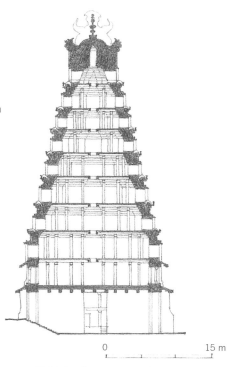

0   15 m

15.62 **Section: The summit of a *gopuram***

JAIPUR

The Mughal emperor Akbar's policy to subjugate the Rajputs was to offer them conciliatory alliances, preserving their cultural and political independence, subject to a military tax; and to invade only if they rejected that offer. The Rajput king Raja Bharmal of Amer was the first to accept this alliance, which enabled his state to prosper during the Mughal tenure. Amer was one of the critical ports on the highway from Agra to the Kutch coast, so its defense and the taxes that it generated were important for the Mughals. For their loyalty, Amer maharajas were often appointed viceroys to Mughal territories such as Malwa in peninsular India.

After Aurangzeb's death in 1707, the then maharaja of Amer, Sawai Jai Singh, realized that the Mughal Empire was beginning to break down, and went on an aggressive campaign to modernize and weaponize his own state. In particular, he modernized his forts' defenses to better withstand artillery and invested in large amount of artillery as well, with a massive reserve of ammunition—at the cost of cavalry, which was the traditional strength of the Rajputs. Because of this militarization, Amer quickly emerged as a strong and stable regional power, highly protective of trade routes and commercial activity, and in the waning days of the Mughals attracted a large amount of migration from Mughal cities.

In 1727, Sawai Jai Singh felt sufficiently secure that he moved his palace out of the big fort at Amer and down the hill onto an open field, where he already had a built a large garden. This was quite a risk, for the location of the new city made it vulnerable not only to artillery but even to a strong cavalry attack. Jai Singh's solution was to build a fort on the hillock immediately behind the new city, called Nahargarh, to which the royal family at least could retreat in case of a sudden attack. Nahargarh had the particular advantage of an artesian spring, around which a fantastic asymmetrical tank was built. But as it happened, Nahargarh never had to be used.

Jai Singh called his new city Jaipur, and he put the architect Vidyadhar, the head of his *imarat*, or building department, in charge of building it. Vidhyadhar is the first recorded

15.63 Plan of Jaipur, India

individual town planner in South Asian history in charge of building a brand-new city (although Mughal court names are also documented as being in charge of various projects, such as Fatehpur Sikri).

Fortunately, Vidyadhar proved equal to the task. He first built a master plan for the city expanding outward in blocks from the existing garden. This gave him five additional squares—one short, since the Nahargarh hill butted into the garden in one corner. To compensate, Vidyadhar added another neighborhood square, called a *chokri*, at the other end of the city. Around the boundary of the new city he built a wall—not strong enough to hold back artillery fire, but high enough to designate the urban boundary and to control access through designated gates. Since the city stood on an important trade route, controlling access was vital to collecting *octroi* (taxes).

Within the city walls, Vidyadhar invested heavily in building the drainage infrastructure of the city and, more importantly, in constructing rows of markets along the main arteries of the city. By building up the street

edges of the main avenues, Vidyadhar was not only able to construct a unified street picture, he also immediately had a large amount of commercial street-front property available for sale, which attracted merchants fleeing the declining Mughal cities. Behind the main streets, the interiors were built up around the settling populations, who largely clustered around trades. Street intersections were cut at the corners to create *chokris*. The street section of the shopswas set up such that people could gather on shop rooftops and view the street processions that were commonpace then as today on festival days.

In the 19th century, all of Jaipur's main streets were painted a uniform color—a pink pigment derived from the local sandstone—to welcome a visiting colonial prince. This added significantly to the strong urban street picture of the city. Sawai Jai Singh patronized Jesuit priests alongside Islamic scientists and Hindu and Jain scholars in his court. He had an extensive library, and is famous for building the most accurate observatories in the world of the time, called *Jantar Mantar*.

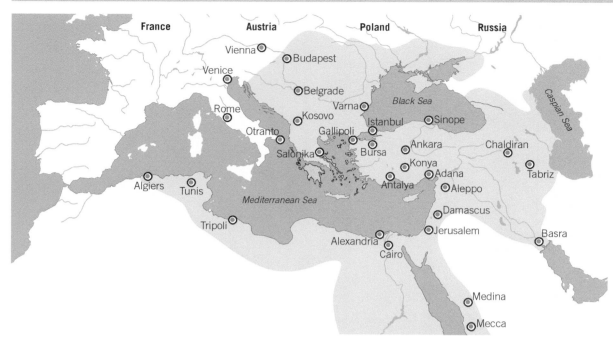

15.64 Ottoman Empire

NUROSMANIYE MOSQUE, ISTANBUL

Faced with the transforming world economy, the Ottomans allied themselves with the French against England, Austria, and Russia. Although the Ottomans had lost their military advantage in Europe, they continued to be very strong financially. In fact, around 1700, they dominated the life and culture of the eastern half of the Mediterranean, controlling a vast territory that stretched from the Persian Gulf to Algeria. In 1703 Ahmed III moved the capital of the Ottoman Empire back to Istanbul (it had been in Bursa), which precipitated a major building boom. Instead of following the Suleymaniye canon established by Sinan, the architecture looked to external influences to generate new architectural expressions. For this reason, 18th-century Ottoman architecture is often described as being Westernized. But as scholars have noted, it is better thought of as an early modern architecture in which Sinan's "classicism" was hybridized with European—and particularly French—Baroque architectural sensibilities and then mixed together with Persian and Indian precedents, the latter especially in palaces and gardens, such as the Sa'dabad Palace and the garden at Kagithane, Istanbul. This amalgam contrasts with Russia's more aggressive attempt to modernize the state through the singular importation of French taste.

Mahmud I's Nurosmaniye Mosque (1749–55) combined a standard centralized domed plan with an unusually wide, highly fenestrated facade under a massive arch. A tightly clustered sequence of engaged pillars with capitals that unexpectedly merged with the cornice are complemented by European Baroque details such as scrolls, shells, cable and round moldings, engaged pillars, and fluted capitals.

15.65 Nurosmaniye Mosque, Istanbul

15.66 St. Paul's Cathedral, London

THE ANGLICAN CHURCH

In 1536, in order to annul his marriage to his Catholic Spanish queen, Catherine of Aragon, the English king Henry VIII dissolved the Catholic monasteries and abbeys and created the Church of England, or Anglican Church, with himself as its head. However, this new church maintained many liturgical similarities to the Catholic Church, a fact that came to be vociferously opposed by the Puritans, who, influenced by Protestants such as the Calvinists, wanted a purer form of worship freed of all Catholic influence. The Puritan influence in Parliament became so strong that during the English Civil War (1642–51) they executed Charles I in 1649 and set up the Puritan Oliver Cromwell (1599–1658) as ruler of a self-proclaimed Protestant Republic. This was, however, a short-lived revolution, and in 1660 the monarchy was able to reinstate itself. The Puritans found themselves marginalized in English society, and many left to join their compatriots already settled on the shores of New England.

In 1665 a great fire destroyed most of central London, including eighty churches. The rebuilding of the churches became an opportunity to place a strong Anglican imprint on the city. Dominated by the landed gentry, the Anglican Church effectively functioned as an extension of the interests of the ruling class. Sir Christopher Wren, an English nobleman trained as an astronomer, was asked to design almost all of these churches. Wren studied contemporary French architecture but seemed to have been more impressed with Italianate examples and literature, particularly Palladian simplicity. Anglicanism placed considerable emphasis on the dignity of the service as prescribed in the Book of Common Prayer, but unlike Italian Counter-Reformation churches, which emphasized the spectacle of devotion, Wren's churches possess some of the simplicity and openness of Protestant churches. The color palette of their interiors was restrained; almost everything was white, with a few accents like gilded column capitals, string courses, and rosettes set against the dark wood of the altarpiece and furniture. Large windows brought in ample light.

After the destruction of St. Paul's Cathedral in the Great Fire of London, many wanted to rebuild it in the old Gothic style. Wren, however, envisioned a building up to date with European neoclassical sensibilities. Several plans and revisions were made, including one known as the "great model," which had highly original, large concave exteriors. It was rejected for a more conventional plan. The church fathers accepted the modern exterior but insisted on a medieval-style section, with low side aisles and a tall nave.

The building (1675–1709) is in the shape of a cross, with the dome, one of the largest in the world, over the crossing. It is surrounded by three galleries on different levels. To disguise the low side aisles, Wren created a blind second story that also concealed the buttresses holding up the vaults. Without the false second story, the dome would have looked astonishingly out of scale. Even so, it looms large, resting on a ring of columns with eight cleverly disguised buttresses. On the interior is a giant pilaster order for the nave and a lower order for the secondary spaces, modeled loosely on St. Peter's Basilica in Rome.

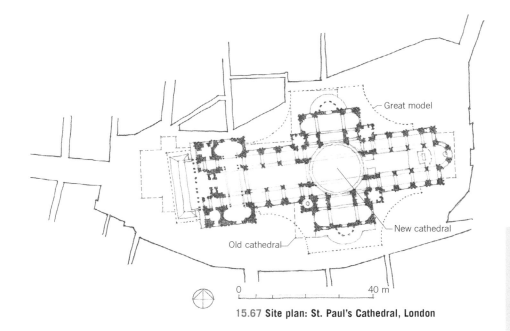

15.67 **Site plan: St. Paul's Cathedral, London**

A catenary arch is the mirrored upward projection of a suspended chain. It is the most ideal form of vault, as it supports itself without the need for buttressing. This form of curve was derived from the mathematics of Jacobus Bernoulli.

But unlike Michelangelo's lower drum, which fits compactly onto the body of the building, St. Paul's drum is both lofty and airy, rising almost incomprehensibly out of the center of the building. While Michelangelo's lantern appears as a bundle of forces collected into a relatively tightly wound package, Wren's lantern sits serenely on top of the dome as a small centralized tempietto.

The semispherical dome (flattened on top) consists of a wooden frame with a lead surface supported by an invisible conical masonry structure. Below that is an almost spherical vault. To create the impression of height so that the inner and outer dome appear to match, the columns supporting the dome lean toward the center.

During the Baroque period, the dome became one of the dominant themes for churches and even for secular buildings, like the U.S. Capitol. There are several variations, but unlike Palladio's dome, which has no drum, most post-Renaissance architects preferred the model set out by Donato Bramante, which was a dome resting on a short drum. Wren's dome for St. Paul in London is clearly an adaptation of Bramante's theme.

15.68 **Dome, St. Paul's Cathedral**

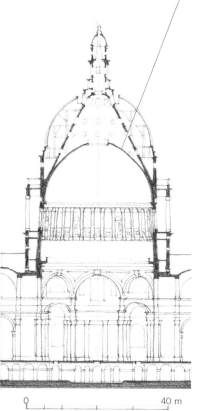

15.69 **Section through dome of St. Paul's Cathedral**

15.70 **St. Mary Woolnoth, London**

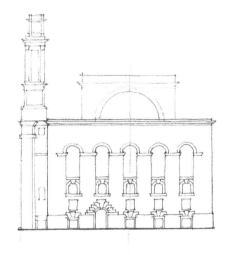

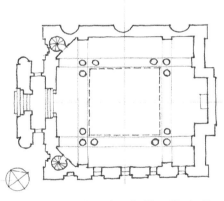

15.71 **Plan and section: St. Mary Woolnoth**

St. Mary Woolnoth

The most imaginative of the English architects of the early 18th century was undoubtedly Nicholas Hawksmoor (1661–1736), Wren's apprentice. Wren shared with his apprentice an interest in the architecture of Asia Minor and in the then still barely known architecture of Greece and Egypt. But if Wren had an eye for compositional unity, Hawksmoor aimed to bring the elements of architectural composition into dynamic interrelationship. He pried features out of their expected contexts.

The strangeness of Hawksmoor's buildings is a result of a design process that emphasized esoteric historical and philosophical meanings. In that sense, Hawksmoor spoke to a generation of designers that attempted to distance itself from amateur architects and questioned the normative production of aesthetic ideals as public spectacle. His St. Mary Woolnoth (1716–24) is an astonishing building when compared with the stiff linearity of the English Palladian style that was starting to make its presence felt. The double-tower front facade appears to be two buildings stacked on top of each other, the entirety surmounted by two symmetrically placed small bell housings. In the lower zone, the voussoirs around the openings are connected to horizontally banded rustication grooves that continue even around the corner columns. Over this structure, Hawksmoor placed a "base" on which rests an entablatured blind portico.

It would be wrong to read Hawksmoor's architecture as simply playful or baroque, however. He was not just playing with formal composition but also citing less well-known references from antiquity. Not adhering to the limited Palladian interpretation of the antique, Hawksmoor studied buildings such as the Roman tomb of the Julii at St.-Rémy, France. The two columns flanking the entrance are esoteric references to the Temple of Solomon, the reconstruction of which preoccupied many architects of the time, including Wren. Anglican theologians of the day were also interested in the Second Temple of Solomon as a way to reconnect to both biblical authenticity and the ethos of early Christianity. The upper portico was a reference to the Mausoleum of Halicarnassus, one of the seven ancient wonders of the world, which had been destroyed but for which Hawksmoor made a sketch based on descriptions by Pliny and Vitruvius. In this way, Hawksmoor opened a brief window to the possibility that antiquity could be a source of architectural heterogeneity—contrary to the rush to exemplify, as with the spread of the Baroque style throughout colonial Europe.

15.72 Stratford Hall Plantation, near Montross, Virginia

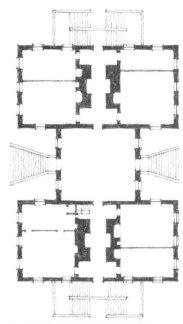

15.73 Plan: Stratford Hall Plantation

WHIGS AND THE PALLADIAN REVIVAL

By the early 18th century, the older puritanical interests of England had been channeled into the rise of the Whig party, which, with Robert Walpole as prime minister under kings George I and George II, pursued a policy of aggressive mercantile capitalism focused on protecting British interests in the colonies, accompanied by anti-Catholic and anti-slavery policies, and a strong anti-Tory push for constitutional monarchy. Continuing the Whigs' puritanical leaning, the Georgian architecture of this time was overtly simple and understated. Walls were usually of unadorned brick, and windows and doorways were framed in wood painted white. Facades were symmetrically arranged around the ground-level entrance or, on occasion, accessed by a short flight of steps. Grander houses might have a portico, pilasters, or corner quoins.

The Georgian style was England's first truly national style; it was unique to England and its colonies and arose out of the Protestant ethic of nondemonstrative simplicity. Functional and serviceable, it was adopted by the newly emerging mercantile class, which was heavily involved in coal and agricultural ventures, not only in England but also abroad. Unlike the French aristocracy, the English upper classes actively invested in

the colonies. Stratford Hall Plantation (1738) in Virginia, at the head of a large estate that grew tobacco for export to England, was designed for Thomas Lee, a businessman in the Virginia colonies and for a time acting governor of the state.

Palladian Revival architecture blossomed after the 1715 publication of *Vitruvius Britannicus*, written by the Scottish lawyer and architect Colen Campbell, who proclaimed the superiority of antiquity over what he argued were the affected and licentious forms of the Baroque. The work of Inigo Jones, in his eyes, should have been held in just as high an esteem as that of Palladio. *Vitruvius Britannicus*, together with the publication of the three volumes of *The Architecture of A. Palladio* (1715, 1717, and 1725) by the Venetian Giacomo Leoni, sparked a movement that invested a great deal of energy in substantiating the idea of the primacy of the natural law of proportion, still a rather novel idea in English design practice. Facade, plan, and volume had to be unified into a formal whole. Yet despite this penchant for abstraction, the external detailing had to adhere closely to Palladio's own works—thus the frequent use of rusticated bases, pilastered upper elevations, and pedimented entrances in the emerging Georgian style. Palladio's legacy

bore an aura of authority and exclusion, yet, being of farming origin, also played into the Whig ideology of the time. Moreover, Campbell's treatises offered relatively cheap but prestigious models to imitate. The printed distribution of plans, plates, and treatises helped to further Palladianism, a style that could be easily taught, mastered, and copied.

The Palladian movement reached its height in the hands of Richard Boyle, otherwise known as Lord Burlington (1694–1753), an influential Whig politician. Upon inheriting a fortune from his grandfather, and after trips to Italy in 1714 and 1719, he began his career as a gentleman architect, hoping to promote neo-Palladianism as a nationally accepted style by influencing the Office of the Works to pick candidates of his choice for commissions. The most important of his buildings was his own Chiswick House (1723–29), which was not actually a house but rather a pavilion to house his library and entertain friends. Its basic model is that of Palladio's Villa Rotonda, though the facade is modeled on the Villa Foscari, which faces the Brenta canal in the Veneto. Certain features were also taken from Vincenzo Scamozzi, such as the obelisk chimneys, the octagonal rather than circular main hall, and the string course at the balustrade level that wraps around the entire building.

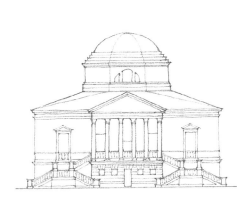

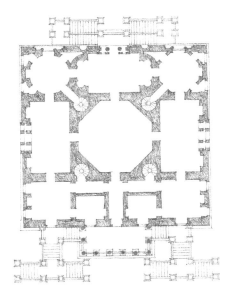

15.74 Plan and elevation: Chiswick House

15.75 Chiswick House, near London

Palladian motifs also became common in the palaces on the Strand, a long street that ran along the north side of the Thames River and linked the old walled city of London, the country's economic capital, with Buckingham Palace (though it was still relatively modest at that time) and Westminster, the symbolic and political capital of the country. With Greece itself firmly under Ottoman control, Palladian orders took on the authority of a prime source of classicism and influenced many designs, including that of Thomas Jefferson for the University of Virginia.

Touro Synagogue, Newport

The Puritans in New England sought to establish a new church in the New World. Religious tolerance and separation of church and state were not part of their core ideology, which produced many dissenters, including Roger Williams. A severe critic of the Church of England, Williams, influenced by the Puritans, moved to Boston to join the Pilgrims but quickly found them lacking as well. In particular, Williams's contact and friendship with the Native American tribes ran counter to the policies of both the Crown and the settlers. In response, Williams founded his own colony in Providence, Rhode Island, in 1636, with religious tolerance as one of its pillars.

In 1740, Rhode Island resident Peter Harrison went to England to receive formal training as an architect. By using pattern books, taking grand tours of Italy, and learning drafting skills, Harrison became America's first trained architect and a strong advocate of the principles of neo-Palladianism as the appropriate expression of the new ideals of the time. In Newport, Rhode Island, Harrison built the Redwood Library (1748–50) and the Touro Synagogue (1759–63), the latter commissioned by descendants of Sephardic Jews who had been expelled from Spain, Portugal, and France with the Muslims

in the 15th and 16th centuries. The members of the small congregation were attracted to Newport because Rhode Island's founder, Roger Williams, had guaranteed religious freedom there. Harrison drew on the Bevis-Marks Synagogue of London (1701), which was a simple box with surrounding galleries on three sides; it, too, was designed for a Sephardic community. The twelve columns supporting the women's galleries on the interior represent the twelve tribes of Israel. They are each made of a single tree trunk; the lower ones are Ionic, and the upper ones Corinthian. There were no pews. Instead, the floor at the center was reserved for a table for the reading of the law. The men sat along the perimeter on the ground floor, and the women above in the balconies. The building has a sense of intimacy and openness that Harrison had not been able to achieve in the King's Chapel in Boston. Harrison, a staunch loyalist, ran afoul of the American revolutionaries, and his house and library were burned by them in 1775, soon after his death.

15.76 **Great House of Shirley Plantation, near Hopewell, Virginia**

Shirley Plantation, Virginia

If Georgian neo-Palladianism was associated with some of the most progressive thinkers in New England, it was also, simultaneously, the style of choice for the great houses of the slave-based plantations of Virginia. Early in the 17th century, the British tobacco plantations relied on indentured workers and convicts for labor, but this system had limited economic viability. Meanwhile, tobacco started to become a lucrative cash crop as most of the male population of England began to smoke daily. This led to a labor crisis, and an indentured labor rebellion in 1675 pushed Virginia to pass a new series of laws that legislated slavery into the institution that made it infamous. First, Virginia slave laws linked slavery to race: only Africans could be enslaved. Second, they specified that all children born to an enslaved mother, regardless of the father, would also be slaves. This made slavery hereditary and made children, often even those with white fathers, enslavable. It was as a consequence of the Virginia laws that slave trade really took off, with slave populations multiplying tenfold. Virginian owners also invested in keeping slave families together and maintaining their health to maximize the production of children.

The plantation mansion shared a kinship with Palladio's villas in that both were based on farming. Shirley Plantation, settled in 1613, was Virginia's first and largest plantation. Its mansion, called the Great House (1738), was made from locally prepared brick in Flemish bond. It had a two-story portico with Doric columns on two sides of the house, so as to present an entrance for both visitors arriving by the James River and those arriving by land, on the plantation side. Inside the mansion a "flying" or square rigged staircase rose three floors. The house was surrounded by eleven supporting buildings, also of brick, arranged symmetrically on a 4-meter grid. Two immediately in front were the laundry and kitchen, designed to symmetrically match and stage the mansion. Others were the storehouse, the icehouse, the smokehouse, the dovecote, and stables.

The slaves lived in the Great Quarters, about 1.5 kilometers from the mansion. These dwellings were duplex wood-frame cabins, about 6 by 12 meters, arranged in a simple row. Each duplex had a double brick chimney that served both sides. The Shirley mansion has been continuously occupied by the Hill Carter family since 1738. Ann Hill Carter married Henry Lee in the mansion's parlor in 1793; they were the parents of Confederate general Robert E. Lee.

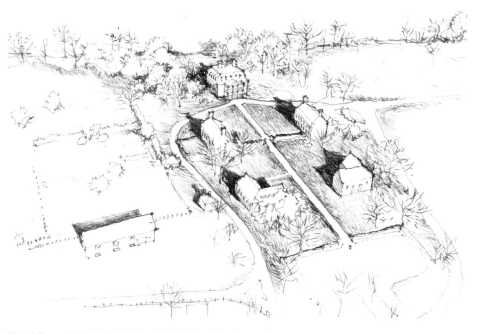

15.77 **Plan of Shirley Plantation showing location of mansion, fields, and Great Quarters of the slaves**

1800 CE

INTRODUCTION

The start of the 19th century was a watershed moment in the advent of modernity. In 1800, the world's wealth was about the same it had been a millennium before; China's wealth was greater than that of the entire Western world; and less than 2 percent of the world's population lived in cities. Today, a little over two centuries later, the world's wealth has increased more than sixteenfold; the West's share of that wealth is almost 75 percent; and about 50 percent of the world's population lives in cities.

Momentous events around 1800 unleashed this radical transformation. The European Enlightenment, particularly its emphasis on nature, science, reason, and egalitarianism, circulated in the colonial world and eventually captured the global imagination. Two major social revolutions—the American and the French—translated the Enlightenment into political form, creating new democracies that charted the path, however circuitous and fitful, that led to the decline of the monarchic institution, which was replaced by that of the nation-state. And at the center of it all, the Industrial Revolution, particularly the invention of the cotton gin, transformed a global mercantile economy into a mass-manufacturing industrial economy, which made consumer goods the new focus of the global economic system. One of its lesser consequences was a global building boom, and with it the steady emergence of a new sensibility regarding the purposes and forms of architecture.

But that was still in the future; in its time this entire transformation was more gradual and fraught with contradictions. Europe was still oriented primarily toward accumulating wealth from far-flung global territories; its own historical identity was as yet episodic, and its sense of manifest destiny only just beginning to emerge. Thus the call for egalitarianism, for instance, cohabited with the defense of slavery and colonization: Jefferson's home in Virginia was both a model of Neoclassical utopianism and a site of slavery. As a consequence of the fractures between ideality and reality, the Enlightenment was slow to catch on. The establishment of democracies was met with trepidation and uncertainty, with most nations seeking a balance between representative democracy and a continuation of the rule of the privileged.

Napoleon fought to spread the ideals of the French Revolution, yet also crowned himself monarch. The U.S. Constitution sought to balance the House of Representatives with the Senate and Supreme Court; and England and Prussia worked hard to oppose revolution by adjusting monarchy to the ideals of the Enlightenment.

Revolution in France—which had taken the principles of liberty, equality, and fraternity to a much bloodier extreme than revolution had done in the United States—was opposed by the allied forces of England and the Prussian Empire. For most of the first quarter of the 19th century, determined battles were waged across Europe to choke the cry of the French Revolution in its cradle. Napoleon and his armies forced change not only in France but also in Italy, Austria, and Germany. The United States, caught in the middle, tried to steer a neutral path—although its traditional allegiance was to England, while the likes of Jefferson and Benjamin Franklin were ardent defenders of new French ideals.

The utopianism of the Enlightenment was generally tempered, if not co-opted outright, by the lingering traditions of aristocratic privilege. This produced an architecture generally known as Neoclassical, the history of which took many turns and in some cases retreated toward more conservative stances. Nonetheless, traces of a more vigorous and austere Neoclassicism, such as that pursued by the French architects Claude Nicholas Ledoux and Étienne-Louis Boullée, are to be found throughout Europe from 1800 onward. Classicism, which had started during the Renaissance as a quest to relearn from a lost past, now emerged as a claimant to a privileged cultural imperative, the roots of which came to be castigated as Eurocentrism. The liberation of Greece from Ottoman occupation in 1829 spawned a vigorous neo-Greek movement not only in the United States but also in Germany and Scotland, as well as in British India. Architects began to stress not the willful play of forms that Baroque architecture enjoyed, but a reasoned and principled revival of original classical idioms.

Competing with classicism, there emerged a new interest in nature and the non-classical heritage—that is, the Gothic. The Romantics, particularly in England, sought alternative narratives from the past in a quest to define a more specifically English heritage. In Berlin, the capital of the Protestant Prussian Empire, the architect Karl Friedrich Schinkel (1781–1841), influenced by the likes of Goethe and Schiller, looked to create a more austere classicism as an expression of nationalism. The German Romantic movement envisioned nature as a manifestation of the divine. Painter Caspar David Friedrich created meditative landscapes that hover between mysticism and a sense of melancholy and solitude. Goethe and Schiller linked nationalism to the ideals of ancient Greece, giving the German movement a different tenor than the nationalism of France, which emphasized the idealization of political institutions and social arrangements. And in the United States, the gentleman architect Thomas Jefferson designed a university in Virginia based on the best classical information he had access to, while Charles Pierre L'Enfant laid out the capital of the world's first modern democratic republic in Washington, DC, an urban vision that used axial planning to merge urban spectacle with the idea of the balance of powers.

At the same time, classicism was challenged by more trenchant critiques that sought evermore pristine origins for architecture—in nature, primitive civilizations, or universal "science." The French Jesuit priest Marc Antoine Laugier converted the theoretical claims of the political philosopher Jean-Jacques Rousseau into new architectural theory. If nature made man noble, then for Laugier it was the "savages" of America who represented that nobility. Other "authenticities" were also sought; J. L. Durand looked to interrogate the orders of antiquity to extract their underlying geometric principles, rather than just accept them as privileged points of origin. Eugène-Emmanuel Viollet-le-Duc was the first to use steel as an exposed material, while Étienne-Louis Boullée published a series of theoretical works embodying the thinking of men of reason such as Isaac Newton.

In the wake of the American Revolution, Latin American colonies in Central and South America also began to declare independence. The failed Haitian slave revolution against

the French (1791–1804) was first, and far ahead of its time. When Napoleon invaded Spain and Portugal in 1808, their Latin American colonies used the opportunity to give the Latin American independence movement some momentum. The Portuguese monarchy relocated to Brazil during Portugal's occupation by Napoleon. After the court returned to Lisbon, the viceroy, who remained in Brazil, declared independence successfully in 1822. In general, however, the Latin American transition to nation-states was tumultuous, and it would take almost half a century before a series of long civil wars settled down enough to permit the creation of stable administrations. For two decades these erstwhile colonies tried unsuccessfully to fashion a united federation. Eventually they settled on the separate nations of today's South America.

When the U.S. Declaration of Independence and Constitution were written, their authors, with all their idealism, likely believed slavery was on the decline and would to die a natural death. Tobacco fields were exhausted from overuse, slave revolts were endemic, and financing for plantation expansions was becoming increasingly scarce. Not wanting to confront the Southern states that produced a majority share of the plantation wealth of the newly minted United States, the Founding Fathers left the topic of slavery untouched, at the mercy of the forces of history. And as history would have it, the Industrial Revolution—which itself had to rely on water, coal, and steam for power—revitalized the economic value of slavery like never before. As the demand for raw cotton skyrocketed, the slave plantations of the American South prospered—even as the earliest industrial manufacturing towns of England, such as Manchester and Liverpool, created a new industrial working-class culture that pointed to the end of rural, agricultural civilization. With industrialization came industrial infrastructure—factories, ports, warehouses, and shipyards, all built at the speed and size of utility, using the materials closest at hand—as well as the first public institutions designed to deal with urban citizenship: hospitals, prisons, and lunatic asylums.

In the midst of this fundamental transformation in thought, political ordering, and economic production, the European powers also commenced a colonial expansion project of a kind that had never been seen before. England led the way. The "loss" of America to independence meant first and foremost that British traders no longer enjoyed monopolistic rights and had to pay market price for American products. While this was still quite a viable proposition, the English government decided on a policy of aggressive expansion in the Old World to offset the American losses. Unlike the first period of colonization, when the Western European powers were looking for alternatives to the Ottoman and northern Italian stranglehold on the spice trade; now, in the late 18th century, the European powers were on the ascendant, flush with wealth from the plantation trade in the American colonies and powered by the Industrial Revolution. British warships in particular sailed the deep oceans largely unchallenged.

The big colonial story of the time was the unexpected ease with which the English were able to take over most of the Indian subcontinent in just a few decades, after two centuries of trying and succeeding only in building coastal ports. As the Mughal Empire declined, the officers of the British East India Company became increasingly bold and began to find spectacular success in their confrontations with local rulers. All this took place precisely when the main cadres of the British forces were being repeatedly defeated by George Washington's revolutionary forces, with some help from the French. The contrasting performances of the two armies possessed the British public imagination, and the British government decided to develop India as the counter-colony to the United States. In 1773 the Crown appointed the first official governor general of India to oversee the operations of the private British East India Company, and with that began the so-called Raj, the British effort to bring the best of the Enlightenment to India while pursuing an aggressive mercantile policy to feed the British mill and trade objectives. Calcutta (now Kolkata), once a swamp, was transformed by the newfound wealth of the

British East India Company into a massive port city that—if only in its pretentions—tried to vie with London by building plastered colonial governmental structures and mansions.

Meanwhile, East Asia, particularly China, continued to advance economically. China under the Qing dynasty extended its borders the old-fashioned way, conquering Tibet, Turkestan, and Mongolia. In size, population, production, and raw wealth, it had no equal. Its bold-thinking ruler, the Qianlong Emperor, aimed to create a pan-Asian empire, unified around the Indic origin ideal of *chakravartin*. He declared several religions and languages official. (Napoleon did the same after the French Revolution.) The Qianlong Emperor's purposeful use of imitation in constructing his new capital city, Chengde, was driven by the ideological innovation of constructing a vision of China as the center of a pan-Asian world. He also undertook a massive agricultural reform policy that involved the relocation of over 5 million Chinese peasants to Sichuan Province. The Chinese peasant was technologically advanced for his time and highly mobile, not quite as wedded to his land as the stereotypical provincial Western farmer. Later in the century China would come to be viewed stereotypically in the West as tradition-bound and moribund, but in 1800 China was still the object of global envy.

Apart from China, Europe, and the European-controlled colonies, there were two other areas that continued to develop architecturally but in very different ways—Japan and Thailand. In Japan, the Tokugawa shoguns, witnessing the havoc caused by the influx of silver in China, aimed to strictly regulate access by the expanding colonial world; only some Chinese and occasional European vessels were allowed into the port of Nagasaki. At the same time, Shogunate Japan tried to transform itself internally, developing a "modern" architecture of the middle class for Kabuki theater. Thailand, which was never colonized, was, by contrast, more than willing to open itself up to Western influence, unifying borrowed elements into regionally developed forms of practice. In that sense the story of 19th-century urbanism has to include not only such new cities such

as Washington, DC, and the redesigning of such older cities as Berlin, London, Paris, Dublin, and Athens; but also Bangkok, the newly founded capital of Thailand, which provides a glimpse of modern Southeast Asia architecture in a city that was neither colonized by the Europeans nor closed off in the name of tradition.

Napoleon was first to liberate the Jews in Europe. With that, and with the establishment of various Jewish reform movements, there was a global movement to build synagogues, an activity that had long been suppressed.

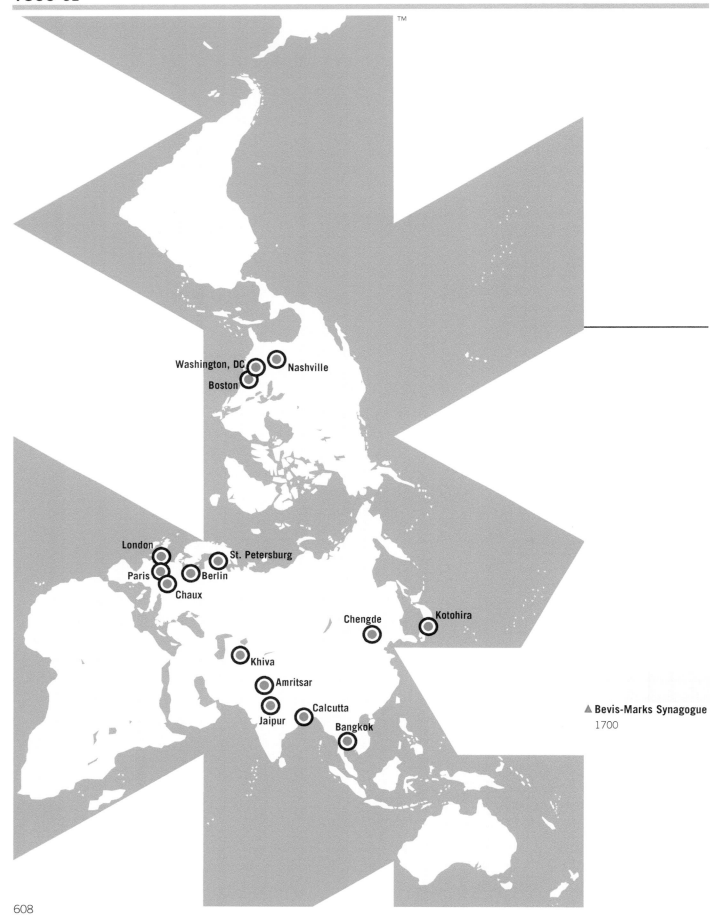

Washington, DC
Nashville
Boston

London
St. Petersburg
Paris
Berlin
Chaux

Chengde
Kotohira

Khiva

Amritsar

Jaipur
Calcutta

Bangkok

▲ Bevis-Marks Synagogue
1700

▲ Tash-Khovli
1830s

South Asia: Mughal Dynasty
1526–1858

▲ Jantar Mantar
Completed 1734 ▲ **Darbar Sahib**
1764

▲ **Hawa Mahall**
1799

Japan: Edo Period
1615–1868

▲ **Kanamaru-za**
1835

China: Qing Dynasty
1644–1911

▲ **Imperial Palace at Chengde**
1703–80 ▲ **Putuo Zongcheng Temple**
1771

Opium War
1839–1842

▲ **Wat Pra Kaew**
Completed 1784

1750 CE   **1800 CE**   **1850 CE**

Neoclassicism
Mid-18th to mid-19th centuries

▲ **Strawberry Hill**
Rebuilt 1749–77 ▲ **Shelburne House**
Begun 1763

▲ **Government House**
Begun 1803

Writers' Building ▷
1870

▲ **Ste. Geneviève**
1757 ▲ **Bibliothèque Nationale**
1788

▲ **Valhalla**
1830–42

▲ **Salt Works of Chaux**
1775–79 ▲ **Père Lachaise**
1804

Schauspielhaus ▲   ▲ **Altes Museum**
1818–21   1823–30

▲ **St. Madeleine Church**
1845–51

Royal Scottish Academy ▲
1835 ▲ **Tennessee State Capitol**
1845–59

▲ **Beth Elohim Synagogue**
1840

▲ **Bibliothèque St. Geneviève**
1845–51

Industrial Revolution
17th to 18th centuries

England: Hanoverian Rule
1714–1901 French Revolution
1789–1799 Napoleonic Wars
1795–1815

Victorian Era
1830–1901

American War of Independence
1775–1783 Haitian Slave Revolution
1791–1804

Joseph Bramah invents the water closet. ◉
1778 ▲ **Suffolk House of Correction**
1803 ▲ **Pentonville Prison**
1844

16.1 **Khiva, former capital of Khwarezmia**

TASH-KHOVLI

By 1800 the old land-based Silk Route was so completely in decline that one of the ways in which profit was extracted from it was by raiding, enslaving, and reselling traders who still plied that route. Khiva became the site of a notorious slave market. The city (now in Uzbekistan) is split into two parts. The outer town, called Dichan Kala, was formerly protected by a wall with eleven gates. The inner town is encircled by brick walls whose foundations are believed to have been laid in the 10th century. In the 1830s, Alla-Kulli-Khan built a palace, Tash-Khovli ("Stone Country Estate") in the eastern part of the inner city, just to the west of a large market. This complex has three yards arranged in a U with secondary spaces filling in the gaps. The southernmost is the receiving yard, where important visitors would be met; in the middle is a yard for entertainment; and the last and most private yard was occupied by the harem. Typically, the outside walls of the palace were left plain, but the walls of the courtyards were decorated with blue and white majolica tile. The wooden pillars have distinctive bulbous bases carved with geometrical and plant decorations, and the ceilings are painted in a golden-red color. In 1873, the Russians, eager to control the trade routes to the south and east, took the city and created a quasi-independent state under their control.

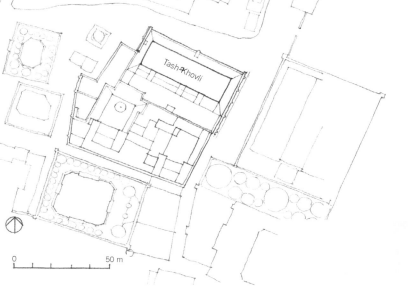

16.2 **Area plan: Tash-Khovli, Khiva, Uzbekistan**

16.3 **Courtyard: Tash-Khovli**

JAIPUR AND THE END OF THE MUGHAL EMPIRE

The Mughal Empire was at its largest under Aurangzeb (r. 1658–1707), who annexed all the Deccan Sultanates. After his death in 1707, however, the empire quickly began to crumble. Taking advantage of the situation, a number of Mughal governors, particularly the Rajput ones, either moved toward independence or declared independence outright. The prosperity of South Asia actually increased at this time with growth in trade, including from the newly established European trading ports. If modernity can be understood as the forward thrust of transformation and as the production and exploration of the possibilities of the new in negotiation with the values of the status quo, then this was indeed a period of modernity.

Sawai Jai Singh II (r. 1699–1743) utilized this opportunity to secure more autonomy for his own Kingdom of Amer (Jaipur). Since the 10th century, Amer had existed as a fortress town guarding an important pass on a trade route linking western India to Delhi. Amer palace, located halfway up a hill, consisted of a series of interconnected courtyards protected by a fort. Three additional forts, strategically placed on adjoining hilltops, guarded the city. But in 1727, Sawai Jai Singh felt sufficiently secure to establish a new capital on the unprotected plain, on the site of one of his garden palaces. Designed with the help of the architect Vidyadhar, Jaipur abuts the Amer hill on one side. The city was laid out on a grid to create a series of square neighborhoods divided by major arterials. Public amenities and market hubs were located at the intersections, called *chokris*. The main east-west street was laid out to visually align on axis with temples located on nearby hilltops. To entice settlers, Sawai Jai Singh ordered that shops be constructed along the entire length of main streets so that the main arteries of the city were well defined. A consistent street section was maintained and, to a visitor, the city appeared to be well inhabited and complete. The strategy worked, and Jaipur was fully inhabited in twenty-five years.

16.4 **Amber Fort, Amer, India**

16.5 **Jantar Mantar, Jaipur, India**

16.6 Hawa Mahall, Jaipur, India

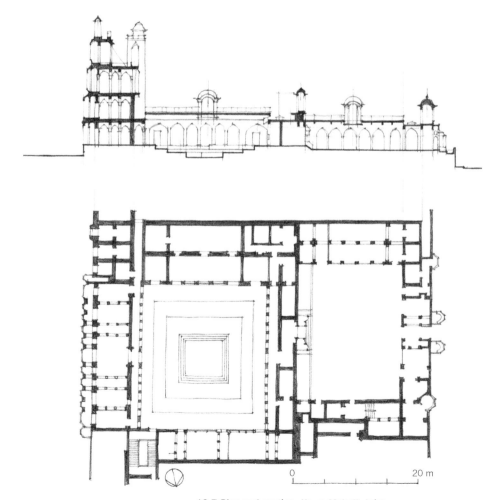

16.7 Plan and section: Hawa Mahall, Jaipur

There is a theory that Jaipur was based on a nine-square mandala. Although not verifiable, the story is given credence because Sawai Jai Singh was an avid follower of Hindu astrology. In fact, to obtain the most precise observations of the planetary bodies, he built state-of-the-art observatories in Jaipur, Delhi (built for the Mughal emperor), Varanasi, Ujjain, and Mathura. Sawai Jai Singh's observatories were based on similar ones built by Ulugh Beg in the 15th century in Samarkand, only these were larger, and since they were spread apart, their observations could be cross-referenced for greater accuracy. Named Jantar Mantar, they make for a stunning, astonishingly modern sculpture park. (*Jantar Mantar* is a corruption of *yantra*, which means "instrument.")

In 1799, Sawai Jai Singh's grandson, Sawai Pratap Singh, built the Hawa Mahall, considered to be one of Jaipur's signature monuments. The Hawa Mahall ("Wind Palace") gets its name because, as a palace, it was considered to be insubstantial—or made of wind. It earned this title because the structure is essentially a five-story-high screen wall. Constructed at the edge of the palace complex, facing the street, it was built to enable the women of the royal household to watch festival processions on the street while remaining unobserved themselves. Designed by Lal Chand Ustad, this structure derives from elements of Mughal palaces and mosques that often contained screened sections for women. At the Hawa Mahall, however, Ustad transformed the concept into a grand urban structure. Sawai Pratap Singh also constructed a palace on one of the artificial lakes of Jaipur.

16.8 Darbar Sahib, Amritsar, Punjab, India

DARBAR SAHIB

In the 18th century, the Sikhs, under Maharaja Ranjit Singh (r. 1801–1839), expanded into an empire encompassing the region of the five tributaries of the Indus, or the Punjab (literally, "five rivers"). Founded by Guru Nanak in the 15th century, Sikhism was a mix of Islamic Sufi concepts and Hindu bhakti ideas. Critical of some Hindu practices, it eliminated idol worship and caste distinction and emphasized the unity of God and the necessity of an intimate experience with the divine. The Sikhs offered themselves as an alternative to both Islam and Hinduism and accepted converts from both. Sikh involvement in the political affairs of the Mughals was complex; they fell in and out of favor with the Mughal court at various times. In 1699, Guru Gobind Singh (1675–1708), the last of their gurus, formalized the Sikh religion, enjoining the faithful to defend it by arms if necessary.

Darbar Sahib, or Golden Temple, built in Amritsar in 1764 during the reign of Maharaja Ranjit Singh, had long been an important place of Sikh pilgrimage and learning. It was here that, in 1604, Guru Arjan Das installed the Granth Sahib, the Sikh holy book after its compilation. It sits in the center of a square sacred pool, 150 meters on each side, that is surrounded by a marble walkway (for ritual circumambulation), which in turn is separated from the outside world by buildings that house the various functions of the institution, such as its administrative offices, galleries, and dining halls. A causeway leads from the Darbar Sahib to the edge, where one finds a three-story structure with a single dome, the Akal Takht, where the highest priests have their offices. Every morning the Granth Sahib is ceremoniously carried from the Akal Takh to the Darbar Sahib to be installed; it is returned in the evening. Among the several affiliated structures that lie outside the compound is the Guru-ka-langar, a three-storied building where 35,000 people are fed daily at no charge.

The Darbar Sahib itself has doorless entrances on all four sides as an indication of the building's accessibility to all. No formal rituals are conducted here, but hymns are sung day and night. The lower story of the main structure is made of marble, whereas the upper story and domes are covered with plates of gilded copper. An off-center low fluted dome is partially obscured by a high parapet with four *chattris* at the four corners. Its ornamentation and formal outlines are based on Mughal precedents, though the easy informality of their orchestration gives the Darbar Sahib a fluidity of expression associated more with complex Hindu and Jain temples than with the stately tombs and mosques of the Mughals. It is a unique structure, a product of one of the most determined attempts to bridge the differences between Islamic and Hindu thought to create a new synthesis.

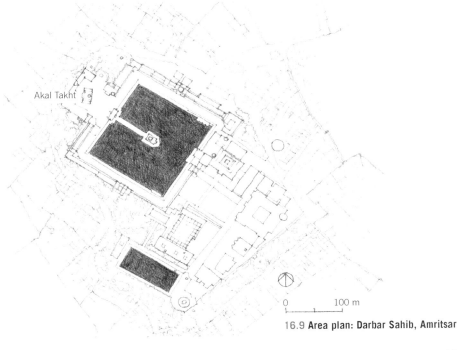

Akal Takht

0   100 m

16.9 **Area plan: Darbar Sahib, Amritsar**

16.10 **Wat Pra Kaew, Bangkok, Thailand**

16.11 **Wat Pra Kaew**

WAT PRA KAEW

By the late 18th century, the history of architecture becomes largely the history of European architecture, of European colonial architecture, and of Chinese architecture. Islamic architecture was on the wane, as was noncolonial architecture in India and elsewhere. There was one important and remarkable exception: Thailand. Thailand, or Siam, emerged as an important regional force in the 14th century under King Sukhothai, who controlled the area roughly covered by modern Thailand. His capital was the island city of Ayutthaya, about 100 kilometers north of Bangkok. Though the Thai culture was largely Indic in origin (*Ayutthaya* is Thai for Ayodhya, the sacred capital of Lord Rama), the Thai learned their Sanskrit and scripture from the Khmer of Cambodia, building several Angkor-inspired temples and stupas in Ayutthaya. The Chinese admiral Zheng He came to Ayutthaya and left behind a Chinese princess and her attendant, whose descendants still survive in Thailand as a distinct community and worship the princess and the admiral in a temple at Ayutthaya. In the mid-15th century, the Thai sacked Angkor, and then in 1782, under King Rama I (r. 1782–1809) of the Chakri dynasty, established as their capital the city of Bangkok, or Ratanakosin, on the Chao

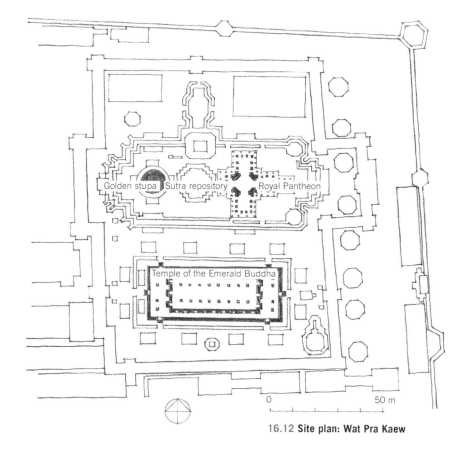

Golden stupa Sutra repository Royal Pantheon

Temple of the Emerald Buddha

0   50 m

16.12 **Site plan: Wat Pra Kaew**

16.13 **Golden stupa, Wat Pra Kaew**

Phraya River. The new Royal Palace was created as its symbolic core in a compound a few hundred meters from the river's edge. Looking beyond the borders there was Cambodia, with Phnom Penh as its capital, and Vietnam whose capital became Hué in 1802 under the Nguyen dynasty.

In the eastern section of the compound, a special structure was created to house the Emerald Buddha, a jade Buddha dated to 1434. Much venerated, it was brought to Bangkok in 1778 from northern Thailand. The compound is defined by a rectangular perimeter colonnade, with projections in the east and west, that contains a continuous wall fresco, painted on dry plaster, narrating the story of the Ramayana, the Hindu sacred text. At the center of the compound, on a raised platform running east-west, are three huge closely spaced buildings, a golden stupa, a square sutra repository, and a temple structure known as the Royal Pantheon. Also on the platform is a large stone model of Angkor Wat. Rama I had wanted the entire abandoned structure from Cambodia to be transferred to Bangkok, but when his emissaries returned with descriptions of its immensity, he decided to settle for a model. Angkor Wat is itself, like any Hindu temple, a model of the cosmos, and as such the model is almost equivalent, in its philosophical significance, to the original.

The close proximity of these buildings is not due to lack of space. Each building in well-established Mahayana Buddhist symbolism is a representation of the other, and the proximity of each was intended to keep them from being seen as autonomous structures; instead they were to be viewed as substitutes or even as metaphors for each other.

Whereas the stupa is completely gilded, the other two buildings are lavishly decorated on the outside with mosaics made of red, blue, and green tiles as well as fragments of glass and mirrors. The Wat Pra Kaew ("Temple of the Emerald Buddha") stands to the south of the platform. It has a single interior space undivided by partitions, with the Buddha placed at the far end in a resplendent setting, high above human height, enshrined in a small golden temple. The walls are covered with frescoes, and the roof trusses are made of wood.

The building, and indeed the entire architectural ensemble, was one of the most important of its time in Southeast Asia, reflecting the cosmopolitan taste of its patron. The tiles on the outside of the building are done in a Persian style, while the mosaics were made by Byzantine craftsmen, and the Buddha hall is a type of Sistine Chapel, its walls painted with religious murals. The placement of the Buddha on

top of a golden structure appears almost Baroque. This should not be interpreted as a sign of "Oriental" eclecticism in the face of the rigorous historicism of the European Enlightenment, but rather as a modern fusion of different elements into something unique. Thailand was never colonized—a rarity in that part of the world—and thus its rulers had the freedom to explore and develop contemporary architectural ideas that were denied those countries placed under colonial imprint. Whereas native architectural traditions began to dry out or became fossilized with the introduction of European-style buildings in India, for example, such traditions continued to develop with a sense of freedom in Thailand, unfettered by any colonial overlords' offended eyes.

16.14 Print from the *Carceri* series by Giambattista Piranesi

16.15 Drawing made from a Piranesi print of Roman ruins

NEOCLASSICISM VS. ROMANTICISM

The term *Neoclassicism*, in wide use today, was actually invented in the mid-19th century. Until then, critics, theorists, and artists called it simply the "true style" that challenged the fluctuations of taste and, particularly, the extravagances of Baroque space. The heady mercantile era of the preceding century gave way to a desire for something perceived as authentic and stable. At its best, Neoclassicism shared the Enlightenment's spirit of reform, whether it was scientific advancement in the Age of Reason or the new political philosophy that stressed the principles of a socially regulated human action. But Neoclassicism was also connected to Eurocentrism, the idea that European heritage conferred special standing in the history of civilization. Although Neoclassicism was originally a broad movement encompassing all the arts and the humanities, by the middle of the 19th century it had mostly died out except in architecture, where it survived into the 20th century.

The Adam brothers were already successful architects when Robert Adam (1728–92) made his first European trip. In Rome he met and befriended Giambattista Piranesi (1720–78), whose etchings of dilapidated Roman scenery were then wildly popular. Copperplate engravings were all the rage at the time, but Piranesi elevated the art into an idiom all its own. Scouring the often malaria-infested Roman *campagna* for pictorial possibilities, Piranesi created etchings of haunting intensity, bringing into view unexpected and revealing angles, with broken stones, crumbling bricks, collapsed vaults, and overgrown facades. This was a Rome far different from the one imagined in England, where it was embedded in a rhetoric of order and manliness. Piranesi envisioned a cataclysmic end of time, with nothing left to show for Rome's erstwhile grandeur. The Colosseum is an empty crater, the foundation wall of Hadrian's Tomb a vast battered cliff.

Adam and Piranesi represented the two sides of the Romantic movement. Both admired the heroic, but from different political perspectives. Adam saw the Roman past as the legitimization of European—and particularly English—civilizational supremacy in a diverse global world, while Piranesi rendered it as a meditative reflection on the short-sightedness of the powers currently in charge. Whereas Adam privileged a sustained investment in the "eternal principles" of the "true style"—that is, classicism—Piranesi pointed toward a more conflicted reading of history, one less sure of its certainties and more mindful of its losses.

In the European colonial environment, where global realities had increasingly become part of upper-class life, Neoclassicism, as the work of Adam demonstrates, provided a language of stability and order that also reinforced the search for European self-understanding in the wake of the colonial experience. But Neoclassicism, as a language of self-mastery, was also a language of the master over the production of others. Neoclassicism thus all too easily legitimized empire as a

16.16 Entrance facade: Shelburne House, London

16.17 Interior: Syon House, London

structure imposed over colonialism, harboring an underlying, suppressed contradiction between a civilizational ideal and the political expediencies that were necessary to realize that ideal.

Adam's belief in the "true style" meant a rigorous investment in accurate antique precedent, not Renaissance transmissions. He sought to create a totally integrated architectural and spatial environment. The facade of Shelburne House in London (begun 1763) comprised a seven-bay, three-story central block with a four-columned pedimented temple front. It is a combination of Palladio's Villa Foscari and his Palazzo Thiene. The central temple front is set between two-story, three-bay pavilions. A rusticated, false-arcaded ground floor unifies the composition. The ornamentation of the frieze was taken from the Temple of Concord in Rome. Some of the most important people in London society gathered at the Shelburne House, among them Benjamin Franklin and David Hume. Much of the house was demolished in the 1930s. The eating room was rebuilt and is in the Metropolitan Museum of Art in New York.

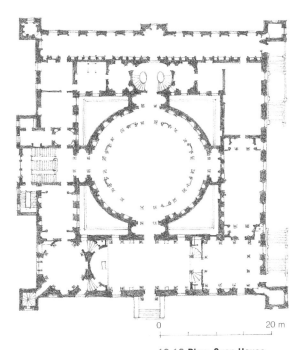

0   20 m

16.18 Plan: Syon House

16.19 **Strawberry Hill, Twickenham, England**

16.20 **Interior: Strawberry Hill**

The Romantics, in opposition to the Neoclassicists, invested in the Middle Ages, rather than Rome, as the more authentic and more emotional home in antiquity. Horace Walpole (1717–97), builder of Strawberry Hill (1749–77), used the term *Gothic picturesque* to define this style. Walpole was in many respects a counterculturalist. His principal passion was writing Gothic novels, such as *The Castle of Otranto*. He also wrote a four-volume history of art entitled *Anecdotes of Painting* (1761–71), as well as an essay entitled "History of the Modern Taste in Gardening" (1771). Upon the death of his famous father in 1745, Walpole settled at Strawberry Hill, an estate of some 16 hectares at Twickenham, southwest of London, set among fashionable villas overlooking the Thames River and near the residence of his friend, the poet and garden enthusiast Alexander Pope. Rather than delve deep into classicism, Walpole was among the first English intellectuals to amass a vast collection of objects from around the world, building in essence one of the first museums. To hold and display his collection he expanded the existing house and built a library, an armory, a gallery, a "star chamber," a "tribune," a sort of shrine, a china closet, bedrooms in several colors, and an oratory.

The structure itself was made in a kind of an experimental Gothic idiom, searching not for a singular expression but playing with the collaging of forms. There were towers, battlements, and stained glass rescued from demolished buildings.

While Robert Adam was an ideologue and consummate tastemaker for the metropolitan gentry, Walpole created a willful aesthetic environment reflecting his personal choices. Strawberry Hill became celebrated in its time; after 1763 Walpole even began selling entrance tickets. The house became a showpiece, while Adam's work represented the profession of an ideal. Adam and Walpole represent the paradoxes associated with emerging modernism: in the former, professionalism, or at least the beginnings of what might be called a professional practice; and in the latter, the deliberate and self-conscious search for personal expression in a diverse world.

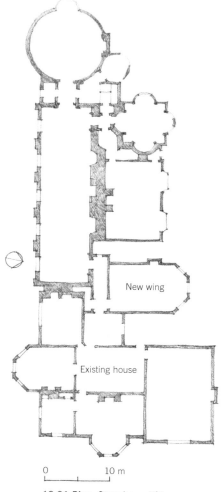

New wing

Existing house

0   10 m

16.21 **Plan: Strawberry Hill**

16.22 Reproduction of the frontispiece to Marc-Antoine Laugier's *Essai sur l'architecture*, from *Allegory of Architecture Returning to its Natural Model* by Charles Eisen

Laugier, Rousseau, and the Noble Savage

Whereas in England, Neoclassicism was generally seen as the proper environment for the elite, the tone in France was more strident, assuming a subtext of antimonarchism driven in part by an emerging interest in rationalism and legalism and a desire to rethink the role of civic institutions. In architectural circles, all this came into the open with the publication in 1753 of Marc-Antoine Laugier's *Essai sur l'architecture*. Translated into English in 1775, it was a flashpoint of discussion about the nature of architectural production. Unlike Leon Battista Alberti's *Ten Books on Architecture*, Andrea Palladio's *Four Books on Architecture*, and Claude Perrault's French translation of Vitruvius, Laugier's work pointed not to a classical past, but rather to an earlier, "rustic" past.

Here we have the beginnings of primitivism in modern art and architecture. Laugier wrote neither as an architect nor as a gentleman connoisseur. He was a Jesuit priest and impassioned orator, in a climate of approaching revolt. Unlike previous writers, Laugier frowned on the use of pilasters as "fakes" that did not contribute to the actual solidity of the object. Even though his image of the ideal building was not based on Roman models, Laugier admired the Maison Carrée at Nîmes, France, as the most perfect building of antiquity: "Thirty columns support an entablature and a roof which is closed at both ends by a pediment—that is all; the combination is of a simplicity and a nobility which strikes everybody." But critically for Laugier, unlike Adam and the other Neoclassicists, it was not the classical temple as such that needed to be imitated, but that which lay behind its design, the original "rustic hut," or *cabane rustique*, as he called it (widely mistranslated into English as "primitive hut"). This hut, according to Laugier, consisted only of columns, entablatures, and pediments. Vaults, arches, pedestals, and pilasters were not part of that system and, he argued, should therefore not be used. Even arcades, another important element in classical architecture, were listed by Laugier as "abuses."

Laugier's book was highly controversial. He argued that architecture should not be seen as representing a magical transition from the worldly to the heavenly, as had been implied by the Baroque style, or a search for classical truths in the architecture of Greece and Rome, but rather as a medium that told nothing less than the story of the "origins" of mankind—all mankind. This is why Laugier is often cited as one of the key precursors of the discourses of modern architecture, still more than a century away. These origins had to remain embedded in architecture. They were similar to the notion of grace—a sign of divine approval that for Catholics is embedded in the human soul.

In this sense, Laugier's argument echoed the 15th-century debate between Bartolomé de las Casas and Juan Ginés de Sepúlveda in Madrid on the question of the status of Native Americans. The Jesuits had studied and written about the life and work of the Native Americans and had lived more with them in the farthest reaches of the Americas than had any other colonists. While Walpole collected objects from around the world to glean in them meaning from the world's civilizations, Laugier's hut sought to bring home to Europe what the Jesuits had learned from people, who in their eyes were not "primitive" as in barbarians, but "noble" primitives. It was this, the Jesuits argued, that prepared them for Christ.

Influencing Laugier's writings was the just-published *Discourse sur les arts et les sciences* (1750) by Jean-Jacques Rousseau (1712–78). In this astonishing book, Rousseau critiqued what he saw as the naïveté of the Enlightenment's careless atheism. Not only had reason in the hands of the more powerful crushed individual liberty, but it had also replaced simple virtues with a labyrinth of false truths. The arts and sciences did not lead to knowledge but to hypocrisy, and civilization led to class division, slavery, serfdom, robbery, war, and injustice. The only real progress, he argued, was moral progress. It was a powerful and controversial critique of everything that the French intelligentsia had built up over the previous century. Rousseau, a native of the Calvinist city of Geneva, marveled at the civilizational and devotional virtues of Swiss farmers and Native Americans. It was Rousseau who coined the famous term *the noble savage* to describe the innate nobility of people like the Iroquois.

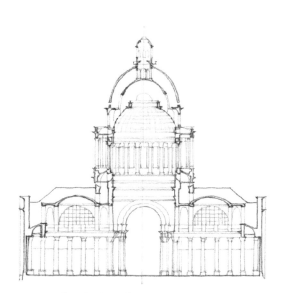

16.23 Section: St. Geneviève, Paris

16.24 St. Geneviève

St. Geneviève

Jacques-Germain Soufflot (1709–80) saw
in Laugier's argument the opportunity
for experimentation. The dome of his St.
Geneviève (Paris, 1757)—now known as the
Panthéon—was derived from Bramante's
San Pietro in Montorio and is Baroque in its
overscaled relationship to the building on
which it rests. The church, as a centralized
Greek cross, fulfilled a Renaissance
aspiration. Novel, however, and influenced by
Laugier, was the clean-cut, though gigantic,
Neoclassical temple front with Corinthian
capitals modeled on the Pantheon in Rome,
though with six rather than eight columns. On
the interior, Soufflot adhered to Laugier's call
for an architecture in which every element
has a structural rationale. There are pilasters,
but they are clearly linked to the structural
grid established by the columns. The vaults
have a billowing lightness and are illuminated
from the side through large windows,
concealed on the exterior behind a parapet.
The contrast between the building's severe,
cliff-like exterior and the luminous, airy
interior was meant to be a literal evocation
of the Enlightenment's transformative power.
The building was originally attached at its rear
to a monastery but was made freestanding in
the 19th century.

16.25 Interior: St. Geneviève

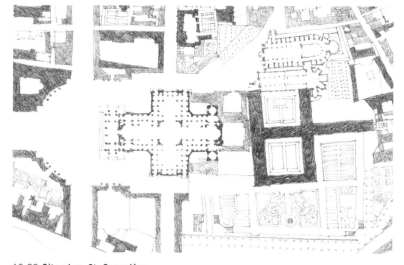

16.26 Site plan: St. Geneviève

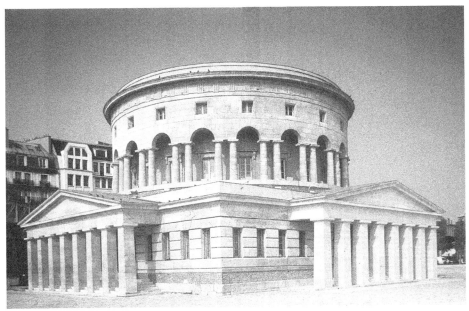

16.27 **Barrière de la Villette, Paris**

16.28 **Column of Director's House: Salt Works of Chaux, Arc-et-Senans, France**

Ledoux and Boullée

Claude Nicholas Ledoux and Étienne-Louis Boullée are often called revolutionary architects, but this is based on their architecture rather than their politics. Both architects straddled the fence in the French Revolution, even though they set in motion much of the aesthetic that for a short while governed the sensibilities of the age. Boullée probably made the transition to the postrevolutionary world better than Ledoux. He built little after the Revolution, but his place was more secure, and it was his vision that young architects in the Academy of Architecture, where Boullée taught, aspired to emulate. After the French Revolution, the history of Neoclassicism took many turns, fusing with the Greek Revival in Germany and Scotland and blending in with the eclectic stylistic preferences of the Victorians. Despite all this, traces of a vigorous and austere Neoclassicism as pursued by Ledoux and Boullée could be found throughout Europe from 1800 onward.

Claude Nicholas Ledoux (1736–1806) designed a series of gates and tollhouses for the French crown before the revolution—forty-five buildings in all—to mark the boundary of Paris and to impress approaching visitors. The stations also served as toll collection places for a much-hated tax on the importation of salt (which

had become very expensive) into the city. Like Christopher Wren's churches, each of Ledoux's gatehouses was different from the next and in its own way varied and forceful. A few are still extant, including the Barrière de la Villette (1785–89), which provides a good sense of Ledoux's austerely simplified architectural vocabulary. The central drum is supported by column pairs that serve as a screen holding the arcaded bottom of a cylinder, which is basically a circular building around a cylindrical light well at its core. Windows are without moldings and ornamentation is held to a minimum. The wide and low pediment—compared with the more historically accurate pediment of St. Geneviève—and the astonishing, domeless drum are far outside the norms of classicism, but Ledoux, probably more than any other architect of his generation, was seeking to redefine architectural typology from top to bottom.

Ledoux also designed various buildings for the Salt Works of Chaux (1775–79), located in the east of France in the Franche-Comté region between two villages near the forest of Chaux, not far from Besançon. The nearby forest supplied the wood needed to fire the kilns in which the salt was extracted from the brine. The factory replaced a previous installation that consisted of little more than a ramshackle assortment of

sheds. The brine was brought to the site from its source kilometers away by means of wooden pipes. Ledoux's plan called for a semicircular arrangement of buildings with the house of the director at the center and the salt-extracting buildings to both sides. The circumference is occupied by storage buildings, with the main entrance to the facility in the circle directly opposite the director's house. The salt trade was among the grimmest aspects of life in 18th-century France; the forcible imposition of a tax gave rise to widespread smuggling and robbery, as salt was very much cheaper outside the country. The security of the salt works was therefore essential. The entrance contained guardrooms and a small prison and is marked by a dense peristyle of six baseless Tuscan columns, with a squat attic above. Along the walls are openings out of which flows, in a sculptural mass, the thick, saline water. The columns, with their alternating round and square stones, were quite novel. Interpretations vary, but it seems that Ledoux wanted to show them as if they were in the process of being formed. This is perhaps the first architect-designed factory in history; what Ledoux hoped to demonstrate was the advantage of a rational and comprehensive solution to an industrial problem elevated to the level of the symbolic. Salt was produced there until 1895.

16.29 Salt Works of Chaux, Arc-et-Senans, France

More than any other architect, Étienne-Louis Boullée (1728–99) managed to straddle these complex political times. He won widespread acclaim during his lifetime for his series of inspired drawings that seemed to envision a postrevolutionary world. Boullée's buildings have simple geometrical shapes, are monumental in scale, and often serve as backdrops for uncluttered, neo-pagan devotions. His project for the Bibliothèque Nationale (1788), though often classified as an example of the Neoclassical sensibility, has actually no standard classical features on the surfaces except for the entablature and the frieze of garlands. The main entrance, guarded by two large figures of Atlas, gives admittance to a vast barrel-vaulted space boldly slit open at the top. The books are arranged on shelves against the walls of continuous terraces on the two sides of the interior of the building. Even more spectacular is Boullée's cenotaph for Sir Isaac Newton (1784). A sphere that represents the earth on the outside is on the inside a planetarium, with small holes forming the constellations. The entrance leads to a passageway that opens onto a shrine at the base of the inner void. Boullée's structures are always grand, both inside and out. For a theater, he designed a building within a building, a Pantheonesque interior placed inside a vast structure that was itself encased in a dome.

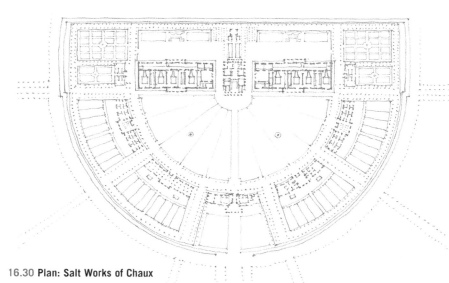

16.30 Plan: Salt Works of Chaux

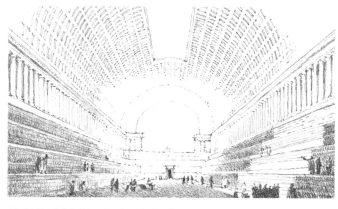

16.31 Boullée's idea for the Bibliothèque Nationale

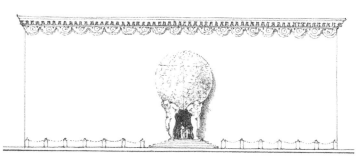

16.32 Facade: Bibliothèque Nationale

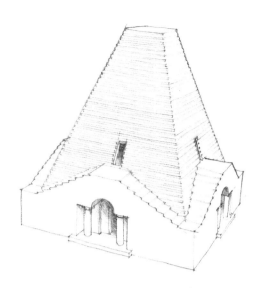

16.33 Ledoux's pyramid building, a project for a cannon forge

16.34 Ledoux's house of supervisors of the source of the Loue, a project for the ideal city of Chaux

16.35 Ledoux's project for an agricultural lodge

16.36 Ledoux's House of Circles, a project for an artist's studio

16.37 View of the Cemetery of Père Lachaise. Paris

16.38 Mt. Auburn Cemetery, Cambridge, Massachusetts

Napoleonic Cemeteries

After the French Revolution, Napoleon sought to rebuild not only France but all of Europe along Enlightenment lines. He eventually succumbed to his overreaching ambition, making enemies of the Austrians, Russians, and English, who were all eager to keep Napoleonic ideas as far as possible from their domains. The impact of the Napoleonic era was, however, profound, bringing into parlance concepts like liberty and justice, abstractions that were presumed universal and strong enough to replace the defunct and self-serving regimes of the aristocracy. Napoleon proved that nations could function without the paternalism of kings and princes. Socially, he introduced many Enlightenment-influenced notions—the Napoleonic Code of 1804, for example, brought about the emancipation of the Jews in many of the lands under his control; it also modernized the school system.

One of his important contributions to architecture was in cemeteries. Prior to then Napoleon, the well-to-do were buried in or near a parish church. The poor were buried in paupers' graves. As for soldiers, they were easily dispensable figures, often fighting as conscripts or mercenaries. They were buried in unmarked graves on the battlefield. But in Napoleon's army, death in battle took on a new dignity, a notion that would gain in importance in the Romantic period to come. Consequently, military death achieved an honorable connotation that it had not had since antiquity. As a result of these changes, the cemetery known as Père Lachaise, which was laid out in 1804 outside of Paris, was open to all citizens. Graves, however, were to last for only five years unless the plot was bought by the deceased's relatives, who were also required to endow certain architectural features of the cemetery. The cemetery was among the first examples of a "garden cemetery," laid out with trees, bushes, and winding paths; it had a central esplanade ending in a funerary monument. Père Lachaise became the model for cemeteries all over the world: the Glasgow Necropolis (1820), the South Metropolitan Cemetery at Norwood in London (1830s), and the Mt. Auburn Cemetery in Cambridge, Massachusetts (1831), are just a few examples.

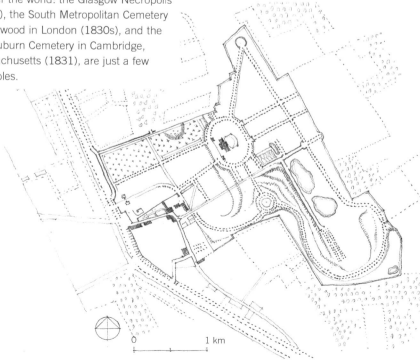

0   1 km

16.39 Plan: Cemetery of Père Lachaise

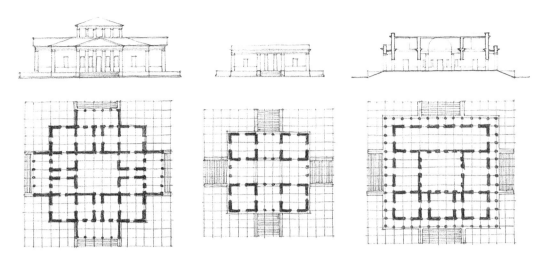

16.40 Horizontal combinations from Durand's *Précis*

Jean-Nicolas-Louis Durand

In France, the Romantic movement had many representatives among painters. Théodore Géricault (1791–1824), for example, used dramatic compositional techniques to bring out the themes of heroism, suffering, and endurance. In architecture, Romanticism was slower to develop. This was largely because architecture in France, unlike in England and Germany, remained under state sponsorship. For that reason, post-Napoleonic French architecture maintained the course of Enlightenment rationalism. The most important proponent of this tendency was Jean-Nicolas-Louis Durand (1760–1834), a pupil of Étienne-Louis Boullée and a professor at the École Polytechnique (founded in 1794) whose work set the tone for more than a generation. The purpose of the École Polytechnique was to graduate engineers capable of meeting the needs of the revolutionary armies as well as providing plans for civilian public works in the remote corners of the new republic. No such school existed in England, where the evolution of taste, remaining in the hands of the elite, was decentralized and thus often eclectic. Durand's book *Précis*, first published in 1802, became a reference book used throughout Europe for half a century. In it, he rejected the standard Neoclassical emphasis on historical relationship between contemporary architecture and classical

antiquity, and instead argued that even classical antiquity needed to be regularized according to the eternal principles of geometry. Durand was opposed to historical classicism that only copied surface classical elements but that in plan was anything but rational—like the Capitol Building in Washington, DC, for example. He wanted the plan to be laid out on a grid and the function clearly expressed. "To please," he wrote, "has never been the purpose of architecture." Instead, the architect should provide "public and private utility," while aiming to serve "the well-being and the maintenance of individuals and of society." Durand's designs for walls, following Laugier, were freed from pilasters, moldings, quoins, and rustications. This was not stripped-down

classicism, but rather a linking of architecture with nature and reason. The square, which has no dominant axis, constituted Durand's ideological and figural building block, serving to link the columns in a grid and stabilizing the architectural formation. Like an ideal military unit, a building had to reflect order, clarity, and hierarchy. Rationalism and civic dispassion had to be evinced to demonstrate architecture's independence from aristocratic whim. In this respect, Durand represents a break from insistence on tradition and literal historicism. Unlike Picturesque and Romantic notions of history as the ground on which the future projects itself, Durand's architecture was strikingly "modern," insisting on the primacy of program in the service of the state.

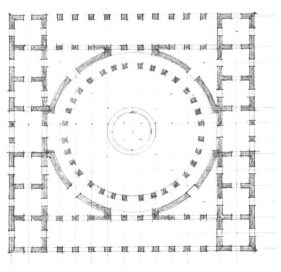

16.41 **A design by Durand**

16.42 Virginia State Capitol, Richmond

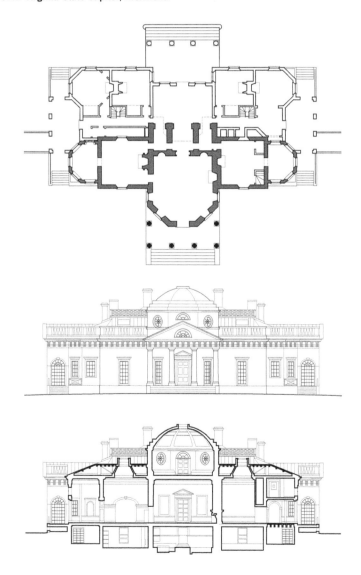

16.43 Plan, main facade, and section: Monticello plantation, near Charlottesville, Virginia

Jeffersonian Neoclassicism

When the sons, daughters, and grandchildren of the European settlers revolted against English rule, what had started as a search for economic freedom became one of the Enlightenment's greatest moments. Historically, in their search for antecedents, the American taste-setters saw themselves as paralleling the early Roman Republic rather than the Roman Empire. It was a subtle but important distinction, based more on fantasy than historical accuracy. The style of French postrevolutionary Neoclassicism was picked up in particular by Thomas Jefferson (1743–1826), the drafter of the Declaration of Independence and the third president of the United States, who left a lasting imprint on American architecture of the period. Having lived in Paris for five years (1784–89) as ambassador to France, he came to admire philosophical developments in Europe, which instilled in him the idea that architecture was directly related to social reform. He was also the consummate gentleman architect, amassing a library of 130 books on the fine arts—certainly the largest in the United States at the time. As an amateur architect, Jefferson, together with Charles-Louis Clérisseau, fused the styles of Laugier and Adam in the design of the Virginia State Capitol (1785–92). It was modeled on the Maison Carrée of Nîmes, one of the few Roman buildings that was accepted by Laugier as true to the standards of the "rustic hut."

Monticello

Thomas Jefferson designed most of Monticello, his plantation and primary residence, himself. He designed the house along neo-Palladian lines, with a prominent pedimented portico fronting an octagonal rotunda dome as the centerpiece. Within, Jefferson devoted most of his attention to his library and living room, reserving the central space as a kind of a museum for the waiting guests, where they were regaled with displays of Jefferson's scientific experiments and re-creations of objects from Lewis and Clark's expedition through the Western territories that had been acquired from Napoleon in 1805 during Jefferson's presidency.

Tobacco was the primary product of the Monticello plantation. Jefferson was a slave-owner, and, unlike George Washington, did not free his slaves on his death—except the children of Sally Hemings, his domestic help slave, with whom he almost certainly had six children. Hemings's family lived under the kitchen at Monticello, and the rest of the slaves lived in cabins along a prominent lane called Mulberry Row. Jefferson died about $130,000 in debt; his daughter sold Monticello and the slaves to settle his estate.

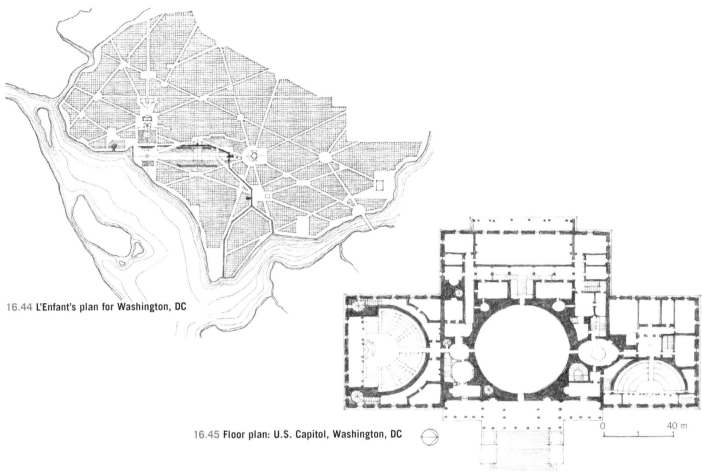

16.44 L'Enfant's plan for Washington, DC

16.45 Floor plan: U.S. Capitol, Washington, DC

0   40 m

WASHINGTON, DC

The design of Washington, DC, was the first attempt to spatialize a new capital city as an embodiment of the nation-state. Charles Pierre L'Enfant, a French engineer who served in the American Revolutionary War, worked at the direction of George Washington to prepare the plan. While Jefferson had a more modest vision for the capital, L'Enfant, presumably reflecting Washington's conception, designed something more grandiose—a city for the ages.

Over the base pattern of the urban grid, L'Enfant imposed a Baroque-style web of avenues that is surprisingly idiosyncratic and that adjusts to the landscape and to the turns of the Potomac River. Together they form fifteen squares, intended to be divided among the states. Over this, he imposed a third order, with the Capitol Building and the White House not facing each other across an open mall but placed at the ends of an L, with the capitol at the longer arm of the east-west-facing L. The intersection of the

two arms lies along the Potomac so that the two buildings, backing their way into the urban fabric from the river's edge, achieve a sense of parallel prominence when approached from the riverside—one of the major ways by which the city would have been accessed at the time.

L'Enfant's design calls to mind the gardens of Versailles because the grand avenues of the former are like the allées of the latter. However, the Capitol and the White House are also connected by one of several diagonals—Pennsylvania Avenue is a Baroque device first articulated for Rome under Sixtus V in his attempt to link the great pilgrimage sites of that city. In that sense the city blends aspects of Versailles and Rome, bringing the Counter-Reformation ideal of the freestanding monumental building into line with the notion of a city as a landscape traversed by grand ceremonial approaches.

The siting of both the Capitol and the White House away from the river's edge and fronted by lawns derives from English country house prototypes. It might also point

to the Hôtel des Invalides (begun 1671) in Paris, which, unlike the Louvre, was set at 90 degrees to the Seine River at the end of a park, connecting building and river. (At St. Petersburg, the Winter Palace, which is modeled on the Louvre, sits alongside the Neva River.)

L'enfant was dismissed from service in 1792, and he left for Paris with all his drawings. The plan as executed was based on the drawings of Benjamin Banneker, a former slave and self-taught astronomer.

The U.S. Capitol Building, begun in 1793, went through several stages involving the architects William Thornton, Henry Latrobe, and Charles Bulfinch, in that order. It was a difficult building to design, since there was no clear prototype for a building with such a complex program. In the Thornton plan, the House chambers and the Senate chambers were placed right and left of a great rotunda that was envisioned as a museum, with niches sheltering statues of revolutionary heroes. The building seamlessly integrated

16.46 The U.S. Capitol today

allusions to a mythical Roman Republic, to universal geometries, and to great historical events. The entrance was defined by a temple front with eight columns, modeled on the Pantheon, flanked somewhat unusually by columnar porches. Though the building was symmetrical on the exterior, it was not on the interior, where there was no attempt to balance the two chambers. This went against the Neoclassical tendencies of the time. The building, set on a high ground-floor plinth, was topped by a Pantheonesque dome resting on an octagonal drum—higher than that of its Roman model, so it would be easily visible from the surroundings. Beginning in 1855, the west front of the Capitol was rebuilt and a new dome, held up by a steel frame, was designed to rest on a high drum. Compared to the conventions established by Michelangelo's dome for St. Peter's in Vatican City, the dome is far out of proportion to the building below. Perhaps it is this strangeness that keeps the building from looking like a cathedral and imparts to it an unmistakable uniqueness.

Bulfinch, when left to his own devices, as at the Massachusetts State House (1795-98), was closer to the tradition of Palladio and Inigo Jones. Sited prominently on a hill, the state house is a brick structure with white woodwork and trim in the Georgian manner, but modeled loosely on Palladio's Pallazo Thiene and Robert Adam's Shelburne House. The upper floor is accessed by parallel stairs that flank the central space. A broad loggia with paired pilasters provide vistas down to the city and harbor. The wooden dome, originally painted gray to make it look like stone, was gilded in the 1890s. The style of the building is known as Federal, referring to buildings designed between 1780 and 1830 in the United States.

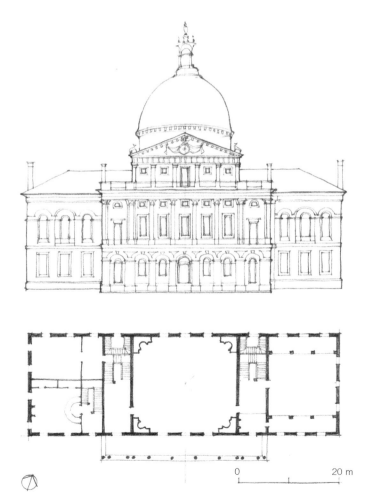

0   20 m

16.47 Plan and elevation: Massachusetts State House, Boston

16.48 19th-century Europe

16.49 Church of the Savior on Blood, St. Petersburg, Russia

NATIONALISM

Nationalism is presently such a ubiquitous concept that one forgets that it is actually a modern concept, springing from the end of the Napoleonic wars. As important as Napoleon Bonaparte was in spreading the ideas of liberty and justice throughout Europe, the consequences of decades of war left Europeans in desperate need of stability. In 1813, Europe's diplomats met in Vienna to discuss the political future of Europe in the hope that the borders could be stabilized. The Vienna Congress stipulated that countries were to create constitutions, if they had not already done so—a promise some rulers broke to create stronger bonds between the aristocracy and the bourgeoisie. Prior to the Vienna Congress, that bond was achieved mainly through the antiquated custom of marriage, which only tended to splinter and fragment the political landscape. It was hoped that countries with fixed national boundaries and with a working legal infrastructure would avoid war or have the means and recourse to avoid it. Though the ideals proved to be elusive, there is no doubt that the Vienna Congress helped create the modern notion of a nation-state, and it was certainly successful in determining the future national boundaries in Europe—boundaries that drive European politics to this day.

The new spirit of nationalism found an easy alliance with Romanticism. For the nationalists, history was more than just a gentleman's pastime. State boundaries had to make sense historically, linguistically, geographically, and now ethnically, and this led to an interest in local history and the development of regional antiquarianism. Russia experienced a revival of the Russian language (until the defeat of Napoleon, the Russian aristocracy had spoken mainly French). In Germany, there was a fascination with the medieval and with the imagery of the forest, as well as with the ancient Greeks, with whom many Romantics felt an affinity. Romantic nationalism also emerged in Scandinavia as a protest against Russian occupation and took the form of a revival of Nordic mythology. Apart from the development of national languages, Romantic nationalists were interested in folklore and local customs, even if these had to be enhanced. A case in point is the "discovery" of *Beowulf* in a single manuscript, first transcribed in 1818, after the manuscript had lain as an ignored curiosity in scholars' collections for two centuries. *Beowulf* quickly came to be seen as an English national epic. In architecture, Romantic nationalism was slower to take hold due to the entrenched dominance of Neoclassicism, but as the century progressed, more and more examples could be found. One such, the Church of

the Savior on Blood in St. Petersburg (1883–1907), was clearly meant to give impetus to a revival of Byzantine forms.

In recent decades, with the post–Cold War multiplication of new countries, Romantic nationalism has become a global phenomenon. Though it heralds the farmer and the workers, it often develops into an aesthetic that appeals to upper-class tastes. As a result, Romantic nationalism is generally a conservative response in the context of the lower classes and a seemingly liberal response in the context of the upper classes. The traits are clearly identifiable: passion for one's country combined with a feeling—fact-based or not—of past injustices at the hands of others. The past that Romantics point to is often bucolic and pre-modern—a cleaned-up fiction more than a reality.

16.50 **Neue Wache, Berlin**

16.51 **Schauspielhaus, Berlin**

Altes Museum

During the 17th century, the electors of Brandenburg expanded their territory so that by the end of the century Prussia had grown from a regional principality to a major state. And with the defeat of Napoleon at Leipzig in 1813, it became an important European power. Despite the difficulties with France, infatuation with Napoleonic ideas led to a generation of German thinkers who hoped to retool the Enlightenment to fit the German context.

Energetic reformers, including the noted scientist Wilhelm von Humboldt, head of Prussia's department of education and arts, helped transform Prussia into a progressive state by abolishing serfdom and curtailing the privileges of the nobility, introducing agrarian and other social and economic reforms, and creating an exemplary system of universal education. Among the leading literary figures in Germany at the time were Johann Wolfgang von Goethe (1749–1832) and Friedrich von Schiller (1759–1805), who wanted to link German nationalism to the ideals of ancient Greece. This gave the German movement a different tenor than the nationalism in France, which emphasized the idealization of political institutions and social arrangements.

The person who gave architectural shape to Romantic neo-Greek ideals was Karl Friedrich Schinkel (1781–1841). He completed his training as an architect in 1803 in Rome, where he met Wilhelm von Humboldt, with whom he became friends. It was Humboldt who helped secure Schinkel's position in the Prussian bureaucracy; one of his first public projects was the design of the Neue Wache, or New Guardhouse (1816–18), a monument to the new citizen's army of Prussia. Until then, the only significant Neoclassical building in Berlin was the Brandenburg Gate, inspired by the Athenian Propylaea. The Neue Wache is an austere building with a Doric porch flanked by two tower bases (rather than towers) that make the building appear to be a temple-gate combination. The tympanum shows the Goddess of Victory controlling and deciding a battle. The interior is a simple square room without a dome but with a round skylight at the center.

A few of Schinkel's other prominent works included a theater, the Schauspielhaus (1818–21); the Altes Museum at Berlin (1823–30); Schloss Glienicke (completed 1827); and the Bauakademie (1831–36). No other architect in Europe, with perhaps the exception of John Nash, wielded so much influence. Schinkel's most visible commission was for a public art museum (1822–30) sited very prominently opposite the Schloss, or Royal Palace, in the very heart of Berlin. Now called the Altes Museum, it embodies Schinkel's commitment to monumental civic architecture as a vehicle of the Enlightenment's cultural imperative. Though museums were beginning to appear, most were refurbished palaces; the building type, as an institutional element in the urban landscape, did not yet exist, as up until this period art collecting had largely been an aristocratic privilege. Schinkel designed the building as a great block with two interior courtyards and a central space. The surmounting Pantheonesque dome, clamped into the frame of the building, was not visible from the front; instead, the front consists of a row of columns, like a great Greek stoa, elevated on a platform above the surroundings. At the top of the stairs, before entering the rotunda, there is a loggia with large open-air staircases to the right and left of the principal axis. Art works were exhibited in long rectilinear rooms with column pairs forming a passage down the middle. This was not a temple or sanctuary, but rather a type of civic warehouse resembling an agora, with the central space fitted out with statues. The gallery spaces were designed for perambulating and conversing about art as much as for looking at it. The plan was clearly influenced to some extent by Durand's call for the systematization between structure and program.

16.52 Altes Museum, Berlin

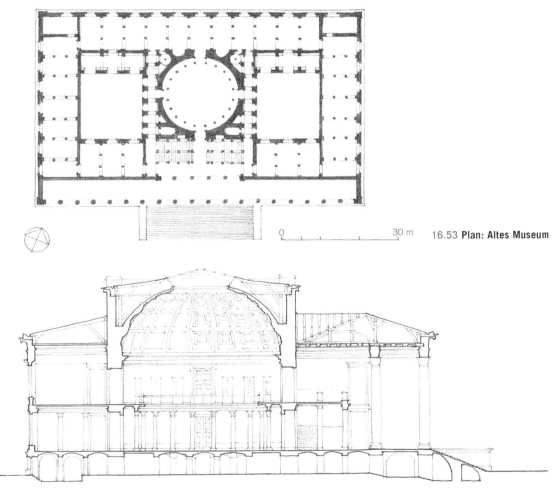

16.53 Plan: Altes Museum

16.54 Section: Altes Museum

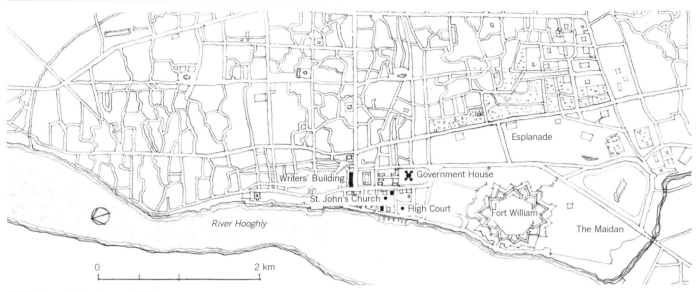

16.55 Map of Calcutta, ca. 1850
Redrawn from 1842 map in the David Rumsey Historical Map Collection

COLONIAL CALCUTTA: THE ESPLANADE

While the Americans were building Washington, DC, as their new federal capital, and while Napoleon's armies were bringing France's revolution to the rest of Europe, the English began their counterproposition to these movements by beginning the large-scale construction of what effectively became their capital in colonial India.

The early days of the English colonists in India were far from idyllic. Calcutta (now Kolkata) was awarded to the British by the Mughals because it sat on one of the least desirable pieces of land—a marshy swampland. Cholera, typhoid, malaria, and tuberculosis were endemic. Particularly feared were the monsoons, when flooding increased health risks exponentially. But the deep waters of the river Hooghly enabled ocean-faring ships to travel 96 miles inland, and Calcutta developed into a busy port. By the 1780s the British East India Company army had become so large that only military personnel were allowed to reside within the fort, and new public buildings had to be constructed outside the fort. A huge open space was created all around the fort to maintain defensive sightlines. This made the avenues lining the edge of the Maidan, as the open space was called, into prime sites for new mercantile and civic establishments. As Calcutta grew in prestige and wealth,

two-, three-, and even four-story mercantile establishments quickly filled in the avenue's edges, creating a continuous facade around the Maidan. Very visible and meant to be seen, monumental loggia, pilasters, and the occasional pedimented portico rubbed shoulders with one another, as crisp, white, Italianate and Neoclassical buildings lined up to announce the English presence, forming what was called the Esplanade. Little of the Esplanade was made from stone, however. Most of it was brick-based indigenous construction with a generous coating of painted *chunar* plaster. The *chunar* looked good and shined in the sun but had to be constantly repaired, especially after the monsoons, when it often peeled away, exposing the "sham" of the buildings—and by implication, of their nouveau riche

occupants—much to the chagrin and derision of colonial commentators from the homeland. (This discourse of pride and shame as a function of appearance lingered around colonial architecture to its very end.)

Writers' Building

Faced with huge financial losses with the impending American independence, the English parliament focused its attention on its colonies in the East, particularly in India, and found that in spite of its political successes and ample displays of wealth, the British East India Company was nonetheless badly in debt, according to the banking statements in London. Its officers were accused of corruption and profiteering, and in 1773, the company was reorganized in the hopes of establishing accountability. A governor

16.56 View of *chunar* Calcutta from the Esplanade, ca. 1850

16.57 Writer's Building, as originally built and as reskinned, Calcutta

16.58 St. John's Church, Calcutta

general was appointed to ensure that besides becoming profitable, the company's administration over its territories was just and in consonance with British ideals. A fair government in India was necessary not only to legitimize colonization but to also to soften protest back in England. Thus was born the ideological project of colonization.

Warren Hastings, the first governor general of India (1772–85), was a capable and responsible administrator. He increased revenues exponentially (mostly from opium production, set for export to China), expanded territories, and, most importantly, ruthlessly enforced a strict administration with detailed accounting. Hastings's approach to the problem of "just governance" was supremely pragmatic. It was imperative that the English learn local languages, customs, and systems of government, he proposed, because that would enable them to know the people better and to govern them with those systems. In 1784 he created the Asiatic Society of Bengal, with William Jones as its president, to study and translate the culture. For Hastings, Indian culture and civilization was a real and living thing that he was not interested in transforming or reforming, only

in governing—which he was wont to do with personal discretion and an iron hand.

His signature building was the gigantic secretariat and training school he had built for the clerks of the British East India Company. Known as the Writer's House (1780)—the "writers" were the clerks—this interminably long three-story structure lines one entire length of Calcutta's water tank. Given that it was the writers who enabled the rationalization of the company's presence in India, it is only fitting that their domain was a remarkable essay in rationalization and functionalism, with a single cornice running the entire length of the perimeter, interrupted only slightly by the central facade. It was designed by a civil architect, John Fortnom, and Thomas Lyon, a carpenter and amateur architect.

St. John's Church

At the turn of the 19th century, English colonial policy changed again, this time influenced by the Enlightenment's critique of the arbitrariness of power. Warren Hastings was impeached by Edmund Burke (1729–97), who argued that parliamentary oversight was not enough: there had to be

a social contract attached to the principle of divine sanction; the purpose of the colonial administration had to be consonant with the "eternal laws" of good governance. For the Tories, good governance was ensured by the abiding prestige of the king and his aristocracy. Lord Charles Cornwallis, the new governor general (1786–93), in an attempt to replicate European aristocracy in India, created a new class of landowners called zamindars.

The results were disastrous. In the Mughal administration, land had been collectively owned at the village level, and zamindars were only tax collectors. Now that they owned the land, they could sell it in response to market opportunities. The peasantry were completely disempowered. Enterprising company officers exploited the opportunity, making quick fortunes. Colonial architecture was called upon to signify the new "eternal laws." The Writer's Building was reskinned and acquired Doric porticoes. St John's Church (1787) built was based on the late Georgian high steeple of St. Martin-in-the-Fields in London. A simple box (a three-bay nave and galleries) with a Tuscan portico and a stone steeple and spire, its symbolic importance equaled that of King's Chapel in Boston as a visible reminder of the authority of church and king. And this time it was made from real stone, and not just *chunar*.

16.59 Government House, Calcutta, India
Based on a map in in the David Rumsey Historical Map Collection

Government House

By 1800, a new generation of company officers under the influence of the Romantics took issue with the Whig-backed zamindari system. They admired the Indian village (the country's ancient urban culture notwithstanding), thus enhancing the impression in Europe that the distinction between Europe and the colonies was a difference between cities and villages. They placed their faith in the paternalistic figure of the British officer, a man with great and concentrated authority who was highly paid but barred from obtaining any profit from company activities—and who was expected to be educated, enlightened, knowledgeable, and sympathetic. The highest British officer was the governor general.

In 1798, when Lord Richard Wellesley replaced Cornwallis as governor general, he began construction of a new Government House (1803) to embody his authority. Its design, prepared by Charles Wyatt, was created with spectacle in mind. With a tall Pantheonesque central dome, each side of the facade is symmetrical and complete, and stands as an idealized object in space. The strict Neoclassical portico set up on a broad and imposing staircase sealed its identification with the eternal principles of Vitruvius, even though the entire structure was made in brick and *chunar*, not Italian marble. However, as Chattopadhyay has argued, the Government House's interior—unlike Kedleston Hall, which was segmented into rooms for privacy—was divided by

perforated colonnades designed to ensure that the retinue of servants had constant, but screened, access to all spaces. Cornwallis's wife complained that the Government House had no place she could call her own.

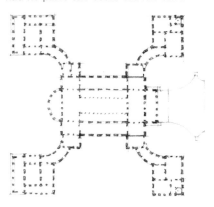

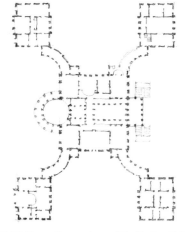

16.60 Plans: Comparison of Kedleston Hall, Derbyshire, England, and Government House, Calcutta

GREEK REVIVAL

Although today the Parthenon is one of the most revered ancient buildings in Europe, its artistic prominence only slowly came into focus during the 19th century. In 1805, when Thomas Bruce, 7th Earl of Elgin, who had purchased the Parthenon frieze from the Ottomans, first approached the British Museum about buying the pieces, he encountered hesitation on the part of the authorities. A few years later, when Charles Robert Cockerell took the sculptures from the temple of Aegina, the English showed no interest in their purchase, and he sold them to Ludwig I of Bavaria, where they now form the kernel of the Glyptothek Museum in Munich.

The fascination with Greece received a boost when hostilities ended between England and France in 1814, allowing Europeans to flock to Greece in unprecedented numbers. The country became all the more alluring in the 1830s, following the liberation of Greece from Turkish occupation. In 1830, England, Germany, and Russia signed the London Protocol, which recognized the independence of Greece. The Germans and the Bavarians placed themselves in charge of the military operation that eventually freed Greece from the Ottoman Empire in 1833, putting Otto von Wittelsbach on the throne, his reign guaranteed by the European powers. The impact of the liberation of Greece on the European consciousness was profound. It breathed new life into the Neoclassical movement and into Enlightenment notions about freedom and progress. As a result, Neoclassicism, once associated with the heavy-handed world of imperial institutions, was now linked to the optimistic and progressive world of bourgeois industry.

Neo-Greek architecture took on a more strident form near Regensburg, Germany, at Valhalla (1830–42), designed by Leon von Klenze (1784–1864) as a hall of fame for German luminaries. Klenze, who had studied in Paris under Jean-Nicolas-Louis Durand, also designed the Glyptothek Museum (1816–30) in Munich with an archaeologically correct Greek front and a Roman-style interior, following Durand's methodology.

16.61 **St. Madeleine Church, Paris**

16.62 **View of Valhalla, near Regensburg, Germany**

Valhalla, sited on a bluff over the Rhine River, was a relatively correct Greek-styled temple placed on a series of terraces. Ludwig I also sent Klenze to help design Greece's new capital city, Athens, located to the largely uninhabited west and south sides of the ancient Acropolis. It became the first capital city built to reflect the fusion of Enlightenment and Romantic ideals. The neo-Greek movement was relatively short-lived on the Continent, where it had to compete with other styles. But in Scotland, where the economy had rapidly developed in the middle of the 19th century due to its expanding hold on cotton trade and shipbuilding—Glasgow ships accounted for 85 percent of Britain's total tonnage—the country was eager to express itself as autonomous, even though it was part of England. The Greek style was thus an important expression of its national romantic fervor, as can be seen in the Royal Scottish Academy building (William Henry Playfair, 1835) in Edinburgh, and St. Vincent Street United Presbyterian Church (Alexander Thomson, 1857–59) in Glasgow.

Tennessee State Capitol

The most impressive examples of the Greek Revival were in the United States, where a particularly strong connection was made between Greece and America's own newfound nationhood. This was not a case of history simply being imported into the open landscape of the Americas. The Americans saw their nation as the land of opportunity, where they could return to classical values

without encumbrance of custom. The *Modern Builder's Guide*, which appeared in 1833 and ran through five editions until 1855, presented detailed engravings of the classical orders and their sources in ancient temples. The Greek Revival in the United States expanded on the Hellenistic leanings of the architecture of the so-called Federal Era (1780–1830), but unlike the Federal style, which was best expressed in the great houses of the well-to-do, the Greek Revival was applied to institutional

and governmental buildings, including the Patent Office in Washington, DC (1836), with a copy of the front of the Pantheon as part of its facade; the Old Shawneetown Bank (1836) in Old Shawneetown, Illinois; the James Dakin Bank of Louisville (1834–36) in Louisville, Kentucky; the Market Hall (1840) in Charleston, South Carolina; and William Strickland's Tennessee State Capitol (1845–59) in Nashville, Tennessee, which combined a temple with a huge version of the Greek Choragic Monument of Lysicrates in Athens.

16.63 **Royal Scottish Academy, Edinburgh**

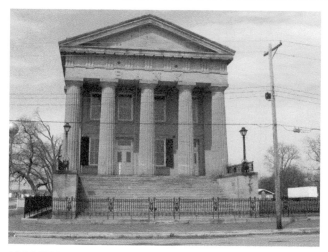

16.64 Old Shawneetown Bank, Shawneetown, Illinois

16.65 Market Hall, Charleston, South Carolina

These were not isolated examples but part of a wave of neo-Hellenism that lasted for decades and that stretched up into Canada; it can be felt in even humble buildings as far away as Oregon. When the Native Americans in the western half of New York State were conquered, place names were literally taken out of the *Iliad*; today one can travel to Ithaca, Troy, Syracuse, Athens, Rome, Carthage, and even to Homer without ever leaving the state. In Nashville, Tennessee, a full-scale replica of the Parthenon was built in 1897. It was not painted in the vibrant colors of the ancient Greeks but remained white, as the neo-Greeks preferred. The columnar

Grecian mode was also easily adopted for plantation houses, especially in Mississippi and Louisiana, where circumferential porches had been customary since the 18th century. Oak Alley (1836), the home of planter Alexander Roman, near Vacherie, Louisiana, is a well-known example of this mode. The massive encircling columns support a continuous veranda on the second-floor level, and the twenty-eight columns are matched by an equal number of live oaks that line the formal approach to the house from the Mississippi River, literally playing out the relationship between nature and form—and reinforcing the ideology of elitism.

Metcalfe Hall

From 1800 onward, great surveys were conducted to map every bit of land in colonial India, so that landholdings could be transferred to individual peasants. But this system could not be strictly enforced, since land was held collectively in village trusts. As corruption again grew, the critics of the Romantics arose: the new liberals who, from 1828 to 1856—the period of the governorships from Lord William Bentinck to the Earl of Dalhousie—drew inspiration from the Benthamite utilitarians. They believed that human nature was intrinsically the same everywhere and that it could be brought forth by education, law, and free trade. For them, passing on English civilization to the Indians, whose civilization was seen as defective, had a singular objective. They saw themselves as custodians of the Indian civilization until the Indians were sufficiently "civilized" and self-disciplined to maintain it themselves. This task was commonly characterized as the "white man's burden."

In architecture the favored style was now the Greek Revival. Since the liberation of Greece from the Turks in 1830, English and continental archaeologists had been poring over Greek ruins, measuring, copying, and studying them in great detail. Building from these accurate style sheets became the new clarion call of the 1840s. Sir Robert Smirke designed the British Museum in London (1823–47) in studied classicism. In Calcutta, C. K. Robinson designed Metcalfe Hall (1840–44) as a fine Greek Revival building, with thirty huge Corinthian columns supporting a massive entablature.

16.66 Tennessee State Capitol, Nashville

16.67 Metcalfe Hall, Calcutta, India

16.68 View of Manchester factories depicted in a painting by William Wylde in 1857

INDUSTRIAL REVOLUTION

By the second decade of the 19th century, industrialization in England began to have global implications. A whole new society was being created, taking shape in a new type of city and new types of political and power relations. Unlike the great metropolises of old, factory towns like Manchester, Leeds, and Liverpool were not urban to begin with. There was no core of elegance—no great boulevards, no parks, churches, palaces, or cultural institutions. And yet these were cities competing in size and population with the likes of London and Paris. Manchester, nicknamed Cottonopolis because of all its cotton mills, became the second-largest city in England after London. The industrial city was a novel urban landscape of people, traffic, and commerce—with a level of squalor never witnessed before. There was no urban planning; there was no sewage system; and water delivery was haphazard. Typhoid and tuberculosis outbreaks were common. Air pollution from the foul smells of factories, sewage, and slaughterhouses was a given. (In London, the stench from the Thames River was so severe that work in the Parliament building, which is located right next to the river, was often impossible.) The cramped conditions of the workers were startling; life expectancy was twenty-eight years. During the Napoleonic wars, the government paid little attention to these problems, and even after the war, despite growing unrest, the conservative Tory Party was resistant to change.

When the Whig Party gained a majority in the 1830 elections, things began slowly to change. The Reform Bill of 1832 reapportioned city districts to reflect changes in the population; it also liberalized voting qualifications and defined the idea of democracy as we understand it today, even though voting rights were, for a long time, still reserved for men only. The Factory Acts of the 1830s reduced the hours of child labor; the Mines Act of 1842 prohibited underground work for all women and for boys under the age of ten; and the Ten Hours Act of 1847 limited the workday for women and young people to ten hours. Despite these improvements, factory life remained dire and a major point of contention and political strife. Efforts were made to control sanitation. In the 1860s, Joseph Bazalgette, chief engineer of the Metropolitan Board of Works, designed an extensive series of underground sewerage pipes to that diverted waste downstream of the population center. The modern notion of infrastructure was therewith born, and the system was soon expanded to include electricity and water.

The most important change to the landscape was the emergence of the factory—in particular cotton and clothing factories located near streams used drive waterwheels. Established in 1771, Arkwright's Mill at Cromford (just south of Matlock Bath) was the world's first successful large-scale cotton-spinning mill based on waterpower. Arkwright, who has become known as the father of the factory system, built the village of Cromford in order to house his mill's workforce. By 1790, the main buildings had been completed. The buildings were uniform in look, mostly rectangular blocks of unadorned brick or stone with wooden floors and usually four to six floors high. The power from the waterwheel was distributed through the building by means of a system of shafts, gears, and beltings. From the main shaft on each floor, power was distributed to smaller shafts. Belts from the shafts drove the individual machines. The longer the shaft, the more vulnerable it was to breakage. The maximum length was about 30 meters, which limited the overall length of the mills. The problem of mechanically distributing power over long distances was solved with the introduction of wire rope, introduced around 1850. The development of electrically powered machines at the end of the century allowed factories to be designed with greater flexibility, and they no longer had to be placed next to rivers.

At first these factories provided for local markets, but by the 1830s factories were oriented toward national and international markets. The early small factories employed families, relying often on the labor of children; larger factories often employed young women, usually between the ages of thirteen and twenty-five. Their lives were highly regularized, most living in boardinghouses that had strict rules of behavior. The scale of production can be best demonstrated by numbers: In 1860, England laid 27,000 kilometers of new railroad track, compared to 16,000 kilometers in France. By 1870, England controlled one-third of the world's overall production. English factories had 39.5 million cotton spindles in its factories, compared with just 5 million in France.

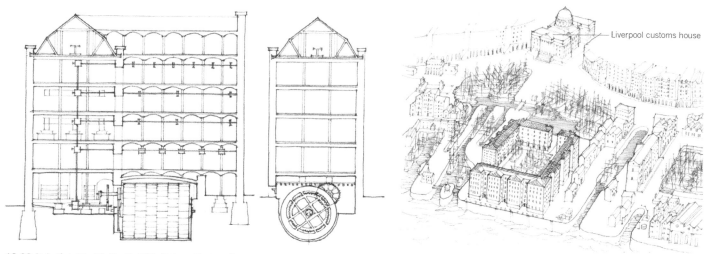

16.69 Jedediah Strutt's North Mill, Belper, Derbyshire, England

16.70 Aerial view: Albert Dock, Liverpool, England

Liverpool customs house

Albert Dock

The English ports of London and Liverpool constituted cities unto themselves. The London docks at midcentury, which were continually being improved and expanded, employed 30,000 people. Liverpool witnessed a series of expansions cementing its status as a global commercial power. By the 1890s, it had become the second-largest port in England, after London. It now became England's main slave port. Cotton, tea, rice tobacco, sugar, and grain passed through this port—as did immigrants. Specialized docks were built to house different types of merchandise, from palm oil, cocoa, and cotton to ivory and timber.

The Albert Dock (1846) in Liverpool, built of cast iron, brick, and stone with no structural wood, was the first fireproof warehousing system in the world. It also had the world's first hydraulic warehouse hoist system. Sited around a rectangular basin, the inner side had a ground-level colonnade of hollow cast-iron columns filled with masonry, with warehouses on the floors above. Tall windows allowed cranes to load and unload from and to the floors. To make the building fully fireproof, the cast-iron columns and beams supported shallow brick-arched floors. At a cost of £700,000, the Albert Dock was probably the most expensive structure in the world of that time. But within two decades, the entrance was too small for the ships, which had kept getting larger, so it

was converted to a warehouse. Next to the dock was a new customs house (no longer extant) designed by John Foster, with a grand and severe Ionic pedimented temple front (modeled on the Pantheon, but with Ionic capitals) with a Renaissance style dome at its core.

16.71 Albert Dock

16.72 **Eastern State Penitentiary, Philadelphia**

16.73 **Suffolk House of Correction, Bury St. Edmunds, England**

Panoptic Prisons

As the ideas of the Enlightenment were adopted in the new industrial cities of the 19th century, the definition of criminality changed considerably. In the 18th century, criminals, the insane, the poor, and the indigent—all the "unwanteds"—were thrown together in large halls and corridors. The Lunatics Tower in Vienna (1784) was nothing more than a cylindrical fortress. Overcrowding, filth, and brutal conditions made them into exceptionally terrifying places. In England around 1819, there were 220 capital offenses, ranging from murder to stealing bread. With the Enlightenment came the attempt to refine the law, but it was not so much the terror of the prisons that so appalled the early 19th-century moralists as the fact that humanity could, in essence, be placed outside the reach of the moral life. A connection had to be made between the reform of the body and mind of the prisoner and the legitimacy of the state. This engendered the first modern jails, such as the Virginia Penitentiary (1798) by Benjamin Latrobe and the Suffolk House of Correction in Bury St. Edmunds, England (1803), where the governor's house was at the prison's center to demonstrate the new force of law that now ostensibly protected the prisoners from abuse while enforcing its own code of behavior.

These new prisons were designed with isolated cells for the inmates grouped along open corridors of buildings that were like the spokes of a wheel, giving rise to the name panoptic prison. An exemplar of the panoptic system can be found at the Eastern State Penitentiary in Philadelphia (begun 1821), organized according to a philosophy set out by the Pennsylvania Quakers that presumed that isolation would promote monastic self-reflection. Prisoners lived in a cell and could go outside into a small private courtyard. They were allowed out only for infrequent baths or medical emergencies. Visits were permitted only from officials. Masks and the use of numbers rather than names ensured anonymity if inmates had to be removed from their cells. Even the sewer pipes were arranged to prevent communication from

cell to cell. All the while, the prisoner's every movement was observed, either through the corridor or from the towers during exercises. Prisoners who were able were allowed to choose to perfect a few skills, such as shoemaking, basket-weaving, and broom-making; it was thought that these humble activities would reconnect them with the principle that service to society was the primary reason for existence. This system was much admired despite the fact that it soon became obvious that quite a few inmates went insane. Its English equivalent, the Pentonville Prison in London (1844), designed by Jeremy Bentham, had five radiating arms extending from a central hall, from which the prisoners could be observed. Pentonville became the most copied prison in the world.

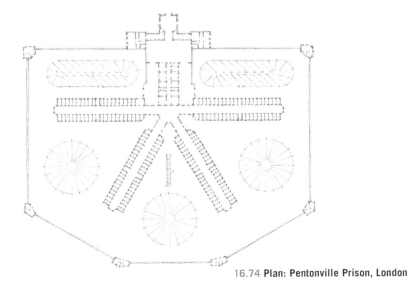

16.74 **Plan: Pentonville Prison, London**

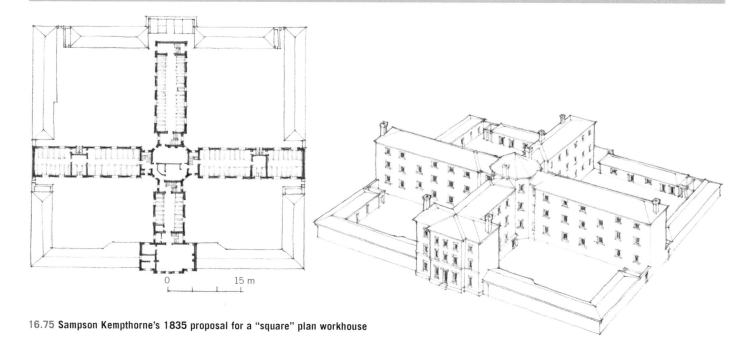

16.75 Sampson Kempthorne's 1835 proposal for a "square" plan workhouse

Workhouses

Many English cities had so-called workhouses that gave the poor work but also served as religious boarding schools. The institutions were run by a parish as a type of charity work. From the perspective of their patrons they were designed as "large, spacious and we may say fairly elegant buildings," but the truth was far different. Frederick Engels wrote the following in his 1845 *Condition of the Working Class in England*:

> Below the bridge you look upon the piles of debris, the refuse, filth, and offal from the courts on the steep left bank; here each house is packed close behind its neighbor and a piece of each is visible, all black, smoky, crumbling, ancient, with broken panes and window-frames. The background is furnished by old barrack-like factory buildings. Here the background embraces the pauper burial-ground, the station of the Liverpool and Leeds railway, and, in the rear of this, the Workhouse, the "Poor-Law Bastille" of Manchester, which, like a citadel, looks threateningly down from behind its high walls and parapets on the hilltop, upon the working-people's quarter below.

Workhouses came in different formats. Most were exercises in social geometry: square or rectangular, with courts that separated the men, women, and children; and a chapel, infirmary, and administration offices at the center. By the 1830s there was a good deal of opposition to workhouses, given the hardship and brutality that they engendered. Though the government periodically attempted to reform their practices, their existence ended officially only in 1929.

16.76 Plan: Bridge Street Workhouse, Manchester, England

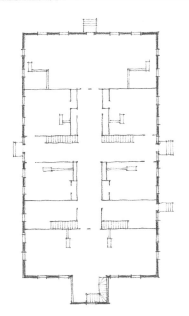

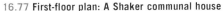

16.77 First-floor plan: A Shaker communal house

16.78 Interior of a Shaker house

SHAKERS

The growing dissatisfaction with the grand Enlightenment aspirations about the unity of reason and nature spawned a generation of utopian thinkers, social philosophers, and cultural critics. Chief among these in France was Claude Henri de Rouvroy, Comte de Saint-Simon, an aristocrat, an officer in the American Revolutionary War, a real estate speculator, and a journalist. His writings, including *Memoire sur la science de l'homme* (1813), *De la réorganisation de la société Européene* (with Augustin Thierry, 1817), and *Le nouveau Christianisme* (1825), were highly influential. He advocated a semi-mystical "Christian-scientific" socialism envisaged around an elite of philosophers, engineers, and scientists who would tame the forces of industrialization by means of a rational Christian humanism. Though Saint-Simon had adherents in Europe and even influenced the thinking of Karl Marx, his movement to create new communities was rarely brought to fruition. In the United States, on the other hand, utopian ideals found a ready audience, with the founding of utopian communities reaching its height around 1840. Why? Many utopian thinkers were U.S. citizens, but a substantial minority were emigrants from England, France, Germany, and Scandinavia. For most, the ideal was a small tidy village with a range of craft industries.

The Shakers aimed at nothing less than transforming earth into heaven. They were celibate, and their daily work and religious rituals were designed to foster a belief in both the earthly sphere, envisioned as a rural settlement, and a heavenly sphere, envisioned as a New Jerusalem. Between 1780 and 1826 the Shakers founded twenty-five settlements from Maine to the Ohio frontier. Communities were organized into communal households called families, which consisted of thirty to one hundred persons. Shaker communities adopted names such as City of Peace, City of Love, Holy Land, and Pleasant Grove. Discipline was not imposed but was a condition of divine respect. For example, anyone who slouched or nodded off was required to make a public apology. Law also required that one sleep straight. Furniture reinforced the requirement for posture; chairs were light and sturdy but had tall backs.

Shaker life was highly regulated. The women were responsible for sweeping the house, whereas the men cleaned the workshops. Drawers were often installed recessed into walls so as not to collect dust or create clutter. In the houses, an invisible boundary separated the men's rooms on the west from women's rooms on the east. Double sets of stairs and doors articulated the division between male and female brethren. The furniture, clothing, and even the buildings themselves were made by members of the community, who were therefore physically surrounded by the handiwork of other believers. Despite these constraints, Shaker rituals involved dance and pantomime. Imaginary garments were donned; and "visitors" appeared with particular messages to tell. Members who never raised their voices would suddenly begin singing, shouting, and whirling in dizzy spirals—hence the name of their sect.

The well-built and prosperous Shaker villages greatly enhanced the credibility of the communitarian strategy for social change. But the Shakers' unwillingness to engage in heavy industry eroded their prosperity after the Civil War, and their numbers declined sharply—due in large part because of their belief in celibacy and the resulting lack of descendants.

AUGUST WELBY PUGIN AND THE ENGLISH PARLIAMENT BUILDING

It is perhaps not coincidental that the two most important architectural theoretical works of the time came not from secularists but from secularism's—and industrialism's—critics: Marc-Antoine Laugier and August Welby Pugin (1812–52). Pugin's father, August Charles, Comte de Pugin, fled France during the revolution and, as an authority on the Gothic style, took up work in the office of John Nash, who had to accommodate the growing demand for Gothic-style architecture even though he personally found it troublesome. The younger Pugin was already saturated in Gothic architecture and had even converted to Catholicism as the only true religion. With little hope for a commission, he set about writing *Contrasts*, which he published in 1836 at his own expense because no publisher would agree to put out such an explosive work. The book made his reputation, and soon commissions for chapels, churches, and even private houses came his way. "The history of architecture is the history of the world," he wrote, and, turning to the work of his own day, he asked whether "the architecture of our times, even supposing it solid enough to last, hand[s] down to posterity any certain clue or guide to the system under which it was erected? Surely not.... It is a confused jumble of styles and symbols borrowed from all nations and periods." At stake was not just a style, he believed, but the history of civilization. Industrialism, greed, and secularism had isolated man from his fellow man.

Contrasts set the tone for a critique of industrialism that focused not on repairing the inequities that it precipitated by means of law and politics, but by proposing a quasi-utopian alternative—one harkening back to the Middle Ages, for Pugin a time during which a vibrant social conscience had existed that he felt had since been lost. The architect, he argued, should therefore not just adopt any style the client wanted. That would be equivalent to endorsing the arbitrariness of the modern world. *Contrasts* has a plate showing a town as Pugin imagined it in 1440, and another one showing it again in 1840. The former portrays a coherent city with intact walls and a church in the foreground;

16.79 **A plate redrawn from Pugin's *Contrasts*, showing a town in 1440**

16.80 **A plate redrawn from Pugin's *Contrasts*, showing the same town illustrated above in 1840**

the latter shows a cluttered river, a jumble of church spires and smokestacks, and in the foreground a prison; the church is still there but now overgrown and neglected. It was an accusation against rationalism that remains embedded in the image of modernity to this day, easily retrieved by those who see modern life as a downward spiral into ethical and moral decline. Architecture had to be based on principles (and in this he was the child of the Enlightenment), including the use of local materials in accordance with local traditions. This was what made "true" Gothic different from what he saw as the shallow Gothic of Horace Walpole or, worse, the cold rationalism of the Neoclassicists. Only Gothic, he argued, could provide the moral compass that one should expect from a Christian society.

Despite Pugin's conservatism, he should not be seen as naively antimodern. His convictions in respect to regional traditions and local climate, as well as his belief in "honest" construction, were all taken up by modernists once the Gothic imperative had played itself out. One of his arguments against Italianate architecture was that it did not suit England. A building, he maintained, had to show its various purposes, and this led to an appreciation for asymmetry and to an emphasis on articulating the differing parts of a building, an argument that modernists would later take up as well.

It was because of this growing confidence in the legitimacy of the neo-Gothic as a genuinely English format that, after the old palace at Westminster burned in 1834, a parliamentary committee decided to rebuild in the Gothic style. Two hundred years earlier, a similar body had decided to rebuild old St. Paul's in the Neoclassical style.

A competition for the commission for the new Parliament building was announced; it was eventually given to Charles Barry, who worked closely with Pugin. Few can deny the brilliance of the plan, with its lucid hierarchies that differentiate between public and private areas and the grandeur of the approaches to the great octagonal hall that separates the House of Lords to the north from the House of Commons to the south. An internal spine, which allows for a special sovereign's entrance at the southeast corner of the building, was buffered by a number of open-air courts that allowed light into the various rooms. Offices, libraries, and meeting rooms were lined up along the principal facade toward the river. The exterior—done almost uniformly in a soft, yellowish limestone—was designed in a Perpendicular Gothic style that replicated the taste of the 15th century. Despite the monotone treatment of the building's external mass, Barry was able to introduce picturesque elements to the skyline through the asymmetrical positioning of the vertical elements—the Victoria Tower, the lantern over the octagonal room, and the spectacular Big Ben, Parliament's now-famous clock tower. The debates that swirled around this building concerning the role and purpose of architecture were remarkable. The history of modern architecture is intertwined with the history of polemics, beginning with Charles Perrault's attack on beauty, carried forth by Marc-Antoine Laugier's attack on the classical orders, and extended into the 19th century by Pugin, the greatest defender of the Gothic at the time, who envisioned the building as a showcase of the Gothic style, a moral and aesthetic exemplar. Neoclassicism, with its cosmopolitan allusions that had met the expectations of the old elite, had here given way to a style that was associated not only with the new moralists but also with the monarchy of Queen Elizabeth I (1533–1603), whose rule was increasingly considered to be a golden age in which England saw the first flush of its global power. In other words, Neoclassicism, though once the favorite language of colonial authority, was increasingly seen as too generic and undifferentiated—as too Continental—to differentiate England, which was now the single most powerful colonial empire in the world, from its competitors.

16.81 Houses of Parliament, Westminster, London

1. Clocktower
2. Westminster Hall
3. Chamber of the House of Commons
4. Central hall
5. Chamber of the House of Lords
6. Royal gallery
7. Sovereign's entrance

0   80 m

16.82 Plan: Houses of Parliament

16.83 **Oriel Chambers, Liverpool, England**

EUGÈNE-EMMANUEL VIOLLET-LE-DUC

The mid-19th century saw the rapid expansion of the middle class, the fitful demise of the influence of the landed gentry, and the rise of a professional class. The Geological Society upgraded its membership from the "interested" gentry to one based on merit and scholarly accomplishment. Arguments that fossils were planted in the ground by God, still a viable theory in the 1830s, were no longer accepted in 1850.

In architecture a similar revolution was taking place, led by a generation of theorists that included Eugène-Emmanuel Viollet-le-Duc (1814–79) in France, Gottfried Semper (1803–79) in Germany, and John Ruskin (1819–1900) in England. Though different in many respects, each tried to rethink the principles of rationalism and technology, and all were writing at the same time. Ruskin's *Stones of Venice* appeared first in 1851, on the same date as Semper's *Die vier Elemente der Baukunst*. Viollet-le-Duc's *Dictionnaire raisonné de l'architecture française du XIe au XVe siècle*, which was published in several editions, first appeared in 1854. Without doubt, the period represented a turning point in architectural discourse. Viollet-le-Duc was a strong advocate of the modern material of iron. Unlike other architects of his time, who were giving cast iron a Gothic flavor to appease the demands of the followers of

August Welby Pugin, Viollet-le-Duc made no such demand.

Neither was he advocating the technological rationalism of Sir Joseph Paxton in the Crystal Palace in London. Cast iron, and then iron, had emerged relatively quickly on the architectural scene, but the application proper to its aesthetic was not yet obvious to mid-century architects. In the 17th and 18th centuries, Baroque architects, because of the large domes and complex lighting effects, operated in a realm between architecture and technology. Neoclassicism, with its emphasis on image, made significantly fewer technical demands on the architect. But with the introduction of cast iron, that changed rapidly. The catalogues of architectural components published by the design offices of British foundries began to grow thicker, and it was a short step from adding cast-iron balconies (excellent examples of which abound in the French Quarter of New Orleans, Louisiana) to designing entire houses and structures out of cast iron.

By 1850 some were arguing for a congruence between material and form, as can be seen in the remarkable Oriel Chambers (1864) in Liverpool, England, by the architect Peter Ellis. The thin cast-iron frame holds glazed bay windows with no concession to ornamentation. At the time, it

was not well received; architects preferred to use cast iron mainly for floor supports. In that sense, the general approach of Quatremère de Quincy, who taught at the École des Beaux-Arts, still prevailed. He critiqued the use of exposed iron in anything other than industrial buildings, setting a tone with long-lasting consequences. Iron received strong support, however, from the Romantics, who saw it as an opportunity to escape the strictures of the classical orders and to introduce a more local or regional flavor to architecture. Viollet-le-Duc tried to hold a middle ground, arguing against both the academy, with its Neoclassical allegiances, and the autonomy of rational engineering. For him, rationalism was a question not of numbers and efficiency but of style—a style that emerged from a thorough familiarity with the history of architecture and with the visual and functional needs of the program.

Viollet-le-Duc's approach is best exemplified in his design for an iron armature for a concert hall (1886), which even today strikes one as astonishing. Using the idea of a buttress but inverting it and placing it on the inside instead of the outside, he holds up a steel frame that in turn supports a thin masonry roof.

16.84 **Viollet-le-Duc's design for a concert hall**

16.85 **Abbey of Vézelay, France**

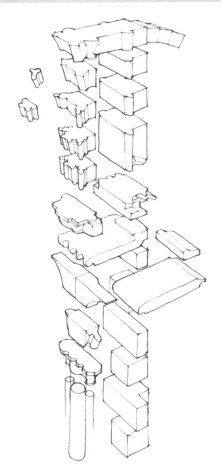

16.86 **Viollet-le-Duc's analysis of a Gothic column**

ARCHITECTURAL PRESERVATION

Today, architectural preservation is a major part of the architectural profession, but that was not always the case. Medievalists were especially concerned about the bad conditions many cathedrals were in, and the first preservation efforts were concerned with medieval buildings. Viollet-le-Duc played a large part in this movement, having been asked in 1835 to restore the Romanesque Abbey of Vézelay in France. This led to restorations at Notre-Dame in Paris, Mont St.-Michel in Normandy, and the town of Carcassone in Provence. Whereas John Ruskin advocated a restoration that preserved only the building's status quo, Viollet-le-Duc advocated a more aggressive form of preservation that included the possibility of rebuilding and even extending a building in the same stylistic manner. At Carcassone, the high-pitched roofs and the Cathedral of Vézelay are basically his designs. In France, many cathedrals had been damaged during the French Revolution or had fallen into disrepair. On some buildings, Baroque and Neoclassical additions had been added. In dealing with such complex situations—and given that a medieval church might have taken centuries to complete and thus exhibited numerous styles—his approach was not to pick a particular time and restore it to that moment, but rather to synthesize the building and make the restoration a completion. This put a lot of power in the hands of the designer; the final result might have been a building that could never have existed prior to that moment. To advance his cause, Viollet-le-Duc made extensive studies of medieval building practices—not only so that the restoration could be accurate, but also to show how this knowledge could ensure the conceptual and perceived authenticity of the new parts of the building.

16.87 **Restoration in Carcassonne, France, by Viollet-le-Duc, begun in 1853**

16.88 Bibliothèque Ste.-Geneviève, Paris

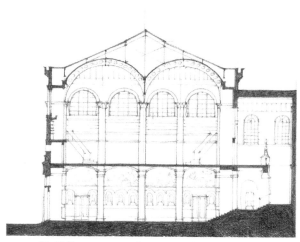

16.89 Transverse section: Bibliothèque Ste.-Geneviève

BIBLIOTHÈQUE STE.-GENEVIÈVE

Among those who argued in favor of the use of iron in France was Henri Labrouste (1801–75). His Bibliothèque Ste.-Geneviève (designed 1843, built 1845–51), with its slender columns and billowing domes, coexists with stone walls, themselves without any trace of classical columns and pilasters. The distinction between the two floors is made on the outside by a thin entablature, with a continuous row of garlands suspended beneath it. Below, the wall is punctuated by relatively small, Romanesque-style round-headed windows. Above, from end to end, runs an arcade, with pilasters forming a regular rhythm across the facade; it is distinctly Roman in flavor. The lower two thirds of the arcade are filled in to allow for a window in each bay. The whole is topped by a stripped-down cornice, lightly decorated in a neo-Greek manner. The building thus makes numerous historical references, but is in no way historicist. Labrouste attempted to create an idiom that, through its reductivist aesthetic, could demonstrate a fluid connection between the old and the modern. To indicate the iron used on the interior for those with a keen eye, Labrouste articulated the end bolts of the tie rods with round panels nestled between the archivolts. The building also has a Picturesque component, for inscribed on the panels in the arcades are the names of the authors of the books on the shelves within.

In Labrouste's hands, iron was a significant enrichment of the architect's toolbox. In the vestibule, for example, the tall and solid piers contrast with the spindly cast-iron arches. But these arches were meant to evoke the branches of a sacred grove, an image reinforced by wall frescoes that show treetops over the busts of famous literary figures. The vestibule thereby becomes a reference to the fabled Elysian Fields. Because Labrouste's position was not in line with the more conservative tastes of the academy, his career did not advance as fast as did those of his contemporaries. His use of iron as a form of vaulting became more common in the next decades and was used, for example, at Notre-Dame de la Croix (1870) in Paris. The building is sited with its back against the urban fabric and its long facade facing into the open square that flanks the Pantheon.

Semper made an equally bold argument: that the origins of architecture lay not in the Greek post and lintel and not even in the need to add a roof to the post and lintel, as Laugier had argued. Architecture began, so he argued, with weaving and the fashioning of clothes. From weaving a basket, primitive humans learned how to weave branches into walls and then close off the gaps with mud. From pottery, they learned how to make tiles and bricks. Thus, the beginning of architecture has less to do with myth and archaeology than with anthropology. It was a radical rethinking of the question,

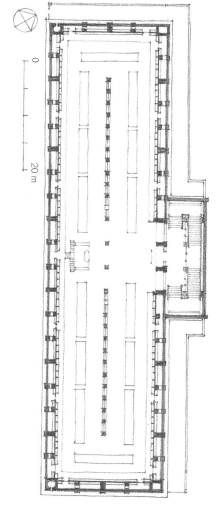

16.90 Plan: Bibliothèque Ste.-Geneviève

16.91 Swiss Polytechnical School, Zurich

much discussed at the time, about the origins of architecture. For Semper, nature was not an abstraction producing regular geometries that needed to be emulated; nor was it a biological force in the sense that Gothic architects understood it when, for instance, they modeled their vaults on tree branches. Instead, nature was wrapped up with our basic human instinct for making things, which Semper understood as having both economical and moral components. At the Great Exhibition of 1851, he lavished praise not on Sir Joseph Paxton's amazing technologically driven design of the Crystal Palace but on the display of houses from Trinidad, whose production yielded glimpses of an early stage of cultural development before industrialization derailed the processes by which craft develops form.

His theoretical opinions aside, when it came to architecture, Semper drew heavily on motifs from the Roman Baroque, using rusticated ground floors and pilastered upper floors. This is apparent in his design for the Swiss Polytechnical School (1858–64) in Zurich, where the domed rotunda, used as a reading room, is placed not at the center of the composition, as might have been expected, but along its facade as a dramatic accent to the entrance. It leads to a central hall defined by a restrained classical vocabulary.

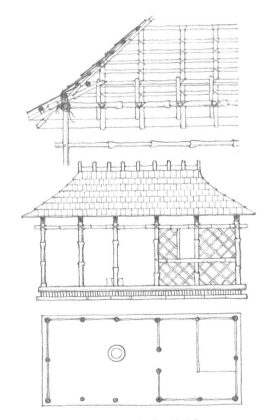

16.92 Caribbean hut, by Gottfried Semper

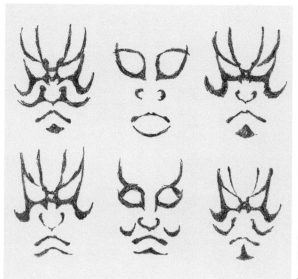

16.93 Examples of Kabuki makeup

16.94 Facsimile of Nishimura Shigenaga's *Interior of a Kabuki Theater*

KANAMARU-ZA

The cultures of Korea and Japan, influenced no doubt by the strict regulations of Qing China, were also highly controlled. One of the inevitable manifestations of a ritualized and regulated social order, as Michel Foucault wrote based on his studies of similar conditions in Europe, is the symptomatic creation of spaces of sanctioned exclusion, or heterotopias—that is, sites where the prohibited is provisionally allowed. In the West, these include prisons, hospitals, mental asylums, fairs, and carnivals. In Kyoto, the Shimabara district of prostitution was such a site. A parallel consequence of strict regulation was the emergence of a theatrical form called Kabuki. The word *Kabuki* connotes "out-of-the-ordinary" and "shocking." This type of theater was a mix of the acrobatic, the comical, and the sensual with theatrical special effects—a fusion that had developed in the Shimabara district and had already been banned by the shoguns in 1652. However, the scandal associated with the notorious Kabuki only assured its popularity. In the Shimabara, high officials interacted with theater people who, though beautiful, accomplished, and expensively dressed, were otherwise viewed as social outcasts.

The earliest theaters were temporary structures similar to those used for special public Noh performances, except that they were more plebeian than the high-class stages of the Noh. The Kabuki stages were fenced-off outdoor areas focused on a temporary stage with a gabled roof. Their placement was casual and improvised, taking advantage of already existing situations or props, such as the Sumiya's removable screens that enabled the street to suddenly become a stage for the audience seated in its front rooms. The stages became more permanent when a wooden wall was added behind the stage. As Kabuki became popular with more elite audiences, a separate space for them above that of the commoners in the form of raised boxes (*sajiki*) was added along the sides. These early theaters were equipped with dressing rooms, viewing boxes, teahouse additions, and corollary entertainments.

The mature form of the Kabuki theater emerged in the late 17th century. With a solid wall running around the perimeter, it had only a single entrance, low and small, to regulate access. Only one person at a time could enter or exit, and then only by bending, as one entered a teahouse. The facade had shoji screens and wooden slats to control sight lines. A small tower with a drum, vertical banners, and platforms extending into the streets furnished a framework for advertising. There was no lobby. The audience entered directly into the main space, known as the

doma, which was basically an open lawn. In front was the main stage, roughly 12 meters square. To the sides, lifted on stilts, were the cubicles, with passages behind to admit the higher-class clients. The stage and the cubicles all had individual gabled roofs. The stage roof was held up by corner pillars with the gable end facing the audience, as in Noh stages. The stage, however, had an extensive backstage area, including side wings of different sizes, and an extensive preparation area almost twice as large as the stage itself. The backstage was independently roofed. The seating was divided into individual spaces, called *masu*, by means of low wooden separators arranged in a grid. By the 1740s, ever-larger Kabuki stages were built throughout Japan. Over time, the entrance facades became more elaborate, with up to three entrances—two large ones for the elite and a smaller one for commoners. An angled raised corridor led to the stage front. The stage became equipped with a revolving segment that could be used to execute quick scenery changes. There are only a few extant Kabuki theaters from the 17th and 18th centuries, among which the Kanamaru-za (1835) is the best preserved.

16.96 Interior of Kanamaru-za, Kotohira, Japan

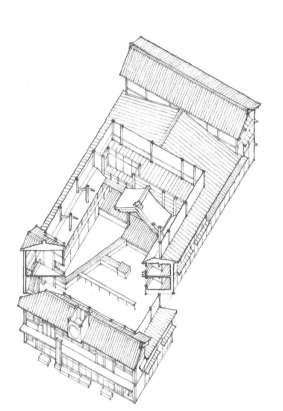

16.95 Pictorial view: A Kabuki theater similar to Karamaru-za

16.97 Kanamaru-za, Kotohira

16.98 Plan: A Kabuki theater

16.99 19th-century China

QIANLONG'S UNIVERSAL VISION

Though China increased its export of tea by more than 50 percent in the first third of the 19th century and quadrupled its silk exports, Chinese traders showed little interest in European merchandise. Indeed, they demanded hard currency payment in silver. The result of this asymmetrical trade relationship was that by 1800, almost half of the Spanish silver mined in America ended up in Chinese coffers. England, meanwhile, was having serious financial problems and began to force Chinese traders to accept opium in exchange for tea, a policy they pursued so relentlessly that by the end of the 19th century, the Chinese economy went into a long-lasting tailspin. This is arguably one of the great civilizational tragedies created by European colonialism.

Back in the 18th century, the eventual reversal of China's fate would not have been conceivable. At that time, China under the Qianlong Emperor (r. 1736–96) was the largest and richest empire in the world, and from the Chinese perspective, trade with the new European mercantile world had to be severely regulated to minimize disruption. Qianlong saw himself as a pan-Asian emperor, not dissimilar to his contemporary Napoleon Bonaparte, who pursued a pan-

European ideal. And like Napoleon, he was a military commander of great skill. In ten campaigns between 1755 and 1790, Qianlong expanded the Chinese empire to its greatest extent ever, bringing Mongolia, Chinese Turkestan, and Tibet under his control. Ruling over such a diverse population and being a ruler of foreign origin himself, Qianlong aspired to establish a model of governance both pluralistic and moral. Qianlong's grandfather, the Kangxi Emperor, who was of Manchu origin, had chosen to practice Tibetan Buddhism in private, even though his governmental policy was based on Confucian ethics. Unsatisfied by this arrangement, Qianlong sought to project himself as a *chakravartin*—a "universal

ruler"—under the guidance of Rolpay Dorje, a Tibetan monk who became the grand lama of Beijing in 1736.

Qianlong tried to fit this role by casting himself as the mediator between the different peoples of his vast kingdom. To the Tibetans, Qianlong represented himself as a reincarnation of Manjusri, an important Tibetan bodhisattva. To the Mongols, he was always one of their own, steeped in their traditions. And, most importantly, to the Han Chinese he ensured that he was renowned as a great scholar and patron of the arts. Qianlong spoke several languages, and the court was officially polyglot: edicts were issued in at least three languages. He also commissioned compendia of all the great literary works of the time, and the number of ancient Chinese paintings and artifacts collected during the Qianlong Emperor's reign was unprecedented. The collections of the national palace museums in both Beijing and Taipei were largely formed under the Qianlong Emperor and are the largest repositories of important Chinese artifacts extant today.

As *chakravartin*, Qianlong offered a complex, multinucleated conception of empire and universality that contrasted with the European Enlightenment–based colonial model of empire and universal modernity unfolding at the same time. Although there were some crossovers, such as the influence Chinese social orders had on Enlightenment thinkers such as Voltaire, the English-European model eventually overwhelmed Qianlong's model, largely due to the rising tide of European prosperity. The policies of China today, with their rush to prosperity and global influence, could arguably seek to reinstate Qianlong's pan-Asian vision.

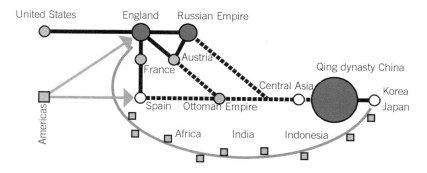

16.100 Eurasian trade diagram, ca. 1800

Chengde

As part of that pan-Asian vision, Qianlong staged Chengde as the symbolic capital of this new world (while government continued to be run from Beijing). Originally built as a royal summer residence, Chengde, located north of the Great Wall—outside the wall—affirmed the universality of Qianlong's rule. In addition to building a road from Bejing to Chengde that continued into Mongolia and a dam to control the Wulie River that ran through the city, Qianlong enlarged the palaces and gardens, and founded several temples in surrounding areas, including the Puningsi (1755), the Puyousi (1760), the Anyuanmiao (1764), the Pulesi (1767), the Putuo Zongcheng (1771), the Shuxiangsi (1776), and the Xumifushoumiao (1780).

The Chengde temples, dedicated to a range of Confucian and Buddhist deities, are drawn from—and meant to represent—various parts of the empire. Together they form an arc that can be taken in at once from the main hill north of the palace. A self-conscious visual ensemble, Chengde was a veritable microcosm of the Qing Empire, a map of the land. But Chengde was also an ordering of that map according to a Buddhist mandala. A critical feature of Chengde's landscape is a 60-meter-high rock formation called the Qingchui Peak. Wider at the top

than at the bottom, Qingchui looks like a huge pillar perched unbelievably at the summit of one of the eastern hills. Using the Qingchui "pillar" as the center, all the local Tibetan Buddhist temples and the palace complex can be interpreted as "facing" Qingchui, not literally but by the geomantic logic of Chinese and Tibetan landscape architecture. In this reading, Chengde as a whole was a mandala, with Qingchui standing in for Sumeru, the sacred mountain at the center.

The palace had three main groups of halls: the Main Palace (Zhenggong), the Pine and Crane Studio (Songhezhai), and the Eastern Palace (Donggong). The Main Palace, the principal living quarters, had nine courtyards representing the nine divisions of the celestial sphere. A wall enclosed a 4-square-kilometer area with several discrete landscape zones. The lake district had an island with buildings and courtyards that housed officials and was used for private activities. North of the Garden District was a site known as the Garden of Ten Thousand Trees, which was laid out beginning in 1703 and improved for decades. It contained a Prairie District that was meant as a type of replica of the Mongolian steppe. Though used for horse races, military exercises, and fireworks, it had important political and

16.101 **Qinqchui Peak at Chengde, Hebei Province, China**

ceremonial functions as well. On special occasions, the Qing created a simulated Mongolian campsite, complete with yurts.

The twelve temples, of which only nine survive today, were designed as representations of other temples. The Pulesi ("Temple of Universal Happiness," 1767), for instance, is a hybrid building that merges the Tibetan conceptual order with Chinese formal expression. In appearance, the Pulesi is like the shrine at the Temple of Heaven in Beijing; it is a round temple with a double eave and conical roof. In plan, however, it replicates a Buddhist mandala with a series of stepped terraces. Chengde's most visible structure, the Putuo Zongcheng (1771), is a small-scale replica of Lhasa's famed Potala Palace. Like the Potala, the Putuo consists of a series of low white buildings rising up the side of a hill, culminating in the central red structure, the Dahongtai ("Great Red Terrace"), with the golden temple's roofs projecting over the summit. But the Putuo is not a pure copy. The original Potala's massive white walls enclosed a small courtyard. The walls of the Putuo, by contrast, enclose the Great Red Terrace, within which stood a huge Chinese-style temple pavilion more suitable for royal receptions than a hidden spiritual practice.

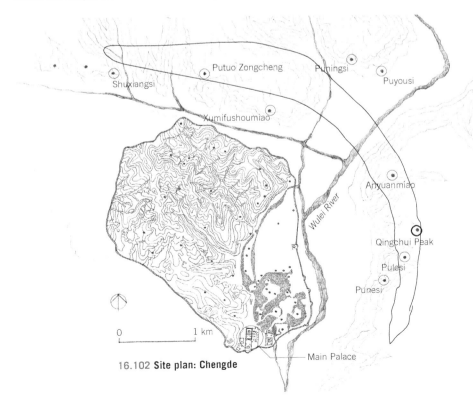

Putuo Zongcheng
Shuxiangsi
Puningsi
Puyousi
Xumifushoumiao
Wulei River
Anyuanmiao
Qingchui Peak
Pulesi
Punesi
Main Palace

0   1 km

16.102 **Site plan: Chengde**

16.103 Pulesi, Chengde, Hebei Province, China

16.104 Putuo Zhongcheng, Chengde

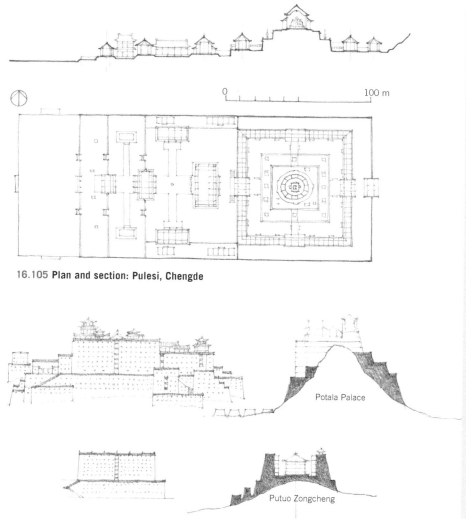

16.105 Plan and section: Pulesi, Chengde

16.106 Diagrammatic comparisons of the Potala Palace at Lhasa and the Putuo Zongcheng at Chengde
Based on drawings by Anne Chayet

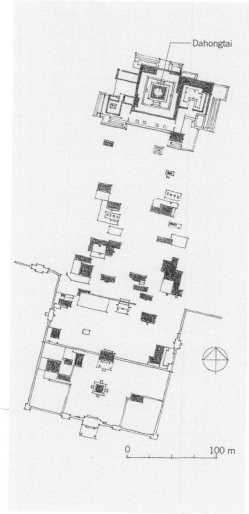

16.107 Site plan: Putuo Zongcheng

16.108 **View from Qingyi's stroll path, Qingyi Garden, Beijing**

largest element, the island is in the middle and constantly attracts the eye. Yet while walking around, the pagoda in the distance always remains in view, becoming the best-remembered part of the garden.

The compositional ideas were derived from principles described in texts such as the Ji Cheng's *Yuan Zhi* ("Gardening"), written in the early 17th century. Ji Cheng invoked design concepts such as "suitability," "refinement," "simplicity," and "changeability or unexpectedness," which were to be used to create places that have qualities such as "the real and the false," "assembling and spreading," "unevenness and neatness," "connecting and separating," "open and closed," and "level and solid."

Qingyi Garden

One of Qianlong's additions was a new garden, originally called Qingyi Garden (1750–64) and now known as the Summer Palace. It was designed as a series of palaces and pavilions around a large oval lake that is separated from two smaller lakes by long narrow islands. A stroll path goes around the lake and across all the small islands. In the middle of the main lake is a small artificial island, connected to the edge on the east by a long, arched, graceful bridge. The north edge of the lake is dominated by a huge palace and a Buddhist shrine complex, raised high on a solid stone platform, on axis with the central island. In the west, the horizon is filled with a series of long mountains with distinct peaks. A pagoda and several pavilions were built on the crests of the peaks.

Chinese gardens were intended to evoke the order of nature distilled to its essence. The design skill lay in ensuring that every element functioned in a way that was harmonious with the whole from the perspective of viewing sites along the strolling paths. A garden's quality was described as a function of its scenic spots, which were thought of as embodied poems and three-dimensional paintings. Symmetry was abhorred.

At the same time, all the expectations and conveniences of a royal palace and seat of government were to be fulfilled. There are three palpable visual foci at the Summer Palace: the island in the middle of the lake, the Buddhist shrine at the northern edge, and the tall pagoda on the hills in the west. Although the Buddhist shrine is the

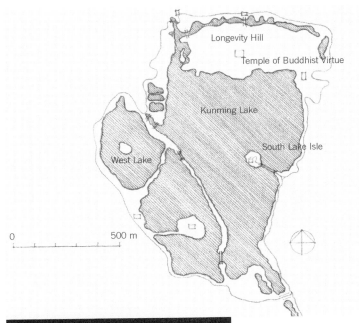

16.109 **Plan of Qingyi Garden**

16.110 **View from pavilion: Qingyi Garden**

16.111 **Touro Synagogue, Newport, Rhode Island**

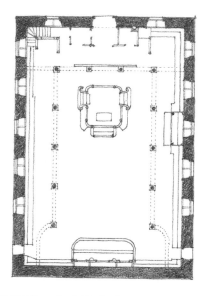

16.112 **Plan: Bevis-Marks Synagogue, London**

SYNAGOGUES

Until the end of the 15th century, most Jews lived within the footprint of the old Roman Empire, whether in Trastevere in Rome, in Spain, or in Thessalonica in Greece. This was the result of the great diaspora imposed on the Jews by the Roman emperor Titus, after his victory over the Jews and the destruction of the Second Temple in 70 CE. Beginning with the Christian era, restrictions were imposed on Jews wherever they lived. They were not allowed to own land and were excluded from affairs of the military, thus denying them access to aristocratic privileges. Since banking was one of the few trades they were permitted to engage in, Jews were able to create a network that transcended local rivalries, and in that capacity were often protected by kings and princes, who used them as private bankers. In Venice, Jews were allowed to come to the city principally because of their banking associations. They were assigned to live in an area known as the ghetto, a term from then on used to designate where Jews were required to live. An exception was in Lithuania, where, from 1316 onward, Jews had a surprising amount of freedom.

With their expulsion by the Spanish in 1492 and by the Portuguese in 1496, the Sephardic Jews were forced to seek sanctuary in Poland, Amsterdam, Venice, Greece, Istanbul, and even Rome. In Amsterdam, a Sephardic synagogue was built in 1675 that has remained largely unchanged, and is today one of the few tangible remnants of Amsterdam's once-thriving Jewish community. It is a large rectangular brick building, with large round-headed windows on all sides that emphasize its vast interior space. It became the model for several later synagogues, including the Bevis-Marks Synagogue in London (1700) and the smaller Touro Synagogue in Newport, Rhode Island, the oldest synagogue in the United States. Jewish life in Germany improved slightly in the 18th century when courts invited Jews to come and serve as financial agents. In 1714, King Frederick William I of Prussia permitted the construction of a synagogue in Berlin.

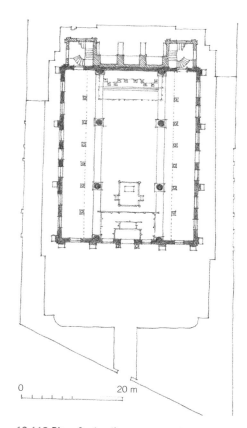

0   20 m

16.113 **Plan: Sephardic synagogue, Amsterdam**

16.114 Interior: Beth Elohim Synagogue, Charleston, South Carolina

The fate of Jews significantly improved under Napoleon, who passed a number of measures supporting the position of Jews in the French Empire and Austria—and, just as importantly, in conquered countries. He abolished laws restricting Jews to ghettos or to certain professions. In 1797 when he invaded Italy, he threw open the gates to the ghettos. In 1807, like his contemporary Qing emperors of China, he sanctioned several religions as "official"—a first for a European ruler; these included Judaism, Roman Catholicism, Lutheranism, and Calvinism. As a result of Napoleon's initiatives, Jews in other lands sought and eventually received emancipation in Germany in 1848, in Great Britain in 1890, in Russia in 1917, and finally in Spain in 1930.

The response by Jews to German emancipation was a building boom of unprecedented proportion. During the 19th century, more than two hundred large synagogues were built. It would be shortsighted to see synagogue architecture as part of the general European trend toward eclecticism. Synagogue eclecticism was a direct response to the new freedom from restrictions on what could be built. Furthermore, most of the architects were non-Jews who brought their own, often romanticized, expectations of what a Jewish space should look like. Gottfried Semper (1803–79) designed a synagogue in Dresden (1840) that was on its exterior Carolingian-Romanesque, presumably to emphasize the aspirations of assimilation, but on the inside there was an order of columns with deep impost blocks copied from the Alhambra at Granada.

The emergence of the Reform Judaism, intended to appeal to urban Jews, had a major influence on synagogue design. Reform Jews stressed the universal teachings of Judaism but also sought to modernize rituals that were difficult to maintain in a modern world. Reform Jews held that Jewish people were not in a state of permanent exile but were contributing members of their community and nation. They considered every house of worship a temple, as holy as the original temple in Jerusalem. Pews were permitted, and prayer was in German. The organ was introduced. The first Reform synagogue was opened in Seesen in central Germany in 1810 and was called a "temple," in keeping with Enlightenment ideals. Some synagogues took up the classical theme and were designed almost literally as temples, as in the Seitenstettengasse Synagogue in Vienna (1826) and the Beth Elohim Synagogue in Charleston, South Carolina (1840).

16.115 Beth Elohim Synagogue, Charleston, South Carolina

16.116 Tempio Israelitico, Rome

Others were in keeping with the general 19th-century preoccupation with history and were developed along Egyptian and Byzantine lines, as, for example, the Princes Road Synagogue (1874) in Liverpool, which is a type of Norman Gothic with Oriental touches; and the Tempio Israelitico (1882) in Florence, whose prayer hall is almost square, with galleries on three sides supported by columns with Moorish cusped arches. Every inch of surface is covered with patterns and colored designs of abstract Islamic configurations, creating a soft reddish-golden atmosphere. Synagogues, like mosques, did not display human figures.

16.117 Princes Road Synagogue, Liverpool, England

1900 CE

INTRODUCTION

As the 19th century wore on, the forms, institutions, and modes of representation that can be retrospectively identified as being modern or modernist eventually started to coalesce. But that was a long time coming.

By the middle of the 19th century, the new nation-states of Europe and the Americas were jockeying with each other to envision and establish the institutions and the accompanying social, political, and economic practices of modernity. The burgeoning colonial industrial economy fueled slow but steady growth. British supremacy on the sea continued to flourish, and by the end of the century England was the dominant global force, controlling land all around the world. As other European nations scrambled to compete with the English, the rest of the world began to adapt to, and challenge, the new global imperatives of the colonial world. At the same time, the social costs of industrial concentration became more apparent—devastation of old rural economies; development of massive, subsistence-level working classes; and rapid growth in urban populations—creating cities that were woefully underprepared to deliver the services that were suddenly expected of them. The consequent urban upheavals, accompanied by a chorus of criticism from the likes of as Ruskin, Morris, Marx, and Engels, were met with the establishment of a series of new urban institutions designed to cope with the new city. For the first time, what we now recognize as public-sector works—such as hospitals, fire stations, law courts, and the like—were undertaken by European municipal bodies. Soon, these bodies began also to take pride in their work and in their cities and began to build larger public works that sought to establish the identity of the city as a civic space. Particularly celebrated were railroad stations that moved the people and goods necessary to the new economy; law courts that signified the new, more public-minded jurisprudence of the city; and museums that catered to new conceptions of an educated citizenry. New public societies that debated the meaning of the public, such as libraries and athenaeums, began to be established; and as the ultimate democratic civic space accessible to all, the large urban park in the midst of the city became a central part of the urban experience. This was especially true in the United States, spearheaded by the creation of Central Park in Manhattan in the 1850s, designed by the landscape architect Frederick Law Olmsted in collaboration with Calvert Vaux, a European-trained architect. Central Park, former site of immigrant slums and squatter settlements, soon came to embody the idea of massive public works as the signature mark of a prosperous city, even though it would still take more than half a century before the park was fully established as the heart of the city.

In terms of architectural expression, the 18th-century Enlightenment ideal—which held up a restatement of the Greco-Roman classical ideal as the specific European heritage that best expressed the new institutions of modernity—for the most part continued to hold sway. Classicism and classical revivalism, however, had their critics. The proponents of the Arts and Crafts movement in particular felt that the true expression of an architectural style must be derived only from expressions of handwork, as in the past, and favored a more Gothic-inspired vocabulary. Early modernist opinions that eschewed all styles were also beginning to surface. An important flashpoint in this debate was the first world's fair ever held, the Great Exhibition of 1851 in Hyde Park, London. Eventually remembered as the Crystal Palace Exhibition on account of the massive temporary pavilion of steel and glass that was designed for it by the engineer Joseph Paxton, this event was intended to showcase the global demand for British goods. Instead, Arts and Crafts enthusiasts used it to stage a political demonstration showcasing the shoddiness of those goods and extolling in their place the exotic handcrafted indigenous goods of the colonies. The demonstrators called on the British Empire to protect crafts and a craft ethic in England, as in its territories.

The Arts and Crafts revolution, as a consequence, became one of the first truly global transformative movements, intended to revolutionize lives by rethinking livelihoods and ways of working. In the United States, the ethics of Arts and Crafts, if not always its aesthetic, permeated the complete array of architectural explorations, fueled in part by a nascent sense of American exceptionalism that sought to generate an original American architectural expression. The craft-based ideal, though still significantly derivative of European styles, catered to this desire. The strong sense of rustication and the attention to detail and ornament that can be found in work by H. H. Richardson as well as some early work by McKim, Mead & White can be understood in this context. And certainly the bungalow, which began as a white man's domestic space in colonial India but then spread through the colonial world, and particularly the United States, as the symbol of the good life, was widely proselytized as an expression of the craft aesthetic.

Concomitantly, Arts and Crafts enthusiasts also built the first set of design schools in colonial India as part of their effort to preserve and revive the crafts against the standardization that was the staple of the colonial Public Works Department. In the process they invented a new architectural style that sought expressly to modernize Mughal building and aesthetic traditions, known as the Indo-Saracenic. This was particularly popular in some of the so-called princely states, such as Jaipur, where a former military engineer, Colonel Swinton Jacobs, organized the massive *Jeypore Portfolio of Architectural Details* as something of a catalogue of Indic styles curated for reuse. The Yankee blockade of the Southern ports during the American Civil War (1861–65) prompted the British to source its raw cotton from western India, which had suitable volcanic soil for cotton production; this resulted in the establishment of Bombay (now Mumbai) as a major port. The Suez Canal was cut by the British primarily to shorten the passage from Bombay to the cotton mills of Manchester. The cotton trade brought new wealth to Bombay, whose new architecture, to suit the extant Arts and Crafts trends in England, was of course built in the Venetian Gothic style.

In a different register, however, the critiques of strict classicism also led to eclecticism—that is, appreciation and skillful reuse of the vast diversity of architectural styles from European history and beyond. The eclectic assertion that architectural languages were more a question of materials and aesthetics than of political ideology was fueled in particular by the rise of the architect, in the late 19th century, as an

independent professional, riding on the coattails of similar movements by doctors and lawyers. The move to professionalize was centered in Paris. In spite of England's dominance in the 19th century, Paris was the more influential center of the new urban culture of the times. Its center was thoroughly rebuilt during the Second Empire under Napoleon III and became the model for urban redesigns in Europe and around the world. Argentina's exports, for example, may have largely gone to England, but when it came to designing streets and public buildings, Argentina's elite turned to Parisian models. The French Beaux-Arts, as a voice that combined bourgeois elegance and professional expertise (also known as the Second Empire style), was an international movement in its own right. Although the École des Beaux-Arts had already been in existence for almost a century, in the late 19th century it became a central powerhouse for architectural thinking, moving the discourse away from the drawing rooms and boudoirs of the gentlemen architects of the past. Its compositional strategies—strongly axial, eclectic, and focused on the production of the framed spectacle—came to embody the expressions of the new urban world that was emerging at the time. Beaux-Arts aesthetics were widely adopted not only in Europe and North America but also in many other parts of the world, including Japan, Argentina, and China, as the international standard of the global-colonial world.

One influential manifestation of the Beaux-Arts ideal was the City Beautiful movement. It began with Chicago-based architect Daniel Burnham's iron-fisted production of the spectacle of the extremely successful Chicago's World's Fair of 1893. With the buildings all painted in white, Burnham's vision permanently imbricated into the modern sensibility the suggestion that monochromatism, and particularly white monochromatism, successfully liberated architecture from the weight of history and suspended it in an eternal present where it was only the composition that mattered. When the National Mall in Washington, DC, was redesigned according these principles in 1901, the Burnham vision became a movement and was adopted by cities across the United States. In 1905 Burnham also

prepared a proposal for Manila, which had just become a U.S. territory.

By 1900, European territorial expansion, with its larger global sphere of influence, was at its very height. English successes in Southeast Asia and China, along with its continued domination of India, initiated a new sphere of economic migration between those areas that paid some small local dividends for the colonized populations—as in the example of the Chettinad mansions—while driving most of the profit back to London. The British also built out an extensive utilitarian infrastructure orchestrated around railroads to enable the extraction of raw materials, and to distribute the manufactured goods. The imperial Public Works Department commanded a mini-army in its own right.

But the centerpiece of the new European colonial expansion was the tragic land-grab of the African continent. Largely defenseless against European armaments, Africa had hitherto been protected by the sheer lack of knowledge of its hinterland. As accurate cartography revealed its true size, all the major European powers rushed to claim African territory by any means they could. The African land-grab epitomizes the proverbial heart-of-darkness at the center of the colonial 19th century. While the old colonial powers—the English, French, Spanish, Portuguese, and Dutch—continued to dominate distant shores, the remaining European nations, the latecomers to the colonial game, in particular the Germans, Belgians, and Italians, rushed to grab the lands that were still "available," mostly in Africa. Africa was literally divided up at a conference held in Berlin in 1884. Even so, there were battles. South Africa was a particularly contested prize, with its newfound mineral wealth, which pitted the earlier Dutch settlers against the British.

Late in the 19th century, Germany under Otto von Bismarck had been particularly determined to catch up with, and surpass, England and France in wealth and power. Bismarck pushed through a process of aggressive industrialization that saw Germany's output rival that of England in less than a generation. By the early 20th century, Germany was a significant power to be reckoned with. Somewhat free of the long discussions of style and modernity that had dominated earlier discourses in places like England and France, late 19th-century Germany sought to embody its own vision of an incipient modernism. Thus, the factories of Peter Behrens, the Deutsche Werkbund, and the new uses of concrete looked to American factories for inspiration, rather than to Beaux-Arts academies.

Germany's success at bootstrapping itself without the advantage of a far-flung colonial empire (and without the vast reserves of a United States) made it into a model for other parts of the world that were looking for non-colonial models of growth. Japan in particular took Germany as its role model. Anticipating a colonial incursion, and tired of the old practices of the Bakafu code, Japan's elite orchestrated a revolt against the reigning shogunate. The consequent so-called Meiji Restoration of 1868 aggressively worked to import Western knowledge, skills, and institutions to Japan, launching it as an industrial and economic power. The Meiji Restoration positioned Japan as a counterforce to European colonial expansion, thereby transforming Japan into a colonial power in its own right.

Inescapably, the watershed event of these times was World War I. Germany, in collaboration with the Old World empires—the Austro-Hungarian and Ottoman—went to war with a world that had grown powerful on colonial riches. The consequence was a long stalemate, and a particularly bloody one because of the extensive use on both sides of new industrial technologies to develop weaponry. The fallout of World War I permanently eradicated all vestiges of the preindustrial, pre-colonial world and ultimately even spelled the death of the colonial world. Thenceforth, industrial technologies and capital reigned, and the whole world decisively advanced toward nation-statehood. Architecturally speaking, these transformations put modernity, and the continued search for a distinctive new architectural modernism, firmly in the driver's seat. The 1926 competition for the new League of Nations embodied the contentions of this new world order.

After World War I, the United States' emergence as the global economic superpower of the 20th century seemed assured. Its industrial might, vast natural and land resources, and sense of opportunity gave it a decisive edge. Besides its industrial forms, the new skyscrapers of its cities like Chicago and New York, although dressed in various neoclassical garbs, had already demonstrated the possibilities of new materials, structures, and ways of living. Frank Lloyd Wright shone forth as the main American figure with a comprehensive vision of how to articulate a new architectural order, complete with ornamentation, based on new materials and his own vision of a land-based agro-rural lifestyle. Working in a milieu that was almost completely isolated from the early modernists of Europe, Wright began to outline his vision first in Wisconsin and then in the American Southwest and Japan, searching for what he was to later describe as a comprehensive, "organic" aesthetic order that integrated all aspects of design—painting, furniture, architecture, ornamentation, landscape, and even urbanism. His sources were diverse—Richardson and Sullivan by direct influence, the American prairie by context, the Celtic world by personal connection, and the pre-Columbian and Japanese realms by affinity. Divorced from the European modernist milieu, Wright constructed an alternate modernist universe whose potential may still be unfulfilled.

The early 20th-century American architectural academy, however, was still dominated by the Beaux-Arts teaching model, as it was in Europe. This was decisively challenged on multiple fronts, especially by the establishment of the Bauhaus in Germany in 1919, led by Walter Gropius; the irruption of a diverse range of modernist idioms to express the communist ideals of the new Soviet Union after the Communist revolution in Russia and, emanating from Paris starting in 1917, the Cubist-inspired writings and projects by the Swiss-born architect and painter Le Corbusier.

Determinedly seeking to reboot design discourse in Germany, Gropius's Bauhaus was initially strongly influenced by early modern German and Viennese discourses, in particular Art Nouveau and Expressionism. With figures like Johannes Itten central to the teaching staff, early Bauhaus looked to diverse sources, including a kind of emotional mysticism, to find a path to a new modern aesthetic. But soon after it moved to Dessau in 1925, Bauhaus became rigorously devoted to a strict machine aesthetic, embodied in particular by Gropius's design of the new school building and dormitory.

The Soviet world was by far the most diverse and experimental, actively seeking to invent new forms, idioms, and ideologies for what, at that time, seemed like a brave new frontier for humankind. Pushing modernist ideas to their limits, the Soviets assembled themselves into loose groups under intentionally avant-garde titles such as the Constructivists, the Suprematists, and, by contrast, the Rationalists. Their explorations and propositions advanced many new frontiers in architectural thinking, the diversity of which has only recently begun to be fully accounted for.

But the loudest and most distinctive bell announcing the birth of a new era was sounded in Paris by Le Corbusier, who, in the 1920s, published his ideas of a focused agenda for a new modernism in a series of books and conceptual projects, the most influential of which was *Vers une Architecture*, translated into English as "Towards a New Architecture." *Vers* offered a succinct vision of modernism, delineated into clear principles, aphoristic assertions, and tabulated principles, such as the "five points" of a new architecture. Le Corbusier skillfully backed these up with dramatic theoretical projects, such as replacing the architectural fabric of Paris with crystalline towers, which quickly captured the international imagination and sparked strong reactions, catapulting Le Corbusier into iconic status.

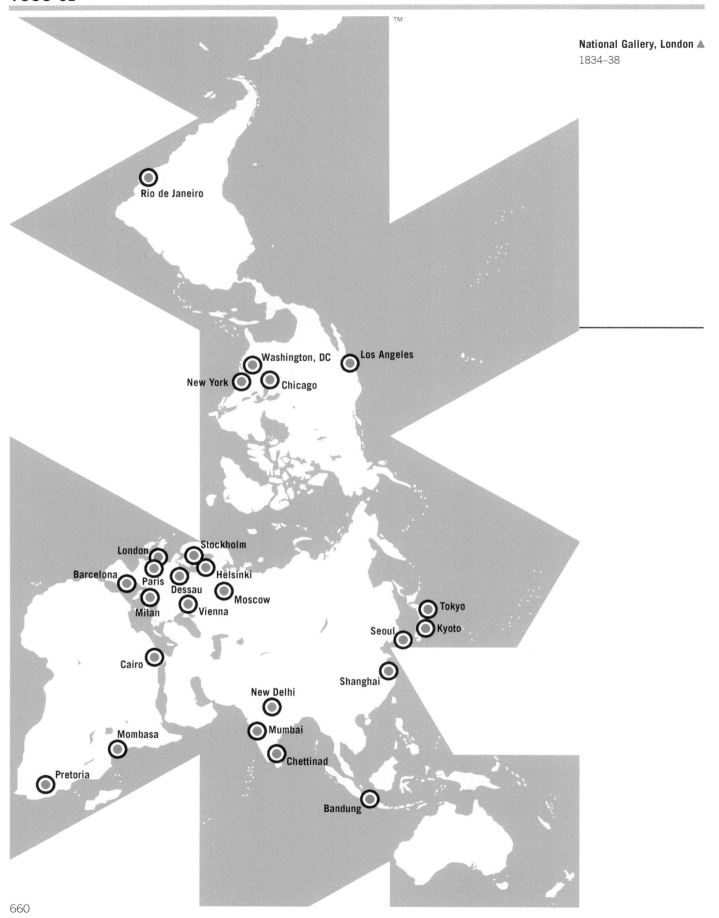

National Gallery, London ▲
1834–38

Rio de Janeiro

Washington, DC   Los Angeles
New York   Chicago

London   Stockholm
Barcelona   Helsinki
Paris
Dessau   Moscow
Milan   Vienna
Tokyo
Seoul   Kyoto
Cairo
Shanghai
New Delhi
Mombasa   Mumbai
Chettinad
Pretoria
Bandung

▲ Crystal Palace
1850–51

▲ St. Pancras Station
1863–76

▲ Bandung Institute of Technology
1920

▲ Galleria Vittorio Emanuele II
1865–67

▲ Victoria Terminus
1878–88

▲ Shanghai Bank
1923–25

▲ Central Park
1853–83

▲ Reliance Building
1890–95

▲ Wrigley Building
1920–24

▲ Trinity Church
1872–77

▲ Boston Public Library
1888–95

▲ Pennsylvania Station
1904–10

▲ Paris Opera House
1861–75

▲ Al-Rifa'i Mosque
1869–80 and 1906–11

▲ Mubarak Mahal
1899

1850 CE	1900 CE	1950 CE

American Civil War
1861–65

World War I
1914–18

Great Depression
1929 to late 1930s

World War II
1939–45

▲ Cornell University
Founded 1865

▲ Winslow House
1893

▲ Robie House
1908–10

▲ Gamble House
1908–9

▲ Taliesin
Begun 1911

▲ Hollyhock House
1921

▲ Isaac Bell House
1882–83

▲ Maison Tassel
1892–93

▲ Glass House
1914

▲ Moller House
1927–8

▲ Casa Batlló
1904–6

▲ 25b, rue Franklin
1902–4

▲ Einstein Tower
1917–21

▲ Keith Arcade
1927

▲ Stockholm Public Library
1920–28

▲ Woodland Cemetery Chapel
1918–20

▲ Friedrichstrasse Office Building
1921

▲ Tatlin's Tower
1919

▲ Bauhaus, Dessau
1924–26

▲ Villa Savoye
1928–31

PUBLIC SECTOR ARCHITECTURE

In London, prior to 1850, grand public buildings were rare, apart from an occasional guildhall or market house from the 17th century that had escaped the conflagration of 1666. It was only in the 1820s that a civic presence made itself noticeable again, with the new Privy Council and Board of Trade Building (1822–27), the General Post Office (1823–28) by Robert Smirke, and the British Museum (1823–46), also by Smirke. But the amount of civic architecture was still meager at best, and metropolitan improvements were largely haphazard and impromptu affairs—London was basically run as a medieval corporation, with dozens of committees and organizations defending their turf and rarely working in unison. In 1855, in an attempt to rectify the situation, the government created the Metropolitan Board of Works to improve the process by which decisions regarding the commissioning and building of public buildings could be made. The result was immediate. In fact, most public buildings in Great Britain, whether municipal offices, post offices, fire stations, schools, or libraries, date from after this time. Among the most important Victorian-era governmental buildings that put a new bureaucratic face on the empire were the Admiralty (proposed 1852, built 1887), South Kensington Museum (1857), Colonial Office (1870–74), Home Office (1870–75), New Law Courts (1871–82), War Office (1898–1906), and New Public Office (completed 1908). The massing of these buildings tended to be heavy, usually in a Renaissance-Italianate manner, with well-articulated quoins and voussoirs, such as at the India Office (1863–68) and the New Government Offices (1868–78).

17.1 **Foreign and Commonwealth Office, London**

17.2 **Interior courtyard, Foreign and Commonwealth Office**

17.3 **Manchester City Hall, England**

Cities began to compete for the top architects for their town halls, railroad stations, and commodity exchange buildings. Manchester, the great port city infamous for its gritty mills and open sewers, took the lead in the attempt to reform its urban image. Its grand city hall was designed by Alfred Waterhouse (1830–1905) in a restrained Romanesque style, with a tall bell tower purposefully modeled on the Parliament Building in London. The city of Leeds followed suit in 1858 with a city hall designed by Cuthbert Brodrick. Four law courts were placed at the corners. Offices for the lawyers were located between the front and back facades. The building opened with much fanfare—even Queen Victoria attended—and soon became the center of civic life in Leeds. Its design featured a monumental Corinthian order with unpedimented entrances on all sides. It is reminiscent of the Grand Theatre building (1773–80) by Victor Louis in Bordeaux, and indeed its attempt to recall the virtues of the Enlightenment are quite evident. Different from the Grand Theatre, however, was the addition of a huge tower modeled on the Hellenistic mausoleum at Halicarnassus, which, oddly, was surmounted by a slightly Rococo domed top. This eclecticism, which was later to be much critiqued, was, however, part of the exuberance of this new industrial era, which was seeking freedom from a slavish commitment to history.

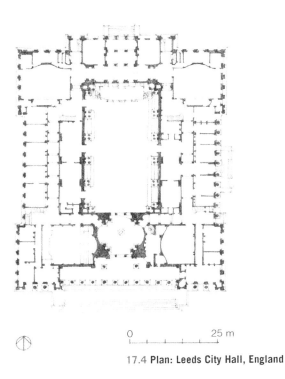

17.4 **Plan: Leeds City Hall, England**

17.5 **Grand Theatre, Bordeaux, France**

17.6 **Leeds City Hall**

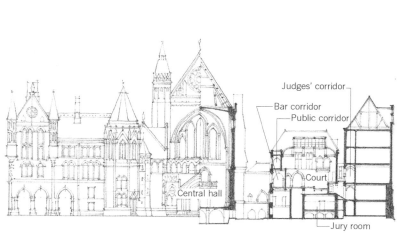

17.7 **Elevation-section: London Law Courts**

17.8 **London Law Courts**

London Law Courts

The Victorian era on the whole was still tied to the Picturesque ideal that architecture had to be linked creatively to the past in order to dignify the present. But the Victorians tended to be less attached to the purity of Roman or Greek prototypes than the generation of Robert Adam and John Nash. They experimented with historical styles that resonated with the increased archaeological erudition of the time and with the diverse philosophical persuasions of their clientele. George Edmund Street (1824–81), who designed the London Law Courts (1870–81), for example, used an early medieval style, not August Welby Pugin's high Gothic. Street chose this style for its more stern and primitive associations. He and many of the young architects of the time were enthralled with the ideals of Gallic toughness. What today might be seen as medieval, they saw as Saxon. The Saxons were not known for their architectural accomplishments, however, and here the added problem is that the precedents are more Franco-Norman than English.

With four different systems of circulation, the Law Courts building was quite complex and mirrored the new and expanded horizons of law. It had eighteen courtrooms, two of them larger than the others for the more prominent trials. A private corridor for the bar circled the building between the courts and the central hall. Judges were provided

with their own corridor circuit, one-half level higher than that of the bar; it ran behind the courtrooms and gave direct access to the raised daises on which the judges sat in the courts. A circumferential corridor running just under that of the judges accommodated attorneys and had its own doorways into the courtrooms. The public, considered to be troublesome and boisterous, was segregated in its own corridor, which connected to the upper galleries of the courtroom. The large portal opening onto the Strand was used only infrequently for ceremonial purposes. One entered the building at specialized and

monitored entrances that led to staircases and thus to the proper corridors. The great hall was not the central element of the circulation system but was used only by those already inside the building. Given the tight packing of rooms and corridors, ventilation was a major concern, and so spaces and gaps were left in the composition to allow for outdoor ventilation and ventilation shafts. Whether the building lived up to its ideology of transparency or obfuscated it in a labyrinthine system remains a topic of discussion.

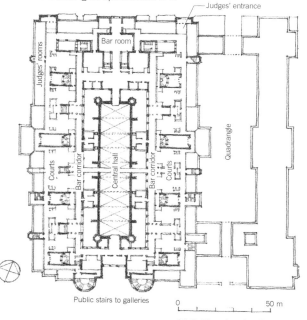

17.9 **Plan: London Law Courts**

17.10 **Plan of Zurich, Switzerland**

17.11 **Anhalter Bahnhof, Berlin, Germany**

RAILROAD STATIONS

For most people in England and Europe, iron, a new material, was best seen in the spectacular railroad stations of the time. Representing a new culture of mobility and exchange, these buildings were not only marvels of engineering but also new and imposing additions to the urban environment. Civil engineers began to compete with architects as arbiters of taste. St. Pancras Station in London (1863–76), for example, contained a volume of space within its 80-meter span that defied anything architecture could have striven for previously. The large steel members were brought to the construction site by the railroad itself. In front of the shed, facing the city, was a building that contained baggage facilities, waiting rooms, and offices for various functions. By the 1880s, terminals in England, Germany, France, the United States, and even in the colonies, such as Victoria Terminus in Mumbai (1888), had become the symbol of the age, leading one commentator to write that train stations were to the European 19th century what monasteries and cathedrals had been to the 13th century. Railroad stations significantly changed the orientation and configuration of many cities, as railroad lines usually had to go near cities rather than through them because of the trains' smoky steam engines. Many of these peripheral railroad stations subsequently developed into urban hubs in their own right, with boulevards and rectangular urban blocks.

In Paris, for example, were the Gare de Lyon (*gare* is the French word for "station"), the Gare du Nord, the Gare de l'Est, the Gare d'Austerlitz, the Gare Montparnasse, and the Gare St. Lazare, all of which changed the economic and social environment of the city.

The rise of the railroad station in England can be further explained by the fact that railroads were private companies in competition with each other, and therefore needed grand structures to distinguish them from their competitors. Although there were differences in the styles of the front building, with its portico and waiting rooms, the main prototype of shed-and-front building remained unchanged until well into the 20th century. The Anhalter Bahnhof (1872–80) in Berlin is another classic example of the type.

In the colonies, where the English were monopoly owners of the railways, the stations were projected as symbols of civilizational advancement enabled by colonial rule. The Public Works Department of colonial India, staffed by officers of the trained English Corps of Engineers, took great pride in designing not only the large terminus stations but also the thousands of smaller stations that were needed throughout India for material extraction and transportation of goods and people. While the larger stations were equipped with wide spans and rich decoration, the smaller ones were built using standardized and rationalized design schemes both to optimize functionality and to project a sense of militaristic order.

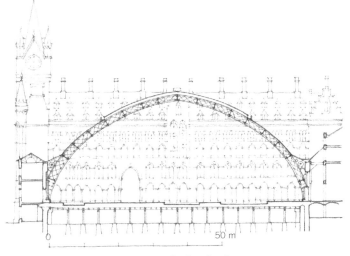

17.12 **Section: St. Pancras Station, London**

17.13 Finnish Athenaeum, Helsinki

THE ATHENAEUM

By the turn of the century, the idea of associations—citizens coming together around a particular set of common interests—had become a social movement unto itself, reaching into the middle class. The theoretical underpinnings of this development can be found in the writing of Alexis de Tocqueville (1805–59), the French philosopher and social scientist. He argued that associations were an important part of a healthy civil society. Given the contrary propensity for isolation in the modern world, society needed to be bound together, he argued, not through the abstract authority of the state but through voluntary associations, educational institutions, newspapers, and even commercial and manufacturing associations.

Building on the older mercantile culture of coffeehouses, the new associations of the 19th century tended to be pro-urban, seeing the city, despite its faults and ugliness, as the symbol of civilization and the place where the virtues of polity, politeness, and urbanity could be exercised and maintained. Associations took many forms: some were social, others political; some secular, others religious. Among them were the Natural History Society, the Mechanic's Institute, the Architectural Association, the Royal Victoria Gallery for the Encouragement of Practical Science, and a rich array of musical groups, library societies, and philosophical and charitable organizations.

Before the public library came the athenaeum. Inspired by Hadrian's Athenaeum in Rome, which was meant to emulate the culture of learning associated with temples dedicated to Athena, 19th-century athenaeum societies sought to promote a culture of literary and scientific learning focused on books, poetry, criticism, and the like. Their roots were in the Enlightenment, probably in the 1798 literary magazine called the *Athenaeum* that was started by the brothers August and Karl Friedrich Schlegel, pioneers of Indo-European studies and active advocates of the German Romantic movement.

A wide diversity of athenaeums sprang up all over Europe and the United States. Rather than stick to a specific visual heritage, athenaeums sought to be very current and in tune with extant intellectual cultures. They were modern-day temples of Athena. Many were designed in the Italianate manner, while others were Greek Revival. Some were a mix, such as those in London and Boston. The Wadsworth Atheneum in Hartford, Connecticut, is the oldest in the United States and exhibits a fascinating blend of diverse architectural idioms. Its original building, designed by Alexander Jackson Davis and Ithiel Town in 1842, was a neo-Gothic building complete with turrets and a crenelated roofline. Besides a large fine arts collection, this building housed the beginnings of what later became the Hartford Public Library and the Connecticut Historical Society. In 1910 and 1915, two new wings were added to house the growing art collection, one in Tudor Revival style and the other in a more Italianate Renaissance mode, both designed by Benjamin Wistar Morris. In 1934, the museum chose a strong modernist idiom for its new wing—the first museum in the United States to adopt modernism—making the entire structure an eclectic assemblage.

The athenaeum was an international movement, with institutions appearing in the United States, in England, and in other parts of Europe. The Finnish Athenaeum (1887) in Helsinki, designed by Theodor Höjer, demonstrates the emerging scale and importance of these institutions. The facade is decorated with statues and reliefs along with busts of the architect Bramante, the painter Raphael, and the sculptor Phidias. On the third floor, the caryatids that support the pediment symbolize the four classical art forms: architecture, painting, sculpting, and music. Between the second-floor windows are reliefs that represent Finnish and international artists.

17.14 **National Gallery, London**

17.15 **French-Egyptian Museum, Cairo**

NATIONAL MUSEUMS

Before the European Enlightenment, history was more often than not explained as mythical genealogies, and as a sequence of great kings, queens, and military events. But beginning in the Enlightenment, history began to be perceived in terms of a civilizational dynamic and verifiable data. The original fixation on Rome and Greece expanded into a fascination with global history—particularly that of Egypt, Mesopotamia, China, and India—with nations such as England, France, and Germany seeing themselves as the protectors and heirs of antique values. With William Jones's 1786 discovery of the linguistic continuity between Sanskrit and Greek and Latin, comparative histories, along with theories of "originary" nations, also began to circulate.

The national museums that now came into being exemplified the Victorian's desire—and capacity—to master the logic of the expanding concept of history. The Louvre was among the first of these new museums, having been transformed in 1793 from a private royal collection into a public art museum open to all citizens free of charge. Subsequently, Napoleon transformed the Louvre into an instrument of the state to strengthen the link between national identity and the history of civilization. The idea of the national museum was taken up by the Prussian king Friedrich Wilhelm II, who built the Altes Museum in Berlin in 1829. By the end of the 19th century, the European Enlightenment conception of nation and empire was inextricably intertwined with museum displays and exhibitions.

The discovery of dazzling, forgotten ruins, such as those found at Angkor Wat by the French in the 1860s, became almost a competitive sport among nations. The principle of these discoveries was "finders keepers," with the finders becoming more famous than their discoveries: the Elgin Marbles, from the frieze of the Parthenon, were named not after the temple but after the man who had dismantled them and sold them to the British Museum—Thomas Bruce, the 7th Earl of Elgin.

The span of time encompassing the construction of the National Gallery in London (1861), the Kyoto National Museum (1898), the Estonian National Museum (1909), and the National Gallery of Art in Washington, DC (1931), demonstrates the expanding role of history in the construction of national ideologies. At the same time, museums were built in the colonies to stress the legitimacy of the colonizer's presumed civilizing mission and to enable native peoples to recognize themselves as differentiated subjects under the overarching and unifying umbrella of empire. India's Government Museum of Chennai (1851) and Prince of Wales Museum in Mumbai (1914), as well as the French-Egyptian Museum in Cairo (1858), are but a few examples of the complex aspects of the history of colonialism.

In most cases, these museums were conceived as Neoclassical structures, because the claim to classicism and its associated principles of order and system were so central to the concept of nationalism in the 19th century. The National Gallery

of England had an octastyle temple front. The imprint of Neoclassicism was so strong that even in the 20th century, modernism—apart from a few exceptions—could do little to challenge it, at least in Europe and the Americas. In Europe, until the advent of postmodernism there were few examples of museums not built in a Neoclassical style.

17.16 **Prince of Wales Museum, Mumbai, India**

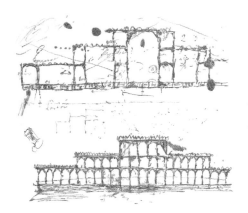

17.17 Sir Joseph Paxton's sketch for the Crystal Palace, London

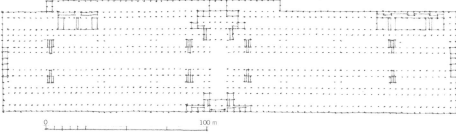

17.18 Plan: Crystal Palace

WORLD'S FAIRS

The first industrial exhibition was held in France in 1801 to search for buyers of products during an economic depression that followed the French Revolution. The English also had such fairs, but on a smaller scale. The success of these fairs led Henry Cole (1808–82), a leading advocate of the necessity for improvement in industrial design and well-known through his *Journal of Design and Manufactures* (1849–52), to argue that what was needed was not a national exhibition but a large international one that could assemble the best goods from the world over and, at the same time, showcase England's unique influence in the global economy. The fair he organized was held in 1851 and took place in a building that came to be called the Crystal Palace.

The Crystal Palace was designed and engineered by Sir Joseph Paxton, an innovative designer of steel and glass greenhouses. Unlike Henri Labrouste's Bibliothèque St.-Geneviève with its custom-detailed iron elements, or St. Pancras Station with its massive beams, the Crystal Palace was composed of thin, lightweight elements that were mass-produced and assembled on-site. Tension wires kept the structure from falling over. The effect was of a building that seemed almost to be woven; compression and tension forces were brought into the open as no other building had ever done before. Paxton also understood that the

structure had to be inspiring and so designed its central element in the form of a long nave filled with exhibits, trees, and gardens. On display were the first English mass-produced machines and products, alongside intricate handcrafted products from the colonies. The contradiction between the two reflected the intellectual mindset of the time. The industrial bosses marveled at the engineering and mass production; the Arts and Crafts enthusiasts pointed to the colonial products as evidence of what was lost to England. John Ruskin and Owen Jones decried the building and its industrial contents as representing the superficiality of modern culture, while extolling the colonial products for their beauty.

No one had ever seen such a spectacle. The fair was a phenomenal success: 6 million people visited in the six short months the exhibition was open. The fair's unprecedented triumph set the stage for a seemingly endless series of repeats: the Great Industrial Exhibition of Dublin (1853), the New York Crystal Palace (1853), the International Exhibition of London (1862), the Dublin International Exhibition (1865), and London's Colonial and Indian Exhibition (1886). There were still others: the international exhibitions in Paris in 1855, 1867, 1878, 1889, and 1900; the Centennial Exhibition in Philadelphia (1876); the World's Columbian Exposition in Chicago (1893), and the World's Exposition at Melbourne,

Australia (1880). And then there were countless exhibitions held in the colonies and in non-European countries: in Calcutta and Jaipur, India (both in 1883); in South Africa (1887, 1893); in Belgium (1894); in Jamaica (1891); and in Guatemala (1897). A cultural history of these exhibitions would map out the core topics of 19th-century modernity, including the mass-production of space and goods; the spectacle of display; the rituals of consumption; and the relationship between capital, nationalism, imperialism, and entertainment.

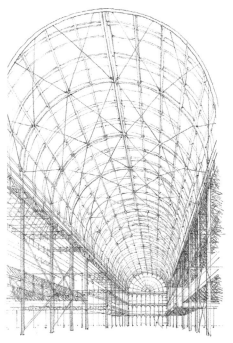

17.19 Interior: Crystal Palace

17.20 **Memorial Hall of Harvard University, Cambridge, Massachusetts**

17.21 **Museum of Natural History, Oxford, England**

GLOBAL ARTS AND CRAFTS MOVEMENT

No Victorian-era theorist was as widely read and discussed as John Ruskin. Ruskin preferred the simpler Italian medieval style to the more complicated northern Gothic, because form, he argued, should be determined by the material of which it consists and of the way in which it is constructed. The early medieval period, he felt, embodied this ethos. Unlike Pugin, Ruskin was not opposed to the use of iron, but he much preferred conventional materials. Disturbed by the rawness of industrialism, he wanted to bring a new awareness to the aesthetic intensity of the architectural surface. The fact that a wall is a series of layers, he argued, should be shown as distinctly as possible on the surface. He was not opposed to thin walls, for example, but wanted the thinness to be expressed in the paneling or in the use of a checkered pattern. Ruskin also asked his readers to rethink their attitude to the past, looking not at the question of proportion and order in the neoclassical sense, nor at the question of Roman versus non-Roman motifs, but rather at the physical and material rationale that underlies architectural reasoning.

Ruskin's concern for the visual led him to prefer monolithic columns. He rejected the use of piers and buttresses, as they interfered with the visual impact of a form. Mass was not to be constricted by cold geometry;

rather, it was something to be molded freely with simple and grand outlines. He very rarely dealt with interiors and thus rarely asked questions about program and function. For Ruskin, the shape of a building—as would have been significant for Durand—was less important than the architect's attitude toward designing it; and a building's tactile surface and detail were just as important as the plan.

After Ruskin, a generation of architects began to design in a way that they thought conformed to his vision of the constructed world. This entailed a shift away from the enforced medievalism of Pugin to a more inventive style for which there is no particular name apart from the term *Ruskinian Gothic*. Among those who worked in this direction was the firm of Deane and Woodward, which designed the interior of the Museum of Natural History at Oxford University (1853) using exposed Gothic-styled iron, demonstrating its expressive qualities down to the rivets holding the elements together. The industrial feel is offset by individually designed capitals with inventive floral motifs and the use of column clusters to create a light, transparent appearance. In the United States, one of the best examples of Ruskinian Gothic is Memorial Hall (1865–68) at Harvard University in Cambridge, Massachusetts. Housing a theater and dining hall, it was designed by William Robert Ware and Henry Van Brunt. Most of the building is in red brick accented in a lively manner with yellowish

limestone. The roof is stripped in grays, whites, and reds, with a massive tower rising over the ensemble.

In this context, a movement sprang up that defined a middle ground between socialism and capitalism. Known as the Arts and Crafts movement, it appealed to individuality, novelty, and good taste; but it refined these tendencies into a social and philosophical position that revolved around the critique of what many saw as the ethical vacuum at the center of England's mercantile culture. The concern of the Arts and Crafts was not with the end product of design, and certainly not with efficiency, but with the processes shaping the design—there had to be an intimate connection between design and production. This position was to have significant influence on later modernists, such as Henry Van de Velde, Hermann Muthesius, Adolf Loos, and Walter Gropius.

17.22 **William Morris textile design**

17.23 **Government Secretariat, Mumbai, India**

Arts and Crafts artists were, for the most part, resistant to making connections to industry, as they were frustrated by what they perceived as the drift toward mechanization. Perfection of finish, symmetry, and precision were suspect, since they represented the denial of the human element. But just because the movement critiqued capitalism and industrialism did not mean it was a friend of the socialists, who for their part paid little regard to the Arts and Crafts movement; the socialists' weapons were the trade unions, not guilds of bookbinders and furniture makers. In reality, the Arts and Crafts appealed more to the disenfranchised bourgeoisie, social utopians, and upper-class aesthetes than to members of the working class. In this it was, in essence, an extension of Victorian ideals that tried to educate the middle class on the question of taste. Ruskin, for example, created a museum in Sheffield that contained carefully assembled objects intended for the edification of local laborers and schoolchildren; it displayed paintings, sculptures, prints, and casts.

Arts and Crafts in India: Indo-Saracenic Style
The Arts and Crafts movement became quite widespread, reaching Belgium, France, Germany, the United States, and even some of the English colonies, particularly India. in fact, some Arts and Crafts enthusiasts, like John Lockwood Kipling (father of the author Rudyard Kipling), moved to India to dedicate themselves to the cause of preserving and promoting Indian crafts. Kipling promoted a new journal on Indian crafts and even started a school to train young craftsmen.

Late in the 19th century, Gothic Revival architecture, with its overt message of English nationalism, seemed increasingly out of place in India. It was now clear to the English that India had an architectural history that was as deep as it was complicated. With scholars now studying Indian art and architecture, a new generation of architects began to experiment with a style that came to be known as Indo-Saracenic, which adapted the architectural vocabulary of Islamic or "Saracenic" architecture to create buildings such as town halls, libraries, and schools. The Indo-Saracenic paralleled the attempt in Egypt to create a neo-Mamluk style. Part of the Indo-Saracenic ideal was lodged in the colonial stereotype of the putative "decline" of Indian civilization. The English claimed that they had succeeded in conquering India because Indian civilization in general had

gone into decay. One of the chief proponents of this idea was James Fergusson, the first historian of Indian architecture. Without any understanding of the functional or conceptual basis of Indian architecture, Fergusson classified and evaluated Indian buildings based on their formal properties and proposed that Indian architecture periodically went into decline and that it had thus to be revived by contact with foreigners.

For John Ruskin, the crucial index of decline could be mapped by differentiating between Indian craft and Indian art. While craftsmen, working in their native "innocence," were seen as a positive example for the English, the Indian arts had, in his opinion, gone into a decline accompanied by a downslide in morality. Fearing that this decline might be due to the corrupting influence of Europeans, his prescription was to educate Indian craftsmen in European aesthetics while preserving and reviving their craft traditions. European art with Indian craft in the service of modern colonial buildings was, therefore, the 19th-century recipe for a "modern" Indian architecture.

17.24 **Victoria Terminus, Mumbai**

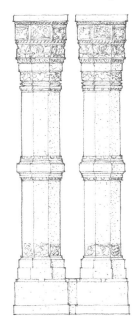

17.25 **National Art Gallery, Government Museum of Chennai, India (formerly the Victoria Technical Institute Building)**

At this time Bombay (Mumbai) emerged as the primary port of British India, especially after the opening of the Suez Canal in 1869. The Northern blockade of Southern cotton during the U.S. Civil War (1861–65) suddenly made Bombay the prime exporter of Indian cotton. New wealth made for new civic buildings. For the most part, colonial architects continued to believe that the English national style of architecture was still the appropriate style for the buildings of British India; and in Victorian England, in the wake of Pugin's critiques, Ruskinian Gothic was championed as the special preserve of Great Britain and its global colonial culture. All of Bombay's major civic structures were Ruskinian Gothic: St. Clair Wilkins's Secretariat (1867–74) and his public Works Offices (1869–72) were followed by John Begg's Post and Telegraph offices (1871–74), and finally by the Law Courts (1871–78) by Colonel J. A. Fuller. Sir Gilbert Scott designed the University Hall (1869–74) with a semicircular apse and a rose window in the French decorative style of the 15th century. His design of the nearby library was completed with a clock tower (1878) 80 meters high, modeled after Giotto's campanile at Florence. With high-pitched roof, crenellations, towers, dormers, and Venetian arches, all these buildings assembled in a row defined Bombay's image as a distinguished colonial outpost.

The most spectacular of the Gothic Revival buildings was F. W. Stevens's Victoria Terminus (1878–88), the grand terminus and offices of the Central Railway. The design derives from Gilbert Scott's St. Pancreas Station in London, although with its fanciful Gothic detailing, polychromatic stone, decorative tile, marble, and stained glass, it arguably exudes a certain un-English exuberance and excess, symptomatic perhaps of growing English interest in Indian ornamental details. The largest British building in India at that time, Victoria Terminus was a success with the English public and, quite appropriately given the city's success as a center of import and export, immediately became the iconic image of Bombay.

One of the most celebrated attempted translations of Arts and Crafts ideals into the practice of architecture in India was undertaken by Colonel Swinton Jacobs. An engineer by training, Jacobs worked in the "princely state" of Jaipur, in Rajasthan, for more than forty years, from 1867 to 1912. (Princely states were nominally independent but governed by local rulers who were subject to the oversight of the British Empire.) Jacobs believed that draftsmen trained to accurately copy full-size details from examples of Indian architectural history would come to appreciate the intrinsic quality of their own culture. His *Jeypore Portfolio of Architectural*

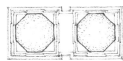

17.26 **Sample drawing from the** *Jeypore Portfolio of Architectural Details*

Details (1890) was a collection of individual folio sheets that a craftsman could look at and study. All the examples, however, were drawn from Islamic architecture.

17.27 **Mubarak Mahal, Jaipur, India**

17.28 **Jaipur Town Hall, India**

A building often attributed to Jacobs but probably designed by one of his personally trained disciples, Lala Chiman Lal, was the Mubarak Mahal (1899), located within the palace compound of Jaipur. A ceremonial reception hall, the Mubarak Mahal was also a museum comprising a two-story cubic volume with projecting porches. It is a case study in Indo-Saracenic ornamentation: on the upper story, a fanciful filigree of carefully executed embellishment outlines the cantilevered balcony that runs around the entire perimeter of the structure, and on the lower story individual bays, conceived as display cases, self-consciously stage distinct ornamental details. The entire program, layout, and proportions and divisions of the structure—in short, its aesthetic—derived from the European tradition. Only in its details was it Indian.

Robert F. Chisholm (1840–1915) belonged to the generation of professional architects who believed more in exploring their professional freedom than in following designs from ideological strictures. It was this search that led him inevitably to eclecticism. His unbuilt design for the Bombay Municipal Hall competition, for example, called for a three-story volume with a large central dome that was based on the Taj Mahal. Chisholm did not hesitate to open up the dome at the base with tall arched openings that necessitated an internal structural system made of steel. Smaller domes on octagonal bases terminated the corners of the main

cubic volume. The corners were further emphasized by the suggestion of turrets created by faceting the edges, with a string of moldings close to the ground that flare out slightly at the base, as, for instance, in the Hindu Victory Tower at Chittorgarh. The overall conception of the massing is reminiscent of Henry Hobson Richardson's Trinity Church in Boston. The centerpiece of the elevation changes at every level: a porch supported by paired columns on the ground floor, surmounted by a narrow balcony on the second floor and finished with a wide, double-height arch surmounted by a Bengal-style drooping roof integrated into the cornice line. No part of the design was left untouched by careful attention to detail.

Arts and Crafts enthusiasts and the Indo-Saracenics did not make much of an impression on the local Indian maharajas in their personal commissions. Sawai Ram Singh (r. 1835–80) brazenly continued to have his workmen build imitation, hybridized, European-style buildings, such as his Town Hall in Jaipur. Singh was a wily character. He had used the typical colonial misrecognition of his relationship with his feudatories to his advantage, making his feudatories, who usually served as checks on his authority, submissive to him on the basis of the representation he had among his English backers. For maharajas who, like the babus, had no paternalistic project in mind, the identifiable style of power was European.

17.29 **Robert F. Chisolm's winning entry for the Bombay Municipal Hall**

17.30 Gamble House, Pasadena, California

Arts and Crafts in California

In California, Arts and Crafts underwent its most vigorous transformation and its longest period of vibrancy, fusing with Spanish-Mexican motifs as well as elements from the Italian Mediterranean and the Far East. Linked to its development was a public school system strongly committed to manual-arts education and in particular to the belief that the union of head and heart through handicraft yielded therapeutic benefits. Local libraries organized sketch clubs and hosted exhibitions of local craft production.

Elements from the local landscape and flora were also quite strong in the California Arts and Crafts. Whether depicting golden poppies, the Torrey pines, the redwoods, or the sublime majesty of the Yosemite Valley, California's Arts and Crafts artists extolled the state's natural beauty and were much more intimately associated with the outdoors than their counterparts in England and the northeastern United States. Many of their houses exploited the fine views and outdoor living afforded by the natural settings. These Arts and Crafts houses featured deliberate blurring of interior and exterior space through the use of decks, pergolas, porches, and terraces. The English-style medievalism in these houses gave way to an aesthetic of primitivism embodied, for example, in the writings of Jack London, author of *The Call of the Wild* (1903). London's own house in Sonoma's Valley of the Moon was a prime example of Arts and Crafts domestic architecture: redwood, timber with bark left

on, huge halls, and giant fireplaces. The Gamble House by Charles Sumner Greene and Henry Mather Greene (Pasadena, California, 1908–9) is an excellent example of the use of Japanese motifs. The stepping-stone path across the yard, the battered retaining wall, and an airy elevated porch are all inspired by Japanese precedents. The house rests on a broad terrace that extends the space of the living rooms outward toward the gardens and lawns. The house also was designed in relationship to the existing majestic eucalyptus trees. Inside, from lamps to furniture to carpets, not a single detail is left unattended. As was common in Arts and Crafts, but rarely achieved on this scale, furniture, built-in cabinetry, paneling, wood carvings, rugs, lighting, and leaded stained glass were all custom-designed by the architects.

The plan was unusual. A hall with a staircase bisected the entire building, with the living room and den on one side and the dining room, kitchen, and a guest bedroom on the other side. The principal upstairs bedrooms had sleeping porches overlooking the garden. Unlike Shingle Style houses with their steeply pitched roofs, the roofs here are very flat, seeming to float over the building; the shadows from the overhangs emphasize the horizontal layering of space. On the interior, the heavy wooden beams were left exposed, but they were smoothed and polished to bring out the material's yellowish warmth. The ceilings are plain white in the Japanese style and stand out against the wood framing. Art Nouveau touches on the lamps, stained glass, and rugs add a layer of urban sophistication. The house was designed as a retirement residence for David and Mary Gamble of Cincinnati, Ohio. David, a second-generation member of the Procter & Gamble Company, a leading soap manufacturer, had retired in 1895.

0   10 m

17.31 First-floor plan: Gamble House

17.32 Interior: Gamble House

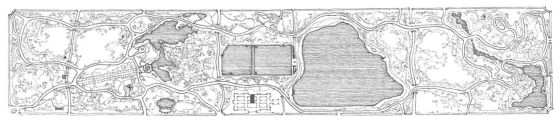

17.33 Plan of Central Park, New York City

CENTRAL PARK

Building on the Romantic associations with nature as integral to the development of citizenship, by the early 19th century urban parks were widely recognized as an important indicator of a city's livability. Although not included in the original Commissioners' Plan of 1811, New York City's Central Park (1853–83) was not only the nation's first and largest urban park, but it also became the model of American landscape design. Won in an open competition, Central Park was the very first commission of the famous landscape architect Frederick Law Olmsted (1822–1903). Olmsted began his career as a journalist and was influenced first by his dispatches from Europe, where he was particularly impressed by the new urban parks, such as Birkenhead Park in England by Joseph Paxton of Crystal Palace fame, and subsequently by his travels in the South, where he carefully documented and commented on the adverse effects of the slave economy.

Central Park was championed by Andrew Jackson Downing, an advocate of landscape design and a famous critic of industrialization and urbanization, as well as a mentor to Olmsted. Downing (1815–52), influenced by Picturesque ideas as well as the growing moralism of the early Victorian era, saw in landscapes more than just beauty. He saw the garden as something more than a convenient stage for setting up monuments to heroes, as it was at Stowe Gardens in Buckinghamshire, England. Landscape, so Downing held, strengthened character and supported the integrity of the family. The intimate house garden, he argued, served as a civilizing and protective veil around the house and helped it to blend as naturally as possible into the landscape. At the time, the area around most large cities in the United States had been radically deforested to make way for farms. In 1845, when Henry David

Thoreau lived for two years in solitude next to Walden Pond in Massachusetts in an attempt to immerse himself in nature, the pond was one of the few areas for many miles around surrounded by trees. Downing believed that one could bring nature to the city in the form of parks, but only if they were big enough to simulate a landscape—albeit one that had been tamed and brought into balance with human needs.

When Downing was killed in a steamboat explosion on the Hudson River in 1852, Olmsted joined with Calvert Vaux to submit the competition entry for the park. Vaux was an English architect who had come to the United States to work with Downing. The 3.4-square-kilometer park, in the heart of Manhattan, was built on land occupied by free slaves and Irish immigrants, who were forcibly evicted. The park was not raw nature, but a carefully constructed vision of it. This involved vast amounts of cut and fill work, the planting of millions of trees, the construction of thirty-six bridges, and the creation of meadows, forests, hilltop lookouts, castles, sheep farms, skating rinks, and eateries. In keeping with the Romantic Picturesque tradition, a flock of pedigreed Dorset sheep were maintained in a specially designated meadow. Two major reservoirs stored water for the city. Underneath was an elaborate drainage system.

Olmsted and Vaux were at constant loggerheads with the park's commissioners to ensure that the park was maintained as a democratic space accessible to all. Although Central Park attracted 10 million visitors in its first years, it went into severe decline around the turn of the century. In 1934, Robert Moses cleaned up and restored the park as part of his drive to transform New York City.

Olmsted, Vaux and Company, founded in 1861, also designed parks in Milwaukee, Wisconsin; Buffalo, New York; and other cities. The firm was inherited by Olmsted's

sons, John Charles Olmsted (1852–1920) and Frederick Law Olmsted Jr. (1870–1957), who developed it into one of the largest and most influential landscape firms of the time. They designed numerous well-known projects such as Acadia National Park, Yosemite National Park, and Atlanta's Piedmont Park, as well as the complete park systems of cities such as Portland and Seattle.

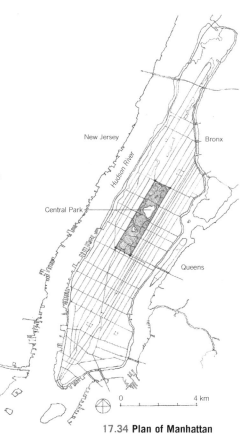

17.34 Plan of Manhattan

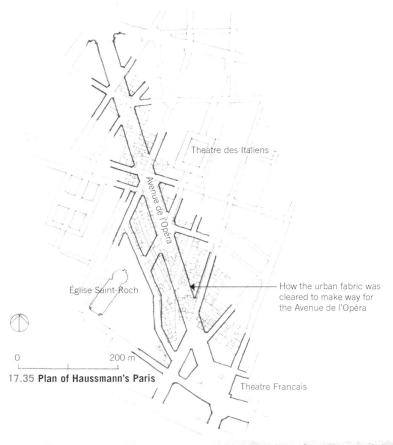

Theâtre des Italiens

Avenue de l'Opéra

How the urban fabric was cleared to make way for the Avenue de l'Opéra

Église Saint-Roch

0   200 m

17.35 Plan of Haussmann's Paris

Theatre Francais

17.36 Street view: Haussmann's Paris

PARIS AND HAUSSMANN

After Napoleon's defeat in 1815, the monarchy was restored in France and lasted in various forms until 1848, when another major popular revolt in the streets of Paris—immortalized by Victor Hugo in *Les Miserables*—led to the establishment of the Second Republic. Louis-Napoleon Bonaparte was elected president of the Second Republic, and in 1852 a plebiscite was held that gave him supreme power, with the title of emperor, as Napoleon III (1808–73). He promptly canceled the independence of parliament and rolled back advancements that had been made in the name of universal suffrage, free press, and education. Public institutions were strictly supervised, the teaching of philosophy in the high schools was suppressed, and the power of the government was increased.

Initially, the fortunes of France seemed restored. The country emerged victorious in the Crimean War (1854–56) and then went on to build the Suez Canal (1854–69). Napoleon III was eager to translate these successes into architectural form and, even more, to make Paris into the "capital of the 19th century." His agent of change was Georges-Eugène Haussmann (1809–91), whose vision for Paris, like Napoleon III's, was unmistakably big. Unlike earlier urban design approaches—as in Rome under Sixtus V, and in Washington, DC—that used straight boulevards in relationship to major buildings such as palaces and churches, Haussmann's new streets were laid out according to pragmatic and economic considerations. They had to be built, however, by destroying large parts of medieval Paris and displacing thousands of inhabitants, mainly from the lower classes.

17.37 **Paris Opera House, France**

17.38 **Grand Staircase: Paris Opera House**

Though there was some attempt to integrate the new streets with the old, little was spared and entire neighborhoods were wiped out. The new streets were lined with apartments and provided with sewage pipes and gas lines. To forestall conflagrations, the use of stone for buildings, once the privilege of the rich, was now common throughout the new parts of the city. Haussmann's Paris would become the model for cities around the world, such as Buenos Aires, Cairo, Rome, and Saigon. "Haussmannization," which impeded effective blockading of streets, is sometimes blamed for the suppression of the Paris Commune in the street revolts of 1871.

One of the centerpieces of the new Paris was the Opera House (1861–75), set at the intersection of several radiating streets. It was designed by Charles Garnier (1825–98), a young architect who was only thirty-six years old when he won the competition. Earlier, he had won the Prix de Rome, demonstrating that even a workingman's son could gain access to the new professional class. Garnier's design combines the double columnar colonnade from the Louvre with elements from Michelangelo's facade on the Campidoglio, blending the royal symbolism that would have appealed to Napoleon III with the republican symbolism of Michelangelo's work. The front, when taken as a whole, could also be seen as a very wide triumphal arch. In this way, the building successfully

negotiated the complex political situation of its times without referring to Rome or Greece in any direct way. Like the London Law Courts, this building had multiple programs and circulation systems. The impressive front entrance was for the public arriving on foot. Those arriving by coach entered on the right-hand side. Performers and members of the opera administration entered at the rear. There was a special side entrance for

the emperor, to which he could roll up in his coach and go directly indoors. Structurally the building is of steel, but the steel is rendered invisible by stone and brick. The staircase that lies between the entrance narthex and the theater is itself a three-dimensional theater intended to allow opera goers to see and be seen, the encounters themselves constituting an elaborate social ritual.

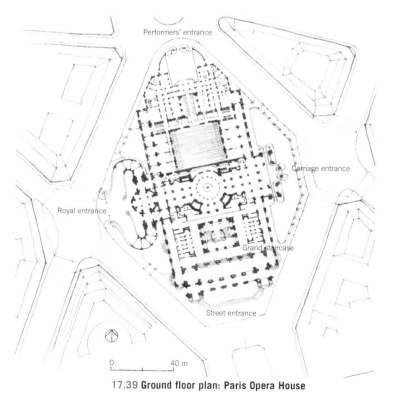

17.39 **Ground floor plan: Paris Opera House**

17.40 **Galleria Vittorio Emanuele II, Milan, Italy**

17.41 **Piazza del Duomo, Milan**

THE *PASSAGE*

Besides train stations and industrial fairs, the building type that perhaps best epitomized the Industrial Revolution and its new culture of mass consumption was the shopping gallery. These buildings were places where one could see firsthand not only the wealth of the global marketplace but also the use of new building materials, metal and glass. At the beginning of the 19th century, most shops differed very little from those of medieval times—a window or counter faced the street, and there was a small enclosure where business could be transacted. The fall in the price of glass made large shop windows possible, and they appeared at the end of the 1820s in London, Paris, and New York. In Paris, shopping streets—called *galeries* or *passages*—were soon designed with rows of shops under a single glazed roof. By the end of the 19th century, *passages* or their equivalents could be found in most European cities. At first they were on a single floor, but soon they were built on two or more levels. They provided security for shop owners as well as convenience for shoppers: most 19th-century cities were noisy and chaotic, and the streets unpaved. *Passages* offered protected enclaves for bourgeois patrons.

Marking the zenith of this building type was the Galleria Vittorio Emanuele II in Milan, a building that became a symbol of the young nation. Its entrance was located facing the piazza in front of the Duomo, the facade of which had only been finished in 1806. The planning of the piazza had stalled for decades, but it was revived with the unification of Italy in 1859. Almost immediately the designing of the galleria was put into motion, and when it was opened in 1867, it was seen as an engineering and urban marvel.

The building, whose four wings meet at a great, glassed dome, is completely regular on the interior, but it dovetails with the older existing structures around it. There are seven floors, not including the cellar, with a network of concealed intersecting supports that allow for a flexible use of space. Staircases are located at the rear and are accessible through courtyards so as not to disturb the visual unity of the facades. The main staircases are located at the reentrant angles of the crossings. The third floor is reserved for club rooms, offices, and studios, while the uppermost floors are residential. More than just a shopping arcade, this building is an urban entity in itself.

17.42 **Friedrichstrassenpassage, Berlin**

17.43 **Galeries St. Hubert, Brussels**

ÉCOLE DES BEAUX-ARTS

Throughout the 19th century, Europe's prime school for the study of architecture was the École des Beaux-Arts in Paris. Though intended for French citizens, it was by the end of the 19th century visited by students from around the world, creating a cadre of devotees who spread the school's pedagogical system and architectural style to places around the globe. Its influence could still be felt in American architectural schools well into the 1940s. The Beaux-Arts was originally founded as the Académie Royale d'Architecture in Paris in 1671 by Jean-Baptiste Colbert, minister of Louis XIV, who envisioned it as a place that would create the talent necessary for the king's complex building program. The French Revolution ended the royal academies, but in 1803, architectural education resumed, mainly to prepare students for state-sponsored architectural competitions. The founding of the Société Centrale des Architects in 1840 made architecture into an academic profession similar to law and medicine. The Société ended the aristocratic system of patronage. It was also the death knell of the gentleman architect (though that tradition had always been stronger in England than in France). This is important to note, because even though the academic style of the French was much criticized by the moderns of the 20th century, the École elevated architecture to an autonomous and structured discipline.

With that autonomy came new and complex theoretical questions about the nature of architectural production. Should one use new materials like steel and glass? And if so, how? What is the relationship between the identity of a nation, its history, and its architecture? By mid-century these issues became quite divisive. On the one side stood defenders of idealized classicism such as Quatremère de Quincy; on the other were the Romantics such as Henri Labrouste, with their flexible understanding of history. The conflict broke into the open with the appointment of Eugène-Emmanuel Viollet-le-Duc in 1863 as professor of the history of art and aesthetics. He supported the use of iron in buildings, which many French architects resisted.

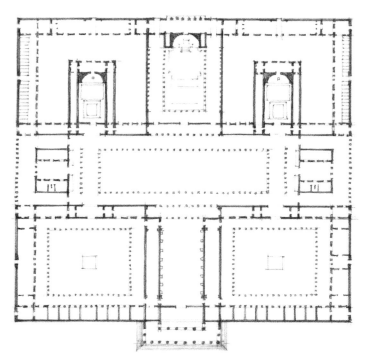

17.44 Design for a supreme court, Henri Labrouste, awarded the Prix de Rome in 1824

His appointment was short-lived, however, and by the 1880s the school became known as a champion of an eclectic style that was Picturesque in its massing but that, nevertheless, remained committed to the tradition of clean and rectilinearly organized plans. Students who were enrolled in the school received much of their education outside of its walls. In fact, their principal learning took place in the atelier. The senior members of the field all employed students as cheap labor; in return, they educated them in the principles of design. Naturally, quality varied, as did style, and students therefore tended to choose those with whom they felt most compatible. Lectures were given at the school, yet attendance was voluntary, and no course examinations were given. Advancement depended on winning points in the monthly competition in composition, construction, perspective, and mathematics.

For a student, the pinnacle of success was winning the annual Prix de Rome, permitting him to live and study at the Villa Medici for one year. The competition took place in three stages and lasted for several months. Students had to develop a twelve-hour sketch (or *esquisse*) solving a design problem that had been set out by the professor of theory, leading to a more substantial presentation (or *charrette*), named for the carts in which the students carried their material to the school. The authors of the best eight were then given about three months, usually until the end of July, to develop a *projet rendu* (finished drawing). It was from these that a winner was chosen. Drawings made for the final stage of the competition could be very large; some measured 5 meters in length.

Of particular importance to the Beaux-Arts conception of design was the ground plan. It had to be functionally clear and formally coherent, and it was usually composed of intersecting rectangles organized symmetrically along a central axis. There was a strong desire to balance buildings with courtyards and solids with voids. The arrangement of spaces—the differentiation between primary and secondary—was known as the *parti*.

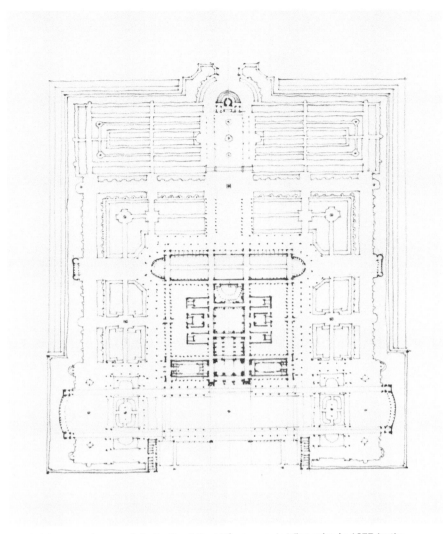

17.45 Athenaeum for a capital city, Henri-Paul Nénot, awarded first prize in 1877 by the École des Beaux-Arts in a competition for assembly rooms, a library, and a greenhouse

Beaux-Arts plans have a set of unique characteristics:

1. Symmetry is stressed, and where there is asymmetry, it must be worked into the larger whole.
2. Axiality is important; the most important spaces must be on axis and clearly emphasized in space and proportion.
3. Cross-axes are used to distribute and organize the program.
4. There should be a clear hierarchy of the major and minor parts of the program. There should be no hidden spaces, but a gradation of importance.
5. At the center of the composition should be a great hall, the dimensions of which relate to the building's overall proportions.
6. Repeating elements should be unified to support the overall planning.
7. The relationships between open and closed spaces and among buildings, courtyards, and surrounding gardens should be resolved into an integrated whole.
8. The decorative elements should be in accordance with the program. Civic buildings should show restraint; opera houses, ebullience.

Henri Labrouste's proposed design for a supreme court from 1824 and Henri-Paul Nénot's design for an athenaeum from 1877 exhibit similar characteristics. Nénot's project is designed around an assembly room that opens onto a grand longitudinally placed plaza that provides the outer dimension for the scheme. The assembly room is placed at the end of a series of halls to emphasize its importance. Secondary reading rooms are placed to the right and left of the main halls. The asymmetrical elements are balanced, and the gardens, which frame the entire building, are integrated into the scheme. The building, set off from the boulevard by its grand plaza, is sited at a street intersection and is the culminating axial element of that street. Yet the presence of all these elements alone does not necessarily declare the building as an example of Beaux-Arts. The design for the U.S. Capitol (1793) by Charles Bulfinch, for example, is Neoclassical but has an asymmetrical interior with an oval space rather awkwardly lodged between the rotunda and the senate chamber. From the perspective of a Beaux-Arts architect, this would be unacceptable.

17.46 A Chettinad mansion, India

CHETTINAD MANSIONS

After the fall of the Cholas in the 14th century, the Chettiars, originally gem dealers, ship chandlers, and salt merchants in the Chola Empire, settled in about seventy-five villages around a single temple near present-day Karaikudi in south-central India, in an area called Chettinad. They were among the first local communities to befriend the new English traders, and in the late 19th century they spread into Southeast Asia—particularly into Burma, Malaysia, Indonesia, and Ceylon—becoming wealthy money lenders and diamond merchants and often working as official agents of the British East India Company. After World War II, when the British withdrew, the Chettiars were deported in large numbers from the newly independent countries of Southeast Asia; some returned to India, and many others settled in the United Kingdom. Through the late 19th and early 20th centuries, the Chettiars repatriated significant sums of money back to their Chettinad villages, resulting in the construction of thousands of mansions. Designed to look European on the outside, they were on the interior distinctly more local, with a touch of the Indonesian in feel and design. The exteriors of the typically two-story structures were often Italianate in style, with columns, and entablatures in painted stucco on brick. Inside there was usually a long *impluvium*-style courtyard with columns made of Burmese teak, polished or lacquered in black or blue. Some columns were of Italian marble. The interior space was dominated by a high-pitched roof that dramatically sloped into the central courtyard.

17.47 Courtyard, Chettinad House, Tamil, India

17.48 Sultan Hassan, Al-Rifa'i, and Mahmoud Pasha Mosques, Cairo

17.49 Plan of Cairo, ca. 1874

COLONIAL MODERNISM

Though the history of non-European modernism is generally thought to begin early in the 20th century with the spread of Art Deco (along Mumbai's Marine Drive, for instance), it actually commences in the second half of the 19th century, often still under the shadow of colonialism. The interrelated concepts of a "colonial modernity" and a "colonial modernism"— as the global crucibles of the genesis of modernism—are only just beginning to be theorized and understood.

This was true for Egypt, one of the first Arab countries to attempt to reinvent itself by means of modern ideas. The neo-Mamluk style began to develop when Egypt proclaimed itself independent from the Ottoman sultanate in 1833 and needed an image that was both modern and Egyptian. Sa'id Pasha (r. 1854–63), Muhammad 'Ali's son and third successor, and especially Isma'il Pasha (r. 1863–79), his grandson, were the architects of Egypt's freedom from the Ottomans. Isma'il was fascinated by French culture, so much so that he adopted French manners in his personal life and encouraged his entourage to follow suit. He also was an impatient modernizer who wanted to turn Egypt into an extension of Europe, despite adverse economic circumstances. The country's foreign debt, however, spun out of control. Bankruptcy was declared in 1879, leading to its occupation by the British in 1882.

Isma'il's passion for Europeanization can be understood as mimicry or as local modernism, as in any other part of the world. Inspired by his visit to the Exposition Universelle in Paris in 1867, he tried to turn his own capital into another Paris, complete with wide, straight avenues planted with trees, planned gardens, pavilions, and all the amenities of modern city life, such as theaters, cafés, and even an opera house. He commissioned his minister of public works, Ali Pasha Mubarak, a member of the academic mission of 1844–49 to France and one of the most influential figures in modern Egyptian history, to draw up the city's new master plan.

With the exception of two boulevards— Shari Muhammad 'Ali and al-Sikka al-Jadida (New Avenue or Shari' al-Muski)—that cut across the old city's dense fabric and required the razing of many medieval structures, the new city extended westward toward the Nile along a north-south axis, with streets radiating from central squares to form star patterns à la Haussmann. This Parisian-style Cairo was built in haste to impress the European monarchs who had been invited to Egypt for the inauguration of the Suez Canal in 1869—among them Empress Eugénie, wife of Napoleon III.

After the English set up a puppet state in 1882, the neo-Mamluk style, also known as neo-Islamic, remained dominant, relating contemporary Egyptian architecture to a glorious phase of its history. One of the

monumental examples, as studied by Nasser Rabbat, the noted scholar of Islamic history, is al-Rifa'i Mosque, constructed in two stages, between 1869 and 1880, and 1906 and 1911. The first stage was designed and supervised by the Egyptian architect Hussein Fahmi, the second by the Austro-Hungarian Max Herz, with others hired as consultants and interior designers. The plan is a rendering of Beaux-Arts ideas: axiality, the rationalization of the spaces, and the interlocking of solids and voids.

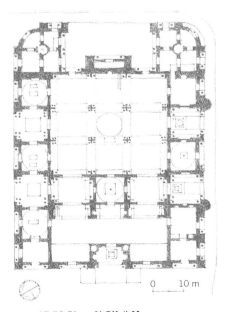

17.50 Plan: Al-Rifa'i Mosque

17.51 Trinity Church, Boston

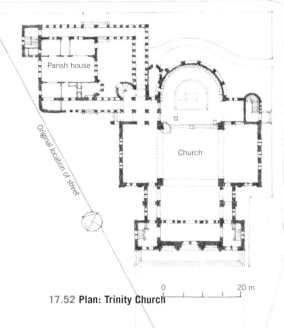

17.52 Plan: Trinity Church

0   20 m

HENRY HOBSON RICHARDSON

By the late 1830s, the Greek Revival had become without question the adopted style of the United States, and it remained so up to the Civil War. The simplicity, ideological coherence, and the ease with which its forms could be copied in brick and wood by local carpenters contributed greatly to its success. It had little competition from the Gothic style, which in the United States, unlike in Europe, had few major representatives. The result was a fluid movement from the Greek Revival to a French-derived style known as Second Empire. With its compositional emphasis on vertical pavilions and classically derived ornamentation, the Second Empire remained an important subcurrent until well into the advent of modernism. In the 1880s and 1890s, a group of architects began to chart their own way, however, bringing out latent ideas of the Picturesque while trying to match this aesthetic with the needs of rising the mercantile class. These architects were Frank Furness in Philadelphia, Louis Sullivan in Chicago, and Henry Hobson Richardson in Boston. All developed very distinctive approaches. Furness brought to the United States many of Viollet-le-Duc's ideas about integrating iron into design. Sullivan stressed bold simplicity combined with rich ornamentation in his buildings. And Richardson's work from the late 1870s to the mid 1890s came to be seen by many as a style unto itself.

When Richardson (1838–86) was young he had intended to become a civil engineer, but he switched to architecture while studying at Harvard. In 1859, he began to study at the École des Beaux-Arts and remained in Paris for five years. Because of his Parisian training, Richardson was well suited to serve the needs of the rising class of new businessmen who wanted to see their success endorsed by the currently fashionable style of cosmopolitan Paris. But by the 1870s, Richardson was increasingly drawn to the English medieval style and to the Picturesque, attempting to synthesize their disparate and even contradictory aspects. Richardson's plans, for example, maintain the clarity typical of the Beaux-Arts, while his attention to the tactility and color of the building's stone surface evoke a tactility more in line with Queen Anne style and Ruskinian Gothic. Richardson closely collaborated with landscape architect Frederick Law Olmsted on many of his projects.

In 1872 Richardson achieved national prominence by having been selected to build Trinity Church in Boston. It was set on a triangular site, designed in a soft pink limestone accented by dark brown stones for the columns, entablatures, and cornices. Though a small building, the generously scaled windows of the facade, compared to the small windows of the tower, make the composition seem both

17.53 Porch, Trinity Church

17.54 **Winn Memorial Public Library, Woburn, Massachusetts**

17.55 **Capitals, Winn Memorial Public Library**

intimate and dynamic. Trinity Church's porch, facade, and crossing tower step back in clear volumetric hierarchy. The porch, added after the building's completion but built to Richardson's specifications, was modeled loosely on the church of St. Trophime in Arles, France, whereas the tower, very wide and spanning the entire width of the nave, was modeled on French and Spanish medieval buildings, including the 12th-century tower of the Cathedral of Salamanca in Spain. Though the building's style, in its massing and detailing, is neo-Romanesque, its plan is a Latin cross, with an apse at the eastern end. The focus of the church is the tall and airy crossing of the interior which is one of the best preserved examples of the Arts and Crafts style, consciously infused here with a neo-Byzantine element. The interior, though relatively dark, is permeated by the muted light of stained glass windows in red, blue, and brown tones that wash against the wall's golden surfaces. Originally, a huge candelabra hung from the center of the crossing. Overall, the building is an excellent example of a blend between the neo-Romanesque and the Arts and Crafts movement.

Richardson was fortunate that his mature career coincided with the rise of the American public library movement. The flowering of public education and the spread of interest in cultural developments

in England and the United States led to the creation of many towns' lending libraries. It was a highly successful experiment in making the printed word accessible to a general audience—a unique idea in the world at the time. Richardson's libraries have a loose exterior picturesqueness meant to contrast with the clarity of the plan, as, for example, at the Winn Memorial Public Library in Woburn, Massachusetts (1876–79).

The plan is organized around a barrel-vaulted longitudinal library space with book-lined alcoves along the sides. It is adjoined by a transept-like reading room, at the head of which is a picture gallery and an octagonal museum. The building is entered from the side along a tall tower with Gothic-style tracery in its upper ranges. For the walls, Richardson, meticulous in his choice of materials, ordered red sandstone from a quarry in Massachusetts. The column bases and horizontal bands are of a cream-colored sandstone from Ohio, all set on a granite base. For the ornamental carvings of the capitals and corbels, Richardson brought in a Welsh sculptor.

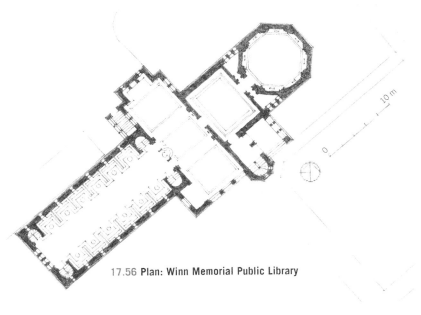

17.56 **Plan: Winn Memorial Public Library**

17.57 Typical bungalow floor plan

17.58 Typical block of bungalows

THE GLOBAL BUNGALOW

One of the most visible manifestations of the global colonial economy was the development and spread of the bungalow. The bungalow (the word derives from the Bengali word *bangla*) was first used by the English colonists in India as a type of garden and plantation house. Most had a single ridge roof that overhung the house, creating a porch called the verandah (originally a Hindi word). The verandah served as an intermediate space where colonizer and colonized could interact. In tropical climates it was also the most comfortable space of the house. In time, bungalows added an entrance porch, which had to be large enough to receive a carriage. The interior space was designed around a central room with bedrooms directly off to the sides, and toilets and kitchens in the back so that they could be serviced by the local staff. Servant quarters were built at a distance in the back of the garden. The colonial bungalow spread as a type throughout the tropical colonies in the late 18th and early 19th centuries.

As a symbol of the good life, the bungalow was exported back to England and soon could be found in the United States as well, in the form of the detached, single-family residential dwelling that could be easily built on small parcels. Climate and lifestyle dictates did not allow the core properties of the colonial bungalow to be exported, but its

image was variously translated as it spread. The noncolonial bungalow was usually a single-story house (though sometime it had two floors) of modest scale, with a low overhanging roof and a porch running along its front. Many subcategories evolved. The California bungalows—which were among the earliest in the United States, dating from about the 1880s onward—commonly have wood shingles, horizontal siding, or stucco exteriors, as well as brick chimneys. The so-called Chicago bungalow, which was popular between 1910 and 1940, was often made of brick. In many cases, the bungalow was inexpensive to build and did not need an architect. Furthermore, with its space-saving layout, it appealed to middle-class owners who could not afford live-in servants. The kitchen was compact and located next to the dining room. The walls were usually wallpapered, whereas the trim for the doors and windows was dark-stained oak.

In the 1880s, the bungalow became associated with the Arts and Crafts movement, and indeed many bungalows were built in the so-called American Craftsman style, which was a reaction against the overdecorated aesthetic of the Victorian era. Though the Arts and Crafts emphasized the handmade over the mass-produced, and some early bungalows followed in this aesthetic, the bungalow was soon nothing less than an industrialized product. In fact,

by the turn of the 20th century, an entire house could be ordered through catalogues; the bungalow was then shipped by rail or boat to be assembled on-site. Doors, windows, and built-in furnishings such as bookcases, desks, and folding beds could also be purchased from mail-order catalogues. The bungalow was spread as part of the suburbanization of the American city, with whole bungalow districts appearing in many U.S. cities.

SHINGLE STYLE

Unique to the United States, and parallel to the Arts and Crafts movement, but more closely allied with the Queen Anne style, was the development of what is now called the Shingle Style. Houses designed in this manner—often as summer homes for the New England elite—show an inventiveness in plan, with elements not merely touching each other but seeming to pass through or overlap with each other. The firm that developed this style more than any other was McKim, Mead & White (founded 1879), which eventually became one of the leading design firms in the United States.

William Rutherford Mead (1846–1928), who had an affinity for the Renaissance, and Stanford White (1853–1906) had little formal training, but they worked their way up as apprentices. Charles Follen McKim (1847–1909), by contrast, had studied at the

17.59 Isaac Bell House, Newport, Rhode Island

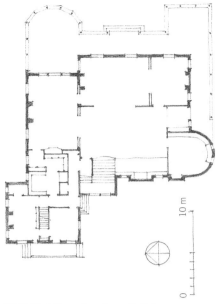

17.60 First-floor plan: Isaac Bell House

École des Beaux-Arts. Between the three they produced a style of architecture that brought out the best in each of them. One of their innovations in their Shingle Style homes was to take the rooms of the servants' quarters out from under the attic and place them in a compact block or wing, against which the more openly designed living rooms of the first floor were contrasted. This can be seen in the Isaac Bell House (1882–83) in Newport, Rhode Island, where the staircase was situated in a large room that served as a circulation center and as a spatial extension of the neighboring study and drawing rooms. This makes it different from the more controlled and boxy spaces of Arts and Crafts houses. Even though it was common to raise the first floor above the level of the ground, the use of porches made the house appear as if were resting on an elevated terrace, protected from the sun and rain by generously proportioned overhangs and roofs. The vertical surfaces of the houses were completely clad in wooden shingles, using a variety of possible patterns to differentiate certain elements like the gable front. The interior surfaces were usually covered with dark wooden paneling in combination with stucco, usually wallpapered but sometimes left plain.

In contrast, the Watts Sherman House (1874) in Newport, Rhode Island, by Henry Hobson Richardson, is closer to the Queen Anne and the Arts and Crafts styles. The rooms are arranged in a more formal way and less open to the hall, and the servants lived in the attic. The overall massing is much more complex than the more volumetrically simple Isaac Bell House.

The Shingle Style began to fade in the late 1890s, by which time U.S. architects who had trained in Paris at the École des Beaux-Arts were returning home with a notion of architectural space that did not conform to the style's relaxed openness. The new preoccupation with monumentality in the United States met the expectations of the more class-conscious elite and ultimately put an end to Arts and Crafts and its related aesthetic phenomena. McKim, Mead & White played a dominant role in this shift, becoming the leading representative in the United States of the Beaux-Arts neoclassical style.

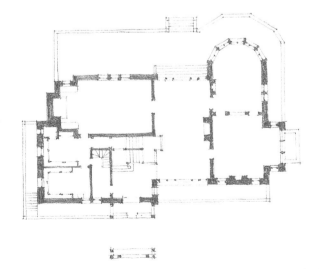

17.61 First-floor plan: Watts Sherman House, Newport, Rhode Island

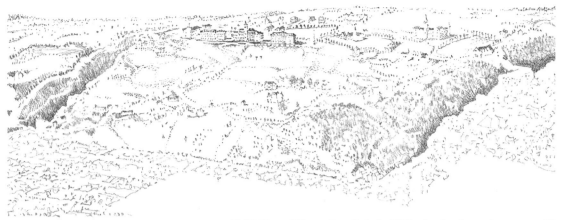

17.62 **View of Ithaca, New York, in 1882, showing the early campus of Cornell University**

CAMPUS ARCHITECTURE IN THE UNITED STATES

The Land Grant Act of 1861, signed into law by President Abraham Lincoln, had a major impact on the history of U.S. education. It stipulated that each state was to have its own university, paid for by the sale of government land. No such educational policy had ever been attempted before, and no one could have foreseen its consequences in shaping advanced education in the United States. Despite differences from state to state, the early schools (known as land-grant schools) shared certain basic goals, including the promotion of practical education, the right of education for all social classes, and the freedom of students to choose their course of study. By the 1870s almost every state had one such university. Among the earliest were Cornell University in Ithaca, New York, and the University of California, Berkeley. By the turn of the century, dozens of private universities had also been built, and because of the rapid professionalization of the sciences in the 1880s, a new generation of technical institutions emerged. The Massachusetts Institute of Technology (MIT), founded in 1863, was among the first, but soon there were also the Illinois Institute of Technology (1890); the Carnegie Technical Institute (1900), which later became Carnegie Mellon University; and the California Polytechnic State University (1901). The net result of this combination of public, private, and technical universities was a university system unique in the world.

In terms of architecture, many U.S. universities looked to English precedents, such as Cambridge and Oxford, but toward the end of the 19th century, the upper classes began to see higher education in a broader context as a maturing experience. This led to the design of campuses with sports facilities, dormitories, and a parklike atmosphere such as the rural environs Jefferson specifically chose for the University of Virginia.

Universities built in this period by the top firms in the country are still today some of the most impressive accomplishments of that era. Designs came in three basic styles: Georgian, neo-Gothic, and Neoclassical. The Georgian style, leaning on the tradition of Harvard University, had individual buildings, usually raised in brick, arranged around a quad or "green," as at Cornell University. Differing from that was the neo-Gothic style that offered an integration of life, study, and sports; examples can be found at Princeton University in New Jersey and at the University of Chicago, where there was no central quad but a loose arrangement of buildings in the landscape. The Neoclassical was also frequently used—as for example at Columbia University in New York City, with its centerpiece, Low Memorial Library, designed by McKim, Mead & White (1903); the University of Michigan (1904–36) by Albert Kahn; and MIT (1913–16), designed by William Bosworth, with buildings arranged around a central axis, and a domed library modeled on the Pantheon at the symbolic head of the composition.

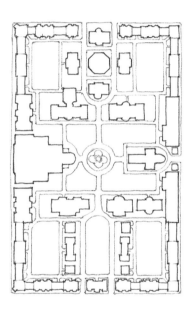

17.63 **Early plan for the University of Chicago campus**

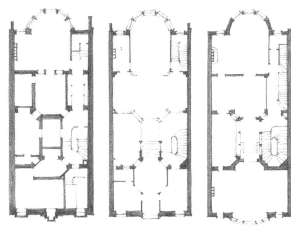

17.64 Floor plans: Maison Tassel, Brussels

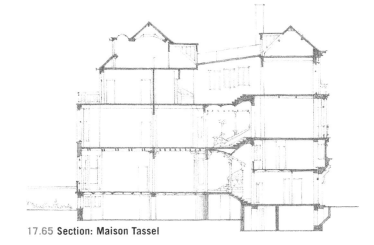

17.65 Section: Maison Tassel

ART NOUVEAU'S MAISON TASSEL

Though Westerners had purchased Chinese and Japanese tea sets, plates, and bowls for well over a hundred years and had tried to imitate certain Chinese building types like the garden pavilion, Art Nouveau artists were stimulated by Japanese art, with its sinuous ornamental patterns. Indeed, the movement is named after d'Art Nouveau, the shop of Siegfried Bing, a Parisian importer of Japanese art and himself the owner of one of the important private collections of japonaiserie. In London, James Whistler was a brilliant promoter and adaptor of the Japanese style. He and others admired, in particular, the work of Kitagawa Utamaro, whose woodcuts were known for their curving lines, asymmetrical distribution of masses, and boldness of composition. Furthermore, the idea of coordinating a painting, its frame, its artistic effect on the room, and even the shape and proportion of the whole room, already put forward by William Morris, was reinforced by the perceived coordinated unity of Japanese architecture. For Art Nouveau, exclusive purity of style was not important. Japanese themes could be fused with Greek, Celtic, and—after Knossos had been excavated in 1900—Minoan motifs.

Though Art Nouveau expressed itself in the surface, it was far from superficial. In its rejection of depth and perspective and its insistence on flatness, it foreshadowed future dialogues on the validity of the representation of illusionary depth. Nature was no longer a remote system of regulating realities, as it was for the Enlightenment, but a sensuous play of living forms. Biological forms were eagerly embraced. Ornamentation was no longer a sin but the means by which one could reach behind the static world of appearances. A door handle by Victor Horta (1861–1947) loops in and around itself like a piece of soft candy, one strand of which springs out into space to almost accidentally form a handle.

Art Nouveau had parallels with the Arts and Crafts movement in England, but there were important differences. Whereas the Arts and Crafts movement aimed to heal the alienation that had arisen between man and his products as a consequence of industrialization, Art Nouveau stressed creativity. While the products promoted by Arts and Crafts were by no means inexpensive, the movement carried with it spiritual and therapeutic connotations and a back-to-the-land naturalness that was ostensibly accessible to all; Art Nouveau appealed mainly to the wealthy.

Victor Horta, active in Belgium, was probably the greatest of the Art Nouveau architects. In Maison Tassel (1893), Horta brought out the expressive quality of iron, which he used both inside and outside of the house in the form of ribbons that appear weightless, spiraling and twisting into space. Since the floors were supported for the most part by iron columns, rooms could open into one another and be distributed in a novel manner. Horta rejected the standard Brussels building type, with the staircase to one side of the building. Instead, the staircase, combined with a lightwell, is placed at the center. This allowed him to vary the elevations of the floors in the front and back, with four floors in the front along the street and three in the back, and the main rooms oriented in the center. Interpenetrating space, as well as the use of mirrors to enhance the feeling of space, make the interior seem a world unto itself—a sanctuary from outside life.

17.66 Maison Tassel

RISE OF PROFESSIONALISM

Medicine and law were among the first fields to be professionalized, starting around 1860. Architecture lagged behind, long considered to be more of a gentleman's occupation. By the middle of the 19th century, the professionalization of the field was gradually winning converts, especially since the Beaux-Arts system was so successful. In England, The Royal Institute of British Architects (RIBA) was founded in 1834, and with it came increased attention on the education of the architect, with the RIBA sponsoring lectures and publications on a variety of subjects. Professionalism discouraged ad hoc, on-the-spot solutions in favor of precise architectural drawings. This is clearly demonstrated in the case of William Butterfield (1814–1900), who is often associated with the aesthetics of John Ruskin. The first church he built required only nine drawings; but for the chancel of St. Mark's Dundela in Belfast (completed 1891), the contract was accompanied by about forty drawings, including working details and fittings down to the boot scrapers. The new prerequisite for explicitness such as detailed specifications and drawings had its effect on the contractual relationship between client, architect, and craftsmen. By the middle of the 20th century, a building of any magnitude would require perhaps one thousand drawings, accompanied by a detailed book of specifications.

In the United States, the American Institute of Architects (AIA) had already been formed in 1836. But, interrupted by the Civil War and handicapped by the very immensity of the far-flung continent and the commensurate communications difficulties, architectural professionalism did not really blossom until after the World's Columbian Exposition of 1893 (also known as the Chicago World's Fair). The exposition buildings, designed on a monumental scale and integrated into a master plan, served to demonstrate what professional architects could accomplish. These architects included AIA leaders Daniel Burnham, Richard M. Hunt, Henry van Brunt, and Charles F. McKim.

17.67 View of an architect's office

The Tarsney Act passed by Congress that year established the requirement for limited competitions for federal commissions, with institute members advising the treasury secretary, the federal official responsible for governmental building appropriations. Though the Tarsney Act was never fully implemented, the status of the professional—as opposed to an architect working as an employee of the government—was increasingly secure. By 1895, the AIA had more than seven hundred members. In the first decade of the 20th century, Daniel Burnham's architectural firm was the world's largest and had become, as discussed by the historian Mary Woods, the model for countless later firms that utilized global business techniques. This new professional class had little patience with the mid-century battle between classical and medieval revival styles. That does not mean that Hunt, for example, who was schooled at the École des Beaux-Arts in Paris and who was a major advocate of architecture as a profession, was indifferent to style; rather, he had left the sectarian debates for a more fluid and individualist appropriation of the architectural vocabulary of the time.

INTERNATIONAL CITY BEAUTIFUL PLANS

The exceptional success of the Crystal Palace exposition in London of 1851, attended by an estimated 6 million visitors, triggered a series of imitation events around the world designed to showcase their global reach. The Exposition Universelle of 1867 and 1878 in Paris boasted 15 million and 16 million visitors, respectively, while the Centennial Exhibition in Philadelphia in 1876 had 10 million. Finally, at Paris's 1889 Exposition Universelle, the Eiffel Tower reported 32 million visitors—and in response, the United States launched the Columbian Exposition of 1893 in Chicago, ostensibly to celebrate the four hundredth anniversary of Christopher Columbus's arrival in America.

Designed by Daniel Burnham, the Columbian expo ushered in the golden era of Beaux-Arts design and planning in the United States, with carefully detailed Neoclassical buildings orchestrated along long and dramatic axial lines, all designed to generate a spectacular sense of the civic.

Inspired by the exhibition, city fathers around the country began to draw up plans following some of its principles in a movement that came to be known as City Beautiful. These cities included Cleveland, San Francisco, Chicago, Detroit, Baltimore, and St. Louis. Although few plans were

17.68 Boston Public Library

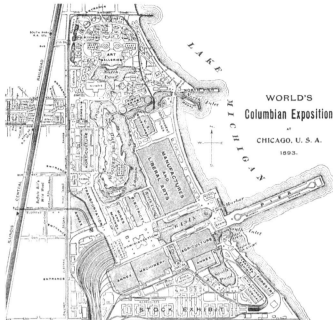

17.69 Plan of World's Columbian Exposition, Chicago

actually implemented in their totality, those that were completed were very influential. In 1900, Congress formed a special committee to redesign Washington, DC. Committee members included Daniel Burnham, Frederick Law Olmsted Jr., and Charles F. McKim of McKim, Mead & White. Their plan created the National Mall as we know it now, with the Lincoln and Grant Memorials, along with Union Station, which was designed by Daniel Burnham. The plan also cleared slums and established a new citywide park.

Pennsylvania Station in New York City (1904–10) featured a block-long Doric columnar screen, a drive-in unloading street, a central waiting room modeled on Diocletian's baths in Rome, and a steel-and-glass hall and circulation platform leading down to the various levels. The building was designed by McKim, Mead & White, one of the leading champions of the Beaux-Arts. Another example of their work is the Boston Public Library (1895), which faces Richardson's Trinity Church across Copley Square. Drawing on Henri Labrouste's Bibliothèque St.-Geneviève in Paris, its arcade, set up on a high base, has the names of famous authors etched into the spandrels. With its use of exquisite marbles and mosaics, it was one of the finest U.S. public buildings at that time. Its monumental entrance leads up to the main barrel-vaulted

reading room, which spans the entire length of the building, and its central courtyard is surrounded by an arcaded gallery in the manner of a Renaissance cloister. The library also features thin tile vaults by the Catalan master builder Rafael Guastavino.

In 1898, the Philippines was acquired by the United States following its victory over the Spanish forces in the Pacific. This gave Daniel Burnham an opportunity to internationalize his urban vision in the form of plans he made for Manila and Baguio, though these were also not fully implemented. Nonetheless, Burnham acquired a formidable reputation in the Philippines and around the world.

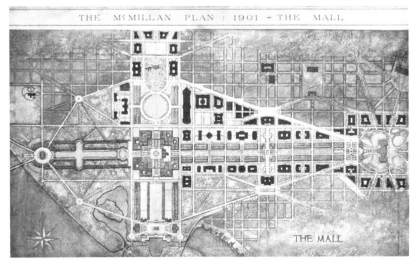

17.70 Plan of Washington, DC

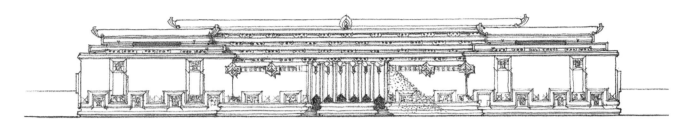

17.71 Lucknow University Library, India

Walter Burley Griffin

Newly united in 1901, Australians, under Prime Minister Edmund Barton, were looking for a style suitable to express their national aspirations. Some attempts at transforming an Arts and Crafts– and Art Nouveau–derived interpretation of Australian flora and a Richardsonian-derived idea of civic buildings (such as Edward Raht's Equitable Life Assurance Society Building in Sydney, 1895) were finally rejected in favor of a more progressive modernism, as can be seen in the design of Canberra, Australia's new national capital. The winning entry of the 1912 competition was by a young, little-known architect from Chicago, Walter Burley Griffin. Strongly influenced by Frank Lloyd Wright's houses and Daniel Burnham's master plans, Griffin called himself a landscape architect to emphasize what he claimed was the organic derivation of his design. His proposal also drew on the City Beautiful Movement insofar as it featured a picturesque ordering of the landscape with intersecting axial geometries. He proposed to use the irregular basin from the site to create a series of interconnected water tanks and even a lake, showcasing the main government center and capital. The rest of the city was spread out axially, with star-shaped intersections forming the highly visible civic centers and nodes of residential suburbs.

Although Canberra was not developed until after World War II, Griffin created a

successful practice in Australia, designing several houses and institutional buildings. His architecture was derived largely from Wrightian sources, particularly the latter's California houses. Griffin's Creswick Residence in Castlecrag (1926), his ten-story office building in Melbourne, and the Keith Arcade (1927), also drew on the decorative motifs of local flora.

In 1935, Griffin took an opportunity to design a library in India and left Australia. His last set of buildings, therefore, are in Lucknow, India, where he unexpectedly died in 1937. As in Australia, Griffin tried to invent a new architectural vocabulary—this time suitable for modern India. He did not try to copy Wright so much as to translate Wright into a new national style and an alternative to both the Beaux-Arts and European modernism.

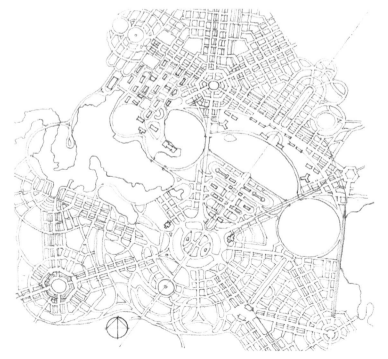

17.72 Walter Burley Griffin's plan for Canberra, Australia

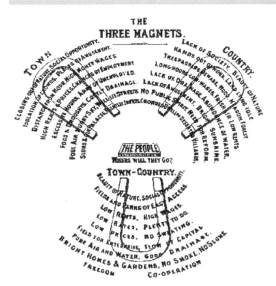

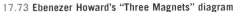

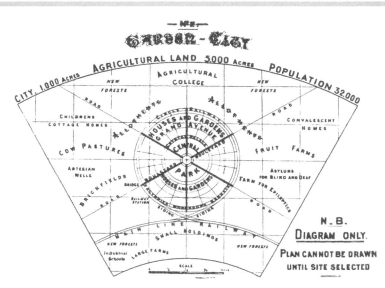

17.73 Ebenezer Howard's "Three Magnets" diagram

17.74 Ebenezer Howard's diagram of the garden city concept

THE GARDEN CITY MOVEMENT

By the late 19th century, the great new industrial Victorian cities of the world like New York had, despite their significant financial success and clout, become overcrowded, dirty, and violent. Many in the middle and upper classes preferred to turn their backs on the city for the comfort and security of the suburbs, with their socially and economically stratified neighborhoods. The results shaped the debate about the nature of a city. On one hand, there was the uncomfortable density of life, the cagey interaction between the classes, and the persistence of poverty and grime; but side by side with these negatives were the benefits of urbanity: the centers of learning, the theaters, the libraries, and the concert halls. For every theory that decried the city as an uncontrollable behemoth, there were those who were deplored the blandness and false security of the suburbs.

It was in an attempt to solve this controversy that Ebenezer Howard wrote his book *Tomorrow: A Peaceful Path to Real Reform* (1892), republished as *Garden Cities of To-morrow* (1902). The city suggested therein was to have the virtues of both the city and the suburbs, but in a highly controlled way that controlled or abolished the contested extremes and made for pleasant surroundings. Howard's garden city was not a suburb but a type of mini-city with a core and a perimeter. It was not meant to be fully dependent on a nearby great metropolis as a suburb would be, but it was

no mere village either. The size was set at a comfortable 6,000 acres, which were not owned by individual citizens but held in a trust. The town was to consume only 1,000 acres at the center, where there would be a park with public buildings, surrounded by shops. Running all around this central park would be a wide glass arcade or "crystal palace" where purchases could be made. The population of the town was to be kept at 30,000. Factories, warehouses, and the like, fronting on a circular railway, were on the outer ring of the town, and beyond that were the farms. Since there was no land ownership, the town was run as a corporation. The rents would provide income for the company, which would then be invested back into the community.

Howard's vision did not arise in a vacuum. There had been already several attempts to create somewhat similar towns, but most of these were factory towns built by factory owners who wanted to convenient access to the workforce. The societal benefit in such a solution was the creation of a stable working class. The "company stores" often associated with such schemes were run by the factory owners. Port Sunlight (1888), for example, not far from Liverpool, was founded by the owners of a soap manufacturing business; in addition to factory-owned stores and businesses, the town had schools, churches, and training centers.

Letchworth (1903) north of London, was the first garden city to be actually built on

Howard's model. Though it did not develop altogether as planned, it was not a failure, as many had predicted it would be; it attracted factories like the Spirella Company (1912), which manufactured corsets. Ultimately, the Garden City movement produced more than thirty communities in England. Howard's book also shaped the development in England of the so-called New Towns built after World War I. Canberra, the Australian capital, was also influenced by Howard's design concepts.

17.75 Plan of Letchworth, England

17.76 Municipal Theater, Rio de Janeiro

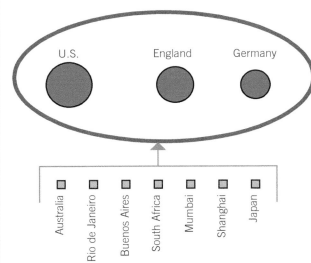

17.77 Global trade diagram, ca. 1900

INTERNATIONAL BEAUX-ARTS

Between 1870 and 1910 the global economic situation changed considerably. England was at such heights that its slide was not immediately noticeable, but by 1900, England had to share its economic power with the United States and, increasingly, with the economic might of Germany. The rise of Germany was not accidental. Its educational system was first rate: by the end of the century, Germany possessed a literacy rate of 99.9 percent, an educational level that provided Germany with engineers, chemists, opticians, skilled workers for its factories, skilled managers, knowledgeable farmers, and skilled military personnel. In comparison, literacy in Britain, France, Norway, Sweden, and Australia was 30 to 50 percent. France was certainly the world's cultural leader, but by 1880 it produced only 7.8 percent of world manufacturing output, and by 1900 this had dropped to 6.8 percent; that year, Italy had only a 2.5 percent share of the global market. Meanwhile, Germany's output had risen to 13.2 percent due to its greatly expanded heavy industry; this, ominously, gave it military capabilities that in time led to World War I.

The most important rising economy of the time, however, was that of the United States, which grew considerably beginning in the last decade of the 19th century. Following the Civil War, the United States had already begun to industrialize on a massive scale. Raw materials were plentiful. Coal was

found in abundance in the Appalachian Mountains. Large iron mines opened in the Lake Superior region of the upper Midwest. Steel mills thrived in places where these two important raw materials occurred together or in proximity. Large copper and silver mines opened, followed by lead mines and cement factories. The largest salt reserves in the world were found in New York and Pennsylvania. Mass-production methods developed at a fast pace.

American-engineered tall buildings, complete with Beaux-Arts cladding, went up from Buenos Aires to Shanghai. U.S.-designed bridges were soon appearing in New Zealand, Taiwan, Manchuria, Japan, Mexico, and South America; and by 1910, skyscraper components produced in the United States were shipped to East Asia, South Africa, and Central America. Milken Brothers, a leading U.S. steel firm, established branch offices in London, Mexico, Havana, Cape Town, and Sydney, erecting office buildings, mills, and factories with steel framing.

With the global economy centered on England and the United States, formerly peripheral countries underwent an economic upturn of their own, as materials and products could now be advantageously exported. This modernization at the global periphery, however, went hand in hand with the increasing disempowerment of the underclasses. In South America, the new upper class may have had factories

built with American steel, but on matters of the material culture, they more often than not flaunted the latest of French fashions; French urban design was also imported as a visible substantiation of their policies. One of the consequences was that Beaux-Arts eclecticism, with its associations with the professional class, developed into an international movement. There were few major metropolises that were not touched by this phenomenon.

These global realities left their most dramatic imprint in Argentina and Brazil, with most of its exports of beef, wool, and wheat supported by heavy investments from England. Rio de Janeiro, during its Republican phase from the 1880s to 1910s, was significantly rebuilt under its mayor, Pereira Passos, who came to be regarded as the "Haussmann of the Tropics," relying on architects such as Ricardo Severo (1869–1940), who was greatly influenced by Beaux-Arts academicism. The Municipal Theater (1905) by the Brazilian architect Oliveira Passos was designed to be reminiscent of the Paris Opera.

The building of these structures coincided with the development of pubic hygiene and the introduction of electrical and gas services. As in Egypt, where debate still rages today as to the Egyptian authenticity of the neo-Mamluk style, in Rio de Janeiro, a camp developed in 1910 that argued that Brazil's true national style was the early 19th-century Portuguese colonial architecture

17.78 Presidential Palace, Havana

SKYSCRAPERS

If there is one building type that represents the confluence of new materials, new strategies of construction, and new attitudes to capital and representation in the early 20th century, particularly in the United States, it is the skyscraper. It did not appear suddenly, for it took considerable time for its function, production, design, and even its purpose to be synthesized. The most significant contributing factor was the improved quality of steel, which allowed prefabricated elements to be brought to the construction site and erected with relative rapidity. The technology of steel framing was well established by 1890; in fact, during construction, many buildings of that time would look as modern as buildings of today.

Questions about how to design the steel frame were, however, the least problematic part of the building. Elevators needed to be improved and their operation guaranteed. The same was true of the plumbing, electrical, and heating systems and the integration of all these systems with each other. At the 1900 Paris Exposition, the designers of the U.S. exhibition chose to emphasize just this, using as an example the recently erected eighteen-story Broadway Chambers Building in New York City. The exhibition presented a 4-meter-high model of the building with an exterior skin in plaster that could be removed to show the underlying steel frame, complete with mechanical systems, boilers, pipes, and furnaces. It was an eye-opening lesson in an emerging architectural ideal.

From a financial standpoint, the idea was relatively straightforward. An investor, typically a bank, insurance agency, or newspaper, would finance the building and use it as home office, occupying the lower, walk-in floor while renting out the rest to business tenants. Besides having a stately home office, the owner would have made a good investment in a booming rental market hungry for representative office space. The owner company's logo would be affixed to the top of the building and beam forth its message.

because those structures were built by local craftsmen, whereas the late 19th-century buildings belonged to a more alienated age. Today some ascribe Rio's urban difficulties to the aggressive modernization of the city under Passos. Others praise him for his foresight.

The former Presidential Palace in Havana, Cuba, was designed by the Cuban architect Carlos Maruri and the Belgian architect Paul Belau. It was inaugurated in 1920. Modeled loosely on the Palazzo Madama (1718–21) in Turin, Italy, by Filippo Juvarra, it sports an eclectic addition.

17.79 Modern steel construction, Woolworth Building, New York City

17.80 Woolworth Building

17.81 Reliance Building, Chicago

The Woolworth Building (1911–13) in New York City, designed by Cass Gilbert in a Gothic style, was at the time of its construction the world's tallest building. It was built for Frank W. Woolworth, owner of the famous five-and-dime chain. The whole was sheathed in elaborate terra-cotta tiles with equally elaborate Gothic-inspired detailing. The interior lobby had mosaic-covered vaults.

This commercialization of styles resulted in an increased need to outdo the competitor. Many early designers assumed that a classical or Gothic front was still the appropriate response, but in Chicago, which in the 1890s had more tall buildings than any other city in the world, a group of designers were beginning to challenge that notion. Among the most innovative was the firm of Daniel Burnham & Company, which designed the fifteen-story steel-and-glass Reliance Building in 1894, with the principal design credits going to John Root and Charles B. Atwood.

Instead of the heavy cornice that is seen in buildings like Dankmar Adler and Louis Sullivan's Wainwright Building in St. Louis, Missouri (1890), the Reliance Building is topped with a thin square lid, and the top floor, which houses machinery for heating and other utilities, converts into a type of frieze. Bay windows reach out into space, giving the building an inner dynamic. The insistent verticality of the Wainwright Building has been replaced by a layered look; but instead of appearing heavy, one floor almost seems to float over the next, assisted in this effect by the building's spandrels, which are lined with delicately ornamented white terra-cotta tiles that give it an ethereal presence.

Wrigley Building

The Reliance Building was more the exception than the rule. A look of modernity in tall buildings was not insisted upon and, in fact, went counter to the idea that these buildings were meant to advertise old wealth and culture. For that very reason, most tall buildings after the World's Columbian Exposition were clad in historical styles. A typical example is the headquarters building of AT&T, the largest and most innovative

corporation in the United States, in New York (1912). It was designed by the Beaux-Arts–trained architect William Welles Bosworth, an American who had also studied at MIT, one of the first institutions in the United States to model itself on the Beaux-Arts system of education. Corporate representation at the turn of the century was a form of modernity in its own right. In that sense, the skyscraper was similar to the train stations of the 1860s, and much like the train stations of the period, skyscrapers competed against each other in size and lavishness.

It is often argued that Beaux-Arts modernism survived so long in the United States because of the hold that the system had on academe—but that is not the only reason. Beaux-Arts modernism had become the language par excellence of corporations eager to promote themselves. Historical awareness and reference to great architectural accomplishments of the past were an integral part of this ambition. That was the reason Bosworth chose to model his columns in the lobby of the AT&T building on those of the Parthenon and also why, at

17.82 Wrigley Building, Chicago

17.83 Casa Batlló, Barcelona

the top of the Wrigley Building (1920–24) in Chicago, which was designed for the well-known manufacturer of chewing gum, the architects placed a reconstruction of the Monument of Lysicrates in Athens (334 BCE). Would Lysicrates turn over in his grave, or smile indulgently? It was not only the monument as a token of Athenian sophistication that was at stake here but also the fact that the French government had just completed its restoration in 1887. The clock tower presented the image that capitalism wanted to make history whole again by brazenly co-opting ancient history as a consumer brand.

CASA BATLLÓ

Antonio Gaudí (1852–1926), despite his obvious talent, was not a particularly good student at the school of architecture at Barcelona. The Beaux-Arts academic styles and rationalization of construction did not appeal to him; he preferred history and economy. After a period in which he apprenticed with various local architects, he set out on his own. One of the characteristics of his work was his use of color. His architecture, more than any produced in the 20th century, must be experienced in person in order to be fully understood. Le Corbusier and Frank Lloyd Wright were consummate colorists, but for Wright, color was a question of patina, and for Le Corbusier, color served spatial articulation. For Gaudí, color was a tactile experience and sprang, as César Martinell has pointed out in his research, from the immediacy of folk sensibilities, Mediterranean mosaic art, and Spain's Islamic past. Gaudí experimented with colored stone and glass, polychrome glazes, and broken tiles and plates, and exploited the shadings of stone and brick.

Despite the seemingly impromptu character of his buildings, Gaudí was very much a perfectionist, working out every project in great detail. The facade of Palau Güell (1886–90) was completely redrawn twenty-eight times, and some of its details changed completely. This explains why it took him four years to perfect the columns of the nave of Sagrada Familia (1882–1926). The richness of Gaudí's forms might make his work seem preeminently sculptural, but according to him, his priorities were situation, measure, material—and only then form. Already in his first works, he was creating hyperbolic and trumpet-shaped helical forms, but always in combination with his refined sense of construction. As a young architect, he could imagine structural possibilities that seemed to defy conventional wisdom. One worker once waited hours after a particularly precarious-appearing corbel had been constructed to see if it would fall. It still stands today.

In the late 19th century, Barcelona had become one of the leading Mediterranean ports, specializing in the trade of cotton and metal. The wealth of the local bourgeoisie resulted in commissions such as the one for the Casa Batlló (1904–6) for Josep Batlló, a textile manufacturer, which involved renovating an existing building. Gaudí modified the inner court, introducing a staircase with a tautly undulating outline. The facade shows wavy forms surfaced with ceramics in shades of blue. The enigmatic, mask-like balconies and the stained-glass windows evoke floral, animal, and geological motifs. The roof of glazed brick looks like the scales of a dragon pierced by the tower, which has at its top a head of garlic that morphs into a three-dimensional cross—perhaps an allusion to St. George and the killing of the dragon, a story with much local resonance. At the level of the *piano nobile*, the malleable forms that seem to be made more of mud than of stone are held up by thin, bony colonnettes "deformed" in the middle and ornamented by vines.

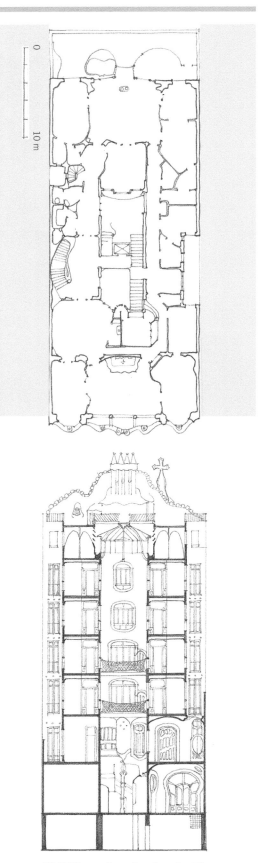

17.84 Roofscape: Casa Batlló

17.85 Plan and section: Casa Batlló

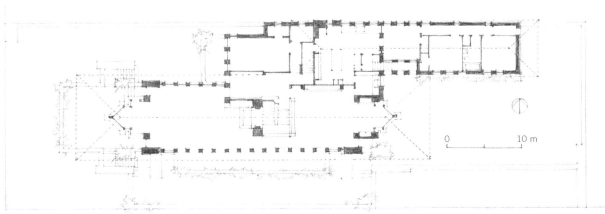

FRANK LLOYD WRIGHT

The long and complex career of Frank Lloyd Wright (1867–1959) can be divided into several phases: from the time he opened his office in 1893 to the Robie House (1908–10); the Taliesin phase (1911–14); the period from the design of the Imperial Hotel to Falling Water (1934) and Taliesin West (1938); and the period from the Johnson Wax Administration Building (1936) to the Marin County Civic Center (1957) and the end of his life in 1959. His production was vast and includes about four hundred houses and a dozen or so other major buildings. By the time Wright designed the Robie House in Chicago, his style had become quite distinct when compared to the Victorian mansions that were then in vogue. Furthermore, unlike other architects who changed style slowly or at the behest of a client, Wright's break with tradition was driven by a personal stylistic development in search for ever greater abstraction. At the Robie House, its Shingle Style origins can still be seen in the service rooms, which are packed into a massive block against which the building rests. The hip roofs have been flattened so that they practically disappear. The fireplace has now become the spatial and visual hub of the building, freed from encroaching walls and linked only to a staircase.

The house is screened against the street and no staircase is visible; it seems almost defensive while, at the same time the design emphasizes the linearity of the street. The bands of white stone parapets form a series of striations that rise to meet the dark-edged roof lines, with the bands of windows recessive in the shadows. The main floor opens onto a balcony that runs along the entire southern exposure. And in good Arts and Crafts fashion, every aspect of the house was designed by Wright himself, from the carpets to the light fixtures.

A comparison of the Robie House with the Steiner House by Adolf Loos yields more similarities than are obvious at first glance. Both give the client an interior environment that is intimate, richly detailed, and crafted down to the last detail. Both are also abstract and mute to the outside world. The principal difference, and one that was to remain a difference between European- and American-style modernism, is their relationship to the outside. The American tradition, whose way had been paved by the Shingle and bungalow styles as well as by the philosophy of Andrew Jackson Downing, was not averse to incorporating porches and platforms into the living space of the building, an idea relatively rare in European domestic design until after World War II.

17.87 **Robie House, Chicago**

Taliesin

After a trip to Italy in 1909, Wright began to build at first a retreat and then a home in Spring Green, in southern Wisconsin, that came to be called Taliesin (1911–14). The name refers to the *Book of Taliesin*, a collection of poems and prophecies attributed to a 6th-century CE Welsh court poet. The building marked a significant departure from Wright's earlier homes, which were constrained by their suburban lots and tended to be designed to move from formal to informal spaces. Taliesin, which sits on top of a broad hill with views in three directions and had ample space to expand, was designed without this polarity. It was a highly personal expression, but it was also infused with what Wright thought was a uniquely American receptivity to the landscape. It was not "on" the hill, he claimed, but "of" the hill, for it was not easy "to tell where pavement and walls left off and ground began," surrounded as it was by low walled-garden courts reached by stone steps. The house reflects Wright's experiences in Italy, where he saw for the first time the great Renaissance and Baroque villas and gardens. It was, therefore, not just a house but a country estate, house, farm, studio, workshop, and family seat all in one.

The house, low and horizontal, with ungabled hip roofs, rhythmically seems to respond to the surrounding hills. The walls are of roughly dressed stone laid in textured horizontal courses, as if partially natural and partially manufactured. The house, with its broad, hooded roofs, gave the occupants a sense of being embedded in the landscape. It was, Wright explained, a "natural house," by which he meant not that it was like a cave or log cabin but that it was "native in spirit." Taliesin's plan organization is a geometric ordering of the landscape, with each part joined to the next in a meandering pattern of solids and voids that winds its way down the hill. The principal living block is a rectangle that has been eaten into by voids or expanded outward by terraces and rooflines. Subtle shifts of alignments create a dynamic within the house that is enhanced by placing the access points to the rooms in their corners.

In the 1930s, Wright built another home and office for himself in the Arizona desert called Taliesin West. He lived and taught there from 1937 until his death in 1959.

17.88 Taliesin East, Spring Green, Wisconsin

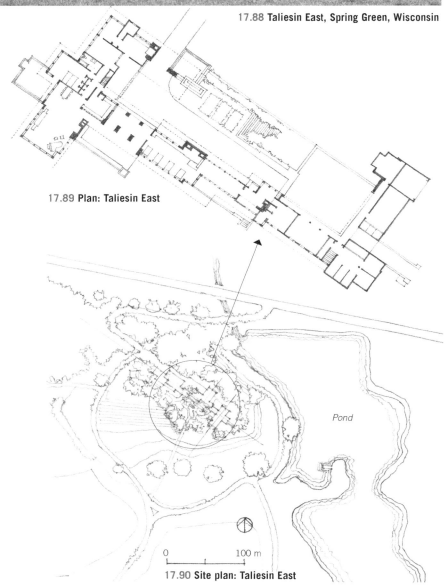

17.89 Plan: Taliesin East

Pond

0   100 m

17.90 Site plan: Taliesin East

17.91 Union Buildings, Pretoria, South Africa

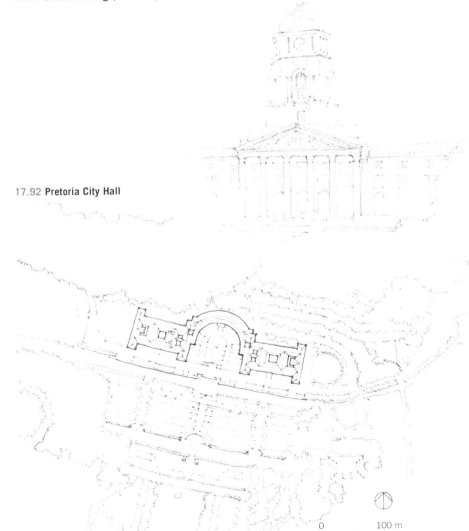

17.92 Pretoria City Hall

0   100 m

17.93 Site plan: Pretoria City Hall

AFRICAN LAND GRAB

Between 1870 and 1900, European powers rushed to colonize Africa, and by the early 20th century, much of Africa, except Ethiopia and Liberia, had been colonized. Since slavery was by then illegal, it was the hunt for sources of raw materials and expanding industrial markets that spurred this scramble. Besides Britain and France, Germany, Belgium, and Italy—countries that had hitherto been denied a piece of the colonial pie—rushed to stake a claim. The competition was so intense that fears of rampant inter-imperialist conflicts led to the infamous diplomatic summit of European powers known as the Berlin West Africa Conference (November 1884–February 1885). Designed to regulate the colonial carving up of Africa, the Berlin Treaty drawn up at this conference was made without any African participation.

The discovery of gold in South Africa in 1876, at a time when gold prices had risen, was a boon for that country's colonial Dutch population, but it also attracted the British, who were eager to control the world gold market. In a bitter conflict, the Second Boer War (1899–1902), the British took possession of Cape Colony, Natal, and Transvaal. In 1910 they officially created the Union of South Africa. The English architect Sir Herbert Baker (1862–1946) designed numerous buildings in the new dominion, including cathedrals, churches, schools, universities, and the Union Buildings in Pretoria (1910–13). The structure, in the English monumental style, was planned as the government center of the South African nation and as a gesture of reconciliation with the Boers after the terrors and disasters of the war. It is convex, with the main program, such as committee chambers, in the middle. The two side wings represented the Boer and the English part of the population; Africans were not represented. (After the first free elections in 1994, it became the residence of the president.) Baker took the lessons he learned in South Africa to New Delhi, where he partnered with Sir Edwin Lutyens in the design of British-ruled India's new capital.

17.94 **Kyoto National Museum, Japan**

17.95 **Hong Kong & Shanghai Banking Corporation Building, Shanghai**

KYOTO NATIONAL MUSEUM

While colonization had already introduced many parts of Asia to Europe and modernization, Japan was the first country to embark on a self-initiated process of modernization and Westernization. This was done under the Meiji Restoration (1868), which reinstated the monarchy following the demise of the last shogunate. Anxious about possible invasion and conscious of the weakness of the shogunate that had aggressively worked to keep the colonists at bay, the Japanese upper class forced the return of power to the emperor and embarked on a course of aggressive industrialization and militarization. Delegations from Japan were sent to European world exhibitions to learn the latest technological developments. Japan particularly cultivated a relationship with Germany under Bismarck. The Japanese also studied the Egyptian modernization program under Isma'il Pasha. Japan invaded China and Taiwan in 1895, then parts of Russia, and then annexed Korea in 1910.

The Kyoto National Museum (1897), built in a French Baroque style, was meant to mark the emergence of Japan onto the world stage. This rapid introduction of Western styles—even though it was made as a way to compete in the rapidly expanding global economy—engendered a backlash from traditionalists. Nationalists denounced Western customs and by World War II had forced the government to return to a more traditional modality, at least in outer appearance, for underneath the call for tradition was a policy that continued the modernization of Japan's military machine.

MYONGDONG CATHEDRAL

As with Japan, Beaux-Arts eclecticism arrived in Korea largely through the opening of its ports in 1876, leading to the building of Myongdong Cathedral (1898) in the Gothic style and the Toksugung Palace (1909) in the Renaissance style. During the 1910 Japanese annexation of Korea, Japan continued this Westernization, using Western styles as a symbol of their own colonial footprint. The Bank of Korea Headquarters (1912) was built in a Renaissance style, and the Seoul Anglican Church (1916) in the Romanesque. Formal education in Western architectural concepts and engineering was first introduced to Korea in 1916.

17.96 **Myongdong Cathedral, Seoul, South Korea**

HONG KONG AND SHANGHAI BANKING CORPORATION BUILDING

Shanghai came into existence in the late Song dynasty as a small town of merchants and fishermen, but with the Treaty of Nanjing in 1842, which followed China's defeat in the Opium War of 1841 by the British forces in Canton, its character changed radically. The Chinese were forced to open their ports—along with other cities—to British, French, American, and other foreign occupants, who brought along with each of the city's expansions new buildings, roads, and management practices. By the 1920s, Shanghai was called the Paris of the East. The earliest buildings erected by Westerners in Shanghai were a hybrid of Western and Chinese motifs, of which the Francisco Xavier Church in Dongjiadu (1853) is one of the few remaining examples. Others, like the Hong Kong and Shanghai Banking Corporation Building (1923), with its broad colonnaded neo-Grecian front, were more properly Western. Built for the second-largest banking house in the world in 1925, the building represents the apex of Shanghai's commercial prosperity. Upon its completion it was advertised as the "most beautiful building from the Suez Canal to the Bering Sea." Divided vertically into three portions in classical proportions of 2:3:1, the base of the first story centers on three arches that carry above it three stories of six colonnades topped by the pediment.

17.97 **United Shoe Machinery Company, Beverly, Massachusetts**

CONCRETE

Portland cement was named after the tiny island of Portland in Dorset, England, where a desirable limestone used in its manufacture was found. But by 1900, U.S. manufacturers were outproducing the English. as well as perfecting new ways to integrate concrete with steel. By the end of the second decade of the 20th century, the demand for cement was staggering, as manufacturers competed with each other for stronger materials.

Initially, concrete was thought to be advantageous over other materials, since it was believed that it did not require skilled labor, and thus not a few early concrete buildings are in the English colonies, such as the Secretariat and Army Headquarters at Shimla, India (1886). To build with a single material with a single technique required fewer specifications and less site supervision. As it turned out, while pouring concrete did not require great skill, the production and quality control of the material itself required highly developed technical competencies. What eventually spurred the broad acceptance of concrete was not its cost (for it turned out to be more expensive than one thought) but its fire resistance. The problem of how to attach the bars to each other was solved in 1884 by Ernest Leslie Ransome, superintendent of the Pacific Stone Company of San Francisco, who patented a special machine that could twist iron bars into the necessary three-dimensional steel armatures. Ransome's design for the United Shoe Machinery Company (1903–6) set the tone for this technique, which allowed for a continuous band of windows from floor to ceiling.

The Kahn System of reinforced concrete developed by Albert Kahn had, by 1907, already been used in 1,500 U.S. buildings, 90 English ones, and dozens of others around the globe. Kahn developed these ideas for new large-scale manufacturing enterprises, such as the Packard Motor Car Company manufacturing plant in Detroit, Michigan; the Dodge Brothers Motor Car Company plant in Hamtramck, Michigan; and the Pierce Arrow plant in Buffalo, New York. He went on to build more than one thousand buildings for Ford Motor Company and hundreds for General Motors. In 1923, he built a fifteen-story building in Detroit for Ford Motor Company, which was at the time the largest manufacturing corporation in the world.

In Spain, the young Antonio Gaudí experimented freely with concrete, producing forms that are still staggeringly fresh today, as in the strange vase- and bottle-shaped skylights of the Casa Mila (1905–10) in Barcelona. By contrast, the more rationalized and orthogonal vision for the use of exposed concrete was pushed by Auguste Perret (1874–1954).

17.98 **Dodge Brothers Motor Car Company, Hamtramck, Michigan**

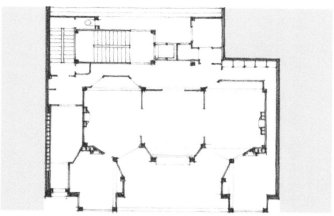

17.99 Plan: 25b, rue Franklin, Paris

17.100 25b, rue Franklin

Not as free and expressionistic a form-maker as Gaudí, Perret argued that the visual expression of concrete's load-bearing identity were just as important as its structural properties. Working in the spirit of Eugène-Emmanuel Viollet-le-Duc, Perret aimed to integrate architecture and civil engineering, rather than exploring its possibilities in ways that others, such as Max Berg and Gaudí, were doing. Perret, as a civil engineer, had a deep distrust of architectural freedoms. When asked to engineer a theater in Paris that was designed by Henry van de Velde, he complained that the building was structurally inconsistent and forced Van de Velde to resign. Van de Velde had originally been a painter, and, in teaching himself to design buildings, he had come to see architecture as creatively autonomous from engineering. It was Le Corbusier, his employee for a while, who, more than anyone else, understood and theorized the need to integrate the innovations of structure with those of living. The tension, however, between the requirements of engineering and those of design, which was here opened up, remains a point of theoretical contention to this day.

Perret's 25b, rue Franklin, in Paris (1902–4), a speculative apartment building in a fashionable quarter of the city, aimed to demonstrate that concrete could be adapted to domestic architecture in an age when most thought it suitable only for factories and warehouses. Due to concerns about its weather-worthiness, the concrete was, however, not visible on the outside.

Smooth, colored bricks covered the concrete elements, while tiles depicting chestnut leaves were applied to the thin brick walls that filled the spaces between the columns. Each floor consisted of a six-room apartment with a bathroom, staircase, and elevator at the rear. The five principal rooms were arranged symmetrically around a central salon. Despite the conventionality of the plan, the design's novelty lay in the allocation of all internal load bearing to slender columns.

17.101 Detail: 25b, rue Franklin

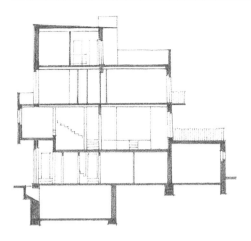

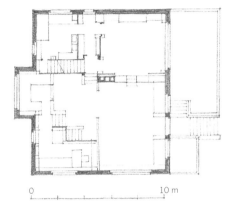

0 _____ 10 m

17.102 Section and plan: Moller House, Vienna

17.103 Moller House, Vienna

17.104 Loos Haus on Michaelerplatz, Vienna

ADOLF LOOS

A stonemason's son, Adolf Loos (1870–1933) was born in rural Moravia, 100 kilometers north of Vienna. When he was nine, his father whom he idolized, died. Loos's relationship with his mother, Maria Hertl, was strained at best, and when he was twenty-three she cut him off from the family, with just enough money for a passage to the United States. In the United States, Loos was enraptured by the Chicago exposition, American industrial infrastructure, and the writings of Louis Sullivan. After returning to Austria, he settled in Vienna, where at first he evinced much enthusiasm for the Secessionists. But then he began to denounce Secessionist art and architecture, along with other modern decorators such as the Deutsche Werkbund, for their moral degeneration. In 1908 Loos wrote a now-famous article entitled "Architecture and Ornament" in which, relying on Jean-Jacques Rousseau's critique of civilization, he railed against the use of ornament as a degenerate form of art not suitable for advanced European cultures. For Loos, ornament was appropriate in tribal societies, where it played an important part in social interaction, but for an advanced civilization, ornament was no longer a relevant form of communication. Loos was not opposed to using the color and texture of natural materials for their ornamental quality, however. His opinions put a damper on his career, but he did secure a number of jobs leading up to the design for a commercial building in Vienna in a style now called the

Wiener Moderne; popularly, the building is called the Loos Haus (1909–10).

By the time Loos designed the Steiner House (1910), even the residual classical motifs of his earlier work were gone, leaving only a pure white exterior. The building certainly anticipates—and indeed was highly influential in—the modernist aesthetic that would become the norm from the 1930s onward, although it differed markedly from later functionalist buildings. Here the stark exterior was meant to contrast with the lush and almost sensual interior. "On the outside, the building must remain dumb and reveal all its richness only on the inside," Loos wrote in 1914.

The Moller House (1927–8) is paradigmatic of Loos's approach. Its facade is simple and rather forbidding, with the entrance, balcony, and windows bound together into a tight compositional unit. Since the windows on the top floor face the rear, the number of windows on the facade is limited. Despite the external symmetry, the interior is labyrinthine. The living and family rooms on the second floor are separated by steps and framed openings to create a range of areas, some more private than others. The interiors of the principal rooms are richly outfitted with light-colored wood veneers on the walls and oriental carpets on the floors, creating a sense of sumptuous elegance. In this respect, though Loos is seen as the harbinger of the modern movement, his work maintained a strong allegiance to the Arts and Crafts ideal of interiority and intimacy.

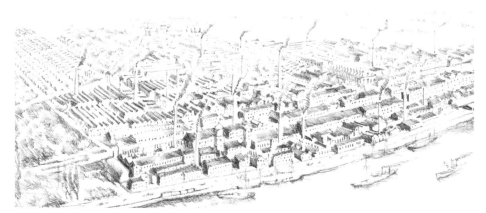

17.105 **View of Ludwigshafen, Germany**

The latter was seen—at least until the advent of modernism—as not really part of the architect's concern. The freedom engineers achieved had resulted in a type of building that was designed around the concepts of function and utility. Decoration was eschewed, but there was a desire to express strength and stability. There was also a contradictory desire for light, and the creation of long steel and glass walls paved the way for what later came to be known as the curtain wall, used extensively in skyscrapers in the 1950s.

THE FACTORY AESTHETIC

By the early 20th century, factory design had changed considerably over the previous century. The introduction of electricity in the 1880s freed the factory floor from the cumbersome system of pipes, gears and belts that had driven the coal and steam powered machines during most of the 19th century. Advances in steel engineering allowed factory buildings to become larger and spaces wider. Glass was used extensively to permit illumination. Skylights were common, sometimes in saw tooth form or as part of a Pratt truss. Flat roofs were also adopted, since it was easy for fire to develop in the old gable roof system, with its complex wood supports. The development of concrete provided a fireproof—although expensive—alternative to buildings that were of brick, stone, or terra-cotta. Standardized building types became widely available in the form of iron- and steel-framed structures.

The late 19th century also saw the emergence of a search for a factory aesthetic once it became clear that the building was—or could be—used for advertising. Some factories had main buildings that were in a type of Gothic or Romanesque—and occasionally classical—style. The Yenidze Tabakfabrik (1907–9) in Dresden, Germany, bloomed forth in an Oriental style, even using simulated minarets and a glazed dome to conform to the branding of its cigarettes. Usually, such buildings were designed without an architect. But even when an architect was involved, there was a noticeable difference between the image of the building that the architect designed and the factory itself, designed by engineers.

17.106 **Yenidze Tabakfrabik, Dresden, Germany**

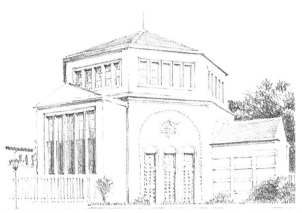

17.107 **AEG Pavilion, German Shipbuilding Exhibition of 1908, Berlin**

17.108 **Tea kettle by Peter Behrens, 1909**

DEUTSCHE WERKBUND

The transformation of Germany from an agricultural society into an industrial one and from a country with limited national and military goals to a world power on par with England occurred at an astonishing pace. Between 1894 and 1904, the value of Germany's foreign trade doubled, and by 1913 Germany overtook Great Britain in percentage of world industrial production—and did all this without a colonial empire. Large companies like Friedrich Krupp Werke (munitions, cannons, steel, and ships), the Allgemeine Elektrikitäts-Gesellschaft, or AEG (turbines, electric railroads, and equipment for the new German navy), and Siemens-Schuckert Werke (railroad and electrical equipment) were supported by the government through lucrative military contracts and protected from international competition by tariffs. Beginning in the mid-1890s and continuing until the outbreak of World War I, urban officials, functioning under the tight control of the imperial government and learning, belatedly, the lessons of England and France, organized special exhibitions to promote and glorify German production.

Though the architecture and architectural quality of these exhibitions varied, they were, for those who noticed, a bold showcase for innovation. German architects were not hampered by the Beaux-Arts system, which was never implemented in Germany. For the Nordwestdeutsche Kunstausstellung in Oldenburg in 1905, Peter Behrens designed a highly abstracted and formal exhibition layout with square structures, their surfaces incised with simple geometrical forms; an octagonal, domed garden pavilion; and a rigorously symmetrical exhibition hall with a central cubical space to which four smaller skylight boxes were attached at the corners. At the German Shipbuilding Exhibition of 1908, Behrens built an octagonal, baptistery-like structure for the AEG. The high altar was actually a ship's deck on which stood a great searchlight, the most advanced of its kind in the world and the pride and joy of the German navy. At a 1910 exhibition of concrete manufacturers, visitors saw Behrens's all-concrete pavilion for Zementwahrenfabrikanten Deutschlands (German Concrete Manufacturing Association).

At the 1914 Werkbund Exhibition in Cologne, the dramatic Glass House by Bruno Taut, who had a quasi-mystical fascination with glass, was on display. It consisted of two spaces: a type of crypt below, set within a cylindrical concrete plinth, and a domed space above. The crypt contained a pool at its center, with water cascading down small terraces decorated with pale yellow glass. Access to the dome above was by means of curving stairs at the top of the plinth, on which rested a fourteen-sided structure of concrete beams. On top of that structure, Taut set the prismatic dome with a double skin of glass—an outer protective layer of reflective glass, and an inner layer of colored glass—as if in a three-dimensional explosion of light, color, and geometry. Apart from the structure itself, all its surfaces were made of glass, in keeping with the pavilion's purpose as an advertisement for the glass industry. Walls were made of shiny glass tiles, transparent glass bricks, and translucent colored glass. Even the steps were made of glass.

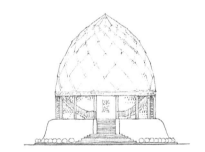

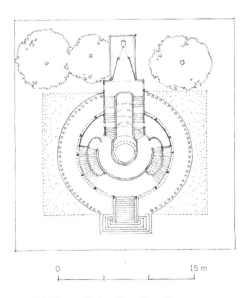

17.109 **Plan and elevation: Glass House, Werkbund Exhibition, Cologne, Germany**

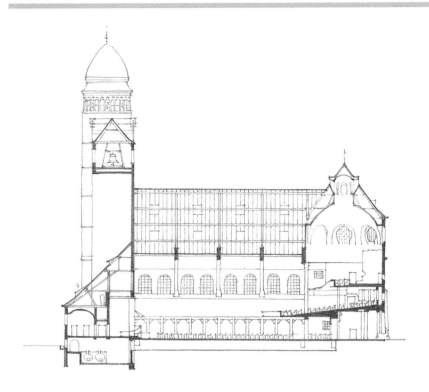

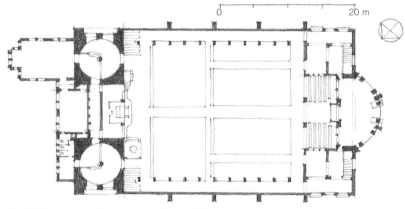

17.110 Plan and section: Garnisonskirche, Ulm, Germany

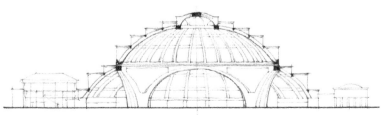

17.111 Section: Breslau Jahrhunderthalle, Breslau, Germany

GERMAN CONCRETE

Even though Ford's factories brought to the fore the radical modernity of reinforced concrete from the point of view of civil engineering, the architectural question still remained open. While the expressive potential in concrete's ability to take any form languished in England—suffering in part under Ruskinian proscriptions—it flourished in France and Germany. If the French contribution consisted of attempting to integrate concrete into the conventions of architectural practices, the Germans contributed toward its engineering. One of the earliest uses of concrete in a major public building in Germany was the Garnisonskirche in Ulm (1906–8), a Protestant church that, as its name implies, was made for and by a military base. It was designed by Theodor Fischer (1862–1938), a prolific architect and noted educator, and one of the founders of the Deutsche Werkbund. He argued for a contextual modernity, and his work therefore seems more neo-medieval than modern today. Nonetheless, the building is a landmark in the history of modern architecture. The body of the church consisted of a reinforced-concrete skeleton with brick infill. The towers are huge empty silos 55 meters high, with a bell chamber suspended between them.

A second important building was the Breslau Jahrhunderthalle (1913), which showed off the virtuosity and elegance of concrete. Part of a campaign by the city to define itself as the "Metropolis of the East," it was designed by Max Berg, Frankfurt am Main's building department director, to serve as both an exhibition hall and assembly hall. The Jahrhunderthalle (literally "Centennial Hall") was an enormous building, with an enclosed floor space of over 5,600 square meters that could hold ten thousand people. Due to the fires that had broken out at a building of the 1910 world's fair in Brussels, the builders decided to use concrete—the first attempt ever to use the material for a building on that scale. The structure consisted of four large curved arches that formed a continuous ring on which rested the dome. To provide a more secure environment against weather, the glazing was not laid in the interstices of the ribs. Instead, Berg designed a system of stepped glazing applied to the outside of the dome in the form of vertical windows and horizontal roofs. From the inside, the small horizontal roof planes disappear in the light that streams through the vertical apertures of glass.

EXPRESSIONISM

Architecture before and after World War I was surprisingly imaginative and experimental. Expressionism, as it soon came to be known, had begun to develop before World War I in the work of Bruno Taut and a few others. Particularly influential were the writings of Paul Scheerbart, who in 1914 published *Glass Architecture*, a book describing a utopian architecture of colored glass in combination with sparkling jewels and enamel. The Expressionists, despite their differences, all envisioned an architecture as far removed from classicism as could be imagined at that time. The old notion that architecture reembodied the power of the past gave way to a desire to create an architecture that spoke to the immediacy of perception and the psychology of the beholder. As one commentator, Heinrich de Fries, explained, "Buildings are in the highest degree alive…. We can only guess at the extent to which the art of spatial articulation will one day transcend the art of pictorial creation." Expressionism rejected the duality of interior and exterior, and of building and landscape. It also opened architecture to influences from the other arts—in opposition to the Arts and Crafts movement, which had hoped to integrate the artistic conception within the framework of craftmaking.

The movement was particularly strong in Prague between 1910 and 1914. In the 1880s, Czech artists, dissatisfied with the poor standards of the Prague Academy of Painting, departed en masse for Munich, a leading center for the German Arts and Crafts movement. Many others went to Paris, where they encountered the work of Auguste Rodin, whom many Czechs admired for the spontaneity and expressiveness of his work. Other sources of inspiration were found in French Cubism, which began to be exhibited in 1908. But despite the pictorial innovations of Pablo Picasso and Georges Braque, the possibility of a Cubist architecture was not pursued in France until the arrival of Le Corbusier in the 1920s—and certainly not in Germany, where French developments were generally viewed with suspicion. The introduction of Cubism into architecture in Prague was, therefore, path-breaking.

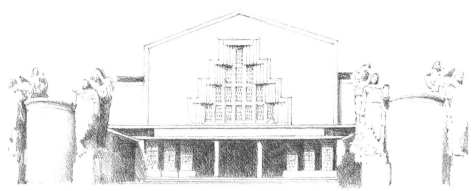

17.112 **Pavilion of Commerce, 1908 Jubilee Exhibition, Prague**

One of the leading architects among the Czech Cubists was Jan Kotera (1871–1923), a professor at the Prague School of Decorative Arts, who actively collaborated with Czech sculptors like Jan Štursa and Stanislav Sucharda on his architectural designs. He saw prismatic shapes as appropriate to the intellectual vitality of the modern age. For him, structure had to give way to the logic of visual dynamics. This was also true for Pavel Janák (1882–1956), whose idiosyncratic interpretation of Cubism led him to shift toward tapered, slanted, and triangular forms. He argued that the orthogonal architecture reflected its dependency on matter and weight, whereas the new Cubist style, with its angles, expressed the active nature of the human spirit and its ability to prevail over matter.

After World War I, with the downfall of the aristocratic regime in Germany, Expressionist architecture found one of its more realistic voices in Hans Poelzig (1869–1936), whose first major commission, the Grosse Schauspielhaus ("Large Performance Hall") in Berlin, had a plaster ceiling, hung from the rafters, that looked like cave stalactites. Thousands of light bulbs, variously colored in shades of yellow, green, and red, were embedded in the vault so that the whole thing resembled both a cave and, when the lights were dimmed, a starry night sky. The foyer was supported by a single column that, like a fusion between a fountain and a plant, spread successive rings of colored petals —also illuminated by recessed colored light bulbs—until it reached the vault above.

17.113 **Pavel Janák's study for a facade**

17.114 Interior: Grosse Schauspielhaus, Berlin

17.115 A drawing for a futurist Città Nuova ("New City") by Antonio Sant'Elia

Another important figure in the Expressionist camp was Hans Bernhard Scharoun (1893–1972), who rejected the crystalline shapes of some of the other Expressionists in favor of soft, rubbery forms. In his design for a stock exchange building (1922), he warped and bent space around the central lobby, giving the appearance of a building that had ingested the various aspects of the program.

In Italy, Expressionism took an even stronger form under the name of Futurism, initially a literary movement created by Filippo Tommaso Marinetti in 1909—it was his manifesto, *Le futurisme*, published in Paris, that coined the name of the movement. Marinetti was a keen follower of the Cubist movement and even took a group of Italian painters to Paris to show them recent work. Soon, however, the Italians developed their own distinctive style, significantly more aggressive in tone in comparison to the quiet utopianism of Scheerbart. The Futurists were particularly enamored of technology, speed, and machinery and expressed this in their painting and poetry. They saw the outbreak of World War I as a positive development for the Italians and hoped it would propel the young country into the modern age. "Art," so Marinetti stated, "can be nothing but violence, cruelty, and injustice." The movement eventually came to include architecture, and in a 1914 manifesto, Umberto Boccioni proclaimed the movement's antipathy to the classical styles.

Boccioni argued instead for an architecture of "dynamic awareness." The leading architect among the group was Antonio Sant'Elia (1888–1916), who built little but who made influential visionary drawings of massive buildings with soaring heights.

In Germany, the Expressionists formed several groups, such as the Arbeitsrat für Kunst ("Worker's Council for Art") and the Novembergruppe ("November Group," named after the 1917 Russian Revolution). In 1918, the November Group, in its first manifesto, called upon Cubists, Futurists, and Expressionists to join together in the regeneration of Germany after its defeat in World War I.

The architect most associated with Expressionism was Eric Mendelsohn (1887–1953), as famous for his drawings as for his buildings. His sketches, many unrelated to any commission, emphasized the building's flowing silhouette. There are no pictorial enhancements, no landscape features—just the building without context, drawn in dark lines on a white sheet of paper. Despite his seemingly impossible and grandiose ambitions for the field of architecture, Mendelsohn was an extremely successful architect, even during the 1920s, and was one of the first professionally successful modernist architects, employing as many as forty people in his office.

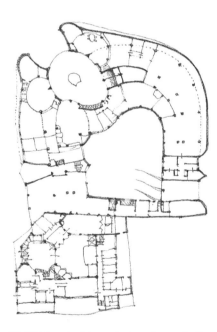

17.116 A project for a stock exchange by Hans Bernhard Scharoun

17.117 **Einstein Tower, Potsdam, Germany**

17.118 **Interior: Einstein Tower**

Mendelsohn was naturally drawn to concrete, but the technology at that time was still rather limited, and even though he first conceived of the Einstein Tower in Potsdam, Germany (1917–21), as a concrete building, it was in actuality a brick structure with a concrete-stucco exterior. The tower, his first major commission, was built for the Astrophysical Institute in Potsdam and is still in use today. The building, surrounded by a forest, was sited in a clearing on a plateau at the edge of a drop-off. (The site is now somewhat altered.)

The form of the building's exterior in some places seems to have been carved out; in other places, it seems to have been molded. In the vicinity of the windows, it seems to be a soft encasement of a mysterious, angular metallic structure within. In the approach to the building, a set of steps leads to an elevated deck that opens to the entrance lobby, with one stair leading down and another leading up the tower. The telescope at the top of the tower transmits light to instruments in the basement laboratory. Between the shaft and the base, to the rear of the building, are study and sleeping quarters for the scientists.

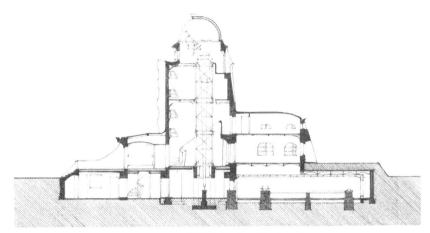

17.119 **Section: Einstein Tower**

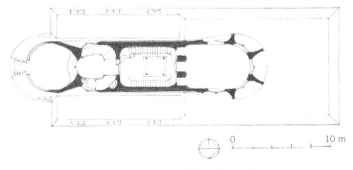

0   10 m

17.120 **Plan: Einstein Tower**

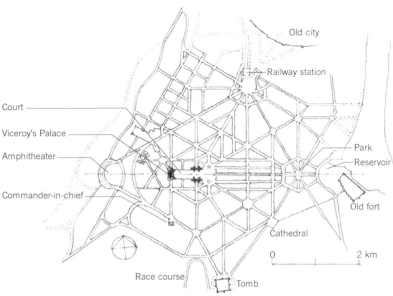

17.121 **Plan of New Delhi, India, by Sir Edwin Lutyens, 1911**

NEW DELHI

In 1911, at a coronation *darbar* ("court") in Delhi, India, George V announced his decision to build a new capital for imperial India, one that could unfalteringly display the English determination to maintain British rule in India in perpetuity. Calcutta had always been the seat of the colonial government, but this was an accident of history. The English chose Delhi to ensure the identification of the new capital with the onetime Mughal seat of power. A debate immediately raged over whether the architecture should acknowledge an indigenous idiom or reflect the conventions of colonial neoclassicism. After intense lobbying by advocates of both sides, Viceroy Lord Charles Hardinge decided that a design that was "plain classic" with a "touch of Orientalism" would be best. His solution was not much different from that of a century earlier, when a classical revival had been advocated based on the eternal principles of classical architecture. With that, the colonial ideologues were back to where they had started—except for the "touch of Orientalism."

New Delhi's master plan and the design of its principal building, the Viceroy's Palace (1921–27), was executed by Sir Edwin Lutyens. The Secretariat buildings were designed by Herbert Baker, who had just completed the Union Buildings in Pretoria to great success. The master plan reflected Beaux-Arts academicism; a series of radial

spokes were elegantly stitched together over 85 square kilometers to create an expansive vision of a capital city. Different classes of bungalows appropriate for various levels of officers were distributed around its expanse. At its center was the grand east-west path, King's Way, with the Viceroy's Palace and Secretariat raised on a hill at its western terminus. The other end of King's Way was marked by a diminutive memorial to the unknown soldier, designed by Lutyens.

17.122 **Viceroy's Palace, New Delhi**

Although they had a personal falling out, Lutyens's and Baker's designs harmonized well. Finished in red and yellow Rajasthan sandstone, both sets of designs stress the horizontal, utilizing the Indian *chajja*, or overhang, to cast long, continuous shadows that contrast sharply with the bright Indian sun. Small *chattris*, campaniles, and domes provide the vertical counterpoints. Baker, ever more the imperialist than Lutyens, did not hesitate to incorporate some elephants and sandstone screens to make his designs more "Oriental" in tone. But the general impression of the entire viceroyal complex displays the restrained and accomplished use of a stripped-down neoclassical vocabulary, arguably some of Lutyens's and Baker's best work. Indeed, the greatest impact is from the distance at the terminus of King's Way (now called Raj Path), where the broad horizontal sweeps off the complex effectively emphasize the three domes and two campaniles.

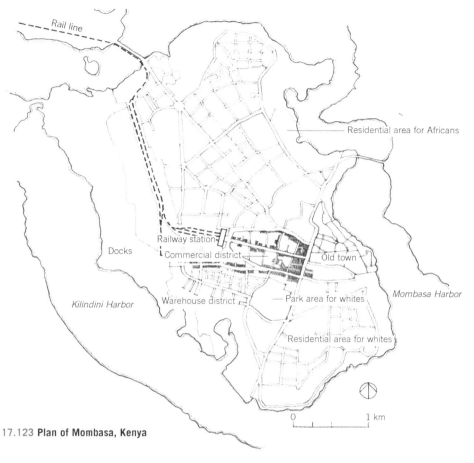

17.123 **Plan of Mombasa, Kenya**

Rail line

Residential area for Africans

Railway station
Docks
Commercial district
Old town
Kilindini Harbor
Warehouse district
Park area for whites
Mombasa Harbor
Residential area for whites

0   1 km

MOMBASA

With the exception of a few countries such as Ethiopia, most of Africa prior to World War I was still under colonial rule, with the occupying powers primarily interested in the extraction of goods. As a result, the principal building projects were train stations, port facilities, and urban layouts that separated whites from blacks. Mombasa is an excellent example. It had long been a busy port with a complex multiethnic character. Its harbor, on the eastern side of the island, had a narrow entrance and afforded good protection. In the 16th century, the Portuguese had hoped to control the city but were never able to assert their domination over the sultan of Mombasa, who reigned over the relatively independent city until the middle of the 19th century, when it became a British protectorate. In 1887, the city's administration was relinquished to the British East Africa Association, which envisioned it as the sea terminal of the Uganda Railway (started in 1896). The aim was to connect the city with Buganda (part of present-day Uganda), a wealthy kingdom on the north shore of Lake Victoria that the colonial powers were eager to exploit for coffee and tea; white settlers also hoped to set up cotton farms.

Construction of the line started at Mombasa and reached Lake Victoria in 1901. Indian traders set up corporations alongside the British, dealing in rice and coffee in particular. In the 1920s, Mombasa became Africa's leading harbor for kerosene and gasoline. Because the old city was compact and not very large, the rest of the island was relatively free for development. The English built a new harbor, Kilindini Harbor, on the island's west side, which could accommodate berths for large ships. In 1926, Walton Jameson, a town planning expert, laid out the new colonial city. Predictably, the train station was at the conceptual apex of the design. A tri-pronged set of streets formed a business center running eastward, connecting to the old town. To the north and south of the business center, the city was divided according to race and class, with separate African and Swahili quarters; the more elite section was to the south, with its oceanfront, and was separated from the business center by a zone of schools, a golf course, parks, and sports areas.

17.124 **Old town, Mombasa**

17.125 **Lister County Courthouse, Sölvesburg, Sweden**

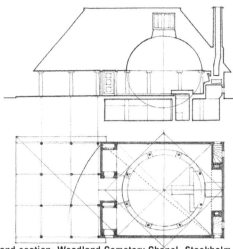

17.126 **Plan and section: Woodland Cemetery Chapel, Stockholm**

ASPLUND AND LEWERENTZ

Sweden had been fortunate to escape the ravages of World War I, and the comparative postwar prosperity left the young Gunnar Asplund (1885–1940) in an excellent position to make a name for himself with his design of the Woodland Cemetery (1918–20) in Stockholm (codesigned with Sigurd Lewerentz) and the Lister County Court House (1917–21) in Sölvesborg, Sweden. The latter building is a simple rectangle with a circular courtroom embedded in the plan to the rear. From 1913 to 1914, Asplund had taken a trip to Rome, Ravenna, and Sicily that brought him into contact with the great architectural works of the past. He was drawn less to the most famous monuments than to simple medieval churches, nestled against other buildings or silhouetted against the open sky. Though he can be considered a modernist, his interest in nonmachine aesthetic monumentality has led many to view him as a classicist, but such distinctions are not clear-cut; Asplund's work is, in fact, a continuation of late 19th-century Romanticism.

Under Asplund, Swedish national Romanticism shed its overt allegiance to the Middle Ages and sought out an abstract formalism, as, for example, in the Stockholm Public Library (1920–28), a building of absolute functional clarity. It is composed of a cylindrical reading room within a U-shaped building, a restatement of Schinkel's Altes Museum in Berlin—which was later restated

again in Le Corbusier's Assembly Building in Chandigarh, India, and in James Stirling's Neue Staatsgalerie museum in Stuttgart, Germany. From the entrance, the visitor is conducted upward by a dramatic but simply designed staircase, framed by an Egyptian-style portal. Within the reading room, above the three open tiers of books, rise the rough surfaces of the cylindrical walls, ending in a row of windows and a flat ceiling. On the exterior, the facade is divided in two, with the base almost as tall as the upper part. Dividing the sections is an Egyptian-style frieze filled with mysterious symbols that refer to learning and the arts.

Asplund and Lewerentz designed the Stockholm Exhibition in 1930, by which time they had both expressly adopted modernism. The exhibition's slogan, "Accept!", was a call to accept modernism in Scandinavian life, including the mass factory production of food.

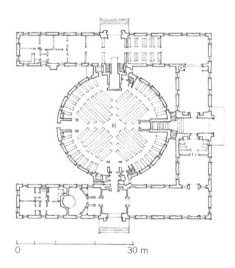

0   30 m

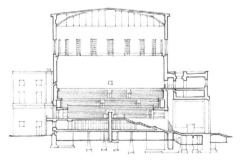

17.127 **Plan and section: Stockholm Public Library**

17.128 Hollyhock House, Los Angeles

17.129 Interior fireplace, Hollyhock House

FRANK LLOYD WRIGHT AND THE MAYAN REVIVAL STYLE

By the early decades of the 20th century, Frank Lloyd Wright's interests in architecture had become more eclectic. He began to design a series of houses in California and received his most important commission to date, the design of the new Imperial Hotel in Tokyo. What distinguishes this work is Wright's attempt to revivify not European but pre-Columbian sources. Wright had had a childhood fascination with pre-Columbian architecture, and it suddenly emerged in this work in what is sometimes called Mayan Revival style, although the references are diverse and not limited to Mayan sources.

Hollyhock House, located in the Hollywood section of Los Angeles and constructed at the peak of excitement over the city's role in the fast-growing motion picture industry, was built for Aline Barnsdall, a wealthy oil heiress and supporter of left-wing causes. The basic diagram of the house is relatively simple, laid out as a U opening to the east, with the garden moving down the slope. At the head of the U is the living room, with the bedroom area to the south and the more public rooms to the north, close to the garage. The whole creates a complex set of closed and open spaces operating on different levels, with some of the roofs accessible as terraces. The house was built of stuccoed hollow tile and wood.

Wright prepared over seven hundred drawings for the Imperial Hotel in Tokyo, a 250-room extravaganza that was lavished with delicate and carefully articulated detailing. Made from poured concrete, concrete block, and carved oya stone, Wright's building was a tour de force in modernist ornamentation and integrated design, quite the counterpoint to the contemporary puritanical injunctions in modernist Europe of the likes of Adolf Loos. It replaced a Meiji-era structure built

for international guests visiting Japan. The hotel is famous for having withstood the great Tokyo earthquake of 1923 on account of its "floating" foundations, although a series of other structural factors, such as the quantity of steel in the overhangs, may also have played a role. The hotel was damaged during World War II, but Wright refused to be involved in its repair and expansion after the war. The building was demolished in the 1960s.

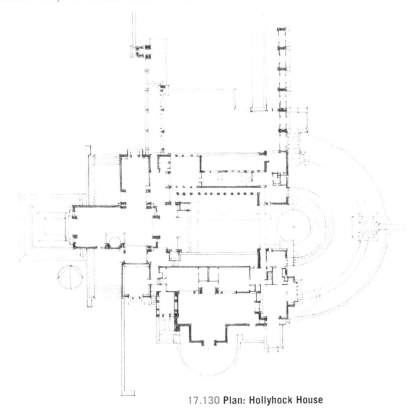

17.130 Plan: Hollyhock House

17.131 Bandung Institute of Technology, Bandung, Indonesia

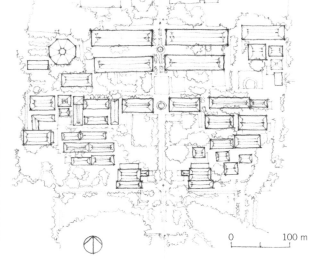

17.132 Site plan: Bandung Institute of Technology

DUTCH KAMPUNG

While the English controlled India and most of the China trade, the Dutch retained their hold on Indonesia, in spite of several English and French attempts to dislodge them. However, late 19th-century wars with the French, the Acehnese, and the Javanese put the Dutch colonial government deeply into debt. In response, the Dutch set production quotas, fixed prices, restricted travel, and raised taxes. These policies were a disaster and led to massive starvation in the midst of bumper crops of export commodities. A disgruntled young Dutch colonial officer, Eduard Douwes Dekker, captured the hardships of these years for the Dutch public in the 1859 novel *Max Havalaar*. The ensuing outrage back in the Netherlands forced the hand of the colonial authorities, and in a series of legislative changes starting in 1870, the so-called Liberal Policy dismantled the forced cultivation of export commodities and opened the colonial economy to Dutch private enterprise. The policy sparked a large migration of Dutch to the East Indies, leading to a forceful spatial assertion of European identity against Indonesian and immigrant Asian societies. Using the Garden City model, the Dutch carved their colonial space out of what they saw as the congestion and filth of neighborhoods in the colonial towns across Java and Sumatra, building Indian-style bungalows set in spacious gardens with outbuildings for kitchens and servants.

In 1901, the Dutch queen, Wilhelmina, announced that the Netherlands would from then on accept an ethical responsibility for the welfare of its Indonesian subjects. This announcement was a sharp contrast with the former doctrine of profit-making. The result, architecturally, was a search for hybrid styles. In fact, the Indies-born but ethnically Dutch architect Henri Maclaine Pont was one of the progenitors of the Indische style, an architecture dedicated to the fusion of Dutch and indigenous approaches. Hendrik Petrus Berlage, the noted Dutch architect, characterized the challenge as one of pulling together the universal qualities of Western modernism with "the local spiritual aesthetic elements of the East," an early interpretation of what later came to be characterized as "critical regionalism."

An exemplar of this approach was Pont's design for the Bandoeng Technische Hoogeschool (Bandung Institute of Technology, 1920). The twenty buildings were laid out crossways to the site's principal axis in a Beaux-Arts manner. The wood trusses of the buildings were left exposed on the interiors of the halls in keeping with the strictures of the Arts and Crafts movement, while the roof form is a free interpretation of the traditional Sumatran *minangkabau* roof system found in many regions of Southeast Asia.

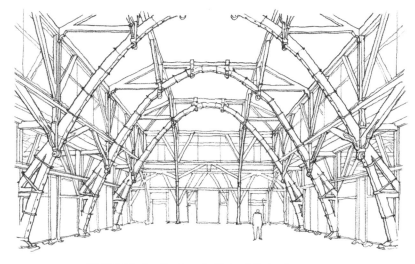

17.133 Interior: Bandung Institute of Technology

17.134 Theo van Doesburg's color design for Amsterdam University Hall, Netherlands

DE STIJL MOVEMENT

After World War I, Expressionism in Holland gave way to a vibrant avant-garde culture that focused on issues of abstraction and color; at the center of it were Piet Mondrian and Theo van Doesburg. The latter still had ties to the Expressionist cause insofar as he advocated a form of three-dimensional color environment. As Van Doesburg explained in several essays published in *de Stijl* between 1926 and 1928, the essence of the countercomposition was its opposition to the orthogonal character of architecture and nature. Art, he argued, in aspiring to the spiritual, must provide for architecture an additional dimension—the oblique—that architecture by itself was not capable of creating, given that it was shackled to weight and gravity. In that sense, art, for him, was opposed to functionality as well as to construction.

Van Doesburg was deeply influenced by the work of painter Piet Mondrian. His designs for a cinema/dance hall, the Café Aubette in Strasbourg (1926–28), which involved broad compositions of colored rectangles in relief, oriented at 45-degree angles. Mirrors were placed between the windows to reflect the ceiling and the three other walls, all treated in a manner that turned the architectural surface into a kind of plastic relief sculpture.

One of the few examples of de Stijl architecture is the Schröder House (1924), designed by Dutch architect Gerrit Thomas Rietveld, who lived and worked in Utrecht. The client, Truus Schröder-Schräder, the wife of a noted lawyer, wanted a house with as few walls as possible. It is built at the end of a block of conventional 19th-century attached row houses, giving it views in three directions. Rietveld exploited this to create a house in which the volumes seem to be composed of plains, some hanging free from the facade. The principal colors were white and gray, with red, yellow and blue serving as accents. The ground floor was relatively conventional but the upper floor had numerous movable walls that allowed for spaces to be opened or closed as desired.

Walter Gropius rejected Van Doesburg's position, as did architect Jacobus Johannes Pieter Oud (1890–1963). They argued that architecture needed to focus on social and economic realities, rather than abstract spiritual speculations.

17.135 Schröder House, Utrecht, Netherlands

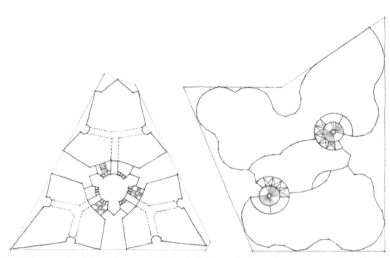

17.136 Plans for Friedrichstrasse Office Building and glass skyscraper projects, Berlin

17.137 Friedrichstrasse Office Building project

FRIEDRICHSTRASSE OFFICE BUILDING

In 1921 a competition was held for a tall office building along the Friedrichstrasse in Berlin, and though Mies van der Rohe (1886–1969) did not win, largely because he flouted all the rules of the prospectus, his design has entered the lore of skyscraper history for its radical innovation. Mies began his training with his father as a stonemason, but his talent led him to Berlin, where he worked for a while for Bruno Paul, one of Germany's most influential Art Nouveau architects, and then for the more modernist-oriented Peter Behrens. The houses Mies built during the 1920s were certainly competent but hardly imaginative. They stood in sharp contrast with his unbuilt work, which was an evocative and imaginative expression of the emerging modernist aesthetic. His submittal for the office tower competition, for example, shows a building composed of three angular prismatic towers linked in the middle by a circulation core, with an open cylindrical space left free all the way from bottom to top. The steel skeleton with cantilevered floor slabs was sheathed completely in glass. The design reduced the building to its fundamental elements: the circulation core and the office pods. The core that contains the stairways, elevators, and lavatories constitutes a type of trunk clearly visible in the plans. Mies did not, as was conventional, see each floor as filling the site

to maximum capacity. Instead, the building breaks apart the block into three separate thirty-story towers that only at the buildings' tangents touch the perimeter of the site. The competition drawings showed the buildings rising high above the haphazard townhouse-apartment blocks.

This project, along with his contemporary design for a country house in brick, placed Mies firmly within the emerging modernist movement that was aiming beyond Expressionism, which was still the prevailing post–World War I aesthetic. He joined the Novembergruppe in 1922. The original political motivation of the group by that time had been lost, but the organization remained important because of its architectural exhibitions, of which Mies soon became the director in charge. In a series of blunt and

terse texts, he laid out his ambitions: "We refuse to recognize the problem of form, but only the problems of building." To this he added, "Essentially the task is to free the practice of building from the control of aesthetic speculators and restore it to what it should exclusively be: Building." This declaration of purpose was published in a journal called G, which appeared in July 1923 under the editorship of Hans Richter, El Lissitzky, and Werner Graeff, and which announced its hostility toward romance and subjectivity in art. Though these skyscrapers, and the Brick Country House, had a minimal investment in their structural logic, Mies, by the mid-1920s, was moving toward a position that placed structure—stripped of allusions, illusions, and the raw realities of building—into the center of architectural production.

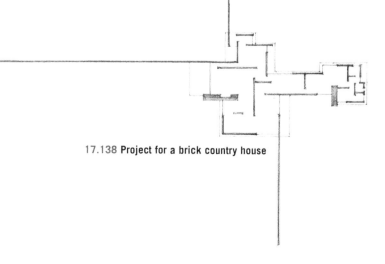

17.138 Project for a brick country house

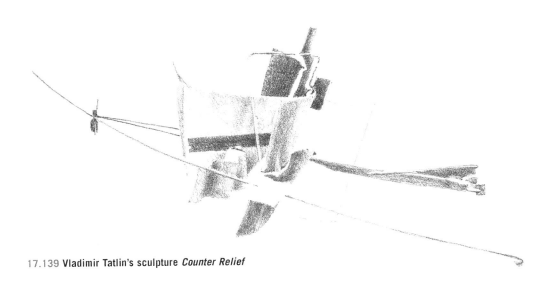

17.139 Vladimir Tatlin's sculpture *Counter Relief*

RUSSIAN CONSTRUCTIVISM

When Karl Marx, in the 1860s, critiqued capitalist society and proposed an alternative world controlled by the proletariat, he assumed that change would take place in industrialized Europe. But when the revolution did come in 1917, it was in the under-industrialized country of Russia with a small working class. The Russian Revolution capitalized on the prevailing anti-czarist sentiment to forge a communist vision that, like postcolonial modernist attempts, sought to skip over the capitalist age straight into communism. The Russian avant-garde wanted a clean slate, seeing in the new situation a singular opportunity for manifesting the arts as politically purposeful reality. Thus, the Soviet experiment, as long as it lasted, was possibly modernism's very best opportunity to constitute and express itself as a cross-disciplinary social, political and aesthetic movement. It therefore catalyzed modernists across Europe and beyond and became, for a while, the sounding board of international modernism.

The Russian Constructivists sought to push modernist claims to their limits. The term *Constructivism* emerged at the beginning of the 1920s and was closely associated with the Society of Contemporary Architects (OSA). This movement was, among the various tendencies, the closest to the tenets of the European New Architecture, and to the work of Le Corbusier in particular. It was led by Moisei Ginzburg (1892–1946), whose structures aimed to embody the ideals of the new socialist order. For Ginzburg and the Constructivists, art for art's sake was dead: art now had to reflect the newly established truth of the world. To sever art and by extension architecture from their subservience to the bourgeois class, artists and architects had to draw their aesthetic from factory production, given that industrialization, now controlled by the communists, would, so it was presumed, become the springboard for a truly universal human culture. Constructivism, though it was grounded in an image of industrial labor, was not a one-to-one translation of industry into aesthetics, but it was the first modernist aesthetic that admitted, and in fact glorified, the mass-produced object. Constructivists used the term *laboratory work* to describe their formal investigations and to emphasize their solidarity with both science and labor. Laboratory work was, however, not to be equated with the pragmatism of problem solving, for the Constructivists, though they admired utilitarianism, also spoke of the need for a formal language that was imbued with an aura of heroism.

Constructivism, the best-known movement outside of Russia, is often, but mistakenly, associated with the entirety of Russian revolutionary art, but not all Russian art of the time was Constructivist: there were also Rationalists and Suprematists. The theme of heroism was tackled in the work of a group headed by a charismatic figure, Nikolai Ladovsky, whose ASNOVA group (Association for the New Architecture), founded in 1923, attributed to the new forms of architecture the power of acting in revolutionary ways on the psyche of the masses. Also known as Rationalists, they differentiated themselves from the Constructivists; despite certain similarities, they intended to develop a more purely scientific foundation for the aesthetics of modern architecture.

The third major group, the Suprematists, focused on fundamental geometric forms such as squares and circles. In art, their best-known representative was Kazimir Malevich, who painted simple geometric shapes on his canvases; in architecture, it was El Lissitzky (1890–1941). Lissitzky, who designed exhibition displays and propaganda works, was also greatly influenced by the aesthetics of the Bauhaus and de Stijl. Projects like his Wolkenbügel, however, which had towers supporting vast cantilevered buildings in the sky, show his daring formal vision.

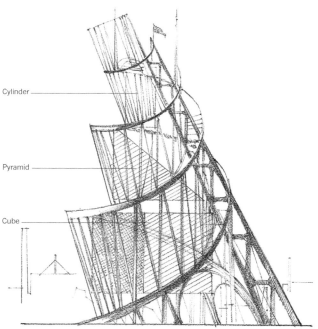

17.140 Drawing of the Monument to the Third International

Tatlin's Tower

Together with the Vesnin brothers and Moisei Ginzburg, Vladimir Tatlin (1885–1953) occupies a central position in early Constructivism and became, along with Malevich and El Lissitzky, an important catalyst in the modernist movement of the 1920s. Tatlin studied art in Moscow and after a long journey working on ships as a sailor, he went to Paris, where he met Picasso and other Cubists. During this period, his work moved away from painting to begin three-dimensional explorations into material and gravity. Some of his more interesting works were installed in the corners of a room in a type of dialogue with the walls and a diagonally redirected space—an experiment with the formalist concept of "defamiliarization." Later in the decade, Tatlin defined his efforts as aiming at synthesizing the various branches of art with technology. His artistic explorations and utopian theory coalesced in his project for a huge 400-meter-high tower (designed in 1919) that was meant to straddle the Neva River in the center of Petrograd (St. Petersburg) in celebration of the newly founded Third (Communist) International. The monument, of which a 5-meter-high model was built, consisted of three volumes of glass suspended in a vast double spiral structure stiffened along its slope by a leaning truss.

The lower space, a cube, was to complete one rotation per year on its axis to correspond to the frequency of the Communist International General Assembly meetings. The second space, a pyramid, was to rotate on its axis once per month, corresponding to the meeting frequency of the Secretariat. The third and smallest room, a cylinder, was to rotate once per day to match the daily operations of the International. It contained, among other spaces, offices for a newspaper that issued pamphlets and manifestoes. Radio masts rose from the peak of the monument, not unlike those at the Eiffel Tower, which Tatlin's edifice emulated implicitly.

The tower became a symbol of the young Soviet Republic, and smaller versions of it were carried in processions through Moscow like religious objects and presented at various exhibitions abroad. El Lissitzky was moved to write that the tower was the modern equivalent to Sargon's ziggurat but created in a new material for a new context. The iron, he added, represented the will of the proletariat, whereas the glass was a sign of a clear conscience. Another commentator saw the spiral as the symbol par excellence of modern times, whereas the Formalist Viktor Shklovsky called it, in semiological terms, a monument "made of steel, glass and revolution."

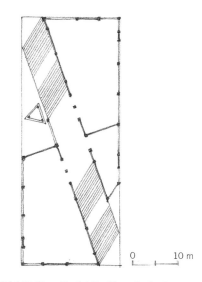

17.141 Plan: Soviet Pavilion, Paris, France

17.142 **Rusakov Factory Club, Moscow**

0   10 m

17.143 **Plan and section: Rusakov Factory Club**

Soviet Pavilion

Konstantin Stepanovich Melnikov (1890–1974), one of the most productive of the Russian avant-garde architects, has been hailed as one of the twelve great architects of the contemporary world. He adamantly refused, however, to be associated with any ism, and his highly idiosyncratic œuvre featured works that radically differed from each other. He built about twenty structures, of which only a few survive. Like Tatlin, he began his career studying painting but widened his scope to include architecture, graduating from the Moscow School of Painting and Sculpture in 1917. He was trained in a neoclassical style, as was typical prior to the revolution.

One of his first major works was the Soviet Pavilion in Paris, which was built for the 1925 International Exhibition of Modern Industrial and Decorative Arts; the displays were designed by Rodchenko. Melnikov, starting with a building made of pyramids and spirals in a Tatlinian manner, eventually created a startling angular composition with a staircase running diagonally up and then down the entire building. Though a relatively small building, the staircase gave to it a monumental cast. The structure was built not of steel but of wood fitted in Moscow by peasants wielding traditional Russian axes,

and shipped to Paris for assembly by French carpenters. The flying roof panels were painted red, the walls gray, and the window mullions white.

There was a debate in the USSR at the time about whether the new Soviet architecture should aspire to be technologically advanced or reflect local craft traditions. Melnikov favored the latter, but he was more than flexible when it came to larger commissions, such as the Rusakov Factory Club (1927). Workers' clubs had been created after the revolution to elevate the workers' culture and literacy while providing leisure places after their daily toils, but by 1924 most workers had shown themselves to be less than zealous for such uplift. A new generation of workers' clubs came into being that focused more on club activities than ideology.

At a time when living space in Moscow averaged 5 square meters per capita, the clubs were one of the few places outside of the factory where workers could congregate. Melnikov went even further and interpreted them as an expression of a group individuality against the backdrop of urban anonymity. Melnikov's Rusakov Factory Club is highly expressive, despite the symmetry and simplicity of its plan. The lecture hall that was its main programmatic element was

divided into three subunits that seemed to break through the building's exterior and to hover dangerously above the entrance. Each auditorium box seated 190 people, and each faced a large common stage. Three rooms for club functions were located in a mezzanine just below the seating.

17.144 **Soviet Pavilion, Paris**

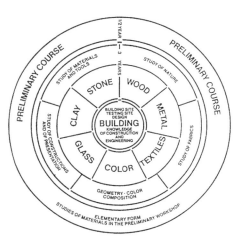

17.145 Diagram of the Bauhaus curriculum

17.146 The Bauhaus, Dessau, Germany

THE BAUHAUS

In 1919 Walter Gropius (1883–1969) was made the head of a new school of architecture formed by the merger of two older schools of arts and crafts. Significantly less pragmatically oriented than the Deutsche Werkbund, the Bauhaus sought to engender a new unified pedagogy and vision that unified the arts and crafts, in collaboration with industry. Though nominally a national school, the Bauhaus was always cosmopolitan in orientation, open to all students regardless of gender, nationality, or previous qualifications. Initially the Bauhaus's purpose was to produce a new "guild of craftsmen," but that does not mean it was reactionary, for Gropius also wanted a school that could unify the arts and close the gap between industry and craft. In that sense, unlike William Morris, who saw craft as a bulwark against industry, or the Werkbund, which was seeking an industrialized craft, Gropius was seeking to discover the internal ethos of industrial production itself. The question was not just how to make things, but how to perceive and experience things as well. For that reason, Gropius brought in painters, including Lyonel Feininger, Paul Klee, and Johannes Itten. The celebration of painters as form-makers reflected a not-so-subtle shift away from the social (and thus from the contentious political issues of the time), toward the language of abstraction and design. Itten was placed in

charge of the basic course required of all incoming students. Its purpose was to free the students' creative powers and guide them toward a suitable direction in their later studies.

In 1924, the reduction of funding from Weimar, its host city, forced the school to move to Dessau, where the Junkers aircraft factory was located. Gropius used this opportunity to reinvent the Bauhaus, purging its faculty and stripping the curriculum of its more expressionistic and mystical elements, to focus more single-mindedly on an industrial aesthetic inspired in part by the Junkers factory. Johannes Itten left and was replaced by the Russian Wassily Kandinsky.

17.147 Joost Schmidt's poster for the 1923 Bauhaus exhibition in Weimar

The city of Dessau helped finance a new campus, which was designed by Gropius as a signature, representative work. The program of the Dessau building (1919–25) included workshops, administrative offices, a lecture hall, and a stage, as well as workrooms, a canteen, and student accommodations. Gropius divided the program into two major elements separated by a road and connected by a bridge. The bridge, fittingly, was where Gropius had his office: to go from the classrooms to the studio spaces, one had to pass by Gropius's office. The building was not particularly unified in the classical sense, for each element had its own programmatic logic. The dormitory at the east end stood

17.148 **Corner of the Bauhaus building, Dessau**

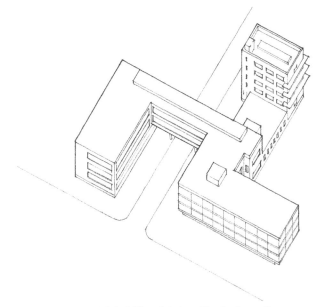

17.149 **Pictorial view: The Bauhaus, Dessau**

awkwardly connected to the long, one-story space that contained the lecture hall and canteen, which in turn was linked to the main building, whose two stories of studio spaces were transformed into a glazed box. The L-shaped area containing offices and classrooms, on the other hand, was designed with horizontal banding of white stucco that contrasted with the windows. The only two colors in the whole composition were white and black.

In 1928, Gropius stepped down as head of the Bauhaus and appointed Hannes Meyer (1889–1954), a Swiss architect, to take over. Meyer's socialist political allegiances led to conflict with the government, and he was forced to resign in 1930. The position then went to Mies van der Rohe, who kept the school afloat until it was officially closed by the Nazis in 1933.

The Bauhaus, though it lasted only fourteen years, became a lightning rod for debates that enabled the furthering of modern architecture in the brief moment in time between the early 1920s and the return of neoclassicism and nationalism in the 1930s. Criticism of the school came not only from conservative factions but from modernists as well. Le Corbusier, though he would change his mind later, argued that modern architecture could be taught

aesthetically, as it was allied primarily with industry. For him, architecture should not emerge out of decorative design. Similarly, Theo van Doesburg, the Dutch artist, argued that the Bauhaus, in emphasizing individual creativity, had abandoned the all-important search for a relationship between artist and society. Despite these difficulties the Bauhaus remained the leading school of modernist design in Europe.

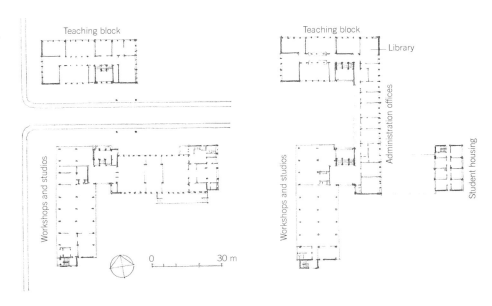

17.150 **Ground- and second-floor plans: The Bauhaus, Dessau**

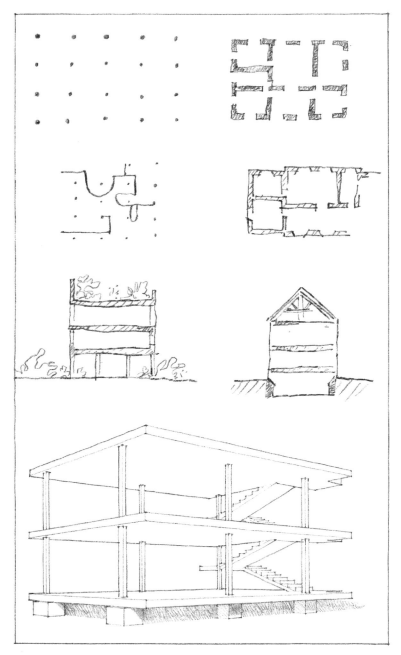

17.151 Facsimile of sketches illustrating Le Corbusier's Five Points toward a New Architecture

LE CORBUSIER AND *VERS UNE ARCHITECTURE*

Due to the dominance of the Beaux-Arts system, the innovations in design that were taking place in other parts of Europe and in the United States had only minimal resonance in France. For modernism to develop it needed someone who could break its cultural isolation and provide a suitable alternative. That person was Charles-Édouard Jeanneret-Gris, who later changed his name to Le Corbusier (1887–1965). A Swiss-born architect who worked briefly in the offices of Auguste Perret and Peter Behrens, Le Corbusier moved permanently to Paris in 1916, at the age of twenty-nine. Le Corbusier's articles in *L'Esprit nouveau*, as well as his epochal 1923 book *Vers une architecture* (*Towards a New Architecture*), became the most significant summary statements of the ideals of the modernist movement to appear since World War I.

Jeanneret began his career designing houses in the Art and Crafts style in his native city of La Chaux-de-Fonds in Switzerland. But once in Paris, and after a travel tour to Turkey, Greece, Italy, and other parts of Europe and the Mediterranean in 1911, he allowed his unique style to develop rapidly. He was strongly influenced by the modern painters, particularly the Cubists. In 1920, he took on the name Le Corbusier. *Vers une architecture* outlined Five Points toward a New Architecture: the *pilotis* (stilts) that support the building, the free plan with the only structural support coming in the form of columns, the free facade, the strip window, and the roof terrace. These features, he argued, were based on structural properties of reinforced concrete as well as the increasing availability of mass-produced architectural elements. They also allowed the architect to work with pragmatic forms. The idea of the *pilotis* was to remain with Le Corbusier throughout his career. Inspired by Rousseauesque thinking that invested undisturbed nature with an ideal of plenitude, Le Corbusier's *pilotis* were meant to liberate the land from the oppression of a building that interrupted its flow and rhythm.

Villa Savoye

In the 1920s, Le Corbusier designed a series of houses in Paris and its suburbs that explored and demonstrated the possibilities of his Five Points. The Maisons La Roche-Jeanneret (1923), which now houses the Fondation Le Corbusier, was a combined set of houses for two different clients. Le Corbusier responded to the spatial

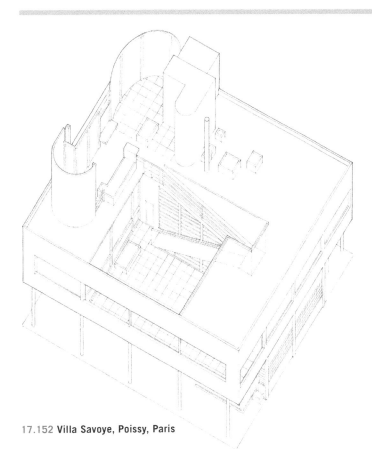

17.152 Villa Savoye, Poissy, Paris

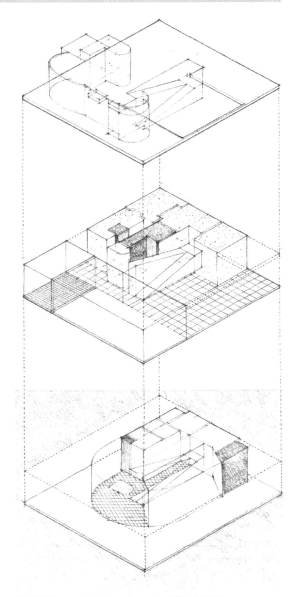

17.153 Expanded view of spaces: Villa Savoye

17.154 Villa Savoye

demands of the different households by designing interweaving layers of spaces, connected by a central court. The house was painted white, but on the inside, walls were painted in a variety of soft hues of red, yellow, and blue, as well as white.

His most influential work from this time was the Villa Savoye (1931) at Poissy, a suburb of Paris, where the client owned a large parcel of land that swelled up to a gentle hill. At its apex, Le Corbusier placed a cubic volume, lifted on *pilotis*, a column-and-slab construction in reinforced concrete. The walls were built of brick and stuccoed over. The plans on every floor were customized to their functional requirements, and a simple strip window was the centerpiece of the elevation.

The ground-floor plan was designed around the turning radius of the client's automobile, which, after dropping off his employer at the entry on axis with the center, was to be parked by the chauffeur in parking slots located around the curve. (In *Vers une architecture*, Le Corbusier had praised the design of the modern French automobile as an aesthetic achievement as great as the Parthenon.) Inside the front door and past the chauffeur's quarters, a carefully designed ramp rises up the middle of the villa. Living spaces were arranged around the ramp on three sides on the first floor. A terrace fills up the rest. The ramp reverses direction and ends on the roof, where a freestanding wall with a single window self-consciously frames the landscape. Although Le Corbusier celebrated the automobile, he also designed the building as a promenade with experiences unfolding at every turn. Once again, though the exterior was white (apart from the red entrance door), some of the interior walls were painted in pastel hues of beige, rose, and blue.

17.155 **Lovell Beach House, Newport Beach, California**

17.156 **Lovell House, Hollywood Hills, Los Angeles**

LOVELL HOUSE

Modernist architecture did not produce any major inroads in the United States until the 1940s, with the arrival of Walter Gropius and Mies van der Rohe. There are two principal reasons for American resistance to modernism: Beaux-Arts architecture was still strong and taught in architecture schools; and Frank Lloyd Wright, the dominant American architect of the time, was a trenchant critic of the Europeans' boxy, unadorned aesthetic.

Early examples of European modernist architecture in the United States are thus few and center on the work of two architects, Rudolf Michael Schindler (1887–1953) and Richard Neutra (1892–1970). Schindler, whose work was very much underappreciated at the time, was born in Austria but moved to the United States in 1914. He found employment in the office of Wright until branching out on his own, setting the tone for an architecture that had never been seen in the United States with his Lovell Beach House (1922–26). It was not a house in any traditional sense; nor was it a house in the Corbusian sense, with floor slabs and columns. Instead, a series of five concrete wall elements elevated the living quarters high above the ground to catch the sea breezes. The house appeared from below like the underside of a bridge. The floors, roofs and walls were built of wood.

The same clients commissioned Neutra to design their principal residence (1927–29) in the Hollywood Hills in Los Angeles. It was built against a steep hill with views to the city to the south. The entrance was at the top level, where the family bedrooms and sleeping porches were also located. A staircase, enclosed on two sides by glass and with spectacular views, led down to the main floor and the living room, which faces south. The guest room and kitchen were to the north. It was the first completely steel-framed residence in the United States, the prefabricated elements bolted together in less than forty hours. The house was not a box, however, but rather a complex structure with extended balconies and sleeping porches on the upper floor suspended from powerful roof beams above. The dominant interior colors were blue, gray, white, and black. Carpets and draperies were in shades of gray. The metal trim was gray and the woodwork black. Potted plants softened the hard lines. The surface of the building was defined by glass and white steel panels.

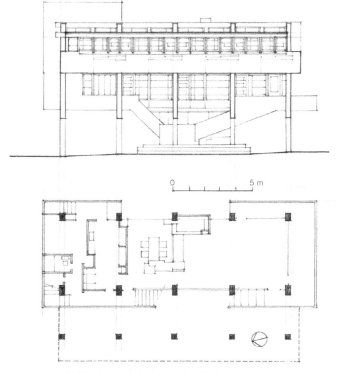

17.157 **Plan and elevation: Lovell House**

1950 CE

INTRODUCTION

By the middle of the 20th century, the great expectations of the European Enlightenment and its modernist institutions were being pursued with greater zeal than ever—and being widely critiqued for their contradictions and failures. It was High Modernism's heyday, but it was also its watershed point: from mid-century it went into steady decline, severely challenged and eventually supplanted by its postmodern critics in the late 1970s and early 1980s.

The defining event of the era was, of course, World War II. Although World War I had been bloody and expensive, the ensuing peace had given rise to the hope that the utopian aspirations of modernism could now be realized. Although the interwar years were marked by political chaos and financial instability—including the turmoil of the Weimar Republic in Germany and the Great Depression of 1929 in the United States—they were also characterized by grand projects that sought to finally deliver on the social and aesthetic possibilities of the industrial age. In architecture, significant events of the time included Walter Gropius's new school of design, the Bauhaus (founded in 1919), Le Corbusier's books *Vers une Architecture* (*Toward a New Architecture*), first published in 1923, and *City of Tomorrow and Its Planning* (1929); and Ludwig Mies van de Rohe's Weissenhof Siedlung Exhibition in 1927. The Congrès Internationaux d'Architecture Moderne (CIAM), founded in 1928, also played an important role as it quickly grew into an organization with dozens of members from around the world, all committed to deploying the ideals of functionalism and rationalism in building and urban planning. Even in the early days of the Soviet Republic, the social expectations of modern architecture were broadly vouchsafed, as in the Palace of the Soviets competition of 1931. A major exhibition at the Museum of Modern Art in New York City in 1932 sought to codify this modernism as the International style.

By 1935 Adolf Hitler in Germany and Joseph Stalin in the Soviet Union had put an end to modernism in their respective spheres of influence. World War II brought the utopian aspirations of the modernist project to a screeching halt—not only by putting a stop to construction, but even more by undermining its grounding assumptions.

The fact that the modernist Western world, instead of producing models of social utopias, could just as easily create a model machine for the Holocaust, provoked an era of soul-searching about the collateral consequences of relentlessly pursing a rationalist agenda. Brutalism (from *beton brut*, or "naked concrete") emerged to define a new expression for the modernist work—an aesthetic that was not pure and white but raw and gray, cognizant, it was suggested, of the inescapable brutality that accompanied the modern world. Le Corbusier himself was a leading light of this project that was ultimately embraced all around the globe, particularly in the postcolonial world and Western academia. Many of the new buildings on U.S. university campuses were brutalist, such as the University of California–Berkeley's Wurster Hall (1964) and the University of Washington's Gould Hall (1972).

Modern architecture, like other forms of culture, was impacted by the tumultuous1960s and its aftermath. Team X, formed by a group of disgruntled CIAM members, sought to rearticulate the identity and aspirations of the modern movement into a more human-scaled, softer expression that was more community- and region-based. Instead of celebrating the machine, a more climate-responsive architecture began to take shape. Peter and Alison Smithson bridged the brutalist and Team X camps. Maxwell Fry and Jane Drew codified their work in Africa under the rubric of Tropical Architecture. A group from England, Archigram, whose name came from the banner of the journal it founded, promoted an architecture influenced by pop art and a counterculture that was mobile, flexible, transitory, and youth-oriented. Kenzo Tange built the Yamanashi Press and Broadcasting Center (1966) in Kofu, Japan, and Denys Lasdun the Royal National Theatre (1976) in London.

An indirect consequence of World War II was that it finally dismantled the colonial world. Beginning in 1947 with India, the European colonies in Asia and Africa, one by one, declared independence in the 1950s and 1960s. Many of these newly independent postcolonial nation-states adopted modern architecture as the idiom with which to build their new institutions of state, such as Chandigarh in India, Brasília in Brazil, and Islamabad in Pakistan; these were followed by a series of new African capitals, such as

Ibadan in Nigeria and Dodoma in Tanzania. Even in communist Cuba, as in the early days of the Soviet Republic, modern architecture found a unique voice and form. Thus, whereas modernism was highly contested in Europe and the United States, it was more readily embraced in places such as Ankara, colonial North Africa, Latin America, Australia, Japan, and India. In part this was because in the former colonies, modernism, with its claims to universality, represented a path to modernity that, unlike classicism, was not so strongly identified with Eurocentrism.

Of course, the formation of major global institutions, such as the United Nations with all its accessory bodies, also played a major role in the worldwide dissemination of modernism. Not only were the headquarters of major UN institutions such as the General Assembly in New York and UNESCO in Paris designed in the modernist mold, but the UN funded habitat consultants to travel around the world and advocate for modernist urban and rural planning models. At the vanguard of this movement were visionaries such as Buckminster Fuller and structuralist urban thinkers such as Constantinos Doxiadis and his Ekistics group based in Athens, Greece. As part of this new global outlook, the new postwar embassies of the United States, such as Edward Durell Stone's embassy in New Delhi, were also built in modernist style.

European modernism, quite distinct from the homegrown modernism developed by people like Frank Lloyd Wright, was ushered into the United States through the academies, in particular when Mies van der Rohe began teaching at the Illinois Institute of Technology in Chicago, and Walter Gropius at Harvard University. As the American economy boomed in the 1950s and 1960s, private corporations eagerly adopted the new style with its sleek outlines as the new symbol of big business, eschewing their prewar penchant for neoclassicism. The steel-and-glass skyscraper quickly established itself as the new symbol of corporate America, supplanting the stone-clad tower epitomized by the Empire State Building. Lever House (1950–52), designed by Skidmore Owings and Merrill (SOM), and the Seagram Building by Mies van der Rohe, both in New York City, set the tone. SOM specialized in designing corporate headquarters in the United States and abroad, and became one of the largest

architectural firms of the time. As the steel-and-glass skyscraper became established as the symbol of U.S. capitalism, even old iconoclasts like Le Corbusier and Frank Lloyd Wright came to be seen as anachronistic.

Post–World War II architecture also saw the rise of the master-architect and the prestige commission. Many of these came to define the popular identity of the modern movement, such as the town hall in Säynätsalo, Finland (1952) by Alvar Aalto, the Guggenheim Museum (1956–59) by Frank Lloyd Wright, the Berlin Philharmonic Hall (1956–63) by Hans Scharoun, and the Sydney Opera House (1957–73) by Jørn Utzon. A structure-based expression of monumental architecture, exemplified by the work of U.S.-based Eero Saarinen, made for an architecture of distinctive profiles. The standout figure of the late-modernist period, however, was Louis Kahn. This Philadelphia-based self-styled disciple of Le Corbusier developed a distinctive body of work that began as a discourse of "serving" versus "served" spaces, but eventually sought to reintroduce ideas of classical monumentality into a modern architecture, influenced in particular by his idiosyncratic phenomenological reading of the antiquities of Rome.

By the mid-1970s, the critics of modern architecture were well entrenched. What began as a critique of the perceived failures of modernist urban schemes, evolved into a scathing criticism of the formal orthodoxies of modern architecture. Some architects, like Aldo Rossi in Italy, hoped for a return to history; others, like Robert Venturi and Denise Scott Brown, sought out parody and irony; whereas Peter Eisenman in the United States and Oswald Mathias Ungers in Germany aimed for a formalism more rigorous than even that of the modernists. The most enduring aspect of postmodernism was its call for a heightened awareness of a building's context—but how context was to be defined was much debated, and varied from Daniel Libeskind's highly abstract Jewish Museum in Berlin (2001) to the efforts of Prince Charles of England to reawaken an interest in traditional styles. In the 1990s, in opposition to the conservative tenor of much architectural production, a group of avant-garde architects, among them Rem Koolhaas from Holland, called for a revival of

modernist forms and abstractions. Advances in technology and computers also enabled architects to build structures that in previous decades would have been unthinkable. Frank Gehry's Guggenheim Museum (1997) in Bilbao, Spain, with its curved titanium skin, and the blue, bubble-shaped Kunsthaus (2003) in Graz, Austria, by Peter Cook and Colin Fournier, are noted examples.

MODERNISM

An inescapable problem in discussing 20th-century architecture is the definition of such terms as *modernity*, *modernization*, and *modernism*. For example, different artistic fields—and even different practitioners—tend to have contradictory understandings of modernism. In the collages of Kurt Schwitters, modernism might be used to indicate fragmentation; in James Joyce's *Finnegan's Wake*, a heightened sense of subjectivity is implied; and to understand the music of Arnold Schoenberg, objectivity is the precondition. In architecture, modernism is associated with a radical break with past forms. The ballast of literal historical allusions is thrown overboard. In the late 1920s, buildings by LeCorbusier or Mies van der Rohe had white walls and simple forms, with the emphasis on function and structure. Explicitly codifying modernism as a style was Philip Johnson's and Henry-Russell Hitchcock's book, *The International Style*, which followed on the heels of an exhibition at the New York Museum of Modern Art (1932). In the Weimar Republic between 1923 and 1933, there arose the term *Neue Sachlichkeit* ("New Objectivity"); a critique of the overemotional aspects of some forms of Expressionism, it advocated clean lines and matter-of-fact design. The word *functionalism* also came into play, though this term also had several connotations. For Mies van der Rohe, the emphasis was on the clarity of a building's form and detailing; for Walter Gropius, it was on the building's massing and organization. For Le Corbusier, it meant the use of concrete and of the free plan, as defined by his Five Points.

The 1930s, and the period between the world wars in general, was an era of optimism for the modernists in Europe. After World War I had cleared out the detritus of history, a rational reordering of the world seemed possible and desirable. Even small

18.1 **Modern steel construction**

18.2 **Norris Dam, Tennessee Valley Authority; Cling River, Anderson and Campbell Counties, Tennessee**

projects were imbricated with an avant-garde spirit—optimistic harbingers of things to come. Iconic works from this ethos included Gerrit Rietveld's Schröder House (Utrecht, Netherlands, 1924); Alvar Aalto's Viipuri Library (1927–35); Richard Neutra's Lovell House (Hollywood, California, 1927); Karl Ehn's Karl-Marx-Hof (Vienna, Austria, 1927–30); Clemenz Holzmeister's Grand National Assembly Hall (Ankara, Turkey, 1928); Le Corbusier's Villa Savoye (Poissy, France, 1929–31); Ludwig Mies van der Rohe's German National Pavilion (1929); Johannes Duiker's Open Air School (Amsterdam, 1930); and Lúcio Costa's and Oscar Niemeyer's Ministry of Health and Education (Rio de Janeiro, Brazil, 1936–46).

The politics associated with modernization, though firmly anchored in the Enlightenment project, have varied from totalitarianism and elitism to republicanism and radical democracy. An example of modernization impacting aesthetics is the Tennessee Valley Authority, which in the 1930s redesigned a huge area along the Tennessee River to create a series of strikingly modern dams for electricity generation. The tightest relationship between modernism and modernization was to be found in the days of the newly forming Soviet Union, when there was, for a few

years, a sense of excitement about the new social promise of communism. El Lissitzky, Vladimir Tatlin, and Konstantin Melnikov were at the core of this development, which also included Mart Stam, a Dutch architect, as well as Max Taut and Hannes Meyer, both Germans, the latter serving as head of the Bauhaus for a few years before moving to Moscow. For these men, and for like-minded Constructivists, factory life had to find its expression in cubist forms, open steel structures, and the absence of historical references.

The idea of integrating modernism, modernization, and nationalism was particularly attractive to the elites of some non-European countries eager to create a new idiom. These trends appeared early on: in Turkey, as a pro-modernist state formed by Kemal Atatürk; in Tel Aviv, which was to become one of Israel's leading cities after nationhood was established in 1948; and then in Brazil, which had been independent since 1822, but which under Getulio Vargas strove for national self-articulation. It was most vigorously explored in post–World War II South Asia, where several modernist-style cities and capitals were built.

The works of Frank Lloyd Wright and Alvar Aalto have a somewhat unusual position in the discussions about modernism: both men

18.3 **Chairs designed by Mies van der Rohe**

are integral to its history, yet both were critics of its emphasis on functionalism, and both held that architecture should not promote a radical rupture with the past. They also shared a stronger respect for the natural landscape than most modernists of the time.

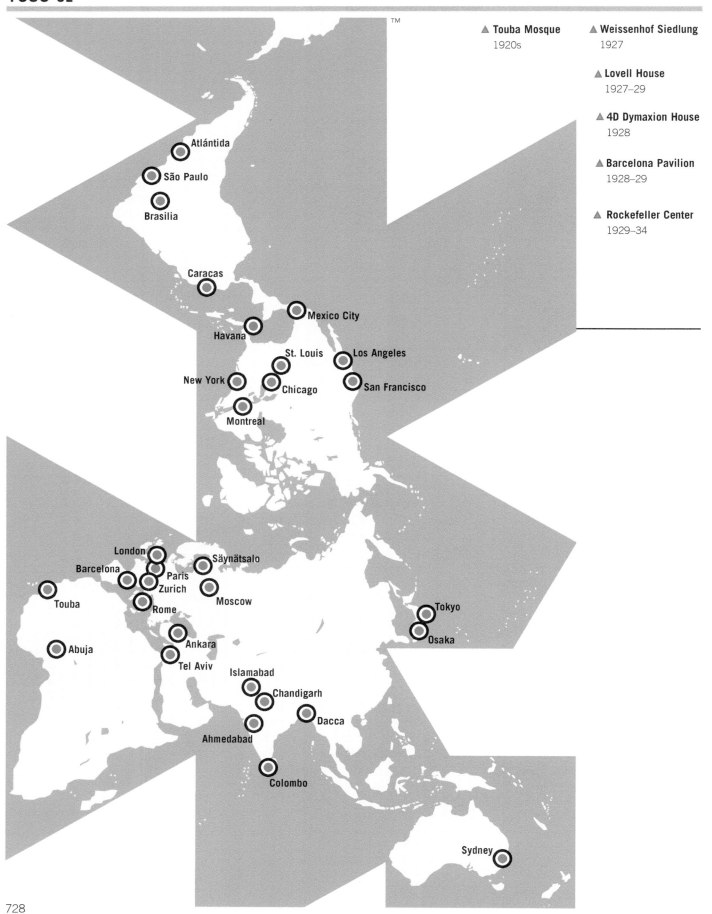

TM

▲ Touba Mosque
1920s

▲ Weissenhof Siedlung
1927

▲ Lovell House
1927–29

▲ 4D Dymaxion House
1928

▲ Barcelona Pavilion
1928–29

▲ Rockefeller Center
1929–34

Atlántida

São Paulo

Brasilia

Caracas

Mexico City

Havana

St. Louis

Los Angeles

New York

Chicago

San Francisco

Montreal

London

Säynätsalo

Barcelona

Paris

Zurich

Moscow

Touba

Rome

Abuja

Ankara

Tokyo

Tel Aviv

Osaka

Islamabad

Chandigarh

Dacca

Ahmedabad

Colombo

Sydney

▲ Pavilion Suisse
1932

▲ Unité d'habitation, Marseille
1947–52

▲ Palace of the Soviets
1931

▲ Säynätsalo Town Hall
1949–52

▲ Fallingwater
1936–37

▲ Yale University Art Gallery
1951–53

▲ Health and Education Ministry, Rio de Janeiro
1936–46

▲ Casa del Fascio
1932–36

▲ Chapel at Ronchamp
1955

▲ Esposizione Universale di Roma (EUR)
1937–42

▲ Brasília
1956–60

1950 CE

▲ Bata Shoe Factory
1937

▲ TWA Terminal
1956–62

▲ Villa Mairea
1938–41

▲ Sydney Opera House
1957–73

▲ Church of Christ the Worker
1958–60

▲ Illinois Institute of Technology Library Building
1944–45

▲ School of Architecture, Ahmedabad
1965

▲ Japanese Pavilion, Paris Expo
1937

▲ Guggenheim Museum
1956–59

▲ Piazza d'Italia
1975–78

▲ Salk Institute
1960–63

▲ Centre Georges Pompidou
1971–77

▲ Eames House
1945–49

▲ Heidi Weber House
1965

▲ AT&T Building
1980–84

▲ Farnsworth House
1946–51

▲ House for Dr. Bartholomew
1961–63

▲ Berlin Social Science Research Center
1981

▲ National Schools of Art, Havana
1961–65

▲ Chapel of Light
1989

▲ Olympic Stadium, Tokyo
1961–64

▲ Magney House
1982–84

▲ Sher-e-Banglanagar
1961–82

▲ Pyramide du Louvre
1989

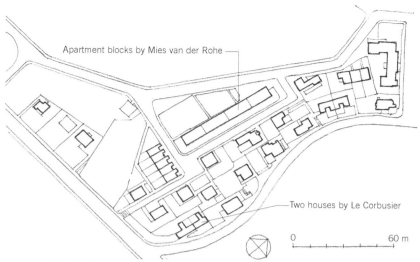

18.4 Site plan: Weissenhof Siedlung, Weissenhof, Germany

Apartment blocks by Mies van der Rohe

Two houses by Le Corbusier

0   60 m

Weissenhof Siedlung

In the late 1920s, with the German economy slowly gaining steam after the inflationary crisis of 1923, housing projects sponsored by municipal and state governments and cooperative building societies had begun to be built across Germany. To support these efforts, the Deutsche Werkbund, at the time under a pro-modernist leadership, sponsored an exhibition of houses to be designed by architects from all over Europe. Stuttgart was chosen as the site because of the progressive politics of its regional government. Ludwig Mies van der Rohe headed the project, which opened in 1927. What was presented to the world was an entire housing estate (or *Siedlung*) dedicated to avant-garde European modernist thinking. Included in the exhibition were buildings by Le Corbusier, Walter Gropius, Adolf Loos, J. J. P. Oud, Hans Scharoun, and Bruno Taut, among others. Initially, Mies even hoped that Erich Mendelsohn and Henry van der Velde would contribute—a wish that did not materialize.

Mies organized the buildings into a loose rectangular composition above a broad, S-shaped road that followed the slope of the land, with the taller buildings at the top. To create a unified image, all the architects had to employ flat roofs and white facades. Included in the exhibition were rowhouses, duplexes, single-family houses, and apartment buildings. The Weissenhof Siedlung marked a turning point in the history of modernism.

Though the movement was hardly uniform—there were important differences among its leading members—the exhibition created for the public, and indeed for the architects themselves, the appearance of a common mission.

The building that Mies designed for the exhibition, an apartment block, showcased the earliest use of structural steel in an apartment building in Europe. The steel allowed Mies to create thin, non-load-bearing walls on the interior. As would become his custom, he combined the walls that contained the water and plumbing pipes with stairwell walls to create a core that repeated itself on the various floors. This core is in the shape of a two-pronged fork, with the staircase between the prongs. The walls contained the plumbing and water pipes for the kitchens and bathrooms. It was a brilliant and simple compression—and unification—of structure, space, and function.

18.5 Mies van der Rohe's apartment block, Weissenhof Siedlung

18.6 Two houses by Le Corbusier, Weissenhof Siedlung

Le Corbusier's building, by contrast, followed the principles of his Five Points. It was elevated against the slope of a hill and had a roof terrace with a pergola and planters. Much as in Mies's plan, Le Corbusier's interior is almost completely open, but in Le Corbusier's case the partition walls do not reach the facade. There are no rooms in the conventional sense, but rather a typically French enfilade organization along the facade. The kitchen, bath, and toilet are lined up against the far wall, which might seem reasonable given the need for pipes and ventilation. But the wall is suspended in space and thus the pipes had to be hidden in the floor.

Both buildings speak to the image of the new, modern man. Mies's building organizes the service elements around their functionality, separating the bodily functions, like eating and bathing, from empty space. Le Corbusier organizes the space around culturally based hierarchies, while bathing and cooking areas are whittled down and placed in marginal spaces. Although the houses of the *Siedlung* (twenty-one in all) were designed for the working class—the intended beneficiary of modernist politics— the actual cost would have been way out of reach for most workers. This disparity between the avowed politics of the modernist house and its actual consumption, only by the rich elite, continues to dog it even today.

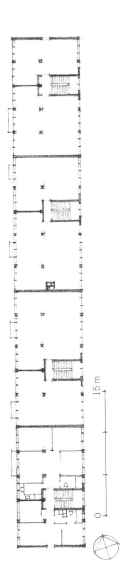

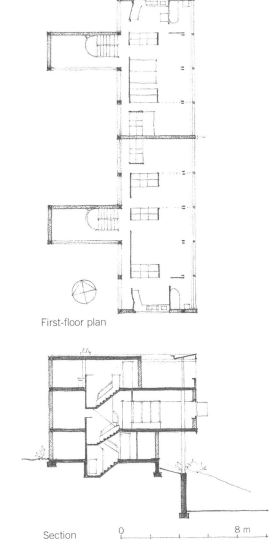

First-floor plan

Section   0   8 m

18.7 First-floor plan: Mies van der Rohe's apartment block, Weissenhof Siedlung

18.8 Two houses by Le Corbusier, Weissenhof Siedlung

18.9 **Hanna House, Palo Alto, California**

Usonian Houses

Throughout the 1930s, Frank Lloyd Wright continued to critique both the Beaux-Arts and modernist styles. Instead, he tried to infuse modernism with a national Romantic sentiment—in his case holding out the ideal of democracy rooted in a simple life closely connected with the land. The traditional city, which derived from Europe, he argued, would eventually be replaced by a dispersed network of habitation. Anticipating this, he designed a futuristic Broadacre City (1932) that was to cover 10 square kilometers. Though Broadacre remained a utopian project, Wright was able to realize certain aspects of it with his Usonian houses. The origin of the name *Usonian* is unknown; but it is likely derived from *U.S.onia*, the name for a reformed American society that Wright tried to bring about for twenty-five years. In the United States there had been a long tradition of pattern-book houses that could be constructed without an architect by local builders, such as the Arts and Crafts bungalows. Wright's Usonian houses extended that tradition, except that what was imitated was not so much the individual plans as the general idea.

The Great Depression of 1929 had left millions homeless in the United States, and Wright was eager to show that his housing, in contrast to that of a Weissenhof, could accommodate the changed economic conditions without loss of integrity. Wright proposed a single-story house that did not require expensive excavations for basements or upper-floor framing. Steel, which was expensive, was not used; instead, the houses were to be made of wood, brick, local stone, and prefabricated blocks. The bricks were not covered with stucco and the wood was left plain, thus reducing finishing costs. The houses were sited not only to make optimal use of the lot, but also to include as much openness as possible from the living room to the backyard. Heating was incorporated into the concrete floor in the form of looped water pipes buried under the slab. The elaborate and expensive millwork needed to conceal radiators in Prairie houses could thus be eliminated.

Wright fused the dining and living rooms and in some cases combined them into a single space. This was a radical departure from his earlier houses, and indeed from centuries of tradition: because of noise, smells, and the activities of servants, the kitchen was always set apart from the dining room. But the owners of these houses were not expected to be wealthy enough to afford a maid. Wright also wanted to create spaces that were conducive to family conversation. The kitchen was placed close to the carport as well, minimizing the distance between the car and the kitchen to facilitate the transportation of groceries.

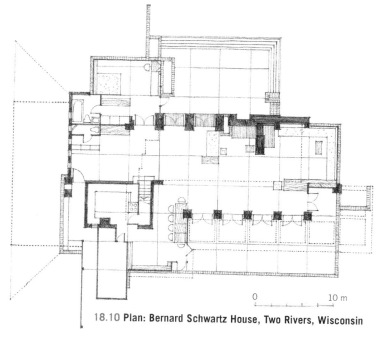

18.10 **Plan: Bernard Schwartz House, Two Rivers, Wisconsin**

18.11 **Unité d'habitation, Marseille, France**

Congrès Internationaux d'Architecture Moderne
From the early 20th century onward, European architects banded together in various organizations to define their position and forward their cause in political and cultural matters. The Werkbund, which still exists today, was founded in 1907 in Munich and had among its members Peter Behrens, Walter Gropius, and Bruno Taut. The Novembergruppe, formed in Berlin in 1918, though short-lived, was more clearly pro-modern, seeing the postwar economy as an opportunity to rethink social relations and architectural expression. The group that had the most important impact on architectural thinking, however, was the Congrès Internationaux d'Architecture Moderne (CIAM, 1928–45), which came into being as a result of the competition for the design of the Palace of the League of Nations in Geneva, Switzerland, in 1927. The competition turned into a contest between modernists and traditionalists, with Le Corbusier's entry rejected in favor of a Beaux-Arts project designed by Henri-Paul Nénot. Though the membership of CIAM was constantly changing—as were its priorities— Le Corbusier played the dominant role in it, along with Walter Gropius and the Swiss architectural historian Siegfried Giedion. From its inception, there were arguments about which direction to take, but the group managed to hang together for almost two decades. Nonetheless, in the five congresses held before World War II, CIAM shifted its

position from an organization that encouraged a plurality of views about modern architecture to one increasingly dominated by the ideas of Le Corbusier.

The first congress, in 1928, produced a manifesto known as the Sarraz Declaration, named after the Château de la Sarraz in France, where the group met. Twenty-four architects signed the document, which attacked the academies for their sterilizing grip on the architectural profession; it instead promoted an architecture based on practical, economic, and sociological considerations. The document held that modern architecture had the obligation to satisfy not only the material needs of the population but also the spiritual and intellectual demands of contemporary life. Modern urbanism, it argued, should be based not on arbitrary aesthetic principles but on a collective and methodological land policy. This realism was eventually replaced by a more utopian ethos emphasizing the question of whether architects should adopt a sociological approach or a more formal one. The urban designers with practical experience tended to favor the former, whereas Le Corbusier, ever the elitist, favored the latter.

At CIAM 3, held in Brussels, Le Corbusier began to gain the upper hand in determining the agenda and in promoting his Ville Radieuse ("Radiant City"). At the fourth CIAM congress, in 1933, the participants published their conclusions as the Athens Charter (so-called because the Congress

was held on board a ship that sailed from Marseille to Athens). It committed CIAM to rigidly functional cities, whose citizens would be housed in high, widely spaced apartment blocks based on CIAM planning principles that called for the separation of living functions. Greenbelts would separate each zone of the city. Generally speaking, it was assumed, as Le Corbusier phrased it, that the positions adopted by CIAM would be accepted by "an enlightened population that would understand, desire and demand what the specialists have envisioned for it."

18.12 **Le Corbusier's vision for the residential quarter of the Radiant City**

18.13 **Pavilion Suisse, Paris**

Pavilion Suisse

Le Corbusier reinvented the ideal industrial city of the modern age. He published his ideas in the form of several utopian proposals to remake Paris, among which were *The Contemporary City* (1922) and *The Radiant City* (1933). Drawn from the viewpoint of a bird or a plane, these cities erased a huge swath of the existing urban fabric of Paris, leaving only some of the more respected monuments and churches in place. The new city consisted of rows of identical cruciform skyscrapers clustered around an airfield in the center. In later schemes, he showed housing organized in long, multistory blocks that twisted and turned to create bounded fields between their curves. Le Corbusier also made a series of perspectives from the human-eye level that showed a continuous green landscape flowing under the skyscrapers, built on stilts, as far as the eye could see. The audacity of Le Corbusier's proposals—particularly the impunity with which he proposed to erase the historic city—provoked loud reactions, both of praise and horror. For his defenders, his urban designs catapulted him into the role of the messiah of a new industrial age. Le Corbusier was never able to realize any of his sweeping urban plans as he wished, even though some of the suggested features eventually came to influence urban planning the world over, especially after World War II.

The Radiant City was an example of social functionalism. Each apartment block was equipped with a catering section and laundry in the basement. The space between the blocks was dedicated to sports and leisure, and the roof was for gardens and day-care centers. Transportation systems were designed throughout the city. All this was part of Le Corbusier's critique of the horizontal spread of the Garden City and the wasted commuting time that engendered. The Pavilion Suisse (1932), a student dormitory that he was able to build at the Cité Universitaire in Paris, was intended as a showpiece for his vision. Two rows of long and narrow rooms were arranged around a central corridor, a plywood closet separated the kitchen from the living area, and the toilets and baths were shared. Most importantly, the building was elevated off the ground by columns that Le Corbusier called *pilotis*.

At Marseille, Corbusier realized one of several Unités d'Habitations (1947–52), structures for up to 1,600 people designed in the form of vertical village, complete with an internal shopping street halfway up, a recreation ground and children's nursery on the roof, and a generous surrounding area of parkland made possible by the density of the accommodation in the slab itself.

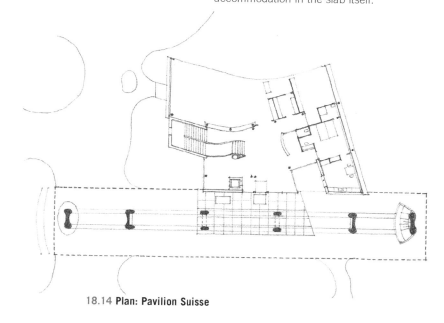

18.14 **Plan: Pavilion Suisse**

18.15 **End court with sculpture, Barcelona Pavilion, Barcelona, Spain**

Barcelona Pavilion

Mies van der Rohe's German National Pavilion, built for the 1929 Barcelona International Exhibition, became an icon of the modernist aesthetic almost from the beginning. It was visited by people from all over the world, showing a side of modernism that many had not expected from Mies, who was normally thought of as a defender of harsh industrial architecture. Here they saw a building that stressed the visual and sensual aspects of surfaces and materials. The building, which rested on a white travertine platform, was entered from the west by a path that led down a forested hill. The view to the immediate left was of a nude female statue by Georg Kolbe, standing in a pool of water framed by walls clad in dramatically veined green marble from the Greek island of Tinos, contrasting with the green of the forested hill above. The south-facing walls would have received the bright Spanish sun, contrasting with the cool hues of the interior surfaces. There were no doors, only a set of walls that defined spaces through which one walked.

Not only was there the physical impression of this free-flowing space but also the visual sensation created by the rich colors, the opulent surfaces, and the dazzling play of reflections off the polished materials; even the columns were encased in highly reflective chrome sheathing. The columns form a structural rhythm of two rows of four, in syncopated relationship with the walls, which are sometimes quite close

to the columns, sometimes farther away. It is impossible to understand the columns as part of a structural-rationalist system; they are, in essence, broken apart to stand in dialogue with both the walls and the viewers of the space. The minimalism of the design draws on the elementarist compositions of Kazimir Malevich and other Constructivists, but Mies was no socialist. The building is, in fact, meant to appeal to an elite clientele. Mies was doing something similar to what Adolf Loos had done in the previous decade: unifying a language of stark modernism on the exterior with lush and sensuous materials on the interior. But unlike Loos, whose

interiors were intimate, Mies's are open and mysteriously shimmering. The building does have, however, a clear and identifiable spatial focus defined by four different walls, the most important one made of a rare marble called onyx dorée, with veins that ranged from dark gold to white. It was flanked by a wall of milk-glass lit from within. In front of the onyx wall was a table and, set side by side, a pair of metal-frame chairs with white leather cushions. Behind the chairs, through a wall of green glass, glimmered the surface of the pool. The view through the glass darkened the marble rising behind the pool and accented its veining.

18.16 **View from pool, Barcelona Pavilion**

18.17 Wall and column juxtaposition, Barcelona Pavilion

Visitors saw a series of conjoining and overlapping visual planes, starting with the horizontal view of the trees behind the building, framed by the roof and the top of the Tinian marble wall, and then descending through various layers to the floor of the building. The floor, surfaced in white travertine and matching to some degree the whiteness of the roof, created for visitors a floating sensation interrupted only in the central room, where the space in front of the great onyx slab was covered by a thin black carpet. On the opposite wall, the glass was covered by drapery of scarlet silk. The central space was thus a type of stage set, with its single column off to one side, standing at a respectful distance from the onyx wall.

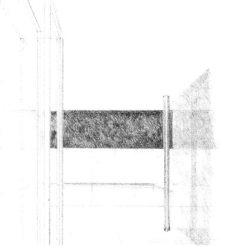

18.18 Column detail: Barcelona Pavilion

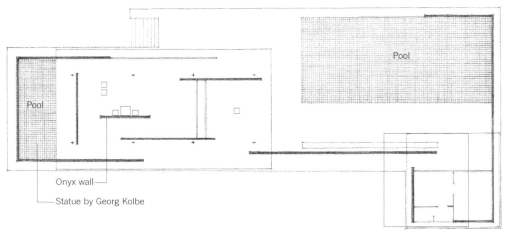

Pool

Pool

Onyx wall

Statue by Georg Kolbe

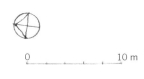

0   10 m

18.19 Plan: Barcelona Pavilion

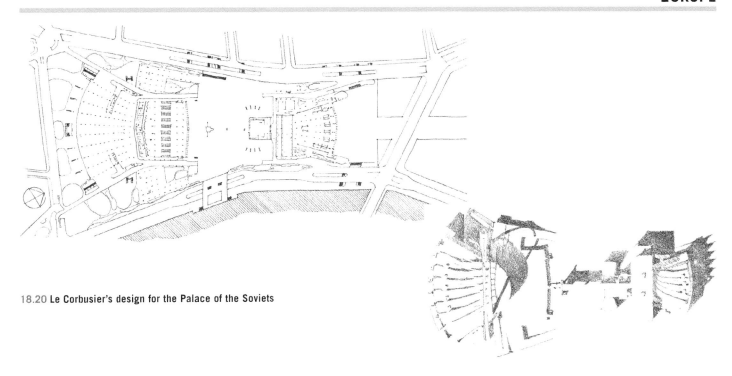

18.20 **Le Corbusier's design for the Palace of the Soviets**

Palace of the Soviets Competition

To celebrate the new Soviet state, Joseph Stalin planned to build a huge Palace of the Soviets in Moscow, Russia. A competition was held in 1931 under the hopeful auspices of the architectural community. It was believed that Russia, as an emerging world power, would continue the trend set by Constructivists. Over 160 Soviet architects and firms and 24 foreigners volunteered designs; among the latter were Le Corbusier, Walter Gropius, Hannes Meyer, Erich Mendelsohn, and August Perret.

The competition was carried out in four phases. The first, open only to the Soviet architects, assisted in the formulation of the exact functions of the palace and only required that the building be conceived as a "people's forum" for mass demonstrations and rallies. The results of this phase, published and exhibited in Moscow, established the guidelines for the second stage of the competition, such as a large auditorium to accommodate 15,000 people, and a series of spaces to serve as a theater and cinema.

The stipulations of the competition stressed "monumental quality, simplicity, integrity and elegance" and the use "both of new methods and the best employed in

classical architecture." Le Corbusier's design was conceived in a Constructivist mold to optimize the functional requirements of the complex, but in a manner that created a striking visual image, especially from above. Unlike most of the competition entries, which tried to squeeze all the functions into a single mass, Le Corbusier distributed the functions into two main volumes. The foci of these volumes were the two wedge-shaped auditoriums, neatly fitted into the irregular site on the banks of the Moscow River. The plans of two auditoriums (designed with Gustave Lyon) were optimized not only for sightlines and acoustics but also for ease of access and egress. The sculptural drama of the design was provided by the auditoriums' roofs, which were suspended from splayed girders. The girders of the larger auditorium were suspended by cables from a soaring parabolic arch. This arch, much like Eero Saarinen's post–World War II arch in St. Louis still to come, would have towered above the Moscow skyline and would have, from certain vistas, framed the bulbous domes of the Kremlin within its curve. The arch was intended as an inscription of modernity on the skyline. It would have been the first modern building with such an ambition, apart perhaps from the Eiffel Tower, which had no

particular program and was conceived as part of the preparations for the Paris World's Fair of 1889.

The modernists, however, were to be sorely disappointed when the top award went to Boris Iofan and Vladimir Shchuko for a design that called for a towering wedding cake concoction of enormous massing and height. It was to be topped by a huge apotheosis of Vladimir Lenin. Despite being an expression of Soviet might, the edifice was much closer in design to contemporaneous icons of capitalism, like the Wrigley Building (1920) in Chicago, than to Russian Neoclassical architecture. In preparation for the construction of Iofan's building, the Cathedral of Christ the Savior was demolished in 1931. However, water from the adjoining Moscow River began to flood the site, delaying construction. By the outbreak of World War II, the steel skeleton was almost complete, but in the course of the war, much of that steel was melted down to make tanks to fight the Nazis. Nikita Khrushchev abandoned the project after Stalin's death in 1953 and had the already existing structure converted into a Moscow metro station and a giant public swimming pool. Recently, the Cathedral of Christ the Savior has been rebuilt at the site; it was consecrated in August 2000.

18.21 **Lower plaza, Rockefeller Center, New York City**

Rockefeller Center

By the late 1920s, New York had risen to the level of a world metropolis. Dozens of tall buildings had been constructed, including new civic and institutional buildings. Skyscraper architects had moved away from overt historicism toward the elegant lines of Art Deco, as at the Chrysler Building (1928–30). The Chanin Building (1927–29) went even further, with a neutral, gridlike facade. Rockefeller Center, designed by Raymond Hood and Wallace K. Harrison, was nothing less than a city within a city, composed of fourteen buildings between Forty-Eighth and Fifty-First Streets in New York City. At the core of the composition was the seventy-one-story RCA Building (1931–32), which faced onto a sunken plaza defined on its flanks by low-rise buildings— the British Empire Building and the Maison Française. The RCA Building was sheathed in a yellowish limestone with aluminum trim, with the windows arranged vertically in slightly recessed strips to emphasize the structure's soaring qualities. In its complete avoidance of references to a classical past, as well as the thinness of its central tower, this building, in many respects, paved the way for the skyscraper aesthetic developed by the modernists. Radio City Music Hall, containing the nation's largest indoor theater, was on the next block. A cross street, Rockefeller Plaza, introduced an innovative division of the central parcel.

Though rarely emulated, the center was much admired for its urban design implications. The setbacks, which were required by zoning regulations, were woven so fluidly into the design that they seemed to be an organic part of the building—a quality different from that found at the RCA Building, the Chanin Building, or even the Empire State Building, with its stockier base. To emphasize the building's towering quality, the lower buildings were designed to look more substantial— almost like stone volumes that also help frame the views of the tower.

Artists were brought in to create sculptures and murals—themselves excellent examples of Art Deco—for placement over the entrance doors and in the lobby. These included Paul Manship, who designed a gilded statue of a recumbent Prometheus. The Mexican socialist artist Diego Rivera was commissioned to create a mural for the lobby, but when it was discovered that it contained a portrait of Vladimir Lenin and other anticapitalist imagery, it was removed.

Tall buildings constructed in New York City from 1920 to 1930 (partial list):

Standard Oil Building (1920–28)
Bowery Savings Bank (1921–23)
Barclay-Vesey Building (1923–27)
Ritz Tower (1925–27)
Paramount Building (1926–27)
Chanin Building (1927–29)
Chrysler Building (1928–30)
RCA Building (1929–31)
McGraw-Hill Building (1930–31)
Empire State Building (1930–31)

18.22 **Rockefeller Center**

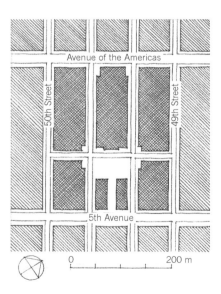

18.23 **Plan diagram: Rockefeller Center**

18.24 **Bata Shoe Factory, Zlín, Czech Republic**   18.25 **Bata Shoe Factory**

Czechoslovakia

In many places in Europe, national Romanticism hindered the advancement of modernist architecture because many nationalists saw modernism—and its associations with industrialism and socially progressive politics—as antithetical to the idyllic past that was central to Romantic ideology. This explains to some extent why the first true example of modernism as a state-sponsored aesthetic flourished in Turkey and some other non-European countries, where Romanticism was not as firmly developed. Nonetheless, nationalism, even in Europe, began to turn to modernism as an expression of a country's search for autonomy and capitalist strength. One of the first places where this new equation was manifest was Czechoslovakia, which in 1918 emerged as an independent state from the dismembered Austro-Hungarian Empire. The small Central European country inherited both a large portion of the former empire's ethnic diversity and its economic strength. In fact, Czechoslovakia became one of Europe's most politically stable and democratic systems during the restless interwar years. This stability is generally attributed to Tomas Garrigue Masaryk (1850–1937), the first president of the republic and an internationally respected scholar-statesman. Though Czechoslovakian government officials never gave state sponsorship to modernism, this did not hamper the younger generation and the educated and prosperous middle class from seeing modernism as an articulation of Czechoslovakia's political emancipation

from the old Austro-Hungarian Empire. The teaching of Otto Wagner disciples like Jan Kotera and Jože Plecnik, who belonged to the same generation as Josef Hoffman and Adolf Loos, was immensely influential.

By 1937, the Bata Shoe Company had become the world market-leader in shoe production, becoming the first manufacturer in Europe to mass-produce good-quality shoes at an affordable price. The company's founder, Tomás Bata, invested in an extensive building program, first in his hometown of Zlín, where he located the company headquarters, and later in factory towns that he and his successor, Jan Bata, established on three continents. Bata had factories and sales organizations in thirty-three countries and was at the time one of the most international companies in the world. Bata systematically hired young Czech architects and engineers with international experience. One of these young professionals was Vladimir Karfik, who had worked for Le Corbusier and Frank Lloyd Wright.

The Bata headquarters, a seventeen-story building designed by Karfik (1937), was one of the first high-rise buildings in Europe. It was built with a structural frame of reinforced concrete on a module of 6.15 by 6.15 meters. This so-called Bata standard was the basis for all Bata buildings, ranging from factories and retail stores to various public buildings. Contrary to traditional dispositions in skyscraper design, three service pods were located on the perimeter of the building. This created an unobstructed rectangle measuring 80 by 20 meters organized as an open-plan

office in which reconfigurable office modules were the only spatial dividers. Electricity and telephone networks with plugs laid in the floor on a 3-by-3-meter grid facilitated flexibility in space organization. The most striking feature of the building was Jan Bata's office in the form of an elevator. The vertically mobile unit allowed Bata to dock on every floor—thereby going wherever he was needed. Bata was also able to communicate with his employees throughout the building by means of an intercom. The interior of the office elevator, designed with wood paneling and double windows, was well lit by natural light. Among the most difficult tasks Karfik faced was how to make a sink with running cold and hot water possible and how to adapt the cabin to quick temperature changes when moving in the shaft.

By the end of the 1930s, European modernism was not moving forward very well. Gropius and Mies had all but disappeared from the scene, and Le Corbusier received few commissions, prompting him to seek work outside of Europe, such as in Ankara, Turkey; in Tel Aviv (then part of the Palestinian Protectorate); and in Casablanca, Morocco, which was a French colony. Though the architects with whom he coordinated in these cities are not well known, they made major contributions to the cause of modern architecture. Turkey and Israel were particularly important in this respect, since modern buildings there were part of a highly visible nation-building effort, rather than the fiat of a colonial administration as in Casablanca.

18.26 Touba Mosque, Senegal

Touba

In 1887, Sheikh Amadou Bamba (1853–1927), a Muslim mystic, founded a homestead later called Touba in an isolated place outside the town of Mbacké, in what is now Senegal. He acquired a reputation as a holy man, and soon followers began to seek him out. He developed a form of Sufism, known as Mouridism, according to which the material world is not complete in and of itself: matter, it teaches, is relevant to life only insofar as it is infused by the divine. Bamba perceived his mission as also a social one; he wanted his adherents to return to the "straight path" of Islam. So Touba became a holy city in which everything frivolous—laughing, dancing, drinking alcohol—was forbidden.

At first the French colonial authorities viewed Bamba's growing popularity as a threat to their authority and sent him into exile, but since his position was one of nonviolence, they released him and eventually gave him their nominal support. In the 1920s, Bamba launched the construction of a large mosque; he was assisted by thousands of faithful volunteers in its construction. The reinforced concrete structure, which has been continuously enlarged, has three domes and five minarets, the central one being quite tall and visible for miles in the flat Senegalese landscape. The roofs of the domes are green and blue, and the walls are clad in a rose-tinted stone;

the interior is richly decorated. Bamba died in 1927 and his successors finished the building in 1963. It was only then that a city was laid out on a grid plan, with broad radiating streets emanating from the central square where the mosque is located.

The cemetery is located opposite the mosque and thus at the city center, which for Islam is unusual, since cemeteries are usually placed outside of a city. Here the cemetery functions as the gate to the hereafter and is an important part of the Sufi mystical experience. It was designed symbolically around an ancient sacred baobab tree (which died in 2003). On the *qibla* side of the mosque is another tree, a palm tree, that marks the spot where the first birth in Touba took place. These trees are called palaver trees by the locals. (*Palaver* derives from the Portuguese *palavra*, which means speech or discussion.) Since ancient times, palaver trees have served as the heart of community meetings and been at the center of civic and religious functions; because of their longevity, the trees are considered the spiritual guarantors of a community's life. The palaver tree tradition can be found across central Africa. In Islamic areas, it is the mosque that serves as the political and social center of the Islamic community, which can bring the mosque into competition with this older tradition. Here, however, the old and the new were fused, the ancient tradition of the baobab tree blending with the Sufi concept of a tree of paradise. Furthermore, the tall minaret is itself meant to be seen as treelike. Touba was recognized as a model "peace city" by the United Nations Human Settlement Division in 1996.

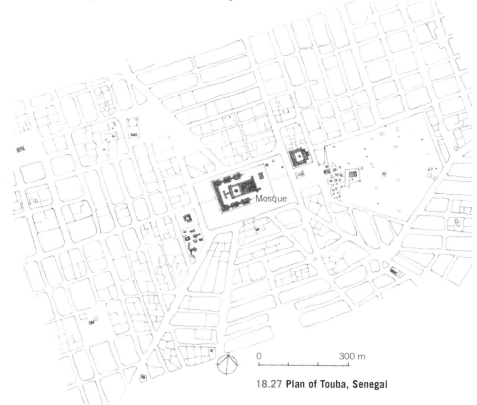

18.27 Plan of Touba, Senegal

National Modernism, Ankara

The transition from the Ottoman Empire to modernity was completed when the Turkish Republic was founded by Mustafa Kemal (also known as Atatürk) in 1923. Atatürk adopted modern architecture as the expression of this new secular nation, starting what is now called national modernism. In contrast to other localities, such as Casablanca, where modernism was imposed by colonial masters, in Ankara it was a triumphant statement that announced Turkey's independence. Atatürk's ambition was to achieve an industrialized nation based on technical and scientific progress, with institutions modeled after those in Europe.

Ankara, at that time a small town in central Anatolia, was chosen as the new capital since it was more or less in the center of the nation. Its design in 1927 by the German planner Hermann Jansen can be considered, along with Canberra, Australia, among the first in a long string of modernist capitals that would include Brasília, Brazil; Chandigarh, India; and Islamabad, Pakistan. The Austrian architect Clemenz Holzmeister (1886–1983), for example, designed the government district, including several ministries, the presidential palace, and the Grand National Assembly Hall. Despite the plain cubic facades, the overall organization was often indebted to classical principles and vocabulary. Nonetheless, the purpose was to visibly and progressively champion the ideals of the new Republic of Turkey. New schools, especially for girls; houses; centers of popular education; and places for physical education, recreation, leisure, and entertainment were among the typologies that became emblematic for the republic's stated aims. The Ismet Pasa Girls' Institute in Ankara, a vocational school, was designed by the Swiss Ernst Egli in 1930. Modern architecture and planning was also employed for model villages, factories, and large infrastructural projects such as the Cubuk Dam outside Ankara (1936). The exhibition hall in Ankara, which also served as an opera house, was designed by Turkish architect Sevki Balmumcu, who won the commission in a competition. It was erected to showcase the technological accomplishments of the Turkish Republic, as were the structures built for the Izmir International Fair.

18.28 Cankaya Presidential Mansion, Ankara, Turkey

National Modernism, Tel Aviv

During the British mandate over Palestine (1920–48), modern architecture became the dominant style among the Jewish people there, who associated it not only with socialist idealism but also with a tabula rasa, free from the memories of the Jewish diaspora. Modern architecture's claim to be founded not on cultural premises but on natural parameters, such as heat, wind, light, topography, and materials, along with a streamlined practicality that accommodated the faster-spaced rhythm of modern life, was welcomed by Jews who were starting out to reshape their lives. There was no shortage of architects, since many were fleeing European fascism. Erich Mendelsohn, Alexander Klein, and Adolf Rading were particularly instrumental in consolidating Zionist and modernist design concepts. Mendelsohn's architecture—for instance, his Hadassah University Medical Center on Mount Scopus in Jerusalem (1936–39)—consists of plain volumes, courtyards, and carefully punched blank walls. It was invested with abstracted, quasi-Oriental imagery, in contrast to the whitewashed international modernist architecture of Ze'ev Rechter's Engle House in Tel Aviv (1933), the city that came to embody Israel's modernism.

Tel Aviv, when founded in 1909, was a small suburb to the north of the Arab city of Jaffa. Unlike Jaffa, with its mixed population, Tel Aviv was designed by Jews for Jews. Its city fathers welcomed the ethos of modernism, and by the late 1930s the city had become one of the few all-modern cities in the world. With the transition to Israeli statehood in 1948, Tel Aviv became the model for future development—especially since it was allied with Israel's massive modernization project, the blueprint for which was prepared by the state planning division headed by Arieh Sharon, a Bauhaus disciple of Hannes Meyer. Sharon's designs were of strict rational modernism cleansed of all Oriental symbolism.

In the 1960s, a new generation of Israeli-born architects began to critique the allegiance to modernism, seeking instead ways to establish communal identity using visceral ties with the past. Aligning themselves with post–World War II criticism, particularly the teaching of Team X and Louis Kahn, their architecture sought local expression in shaded communal spaces, hierarchical layouts, broken volumes, and local building materials, as was evident in the early example of Ram Karmi's Negev Center (1960).

18.29 Ground-floor plan: Japanese Pavilion, 1937 Paris International Exposition   **18.30** Japanese Pavilion, 1937 Paris International Exposition

Japanese Pavilion

The Japanese investment in industrialization began during the years of the Meiji period (1869–1912), which was characterized not only by rapid industrialization and mechanization but also by the complete adoption of Western clothes, habits, and manners. Germany under Bismarck was the role model. In the years leading up to World War II, the country's avante-garde began experimenting with modernism. Young Japanese architects traveled in Europe or took up apprenticeships with European architects; among them was Mamoru Yamada. He traveled to Europe, spending a considerable amount of time in Germany, after having completed the Electrical Laboratory for the Ministry of Public Works (1929), the only Japanese work to be included in Hitchcock and Johnson's International Style Exhibition of 1932. His later work, Tokyo Teishin Hospital (1938), with its white tiled exterior finish, large standardized windows, and minimal ornamentation, is representative of Japanese rationalist architecture of the prewar period.

A successful example of a modernist Japanese design in Europe is the Japanese Pavilion designed for the Paris International Exposition of 1937 by Junzo Sakakura, who had trained under Le Corbusier in Paris from 1931 to 1936. Initially, he had been commissioned to oversee the construction of a traditional-style pavilion, but he surreptitiously modified that design to create a delicate structure of steel, glass, and concrete that was well integrated into its sloped and wooded site. The building was a distinctly Japanese rendering of modernism. Rather than the literal use of a traditional Japanese architectural vocabulary, Sakakura incorporated a steel frame that reinterpreted the rhythms of traditional Japanese wooden structures in a modernist manner.

Villa Mairea

Alvar Aalto (1898–1976), a Finnish architect, came to modernism more cautiously than did the architects in Turkey and Brazil, where national interests propelled modernism forward aggressively. In Finland, a vibrant national Romantic tradition was popular at the time; it idealized village life, which Alto linked, somewhat incongruously, with his unbounded enthusiasm for Italy and in particular for its rural towns. "The curving, living, unpredictable line which runs in dimensions unknown to mathematicians," is the incarnation, Aalto wrote, of "everything that forms a contrast in the modern world between brutal mechanization and religious beauty in life." This vision was embodied in the Villa Mairea (Noormarkku, Finland, 1938–41).

The overall planning of Villa Mairea can be seen as Wrightian, and early sketches show a relationship to Wright's later Fallingwater. But in terms of composition, Aalto's design has a more Cubist understanding of space— not in an obvious sense, as in Pavel Janák's work in Czechoslovakia, but in the asymmetrical tensions that exist in the plan between solid and void and between the implied square of the garden and the house, which is clamped against one corner. But what could be seen as Cubism can also be read as the introduction of a temporal coefficient into the design: the house appears to have grown and expanded over time. Aalto also allowed for an

18.31 Villa Mairea, Noormarkku, Finland

18.32 Living room: Villa Mairea

overt regional gloss in his choice of the wood for the exterior and the use of rustic wooden rails for the balconies. These are, however, offset by steel railings that look like they've been borrowed from a ship and contrast with the smooth bamboo railings used for the interior staircase.

Because of its almost eclectic fusion of different motifs, Villa Mairea could be seen as breaking the mold of modernist reserve. But it could also be perceived as an extension of the late 19th-century approaches of Greene & Greene, Antonio Gaudí, Victor Horta, and Adolf Loos. Though all the modernists had unique styles, Aalto was consistently viewed as less beholden to rationalism and functionalism because of his use of curved lines, contrasting materials, and a penchant for picturesque massing. Aalto worked closely with his wife, Aino (1894–1949), who was also Finnish. Much of the Villa Mairea's interior, in fact, was designed by her. They collaborated on the design of chairs made with bent plywood, a new technology at the time and far different from the heavy steel-frame chairs of most modernists. Aalto was a CIAM member, attending the second congress in Frankfurt in 1929 and the fourth congress in Athens in 1933. His reputation grew as a consequence of the Finnish Pavilion at the 1939 New York World's Fair, and Baker House Dormitory (1947) for the Massachusetts Institute of Technology in Cambridge.

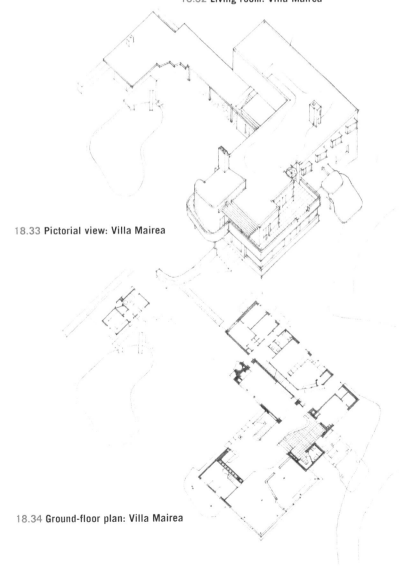

18.33 Pictorial view: Villa Mairea

18.34 Ground-floor plan: Villa Mairea

18.35 Fallingwater, Bear Run, Pennsylvania

Fallingwater

Edgar J. Kaufmann had made a fortune on his department stores. On the advice of his son, who was a student at the Taliesin School of Architecture, he engaged Wright in 1935 to design a family weekend and summer retreat on their woodland property at Bear Run in western Pennsylvania. (Their permanent residence was in Pittsburgh.) Unlike the bread-and-butter Usonian houses, Fallingwater (1936) is a dramatic statement on the possibilities of reinforced concrete and demonstrates a very un-Aalto-esque relationship to nature, expressed most memorably by a triple set of deeply overhanging cantilevered terraces that appear to float over a dramatic waterfall. The Kaufmanns had wanted a house from which they could look at the waterfall, but instead Wright built them one that was literally over the waterfall. A stair in the living room leads down to the top of the waterfall and to a small platform where people can sit and dangle their feet in the water.

Wright's justifications for his design lay in his conception of "organic architecture," a decidedly subjective term that for him indicated a building integrated into its site and context in the form of a sympathetic counterstatement. The diagonal plan and stepped section, for example, is a response to the contours of the site, a point particularly important to Wright and anticipated in part in earlier projects like the Freeman House

(1924–25). Here the ornamenting of the building's surface has given way to rustic, horizontally coursed yellowish stones that contrast with the smooth, stuccoed surfaces of the balconies and roof lines. Windows are hidden in recesses, with thinly mullioned glazing capturing some of the spaces in between the floor and roof to create indoor-outdoor rooms.

When viewed from below the waterfall, the house seems to hover provocatively over the site, its straight lines contrasting with the huge boulders, and the white balconies contrasting with the rich foliage of the forest. The stone walls that anchor the cantilevers mimic the stratified pattern of the rock ledges and rise up into the house in the form of towers that anchor the composition and seem almost like ancient ruins. Since the site is quite remote, Wright built a separate servants' quarter and garage just up the hill from the house. Today the site is much more forested than it was originally, concealing the building more than Wright probably would have liked.

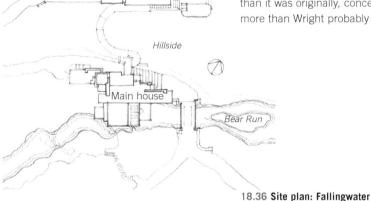

18.36 Site plan: Fallingwater

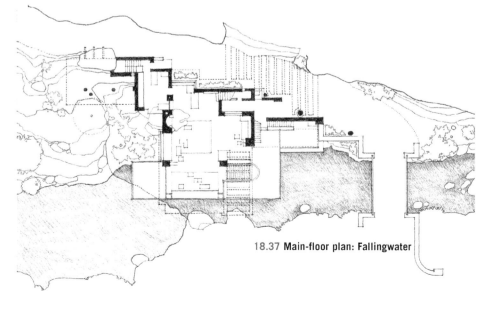

18.37 Main-floor plan: Fallingwater

18.38 Residential building, Rio de Janeiro, by Lúcio Costa

Brazilian Modernism

After the economic crash of 1929, Brazil's export-oriented economy was shattered, paving the way for President Getulio Vargas (1883–1954), who, as a virtual dictator (r. 1930–45), created a developmentalist, state-sponsored program of modernization. Much as in Kemal Atatürk's Turkey, modern architecture was to be the visible imprint of his nationalist project. In 1930, the young architect Lúcio Costa was appointed director of the Escola Nacional de Belas Artes. Though Costa initially knew little about modern architecture, he soon became its leading advocate, bringing in a Russian émigré, Gregori Warchavchik (1896–1972), who presented his "modernist house" at an exhibition that was opened to the public in 1930. It had a white, cubic volume (though a parapet concealed a pitched, tiled roof) that earned the architect a place in the 1930 CIAM congress.

Early in his own career, Costa had little work and had spent his time studying books on the architecture of Walter Gropius, Ludwig Mies van de Rohe, and, most of all, Le Corbusier. Le Corbusier himself had built little other than his "white" houses, but his books *Towards a New Architecture*, *The Contemporary City*, and *Precisions* were widely influential. In 1936, Gustavo Capanema, the thirty-three-year-old minister of education and health, took the bold step of commissioning Costa to build the ministry's official headquarters. Costa's initial design was a merger of the two halves of Le Corbusier's competition entry for the League of Nations project (1927). His final design, prepared in collaboration with Oscar Niemeyer (in consultation with Le Corbusier), was a fourteen-story tower set in the middle of a rectangular site. Ten-meter-high *pilotis*—much higher than Le Corbusier had proposed—vehemently lift the structure off the ground. On the cross-axis, along one length of the site is the double-height block of the auditorium and the public spaces. Its most dramatic statement was the use of a curtain wall on the south side and a system of *brise-soleils*, or sunshades, on the other. Two towering curved shapes, covered with blue tiles, functioned as vents and storage for mechanical services. There was a restaurant on the roof terrace as well.

Costa and Niemeyer also collaborated on the design of the Brazilian Pavilion for the New York World's Fair of 1939, whose slogan was "The World of Tomorrow." Costa wanted a building that would stand out not for its scale (the site was not big), nor for its luxury (Brazil was still poor), but for its inherent formal qualities. Simplicity and the suggestion of direct functionalism was its message. The two-story design lifted the main volume of the pavilion above the ground and made a statement out of its access ramp, whose large sweeping curve seemed to forcefully wedge itself into the upper floor. The ground floor was partially enclosed and had freestanding displays for national beverages like coffee, maté, and guarana. The garden to the rear showed off Brazilian flora. The upper floor, with the main auditorium, had an exhibition space with double-height steel columns that partially supported a free-plan mezzanine. Its facade had a *brise-soleil*, whereas the rear was glazed from top to bottom. The building became the icon for Brazilian modernism.

18.39 Ministry of Health and Education, Rio de Janeiro

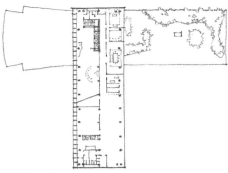

Third-floor plan

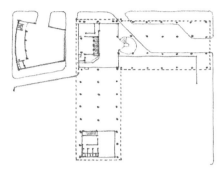

Ground-floor plan

18.40 Plans: Ministry of Health and Education Building, Rio de Janeiro

18.41 **São Paulo Museum of Art, São Paulo, Brazil**

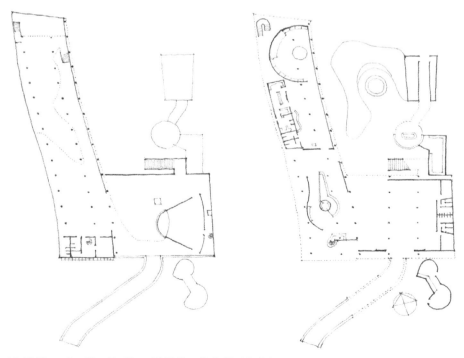

18.42 Plans: Brazilian Pavilion, 1939 New York World's Fair

Not everything in Brazil was European modernism and structural expression. Lina Bo Bardi (1914–92), for instance, designed a house made of adobe and straw, and Bernard Rudofsky, who lived in Brazil for three years (1938–41) and later wrote *Architecture Without Architects*, built a house for Joan Arnstein organized around five internal garden courtyards that extended the spaces of the living room, dining room, master bedroom, and children's bedrooms.

Bo Bardi was one of the few independently practicing women architects among the early modernists. She was born in Italy. After graduating in Rome, she opened her own office, was involved in the Italian Communist Party, and after World War I created an influential journal, *A Cultura della Vita*, with Bruno Zevi. In 1946, she moved to Brazil and became a citizen in 1951. There she cofounded the journal *Habitat* with her husband, the art critic Pietro Maria Bardi. Her most important commission was for the São Paulo Museum of Art (1947), a dramatic Brutalist creation. Sited at the top edge of a slope, she suspended the entire building in the form of a box from enormous concrete beams in order to open vistas to the horizon.

18.43 Palace of Italian Civilization, Esposizione Universale di Roma (EUR), Rome

of the Renaissance, and beyond that to the Roman Empire. Members of the Italian Movement for Rational Architecture (MIAR), founded in 1928, looked for inspiration in Greco-Roman classicism as well as in the vernacular traditions of the Mediterranean region.

Some of the most significant examples of large-scale urban renewal requiring demolition in Rome, Milan, Turin, Bergamo, and Genoa were overseen by Mussolini's architect, Marcello Piacentini. He was also responsible for two significant new urban schemes: Città Universitaria (1932–35) and the Esposizione Universale di Roma (EUR, 1937–42), originally intended as the site of the 1942 Universal Exposition in Rome. The onset of World War II eclipsed plans for the exposition, but several pavilions were realized, including Ernesto La Padula's metaphysical and iconic Palace of Italian Civilization (1937–40). It was a glass box protected from the outside by a facade that consisted of six horizontal registers of identical arched loggias clad in travertine.

Fascist Modernism, Italy

With the end of the World War I, Italian architecture entered a new phase of self-awareness, especially in light of the rise of Fascism following Benito Mussolini's coup in 1922. Due to the strong nationalistic impulse at the core of Fascist ideology, Italian architects found themselves reflecting upon the role of tradition in their architecture. But this return to tradition, with its links to national Romanticism, had a very different character in Italy than it did in Germany. Italy's implementation of a vast state-sponsored building program that included the construction of post offices, train stations, civic buildings, and even small towns placed the country closer in spirit to Turkey. For many architects, the Fascist critique of passivity seemed to legitimate modernism. Italian Fascist architecture, therefore, did not see itself as antithetical to clean geometries and white surfaces. There was, however, a fierce debate over the precise style that was to best represent the Fascist ethos. As a result, the avant-garde ideal of merging life and art fused in Italy with the sinister ambitions of totalitarianism, with artists and architects drawing numerous parallels between Mussolini and the great patrons

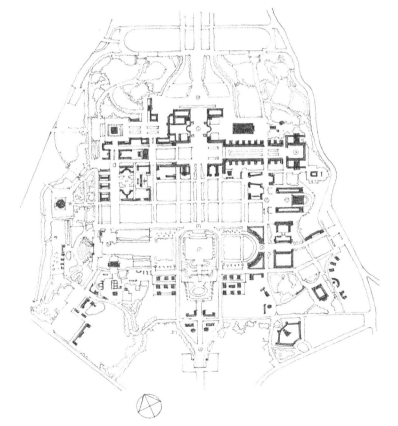

18.44 Site plan: Esposizione Universale di Roma (EUR)

18.45 **Casa del Fascio, Como, Italy**

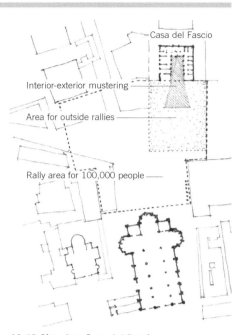

18.46 **Site plan: Casa del Fascio**

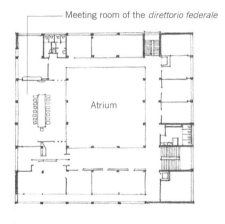

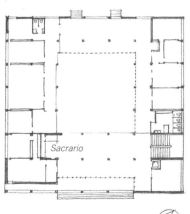

18.47 **Ground- and first-floor plans: Casa del Fascio**

Among the many representatives of the modernist movement in Italy, Giuseppe Terragni (1904-43) was certainly the most prominent. He studied architecture at the Milan Polytechnic and became a member of Gruppo 7 (founded 1926), which consisted of seven architects unified in their advocacy of rationalism and Fascism. Giuseppe Terragni's Casa del Fascio (1932–36) in Como, designed as the regional headquarters of the Fascist Party, is not, despite its white boxy form, as ahistorical as it appears, for it fuses the model of the socialist meeting hall with the principle of an Italian palazzo by adhering to the traditional courtyard plan. The building was designed as a "house of glass," a descriptive term more apparent from the inside than the outside. Some 20 percent of its surface is glass, with large windows framing the city; the array of glass doors between the piazza and the atrium could all be swung open on demand. The meeting room of the *directorio federale* (provincial directorate) also overlooks the central atrium through a glass wall. This transparency symbolically implies that the Fascist government wanted to be viewed as accessible and transparent, and its leader and the people to be seen as a single continuum.

Unlike Le Corbusier's idea of architecture, which favored column grids, thin walls, and horizontal windows, Terragni created a complex, layered geometric architecture that allowed the building to be axial in approach and entry and yet have an interior of interpenetrating asymmetries that fit together almost like a puzzle. The plan is organized with offices along the eastern facade and meeting rooms along the opposite facade, separated by an atrium. On the front there is a balcony that faces onto the large piazza but that allows speakers to address the crowds inside the building as well. The spiritual core of the building is the *sacrario*, or chapel, which is dedicated to the fallen heroes of the "Fascist Revolution." It is located to the left of the entrance foyer. To heighten the impression of entering a sacred precinct, Terragni made the floor level of the *sacrario* slightly lower than that of the atrium. The ceiling of the foyer is covered with black marble, whereas walls are covered in red granite. The main hall is defined by an open structural system, with columns holding up large concrete beams on which are placed horizontal louvers that filter the light, while a gap in the center allows a controlled beam of direct light.

18.48 **Exterior view: Säynätsalo Town Hall, Finland**

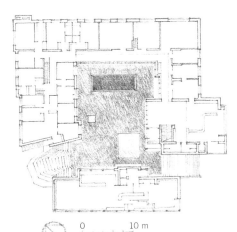

0   10 m

18.49 **Plan: Säynätsalo Town Hall**

18.50 **Site plan: Säynätsalo Town Hall**

Säynätsalo Town Hall

By the time Alvar Aalto designed the Säynätsalo Town Hall (1949–52), his reputation was secure, largely due to the acclaimed Finnish Pavilion at the Paris World's Fair in 1937. In this town hall he began to move away from the modernist-Cubist complexity of his early work toward the imagery of ancient Crete and medieval Italy that had fascinated him as a youth. The space, for that reason, is less a courtyard than a civic enclave raised above the lower slope. One enters it at a corner by means of a staircase molded into the landscape. The council chamber, visible through a gap, is housed in a structure that is square in plan and surmounted by a pitched roof that is, apart from a razor thin line of dark flashing, not visible from the ground, making the volumes appear as abstract shapes. The external surfaces are all of textured brick in Flemish bond. The picturesque qualities of the composition are obvious. The staggers, angles, and shifts enhance the three-dimensional quality of the building, as do the windows of different sizes and proportions. In some places, the brick, where it touches the ground, rests on black tiles that cover the foundation; in other places, the brick appears to float effortlessly over the windows.

More modernist in flavor is the Seinäjoki Town Hall (1958), where Aalto returns to the Cubist format, with its play of volume and solid, and of frame and opening. The site consists of two parcels straddling a busy road. Aalto created an esplanade through the site, with the buildings defining and expanding its spatial elements.

18.51 **Town Hall, Säynätsalo**

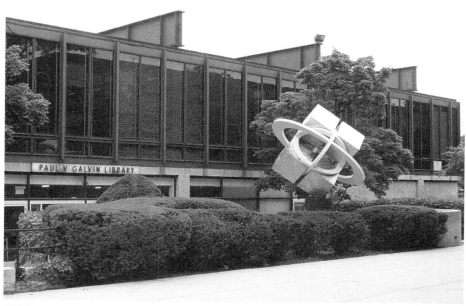

18.52 **Illinois Institute of Technology Library Building, Chicago**

Illinois Institute of Technology Library Building

International modernism in the United States, and globally, would have developed far differently had not some of its leading proponents emigrated to the U.S. during Hitler's regime. Mies van der Rohe came in 1937 to head Chicago's Armour Institute of Technology (later renamed the Illinois Institute of Technology). The same year saw the arrival of Walter Gropius, who taught at the Harvard Graduate School of Design. Marcel Breuer came to the United States as well and began a collaboration with Gropius before launching his own office in 1941. The publication in 1941 of the seminal *Space, Time and Architecture* by the Swiss historian and critic Sigfried Giedion was hugely influential; his book gave intellectual and historical depth to the modern movement. Giedion argued that modernism was the only style that was in tune with the times since it could translate concrete, steel, and glass into an aesthetic of clean surfaces and visual transparency.

Mies was not only appointed head of the architecture department of the Illinois Institute of Technology (IIT) but was given the commission to lay out the campus. It became the first truly modern campus in history with all buildings made of steel, brick, and glass. The site was laid out on a 7.3-meter grid, that being the dimension of the standard

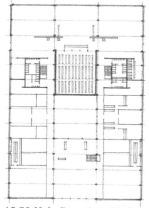

18.53 **Main-floor plan: IIT Library Building**

U.S. classroom. The grid system also guaranteed that if only a part of the campus were constructed, future architectural unity could be preserved. The buildings were all rectangular and more or less of the same height but varied in shape, according to program.

In designing the buildings, a new type of space became central to Mies's aesthetics. Whereas in earlier decades, his spaces flowed along walls and columns, here he became interested in large, vacuous spaces defined by a simple symmetry of form and bounded at the perimeter by columns conceived in rigorous geometrical order. Mies realized the potential of these ideas in the plans for his unbuilt library building (1942–43), where, however, he did not abandon his notion of a conceptual core, formed here by the book stacks placed in a square toward one end of the building and flanked by bathrooms and stairs. This conceptual mass was contrasted with an open courtyard that was to be fronted by an interior waiting room. The plan was flexible, but not "free" as Le Corbusier would define it. It was layered, thickened, and thinned. Since this was to be a one-story building, the fire code permitted the use of unencased steel, allowing Mies to reveal the structural elements inside and out with maximum clarity. Mies elaborated on the theme again in the Crown Hall at IIT (1950–56) and later in his career at the National Gallery in Berlin (1962–67).

18.54 **Crown Hall, IIT, Chicago**

Farnsworth House

Of Mies van der Rohe's few commissions for private residences, the best known was the Farnsworth House (1946–51) in Illinois. Because the site, not far from a river, was prone to flooding, Mies elevated the house 2.2 meters above ground level. Entrance was gained by a broad flight of steps interrupted by a large, open podium without railings. Two sets of four columns support a roof cantilevered at both ends. There are no walls, but rather sheets of glass between the columns that span from floor to ceiling. The kitchen and bathrooms were unified into a single core element set to one side of the space to define two separate zones. The floors of white travertine and the white painted steel frame created a sense of grace and refinement. The curtains were of natural shantung silk and the woodwork of teak, Mies being very luxury-conscious when it came to the sparse interior furnishings. There were difficulties, however, in actually living in the house (Mrs. Farnsworth complained of feeling like she was in a fish bowl). The house nonetheless became the model for several other experiments, the most notable being the private residence designed by Philip Johnson on his estate in New Canaan, Connecticut (1949). The Johnson house used steel for the posts but the roof was of wood, which was significantly easier to construct and repair. Johnson separated the bathroom core from the kitchen, which he reduced to the level of furniture.

18.55 **Farnsworth House, Plano, Illinois**

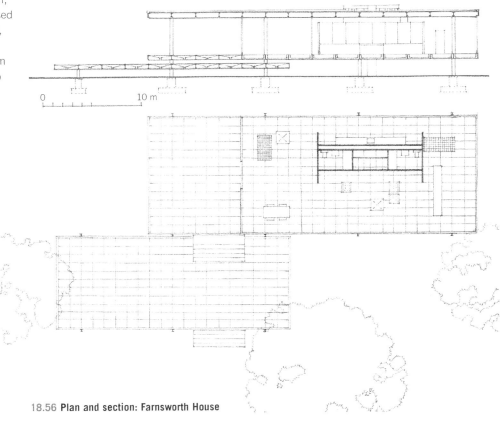

0   10 m

18.56 **Plan and section: Farnsworth House**

18.57 **Eames House, Pacific Palisades, California**

18.58 **Eames House**

Eames House

In the United States, John Entenza (1905–84), editor of the influential Los Angeles–based *Arts and Architecture* magazine, was an important but much-overlooked sponsor of modern architecture in America, bringing the works of many artists and architects to public attention. To combat the housing shortage after World War II, he started a drive to assemble well-designed houses rapidly and inexpensively using wartime technologies and materials. In January 1945, to speed his project along, he invited architects to construct prototype houses in Los Angeles to explore the feasibility of his idea. Of the twenty-four houses completed by 1966, one of the most innovative was a project by Charles and Ray Eames, a husband-and-wife team who designed a residence for themselves.

Born in St Louis and trained in architecture at Washington University, Charles had taught in Michigan, where, at the Cranbrook Academy of Art, he met Eero Saarinen, with whom he entered into

a competition project—Organic Design in Home Furnishings—that was sponsored by the Museum of Modern Art in New York City. The Eameses had initially conceived of a pristine, Mies-like cube standing on two slender steel columns, cantilevered out from the slope of a hillside lot. However, in 1947, they designed it to enclose more space using the same amount of steel, and put it at the perimeter of the site rather in its center. The house, anchored by a retaining wall, nestles against the hillside, parallel to its contours, making it a statement as much about the site, the location, and the inhabitants as about the deployment of prefabricated industrial materials. The house featured extremely thin steel framing with exposed corrugated metal roofing, and consisted of 18 bays—each 2.3 meters wide, 6 meters long, and 5 meters high—that determined the rhythm of the structure. Glazed panels—transparent, opaque, or translucent, as the situation demanded, and occasionally interrupted by painted panels in bright primary colors—gave the house a vibrant and playful character.

The Eameses filled the house with a collection of items they had accumulated from around the world. They made a film called *House after Five Years of Living*, implying that their house was not so much a designer display but an organic organism with the patina of lived-in existence that reflects the character and preferences of the inhabitants. Other than designing plans for houses, the Eameses designed exhibitions, made films, and built toys and furniture. One of their earliest successes was a technique for bending plywood, which was used in World War II field hospitals for making leg splints and, later, for chair seats. They also designed a chaise lounge and ottoman manufactured by the Herman Miller Company, whose headquarters they also designed. Their films were experimental and conceptual; their best known film, *Powers of Ten*, attempted to show a post-Einsteinian universe.

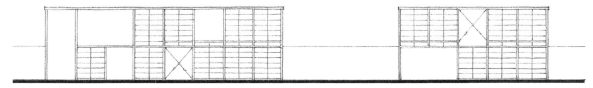

18.59 **Elevation: Eames House**

18.60 **Yale University Art Gallery, New Haven, Connecticut**

Yale University Art Gallery

Louis Kahn (1901–74), like Wright before him, developed an aesthetic outside of the developing norms of international modernism. But that does not mean that his work was not influenced by modernism and its drive to master abstraction. The Yale University Art Gallery in New Haven, Connecticut (1951–53) is remarkably unrhetorical with horizontally marked brick walls defining one direction and the aluminum glazing of the windows defining the other. He placed the building's programmatic needs within this very simple framework by organizing them into cylinders and rectangles. The idea is not unlike the way Mies attempted to unify secondary program elements into a vertical spine, except that here they become almost sculptural. Kahn was intrigued by the interaction between humans and the technical systems that service them—and that are therefore an integral part of the architectural world. So he chose to make a virtue out of electrical wiring, outlets, lighting fixtures, and ductwork, all of which are allowed to remain visible. The entrance is almost invisible from the street as it is on a higher level and separated by a wall and a set of stairs. Mies, more likely than not, would have made the entrance at street level with lots of glass; Gropius might have made a thin canopy. But Kahn's entrance is something one finds somewhat unexpectedly—perhaps like in a medieval European town. Even

the steps seem to indicate a change in the urban elevation. It is a subtle homage to the power of a type of space that is both intimate and urban. Kahn continually downplayed entrances in his architecture, deemphasizing the ceremonial aspect of approach. The uncompromising bluntness of the building foreshadows an aesthetic that came to be known as brutalism, which was to take root in the late 1960s.

Kahn studied at the American Academy in Rome in 1950, followed by travels to Italy, Egypt, and Greece in 1951. Unlike most modernists, who rejected the architecture of antiquity, he saw in it a struggle to make the building hold its own against the overwhelming grandeur of the landscape. For this reason, he preferred the archaic Temple of Paestum to the refined proportions of the Parthenon. His study of Greek and Roman architecture led Kahn to use simple but arresting forms—and even symmetries—at a time when these would have been frowned upon by functionalists.

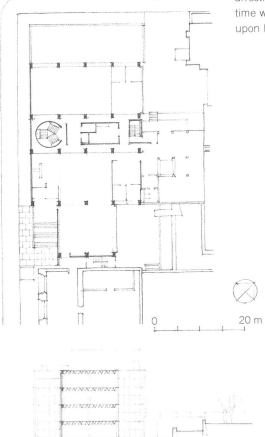

18.61 **First-floor plan and section: Yale University Art Gallery**

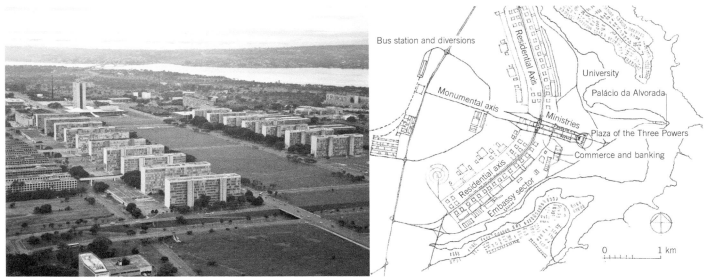

18.62 Brasília, Brazil

18.63 Site plan: Brasília

National Modernism, Brasília

In Brazil, modern architecture served as an expression of national identity and reached its zenith with the creation of Brasília in 1956 (inaugurated 1960). A hinterland capital had been proposed for Brazil since the late 19th century as a way to shift focus from the coastal towns and create a geographically accessible capital for the whole country. President Juscelino Kubitschek, who advocated rapid industrialization and who made the decision to go ahead with the new capital, invited the Brazilian-born and -trained architect Oscar Niemeyer (1907–2012) to design the main buildings and, after a competition, Lúcio Costa to prepare the master plan. It was to be accessible mainly by airplane, and thus was meant to be the supreme manifestation in the processes of modernization. Costa's plan, which itself looked like a plane, was based on the CIAM principles separating habitation, recreation, work, and circulation. Designed around two axes intersecting to form a cross, Brasília was an automobile city. Long, high-speed roads, with three multilane systems on each axis and over- and underpasses at intersections, were designed to enable rapid transportation. A dam built across the River Paranoa created long finger lakes around the southern, eastern, and northern edges of a U-shaped plateau on which the city was located. The main monumental axis of the city ran east-west, bisecting the plateau.

On the north-south cross-axis, arranged in a gentle curve, were the main residential units—the "superblocks"—organized in three layers, with parking at the eastern edge. Each superblock, 240 by 240 meters, was conceived as a grouping of six-story apartment units, raised on *pilotis*, with play space for children within inner courts. Private dwellings were nestled between the fingers of the lakes in the north and south, and farther inland to the west were the airport and the train station.

The functional, ceremonial, and visual focus of the city is the so-called Plaza of the Three Powers, at the eastern edge of the plateau. Approaching from the west, the eleven towers of the ministries start a grand procession culminating in the rectangular blocks of the Foreign Ministry and the Treasury, beyond which, at the center of the

axis, is the National Congress. This building is singular in the history of modern architecture. It houses two major chambers, the larger one for the Chamber of Deputies and the smaller one for the Senate. The raked visitors' seating of the round Chamber of Deputies is expressed in the roofline in the form of an upward turned bowl. The senate chamber has a traditional dome over it. Together, the saucer and dome, lifted clear above the ground on a giant platform, make for a memorable skyline, self-consciously designed as the icon of Brasília. Below, in two stories, accessed by a ramp, are all the offices.

Farther east, in line with the ramp, rise twin towers, linked by the walkway of the Secretariat. They sit in the middle of a rectangular reflective pool, at the eastern edge of which is the climax of the whole complex: a gigantic plaza, with the executive

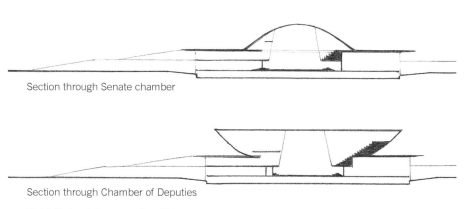

Section through Senate chamber

Section through Chamber of Deputies

18.64 National Congress, Brasília

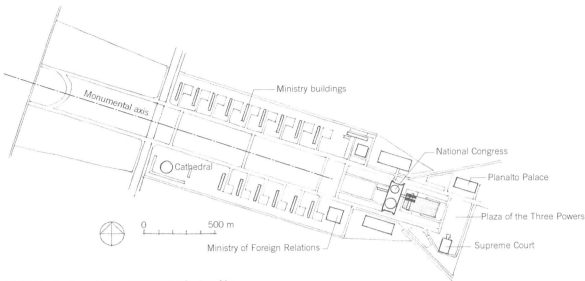

18.65 **Termination of the monumental axis, Brasília**

office of the president (the Planalto Palace) and the Supreme Court at either end. One of the multilane highways cuts through the plaza next to the Planalto Palace, connecting to the peripheral roads and the residence of the president, the Palácio da Alvorada, at the water's edge.

These three buildings, all designed by Niemeyer, represent a monumentalization of the Brazilian national modern style. All are concrete slab structures, glazed all around and sandwiched between deep overhanging roofs and floor slabs. In the Planalto Palace, a whole story lies below the ground slab, and in the other two buildings the ground slab lifts the main floor above the ground. Within, the plans are more reminiscent of Mies's precise geometries than Le Corbusier's sensuous curves. The colonnades lining the expressive edges of the buildings (always only on two opposite sides, except in the later Foreign Ministry building, where they are on all four sides) were designed as delicately wrought curvilinear forms, expressive less of their character as load-bearing members and more as tie beams stretched thin by tension, almost to the point of disappearing at their edges. (Joaquim Cardoso did the structural calculations.) In the Planalto Palace, the colonnades face the plaza; in the Supreme Court, they are located toward the side; and in the Palácio da Alvorada they are turned laterally, forming a string of inverted arches across the facade.

After World War II, Brazilian modern architecture became widely influential in the development of modern architecture around the world, though it had begun initially as a derivative of European modernism. Brasília's foreign ministry building was the model for New York City's Lincoln Center. Oscar Niemeyer effectively became the chief architect of the United Nations Headquarters (1947), also in New York City, after Le Corbusier was removed from the project and Wallace Harrison was appointed head of the United Nations Board of Design. Harrison's design of the Albany Civic Center (1962–68), one of the largest modernist-style civic centers in the United States, was inspired by Costa's and Niemeyer's Plaza of the Three Powers in Brasília.

18.66 **Ministry of External Relations, Brasília**

National Modernism, Chandigarh

When India attained independence in 1947 it was divided into two countries along religious lines, resulting in the creation of the new Islamic nation of Pakistan. In that division, the Indian state of Punjab lost its capital, Lahore, to Pakistan, so Jawaharlal Nehru, the first prime minister of independent India, decided to construct a new capital, Chandigarh. Like Brazil's Getulio Vargas and Juscelino Kubitschek, Nehru modeled his development plans on Franklin Delano Roosevelt's New Deal and initiated a series of state-sponsored industrialization projects. His sentiment was expressly anti-nostalgic. He wanted Chandigarh to be a "new city, unfettered by the traditions of the past, and a symbol of the nation's faith in the future."

When Le Corbusier joined the project in 1952, the urban plan had already been prepared by Albert Mayer, an American town planner, on the principles of the City Beautiful movement, with superblocks accessed by gently curving roads. Le Corbusier shrunk the superblocks into 800-by-1,200-meter rectangular neighborhood units or sectors serviced by a diminishing hierarchy of roads and bicycle paths, according to CIAM principles. Within these sectors, Le Corbusier wanted to design multistory residential units (perhaps like those in Brasília, or in his Unités d'Habitations, the first of which had just been constructed in Marseille), but that idea was immediately dismissed by the officers in charge of the project who were committed to a low-rise suburban image, inspired in part by the sprawling cantonments the British had built for their officers in colonial India. The state housing, therefore, was done not by Le Corbusier, but by his cousin, Pierre Jeanneret (who was the project architect), and the English husband-and-wife team Maxwell Fry and Jane Drew (who had been working in Africa), assisted by a team of nine Indian architects and planners. Most of the construction was made of load-bearing exposed brick walls, accented by random rubble-stone porticoes and concrete window protectors, plastered and painted white.

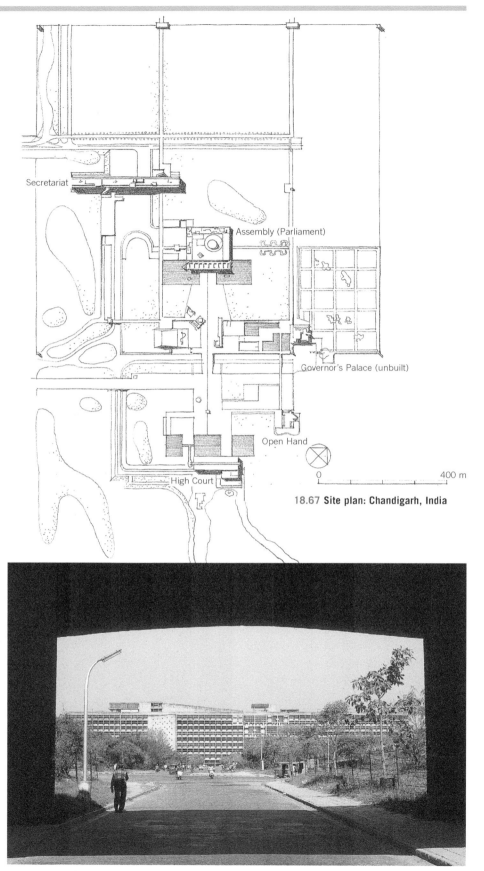

18.67 Site plan: Chandigarh, India

18.68 Secretariat, Chandigarh

Le Corbusier's Capitol Complex for Chandigarh (1951–62)—containing the High Court, Assembly, and Secretariat for the states of Punjab and Haryana—was located at the northern end of the city on a vast open plain, visually bound only by the distant Himalayan foothills. The boundaries are loosely defined by two adjoining 800-meter squares that contain two 400-meter squares. The vehicular roads are located somewhat below grade; the excavated earth was used to create the artificial hills that screen the Capitol from the rest of the city. An irregularly shaped pedestrian plaza, linking the Assembly and the High Court, studded with a set of symbolic follies, forms the conceptual center of the Capitol. The High Court, the first building to be constructed, is contained within a tight frame and endowed with a second roof (with suspended arches) built above the first one to provide shade. Three huge pylons create a monumental gateway fronted by two reflecting pools. The building's elevation has a rhythm determined by the divisions of the nine courts. The elevation, in fact, is almost the same as its plan. Although made of cast-in-place rough concrete, the High Court, with the pylons painted in soft pastels, appears lightweight and airy, particularly when reflected in the pools.

The Secretariat has a very different character. In the context of the larger composition, it functions as a backdrop to the Assembly, taking the form of a long slab with a dramatic roofline and a facade completely composed of *brise-soleils*. Staircases appear as attached towers with small windows. With its long double-loaded corridor, the building was a restatement of Le Corbusier's idea of a collective living solution, the Unité d'Habitation. But while the Unité was raised on robust concrete *pilotis*, the Secretariat sits directly on the ground.

18.69 **High Court, Chandigarh**

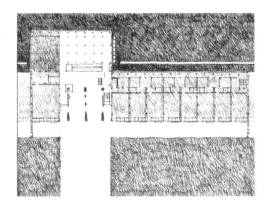

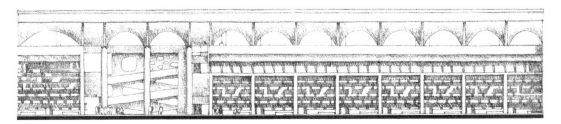

18.70 **Plan diagram and elevation: High Court, Chandigarh**

18.71 Assembly Building, Chandigarh

Le Corbusier also gifted to Chandigarh the Open Hand Monument, which he devised as the city' symbol. Standing in the Capitol, it is a 23-meter-high sculpture of burnished steel. While the aesthetic origins of the sculpture are diverse, Le Corbusier articulated his most ambitious hope for the Open Hand in a letter to Nehru from 1955, when he proposed the sculpture as a symbol of the Non-Aligned Movement (NAM). Nehru's brainchild, NAM was an attempt to propose a third alternative to the divisive two-world—communist versus capitalist—hegemony of the Cold War. Although not adopted for NAM, the Open Hand did become the symbol of Chandigarh as a city embodying Nehru's hopes for a modern India.

Le Corbusier's Assembly Building (1953–63) is a skillful essay in organization and monumentality. On a trip to Ahmedabad in western India, Le Corbusier saw the form of a hyperbolic paraboloid arch under construction for a thermal power station and, mesmerized, immediately decided to use it as a motif in the Assembly Building. At this time he was also working, in conjunction with the mathematician and musician Iannis Xenaxis, on several projects in France, all of which explored the sculptural possibilities of ruled surfaces. For the design of the Assembly Building, Le Corbusier seems to have literally dropped the hyperbolic paraboloid arch into a box. Around the hall, a forest of columns, rising high into a black ceiling, created the foyer. The three edges of the box were given over to offices. *Brise-soleils* functioned as the skin. On the fourth edge of the box, the side facing the plaza, Le Corbusier built a monumental portal, opposite to and facing the portal of the High Court across the vast plaza. A row of thin pylons holds up a free-form roof that looks like the horns of a bull in outline, giving the Assembly Building the appearance of a majestic bull standing firm on the vast Indian plain—quite in contrast to Niemeyer's palaces in Brasília, which barely touch the ground and seem to fly above it in defiance of gravity.

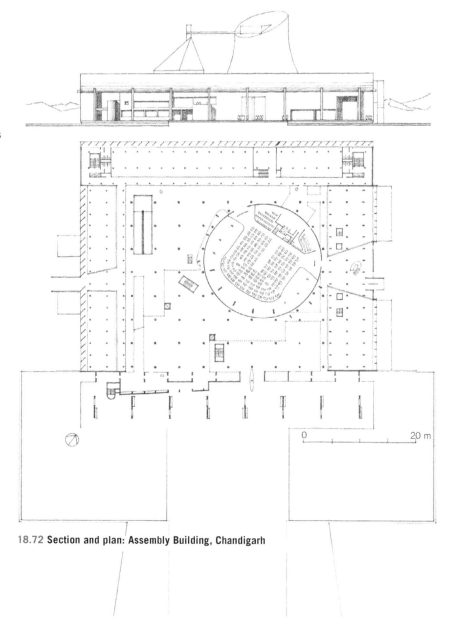

18.72 Section and plan: Assembly Building, Chandigarh

18.73 **Notre Dame de Haut, Ronchamp, France**   18.74 **Plan and section: Notre Dame de Haut**

Chapel at Ronchamp

Le Corbusier accepted two commissions from religious institutions. One was for a chapel, Notre Dame de Haut at Ronchamp (1955), in the Jura Mountains of eastern France. The other for a monastery at La Tourette (1957–60), near Lyon, France. Both commissions were made by a reformist wing of the Catholic Church trying to reestablish the relevance of their institution in the wake of faltering attendance. Appealing to the younger generation by adopting modern architecture was part of this effort. It was not only a bold experiment but also demonstrated that modernism could indeed create the kind of inward-oriented atmosphere conducive to contemplation. Although Le Corbusier was not a churchgoing Catholic, he welcomed the commissions because they allowed him to experiment with symbolic forms, which he had never done before in a European context.

The chapel, which astonished many people when it was built, is a singular and memorable edifice and stands today, along with the Rosaire Chapel (1949–51) by Henri Matisse, as one of the outstanding modern religious expressions of the 20th century. Fundamentally, the building is a sculpture; its principal design element is the curve deployed repeatedly to form a dramatic set of intersections and trapped, cavelike spaces. Three continuous walls, changing direction, thickness, and height, create a volume that defies the conventional expectations of facade and interior. Two convex curves bulge out on the north and west, creating a backside, while two concave indents to the south and east represent the front. On top of the walls, on columns hidden in the walls, floats a thick, organic-appearing roof that comes to a sharp point at one end. It has been compared by some to a cushion, and by others to a hat.

Three towers, clustered together with hooded tops, rise above the roof, forming vertical counterpoints to the general horizontality and earth-bound appearance. Light washes down into the inner space of these towers and spills into the inner sanctum. Each tower has a specific function, serving as chapel, sacristy, and baptistery, respectively. The west wall is punctured by a series of irregularly placed, punched-out windows of various sizes and depth that bring spots of intense light into the interior. Inside, the roof hangs like a sail over the nave while sloping gently to the south toward the altar. A statue of the Virgin Mary stands in an alcove in the eastern wall and was designed so that it can be rotated to face both inside and outside, for those occasions when church services are held outdoors. Near the church, using stones from the site, Le Corbusier constructed a small, stepped pyramid. The church bells are placed in a steel-framed structure to one side. Sited on the flat top of a hill in a forested area of the Jura Mountains, the building is reached by a gently curving road that leads up the hill and passes a low meeting and service building. From the top, serene views range in all directions, imparting to the church the aspect of a pilgrimage site. (Indeed, on the site there once stood a pilgrimage chapel, destroyed in World War II, that had been dedicated to the Virgin Mary.)

18.75 **Interior: Notre Dame de Haut**

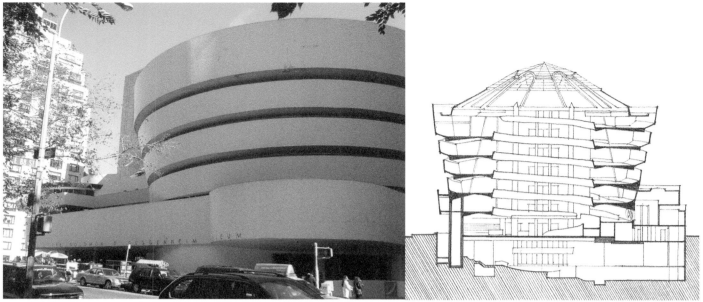

18.76 Guggenheim Museum, New York City

18.77 Section and plan: Guggenheim Museum

Guggenheim Museum

After World War II, modern architecture's insistence on a rationalized functional aesthetic ran up against the need to express monumentality, particularly in large civic structures. Frank Lloyd Wright's design for the Guggenheim Museum (1956–59) in Manhattan was particularly innovative in this respect, with a dramatic exterior form and the large interior space at its center that is formed by a curving ramp. The sides of the building are fully occupied by this gently spiraling ramp, designed to allow visitors to view art continuously, without interruption. It also enables everyone viewing the art to be seen, an idea close to the sensibility of Charles Garnier's Paris Opera House. The ramp, expanding in diameter as it ascends—or shrinking as it descends, as the case may be—generates an external profile that contrasts sharply with the rectilinear geometry of the surrounding Manhattan blocks. Wright defended the spiral by arguing that abstract art no longer needed to be seen in the traditional framework of rooms and walls. But as innovative and controversial as Wright's exhibition ideas were, there is no debate about the building's impressive central space. Accessed virtually directly from the street, it was conceived as an extension of the urban site. In that respect it constituted an important breakthrough in the relationship of modernism to civic space. Though the Museum of Modern Art (1938–39) by Philip

Goodwin and Edward Durell Stone was technically the first modern building in New York, the Guggenheim was the city's first truly modernist civic structure.

The project went through several permutations. At first the building was to be a type of private gallery, showing the works of Solomon R. Guggenheim, but later in 1952 the museum expanded its definition to become something much broader, rivaling the Museum of Modern Art as an institution of experimentation and taste-making across the whole range of modern art. The expanded program forced Wright to make amendments and concessions, but he did not change his stance that flat paintings would be well served by hanging against curving walls, and the public's positive reception of the building offset complaints by curators and painters. The building was based on an innovative structural system of radially splayed concrete ribs that held the floor plates and came together at the top to form the dome. While the building soon became a Manhattan landmark, the success of its functional purpose—the display of paintings—remains questionable and was never imitated. One complaint is that the building competes by claiming artwork status itself and thus may distract from the display; another is that visitors cannot really come to rest, as they are is in motion on a ramp that urges movement rather than repose.

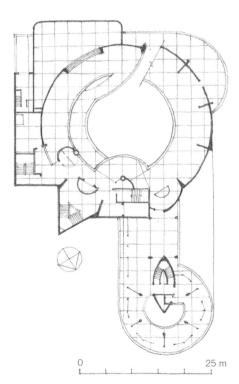

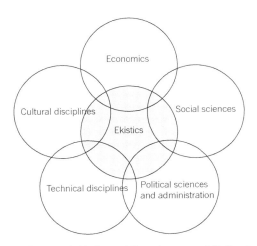

18.78 Diagram of ekistics and the sciences contributing to it

Ekistics

Constantinos Doxiadis (1913–75), former chief town planning officer of Athens, Greece, started his own firm in 1951 and after that built in dozens of countries, including India, Bangladesh, Ethiopia, France, Ghana, Iran, Iraq, Italy, Jordan, Pakistan, and Syria. His was one of the largest international practices at the time. Doxiadis introduced issues like regional climate and geography into the discussion of modernism at a time when such considerations were still rare. He coined the term *ekistics*, derived from the Greek *oikos*, meaning "house," to refer to the science of human settlements. Doxiadis aspired to expand the scientific basis of architecture, urban design, and planning in order to reject arbitrary self-expression and monotonic versions of rationalism and also to embrace extratechnological and nonfunctionalist concerns. He soon surrounded himself with an international and interdisciplinary group that included global visionaries (like Buckminster Fuller and Margaret Mead), architects, planners, and United Nations consultants (such as Jaqueline Tyrwhitt and Charles Abrams), economists and environmental thinkers (including Barbara Ward and Renee Dubos)—all of whom, to some degree, supported Doxiadis's vision.

His planning model was called Dynapolis, a term signifying a dynamic city that would change over time and allow its urban core to expand continually in a unidirectional manner in order to avoid congestion and do away with the permanence and monumentality of stationary city centers. The business district and residential areas would also grow along this axis, and industrial areas would be pushed to the edges. This logic of functional separation extended to the system of social ordering, so that each residential sector was broken down into smaller communities arranged hierarchically.

The model of Dynapolis informed many plans for urban restructuring—from Baghdad, Iraq (1958), to Athens, Greece (1960), to Washington, DC—and became the basis for the creation of Islamabad, the new capital of Pakistan (1960). Doxiadis designed Islamabad's master plan and the prototypes of the major housing types, but the design of the individual buildings was assigned to local and foreign architects. The master plan was based on his concept of a moving core—the idea that the commercial hub of the city would continue to move and grow as necessary, creating a linear city in its wake.

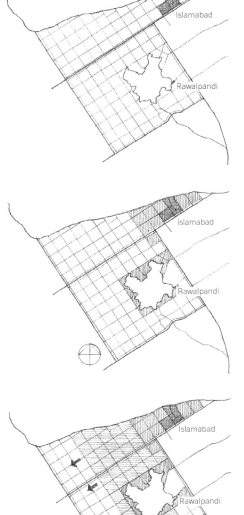

18.79 Islamabad, Pakistan: A growing dynametropolis

18.80 Sydney Opera House, Australia

Sydney Opera House

Jørn Utzon's Sydney Opera House (1957–73) was another early prestige commission. Located right on the water's edge, with the graceful curve of the Sydney Harbor Bridge as a backdrop, Utzon's prizewinning entry imagined a series of successive interlocking shells of different heights hovering above a vast stepped platform, conjuring an image of ships' sails through outright technological virtuosity. Supported on 580 concrete piers sunk up to 25 meters below sea level, the shells are sheathed in white ceramic tile and contain five performance spaces. Although Utzon never completed the project himself, it quickly became the signature project of Australia and a national icon.

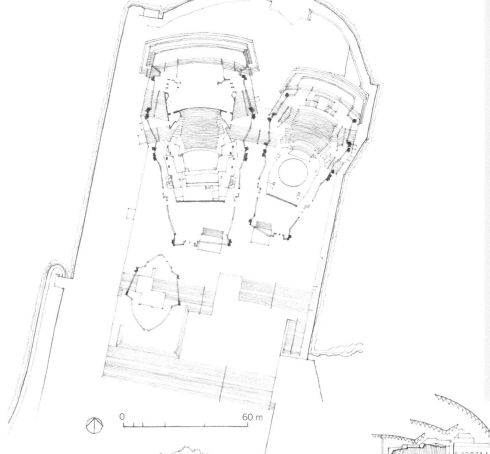

18.81 Site plan and section: Sydney Opera House

First generation of post–World War II prestige buildings:

- Berlin Philharmonic Hall, 1956–63, Hans Scharoun
- Sydney Opera House, 1957–73, Jørn Utzon
- Lincoln Center for the Performing Arts, New York City, 1962–65, Max Abramovitz, Pietro Belluschi, Philip Johnson, Eero Saarinen, and others
- John F. Kennedy Center for the Performing Arts, Washington, DC, 1964–71, Edward Durell Stone
- Tokyo Olympic Stadium, 1964, Kenzo Tange
- Kimbell Art Museum, Fort Worth, Texas, 1967–72, Louis Kahn
- New National Gallery, Berlin, 1972–78, Ludwig Mies van der Rohe
- Palast der Republik, East Berlin, 1973–76, Heinz Graffunder and Karl-Ernst Swora
- East Wing, National Gallery, Washington DC, 1974–78, I. M. Pei

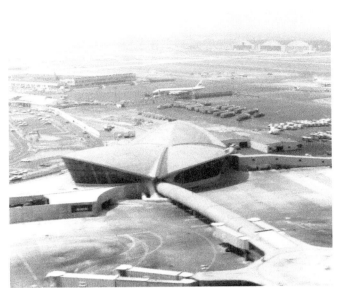

18.82 **TWA Terminal, John F. Kennedy International Airport, Queens, New York**

18.83 **TWA Terminal, John F. Kennedy International Airport**

Eero Saarinen

Born in 1910 in Finland, Eero Saarinen injected poetry into the structural possibilities of reinforced concrete. Though Erich Mendelsohn had attempted this in the 1930s, he had built relatively little during a time when concrete was still rather experimental. Eero Saarinen's career ended prematurely with his death in 1961, but in the short space of eleven years, he had already worked on nearly thirty projects in Europe and the United States, some of which became international icons and symbols of the United States' postwar identity as a technological superpower. Among his works are the St. Louis Gateway Arch (1948–64), the General Motors Technical Center (1948–56) in Detroit, and the TWA Terminal (1956–62) at New York's John F. Kennedy International Airport.

Saarinen's 1947 competition-winning entry for the Gateway Arch at St. Louis, Missouri (1961–66), was conceived as a huge structure located on the banks of the Mississippi River. It was a monument meant to match—if not exceed—in scale, technological prowess, and symbolic stature, Paris's Eiffel Tower. Because it represented the gateway to the West, it was seen as a dramatic reference to America's origins, putting St. Louis on the international map. A catenary curve, the arch's span and rise are both 192 meters. It consists of a double skin of steel—stainless steel without and carbon steel within—reinforced where required by concrete. The two legs in section are equilateral triangles, 16.5 meters to a side at the ground tapering off to 5 meters at the summit. A Museum of Westward Expansion is located at the ground level, and a viewing deck can be accessed at the top by elevator. Saarinen's TWA Terminal (1956–62) at New York's John F. Kennedy International Airport was conceived as a bird with wings spread and poised to take off. He designed the terminal largely by using models rather than drawings. It has no facade or right angles. Instead, its captivating forms and undulating interiors—along with its dramatic TWA-red carpeted floors—were meant to evoked a vision of grace and lightness.

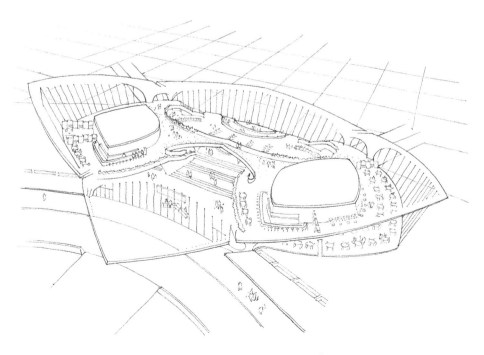

18.84 **Pictorial view: TWA Terminal, John F. Kennedy International Airport**

Steel and Glass Skyscraper

Skyscrapers had long been the primary symbol of the U.S. metropolis. In their early days, architects sought out a great deal of differentiation, but by the late 1920s, the look of tall buildings began to be more standardized, with the exception perhaps of a crowning element, like in the Chrysler Building (1928). Skyscraper design underwent its most dramatic change with Mies van der Rohe's Seagram Building (1958) in Midtown Manhattan, designed in collaboration with Philip Johnson and built as the headquarters for the Canadian distillers Joseph E. Seagram & Sons. The thirty-eight-story building is a vertical box with clean and sharp edges. Unlike early skyscrapers, whose bodies were punctuated by windows, here glass reaches from floor to ceiling and serves as the skin of the building. The visible edge of the floor plate is covered by bronze spandrels that give a light horizontal zippering effect to the floors during the day, when light reflects off the glass—an effect even more pronounced at night, when the reflection contrasts with the interior illumination.

Although the building seems to be all structural steel and glass, this is not exactly true. Fire code prohibited exposed steel, meaning that the steel supports had to be covered in fireproof concrete. Since this is not how Mies wanted the building to read on the outside, he used nonstructural, bronze-toned Ibeams running vertically, like mullions, down the facades. These vertical mullions are equally spaced across the entire facade. Together with the horizontal spandrels, they create a pronounced grid pattern. This surfacing does not extend to the ground, however, allowing the building's real structure—the concrete-encased beams—to be visible in the lobby. The glass is not purely transparent, but tinted bronze, so that in certain lighting conditions, the whole building—its structure and its glass—seem to have a golden hue, perhaps, it has been argued, subtly suggesting the color of whiskey, one of the building owner's products.

In the 1960s, Chicago's skyline began to change as a consequence of the relaxation of height limits previously imposed by the city. Many towers were built, including several by Mies in his usual boxy style, such as the Lake Shore Drive Apartments (1948–51) and the Chicago Federal Center (1959–74). These buildings stimulated a vibrant and still ongoing discussion about the surface treatment of a tall building. Some architects developed the grid pattern by emphasizing different aspects of its composition; others worked with the reflective conditions of glass. Perhaps the culmination of the Miesian interrogation of the surface was the John Hancock Tower (1976) in Boston by I. M. Pei and Henry N. Cobb.

18.85 Seagram Building, New York City

18.86 Lobby, Seagram Building

18.87 Alcoa Building, San Francisco

By the 1970s, Skidmore, Owings & Merrill (SOM), founded in 1936, employed about a thousand architects, engineers, and technicians who provided complete planning, designing, engineering, and construction services. It was one of the world's first multitasking architectural corporations. The firm had seven principal offices, located in New York City, Chicago, San Francisco, Paris, Los Angeles, Washington, DC, and Portland, Oregon. Commissions ranged from presidential libraries to routine industrial buildings. Though there was diversity in aesthetic production, perfecting the Miesian paradigm and making modernism the language par excellence for corporations was an important concept behind the firm's reputation. This can be seen in the headquarters of the Business Men's Assurance Company of America in Kansas City, Missouri (1963), situated outside the city on the edge of a park. Unlike the Miesian preference for steel and glass, here the steel frame is clad in white Georgian marble. The windows are set back to create a stark, minimalist effect. The Alcoa Building in San Francisco (1964) took this design idea one step further with its exoskeletal cross-bracing, which both serves a structural purpose and provides a symbolic message. Although the unrelenting and uncompromising abstraction of the cross-bracing seems to make it mute and faceless, the absence of rhetorical messages is belied by the idea that the form is the expression not of technological efficiency but of technological elegance.

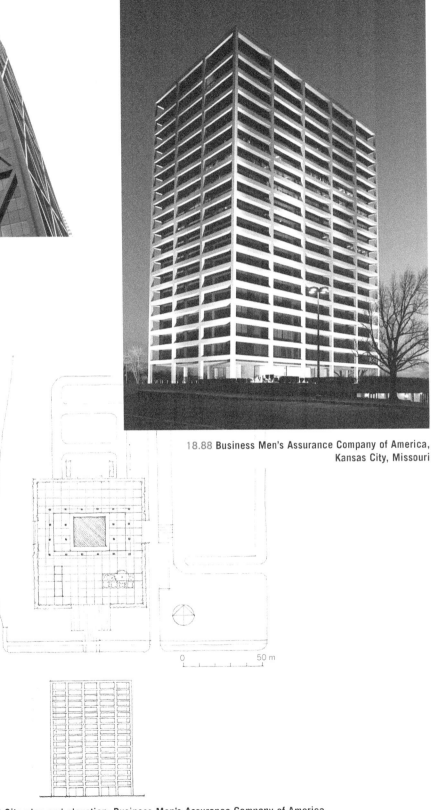

18.88 Business Men's Assurance Company of America, Kansas City, Missouri

18.89 Site plan and elevation: Business Men's Assurance Company of America

18.90 Aula Magna, La Ciudad Universitaria de Caracas, Venezuela

18.91 Diego Rivera House, Mexico City

Latin-American Modernism

In many parts of the Latin American world, modernism was not so much a state-sponsored nationalist sentiment as a search for expression by the artistic avant-garde. It was first propounded not by architects but by poets and writers, including Rubén Darío (Panama), José Asunción Silva (Colombia), Manuel Gutiérrez Nájera (Mexico), José Enrique Rodó (Uruguay), José Martí (Cuba), Bienvenido Nouel (Dominican Republic), and Luis Lloréns Torres (Puerto Rico). It was not until the 1940s and 1950s that what is now also sometimes called tropical modernism emerged as the language of autonomy and independence. Though strongly influenced by Le Corbusier, this Latin American rendition of modernism emphasized not only clean lines but also the need for shaded surfaces, wide windows, surrounding gardens, and lightweight construction. Among its proponents were Guillermo González-Sánchez in the Dominican Republic; Antonin Nechodoma and Henry Klumb in Puerto Rico; and Juan O'Gorman and Felix Candela, among others, in Mexico.

La Ciudad Universitaria de Caracas (1944–70), by the Venezuelan architect Carlos Raúl Villanueva, is one of the boldest interpretations of modern architecture in Latin America. Built as an autonomous urban assemblage next to Plaza Venezuela, this compendium of more than forty buildings was developed over a period of radical economic, social, and political changes. At the center

of the campus was a succession of spaces where inside and outside merge seamlessly into one another. Villanueva visualized a system of flows and paths, or "movements," as a fundamental design criterion; it was realized in his conception of the university's covered plaza, with its large canopy of irregular shape and varying height, protecting

the shaded space within. Here Villanueva incorporated the work of several avant-garde artists of the time, including Fernand Léger, Antoine Pevsner, Victor Vasarely, Jean Arp, and Henri Laurens, as well as a group of Venezuelan geometric abstract artists, such as Mateo Manaure, Pascual Navarro, Oswaldo Vigas, and Armando Barrios.

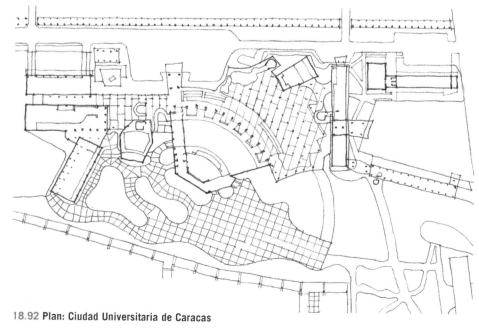

18.92 Plan: Ciudad Universitaria de Caracas

18.93 **Church of Christ the Worker, Atlántida. Uruguay**

The high-tech structural achievements of architects such as Eero Saarinen and Jørn Utzon can be contrasted with the work of the Uruguayan architect Eladio Dieste, who had been practicing since the early 1960s. An engineer by training, Eladio Dieste made his reputation building a whole range of structures, from grain silos, factory sheds, markets, maintenance hangars, fruit-packing plants, warehouses, and bus terminals to a handful of churches of exceptional spans and beauty. In most of his buildings he used Gaussian vaults, which are self-supporting shells that stand up not only because they are light but also because they are bent or folded in such a way that they are subject to limited lateral thrusts. Dieste also perfected techniques of reinforced masonry with the objective of minimizing the use of materials and maximizing the size of openings.

Dieste's Church of Christ the Worker, (1958–60) in Atlántida, Uruguay, is a simple rectangle, with sidewalls rising up in undulating curves to the maximum amplitude of their arcs. The undulation enables the thin walls to be self-stabilizing, much as a bent sheet of paper does. At the top, the geometry of the wall is merged with the continuous double curvature of the ceiling (reinforced with tie-rods concealed in troughs). The beauty of the forms is augmented by the subtle interplay of light: while small, punched rectangular openings diffuse light through the interior, a triple row of baffles above the entrance, opening in opposite directions, flood the space with indirect light. His warehouse for the fruit-packing plant in Salto (1971–72) consists of a series of large discontinuous double-curvature vaults spanning approximately 150 feet. Not only do the vaults make the span seem effortless, but the glazed slits light up the vaults and space to create a space of rare sensuality.

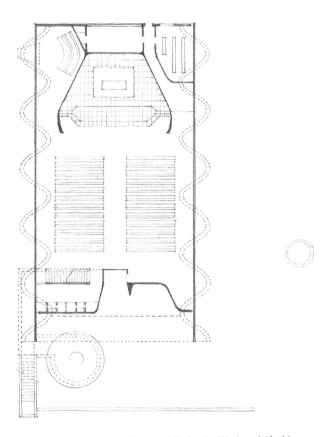

18.94 **Section and plan: Church of Christ the Worker, Atlántida**

18.95 School of Music, National Schools of Art, Havana

18.96 School of Ballet, National Schools of Art, Havana

National Modernism, Cuba

In 1961, two years after the Cuban Revolution, Fidel Castro and Ernesto "Che" Guevara decided to transform the golf course of the Havana Country Club into an experimental project that would make art available to all. The master plan for the National Schools of Art (1961–65) was given to the young Cuban architect Ricardo Porro, who had just returned from exile. Porro invited his Italian colleagues Vittorio Garatti and Roberto Gottardi, in Caracas, Venezuela, to collaborate. The three architects initiated a unique process: the design and construction of the schools occurred simultaneously with the beginning of the schools' academic activities. Porro designed the School of Plastic Arts and the School of Modern Dance; Gottardi, the School of Dramatic Arts; and Garatti, the School of Music and the School for Ballet. Even though each has its particularities, the five schools followed three common guiding principles: first, a response to the tropical landscape that allowed for an intimate relationship between nature and architecture; second, the use of earthen materials produced on the island instead of steel and cement; and third, the use of the *bóveda catalana*, or Catalan vault, as the primary structural system.

Though this ancient and versatile technique required very little by way of resources and materials and was chosen partially in response to the economically

austere circumstances of Cuba—made especially acute after the blockade imposed by United States in October 1960—it conferred on the architecture the sensuality and the eroticism that Porro claimed was prototypically Cuban. By 1965 the schools, still unfinished, began to generate controversy. They were accused

of being examples of an individualism that contradicted the increasingly influential standardized models of the Soviet-functionalist style. This eventually led to the project's abandonment. Castro's government, however, has since initiated a process of restoration, with Gottardi, the only one of the three architects still in Cuba, as its director.

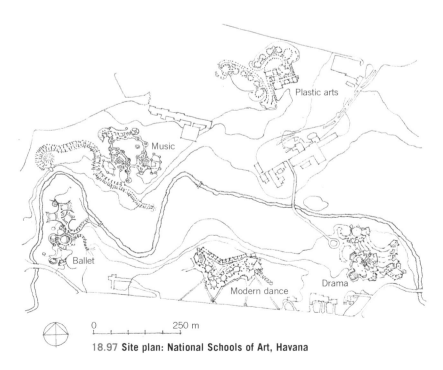

18.97 Site plan: National Schools of Art, Havana

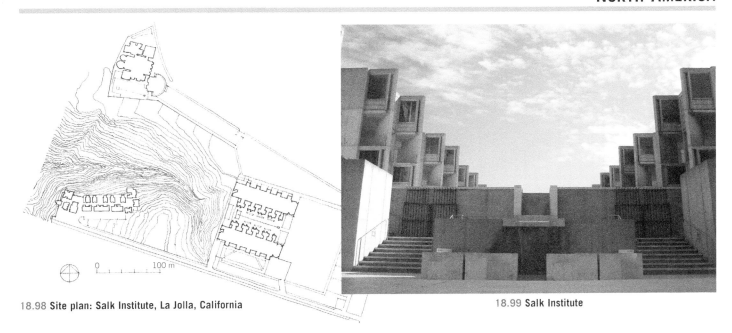

18.98 **Site plan: Salk Institute, La Jolla, California**

18.99 **Salk Institute**

Salk Institute

For Dr. Jonas Salk, the discoverer of the polio vaccine, medical research was not entirely the domain of scientists and administrators; it belonged to the public, and in Louis Kahn, Salk found the architect who could transform that ideal into architectural form. The Salk Institute building (1960–63) in La Jolla, near San Diego, California, is close to a bluff overlooking the Pacific Ocean. Three floors of laboratories, completely open in all directions, are separated by half-floors dedicated to mechanical ducts. As was typical of Kahn, the building went through several design permutations before its final form was agreed upon. In its final configurations it consisted of two rectangular laboratory blocks separated by a courtyard, with towers housing the scientists' study rooms projecting from the laboratories but sitting in the courtyard space. Circulation towers were located on the other side of the laboratories, aligned to the study towers that were separated from the laboratories by bridges to declare a physical and psychological differentiation. Whereas from the outside the building is austere and windowless, the courtyard, elevated one floor above the level of the site, captures the dramatic views toward the ocean. The diagonal walls of the towers allow each office to have an ocean view. Originally, Kahn had envisioned the court as a lush garden, but in 1966, after seeing the work of Luis Barragán,

Kahn invited him to see the designs, and it was Barragán who came up with the idea of an empty plaza. The plaza is entered from the east, through a quiet garden. A narrow waterway slices through the courtyard on its axis and ends in the quiet waterfall of a sunken viewing terrace—an area of repose.

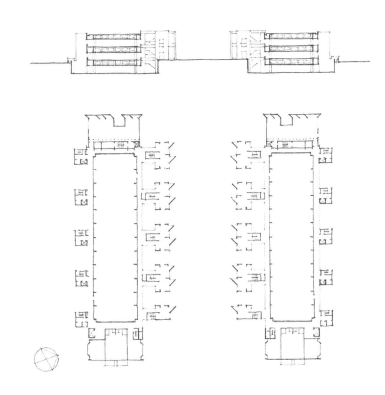

18.100 **Section and plan of laboratory buildings, Salk Institute**

18.101 **Plan: Sher-e-Banglanagar, Dacca, Bangladesh**

18.102 **Sher-e-Banglanagar**

National Modernism, Bangladesh

Louis Kahn spent more than a decade working on Sher-e-Banglanagar (1961–82) in Dacca (as it came to be called after Bangladesh became independent in 1971) and almost went bankrupt in the process. It was completed well after Kahn's death in 1974, but when it was finished in the late 1980s, it instantly captured the attention of the Bangladeshi populace and was celebrated as a triumphant display of their independence. What the Bangladeshi citizens see is a closely clustered assembly of monolithic concrete towers, slashed open, with huge triangular, rectangular, and semicircular openings. Together they form the outer envelope—the serving zone—to the central chamber of the parliament, with the trusses of the gigantic roof structure just visible from a distance.

The entrance to the building is from the north, through a large square building with grand staircases. The four buildings for offices are packaged between this building and the other axially placed elements, which are the minister's offices to the west, lunchrooms to the east, and a mosque to the south. The mosque, preceded by a circular ablution space, is formed by four round towers clamped against a rotated square; it is tilted a few degrees from the axis in order to orient it toward Mecca. Within, Sher-e-Banglanagar, much as the Pantheon's oculus, is a studied essay in the use of natural light to illuminate monumental spaces—split,

spliced, and reimagined through a series of cubist transformations. From the outside, however, Sher-e-Banglanagar sits in silent dignity, with a vast swath of land cleared all around it, first to make a reflecting pool and then a giant plaza. Unlike the great plazas of Brasília and Chandigarh, Bangladesh's plaza became an instant success. Every day thousands of people throng its vast expanse, playing, picnicking, protesting, or otherwise participating in the public affairs of civic life. Kahn's Sher-e-Banglanagar, like Le Corbusier's Chandigarh, was his largest and

final project, and along with the Kimball Art Museum in Fort Worth, Texas, and the Salk Institute in La Jolla, California, certainly the finest of his later work. Where the Kimball Art Museum is about the invention of the section and the very precise and subtle measurement of light in its galleries, and the Salk Institute is a singular and profound meditation on the framing of a view, Sher-e-Banglanagar, though of much cruder workmanship, is Kahn's most complex essay on the interplay of light and mass in a tightly controlled formal order.

18.103 **Interior: Sher-e-Banglanagar**

18.104 **Totsuka Country Club, Yokohama, Japan**

18.105 **Nichinan Cultural Center, Nichinan, Japan**

Metabolism

On the basis of the design for his internationally acclaimed Hiroshima memorial, Kenzo Tange (1913–2005) was invited to attend the 8th CIAM meeting held in England in 1951, where he met Le Corbusier, Siegfried Giedion, Walter Gropius, and Jose Luis Sert, among others. It was at this congress that the question of the "urban core" was raised, rekindling Tange's interests in urban planning. Tange became a member of Team X after the dissolution of CIAM in 1956 and presented his design for the Tokyo City Hall (1957) at their Otterlo, Netherlands, meeting in 1959. To this meeting he also brought Kiyonori Kikutake's drawings for the reorganization of Tokyo, which envisioned tall, circular residential towers on land and factories on giant cylinders in the bay. This was the beginning of his interest in urbanization as an organic system and led to the development of Metabolism.

Tange presented his Metabolist concepts at the World Design Conference held in Tokyo in 1958. This conference was conceived as an alternative to Team X and was attended by, among others, Kikutake, Kisho Kurokawa, Noboru Kawazoe, Fumihiko Maki, Peter and Alison Smithson, Jacob Bakema, Paul Rudolph, Ralph Erskine, Louis Kahn, Jean Prouvé, Minoru Yamasaki, Balkrishna V. Doshi, and Raphael Soriano.

Unlike Team X, which approached urban design and planning by trying to solve problems at the human scale, the Metabolists worked at the largest scale conceivable, seeing their structures through a biological metaphor as an expression of the city's new life force. Despite this large scale, Metabolism was a philosophical proposition about inhabiting the earth in harmony with the forces of nature.

While Tange's urban plans bore little fruit, his architectural practice, patronized by Japan's elite, flourished. With an uncanny aesthetic sense rivaled by few who worked with exposed concrete at such large scales, Tange built a celebrated body of work in the 1960s and 1970s. The Totsuka Country Club (1960–61) acquired its upward-turning profile from Chandigarh's Assembly; the Nichinan Cultural Center (1960–62), with its forceful fins, was a beast unto itself; and finally, the Olympic Stadium in Tokyo was a stellar display not only of the structural possibilities of concrete and tensile cable but also of the ability of structure to generate poetic forms such as had been rivaled only by Santiago Calatrava in the recent past.

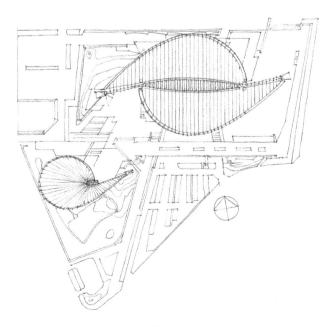

18.106 **Site plan: Olympic Stadium, Tokyo**

18.107 Trellick Tower, London

18.108 Foundling Estate, London

Brutalism

In the mid-1960s, numerous architects, led by Kenzo Tange, became interested in megastructures that consisted of simple, large-scale repetitive structures packed with program. Cultural contexts were meant to play only a limited role in these buildings. Instead, the buildings emphasized material simplicity and secular anonymity. They spoke of the ethos of managerial grandness and implied a transnational utopianism. The Foundling Estate in London (1973) has long lines of housing stacked on massive piers. Though structures like these were soon maligned, they brought modernism to a new pitch in their fearless acceptance of large-scale realities.

Brutalism was particularly popular among university administrators, and many campuses in the United States have at least one example of late 1960s Brutalism, such

as Kane Hall at the University of Washington, Seattle, designed by Walker & McGough (1969) and the Stratton Student Center at the Massachusetts Institute of Technology in Cambridge by Eduardo F. Catalano. Similar, but much larger, is the Rand Afrikaans University in Johannesburg, South Africa (1975), designed by William Meyer, which fused the latest trends in megastructure with ideas that were seen as specifically African. Trellick Tower (1967–73) by Erno Goldfinger in London is similarly vast and imposing.

Chinese-born I. M. Pei (1917–) refined the brutalist aesthetic by developing a distinctive style that appealed to many city leaders during the days in which museums and cultural buildings were coming to be seen as an established aspect of a city's profile. His Herbert F. Johnson Museum of Art on the campus of Cornell University (1970–73) in Ithaca, New York, consisted of a set of distinct vertical concrete masses holding the main mass of the gallery high in the air; huge panes of glass fill in the open volumes, making the whole structure unexpectedly transparent. Pei's East Building, National Gallery (1974–78), in Washington, DC, has numerous brutalist motifs, such as the stark masses, deep recesses, sharp edges, and wide openings, but it was clad in a white sandstone that foreshadowed a new generation of elegant, modernist civic structures.

18.109 East Building, National Gallery, Washington, DC

18.110 Herbert F. Johnson Museum of Art, Cornell University, Ithaca, New York

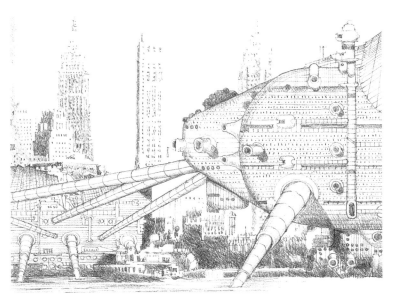

18.111 **A portion of Ron Herron's Walking City**

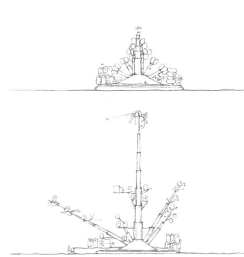

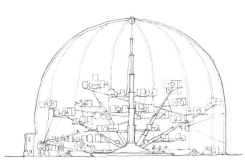

18.112 **Peter Cook's Blow-out Village**

Archigram

Archigram was a publication, begun in 1961, that quickly became known for its alternative ideas. Short for "Architectural Telegram," *Archigram* was produced by the young English architects Peter Cook, David Greene, Michael Webb, Ron Herron, Warren Chalk, and Dennis Crompton. The full *Archigram* group later included Colin Fournier, Ken Allison, and Tony Rickaby. Though the actual collaborations between these architects were often sporadic and difficult, the magazine's agenda called for a holistic vision of the city and its parts as a living, flowing, pulsing, flexible organism. Challenging the grid established by Le Corbusier, *Archigram*'s texts, collages, and comic book–style designs emphasized the use of anything but 90-degree angles and thematized the curving and twisting of Le Corbusier's straight lines. Using bright colors, a nonstandard format, and an explicitly cut-and-paste style of assembly, *Archigram* delivered visions of technologically advanced cities that walked on four legs, so-called Plugin Cities that could be stacked and changed like cords in an outlet, and Instant Cities that could be flown in and made to sprout like spring flowers in the hands of any eager architect, critic, or admirer. Though many of the *Archigram* structures were unbuildable, Peter Cook's recently built Kunsthaus in Graz, Austria, with its amorphous blue shape contrasting with the traditional architecture around it, gives some indication of the *Archigram* aesthetic and the excitement that it can generate.

The work of one member of the *Archigram* group, Mark Fisher, a student of Peter Cook at the Architectural Association (AA) in London, embraced the language and images of the youth culture that was blooming in England and abroad. His investigations into inflatable technology led to the Automat in 1968. It was a user-responsive pneumatic structure supported by internal bracing cables, which, attached to high-pressure jacks, allowed the structure to expand and contract in response to a user's weight requirements. Fisher improved the Automat in his design of the Dynomat, the surface of which was controlled by a series of valves, again responding to user interactions. The structure could be deflated and folded to fit in the back of a car.

In 1977, Mark Fisher was asked to design inflatable stage props for the Animals tour of the rock group Pink Floyd. During the design process, Fisher created the theme of two towering pneumatic icons. For the first show, he also designed a bloated, inflatable "nuclear family"—including 2.5 children. The most memorable of the Animals tour inflatables were the series of pigs, which flew over the audiences' heads, snorting and ultimately exploding above and behind Pink Floyd's stage. From his success with Pink Floyd's Animals tour, Mark Fisher went on to develop many of rock and roll's most memorable sets, including Pink Floyd's Wall and Division Bell sets and Lisbon's Expo '98.

Buckminster Fuller

Among the modernists, the one who most radically rethought the question of technology was Buckminster Fuller (1895–1983). In 1929, at the age of thirty-two, Fuller decided to study what he called the ecological principles of life. His goal was to analyze nature's resources and think of ways to make them available to all of humanity through an informed, efficient, flexible, and responsible attitude toward design. His key concepts were synergetics, which is what he called the underlying coordinate system of both physical and metaphysical nature; and ephemeralization, which essentially is doing more with less. Unlike some European modernists, who saw housing as primarily a question of social needs allied loosely with industrial realities, Fuller saw housing as tightly interwoven with industrialization and social utopian thinking.

What resulted in 1928, after a series of experiments with large-scale towers and multiple-family housing systems, was the project for a prefabricated, mass-produced 4D Dymaxion House, in which plumbing and electrical networks, as well as appliances, were contained in the central mast. The house could therefore operate independently of any utility network, which made it flexible enough to be located anywhere in the world. It was enclosed by transparent, shuttering walls made of vacuum-pane glass, which eliminated the need for windows. A specially designed ventilation system made dusting unnecessary, as air drawn through vents was filtered and then heated or cooled as desired. An in-home laundry facility was designed to wash, dry, fold, and place clean laundry in appropriate compartments. The entire structure was to be mass-produced and flown to its site by blimps, with installation requiring only a single day. All of this, Fuller estimated, would cost only slightly more than a 1928 Ford or Chevrolet automobile. The 4D Dymaxion House, however, was never realized.

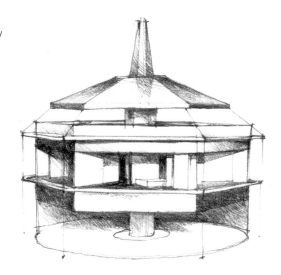

18.113 Drawing of a 4D Dymaxion House

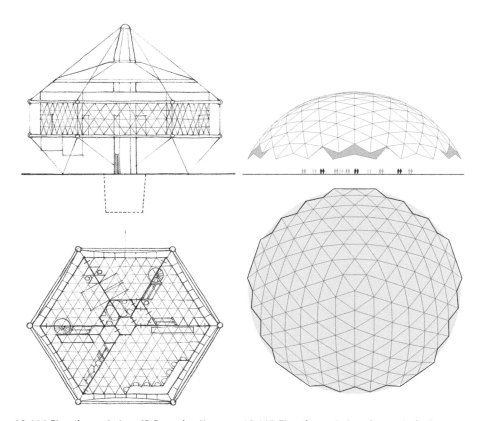

18.114 Elevation and plan: 4D Dymaxion House   **18.115 Elevation and plan of a geodesic dome**

18.116 **U.S. Pavilion, Montreal Expo, Canada**

Fuller also had a great interest in geography and produced the Dymaxion map (1941), as an icosahedron that could be unfolded in different ways. (The term *Dymaxion* was derived from a mixture of *dynamism*, *maximum*, and *ions*.) From the advent of the Dymaxion map to the geometries that led Richard Smalley and others to the Nobel Prize–winning discovery of carbon buckyballs (the most symmetrical large molecules known, they are named for Fuller, who was affectionately known as Bucky), Buckminster Fuller influenced a whole generation of architects, scientists, and visionary thinkers. He was one of the earliest advocates of renewable energy sources—solar, wind, and waves—and coined the term *Spaceship Earth* to emphasize the fact that we live on an ecologically interconnected planet.

Fuller's breakthrough discovery—and this one was fully practical—was the geodesic dome, which was designed to have the best possible ratio of volume to weight. Fuller determined that a network of triangular struts arranged on great circles (geodesics) would create local triangular rigidity and distribute the stress in a manner that would result in the most efficient structure ever designed. Geodesic domes, in fact, become stronger as they increase in size. Industry and the U.S. military immediately saw the potential of geodesic domes, and they were built by the hundreds around the world. The U.S. Pavilion at the 1967 Montreal Expo was, for example, a giant geodesic dome.

18.117 **Buckminster Fuller's Dymaxion map**

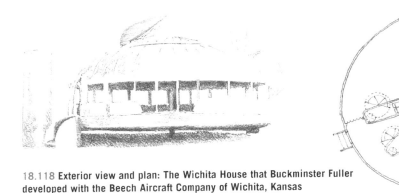

18.118 **Exterior view and plan: The Wichita House that Buckminster Fuller developed with the Beech Aircraft Company of Wichita, Kansas**

18.119 **House by Art Beal, Cambria, California**

18.120 **A homemade dome**

Counterculture Architecture

Beginning in the early 1960s and escalating toward the end of the decade, numerous young architects, builders, and artists—mainly in the United States—began to seek out alternatives to professional architecture, building with sod or discarded building elements and studying vernacular practices around the world. They were part of a broader counterculture of the times that criticized the social norms of the age, including the suburban lifestyle and the exploitation of natural resources. Though many of these people's names remain obscure, their efforts were sometimes spectacular, such as the house built by Bob de Buck and Jerry Thorman in New Mexico, a freeform maze of spaces gathered around central shafts of concrete columns that are actually the chimney flues. The structure was decorated with hubcaps and built with wood scavenged from construction sites. The framing was plastered, giving it an organic feeling. According to de Buck: "Tools not to have: straightedge, square, level, plumb."

In 1965, an artist community called Drop City was founded in southern Colorado and attempted to combine innovative architectural form with social utopianism. The original founders were Gene Bernofsky, JoAnn Bernofsky, Richard Kallweit, and Clark Richert, art students and filmmakers from the University of Kansas and the University of Colorado. Their intention was to create a live-in work inspired by the "happenings" of painter and performance artist Allan Kaprow and the impromptu performances of John Cage, Robert Rauschenberg, and Buckminster Fuller. Residents constructed domes and zonohedra, using geometric panels made from the metal of automobile roofs and other inexpensive materials. The property deed stipulated that the land on which the commune was built was "forever free and open to all people." Eventually,

tensions and personality conflicts developed, leading many of the occupants to leave. Nonetheless, there were several attempts to repeat the experiment, such as the Criss-Cross artists' colony in Colorado. Though dispersed and fragmented, this movement played an important part in demanding that architects developed greater ecological awareness.

Another example of counterculture architecture is a building that, once the scourge of the neighborhood, is now a tourist attraction. It was made by Art Beal, a garbage collector for the town of Cambria, California. Known also known as Captain Nitt Witt or Dr. Tinkerpaw, he spent his life constructing a residence on the side of a hill from salvaged materials using only hand tools. The structure is made from car parts, cans, shells, TV antennas, driftwood, and local rocks.

18.121 **Structures in Drop City, Colorado**

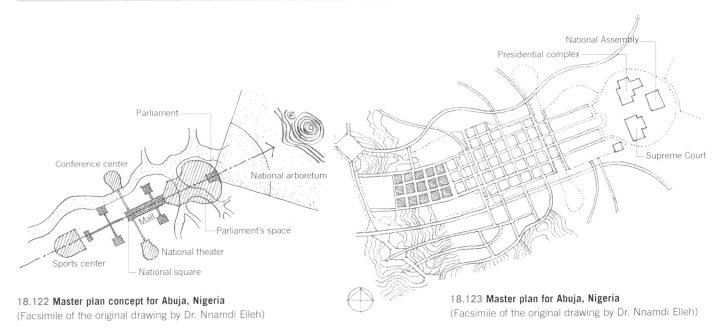

18.122 Master plan concept for Abuja, Nigeria
(Facsimile of the original drawing by Dr. Nnamdi Elleh)

18.123 Master plan for Abuja, Nigeria
(Facsimile of the original drawing by Dr. Nnamdi Elleh)

National Modernism, Nigeria

World War II left England and France considerably weakened. By the mid-1960s, almost all of the English colonies in Africa had achieved independence, including Uganda in 1962 and Zanzibar and Kenya in 1963. Most immediately embarked on an aggressive campaign of modernization. New capitals, schools, and hospitals had to be built, but since traditional architecture had been neglected, skilled builders and craftspeople were rare. In 1945, in all of Africa, including Egypt, there were only 26 cities with a population over 100,000. By the 1970s there were 120 such cities, but architectural development remained spotty.

After Nigeria's independence in 1960, several modernists arrived in Lagos, including the husband and wife team of Maxwell Fry and Jane Drew, who designed the University of Ibadan in the early 1960s, after having worked in Chandigarh, India. The university's nucleus is a series of connected buildings consisting of a ring of residential colleges arranged around a core of buildings devoted to teaching and administration. Open balconies, screens, and covered passageways make use of prevailing winds. The plan can be described as loosely hierarchical, with sports and residential complexes at one end and the class and administration buildings at the other.

By 1991 new oil revenues created wealth and stability, and Nigeria's capital was moved to a new city, Abuja, located on the Gwanga Plains in the middle of the country. Abuja's master plan (1976) was designed by Kenzo Tange, blending Lúcio Costa's airplane plan for Brasília with the circulation pattern of Tokyo. Anthropomorphically conceived, it had the shape of a body with head, torso, arms, and tail. The head contained the three principal government buildings, the torso the main body of the city, and the arms the conference center and theater. Though it was designed as a site for a democratic government, the head can be easily barricaded in times of civil disturbances. Abuja is currently far from complete.

18.124 University of Ibadan, Nigeria

18.125 School of Architecture, Ahmedabad, India

18.126 Gandhi Ashram Museum, Ahmedabad, India

South Asian Modernism

The Brazilian government was toppled by a military coup in 1965, arresting the development of Brazilian modernism. However, in South Asia, as in other parts of the postcolonial world, a more regional modern architecture continued to flourish. The Indian team of architects that had worked with Le Corbusier in Chandigarh continued to build throughout northern India. Aditya Prakash, for instance, was responsible for designing many new campuses and universities, such as those in Ludhiana and Hissar in the 1960s. Shivnath Prasad, in

New Delhi, developed Le Corbusier's brutalist vocabulary at the Akbar Hotel (1965–69) and at the Sri Ram Center for Performing Arts (1966–72). In Bangladesh, Mazharul Islam used brick and concrete for his dormitory at Jahangir University (1969). In general, building was done with load-bearing brick walls, with concrete lintels and slabs and deep overhangs as protection from the sun. Thus, unlike Brazil, where structural innovation became an integral part of the national modern style, architects in India, related perhaps more to the work of Dieste in Uruguay, developed a vocabulary using exposed brick and concrete constructed with simple technical skill and inexpensive finishes.

Balkrishna V. Doshi (1927–) and Charles Correa (1930–2015) were among the most prominent Indian architects. One of Doshi's successful early projects was the School of Architecture in Ahmedabad (1965), a reworking of Le Corbusier's design for the College of Art in Chandigarh. Unlike Le Corbusier's design, which was closed off and

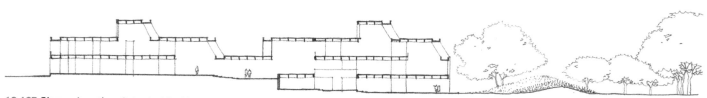

18.127 Plan and section: School of Architecture, Ahmedabad

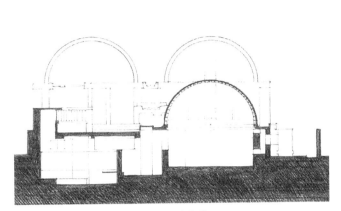

18.128 **Section: Sangath, Ahmedabad, India**

18.129 **Sangath, Ahmedabad**

regulated by a very strict circulation system, Doshi's school maintained the principle of north light, but he opened the building up so that it operated as a multifunctional space. Later in life, Doshi moved more in the direction of Louis Kahn, asking more fundamental questions of materials and assembly. The design of Sangath (1979), his own office, took on the work of rethinking a climatic response from first principles. The consequence was a structure that was just as much below ground as above, with a series of vaulted roofs (covered with broken china) derived from the original shed that stood on the site.

Correa extended Le Corbusier's fascination with sunlight to create a series of houses made of brick and concrete that used the concept of sections as well as a pergola roof to create microclimatic conditions. His Parekh House (1967–68) in Ahmedabad, for instance, had two sections: one for the summer and the other for the winter. The distant influence of Kahn's Trenton Bath Houses can be seen in Correa's design for the Gandhi Ashram Museum (1958–63), intended to house artifacts and an exhibition of the life of Mahatma Gandhi. Here Correa used a 6-meter grid composed of I-shaped brick piers to set up an interconnected network of spaces—some open to the sky, some covered but open, and some fully enclosed—that showed an early skill in developing courtyard-like spaces to

advantage. Correa used a mud-tile roof, held up on concrete beams, that drains rainwater into channels in the concrete slabs. The water is then collected in a central pond through huge concrete gargoyles, reminiscent of Le Corbusier's High Court in Chandigarh. Operable wooden louvers enabled air circulation in the enclosed spaces.

Correa's later work developed his climatic solutions for different sites and programs. For his residential tower in Bombay, the Kanchenjunga apartments (1970–83), for instance, he punched out double-height spaces in the corners to create an open feeling and to set up air circulation through each apartment. His Kovalam Beach Resort (1969–74) utilized the natural slope of the ocean-facing hill to create a rhythm of rooms and terraces open to the sky.

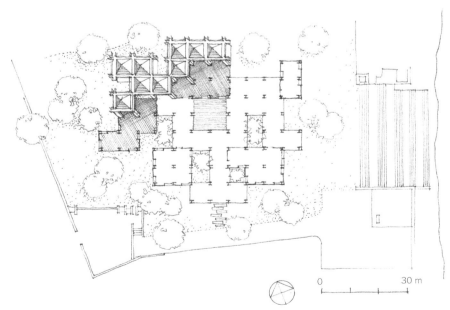

18.130 **Plan: Gandhi Ashram Museum**

779

But even in the United States, vast housing blocks shot up that exacerbated post–World War II social and racial tensions. This led to the announcement of the "death of modernism" with the destruction in 1972 of the Pruitt-Igoe Housing Project (1952–55) in St. Louis, Missouri, which opened to a great deal of optimism but, because of mismanagement and endemic racist policies, became the very symbol of urban blight and racial imbalance. Beginning in the late 1960s, architects began to return to the question of context, history, traditions, and form as a way to revitalize the purpose and meaning of their profession. The protest against modernism began in the United States but quickly morphed into a global movement that eventually dampened the spread of international modernism.

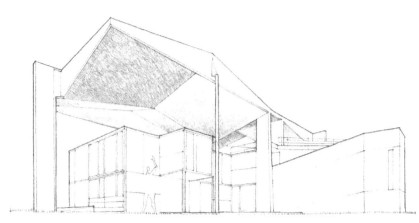

18.131 Heidi Weber House (Centre Le Corbusier), Zurich

POSTMODERNISM

The word *postmodernism* does not refer to a particular definable style, and in this it is very different from other designations, like Georgian or Shingle Style or even the International style, which, despite its multiple meanings and origins in architecture, by the 1950s described a set of practices loosely defined around the ideals of CIAM. But what had seemed so promising in 1950 was by 1970 seen not only as constricting but also as failing to live up to its promises. More and more, critics began to associate modernism with capitalism, bureaucracy, and failed social housing. And for Europeans, modernism after World War II meant endless rows of hastily built, drab housing blocks. There were no Brasílias, Chandigarhs, or Daccas in Europe, and few examples of successful civic modernism. In the United States, modernism was more successful. It had made significant inroads in domestic architecture, had thoroughly transformed the corporate landscape, and even had a few successful civic projects to show for itself, such as the Lincoln Center (1956) in New York City and Civic Center Plaza (1965–66) in Chicago.

18.132 AT&T Building, New York City

18.133 **Piazza d'Italia, New Orleans**

Certainly one of the most intriguing aspects of postmodernism was its interest in irony. No architecture before or after has allowed the designer to experiment with cultural and historical images with as free a hand as postmodernism. Examples include the Piazza d'Italia in New Orleans (1975–78) by Charles Moore; the AT&T Building in New York City (1984) by Philip Johnson, the National Collegiate Football Hall of Fame (1967; unbuilt) by Venturi, Scott Brown & Associates, and the Animal Crackers House in Chicago (1976–78) by Stanley Tigerman. Tigerman, influenced by inflated pop art forms, built an addition to a house that looks like a series of rollers that can be turned by using the ventilators on the sides as knobs. It is half industrial and half cartoonish in character. Even more provocative were the designs of the New York–based firm known as SITE (Sculpture in the Environment), which received commissions from Best, a forward-looking supermarket chain. In one project, SITE peeled the brick facade from the box, and in another, they designed the facade to appear as if it were in a state of decay and ruin. The irony was aimed at the strangeness of suburban architecture. It was the first firm to engage the question of the shopping mall through criticism and humor simultaneously.

Charles Jenck's 1977 book *The Language of Postmodern Architecure* sought to establish a canon for postmodernism by linking architectural vocabulary to structuralism, or the study of the structure of language. Michael Graves (1934–2015) was singled out by Jencks. His buildings used color, stripped down classical vocabularies, and applied the methodology of the collage. Other architects moved in the direction of social realism, such as Robert Venturi (1925–) and Denise Scott Brown (1931–), who were influenced by pop art and who turned their gaze at highway architecture and most specifically to Las Vegas, Nevada. Charles Moore (1925–93), by way of contrast, sought a deeper personal commitment to architecture than that which could be provided by a standard professional practice. In his writings we see the beginnings of an interest in phenomenology, a movement that was to grow steadily in the United States and abroad and that was linked to a trend toward political conservatism in architecture.

Moving from Philip Johnson to Charles Moore, one can begin to recognize the inherent and unresolved complexity of postmodernism, for though it heralded a release from the strictures of modernism and was thus a liberating movement, it also had conservative leanings, as was brought to the fore by the phenomenologists, who, in the United States and elsewhere, began to replace the socially oriented architects in academia. Those who wanted to take up the issue of community-oriented architecture often left the field of architecture for the rapidly expanding discipline of urban planning. Among the very early phenomenologists, Christian Norberg-Schultz (1926–2000) was strongly influenced by the German philosopher Martin Heidegger and argued for a regionally-based aesthetic, whereas Moore argued that architecture needed to integrate a sensitivity to landscape with an aesthetic determined by psychology and memory. At the opposite extreme from phenomenology was psychoanalysis, which among architects, unlike artists at the time, received very little interest.

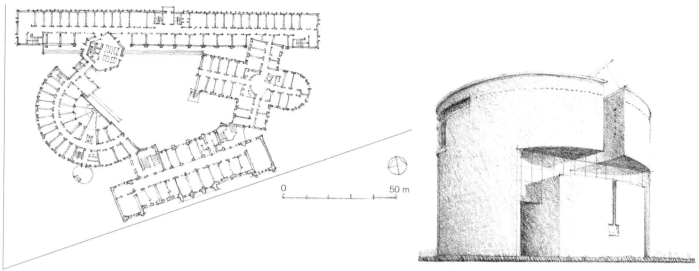

18.134 Plan: Social Science Research Center, Berlin

18.135 House at Stabio, Switzerland

Robert Stern (1939–) also interrogated the image of the American suburb in his Point West Place office building in Framingham, Massachusetts (1983–84), which in essence placed an Egyptianesque facade onto an otherwise generic office building. James Stirling's project for the Berlin Social Science Research Center (1981) begins with an existing building; appended behind it are buildings in the form of a collage—an amphitheater, a castle, an octagonal baptistery, and even a church. Through this historicism, which relies on precedents from the classical to the Renaissance, Stirling poked fun at a city that, unlike other European capitals, only began in the late 18th century. This instant Europeanization of Berlin was also meant to thumb its nose at Europe's fascination with its own past.

Buildings like the Berlin Social Science Research Center led many to criticize postmodernism as a style without rules. But there were many postmodernists who rejected irony and the open-endedness of the design process in favor of a claimed authenticity and seriousness. This movement was particularly strong in Europe. The German architect and theorist Leon Krier (1946–), a particularly strident critic of modernism, argued for a new Hellenism; in England, Prince Charles called for a return to pre-modern, homegrown

English styles. In Italy, Aldo Rossi (1937–97) argued for a typological coherence to architecture and challenged both modernists and postmodernists by staying within the brutalist aesthetic. At the Gallaratese (1969–73), a large apartment building project on the outskirts of Milan, for example, Rossi designed one of the blocks with a rhetoric of extreme formalist stoicism. The result was the emergence of an ethos of "regionalism" which had many defenders since it allowed for a criticism of modernism, on the one hand, and of postmodernism's penchant for irony and arbitrariness on the other. Regionalism was particularly strong outside of the West, where it tapped into nationalist and anticolonialist sentiments. But there were also a handful of European regionalists, such as the Swiss architect Mario Botta (1943–), whose work drew somewhat vaguely on local, historical forms. Nonetheless, his buildings' plans remained in some sense modern, as did their massing.

Whereas many of the more conservative postmodernists attempted to orient architecture back to its temporal, contextual, and historical roots, Peter Eisenman (1932–), along with John Hedjuk (1929–2000) and a few others, rejected any softening of architecture in the direction of culture. Architecture, to maintain itself as a discipline,

had to remain aloof from cultural traditions and bourgeois demands. Eisenman thus created for his buildings a set of formal constraints that had nothing to do with function or program. His radical formalism lies at the opposite end of the spectrum from Robert Venturi's pop contextualism. Nonetheless, both celebrated the disjuncture of expectations in the understanding of what is architecture. Eisenman's architecture, however, maintained a focus on the design process by seeking out a self-referential language that excluded the traditional priority of client needs. For the design of a house he created a type of game in which a cube was cut, rotated, sliced, and otherwise manipulated, so that what was left over was the "house": function, siting, weather, and use were given no consideration at all. He wanted to demonstrate that function is just as flexible as form and that a "house" is a semantic indicator of an architectural object, not its typology. This is different from the views of Rossi, who wanted functionalism to bend to the primacy of type.

18.136 **Centre Georges Pompidou, Paris, France**

Postmodernism, through the influences of pop art, also began to accommodate itself to the new medium of signage and advertising. The Centre Georges Pompidou (1971–77) in Paris, designed by the firm Piano & Rogers, was about "legibility." It was originally to have large billboards suspended from its metal structure. The service conduits, too, had to be legible. Air-conditioning ducts are blue, electricity conduits are yellow; elevator cables are red, staircases gray, and the structure itself is white. Putting so much emphasis on visual impact, postmodern architects had little to contribute to the topic of technology, but in his State of Illinois building in Chicago (1979), Helmut Jahn left elements of the structure exposed, especially on the interior, to better reveal the workings of the building, and experimented with new forms of skyscrapers that foreshadowed the skyscraper revival of the 1990s.

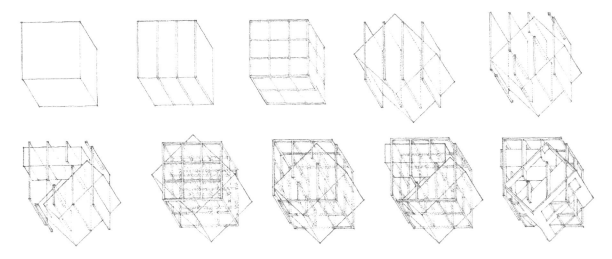

18.137 **Peter Eisenman's drawings for House III for Robert Miller**

18.138 Chapel of Light, Ibaraki Kasugaoka Kyokai Church, Osaka, Japan

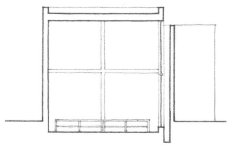

18.139 Section: Chapel of Light, Osaka, Japan

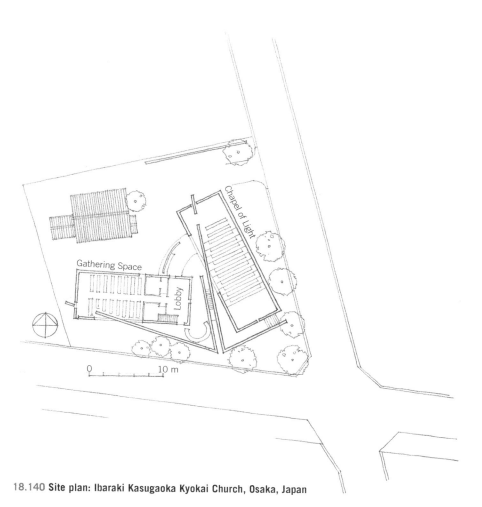

18.140 Site plan: Ibaraki Kasugaoka Kyokai Church, Osaka, Japan

Postmodernism had such a profound impact on the non-Western world that in the 1980s and early 1990s it found itself reassessing its claims to modernity and nationalism. Japanese architecture, for example, moved away from Metabolism and other forms of modernist expression. Arata Isozaki (1931–) became more literal in his references to Japanese forms, whereas younger, self-trained architects like Tadao Ando (1941–) gravitated toward elemental forms that stressed the interplay of light and materials in the experience of minimalist, poetic creations. His work became the hallmark of a new and very successful Japanese aesthetic that was highly modern and abstract and that also found common cause with traditional Japanese forms. His work in concrete, the predominant material of his expression, was immaculately poured. The Shingonshu Honpukuji ("Water Temple," 1991), for instance, focused on an singular moment where a stair descended through a round pond with a smattering of water lilies. At his Chapel of Light, the main chapel at Ibaraki Kasugaoka Kyokai Church (1989), the altar wall is composed of four pieces of concrete that hover weightlessly next to each other to create a luminous cross; at the rear, in another tour de force, the slight gap between the walls allows a blinding sliver of light to penetrate the dark stillness.

Japanese postmodernism could be seen as a highly refined form of modernism, and not really as postmodernism at all, since it is stripped of all except the most basic of cultural references. But the rise of postmodernism in other places was significantly messier and was often accompanied by the erosion of the secular nation-state as the common reference point for diverse communities. Since postmodernism allowed alternative claims to the conventions of nationalism, irony was almost never brought into play: on the contrary, the search was usually for some form of regional authenticity based on traditions. Just what constituted "tradition" then became highly contested, particularly in places like South Asia, where different claims, due to India's complex past, could be made upon history and its associated aesthetics. For example, right-wing Hindu nationalists demolished a mosque in northern India in the early 1990s on the grounds that it had been built on the foundations of a Hindu temple a millennium ago; the incident sparked religious riots. Similarly, the Islamic world saw a resurgence of orthodox claims to Islamic identity in cultural expression, forcing the rollback of national modernism in places such as Turkey and Egypt. Often, however, the tendency to see everything before modernism as traditional—that is, as firmly established and permanent—has left a gap in how to engage earlier aesthetic modalities in the modern world.

A long list could be made of architects of the postcolonial and non-Western world who are searching for a way to resolve this issue without resorting to, or endorsing, regressive, nationalist politics. For the most part, such architects, deeply steeped in the sensibilities of modern architecture, have attempted to reimagine their practices by referencing easily accessible and often somewhat stereotypical claims to mandalas, and other traditional or iconesque construction systems. Others talk of urban morphologies, place-making, and even *genius loci*, a term that has its origins in European Romantic philosophy of the early 19th century. More realistic was the work of Hassan Fathy (1899–1989) in Egypt. He utilized ancient design methods and materials to create low-cost architecture. He also trained locals to make their own materials

18.141 **San Cristobal Stables, Los Clubes, Mexico City**

and build their own buildings. Climatic conditions, public health considerations, and ancient craft skills also affected his design decisions.

Geoffrey Bawa (1919–2003), an architect from Sri Lanka trained at the Architectural Association in London, engaged problems of managing large land and water systems while building with masons who know nothing of modern building techniques. He drew, nonetheless, on local solutions and developed an aesthetic that is freely eclectic in its expression. His house for Dr. Bartholomew (1961–63) utilized a mixture of locally available materials, including coconut trunks, granite, and fired-earth tiles, as well as concrete for the foundation. He also introduced water pools, not only for cooling

but also to serve as visual beacons along a circulation path.

In Mexico, Luis Barragán (1902–88), who had collaborated with Louis Kahn on the design for the plaza at the Salk Institute building, developed a design vocabulary of simple forms, their elegance heightened by the use of color. Somewhat like Ando, he maintained a minimalist aesthetic insisting on stark planes in studied juxtapositions. As a consequence, his work has a strong poetic appeal. In his own house, he differentiated windows that were meant for framing a view from those that just were there to admit light. Barragán was little known in the world until a retrospective at the Museum of Modern Art in New York in 1975 made him famous.

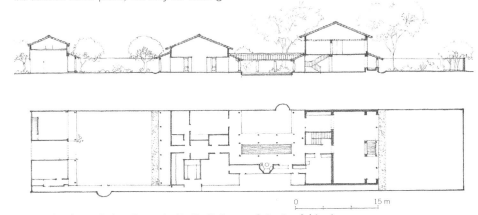

18.142 **Section and plan: House for Dr. Bartholomew, Colombo, Sri Lanka**

18.143 Simpson-Lee House, Mt. Wilson, Australia

18.144 Marie Short House, Kempsey, Australia

MAGNEY HOUSE

One of the most consistent explorations of a localized modernism was undertaken by Australia's Glenn Murcutt. Beginning with a sensibility strongly impressed by Mies van der Rohe's minimalist architecture, Murcutt's one-man practice has taken up small projects in the manner of California's Case Study Houses. His designs minimize the use of material while maximizing their effectiveness in controlling climate. His buildings disturb the land as little as possible and are constructed as efficiently as possible. A deep-seated knowledge of the site and of local conditions is cardinal to Murcutt's ethic; by choice, he has never practiced outside of Australia, although he teaches worldwide.

Murcutt's Magney House (1982–84), located 500 meters from the southern Pacific coast of Australia, has a masonry wall 2.1 meters high to the south to buffer the building against cold ocean winds. By contrast, the northern facade is completely glazed, though protected by retractable louvers, to take in the light and views. A continuous band of glazing about 2 meters off the ground encircles the house to admit ambient light and to make the sky visible from inside. Above this, two asymmetrical curves built with corrugated metal sheets not only protect the glazing and collect water that is stored in subterranean tanks but also give the house its signature roof profile as a "machine for living." Two vents from the kitchens hover above the roof like periscopes. Taut, V-shaped steel struts hold the roof overhang, calculated to keep the summer sun out and let the winter sun in. The plan is simple: a thin band of serving spaces to the south are separated from the northern bank of living spaces by a corridor, located exactly where the gully collecting water from the two roofs runs. Murcutt's Simpson-Lee House (1989–94) is built on the same principles but with a very different expression.

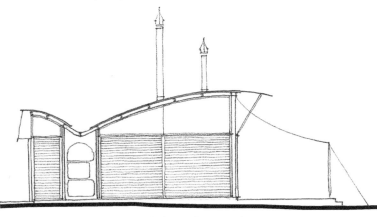

18.145 Section: Magney House, Bingie Bingie, Australia

Globalization Today

19.1 **Aerial view of Shenzhen Special Economic Zone, China**

INTRODUCTION

The awareness that we live in a world of global relationships is now itself global. Fifty years from now, it is likely that the end of the Cold War, the rise of China, and the onset of global warming will be remembered as the definitive events of the late 20th century, not the spectacle of 9/11 or the rise of ISIS. Since the fall of the Berlin Wall in 1989, the fruits of victory in the Cold War for the capitalist bloc led by the United States have taken the form of globalization, or the determined push to dominate global markets via the enforcement of favorable trade and tariff regimes.

Unshackled by the structural reforms initiated by Deng Xiaoping in 1978, China has stepped up to the opportunity of globalization to corner much of the market, pioneering the concept of the special economic zone (SEZ), an updated version of the colonial port treaties that were once signed to enable special places like Hong Kong to operate. Since the mid-1990s, formerly Third World countries have jostled to emulate the Chinese economic model, creating a new intermediate class of nations in the global hierarchy. Today they are known as the BRICS—Brazil, Russia, India, China, and South Africa—but others, such as Nigeria and Mexico, are clamoring to join in.

The keystone in the infrastructure of globalization is the containerization that has optimized international shipping in an unprecedented way, accompanied by massive purpose-built ships, automated ports, and radically rationalized truck and rail transport. None of this would have been possible without the concomitant spread of the new digital network, the Internet, which has not only generated the sense of a self-aware global community but has also enabled instantaneous financial transactions across national boundaries, transactions that power the engines of globalization. To support this network of global finance, a new empire of global cities has emerged—major cities that compete and collaborate to control global finance. Generic infrastructural buildings such as airports, airport malls, transit systems, and convention centers are also being built around the world to smooth the movement of the agents of global finance.

Global self-consciousness has also been spurred by two global crises: climate change and terrorism. Two centuries of relentless industrialization, powered by fossil fuels, has produced more wealth than ever before but has also ended up threatening the delicate equilibrium that is the atmosphere of planet

19.2 **Container ships in port, Seattle**

19.3 **Bollards protecting the U.S. Capitol in Washington, DC**

Earth. Architecture's role in this process is certainly not without blame; buildings are the largest consumers of energy in the United States, for instance. But the new crisis of terrorism can only be indirectly indexed to architecture. In the face of the overwhelming military might of today's dominant nation-states, insurgencies around the world have found a way to use the power of media—and more recently the Internet—to globalize the impact of guerilla warfare, originally a very localized and supplementary military tactic. Architecture plays the role of collateral damage in this war. More than the destruction of habitats that conventional warfare brings about, the bombing of iconic architecture like the Twin Towers in New York captures global attention, reminding us that architecture, in spite of all its materiality and massive capital expenditures, is ultimately just as subject to its media image as a supermodel. Architecture's supermodel-like qualities have resulted, on the one hand, in the fortification of significant public buildings such as embassies with bollards, high-perimeter walls, and other security features; and, on the other hand, in a global obsession with super-iconic buildings, recognizable worldwide, designed by a dazzling class of storied "starchitects."

In spite of all the razzle-dazzle, the critical architectural response to globalization is characterized by uncertainty and constant reinvention. Every year a new conference announces the establishment of a new ism; if it is Deconstructivism one day, it is the New Pragmatism the next, and then a New Regionalism the day after. New Urbanism is followed by New Landscape Urbanism, close on the heels of which comes Planetary Urbanization, accompanied by the Global Cities Network. In a sense, this is a sign of a rich discourse and the abandoning of orthodoxies. And yet, while the certainties of modernism are routinely criticized, the search for new ecological utopias is still a professional obsession. And while it is the unknown possibilities of technologically imbued architecture that get the most press and research funding, it is the postmodern-like quests for identity, place, and local empowerment that still find currency among alternative designers.

If the psychological response to uncertainty is preservation, it is no surprise that the movement for preservation—or conservation, as it is also termed—has emerged as a major force in the architectural community. Much more than the old modernist distinction between the new and the old, preservation today is a multivalent movement that includes strategies as diverse as building resilient social networks and banking the world's seeds to ensure biodiversity in the future. From World Heritage to DOCOMOMO to local activist groups, preservation is enjoying an unexpected renaissance. And in its midst, the city—as the ancient, evanescent Greek ideal of diverse communities sustained in an egalitarian matrix—has emerged as the focus of the civic objectives of professional architects. In 2009 half the world's population lived in cities, indicating the global trend toward urbanization—a statistic that was celebrated by both advocates and critics of globalization.

There is no one equation that can describe today's architecture, in spite of the whitewashing of the world that is implied by the term *globalization*. Instead, the global and the local have become so intertwined that perhaps the neologism *glocal* best describes the world that architects design for today. Rather than painting global architecture with a single brush, we would like to suggest an overlay of seven different global trends, each coming to terms with contemporary reality in a different way. And even though there are overlaps, each is governed by a set of circumstances, ideologies, and politics that differentiates it from the others.

19.4 **Map of the Global Cities Network**

1

In 2016, construction activity around the globe was worth over $7 trillion, constituting about 10 percent of the world's economy. These numbers will only increase, expected to grow to about $10 trillion by 2020, thanks to the economic developments taking place mostly in Asia, but also in Africa, Latin America, and eastern Europe. Though a vast proportion of these construction dollars are filtered through large, anonymous real-estate and engineering firms, whether owned privately or by the state, there are a host of large firms that provide architectural services at this level. One of these, Kohn Pedersen Fox Associates (KPF), founded in 1976 and originally working mainly in the United States and Europe, has in recent decades designed the Tigamas master plan (1990), the Kuwait International Hotel (1991), the Singapore Arts Center (1992), the Tel Aviv Peninsula master plan (1996), and the De Hoftoren/ Ministry Headquarters of Education, Culture, and Science for the Hague (2003), to list only a small fraction of their work. Seattle-based Callison Architecture, with five hundred people under a single roof, is the retail expert of the world, having designed in the Philippines (Ayala Center Greenbelt), China (Bank of China, Shangdi Center), Japan (Seibu Department Stores), India (Gardens Galleria), Qatar (Pearl of the Gulf), Dubai (Diera City Centre), and Russia (Ikea stores).

19.5 **Facade of old building surrounded by scaffolding during restoration**

19.6 Heavily urbanized megacity

demand has slowed recently. While the material effects of this transformation were felt worldwide, another kind of competition for supremacy is being waged in Asia in the race to claim the world's tallest building. In less than ten years, this title has shifted from Kuala Lumpur to Shanghai to Taipei and back to Shanghai. The power of tall buildings as a global icon was verified by the destruction of Minoru Yamasaki's twin towers at the World Trade Center by terrorists on September 11, 2001. That a handful of fanatical religious zealots planning vengeance in a remote field in the middle of Afghanistan could focus so precisely on these skyscrapers as the embodiment of the United States testifies to the continuing hold of architecture as an icon in the global imagination—as well as its perishability. New York has recently completed the construction of another tall tower at the World Trade Center complex, designed by Daniel Libeskind and David Childs of SOM, at a cost of almost $4 billion.

The St. Louis–based firm Hellmuth, Obata & Kassabaum (HOK) is another megafirm, with 2,500 employees worldwide. Its general style is a clean, professionalized version of postmodernism, with a flair for color and design. The Japanese megafirm Nikken Sekkei, like New Delhi's Morphogenesis, is more straightforwardly modernist: many of its buildings are infused with a clean, rectilinear sensibility; its presentation and designs predicated on new computing possibilities. Gensler, NBBJ, RTKL, and Ellerbe Beckett, now part of AECOM, are other large firms practicing worldwide. Some of these firms are so large that they conduct their own internal annual design awards competition with external juries, such as the GDEA, the Gensler Design Excellence Awards.

China has been a big draw since it opened to foreign investment in a massive industrialization and capitalization program the likes of which had never been seen before. By 2020, many of the world's twenty largest cities are going to be in China. (India is not far behind.) During the first decade of the 21st century, the worldwide price of steel doubled because of the demand from China, raising the cost of tall buildings in the rest of the world appreciably, although Chinese

19.7 Skyline of modern Shanghai

19.8 The new One World Trade Center tower, New York

2

A second way to map architecture at the global level is to follow the careers of those who self-consciously infiltrate the global economy with the principles of high design. Frank Gehry is the leader in this respect, designing opera houses, museums, and institutional headquarters the world over. These buildings are meant to be high profile and are readily used in tourist brochures. They are prestige commissions. This tendency began after World War II with such commissions as Jørn Utzon's Sydney Opera House (1957–73), but the most recent examples include the construction in Seoul of the Leeum Samsung Museum of Art, with buildings by Rem Koolhaas, Mario Botta, and Jean Nouvel. Qatar is being transformed into a world-class cultural center with the completion of five new museums, including the Islamic Museum by I. M. Pei and another by Santiago Calatrava, the renowned Spanish architect-engineer.

The global commodification of prestige buildings should not lead us to dismiss the potential importance of these buildings in the history of architecture, for they are places where architects can experiment not only with new technologies but also with new ideas about program and function. For the public, these buildings are also the most accessible and visible examples of avant-garde architectural production. Nonetheless, these projects are not unambiguous. The Guggenheim Museum in Bilbao, Spain, has brought in millions in tourist dollars, and the advantages and disadvantages need to be continually kept in mind. But even this is not a new phenomenon. The "Bilbao effect" is today what the great international exhibitions were to the 19th century—economic engines that promise an enhancement of awareness and knowledge but also extend the flattening process of capital. The Qatar museums are specifically aimed at tourists, whom officials hope will be lured to beach resorts and expansive desert landscapes—"all in a very safe environment." According to one official, "We expect tourism growth to more than double in the next six years, from the four hundred thousand visitors that presently visit Qatar to more than one million tourists in 2010."

19.9 Frank Gehry's iconic Guggenheim Bilbao, Spain

19.10 **Interior view: Santiago Calatrava's Quadracci Pavilion, Milwaukee Art Museum, Wisconsin**   19.11 **Quadracci Pavilion, Milwaukee Art Museum**

Among the elite designers who work at the global scale of prestige commissions, only Rem Koolhaas, a Dutch architect, has a well-articulated theory about the status and future of a globalized architecture. His 1,376-page book, *S,M,L,XL*, written together with Bruce Mau, Jennifer Sigler, and Hans Werlemann (1995), combines essays, manifestos, diaries, fiction, travelogues, and meditations on the contemporary city. The book's large color graphics transformed architectural publishing. One of its themes was "bigness," part of an attempt to address the concerns of scale in the modern, global world. An essay in the book, "The Generic City," declares that the usual differences between architecture, the street, and the city are things of the past. Instead, architecture has to embrace and combine all of these. Furthermore, the anonymity of the city and its architectural components is an inevitable consequence of modern life—and perhaps an ideal to strive for. In 2014 Rem Koolhas curated the Venice Architecture Biennale, in which he dispensed with the tradition of celebrating the work of famous architects and instead catalogued the mundane registers of construction—walls, flooring, paneling, and the like—that make up the bulk of the work of architectural design.

19.12 **The Office for Metropolitan Architecture's Central Public Library, Seattle, Washington**

19.13 **2014 Venice Architecture Biennale**

19.14 **Couture by Alexander McQueen (above) and Frank Gehry's Louis Vuitton concept model (below)**

Despite this position, Koolhaas, like others, has become the favored architect of the governmental and capitalist elite, or at least those who want to think fast and preferably big, whether it be the Dutch for their embassy in Berlin; the Chinese and their CCTV tower in Beijing; the European Union and its headquarters in Brussels; Samsung, with its Leeum Museum in Seoul; or Prada, with its elegant store in New York City. The difference between KPF and Rem Koolhaas is thus blurry, for both operate at the intersection of high capital and high design. Koolhaas, however, has a practice that seeks to articulate much more strongly than KPF the autonomy of the architect and the symbolic celebration of the architect's name. To this effect, Koolhaas founded the Office for Metropolitan Architecture (OMA) in 1975, a pure design corporation that in his own words blends "contemporary architecture, urbanism, and cultural analysis" and tries to address the problems associated with contemporary globalization with truly innovative and radical solutions. Besides institutional buildings in Europe, the United States, and Asia, OMA has designed urban plans for large cities, proposed a new logo for the European Union, and even prepared the digital identity for global high-fashion retail giant Prada.

The 21st century, in fact, has seen the increasing intersection of the world of haute couture and architecture. Not only do several iconic fashion designers, such as Tom Ford, have architectural backgrounds, but the design of fashion shows and flagship stores, such as those of Louis Vuitton, has emerged as a distinctive genre in itself. Fashion designers like Hussein Chalayan and Comme des Garçons self-consciously refer to architectural structure in their designs—and, conversely, some architects, such as Zaha Hadid, also crossed over into fashion design.

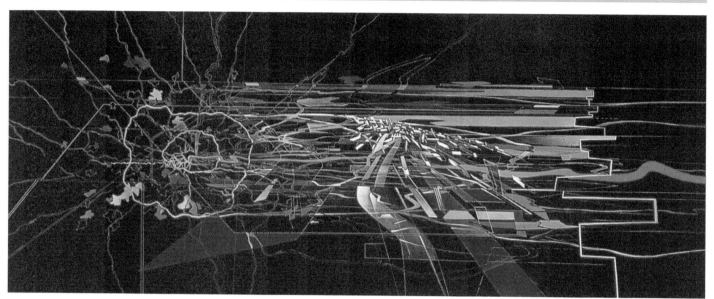

19.15 *Vision for Madrid*, drawing by Zaha Hadid

Zaha Hadid (1950–2016) occupies a special place in this spectrum. As a woman architect born in Iraq, Hadid broke many of the glass ceilings and stereotypes of architecture culture. Eschewing the formal shibboleths of both modernism and postmodernism, she quickly developed a distinctly individualistic style that emphasized bold forms and sensuous lines, which was at first described as being deconstructivist but came into its own with the ascent of computer-based parametric modeling in the 1990s. As a woman of color, Zaha Hadid gave expression to the aspirations of women architects worldwide, including those of earlier generations such as Eileen Gray of France, Minnette de Silva of Sri Lanka, and U. E. Chowdhury of India.

One of the problems with "starchitects" is that once they retire or die, their work cannot be sustained, as happened with the firms of the earlier generation of modernist masters such as Le Corbusier, Frank Lloyd Wright, and Ludwig Mies van der Rohe. Benedetta Tagliabue's work at EMBT in Barcelona is a notable exception in this regard: not only has she completed and continued the work she began with Enric Miralles (1955–2000), she has also been able to create a distinctive new identity for herself that builds on the legacy of the firm.

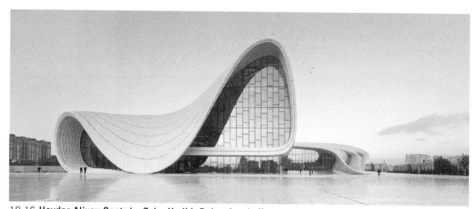

19.16 **Heydar Aliyev Centr by Zaha Hadid, Baku, Azerbaijan**

19.17 **Clichy-Montfermeil Metro Station competition drawings by Benedetta Tagliabue**

19.18 **A courtyard of Sardarnagar**

3

In contradistinction to the approach just outlined are the architectural practices that come from the direction of nongovernmental organizations (NGOs) that aim to solve pressing social and economic problems. Globally, one in seven people lives in a slum settlement. By 2020, that number will increase to one in three. NGOs are an important part of the solution to this pending crisis, since they are more flexible than government bureaucracies and thus often more capable of identifying problems and suggesting solutions that are acceptable to local communities.

Though the idea of the NGO dates to the early 20th century, the phrase *nongovernmental organization* only came into broader use with the establishment of the United Nations in 1945, when provisions were made for the creation of such organizations. Today, the amount of unacknowledged work done by NGOs around the world is staggering. An example is the building effort undertaken by Kutch Nav Nirman Abhiyan, a collection of forty NGOs in Kutch, in western India, which came together after the devastating earthquake of January 26, 2000, to undertake a range of development initiatives in the areas of social work, primary education, and disaster management. It has also helped construct more than twenty thousand dwellings built by the local communities themselves. The new structures used reinforcement techniques to make the buildings more earthquake resistant. Such work by "barefoot architects," as they have sometimes been called, is the other side of the world of global capital. Another organization, Architecture for Humanity, a San Francisco–based NGO, provides volunteered professional design services to community groups, social entrepreneurs, and other not-for-profit organizations the world over. It helps underprivileged communities plan and develop schools, clinics, and sports fields, among other things.

4

A fourth type of architecture operating at the global level is produced by local architects with small firms that, despite varying design methodologies, advocate a carefully crafted and well-thought-out relationship between program and the constraints formed by climate, site conditions, and materials. Though explicitly local by orientation, these architects constitute a global movement due to their shared ethic of design, which can be described broadly as one derived from modern architecture. At Atelier Feichang Jianzhu's Split House near Beijing, for example, the architect uses rammed earth not only for its natural thermal insulating properties but also because rammed earth has been a part of Chinese architecture in history. Framed against the backdrop of the nearby cliffs, it can even be seen through a Ruskinian ethos as a commentary on the nature of material and geology. In Adirá & Broid & Rojkind's F-2 House, volcanic basalt, a common local material in Mexico City, is used as a visual and tactile contrast to the cast-in-place concrete. The aesthetic is close to that of Marcel Breuer, who helped create a form of modernism compatible with the open landscape and the need to capture the breeze. Both these houses are therefore high modernist in style—but that should not be any reason to condemn them.

19.19 Antioch Baptist Church, a project of Auburn University's Rural Studio, Perry County, Alabama

19.20 Anupama Kundoo's own house in Auroville, India

5

Irony is particularly remote in today's aesthetic and will, sadly, remain so, given the penchant for appearing respectful to the ideologies of tradition and inheritance. For that reason, we would like to point to a fifth global phenomenon: architecture produced locally but by amateurs and architects with an open sensibility to the potential in ready-mades—a house in Massachusetts made completely out of newspaper (including the furniture), a house in Nevada using automobile tires, complete buildings made out cardboard tubes, squatter settlements in Mexico that make use of discarded building materials, architects who use off-the-shelf technologies to subvert expectations, and those who build houses with shipping containers. This type of architecture burst onto the scene in the late 1960s with Drop City in Colorado, which was a center of the counterculture movement. Since then, it has expanded into an informal movement all its own. Sean Godsell's Future Shack, for instance, combines a sun-shading device with a shipping container to design a mass-produced, relocatable house. The Rural Studio, developed by Samuel Mockbee (1944–2001) at Auburn University in Alabama, is particularly exemplary. Working with the basic principle that even the poorest deserve the dignity of good architecture, Mockbee and his students designed and built a host of inexpensive and imaginative structures, advancing the frontier of architectural practice with such innovations as sidings made from salvaged automobile windscreens and license plates.

Designing within the context of "the local" does not require using or replicating ancient techniques or falsely aestheticizing local customs, as is so often done, for example, by those who reduce the Chinese tradition of screens to working with metal screens.

The architecture of small firms is important to the development of architectural thinking, as small firms can often be more experimental and open-ended in their approach. Atelier Bow Wow in Tokyo, established by Yoshiharu Tsukamoto and Momoyo Kaijima, made a name for itself designing unusual structures like the Mado Building in Tokyo (2006) in the tight urban environments of Japanese cities. Anupama Kundoo developed innovative design techniques in Auroville, India. In Barcelona, the mid-19th-century Santa Caterina Market was remodeled (1997–2005) by architects Enric Miralles and Benedetta Tagliabue of EMTB Associates. They added a wavy wooden roof over the whole building, practically filling the piazza. The colorful roof tiles are decorated to emulate the vibrant colors of the vegetables and fruits in the market stalls. The structure has brought new life to the economically depressed area of Barcelona's Gothic Quarter. Another architect, Teddy Cruz, works with the migrant communities of Los Angeles, as well as the Mexican communities across the border, to develop innovative housing solutions.

6

A sixth category of global production revolves around the question of environment. It was only recently that mainstream architectural professionals began to acknowledge the impact buildings have on the environment. The production of materials like rubber, steel, and glass is highly polluting. There are also issues of how much energy a building requires for heating and cooling, and the question of a building's life span. The U.S. Environmental Protection Agency estimates that architectural debris comprises 25 percent of the nation's overall waste stream. This waste often contains materials such as lead paint, asbestos, fluorescent light bulbs, light ballasts, treated lumber, and other items that pollute the environment.

The impact of industrialism on the environment and society began to be critiqued in the late 19th century. Frederick Law Olmsted designed parks that were oases of nature in the urban context, and Frank Lloyd Wright and others attempted to integrate the mechanical and the natural. But it was only with the ecology movement of the 1960s that environmentalism became a political issue. The slow success of that movement led to the emergence of the field of environmental management in the 1980s. Most of the issues involved law, government, and industry, and architecture has only recently begun to find a role within the debates. Today, some architects specialize in low-budget design-build projects; others, in green housing projects, self-sufficient houses, solar houses, eco-villages, and now, so-called health houses.

The central term in this movement is the word *sustainability*, but it can mean different things to different groups. In the context of environmental management, the issues revolve around questions of politics, government, law, planning, and banking. Architectural design, as such, is often left until the end of the process. But this has begun to change, and most large firms now offer a specialization in green architecture. As a common standard of measurement of the sustainable character of a building, U.S. architects now use the Leadership in Energy and Environmental Design (LEED) Green Building Rating System.

19.21 **Commerzbank, Frankfurt, Germany**

The LEED system evaluates buildings along a wide spectrum of criteria but usually favors more technologically advanced solutions. Among architects who work with low budgets is Thomas Herzog in Germany, who combines conventional methods of environmental design—high spaces to reduce air-conditioning costs, for example—with high-end technology such as specially designed types of glass and cooling systems. William McDonough has championed the ideological imperative that sustainability should have for the world's leading corporations. His headquarters for Volkswagen and his projected 65,000-square-meter plant, built on 130 hectares of former rain forest in Brazil, are just two of his larger commissions. At the high end of green architecture is Foster & Partners' design for the Commerzbank in Frankfurt, Germany, now the tallest building in Europe. Interspersed throughout the tower are sky gardens. There are now firms that specialize in the greening of architectural projects, just as there are firms that specialize in developing green master plans that look to future needs.

19.22 **Cast of pollution from the Louis Vuitton factory in Paris, by Jorge Otero-Pailos**

7

A final but increasingly important global formation centers on the World Heritage List to preserve buildings and building environments, created under the auspices of the United Nations Educational, Scientific and Cultural Organization (UNESCO) in 1972. Only forty-odd years old, the list now consists of more than eight hundred properties in 134 countries. The list is continually expanded, and even modernist sites like Chandigarh, India have recently been added to it. The amount of space worldwide that is now curated, or under some form of protection, has increased exponentially since the list's inception—entire valleys, villages, and landscapes are now under protection.

As valuable as this movement for preservation is, it is the lure of tourist dollars, as much a need to preserve identity, that drives the search for heritage. The Dogon cities of Djenné were inscribed on the UNESCO Heritage List in 1988, and now a road is being planned to reach the remote location. Being "protected" will certainly be a mixed blessing, given that this is a living community and not a set of fossilized ruins. More conventional is the protection of archaeological sites. More than four hundred thousand people visit the remote site of

Machu Picchu in Peru every year. A road has now been built to carry tourists almost to the top of this remote mountain. In 1994, a new category was created by UNESCO: "cultural landscapes" were introduced to broaden the representation of what UNESCO calls human heritage, but the delimitations of this term will become increasingly complex as such cultural landscapes become increasingly entangled with politics.

The preservation of the modern architecture of the world has been championed by DOCOMOMO, an organization that started in Europe in 1988 and has established itself as a major force worldwide. As most of the world's modern architecture is now at least half a century old, it is increasingly under threat of destruction. Through publications, awards, conferences, and local activism, DOCOMOMO's regional chapters have sought to make the case that modern architecture is as deserving of preservation as the pre-modern architecture of the world.

Preservation is a global force in the architectural community today. While it is largely devoted to fighting imminent destruction, a more critical approach to thinking about preservation can be found

in the work of people like Jorge Otero-Pailos, who made the casting of pollution into an interrogation of the conventions of preservation practice.

Global heritage is most certainly a form of global intermixing. Whether that intermixing is to be understood as a form of cultural liberation from the hegemony of the local or as cultural contamination by the hegemony of the global is a question that can only be resolved in each particular situation.

In the last decade, architectural educators have been asking for a textbook that looks beyond the Eurocentric approaches of the past. Ironically, recent decades have also seen the rising specter of nationalism, which has become a global phenomenon in its own right as countries seek to establish their credentials in global historical narratives. This new nationalism, though it has played some role in awakening an awareness about local realities, has had, and continues to have, a dampening effect on learning about what lies over the horizon. The tension between the global and the national is the fundamental paradox of our age.

Today we live in a world that is significantly more static than in centuries before—boundaries are controlled by international law and political alliances, UNESCO protects architectural and urban marvels of the past, and local and national regulations govern what can and cannot be built. We control our actions for the sake of global tranquility. But inequities and injustices in the location of boundaries persist, and so, too, do the tensions that result from inward-looking ideologies. In this environment, the maxim "know your neighbor" is all the more important but at the same time all the more elusive, since we can all, no matter our country of origin, easily revel in our singularity—in the presumed uniqueness of our history.

This is something we need to guard against. A global history is not the history of all the modern nations added up like beads on an abacus, but neither is it a history that assumes a universal aspect to mankind and its productions. For a global history to be more than just dates and facts, it has to be rooted in the principle that each of us learns how he or she is indeed different in the eyes of others.

19.23 **Cast of pollution from Trajan's Column at the Victoria and Albert Museum in London, by Jorge Otero-Pailos**

Glossary

abacus The rectangular stone slab forming the top of a column capital, plain in the Doric style but molded or otherwise enriched in other styles.

abbey 1. A monastery under the supervision of an abbot, or a convent under the supervision of an abbess. 2. The church of an abbey.

acanthus A Mediterranean plant whose large, toothed leaves became a common motif in the ornamental program of Corinthian and composite capitals and friezes.

accouplement The placement of two columns or pilasters very close together.

acropolis 1. The fortified high area or citadel of an ancient Greek city, typically marked by an important temple. 2. [Acropolis] The citadel of Athens and site of the Parthenon.

adobe Sun-dried brick made of clay and straw, commonly used in countries with little rainfall.

adyton A restricted area within the *cella* of a Greek or Roman temple.

aedicule (pl: aediculae) A small construction designed in the form of a building—like a canopied niche flanked by colonnettes or a door or window opening—framed by columns or pilasters and crowned with a pediment.

ageya A Japanese pleasure house.

aggregate From the Latin *aggregare*, to add together. Any of various hard, inert mineral materials, such as sand and gravel, added to a cement paste to make concrete or mortar.

agora A marketplace or public square in an ancient Greek city, usually surrounded by public buildings and porticoes and commonly used as a place for popular or political assembly.

alameda 1. A public promenade lined with shade trees. 2. In Latin America, a boulevard, park, or public garden with such a promenade.

Alcazar A castle or fortress of the Spanish Moors, specifically the palace of the Moorish kings in Seville, Spain, which was later used by Spanish kings.

altar 1. An elevated place or structure upon which sacrifices are offered or incense burned in worship or before which religious rites are performed. 2. The table in a Christian church upon which the Sacrament of the Eucharist is celebrated.

amalaka The bulbous, ribbed stone finial of a *shikhara* in Indian architecture.

ambo Either of two raised stands from which the Gospels or Epistles were read or chanted in an early Christian church.

ambulatory 1. The covered walk of an atrium or cloister. 2. An aisle encircling the end of the choir or chancel of a church, originally used for processions.

amphitheater 1. An oval or round building with tiers of seats around a central arena, like those used in ancient Rome for gladiatorial contests and spectacles.

ang A lever arm in traditional Chinese construction, placed parallel to the rafters and raked at an angle to counterbalance the forces applied by the inner and outer purlins. The ang supports the outermost purlin by means of a bracket or crossbeam and is pinned at the inner end against a purlin. The ang first appeared in the 3rd century CE but served purely as a decorative element after the Song dynasty.

annular Having the shape of a ring.

anta In Greek temples, a rectangular pier or pilaster formed by thickening the end of a projecting wall.

apadana The grand columnar audience hall in a Persian palace.

apse A semicircular or polygonal projection of a building, usually vaulted and used especially at the sanctuary or the east end of a church to define the space for an altar. Also called an exedra.

apteral 1. Without a colonnade along the sides. 2. Having no aisles, as a church. 3. Revealing no aisles, as a church facade.

aqueduct A conduit or artificial channel for conducting water from a remote source, usually by gravity, especially an elevated structure constructed by the Romans to carry a water channel across a valley or over a river.

arabesque A complex and ornate design that employs flowers, foliage, and sometimes geometric figures and the figures of animals to produce an intricate pattern of interlaced lines.

arcade 1. A range of arches supported on piers or columns, this composition dates back to Hellenistic times and was used mainly in Islamic and Christian architecture. 2. An arched, roofed gallery or passageway with shops on one or both sides.

arch A curved structure for spanning an opening and designed to support a vertical load primarily by axial compression.

architecture parlante "Speaking architecture," a term used in 18th-century France to describe the architecture of buildings that, in their plans or elevations, create an image that suggests their functions.

architrave 1. The lowermost division of a classical entablature, resting directly on the column capitals and supporting the frieze. 2. A molded or decorative band framing a rectangular door or window opening.

arcuate Curved or arched like a bow: a term used in describing the arched or vaulted structure of a Romanesque church or Gothic cathedral, as distinguished from the trabeated architecture of an Egyptian hypostyle hall or a Greek Doric temple.

arris A sharp edge or ridge formed by two surfaces meeting at an exterior angle, like that formed by the adjoining flutes of a classical column.

ashlar A squared building stone finely dressed on all faces adjacent to those of other stones so as to permit very thin mortar joints.

ashram In Indian architecture, a house for resting.

atrio In Mexican architecture, a large open court that is walled along the edges.

atrium 1. The main or central inner hall of an ancient Roman house, open to the sky at the center and usually having a pool for the collection of rainwater. Also called a *cavaedium*. 2. The forecourt of an early Christian church, flanked or surrounded by porticoes. 3. An open, skylit court around which a house or building is built. 4. A skylit central court in a building, especially a large interior one having a glass roof and surrounded by several stories of galleries.

attic 1. A low story or decorative wall above an entablature or the main cornice of a classical facade. 2. A room or space directly under the roof of a building, especially a house; a garret.

axis 1. The line about which a rotating body turns. 2. A line about which a three-dimensional body or figure is symmetrical. 3. Any line used as a fixed reference in conjunction with one or more other references for determining the position of a point or of a series of points forming a curve or a surface. 4. A straight line to which elements in a composition are referred for measurement or symmetry.

bagh A garden in Indian architecture.

baldachino 1. A canopy of fabric carried in religious processions or placed over an altar or throne. 2. An ornamental canopy of stone or marble permanently placed over the high altar in a church.

balustrade A series of balusters used to support a rail in a stair or balcony. Also called a banister.

bangla In Bengal, a hut with a curved thatched roof, the form of which was emulated in brick temples.

banister See balustrade.

baptistery A part of a church or a separate building in which the rite of baptism is administered.

baradari A Mughal pavilion with triple arcades on each of its four sides, hence the translation of the word as "twelve-doored"; a summer house.

baray A large, shallow water tank in Southeast Asia.

barrel vault A vault having a semicircular cross-section.

base The lowermost portion of a wall, column, pier, or other structure, usually distinctively treated and considered as a separate architectural unit.

basilica 1. A large oblong building used as a hall of justice and public meeting place in ancient Rome, typically having a high central space lit by a clerestory and covered by timber trusses, as well as a raised dais in a semicircular apse for the tribunal. The Roman basilica served as a model for early Christian basilicas. 2. An early Christian church, characterized by a long, rectangular plan, a high colonnaded nave lit by a clerestory and covered by a timbered gable roof, two or four lower side aisles, a semicircular apse at the end, a narthex, and often other features, as an atrium, a bema, and small semicircular apses terminating the aisles.

bastion The projecting part of a rampart or other fortification, typically forming an irregular pentagon attached at the base to the main work.

batter A backward slope of the face of a wall as it rises.

bay 1. A major division—usually one in a series—marked or partitioned off by the principal vertical supports of the structure. 2. Any of a number of principal compartments or divisions of a wall, roof, or other part of a building part marked off by vertical or transverse supports.

bazaar A marketplace or shopping quarter, especially in the Middle East, where goods are set out for sale. A bazaar is often comprised of rows of small shops or stalls in a narrow street, or of a certain section of town divided into narrow passageways.

beacon tower Any of the high towers built along a great wall at regular intervals from which warning signals or alarms could be sent back and forth by means of fire and smoke.

bekhnet The Egyptian word for "pylon" meaning "to be vigilant."

belvedere A building or architectural feature of a building designed and situated to look out upon a pleasing scene.

bema 1. The sanctuary space surrounding the altar of an Eastern church. 2. A transverse open space separating the nave and the apse of an early Christian church, developing into the transept of later cruciform churches.

bhumi 1. Earth in Indian architecture. 2. The horizontal relief of a *shikhara* or temple tower.

biyong Literally, "jade ring moat," a ritual structure in Chinese architecture enclosing a space in the shape of the *bi*, a flat jade ceremonial disk. Originally a separate structure, the *biyong* later became part of a single ritual complex with the *mingtang*.

blind arcade A series of arches simulating the pattern of the arcade on a wall surface.

bouleuterion A place of assembly in ancient Greece, especially for a public body.

boulevard Originally, the flat summit of a rampart; later, any major tree-lined thoroughfare, often laid out over an old fortification.

bracket A support projecting horizontally from a wall to bear the weight of a cantilever or to strengthen an angle, as along an eave or under a bay window.

Brahmin Any of the priests belonging to the Indian upper class.

brise-soleil A screen, usually of louvers, placed on the outside of a building to shield the windows from direct sunlight.

broken pediment A pediment with its raking cornices interrupted at the crown or apex; the gap is often filled with an urn, a cartouche, or other ornament.

bungalow 1. In India, a one-story thatched or tiled house, usually surrounded by a veranda. The word derives from the Bengali word *bangla* and was first used by the English colonists in India as a type of garden and plantation house. 2. In the United States, a derivative of the Indian bungalow, popular especially in the first quarter of the 20th century, usually having one or one and a half stories, a widely bracketed gable roof, and a large porch, and often built of rustic materials.

buttress An external support built to stabilize a structure by opposing its outward thrusts, especially a projecting support built into or against the outside of a masonry wall.

cai One of eight grades of modular timber sections in traditional Chinese construction, based on the size and span of a building.

caitya A Buddhist shrine in India, usually carved out of solid rock on a hillside, having the form of an aisled basilica with a stupa at one end.

caldarium The room in an ancient Roman bath containing hot water.

camber A slight convex curvature intentionally built into a beam, girder, or truss to compensate for an anticipated deflection.

campanile The Italian word for a tower, usually a bell tower near but not attached to the body of a church.

candi A temple in Southeast Asian architecture.

cantilever A beam or other rigid structural member extending beyond a fulcrum and supported by a balancing member or a downward force behind the fulcrum.

cao A space in Chinese architecture.

capital The distinctively treated upper end of a column, pillar, or pier that crowns the shaft and takes the weight of the entablature or architrave.

cardo The main north-south route in an ancient Roman town.

caryatid A sculptured female figure used as a column, especially in ancient Greece.

castellated Having turrets and battlements, like a castle.

castrum An ancient Roman military camp having streets laid out in a grid pattern.

catacomb 1. An underground cemetery consisting of linked galleries and chambers with recesses for coffins and tombs. 2. The subterranean complex of layered corridors with burial vaults, chambers, and niches, covered with inscribed tablets and often decorated with frescoes, built by the early Christians in and near Rome.

cathedral The principal church of a diocese, containing the bishop's throne, called the cathedra.

causeway 1. A road or path raised above surrounding low or wet ground. 2. A raised passageway ceremonially connecting the valley temple with an ancient Egyptian pyramid.

cella Latin for the Greek word *naos*: the principal chamber or enclosed part of a classical temple where the cult image was kept.

cement A calcined mixture of clay and limestone, finely pulverized and used in concrete and mortar.

cenotaph A monument erected in memory of a deceased person whose remains are buried elsewhere, often having the form of a domed pavilion or temple replica.

cenoté The Mayan word for the deep water-filled sinkholes that the Itzá associated with the underworld.

centering A temporary structure or framework for supporting a masonry arch or vault during construction until the work can support itself.

central plan The plan for a building organized around a large or dominant space, usually characterized by two axes crossing each other at right angles.

chamfer A beveled surface, usually formed or cut at a 45-degree angle to the adjacent principal faces.

chan Chinese for "meditation" (based on the Sanskrit word *dhyan*); zen in Japanese.

chancel The space about the altar of a church for the clergy and choir, often elevated above the nave and separated from it by a railing or screen.

chapel A separately dedicated part of a church for private prayer, meditation, or small religious services.

char bagh The quadrangular design of Islamic gardens.

chattri In Indian architecture, a rooftop kiosk or pavilion having a dome, usually supported on four columns.

cheng The walling of a Chinese city.

chih In Chinese architecture, the bronze or stone disk between a column's base and its foot.

choir That part of a church, usually part of the chancel, set apart for clergy and singers.

chorten A memorial mound of earth in a Tibetan Buddhist religious center.

choros A group of minor actors offering commentary in classical Greek plays.

chu A column in Chinese architecture.

ci A Chinese shrine.

citadel A fortress in a commanding position in or near a city, used in controlling the inhabitants and in defense during attack or siege.

classical Of or pertaining to the art or architecture of ancient Greece and Rome, on which the Italian Renaissance as well as other styles, such as the Baroque, were based.

clerestory The uppermost section of a Gothic nave characterized by a series of large windows rising above adjacent rooftops to admit daylight to the interior.

cloister A covered walk having an arcade or colonnade on one side that opens onto a courtyard.

cloister vault A compound vault formed by four coves meeting along diagonal vertical planes.

coffer Any of a number of recessed, usually square or octagonal panels in a ceiling, soffit, or vault.

colonnade A row of regularly spaced columns carrying an entablature and usually one side of a roof structure.

colonnette A small, slender column used more often for visual effect than structural support.

colossal order An order of columns more than one story in height. Also called giant order.

column 1. A rigid, relatively slender structural member designed primarily to support compressive loads applied at the member ends. 2. A cylindrical support in classical architecture consisting of a capital, shaft, and usually a base, either monolithic or built up of drums the full diameter of the shaft.

composite order One of the five classical orders, popular especially since the beginning of the Renaissance but invented by the ancient Romans, in which the Corinthian order is modified by superimposing four diagonally set Ionic volutes on a bell of acanthus leaves.

compression A force that acts to press and squeeze together, resulting in a reduction in size or volume of an elastic body; many materials (e.g., masonry) are stronger in compression than in tension.

concrete An artificial, stonelike building material made by mixing cement and various mineral aggregates with sufficient water to cause the cement to set and bind the entire mass. Concrete is weak in tension, but the insertion of steel bars helps reinforce concrete to withstand tensile forces.

corbel A brick or stone projecting from within a wall, usually to support a weight.

Corinthian order The most ornate and least used of the five classical orders, developed by the Greeks in the 4th century BCE but used more extensively in Roman architecture; similar in most respects to the Ionic but usually of slenderer proportions and characterized especially by a deep bell-shaped capital decorated with acanthus leaves and an abacus with concave sides.

cornice 1. The uppermost member of a classical entablature, consisting typically of a *cymatium*, corona, and bed molding. 2. A continuous, molded projection that crowns a wall or other construction, divides it horizontally for compositional purposes, or conceals lighting fixtures, curtain rods, and the like.

corps de logis In French architecture, a term describing the central element of a building as opposed to its subsidiary wings and pavilions.

crenel Any of the open spaces alternating with the merlons of a battlement.

crennelation The regular alternation of merlons and crenels, originally for defense but later used as a decorative motif.

cromlech A circular arrangement of megaliths enclosing a dolmen or burial mound.

crossing The intersection of the nave and transept in a Latin cross-plan church, over which a tower or dome was often built.

cross-in-square A typical Byzantine church plan having nine bays. The center bay is a large square surmounted by a dome. The smaller square corner bays are domed or vaulted, and the rectangular side bays are barrel vaulted.

crypt An underground chamber or vault used as a burial place, especially one beneath the main floor of a church.

cupola A light structure on a dome or roof, usually crowned with a dome and serving as a belfry, lantern, or belvedere.

curtain wall An exterior wall supported wholly by the structural frame of a building and carrying no loads other than its own weight and wind loads. Often consisting of glass panels, this modern innovation made possible other inventions like the *plan libre*, or free plan.

cyclopean wall A wall formed with enormous, irregular blocks of stones fitted closely together without the use of mortar. The methods of its construction were so hard to fathom that it was thought to have been erected by a race of giants—the Cyclops.

cyma recta A projecting molding having the profile of a double curve with the concave part projecting beyond the convex part.

cymatium 1. The crowning member of a classical cornice, usually a *cyma recta*. 2. See echinus.

dado 1. The part of a pedestal between the base and the cornice or cap. 2. The lower portion of an interior wall when faced or treated differently from the upper section, as with paneling or wallpaper.

darwaza An entrance gate in Indian architecture.

Decorated style The second of the three phases of English Gothic architecture from the late 13th through the late 14th centuries, characterized by rich tracery, elaborate ornamental vaulting, and refinement of stonecutting techniques.

dentil Any of a series of small, closely spaced, rectangular blocks forming a molding or projecting beneath the coronas of Ionic, Corinthian, and composite cornices.

deul A shrine in Orissan architecture.

diwan-i am In architecture of the Indian subcontinent, a hall for public meetings.

diwan-i khas In architecture of the Indian subcontinent, a hall for private meetings.

dolmen A prehistoric monument consisting of two or more large upright stones supporting a horizontal stone slab, found especially in Britain and France and usually regarded as a tomb.

dome A vaulted structure having a circular or polygonal plan and usually the form of a portion of a sphere, so constructed as to exert an equal thrust in all directions.

Doric order The oldest and simplest of the five classical orders, developed in Greece in the 7th century BCE and later imitated by the Romans. It is characterized by a fluted column having no base, a plain cushion-shaped capital supporting a square abacus, and an entablature consisting of a plain architrave, a frieze of triglyphs and metopes, and a cornice, the corona of which has *mutules* on its soffit. In the Roman Doric order, the columns are slenderer and usually have bases, the channeling is sometimes altered or omitted, and the capital consists of a bandlike necking, an echinus, and a molded abacus.

dormer A projecting structure built out from a sloping roof, usually housing a vertical window or ventilating louver.

dou-gong A bracket system used in traditional Chinese construction to support roof beams, project the eaves outward, and support the interior ceiling. The absence of a triangular tied frame in Chinese architecture made it necessary to multiply the number of supports under the rafters. To reduce the number of pillars would normally require the area of support afforded by each pillar to be increased by the *dou-gong*. The main beams support the roof through intermediary queen posts and shorter upper beams, enabling the roof to have a concave curve. This distinctive curve is believed to have developed at the beginning of the Tang period, presumably to lighten the visual weight of the roof and allow more daylight into the interior.

dromos A corridor in Mycenean architecture.

drum 1. Any of several cylindrical stones laid one above the other to form a column or pier. 2. A cylindrical or faceted construction, often pierced with windows, supporting a dome.

du Chinese for "capital"; hence, a city in Chinese architecture.

duomo The Italian designation for a true cathedral.

durbar 1. The court of a native prince in India. 2. The audience hall in which an Indian prince or British governor gave a state reception in India.

durga An Indian term for a fort.

echinus 1. The prominent circular molding supporting the abacus of a Doric or Tuscan capital. 2. The circular molding under the cushion of an Ionic capital, between the volutes, usually carved with an egg-and-dart pattern.

eclecticism A tendency in architecture and the decorative arts (particularly during the second half of the 19th century in Europe and the United States) to freely mix various historical styles with the aim of combining the virtues of diverse sources or of increasing allusive content.

elevation An orthographic projection of an object or structure on a vertical picture plane parallel to one of its sides, usually drawn to scale.

enfilade An axial arrangement of doorways connecting a series of rooms so as to provide a vista down the entire length of the suite.

engaged column A column built to be truly or seemingly bonded to the wall before which it stands.

entablature The horizontal section of a classical order that rests on the columns, usually composed of a cornice, frieze, and architrave.

entasis A slight convexity given to a column to correct an optical illusion of concavity that would occur if the sides were straight.

exedra See apse.

facade The front of a building or any of its sides facing a public way or space, especially one distinguished by its architectural treatment.

fang 1. A tie beam in the *dou-gong* system of traditional Chinese construction. 2. A ward or district of a Chinese city.

fascia 1. One of the three horizontal bands making up the architrave in the Ionic order. 2. Any broad, flat, horizontal surface, as the outer edge of a cornice or roof.

fazenda "Hacienda" in Portuguese.

fen A modular unit in traditional Chinese construction, equal to one-fifteenth of the height and one-tenth of the width of a *cai*.

finial A relatively small, usually foliated ornament terminating the peak of a spire or pinnacle.

Flamboyant style The final phase of French Gothic architecture from the late 14th through the middle of the 16th centuries, characterized by flamelike tracery, intricate detailing, and frequent complication of interior space.

fluting A decorative motif consisting of a series of long, rounded, parallel grooves, like those on the shaft of a classical column.

flying buttress An inclined bar of masonry carried on a segmental arch and transmitting an outward and downward thrust from a roof or vault to a solid buttress that, through its mass, transforms the thrust into a vertical one; a characteristic feature of Gothic construction.

folly A whimsical or extravagant structure built to serve as a conversation piece, lend interest to a view, or commemorate a person or event, found especially in 18th-century England.

forum The public square or marketplace of an ancient Roman city, the center of judicial and business affairs, and a place of assembly for the people; it usually included a basilica and a temple.

frieze 1. The horizontal part of a classical entablature between the cornice and architrave, often decorated with sculpture in low relief. 2. A decorative band, as one along the top of an interior wall immediately below the cornice, or a sculptured one in a stringcourse on an outside wall.

frigidarium The room in an ancient Roman bath containing unheated water.

fu-chiao lu-tou In traditional Chinese construction, the system for supporting a corner condition with bracket supports.

gable The triangular portion of wall enclosing the end of a pitched roof from cornice or eaves to ridge.

gable roof A roof sloping downward in two parts from a central ridge so as to form a gable at each end.

gallery 1. A long, relatively narrow room or hall, especially one for public use and having architectural importance due to its scale or decorative treatment. 2. An upper-level passage in a medieval church above the side aisle and below the clerestory window used for circulation, seating, and even the display of art.

garbha-griha A "womb chamber," the dark, innermost sanctuary of a Hindu temple where the statue of the deity is placed.

ghana-dwaras Literally "blind doors," the implied doors in Hindu architecture.

ghat A broad flight of steps descending to a river in India, especially a river used as a sacred bathing site.

giant order See colossal order.

golden section A proportion between the two dimensions of a plane figure or the two divisions of a line in which the ratio of the smaller to the larger is the same as the ratio of the larger to the whole: a ratio of approximately 0.618 to 1.000.

gompa A Tibetan Buddhist monastery.

gong 1. A cantilevered bracket in traditional Chinese construction. 2. A Chinese palace.

gopuram A monumental, usually ornate gateway tower to a Hindu temple enclosure, especially in southern India.

Greek cross A centralized church plan having the form of a cross whose arms are identical and symmetrical about the central space.

groin vault A compound vault formed by the perpendicular intersection of two vaults, forming arched diagonal arrises called groins.

guan A Chinese monastery.

hacienda 1. A large, landed estate for farming and ranching in North and South American areas once under Spanish influence. 2. The main house on such an estate.

haniwa A terra-cotta statue made for ritual use and buried with the dead as a funerary object during the Kofun period of Japan.

hashira 1. A sacred post in Shinto architecture, shaped by human hands. 2. A column, post, or pillar serving as the basic vertical member of a traditional Japanese wooden structure.

henge A circular arrangement of vertically oriented wooden posts or stones.

hipped roof A roof having sloping ends and sides meeting at an inclined projecting angle called a hip.

hippodrome An open-air stadium with an oval track for horse and chariot races in ancient Greece and Rome.

historicism 1. The reference to a historical

moment or style. 2. In architecture, a building whose form adheres to the stylistic principles of an earlier period.

hôtel An 18th-century French townhouse having one or two stories oriented horizontally in a large suburban estate setting.

hypocaust A system of flues in the floor or walls of ancient Roman buildings, especially baths, that provided central heating by receiving and distributing the heat from a furnace.

hypostyle Of or pertaining to a hall having many rows of columns carrying the roof or ceiling.

icon A representation of a sacred Christian personage, as Christ or a saint or angel, typically painted on a wood surface and itself venerated as sacred, especially in the tradition of the Eastern Church.

imam A mosque's leader of group prayer.

insula A block of buildings or space surrounded by four streets in an ancient Roman town.

intihuatana The "hitching post of the sun" in Incan settlements.

Ionic order A classical order that developed in the Greek colonies of Asia Minor in the 6th century BCE, characterized especially by the spiral volutes of its capital. The fluted columns typically had molded bases and supported an entablature consisting of an architrave of three fascias, a richly ornamented frieze, and a cornice corbeled out on egg-and-dart and dentil moldings. Roman and Renaissance examples are often more elaborate and usually set the volutes of the capitals 45 degrees to the architrave.

iwan A large vaulted hall serving as an entrance portal and opening onto a courtyard, prevalent in Parthian, Sassanian, and later in Islamic architecture.

jami masjid "Friday mosque": a congregational mosque for public prayer, especially on Fridays.

jian 1. A standard unit of space in Chinese architecture, marked by adjacent frame supports. The nature and appropriate scale of a building determine the number of *jian* to be allotted; the resulting width, depth, and height of the building then determine the number of *fen* required for the cross-section of each structural member. 2. The spatial unit that serves as the basis for the modular structure of a Chinese city: a number of *jian* connected become a building; several buildings arranged along the sides of a lot frame a courtyard; a number of courtyard units side by side become an alley; several alleys line up to create a small street district; a number of such districts form a rectangular ward; wards surround the palace-city and create a grid of streets.

jiangren A master craftsman in Chinese architecture.

jikido A dining hall in Japanese architecture.

jing In Chinese architecture, a room for private prayer.

Ka'aba A small, cubical stone building in the courtyard of the Great Mosque at Mecca containing a sacred black stone and regarded by Muslims as the house of God. It is the objective of Muslims' pilgrimages and the point toward which they turn in prayer.

kairo A roofed, semi-enclosed corridor in Japanese architecture.

kalan A shrine in Southeast Asian architecture.

kalyan mandapa In India, a hall with columns in which the marriage of the temple deity and his consort is ritually performed.

kami Sacred spirits related to Japanese architecture.

ke A Chinese pavilion of many stories.

ken A linear unit for regulating column spacing in traditional Japanese construction, equal to 6 *shaku* (5.97 feet or 1.818 meters) in the *inaka-ma* method, and in the *kyo-ma* method, initially set at 6.5 *shaku* (6.5 feet or 1.97 meters) but later varying according to room width as determined by tatami units.

keystone A voussoir at the crown of an arch serving to lock the other voussoirs in place. Until the keystone is in place, no true arch action is incurred.

kgotla The public meeting or traditional law court of a Botswana village.

kiva A square-walled underground chamber used by Native Americans for spiritual ceremonies.

kodo A lecture hall in Japanese architecture.

kondo The "golden hall": the sanctuary where the main image of worship is kept in a Japanese Buddhist temple. The Jodo, Shinshu, and Nicheiren sects of Buddhism use the term *hondo* for this sanctuary; the Shingon and Tendai sects use *chudo*; and the Zen sect uses *butsuden*.

kovil A Tamil temple.

kyozo The sutra repository in Japanese architecture.

Lanzón A column of rock portraying a Chavín mythical being who provided the god's oracular declamations.

lathe-turned Of or pertaining to a column whose cylindrical shaft is ornamented with incisions revealing its construction, during which it was laid on a lathe and then carved.

Latin cross A dominant church plan type in Western medieval architecture. Such a church is in the shape of a cross with a nave longer than the intersecting transept.

ling A purlin in traditional Chinese construction.

lingam A phallus; the symbol of the god Shiva in Hindu architecture.

lintel A beam supporting the weight above a door or window opening.

loggia A colonnaded or arcaded space within the body of a building that is open to the air on one side, with views into a public square or garden. Loggias can be built on either the ground floor or the upper floors of a building.

lotus A representation of various aquatic plants in the water lily family, used as a decorative motif in ancient Egyptian and Hindu art and architecture.

lou A Chinese multistoried pavilion or tower.

lu-tou In traditional Chinese construction, the base or lowest member in a set of brackets.

madrasa A Muslim theological school arranged around a courtyard and usually attached to a mosque, found from the 11th century on in Egypt, Anatolia, and Persia.

maharaja A great Indian king.

mahajanapadas Kingdoms of the Aryans.

mahastupa "Great stupa."

maidan The large open square of a city used as a marketplace or parade ground, especially in the Indian subcontinent.

mandala A Hindu or Buddhist diagram of the cosmos, often used to guide the design of Indian temple plans.

mandapa A large, porchlike hall leading to the sanctuary of a Hindu or Jain temple and used for religious dancing and music.

mandir A temple or palace in Indian architecture.

mani A Tibetan Buddhist wall of inscribed stones.

martyrium 1. A site that bore witness to important events in the life of Christ or one of his apostles. 2. A place where the relics of a martyr are kept. 3. A church erected over the tomb of a martyr or in honor of a martyr.

masjid A mosque.

masseria A system of plantation estates in Italy.

mastaba An ancient Egyptian tomb made of mud brick, rectangular in plan with a flat roof and sloping sides, from which a shaft leads to underground burial and offering chambers.

megalith A very large stone used as found or roughly dressed, especially in ancient construction work.

megaron A building or semi-independent unit of a building typically having a rectangular principal chamber with a center hearth and a porch, often of columns in antis. *Megarons* were traditional in Greece since Mycenaean times and believed to be the ancestor of the Doric temple.

men A gate in Chinese architecture.

menhir A prehistoric monument consisting of an upright megalith, usually standing alone but sometimes aligned with others in parallel rows.

merlon One of the solid parts between the crenels of a battlement.

metope Any of the panels, either plain or decorated, between triglyphs in the Doric frieze.

miao A Chinese temple. Also called a *shi*.

mihrab A niche or decorative panel in a mosque designating the *qibla*.

minaret A lofty, slender tower attached to a mosque with stairs leading up to one or more projecting balconies from which the muezzin calls the faithful to prayer.

minbar A pulpit in a mosque, recalling the three steps from which Mohammed addressed his followers.

mingtang "Bright hall": a ritual structure in Chinese architecture that serves as the symbolic center of imperial power. The first is presumed to have been built under the Zhou dynasty in the first millennium BCE.

minster Originally, a monastery church; later, any large or important church, as a cathedral or the principal church of a town.

miyan Eaves in Chinese architecture.

module A unit of measurement used for standardizing the dimensions of building materials or regulating the proportions of an architectural composition.

mortar A plastic mixture of lime or cement (or both) with sand and water, used as a bonding agent in masonry construction.

mortuary temple An ancient Egyptian temple for offerings and worship of a deceased person, usually a deified king. In the New Kingdom, cult and funerary temples had many features in common: an avenue of sphinxes leading to a tall portal guarded by a towering pylon; an axial plan with a colonnaded forecourt and a hypostyle hall set before a dark, narrow sanctuary in which stood a statue of the deity; and walls lavishly decorated with pictographic carvings in low or sunken relief.

mosaic A decorative pattern or figural image or narrative made of small, usually colored pieces of tile, enamel, or glass set in mortar.

mosque A Muslim building or place of public worship.

mudra A stylized hand gesture intended as a symbol in Buddhist and Hindu sculpture.

mullion 1. A vertical member between the lights of a window or the panels in wainscoting. 2. One of the radiating bars of a rose window.

muqarna A system of decoration in Islamic architecture created by the intricate corbeling of brackets, squinches, and inverted pyramids. Sometimes wrought in stone, it is more often found in plaster.

musalla In Islamic architecture, a temporary place in which worshippers congregate to perform their prayers.

nandaimon The principal south gateway to a Japanese temple or shrine.

naos See *cella*.

narthex 1. The portico before the nave of an early Christian or Byzantine church, appropriate for penitents. 2. An entrance hall or vestibule leading to the nave of a church.

nave The principal or central part of a church extending from the narthex to the choir or chancel and usually flanked by aisles.

necropolis A historic burial ground, especially a large, elaborate one of an ancient city.

neoclassicism The classicism prevailing in the architecture of Europe, America, and various European colonies during the late 18th and early 19th centuries, characterized by the introduction and widespread use of Greek and Roman orders and decorative motifs; the subordination of detail to simple, strongly geometric compositions; and the frequent shallowness of relief in ornamental treatment of facades.

niche An ornamental recess in a wall, often semicircular in plan, surmounted by a half-dome, and used for a statue or other decorative object.

nuraghe Any of the large round or triangular stone towers found in Sardinia and dating from the second millennium BCE to the Roman conquest.

obelisk A tall, four-sided shaft of stone that tapers as it rises to a pyramidal point. Obelisks originated in ancient Egypt as a sacred symbol of the sun god Ra and usually stood in pairs astride temple entrances.

oculus A circular opening, especially one at the crown of a dome.

ogee A molding having a profile of a double curve in the shape of an elongated S.

ogive A rib crossing a compartment of a rib vault on a diagonal.

open plan A floor plan having no fully enclosed spaces or distinct rooms.

opet A secret chamber in Egyptian architecture.

opus incertum Ancient Roman masonry formed of small rough stones set irregularly in mortar, sometimes traversed by bands of bricks or tiles.

opus reticulatum An ancient Roman masonry wall faced with small pyramidal stones set diagonally, with their square bases forming a netlike pattern.

oriel A bay window supported from below by corbels or brackets.

pagoda A Buddhist temple in the form of a square or polygonal tower with roofs projecting from each of its many stories, erected as a memorial or to hold relics. From its Indian prototype the stupa, the pagoda gradually changed in form to resemble a traditional multistoried watchtower as it spread with Buddhism to China and Japan. Pagodas were initially made of timber, but from the 6th century CE on were more frequently of brick or stone, possibly due to Indian influence.

pai lou A monumental gateway in Chinese architecture, having a trabeated form of stone or wood construction with one, three, or five openings and often boldly projecting roofs. *Pai lou* were erected as memorials at the entrances to palaces, tombs, or sacred places; related to the Indian *toranas* and the Japanese torii.

Palladian motif A window or doorway in the form of a round-headed archway flanked on either side by narrower compartments. The side compartments are capped with entablatures on which the arch of the central compartment rests.

palmette A stylized palm leaf shape used as a decorative element in classical art and architecture.

panopticon A building such as a prison, hospital, or library arranged so that all parts of the interior are visible from a single point.

pantheon 1. A temple dedicated to all the gods of a people. 2. A public building serving as the burial place of, or containing the memorials to, the famous dead of a nation.

parapet A low protective wall at the edge of a terrace, balcony, or roof, especially that part of an exterior wall, firewall, or party wall that rises above the roof.

parti Used by the French at the École des Beaux-Arts in the 19th century, the design idea or sketch from which an architectural project will be developed.

passage grave A megalithic tomb of the Neolithic and early Bronze Ages found in the British Isles and Europe consisting of a roofed burial chamber and narrow entrance passage covered by a tumulus. They are believed to have been used for successive family or clan burials spanning a number of generations.

pavilion A central or flanking projecting subdivision of a facade, usually accented by more elaborate decoration or greater height and distinction of skyline; used frequently in French Renaissance and Baroque architecture.

pediment 1. The low-pitched gable enclosed by the horizontal and raking cornices of a Greek or Roman temple. 2. A similar or derivative element used to surmount the major division of a facade or crown an opening.

pendentive A spherical triangle forming the transition from the circular plan of a dome to the polygonal plan of its supporting structure.

pergola A structure of parallel colonnades supporting an open roof of beams and crossing rafters or trelliswork, over which climbing plants are trained to grow.

peripteral Having a single row of columns on all sides.

peristyle 1. A colonnade surrounding a building or a courtyard. 2. The courtyard so enclosed.

Perpendicular style The final phase of English Gothic architecture, prevailing from the late 14th through the early 16th centuries, characterized by perpendicular tracery, fine intricate stonework, and elaborate fan vaults. Also called rectilinear style.

piano nobile The principal story of a large building, such as a palace or villa, usually one flight above the ground floor, with formal reception and dining rooms.

piazza An open square or public place in a city or town, especially in Italy.

Picturesque The late 18th-century term describing irregular and uncultivated landscapes and designs.

pilaster A shallow rectangular feature having a capital and a base and projecting from a wall, treated architecturally as a column.

piloti A column of steel or reinforced concrete supporting a building above an open-ground level, thereby leaving the space available for other uses.

piye A Mexican ritual calendar composed of twenty hieroglyphs or "day signs," which combined with thirteen numbers to produce a cycle of 260 days.

plinth 1. The usually square slab beneath the base of a column, pier, or pedestal. 2. A continuous, usually projecting course of stones forming the base or foundation of a wall.

podium 1. A low wall serving as the base for a colonnade or dome. 2. A raised platform encircling the arena of an ancient Roman amphitheater, where the seats for the privileged spectators were located.

pol A gateway in Indian architecture.

polis A Greek city-state.

portcullis A strong grating of iron or timber hung over the gateway of a fortified place in such a way that it could be lowered quickly to prevent passage.

porte cochere 1. A porch roof projecting over a driveway at the entrance to a building and sheltering those getting in or out of vehicles. 2. A vehicular passageway leading through a building or screen wall into an interior courtyard.

portico A porch or walkway with a roof supported by columns, often leading to the entrance of a building.

propylaeum A vestibule or gateway of architectural importance before a Greek temple precinct or other enclosure.

propylon A freestanding gateway in the form of a pylon that precedes the main gateway to an ancient Egyptian temple or sacred enclosure.

proscenium The front part of the stage of an ancient Greek or Roman theater upon which the actors performed.

pteron Greek word for "wing," but also "oar" and "sail": an early form of a peristyle raised on a lofty podium.

pu The distance between purlins in traditional Chinese construction.

puan A roof purlin in Chinese architecture.

pueblo A communal dwelling and defensive structure of the Native Americans of the southwestern United States. Built of adobe or stone and typically many-storied and terraced, pueblos were entered through the chambers' flat roofs by ladders. Pueblo structures were built on the desert floor, in valleys, or in the more easily defended cliff walls of mesas.

purlin A longitudinal member of a roof frame for supporting common rafters between the ridge and eaves.

pylon A monumental gateway to an ancient Egyptian temple, consisting either of a pair of tall truncated pyramids and a doorway between them, or of one such masonry mass pierced with a doorway, often decorated with painted reliefs.

qibla 1. The direction toward which Muslims face to pray, specifically the Ka'aba at Mecca in Saudi Arabia. 2. The wall in a mosque in which the mihrab is set, oriented to Mecca.

qin Sleeping chambers in Chinese architecture.

que A Chinese watchtower, also called a *hua biao*.

quoin One of the stones forming the external angle of a wall, usually differentiated from the adjoining surfaces by material, texture, color, size, or projection.

rammed earth A stiff mixture of clay, sand, or other aggregate and water compressed and dried within forms as a wall construction.

ratha A Hindu temple cut out of solid rock to resemble a chariot.

Rayonnant style The middle phase of French Gothic architecture from the end of the 13th through the late 14th centuries, characterized by circular windows with radiating lines of tracery.

rectilinear style See Perpendicular style.

rekha deul The sanctuary and convexly tapered tower of an Orissian temple.

rib Any of several archlike members supporting a vault at the groins and defining its distinct surfaces or dividing these surfaces into panels.

ribat An Islamic fortified monastery-like building providing soldiers with an opportunity to exercise their religion.

rose window A large, circular window, usually of stained glass and decorated with tracery, symmetrical about the center.

rotunda A round, domed building, or a large and high circular space in a building, especially one surmounted by a dome.

rustication Ashlar masonry having the visible faces of the dressed stones raised or otherwise contrasted with the horizontal and usually the vertical joints, which may be rabbeted, chamfered, or beveled.

sacristy A room in a church where the sacred vessels and vestments are kept.

sanctuary 1. A sacred or holy place. 2. The most sacred part of a church, in which the principal altar is placed. 3. An especially holy place in a temple. 4. A church or other sacred place where fugitives are immune from arrest.

sangha A Buddhist community.

scaenae frons The highly decorative wall or backdrop at the rear of the stage of a Roman theater.

schist A crystalline metamorphic rock that has a parallel or foliated arrangement of mineral grains.

section An orthographic projection of an object or structure as it would appear if cut through by an intersecting plane to show its internal configuration, usually drawn to scale.

sha In Chinese architecture, the finial atop a pagoda.

shaft 1. The central part of a column or pier between the capital and the base. 2. A distinct, slender vertical masonry feature engaged in a wall or pier and supporting or feigning to support an arch or a ribbed vault.

shi See *miao*.

Shi'ite A Muslim sect that believes Ali to be the successor to Mohammed.

shikhara The tower of a Hindu temple, usually tapered convexly and capped by an *amalaka*.

shinbashira The heart pillar or central pillar of Japanese castles.

shiva lingam Another term for lingam.

shoro One of a pair of small, identical, symmetrically placed pavilions in a Japanese Buddhist temple structure from which the temple bell is hung.

sobo The priests' quarters in a Japanese Buddhist temple.

spandrel 1. The triangular, sometimes ornamented area between two adjoining arches or between an arch and the rectangular framework surrounding it. 2. A panel-like area in a multistory frame building, between the sill of a window on one level and the head of a window immediately below.

sphinx A figure of an imaginary creature having the body of a lion and the head of a man, ram, or hawk, commonly placed along avenues leading to ancient Egyptian temples or tombs.

 # GLOSSARY

spire A tall, acutely tapering pyramidal structure surmounting a steeple or tower.

splay A surface that makes an oblique angle with another, such as where a window or door opening widens from the frame toward the face of the wall.

squinch An arch or corbelling built across the upper inside corner of a square tower to support the side of a superimposed octagonal structure.

stambha In Indian architecture, a freestanding memorial pillar bearing carved inscriptions, religious emblems, or a statue.

stele An upright stone slab or pillar with a carved or inscribed surface, used as a monument, a marker, or a commemorative tablet in the face of a building.

stoa An ancient Greek portico, usually detached and of considerable length, used as a promenade or meeting place around public places.

stucco A coarse plaster composed of portland or masonry cement, sand, and hydrated lime mixed with water and applied in a plastic state to form a hard covering for exterior walls.

stupa A Buddhist memorial mound erected to enshrine a relic of the Buddha and to commemorate some event or mark a sacred spot. Modeled on a funerary tumulus, it consists of an artificial dome-shaped mound raised on a platform, surrounded by an outer ambulatory, with a stone *vedika* and four *toranas*, and crowned by a *chattri*. In Sri Lanka, the name for *stupa* is *dagoba*; and in Tibet and Nepal, it is *chorten*.

stylobate A course of masonry forming the foundation for a row of columns, especially the outermost colonnade of a classical temple.

suarloka A decorated frieze in Southeast Asian architecture.

Sufi A Muslim mystic.

sultan The ruler of a Muslim country.

Sunni A Muslim sect that considers Abu Bakr to be the successor to Muhammad.

synagogue A building or place of assembly for Jewish worship and religious instruction.

ta A Chinese pagoda in which a deceased high priest is buried.

tablero The rectangular panel sitting atop a sloping panel or *talud* in Mexican architecture.

takht The throne or elevated platform used by royalty in a mosque.

talud The sloping panel beneath the rectangular panel or *tablero* in Mexican architecture.

taypi In South America, the zone of convergence between the principles of *urco* (the west, high, dry, pastoral, celestial, male) and *uma* (the east, low, agricultural, underworld, female).

temenos In ancient Greece, a piece of ground specially reserved and enclosed as a sacred place.

tension A structural force that acts to stretch or pull apart a material, resulting in the elongation of an elastic body. Ductile materials like steel effectively resist tension.

tepidarium A room of moderately warm temperature in an ancient Roman bath, between the *frigidarium* and the *caldarium*.

thalassocracy A maritime trading economy initially defined by Aristotle.

thermae An elaborate public bathing establishment of the ancient Greeks and Romans, consisting of hot, warm, and cool plunge pools, sweat rooms, and athletic and other facilities.

thrust The outward force or pressure exerted by one part of a structure against another.

tianming The "mandate of heaven" as described by members of the Zhou dynasty. Rites of worship, an ideology of "harmony," and sacrifices to ancestral deities all served to link political and religious authority under *tianming*.

ting A courtyard in Chinese architecture: the site of large, often ceremonial gatherings.

tirtha A place or site considered holy in Indian architecture.

tokonoma Picture recess: a shallow, slightly raised alcove for the display of a kakemono or flower arrangement. As the spiritual center of a traditional Japanese house, the tokonoma is located in its most formal room.

torana An elaborately carved, ceremonial gateway in Indian Buddhist and Hindu architecture, having two or three lintels between two posts.

torii Derived from *torana*, a torii is a gateway in Japanese architecture.

torsion The twisting of an elastic body about its longitudinal axis caused by two equal and opposite torques, producing shearing stresses in the body.

trabeated Of or pertaining to a system of construction employing beams or lintels.

transept 1. The major transverse part of a cruciform church, crossing the main axis at a right angle between the nave and choir. 2. Either of the projecting arms of this part, on either side of the central aisle of a church.

triforium An arcaded wall corresponding to the space between the vaulting and the roof of an aisle, usually opening onto the nave between the nave arches and the clerestory.

triglyph One of the vertical blocks separating the metopes in a Doric frieze, typically having two vertical grooves or glyphs on its face, and two chamfers or half channels at the sides.

tumulus An artificial mound of earth or stone, especially over an ancient grave.

turret A small tower forming part of a larger structure, frequently beginning some distance above the ground.

tympanum 1. The recessed triangular space enclosed by the horizontal and raking cornices of a triangular pediment, often decorated with sculpture. 2. A similar space between an arch and the horizontal head of a door or window below.

tzompantli A skull rack in Central American architecture.

ulu Jami A Friday mosque having a large *sahn* for large congregations, dating from the 7th to the 11th centuries CE.

vahana Literally, a "vehicle" of Hindu gods, usually in the form of an animal.

vault An arched structure of stone, brick, or reinforced concrete forming a ceiling or roof over a hall, room, or other wholly or partially enclosed space. Because it behaves as an arch extended in a third dimension, the longitudinal supporting walls must be buttressed to counteract the thrusts of the arching action.

vav An Indian step well.

Vedas The oldest sacred writings of Hinduism, composed between 1500 and 800 BCE, incorporating four collections of hymns, prayers, and liturgical formulas: Rig-Veda, Yajur-Veda, Sama-Veda, and Atharva-Veda.

vedika 1. A hall for reading the Vedas. 2. A railing enclosing a sacred area, as a stupa.

vihara A Buddhist monastery in Indian architecture, often excavated from solid rock, consisting of a central pillared chamber surrounded by a veranda onto which open small sleeping cells. Adjacent to this cloister was a courtyard containing the main stupa.

volute A spiral, scroll-like ornament, as on the capitals of the Ionic, Corinthian, and composite orders.

voussoir Any of the wedge-shaped units in a masonry arch or vault that has side cuts that converge at one of the arch centers.

wainscot A lining of wood, usually in the form of paneling, covering the lower portion of a wall.

wat A Buddhist monastery or temple in Thailand or Cambodia.

westwork The monumental western front of a Romanesque church, treated as a tower or towers containing a low entrance hall below and a chapel open to the nave above.

wetu Hut-shaped Native American houses.

xanadu A place of idyllic beauty and contentment; S. T. Coleridge's modification of Xandu, modern Shangtu and the site of Kublai Khan's summer residence in southeastern Mongolia.

xieshan The simple hip-and-gable style roof in Chinese architecture.

yin and yang In Chinese philosophy and religion, the interaction of two opposing and complementary principles—one that is feminine, dark, and negative (yin) and the other that is masculine, bright, and positive (yang)—that influences the destinies of creatures and things.

yingbi A screen wall in Chinese architecture that protects the main gate to a monastery or house against evil spirits, which were believed to only move in a straight line.

Yingzao Fashi A compendium of Chinese architectural tradition and building methods, compiled by Li Jie and printed in 1103 CE. It has thirty-four chapters devoted to technical terms, construction methods, measurements and proportions of architectural elements, labor management, building materials, and decoration.

zhi During the Han and Jin dynasties, a Taoist cave dwelling for the practice of asceticism and sacrificial offerings to the gods.

ziggurat A temple tower in Sumerian and Assyrian architecture, built in diminishing stages of mud brick with buttressed walls faced with burnt brick, culminating in a summit shrine or temple reached by a series of ramps. Thought to be of Sumerian origin, dating from the end of the 3rd millennium BCE.

Bibliography

General Sources

Alfieri, Bianca Maria. *Islamic Architecture of the Indian Subcontinent.* London: Laurence King Publishers, 2000.

Barraclough, Geoffrey. *Hammond Atlas of World History.* Maplewood, NJ: Hammond, 1999.

Chihara, Daigoro. *Hindu-Buddhist Architecture in Southeast Asia.* New York: E. J. Brill, 1996.

Chinese Academy of Architecture. Beijing: China Building Industry Press; Hong Kong: Joint Publishing Co., 1982.

Coaldrake, William Howard. *Architecture and Authority in Japan.* London, New York: Routledge, 1996.

Coe, Michael D., and Rex Koontz. *Mexico: From the Olmecs to the Aztecs.* London: Thames & Hudson, 2002.

Crouch, Dora P., and June G. Johnson. *Traditions in Architecture: Africa, America, Asia, and Oceania.* New York: Oxford University Press, 2001.

Evans, Susan Toby, and David L. Webster, eds. *Archaeology of Ancient Mexico and Central America: An Encyclopedia.* New York: Garland, 2001.

Ferguson, William M., and Richard E. W. Adams. *Mesoamerica's Ancient Cities: Aerial Views of Pre-Columbian Ruins in Mexico, Guatemala, Belize, and Honduras.* Albuquerque: University of New Mexico Press, 2001.

Grube, Nikolai. *Maya: Divine Kings of the Rain Forest.* Assisted by Eva Eggebrecht and Matthias Seidel. Cologne, Germany: Könemann, 2001.

Huntington, Susan L. *The Art of Ancient India: Buddhist, Hindu, Jain.* With contributions by John C. Huntington. New York: Weatherhill, 1985.

Jarzombek, Mark. Architecture of First Societies: A Global Perspective. New York: John Wiley & Sons, 2013.

The Kodansha Bilingual Encyclopedia of Japan. Tokyo: Kodansha International; New York: Kodansha America, 1998.

Kostof, Spiro. *A History of Architecture: Settings and Rituals.* Revisions by Greg Castillo. New York: Oxford University Press, 1995.

Kowalski, Jeff Karl, ed. *Mesoamerican Architecture as a Cultural Symbol.* New York: Oxford University Press, 1999.

Kubler, George. *The Art and Architecture of Ancient America: The Mexican, Maya, and Andean Peoples.* New Haven, CT: Yale University Press, 1990.

Lang, Jon T., Madhavi Desai, and Miki Desai. *Architecture and Independence: The Search for Identity—India 1880 to 1980.* Delhi: Oxford University Press, 1997.

Loewe, Michael, and Edward L. Shaughnessy, eds. *The Cambridge History of Ancient China: From the Origins of Civilization to 221 BC.* Cambridge, UK, and New York: Cambridge University Press, 1999.

Meister, Michael W., ed. *Encyclopedia of Indian Temple Architecture, vols. 1 and 2.* Coordinated by M. A. Dhaky. New Delhi: American Institute of Indian Studies; Philadelphia: University of Pennsylvania Press, 1983.

Michell, George. *Architecture of the Islamic World: Its History and Social Meaning.* New York: Thames & Hudson, 1984.

Nishi, Kazuo, and Kazuo Hozumi. *What Is Japanese Architecture?* Translated, adapted, and with an introduction by H. Mack Horton. Tokyo, New York: Kodansha International, 1985.

Schmidt, Karl J. *Atlas and Survey of South Asian History: India, Pakistan, Bangladesh, Sri Lanka, Nepal, Bhutan.* New Delhi, India: Vision, 1999.

Sickman, Laurence, and Alexander Soper. *The Art and Architecture of China.* Harmondsworth, UK: Penguin, 1971.

Steinhardt, Nancy Shatzman. *Chinese Architecture.* New Haven, CT: Yale University Press; Beijing: New World Press, 2002.

———. *Chinese Imperial City Planning.* Honolulu: University of Hawaii Press, 1990.

Tadgell, Christopher. *Antiquity: Origins, Classicism and the New Rome.* Abingdon, UK: Routledge, 2007.

———. *The East: Buddhists, Hindus and the Sons of Heaven.* Abingdon, UK: Routledge, 2008.

———. *The History of Architecture in India: From the Dawn of Civilization to the End of the Raj.* London: Architecture Design and Technology Press, 1990.

———. *Islam: From Medina to the Magreb and from the Indies to Istanbul.* Abingdon, UK: Routledge, 2008.

Thapar, Romila. *Early India: From the Origins to AD 1300.* Berkeley: University of California Press, 2002.

Tignor, Robert L., Jeremy Adelman, Stephen Aron, Stephen Kotkin, Suzanne Marchand, Gyan Prakash, and Michael Tsin. *Worlds Together, Worlds Apart: A History of the Modern World from the Mongol Empire to the Present.* New York: W. W. Norton, 2002.

Trachtenberg, Marvin, and Isabelle Hyman. *Architecture, from Prehistory to Postmodernity.* New York: Harry N. Abrams, 2002.

Online Resources

Great Buildings Online: www.greatbuildings.com/

Grove Art Online: www.oxfordartonline.com. Web access to the entire text of *The Dictionary of Art*, edited by Jane Turner (34 vols., 1996), and *The Oxford Companion to Western Art*, Hugh Brigstocke, ed. (2001).

Metropolitan Museum of Art Timeline of Art History: www.metmuseum.org/toah/

Taj Mahal: http://www.tajmahalindia.net/taj-mahal-monument.html

Wikipedia: The Free Encyclopedia: wikipedia.org/

3500 BCE

Arnold, Dieter. *The Encyclopedia of Ancient Egyptian Architecture.* Edited by Nigel and Helen Strudwick. Translated by Sabine H. Gardiner and Helen Strudwick. Princeton, NJ: Princeton University Press, 2003.

Burl, Aubrey. *The Stone Circles of the British Isles.* New Haven, CT: Yale University Press, 1976.

Clark, Grahame. *The Earlier Stone Age Settlement of Scandinavia.* London: Cambridge University Press, 1975.

Hawkins, Gerald S., and John B. White. *Stonehenge Decoded.* New York: Dorsett, 1965.

Hewitt, Roger L. *Structure, Meaning and Ritual in the Narratives of the Southern San.* Hamburg: Buske. 1986.

Jia, Lanpo. *Early Man in China.* Beijing: Foreign Languages Press, 1980.

Marlowe Frank W. *The Hazda: Hunter-Gatherers of Tanzania.* Berkeley: University of California Press. 2010

McBurney, Charles, and Brian Montagu. *The Stone Age of Northern Africa.* Harmondsworth, UK: Penguin Books, 1960.

Mysliwiec, Karol. *The Twilight of Ancient Egypt, First Millennium B.C.E.* Ithaca, NY: Cornell University Press, 2000.

Nicholson, Paul T., and Ian Shaw, eds. *Ancient Egyptian Materials and Technology.* Cambridge, UK: Cambridge University Press, 2000.

Phylactopoulos, George A., ed. *History of the Hellenic World.* University Park, PA: Pennsylvania State University Press, 1974.

Possehl, Gregory L. *Harappan Civilization: A Recent Perspective.* New Delhi: American Institute of Indian Studies; Columbia, MO: Oxford and IBH, 1993.

Price, Theron Douglas. *Europe's First Farmers.* New York: Cambridge University Press, 2000.

BIBLIOGRAPHY

Shafer, Byron E., ed. *Religion in Ancient Egypt: Gods, Myths and Personal Practice.* Ithaca, NY: Cornell University Press, 1991.

Walter, Mariko Namba, Eva Jane, and Neumann Friedman, eds. *Shamanism: An Encyclopedia of World Beliefs, Practices and Cultures.* Santa Barbara, CA: ABC-CLIO, 2004.

Wilson, Peter J. *The Domestication of the Human Species.* New Haven: Yale University Press, 1988.

Youkanna, Donny George. *Tell es-Sawwan: The Architecture of the Sixth Millennium BC.* London: Nabu, 1997.

2500 BCE

Crawford, Harriet E. W. *The Architecture of Iraq in the Third Millennium B.C.* Copenhagen: Akademisk Forlag, 1977.

Downey, Susan B. *Mesopotamian Religious Architecture: Alexander through the Parthians.* Princeton, NJ: Princeton University Press, 1988.

Fairservis, Walter Ashlin. *The Roots of Ancient India: The Archaeology of Early Indian Civilization.* New York: Macmillan, 1971.

Kemp, Barry J. *Ancient Egypt: Anatomy of a Civilization.* London, New York: Routledge, 1991.

Kenoyer, Jonathan M. *Ancient Cities of the Indus Valley Civilization.* Karachi: Oxford University Press; Islamabad: American Institute of Pakistan Studies, 1998.

Kubba, Shamil A. A. *Mesopotamian Architecture and Town Planning: From the Mesolithic to the End of the Proto-Historic Period, ca. 10,000–3,500 BC.* Oxford, UK: B.A.R., 1987.

Oppenheim, A. Leo. *Ancient Mesopotamia: Portrait of a Dead Civilization.* Chicago: University of Chicago Press, 1977.

Rossi, Corinna. *Architecture and Mathematics in Ancient Egypt.* Cambridge, UK, and New York: Cambridge University Press, 2004.

Sarianidi, Victor. *Necropolis of Gonur.* Translated by Inna Sarianidi. Athens: Kapon, 2007.

Shady, Ruth, and Carlos Leyva, eds. *La Ciudad Sagrada de Caral-Supe: Los Orígenes de la Civilización Andina y la Formación del Estado Prístino en el Antiguo Perú.* Lima: Instituto Nacional de Cultura: Proyecto Especial Arqueológico Caral-Supe, 2003.

1500 BCE

Anthony, David W. *The Hose, The Wheel and Language: How Bronze Age Riders from the Eurasian Steppes Shaped the Modern World.* Princeton, NJ: Princeton University Press, 2007.

Byrd, Kathleen M. *The Poverty Point Culture: Local Manifestations, Subsistence Practices, and Trade Networks.* Baton Rouge, LA: Geoscience Publications, Department of Geography and Anthropology, Louisiana State University, 1991.

Chang, Kwang-chih. *Shang Civilization.* New Haven, CT: Yale University Press, 1980.

Clarke, Somers, and R. Engelbach. *Ancient Egyptian Construction and Architecture.* New York: Dover Publications, 1990.

Gibson, Jon L. *The Ancient Mounds of Poverty Point: Place of Rings.* Gainesville: University Press of Florida, 2000.

Moore, Jerry D. *Architecture and Power in the Ancient Andes: The Archaeology of Public Buildings.* Cambridge, UK, and New York: Cambridge University Press, 1996.

Oates, Joan. *Babylon: Ancient Peoples and Places.* London: Thames & Hudson, 1979.

Rossi, Corinna. *Architecture and Mathematics in Ancient Egypt.* Cambridge, UK, and New York: Cambridge University Press, 2004.

800 BCE

Bell, Edward. *Prehellenic Architecture in the Aegean.* London: G. Bell & Sons, 1926.

Burger, Richard L. *The Prehistoric Occupation of Chavín de Huántar, Peru.* Berkeley and Los Angeles: University of California Press, 1984.

Castleden, Rodney. *The Knossos Labyrinth: A View of the Palace of Minos at Knossos.* London: Routledge, 1990.

Coe, Michael D. *The Olmec World: Ritual and Rulership.* Princeton, NJ: Art Museum, Princeton University, and New York: In association with Harry N. Abrams, 1996.

Damluji, Salma Samar. *The Architecture of Yemen: From Yafi to Hadramut.* London: Laurence King, 2007.

Diehl, Richard A. *The Olmecs: America's First Civilization.* London: Thames & Hudson, 2004.

Eck, Diana L. *Banaras, City of Light.* New York: Columbia University Press, 1999.

El-Hakim, Omar M. *Nubian Architecture: The Egyptian Vernacular Experience.* Cairo: Palm, 1993.

Jastrow, Morris. *The Civilization of Babylonia and Assyria: Its Remains, Language, History, Religion, Commerce, Law, Art, and Literature.* Philadelphia and London: J. B. Lippincott, 1915.

Li, Hsüeh-ch'in. *Eastern Zhou and Qin Civilizations.* Translated by K. C. Chang. New Haven: Yale University Press, 1985.

Moore, Jerry D. *Architecture and Power in Ancient Andes: The Archaeology of Public Buildings.* Cambridge: Cambridge University Press, 1996.

Moseley, Michael Edward. *The Maritime Foundations of Andean Civilization.* Menlo Park, CA: Cummings, 1975.

Pfeiffer, John E. *The Emergence of Society: A Pre-history of the Establishment.* New York: McGraw-Hill, 1977.

Ricke, Herbert, George R. Hughes, and Edward F. Wente. *The Beit el-Wali Temple of Ramesses II.* Chicago: University of Chicago Press, 1967.

Scoufopoulos, Niki C. *Mycenaean Citadels.* Gothenburg, Sweden: P. Åström, 1971.

Willetts, Ronald F. *The Civilization of Ancient Crete.* Berkeley and Los Angeles: University of California Press, 1976.

400 BCE

Ball, Larry F. *The Domus Aurea and the Roman Architectural Revolution.* Cambridge, UK: Cambridge University Press, 2003.

Barletta, Barbara A. *Ionic Influence in Archaic Sicily: The Monumental Art.* Gothenburg, Sweden: Åström, 1983.

———. *The Origins of the Greek Architectural Orders.* Cambridge, UK: Cambridge University Press, 2001.

Berve, Helmut. *Greek Temples, Theatres, and Shrines.* London: Thames & Hudson, 1963.

Camp, John M. *The Archaeology of Athens.* New Haven, CT: Yale University Press, 2001.

Clark, John E., and Mary E. Pye, eds. *Olmec Art and Archaeology in Mesoamerica.* Washington, DC: National Gallery of Art; New Haven, CT: distributed by Yale University Press, 2000.

Coulton, John James. *Ancient Greek Architects at Work: Problems of Structure and Design.* Ithaca, NY: Cornell University Press, 1977.

Detienne, Marcel. *The Cuisine of Sacrifice Among the Greeks.* With essays by Jean-Louis Durand, Stella Georgoudi, Françoise Hartog, and Jesper Svenbro. Chicago: University of Chicago Press, 1989.

Dinsmoor, William Bell. *The Architecture of Ancient Greece: An Account of Its Historic Development.* New York: Norton, 1975.

Frye, Richard Nelson. *The Heritage of Persia.* Cleveland, OH: World Publishing, 1963.

Fyfe, Theodore. *Hellenistic Architecture: An Introductory Study.* Cambridge, UK: Cambridge University Press, 1936; Oakville, CT: Aarhus University Press, 1999.

Grant, Michael. *The Etruscans*. New York: Scribner, 1980.

Hurwit, Jeffrey M. *The Art and Culture of Early Greece, 1100–480 BC*. Ithaca, NY: Cornell University Press, 1985.

Martienssen, Rex Distin. *The Idea of Space in Greek Architecture, with Special Reference to the Doric Temple and Its Setting*. Johannesburg: Witwatersrand University Press, 1956.

Scully, Vincent Joseph. *The Earth, the Temple, and the Gods: Greek Sacred Architecture*. New Haven, CT: Yale University Press, 1962.

Taylour, William Lord. *The Mycenaeans*. London: Thames & Hudson, 1964.

Thapar, Romila. *As´oka and the Decline of the Mauryas*. New Delhi and New York: Oxford University Press, 1997.

Warren, John. *Greek Mathematics and the Architects to Justinian*. London: Coach, 1976.

Winter, Frederick E. *Greek Fortifications*. Toronto: University of Toronto Press, 1971.

0

Ball, Larry F. *The Domus Aurea and the Roman Architectural Revolution*. Cambridge, UK, and New York: Cambridge University Press, 2003.

Boatwright, Mary Taliaferro. *Hadrian and the City of Rome*. Princeton, NJ: Princeton University Press, 1987.

Chase, Raymond G. *Ancient Hellenistic and Roman Amphitheatres, Stadiums, and Theatres: The Way They Look Now*. Portsmouth, NH: P. E. Randall, 2002.

Dallapiccola, Anna Libera, with Stephanie Zingel-Avé Lallemant, eds. *The Stúpa: Its Religious, Historical and Architectural Significance*. Wiesbaden, Germany: Steiner, 1979.

Hansen, Richard D. *Excavations in the Tigre Complex, El Mirador, Petén, Guatemala*. Provo, Utah: New World Archaeological Foundation, Brigham Young University, 1990.

Lawton, Thomas. *Chinese Art of the Warring States Period: Change and Continuity, 480–222 BC*. Washington, DC: Published for the Freer Gallery of Art by the Smithsonian Institution Press, 1983.

MacDonald, William Lloyd. *The Architecture of the Roman Empire*. New Haven: Yale University Press, 1982.

Rykwert, Joseph. *The Idea of a Town: The Anthropology of Urban Form in Rome, Italy and the Ancient World*. Princeton, NJ: Princeton University Press, 1976.

Sarkar, H. *Studies in Early Buddhist Architecture of India*. Delhi: Munshiram Manoharlal, 1966.

Schopen, Gregory. *Bones, Stones, and Buddhist Monks: Collected Papers on the Archaeology, Epigraphy, and Texts of Monastic Buddhism in India*. Honolulu: University of Hawaii Press, 1997.

Snodgrass, Adrian. *The Symbolism of the Stupa*. Ithaca, NY: Cornell University, 1985.

Stamper, John W. *The Architecture of Roman Temples: The Republic to the Middle Empire*. Cambridge, UK: Cambridge University Press, 2005.

Townsend, Richard F., ed. *Ancient West Mexico: Art and Archaeology of the Unknown Past*. New York: Thames & Hudson; Chicago: Art Institute of Chicago, 1998.

Ward-Perkins, John Bryan. *Roman Architecture*. Milan, Italy and London: Electa Architecture, 2003.

200 CE

Aveni, Anthony F. *Between the Lines: The Mystery of the Giant Ground Drawings of Ancient Nasca, Peru*. Austin: University of Texas Press, 2000.

Behrendt, Kurt A. *The Buddhist Architecture of Gandhara*. Leiden, Netherlands, and Boston: E. J. Brill, 2004.

Berrin, Kathleen, and Esther Pasztory. *Teotihuacán: Art from the City of the Gods*. New York: Thames & Hudson and the Fine Arts Museums of San Francisco, 1993.

Litvinsky, B. A., ed. *History of Civilizations of Central Asia, vol. 3: The Crossroads of Civilizations, AD 250 to 750*. Paris: UNESCO, 1992.

MacDonald, William Lloyd. *The Pantheon: Design, Meaning, and Progeny*. Cambridge, MA: Harvard University Press, 1976.

MacDonald, William Lloyd, and John A. Pinto. *Hadrian's Villa and Its Legacy*. New Haven, CT: Yale University Press, 1995.

Munro-Hay, Stuart. *Aksum: A Civilization of Late Antiquity*. Edinburgh, UK: University Press. 1991.

Phillipson, David W. *Ancient Ethiopia: Aksum: Its Antecedents and Successors*. London: The British Museum, 1998.

Romain, William F. *Mysteries of the Hopewell: Astronomers, Geometers, and Magicians of the Eastern Woodlands*. Akron, OH: University of Akron Press, 2000.

Sanders, William T., and Joseph W. Michels, eds. *Teotihuacán and Kaminaljuyu: A Study in Prehistoric Culture Contact*. University Park, PA: Penn State University Press, 1977.

Sharma, G. R., ed. *Kusana Studies: Papers Presented to the International Conference on the Archaeology, History and Arts of the People of Central Asia in the Kusana Period, Dushambe (Tadjikistan) U.S.S.R., September 25–October 4, 1968*. Allahabad, India: Department of Ancient History, Culture and Archaeology, University of Allahabad, 1998.

Silverman, Helaine, and Donald Proulx. *The Nasca*. Oxford, UK: Blackwell, 2002.

Taylor, Rabun M. *Roman Builders: A Study in Architectural Process*. Cambridge, UK, and New York: Cambridge University Press, 2003.

Wang, Zhongshu. *Han Civilization*. Translated by K. C. Chang and collaborators. New Haven, CT: Yale University Press, 1982.

Woodward, Susan L., and Jerry N. McDonald. *Indian Mounds of the Middle Ohio Valley: A Guide to Mounds and Earthworks of the Adena, Hopewell, Cole, and Fort Ancient People*. Blacksburg, VA: McDonald & Woodward, 2002.

400 CE

Aikens, C. Melvin, and Takayasu Higuchi. *Prehistory of Japan*. New York: Academic Press, 1982.

Asher, Frederick M. *The Art of Eastern India, 300–800*. Minneapolis: University of Minnesota Press, 1980.

Bandmann, Günter. *Early Medieval Architecture as Bearer of Meaning*. Translated by Kendall Wallis. New York: Columbia University Press, 2005.

Barnes, Gina Lee. *Protohistoric Yamato: Archaeology of the First Japanese State*. Ann Arbor: University of Michigan Center for Japanese Studies, Museum of Anthropology, University of Michigan, 1988.

Beal, Samuel. *The Life of Hiuen-Tsiang by Hwui Li*. New Delhi: Asian Educational Services, 1998.

Blanton, Richard E., et al. *Ancient Oaxaca: The Monte Albán*. New York: Cambridge University Press, 1999.

Cunningham, Alexander. *Mahâbodhi, or the Great Buddhist Temple under the Bodhi Tree at Buddha-Gaya*. London: W. H. Allen, 1892.

Freely, John. *Byzantine Monuments of Istanbul*. Cambridge, UK: Cambridge University Press, 2004.

Hardy, Adam. *The Temple Architecture of India*. Hoboken, NJ: John Wiley & Sons, 2008.

Harischandra, B. W. *The Sacred City of Anuradhapura*. New Delhi: Asian Educational Services, 1998.

BIBLIOGRAPHY

Holloway, R. Ross. *Constantine and Rome.* New Haven: Yale University Press, 2004.

Imamura, Keiji. *Prehistoric Japan: New Perspectives on Insular East Asia.* London: UCL Press, 1996.

Khandalavala, Karl, ed. *The Golden Age of Gupta Art: Empire, Province, and Influence.* Bombay: Marg, 1991.

Krautheimer, Richard. *Early Christian and Byzantine Architecture.* New York: Penguin, 1986.

Mitra, Debala. *Ajanta.* New Delhi: Archaeological Survey of India, 1980.

Mizoguchi, Koji. *An Archaeological History of Japan: 30,000 BC to AD 700.* Philadelphia: University of Pennsylvania Press, 2002.

Ray, Himanshu P. *The Winds of Change: Buddhism and the Maritime Links of Early South Asia.* New Delhi: Oxford University Press, 1994.

Spink, Walter M. *Ajanta to Ellora.* Ann Arbor: Marg Publications for the Center for South and Southeast Asian Studies, University of Michigan, 1967.

Weiner, Sheila L. *Ajanta: Its Place in Buddhist Art.* Berkeley and Los Angeles: University of California Press, 1977.

Williams, Joanna Gottfried. *The Art of Gupta India: Empire and Province.* Princeton, NJ: Princeton University Press, 1982.

600 CE

Adams, Cassandra. "Japan's Ise Shrine and Its Thirteen-Hundred-Year-Old Reconstruction Tradition." *Journal of Architectural Education* 52, no. 1 (1988).

Berkson, Carmel, Wendy Doniger O'Flaherty, and George Michell. *Elephanta, The Cave of Shiva.* Princeton, NJ: Princeton University Press, 1983.

Bock, Felicia G. "The Rites of Renewal at Ise." *Monumenta Nipponica* 29, no. 1 (1974).

Davies, John Gordon. *Medieval Armenian Art and Architecture: The Church of the Holy Cross, Aght'amar.* London: Pindar, 1991.

Freely, John. *Byzantine Monuments of Istanbul.* Cambridge, UK: Cambridge University Press, 2004.

Goldstein, Paul S. *Andean Diaspora: The Tiwanaku Colonies and the Origins of South American Empire.* Gainesville: University Press of Florida, 2005.

Hardy, Andrew, Mauro Cucarzi, and Patrizia Zolese, eds. *Champa and the Archaeology of My S'on (Vietnam).* Singapore: NUS Press, 2009.

Harrison, Peter D. *The Lords of Tikal: Rulers of an Ancient Maya City.* New York: Thames & Hudson, 1999.

Janusek, John Wayne. *Identity and Power in the Ancient Andes: Tiwanaku: Cities Through Time.* New York: Routledge, 2004.

Kidder, J. Edward. *The Lucky Seventh: Early Horyu-ji and Its Time.* Tokyo: International Christian University and Hachiro Yuasa Memorial Museum, 1999.

Kolata, Alan L. *The Tiwanaku: Portrait of an Andean Civilization.* Cambridge, MA: Blackwell, 1993.

Kramrisch, Stella. *The Presence of Síva.* Princeton, NJ: Princeton University Press, 1992.

Krautheimer, Richard. *Rome: Profile of a City, 312–1308.* Princeton, NJ: Princeton University Press, 2000.

Malmstrom, Vincent H. *Cycles of the Sun, Mysteries of the Moon: The Calendar in Mesoamerican Civilization.* Austin: University of Texas Press, 1997.

Mathews, T. F. *Early Churches of Constantinople, Architecture and Liturgy.* University Park: Pennsylvania State University Press, 1971.

Mizuno, Seiichi. *Asuka Buddhist Art: Horyu-ji.* New York: Weatherhill, 1974.

Ngô Van Doanh. *My Son Relics.* Hanoi: Gioi, 2005.

Robert, Mark, and Ahmet Çakmak, eds. *Hagia Sophia from the Age of Justinian to the Present.* Cambridge, UK: Cambridge University Press, 1992.

Schele, Linda, and Peter Mathews. *The Code of Kings: The Language of Seven Sacred Maya Temples and Tombs.* New York: Scribner, 1998.

Suzuki, Kakichi. *Early Buddhist Architecture in Japan.* Tokyo: Kodansha International, 1980.

Tartakov, Gary M. "The Beginnings of Dravidian Temple Architecture in Stone." *Artibus Asiae* 42 (1980).

Utudjian, Edouard. *Armenian Architecture, 4th to 17th Century.* Translated by Geoffrey Capner. Paris: Éditions A. Morancé, 1968.

Warren, John. *Greek Mathematics and the Architects to Justinian.* London: Coach, 1976.

Watanabe, Yasutada. *Shinto Art: Ise and Izumo Shrines.* New York: Weatherhill/Heibonsha, 1974.

Wharton, Annabel Jane. *Refiguring the Post-Classical City: Dura Europos, Jerash, Jerusalem, and Ravenna.* Cambridge, UK, and New York: Cambridge University Press, 1995.

800 CE

Atroshenko, V. I., and Judith Collins. *The Origins of the Romanesque: Near Eastern Influences on European Art, 4th–12th Centuries.* London: Lund Humphries, 1985.

Chandler, David P. *A History of Cambodia.* Boulder, CO: Westview, 2000.

Coe, Michael D. *The Maya.* London and New York: Thames & Hudson, 1999.

Ettinghausen, Richard. *Islamic Art and Architecture 650–1250.* New Haven, CT: Yale University Press, 2001.

Flood, Finbarr Barry. *The Great Mosque of Damascus: Studies on the Makings of an Ummayyad Visual Culture.* Leiden, Netherlands, and Boston: E. J. Brill, 2001.

Frederic, Louis. *Borobodur.* New York: Abeville, 1996.

Hattstein, Markus, and Peter Delius, eds. *Islam: Art and Architecture.* Translated by George Ansell German. Cologne, Germany: Könemann, 2000.

Horn, Walter, and Ernest Born. *The Plan of St. Gall.* Berkeley and Los Angeles: University of California Press, 1972.

Jackson, John G. *Introduction to African Civilization.* Secaucus, NJ: Citadel, 1970.

Joe, Wanne J. *Traditional Korea, A Cultural History.* Edited by Hongkyu A. Choe. Elizabeth, NJ: Hollym International, 1997.

Kelly, Joyce. *An Archaeological Guide to Northern Central America: Belize, Guatemala, Honduras, and El Salvador.* Norman: University of Oklahoma Press, 1996.

Lassner, Jacob. *The Shaping of Abbasid Rule.* Princeton, NJ: Princeton University Press, 1980.

Michell, George. *Pattadakal.* New Delhi and Oxford, UK: Oxford University Press, 2002.

Milburn, Robert. *Early Christian Art and Architecture.* Berkeley and Los Angeles: University of California Press, 1988.

Stuart, David, and George Stuart. *Palenque: Eternal City of the Maya.* London: Thames & Hudson, 2008.

Tartakov, Gary Michael. *The Durga Temple at Aihole: A Historiographical Study.* New Delhi and New York: Oxford University Press, 1997.

Xiong, Victor Cunrui. *Sui T'ang Ch'ang-an: A Study in the Urban History of Medieval China.* Ann Arbor: Center for Chinese Studies, University of Michigan, 2000.

1000 CE

Asopa, Jai Narayan. *Origin of the Rajputs.* Delhi: Bharatiya, 1976.

Conant, Kenneth John. *Carolingian and Romanesque Architecture, 800 to 1200.* Baltimore: Penguin, 1959.

Dehejia, Vidya. *The Sensuous and the Sacred: Chola Bronzes from South India.* New York: American Federation of Arts; Seattle: University of Washington Press, 2002.

———. *Yogini, Cult and Temples: A Tantric Tradition.* New Delhi: National Museum, 1986.

Desai, Devangana. *Khajuraho.* New Delhi and New York: Oxford University Press, 2000.

Dodds, Jerrilynn D. *Architecture and Ideology in Early Medieval Spain.* University Park: Penn State University Press, 1990.

Grossmann, Peter. *Christliche Architektur in Ägypten.* Leiden, Netherlands, and Boston: E. J. Brill, 2002.

Handa, Devendra. *Osian: History, Archaeology, Art and Architecture.* Delhi: Sundeep Prakashan, 1984.

Kowalski, Jeff Karl. *The House of the Governor: A Maya Palace at Uxmal, Yucatán, Mexico.* Norman: University of Oklahoma Press, 1987.

Michell, George. *Early Western Calukyan Temples.* London: AARP, 1975.

Miller, Barbara Stoler. *The Powers of Art: Patronage in Indian Culture.* New Delhi and New York: Oxford University Press, 1992.

Necipoglu, Gülru. *The Topkapı Scroll: Geometry and Ornament in Islamic Architecture.* Santa Monica, CA: Getty Center for the History of Arts and the Humanities, 1995.

Rivoira, Giovanni Teresio. *Lombardic Architecture: Its Origin, Development, and Derivatives.* New York: Hacker Art Books, 1975.

Spink, Walter M. *Ajanta to Ellora Bombay.* Ann Arbor: Marg Publications for the Center for South and Southeast Asian Studies, University of Michigan, 1967.

Steinhardt, Nancy Shatzman. *Liao Architecture.* Honolulu: University of Hawaii Press, 1997.

Tartakov, Gary M. "The Beginning of Dravidian Temple Architecture in Stone." *Artibus Asiae* 42 (1980).

Young, Biloine W., and Melvin L. Fowler. *Cahokia, the Great Native American Metropolis.* Urbana: University of Illinois Press, 2000.

1200 CE

Bernier, Ronald M. *Temple Arts of Kerala: A South Indian Tradition.* New Delhi: S. Chand, 1982.

Bony, Jean. *French Gothic Architecture of the 12th and 13th Centuries.* Berkeley and Los Angeles: University of California Press, 1983.

Branner, Robert. *Burgundian Gothic Architecture.* London: A. Zwemmer, 1960.

Braunfels, Wolfgang. *Monasteries of Western Europe: The Architecture of the Orders.* Translated by Alastair Laing. London: Thames & Hudson, 1972.

Brumfield, William Craft. *A History of Russian Architecture.* Cambridge, UK: Cambridge University Press, 1993.

Buchwald, Hans Herbert. *Form, Style, and Meaning in Byzantine Church Architecture.* Brookfield, VT: Ashgate, 1999.

Cassidy-Welch, Megan. *Monastic Spaces and Their Meanings: Thirteenth-Century English Cistercian Monasteries.* Turnhout, Belgium: Brepols, 2001.

Chandler, David P. *A History of Cambodia.* Boulder, CO: Westview, 2000.

Coe, Michael D. *Angkor and the Khmer Civilization.* New York: Thames & Hudson, 2003.

Dehejia, Vidya, ed. *Royal Patrons and Great Temple Art.* Bombay: Marg, 1988.

Diehl, Richard A. *Tula: The Toltec Capital of Ancient Mexico.* London: Thames & Hudson, 1983.

Dodds, Jerrilynn D., ed. *Al-Andalus: The Art of Islamic Spain.* New York: Metropolitan Museum of Art and Harry N. Abrams, 1992.

Duby, Georges. *The Age of the Cathedrals: Art and Society, 980–1420.* Translated by Eleanor Levieux and Barbara Thompson. Chicago: University of Chicago Press, 1981.

Enzo, Carli, ed. *Il Duomo di Pisa: Il Battistero, il Campanile.* Florence: Nardini, 1989.

Erdmann, Kurt. *Das Anatolische Kervansaray des 13. Jahrhunderts.* Berlin: Verlag Gebr. Mann, 1976.

Findlay, Louis. *The Monolithic Churches of Lalibela in Ethiopia.* Cairo: Publications de la Société d'Archéologie Copte, 1944.

Fukuyama, Toshio. *Heian Temples: Byodo-in and Chuson-ji.* Translated by Ronald K. Jones. New York: Weatherhill, 1976.

Grabar, Oleg. *The Alhambra.* Cambridge, MA: Harvard University Press, 1978.

Guo, Qinghua. *The Structure of Chinese Timber Architecture: Twelfth Century Design Standards and Construction Principles.* Gothenburg, Sweden: Chalmers University of Technology, School of Architecture, Department of Building Design, 1995.

Kinder, Terryl Nancy. *Cistercian Europe: Architecture of Contemplation.* Grand Rapids, MI: W. B. Eerdmans Publishing and Cistercian Publications, 2002.

Kostof, Spiro. *Caves of God: The Monastic Environment of Byzantine Cappadocia.* Cambridge, MA: MIT Press, 1972.

Kraus, Henry. *Gold Was the Mortar: The Economics of Cathedral Building.* London and Boston: Routledge & Kegan Paul, 1979.

Krautheimer, Richard. *Early Christian and Byzantine Architecture.* Harmondsworth, UK, and New York: Penguin, 1986.

Liu, Dunzhen. *Chinese Classical Gardens of Suzhou.* Translated by Chen Lixian. Edited by Joseph C. Wang. New York: McGraw-Hill, 1993.

MacDonald, William Lloyd. *Early Christian and Byzantine Architecture: Great Ages of World Architecture.* New York: G. Braziller, 1962.

Mannikka, Eleanor. *Angkor Wat: Time, Space, and Kingship.* Honolulu: University of Hawaii Press, 1996.

Moynihan, Elizabeth B. *Paradise as a Garden: In Persia and Mughal India.* New York: G. Braziller, 1979.

Nath, R. *History of Sultanate Architecture.* New Delhi: Abhinav Publications, 1978.

Noma, Seiroku. *The Arts of Japan.* Translated and adapted by John Rosenfield. Tokyo and New York: Kodansha International; New York: Harper & Row, 1978.

Ousterhout, Robert G. *Master Builders of Byzantium.* Princeton, NJ: Princeton University Press, 1999.

Panofsky, Erwin, ed. *Abbot Suger on the Abbey Church of St.-Denis and Its Art Treasures.* Princeton, NJ: Princeton University Press, 1979.

Peroni, Adriano, ed. *Il Duomo di Pisa.* Modena, Italy: F. C. Panini, 1995.

Petruccioli, Attilio, ed. *Bukhara: The Myth and the Architecture.* Cambridge, MA: Aga Khan Program for Islamic Architecture, 1999.

Rabbat, Nasser. "Al-Azhar Mosque: An Architectural Chronicle of Cairo's History." *Muqarnas 13* (1996): 45–67.

Rowley, Trevor. *The Norman Heritage, 1055–1200.* London and Boston, MA: Routledge & Kegan Paul, 1983.

Settar, S. *The Hoysala Temples.* Bangalore, India: Kala Yatra, 1991–1992.

Starza, O. M. *The Jagannatha Temple at Puri: Its Architecture, Art, and Culture.* Leiden, Netherlands, and New York: E. J. Brill, 1993.

BIBLIOGRAPHY

Strachan, Paul. *Imperial Pagan: Art and Architecture of Burma*. Honolulu: University of Hawaii Press, 1990.

Tobin, Stephen. *The Cistercians: Monks and Monasteries of Europe*. Woodstock, NY: Overlook, 1996.

Tozzer, Alfred M. *Chichen Itza and Its Cenote of Sacrifice: A Comparative Study of Contemporaneous Maya and Toltec*. Cambridge, MA: Peabody Museum, 1957.

Von Simson, Otto Georg. *The Gothic Cathedral: Origins of Gothic Architecture and the Medieval Concept of Order*. Princeton, NJ: Princeton University Press, 1988.

Wang, Eugene Yuejin. *Shaping the Lotus Sutra: Buddhist Visual Culture in Medieval China*. Seattle: University of Washington Press, 2005.

1400 CE

Ackerman, James S. *Palladio*. Harmondsworth, UK: Penguin, 1966.

Ballon, Hilary. *The Paris of Henri IV: Architecture and Urbanism*. Cambridge, MA: MIT Press, 1991.

Battisti, Eugenio. *Brunelleschi*. Translated by Robert Erich Wolf. Milan: Electa Architecture; London: Phaidon, 2002.

Blair, Sheila S., and Jonathan M. Bloom. *The Art and Architecture of Islam, 1250–1800*. New Haven, CT: Yale University Press, 1994.

Borsi, Franco. *Leon Battista Alberti: The Complete Works*. London: Faber, 1989.

Bruschi, Arnaldo. *Bramante*. London: Thames & Hudson, 1977.

Burger, Richard L., and Lucy C. Salazar, eds. *Machu Picchu: Unveiling the Mystery of the Incas*. New Haven, CT: Yale University Press, 2004.

Chappell, Sally Anderson. *Cahokia: Mirror of the Cosmos*. Chicago: University of Chicago Press, 2002.

Clarke, Georgia Roman House. *Renaissance Palaces: Inventing Antiquity in Fifteenth-Century Italy*. Cambridge, UK, and New York: Cambridge University Press, 2003.

Evans, Joan. *Monastic Architecture in France, from the Renaissance to the Revolution*. Cambridge, UK: Cambridge University Press, 1964.

Fedorov, Boris Nikolaevich. *Architecture of the Russian North, 12th–19th Centuries*. Translated by N. Johnstone. Leningrad: Aurora Art Publishers, 1976.

Goodwin, Godfrey. *A History of Ottoman Architecture*. London: Thames & Hudson, 1971.

Günay, Reha. *Sinan: The Architect and His Works*. Translated by Ali Ottoman. Istanbul: Yapı-Endüstri Merkezi Yayınları, 1998.

Hall, John W., ed. *Japan in the Muromachi Age*. Ithaca, New York: East Asia Program, Cornell University, 2001.

Hitchcock, Henry Russell. *German Renaissance Architecture*. Princeton, NJ: Princeton University Press, 1981.

Howard, Deborah. *Jacopo Sansovino: Architecture and Patronage in Renaissance Venice*. New Haven, CT: Yale University Press, 1975.

Huppert, A. (2015). *Becoming an Architect in Renaissance Italy: Art, Science and the Career of Baldassarre Peruzzi*. New Haven, CT: Yale University Press.

Jarzombek, Mark. *On Leon Baptista Alberti: His Literary and Aesthetic Theories*. Cambridge, MA: MIT Press, 1989.

Kuran, Aptullah. *The Mosque in Early Ottoman Architecture*. Chicago: University of Chicago Press, 1968.

Lieberman, Ralph. *The Church of Santa Maria dei Miracoli in Venice*. New York: Garland, 1986.

López Luján, Leonardo. *The Offerings of the Templo Mayor of Tenochtitlán*. Translated by Bernard R. Ortiz de Montellano and Thelma Ortiz de Montellano. Albuquerque: University of New Mexico Press, 2005.

Millard, James, ed. *New Qing Imperial History: The Making of Inner Asian Empire at Qing Chengde*. London and New York: Routledge, 2004.

Murray, Peter. *Renaissance Architecture*. Milan: Electa; New York: Rizzoli, 1985, 1978.

Pandya, Yatin. *Architectural Legacies of Ahmedabad*. Ahmedabad, India: Vastu-Shilpa Foundation for Studies and Research in Environmental Design, 2002.

Prinz, Wolfram Schloss. *Chambord und die Villa Rotonda in Vicenza*. Berlin: Mann, 1980.

Rabbat, Nasser O. *The Citadel of Cairo: A New Interpretation of Royal Mamluk Architecture*. Leiden, Netherlands, and New York: E. J. Brill, 1995.

Ryu, Je-Hun. *Reading the Korean Landscape*. Elizabeth, NJ: Hollym International, 2000.

Singh, Upinder (2008). *A History of Ancient and Early Medieval India: From the Stone Age to the 12th Century*. New Delhi; Upper Saddle River, NJ: Pearson Education.

Smith, Christine Hunnikin. *Architecture in the Culture of Early Humanism: Ethics, Aesthetics, and Eloquence, 1400–1470*. New York: Oxford University Press, 1992.

Sumner-Boyd, Hilary, and John Freely. *Strolling through Istanbul: A Guide to the City*. New York: Kegan Paul, 2001; New York: Columbia University Press, 2003.

Tafuri, Manfredo. *Venice and the Renaissance*. Translated by Jessica Levine. Cambridge, MA: MIT Press, 1989.

Talayesva, Don C. *Sun Chief: The Autobiography of a Hopi Indian*. New Haven, CT: Yale University Press, 1942.

Treib, Marc, and Ron Herman. *A Guide to the Gardens of Kyoto*. Tokyo: Shufunotomo, 1980.

Van der Ree, Paul, Gerrit Smienk, and Clemens Steenbergen. *Italian Villas and Gardens: A Corso di Disegno*. Munich: Prestel, 1992.

Vogt-Göknil, Ulya. *Living Architecture: Ottoman*. New York: Grosset & Dunlap, 1966.

Von Hagen, Victor Wolfgang. *The Desert Kingdoms of Peru*. New York: New American Library, 1968.

Waldman, Carl. *Atlas of the North American Indian*. New York: Checkmark, 2000.

Wright, Kenneth R. *Machu Picchu: A Civil Engineering Marvel*. Reston, VA: American Society of Civil Engineers, 2000.

Zhu, Jianfei. *Chinese Spatial Strategies: Imperial Beijing, 1420–1911*. London and New York: Routledge Curzon, 2004.

1600 CE

Argan, Giulio Carlo. *Michelangelo Architect*. Translated by Marion L. Grayson. London: Thames & Hudson, 1993.

Balas, Edith. *Michelangelo's Medici Chapel: A New Interpretation*. Philadelphia: American Philosophical Society, 1995.

Begley, W. E., and Z. A. Desai. *Taj Mahal: The Illumined Tomb: An Anthology of Seventeenth-Century Mughal and European Documentary Sources*. Cambridge, MA: Aga Khan Program for Islamic Architecture; Seattle: University of Washington Press, 1989.

Blake, Stephen P. *Half the World: The Social Architecture of Safavid Isfahan, 1590–1722*. Costa Mesa, CA: Mazda, 1999.

Blunt, Anthony. *Guide to Baroque Rome*. New York: Harper & Row, 1982.

Borsi, Francio. *Bernini*. Translated by Robert Erich Wolf. New York: Rizzoli, 1984.

Coaldrake, William Howard. *Gateways of Power: Edo Architecture and Tokugawa Authority, 1603–1951*. Ph.D. diss., Harvard University, 1983.

Coffin, David R. *The Villa in the Life of Renaissance Rome*. Princeton, NJ: Princeton University Press, 1979.

D'Amico, John F. *Renaissance Humanism in Papal Rome: Humanists and Churchmen on the Eve of the Reformation*. Baltimore: Johns Hopkins University Press, 1983.

De Tolnay, Charles. *Michelangelo: Sculptor, Painter, Architect*. Princeton, NJ: Princeton University Press, 1974.

Dussel, Enrique D. *The Invention of the Americas: Eclipse of "the Other" and the Myth of Modernity.* Translated by Michael D. Barber. New York: Continuum, 1995.

Evans, Susan, and Joanne Pillsbury, eds. *Palaces of the Ancient New World*: *A Symposium at Dumbarton Oaks, 10th and 11th October 1998.* Washington, DC: Dumbarton Oaks Research Library and Collection, 2004.

Gotch, John. *Alfred Inigo Jones.* New York: B. Blom, 1968.

Guise, Anthony, ed. *The Potala of Tibet.* London and Atlantic Highlands, NJ: Stacey International, 1988.

Günay, Reha. *Sinan: The Architect and His Works.* Translated by Ali Ottoman. Istanbul: Yapı-Endüstri Merkezi Yayınları, 1998.

Hersey, George L. *High Renaissance Art in St. Peter's and the Vatican: An Interpretive Guide.* Chicago: University of Chicago Press, 1993.

Hughes, Quentin. *Malta: A Guide to the Fortifications.* Valletta, Malta: Said International, 1993.

Inaji, Toshiro. *The Garden as Architecture: Form and Spirit in the Gardens of Japan, China, and Korea.* Translated and adapted by Pamela Virgilio. Tokyo and New York: Kodansha International, 1998.

Ishimoto, Yasuhiro. *Katsura: Tradition and Creation in Japanese Architecture.* Text by Kenzo Tange. Photos by Yasuhiro Ishimoto. New Haven, CT: Yale University Press, 1972.

Krautheimer, Richard. *Roma Alessandrina: The Remapping of Rome under Alexander VII, 1655–1667.* Poughkeepsie, NY: Vassar College, 1982.

Lazzaro, Claudia. *The Italian Renaissance Garden: From the Conventions of Planting, Design, and Ornament to the Grand Gardens of 16th-Century Central Italy.* New Haven, CT: Yale University Press, 1990.

Lees-Milne, James. *Saint Peter's: The Story of Saint Peter's Basilica in Rome.* Boston: Little, Brown, 1967; Chicago: University of Chicago Press, 1986.

Lev, Evonne. *Propaganda and the Jesuit Baroque.* Berkeley and Los Angeles: University of California Press, 2004.

Mann, Charles C. *1491: New Revelations of the Americas Before Columbus.* New York: Knopf, 2005.

Meek, Harold Alan. *Guarino Guarini and His Architecture.* New Haven, CT: Yale University Press, 1988.

Michell, George. *The Vijayanagara Courtly Style: Incorporation and Synthesis in the Royal Architecture of Southern India, 15th–17th Centuries.* New Delhi and Manohar, India: American Institute of Indian Studies, 1992.

Millon, Henry A., ed. *Triumph of the Baroque: Architecture in Europe, 1600–1750.* New York: Rizzoli, 1999.

Nath, R. *Architecture of Fatehpur Sikri: Forms, Techniques & Concepts.* Jaipur, India: Historical Research Documentation Programme, 1988.

———. *History of Mughal Architecture.* New Delhi: Abhinav, 1982.

Necipoglu, Gülru. *The Age of Sinan: Architectural Culture in the Ottoman Empire.* London: Reaktion, 2005.

Paludan, Ann. *The Imperial Ming Tombs.* New Haven, CT: Yale University Press, 1981.

Partner, Peter. *Renaissance Rome, 1500–1559: A Portrait of a Society.* Berkeley and Los Angeles: University of California Press, 1976.

Rizvi, Kishwar. *Transformations in Early Safavid Architecture: The Shrine of Shaykh Safi al-din Ishaq Ardabili in Iran (1501–1629).* Ph.D. diss., Massachusetts Institute of Technology, 2000.

Sinding-Larsen, Amund. *The Lhasa Atlas: Traditional Tibetan Architecture and Townscape.* Boston: Shambhala; New York: Random House, 2001.

Studio, Fianico. *The Medici Villas.* Florence: Libreria Editrice Fiorentina, 1980.

Summerson, John Newenham. *Architecture in Britain, 1530 to 1830.* Harmondsworth, UK, and New York: Penguin, 1991.

———. *Inigo Jones.* New Haven: Published for the Paul Mellon Centre for Studies in British Art by Yale University Press, 2000.

Thompson, Jon, and Sheila R. Canby, eds. *Hunt for Paradise: Court Arts of Safavid Iran, 1501–1576.* Milan: Skira; London: Thames & Hudson, 2003.

Walton, Guy. *Louis XIV's Versailles.* London: Viking, 1986.

Wescoat, J., Joachim Wolschke-Bulmahn, Dumbarton Oaks, and Arthur M. Sackler Gallery. *Mughal Gardens: Sources, Places, Representations, and Prospects.* Washington, D.C.: Dumbarton Oaks Research Library and Collection, 1996.

Zhao, Lingyang. *Zheng He, Navigator, Discoverer and Diplomat.* Singapore: Unipress, 2001.

1700 CE

Arciszewska, Barbara, and Elizabeth McKellar, eds. *Articulating British Classicism: New Approaches to Eighteenth-Century Architecture.* Hants, UK: Aldershot, 2004.

Arshi, Pardeep Singh. *The Golden Temple: History, Art, and Architecture.* New Delhi: Harman, 1989.

Banerjea, Dhrubajyoti. *European Calcutta: Images and Recollections of a Bygone Era.* New Delhi: UBS, 2004.

Berger, Patricia Ann. *Empire of Emptiness: Buddhist Art and Political Authority in Qing China.* Honolulu: University of Hawaii Press, 2003.

Blunt, Anthony, ed. *Baroque and Rococo: Architecture and Decoration.* London: Elek, 1978.

Bourke, John. *Baroque Churches of Central Europe.* London: Faber & Faber, 1962.

Erlanger, Philippe. *The Age of Courts and Kings: Manners and Morals, 1558–1715.* New York: Harper & Row, 1967.

Gollings, John. *City of Victory: Vijayanagara, the Medieval Hindu Capital of Southern India.* New York: Aperture, 1991.

Gutschow, Niels, and Erich Theophile, eds. *Patan: Architecture of a Historic Nepalese City: Excerpts from a Proposed Research and Publication Project (1998–2000) of the Kathmandu Valley Preservation Trust.* Kathmandu, Nepal: Kathmandu Valley Preservation Trust, 1998.

Harman, William. *The Sacred Marriage of a Hindu Goddess.* Bloomington: Indiana University Press, 1989.

Herrmann, Wolfgang. *Laugier and Eighteenth-Century French Theory.* London: A. Zwemmer, 1962.

———. *The Theory of Claude Perrault.* London: A. Zwemmer, 1973.

Metcalf, Thomas R. *Ideologies of the Raj.* Cambridge, UK, and New York: Cambridge University Press, 1994.

Otto, Christian F. *Space into Light: The Church Architecture of Balthasar Neumann.* New York: Architectural History Foundation, 1979.

Pierson, William H., Jr. *The Colonial and Neocolassical Styles.* Oxford, UK: Oxford University Press, 1970.

Roy, Ashim K. *History of the Jaipur City.* New Delhi: Manohar, 1978.

Sachdev, Vibhuti, and Giles Tillotson. *Building Jaipur: The Making of an Indian City.* London: Reaktion Books, 2002.

Sarkar, Jadunath. *A History of Jaipur, c. 1503–1938.* Hyderabad, India: Orient Longman, 1984.

Singh, Khushwant. *A History of the Sikhs.* New Delhi and Oxford, UK: Oxford University Press, 2004.

Sitwell, Sacheverell. *Baroque and Rococo.* London: Weidenfeld & Nicolson, 1967.

Smith, Bardwell, and Holly Baker Reynolds, eds. *The City as a Sacred Center: Essays on Six Asian Contexts.* Leiden, Netherlands, and New York: E. J. Brill, 1987.

BIBLIOGRAPHY

Smith, Charles Saumarez. *The Building of Castle Howard*. London: Faber & Faber, 1990.

Smith, Woodruff D. *Consumption and the Making of Respectability, 1600–1800*. New York: Routledge, 2002.

Wittkower, Rudolf. *Palladio and Palladianism*. New York: G. Braziller, 1974.

1800 CE

Aasen, Clarence T. *Architecture of Siam: A Cultural History Interpretation*. Kuala Lumpur, Malaysia, and New York: Oxford University Press, 1998.

Atterbury, Paul, ed. *A. W. N. Pugin: Master of Gothic Revival*. New Haven, CT: Published for the Bard Graduate Center for Studies in the Decorative Arts, New York, by Yale University Press, 1995.

Ayres, James. *Building the Georgian City*. New Haven, CT: Yale University Press, 1998.

Bastéa, Eleni. *The Creation of Modern Athens: Planning the Myth*. Cambridge, UK, and New York: Cambridge University Press, 2000.

Bergdoll, Barry. *Karl Friedrich Schinkel: An Architecture for Prussia*. New York: Rizzoli, 1994.

Brandon, James R., William P. Malm, and Donald H. Shively. *Studies in Kabuki: Its Acting, Music, and Historical Context*. Honolulu: University Press of Hawaii, 1978.

Brooks, Michael W. *John Ruskin and Victorian Architecture*. New Brunswick, NJ: Rutgers University Press, 1987.

Charlesworth, Michael, ed. *The Gothic Revival, 1720–1870: Literary Sources and Documents*. The Banks, Mountfield, UK: Helm Information, 2002.

Chattopadhyay, Swati. *Representing Calcutta: Modernity, Nationalism, and the Colonial Uncanny*. London and New York: Routledge, 2005.

Conner, Patrick. *Oriental Architecture in the West*. London: Thames & Hudson, 1979.

Crook, Joseph Mordaunt. *The Dilemma of Style: Architectural Ideas from the Picturesque to the Post-Modern*. London: Murray, 1987.

Drexler, Arthur, ed. *The Architecture of the École des Beaux-Arts*. New York: Museum of Modern Art; Cambridge, MA: MIT Press, 1977.

Du Prey, Pierre de la Ruffinière. *John Soane, The Making of an Architect*. Chicago: University of Chicago Press, 1982.

Forêt, Philippe. *Mapping Chengde: The Qing Landscape Enterprise*. Honolulu: University of Hawaii Press, 2000.

Gosner, Pamela W. *Caribbean Georgian: The Great and Small Houses of the West Indies*. Washington, DC: Three Continents, 1982.

Herrmann, Wolfgang. *Gottfried Semper: In Search of Architecture*. Cambridge, MA: MIT Press, 1984.

Hitchcock, Henry Russell. *Early Victorian Architecture in Britain*. New Haven: Yale University Press, 1954.

Kaufmann, Emil. *Architecture in the Age of Reason: Baroque and Post-Baroque in England, Italy, and France*. New York: Dover Publications, 1968.

Leiter, Samuel L. *Kabuki Encyclopedia: An English-Language Adaptation of Kabuki Jiten*. Westport, CT: Greenwood, 1979.

———, ed. *A Kabuki Reader: History and Performance*. Armonk, NY: M. E. Sharpe, 2002.

McCormick, Thomas. *Charles-Louis Clérisseau and the Genesis of Neo-Classicism*. New York: Architectural History Foundation; Cambridge, MA: MIT Press, 1990.

Metcalf, Thomas R. *An Imperial Vision: Indian Architecture and Britain's Raj*. Berkeley and Los Angeles: University of California Press, 1989.

Mitter, Partha. *Much Maligned Monsters: History of European Reactions to Indian Art*. Oxford, UK: Clarendon, 1977.

Moore, Elizabeth H., Philip Stott, and Suriyavudh Sukhasvasti. *Ancient Capitals of Thailand*. London: Thames & Hudson, 1996.

Port, Michael Harry. *Imperial London: Civil Government Building in London 1850–1915*. New Haven, CT: Published for the Paul Mellon Centre for Studies in British Art by Yale University Press, 1995.

Pundt, Hermann G. *Schinkel's Berlin: A Study in Environmental Planning*. Cambridge, MA: Harvard University Press, 1972.

Schumann-Bacia, Eva. *John Soane and the Bank of England*. London and New York: Longman, 1991.

Stewart, David B. *The Making of a Modern Japanese Architecture: 1868 to the Present*. Tokyo and New York: Kodansha International, 1987.

Summerson, John Newenham. *Georgian London*. New York: Scribner, 1946.

Unrau, John. *Ruskin and St. Mark's*. London: Thames & Hudson, 1984.

Upton, Dell. *Architecture in the United States*. Oxford, UK, and New York: Oxford University Press, 1998.

Vernoit, Stephen. *Occidentalism: Islamic Art in the 19th Century*. New York: Nour Foundation, in association with Azimuth Editions and Oxford University Press, 1997.

Vidler, Anthony. *The Writing of the Walls: Architectural Theory in the Late Enlightenment*. New York: Princeton Architectural Press, 1987.

Watkin, David. *German Architecture and the Classical Ideal*. Cambridge, MA: MIT Press, 1987.

Whittaker, Cynthia Hyla, ed. *Russia Engages the World, 1453–1825*. Cambridge, MA: Harvard University Press, 2003.

1900 CE

Baker, Geoffrey H. *Le Corbusier: An Analysis of Form*. New York: Van Nostrand Reinhold; London: E & FN Spon, 1996.

Blau, Eve. *The Architecture of Red Vienna, 1919–1934*. Cambridge, MA: MIT Press, 1999.

Borsi, Franco. *The Monumental Era: European Architecture and Design, 1929–1939*. Translated by Pamela Marwood. New York: Rizzoli, 1987.

Bozdogan, Sibel. *Modernism and Nation Building: Turkish Architectural Culture in the Early Republic*. Seattle: University of Washington Press, 2001.

Cody, Jeffrey W. *Exporting American Architecture, 1870–2000*. London and New York: Routledge, 2003.

Collins, Peter. *Changing Ideals in Modern Architecture, 1750–1950*. Montreal and Ithaca, NY: McGill-Queens University Press, 1998.

Colomina, Beatriz, ed. *Privacy and Publicity: Modern Architecture as Mass Media*. Cambridge, MA: MIT Press, 1996.

Condit, Carl W. *The Chicago School of Architecture: A History of Commercial and Public Building in the Chicago Area, 1875–1925*. Chicago: University of Chicago Press, 1964.

Cunningham, Colin. *Victorian and Edwardian Town Halls*. London: Routledge & Kegan Paul, 1981.

Curtis, William J. R. *Modern Architecture Since 1900*. Oxford, UK: Phaidon, 1982.

Dernie, David. *Victor Horta*. London: Academy Editions, 1995.

Dutta, Arindam. *The Bureaucracy of Beauty: Design in the Age of Its Global Reproducibility*. New York: Routledge, 2007.

Dwivedi, Sharada and Rahul Mehrotra. *Bombay: The Cities Within*. Bombay: Eminence Designs, 2001.

Egbert, Donald Drew, and David Van Zanten, eds. *The Beaux-Arts Tradition in French Architecture*. Princeton, NJ: Princeton University Press, 1980.

Elleh, Nnambi. *African Architecture, Evolution and Transformation*. New York: McGraw-Hill, 1977.

———. *Architecture and Power in Africa*. Westport, CT: Praeger, 2002.

Evenson, Norma. *The Indian Metropolis: A View Toward the West*. New Haven, CT: Yale University Press, 1989.

Friedman, Mildred, ed. *De Stijl, 1917–1931: Visions of Utopia*. Minneapolis: Walker Art Center; New York: Abbeville Press, 1982.

Golan, Romy. *Modernity and Nostalgia: Art and Politics in France between the Wars*. New Haven, CT: Yale University Press, 1995.

Guha-Thakorte, Tapati. *The Making of a New "Indian" Art: Artists, Aesthetics and Nationalism in Bengal, c. 1850–1920*. Cambridge, UK: Cambridge University Press, 1992.

Hildebrand, Grant. *The Wright Space: Pattern and Meaning in Frank Lloyd Wright's Houses*. Seattle: University of Washington Press, 1991.

Hosagrahar, Jyoti. *Indigenous Modernities: Negotiating Architecture and Urbanism*. London and New York: Routledge, 2006

Irving, Robert Grant. *Indian Summer: Lutyens, Baker, and Imperial Delhi*. New Haven, CT: Yale University Press, 1981.

Jarzombek, Mark. *Designing MIT: Bosworth's New Tech*. Boston: Northeastern University Press, 2004.

Kopp, Anatole. *Constructivist Architecture in the USSR*. Translated by Sheila de Vallée. London: Academy Editions; New York: St. Martins Press, 1985.

Kruty, Paul, and Paul Sprague. *Two American Architects in India: Walter B. Griffin and Marion M. Griffin, 1935–1937*. Champaign-Urbana: School of Architecture, University of Illinois, 1997.

Kultermann, Udo., ed. *Kenzo Tange, 1946–1969: Architecture and Urban Design*. Zürich: Verlag für Architektur Artemis, 1970.

———. *New Directions in African Architecture*. Translated by John Maass. London: Studio Vista, 1969.

Lahuerta, Juan José. *Antoni Gaudí, 1852–1926: Architecture, Ideology, and Politics*. Edited by Giovanna Crespi. Translated by Graham Thompson. Milan: Electa Architecture; London: Phaidon, 2003.

Levine, Neil. *The Architecture of Frank Lloyd Wright*. Princeton, NJ: Princeton University Press, 1996.

Lizon, Peter. *The Palace of the Soviets: The Paradigm of Architecture in the USSR*. Colorado Springs, CO: Three Continents, 1995.

Loyer, François. *Victor Horta: Hotel Tassel 1893–1895*. Translated by Susan Day. Brussels: Archives d'Architecture Moderne, 1986.

Maciuika, John V. *Before the Bauhaus: Architecture, Politics, and the German State, 1890–1920*. New York: Cambridge University Press, 2005.

Markus, Thomas A., ed. *Order in Space and Society: Architectural Form and Its Context in the Scottish Enlightenment*. Edinburgh, UK: Mainstream, 1982.

Martinell, César. *Gaudí: His Life, His Theories, His Work*. Translated by Judith Rohrer. Cambridge, MA: MIT Press, 1975.

Middleton, Robin, ed. *The Beaux-Arts and Nineteenth-Century French Architecture*. Cambridge, MA: MIT Press, 1982.

Moravánszky, Ákos. *Competing Visions: Aesthetic Invention and Social Imagination in Central European Architecture, 1867–1918*. Cambridge, MA: MIT Press, 1998.

Nitzan-Shiftan, Alona. *Isrealizing Jerusalem: The Encounter between Architectural and National Ideologies 1967–1977*. Ph.D. diss., Massachusetts Institute of Technology, 2002.

Oechslin, Werner. *Otto Wagner, Adolf Loos, and the Road to Modern Architecture*. Translated by Lynette Widder. Cambridge, UK, and New York: Cambridge University Press, 2002.

Okoye, Ikemefuna. *"Hideous" Architecture: Feint and Resistance in Turn of the Century South-Eastern Nigerian Building*. Ph.D. diss., Massachusetts Institute of Technology, 1995.

Oldenburg, Veena Talwar. *The Making of Colonial Lucknow, 1856–1877*. Princeton, NJ: Princeton University Press, 1984.

Pawley, Martin. *Buckminster Fuller*. London: Trefoil, 1990.

Pyla, Panayiota. *Ekistics, Architecture and Environmental Politics 1945–76: A Prehistory of Sustainable Development*. Ph.D. diss., Massachusetts Institute of Technology, 2002.

Rabbat, Nasser. "The Formation of the Neo-Mamluk Style in Modern Egypt" in *The Education of the Architect: Historiography, Urbanism and the Growth of Architectural Knowledge*. Edited by Martha Pollak. Cambridge, MA: MIT Press, 1997.

Rowland, Anna. *Bauhaus Source Book*. Oxford, UK: Phaidon, 1990.

Sarnitz, August. *Adolf Loos, 1870–1933: Architect, Cultural Critic, Dandy*. Cologne, Germany, and Los Angeles: Taschen, 2003.

Scriver, Peter. *Rationalization, Standardization, and Control in Design: A Cognitive Historical Study of Architectural Design and Planning in the Public Works Department of British India, 1855–1901*. Delft, Netherlands: Publikatieburo Bouwkunde, Technische Universiteit Delft, 1994.

Scully, Vincent Joseph. *The Shingle Style Today, or, the Historian's Revenge*. New York: G. Braziller, 1974.

Sheaffer, M. P. A. *Otto Wagner and the New Face of Vienna*. Vienna: Compress, 1997.

Siry, Joseph. *Carson Pirie Scott: Louis Sullivan and the Chicago Department Store Chicago Architecture and Urbanism*. Chicago: University of Chicago Press, 1988.

———. *Unity Temple: Frank Lloyd Wright and Architecture for Liberal Religion*. Cambridge, UK: Cambridge University Press, 1996.

Starr, S. *Frederick Melnikov: Solo Architect in a Mass Society*. Princeton, NJ: Princeton University Press, 1978.

Steele, James. *Charles Rennie Mackintosh: Synthesis in Form*. London: Academy Editions, 1995.

Steiner, Hadas. *Bathrooms, Bubbles, and Systems: Archigram and the Landscapes of Transience*. Ph.D. diss., Massachusetts Institute of Technology, 2001.

Stern, Robert A. M. *New York 1930: Architecture and Urbanism between Two World Wars*. New York: Rizzoli, 1987.

Stern, Robert A. M., Gregory Gilmartin, and John Montague Massengale. *New York 1900: Metropolitan Architecture and Urbanism, 1890–1915*. New York: Rizzoli, 1983.

Stewart, Janet. *Fashioning Vienna: Adolf Loos's Cultural Criticism*. London and New York: Routledge, 2000.

Summerson, John Newenham. *The Turn of the Century: Architecture in Britain around 1900*. Glasgow, Scotland: University of Glasgow Press, 1976.

Toman, Rolf. *Vienna: Art and Architecture*. Cologne, Germany: Könemann, 1999.

Turnbull, Jeff, and Peter Y. Navaretti, eds. *The Griffins in Australia and India: The Complete Works and Projects of Walter Burley Griffin and Marion Mahony Griffin*. Melbourne, Australia: Miegunyah, 1998.

Turner, Paul Venable. *Campus: An American Planning Tradition*. New York: Architectural History Foundation; Cambridge, MA: MIT Press, 1984.

———. *The Education of Le Corbusier*. New York: Garland, 1977.

Van Zanten, David. *Designing Paris: The Architecture of Duban, Labrouste, Duc, and Vaudoyer*. Cambridge, MA: MIT Press, 1987.

Woods, Mary N. *From Craft to Profession: The Practice of Architecture in Nineteenth-Century America*. Berkeley and Los Angeles: University of California Press, 1999.

Yaha, Maha. *Unnamed Modernisms: National Ideologies and Historical Imaginaries in Beirut's Urban Architecture.* Ph.D. diss., Massachusetts Institute of Technology, 2004.

Zabel, Craig and Munshower, Susan Scott, eds. *American Public Architecture: European Roots and Native Expressions.* University Park, PA: Penn State University Press, 1989.

1950 CE

Baljeu, Joost. *Theo van Doesburg.* London: Studio Vista, 1974.

Bettinotti, Massimo, ed. *Kenzo Tange, 1946–1996: Architecture and Urban Design.* Milan: Electa, 1996.

Cannell, Michael T. *I. M. Pei: Mandarin of Modernism.* New York: Carol Southern Books, 1995.

Cavalcanti, Lauro. *When Brazil Was Modern: Guide to Architecture, 1928–1960.* Translated by Jon Tolman. New York: Princeton Architectural Press, 2003.

Cohen, Jean-Louis. *Le Corbusier and the Mystique of the USSR: Theories and Projects for Moscow, 1928–1936.* Translated by Kenneth Hylton. Princeton, NJ: Princeton University Press, 1992.

Cohen, Jean-Louis, and Monique Eleb. *Casablanca: Colonial Myths and Architectural Ventures.* New York: Monacelli, 2002.

Colquhoun, Alan. *Modernity and the Classical Tradition: Architectural Essays, 1980–1987.* Cambridge, MA: MIT Press, 1989.

Curtis, William J. R. *Balkrishna Doshi: An Architecture for India.* New York: Rizzoli, 1988.

———. *Le Corbusier: Ideas and Forms.* New York: Rizzoli, 1986.

Doxiades, Konstantinos Apostolouv. *Ecology and Ekistics.* Edited by Gerald Dix. Boulder, CO: Westview, 1977.

Ellin, Nan. *Postmodern Urbanism.* New York: Princeton Architectural Press, 1999.

Fromonot, Francoise. *Glenn Murcutt: Buildings & Projects 1969–2003.* London: Thames & Hudson, 2003.

Ghirardo, Diane Yvonne. *Architecture after Modernism.* New York: Thames & Hudson, 1996.

———. *Building New Communities: New Deal America and Fascist Italy.* Princeton, NJ: Princeton University Press, 1989.

Grigor, Talinn. *Cultivat(ing) Modernities: The Society for National Heritage, Political Propaganda, and Public Architecture in Twentieth-Century Iran.* Ph.D. diss., Massachusetts Institute of Technology, 2005.

Ibelings, Hans. *Supermodernism: Architecture in the Age of Globalization.* Translated by Robyn de Jong-Dalziel. Rotterdam, Netherlands: NAi, 2002.

Jencks, Charles. *The Architecture of the Jumping Universe: A Polemic: How Complexity Science is Changing Architecture and Culture.* London: Academy Editions, 1997.

———. *Kings of Infinite Space: Frank Lloyd Wright & Michael Graves.* New York: St. Martin's Press, 1985.

———. *The Language of Post-Modern Architecture.* New York: Rizzoli, 1991.

Kamp-Bandau, Irmel. *Tel Aviv, Neues Bauen, 1930–1939.* Tübingen, Germany: Wasmuth, 1994.

Khan, Hasan-Uddin. *Charles Correa.* Singapore: Concept Media; New York: Aperture, 1987.

Kirkham, Pat. *Charles and Ray Eames: Designers of the Twentieth Century.* Cambridge, MA: MIT Press, 1995.

Klotz, Heinrich. *The History of Postmodern Architecture.* Translated by Radka Donnell. Cambridge, MA: MIT Press, 1988.

Lodder, Christina. *Russian Constructivism.* New Haven: Yale University Press, 1983.

Loomis, John A. *Revolution of Forms: Cuba's Forgotten Art Schools.* New York: Princeton Architectural Press, 1999.

Makiya, Kanan. *The Monument: Art, Vulgarity, and Responsibility in Iraq.* London: Andre Deutsch, 1991.

McCoy, Esther. *Case Study Houses, 1945–1962.* Los Angeles: Hennessey & Ingalls, 1977.

Merkel, Jayne. *Eero Saarinen.* London and New York: Phaidon, 2005.

Mumford, Eric, ed. *Modern Architecture in St. Louis: Washington University and Postwar American Architecture, 1948–1973.* St. Louis, MO: School of Architecture, Washington University; Chicago: University of Chicago Press, 2004.

Murray, Peter. *The Saga of the Sydney Opera House: The Dramatic Story of the Design and Construction of the Icon of Modern Australia.* New York: Spon Press, 2003.

Neuhart, John. *Eames Design: The Work of the Office of Charles and Ray Eames.* New York: Harry N. Abrams, 1989.

Nilsson, Sten. *The New Capitals of India, Pakistan and Bangladesh.* Lund, Sweden: Studentlitteratur, 1973.

Pommer, Richard, and Christian F. Otto. *Weissenhof 1927 and the Modern Movement in Architecture.* Chicago: University of Chicago Press, 1991.

Portoghesi, Paolo. *Postmodern, the Architecture of the Postindustrial Society.* New York: Rizzoli, 1983.

Prakash, Aditya. *Chandigarh: A Presentation in Free Verse.* Chandigarh, India: Marg, 1980.

———. *Reflections on Chandigarh.* New Delhi: B. N. Prakash, 1983.

Prakash, Vikramaditya. *Chandigarh's Le Corbusier: The Struggle for Modernity in Postcolonial India.* Seattle: University of Washington Press, 2002.

Robson, David. *Geoffrey Bawa: The Complete Works.* London: Thames & Hudson, 2002.

Scriver, Peter, and Amit Srivastava. *India: Modern Architectures in History.* London: Reaktion Books, 2015.

Skidmore, Owings & Merrill. *The Architecture of Skidmore, Owings & Merrill, 1950–1962.* New York: Praeger, 1962.

Smith, Elizabeth A. T., and Michael Darling. *The Architecture of R. M. Schindler.* New York: Harry N. Abrams, 2001.

Stanford Anderson, ed. *Eladio Dieste: Innovation in Structural Art.* New York: Princeton Architectural Press, 2004.

Stäubli, Willy. *Brasília.* London: Leonard Hill Books, 1966.

Steele, James. *Architecture for Islamic Societies Today.* London: Academy Editions; Berlin: Ernst & Sohn; New York: St. Martin's Press, 1994.

———. *An Architecture for People: The Complete Works of Hassan Fathy.* New York: Whitney Library of Design, 1997.

Stewart, David B. *The Making of a Modern Japanese Architecture: 1868 to the Present.* Tokyo and New York: Kodansha International, 1987.

Svácha, Rostislav. *The Architecture of New Prague, 1895–1945.* Translated by Alexandra Büchler. Cambridge, MA: MIT Press, 1995.

Taylor, Jennifer. *Australian Architecture since 1960.* Sydney, Australia: Law Book Co., 1986.

Underwood, David Kendrick. *Oscar Niemeyer and the Architecture of Brazil.* New York: Rizzoli, 1994.

Von Vegesack, Alexander, ed. *Czech Cubism: Architecture, Furniture, and Decorative Arts, 1910–1925.* New York: Princeton Architectural Press, 1992.

Weston, Richard. *Alvar Aalto.* London: Phaidon, 1995.

Zukowsky John, ed. *The Many Faces of Modern Architecture: Building in Germany between the World Wars.* Munich and New York: Prestel, 1994.

Illustration Credits

Unless otherwise noted below, maps and drawings are by Francis D. K. Ching and photographs are by Mark Jarzombek or Vikramaditya Prakash.

1.1 © RURO Photography
1.2 flickr/deedavee easyflow (https://creativecommons.org/licenses/by-sa/2.0/legalcode)
1.3 John Atherton/flickr (https://creativecommons.org/licenses/by-sa/2.0/legalcode)
1.4 flickr/Anthony Tong Lee (https://creativecommons.org/licenses/by-nd/2.0/legalcode)
1.5 © Adriana Muntean
1.7 Courtesy of Deniz Tortum
1.8 CC BY-SA 3.0, https://commons.wikimedia.org/w/index.php?curid=144796
1.20 Milonk/Shutterstock.com
1.26 By User: Roweromaniak—Archiwum "Roweromaniaka wielkopolskiego" No_B19-36, CC BY-SA 2.5, https://commons.wikimedia.org/w/index.php?curid=1724285
1.29 Hassan Janali/U.S. Army Corps of Engineers Digital Visual Library
1.35 Photographer manna Gabana Studios Germany
1.47 Pecold/Shutterstock.com
1.48 By Photo: Myrabella—Wikimedia Commons, CC BY-SA 3.0, https://commons.wikimedia.org/w/index.php?curid=10560289

2.2 meunierd/Shutterstock.com
2.3 flickr/steve deeves (https://creativecommons.org/licenses/by/2.0/legalcode)
2.16 Courtesy of the Oriental Institute of the University of Chicago
2.22, 2.25 David Friedman
2.27 © Greg Martin/December 7, 2006
2.35 © Richard T. Mortel, Al-Imam Muhammad Ibn Saud Islamic University, Riyadh, Saudi Arabia
2.43 By Jvdc—Own work, CC BY-SA 3.0, https://commons.wikimedia.org/w/index.php?curid=13862173
2.46 Jeremy Tilston
2.49 © Edgar Asencios Travel Photography (https://www.flickr.com/photos/edgarasencios/)
2.52 Vladislav T. Jirousek/Shutterstock.com

3.5 Allocricetulus/Shutterstock
3.7 Andrew Holt/Getty Images
3.8 By Gisling—Own work, CC BY-SA 3.0, https://commons.wikimedia.org/w/index.php?curid=24704593
3.9 flickr/Zigg-E (https://creativecommons.org/licenses/by-nd/2.0/legalcode)
3.11 By Michel Wal—Own work, CC BY-SA 3.0, https://commons.wikimedia.org/w/index.php?curid=18277157
3.18 Stuart Eric Watson
3.22 David Friedman
3.24 Insights/Getty Images, http://www.gettyimages.com/license/558030613
3.25 © Paul Hessell
3.35 Rob Corder
3.37 © Simon Wang 2009
3.38 Alan Seideman
3.40 Photographer manna Gabana Studios Germany
3.41, 3.42 flickr/Michael Gaylard (https://creativecommons.org/licenses/by/2.0/legalcode)
3.43 © Michael E. Krupar 2008
3.48 By Klaus-Peter Simon—Own work, CC BY 3.0, https://commons.wikimedia.org/w/index.php?curid=4084876
3.56 flickr/Klearchos Kapoutsis (https://creativecommons.org/licenses/by/2.0/legalcode)

4.6 CC BY-SA 3.0, https://commons.wikimedia.org/w/index.php?curid=525791
4.10 By Ruben Charles (http://www.rubencharles.com) —Flickr, (http://www.flickr.com/photos/rubencharles/385883483), CC BY 2.0, https://commons.wikimedia.org/w/index.php?curid=1795580

4.14 flickr/Taco Witte (https://creativecommons.org/licenses/by/2.0/)
4.26 Visual Resources Collection, CBE © University of Washington, Grant Hildebrand
4.30 Arch-Image Library (www.arch-imagelibrary.com)
4.31 By Marsyas—Own work, CC BY-SA 2.5, https://commons.wikimedia.org/w/index.php?curid=479123
4.41 urosr/Shutterstock.com
4.42 © Eric Lafforgue
4.44 Naeblys/Shutterstock.com
4.46 CC BY-SA 3.0, https://commons.wikimedia.org/w/index.php?curid=658402
4.47 Image copyright © The Metropolitan Museum of Art. Image source: Art Resource, NY
4.48 By Mountain—Own work, CC BY-SA 3.0, https://commons.wikimedia.org/w/index.php?curid=602198
4.49 Ben Heys/Shutterstock.com
4.56 © 2006 by Borayin (Maitreya) Larios
4.57 flickr/Arian Zwegers (https://creativecommons.org/licenses/by/2.0/)
4.58 flickr/Manuel Menal (https://creativecommons.org/licenses/by-sa/2.0/)
4.59 Kurkul/Shutterstock.com

5.1 Lambros Kazan/Shutterstock.com
5.9 Public Domain, https://commons.wikimedia.org/w/index.php?curid=1359777
5.10 Courtesy of the Oriental Institute of the University of Chicago
5.13 Federico Pasimi
5.16 © Marc Hesselink
5.23 PhotoDisc, Inc./Getty Images
5.29 By Thermos. [CC BY-SA 2.5 (http://creativecommons.org/licenses/by-sa/2.5)], via Wikimedia Commons
5.31 Photo by Phyllis Harris
5.39 Visual Resources Collection, CBE © University of Washington, Grant Hildebrand.
5.45 flickr/Sarah Murray (https://creativecommons.org/licenses/by-sa/2.0/legalcode)
5.46 Wally Gobetz (wallyg@flickr)
5.56 Thomas F. Smith
5.60 David Friedlander © 2008
5.66 VasenkaPhotography/flickr (https://creativecommons.org/licenses/by/2.0/legalcode)
5.68 Photo by Evan Lovely (EvanLovely.com). All rights shared. Attribution: Creative Commons
5.78 By User: Vmenkov—Own work, CC BY-SA 3.0, https://commons.wikimedia.org/w/index.php?curid=9997302

6.1 By Radosław Botev—Own work, Attribution, https://commons.wikimedia.org/w/index.php?curid=1411909
6.2 By Diliff—Own work, CC BY-SA 2.5, https://commons.wikimedia.org/w/index.php?curid=2067974
6.9 s74/Shutterstock.com
6.12 By MM—Own work (self-made photo), Public Domain, https://commons.wikimedia.org/w/index.php?curid=1049141
6.19 Kevin A. Wong
6.24 CC BY-SA 3.0, https://commons.wikimedia.org/w/index.php?curid=474277
6.29 Gianni Dagli Orti/The Art Archive at Art Resource, NY
6.30 Photo by Bachir Blidi
6.38 flickr/Benjami Villoslada (https://creativecommons.org/licenses/by-sa/2.0/legalcode)
6.41 Photo taken by Philippe J. Moore
6.45 Corbis Digital Stock
6.54 Anita Haugen
6.55 tuulijumala/Shutterstock.com
6.59 By Michael Gunther—Own work, CC BY-SA 3.0, https://commons.wikimedia.org/w/index.php?curid=33850514
6.60 Photo by Jim Marx
6.64 By Godot13—Own work, CC BY-SA 3.0, https://commons.wikimedia.org/w/index.php?curid=25671212

6.69 © by Wesley Shu
6.75 Rafal Cichawa/Shutterstock.com
6.80 Steps to Sanchi stupa by Jyoti Prakash Bhattacharje, Mumbai. India
6.83 E. Stewart (2003)
6.85 Certain rights reserved with Vinay Anil Bavdekar
6.89 Attila JANDI/Shutterstock.com
6.90 Himanshu Sarpotdar
6.94 By Madman2001—Own work, CC BY 3.0, https://commons.wikimedia.org/w/index.php?curid=3999988
6.104 Julie Hillebrant

7.1 Benh Lieu Song (http://creativecommons.org/licenses/by-sa/3.0/)
7.5 Bryn Mawr College, Lantern Slides of Classical Antiquity
7.7 Photo by Nuno Ventura
7.10 Photo by Adrienne Bassett
7.13 Jens Börner, Dresden
7.17 Visual Resources Collection, CAUP (Grant Hildebrand orig.) © University of Washington
7.18 Stewart Butterfield/Flickr (https://creativecommons.org/licenses/by/2.0/legalcode)
7.27 By Alexander Z. CC BY-SA 3.0, https://commons.wikimedia.org/w/index.php?curid=45301
7.29 Doug Drew, Ottawa, Canada. flickr.com/photos/buster-and-bubby/1252348091/
7.30 photoiconix/Shutterstock.com
7.52 Photograph by John C. Huntington, Courtesy of the Huntington Photographic Archive at The Ohio State University.
7.56 Madhawa Karunaratne, Sri Lanka (flickr.com/mahawak)
7.57 Pam Gillespie
7.63 Brian Kinney/Shutterstock.com
7.65 Flat Earth
7.68 Ricardo Barata, Creative Commons
7.73 By Martin St-Amant (S23678) (Français: Travail personnel English: Own work) [CC BY 3.0 (http://creativecommons.org/licenses/by/3.0)], via Wikimedia Commons
7.75, 7.77 © Jeffrey Li 2010
7.81 By Rdikeman at the English language Wikipedia, CC BY-SA 3.0, https://commons.wikimedia.org/w/index.php?curid=6845597

8.1 By Tango7174—Own work, GFDL, https://commons.wikimedia.org/w/index.php?curid=12008404
8.2 flickr/Kai Hendry (https://creativecommons.org/licenses/by/2.0/legalcode)
8.3 By Ariel Steiner—Own work, CC BY-SA 2.5, https://commons.wikimedia.org/w/index.php?curid=1662053
8.4 Jorge Láscar (http://www.flickr.com/photos/jlascar)
8.6, 8.9, 8.10, 8.11 Kumara Sastry
8.18 © by Wesley Shu
8.20 By Buddha_Bamiyan_1963.jpg: UNESCO/A Lezine; Original uploader was Tsui at de.wikipedia. Later version(s) were uploaded by Liberal Freemason at de.wikipedia.Buddhas_of_Bamiyan4.jpg: Carl Montgomery derivative work: Zaccarias (talk) —Buddha_Bamiyan_1963.jpgBuddhas_of_Bamiyan4.jpg, CC BY-SA 3.0, https://commons.wikimedia.org/w/index.php?curid=8249891
8.24 creativecommons.org/licenses/by/2.0/deed.en
8.26 © Brian Searwar
8.27 Melanie Michailidis
8.28 By Farzad j—Own work, Public Domain, https://commons.wikimedia.org/w/index.php?curid=12875974
8.30 Photo by Madhu Nair (www.10yearitch.com; www.smileokplease.com)
8.33 By Theasg sap—Own work, CC BY-SA 3.0, https://commons.wikimedia.org/w/index.php?curid=24505818
8.35 Photograph by John C. Huntington, Courtesy of the Huntington Photographic Archive at The Ohio State University

ILLUSTRATION CREDITS

ILLUSTRATION CREDITS

Index